SECOND CANADIAN EDITION

Managerial Decision Modeling with Spreadsheets

Barry Render

Charles Harwood Professor of Management Science,
Graduate School of Business, Rollins College

Ralph M. Stair, Jr.

Professor Emeritus of Management Information Systems,
Florida State University

Nagraj (Raju) Balakrishnan

Professor of Management,
Clemson University

Brian E. Smith

Professor of Management Science,
McGill University

Pearson Canada
Toronto

To Haviva—my wife, my love, my friend.
—B.E.S

Library and Archives Canada Cataloguing in Publication

Managerial decision modeling with spreadsheets / Barry Render . . . [et al.].—2nd Canadian ed.

Includes bibliographical references and index.

ISBN 978-0-13-208013-2

   1. Management science—Textbooks.   2. Decision making—Mathematical models—Textbooks.   I. Render, Barry

HD30.25.M35 2010   658.4'03   C2008-905613-2

ISBN-13: 978-0-13-208013-2
ISBN-10: 0-13-208013-3

Vice President, Editorial Director: Gary Bennett
Marketing Manager: Leigh-Anne Graham
Developmental Editor: Rema Celio, Christina Lee
Production Editor: Lila Campbell
Copy Editor: Marg Bukta
Proofreader: Nicole Mellow

Production Coordinator: Avinash Chandra
Composition: Integra
Photo and Permissions Research: Amanda McCormick
Art Director: Julia Hall
Cover and Interior Design: Anthony Leung
Cover Image: Veer, Inc.

1 2 3 4 5   13 12 11 10 09

Printed and bound in the United States of America.

ABOUT THE AUTHORS

Barry Render   is the Charles Harwood Distinguished Professor of Management Science at the Crummer Graduate School of Business at Rollins College in Winter Park, Florida. He received his M.S. in Operations Research and his Ph.D. in Quantitative Analysis at the University of Cincinnati. He previously taught at George Washington University, the University of New Orleans, Boston University, and George Mason University, where he held the GM Foundation Professorship in Decision Sciences and was Chair of the Decision Science Department. Dr. Render has also worked in the aerospace industry for General Electric, McDonnell Douglas, and NASA.

Professor Render has co-authored ten textbooks with Prentice Hall, including *Quantitative Analysis for Management, Operations Management, Principles of Operations Management, Service Management, Introduction to Management Science,* and *Cases and Readings in Management Science.* His more than one hundred articles on a variety of management topics have appeared in *Decision Sciences, Production and Operations Management, Interfaces, Information and Management, The Journal of Management Information Systems, Socio-Economic Planning Sciences,* and *Operations Management Review,* among others.

Dr. Render has also been honored as an AACSB Fellow and named a Senior Fulbright Scholar in 1982 and again in 1993. He was twice vice-president of the Decision Science Institute Southeast Region and served as Software Review Editor for Decision Line from 1989 to 1995. He has also served as Editor of the *New York Times* Operations Management special issues from 1996 to 2001. Finally, Professor Render has been actively involved in consulting for government agencies and for many corporations, including NASA; FBI; the U.S. Navy; Fairfax County, Virginia; and C&P Telephone.

He teaches operations management courses in Rollins College's MBA and Executive MBA programs. In 1995 he was named as that school's Professor of the Year, and in 1996 was selected by Roosevelt University to receive the St. Claire Drake Award for Outstanding Scholarship.

Ralph Stair   is Professor Emeritus of Management Information Systems in the College of Business at Florida State University. He received a B.S. in Chemical Engineering from Purdue University and an MBA from Tulane University. Under the guidance of Ken Ramsing and Alan Eliason, he received his Ph.D. in operations management from the University of Oregon.

He has taught at the University of Oregon, the University of Washington, the University of New Orleans, and Florida State University. He has twice taught in Florida State University's Study Abroad Program in London. Over the years, his teaching has been concentrated in the areas of information systems, operations research, and operations management.

Dr. Stair is a member of several academic organizations, including the Decision Sciences Institute and INFORMS, and he regularly participates at national meetings. He has published numerous articles and books, including *Quantitative Analysis for Management, Introduction to Management Science, Cases and Readings in Management Science, Production and Operations Management: A Self-Correction Approach, Fundamentals of Information Systems, Principles of Information Systems, Introduction to Information Systems, Computers in Today's World, Principles of Data Processing, Learning to Live with Computers, Programming in BASIC, Essentials of BASIC Programming, Essentials of FORTRAN Programming,* and *Essentials of COBOL Programming.*

Professor Stair divides his time between Florida and Colorado. He enjoys skiing, biking, kayaking, and other outdoor activities.

Nagraj (Raju) Balakrishnan   is Professor and Graduate Coordinator in the Department of Management at Clemson University. He holds Bachelors and Masters degrees in Mechanical Engineering from the University of Madras (India) and the University of Kentucky respectively, and a Ph.D. in Management from Purdue University. He previously taught at Tulane University.

Dr. Balakrishnan teaches courses in spreadsheet-based Decision Modeling, Business Statistics, Production and Operations Management, and Project Management. He has won several awards for teaching excellence both at Clemson and at Tulane. At Clemson, these include the MBA Professor of the Year award and the College of Business Graduate Teaching Excellence award (twice). He has also taught in Tulane University's Executive MBA program.

Dr. Balakrishnan's current research focuses on production scheduling, capacity allocation models, and problems related to configurations of supply chains. His articles have been published in leading academic journals such as *Decision Sciences, Production and Operations Management, European Journal of Operational Research, Naval Research Logistics, IIE Transactions, Networks*, and *Computers & Operations Research*. He serves as a Senior Departmental Editor of *Production and Operations Management*, Online Editor for the Production and Operations Management Society, and is the recipient of several awards for his research publications including Best Paper awards from the Decision Sciences Institute and the Institute of Industrial Engineers, the Clemson Department of Management Award for Scholarly Achievement, and the Clemson Board of Trustees Award for Faculty Excellence.

Dr. Balakrishnan is very active in writing proposals and has authored or co-authored successful grant proposals totalling over $400,000 from the National Science Foundation and other funding agencies. Several of these have been in collaboration with faculty from the College of Engineering and Sciences at Clemson University.

Dr. Balakrishnan lives in Clemson, SC with his wife Meena, son Nitin, and daughter Nandita. He enjoys traveling and Indian light music, and is an avid racquetball player.

Brian Smith   has been a member of the Faculty of Management at McGill University for over 20 years. He teaches operations research, optimization methods, and business statistics in the B.Com. and MBA programs. He was previously Professor of Mathematics at Dawson College in Montreal, where he served as Chairman of the Department of Mathematics. He also taught as adjunct professor of mathematics at Santa Monica College, California.

Dr. Smith received his undergraduate education at Trinity College Dublin, where he majored in Pure and Applied Mathematics. He obtained his M.Sc. in Mathematics from the University of Alberta, and his Ph.D. in Mathematics from Queen's University at Kingston, Ontario. He subsequently earned a master's degree in Computer Science at McGill University, specializing in Database Management Systems and Monte Carlo simulation.

Dr. Smith is a member of several academic organizations and has frequently presented at national conferences. He served as chair of the Technology in Mathematics Education Committee of the American Mathematical Association of Two-Year Colleges (AMATYC), and he is currently the Software Editor for the *AMATYC Review*. He has also chaired a statistics education committee at the American Statistical Association.

Professor Smith was appointed to the NASA-AMATYC-NSF projects, which were funded by the National Science Foundation to develop teaching modules in mathematics based on actual NASA applications and has co-authored chapters in the books resulting from that project. He is the author of *Simplifying Mathematics using the TI-82/83 or TI-85/86 Graphing Calculators*. His consulting experience includes sales tracking and forecasting in the Canadian pharmaceutical industry, analysis of real estate sales data in Quebec, and statistical analysis of medical research.

Based in Montreal since 1970, Dr. Smith enjoys the ambience and cultural life of the city, and likes to spend time at the Montreal Jazz Festival and other summer attractions in this vibrant city.

CONTENTS

PREFACE xiii

CHAPTER 1 **Introduction to Managerial Decision Modeling 1**

1.1 *Introduction 3*

1.2 *What is Decision Modeling? 3*
Quantitative versus Qualitative Data 4
Role of Spreadsheets in Decision Modeling 4
Types of Decision Models 5

1.3 *Steps Involved in Decision Modeling 6*
Step 1: Formulation 6
Step 2: Solution 8
Step 3: Interpretation and What-If Analysis 9
Decision Modeling in the Real World 9

1.4 *Spreadsheet Example of a Decision Model: Tax Computation 11*

1.5 *Spreadsheet Example of Another Decision Model: Break-Even Analysis 13*
Using Goal Seek to Find the Break-Even Point 14

1.6 *Possible Problems in Developing Decision Models 16*
Defining the Problem 16
Developing a Model 17
Acquiring Input Data 17
Developing a Solution 18
Testing the Solution 18
Analyzing the Results 18

1.7 *Implementation—Not Just the Final Step 18*
Summary 19
Glossary 19
Key Equations 20
Self-Test 20
Discussion Questions and Problems 21
Bibliography 22

CHAPTER 2 **Linear Programming Models: Graphical and Computer Methods 24**

2.1 *Introduction 26*

2.2 *Development of a Linear Programming Model 27*
Formulation 27
Solution 27
Interpretation and Sensitivity Analysis 27
Properties of a Linear Programming Model 27
Basic Assumptions of a Linear Programming Model 28

2.3 *Formulating a Linear Programming Problem 30*
Linear Programming Example: Flair Furniture Company 30
Decision Variables 30
The Objective Function 31
Constraints 31
Nonnegativity Constraints and Integer Values 32
Guidelines to Developing a Correct LP Model 32

2.4 *Graphical Solution of a Linear Programming Problem with Two Variables 34*
Graphical Representation of Constraints 34
Feasible Region 37
Identifying an Optimal Solution by Using Level Lines 37
Identifying an Optimal Solution by Using All Corner Points 40
Comments on Flair Furniture's Optimal Solution 41
Extension to Flair Furniture's Linear Programming Model 41

2.5 *A Minimization Linear Programming Problem 42*
Alberta Plains Turkey Farm 43
Graphical Solution of the Alberta Plains Turkey Farm Problem 44

2.6 *Summary of the Graphical Solution Methods 46*

2.7 *Special Situations in Solving Linear Programming Problems 47*
Redundancy 47
Infeasibility 47
Unboundedness 48
Alternate Optimal Solutions 49

2.8 *Setting Up and Solving Linear Programming Problems Using Excel's Solver 50*
Using Solver to Solve the Flair Furniture Problem 51

Changing Cells   52

Target Cell   53

Constraints   54

Entering Information in Solver   55

Using Solver to Solve the Alberta Plains Turkey Farm Problem   60

2.9   *Premium Solver for Education*   62

2.10   *Algorithmic Solution Procedures for Linear Programming Problems*   64

Simplex Method   64

Karmarkar's Algorithm   65

Summary   65

Glossary   66

Solved Problems   67

Self-Test   71

Discussion Questions and Problems   72

Case Study 2.1: Interactions 98   77

Case Study 2.2: Golding Landscaping and Plants, Inc.   78

Case Study 2.3: International Pharma Inc.   79

Bibliography   80

CHAPTER 3   **Linear Programming Modeling Applications: With Computer Analyses in Excel**   **81**

3.1   *Introduction*   83

3.2   *Marketing Applications*   84

Media Selection   84

Marketing Research   87

3.3   *Manufacturing Applications*   89

Product Mix   89

3.4   *Employee Scheduling Applications*   91

Labour Planning   91

Assignment Problems   93

3.5   *Financial Applications*   94

Portfolio Selection   94

3.6   *Packing Applications*   96

Truck Loading Problem   96

Knapsack and Transportation Problems   100

3.7   *Ingredient Blending Applications*   100

Diet Problems   100

Ingredient Mix and Blending Problems   101

3.8   *Multiperiod Applications*   104

Production Scheduling   104

Sinking Fund   108

Summary   112

Self-Test   112

Problems   113

Case Study 3.1: Dofasco Fuel Management   120

Case Study 3.2: Canadian Military Electronics   122

Bibliography   123

CHAPTER 4   **Linear Programming Sensitivity Analysis**   **124**

4.1   *Introduction*   126

Why Do We Need to Study Sensitivity Analysis?   126

4.2   *Sensitivity Analysis Using Graphs*   127

Types of Sensitivity Analysis   128

Impact of Changes in an Objective Function Coefficient   129

Impact of Changes in a Constraint's Right-Hand-Side Value   131

4.3   *Sensitivity Analysis Using Solver Reports*   135

Solver Reports   136

Sensitivity Report   137

Impact of Changes in a Constraint's Right-Hand-Side Value   138

Impact of Changes in an Objective Function Coefficient   139

4.4   *Sensitivity Analysis for a Larger Maximization Example*   142

Anderson Electronics Example   142

Some Questions We Want Answered   142

Alternate Optimal Solutions   146

4.5   *Analyzing Simultaneous Changes Using the 100% Rule*   146

Simultaneous Changes in Constraint RHS Values   146

Simultaneous Changes in OFC Values   147

4.6   *Pricing Out New Variables*   147

Anderson's Proposed New Product   148

4.7   *Sensitivity Analysis for a Minimization Example*   150

Burn-Off Diet Drink Example   150

Burn-Off's Excel Solution   151

Answering Sensitivity Analysis Questions for Burn-off   152

Summary   154

Glossary   154

Solved Problem   155

Self-Test   157

Discussion Questions and Problems   158

Case Study 4.1: Red Brand Canners   168

Case Study 4.2: Vytec Corporation: Warehouse Layout Planning   171

Case Study 4.3: Airy Dairy   173

Bibliography   174

CHAPTER 5   Transportation, Assignment, and Network Models   176

5.1   *Introduction   178*

Transportation Model   178

Transshipment Model   178

Assignment Model   178

Maximal-Flow Model   178

Shortest-Path Model   179

Minimal-Spanning Tree Model   179

5.2   *Characteristics of Network Flow Problems   179*

5.3   *Transportation Model   180*

LP Model of Executive Furniture's Transportation Model   183

Solving the Transportation Model Using Excel   184

Alternate Excel Layout for the Model   185

Unbalanced Transportation Problems   187

More Than One Optimal Solution   188

5.4   *Facility Location Analysis   188*

Locating a New Factory for Hardgrave Machine Company   188

5.5   *Transshipment Model   191*

Executive Furniture Corporation Example— Revisited   191

LP Model for Executive Furniture's Transshipment Problem   192

5.6   *Assignment Model   193*

Fix-It Shop Example   193

Solving Assignment Models   194

LP Model for Fix-It Shop's Assignment Problem   195

5.7   *Maximal-Flow Model   196*

Road Network in Cornwall, PEI   197

LP Model for Cornwall Road System's Maximal-Flow Problem   197

5.8   *Shortest-Path Model   201*

Ray Design, Inc. Example   201

LP Model for Ray Design, Inc.'s Shortest-Path Problem   202

5.9   *Minimal-Spanning Tree Model   203*

Lauderdale Construction Company Example   203

Summary   207

Glossary   207

Key Equation   207

Solved Problems   208

Self-Test   213

Discussion Questions and Problems   214

Case Study 5.1: Ste-Agathe Wood Store   223

Case Study 5.2: Custom Vans of Canada, Inc.   224

Case Study 5.3: Bonnie Bagels   225

Bibliography   226

CHAPTER 6   Integer Programming Models   227

6.1   *Introduction   229*

Integer Programming Models   229

6.2   *Models with General Integer Variables   230*

Lightwell Chandelier Company   230

Using Solver to Solve Models with General Integer Variables   232

How Solver Solves IP Models   235

Solver Options   235

6.3   *Solving IP Problems: Branch-and-Bound   237*

Stopping Rules in the B&B Method   241

Setting Upper and Lower Bounds   241

6.4   *Models with Binary Variables   243*

Hi-tech Portfolio Selection   244

Solution to the Hi-tech Portfolio 0–1 Model   246

Specifying the Binary Requirement   247

6.5   *Mixed Integer Models: Fixed-Charge Problems   248*

Locating a New Factory for Hardgrave Machine Company   248

The Big-M Method   252

Summary   254

Glossary   254

Key Equation   255

Solved Problems   255

Self-Test   257

Discussion Questions and Problems   258

Case Study 6.1: St. Lawrence River Bridge   262

Case Study 6.2: Jackpine Mall   263

Bibliography   264

CHAPTER 7   Multicriteria and Nonlinear Programming Models   265

7.1   *Introduction   266*

Analytic Hierarchy Process Models   266

Goal Programming Models   267

Nonlinear Programming Models   267

7.2   *The Analytic Hierarchy Process* 267
Synthesis Is the Process of Prioritizing Decision Alternatives 270

7.3   *Goal Programming Models* 276
Goal Programming Example: Wilson Doors Company 277
Solving Goal Programming Models with Weighted Goals 279
Solving Goal Programming Models with Ranked Goals 282

7.4   *Nonlinear Programming Models* 287
Why Are NLP Models Difficult to Solve? 288
Nonlinear Objective Function and Linear Constraints 294
Both Nonlinear Objective Function and Nonlinear Constraints 296
Linear Objective Function and Nonlinear Constraints 297
Computational Procedures for Nonlinear Programming Problems 298
Summary 299
Glossary 299
Solved Problems 300
Self-Test 305
Discussion Questions and Problems 305
Case Study 7.1: Schank Marketing Research 311
Case Study 7.2: The Whom Should We Hire Case 311
Bibliography 313

CHAPTER 8   Project Management   314

8.1   *Introduction* 316
Phases in Project Management 316
Use of Software Packages in Project Management 319

8.2   *Project Networks* 319
Identifying Activities 319
Identifying Activity Times and Other Resources 321
Project Management Techniques: PERT and CPM 321
Project Management Example: General Foundry, Inc. 322
Drawing the Project Network 323

8.3   *Determining the Project Schedule* 326
Forward Pass 327
Backward Pass 329
Calculating Slack Time and Identifying the Critical Path(s) 330
Total Slack Time versus Free Slack Time 332

8.4   *Using Linear Programming to Identify the Critical Path* 333
Linear Programming Model to Determine the Earliest Times 333
Linear Programming Model to Determine the Latest Times 335

8.5   *Variability in Activity Times* 335
PERT Analysis 337
Probability of Project Completion 338
Determining Project Completion Time for a Given Confidence Level 340
Variability in Completion Time of Noncritical Paths 341
What Project Management Has Provided So Far 341

8.6   *Managing Project Costs and other Resources* 342
Planning and Scheduling Project Costs: Budgeting Process 342
Monitoring and Controlling Project Costs 344
Managing Other Resources 346

8.7   *Project Crashing* 347
Crashing General Foundry's Project (Hand Calculations) 348
Crashing General Foundry's Project Using Linear Programming 350

8.8   *Using Microsoft Project to Manage Projects* 352
Creating a Project Schedule Using Microsoft Project 353
Tracking Progress and Managing Costs Using Microsoft Project 356
Summary 359
Glossary 360
Key Equations 360
Solved Problems 361
Self-Test 363
Discussion Questions and Problems 364
Case Study 8.1: Haygood Brothers Construction Company 371
Case Study 8.2: Family Planning Research Center of Nigeria 372
Bibliography 374

CHAPTER 9   Decision Analysis   375

9.1   *Introduction* 377

9.2   *The Five Steps in Decision Analysis* 377
Thompson Lumber Company Example 377

9.3   *Types of Decision-Making Environments* 379

9.4 *Decision Making Under Uncertainty* 381
Maximax Criterion 382
Maximin Criterion 382
Criterion of Realism (Hurwicz) 382
Equally Likely (Laplace) Criterion 383
Minimax Regret Criterion 383
Using Excel to Solve Decision-Making Problems under Uncertainty 384

9.5 *Decision Making Under Risk* 386
Expected Monetary Value 386
Expected Opportunity Loss 387
Expected Value of Perfect Information 387
Using Excel to Solve Decision-Making Problems under Risk 388

9.6 *Decision Trees* 390
Folding Back a Decision Tree 391

9.7 *Using Treeplan to Solve Decision Tree Problems with Excel* 392
Loading TreePlan 392
Creating a Decision Tree Using TreePlan 392

9.8 *Decision Trees for Multistage Decision-Making Problems* 397
A Multistage Decision-Making Problem for Thompson Lumber 398
Expanded Decision Tree for Thompson Lumber 398
Folding Back the Expanded Decision Tree for Thompson Lumber 400
Expected Value of Sample Information 402

9.9 *Estimating Probability Values Using Bayesian Analysis* 403
Calculating Revised Probabilities 404
Potential Problems in Using Survey Results 405

9.10 *Utility Theory* 406
Measuring Utility and Constructing a Utility Curve 407
Utility as a Decision-Making Criterion 410
Summary 412
Glossary 412
Key Equations 413
Solved Problems 413
Self-Test 417
Discussion Questions and Problems 418
Case Study 9.1: Ski Right 426

Case Study 9.2: Blake Electronics 427
Case Study 9.3: Jupiter Corporation 428
Bibliography 429

CHAPTER 10   Queuing Models   431

10.1 *Introduction* 433

10.2 *Queuing System Costs* 433

10.3 *Characteristics of a Queuing System* 436
Arrival Characteristics 436
Queue Characteristics 438
Service Facility Characteristics 438
Service Time Distribution 439
Measuring the Queue's Performance 441
Kendall's Notation for Queuing Systems 441
Variety of Queuing Models 442

10.4 *Single-Server Queuing System with Poisson Arrivals and Exponential Service Times (M/M/1 Model)* 443
Assumptions of the M/M/1 Queuing Model 443
Operating Characteristic Equations for an M/M/1 Queuing System 444
Arnold's Muffler Shop Example 445
Using ExcelModules for Queuing Model Computations 445
Increasing the Service Rate 449

10.5 *Multiple-Server Queuing System with Poisson Arrivals and Exponential Service Times (M/M/s Model)* 450
Operating Characteristic Equations for an M/M/s Queuing System 450
Arnold's Muffler Shop Revisited 451
Cost Analysis of the Queuing System 453

10.6 *Single-Server Queuing System with Poisson Arrivals and Constant Service Times (M/D/1 Model)* 453
Operating Characteristic Equations for an M/D/1 Queuing System 453
Garcia-Golding Recycling, Inc. 454
Cost Analysis of the Queuing System 455

10.7 *Single-Server Queuing System with Poisson Arrivals and General Service Times (M/G/1 Model)* 455
Operating Characteristic Equations for an M/G/1 Queuing System 455
Meetings with Professor Crino 456
Using Excel's Goal Seek to Identify Required Model Parameters 457

10.8   *Multiple-Server Queuing System with Poisson Arrivals, Exponential Service Times, and Finite Population Size (M/M/S/∞/N Model)   458*

Operating Characteristic Equations for the Finite Population Queuing System   459

Government Agency Example   460

Cost Analysis of the Queuing System   461

10.9   *More Complex Queuing Systems   462*

Summary   462

Glossary   462

Key Equations   463

Solved Problems   465

Self-Test   467

Discussion Questions and Problems   468

Case Study 10.1: Winnipeg Ambulance Problem   472

Case Study 10.2: Winter Park Hotel   473

Bibliography   473

CHAPTER 11   Simulation Modeling   474

11.1   *Introduction   476*

What Is Simulation?   476

Advantages and Disadvantages of Simulation   477

11.2   *Monte Carlo Simulation   478*

Step 1. Establish a Probability Distribution for Each Variable   478

Step 2: Simulate Values from the Probability Distributions   480

Step 3: Repeat the Process for a Series of Replications   482

11.3   *Role of Computers in Simulation   482*

Types of Simulation Software Packages   483

Random Generation from Some Common Probability Distributions Using Excel   484

11.4   *Simulation Model to Compute Expected Profit   489*

Setting Up the Model   489

Replication by Copying the Model   492

Replication Using a Data Table   492

Analyzing the Results   494

11.5   *Simulation Model of an Inventory Problem   495*

Simkin's Hardware Store   496

Setting Up the Model   497

Computation of Costs   500

Replication Using Data Table   500

Analyzing the Results   501

Using Scenario Manager to Include Decisions in a Simulation Model   501

Analyzing the Results   504

11.6   *Simulation Model of a Queuing Problem   504*

Denton Savings Bank   504

Setting Up the Model   505

Replication Using Data Table   507

Analyzing the Results   507

11.7   *Simulation Model of a Revenue Management Problem   507*

Judith's Airport Limousine Service   508

Setting Up the Model   509

Replicating the Model Using Data Table and Scenario Manager   511

Analyzing the Results   511

11.8   *Simulation Model of an Inventory Problem Using Oracle Crystal Ball   512*

Reasons for Using Add-in Programs   512

Simulation of Simkin's Hardware Store Using Oracle Crystal Ball   513

Replicating the Model   515

Using Decision Table in Oracle Crystal Ball   518

11.9   *Simulation Model of a Revenue Management Problem Using Oracle Crystal Ball   521*

Setting Up the Model   522

Using Decision Table to Identify the Best Reservation Limit   523

11.10   *Other Types of Simulation Models   525*

Operational Gaming   525

Systems Simulation   525

Summary   526

Glossary   526

Solved Problems   527

Discussion Questions and Problems   536

Case Study 11.1: OntAir Airlines   545

Case Study 11.2: Smyth Transport Company   546

Case Study 11.3: Muskoka Land Development   546

Bibliography   548

CHAPTER 12   Forecasting Models   549

12.1   *Introduction   551*

12.2   *Types of Forecasts   551*

Qualitative Models   552

Time-Series Models   552

Causal Models   552

12.3   *Qualitative Forecasting Models*   *553*

12.4   *Measuring Forecast Error*   *554*

12.5   *Basic Time-Series Forecasting Models*   *555*

Components of a Time Series   555

Stationary and Nonstationary Time-Series Data   556

Moving Averages   556

Using ExcelModules for Forecasting Model Computations   557

Interpreting Forecast Errors   561

Weighted Moving Averages   561

Exponential Smoothing   564

12.6   *Trend and Seasonality in Time-Series Data*   *568*

Linear Trend Analysis   568

Scatter Diagram   569

Least-Squares Procedure for Developing a Linear Trend Line   570

Seasonality Analysis   575

12.7   *Multiplicative Decomposition of a Time Series*   *577*

Sawyer Piano House Multiplicative Decomposition Example   577

Using ExcelModules for Multiplicative Decomposition   578

12.8   *Causal Forecasting Models: Simple and Multiple Regression*   *582*

Causal Simple Regression Model   582

Causal Simple Regression Using ExcelModules   584

Causal Simple Regression Using Excel's Analysis ToolPak (Data Analysis)   589

Causal Multiple Regression Model   592

Causal Multiple Regression Using ExcelModules   593

Causal Multiple Regression Using Excel's Analysis ToolPak (Data Analysis)   596

Summary   *601*

Glossary   *601*

Key Equations   *601*

Solved Problems   *602*

Self-Test   *607*

Discussion Questions and Problems   *608*

Case Study 12.1: Quantico Computerware   *615*

Case Study 12.2: Forecasting Ticket Sales at CineBarn   *616*

Bibliography   *617*

CHAPTER 13   **Inventory Control Models** *(on CD-ROM)*   **618**

APPENDIX A   **Useful Excel Commands and Procedures for Installing ExcelModules   620**

A.1   *Introduction*   *620*

A.2   *Getting Started*   *620*

Organization of a Worksheet   620

Navigating through a Worksheet   620

Toolbars   621

Office Assistant   623

A.3   *Working with Worksheets*   *624*

Working with Rows and Columns   624

Formatting Worksheets   625

A.4   *Using Formulas and Functions*   *625*

Errors in Using Formulas and Functions   626

A.5   *Printing Worksheets*   *627*

A.6   *Installing and Enabling Excel Add-Ins*   *628*

A.7   *Installing and Using ExcelModules*   *629*

The Program Group   630

Starting the Program   630

Technical Support   630

APPENDIX B   **Probability Concepts and Applications   630**

B.1   *Fundamental Concepts*   *630*

Types of Probability   631

B.2   *Mutually Exclusive and Collectively Exhaustive Events*   *632*

Adding Mutually Exclusive Events   633

Law of Addition for Events That Are Not Mutually Exclusive   633

B.3   *Statistically Independent Events*   *634*

B.4   *Statistically Dependent Events*   *635*

B.5   *Revising Probabilities With Bayes' Theorem*   *637*

General Form of Bayes' Theorem   638

B.6   *Further Probability Revisions*   *639*

B.7   *Random Variables*   *640*

B.8   *Probability Distributions*   *641*

Probability Distribution of a Discrete Random Variable   642

Expected Value of a Discrete Probability Distribution   642

Variance of a Discrete Probability Distribution   643

Probability Distribution of a Continuous Random Variable   644

B.9   *The Normal Distribution*   645
Area under the Normal Curve   646
Using the Standard Normal Table   648
Haynes Construction Company
Example   649

B.10   *The Exponential Distribution*   651

B.11   *The Poisson Distribution*   652
Glossary   653
Key Equations   653
Discussion Questions and Problems   654

APPENDIX C   **Areas Under the Standard Normal
Curve   658**

APPENDIX D   **Solutions to Selected Problems   659**

APPENDIX E   **Solutions to Self-Tests   663**

INDEX   **666**

PREFACE

In recent years, the use of spreadsheets to teach decision modeling (alternatively referred to as management science, operations research, and quantitative analysis) has become standard practice in many business programs. This emphasis has revived interest in the field significantly, and several textbooks have attempted to discuss spreadsheet-based decision modeling. However, some of these textbooks have become too spreadsheet oriented, focusing more on the spreadsheet commands to use than on the underlying decision model. Other textbooks have maintained their algorithmic approach to decision modeling, adding spreadsheet instructions almost as an afterthought. In the second edition of Managerial Decision Modeling with Spreadsheets, we have continued to build on our success with the first edition in trying to achieve the perfect balance between the decision modeling process and the use of spreadsheets to set up and solve decision models.

It is important that textbooks that support decision modeling courses try to combine the student's power to logically model and analyze diverse decision-making scenarios with software-based solution procedures. Therefore, this second edition continues to focus on teaching the reader the skills needed to apply decision models to different kinds of organizational decision-making situations. The discussions are very application oriented and software based, with a view toward how a manager can effectively apply the models learned here to improve the decision-making process. The primary target audiences for this textbook are students in undergraduate- and graduate-level introductory decision modeling courses in business schools. However, this textbook will also be useful to students in other introductory courses that cover some of the core decision modeling topics, such as linear programming and simulation.

Although the emphasis in this second edition is on using spreadsheets for decision modeling, the textbook remains, at heart, a decision modeling textbook. That is, while we use spreadsheets as a tool to quickly set up and solve decision models, our aim is not to teach how to blindly use a spreadsheet without understanding how and why it works. To accomplish this, we discuss the fundamental concepts, assumptions, and limitations behind each decision modeling technique, show how each decision model works, and illustrate the real-world usefulness of each technique with many applications from both for-profit and not-for-profit organizations.

We have kept the notation, terminology, and equations standard with other textbooks, and we have tried to write a textbook that is easy to understand and use. Basic knowledge of algebra and Excel are the only prerequisites. For your convenience, we have included a brief introduction to Excel as an appendix.

This textbook's chapters, supplements, and software packages cover virtually every major topic in the decision modeling field and are arranged to provide a distinction between techniques that deal with deterministic environments and those that deal with probabilistic environments. Even though we have produced a somewhat smaller textbook that covers only the most important topics, we have still included more material than most instructors can cover in a typical first-year course. We hope that the resulting flexibility of topic selection is appreciated by instructors who need to tailor their courses to different audiences and curricula.

OVERALL APPROACH

While writing this second edition, we have continued to adhere to certain themes:

■ First, we have tried to separate the discussion of each decision modeling technique into three distinct issues:

1. Formulation or problem setup
2. Model solution
3. Interpretation of the results and what-if analysis

In this three-step framework, steps 1 and 3 (formulation and interpretation) call upon the manager's expertise. Mastering these steps now will give students a competitive advantage later, in the marketplace, when it is necessary to make business decisions. We therefore emphasize these steps.

■ Second, we recognize that business students are primarily going to be users of these decision modeling techniques rather than their developers. Hence, to deal with step 2 (model solution), we have integrated our discussions with software packages so that students can take full advantage of their availability. In this regard, the textbook exploits the wide availability and acceptability of spreadsheet-based software for decision modeling techniques.

Excel is a very important part of what most instructors consider the two main topics in any basic decision modeling textbook: linear programming and simulation. However, we recognize that some topics are not well suited for spreadsheet-based software. A case in point is project management, where Excel is generally not the best choice. In such cases, rather than try to force the topic to suit Excel, we have discussed the use of more practical packages, such as Microsoft Project.

■ Third, although we use software packages as the primary vehicle to deal with step 2, we try to ensure that students focus on what they are doing and why they are doing it, rather than just mechanically learning which Excel formula to use or which Excel button to press. To facilitate this, and to avoid the "black box syndrome," we also briefly discuss the steps and rationale of the solution process in many cases.

■ Fourth, we recognize that in this introductory textbook, the material does not need to be (and should not be) too comprehensive. Our aim here is to inform students about what is available with regard to decision modeling and pique their interest in the subject material. More detailed instruction can follow, if the student chooses, in advanced elective courses that may use more sophisticated software packages.

■ Finally, we note that most of the students in decision modeling courses are likely to specialize in other functional areas, such as finance, marketing, accounting, operations, and human resources. We therefore try to integrate decision modeling techniques with problems drawn from these different areas so that students can recognize the importance of what they are learning and the potential benefits of using decision modeling in real-world settings. In addition, we have included summaries of selected articles from journals such as *Interfaces* that discuss the actual application of decision modeling techniques to real-world problems.

MAJOR CHANGES IN THE SECOND EDITION

We have made the following major changes in this second edition of *Managerial Decision Modeling with Spreadsheets:*

- Significant number of new end-of-chapter exercises. Many of these exercises include multipart questions, giving instructors a rich pool of questions from which to select.

- The following new cases have been added: Chapter 2 (International Pharma), Chapter 3 (Bonnie Bagels, adapted from the U.S. second edition), Chapter 4 (Airy Dairy), Chapter 9 (Jupiter Corporation), Chapter 11 (Muskoka Land Development), and Chapter 12 (Forecasting Ticket Sales at CineBarn). In addition, the Canadian Military Electronics case in Chapter 3 has been expanded.

- More challenging chapter examples and end-of-chapter exercises—Many of the existing chapter examples and end-of-chapter exercises have been revised significantly to make them more rigorous and better suited to a computer-based solution environment.

- Expanded coverage of simulation (Chapter 11)—This textbook now includes additional chapter examples in revenue management, queuing, and project management. It continues to illustrate simulation in Excel both with and without Oracle Crystal Ball. It also discusses the use of Excel's Scenario Manager to vary multiple decision parameters simultaneously (in simulation without Oracle Crystal Ball).

- Expanded coverage of regression (Chapter 12)—This textbook now includes detailed discussion of how Excel's Data Analysis add-in can be used to develop simple and multiple regression models. It includes coverage of the statistical significance of the relationship, the standard error of the regression estimate, confidence intervals of the slopes, the confidence interval of the regression estimate, and multicollinearity.

- Expanded discussion of linear programming formulation (Chapter 2)—This textbook now includes a detailed set of guidelines designed to answer a frequent question that many students have: "How do I know my LP model is right?"

- Expanded discussion of nonlinear programming (Chapter 7)—This textbook now includes coverage of issues such as why nonlinear programming models are difficult to solve, local versus global optimal solutions, and ways to identify these solutions by using Solver.

- Expanded discussion of utility theory (Chapter 9)—This textbook now includes a discussion of the construction of utility curves, risk premiums, and exponential utility functions.

- Chapter 13 (Inventory Control Models) moved to the CD-ROM—Many of our adopters and reviewers indicated that this topic is usually taught as part of Operations Management courses at their institutions. Therefore, we have moved the entire chapter to the CD-ROM in an effort to improve and develop the content of the textbook without increasing its size.

UPDATED FEATURES IN THIS TEXTBOOK

The features of the first edition of this textbook that have been well received as effective aids to the learning process have been updated and expanded in this second edition. We hope that these features will continue to help us to better adhere to the themes listed previously and help students better understand the material. These include the following features:

- Consistent layout and format for creating effective Excel models—We use a consistent layout and format for creating spreadsheet models for all linear, integer, goal, and nonlinear programming problems. We strongly believe such a consistent approach is best suited to the beginning student of these types of decision models.

- Functional use of colour in the spreadsheets to clarify and illustrate good spreadsheet modeling—As part of the consistent layout and format for the spreadsheet models, we have standardized the use of colours so that the various components of the models are easily identifiable. For an excellent illustration of this feature, please see the front end papers of this edition.

- Description of the algebraic formulation and its spreadsheet implementation for all examples—For each model, we first discuss the algebraic formulation so that the student can understand the logic and rationale behind the decision model. The spreadsheet implementation then closely follows the algebraic formulation for ease of understanding.

- Numerous screen captures of Excel outputs, with detailed callouts explaining the important entries. Each screenshot has been annotated with detailed callouts explaining the important entries and components of the model. The front end papers of this edition provide a detailed illustration of this feature also. Excel files are included on the Student CD-ROM and, for your convenience, the callouts are shown as comments on appropriate cells in these Excel files.

- Ability to teach topics both with and without the use of additional add-ins or software—We have discussed several topics so that they can be studied either using Excel's standard built-in commands or using additional Excel add-ins or other software. For example, we have discussed how Excel's built-in Data Table and Scenario Manager procedures can be used to analyze and replicate even large simulation models. We have also discussed how Oracle Crystal Ball can be used to develop models in a more convenient manner, for students who want to install and use this software. Likewise, we have discussed how Microsoft Project can be used to effectively manage large projects.

- Extensive discussion of linear programming sensitivity analysis, using the Solver report—The discussion of linear programming sensitivity analysis in this textbook is more comprehensive than that in any competing textbook.

- Decision Modeling in Action boxes—These boxes summarize published articles that illustrate how real-world organizations have used decision models to solve problems.

- Chapter Vignettes—each chapter opens with an illustrative opening vignette based on real Canadian applications of the specific decision modeling technique introduced in the chapter. Vignettes have been updated to ensure that they faithfully reflect the nature of the application.

- Modeling in the Real World boxes—These boxes help students apply the steps of the decision modeling approach, first presented in Chapter 1, to every technique discussed in the textbook. In most chapters, real Canadian examples are discussed.

- History boxes—These boxes briefly describe how some decision modeling techniques were developed.

- Margin notes—These notes make it easier for students to understand and remember important points.

- Glossaries—A glossary at the end of each chapter defines important terms.

- Self-Tests (with answers) and Key Equations—These end of chapter features allow students to test their knowledge of important terms and concepts to help prepare for quizzes and examinations. The Key Equations list all the mathematical equations in a chapter for student reference and review.

- End-of-chapter bibliographies—Each chapter's bibliography provides a selection of more advanced textbooks and interesting articles. The bibliographies include several classic references that give students a flavour of the history and development of the decision modeling field.

- Companion Website—This textbook's Companion Website, at **www.pearsoned.ca/ render** contains interesting Internet links and several additional cases.

- Featured software tools—Microsoft Excel is the featured software tool in this textbook. Excel's Solver add-in is used extensively in several chapters to solve optimization decision modeling problems. For those choosing to use it, an expanded version of Solver called Premium Solver for Education is available on the Student CD-ROM. In addition, the textbook illustrates how powerful Excel add-ins such as Oracle Crystal Ball and TreePlan can be used to solve simulation and decision analysis models, respectively. These add-ins are also available on the Student CD-ROM. Other Excel procedures, such as Goal Seek, Data Table, and Scenario Manager, have also been explained in detail and used extensively.

- ExcelModules—This program from Professor Howard Weiss of Temple University solves problems and examples in the queuing models (Chapter 9), forecasting models (Chapter 11), and inventory control models (Chapter 12) chapters in this textbook. Students can see the power of this software package in modeling and solving problems in these chapters. ExcelModules is menu driven and easy to use, and it is available on the Student CD-ROM.

- Microsoft Project—This software is featured in the project management (Chapter 7) chapter to set up and manage projects. Readers can go to www.microsoft.com to get more information about this popular software.

COMPLIMENTARY SOFTWARE AND DATA FILES ON THE CD-ROM

As a convenience, the following items are conveniently packaged on the Student CD-ROM that is included as part of this textbook:

1. Premium Solver for Education Version 7.0

2. Access to a 140-day student version of Oracle Crystal Ball Version 11.0

3. TreePlan Version 1.70

4. ExcelModules

5. Excel files for all examples discussed in the textbook (For easy reference, the relevant file names are printed on the margins at appropriate places in the textbook.)

6. Chapter 13: Inventory Control Models

SUPPLEMENTS

- *Companion Website.* The Companion Website at **www.pearsoned.ca/render** contains an interactive study guide for students, which contains additional study questions, resource material and links to additional case studies.

The Instructor's Resource CD-Rom includes the following instructor supplements:

- *Instructor's Solutions Manual.* The Instructor's Solutions Manual includes all relevant Excel files and solutions for the end-of-chapter exercises and cases.

- *PowerPoint Presentation.* An extensive set of PowerPoint slides is available to adopters. The slides are oriented toward text learning objectives and build upon key concepts in the text.

- *TestGen.* This test-generating software allows instructors to custom design, save, and generate classroom tests. The test program permits instructors to edit, add, or delete questions from the test banks; edit existing graphics and create new graphics; analyze test results; and organize a database of tests and student results. This new software allows for greater flexibility and ease of use. It provides many options for organizing and displaying tests, along with a search and sort feature.

All of these instructor supplements are also available for download from a password-protected section of Pearson Education Canada's online catalogue (**www.pearsoned.ca/highered**). Navigate to your book's catalogue page to view a list of those supplements that are available. See your local sales representative for details and access.

ACKNOWLEDGMENTS

There are several people at Pearson Education Canada who worked very hard to bring the textbook through the publication process. First, we would like to give a special thanks to Gary Bennett, Vice President and Editorial Director, for all his help. His guidance and suggestions have been invaluable in making this textbook a reality and it has been a pleasure to work with him. We would also like to gratefully acknowledge the outstanding help provided by Rema Celio, the developmental editor; Lila Campbell, the production editor; and Marg Bukta, the freelance copy editor. I also wish to extend thanks to Avinash Chandra, Leigh-Anne Graham, Anthony Leung, Amanda McCormick, Nicole Mellow, and Laurel Sparrow for their excellent guidance and untiring efforts in the preparation of the second Canadian edition.

I would also like to thank my dear wife Haviva for her encouragement, her patience, and her many helpful suggestions. To my children, Tanya, Dov, Elana, and Danny, you are my best fans and I thank you for your steadfast love, support and encouragement while I worked on this project.

I would like to extend a special thanks to Ron Craig of Wilfrid Laurier University who provided two of the new case studies included in this edition (Chapters 2 and 11).

Finally, I would also like to express our sincere appreciation to the following reviewers:

Phil Troy, *McGill University*
Danny Cho, *Brock University*
Dan Phillips, *Georgian College*
Wojtek Michalowski, *University of Ottawa*
Rick Menking, *Trinity Western University*
Jim Watson, *Humber Institute of Technology and Advanced Learning*
Louie R. D'Orazio, *Mohawk College*

Brian Smith
514-398-4038 (phone)
514-398-3876 (fax)
brian.smith@mcgill.ca (email)

A Great Way to Learn and Instruct Online

The Pearson Education Canada Companion Website is easy to navigate and is organized to correspond to the chapters in this textbook. Whether you are a student in the classroom or a distance learner you will discover helpful resources for in-depth study and research that empower you in your quest for greater knowledge and maximize your potential for success in the course.

Companion Website

[www.pearsoned.ca/render]

Prentice Hall

Companion Website

Jump to... http://www.pearsoned.ca/render | Home Search Help Profile

Home >

Companion Website

Managerial Decision Modeling with Spreadsheets,
Second Canadian Edition, by Render, Stair, Balakrishnan, and Smith

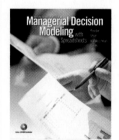

Student Resources

The modules in this section provide students with tools for learning course material. These modules include:

- Chapter Objectives
- Self-Study Questions: Multiple Choice, and Problem Set
- List of Key Terms
- Link to Internet Cases

In the self-study modules, students can send answers to the grader and receive instant feedback on their progress though the Results Reporter. Coaching comments and references to the textbook may be available to ensure that students take advantage of all available resources to enhance their learning experience.

Instructor Resources

A link to the protected Instructor's Central site provides instructors with additional teaching tools. Downloadable PowerPoint Presentations, and an Instructor's Manual are just some of the materials that may be available in this section. Where appropriate, this section will be password protected. To get a password, simply contact your Pearson Education Canada Representative or email Faculty Sales and Services at facultyservice@pearsoned.com.

CHAPTER 1

Introduction to Managerial Decision Modeling

LEARNING OBJECTIVES

After completing this chapter, students will be able to

1. Define a decision model and describe its importance.
2. Understand the two types of decision models: deterministic and probabilistic models.
3. Understand the steps involved in developing decision models in practical situations.
4. Understand the use of spreadsheets in developing decision models.
5. Discuss possible problems in developing decision models.

CHAPTER OUTLINE

1.1 Introduction

1.2 What Is Decision Modeling?

1.3 Steps Involved in Decision Modeling

1.4 Spreadsheet Example of a Decision Model: Tax Computation

1.5 Spreadsheet Example of Another Decision Model: Break-Even Analysis

1.6 Possible Problems in Developing Decision Models

1.7 Implementation—Not Just the Final Step

Summary • Glossary • Key Equations • Self-Test • Discussion Questions and Problems • Bibliography

Management Science Saves Millions at Canadian Pacific Railway

In the mid-1990s Canadian Pacific Railway (CPR) was struggling with high operating costs, low productivity, and rising service requirements.

The CPR network includes 22 000 kilometres of track, stretching from Montreal to Vancouver, and 250 rail yards. The company employs 15 000 people (including 5000 crew members) and has a fleet of 16 000 locomotives and 65 000 rail cars. Every day, CPR's 6000 customers provide about 7000 new shipments heading to 10 000 distinct pairs of origins and destinations.

Source: © Colin Garratt; Milepost 92 1/2 /Corbis

A major paradigm shift was envisaged that would change CPR's traditional operating strategies for moving freight. Like all major North American freight railroads, CPR relied heavily on a tonnage-based operating system in which trains ran only when enough traffic was accumulated to justify the expenses. The new game plan was to change to a schedule-based system in which customer needs drove operations. This was a radical concept for freight rail.

CEO Robert Ritchie admits that he didn't have all the answers, but something in his background told him that operations research and management science held the key. Consequently, he contacted MultiModal Applied Systems, which started by breaking down the enormous operating plan problem into a series of subproblems, which they then attacked sequentially, using MultiRail. MultiRail is MultiModal's unique software solution packed with tools and techniques based on management science and operations research (MS/OR), including heuristic algorithms, optimization, network flow models, and simulation.

Traffic data from the previous year, combined with a forecasting model, gave MultiModal direct access to details of CPR's traffic volume, reflecting both marketing projections and seasonal effects. Working with MultiModal, CPR developed an operating plan that was matched to traffic patterns, optimizing the routing and classification plan for each railcar movement while determining which trains to run.

MultiRail generates up to one million trip plans at a time and produces a viable solution in a matter of minutes. Here are some statistics associated with a "perfectly" executed solution:

- 41% improvement in railcar velocity (time required to move from Point A to Point B);
- 40% increase in labour productivity;

- 16% reduction in fuel consumption;
- 35% improvement in locomotive productivity;
- 19% increase in profits.

Overall, the model-driven operating plan reduced CPR's cost base by $300 million. A subsequent audit of fuel and crew costs identified another $200 million in savings, pushing the total cost savings to more than half a billion dollars.

Peter Horner. "On the Right Track," *OR/MS Today* 30, 3 (June 2003).

1.1   INTRODUCTION

Just like Canadian Pacific Railway in the preceding application, organizations such as Air Canada, IBM, and Bell Telephone frequently use decision models to help solve complex problems. Although mathematical tools have been in existence for thousands of years, the formal study and application of quantitative (or mathematical) decision modeling techniques to practical decision making is largely a product of the twentieth century. The decision modeling techniques studied here have been applied successfully to an increasingly wide variety of complex problems in business, government, health care, education, and many other areas. Many such successful uses are discussed throughout this textbook.

It isn't enough, though, just to know the mathematical details of how a particular decision modeling technique can be set up and solved. It is equally important to be familiar with the limitations, assumptions, and specific applicability of the model. The correct use of decision modeling techniques usually results in solutions that are timely, accurate, flexible, economical, reliable, easy to understand, and easy to use.

1.2   WHAT IS DECISION MODELING?

The types of models include physical, scale, schematic, and mathematical models.

In general, a **model** refers to an abstract or physical construct that represents some real phenomenon or object. We study the model not for its own sake, but because it represents something of interest in the real world. For example, an architect may first draw a two-dimensional diagram to represent a building project. The diagram is a model of the building that can be studied, critiqued, and improved upon. Subsequently, a three-dimensional scale model can be constructed to more closely approximate the final project. In management science we use mathematical models that describe a system by means of variables whose values represent some properties of the system being studied. The actual model is the set of functions that describe the relations between the different variables. Management science models can be *deterministic* (i.e., they work the same way for a given set of initial conditions), or *probabilistic* or *stochastic* (i.e., an element of randomness means different results can be reached from the identical set of initial conditions).

Decision modeling is a scientific approach to decision making.

There are several definitions for **decision modeling**. We define it here as a scientific approach to managerial decision making. Alternatively, we can define it as a representation (usually mathematical) of a practical problem scenario or environment. The resulting model should typically be such that the decision-making process is not affected by personal bias, whim, emotions, and guesswork. Decision modeling is also commonly referred to as *quantitative analysis, management science,* or *operations research.* In this textbook, we prefer the term *decision modeling,* since we will discuss all modeling techniques in a managerial decision-making context.

Any decision modeling process starts with data. Like raw material for a factory, these data are manipulated or processed into information that is valuable to people making

The decision modeling process starts with data.

decisions. This processing and manipulating of raw data into meaningful information is the heart of decision modeling.

Quantitative versus Qualitative Data

Both qualitative and quantitative factors must be considered.

In dealing with a decision-making problem, managers may have to consider both qualitative and quantitative factors. For example, suppose we are considering several different investment alternatives, such as certificates of deposit (CDs), the stock market, and real estate.

We can use *quantitative* factors such as rates of return, financial ratios, and cash flows in our decision model to guide our ultimate decision. In addition to these factors, however, we may also want to consider *qualitative* factors such as pending provincial or territorial and federal legislation, technological breakthroughs, and the outcome of an upcoming election. It be difficult to quantify these qualitative factors.

Data that are used in a model to arrive at a final solution.

Due to the presence (and relative importance) of qualitative factors, the role of quantitative decision modeling in the decision-making process can vary. When qualitative factors are not involved, and when the problem, model, and **input data** remain reasonably stable over time, the results of a decision model can automate the decision-making process. For example, some companies use quantitative inventory models to determine automatically when to order materials and how much to order. In most cases, however, decision modeling will be an aid to the decision-making process. The results of decision modeling will be combined with qualitative information to make decisions in practice.

Role of Spreadsheets in Decision Modeling

Spreadsheet packages are capable of handling many decision modeling techniques.

Computers have become an integral part of the decision modeling process in today's business environments. Until the early 1990s, many of the modeling techniques discussed here required specialized software packages. However, spreadsheet packages such as Microsoft Excel can now handle most of the techniques commonly used in practical situations. For this reason, the current trend in college and university courses is to focus on spreadsheet-based instruction. In keeping with this trend, we discuss the role and use of spreadsheets (specifically Microsoft Excel) during our study of the different decision modeling techniques presented here.

Several add-ins for Excel are included in your CD-ROM.

In addition to discussing some of Excel's built-in functions and procedures (e.g., Goal Seek, Data Table, and Chart Wizard), we also discuss several add-ins for Excel. The Solver add-in comes standard with Excel; others are included in the CD-ROM that accompanies this textbook. Table 1.1 lists these add-ins and indicates the chapter and topic in which each one is discussed and used.

HISTORY   The Origin of Decision Modeling

Decision modeling has been in existence since the beginning of recorded history, but it was Frederick W. Taylor who, in the early twentieth century, pioneered the principles of the scientific approach to management. During World War II, many new scientific and quantitative techniques were developed to assist the military. These new developments were so successful that, after World War II, many companies started using similar techniques in managerial decision making and planning. Today, many organizations employ a staff of operations research or management science

personnel or consultants to apply the principles of scientific management to problems and opportunities. The terms *management science, operations research*, and *quantitative analysis* can be used interchangeably, though here we use *decision modeling*.

The origin of many of the techniques discussed in this book can be traced to individuals and organizations that have applied the principles of scientific management first developed by Taylor; they are discussed in *History* boxes scattered throughout the book.

TABLE 1.1	EXCEL ADD-IN USED IN TOPIC		
Excel Add-ins Included in Your CD-ROM	Premium Solver for Education v7.0 (enhanced version of the Solver add-in that is included with Microsoft Excel)	Chapters 2–8	Linear programming, Network flows, Integer programming, Goal programming, Nonlinear programming, and Project management
	TreePlan v1.70	Chapter 9	Decision theory
	Oracle Crystal Ball v11.0	Chapter 11	Simulation
	Excel Modules (custom software provided with this textbook)	Chapters 10, 12, and 13	Queuing models, Forecasting models, and Inventory control models

A knowledge of basic Excel commands and mechanics will facilitate understanding of the techniques and concepts discussed here. If you are not familiar with Excel, we recommend reading Appendix A, which provides a brief overview of those Excel features most useful in decision modeling. In addition, throughout this textbook we discuss Excel functions and procedures specific to each decision modeling technique.

Types of Decision Models

Decision models can be broadly classified into two categories based on the type and nature of the problem environment under consideration: (1) deterministic models and (2) probabilistic models. The following sections define each of these types of models.

Deterministic means with complete certainty.

Deterministic Models   Deterministic models assume that all the relevant input data are known with certainty; that is, they assume that all the information needed for modeling the decision-making problem environment is available, with fixed and known values. An example of such a model would be the case of Dell Corporation, which makes several different types of PC products (e.g., desktops, laptops), all of which compete for the same resources (e.g., labour, hard disks, chips, working capital). Suppose Dell knows the specific amounts of each resource required to make one unit of each type of PC and the expected profit contribution per unit of each type of PC. In such an environment, if Dell decides on a specific production plan, it is a simple task to compute the quantity required of each resource to satisfy this production plan. For example, if Dell plans to ship 5000 units of a specific model and each unit includes two speakers, then Dell will need 10 000 speakers. Likewise, it is easy to compute the total profit that will be realized by this production plan (assuming that Dell can sell all the PCs it makes).

Resources include labour, raw materials, machine time, and working capital.

The most commonly used deterministic modeling technique is linear programming.

Perhaps the most common and popular deterministic modeling technique is linear programming (LP). In Chapter 2, we first formulate small LP models. Then we show how these models can be set up and solved using Excel. We extend our discussion of LP in Chapter 3 to more complex problems, which are drawn from a variety of business disciplines. In Chapter 4, we study how the solution to LP models produces, as a byproduct, a great deal of information that is useful for managerial interpretation of results. Finally, in Chapters 5, 6, and 7, we study a few extensions to LP models. These include several different network flow models (Chapter 5), and integer, nonlinear, and multi-objective (goal) programming models (Chapters 6 and 7).

As we demonstrate during our study of deterministic models, a variety of important managerial decision-making problems can be set up and solved using these techniques. Moreover, it is possible to solve very large models of this type very quickly using available software packages.

Some input data are unknown in probabilistic models.

Probabilistic models use probabilities to incorporate uncertainty.

Probabilistic Models In contrast to deterministic models, **probabilistic models** (also called *stochastic models*) assume that some input data are not known with certainty. That is, they assume that the values of some important variables will not be known *before* decisions are made. It is therefore important to incorporate this "ignorance" into the model. An example would be deciding whether to start a new internet-based venture. As we saw during the slump in technology stocks in 2000–2002, the success of such ventures is uncertain. However, the investors (e.g., venture capitalists, founders) have to make decisions regarding this venture based on their expectations of future performance. Clearly, there is no guarantee that such expectations will be fulfilled. In recent years, we have seen several examples of firms that have lived up to their expectations (e.g., eBay) and several that have not (e.g., EToys).

Probabilistic modeling techniques incorporate uncertainty by using probabilities on these "random" or unknown variables. Probabilistic modeling techniques discussed in this textbook include decision analysis (Chapter 9), queuing models (Chapter 10), simulation models (Chapter 11), and forecasting (Chapter 12). Two other techniques, project management (Chapter 8) and inventory models (Chapter 13), include aspects of both deterministic and probabilistic modeling.

For each modeling technique, we discuss what kinds of criteria can be used when there is uncertainty and how to use spreadsheets to find optimal decisions. In this context, we use Excel add-ins such as Oracle Crystal Ball, TreePlan, and Excel Modules (see Table 1.1).

Since uncertainty plays a vital role in probabilistic models, some knowledge of basic probability and statistical concepts is useful here. Appendix B provides a brief overview of this topic as a refresher.

1.3   STEPS INVOLVED IN DECISION MODELING

The decision modeling process involves three steps.

It is common to iterate between the three steps.

Regardless of the size and complexity of the decision-making problem at hand, the decision modeling process involves three distinct steps: (1) formulation, (2) solution, and (3) interpretation. Figure 1.1 provides a schematic overview of these steps along with the components or parts of each step. We discuss each of these steps in the following sections.

It is important to note that it is common to have an iterative process between these three steps before the final solution is obtained. For example, testing the solution (see Figure 1.1) might reveal that the model is incomplete or that some of the input data are being measured incorrectly. This means that the formulation needs to be revised. This, in turn, would cause all of the subsequent steps to be changed.

Step 1: Formulation

Formulation is the most challenging step in decision modeling.

Formulation is the process by which each aspect of the problem scenario is translated and expressed in terms of a mathematical model. This is perhaps the most important and challenging step in decision modeling, since the results of a poorly formulated problem will almost surely be wrong. It is also in this step that the decision maker's ability to analyze a problem rationally comes into play. Even the most sophisticated software program will not automatically formulate a problem. The aim in formulation is to ensure that the mathematical model completely addresses all the issues relevant to the problem at hand. Formulation can be further classified into three parts: (1) defining a problem, (2) developing a model, and (3) acquiring input data.

Defining the problem can be the most important part of formulation.

Defining the Problem The first part of formulation (and in decision modeling) is to develop a clear, concise statement of the **decision problem**. This statement will give direction and meaning to all the parts that follow it.

Defining the problem is perhaps the most important, and often the most difficult, part. It is essential to go beyond just the symptoms of the problem at hand and identify the true

FIGURE 1.1

**The Decision Modeling
Approach**

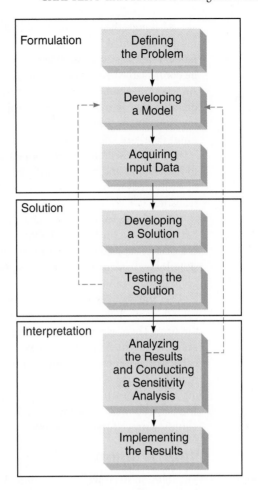

causes behind it. One problem may be related to other problems, and solving a problem without regard to related problems can actually make the situation worse. Thus, it is important to analyze how the solution to one problem affects other problems or the decision-making environment in general. Experience has shown that bad problem definition is a major reason for the failure of management science groups to serve their organizations well.

When the problem is difficult to quantify, it may be necessary to develop *specific, measurable* objectives. For example, say a problem is defined as inadequate health care delivery in a hospital. The objectives might be to increase the number of beds, reduce the average number of days a patient spends in the hospital, increase the physician-to-patient ratio, and so on. When objectives are used, however, the real problem should be kept in mind. It is important to avoid choosing specific and measurable objectives that do not solve the real problem.

Developing a Model   Once you select the problem to be analyzed, the next part is to develop a decision model. Even though you might not be aware of it, you have been using models most of your life. For example, you may have developed the following model about friendship: Friendship is based on reciprocity, an exchange of favours. Hence, if you need a favour such as a small loan, your model would suggest that you ask a friend.

What sets decision modeling apart from other modeling techniques is that the models we develop here are mathematical. A *mathematical model* is a set of mathematical relationships. In most cases, these relationships are expressed as equations and inequalities, as they are in a spreadsheet model that computes sums, averages, or standard deviations.

A variable is a measurable quantity that is subject to change.

A parameter is a measurable quantity that usually has a known value.

Although there is considerable flexibility in the development of models, most of the models presented here contain one or more variables and parameters. A **variable**, as the name implies, is a measurable quantity that may vary or is subject to change. Variables can be controllable or uncontrollable. A controllable variable is also called a *decision variable*. An example would be how many inventory items to order. A **parameter** is a measurable quantity that is inherent in the problem, such as the cost of placing an order for more inventory items. In most cases, variables are unknown quantities, whereas parameters (or input data) are known quantities.

All models should be developed carefully. They should be solvable, realistic, and easy to understand and modify, and the required input data should be obtainable. The model developer has to be careful to include the appropriate amount of detail to be solvable yet realistic.

Acquiring Input Data   Once we have developed a model, we must obtain the input data to be used in the model. Obtaining accurate data is essential, since even if the model is a perfect representation of reality, improper data will produce misleading results. This situation is called **garbage in, garbage out (GIGO)**. For larger problems, collecting accurate data can be one of the more difficult aspects of decision modeling.

"Garbage in, garbage out" means that improper data will produce misleading results.

Several sources can be used for collecting data. Company reports and documents provide some data. Another source is interviews with employees or other people related to the firm. Their experience and judgment can be invaluable. A production supervisor, for example, might be able to tell you very accurately how long it takes to manufacture a particular product. Sampling and direct measurement are other sources of data for the model. You may need to know how many kilograms of a raw material are used in producing a new photochemical product. This information can be obtained by going to the plant and actually measuring the amount of raw material being used. In other cases, statistical sampling procedures can be used.

Step 2: Solution

In the solution step, we solve the mathematical expressions in the formulation.

The solution step involves actually solving the mathematical expressions resulting from the formulation process to identify the optimal solution. Until the mid-1990s, typical courses in decision modeling focused a significant portion of their attention on this step, since it was the most difficult aspect of the modeling process. The focus today has shifted from the detailed steps of the solution process toward the availability and use of software packages. The solution step can be further broken down into two parts: (1) developing a solution and (2) testing the solution.

An algorithm is a series of steps that are repeated.

The input data and the model determine the accuracy of the solution.

Developing a Solution   Developing a solution involves manipulating the model to arrive at the best (or optimal) solution to the problem. In some cases, this may require that a set of mathematical expressions be solved for the best decision. In other cases, you can use a trial-and-error method, trying various approaches and picking the one that results in the best decision. For some problems, you may want to try all possible values for the variables in the model to arrive at the best decision. This is called complete enumeration. For difficult, complex problems you may be able to use an algorithm. An **algorithm** consists of a series of steps or procedures that are repeated until you find the best solution. Regardless of the approach used, the accuracy of the solution depends on the accuracy of the input data and on the decision model itself.

An alternative approach that recognizes the difficulty of developing algorithms to solve computationally intractable problems in a reasonable amount of time is the **heuristic** approach. This approach attempts to find very good, but not necessarily optimal, solutions by using a combination of techniques involving empirical methods and trial and error.

Analysts test the data and model before analyzing the results.

Testing the Solution   Before a solution can be analyzed and implemented, it must be tested completely. Since the solution depends on the input data and the model, both require testing. There are several ways to test input data. One is to collect additional data from a different source and use statistical tests to compare these new data with the original data. If there are significant differences, more effort is required to obtain accurate input data. If the data are accurate but the results are inconsistent with the problem, the model itself may not be appropriate. In this case, the model should be checked to make sure that it is logical and represents the real situation.

Step 3: Interpretation and What-If Analysis

Assuming the formulation is correct and has been successfully implemented and solved, how does a manager use the results? Here again the decision maker's expertise is called upon, since it is up to him or her to recognize the implications of the results that are presented. We discuss this step in two parts: (1) analyzing the results and conducting a sensitivity analysis and (2) implementing the results.

Analyzing the Results and Conducting a Sensitivity Analysis   Analyzing the results starts with determining the implications of the solution. In most cases, a solution to a problem will result in some kind of action or change in the way an organization is operating. The implications of these actions or changes must be determined and analyzed before the results are implemented.

Sensitivity analysis determines how the solutions will change with a different model or input data.

Because a model is only an approximation of reality, the sensitivity of the solution to changes in the model and input data is an important part of analyzing the results. This type of analysis is called **sensitivity analysis** or **post-optimality analysis**. It determines how much the solution will change if there are changes in the model or the input data. When the optimal solution is very sensitive to changes in the input data and the model specifications, additional testing must be performed to make sure the model and input data are accurate and valid.

The importance of sensitivity analysis cannot be overemphasized. Because input data may not always be accurate or model assumptions may not be completely appropriate, sensitivity analysis can become an important part of decision modeling.

Implementing the Results   The final part is to *implement* the results. This can be much more difficult than you might imagine. Even if the optimal solution will result in millions of dollars in additional profits, if managers resist the new solution, the model is of no value. Experience has shown that many decision modeling teams have failed because they did not implement a good, workable solution properly.

The solution should be closely monitored even after implementation.

After the solution has been implemented, it should be closely monitored. Over time, there may be numerous changes that call for modifications of the original solution. A changing economy, fluctuating demand, and model enhancements requested by managers and decision makers are only a few examples of changes that might require the analysis to be modified.

Decision Modeling in the Real World

The decision modeling approach discussed so far is not just a series of theoretical steps. These steps, shown in Figure 1.1, are the building blocks of any successful use of decision modeling. As seen in our first **Modeling in the Real World** box (on page 10), the steps of the decision modeling approach can be used to help a large country such as China plan for critical energy needs now and for decades into the future. Throughout this textbook, you will see how this approach is being used to help countries and companies of all sizes save millions of dollars, plan for the future, increase revenues, and provide higher-quality products and services. The Modeling in the Real World boxes in every chapter demonstrate the power and importance of decision modeling in solving real problems for real organizations. Using the steps of decision modeling, however, does not guarantee success. These steps must be applied carefully.

MODELING IN THE REAL WORLD

Assigning Locomotives and Railway Cars at VIA Rail Canada

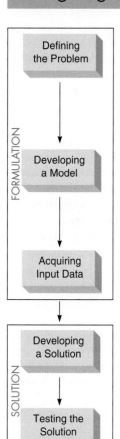

VIA Rail Canada operates a periodic train schedule and maintains a fleet consisting of several types of equipment. VIA Rail has to ensure that every train is assigned appropriate equipment, safety regulations and repair schedules are met, and idle time is minimized for train cars.

A large-scale assignment model was implemented at VIA Rail Canada to solve the simultaneous locomotive and car assignment problem. The model is quite versatile and can be applied to similar railcar assignment problems. (An assignment model is a particular type of LP model that will be covered in depth in Chapters 2 to 6. The assignment model itself is presented in Chapter 5, Section 6.)

Historical data on train departure and arrival times as well as customer demand for first-class and second-class passenger seats were collected.

The locomotive and car assignment problem is solved every few months when the train schedule is updated. The data acquired from these updates can be used for planning train schedules over shorter periods.

The periodic nature of the problem ensures that solutions produced by the assignment model are subject to ongoing inspection and evaluation.

The model assumes that several inputs (e.g., the number of cars a locomotive can pull, seating capacity for passenger cars, etc.) are fixed, when in fact there is considerable variation in these parameters. Sensitivity analysis is used to explore the impact of changes in the parameters.

The model is used on a regular basis to determine the optimal assignment of locomotives and railcars at VIA Rail Canada.

Source: Jean-François Cordeau, Guy Desaulniers, Norbert Lingaya, François Soumis, and Jacques Desrosiers. "Simultaneous locomotive and car assignment at VIA Rail Canada," *Transportation Research* Part B 35, 8 (September 2001): 767–787.

Now that we have explained what a decision model is, let us develop a simple model for a real-world situation that we all face each year, namely, paying taxes. Bob Miller has just completed his B.Com. degree and will be working as an independent consultant. In 2009 he will be filing his income tax for the first time as a self-employed person. However, since his income is not taxed at the source, he wants to start making quarterly payments in 2008 based on projected income, so he is not hit with a huge tax bill in 2009. Bob's income is subject to variability, but he decides to do a rough estimate of his expected federal tax contribution for 2008. (This calculation will not strictly adhere to Canadian tax principles; Bob will perform a more detailed tax computation in consultation with his accountant before filing his tax return at the end of April.) Bob has the following information available to help in developing his decision model:

- He would like to put away 5% of his gross income in a registered retirement savings plan (RRSP), up to a maximum of $5000.
- He does not have any income from dividends or capital gains.
- He is entitled to a personal deduction of $7634.
- He can claim as a nonrefundable tax credit medical expenses that are more than 3% of his net income or $1728, whichever is less.
- He does not anticipate having any other deductions from his income for tax purposes.
- The tax brackets are 16% up to $30 745, 22% between $30 746 and $61 509, 26% between $61 510 and $100 000, and 29% for incomes greater than $100 000. Bob Miller does not believe the higher tax brackets are relevant for him in 2008. He is sure, however, that he will have taxable income in the 22% tax bracket.

To help decide the estimated taxes he should pay to the Canada Revenue Agency each quarter, Bob would like to set up a spreadsheet-based decision model. Screenshot 1.1A shows the formulas that we can use to develop this model.

File: 1-1.xls

SCREENSHOT 1.1A

Formula View of the Excel Layout for Bob Miller's Tax Computation

	A	B	C	D
1	**Bob Miller's Quarterly Tax Computation**			
2				
3	**Problem Parameters**			
4	Retirement Savings % of gross income	0.05		
5	Maximum RRSP contribution	5000		
6	Personal exemption	7634		
7	Maximum medical exemption	1728		
8	Tax brackets	0.16	up to	30745
9		0.22	up to	61509
10				
11	**Input Data**			
12	Gross income			
13	Medical expenses			
14				
15	**Tax Computation**			
16	RRSP contribution	=MIN(B4*B12,B5)		
17	Personal exemption	=B6		
18	Net Income	=B12-SUM(B16:B17)		
19	Tax @ 16% rate	=B8*MIN(B18,$D$8)		
20	Tax @ 22% rate	=IF(B18>D8,B9*(B18-$D$8),0)		
21	Total tax before medical deduction	=SUM(B19:B20)		
22	Medical deduction	=MIN($B$13-0.03*B18,$B$7)		
23	Total tax after medical deduction	=B21-B22		
24	Estimated tax per quarter	=B23/4		

This box shows all the *known* input parameters.

This box shows the two input variables.

Minimum of 5% of income, or $4000.

16% tax up to $30 745

22% tax between $30 745 and $61 509

Quarterly tax payments

Excel Notes

■ The CD-ROM that accompanies this textbook contains the Excel file for each example problem discussed here. The relevant file name is shown on the margin next to each example.
■ In each of our Excel layouts, for clarity, we colour-code the cells as follows:
  ■ input cells, in which we enter the problem data, are shaded yellow.
  ■ output cells, showing the results of our analysis, are shaded green.

The known problem data (i.e., constants) are shown in the box labelled Problem Parameters. Rather than use these known constant values directly in the formulas, we recommend that you develop the habit of entering each known value in a cell and then using that cell reference in the formulas. In addition to being more "elegant," this way of modeling has the advantage of making any future changes to these values easy.

Cells B12 and B13 denote the input data, namely, Bob's projected gross income and projected medical expenses for 2008. These entries represent the only two variables in this decision model. Using these variables, the results are now computed in cells B17:B25 and presented in the box labelled Tax Computation in Screenshot 1.1B.

Cell B17 calculates Bob's tax-deductible contribution to the RRSP. Note that this amount is the smaller value of 5% of his gross income, or $5000. Cell B18 specifies his personal exemption, and cell B19 calculates his net income as the difference between his gross income and the sum of his RRSP contribution and his personal exemption. The taxes payable at the 16% rate and 22% rates are then calculated in cells B20 and B21, respectively. Cell B22 shows the total tax before medical expenses. Cell B23 calculates Bob's allowable medical deduction and the total tax after subtracting the medical exemption is computed in cell B24. Finally, the estimated quarterly tax contribution is computed in cell B25.

Now that we have developed this decision model, how can Bob Miller actually use it? Suppose Bob estimates his income in 2008 at $45 000 and, based on last year's medical expenses, he estimates his medical expenses for 2008 at $2000. When we enter these values

SCREENSHOT 1.1B   **Excel Decision Model for Bob Miller's Tax Computation**

	A	B	C	D
1	**Bob Miller's Quarterly Tax Computation**			
2				
3	**Problem Parameters**			
4	Retirement Savings % of gross income	5.0%		
5	Maximum RRSP contribution	$5,000		
6	Personal exemption	$7,634		
7	Maximum medical exemption	$1,728		
8	Tax brackets	16%	up to	$30,745.00
9		22%	up to	$61,509.00
10				
11	**Input Data**			
12	Gross income	$45,000.00		
13	Medical expenses	$2,000.00		
14				
15				
16	**Tax Computation**			
17	RRSP contribution	$2,250.00		
18	Personal exemption	$7,634.00		
19	Net Income	$35,116.00		
20	Tax @ 16% rate	$4,919.20		
21	Tax @ 22% rate	961.62		
22	Total tax before medical deduction	$5,880.82		
23	Medical deduction	$946.52		
24	Total tax after medical deduction	$4,934.30		
25	Estimated tax per quarter	$1,233.58		

Projected incomes and expenses for 2008.

Bob Miller should pay $1233.58 in taxes each quarter.

in cells B12 and B13, respectively, the decision model lets us know that Bob should pay estimated federal taxes of $1233.58 each quarter. These input values, and the resulting computations, are shown in Screenshot 1.1B. We can use this decision model in a similar fashion with any other projected income values for Bob Miller.

Observe that the decision model we have developed for Bob Miller's example does not optimize the decision in any way. That is, the model simply computes the estimated taxes for a given income level. It does not, for example, determine whether these taxes can be reduced in some way by better tax planning. Later in this textbook, we discuss decision models that will not only help compute the implications of a particular specified decision, but also help identify the optimal decision, based on some objective or goal.

DECISION MODELING IN ACTION
Management Science/Operations Research in Canada

In Canada, people with operations research (O.R.) training are found in special O.R. teams in many areas of both public and private organizations. Also, O.R. methodology is applied by economists, engineers, scientists, administrators, and executives in solving management and policy problems. The O.R. approach is currently used in at least 30 federal departments or agencies, 50 provincial ones, and 20 or more city or municipal governments. It is being heavily used in many Canadian management and consulting companies, in several hundred commercial and industrial companies, in many provinces in Canada, in Canadian banks, insurance and trust companies, and in councils, foundations, and research institutes.

Since its introduction in Canada almost 50 years ago, O.R.

has become widely used by decision makers and managers. Its applications are still expanding.

The breadth and complexity of problems undertaken by O.R. analysts have been increasing, prompting the development of new techniques and methods to meet these new problems. This has stimulated a growing awareness on the part of managers in all sectors of government, business, and industry of the need for such skills and techniques and a growing confidence in what O.R. can do for management and decision making. In both the private and the public sectors, there is an increasing demand, and need, for O.R. services.

Source: Canadian Operational Research Society. Homepage: http://www. ryerson.ca/~vquan/cors/whatisor.htm

1.5   SPREADSHEET EXAMPLE OF ANOTHER DECISION MODEL: BREAK-EVEN ANALYSIS

Expenses include fixed and variable costs.

Let us now develop another decision model—this one to compute the total profit (and associated break-even point) for a firm. We know that the profit is simply the difference between revenues and expenses. In most cases, we can express revenues as the selling price per unit, multiplied by the number of units sold. Likewise, we can express expenses as the sum of the total fixed and variable costs. In turn, the total variable cost is the variable cost per unit, multiplied by the number of units sold. Thus, we can express profit using the following mathematical expression:

$$\text{Profit} = \text{Selling price per unit} \times \text{Number of units} - \text{Fixed cost} \quad (1\text{-}1)$$
$$- \text{Variable cost per unit} \times \text{Number of units}$$

We use the Bill Pritchett clock repair shop example to demonstrate the creation of a decision model to calculate profit (and associated break-even point). Bill's company, Pritchett's Precious Time Pieces, buys, sells, and repairs old clocks and clock parts. Bill sells rebuilt springs for a unit price of $10. The fixed cost of the equipment to build the springs is $1000. The variable cost per unit is $5 for spring material. If we represent the number of springs (units) sold as the variable X, we can restate the profit as follows:

$$\text{Profit} = \$10X - \$1000 - \$5X$$

The BEP results in $0 profit.

Screenshot 1.2A shows the formulas used in developing the decision model for Bill Pritchett's example. Cells B4, B5, and B6 show the known problem parameter values, namely, revenue per unit, fixed cost, and variable cost per unit, respectively. Cell B9 is the lone decision variable in the model and represents the number of units sold (i.e., X). Using these entries, the total revenue, total variable cost, total cost, and profit are computed in cells B12, B14, B15 and B16, respectively. For example, if we enter a value of 1000 units for X in cell B9, the profit is calculated as $4000 in cell B16, as shown in Screenshot 1.2B.

In addition to computing the profit, decision makers are often interested in the **break-even point (BEP)**. The BEP is the number of units sold that will result in total revenue equaling total costs (i.e., profit is $0). We can determine the BEP analytically by setting profit equal to $0 and solving for X in Bill Pritchett's profit expression. That is,

$$0 = \text{Selling price per unit} \times \text{Number of units} - \text{Fixed cost}$$
$$- \text{Variable cost per unit} \times \text{Number of units}$$

which can be mathematically rewritten as

$$\text{Number of units (BEP)} = \frac{\text{Fixed cost}}{\text{Selling price per unit} - \text{Variable cost per unit}} \quad (1\text{-}2)$$

For Bill Pritchett's example, we can compute the BEP as $1000/($10 − $5) = 200 springs. The **BEP in dollars** (which we denote as **BEP$_\$$**) can then be computed as

$$\text{BEP}_\$ = \text{Fixed cost} + \text{Variable cost per unit} \times \text{BEP} \quad (1\text{-}3)$$

For Bill Pritchett's example, we can compute BEP$_\$$ as $1000 + $5 × 200 = $2000.

Using Goal Seek to Find the Break-Even Point

Excel's Goal Seek can be used to automatically find the BEP.

Although the preceding analytical computations for BEP and BEP$_\$$ are fairly simple, the spreadsheet-based decision model shown in Screenshot 1.2B can be used to automatically calculate these values. To do so, we use a feature in Excel called **GOAL SEEK**. This feature allows us to specify a goal or target for a specific cell and the cell that must be automatically manipulated to achieve this target. In our case, we want to manipulate the value of the number of units X (in cell B9 of Screenshot 1.2B) such that the profit (in cell B16 of Screenshot 1.2B) takes on a value of 0. Observe that the formula of profit in cell B16 is a function of the value of X in cell B9 (see Screenshot 1.2A).

Formula View of the Excel Layout for Pritchett's Precious Time Pieces

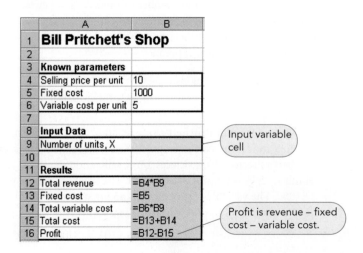

SCREENSHOT 1.2B

Excel Decision Model for Pritchett's Precious Time Pieces

	A	B
1	**Bill Pritchett's Shop**	
2		
3	**Known parameters:**	
4	Selling price per unit	$10.00
5	Fixed cost	$1,000.00
6	Variable cost per unit	$5.00
7		
8	**Input Data**	
9	Number of units, X	1000
10		
11	**Results**	
12	Total revenue	$10,000.00
13	Fixed cost	$1,000.00
14	Total variable cost	$5,000.00
15	Total cost	$6,000.00
16	Profit	$4,000.00

Profit is $4000 if 1000 units are sold.

Screenshot 1.2C shows how the Goal Seek feature works in Excel. Go to Goal Seek by clicking **TOOLS|GOAL SEEK** on Excel's main menu bar. The window shown in Screenshot 1.2C(a) is displayed. Specify cell B16 as the **SET CELL**, with a desired value of 0 for this cell, and cell B9 as the **CHANGING CELL**. Click OK. The **GOAL SEEK STATUS** window shown in Screenshot 1.2C(c) should display, indicating that the target of $0 profit has been achieved. Cell B9 shows the resulting BEP value of 200 units. The corresponding BEP$ value of $2000 is shown in cell B15.

Observe that we can use Goal Seek to compute the sales level needed to obtain any desired profit. For example, see if you can verify that in order to get a profit of $10 000, Bill Pritchett would have to sell 2200 springs.

SCREENSHOT 1.2C

Using Excel's Goal Seek to Compute the Break-Even Point for Pritchett's Precious Time Pieces

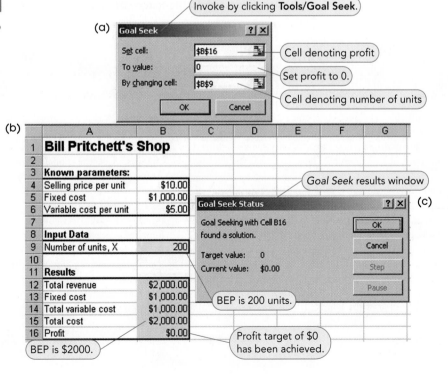

(a) Invoke by clicking **Tools/Goal Seek**.

Goal Seek — Set cell: $B$16 (Cell denoting profit); To value: 0 (Set profit to 0.); By changing cell: $B$9 (Cell denoting number of units)

(b)

	A	B	C	D	E	F	G
1	**Bill Pritchett's Shop**						
2							
3	**Known parameters:**						
4	Selling price per unit	$10.00					
5	Fixed cost	$1,000.00					
6	Variable cost per unit	$5.00					
7							
8	**Input Data**						
9	Number of units, X	200					
10							
11	**Results**						
12	Total revenue	$2,000.00					
13	Fixed cost	$1,000.00					
14	Total variable cost	$1,000.00					
15	Total cost	$2,000.00					
16	Profit	$0.00					

Goal Seek results window

(c) Goal Seek Status — Goal Seeking with Cell B16 found a solution. Target value: 0 Current value: $0.00

BEP is 200 units.

BEP is $2000.

Profit target of $0 has been achieved.

1.6   POSSIBLE PROBLEMS IN DEVELOPING DECISION MODELS

We present the decision modeling approach as a logical and systematic means of tackling decision-making problems. Even when these steps are followed carefully, however, there are many difficulties that can hurt the chances of implementing solutions to real-world problems. We now look at problems that can arise during each of the steps of the decision modeling approach.

Defining the Problem

Real-world problems are not easily identifiable.

In the worlds of business, government, and education, problems are, unfortunately, not easily identified. There are four roadblocks that **decision analysts** typically face in defining a problem. We use an application, inventory analysis, throughout this section as an example.

The problem needs to be examined from several viewpoints.

Conflicting Viewpoints   Analysts may often have to consider conflicting viewpoints in defining the problem. For example, in inventory problems, financial managers usually feel that inventory is too high, since inventory represents cash not available for other investments. In contrast, sales managers often feel that inventory is too low, since high levels of inventory may be needed to fill unexpected orders. If analysts adopt either of these views as the problem definition, they have essentially accepted one manager's perception. They can, therefore, expect resistance from the other manager when the "solution" emerges. So it's important to consider both points of view before stating the problem.

Impact on Other Departments   Problems do not exist in isolation and are not owned by just one department of a firm. For example, inventory is closely tied with cash flows and various production problems. A change in ordering policy can affect cash flows and upset production schedules to the point that savings on inventory are exceeded by

All inputs must be considered.

increased financial and production costs. The problem statement should therefore be as broad as possible and include inputs from all concerned departments.

Beginning Assumptions   People often have a tendency to state problems in terms of solutions. For example, the statement that inventory is too low implies a solution: that

DECISION MODELING IN ACTION
Better Modeling for Better Pollution Control

It is often difficult to balance economic returns with pollution control. When pollution is a problem, modeling industrial facilities can maintain high profitability while achieving pollution control guidelines and laws. This was the situation in Chile.

Chile produced 2 million tonnes of copper in 1994. This large copper production represented about 8% of the country's gross domestic product (GDP). Although private businesses operated about 50% of copper mining operations, Chile controlled most of the refining. Unfortunately, the production of copper produces solid, liquid, and gas byproducts that end up in the environment. As a result, the Chilean government decided to enact pollution and air quality standards for many of the byproducts of the copper mining process.

To help meet pollution and air quality standards, a quantitative optimization model was developed. The objective of

the model was to minimize the costs of copper mining while maintaining pollution and air quality standards set by the Chilean government. The model resulted in a number of changes. First, the model solution was substantially different from the cleanup plans that were developed before the model solution. As a result, many of the early cleanup plans were delayed, redone, or scrapped. In addition, some previously developed pollution and air quality cleanup plans were approved because they were consistent with the solution from the model. Furthermore, the model provided critical input to a computerized decision support system to analyze the impact of various copper mining strategies on total costs and pollution control. The result of this optimization model is a cleaner environment at minimal cost.

Source: Mondschein et al. "Optimal Investment Policies for Pollution Control in the Copper Industry," *Interfaces* 27 (November–December 1997): 69–87.

its levels should be raised. The analyst who starts off with this assumption will likely find that inventory should be raised! From an implementation perspective, a "good" solution to the right problem is much better than an "optimal" solution to the wrong problem.

Solution Outdated   Even if the problem has been specified correctly at present, it can change during the development of the model. In today's rapidly changing business environment, especially with the amazing pace of technological advances, it is not unusual for problems to change virtually overnight. The analyst who presents solutions to problems that no longer exist can't expect credit for providing timely help.

Developing a Model

Even with a well-defined problem statement, a decision analyst may have to overcome hurdles while developing decision models for real-world situations. Some are discussed in the following sections.

Fitting the Textbook Models   A manager's perception of a problem will not always match the textbook approach. For example, most textbook inventory models involve minimizing the sum of holding and ordering costs. Some managers view these costs as unimportant; instead, they see the problem in terms of cash flow, turnover, and levels of customer satisfaction. The results of a model based on holding and ordering costs are probably not acceptable to such managers.

Managers will not use the results of a model they do not understand.

Understanding the Model   Most managers simply will not use the results of a model they do not understand. Complex problems, though, require complex models. One trade-off is to simplify assumptions in order to make the model easier to understand. The model loses some of its reality but gains some management acceptance. For example, a popular simplifying assumption in inventory modeling is that demand is known and constant. This allows analysts to build simple, easy-to-understand models. Demand, however, is rarely known and constant, so the models lack some reality. Introducing probability distributions provides more realism but may put comprehension beyond all but the most mathematically sophisticated managers. In such cases, one approach is for the decision analyst to start with the simple model and make sure that it is completely understood. More complex models can then be introduced slowly as managers gain more confidence in using these models.

Acquiring Input Data

Gathering the data to be used in the decision modeling approach to problem solving is often no simple task. One-fifth of all firms in a recent study had difficulty with data access.

Using Accounting Data   One problem is that most data generated in a firm come from basic accounting reports. The accounting department collects its inventory data, for example, in terms of cash flows and turnover. But decision analysts tackling an inventory problem need to collect data on holding costs and ordering costs. If they ask for such data, they may be shocked to find that the data were simply never collected for those specified costs.

Professor Gene Woolsey tells a story of a young decision analyst sent down to accounting to get "the inventory holding cost per item per day for part 23456/AZ." The accountant asked the young man if he wanted the first-in, first-out figure, the last-in, first-out figure, the lower of cost or market figure, or the "how-we-do-it" figure. The young man replied that the inventory model required only one number. The accountant at the next desk said, "Hell, Joe, give the kid a number." The analyst was given a number and departed.

The results of a model are only as good as the input data used.

Validity of Data   A lack of "good, clean data" means that whatever data are available must often be distilled and manipulated (we call it "fudging") before being used in a model. Unfortunately, the validity of the results of a model is no better than the validity of the data that go into the model. You cannot blame a manager for resisting a model's "scientific" results when he or she knows that questionable data were used as input.

Developing a Solution

There are two potential pitfalls that an analyst may have to face while developing solutions to a decision model.

Hard-to-Understand Mathematics   The first problem is that although the mathematical models we use may be complex and powerful, they may not be completely understood. The aura of mathematics often causes managers to remain silent when they should be critical. The well-known management scientist C. W. Churchman once cautioned that "because mathematics has been so revered a discipline in recent years, it tends to lull the unsuspecting into believing that he who thinks elaborately thinks well."

Hard-to-understand mathematics and giving only one answer can be problems in developing a solution.

The Limitation of Only One Answer   The second problem is that decision models usually give just one answer to a problem. Most managers would like to have a range of options and not be put in a take-it-or-leave-it position. A more appropriate strategy is for an analyst to present a range of options, indicating the effect that each solution has on the objective function. This gives managers a choice as well as information on how much it will cost to deviate from the optimal solution. It also allows problems to be viewed from a broader perspective, since qualitative factors can also be considered.

Testing the Solution

The results of decision modeling often take the form of predictions of how things will work in the future if certain changes are made now. To get a preview of how well solutions will really work, managers are often asked how good the solution looks to them. The problem is that complex models tend to give solutions that are not intuitively obvious. And such solutions tend to be rejected by managers. Then the decision analyst must work through the model and the assumptions with the manager in an effort to convince the manager of the validity of the results. In the process of convincing the manager, the analyst will have to review every assumption that went into the model. If there are errors, they may be revealed during this review. In addition, the manager will be casting a critical eye on everything that went into the model, and if he or she can be convinced that the model is valid, there is a good chance that the solution results are also valid.

Review your assumptions.

Analyzing the Results

Once the solution has been tested, the results must be analyzed in terms of how they will affect the total organization. Even small changes in organizations are often difficult to bring about. If the results indicate large changes in organizational policy, the decision analyst can expect resistance. In analyzing the results, the analyst should ascertain who must change and by how much, whether the people who must change will be better or worse off, and who has the power to direct the change.

1.7   IMPLEMENTATION—NOT JUST THE FINAL STEP

We have just presented some of the many problems that can affect the ultimate acceptance of decision modeling in practice. It should be clear now that implementation isn't just another step that takes place after the modeling process is over. Each one of these steps greatly affects the chances of implementing the results of a decision model.

Even though many business decisions can be made intuitively, based on hunches and experience, there are more and more situations in which decision models can assist. Some managers, however, fear that the use of a formal analytic process will reduce their decision-making power. Others fear that it may expose some previous intuitive decisions as inadequate. Still others just feel uncomfortable about having to reverse their thinking patterns with formal decision making. These managers often argue against the use of decision modeling.

Many action-oriented managers do not like the lengthy formal decision-making process. They prefer "quick and dirty" techniques that can yield immediate results. However, once managers see some quick results that have a substantial payoff, the stage is set for convincing them that decision modeling is a beneficial tool.

Management support and user involvement are important.

We have known for some time that management support and user involvement are critical to the successful implementation of decision modeling processes. A Swedish study found that only 40% of projects suggested by decision analysts were ever implemented. But 70% of the modeling projects initiated by users, and fully 98% of projects suggested by top managers, were implemented.

SUMMARY

Decision modeling is a scientific approach to decision making in practical situations faced by managers. Decision models can be broadly classified into two categories based on the type of problem environment: (1) deterministic models and (2) probabilistic models. Deterministic models assume that all the relevant input data and parameters are known with certainty. In contrast, probabilistic models assume that some input data are not known with certainty. The decision modeling approach includes three major steps: (1) formulation, (2) solution, and (3) interpretation. It is common to iterate among these three steps before the final solution is obtained. Spreadsheets are commonly used to develop decision models.

In using the decision modeling approach, there can be potential problems such as conflicting viewpoints, disregard of the impact of the model on other departments, outdated solutions, misunderstanding of the model, lack of good input data, and hard-to-understand mathematics. Implementation is not the final step. There can be a lack of commitment to the approach and resistance to change.

GLOSSARY

Algorithm. A series of steps that are repeated.

Break-Even Point (BEP). Number of units sold that will result in total revenue equaling total costs (i.e., profit is $0).

Break-Even Point in Dollars (BEP$_\$$). Sum of fixed and total variable cost if the number of units sold equals the break-even point.

Decision Analyst. An individual who is responsible for developing a decision model.

Decision Modeling. A scientific approach that uses quantitative (mathematical) techniques as a tool in managerial decision making. Also known as *quantitative analysis, management science,* and *operations research.*

Decision Problem. A statement, which should come from a manager, that indicates a problem to be solved or an objective or goal to be reached.

Deterministic Model. A model that assumes that all the relevant input data and parameters are known with certainty.

Formulation. The process by which each aspect of the problem scenario is translated and expressed in terms of a mathematical model.

Garbage In, Garbage Out. The principle that improper data will result in misleading results.

Goal Seek. A feature in Excel that allows users to specify a goal or target for a specific cell and automatically manipulate another cell to achieve this target.

Input Data. Data that are used in a model in arriving at the final solution.

Model. A representation (usually mathematical) of a practical problem scenario or environment.

Parameter. A measurable quantity that is inherent in the problem. It typically has a fixed and known value (i.e., a constant).

Probabilistic Model (also called stochastic). A model that assumes that some input data are not known with certainty.

Sensitivity Analysis (also called post-optimality analysis). Determining how sensitive a solution is to changes in the formulation of a problem.

Variable. A measurable quantity that may vary or is subject to change.

KEY EQUATIONS

(1-1)   Profit =   Selling price per unit × Number of units
              − Fixed cost
              − Variable cost per unit
              × Number of units

An equation to determine profit as a function of the selling price per unit, number of units, fixed cost, and variable cost.

(1-2)   Number of units (BEP)

$$= \frac{\text{Fixed cost}}{\text{Selling price per unit} - \text{Variable cost per unit}}$$

An equation to determine the break-even point in units as a function of fixed cost, variable cost, and the selling price per unit.

(1-3)   Break-even point in dollars ($BEP_\$$) =
              Fixed cost + Variable cost per unit × BEP

An equation to determine the break-even point in dollars as a function of fixed cost and variable cost.

⟫ SELF-TEST

- ■ Before taking the self-test, refer back to the learning objectives at the beginning of the chapter, the notes in the margins, and the glossary at the end of the chapter.
- ■ Use the key at the back of the book to correct your answers.
- ■ Restudy pages that correspond to any questions that you answered incorrectly or material you feel uncertain about.

1. In analyzing a problem you should normally study
   a. the qualitative aspects.
   b. the quantitative aspects.
   c. both a and b.
   d. neither a nor b.

2. Decision modeling is
   a. a logical approach to decision making.
   b. a rational approach to decision making.
   c. a scientific approach to decision making.
   d. all of the above.

3. Frederick Winslow Taylor
   a. was a military researcher during World War II.
   b. pioneered the principles of scientific management.
   c. developed the use of the algorithm for decision modeling.
   d. all of the above.

4. The most important and often the most difficult step in the scientific method is
   a. developing a model.
   b. acquiring input data.
   c. defining the problem.
   d. defining a solution.

5. A physical model is an example of
   a. an iconic model.
   b. a schematic model.
   c. a mathematical model.
   d. a stochastic model.

6. An analysis to determine how much a solution would change if there are changes in the model or the input data is called
   a. sensitivity or post-optimality analysis.
   b. schematic or iconic analysis.
   c. futurama conditioning.
   d. both b and c.

7. Decision variables are
   a. controllable.
   b. uncontrollable.
   c. parameters.
   d. constant numerical values associated with any complex problem.

8. Decision models can be classified as
   a. probabilistic and deterministic models.
   b. mathematical and logical models.
   c. simple and complex models.

9. A decision model that assumes all the relevant input data and parameters are known with certainty is a
   a. probabilistic model.
   b. deterministic model.
   c. constant model.
   d. variable model.

10. A decision model that assumes that some input data are not known with certainty is a
   a. probabilistic model.
   b. deterministic model.
   c. constant model.
   d. variable model.

11. The number of units sold that will result in total revenue equaling total costs (i.e., profit is $0) is called the
   a. loss function.
   b. optimal solution.
   c. break-even point.
   d. variable.

12. _____ is the scientific approach to managerial decision making.

13. _____ is the first step in decision modeling.

14. A _____ is a picture, drawing, or chart of reality.

15. A series of steps that are repeated until a solution is found is called a(n) _____.

16. _____ is a representation (usually mathematical) of a practical problem scenario or environment.

17. Decision modeling is also commonly referred to as _____ or _____.

18. Probabilistic models incorporate uncertainty by using _____ on unknown variables.

19. A _____ is a measurable quantity that is inherent in the problem.

20. The decision modeling process involves the following three distinct steps: _____, _____, and _____.

DISCUSSION QUESTIONS AND PROBLEMS

Discussion Questions

1-1 Define *decision modeling*. What are some of the organizations that support the use of the scientific approach?

1-2 What is the difference between deterministic and probabilistic models? Give several examples of each.

1-3 What are the differences between quantitative and qualitative factors that may be present in a decision model?

1-4 Why might it be difficult to quantify some qualitative factors in developing decision models?

1-5 What are the steps involved in the decision modeling process? Give several examples of this process.

1-6 Why is it important to have an iterative process between the steps of the decision modeling approach?

1-7 Briefly trace the history of decision modeling. What happened to the development of decision modeling during World War II?

1-8 What are the different types of models mentioned in this chapter? Give examples of each.

1-9 List some sources of input data.

1-10 Define a decision variable. Give some examples of variables in a decision model.

1-11 What is a problem parameter? Give some examples of parameters in a decision model.

1-12 List some advantages of using spreadsheets for decision modeling.

1-13 What is implementation, and why is it important?

1-14 Describe the use of sensitivity analysis and post-optimality analysis in analyzing the results of decision models.

1-15 Managers are quick to claim that decision modelers talk to them in a jargon that does not sound like English. List four terms that might not be understood by a manager. Then explain in nontechnical language what each term means.

1-16 Why do you think many decision modelers don't like to participate in the implementation process? What could be done to change this attitude?

1-17 Should people who will be using the results of a new modeling approach become involved in the technical aspects of the problem-solving procedure?

1-18 C. W. Churchman once said that "mathematics tends to lull the unsuspecting into believing that he who thinks elaborately thinks well." Do you think that the best decision models are the ones that are most elaborate and complex mathematically? Why or why not?

Problems

1-19 Tom Johnson Manufacturing intends to increase capacity through the addition of new equipment. Two vendors have presented proposals. The fixed cost is $50 000 for proposal A and $70 000 for proposal B. The variable cost is $12 for A, and $10 for B. The revenue generated by each unit is $20.

(a) What is the BEP in units for proposal A?
(b) What is the BEP in units for proposal B?
(c) What is the BEP in dollars for proposal A?
(d) What is the BEP in dollars for proposal B?
(e) If the expected volume is 8500 units, which alternative should be chosen?
(f) If the expected volume is 15 000 units, which alternative should be chosen?

1-20 If the selling price is $8 per unit, variable cost is $4 per unit, and fixed cost is $50 000, calculate the BEP, the $BEP_\$$, and the profit at 100 000 units.

1-21 Angelo Carrera and Jeff Vollmann have opened a copy service on Bathurst Street. They estimate their fixed cost at $12 000 and their variable cost of each copy sold at $0.01. They expect their selling price to average $0.05.

(a) What is their BEP in units?
(b) What is their BEP in dollars?

1-22 Dr. Aleda Roth, a prolific author, is considering starting her own publishing company. She will call it DSI Publishing, Inc. DSI's estimated costs are as follows:

Fixed	$250 000
Variable cost per book	$20
Selling price per book	$30

(a) How many books must DSI sell to break even?
(b) What is DSI's BEP in dollars?

1-23 In addition to the costs in Problem 1-22, Dr. Roth wants to pay herself a salary of $50 000 per year.

(a) Now what is her BEP in units?
(b) What is her BEP in dollars?

1-24 An electronics firm is currently manufacturing an item that has a variable cost of $0.50 per unit and selling price of $1 per unit. Fixed costs are $14 000. Current volume is 30 000 units. The firm can substantially improve the product quality by adding a new piece of equipment at an additional fixed cost of $6000. Variable cost would increase to $0.60, but volume should jump to 50 000 units due to a higher-quality product. Should the company buy the new equipment?

1-25 The electronics firm in Problem 1-24 is now considering buying the new equipment and increasing the selling price to $1.10 per unit. With the higher-quality product, the new volume is expected to be 45 000 units. Under these circumstances, should the company purchase the new equipment and increase the selling price?

1-26 Satish Mehra's company is considering producing, in-house, a gear assembly that it now purchases from Saskatoon Supply, Inc. Saskatoon Supply charges $4 per unit. Mehra estimates that it will cost $15 000 to set up the process and then $1.82 per unit for labour and materials. Either choice would have the same cost at approximately how many units?

1-27 Because hula hoops have come back in style, Hoops Unlimited wants to enter the market quickly. It has three choices: (a) refurbish the old equipment at a cost of $600, (b) make major modifications at the cost of $1100, or (c) purchase new equipment at a net cost of $1800. If the firm chooses to refurbish the equipment, materials and labour would be $1.10 per hoop. If it chooses to make modifications, materials and labour would be $0.70 per hoop. If it buys new equipment, variable costs are estimated to be $0.40 per hoop.

   (a) Which alternative should Hoops Unlimited choose if it thinks it could sell more than 3000 hula hoops?

   (b) Which alternative should the firm use if it thinks the market for hoops would be between 1600 and 2400?

1-28 Jan Anderson and Angela Zhou have joined forces to start A&Z Lettuce Products, a processor of packaged shredded lettuce for institutional use. Jan has years of food processing experience, and Angela has extensive commercial food preparation experience. The process will consist of opening crates of lettuce and then sorting, washing, slicing, preserving, and finally packaging the prepared lettuce. Together, with help from vendors, they feel they can adequately estimate demand, fixed costs, revenue per two-kilogram bag of lettuce, and variable cost per two-kilogram bag of lettuce. They feel that a largely manual process will have monthly fixed costs of $37 500 and variable costs of $1.75 per bag. A more mechanized process will have fixed costs of $75 000 per month with variable costs of $1.25 per bag. They expect to sell the shredded lettuce for $2.50 per bag.

   (a) What is the BEP for the manual process?

   (b) What is the BEP for the mechanized process?

   (c) What is the monthly profit/loss of the manual process if they expect to sell 60 000 bags per month?

   (d) What is the monthly profit/loss of the mechanized process if they expect to sell 60 000 bags per month?

1-29 Christchurch School has 4000 students, each of whom currently pays $1500 per semester to attend. In addition to revenues from tuition, the school receives an appropriation from the church to sustain its activity. The budget for the upcoming semester is $12 million. The church appropriation will be $4.8 million. By how much will the school have to raise tuition to keep from having a shortfall?

1-30 Refer to Problem 1-29. One of the trustees senses that members of the church were resistant to the idea of raising tuition, so he suggests that the 2800 children of members pay $1500 as usual. Children of nonmembers would pay more. What would the nonmember tuition be if Christchurch wanted to continue to plan for a $12 million budget?

1-31 Refer to Problem 1-30. Another trustee believes that if members pay only $1500 in tuition, the most Christchurch can charge nonmembers is $2000 per semester. She suggests that another solution might be to cap nonmember tuition at $2000 and attempt to recruit more nonmember students to make up the shortfall. Under this plan, how many new nonmember students need to be recruited?

1-32 Widget Manufacturing Company must replace a widget machine and is evaluating the capabilities of two systems. A requirement of management is that the machine chosen must be paid for during the first year of operation. The first machine under consideration, machine A, would cost $65 000, and has the capacity to make up to 10 000 widgets per year at a variable cost of $22 per widget. The second machine, machine B, can produce twice as many widgets as machine A and would cost $72 000, but the variable cost is only $17 per widget. Widgets sell for $32 each.

   (a) Find the BEP for each machine.

   (b) Find the $BEP_\$$ for each machine.

   (c) If Widget Manufacturing Company is anticipating a demand of 5500 units in the next year, which machine should it choose?

   (d) If the demand is anticipated at 7500 units, should the company choose a different system?

   (e) At what volume would Widget Manufacturing Company be indifferent to a choice between the two machines? Hint: The total costs will be the same.

BIBLIOGRAPHY

Ackoff, R. L. *Scientific Method: Optimizing Applied Research Decisions.* New York: John Wiley & Sons, Inc., 1962.

Churchman, C. W. "Reliability of Models in the Social Sciences," *Interfaces* 4, 1 (November 1973): 1–12.

———. *The Systems Approach.* New York: Delacort Press, 1968.

Cosares, S., et al. "SONET Toolkit: A Decision Support System for Designing Robust and Cost-Effective Fiber-Optic Networks," *Interfaces* 25 (January 1995): 20–40.

Davis, Joyce. "How to Nurture Creative Sparks," *Fortune* (January 10, 1994): 94. Also see K. MacCrimmon and C. Wagner. "Stimulating Ideas through Creativity Software, "*Management Science* (November 1994): 1514–1532.

Dutta, Goutam. "Lessons for Success in OR/MS Practice Gained from Experiences in Indian and U.S. Steel Plants," *Interfaces* 30, 5 (September–October 2000): 23–30.

Epstein, Rafael, Ramiro Morales, Jorge Seron, and Andres Weintraub. "Use of OR Systems in the Chilean Forest Industries," *Interfaces* 29, 1 (January 1999): 7–29.

Geoffrion, Arthur M., and Ramayya Krishnan. "Prospects for Operations Research in the E-Business Era," *Interfaces* 31, 2 (March 2001): 6–36.

Harris, Carl. "Could You Defend Your Model in Court?" *OR/MS Today* (April 1997): 6.

Horner, Peter. "On the Right Track," *OR/MS Today* 30, 3 (June 2003).

Hueter, Jackie, and William Swart. "An Integrated Labor-Management System for Taco Bell," *Interfaces* 28, 1 (January 1998): 75–91.

Keskinocak, Pinar, and Sridhar Tayur. "Quantitative Analysis for Internet-Enabled Supply Chains," *Interfaces* 31, 2 (March 2001): 70–89.

Kuby, M., et al. "Planning China's Coal and Electricity Delivery System," *Interfaces* 25 (January 1995): 41–68.

Moore, William E., Jr., Janice M. Warmke, and Lonny R. Gorban. "The Indispensable Role of Management Science in Centralizing Freight Operation at Reynolds Metals Company," *Interfaces* 21, 1 (January–February 1991): 107–129.

Salveson, Melvin. "The Institute of Management Science: A Prehistory and Commentary," *Interfaces* 27, 3 (May–June 1997): 74–85.

Vazsoni, Andrew. "The Purpose of Mathematical Models Is Insight, Not Numbers," *Decision Line* (January 1998): 20–21.

Venkatakrishnan, C. S. "Optimize Your Career Prospects," *OR/MS Today* (April 1997): 28.

CHAPTER 2

Linear Programming Models: Graphical and Computer Methods

LEARNING OBJECTIVES

After completing this chapter, students will be able to

1. Understand the basic assumptions and properties of linear programming (LP).

2. Use graphical solution procedures for LP problems with only two variables to understand how LP problems are solved.

3. Understand special situations such as redundancy, infeasibility, unboundedness, and alternate optimal solutions in LP problems.

4. Understand how to set up LP problems on a spreadsheet and solve them using Excel's Solver.

CHAPTER OUTLINE

2.1 Introduction

2.2 Development of a Linear Programming Model

2.3 Formulating a Linear Programming Problem

2.4 Graphical Solution of a Linear Programming Problem with Two Variables

2.5 A Minimization Linear Programming Problem

2.6 Summary of the Graphical Solution Methods

2.7 Special Situations in Solving Linear Programming Problems

2.8 Setting Up and Solving Linear Programming Problems Using Excel's Solver

2.9 Premium Solver for Education

2.10 Algorithmic Solution Procedures for Linear Programming Problems

Summary • Glossary • Solved Problems • Self-Test • Discussion Questions and Problems • Case Study: INTERACTIONS 98 • Case Study: Golding Landscaping and Plants, Inc. • Case Study: International Pharma Inc. • Bibliography

Using Linear Programming in the Canadian Forest Industry

Former Canadian Prime Minister Sir Wilfrid Laurier, speaking about the importance of Canada's forests, once stated: "We must interest the nation, the individual, the farmer, the settler, the lumberman, everybody in the great work which is involved in forestry."

It is hard to imagine the vastness of Canada's forests. The following statement is found on the Interior Lumber Manufacturers' Association's website:

> *Overlaid on a map of Europe, the forests of Canada would cover Great Britain, Ireland, Portugal, Spain, France, the Netherlands, Belgium, Luxembourg, Switzerland, Italy, Albania, Denmark, Norway, Sweden, Finland, Poland, the Czech Republic, Slovakia, Austria, Hungary, Greece and Germany.*

Source: © Corbis/Magma Photo

Fibre allocation optimization is an increasingly important aspect of the forest industry in Canada. Decision making regarding which logs or log segments to make and where to send them (pulp mills, saw mills, or veneer mills) has been shifting from a manual, somewhat imprecise operation to a more formal, scientific endeavour.

Weldwood of Canada implemented this process at its plant in Hinton, Alberta, where it is harnessing resource allocation optimization to manage the flow of fibre to its growing list of mills. Two operations in Hinton lead the list: a pulp mill that produces some high-end grades and a modern two-line sawmill producing 240 million board-feet of lumber targeting Japan and other markets.

Weldwood uses computer-based linear programming models as a way to resolve a myriad of logistical problems by sorting through the variables, quantifying the alternatives, and finding the best bottom-line solution. And bottom line means maximizing profits for the entire Alberta operation, not just each mill separately. Neither linear programming nor this company-wide optimization strategy is new—in fact, these approaches have been applied to the petroleum industry for decades. But advances in computer power, user-friendly interfaces, and, above all, industry consolidation and a pressing need to squeak more margin from every possible source are factors that are causing the industry to focus on fibre industry allocation. In a Canadian industry with exports in excess of $41 billion in 2005, optimization techniques are needed to ensure that profits are maximized.

Sources: Canadian Forest Industries. April 2001, *http://www.halcosoftware.com/difficultdecisions.htm;* Interior Lumber Manufacturers' Association. *http://www.ilma.com/facts.htm;* Natural Resources Canada. *http://cfs.nrcan.gc.ca/sof/sof06/pdf/State-of-Forests_E.pdf*

2.1   INTRODUCTION

Management decisions in many organizations involve trying to make the most effective use of resources. Resources typically include machinery, labour, money, time, warehouse space, and raw materials. These resources can be used to manufacture products (e.g., computers, automobiles, furniture, clothing) or provide services (e.g., package delivery, health services, advertising policies, investment decisions).

In all resource allocation situations, the manager must sift through several thousand decision choices or alternatives to identify the best, or optimal, choice. The most widely used decision modeling technique designed to help managers in this process is called *mathematical programming*. The term **mathematical programming** is somewhat of a misnomer because the modeling technique requires no advanced mathematical ability (it uses just basic algebra) and has nothing whatsoever to do with computer software programming! In the world of decision modeling, programming refers to setting up and solving a problem mathematically.

Linear programming helps in resource allocation decisions.

Within the broad topic of mathematical programming, the most widely used modeling technique designed to help managers in planning and decision making is **linear programming (LP)**. We devote this and the next two chapters to illustrating how, why, and where LP works. Then, in Chapter 5, we explore several special LP models called *network flow problems*. We follow that with a discussion of a few other mathematical programming techniques (i.e., integer programming, goal programming, and nonlinear programming) in Chapter 6.

When developing LP (and other mathematical programming)–based decision models, we assume that all the relevant input data and parameters are known with certainty. For this reason, these types of decision modeling techniques are classified as *deterministic* models.

We focus on using Excel to set up and solve LP models.

Computers have, of course, played an important role in the advancement and use of LP. Real-world LP problems are too cumbersome to solve by hand or with a calculator, and computers have become an integral part of setting up and solving LP models in today's business environments. As noted in Chapter 1, over the past decade, spreadsheet packages such as Microsoft Excel have become increasingly capable of handling many of the decision modeling techniques (including LP and other mathematical programming models) that are commonly encountered in practical situations. So throughout the chapters on mathematical programming techniques, we discuss the role and use of Microsoft Excel in setting up and solving these models.

HISTORY   How Linear Programming Started

Linear programming was conceptually developed before World War II by the outstanding Soviet mathematician A. N. Kolmogorov. Another Russian, Leonid Kantorovich, won the Nobel Prize in Economics for advancing the concepts of optimal planning. An early application of linear programming, by Stigler in 1945, was in the area we today call "diet problems."

Major progress in the field, however, took place in 1947 and later, when George D. Dantzig developed the solution procedure known as the *simplex algorithm*. Dantzig, then an Air Force mathematician, was assigned to work on logistics problems. He noticed that many problems involving limited resources and more than one demand could be set up in terms of a series of equations and inequalities. Although early LP applications were military in nature, industrial applications rapidly became apparent with the spread of business computers. In 1984, Narendra Karmarkar developed an algorithm that appears to be superior to the simplex method for many very large applications.

2.2   DEVELOPMENT OF A LINEAR PROGRAMMING MODEL

Since the mid-twentieth century, LP has been applied extensively to medical, transportation, operations, financial, marketing, accounting, human resources, and agricultural problems. Regardless of the size and complexity of the decision-making problem at hand in these diverse applications, the development of all LP models can be viewed in terms of the three distinct steps, as defined in Chapter 1: (1) formulation, (2) solution, and (3) interpretation. We now discuss each with regard to LP models.

Formulation

Formulation involves expressing a problem scenario in terms of simple mathematical expressions.

Formulation is the process by which each aspect of a problem scenario is translated and expressed in terms of simple mathematical expressions. The aim in LP formulation is to ensure that the set of mathematical equations, taken together, completely addresses all the issues relevant to the problem situation at hand. We demonstrate a few examples of simple LP formulations in this chapter. Then we introduce several more comprehensive formulations in Chapter 3.

Solution

Solution involves solving mathematical expressions to find values for the variables.

The *solution* step is where the mathematical expressions resulting from the formulation process are solved to identify *an* optimal (or best) solution to the model.[1] In this textbook, the focus is on solving LP models using spreadsheets. However, we briefly discuss graphical solution procedures for LP models involving only two variables. The graphical solution procedure is useful in that it allows us to provide an intuitive explanation of the procedure used by most software packages to solve LP problems of any size.

Interpretation and Sensitivity Analysis

Sensitivity analysis allows a manager to answer "what-if" questions regarding a problem's solution.

Assuming that a formulation is correct and has been successfully implemented and solved using an LP software package, how does a manager use the results? In addition to just providing the solution to the current LP problem, the computer results also allow the manager to evaluate the impact of several different types of what-if questions regarding the problem. We discuss this subject, called *sensitivity analysis*, in Chapter 4.

In this textbook, our emphasis is on formulation (Chapters 2 and 3) and interpretation (Chapter 4), along with detailed descriptions of how spreadsheets can be used to efficiently set up and solve LP models.

Properties of a Linear Programming Model

First LP property: Problems seek to maximize or minimize an objective.

All LP models have the following properties in common:

1. All problems seek to maximize or minimize some quantity, usually profit or cost. We refer to this property as the **objective function** of an LP problem. For example, the objective of a typical manufacturer is to maximize profits. In the case of a trucking or railroad distribution system, the objective might be to minimize shipping costs. In any event, this objective must be stated clearly and defined mathematically. It does not matter, by the way, whether profits and costs are measured in cents, dollars, euros, or millions of dollars. An *optimal solution* to the problem is one that achieves the best value (maximum or minimum, depending on the problem) for the objective function.

---

[1] We refer to the best solution as *an* optimal solution rather than as *the* optimal solution because, as we shall see later, the problem could have more than one optimal solution.

2. LP models usually include restrictions, or **constraints,** that limit the degree to which we can pursue our objective. For example, when we are trying to decide how many units to produce of each product in a firm's product line, we are restricted by the available machinery time. Likewise, in selecting food items for a hospital meal, a dietitian must ensure that minimum daily requirements of vitamins, protein, and so on are satisfied. We want, therefore, to maximize or minimize a quantity (the objective) subject to limited resources (the constraints).

    An LP model usually includes a set of constraints known as **nonnegativity constraints.** These constraints ensure that the variables in the model take on only nonnegative values (i.e., ≥ 0). This is logical because negative values of physical quantities are impossible; you simply cannot produce a negative number of chairs or computers.

3. There must be alternative courses of action from which we can choose. For example, if a company produces three different products, management could use LP to decide how to allocate its limited production resources (of personnel, machinery, and so on) among these products. Should it devote all manufacturing capacity to make only the first product, should it produce equal numbers or amounts of each product, or should it allocate the resources in some other ratio? If there were no alternatives to select from, we would not need LP.

4. The objective and constraints in LP problems must be expressed in terms of *linear* equations or inequalities. In linear mathematical relationships, all terms used in the objective function and constraints are of the first degree (i.e., not squared, or to the third or higher power, or appearing more than once). Hence, the equation $2A + 5B = 10$ is a valid linear function, whereas the equation $2A^2 + 5B^3 + AB = 10$ is not linear because variable A is squared, variable B is cubed, and the two variables appear as a product in the third term.

You will see the term **inequality** quite often when we discuss LP problems. By *inequality* we mean that not all LP constraints need be of the form $A + B = C$. This particular relationship, called an equation, implies that the sum of term A and term B exactly equals term C. In most LP problems, we see inequalities of the form $A + B \leq C$ or $A + B \geq C$. The first of these means that A plus B is less than or equal to C. The second means that A plus B is greater than or equal to C. This concept provides a lot of flexibility in defining problem limitations.

Basic Assumptions of a Linear Programming Model

Technically, there are four additional requirements of an LP problem of which you should be aware:

1. We assume that conditions of *certainty* exist. That is, numbers used in the objective function and constraints are known with certainty and do not change during the period being studied.

2. We also assume that *proportionality* exists in the objective function and constraints. This means that if production of 1 unit of a product uses 3 hours of a particular resource, then making 10 units of that product uses 30 hours of the resource.

3. The third assumption deals with *additivity*, meaning that the total of all activities equals the sum of the individual activities. For example, if an objective is to maximize profit = $8 per unit of the first product made plus $3 per unit of the second product made, and if 1 unit of each product is actually produced, the profit contributions of $8 and $3 must add up to produce a sum of $11.

⇒MODELING IN THE REAL WORLD
Setting Crew Schedules at American Airlines

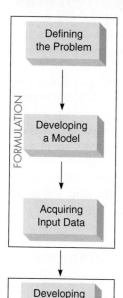

FORMULATION

Defining
the Problem

↓

Developing
a Model

↓

Acquiring
Input Data

SOLUTION

Developing
a Solution

↓

Testing the
Solution

INTERPRETATION

Analyzing
the Results
and Conducting
a Sensitivity
Analysis

↓

Implementing
the Results

American Airlines (AA) employs more than 8300 pilots and 16 200 flight attendants to fly more than 5000 aircraft. The total cost of AA's crews exceeds $1.4 billion per year, second only to fuel cost. Scheduling crews is one of AA's biggest and most complex problems. The Federal Aviation Administration (FAA) sets work-time limitations designed to ensure that crew members can fulfill their duties safely. Union contracts specify that crews will be guaranteed pay for some number of hours each day or each trip.

American Airlines Decision Technologies (AA's consulting group) spent 15 labour years developing an LP model called TRIP (trip reevaluation and improvement program). The TRIP model builds crew schedules that meet or exceed crews' pay guarantee to the maximum extent possible.

Data and constraints are derived from salary information and union and FAA rules that specify maximum duty lengths, overnight costs, airline schedules, and plane sizes.

It takes about 500 hours of mainframe computer time per month to develop crew schedules, which are prepared 40 days prior to the targeted month.

TRIP results were originally compared with crew assignments constructed manually. Since 1971, the model has been improved with new LP techniques, new constraints, and faster hardware and software. A series of what-if studies have tested TRIP's ability to reach more accurate and optimal solutions.

Each year, the LP model improves AA's efficiency and allows the airline to operate with a proportionately smaller work crew. A faster TRIP system now allows sensitivity analysis of the schedule in its first week.

The model, fully implemented, generates annual savings of more than $20 million. AA has sold TRIP to 10 other airlines and one railroad.

Source: R. Anbil et al. "Recent Advances in Crew Pairing Optimization at American Airlines." *Interfaces* 21, 1 (January–February 1991): 62–74.

4. We make the *divisibility* assumption that solutions need not necessarily be in whole numbers (integers). That is, they may take any fractional value. If a fraction of a product cannot be produced (e.g., one-third of a submarine), an integer programming problem exists. We discuss integer programming in more detail in Chapter 6.

2.3   FORMULATING A LINEAR PROGRAMMING PROBLEM

Product mix problems use LP to decide how much of each product to make, given a series of resource restrictions.

One of the most common LP applications is the **product mix problem.** In many manufacturing firms, two or more products are usually produced using limited resources, such as personnel, machines, raw materials, and so on. The profit that the firm seeks to maximize is based on the profit contribution per unit of each product. (Profit contribution, you may recall, is the selling price per unit minus the variable cost per unit.[2]) The firm would like to determine how many units of each product it should produce so as to maximize overall profit, given its limited resources.

Problems with only two variables are uncommon in practice.

We begin our discussion of LP formulation with a simple product mix problem that involves only two variables (one for each product, in this case). We recognize that in most real-world situations, there is very little chance we will encounter LP models with just two variables. Such LP models therefore have little *real-world* value. We nevertheless consider it worthwhile to study these models here for two reasons. First, the compact size of these models makes it easier for the beginning student to understand the structure of LP models and the logic behind their formulation. As we will see, the same structure and logic carries forward even to problems of larger size. Second, and more importantly, as we will see in Section 2.4, we can represent a two-variable model in a graphical form, which allows us to visualize the interaction between various issues in the problem.

Linear Programming Example: Flair Furniture Company

Flair Furniture Company produces inexpensive tables and chairs. The production process for each is similar in that both require a certain number of labour hours in the carpentry department and a certain number of labour hours in the painting department. Each table takes 3 hours of carpentry work and 2 hours of painting work. Each chair requires 4 hours of carpentry and 1 hour of painting. During the current month, 2400 hours of carpentry time and 1000 hours of painting time are available. The marketing department wants Flair to make no more than 450 new chairs this month because there is a sizable existing inventory of chairs. However, because the existing inventory of tables is low, the marketing department wants Flair to make at least 100 tables this month. Each table sold results in a profit contribution of $7, and each chair sold yields a profit contribution of $5.

Flair Furniture's problem is to determine the best possible combination of tables and chairs to manufacture this month in order to attain the maximum profit. The firm would like this product mix situation formulated (and subsequently solved) as an LP problem.

To provide a structured approach for formulating this problem (and any other LP problem, irrespective of size and complexity), we present a three-step process in the following sections.

Decision Variables

Decision variables are the unknown entities in a problem. The problem is solved to find values for decision variables.

Decision variables (or choice variables) represent the unknown entities in a problem— that is, what we are solving for in the problem. For example, in the Flair Furniture problem, there are two unknown entities: the number of tables to be produced this month and the number of chairs to be produced this month. Note that all other unknowns in the problem (e.g., the total carpentry time needed this month) can be expressed as linear functions of the number of tables produced and the number of chairs produced.

Decision variables are expressed in the problems using alphanumeric symbols. When writing the formulation on paper, it is convenient to express the decision variables using

---

[2] Technically, we maximize total contribution margin, which is the difference between unit selling price and costs that vary in proportion to the quantity of the item produced. Depreciation, fixed general expense, and advertising are excluded from calculations.

simple names that are easy to understand. For example, the number of tables to be produced can be denoted by names such as T, *Tables*, or X_1, and the number of chairs to be produced can be denoted by names such as C, *Chairs*, or X_2.

Throughout this textbook, to the extent possible, we use self-explanatory names to denote the decision variables in our formulations. For example, in Flair Furniture's problem, we use T and C to denote the number of tables and chairs to be produced this month, respectively.

Although the two decision variables in Flair's model define similar entities (in the sense that they both represent the number of units of a product to make), this need not be the case in all LP (and other) decision models. It is perfectly logical for different decision variables in the same model to define completely different entities and be measured in different units. For example, variable X can denote the amount of labour to use (measured in hours), while variable Y can denote the amount of paint to use (measured in litres).

Different decision variables in the same model can be measured in different units.

The Objective Function

The objective function represents the motivation for solving a problem.

The objective function states the goal of a problem—that is, why we are trying to solve the problem. An LP model must have a single objective function. In most business-oriented LP models, the objective is to either maximize profit or minimize cost. The goal in this step is to express the profit (or cost) in terms of the decision variables defined earlier. In Flair Furniture's problem, the total profit can be expressed as

Profit = $7 profit per table × Number of tables produced
+ $5 profit per chair × Number of chairs produced

Using the decision variables T and C defined earlier, the objective function can be written as

Maximize $7T + $5C

Constraints

Constraints represent restrictions on the values the decision variables can take.

Constraints denote conditions that prevent us from selecting any value we please for the decision variables. An LP model can have as many constraints as necessary for that problem scenario. Each constraint is expressed as a mathematical expression and can be independent of the other constraints in the model.

In Flair's problem, we note that there are four restrictions on the solution. The first two have to do with the carpentry and painting times available. The third and fourth constraints deal with marketing-specified production conditions on the numbers of chairs and tables to make, respectively.

With regard to the carpentry and painting times, the constraints must ensure that the amount of the resource (time) required by the production plan is less than or equal to the amount of the resource (time) available. For example, in the case of carpentry, the total time used is

3 hours per table × Number of tables produced
+ 4 hours per chair × Number of chairs produced

There are 2400 hours of carpentry time available. Using the decision variables T and C defined earlier, this constraint can be stated as

$$3T + 4C \leq 2400$$

The resource constraints put limits on the carpentry time and painting time needed mathematically.

Likewise, the second constraint specifies that the painting time used is less than or equal to the painting time available. This can be stated as

$$2T + 1C \leq 1000$$

Next, there is the marketing-specified constraint that no more than 450 chairs be produced. This can be expressed as

$$C \leq 450$$

Finally, there is the second marketing-specified constraint that at least 100 tables must be produced. Note that unlike the first three constraints, this constraint involves the $\geq$ sign because 100 is a minimum requirement. It is very common in practice for a single LP model to include constraints with different signs (i.e., $\leq$, $\geq$, and $=$). The constraint on the production of tables can be expressed as

It is common for different constraints to have different signs in an LP model.

$$T \geq 100$$

All four constraints represent restrictions on the numbers that we can make of the two products and, of course, affect the total profit. For example, Flair cannot make 900 tables because the carpentry and painting constraints are both violated if $T = 900$. Likewise, it cannot make 500 tables and 100 chairs, because that would require more than 1000 hours of painting time. Hence, we note one more important aspect of LP models: Certain interactions exist between variables. The more units of one product that a firm produces, the fewer it can make of other products. We show how this concept of interaction affects the solution to the model as we tackle the graphical solution approach in the next section.

A key principle of LP is that interactions exist between variables.

Nonnegativity Constraints and Integer Values

Nonnegativity constraints specify that decision variables cannot have negative values.

Before we consider the graphical solution procedure, there are two other issues we need to address. First, because Flair cannot produce negative quantities of tables or chairs, the nonnegativity constraints must be specified. Mathematically, these can be stated as

$$T \geq 0 \qquad \text{(number of tables produced} \geq 0)$$
$$C \geq 0 \qquad \text{(number of chairs produced} \geq 0)$$

In LP models, we do not specify that decision variables should only have integer values.

Second, it is possible that the optimal solution to the LP model will result in fractional values for T and C. Because the production plan in Flair's problem refers to a month's schedule, we can view fractional values as work-in-process inventory that is carried over to the next month. However, in some problems, we may require the values for decision variables to be whole numbers (integers) in order for the solution to make practical sense. A model in which the variables are restricted only to integer values is called an *integer programming (IP)* model. We will study IP models in detail in Chapter 6. In general, as we will see in Chapter 6, it is considerably harder to solve an IP problem than an LP problem. Further, LP model solutions allow detailed sensitivity analysis (the topic of Chapter 4) to be undertaken, whereas IP model solutions do not. For these reasons, we do not specify the integer requirement in LP models, and we permit fractional values in the solution. Fractional values can then be rounded off appropriately, if necessary.

Guidelines to Developing a Correct LP Model

We have now developed our first LP model. Before we proceed further, let us address a question that many students have, especially at the early stages of their experience with LP formulation: "How do I know my LP model is right?" There is, unfortunately, no simple magical answer for this question. Instead, we offer the following guidelines that students can use to judge on their own whether their model does what it is intended to do. Note that these guidelines do not guarantee that your model is correct. Formulation is still an art that you master only through repeated application to several diverse problems. (We will practise this over the next few chapters.) However, by following these guidelines, you can hopefully avoid the common errors that many beginners commit:

Here are a few guidelines to developing a correct LP model.

■ Recognizing and defining the decision variables is perhaps the most critical step in LP formulation. In this endeavour, one approach we have often found useful and effective is to assume that you have to communicate your result to someone else. When you tell that person "The answer is to do ——————," what exactly do you need to know to fill in the blank? Those entities are usually the decision variables.

■ Remember that it is perfectly logical for different decision variables in a single LP model to be measured in different units. That is, all decision variables in an LP model need not denote similar entities.

■ All expressions in the model (the objective function and each constraint) must use *only* the decision variables that have been defined for the model. For example, in the Flair Furniture problem, the decision variables are T and C. Notice that all expressions involve only T and C. It is, of course, permissible for a decision variable to not be part of a specific expression. For example, the variable T is not part of the constraint $C \leq 450$.

■ At any stage of the formulation, if you find yourself unable to write a specific expression (the objective function or a constraint) using the defined decision variables, it is a pretty good indication that you either need more decision variables or you've defined your decision variables incorrectly.

■ All terms within the same expression must refer to the same entity. Consider, for example, the expression for the carpentry constraint $3T + 4C \leq 2400$. Notice that each term (i.e., $4T$, $3C$, and 2400) measures an amount of carpentry time. Likewise, in the objective function, each term (i.e., $\$7T$ and $\$5C$) in the expression measures profit.

■ All terms within the same expression must be measured in the same units. That is, if the first term in an expression is in hours, all other terms in that expression must also be in hours. For example, in the carpentry constraint $3T + 4C \leq 2400$, the $4T$, $3C$, and 2400 are each measured in hours.

■ Address each constraint separately. That is, there is no single "mega" expression that will take care of all constraints in the model at one time. Each constraint is a separate issue, and you must write a separate expression for each one. While writing one constraint (e.g., carpentry time), do not worry about other constraints (e.g., painting time).

■ Try "translating" the mathematical expression back to words. After all, writing a constraint is just a matter of taking a problem scenario that is in words (e.g., "the amount of the carpentry time required by the production plan should be less than or equal to the carpentry time available") and translating it to a simple linear mathematical expression (e.g., $3T + 4C \leq 2400$). To make sure the translation has been done correctly, do the reverse process. That is, try explaining in words (to yourself) what the expression you have just written is saying. While doing so, make sure you remember the previous guidelines about all terms in an expression dealing with the same issue and being measured in the same units. If your "reverse translation" yields exactly the situation that you were trying to express in mathematical form, chances are your expression is correct.

2.4   GRAPHICAL SOLUTION OF A LINEAR PROGRAMMING PROBLEM WITH TWO VARIABLES

The graphical method works only when there are two decision variables, but it provides valuable insight into how larger problems are solved.

As noted earlier, there is little chance of encountering LP models with just two variables in real-world situations. However, a major advantage of two-variable LP models (such as Flair Furniture's problem) is that they can be graphically illustrated using a two-dimensional graph. This graph can then be used to identify the optimal solution to the model. Although this graphical solution procedure has limited value in real-world situations, it is invaluable in two respects. First, it provides insights into the properties of solutions to *all* LP models, regardless of their size. Second, even though we use a computerized spreadsheet-based procedure to solve LP models in this textbook, the graphical procedure allows us to provide an intuitive explanation of how this more complex solution procedure works for LP models of any size. For these reasons, we first discuss the solution of Flair's problem using a graphical approach.

Graphical Representation of Constraints

Here is a complete mathematical statement of the Flair LP problem.

The complete LP model for Flair's problem can be restated as follows:

$$\text{Maximize profit} = \$7T + \$5C$$

subject to the constraints

$3T + 4C \leq 2400$	(carpentry time)
$2T + 1C \leq 1000$	(painting time)
$C \leq 450$	(maximum chairs allowed)
$T \geq 100$	(minimum tables required)
$T, C \geq 0$	(nonnegativity)

Nonnegativity constraints mean we are always in the graphical area where $T \geq 0$ and $C \geq 0$.

To find an optimal solution to this LP problem, we must first identify a set, or region, of feasible solutions. The first step in doing so is to plot each of the problem's constraints on a graph. We can plot either decision variable on the horizontal (x) axis of the graph, and the other variable on the vertical (y) axis. In Flair's case, let us plot T (tables) on the x-axis and C (chairs) on the y-axis. The nonnegativity constraints imply that we are working only in the first (or positive) quadrant of a graph.

Carpentry Time Constraint   To represent the carpentry constraint graphically, we first convert the expression into a linear equation (i.e., $3T + 4C = 2400$) by replacing the inequality sign ($\leq$) with an equality sign ($=$).

As you may recall from elementary algebra, the solution of a linear equation with two variables represents a straight line. The easiest way to plot the line is to find any two points that satisfy the equation and then draw a straight line through them. The two easiest points to find are generally the points at which the line intersects the horizontal (T) and vertical (C) axes.

Plotting the first constraint involves finding points at which the line intersects the T and C axes.

If Flair produces no tables (i.e., $T = 0$), then $3(0) + 4C = 2400$, or $C = 600$. That is, the line representing the carpentry time equation crosses the vertical axis at $C = 600$. This indicates that if the entire carpentry time available is used to make only chairs, Flair could make 600 chairs this month.

To find the point at which the line $3T + 4C = 2400$ crosses the horizontal axis, let us assume that Flair uses all the carpentry time available to make only tables. That is, $C = 0$. Then $3T + 4(0) = 2400$, or $T = 800$.

The nonnegativity constraints and the carpentry constraint line are illustrated in Figure 2.1. The line running from the point ($T = 0$, $C = 600$) to the point ($T = 800$, $C = 0$) represents the carpentry time equation $3T + 4C = 2400$. We know that any combination of

FIGURE 2.1

**Graph of the
Nonnegativity Constraint
and the Carpentry
Constraint Equation**

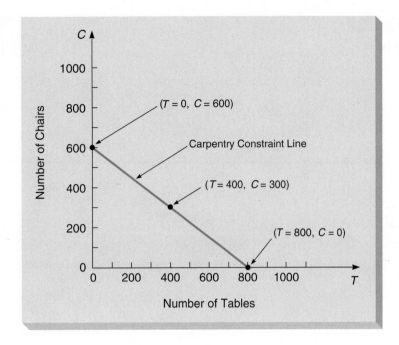

tables and chairs represented by points on this line (e.g., $T = 400$, $C = 300$) will use up all 2400 hours of carpentry time.[3]

Recall, however, that the actual carpentry constraint is the inequality $3T + 4C \leq 2400$. How do we identify all the points on the graph that satisfy this inequality? To do so, we check any possible point in the graph. For example, let us check $(T = 300, C = 200)$. If we substitute these values in the carpentry constraint, the result is $3 \times 300 + 4 \times 200 = 1700$. Because 1700 is less than 2400, the point $(T = 300, C = 200)$ satisfies the inequality. Further, note in Figure 2.2 that this point is below the constraint line.

In contrast, let's say the point we select is $(T = 600, C = 400)$. If we substitute these values in the carpentry constraint, the result is $3 \times 600 + 4 \times 400 = 3400$. Because 3400 exceeds 2400, this point violates the constraint and is, therefore, an unacceptable production level. Further, note in Figure 2.2 that this point is above the constraint line. As a matter of fact, any point above the constraint line violates that restriction (test this yourself with a few other points), just as any point below the line does not violate the constraint. In Figure 2.2, the shaded region represents all points that satisfy the carpentry constraint inequality $3T + 4C \leq 2400$.

Painting Time Constraint   Now that we have identified the points that satisfy the carpentry constraint, we recognize that the final solution must also satisfy all other constraints in the problem. Therefore, let us now add to this graph the solution that corresponds to the painting constraint.

Recall that we expressed the painting constraint as $2T + 1C \leq 1000$. As we did with the carpentry constraint, we start by changing the inequality to an equation and identifying two points on the line specified by the equation $2T + 1C = 1000$. When $T = 0$, then $2(0) + 1C = 1000$, or $C = 1000$. Likewise, when $C = 0$, then $2T + 1(0) = 1000$, or $T = 500$.

There is a whole region of points that satisfies the first inequality constraint.

---

[3] Thus, we have plotted the carpentry constraint equation in its most binding position (i.e., using all of the resource).

FIGURE 2.2

Region That Satisfies the Carpentry Constraint

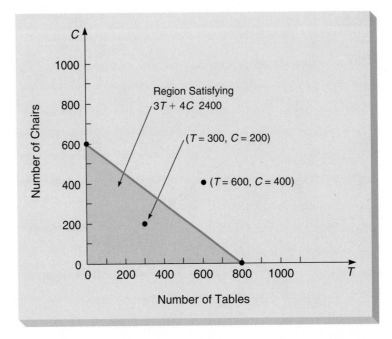

The line from the point ($T = 0$, $C = 1000$) to the point ($T = 500$, $C = 0$) in Figure 2.3 represents all combinations of tables and chairs that use exactly 1000 hours of painting time. As with the carpentry constraint, all points on or below this line satisfy the original inequality $2T + 1C \leq 1000$.

Looking at Figure 2.3, we can see that there are some points, such as ($T = 300$, $C = 200$), that are below the lines for both the carpentry equation and the painting equation. That is, we have enough carpentry and painting time available to manufacture 300 tables and 200 chairs this month. In contrast, there are points, such as ($T = 500$, $C = 200$) and ($T = 100$, $C = 700$), that satisfy one of the two constraints but violate the other. (See if you can verify this statement mathematically.) Because we need the solution to satisfy

FIGURE 2.3

Region That Satisfies the Carpentry and Painting Constraints

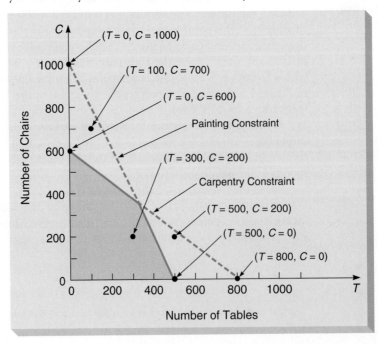

both the carpentry and painting constraints, we will consider only those points that satisfy both constraints simultaneously. The region that contains all such points is shaded in Figure 2.3.

Production Constraint for Chairs   We have to make sure the final solution requires us to make no more than 450 chairs ($C \leq 450$). As before, we first convert this inequality to an equation ($C = 450$). This is relatively easy to draw because it is just a horizontal line that intersects the vertical (C) axis at 450. This line is shown in Figure 2.4, and all points below this line satisfy the original inequality ($C \leq 450$).

Production Constraint for Tables   Finally, we have to ensure that the final solution makes at least 100 tables ($T \geq 100$). In this case, the equation ($T = 100$) is just a vertical line that intersects the horizontal (T) axis at 100. This line is also shown in Figure 2.4. However, because this constraint has the $\geq$ sign, it should be easy to verify that all points to the *right* of this line satisfy the original inequality ($T \geq 100$).

Feasible Region

In all problems, we are interested in satisfying all constraints at the same time.

The feasible region is the overlapping area of all constraints.

The **feasible region** of an LP problem consists of those points that simultaneously satisfy all constraints in the problem; that is, it is the region where all the problem's constraints overlap.

Consider a point such as ($T = 300$, $C = 200$) in Figure 2.4 below. This point satisfies all four constraints, as well as the nonnegativity constraints. This point, therefore, represents a **feasible solution** to Flair's problem. In contrast, points such as ($T = 500$, $C = 200$) and ($T = 50$, $C = 500$) each violate one or more constraints. They are, therefore, not feasible solutions. The shaded area in Figure 2.4 represents the feasible region for Flair Furniture's problem. Any point outside the shaded area represents an **infeasible solution** (or production plan).

Identifying an Optimal Solution by Using Level Lines

When the feasible region has been identified, we can proceed to find the optimal solution to the problem. In Flair's case, the *optimal solution* is the point in the feasible region that

FIGURE 2.4

Feasible Solution Region for the Flair Furniture Company Problem

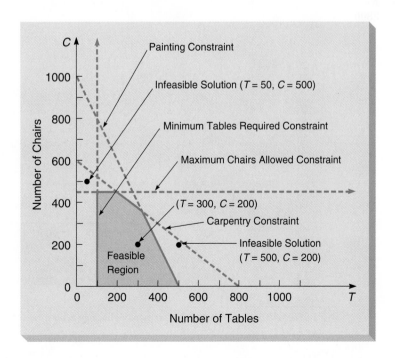

produces the highest profit. But there are many, many possible solution points in the feasible region. How do we go about selecting the optimal one, the one that yields the highest profit? We do this by essentially using the objective function as a "pointer" to guide us toward an optimal point in the feasible region.

Drawing Level Lines   In this method, called the **level, or iso[4], lines** method, we begin by plotting the line that represents the objective function (i.e., $7T + $5C$) on the graph, just as we plotted the various constraints. However, note that we do not know what $7T + $5C$ equals in this function. In fact, that's what we are trying to find out. Without knowing this value, how do we plot this equation?

To get around this problem, let us first write the objective function as $7T + $5C = Z$. We then start the procedure by selecting *any* arbitrary value for Z. In selecting this value for Z, the only recommended guideline is to select a value that makes the resulting equation easy to plot on the graph. For example, for Flair's problem, we can choose a profit of $2100. We can then write the objective function as $7T + $5C = $2100.

Clearly, this expression is the equation of a line that represents all combinations of (T, C) that would yield a total profit of $2100. That is, it is a *level line* corresponding to a profit of $2100. To plot this line, we proceed exactly as we do to plot a constraint line. If we let $T = 0$, then $7(0) + $5C = 2100, or $C = 420$. Likewise, if we let $C = 0$, then $7T + $5(0) = 2100, or $T = 300$.

The objective function line corresponding to $Z = 2100 is illustrated in Figure 2.5 as the line between $(T = 0, C = 420)$ and $(T = 300, C = 0)$. Observe that if any points on this line lie in the feasible region identified earlier for Flair's problem, those points represent *feasible production plans* that will yield a profit of $2100.

What if we had selected a different Z value, say $2800, instead of $2100? In that case, the objective function line corresponding to $Z = 2800 would be between the points $(T = 0, C = 560)$ and $(T = 400, C = 0)$, also shown in Figure 2.5. Further, because there are

> We use the objective function to point us toward the optimal solution.

FIGURE 2.5

Level Profit Lines for $Z = 2100$ and $Z = 2800$

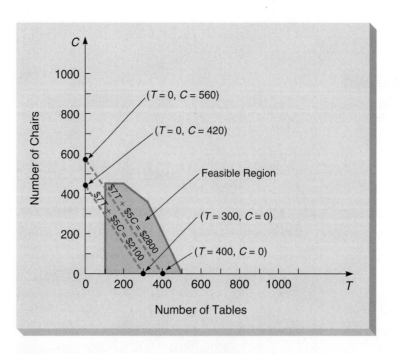

---

[4] Iso means "equal" or "similar." Thus, an isoprofit line represents a line with all profits the same, in this case $2100.

points on this line that lie within the feasible region for Flair's problem, it is possible for Flair to find a production plan that will yield a profit of $2800 (obviously, better than $2100).

Observe in Figure 2.5 that the level lines for $Z = \$2100$ and $Z = \$2800$ are parallel to each other. This is a very important point. It implies that regardless of which value of Z we select, the objective function line that we draw will be parallel to the two level lines shown in Figure 2.5. The exact location of the parallel line on the graph will, of course, depend on the value of Z selected.

We know now that Flair can obtain a profit of $2800. However, is $2800 the highest profit that Flair can get? From the preceding discussion, we note that as the value we select for Z gets larger (which is desirable in Flair's problem because we want to maximize profit), the objective function line moves in a *parallel* fashion away from the origin. Therefore, we can "draw" a series of parallel level lines (by carefully moving a ruler in a plane parallel to the $Z = \$2800$ line). However, as we visualize these parallel lines, we need to ensure that at least one point on each level line lies within the feasible region. The level line that corresponds to the highest profit but still touches some point of the feasible region pinpoints an optimal solution.

From Figure 2.6 below, we can see that the level profit line that corresponds to the highest achievable profit value will be tangential to the shaded feasible region at the point denoted by ④. Any level line corresponding to a profit value higher than that of this line will have no points in the feasible region. For example, note that a level line corresponding to a profit value of $4200 is entirely outside the feasible region (see Figure 2.6). This implies that a profit of $4200 is not possible for Flair to achieve.

Observe that point ④ defines the intersection of the carpentry and painting constraint equations. Such points, where two or more constraints intersect, are called **corner points**, or **extreme points**. From Figure 2.6, note that the other corner points in Flair's problem are points ①, ②, ③, and ⑤.

Corner Point Property   The preceding discussion reveals an important property of LP problems, known as the *corner point property*. This property states that an optimal solution to an LP problem will always occur at a corner point of the feasible region. In Flair's problem, this means that the optimal solution has to be one of the five corner points

> We draw a series of parallel level lines until we find the one that corresponds to the optimal solution.

> An optimal solution to an LP model must lie at one of the corner points in the feasible region.

FIGURE 2.6

Optimal Corner Point Solution to the Flair Furniture Company Problem

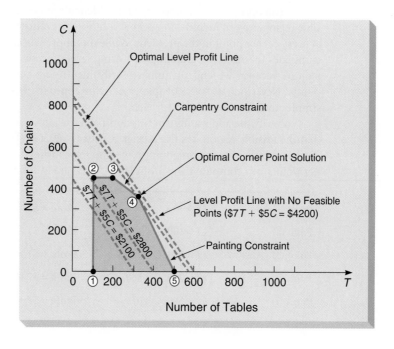

(i.e., ①, ②, ③, ④, or ⑤). For the specific objective function considered here (Maximize $7T + $5C), corner point ④ turns out to be optimal. For a different objective function, one of the other corner points could be optimal.

Calculating the Solution at an Optimal Corner Point   Now that we have identified point ④ in Figure 2.6 as an optimal corner point, how do we find the values of T and C, and the profit at that point? Of course, if a graph is perfectly drawn, you can always find point ④ by carefully examining the intersection's coordinates. Otherwise, the algebraic procedure shown here provides more precision.

To find the coordinates of point ④ accurately, we have to solve for the intersection of the two constraint equations intersecting at that point. Recall from your last course in algebra that you can apply the **simultaneous equations method** to the two constraint equations:

Solving for the coordinates of a corner point requires the use of simultaneous equations, an algebraic technique.

$$3T + 4C = 2400 \qquad \text{(carpentry time equation)}$$
$$2T + 1C = 1000 \qquad \text{(painting time equation)}$$

To solve these equations simultaneously, we need to eliminate one of the variables and solve for the other. One way to do this would be to first multiply the first equation by 2 and the second equation by 3. If we then subtract the modified second equation from the modified first equation, we get

$$\begin{aligned} 6T + 8C &= 4800 \\ -(6T + 3C &= 3000) \\ \hline 5C &= 1800 \qquad \text{implies } C = 360 \end{aligned}$$

We can now substitute 360 for C in either of the original equations and solve for T. For example, if $C = 360$ in the first equation, then $3T + (4)(360) = 2400$, or $T = 320$. That is, point ④ has the coordinates ($T = 320$, $C = 360$). Hence, in order to maximize profit, Flair Furniture should produce 320 tables and 360 chairs. To complete the analysis, we can compute the optimal profit as $7 × 320 + $5 × 360 = $4040.

Identifying an Optimal Solution by Using All Corner Points

Because an optimal solution to any LP problem always occurs at a corner point of the feasible region, we can identify an optimal solution by evaluating the objective function value at every corner point in the problem. While this approach, called the **corner point method**, eliminates the need for graphing and using level objective function lines, it is somewhat tedious because we end up unnecessarily identifying the coordinates of many corner points. Nevertheless, some people prefer this approach because it is conceptually much simpler than the level lines approach.

To verify the applicability of this approach to Flair's problem, we note from Figure 2.6 that the feasible region has five corner points: ①, ②, ③, ④, and ⑤. Using the procedure discussed earlier for corner point ④, we find the coordinates of each of the other four corner points and compute their profit levels. They are as follows:

Point ①	($T = 100$, $C = 0$)	Profit = $7 × 100 + $5 × 0 = $ 700
Point ②	($T = 100$, $C = 450$)	Profit = $7 × 100 + $5 × 450 = $2950
Point ③	($T = 200$, $C = 450$)	Profit = $7 × 200 + $5 × 450 = $3650
Point ④	($T = 320$, $C = 360$)	Profit = $7 × 320 + $5 × 360 = $4040
Point ⑤	($T = 500$, $C = 0$)	Profit = $7 × 500 + $5 × 0 = $3500

Note that corner point ④ produces the highest profit of any corner point and is therefore the optimal solution. As expected, this is the same solution we obtained using the level lines method.

Comments on Flair Furniture's Optimal Solution

The result for Flair's problem reveals an interesting feature. Even though chairs provide a smaller profit contribution ($5 per unit) than tables ($7 per unit), the optimal solution requires us to make more units of chairs (360) than tables (320). This is a common occurrence in such problems. We cannot assume that we will always produce greater quantities of products with higher profit contributions. We need to recognize that products with higher profit contributions may also consume larger amounts of resources, some of which may be scarce. Hence, even though we may get smaller profit contributions per unit from other products, we may more than compensate for this by being able to make more units of these products.

Notice, however, what happens if the profit contribution for chairs is only $3 per unit instead of $5 per unit. The objective is to now maximize $7T + $3C instead of $7T + $5C. Using the level profit lines method, we can determine from Figure 2.6 that the optimal solution will now correspond to corner point ⑤. That is, the optimal solution is to make 500 tables and 0 chairs, for a total profit of $3500. (We strongly recommend that you verify these answers yourself.) Clearly, in this case, the profit contributions of tables and chairs are such that we should devote all our resources to making only the higher profit contribution product, tables.

The key point to note here is that in either situation (i.e., when the profit contribution of chairs is $5 per unit and when it is $3 per unit), there is no easy way to predict *a priori* what the optimal solution is going to be with regard to the numbers of tables and chairs to make. We are able to determine these values only after we have formulated the LP model and solved it in each case. This clearly illustrates the power and usefulness of such types of decision models. As you can well imagine, this issue is going to become even more prominent when we deal in subsequent chapters with models that have more than two decision variables.

Extension to Flair Furniture's Linear Programming Model

As noted in Chapter 1, the decision modeling process is iterative in most real-world situations. That is, the model may need to be regularly revised to reflect new information. With this in mind, let us consider the following revision to the Flair Furniture model before we move on to the next example.

Suppose the marketing department has now informed Flair that all customers purchasing tables usually purchase at least two chairs at the same time. While the existing inventory of chairs may be enough to satisfy a large portion of this demand, the marketing department would like the production plan to ensure that at least 75 more chairs are made this month than tables. Does this new condition affect the optimal solution? If so, how?

Using the decision variables T and C we have defined for Flair's model, we can express this new condition as

$$C \geq T + 75$$

Notice that unlike all our previous conditions, this expression has decision variables on both sides of the inequality. This is a perfectly logical thing to have in an expression, and it does not affect the validity of the model in any way. We can, of course, manipulate this expression algebraically if we wish and rewrite it as

$$C - T \geq 75$$

FIGURE 2.7

Optimal Corner Point Solution to the Extended Flair Furniture Company Problem

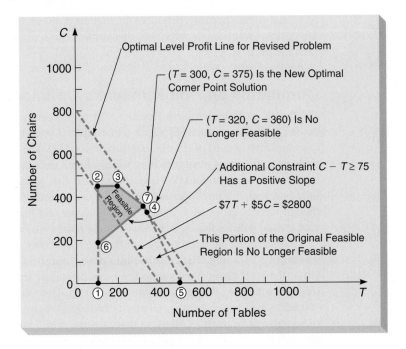

The revised graphical representation of Flair's model due to the addition of this new constraint is shown in Figure 2.7. The primary issue that is noticeably different in drawing the new constraint when compared to the carpentry and painting constraints is that it has a positive slope. All points above this line satisfy the inequality $(C - T \geq 75)$.

Notice the dramatic change in the shape and size of the feasible region just because of this single new constraint. This is a common feature in LP models, and it illustrates how each constraint in a model is important because it can affect the feasible region (and hence, the optimal solution) in a significant manner. In Flair's model, the original optimal corner point ④ ($T = 320, C = 360$) is no longer even feasible in the revised problem. In fact, of the original corner points, only points ② and ③ are still feasible. Two new corner points, ⑥ and ⑦, now exist.

To determine which of these four corner points (②, ③, ⑥, and ⑦) is the new optimal solution, we use a level profit line as before. Figure 2.7 shows the level line for a profit value of $2800. Based on this line, it appears that corner point ⑦ is the new optimal solution. The values at this corner point can be determined to be $T = 300$ and $C = 375$, for a profit of $3975 (see if you can verify these yourself). Note that the profit has decreased due to the addition of this new constraint. This is logical because each new constraint could make the feasible region a bit more restrictive. In fact, the best we can hope for when we add a new constraint is that our current optimal solution continues to remain feasible (and hence, optimal).

2.5 A MINIMIZATION LINEAR PROGRAMMING PROBLEM

Minimization LP problems typically deal with trying to reduce costs.

Many LP problems involve minimizing an objective such as cost instead of maximizing a profit function. A restaurant, for example, may want to develop a work schedule to meet staffing needs while minimizing the total number of employees. A manufacturer may seek to distribute its products from several factories to its many regional warehouses in such a way as to minimize total shipping costs. A hospital may want to provide its patients with a daily meal plan that meets certain nutritional standards while minimizing food purchase costs.

DECISION MODELING IN ACTION
Optimization at Air Transat

Air Transat operates charter flights to vacation spots. In 1993, it had an opportunity to expand, but its manual planning and scheduling system could not support rapid growth. Air Transat acquired the airline operations management system ALTI-TUDE, a three-module optimization package for aircraft routing, crew pairing, and monthly work assignment. The system helped the airline to streamline planning and scheduling and to focus on its core business and expansion rather than internal operational problems. By reducing the planning cycle, increasing operational flexibility, and supporting marketing, the

system helped the company to become the largest charter operator in Canada. ALTITUDE ensures cost-effective solutions by optimizing planning and scheduling problems and allowing easy interfacing among them. It saved the company an estimated 8% to 12% of total costs during the first year and more than a million dollars during the second year in operation.

Source: Desrosiers, Jacques et al. "Air Transat Uses ALTITUDE to Manage its Aircraft Routing, Crew Pairing, and Work Assignment" *Interfaces* 30 (March-April, 2000): 41–53.

Minimization problems that involve only two decision variables can also be solved graphically. To do so, we first set up the feasible solution region and then use either the corner point method or an isocost (level cost) line method (which is analogous to the level profit method in maximization problems) to identify a corner point that yields the minimum objective value. Let's take a look at a common LP problem referred to as the *diet problem*. This situation is similar to the one that the hospital faces in feeding its patients at the least cost.

The official website of the Alberta Turkey Producers (www.albertaturkey.com) tells us that "Turkeys are raised year round in Alberta. Alberta turkey producers raise approximately 2 million turkeys a year producing approximately 14 million kilograms of fresh turkey. Alberta produces 9% of the total Canadian turkey production."

In the next example we show how a fictitious turkey farm (Alberta Plains) can use a linear programming model to blend two different brands of turkey feed to produce a turkey diet at minimum cost.

Alberta Plains Turkey Farm

The Alberta Plains Turkey Farm is considering buying two different brands of turkey feed and blending them to provide a good, low-cost diet for its turkeys. Each feed contains, in varying proportions, some or all of the three nutritional ingredients (protein, vitamin, and iron) essential for fattening turkeys. Each kilogram of brand A contains 5 units of protein, 4 units of vitamin, and 0.5 units of iron. Each kilogram of brand B contains 10 units of protein, 3 units of vitamins, but no iron. The brand A feed costs the farm 2 cents a kilogram, and the brand B feed costs 3 cents a kilogram. The owner of the farm would like to use LP to determine the lowest-cost diet that meets the minimum monthly intake requirement for each nutritional ingredient. Table 2.1 summarizes the relevant information.

TABLE 2.1	COMPOSITION OF EACH KILOGRAM OF FEED (UNITS)		MINIMUM MONTHLY REQUIREMENT PER
Alberta Plains Turkey Farm Data			
INGREDIENT	BRAND A FEED	BRAND B FEED	TURKEY (UNITS)
Protein	5	10	90
Vitamin	4	3	48
Iron	0.5	0	1.5
Cost per kilogram	2 cents	3 cents	

If we let A denote the number of kilograms of brand A feed purchased and B denote the number of kilograms of brand B feed purchased, we can proceed to formulate this LP problem as follows:

$$\text{Minimize cost (in cents)} = 2A + 3B$$

Here is a complete mathematical statement of the LP problem.

subject to the constraints

$$
\begin{array}{lll}
5A + 10B \geq 90 & \text{(protein constraint)} \\
4A + 3B \geq 48 & \text{(vitamin constraint)} \\
0.5A \geq 1.5 & \text{(iron constraint)} \\
A \geq 0 & \text{(nonnegativity constraint on brand A feed)} \\
B \geq 0 & \text{(nonnegativity constraint on brand B feed)}
\end{array}
$$

Before solving this problem, note three features that affect its solution. First, the farmer needs to purchase enough brand A feed to meet the minimum standards for iron. Buying only brand B would not be feasible because it lacks iron. Second, as the problem is formulated, we will be solving for the best blend of brands A and B to buy per turkey per month. If the farm houses 5000 turkeys in a given month, we can simply multiply the A and B quantities by 5000 to decide how much feed to order overall. Third, we are now dealing with a series of greater than or equal to constraints. These cause the feasible solution area to be above the constraint lines, a common situation when handling minimization LP problems.

Graphical Solution of the Alberta Plains Turkey Farm Problem

We plot the three constraints to develop a feasible solution region for the minimization problem.

We first construct the feasible solution region. To do so, we plot each of the three constraint equations as shown in Figure 2.8. Note that in plotting the third constraint, $0.5A \geq 1.5$, it is more convenient to multiply both sides by 2 and rewrite it as $A \geq 3$. Clearly, this does not change the position of the constraint line in any way.

FIGURE 2.8

Feasible Region for the Alberta Plains Turkey Farm Problem

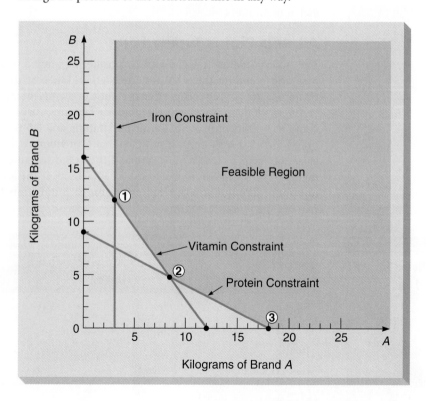

Note that the feasible region of minimization problems is often unbounded (i.e., opens outward).

The isocost line method is analogous to the isoprofit line method we used on maximization problems.

Recall that isocost lines can also be called level cost lines

The feasible region for Alberta Plains's problem is shown by the shaded space in Figure 2.8. Minimization problems are often unbounded outward (i.e., on the right side and on top), but this causes no difficulty in solving them. As long as they are bounded inward (on the left side and the bottom), corner points can be established. Recall that an optimal solution will lie at one of the corner points, just as it did in a maximization problem. In Figure 2.8, the identifiable corner points for Alberta Plains's problem are denoted by ①, ②, and ③.

Isocost Line Method   As with the isoprofit lines we used to solve the Flair Furniture maximization problem, we can draw a series of parallel isocost lines to identify Alberta Plains's optimal solution. The lowest isocost line to touch the feasible region pinpoints an optimal corner point.

For example, we start in Figure 2.9 by drawing a 54-cent cost line, or $2A + 3B = 54$. Obviously, there are many points in the feasible region that would yield a lower total cost. We proceed to move our isocost line toward the lower left in a plane parallel to the 54-cent solution line. The last point touched while still in contact with the feasible region is corner point ②, as shown in Figure 2.9.

To find the coordinates of point ② algebraically, we eliminate one of the variables from the two equations that intersect at this point (i.e., $5A + 10B = 90$ and $4A + 3B = 48$), so that we can solve for the other. One way would be to multiply the first equation by 4, the second equation by 5, and subtract the second equation from the first equation as follows:

$$4(5A + 10B = 90) \text{ implies} \quad 20A + 40B = 360$$
$$-5(4A + 3B = 48) \text{ implies} - \underline{(20A + 15B = 240)}$$
$$25B = 120$$

or

$$B = 4.8$$

We can substitute $B = 4.8$ into either of the two original equations to solve for A. Using the first equation yields $4A + (3)(4.8) = 48$, or $A = 8.4$. The cost at corner

FIGURE 2.9

Graphical Solution to the Alberta Plains Turkey Farm Problem Using the Isocost Line

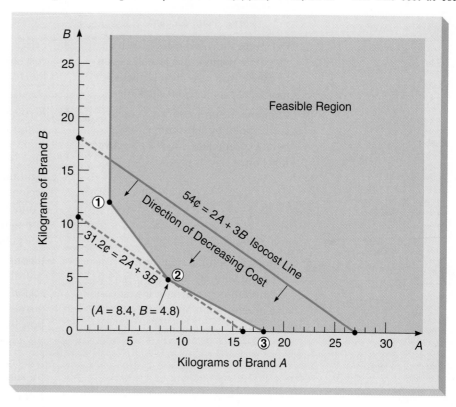

point ② is $2A + 3B = (2)(8.4) + (3)(4.8) = 31.2$ cents. That is, Alberta Plains should use 8.4 kilograms of brand A feed and 4.8 kilograms of brand B feed to make the turkey diet. This will yield a cost of 31.2 cents per turkey. Observe that this solution turns out to have fractional values. In this case, however, these are perfectly logical since turkey feeds can be measured in fractional quantities.

Corner Point Solution Method   Recall from Figure 2.8 that there are three identifiable corner points—①, ②, and ③—for this problem. For point ① we find the coordinates at the intersection of the vitamin and iron constraints, that is, where the line $A = 3$ crosses the line $4A + 3B = 48$. If we substitute $A = 3$ into the vitamin constraint equation, then $4(3) + 3B = 48$, or $B = 12$. Thus, corner point ① has the coordinates $(A = 3, B = 12)$ and a corresponding cost of $2(3) + 3(12) = 42$ cents.

We have already computed the coordinates of point ② as $(A = 8.4, B = 4.8)$, with a cost of 31.2 cents. Finally, we compute the cost at point ③. This is much easier, as it is evident that ③ has the coordinates $(A = 18, B = 0)$. The cost $2(18) + 3(0) = 36$ cents. Hence, as identified earlier with the isocost method, point ② is the optimal corner point.

We must solve for the three corner points algebraically.

2.6   SUMMARY OF THE GRAPHICAL SOLUTION METHODS

As shown in the cases of the Flair Furniture Company and the Alberta Plains Turkey Farm, the graphical methods of solving LP problems involve several steps. Let's review them briefly before moving on:

1. Graph each of the constraint equations.

2. Identify the feasible solution region, that is, the area that satisfies all of the constraints simultaneously.

3. Select one of the two following graphical solution techniques and proceed to solve the problem:

Corner Point Method	*Isoprofit* or *Isocost Method*
4. Determine the coordinates of each of the corner points of the feasible region by either visual inspection or the method of simultaneous equations.	4. Select a specific value for the profit or cost, and draw the *isoprofit* or *isocost* line to reveal its slope or angle.
5. Compute the profit or cost at each corner point by substituting that point's coordinates into the objective function.	5. If you are dealing with a maximization problem, maintain the same slope, through a series of parallel lines, and move the line up and to the right until it touches the feasible region at only one point. If you have a minimization problem, move down and to the left until it touches only one point in the feasible region.
6. Identify an optimal solution as a corner point with the highest profit in a maximization problem or lowest cost in a minimization problem.	6. Identify an optimal solution as the coordinates of a point on the feasible region touched by the highest possible *isoprofit* line or the lowest possible *isocost* line.
	7. Read the optimal coordinates from the graph or compute their values by using the simultaneous equations method.
	8. Compute the optimal profit or cost.

2.7   SPECIAL SITUATIONS IN SOLVING LINEAR PROGRAMMING PROBLEMS

In each of the LP problems discussed so far, all the constraints in the model have affected the shape and size of the feasible region. Further, in each case, there has been a unique corner point that we have been able to identify as the optimal corner point. There are, however, some special situations that may be encountered when solving LP problems: (1) redundancy, (2) infeasibility, (3) unboundedness, and (4) alternate optimal solutions.

Redundancy

A redundant constraint is one that does not affect the feasible solution region.

A **redundant** constraint does not affect the feasible region in any way. In other words, there are other constraints in the model that are more restrictive and thereby negate the need to even consider the redundant constraint. The presence of redundant constraints is quite common in large LP models with many variables. However, it is typically impossible to determine if a constraint is redundant just by looking at it.

Let's illustrate a redundant constraint by considering the following LP problem with three constraints:

$$\text{Maximize profit} = 2X + 3Y$$

subject to the constraints

$$X + Y \leq 20$$
$$2X + Y \leq 30$$
$$X \leq 25$$
$$X,Y \geq 0$$

From Figure 2.10, we see that the first two constraints are so restrictive that they make the third constraint, $X \leq 25$, redundant. That is, it has no effect on the feasible region and can therefore be eliminated from the model without affecting the feasible region or solution in any way.

Infeasibility

There may be no feasible solution region if constraints conflict with one another. This is called *infeasibility*.

Infeasibility is a condition that arises when an LP problem has no solution that satisfies all of its constraints; that is, no feasible solution region exists. Such a situation might occur, for example, if the problem has been formulated with conflicting constraints. This, by the way, is a frequent occurrence in real-world, large-scale LP problems that involve hundreds of constraints. For example, the marketing manager may insist that at least 300 tables be produced to meet sales demand (i.e., $T \geq 300$). At the same time, the production manager may insist that no more than 220 tables be produced due to a lumber shortage (i.e., $T \leq 220$). In this case, an infeasible solution region results. When the decision analyst coordinating the LP problem points out this conflict, one manager or the other must revise his or her inputs. Perhaps the production manager could procure more lumber from a new source, or perhaps the sales manager could lower sales demand by substituting a different model table to customers.

As a further graphic illustration of infeasibility, let us consider an LP problem with the following three constraints:

$$X + 2Y \leq 6$$
$$2X + Y \leq 8$$
$$X \geq 7$$

As seen in Figure 2.11, there is no feasible solution region for this LP problem because of the presence of conflicting constraints.

FIGURE 2.10

Problem with a Redundant Constraint

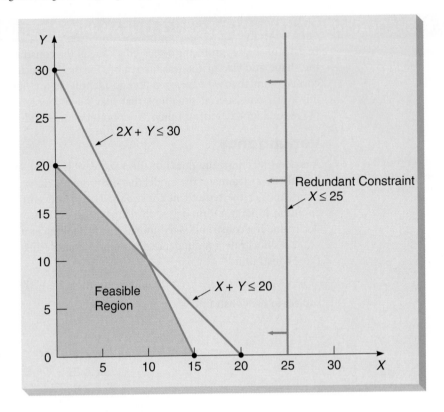

Unboundedness

When the profit in a maximization problem can be infinitely large, the problem is *unbounded* and is missing one or more constraints.

Sometimes an LP model will not have a finite solution. This means that in a maximization problem, for example, one or more solution variables—and thus the profit—can be made infinitely large without violating any constraints. In solving such a problem graphically, you will note that the feasible region is open-ended, or **unbounded**.

FIGURE 2.11

A Problem with No Feasible Solution

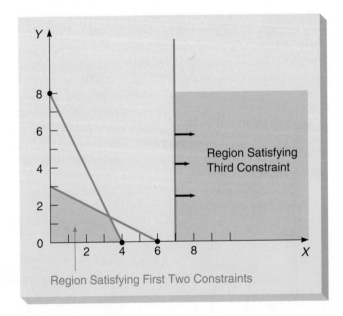

Let us consider a simple two-variable example to illustrate the situation. A firm has formulated the following LP problem:

$$\text{Maximize profit} = \$3X + \$5Y$$

subject to

$$X \geq 5$$
$$Y \leq 10$$
$$X + 2Y \geq 10$$
$$X,Y \geq 0$$

As shown in Figure 2.12, the feasible region extends infinitely to the right and is therefore unbounded. Further, since this is a maximization problem and the feasible region is unbounded in the direction in which profit increases, the solution itself is unbounded; that is, the profit can be made to reach infinity. In real-world situations, the occurrence of an unbounded solution usually means the problem has been formulated improperly. It would indeed be wonderful for the company to be able to produce an infinite number of units of X (at a profit of \$3 each!), but obviously no firm has infinite resources available or infinite demand.

It is important to note that the presence of an unbounded feasible region does not necessarily mean the solution is also unbounded. To demonstrate this, let us revisit the feasible region for the Alberta Plains Turkey Farm problem (refer back to Figure 2.8 if necessary). It is clear this feasible region is unbounded. However, since the Alberta Plains problem had a minimization objective, the fact that the feasible region was bounded inward (on the left side and the bottom) allowed us to identify a corner point as the optimal solution.

Alternate Optimal Solutions

Alternate optimal solutions are possible in LP problems.

An LP problem may, on occasion, have more than one optimal solution. Graphically, **alternate optimal solutions** occur when the isoprofit (or isocost) line runs perfectly parallel to a constraint in the problem that lies in the direction in which the isoprofit (or isocost) line is being moved—in other words, when they have the same slope. To illustrate this situation, let us consider the following simple LP problem:

$$\text{Minimize profit} = \$3X + \$2Y$$

A Feasible Region That Is Unbounded to the Right

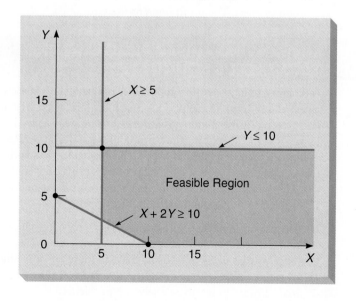

FIGURE 2.13

Example of Alternate Optimal Solutions

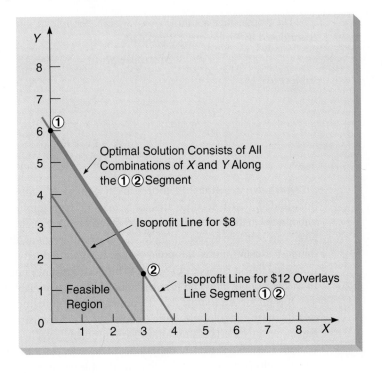

subject to

$$6X + 4Y \leq 24$$

$$X \leq 3$$

$$X, Y \geq 0$$

As shown in Figure 2.13 above, the first isoprofit line of $8 runs parallel to the constraint equation. At a profit level of $12, the isoprofit line will rest directly on top of the first constraint line. This means that any point along the line between corner points ① and ② provides an optimal X and Y combination. Far from causing problems, the presence of more than one optimal solution allows management great flexibility in deciding which solution to select. The profit remains the same at each alternate solution.

2.8   SETTING UP AND SOLVING LINEAR PROGRAMMING PROBLEMS USING EXCEL'S SOLVER

Excel has a built-in solution tool for solving LP problems.

Although graphical solution approaches can handle LP models with only two decision variables, more complex solution procedures are necessary to solve larger LP models. Fortunately, such solution procedures exist. (We briefly discuss them in Section 2.10.) However, rather than using these procedures to solve large LP models by hand, the focus here is on using Excel to set up and solve LP problems. Excel and other spreadsheet programs offer users the ability to analyze large LP problems using built-in problem-solving tools.

There are two main reasons that this book's focus on Excel for setting up and solving LP problems is logical and useful in practice:

- The use of spreadsheet programs is now very common, and virtually every organization has access to such programs.
- Since you are likely to be using Excel in many of your other courses, you are probably already familiar with many of its commands. There is no need to learn any specialized software to set up and solve LP problems.

DECISION MODELING IN ACTION
Linear Programming Model for Catch Allocation in a Commercial Fishery

Fish farming is a growing industry in Canada. Aquaculture products were worth over $526.5 million in 2004, more than double their value a decade earlier. Fish and other seafood products are being farmed in every Canadian province. Some Prairie farmers specialize in growing both grains and rainbow trout!

The aquaculture sector employs more than 14 000 people year-round, both directly and in related industries. In 2004, Canada's fish farmers produced 145 840 tonnes of finfish and shellfish. B.C. and the Atlantic provinces accounted for 92% of the total value of Canadian fish and seafood production in 2004, with 5% located in Quebec and Ontario, and the remaining 3% in the Prairie provinces. Canada exports 85% of the fish and seafood produced in the aquaculture sector. The majority goes to the United States and smaller amounts go to Japan, Taiwan, and France.

JS McMillan Fisheries Ltd. (JSM) is a Vancouver-based commercial fishing, production, and distribution company. As the operations of JSM have evolved, the process of allocat-ing a commercial salmon catch to a set of final products has become complex and time consuming. An LP model was developed to assist JSM management with this allocation decision. The model yields a production plan that maximizes the profit potential of the catch and allows management to carry out "what-if" analyses.

JSM's LP model takes into account many constraints, including Department of Fisheries policies, uncertainty in catch amount, seasonality, and time constraints necessary to limit fish deterioration. The main goal of the LP model is to develop and implement a decision support tool that optimally allocates the catch by producing a feasible production schedule that maximizes profit.

Sources: Begen, Mehmet Atilla and Martin L. Puterman. "Development of a Catch Allocation Tool Design for Production Planning at JS McMillan Fisheries," INFOR, August 2003; http://www.alive.com/1220a4a2.php?subject_bread_cramb=639; http://www.dfo-mpo.gc.ca/Aquaculture/sheet_feuillet/farm_seafood_e.htm

Excel uses an add-in named **SOLVER** to find the solution to LP-related problems. The standard version of Solver that is included with Excel can handle problems with up to 200 decision variables and 100 constraints (not including simple constraints such as the nonnegativity constraints). Larger versions of Solver are available for commercial use from Frontline Systems Inc., which has developed and marketed this add-in for Excel (and other spreadsheet packages). We use Solver to solve LP problems in Chapters 2–5 and integer and nonlinear programming problems in Chapter 6.

There are several other software packages (e.g., LINDO, GAMS) that are capable of handling very large LP models. Although each program is slightly different in terms of its input and output formats, the approach each takes toward handling LP problems is basically the same. Hence, once you are experienced in dealing with computerized LP procedures, you can easily adjust to minor differences among programs.

Using Solver to Solve the Flair Furniture Problem

Recall that the decision variables T and C in the Flair Furniture problem denote the numbers of tables and chairs to make, respectively. The LP formulation for this problem is as follows:

$$\text{Maximize profit} = \$7T + \$5C$$

subject to the constraints

$$3T + 4C \leq 2400 \qquad \text{(carpentry time)}$$
$$2T + 1C \leq 1000 \qquad \text{(painting time)}$$
$$C \leq 450 \qquad \text{(maximum chairs allowed)}$$
$$T \geq 100 \qquad \text{(minimum tables required)}$$
$$T, C \geq 0 \qquad \text{(nonnegativity)}$$

Just as we discussed a three-step process to formulate an LP problem (i.e., decision variables, objective function, and constraints), setting up and solving a problem using

There is no prescribed layout for setting up LP problems in Excel.

Excel's Solver also involves three parts: changing cells, target cell, and constraints. We discuss each of these parts in the following sections.

In practice, there are no specific guidelines regarding the layout of an LP model in Excel. Depending on your personal preference and expertise, any model that satisfies the basic requirements discussed subsequently will work. However, for purposes of convenience and ease of explanation, we use (to the extent possible) the same layout for all problems in this textbook. Such a consistent approach is more suited to the beginning student of LP. As you gain experience with spreadsheet modeling of LP problems, we encourage you to try alternate layouts.

We represent all parameters associated with a decision variable in the same column.

In our suggested layout, we use a separate column to represent all the parameters (e.g., solution value, profit contribution, constraint coefficients) associated with each decision variable in the problem. The objective function and each constraint in the problem is then modeled on separate rows of the Excel worksheet. Although not required to solve the model, we also add several labels in our spreadsheet to make the entries as self-explanatory as possible.

Excel Note

The CD-ROM that accompanies this textbook contains the Excel file for each sample problem discussed here. The relevant file name appears in the margin next to each example.

Changing cells are the decision variables in the problem.

Changing Cells

Solver refers to decision variables as **changing cells**. Each decision variable in a formulation is assigned to a unique cell in the spreadsheet. Although there are no rules regarding the relative positions of these cells, it is typically convenient to use cells that are next to each other.

In the Flair Furniture example, two decision variables need to be assigned to any two cells in the spreadsheet. In Screenshot 2.1A, we use cells B5 and C5 to represent the number of tables to make (T) and the number of chairs to make (C), respectively.

The initial entries in these two cells can be blank or any value of our choice. At the conclusion of the Solver run, the optimal values of the decision variables will automatically be shown here (if found).

File: 2-1.xls, sheet: 2-1A

SCREENSHOT 2.1A   **Formula View of the Excel Layout for Flair Furniture**

These are decision variable names used in the written formulation (shown here for information purposes only).

Names in column A and row 4 are recommended but not required.

	A	B	C	D	E	F
1	**Flair Furniture**					
2						
3		T	C			
4		Tables	Chairs	Solver will place the answers in these cells.		
5	Number of units					
6	Profit	7	5	=SUMPRODUCT(B6:C6,$B$5:$C$5)		
7	**Constraints:**					
8	Carpentry hours	3	4	=SUMPRODUCT(B8:C8,$B$5:$C$5)	<=	2400
9	Painting hours	2	1	=SUMPRODUCT(B9:C9,$B$5:$C$5)	<=	1000
10	Maximum chairs		1	=SUMPRODUCT(B10:C10,$B$5:$C$5)	<=	450
11	Minimum tables	1		=SUMPRODUCT(B11:C11,$B$5:$C$5)	>=	100
12				LHS	Sign	RHS

These are names for the constraints.

Calculate the objective function value and LHS value for each constraint using the SUMPRODUCT function.

The actual constraint signs are entered in Solver. These in column E are for information purposes only.

It is possible, and often desirable, to format these cells using any of Excel's formatting features. For example, we can choose to specify how many decimal points to show for these values. Likewise, the cells can be assigned any name (instead of B5 and C5), using the naming option in Excel. Descriptive titles for these cells (such as those shown in cells A5, B4, and C4 of Screenshot 2.1A) are recommended to make the model as self-explanatory as possible, but they are not required to solve the problem.

Excel Notes

- In all our Excel layouts, for clarity, the changing cells (decision variables) are shaded yellow.
- In all our Excel layouts, we show the decision variable names (such as T and C) used in the written formulation of the model (see cells B3 and C3). These names have no role or relevance in using Solver to solve the model and can therefore be ignored. We show these decision variable names in our models in this textbook so that the equivalence of the written formulation and the Excel layout is clear.

Target Cell

The target cell contains the formula for the objective function.

We can now set up the objective function, which Solver refers to as the **target cell**. We select any cell in the spreadsheet (other than the cells allocated to the decision variables). In that cell, we simply enter the formula for the objective function, referring to the two decision variables by their cell references (B5 and C5 in this case). In Screenshot 2.1A, we use cell D6 to represent the objective function. Although we could use the unit profit contribution values ($7 per table and $5 per chair) directly in the formula, it is preferable to make the $7 and $5 entries in some cells in the spreadsheet and refer to them by their cell references in the formula in cell D6. This is a more elegant way of setting up the problem and is especially useful if subsequent changes in parameter values are necessary.

In Screenshot 2.1A, we have entered the 7 and 5 in cells B6 and C6, respectively. The formula in cell D6 can therefore be written as

$$=B6^*B5+C6^*C5$$

The = at the start of the equation lets Excel know that the entry is a formula. This equation corresponds exactly to the objective function of the Flair Furniture problem. If we had left cells B5 and C5 blank, the result of this formula would initially be shown as 0. As with cells B5 and C5, we can format the target cell (D6) in any manner. For example, because D6 denotes the profit, in dollars, earned by Flair Furniture, we can format it to show the result as a dollar value.

Excel's SUMPRODUCT function makes it easy to enter long expressions.

If there are several decision variables in a problem, however, formulas can become somewhat long, and typing them can become quite cumbersome. In such cases, you can use Excel's **SUMPRODUCT function** to express the equation efficiently. The syntax for the SUMPRODUCT function requires specifying two cell ranges of equal size, separated by a comma.[5] One of the ranges defines the cells containing the profit contributions (cells B6:C6), and the other defines the cells containing the decision variables (cells B5:C5). The SUMPRODUCT function computes the products of the first entries in each range, second entries in each range, and so on. It then sums these products.

Based on the preceding discussion, as shown in Screenshot 2.1A, the objective function for Flair Furniture can be expressed as

$$=SUMPRODUCT(B6:C6,\$B\$5:\$C\$5)$$

---

[5] The SUMPRODUCT function can also be used with more than two cell ranges. See Excel's help feature for details.

Note that this is equivalent to =B6*B5+C6*C5. Also, the $ symbol in the second cell range keeps that cell reference fixed when we copy the formula. This is especially convenient because, as we show next, the formula for each constraint in the model also follows the same structure as the objective function.

Excel Note

In each of our Excel layouts, for clarity, the target cell (objective function) has been shaded green.

Constraints

Constraints in Solver include three entries: LHS, RHS, and sign.

We must now set up each constraint in the problem. To achieve this, let us first separate each constraint into three parts: (1) a **left-hand-side (constraint LHS)** part consisting of every term to the left of the equality or inequality sign, (2) a **right-hand-side (constraint RHS)** part consisting of all terms to the right of the equality or inequality sign, and (3) the equality or inequality sign itself. The RHS in most cases may just be a fixed number—that is, a constant.

Creating Cells for Constraint LHS Values   We now select a unique cell for each LHS in the formulation (one for each constraint) and type in the relevant formula for that constraint. As with the objective function, we refer to the decision variables by their cell references. In Screenshot 2.1A, we use cell D8 to represent the LHS of the carpentry time constraint. We have entered the coefficients (i.e., 3 and 4) on the LHS of this constraint in cells B8 and C8, respectively. Then, either of the following formulas would be appropriate in cell D8:

$$=B8^*B5+C8^*C5$$

or

$$=SUMPRODUCT(B8:C8,\$B\$5:\$C\$5)$$

Here again, the SUMPRODUCT function makes the formula compact in situations in which the LHS has many terms. Note the similarity between the objective function formula in cell D6 [=SUMPRODUCT(B6:C6,$B$5:$C$5)] and the LHS formula for the carpentry constraint in cell D8 [=SUMPRODUCT(B8:C8,$B$5:$C$5)]. In fact, because we have anchored the cell references for the decision variables (B5 and C5) using the $ symbol in cell D6, we can simply copy the formula in cell D6 to cell D8.

Formula in cell D9: =SUMPRODUCT(B9:C9, $B$5:$C$5)

The LHS formula for the painting hours constraint (cell D9), chairs production limit constraint (cell D10), and tables minimum production constraint (cell D11) can similarly be copied from cell D6. As you have probably recognized by now, the LHS cell for virtually every constraint in an LP formulation can be created in this fashion.

Excel Note

In each of our Excel layouts, for clarity, cells denoting LHS formulas of constraints have been shaded blue.

In Solver, the RHS of a constraint can also include a formula.

Creating Cells for Constraint RHS Values   When all the LHS formulas have been set up, we can pick unique cells for each RHS in the formulation. Although the Flair Furniture problem has only constants (2400, 1000, 450, and 100, respectively) for the four constraints, it is perfectly valid in Solver for the RHS to also have a formula like the LHS. In Screenshot 2.1A, we show the four RHS values in cells F8:F11.

The actual sign for each constraint is entered directly in Solver.

Constraint Type   In Screenshot 2.1A, we also show the sign ($\leq$, $\geq$, or =) of each constraint between the LHS and RHS cells for that constraint (see cells E8:E11). Although this makes each constraint easier to understand, note that the inclusion of these signs here is for information purposes only. As we show next, the actual sign for each constraint is entered directly in Solver.

Entering Information in Solver

The default in Solver is to maximize the Target Cell.

After all the constraints have been set up, we invoke the **SOLVER PARAMETERS** window by clicking **TOOLS|SOLVER**.[6] This window is shown in Screenshot 2.1B.

Specifying the Target Cell   We first enter the relevant cell reference (i.e., cell D6) in the **SET TARGET CELL** box. The default is to maximize the target value. (Note that the **MAX** option is already selected.) For a minimization problem, we must click the **MIN** option to specify that the objective function should be minimized. The third option (**VALUE**) allows us to specify a value that we want the target cell to achieve, rather than obtain the optimal solution. (We do not use this option in our study of LP and other mathematical programming models.)

Changing cells can be entered as a block or as individual cell references separated by commas.

Specifying the Changing Cells   We now move the cursor to the box labeled **BY CHANGING CELLS.** We enter the cell references for the decision variables in this box. If the cell references are next to each other, we can simply enter them as one block. For example, we could enter B5:C5 for Flair Furniture's problem. (If you use the mouse or keyboard to highlight cells B5 and C5, Excel automatically puts in the $ anchors, as shown in Screenshot 2.1B.) If the cells are not contiguous (i.e., not next to each other), we can enter the changing cells by placing a comma between noncontiguous cells (or blocks of cells).

SCREENSHOT 2.1B   **Solver Entries for Flair Furniture**

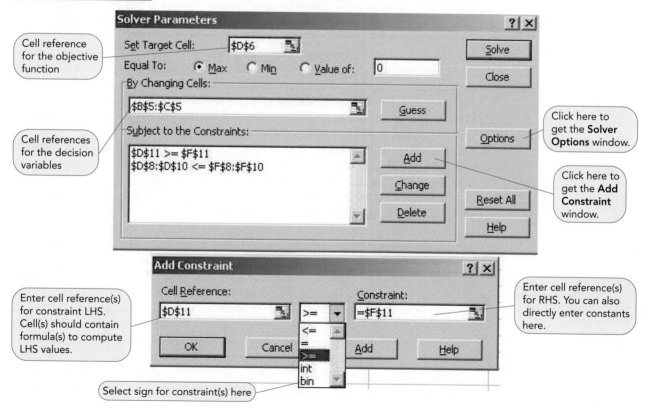

---

[6] If you do not see Solver under the Tools menu in Excel, refer to Appendix B for instructions on how to fix this problem.

Solver includes a button named **GUESS**. We can click this button to get Solver to automatically guess the cell references for the changing cells. This approach is, however, not always reliable, so we recommend that the changing cell references always be entered manually.

The Add Constraint window is used to enter constraints.

Specifying the Constraints   Next, we use the **ADD** constraints feature to enter the relevant cell references for the LHS and RHS of each constraint. The **ADD CONSTRAINT** window (also shown in Screenshot 2.1B) has a box for entering the cell reference of the LHS, a drop-down menu for the sign, and a second box for entering the cell reference of the RHS. The drop-down menu has five choices: ≤, ≥, =, int (for integer), and bin (for binary). (We discuss the last two choices in Chapter 6.)

We can either add constraints one at a time or add blocks of constraints that have the same sign (≤, ≥, or =) at the same time. For instance, we could first add the carpentry constraint by entering D8 in the LHS input box, entering F8 in the RHS input box, and selecting the ≤ sign from the drop-down menu. As noted earlier, the ≤ sign shown in cell E8 is not relevant in Solver, and we must enter the sign of each constraint by using the Add Constraint window. We can now add the painting constraint by entering D9 and F9 in the LHS and RHS input boxes, respectively. Next, we can add the chairs limit constraint by entering D10 and F10 in the LHS and RHS input boxes, respectively. Finally, we can add the minimum table production constraint by entering D11 and F11 in the LHS and RHS input boxes, respectively. Note that in this constraint's case, we should select the ≥ sign from the drop-down menu.

Constraints with the same sign can be entered as a block.

Alternatively, because the first three constraints have the same sign (≤), we can input cells D8 to D10 in the LHS input box (i.e., enter D8:D10) and correspondingly enter F8:F10 in the RHS input box. We select ≤ as the sign between these LHS and RHS entries. Solver interprets this as taking each entry in the LHS input box and setting it ≤ to the corresponding entry in the RHS input box (i.e., D8 ≤ F8, D9 ≤ F9, and D10 ≤ F10).

Using the latter procedure, note that it is possible to have just three entries in the constraints window: one for all the ≤ constraints in the model, one for all the ≥ constraints in the model, and one for all the = constraints in the model. This, of course, requires that the spreadsheet layout be such that the LHS and RHS cells for all constraints that have the same sign are in contiguous blocks, as in Screenshot 2.1A. However, as we demonstrate in several examples in Chapter 3, this is quite easy to do.

At any point during the constraint input process, we can use the **CHANGE** or **DELETE** features to modify one or more constraints, as necessary. It is important to note that we *cannot* enter the formula for the objective function and the LHS and/or RHS of constraints from within the **SOLVER PARAMETERS** window. The formulas must be created in appropriate cells in the spreadsheet before using the Solver Parameters window. Although it is possible to directly enter constants (2400, 1000, 450, and 100 in our model) in the RHS input box while adding constraints, it is preferable to make the RHS also a cell reference (F8, F9, F10, and F11 in our model).

Check the Assume Non-Negative and Assume Linear Model boxes in Solver's options.

Solver Options   When all constraints have been entered, we are ready to solve the model. However, before clicking the **SOLVE** button on the Solver Parameters window, we must first click the **OPTIONS** button to open the Solver Options window (shown in Screenshot 2.1C). For solving most LP problems, we do not have to change any of the default parameters. However, we must check the boxes Assume Non-Negative and Assume Linear Model. Checking the nonnegative box automatically enforces the nonnegativity condition on all the decision variables. Checking the linear model box directs Solver to provide a detailed sensitivity analysis report, which we cover in Chapter 4.

Solver also has another option called **USE AUTOMATIC SCALING** (see Screenshot 2.1C). In practice, it is usually a good idea to scale problems in which values of the objective function

Solver Options Window

Default time allowed. This should be sufficient for most LP models.

Solver Options   ? ✕

Max Time: 100   seconds   OK

Iterations: 100   Cancel

Precision: 0.000001   Load Model...

Tolerance: 5   %   Save Model...

Convergence: 0.0001   Help

Be sure to check both boxes before solving an LP model.

☑ Assume Linear Model   ☐ Use Automatic Scaling
☑ Assume Non-Negative   ☐ Show Iteration Results

Use this option to scale an LP model if necessary.

┌─Estimates─────┐ ┌─Derivatives───┐ ┌─Search──────┐
│ ⦿ Tangent   │ │ ⦿ Forward   │ │ ⦿ Newton   │
│ ○ Quadratic   │ │ ○ Central   │ │ ○ Conjugate │
└───────────────┘ └───────────────┘ └─────────────┘

File: 2-1.xls, Sheet: 2-1D

coefficients and constraint coefficients of different constraints differ by several orders of magnitude. For instance, a problem in which some coefficients are in millions while others have fractional values can be considered a poorly scaled model. Due to the effects of a computer's finite precision arithmetic, such poorly scaled models could cause difficulty for Solver, leading to fairly large rounding errors. Checking the automatic scaling box directs Solver to scale models that it detects as poorly scaled and possibly avoid such rounding problems.

Solving the Model When the Solve button is clicked, Solver executes the model and displays the results, as shown in Screenshot 2.1D. Before looking at the results, it is important to read the message in the **SOLVER RESULTS** window (see Screenshot 2.1D) to verify that Solver found an optimal solution. In some cases, the window indicates Solver's inability to find an optimal solution (e.g., when the formulation is infeasible or the

Excel Layout and Solver Solution for Flair Furniture (Solver Results Window also shown)

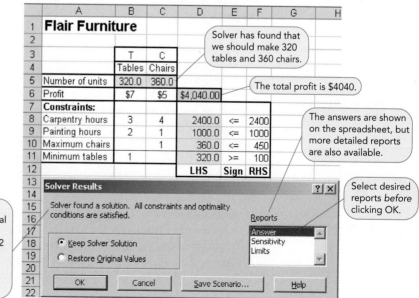

Solver has found that we should make 320 tables and 360 chairs.

The total profit is $4040.

The answers are shown on the spreadsheet, but more detailed reports are also available.

Solver message indicating an optimal solution has been found. See Table 2.2 for the different solver messages possible and their implications.

Select desired reports *before* clicking OK.

	A	B	C	D	E	F	G	H
1	**Flair Furniture**							
2								
3		T	C					
4		Tables	Chairs					
5	Number of units	320.0	360.0					
6	Profit	$7	$5	$4,040.00				
7	**Constraints:**							
8	Carpentry hours	3	4	2400.0	<=	2400		
9	Painting hours	2	1	1000.0	<=	1000		
10	Maximum chairs		1	360.0	<=	450		
11	Minimum tables	1		320.0	>=	100		
12				LHS	Sign	RHS		

Solver Results   ? ✕

Solver found a solution. All constraints and optimality conditions are satisfied.

Reports

⦿ Keep Solver Solution   Answer
○ Restore Original Values   Sensitivity
                                Limits

OK   Cancel   Save Scenario...   Help

TABLE 2.2			
Possible Messages in the Solver Results Window	**MESSAGE**	**MEANING**	**POSSIBLE CAUSE**
	Solver found a solution. All constraints and optimality conditions are satisfied.	Ideal message!	*Note:* This does *not* mean the formulation and/or solution is correct. It just means there are no syntax errors in the Excel formulas and Solver entries.
	Solver could not find a feasible solution.	There is no feasible region.	Incorrect entries in LHS formulas, signs, and/or RHS values of constraints.
	The Set Cell values do not converge.	Unbounded solution.	Incorrect entries in LHS formulas, signs, and/or RHS values of constraints.
	Solver encountered an error value in a target or constraint cell.	Formula error in target or constraint cell.	Most common cause is division by zero in some cell.
	The linearity conditions required by this LP solver are not satisfied.	The Assume Linear Model box is checked in Solver's options, but one or more formulas in the model are not linear.	Multiplication or division involving two or more variables in some cell. *Note:* Solver sometimes gives this error message even when the formulas are linear. This occurs especially when both the LHS and RHS of a constraint have formulas. In such cases, try manipulating the constraint algebraically to make the RHS a constant.

solution space is unbounded). Table 2.2 shows several different Solver messages that could result when an LP model is solved, the meaning of each message, and a possible cause for each message.

Solver provides options to obtain different reports.

The Solver Results window also indicates that there are three reports available: **ANSWER, SENSITIVITY,** and **LIMITS.** We discuss the Answer Report in the next section and the Sensitivity Report in Chapter 4. The Limits Report is not useful for our discussion here, and we therefore ignore it. Note that in order to get these reports, we must select them by clicking the relevant report names to highlight them before clicking OK on the Solver Results window.

Cells B5 and C5 show the optimal quantities of tables and chairs to make, respectively, and cell D6 shows the optimal profit. Cells D8 to D11 show the LHS values of the four constraints. For example, cell D8 shows the number of carpentry hours used.

The Answer Report presents the results in a more detailed manner.

Answer Report   If requested, Solver provides the **Answer Report** in a separate worksheet. The report for Flair's problem is shown in Screenshot 2.1E (we have added grid lines to this report to make it clearer). The report provides the same information as that discussed previously but in a more organized manner. In addition to indicating the values, it also shows the following information for each constraint in the model:

File: 2-1.xls, sheet: 2-1E

Names in Solver reports can be edited, if desired.

1. **Cell.** Cell reference corresponding to the LHS of the constraint. For example, cell D8 contains the formula for the LHS of the carpentry constraint.
2. **Name.** Descriptive name of the LHS cell. We can use Excel's naming feature **(INSERT|NAME|DEFINE)** to define a descriptive name for any cell (or cell range). If we do so, the cell name is reported in this column. If no name is defined for a

SCREENSHOT 2.1E

Solver's Answer Report for Flair Furniture

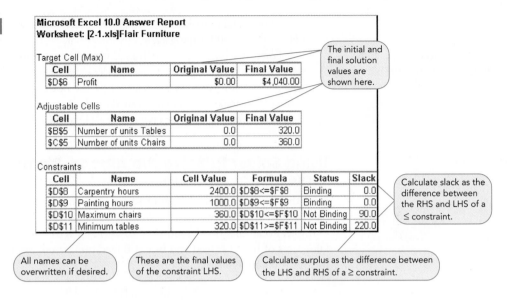

Microsoft Excel 10.0 Answer Report
Worksheet: [2-1.xls]Flair Furniture

Target Cell (Max)

Cell	Name	Original Value	Final Value
$D$6	Profit	$0.00	$4,040.00

The initial and final solution values are shown here.

Adjustable Cells

Cell	Name	Original Value	Final Value
$B$5	Number of units Tables	0.0	320.0
$C$5	Number of units Chairs	0.0	360.0

Constraints

Cell	Name	Cell Value	Formula	Status	Slack
$D$8	Carpentry hours	2400.0	$D$8<=$F$8	Binding	0.0
$D$9	Painting hours	1000.0	$D$9<=$F$9	Binding	0.0
$D$10	Maximum chairs	360.0	$D$10<=$F$10	Not Binding	90.0
$D$11	Minimum tables	320.0	$D$11>=$F$11	Not Binding	220.0

Calculate slack as the difference between the RHS and LHS of a ≤ constraint.

All names can be overwritten if desired.

These are the final values of the constraint LHS.

Calculate surplus as the difference between the LHS and RHS of a ≥ constraint.

cell, Solver extracts the name shown in this column from the information provided in the spreadsheet layout. Solver simply combines labels (if any) to the left of and above the LHS cell to create the name for that cell. Note that these labels can be overwritten manually, if necessary. For example, the name Profit for the target cell (cell D6) can be overwritten to say Total Profit. Observe that the Excel layout we have used here ensures that all names automatically generated by Solver are logical.

3. **Cell Value.** The final value of the LHS of the constraint at the optimal solution. For example, the cell value for the carpentry time constraint indicates that we are using 2400 hours at the optimal solution.

4. **Formula.** The formula specified in Solver for the constraint. For example, the formula entered in Solver for the carpentry time constraint is D8 ≤ F8.

5. **Status.** Indicates whether the constraint is binding or nonbinding. *Binding* means that the constraint becomes an equality (i.e., LHS = RHS) at the optimal solution. For a ≤ constraint, this typically means that all the available amounts of that resource are fully used in the optimal solution. In Flair's case, the carpentry and painting constraints are both binding because we are using all the available hours in either case.

For a ≥ constraint, *binding* typically means we are exactly satisfying the minimum level required by that constraint. In Flair's case, the minimum tables required constraint is nonbinding because we plan to make 320 as against the required minimum of 100.

6. **Slack**. Magnitude (absolute value) of the difference between the RHS and LHS values of the constraint. Obviously, if the constraint is binding, slack is zero (because LHS = RHS). For a nonbinding ≤ constraint, slack typically denotes the amount of resource that is left unused at the optimal solution. In Flair's case, we are allowed to make up to 450 chairs

Binding means the constraint is exactly satisfied and LHS = RHS.

Slack typically refers to the amount of unused resource in a ≤ constraint.

but are planning to make only 360. The absolute difference of 90 between the RHS and LHS (= |450−360|) is the slack in this constraint.

For a nonbinding ≥ constraint, we call this term *surplus* (even though Solver refers to this difference in all cases as slack). A surplus typically denotes the extent to which the ≥ constraint is oversatisfied at the optimal solution. In Flair's case, we are planning to make 320 tables even though we are required to make only 100. The absolute difference of 220 between the RHS and LHS (= |100−320|) is the surplus in this constraint.

Using Solver to Solve the Alberta Plains Turkey Farm Problem

Now that we have studied how to set up and solve a maximization LP problem using Excel's Solver, let us consider a minimization problem—the Alberta Plains Turkey Farm example. Recall that the decision variables A and B in this problem denote the number of kilograms of brand A feed and brand B feed purchased, respectively. The LP formulation for this problem is as follows:

$$\text{Minimize cost} = 2A + 3B$$

File: 2-2.xls

subject to the constraints

$$
\begin{aligned}
5A + 10B &\geq 90 && \text{(protein constraint)}\\
4A + 3B &\geq 48 && \text{(vitamin constraint)}\\
0.5A &\geq 1.5 && \text{(iron constraint)}\\
A, B &\geq 0 && \text{(nonnegativity constraints)}
\end{aligned}
$$

The formula view of the Excel layout for the Alberta Plains Turkey Farm LP problem is shown in Screenshot 2.2A. The solution values and the Solver Parameters window are shown in Screenshot 2.2B on page 61. Note that Solver shows the problem as being solved as a Min problem. As with the Flair Furniture example, all problem parameters are entered as entries in different cells of the spreadsheet, and Excel's SUMPRODUCT function is used to compute the objective function as well as the LHS values for all three constraints (corresponding to protein, vitamin, and iron).

The solved Answer Report obtained for this problem is shown in Screenshot 2.2C. As expected, this result is exactly the same as the one we obtained using the graphical

Formula View of the Excel Layout for Alberta Plains

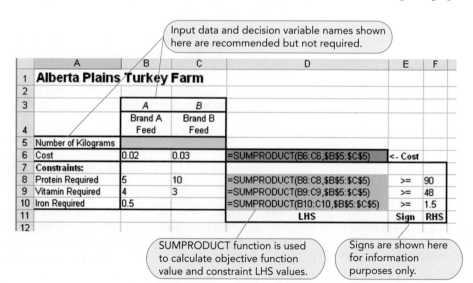

SCREENSHOT 2.2B

Excel Layout and Solver Entries for Alberta Plains

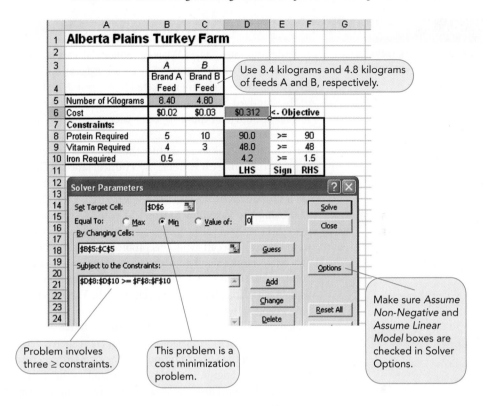

Use 8.4 kilograms and 4.8 kilograms of feeds A and B, respectively.

Problem involves three ≥ constraints.

This problem is a cost minimization problem.

Make sure *Assume Non-Negative* and *Assume Linear Model* boxes are checked in Solver Options.

Surplus refers to the amount of oversatisfaction of a ≥ constraint.

approach. Also, since the constraints in this case are of the "≥" type, we refer to the difference between the LHS and RHS of each constraint as the **surplus** rather than as the **slack** (even though Solver refers to this difference in all cases as slack). Just as the slack denotes the amount of a resource that is left unused in a ≤ constraint by the optimal solution, the surplus denotes the extent to which a ≥ constraint is oversatisfied by the optimal solution.

SCREENSHOT 2.2C

Solver's Answer Report for Alberta Plains

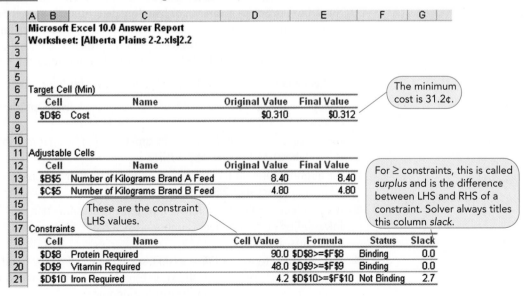

The minimum cost is 31.2¢.

For ≥ constraints, this is called *surplus* and is the difference between LHS and RHS of a constraint. Solver always titles this column *slack*.

These are the constraint LHS values.

2.9   PREMIUM SOLVER FOR EDUCATION (v7.0)

Premium Solver includes several additional options.

Included in your CD-ROM is an enhanced version of the Solver add-in for Excel. This version, called the Premium Solver for Education, is a student version of the powerful Premium Solver software marketed by Frontline Systems Inc. In addition to all the features of the standard Solver that comes with Excel, the Premium Solver for Education includes several options that make it even easier to model and solve LP problems.

As shown in Screenshot 2.3A on the next page, the initial window for Premium Solver for Education looks exactly like the standard Solver window shown in Screenshot 2.1B with the following exceptions: (1) a button labelled Guess is removed, (2) a button labelled Model is added, (3) two toggling buttons labeled Variables and Constraints are added, and (4) a dropdown list to select the solver engine is included.

Using the Variables Button   If your decision variable cells are scattered across your worksheet, selecting all of them in a single multiple selection can become difficult and tedious. In most cases you can avoid this problem by organizing your model so that the decision variable cells occupy a small number of contiguous blocks. But if this is inconvenient, the Premium Solver products allow you to switch to a more flexible method of specifying decision variables, using the Variables button. If you click on the Variables button, the dialog box changes to show the variable selections in a list box, as shown in screenshot 2.3A(b). In this screenshot, you'd click the Add button to get the **ADD VARIABLE CELLS** window (screenshot 2.3A(d)) using which you can select decision variables cells that are scattered across the worksheet.

Selecting the Solver Engine   In the standard Microsoft Excel Solver, the default choice for the Solver engine to optimize a model is the Generalized Reduced Gradient (GRG) Nonlinear Solver. This default setting can be changed using the Solver Options dialog. In the Premium Solver products, selecting the Solver engine is easier. There is a dropdown list that gives the user the choice of three different programs to use:

1. *Standard Simplex LP*. Select this procedure for solving all LP problems and integer programming problems (covered in Chapter 6).

2. *Standard Generalized Reduced Gradient (GRG) Nonlinear*. We go over this procedure, which Solver uses to solve nonlinear programs, in Chapter 7.

3. *Standard Evolutionary*. This procedure is based on the principles of a relatively new optimization technique called genetic algorithms. The standard evolutionary procedure in Solver is capable of handling deterministic as well as nondeterministic models. However, unlike the standard simplex and GRG procedures, there is no way of knowing for certain if a given solution is optimal. Genetic algorithms are beyond the scope of this textbook, and we therefore do not discuss this procedure here.

Other enhancements provided in Premium Solver for Education include the following:

- the option to bypass the creation of reports in the Solver Options window (shown in Screenshot 2.3B(a)),
- the option to return to the Solver Parameters window after a problem has been solved (shown in Screenshot 2.3B(b)),
- the option to present the reports in outline form after a problem has been solved (shown in Screenshot 2.3B(b)),
- if a problem is infeasible, a report indicating constraints that may be causing the infeasibility; or if a problem is unbounded, a report showing a list of non binding constrains, and
- the possibility to use *alldifferent* (dif), *second-order cone* (soc), and *rotated second order cone* (src) constraints (shown in screenshot 2.3A(c); for detail, see the user guide for Premium Solver in the installation folder).

SCREENSHOT 2.3A

Solver Entry Window for Premium Solver for Education

(a)

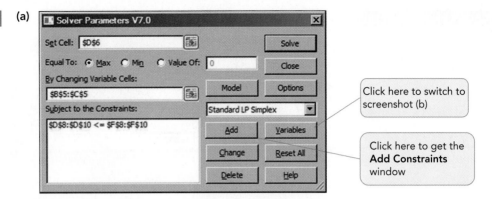

Click here to switch to screenshot (b)

Click here to get the **Add Constraints** window

(b)

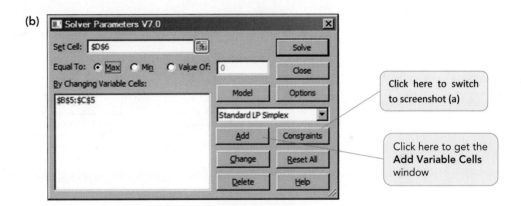

Click here to switch to screenshot (a)

Click here to get the **Add Variable Cells** window

(c)

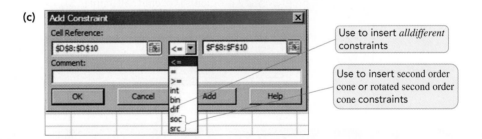

Use to insert *alldifferent* constraints

Use to insert second order cone or rotated second order cone constraints

(d)

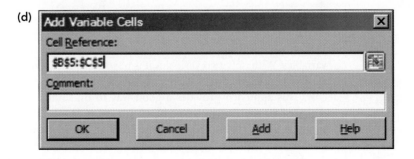

SCREENSHOT 2.3B

(a)

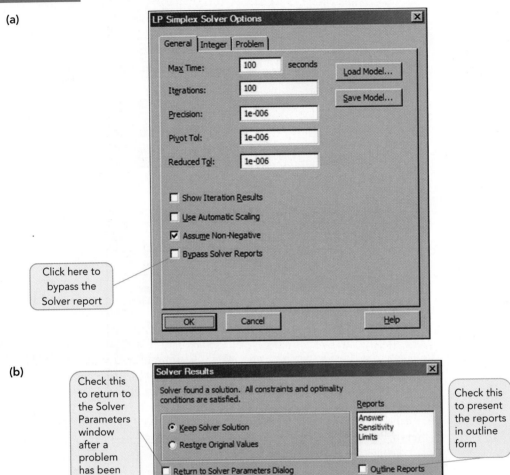

Click here to bypass the Solver report

(b)

Check this to return to the Solver Parameters window after a problem has been solved

Check this to present the reports in outline form

| 2.10 | **ALGORITHMIC SOLUTION PROCEDURES FOR LINEAR PROGRAMMING PROBLEMS** |

Simplex Method

So far, we have looked at examples of LP problems that contain only two decision variables. With only two variables it is possible to use a graphical approach. We plotted the feasible region and then searched for an optimal corner point and corresponding profit or cost. This approach provides a good way to understand the basic concepts of LP. Most real-life LP problems, however, have more than two variables and are thus too large for the simple graphical solution procedure. Problems faced in business and government can have dozens, hundreds, or even thousands of variables. We need a more powerful method than graphing; for this we turn to a procedure called the **simplex method**.

How does the simplex method work? The concept is simple and similar to graphical LP in one important respect: In graphical LP we examined each of the corner points; LP theory tells us that an optimal solution lies at one of them. In LP problems containing

Recall that the theory of LP states the optimal solution will lie at a corner point of the feasible region. In large LP problems, the feasible region cannot be graphed because it has many dimensions, but the concept is the same.

several variables, we may not be able to graph the feasible region, but an optimal solution will still lie at a corner point of the many-sided, many-dimensional figure (called an *n*-dimensional polyhedron) that represents the area of feasible solutions. The simplex method examines the corner points in a systematic fashion, using basic algebraic concepts. It does so in an **iterative** manner, that is, repeating the same set of procedures time after time until an optimal solution is reached. Each iteration of the simplex method brings a value for the objective function that is no worse (and usually better) than the current value. Hence, we are progressively moving closer to an optimal solution.

The simplex method systematically examines corner points, using algebraic steps, until an optimal solution is found.

In most software packages, including Excel's Solver, the simplex method has been coded in a very efficient manner to exploit the computational capabilities of modern computers. As a result, for most LP problems, the simplex method identifies an optimal corner point after examining just a tiny fraction of the total number of corner points in the feasible region.

Karmarkar's Algorithm

In 1984, Narendra Karmarkar developed an alternative to the simplex algorithm. The new method, called Karmarkar's algorithm, often takes significantly less computer time to solve very large LP problems.[7]

Karmarkar's method follows a path of points inside the feasible region.

Whereas the simplex algorithm finds a solution by moving from one adjacent corner point to the next, following the outside edges of the feasible region, Karmarkar's method follows a path of points on the inside of the feasible region. Karmarkar's method is also unique in its ability to handle an extremely large number of constraints and variables, thereby giving LP users the capacity to solve previously unsolvable problems.

Although it is likely that the simplex method will continue to be used for many LP problems, a newer generation of LP software has been built around Karmarkar's algorithm. Delta Air Lines became the first commercial airline to use this software, called KORBX, which was developed and is sold by AT&T. Delta found that the program was capable of effectively handling the monthly scheduling of 7000 pilots who fly more than 400 airplanes to 166 cities worldwide. With increased efficiency in allocating limited resources, Delta saves millions of dollars in crew time and related costs.

SUMMARY

In this chapter we introduce a mathematical modeling technique called linear programming (LP). Analysts use LP models to find an optimal solution to problems that have a series of constraints binding the objective value. We discuss how to formulate LP models and then show how models with only two decision variables can be solved graphically. The graphical solution approach of this chapter provides a conceptual basis for tackling larger, more complex real-life problems. However, solving LP models with numerous decision variables and constraints requires a solution procedure such as the simplex algorithm.

The simplex algorithm is embedded in Excel's Solver add-in. We describe how LP models can be set up on Excel and solved using Solver. The structured approach presented in this chapter for setting up and solving LP problems with just two variables can be easily adapted to problems of larger size. We address several such problems in Chapter 3.

---

[7] For details, see N. Karmarkar. "A New Polynomial Time Algorithm for Linear Programming," *Combinatorica* 4, 4 (1984): 373–395; or J. N. Hooker. "Karmarkar's Linear Programming Algorithm," *Interfaces* 16, 4 (July–August 1986): 75–90.

GLOSSARY

Alternate Optimal Solutions. A situation in which more than one optimal solution is possible. It arises when the angle or slope of the objective function is the same as the slope of the constraint.

Answer Report. A report created by Solver when it solves an LP model. This report presents the optimal solution in a detailed manner.

Assume Linear Model. An option available in Solver that forces it to solve the model as a linear program using the simplex procedure.

Assume Non-Negative. An option available in Solver that automatically enforces the nonnegativity constraint.

Changing Cells. The cells that represent the decision variables in Solver.

Constraint. A restriction (stated in the form of an inequality or an equation) that inhibits (or binds) the value that can be achieved by the objective function.

Constraint LHS. The cell that contains the formula for the left-hand side of a constraint in Solver. There is one such cell for each constraint in the problem.

Constraint RHS. The cell that contains the value (or formula) for the right-hand side of a constraint in Solver. There is one such cell for each constraint in the problem.

Corner (or Extreme) Point. A point that lies on one of the corners of the feasible region. This means that it falls at the intersection of two constraint lines.

Corner Point Method. The method of finding the optimal solution to an LP problem by testing the profit or cost level at each corner point of the feasible region. The theory of LP states that the optimal solution must lie at one of the corner points.

Decision Variables. The unknown quantities in the problem for which optimal solution values are to be found.

Feasible Region. The area satisfying all of the problem's resource restrictions—that is, the region where all constraints overlap. All possible solutions to the problem lie in the feasible region.

Feasible Solution. Any point lying in the feasible region. Basically, it is any point that satisfies all of the problem's constraints.

Inequality. A mathematical expression containing a greater than or equal to relation ($\geq$) or a less than or equal to relation ($\leq$) between the left-hand side and the right-hand side of the expression.

Infeasible Solution. Any point lying outside the feasible region. It violates one or more of the stated constraints.

Infeasibility. A condition that arises when there is no solution to an LP problem that satisfies all of the constraints.

Level (or Iso) Line. A straight line that represents all nonnegative combinations of the decision variables for a particular profit (or cost) level.

Iterative Procedure. A process (algorithm) that repeats the same steps over and over.

Linear Programming (LP). A mathematical technique used to help management decide how to make the most effective use of an organization's resources.

Mathematical Programming. The general category of mathematical modeling and solution techniques used to allocate resources while optimizing a measurable goal; LP is one type of programming model.

Nonnegativity Constraints. A set of constraints that requires each decision variable to be nonnegative; that is, each decision variable must be greater than or equal to 0.

Objective Function. A mathematical statement of the goal of an organization, stated as an intent to maximize or minimize some important quantity such as profit or cost.

Product Mix Problem. A common LP problem involving a decision as to which products a firm should produce given that it faces limited resources.

Redundancy. The presence of one or more constraints that do not affect the feasible solution region.

Simplex Method. An iterative procedure for solving LP problems.

Simultaneous Equations Method. The algebraic means of solving for the intersection point of two or more linear constraint equations.

Slack. Difference between the right-hand side and left-hand side of a $\leq$ constraint. Typically represents the unused resource.

Solver. An Excel add-in that allows LP problems to be set up and solved in Excel.

SUMPRODUCT Function. An Excel function that allows users to easily model formulas for the objective function and constraints.

Surplus. Difference between the left-hand side and right-hand side of a constraint. Typically represents the level of oversatisfaction of a requirement.

Target Cell. The cell that contains the formula for the objective function in Solver.

Unboundedness. A condition that exists when the objective value can be made infinitely large (in a maximization problem) or small (in a minimization problem) without violating any of the problem's constraints.

SOLVED PROBLEMS

Solved Problem 2-1

Personal Mini Warehouses is planning to open a new branch in Manitoba. In doing so, the company must determine how many storage rooms of each size to build. The company builds large and small rental spaces. After careful analysis of the expected monthly earnings of both types of rental space, as well as the constraints (budget, area required for each size space, and projected rental limitations), Personal has formulated the following linear programming model:

$$\text{Maximize monthly earnings} = 50X + 20Y$$

subject to

$$2X + 4Y \le 400 \quad \text{(advertising budget available)}$$

$$100X + 50Y \le 8000 \quad \text{(square metres required)}$$

$$X \le 60 \quad \text{(rental limit expected)}$$

$$X, Y \ge 0$$

where

$$X = \text{number of large spaces developed}$$

$$Y = \text{number of small spaces developed}$$

Solve this LP problem using the graphical procedure and Excel.

Solution

An evaluation of the five corner points of the accompanying graph indicates that corner point C produces the greatest earnings. Refer to Figure 2.14 and the table on page 67.

FIGURE 2.14

Graph for Solved Problem 2-1

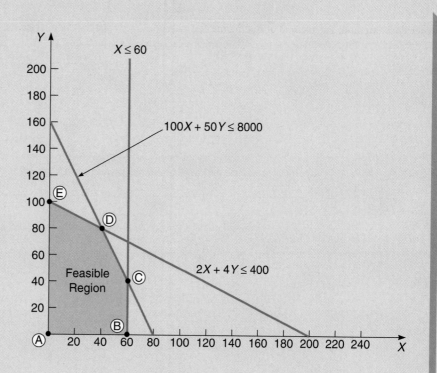

File: 2-4.xls

Corner Point	Values of X, Y	Objective Function Value ($)
Ⓐ	(0, 0)	0
Ⓑ	(60, 0)	3000
Ⓒ	(60, 40)	3800
Ⓓ	(40, 80)	3600
Ⓔ	(0, 100)	2000

SCREENSHOT 2.4

Excel Layout and Solver Entries for Solved Problem 2-1

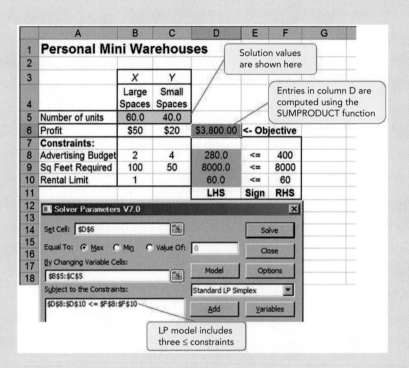

The Excel layout and Solver entries for this problem are shown in Screenshot 2.4 above. As expected, the optimal solution is the same as that found using the graphical approach ($X = 60$, $Y = 40$).

Solved Problem 2-2

Solve the following LP formulation graphically, using the isocost line approach. Also solve using Excel.

$$\text{Minimize costs} = 24X + 28Y$$

$$\text{subject to} \quad 5X + 4Y \leq 2000$$

$$X \geq 80$$

$$X + Y \geq 300$$

$$Y \geq 100$$

$$X, Y \geq 0$$

File: 2-5.xls

Solution

A graph of the four constraints is shown in Figure 2.15. The arrows indicate the direction of feasibility for each constraint. The second graph illustrates the feasible solution region and plots of two possible objective function cost lines. The first, $10 000, was selected arbitrarily as a starting point. To find the optimal corner point, we need to move the cost line in the direction of the lower cost, that is, down and to the left. The last point where a cost line touches the feasible region as it moves toward the origin is corner point Ⓓ. Thus Ⓓ, which represents $X = 200$, $Y = 100$, and a cost of $7600, is optimal.

The Excel layout and Solver entries for this problem are shown in Screenshot 2.5. The optimal solution is $X = 200$, $Y = 100$, and a cost of $7600. As expected, this is the same solution as point Ⓓ in the graph (see Figure 2.15).

FIGURE 2.15

Graphs for Solved Problem 2-2

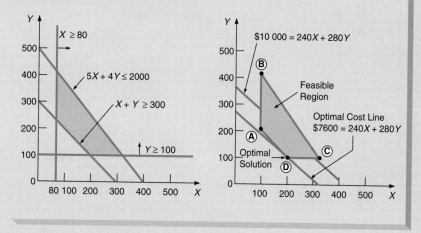

SCREENSHOT 2.5

Excel Layout and Solver Entries for Solved Problem 2-2

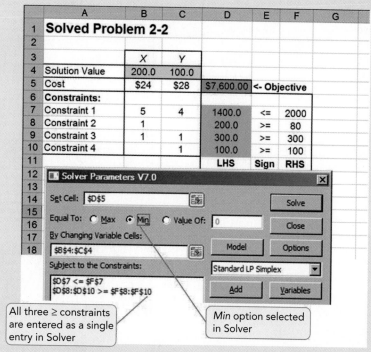

Solved Problem 2-3

Solve the following problem given these constraints and objective function:

$$\text{Maximize profit} = 30X + 40Y$$

$$\text{subject to} \qquad 4X + 2Y \leq 16$$

$$2X - Y \geq 2$$

$$Y \leq 2$$

$$X, Y \geq 0$$

a. Graph the feasible region.
b. Evaluate the objective function at each corner point.
c. Identify the optimal solution.

Solution

a. The graph appears in Figure 2.16 with the feasible region shaded.
b.

Corner Point	Coordinates	Profit ($)
Ⓐ	$X = 1, Y = 0$	30
Ⓑ	$X = 4, Y = 0$	120
Ⓒ	$X = 3, Y = 2$	170
Ⓓ	$X = 2, Y = 2$	140

c. The optimal profit of $170 is at corner point Ⓒ.

FIGURE 2.16

Graph for Solved Problem 2-3

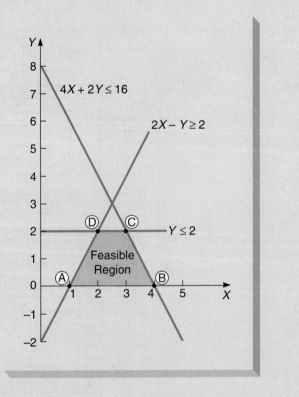

⇢ SELF-TEST

- Before taking the self-test, refer back to the learning objectives at the beginning of the chapter, the notes in the margins, and the glossary at the end of the chapter.
- Use the key at the back of the book to correct your answers.
- Restudy pages that correspond to any questions that you answered incorrectly or material you feel uncertain about.

1. When using a graphical solution procedure, the region bounded by the set of constraints is called
   a. the solution.
   b. the feasible region.
   c. the infeasible region.
   d. the maximum profit region.
   e. none of the above.

2. The corner point solution method can only be used to solve maximization problems.
   a. True
   b. False

3. Using the graphical solution procedure to solve a maximization problem requires that we
   a. move the isoprofit line up until it no longer intersects with any constraint equation.
   b. move the isoprofit line down until it no longer intersects with any constraint equation.
   c. apply the method of simultaneous equations to solve for the intersections of constraints.
   d. find the value of the objective functions at the origin.
   e. do none of the above.

4. The graphical method of LP can only handle _____ decision variables
   a. one
   b. two
   c. three
   d. none of the above

5. Types of graphical solutions to LP include all except
   a. isoprofit line solution.
   b. the corner point solution.
   c. the simplex method.
   d. All are solutions to the graphic approach.
   e. None are solutions to the graphic approach.

6. The graphic method of LP uses
   a. objective equations.
   b. constraint equations.
   c. linear equations.
   d. all of the above.
   e. none of the above.

7. Any LP problem can be solved using the graphical solution procedure.
   a. True
   b. False

8. The set of solution points that satisfies all of an LP problem's constraints simultaneously is defined as the feasible region in graphical LP.
   a. True
   b. False

9. An objective function is necessary in a maximization problem but is not required in a minimization problem.
   a. True
   b. False

10. Which of the following is *not* a property of all LP problems?
    a. the presence of restrictions
    b. optimization of some objective
    c. a computer program
    d. alternative courses of action to choose from
    e. usage of only linear equations and inequalities

11. A feasible solution to an LP problem
    a. must satisfy all of the problem's constraints simultaneously.
    b. need not satisfy all of the constraints, only some of them.
    c. must be a corner point of the feasible region.
    d. must give the maximum possible profit.

12. We can specify more than one Target Cell in Solver.
    a. True
    b. False

13. In Excel, we are required to manipulate constraints so that all variables appear on the left-hand side.
    a. True
    b. False

14. We can enter formulas for constraints directly in the Solver input window.
    a. True
    b. False

15. Changing Cells in Solver refer to the
    a. decision variables.
    b. left-hand side of a constraint.
    c. right-hand side of a constraint.
    d. objective function.

16. Target Cell in Solver refers to the
    a. decision variables.
    b. left-hand side of a constraint.
    c. right-hand side of a constraint.
    d. objective function.

17. To enter decision variables as a block in Solver,
    a. there must be only two decision variables in the problem.
    b. the cells denoting the decision variables must be next to each other.
    c. the decision variables must each be modeled in a separate column.
    d. the problem must have a maximization objective function.

DISCUSSION QUESTIONS AND PROBLEMS

Discussion Questions

2-1 Discuss the similarities and differences between mini-mization and maximization problems, using the graphical solution approach to LP.

2-2 It is important to understand the assumptions underlying the use of any quantitative analysis model. What are the assumptions and requirements for an LP model to be formulated and used?

2-3 It has been said that each LP problem that has a feasible region has an infinite number of solutions. Explain.

2-4 You have just formulated a maximization LP problem and are preparing to solve it graphically. What criteria should you consider in deciding whether it would be easier to solve the problem by the corner point method or the iso-profit line approach?

2-5 Under what condition is it possible for an LP problem to have more than one optimal solution?

2-6 Develop your own set of constraint equations and inequalities and use them to illustrate graphically each of the following conditions:
(a) an unbounded problem
(b) an infeasible problem
(c) a problem containing redundant constraints

2-7 The production manager of a large Vancouver manufacturing firm once made the statement, "I would like to use LP, but it's a technique that operates under conditions of certainty. My plant doesn't have that certainty; it's a world of uncertainty. So LP can't be used here." Do you think this statement has any merit? Explain why the manager may have said it.

2-8 The mathematical relationships that follow were formulated by an operations research analyst at the Smith–Lawton Chemical Company. Which ones are invalid for use in an LP problem, and why?

$$\text{Maximize profit} = 4X_1 + 3X_1X_2 + 8X_2 + 5X_3$$

subject to
$$2X_1 + X_2 + 2X_3 \leq 50$$
$$X_1 - 4X_2 \geq 6$$
$$1.5X_1^2 + 6X_2 + 3X_3 \geq 21$$
$$19X_2 - \tfrac{1}{3}X_3 = 17$$
$$5X_1 + 4X_2 + 3\sqrt{X_3} \leq 80$$

2-9 What is the value of the computer in solving LP problems today?

2-10 Explain why knowing how to use Excel to set up and solve LP problems may be beneficial to a manager.

2-11 What are the components of defining a problem on Excel so that it can be solved using Solver?

2-12 How is the slack (or surplus) calculated for a constraint? How is it interpreted?

2-13 What is an unbounded solution? How does Solver indicate that a problem solution is unbounded?

Problems

2-14 Consider the following LP problem:

$$\text{Maximize profit} = \$1X + \$1Y$$

subject to
$$2X + 1Y \leq 100$$
$$1X + 2Y \leq 100$$
$$X, Y \geq 0$$

What is the optimal solution to this problem? Solve it graphically.

2-15 Graph the following LP problem and find the optimal solution.

$$\text{Maximize profit} = \$3X + \$2Y$$

subject to
$$2X + 1Y \leq 150$$
$$2X + 3Y \leq 300$$
$$X, Y \geq 0$$

2-16 Graphically analyze the following problem:

$$\text{Maximize profit} = \$4X + \$6Y$$

subject to
$$1X + 2Y \leq 8$$
$$6X + 4Y \leq 24$$
$$X, Y \geq 0$$

What is the optimal solution?

2-17 Solve the following LP problem using the corner point graphical method:

$$\text{Maximize profit} = 4X + 4Y$$

subject to
$$3X + 5Y \leq 150$$
$$X - 2Y \leq 10$$
$$5X + 3Y \leq 150$$
$$X, Y \geq 0$$

2-18 Solve the following LP problem by using the graphical procedure and then by using Excel:

$$\text{Maximize} = 5X + 3Y$$

subject to
$$5X + 2Y \leq 40$$
$$3X + 6Y \leq 48$$
$$X \leq 7$$
$$2X - Y \geq 3$$
$$X, Y \geq 0$$

2-19 Solve the following LP problem by using the graphical procedure and then by using Excel.

$$\text{Minimize } X + 2Y$$

subject to

$$X + 3Y \geq 90$$

$$8X + 2Y \geq 160$$

$$3X + 2Y \geq 120$$

$$Y \leq 70$$

$$X, Y \geq 0$$

2-20 Solve the following LP problem by using the graphical procedure and then by using Excel:

$$\text{Minimize } 4X + 7Y$$

subject to

$$3X + 7Y \geq 231$$

$$10X + 2Y \geq 200$$

$$2Y \geq 45$$

$$2X \leq 75$$

$$X, Y \geq 0$$

2-21 Solve the following LP problem by using the graphical procedure and then by using Excel:

$$\text{Maximize } X + Y$$

subject to

$$3X + 6Y \leq 29$$

$$7X + Y \leq 20$$

$$3X - Y \geq 1$$

$$X, Y \geq 0$$

2-22 Solve the following LP problem by using the graphical procedure and then by using Excel:

$$\text{Maximize } 7X + 4Y$$

subject to

$$9X + 8Y \leq 72$$

$$3X + 9Y \geq 27$$

$$9X - 15Y \geq 0$$

$$X, Y \geq 0$$

2-23 Solve the following LP problem by using the graphical procedure and then by using Excel:

$$\text{Minimize } 3X + 7Y$$

subject to

$$9X + 3Y \geq 36$$

$$4X + 5Y \geq 40$$

$$X - Y \leq 0$$

$$2X \leq 13$$

$$X, Y \geq 0$$

2-24 Consider the following four LP formulations. Using a graphical approach, determine

(a) which formulation has more than one optimal solution.
(b) which formulation is unbounded.
(c) which formulation is infeasible.
(d) which formulation has a unique optimal solution.

Formulation 1

Maximize: $10X + 10Y$
subject to: $2X \leq 10$
$2X + 4Y \leq 16$
$4Y \leq 8$
$X \geq 6$
$X, Y \geq 0$

Formulation 3

Maximize: $3X + 2Y$
subject to: $X + Y \geq 5$
$X \geq 2$
$2Y \geq 8$
$X, Y \geq 0$

Formulation 2

Maximize: $X + 2Y$
subject to: $X \leq 1$
$2Y \leq 2$
$X + 2Y \leq 2$
$X, Y \geq 0$

Formulation 4

Maximize: $3X + 3Y$
subject to: $4X + 6Y \leq 48$
$4X + 2Y \leq 12$
$3Y \geq 3$
$2X \geq 2$
$X, Y \geq 0$

Note: Problems 2-25 to 2-38 each involve only two decision variables. Therefore, at the discretion of the instructor, they can be solved by using graphical methods, Excel, or both.

2-25 *(Product mix)* The Sweet Smell Fertilizer Company markets bags of manure labelled "not less than 30 kilograms dry weight." The packaged manure is a combination of compost and sewage. To provide good quality fertilizer, each bag should contain at least 10 kilograms of compost and not more than 20 kilograms of sewage. Each kilogram of compost costs Sweet Smell $1.30 and each kilogram of sewage costs $0.95. Use a graphical LP method to determine the least cost blend of compost and sewage in each bag.

2-26 *(Portfolio selection)* A provincial teachers' pension fund has $250 000 available to invest in a 12-month commitment. The money can be placed in provincial bonds (with a return of 8% and a risk score of 2) or in an equity account (with a return of 9% and a risk score of 3). Pension fund regulations require diversification to the extent that between 50% and 70% of the total investment must be placed in provincial bonds. Also, due to past defaults in other provincial funds, it is decided that the average risk score of the total investment should be no more than 2.42. How much should the teachers' pension fund invest in each security to maximize its return on investment?

2-27 *(Media selection)* The advertising agency promoting the new Breem dishwashing detergent wants to get the best exposure possible for the product within the $95 200 advertising budget ceiling placed upon it. To do so, the agency needs to decide how much of the budget to spend on each of its two most effective media: (1) television spots during the afternoon hours and (2) large ads in the city's Sunday newspaper. Each television spot costs $3200; each Sunday newspaper ad costs $1300. The expected exposure, based on industry ratings, is 30 000 viewers for each television commercial and 20 000 readers for each newspaper advertisement. The agency director, Mavis Early, knows from experience that it is important to use both media in order to reach the broadest spectrum of potential Breem customers. She decides that at least 5 but no more than 10 television spots should be ordered and that the number of newspaper ads should be no more than 8 times the number of television spots. How many times should each of the two media be used to obtain maximum exposure while staying within the budget?

2-28 *(Product mix)* The Electrocomp Corporation manufactures two electrical products: air conditioners and large fans. The assembly process for each is similar in that both require a certain amount of wiring, drilling, and assembly. Each air conditioner takes 3 hours of wiring, 2 hours of drilling, and 1.5 hours of assembly. Each fan must go through 2 hours of wiring, 1 hour of drilling, and 0.5 hours of assembly. During the next production period, 240 hours of wiring time, 140 hours of drilling time, and 100 hours of assembly time are available. Each air conditioner sold yields a profit of $25. Each fan assembled can be sold for a $15 profit. Formulate and solve Electrocomp's problem to find the best combination of air conditioners and fans that yields the highest profit.

2-29 *(Product mix)* Electrocomp's management realizes that it forgot to include two critical constraints (see Problem 2-28). In particular, management decides that to ensure an adequate supply of air conditioners for a contract, at least 50 air conditioners should be manufactured. Because Electrocomp incurred an oversupply of fans in the preceding period, management also insists that no more than 30 fans be produced during this production period. Resolve Electrocomp's problem to find the new optimal solution.

2-30 *(Product mix)* A small magazine publisher wants to determine the best combination of two possible magazines to print for the month of July. *Backyard* magazine, which he has published for years, is a steady seller. The publisher wants to make sure he prints at least 400 copies to meet his demand from the newsstands. *Porch* is a new venture and has received the benefit of a great deal of advance publicity. The publisher is hoping that by positioning it near *Backyard*, he will pick up some spillover demand from his regular readers. Also, he is hoping that the advertising campaign will bring in a new type of reader from a potentially very lucrative market. He wants to print at least 300 copies of *Porch*. The cover price for *Backyard* is $3.50; he is pricing *Porch* at $4.50 because other magazines in this market seem to be able to command this type of higher price. The publisher has 36 hours of printing time available for this production run. He also has 30 hours in the collation department, where the magazines are actually assembled. Each *Backyard* requires 2.5 minutes per copy to print and 1.8 minutes per copy to collate. Each *Porch* requires 2 minutes to print and 2 minutes to collate. How many of each magazine should the publisher print to maximize his revenue?

2-31 *(Product mix)* Personal Mini Warehouses (PMW) is planning to expand its successful Ontario business into Quebec. In doing so, the company must decide how many storage sheds of each size—small and large—to build in its 750 m² facility. Each large shed is 15 m² in size, requires $1 per week in advertising, and rents for $50 per week. Each small shed is 5 m² in size, requires $1 per week in advertising, and rents for $20 per week. PMW has a weekly advertising budget of $100 and estimates that it can rent no more than 40 large sheds in any given week. Formulate PMW's problem as a linear program. Solve by using the graphical procedure, and then by using Excel.

2-32 *(Course planning)* The dean of a business school in Saskatoon must plan the school's course offerings for the next term. Student demands make it necessary to offer at least 20 core courses (each of which counts for 3 credit hours) and 20 elective courses (each of which counts for 4 credit hours) in the term. Faculty contracts also dictate that a total of at least 60 core and elective courses and at least 205 total credit hours be offered. Each core course taught costs the college an average of $2600 in faculty wages, and each elective course costs $3000. How many core and elective courses should be taught so that total faculty salaries are kept to a minimum?

2-33 *(Product mix)* MSA Computer Corporation manufactures two models of computer network routers, the Alpha 4 and the Beta 5. The firm employs five technicians, working 156 hours each per month, on its assembly line. Management insists that full employment (i.e., *all* 156 hours of time) be maintained for each worker during next month's operations. It requires 20 labour hours to assemble each Alpha 4 model and 25 labour hours to assemble each Beta 5 model. MSA wants to see at least 35 total routers made, and it wants the number of Beta 5 routers made to be no more than the number of Alpha 4 routers made. Alpha 4 routers generate a $1200 profit per unit, and Beta 5 routers yield $1800 each. Determine the most profitable number of each model of router to produce during the coming month.

2-34 *(Agriculture planning)* The seasonal yield of olives in a Piraeus, Greece, vineyard is greatly influenced by a process of branch pruning. If olive trees are pruned every two weeks, output is increased. The pruning process, however, requires considerably more labour than permitting the olives to grow on their own and results in a smaller olive. It also permits olive trees to be spaced closer together. The yield of one barrel of olives by pruning requires five hours of labour and half a hectare of land. The production of a barrel of olives by the normal process requires only two labour hours but takes 1 hectare of land. An olive grower has 250 hours of labour available and a total of 75 hectares for growing. Because of the olive size difference, a barrel of olives produced on pruned trees sells for $20, whereas a barrel of regular olives has a market price of $30. The grower has determined that because of uncertain demand, no more than 40 barrels of pruned olives should be produced. Use graphical LP to find

(a) the maximum possible profit.
(b) the best combination of barrels of pruned and regular olives.
(c) the number of hectares that the olive grower should devote to each growing process.

Each valve must go through three separate machines during the fabrication process. After fabrication, each valve is inspected by a human being, who spends 15 minutes per valve. There are 525 inspection hours available for the month. The time required (in hours) by each machine to work on each valve is shown in the following table. Also shown are the minimum number of valves that must be produced for the month and the unit profit for each valve:

| PRODUCT | DEPARTMENT | | | UNIT PROFIT | MINIMUM NEEDED |
	DRILLING	MILLING	LATHE		
X4509	0.40	0.60	1.20	$16	200
X3125	0.30	0.65	0.60	$12	250
X4950	0.45	0.52	0.50	$13	600
X2173	0.35	0.48	0.70	$ 8	450
Capacity (Hours)	700	890	1200		

Determine the optimal production mix for XRP Industries to make the best use of its profit potential.

2-43 *(Product mix)* The Canadian Superior Party Mix Company (CSPM) packages and sells three different 450-gram cans of mixed nuts. The three blends are called Plain Nuts, Mixed Nuts, and Premium Mix. A can of Plain Nuts sells for $2.25, while Mixed Nuts sell for $3.37, and Premium Mix sells for $6.49 per can. A can of Plain Nuts consists of 360 grams of peanuts and 90 grams of cashew nuts. A can of Mixed Nuts consists of 225 grams of peanuts, 135 grams of cashew nuts, 45 grams of almonds, and 45 grams of walnuts. A can of Premium Mix is made up of 135 grams of cashew nuts, 135 grams of almonds, and 180 grams of walnuts. Past demand indicates that customers purchase at least twice as many cans of Plain Nuts as Premium Mix. CSPM has on hand 225 kilograms of peanuts, 125 kilograms of cashew nuts, 45 kilograms of almonds, and 36 kilograms of walnuts. How many cans of each of the three blends should CSPM mix in order to maximize total revenue? What is the maximum revenue?

2-44 *(Product mix)* The Canadian Superior Party Mix Company (Problem 2-43) has discovered that it will only have 525 empty cans available to fill during the next production period. Also, a detailed analysis of historical sales suggests that Mixed Nuts is by far the most popular mix, with the Premium Mix, presumably because of the high price, lagging behind in sales. Consequently, management has decided that the number of cans of Plain Nuts should be one-half the number of cans of Mixed Nuts, but double the number of cans of Premium Mix. Solve the problem again with these new restrictions.

2-45 *(**Investment planning**)* An investor is considering three different railroad stocks to complement his portfolio: B & O Railroad, Short Line Railroad, and Reading Railroad. His broker has given him the following information:

| FACTOR | STOCK ($) | | |
	B & O	SHORT LINE	READING
Short-term growth per $ invested	0.39	0.26	0.42
Intermediate growth per $ invested	1.59	1.70	1.45
Dividend rate	8%	4%	6%

The investor's criteria are as follows: (1) investments should yield short-term growth of at least $1000, (2) investments should yield intermediate-term growth of at least $6,000, and (3) dividends should be at least $250 per year. Determine the least amount the investor can invest and how that investment should be allocated among the three stocks.

ch02_ivey_7A99E018.xls

⇒ CASE STUDY 2.1

Interactions 98

Betsy Little, executive director of the Canadian Medical Hall of Fame (CMHF), and Lindsay Dennison, outreach coordinator for the Faculty of Science at the University of Western Ontario (UWO), were leaving a tiring meeting thinking there had to be a better way to allocate conference space for INTERACTIONS 98.

INTERACTIONS 98

INTERACTIONS 98 was a university-sponsored conference designed to expose high-calibre secondary school students to interesting and innovative research activities. The two-day event introduced about 300 potential university students to the campus environment and activities in the hope of encouraging these students to attend UWO the following fall. One day of INTERACTIONS 98 was devoted to the CMHF Youth Symposium designed to foster appreciation for advances in science and technology.

The youth symposium consisted of a series of sessions highlighting and demonstrating various research activities. Each of the research topics was offered once in the morning and again in the afternoon, with students attending one session in the morning and a

Chris Anderson prepared this case under the supervision of Professor Peter Bell solely to provide material for class discussion. The authors do not intend to illustrate either effective or ineffective handling of a managerial situation. The authors may have disguised certain names and other identifying information to protect confidentiality.

Richard Ivey School of Business
The University of Western Ontario

Ivey Management Services prohibits any form of reproduction, storage or transmittal without its written permission. This material is not covered under authorization from CanCopy or any other reproduction rights organization. To order copies or request permission to reproduce materials, contact Ivey Publishing, Ivey Management Services, c/o Richard Ivey School of Business, The University of Western Ontario, London, Ontario, Canada, N6A 3K7; phone (519) 661-3208; fax (519) 661-3882; e-mail cases@ivey.uwo.ca.

Copyright © 1999, Ivey Management Services; Version: (A) 1999-05-27

different one in the afternoon. Many of the activities were laboratory demonstrations where space was very limited. Because of the space limitations, not all students could attend every topic, and so, prior to the symposium, students submitted a registration form indicating their preference for the sessions they would like to attend. Betsy Little assigned to Lindsay Dennison the task of allocating the students to the sessions in an attempt to satisfy the majority of requests. Table

TABLE 2.4

Students' Indicated Preferences

STUDENT	DATE RECEIVED	SELECTION				
		1-1	1-2	1-3	1-4	1-5
1	February 6	1	5	3	4	2
2	March 13	3	2	4	1	5
3	February 1	5	2	1	4	3
4	March 3	5	3	1	4	2
5	March 7	4	5	3	2	1
6	March 8	2	3	1	4	5
7	March 10	1	2	3	4	5
8	March 3	2	3	5	4	1
9	March 11	2	3	1	4	5
10	February 18	2	3	1	4	5
11	February 21	2	5	1	4	3
12	February 12	2	3	1	4	5
13	March 13	2	5	1	4	3
14	March 23	2	3	5	4	1
15	February 19	4	3	1	2	5
16	February 19	2	5	1	4	3
17	April 3	1	5	3	4	2
18	April 3	5	3	1	4	2
19	April 3	2	4	1	3	5
20	April 3	4	3	5	2	1

2.4 contains an example list of 20 students with their ranking of five sessions, with Table 2.5 indicating the capacity of each session.

Historically, students had been allocated to the sessions as registration forms were received, i.e., on a first-come-first-served basis. This process allowed a manual allocation of space, but sometimes became awkward because the CMHF often received in excess of 300 registrants for limited conference space. Betsy wondered whether there was a better way to assign space while ensuring some degree of fairness and attention towards the order in which registration forms were received.

CHANGING TO A BIDDING SYSTEM

A second issue concerned the way in which student preferences were expressed. Under the current system, students who sent the form in later might be blocked from a session that they really wanted to attend by students who did not much care which sessions they were assigned. One suggestion was that students each be given a number of points and be asked to bid on their preferred sessions by allocating points to sessions. A student who really wanted to attend one session could assign all his or her points to that session, while one who was indifferent could assign an equal number of points to each session. Session spaces could then be allocated to the students bidding the most points.

The assignments of students to sessions were already difficult to handle. Betsy wondered whether changing to such a bidding system would make the assignment problem even more difficult.

TABLE 2.5

Rooms and Capacities

ROOM	CAPACITY
1-1	2
1-2	5
1-3	2
1-4	6
1-5	6

DISCUSSION QUESTION

Would you recommend going to a bidding system? Why or why not?

⟫ CASE STUDY 2.2

Golding Landscaping and Plants, Inc.

Kenneth and Patricia Golding spent a career as a husband-and-wife real estate investment partnership in Vancouver. When they finally retired to a 10-hectare farm in Salt Spring Island, they became ardent amateur gardeners. Kenneth planted shrubs and fruit trees, and Patricia spent her hours potting all sizes of plants. When the volume of shrubs and plants reached the point that the Goldings began to think of their hobby farm in a serious vein, they built a greenhouse adjacent to their home and installed heating and watering systems.

By 2003, the Goldings realized their retirement from real estate had really only led to a second career—in the plant and shrub business—and they filed for a B.C. business licence. Within a matter of months, they asked their lawyer to file incorporation documents and formed the firm Golding Landscaping and Plants, Inc.

Early in the new business's existence, Kenneth Golding recognized the need for a high-quality commercial fertilizer that he could blend himself, both for sale and for his own nursery. His goal was to keep his costs to a minimum while producing a top-notch product that was especially suited to the British Columbia climate.

Working with chemists at a Vancouver-based university, Golding blended "Golding-Grow." It consists of four chemical compounds: C-30, C-92, D-21, and E-11. The cost per kilogram for each compound is indicated in the following table:

CHEMICAL COMPOUND	COST PER KILO
C-30	$0.24
C-92	0.18
D-21	0.22
E-11	0.08

The specifications for Golding-Grow are as follows:
a. Chemical E-11 must comprise at least 15% of the blend.

b. C-92 and C-30 must together constitute at least 45% of the blend.
c. D-21 and C-92 may together constitute no more than 30% of the blend.
d. Golding-Grow is packaged and sold commercially in 50-kilogram lots.

DISCUSSION QUESTION

1. Formulate an LP problem to determine what blend of the four chemicals will allow Golding to minimize the cost of a 50-kilogram lot of the fertilizer.
2. Solve using Excel to find the best solution.

Source: Adapted from J. Heizer and B. Render. *Operations Management* 6/e. Upper Saddle River, NJ: Prentice Hall, Inc. 2001, p. 772.

⫸ CASE STUDY 2.3

International Pharma Inc.

Pharmaceutical drug development is a lengthy and highly competitive process. About one in 5000 drugs that begin clinical testing actually makes it to market. It is an expensive process and the costs continue to increase. The average total research and development (R&D) cost for new drugs in the late '90s was reported to be $897 million (more than double the cost in the '80s, and some five times the cost in the '70s). This rapid rise in R&D costs is driven largely by steep increases in the costs of clinical testing, which have grown five times as fast as preclinical testing costs. Proving the viability of a new drug to national regulatory agencies is time consuming and expensive.

The process of drug development and testing starts at the preclinical level, using tissue cultures and a variety of small animals. Then it goes through three successive phases of human testing. Phase one involves a very small number of healthy volunteers (often 20 to 100) and takes six to nine months. Phase two uses a few hundred patients with the target disease in a controlled study taking six months to three years to complete. Phase three typically requires 1000 to 3000 volunteers and can take between one and five years. New drugs that successfully make it through all stages eventually receive approval. The clinical testing phase (administration of drugs to humans prior to final regulatory approval) is the most critical for drug approval from regulators such as Health Canada or the U.S. Food and Drug Administration. This phase requires global collaboration, with testing being completed in all regions of the world. Once a drug does receive approval, its marketing life is relatively short before coming off patent—approximately 10 years. At that point generic competition enters and profitability is significantly decreased.

To receive regulatory approval in various countries, a number of drug trials need to be conducted within each of several global regions. Most regulatory agencies will only approve a drug if at least some of the clinical studies were conducted within their country or region. Hence, drug companies enroll more patients in regions that will be important once the drugs are commercialized.

International Pharma Inc. (IPI) is an international pharmaceutical developer and manufacturer operating in Canada and elsewhere. With some of its more profitable drugs soon to have their patents expire, the company is eager to bring new drugs to market. Its R&D division is particularly faced with pressures. While the division generates no direct revenue (it is strictly a cost centre), R&D costs account for some 25% of all corporate costs.

PROBLEM STATEMENT

IPI's R&D division estimates it needs at least 20 000 new subjects in the coming year for planned studies. Subjects are recruited into the studies through hospitals by doctors and medical professionals under contract with IPI. These health care workers administer the study drugs and track subjects' responses to the drug treatment. IPI assigns a Clinical Research Associate (CRA) to each subject for oversight of the study and analysis of the data.

The following table shows minimum trial subject requirements by region. It also shows the regional average cost to enroll and complete one patient in a clinical study. Besides internal IPI costs, this figure also includes all external costs (such as hospital fees, medical professional wages, costs of drugs and laboratory tests, and subject recruitment fees).

	NORTH AFRICA & MIDDLE EAST	CENTRAL & SOUTHERN AFRICA	ASIA PACIFIC	SOUTH AMERICA	WESTERN EUROPE	CENTRAL & EASTERN EUROPE	NORTH AMERICA
Number of subjects	500	500	500	500	2500	500	3500
Cost/subject	$12 570	$9764	$12 680	$11 590	$42 980	$24 145	$28 970

The division has 475 CRAs available worldwide to manage subjects. The proportion of their available annual time required by each subject is shown in the following table (note that some geographical areas require considerably more time than others).

	NORTH AFRICA & MIDDLE EAST	CENTRAL & SOUTHERN AFRICA	ASIA PACIFIC	SOUTH AMERICA	WESTERN EUROPE	CENTRAL & EASTERN EUROPE	NORTH AMERICA
CRA per subject	0.06	0.078	0.053	0.043	0.01	0.018	0.014

IPI provides medical supply kits to regions that do not have access to the appropriate supplies and hygiene products. Less-developed countries require more kits per subject than do developed countries. IPI has 65 000 kits available next year. Kit requirements, per subject, are shown in the following table.

	NORTH AFRICA & MIDDLE EAST	CENTRAL & SOUTHERN AFRICA	ASIA PACIFIC	SOUTH AMERICA	WESTERN EUROPE	CENTRAL & EASTERN EUROPE	NORTH AMERICA
Kits per subject	4	9	4	6	1	3	1

YOUR TASK

1. You have been asked by IPI to use LP to determine the least cost solution to its clinical trials problem. Determine the optimal solution and present a short management report to IPI. This report should focus on your recommendations only. As an appendix to this report, show your formulation of the problem and your Solver output.

2. Does this problem meet all the requirements of LP? Why or why not?

3. If you could relax one constraint or increase one resource, would you want to do this? If so, which one would you want to change? Why did you choose this one?

BIBLIOGRAPHY

Bermon, Stuart, and Sarah Jean Hood. "Capacity Optimization Planning System (CAPS)," *Interfaces* 29, 5 (September 1999): 31–50.

Desrosiers, Jacques et al. "Air Transat Uses ALTITUDE to Manage its Aircraft Routing, Crew Pairing, and Work Assignment" *Interfaces* 30 (March-April, 2000): 41–53.

Eliman, A. A., M. Girgis, and S. Kotob. "A Solution to Post-Crash Debt Entanglements in Kuwait's al-Manakh Stock Market," *Interfaces* 27, 1 (January–February 1997): 89–106.

Ferris, M. C., and A. B. Philpott. "On the Performance of Karmarkar's Algorithm," *Journal of the Operational Research Society*, 39 (March 1988): 257–270.

Fletcher, L. Russell, Henry Alden, Scott P. Holmen, Dean P. Angelides, and Matthew J. Etzenhouser. "Long-Term Forest Ecosystem Planning at Pacific Lumber," *Interfaces* 29, 1 (January 1999): 90–111.

Gass, S. I. *An Illustrated Guide to Linear Programming*. New York: Dover Publications, Inc., 1990.

Gautier, Antoine, Bernard F. Lamond, Daniel Pare, and François Rouleau. "The Quebec Ministry of Natural Resources Uses Linear Programming to Understand the Wood-Fiber Market," *Interfaces* 30, 6 (November 2000): 32–48.

Greenberg, H. J. "How to Analyze the Results of Linear Programs—Part 1: Preliminaries." *Interfaces* 23, 4 (July–August 1993): 56–68.

_____. "How to Analyze the Results of Linear Programs—Part 3: Infeasibility Diagnosis," *Interfaces* 23, 6 (November–December 1993): 120–139.

Leach, Howard. "Optimizing the Resources for Several Mills/Products," Presented to the Canadian Woodlands Forum Workshop, "Optimizing Softwood Log Quality," (May 23–24, 2001). Fredericton, N.B., Canada.

Lyon, Peter, R. John Milne, Robert Orzell, and Robert Rice. "Matching Assets with Demand in Supply-Chain Management at IBM Microelectronics," *Interfaces* 31, 1 (January 2001): 108–124.

Orden, A. "LP from the '40s to the '90s," *Interfaces* 23, 5 (September–October 1993): 2–12.

Quinn, P., B. Andrews, and H. Parsons. "Allocating Telecommunications Resources at L. L. Bean, Inc.," *Interfaces* 21, 1 (January–February 1991): 75–91.

Saltzman, M. J. "Survey: Mixed Integer Programming," *OR/MS Today* 21, 2 (April 1994): 42–51.

Schindler, S., and T. Semmel. "Station Staffing at Pan American World Airways," *Interfaces* 23, 3 (May–June 1993): 91–98.

Sexton, T. R., S. Sleeper, and R. E. Taggart, Jr. "Improving Pupil Transportation in North Carolina," *Interfaces* 24, 1 (January–February 1994): 87–104.

Zappe, C., W. Webster, and I. Horowitz. "Using Linear Programming to Determine Post-Facto Consistency in Performance Evaluations of Major League Baseball Players," *Interfaces* 23, 6 (November–December 1993): 107–119.

CHAPTER 3

Linear Programming Modeling Applications: With Computer Analyses in Excel

LEARNING OBJECTIVES

After completing this chapter, students will be able to

1. Model a wide variety of LP problems.
2. Understand major business application areas for LP problems, including manufacturing, marketing, labour scheduling, blending, transportation, finance, and multiperiod planning.
3. Gain experience in setting up and solving LP problems using Excel's Solver.

CHAPTER OUTLINE

3.1 Introduction
3.2 Marketing Applications
3.3 Manufacturing Applications
3.4 Employee Scheduling Applications
3.5 Financial Applications
3.6 Packing Applications
3.7 Ingredient Blending Applications
3.8 Multiperiod Applications

Summary • Self-Test • Problems • Case Study: Dofasco Fuel Management • Case Study: Canadian Military Electronics • Bibliography

Technical Efficiency in Ontario Community Hospitals

Have you ever wondered about the efficiency of your local hospital? Are waiting times in the ER acceptable? How does the hospital compare to others in the same geographic area? Can the efficiency be improved? Researchers in the area of medical management use decision modeling techniques to answer these questions.

Since hospitals in the province of Ontario are funded exclusively by the provincial government, these institutions are particularly well suited to this type of analysis. The Ontario Ministry of Health controls operating and capital budgets for all hospitals and must approve all new services or facilities. Ontario hospitals can be classified by various characteristics—different types of ownership (secular nonprofit, government, religious orders), different sizes, and different locations.

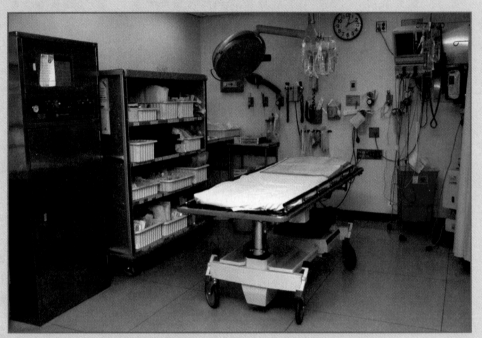

Source: © Bishop/Custom Medical Stock Photo

In order to compare the performance of Ontario hospitals with different types of ownership, sizes, or locations, researchers employed a well established measure of technical efficiency, known as DEA (Data Employment Analysis), that has been used extensively to model the performance of health care institutions such as teaching hospitals, nursing services, nuclear medicine services, and nursing homes.

Input measures are of three major types: (1) human resources (nurses, ancillary staff, administrative staff); (2) purchased services and supplies of all types including drugs and medical/surgical supplies; and (3) the total number of staffed beds.

The primary output is a measure of hospital efficiency that is based on a classification of days of patient care, and costs associated with hospitalization of different types of patients. Canadian data on hospitalized patients were used in the analysis.

A *linear programming* model was developed to compute efficiency scores for each hospital subject to a combination of budgetary, human resources, and supplies constraints. An efficiency score of 1.0 implies that this hospital is as efficient as any linear combination of hospitals in the sample. Efficiency scores less than 1.0 imply that these hospitals can improve their efficiency by increasing outputs and/or decreasing inputs. By analyzing specific variables in the model, a given hospital can determine which inputs/outputs to modify in order to improve efficiency. This model makes an important contribution to the understanding of the determinants of hospital efficiency.

Source: T. S. Gruca and D. Nath. "The Technical Efficiency of Hospitals under a Single Payer System: The Case of Ontario Community Hospitals," *Health Care Management Science* (June 2001): 91–101.

3.1 INTRODUCTION

The preceding hospital efficiency application is an excellent example of the use of linear programming (LP) to model a real-world resource allocation problem and the improvements that can result from using such models. Similar examples exist in other managerial decision-making areas, such as product mix, labour scheduling, job assignment, production scheduling, marketing research, media selection, shipping and transportation, ingredient mix, and financial portfolio selection. This chapter shows how to use LP to model real-world decision-making problems in some of these areas.

For each example discussed, we first briefly describe the development of the written mathematical model and then illustrate its solution using Excel's Solver. Although we use Solver to solve these models, it is critical to understand the logic behind the model before implementing it on the computer. Remember that the solution is only as good as the model. If the model is incorrect or incomplete from a logical perspective (even if it is correct from a mathematical perspective), Excel has no way of recognizing the logical error. Too many students, especially those at the early stages of instruction in LP, hit roadblocks when they try to implement an LP problem directly in Excel without conceptualizing the model on paper first. So we highly recommend that, until you become very comfortable with LP formulations (which takes many hours of practice), you sketch out the layout for each problem on paper first. Then you can translate your written model to the computer.

In developing each written mathematical model, we use the approach discussed in Chapter 2. We first identify the decision variables and then write out linear equations for the objective function and for each constraint in terms of these decision variables. Although some of the models discussed in this chapter are relatively small numerically, the principles developed here are definitely applicable to larger problems. Moreover, the structured formulation approach used here will give you enough practice in paraphrasing LP model formulations and will help develop the skills to apply the technique to other, less common applications.

When implementing these models in Excel, we employ, as much as possible, the same layout presented in Chapter 2. That is, all parameters (i.e., the solution value, objective coefficient, and constraint coefficients) associated with a specific decision variable are modeled in the same column. The objective function and each constraint in the problem are shown on separate rows of the worksheet. Later in this chapter (Section 3.8), however, we illustrate an alternative implementation that may be more compact and efficient for some problems. We encourage you to try alternative layouts based on your personal preference and expertise with Excel.

> It is a good idea to always develop the written LP model on paper first before attempting to implement it in Excel.

> We first identify decision variables and then write linear equations for the objective function and constraints.

Excel Notes

■ The CD-ROM that accompanies this textbook contains the Excel file for each example problem discussed here. The relevant file name is shown in the margin next to each example.

HISTORY   Linear Programming: An Ongoing Success Story

The simplex method, invented by George B. Dantzig in 1947, is still a widely used technique for solving LP problems. While interior point methods and heuristic algorithms are becoming increasingly popular and successful, simplex continues to be a highly effective way of solving LP models. In Dantzig's own words "The tremendous power of the simplex method is a constant surprise to me."

George Dantzig died at the age of 90 on May 13, 1995. In his obituary in the *Washington Post*, Stanford University Professor Arthur F. Veinott Jr. said "For the first time in history, managers were given a powerful and practical method of formulating and comparing extremely large numbers of interdependent alternative courses of action to find one that was optimal."

LP has been used successfully in the airline industry to schedule crews and make fleet assignments, by shipping companies to determine the least expensive way to transport items between locations, and by the oil industry in refinery planning. It is also used in manufacturing, investment planning, advertising, telecommunications, architecture, circuit design, and many other applications.

Sources: http://mail.asis.org/pipermail/asis-l/2005-June/002089.html; http://www2.informs.org/History/dantzig/LinearProgramming_article.pdf; http://www.stanford.edu/group/SOL/dantzig.html

- ■ In each of the Excel layouts, for clarity, Changing Cells are shaded yellow, the Target Cell is shaded green, and cells containing the left-hand-side (LHS) formula for each constraint are shaded blue.
- ■ Also, to make the equivalence of the written formulation and the Excel layout clear, the Excel layouts show the decision variable names used in the written formulation of the model. Note that these names have no role in using Solver to solve the model.

3.2   MARKETING APPLICATIONS

Media Selection

Media selection problems can be approached with LP from two perspectives. The objective can be to maximize audience exposure or to minimize advertising costs.

Linear programming models have been used in the advertising field as a decision aid in selecting an effective media mix. Sometimes the technique is employed to allocate a fixed or limited budget across various media, which might include radio or television commercials, newspaper ads, direct mailings, magazine ads, and so on. In other applications, the objective is the maximization of audience exposure. Restrictions on the allowable media mix might arise through contract requirements, limited media availability, or company policy. An example follows.

Kitchener Electronics has budgeted up to $8000 per week for local advertising. The money is to be allocated among four promotional media: TV spots, newspaper ads, and two types of radio advertisements. Kitchener's goal is to reach the largest possible audience through the various media. The following table presents the number of potential customers reached by making use of an advertisement in each of the four media. It also provides the cost per advertisement placed and the maximum number of ads that can be purchased per week.

MEDIUM	AUDIENCE REACHED	COST PER PER AD ($)	MAXIMUM ADS PER WEEK
TV spot (1 minute)	5000	800	12
Daily newspaper (full-page ad)	8500	925	5
Radio spot (30 seconds, prime time)	2400	290	25
Radio spot (1 minute, afternoon)	2800	380	20

Kitchener's contractual arrangements require that at least five radio spots be placed each week. To ensure a broad-scoped promotional campaign, management also insists that no more than $1800 be spent on radio advertising every week.

The problem can now be stated mathematically as follows. Let

T = number of 1-minute TV spots taken each week

N = number of full-page daily newspaper ads taken each week

P = number of 30-second prime-time radio spots taken each week

A = number of 1-minute afternoon radio spots taken each week

Objective:

$$\text{Maximize audience coverage} = 5000T + 8500N + 2400P + 2800A$$

subject to

$$T \le 12 \quad \text{(maximum TV spots/week)}$$
$$N \le 5 \quad \text{(maximum newspaper ads/week)}$$
$$P \le 25 \quad \text{(maximum 30-second radio spots/week)}$$
$$A \le 20 \quad \text{(maximum 1-minute radio spots/week)}$$

$$800T + 925N + 290P + 380A \le \$8000 \quad \text{(weekly advertising budget)}$$
$$P + A \ge 5 \quad \text{(minimum radio spots contracted)}$$
$$290P + 380A \le \$1800 \quad \text{(maximum dollars spent on radio)}$$
$$T, N, P, A \ge 0$$

File: 3-1.xls

Formulas for LHS of constraints are modeled using the SUMPRODUCT function in Excel.

The formula view of the Excel layout for this problem is shown in Screenshot 3.1A. Observe that in this spreadsheet (as well as in all other spreadsheets discussed in this chapter), the only Excel function we have used to model all formulas is the SUMPRODUCT function (discussed in Section 2.8). We have used this function to compute the objective function value (cell F6) as well as the LHS values for all constraints (cells F8:F14).

SCREENSHOT 3.1A   **Formula View of the Excel Layout for Kitchener Electronics**

> These are the decision variable names used in the written LP formulation, shown here for information purposes only.

> The signs are shown here for information only. Actual signs will be entered in Solver.

	A	B	C	D	E	F	G	H
1	**Kitchener Electronics**							
2								
3		T	N	P	A			
4		TV spots	Newspaper ads	Prime-time radio spots	Afternoon radio spots			
5	Number of Units							
6	Audience	5000	8500	2400	2800	=SUMPRODUCT(B6:E6,$B$5:$E$5)	<-\Objective	
7	Constraints:							
8	Max TV	1				=SUMPRODUCT(B8:E8,$B$5:$E$5)	<=	12
9	Max Newspaper		1			=SUMPRODUCT(B9:E9,$B$5:$E$5)	<=	5
10	Max Prime-Time Radio			1		=SUMPRODUCT(B10:E10,$B$5:$E$5)	<=	25
11	Max Afternoon Radio				1	=SUMPRODUCT(B11:E11,$B$5:$E$5)	<=	20
12	Budget	800	925	290	380	=SUMPRODUCT(B12:E12,$B$5:$E$5)	<=	8000
13	Max Radio $			290	380	=SUMPRODUCT(B13:E13,$B$5:$E$5)	<=	1800
14	Min Radio Spots			1	1	=SUMPRODUCT(B14:E14,$B$5:$E$5)	>=	5
15						LHS	Sign	RHS

> Objective function value (cell F6) and constraint LHS values (cells F8:F14) are computed using the SUMPRODUCT function.

As noted earlier, we have adopted this type of Excel layout for our models in order to make it easier for the beginning student of LP to understand them. Further, an advantage of this layout is the ease with which all the formulas in the spreadsheet can be created. Observe that we have used the $ sign in cell F6 to anchor the cell references for the decision variables (cells B5:E5). This allows us to simply copy this formula to cells F8:F14 to create the corresponding LHS formulas for the constraints.

The entries for the Solver Parameters window for this model, and the resulting solution, are shown in Screenshot 3.1B. The optimal solution is found to be

$$T = 1.97 \quad \text{television spots}$$

$$N = 5.00 \quad \text{newspaper ads}$$

$$P = 6.21 \quad \text{30-second prime time radio spots}$$

$$A = 0.00 \quad \text{1-minute afternoon radio spots}$$

This produces an audience exposure of 67 240 contacts. Observe that this solution turns out to have fractional values. As noted in Chapter 2, since it is considerably harder to solve an integer programming model than an LP model, it is quite common to not specify the integer requirement in many LP models. We discuss problems that require all integer solutions in Chapter 6. In Kitchener's problem, since T and P are fractional, the store would probably round them off to 2 and 6, respectively.

SCREENSHOT 3.1B

Excel Layout and Solver Entries for Kitchener Electronics

Marketing Research

Linear programming has also been applied to marketing research problems and the area of consumer research. The next example illustrates how statistical pollsters can reach strategy decisions with LP.

Canadian Market Research (CMR) is a marketing research firm that handles consumer surveys. One of its clients is a national press service that periodically conducts political polls on issues of widespread interest. In a survey for the press service, CMR determines that it must fulfill several requirements in order to draw statistically valid conclusions on Canadian attitudes to global warming. (Note: the principal wage earner in a family is designated as the head of the family.)

1. Survey at least 2300 Canadian households in total.
2. Survey at least 1000 households whose heads are 30 years of age or younger.
3. Survey at least 600 households whose heads are between 31 and 50 years of age.
4. Ensure that at least 15% of those surveyed live in a large city (population exceeding 1.5 million).
5. Ensure that no more than 20% of those surveyed who are 51 years of age or over live in a large city.

CMR decides that all surveys should be conducted in person. It estimates that the costs of reaching people in each age and region category are as follows:

| | COST PER PERSON SURVEYED ($) | | |
REGION	AGE $\leq$ 30	AGE 31–50	AGE $\geq$ 51
Large city	$7.50	$6.80	$5.50
Not large city	$6.90	$7.25	$6.10

CMR's goal is to meet the five sampling requirements at the least possible cost. We let

L_1 = number surveyed who are 30 years of age or younger and live in a large city
L_2 = number surveyed who are 31–50 years of age and live in a large city
L_3 = number surveyed who are 51 years of age or older and live in a large city
N_1 = number surveyed who are 30 years of age or younger and do not live in a large city
N_2 = number surveyed who are 31–50 years of age and do not live in a large city
N_3 = number surveyed who are 51 years of age or older and do not live in a large city

Objective function:

$$\text{Minimize total interview costs} = \$7.50L_1 + \$6.80L_2 + \$5.50L_3$$
$$+ \$6.90N_1 + \$7.25N_2 + \$6.10N_3$$

subject to

$$L_1 + L_2 + L_3 + N_1 + N_2 + N_3 \geq 2300 \qquad \text{(total households)}$$
$$L_1 + N_1 \geq 1000 \qquad \text{(households 30 years or younger)}$$
$$L_2 + N_2 \geq 600 \qquad \text{(households 31–50 in age)}$$
$$L_1 + L_2 + L_3 \geq 0.15(L_1 + L_2 + L_3 + N_1 + N_2 + N_3) \text{ (large city)}$$
$$L_3 \leq 0.2(L_3 + N_3) \qquad \text{(limit on age group 51+ years who can live in large city)}$$

$$L_1, L_2, L_3, N_1, N_2, N_3 \geq 0$$

The Excel layout and Solver entries for this model are shown in Screenshot 3.2. In implementing this model, we have algebraically modified constraints 4 and 5 to bring all

File: 3-2.xls

DECISION MODELING IN ACTION
LP Modeling in the Forests of Chile

Faced with a series of challenges in making short-term harvesting decisions, Forestal Arauco, a Chilean forestry firm, turned to professors at the University of Chile for LP modeling help. One of the problems in short-term harvesting of trees is to match demand of products—defined by length and diameter—with the supply of standing timber.

The manual system used at the time by foresters led to a significant amount of waste of timber, in which higher diameter logs, suited for export or sawmills, ended up being used for pulp, with a considerable loss in value. An LP model, labelled OPTICORT by the professors, was the logical way to get better schedules.

"The system not only optimized the operational decisions in harvesting but also changed the way managers looked at the

problem," said Professor Andres Weintraub. "The model and its concepts became the natural language to discuss the operations. They had to negotiate the parameters, and the model would do the dirty work. The system had to run in a few minutes to allow discussion and negotiation; that was a critical feature for the success of this tool," he added.

The LP program took about two years to develop, and the researchers were careful to observe two cardinal rules: (1) The solution approach had to be comfortable and clear to the user, and (2) the system had to provide answers to the user in a fast development, so the user could see quick improvements.

Source: J. Summerour. "Chilean Forestry Firm a 'Model' of Success," *OR/MS Today* (April 1999): 22–23.

Constraints can be algebraically modified to bring all variables to the LHS, if desired.

the variables to the left-hand side (LHS) and just leave a constant on the right-hand side (RHS). These are the constraints that ensure that at least 15% of those surveyed live in a large city and that no more than 20% of those surveyed who are 51 years of age or over live in a large city, respectively. For example, constraint 4 is presently modeled as

$$L_1 + L_2 + L_3 \geq 0.15(L_1 + L_2 + L_3 + N_1 + N_2 + N_3)$$

This can be rewritten as

$$L_1 + L_2 + L_3 - 0.15(L_1 + L_2 + L_3 + N_1 + N_2 + N_3) \geq 0$$

which simplifies to

$$0.85L_1 + 0.85L_2 + 0.85L_3 - 0.15N_1 - 0.15N_2 - 0.15N_3 \geq 0$$

SCREENSHOT 3.2   **Excel Layout and Solver Entries for Canadian Market Research**

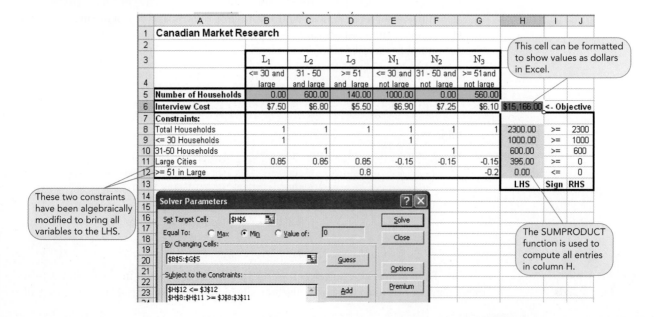

Note that such algebraic manipulations are not required to implement this model in Excel. It is perfectly logical to have cell H11 in Screenshot 3.2 represent the formula $(L_1 + L_2 + L_3)$ and cell J11 represent the formula $0.15(L_1 + L_2 + L_3 + N_1 + N_2 + N_3)$. However, we have included such manipulations in our model since it allows us to make the Excel implementation of each constraint consistent. That is, each cell denoting the LHS value of a constraint will have a SUMPRODUCT function involving the decision variables. Likewise, each cell denoting the RHS value of a constraint will have a constant.

The optimal solution to CMR's marketing research problem costs $15 166 and requires the firm to survey households as follows:

$$\text{Large city and head 31–50 years old} = 600$$
$$\text{Large city and head} \geq 51 \text{ years old} = 140$$
$$\text{Large city and head} \leq 30 \text{ years old} = 1000$$
$$\text{Large city and head} \geq 51 \text{ years old} = 560$$

3.3   MANUFACTURING APPLICATIONS

Product Mix

A popular use of LP is in solving product mix problems.

A fertile field for the use of LP is in planning for the optimal mix of products to manufacture. A company must meet a myriad of constraints, ranging from financial concerns to sales demands to material contracts to union labour demands. Its primary goal is to generate the largest profit possible. We have already studied a simple version of the product mix problem (the Flair Furniture problem) in Chapter 2. Let us now look at a more detailed version of a product mix problem.

Superior Shirts Inc., a Manitoba manufacturer of men's dress shirts, produces four varieties of shirts. One is an expensive, all-silk shirt, one is an all-cotton shirt, and two are blends of polyester and cotton. The following table illustrates the cost and availability (per monthly production planning period) of the three materials used in the production process:

MATERIAL	COST PER METRE ($)	MATERIAL AVAILABLE PER MONTH (METRES)
Silk	18.00	1 000
Polyester	2.60	10 000
Cotton	5.50	30 000

The firm has fixed contracts with several major department store chains to supply shirts. The contracts require that Superior Shirts supply a minimum quantity of each shirt but allow for a larger demand if Superior chooses to meet that demand. (Most of the shirts are not shipped with the name Superior on their label, incidentally, but with "private stock" labels supplied by the stores.) Table 3.1 summarizes the contract demand for each of the four styles of shirts, the selling price per shirt, and the fabric requirements of each variety.

Superior's goal is to maximize its monthly profit. It must decide upon a policy for its product mix. Let

$$S = \text{number of all-silk shirts to produce per month}$$
$$C = \text{number of all cotton-shirts to produce per month}$$
$$B_1 = \text{number of blend 1 polyester–cotton shirts to produce per month}$$
$$B_2 = \text{number of blend 2 polyester–cotton shirts to produce per month}$$

All shirts require 2 metres of material.

TABLE 3.1   **Data for Superior Shirts**

VARIETY OF SHIRT	SELLING PRICE PER SHIRT ($)	MONTHLY CONTRACT MINIMUM	MONTHLY DEMAND	MATERIAL REQUIREMENTS
All silk	$55	500	7 000	100% silk
All cotton	$25	1 000	14 000	100% cotton
Poly–cotton blend 1	$15	10 000	16 000	35% polyester–65% cotton
Poly–cotton blend 2	$20	5 000	8 500	20% polyester–80% cotton

Unlike the Flair Furniture example, in which the unit profit for each product was given (i.e., $7 per table and $5 per chair), the unit profits must be first calculated in this example. We illustrate the net profit calculation for all-silk shirts (S). Each all-silk shirt requires 2 metres of silk at a cost of $18 per metre, resulting in a material cost of $36. The selling price per all-silk shirt is $55, leaving a net profit of $55 − $36 = $19 per shirt. In a similar fashion, we can calculate the net unit profit for all-cotton shirts (C) to be $14, for polyester–cotton blend 1 shirts (B_1) to be $6.03, and for polyester–cotton blend 2 shirts (B_2) to be $10.16. Try to verify these calculations for yourself.

The objective function can now be stated as

$$\text{Maximize profit} = \$19S + \$14C + \$6.03\,B_1 + \$10.16\,B_2$$

subject to

$$
\begin{array}{ll}
2S \leq 1000 & \text{(metres of silk)} \\
2C + 1.3B_1 + 1.6B_2 \leq 30\ 000 & \text{(metres of cotton)} \\
0.7B_1 + 0.4B_2 \leq 10\ 000 & \text{(metres of polyester)} \\
S \geq 500 & \text{(contract minimum for all silk)} \\
S \leq 7000 & \text{(maximum demand for silk)} \\
C \geq 1000 & \text{(contract minimum for all cotton)} \\
C \leq 14\ 000 & \text{(maximum demand for all cotton)} \\
B_1 \geq 10\ 000 & \text{(contract minimum for blend 1)} \\
B_1 \leq 16\ 000 & \text{(maximum demand for blend 1)} \\
B_2 \leq 5000 & \text{(contract minimum for blend 2)} \\
B_2 \leq 8500 & \text{(maximum demand for blend 2)} \\
S, C, B_1, B_2 \leq 0 &
\end{array}
$$

In implementing the model in Excel, we have split the objective function (profit) into two components: a revenue component and a material cost component. For example, the objective coefficient for all-silk shirts (S) is $19. However, we know that the $19 is obtained by subtracting the material cost (2 × $18 = $36) from the revenue ($55). Hence, we can rewrite the objective function as follows:

$$\text{Maximize } (\$55S + \$25C + \$15B_1 + \$20B_2) - (\$36S + \$11C + \$8.97B_1 + \$9.84B_2)$$

We can have the Excel layout show as much detail as desired for a problem.

Whether we model the objective function using the profit coefficients or using the selling price and material cost coefficients, the final solution will be the same. However, in many problems it is convenient, and probably preferable, to have the model show as much detail as possible.

SCREENSHOT 3.3   **Excel Layout and Solver Entries for Superior Shirts**

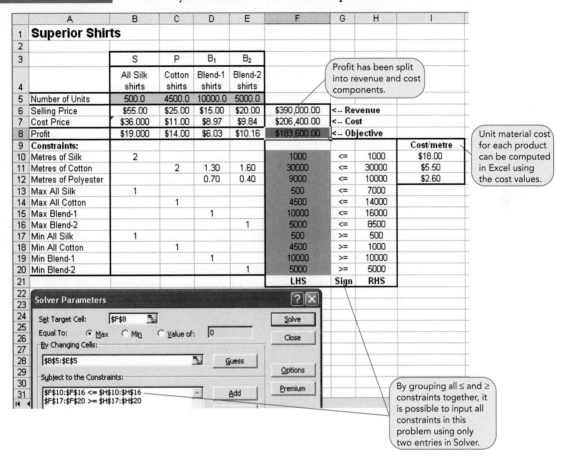

The Excel layout and Solver entries for this model are shown in Screenshot 3.3 above. Cell F6 defines the revenue component of the objective, and cell F7 defines the cost component of the objective function. Cell F8 (the target cell in Solver) is the difference between cells F6 and F7.

Screenshot 3.3 shows that the optimal solution is to produce 500 all-silk shirts, 4500 all-cotton shirts, 10 000 polyester–cotton blend 1 shirts, and 5000 polyester–cotton blend 2 shirts. This results in total revenue of $390 000 and a total material cost of $206 400, yielding a net profit of $183 600.

File: 3-3.xls

3.4   EMPLOYEE SCHEDULING APPLICATIONS

Labour Planning

Labour planning problems address staffing needs over a specific time period. They are especially useful when managers have some flexibility in assigning workers to jobs that require overlapping or interchangeable talents. Large banks frequently use LP to tackle their labour scheduling.

Atlantic Bank of Canada is a busy bank that has requirements for between 10 and 18 tellers, depending on the time of day. The lunch time, from noon to 2 P.M., is usually heaviest. Table 3.2 indicates the workers needed at various hours that the bank is open.

TABLE 3.2	TIME PERIOD	NUMBER OF TELLERS REQUIRED
Atlantic Bank of Canada	9 A.M.–10 A.M.	10
	10 A.M.–11 A.M.	12
	11 A.M.–noon	14
	noon–1 P.M.	16
	1 P.M.–2 P.M.	18
	2 P.M.–3 P.M.	17
	3 P.M.–4 P.M.	15
	4 P.M.–5 P.M.	10

The bank now employs 12 full-time tellers, but many people are on its roster of available part-time employees. A part-time employee must put in exactly four hours per day but can start anytime between 9 A.M. and 1 P.M. Part-timers are a fairly inexpensive labour pool, since no retirement or lunch benefits are provided for them. Full-timers, on the other hand, work from 9 A.M. to 5 P.M. but are allowed one hour for lunch. (Half of the full-timers eat at 11 A.M., the other half at noon.) Full-timers thus provide 35 hours per week of productive labour time.

By corporate policy, the bank limits part-time hours to a maximum of 50% of the day's total requirement. Part-timers earn $10.25 per hour (or $42 per day) on average, and full-timers earn $160 per day in salary and benefits, on average. The bank would like to set a schedule that would minimize its total personnel costs. It will release one or more of its full-time tellers if it is profitable to do so.

We can let

$$F = \text{full-time tellers}$$

$$P_1 = \text{part-timers starting at 9 A.M. (leaving at 1 P.M.)}$$

$$P_2 = \text{part-timers starting at 10 A.M. (leaving at 2 P.M.)}$$

$$P_3 = \text{part-timers starting at 11 A.M. (leaving at 3 P.M.)}$$

$$P_4 = \text{part-timers starting at noon (leaving at 4 P.M.)}$$

$$P_5 = \text{part-timers starting at 1 P.M. (leaving at 5 P.M.)}$$

In the timeline in Figure 3.1, we see that one-half of the full-time employees take their lunch from 11:00 A.M. to 12 noon, and the other half from 12 noon to 1:00 P.M. Part-timers, labeled P_1 to P_5 work a total of four hours, as indicated on the timeline. By

FIGURE 3.1	
Timeline for Scheduling Tellers at Atlantic Bank of Canada	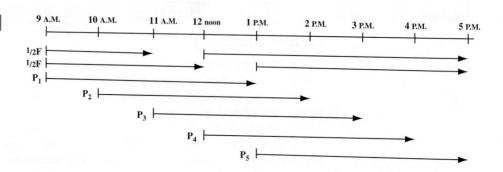

drawing a vertical line through any of the one-hour periods, one can see which employees are working during that period.

Objective function:

$$\text{Minimize total daily personnel cost} = \$160F + \$42(P_1 + P_2 + P_3 + P_4 + P_5)$$

Constraints:
For each hour, the available labour must be at least equal to the required labour hours.

$$
\begin{array}{lll}
F + P_1 & \geq 10 & \text{(9 A.M.–10 A.M. needs)} \\
F + P_1 + P_2 & \geq 12 & \text{(10 A.M.–11 A.M. needs)} \\
\tfrac{1}{2}F + P_1 + P_2 + P_3 & \geq 14 & \text{(11 A.M.–noon needs)} \\
\tfrac{1}{2}F + P_1 + P_2 + P_3 + P_4 & \geq 16 & \text{(noon–1 P.M. needs)} \\
F + \quad P_2 + P_3 + P_4 + P_5 & \geq 18 & \text{(1 P.M.–2 P.M. needs)} \\
F + \quad\quad P_3 + P_4 + P_5 & \geq 17 & \text{(2 P.M.–3 P.M. needs)} \\
F + \quad\quad\quad P_4 + P_5 & \geq 15 & \text{(3 P.M.–4 P.M. needs)} \\
F + \quad\quad\quad\quad P_5 & \geq 10 & \text{(4 P.M.–5 P.M. needs)}
\end{array}
$$

Only 12 full-time tellers are available, so

$$F \leq 12$$

Part-time worker hours cannot exceed 50% of total hours required each day, which is the sum of the tellers needed each hour, so

$$4(P_1 + P_2 + P_3 + P_4 + P_5) \leq 0.50(10 + 12 + 14 + 16 + 18 + 17 + 15 + 10)$$

or

$$4P_1 + 4P_2 + 4P_3 + 4P_4 + 4P_5 \leq 56$$

$$F, P_1, P_2, P_3, P_4, P_5 \geq 0$$

File: 3-4.xls

Alternative optimal solutions are common in many LP applications.

The Excel layout and Solver entries for this model, shown in Screenshot 3.4 on page 94, reveal that the optimal solution is to employ 10 full-time tellers, 7 part-time tellers at 10 A.M., 2 part-time tellers at 11 A.M., and 5 part-time tellers at noon, for a total cost of $2188 per day.

It turns out that there are several alternate optimal solutions that Atlantic Bank can employ. In practice, the sequence in which you present constraints in your model can affect the specific solution that is found. We revisit this example in Chapter 4 (Solved Problem 4-1) to study how we can use Solver's sensitivity reports to detect and identify alternate optimal solutions.

For this problem, one alternate solution is to employ 10 full-time tellers, 6 part-time tellers at 9 A.M., 1 part-time teller at 10 A.M., 2 part-time tellers at 11 A.M., and 5 part-time tellers at noon. The cost of this policy is also $2188.

Assignment Problems

Assigning people to jobs, jobs to machines, and so on, is an application of LP called the assignment problem.

Assignment problems involve determining the most efficient assignment of people to jobs, machines to tasks, police cars to city sectors, salespeople to territories, and so on. The objective might be to minimize travel times or costs or to maximize assignment effectiveness.

The assignment problem is an example of a special type of LP problem known as network-flow problems, and we study these types of problems in greater detail in Chapter 5.

SCREENSHOT 3.4

Excel Layout and Solver Entries for Atlantic Bank of Canada

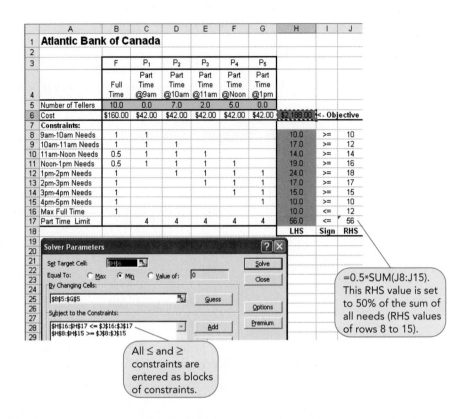

All ≤ and ≥ constraints are entered as blocks of constraints.

=0.5*SUM(J8:J15). This RHS value is set to 50% of the sum of all needs (RHS values of rows 8 to 15).

3.5   FINANCIAL APPLICATIONS

Portfolio Selection

A problem frequently encountered by managers of banks, mutual funds, investment services, and insurance companies is the selection of specific investments from among a wide variety of alternatives. The manager's overall objective is usually to maximize expected return on investment, given a set of legal, policy, or risk restraints.

Maximizing return on investment subject to a set of risk constraints is a popular financial application of LP.

For example, a provincial credit union invests in short-term trade credits, corporate bonds, gold stocks, and construction loans. To encourage a diversified portfolio, the board of directors has placed limits on the amount that can be committed to any one type of investment. The credit union has $5 million available for immediate investment and wishes to do two things: (1) maximize the interest earned on the investments made over the next six months and (2) satisfy the diversification requirements as set by the board of directors.

The specifics of the investment possibilities are as follows:

INVESTMENT	INTEREST EARNED (%)	MAXIMUM INVESTMENT ($ MILLIONS)
Trade credit	7	1.0
Corporate bonds	11	2.5
Gold stocks	19	1.5
Construction loans	15	1.8

In addition, the board specifies that at least 55% of the funds invested be in gold stocks and construction loans, and that no less than 15% be invested in trade credit.

To formulate the credit union's investment decision as an LP problem, we let

$$T = \text{dollars invested in trade credit}$$

$$B = \text{dollars invested in corporate bonds}$$

$$G = \text{dollars invested in gold stocks}$$

$$C = \text{dollars invested in construction loans}$$

Objective:

$$\text{Maximize dollars of interest earned} = 0.07T + 0.11B + 0.19G + 0.15C$$

subject to

$$T \leq 1\ 000\ 000$$

$$B \leq 2\ 500\ 000$$

$$G \leq 1\ 500\ 000$$

$$C \leq 1\ 800\ 000$$

$$G + C \geq 0.55(T + B + G + C)$$

$$T \geq 0.15(T + B + G + C)$$

$$T + B + G + C \leq 5\ 000\ 000$$

$$T, B, G, C \geq 0$$

As in the marketing research problem, before implementing this model on Excel, we have algebraically modified the constraints so that all variables are on the LHS and only a

DECISION MODELING IN ACTION

Using Linear Programming for Flight Scheduling at Air Canada

In 2006, Canada's four largest airports, Toronto Pearson, Vancouver International, Montreal Trudeau, and Calgary International, served over 70 million passengers and recorded almost 1.2 million aircraft movements.

With so much air traffic in Canada's airports, Air Canada, with a fleet of approximately 337 aircraft, has to deal with the complex task of scheduling a large number of daily flights on its domestic and international routes.

"Given the flight schedule of an airline, the fleet assignment problem consists of determining the aircraft type to assign to each flight leg in order to maximize the total expected profits while satisfying aircraft routing and availability constraints." The profit for a leg (route) is a function of passenger demand, the capacity of the aircraft assigned to the leg, and the aircraft operational costs.

LP techniques were employed to determine the weekly fleet assignment in the case where homogeneity of aircraft type (i.e., utilization of the same aircraft type) is sought over routes sharing the same flight number. Homogeneity allows, among other things, easier ground service planning.

The model was tested by examination of two actual Air Canada data sets involving up to 4400 flight legs and produced realistic solutions arising from a trade-off between profits and homogeneity. The comparison with Air Canada's solution shows that the methodology used in this research can be effective in producing realistic schedules, while yielding a significant increase in expected profits.

Sources: N. Belanger, G. Desaulniers, F. Soumis, J. Desrosiers, and J. Lavigne. "Weekly airline fleet assignment with homogeneity," *Transportation Research Part B: Methodological* Vol. 40, No. 4, pp. 306–318; Wikipedia online encyclopedia, May 2006.

SCREENSHOT 3.5   **Excel Layout and Solver Entries for Provincial Credit Union**

These two constraints have been algebraically modified to bring all variables to the LHS.

Cells formatted to show values as dollars.

This LP model can be scaled to show these values in millions of dollars, if desired.

constant is on the RHS. Hence, the constraints dealing with the minimum investments in gold stock and trade credit have been rewritten as follows:

$$-0.55T - 0.55B + 0.45G + 0.45C \geq 0 \text{ Gold stock}$$

$$0.85T - 0.15B - 0.15G - 0.15C \geq 0 \text{ Trade credit}$$

File: 3-5.xls

The Excel layout and Solver entries for this model are shown in Screenshot 3.5 above. The optimal solution is to invest $750 000 in trade credit, $950 000 in corporate bonds, $1 500 000 in gold stocks, and $1 800 000 in construction bonds, earning a total interest of $712 000.

Although we have chosen to implement the decision variables as the number of dollars invested in each choice, we could have set up the decision variables to represent the number of dollars invested in *millions*, for example. In such a case, the solution values would be $0.75 in trade credit, $0.95 in corporate bonds, $1.50 in gold stocks, and $1.80 in construction bonds earning a total interest of $0.712.

Problems with large variability in the magnitudes of parameter and/or variable values should be scaled.

As noted in Chapter 2, it is usually a good idea in practice to scale problems in which typical values of the objective function and constraints differ by several orders of magnitude. One way to do so would be to click the Use Automatic Scaling option available in Solver, discussed in Chapter 2.

3.6   PACKING APPLICATIONS

Truck Loading Problem

The truck loading problem involves deciding which items to load on a truck so as to maximize the value of a load shipped. As an example, we consider Goodman Shipping. One of the company trucks, with a capacity of 5000 kilograms, is about to be loaded.[1]

---

[1] Adapted from an example in S. L. Savage. *What's Best!* Oakland, CA: General Optimization, Inc., and Holden-Day, 1985.

Awaiting shipment are the following items

ITEM	VALUE ($)	WEIGHT (KILOGRAMS)
1	22 500	3750
2	24 000	3750
3	8 000	1500
4	9 500	1750
5	11 500	2000
6	9 750	1750

Each of these six items, we see, has an associated dollar value and weight.

The objective is to maximize the total value of the items loaded onto the truck without exceeding the truck's weight capacity.

There are several ways in which this problem can be formulated. For example, we can define the decision variables as the number of kilograms of each item that is loaded on the truck. There would be six decision variables (one for each item) in the model. In this case, the value of each item needs to be appropriately scaled for use in the objective function. For example, if the total value of the 3750 kilos of item 1 is $22 500, the value per kilo is then $6 (= 22 500/3750). Similar calculations can be made for the other items to be shipped.

Alternate formulations are possible for some LP problems.

Alternatively, we can define the six decision variables as the proportion of each item that is loaded on the truck. Under this approach, let P_i be the proportion of each item i loaded on the truck. The LP model can then be formulated as follows:

$$\text{Maximize load value} = \$22\,500P_1 + \$24\,000P_2 + \$8000P_3 + \$9500P_4 + \$11\,500P_5 + \$9750P_6$$

subject to

$$3750P_1 + 3750P_2 + 1500P_3 + 1750P_4 + 2000P_5 + 1750P_6 \leq 5000 \text{ kg capacity}$$

$$P_1 \leq 1$$

$$P_2 \leq 1$$

$$P_3 \leq 1$$

$$P_4 \leq 1$$

$$P_5 \leq 1$$

$$P_6 \leq 1$$

$$P_1, P_2, P_3, P_4, P_5, P_6 \geq 0$$

These final six constraints reflect the fact that at most one "unit" (i.e., a proportion of 1) of an item can be loaded onto the truck. In effect, if Goodman can load a *portion* of an item (e.g., item 1 is a batch of 1000 folding chairs, not all of which need to be shipped together), the proportions P_i will all have values ranging from 0 (nothing) to 1 (all of that item loaded).

File: 3-6.xls

Screenshot 3.6A shows the Excel layout and Solver entries for Goodman Shipping's LP model. The optimal solution yields a total value of $31 500 and requires Goodman to ship a proportion of 0.33 (i.e., 33%) of item 1 and all of item 2.

The answer leads us to an interesting issue that we deal with in detail in Chapter 6. What does Goodman do if fractional values of items cannot be loaded? For example, if luxury cars were the items being loaded, we clearly cannot ship one-third of a Maserati.

SCREENSHOT 3.6A   **Excel Layout and Solver Entries for Goodman Shipping**

	A	B	C	D	E	F	G	H	I	J
1	**Goodman Shipping**									
2										
3		P_1	P_2	P_3	P_4	P_5	P_6			
4		Item 1	Item 2	Item 3	Item 4	Item 5	Item 6			
5	Proportion	0.33	1.00	0.00	0.00	0.00	0.00			
6	Load Value	$22,500	$24,000	$8,000	$9,500	$11,500	$9,750	$31,500.00	<-- Objective	
7	**Constraints:**									
8	Capacity	3750	3750	1500	1750	2000	1750	5000.0	<=	5000
9	Item 1 Limit	1						0.33	<=	1
10	Item 2 Limit		1					1.00	<=	1
11	Item 3 Limit			1				0.00	<=	1
12	Item 4 Limit				1			0.00	<=	1
13	Item 5 Limit					1		0.00	<=	1
14	Item 6 Limit						1	0.00	<=	1
15								LHS	Sign	RHS

(callout) LP solution permits fractional quantities to be shipped.

(callout) Solution values show proportion of item loaded on truck.

Solver Parameters   [?] [X]

Se_t Target Cell: $H$6

Equal To: (•) Max   ( ) Mi_n   ( ) _Value of: 0

By Changing Cells:

$B$5:$G$5   _Guess

S_ubject to the Constraints:

$H$8:$H$14 <= $J$8:$J$14   _Add

Solve
Close
Options
Premium

If the proportion of item 1 were rounded up to 1.00, the weight of the load would increase to 7500 kilos. This would violate the 5000-kilo maximum weight constraint. Therefore, the fraction of item 1 must be rounded down to zero. This would drop the value of the load to 3750 kilos, leaving 1250 kilos of the load capacity unused. Because no other item weighs less than 1250 kilos, the truck cannot be filled up further.

Thus we see that by using regular LP and rounding the fractional weights, the truck would carry only item 2, for a load weight of 3750 kilos and a load value of $24 000.

As we show in Chapter 6, most LP software packages, including Excel's Solver, are capable of dealing with integer programming problems as well. In fact, using Excel, it turns out that the integer solution to Goodman's problem is to load all of items 3, 4, and 6 for a total weight of 5000 kilos and load value of $27 250.

Screenshot 3.6B shows an alternative model for Goodman Shipping's problem. The decision variables in this model are the weights in kilograms that are shipped, rather than the proportion. The layout for this model is identical to the model shown in Screenshot 3.6A, and you should be able to recognize its written formulation easily. As expected, the solution to this model shows that the maximum load value is $31 500. This load value is achieved by shipping 1250 kilos (= 0.33 of the 3750 kilos available) of item 1 and 3750 (= all of the 3750 kilos available) of item 2.

We observe that the optimal solution requires Goodman to ship 1250 kilos of item 1 and 3750 kilos of item 2 for a maximum load value of $31 500. Suppose that Steven Goodman is informed that the load value of item 3 is expected to increase. At what load

SCREENSHOT 3.6B   **Alternative Excel Layout and Solver Entries for Goodman Shipping**

> Load value is the same as that in Screenshot 3.6A.

> This model shows number of kilos of item loaded on truck.

	A	B	C	D	E	F	G	H	I	J
1	**Goodman Shipping (Alternate Model)**									
2										
3		W₁	W₂	W₃	W₄	W₅	W₆			
4		Item 1	Item 2	Item 3	Item 4	Item 5	Item 6			
5	Weight in Kilos	1,250.00	3,750.00	0.00	0.00	0.00	0.00			
6	Load Value	$6.00	$6.40	$5.33	$5.43	$5.75	$5.57	$31,500.00	<-- Objective	
7	Constraints:									
8	Capacity	1	1	1	1	1	1	5000.0	<=	5000
9	Item 1 Limit (Kilos)	1						1250.00	<=	3750
10	Item 2 Limit (Kilos)		1					3750.00	<=	3750
11	Item 3 Limit (Kilos)			1				0.00	<=	1500
12	Item 4 Limit (Kilos)				1			0.00	<=	1750
13	Item 5 Limit (Kilos)					1		0.00	<=	2000
14	Item 6 Limit (Kilos)						1	0.00	<=	1750
15								LHS	Sign	RHS

Solver Parameters

Set Target Cell: $H$6

Equal To: ● Max ○ Min ○ Value of: 0

By Changing Cells:

$B$5:$G$5

Subject to the Constraints:

$H$8:$H$14 <= $J$8:$J$14

Solve · Close · Guess · Options · Premium · Add

value would Steven first consider loading item 3? If item 3 reaches or surpasses this value, how many units of each item should be shipped?

This is a preliminary example of *sensitivity analysis*, a topic that will be considered in detail in Chapter 4. By experimenting with solver solutions for different load values for item 3, Screenshot 3.6C shows that with a load value of $6 the optimal values of the decision variables and the maximum load value remain unchanged. However, Screenshot 3.6D shows that when the load value of item 3 increases to $6.01, the optimal solution changes to loading 3750 kilos of item 2 and 1250 kilos of item 3, with item 1 not being shipped at all. The maximum load value changes to $31 512.50, an increase of $12.50. Note that the load value for item 1 remains $6.00 so that at $6.01 item 3 is making a larger contribution than is item 1, hence it becomes profitable to ship item 3 instead of item 1.

SCREENSHOT 3.6C   **Excel Solution with Load Value for Item 3 Equal to $6.00**

	A	B	C	D	E	F	G	H	I	J
1	**Goodman Shipping (Alternate Model)**									
2										
3		W₁	W₂	W₃	W₄	W₅	W₆			
4		Item 1	Item 2	Item 3	Item 4	Item 5	Item 6			
5	Weight in Kilos	1,250.00	3,750.00	0.00	0.00	0.00	0.00			
6	Load Value	$6.00	$6.40	$6.00	$5.43	$5.75	$5.57	$31,500.00	<-- Objective	
7	Constraints:									
8	Capacity	1	1	1	1	1	1	5000.00	<=	5000
9	Item 1 Limit (Kilos)	1						1250.00	<=	1250
10	Item 2 Limit (Kilos)		1					3750.00	<=	3750
11	Item 3 Limit (Kilos)			1				0.00	<=	1500
12	Item 4 Limit (Kilos)				1			0.00	<=	1750
13	Item 5 Limit (Kilos)					1		0.00	<=	2000
14	Item 6 Limit (Kilos)						1	0.00	<=	1750
15								LHS	Sign	RHS

SCREENSHOT 3.6D   **Excel Solution with Load Value for Item 3 Equal to $6.01**

	A	B	C	D	E	F	G	H	I	J
1	**Goodman Shipping (Alternate Model)**									
2										
3		W₁	W₂	W₃	W₄	W₅	W₆			
4		Item 1	Item 2	Item 3	Item 4	Item 5	Item 6			
5	Weight in Kilos	0.00	3,750.00	1,250.00	0.00	0.00	0.00			
6	Load Value	$6.00	$6.40	$6.01	$5.43	$5.75	$5.57	$31,512.50	<-- Objective	
7	Constraints:									
8	Capacity	1	1	1	1	1	1	5000.00	<=	5000
9	Item 1 Limit (Kilos)	1						0.00	<=	1250
10	Item 2 Limit (Kilos)		1					3750.00	<=	3750
11	Item 3 Limit (Kilos)			1				1250.00	<=	1500
12	Item 4 Limit (Kilos)				1			0.00	<=	1750
13	Item 5 Limit (Kilos)					1		0.00	<=	2000
14	Item 6 Limit (Kilos)						1	0.00	<=	1750
15								LHS	Sign	RHS

Knapsack and Transportation Problems

Transporting goods from several origins to several destinations efficiently is called the transportation problem.

This problem belongs to a class of problems known as the knapsack problem. The knapsack problem may be stated as follows: Given a selection of items, each with a different weight and value, decide which items should be packed in a knapsack of limited weight capacity in order to maximize the total value of items packed in the knapsack. A related class of problems, known as the transportation or shipping problem, involves determining the amount of goods or items to be transported from a number of origins to a number of destinations. The objective usually is to minimize total shipping costs or distances. Constraints in this type of problem deal with capacities or supplies at each origin and requirements or demand at each destination. Transportation models are covered in detail in Chapter 5.

Like the assignment problem, the transportation problem is also an example of network-flow problems, which we study in greater detail in Chapter 5.

3.7   INGREDIENT BLENDING APPLICATIONS

Diet Problems

The diet problem, one of the earliest applications of LP, was originally used by hospitals to determine the most economical diet for patients. Known in agricultural applications as the feed mix problem, the diet problem involves specifying a food or feed ingredient combination that satisfies stated nutritional requirements at a minimum cost level.

The Perky Puppy Pet Food Company, located in Paradise, Newfoundland, uses three grains to blend a natural dry dog food that it sells in 250-gram packages called the Nutripak. The company advertises that each Nutripak will meet a small (9 – 15 kilogram) adult dog's daily requirement for vitamin A, vitamin D, iron and zinc.

Veterinary sources indicate that for dogs weighing 9 to 15 kilograms, the minimum daily requirement for vitamin A is 250 IU; for vitamin D 300 IU; for iron 12 mg; and for zinc 1 mg. The cost of each grain and the amounts of vitamin A, vitamin D, iron, and zinc supplied by 1 kilogram of each grain are shown in Table 3.3. Perky Puppy wants to know how many grams of each grain should be blended in the 250-gram package so that each Nutripak serving will meet the minimum daily requirements for vitamins A and D, iron, and zinc at a minimum cost.

TABLE 3.3		Perky Puppy's Dog Food Requirements			
GRAIN	**COST/kg**	**VITAMIN A (IU/kg)**	**VITAMIN D (IU/kg)**	**IRON (g/kg)**	**ZINC (g/kg)**
A	$0.80	1200	1060	208	4.4
B	$0.75	1000	1020	220	3.6
C	$0.90	900	1400	150	3.7

We let

$$A = \text{grams of grain A in each 250-gram Nutripak}$$
$$B = \text{grams of grain B in each 250-gram Nutripak}$$
$$C = \text{grams of grain C in each 250-gram Nutripak}$$

Objective function:

Minimize total cost of mixing a 250-gram Nutripak = $0.0008A + $0.00075B
$$+ \$0.0009C$$

subject to

$$1.2A + 1B + 0.9C \geq 250 \quad \text{(vitamin A requirement)}$$
$$1.06A + 1.02B + 1.40C \geq 300 \quad \text{(vitamin D requirement)}$$
$$0.208A + 0.220B + 0.150C \geq 12 \quad \text{(iron requirement)}$$
$$0.0044A + 0.0036B + 0.0037C \geq 1 \quad \text{(zinc requirement)}$$
$$A + B + C = 250 \quad \text{(total mix is 250 grams or 0.25 kilograms)}$$
$$A, B, C \geq 0$$

File: 3-7.xls

Screenshot 3.7 shows the Excel layout and Solver entries for this LP model. The solution to Perky Puppy Pet Food Company's problem requires mixing together 111.67 grams of grain *A*, 31.67 grams of grain *B*, and 106.67 grams of grain *C*. The cost per 250-gram Nutripak is $0.21.

Ingredient Mix and Blending Problems

Diet and feed mix problems are actually special cases of a more general class of LP problems known as *ingredient* or *blending problems*. Blending problems arise when a decision must be

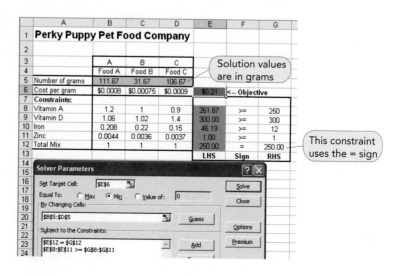

made regarding the blending of two or more products to produce one or more products. Resources, in this case, contain one or more essential ingredients that must be blended so that each final product contains specific percentages of each ingredient. The following example deals with an application frequently seen in the petroleum industry, the blending of crude oils to produce refinable gasoline.

Major oil refineries use LP for blending crude oils to produce gasoline grades.

The Normco Oil Company produces two grades of cut-rate gasoline for industrial distribution. The grades, regular and economy, are produced by refining a blend of two types of crude oil, type $X100$ and type $X220$. Each crude oil differs not only in cost per barrel but in composition as well. The following table indicates the percentage of crucial ingredients found in each of the crude oils and the cost per barrel for each:

CRUDE OIL TYPE	INGREDIENT A (%)	INGREDIENT B (%)	COST/BARREL ($)
$X100$	35	55	30.00
$X220$	60	25	34.80

Weekly demand for the regular grade of Normco gasoline is at least 25 000 barrels, and demand for the economy grade is at least 32 000 barrels per week. *At least* 45% of each barrel of regular must be ingredient A. *At most* 50% of each barrel of economy should contain ingredient B.

Normco management must decide how many barrels of each type of crude oil to buy each week for blending to satisfy demand at minimum cost. To solve this as an LP problem, the firm lets

R_1 = barrels of crude $X100$ blended to produce the refined regular

E_1 = barrels of crude $X100$ blended to produce the refined economy

R_2 = barrels of crude $X220$ blended to produce the refined regular

E_2 = barrels of crude $X220$ blended to produce the refined economy

This problem can be formulated as follows:

Objective:
$$\text{Minimize cost} = \$30\,R_1 + \$30\,E_1 + \$34.80\,R_2 + \$34.80\,E_2$$

subject to

$$R_1 + R_2 \geq 25\ 000 \qquad \text{(demand for regular)}$$
$$E_1 + E_2 \geq 32\ 000 \qquad \text{(demand for economy)}$$

At least 45% of each barrel of regular must be ingredient A.

$R_1 + R_2$ = total amount of crude blended to produce the refined regular gasoline

Thus,

$$0.45(R_1 + R_2) = \text{minimum amount of ingredient } A \text{ required}$$

But

$$0.35\,R_1 + 0.60\,R_2 = \text{amount of ingredient } A \text{ in refined regular gas}$$

So

$$0.35\,R_1 + 0.60\,R_2 \geq 0.45\,R_1 + 0.45\,R_2$$

or

$$-0.10\,R_1 + 0.15\,R_2 \geq 0 \qquad \text{(ingredient } A \text{ in regular constraint)}$$

SCREENSHOT 3.8

Excel Layout and Solver Entries for Normco Oil Company

	A	B	C	D	E	F	G	H
1	**Normco Oil Company**							
2								
3		R₁	E₁	R₂	E₂			
4		X100 in Regular	X100 in Economy	X220 in Regular	X220 in Economy	Optimal blending values		
5	Number of barrels	15,000.00	26,666.67	10,000.00	5,333.33			
6	Cost	$30.00	$30.00	$34.80	$34.80	$1,783,600.00	<- Objective	
7	Constraints:							
8	Min Regular	1		1		25000.00	>=	25000
9	Min Economy		1		1	32000.00	>=	32000
10	Min A in Regular	-0.1		0.15		0.00	>=	0
11	Max B in Economy		0.05		-0.25	0.00	<=	0
12						LHS	Sign	RHS

These two constraints have been algebraically modified to bring all variables to the LHS.

Solver Parameters

Set Target Cell: $F$6

Equal To: ○ Max ⊙ Min ○ Value of: 0

By Changing Cells: $B$5:$E$5   [Guess]

Subject to the Constraints:
$F$11 <= $H$11
$F$8:$F$10 >= $H$8:$H$10   [Add]

[Solve] [Close] [Options]

Similarly, at most 50% of each barrel of economy should be ingredient B.

$$E_1 + E_2 = \text{total amount of crude blended to produce the refined economy gasoline}$$

Thus,

$$0.50(E_1 + E_2) = \text{maximum amount of ingredient } B \text{ allowed}$$

But

$$0.55E_1 + 0.25E_2 = \text{amount of ingredient } B \text{ in refined economy gas}$$

So

$$0.55E_1 + 0.25E_2 \le 0.50E_1 + 0.50E_2$$

or

$$0.05E_1 - 0.25E_2 \le 0 \text{ (ingredient } B \text{ in economy constraint)}$$

Here is the entire LP formulation:

$$\text{Minimize cost} = 30R_1 + 30E_1 + 34.80R_2 + 34.80E_2$$

subject to

$$R_1 + R_2 \ge 25\,000$$
$$E_1 + E_2 \ge 32\,000$$
$$-0.10R_1 + 0.15R_2 \ge 0$$
$$0.05E_1 - 0.25E_2 \le 0$$
$$R_1, E_1, R_2, E_2 \ge 0$$

File: 3-8.xls

Screenshot 3.8 above shows the Excel layout and Solver entries for this LP model. The mix will cost Normco Oil $1 783 600, and require it to blend the following quantities of crude oil:

$$R_1 = 15\ 000.00 \text{ barrels of } X100 \text{ crude oil into regular}$$

$$E_1 = 26\ 666.67 \text{ barrels of } X100 \text{ crude oil into economy}$$

$$R_2 = 10\ 000.00 \text{ barrels of } X220 \text{ crude oil into regular}$$

$$E_2 = 5333.33 \text{ barrels of } X220 \text{ crude oil into economy}$$

3.8   MULTIPERIOD APPLICATIONS

Multiperiod problems are a challenging application of LP.

Perhaps the most challenging application of LP is in modeling multiperiod scenarios. These are situations in which the decision maker has to determine the optimal decisions for several periods (e.g., weeks, months). What makes these problems especially difficult is that the decision choices in later periods are directly *dependent* on the decisions made in earlier periods. We discuss two examples to illustrate this feature in the following sections. The first example deals with a multiperiod production scheduling problem. The second example involves the establishment of a multiperiod financial sinking fund.

Production Scheduling

Setting a low-cost production schedule over a period of weeks or months is a difficult and important management problem in most plants. The production manager has to consider many factors: labour capacity, inventory and storage costs, space limitations, product demand, and labour relations. Because most companies produce more than one product, the scheduling process is often quite complex.

Basically, the problem resembles the product mix model for each period in the future. The objective is either to maximize profit or to minimize the total cost (production plus inventory) of carrying out the task.

Production scheduling is amenable to solution by LP because it is a problem that must be solved on a regular basis. When the objective function and constraints for a firm are established, the inputs can easily be changed each month to provide an updated schedule.

Osgoode Motors, Inc., manufactures two different electrical motors for sale under contract to the Mixwell Company, a well-known producer of small kitchen appliances. Its model GM3A is found in many Mixwell food processors, and its model GM3B is used in the assembly of Mixwell blenders.

Three times each year, the procurement officer at Mixwell contacts Osgoode Motors to place a monthly order for each of the coming four months. Mixwell's demand for motors varies each month based on its own sales forecasts, production capacity, and financial position. Osgoode has just received the January–April order and must begin its own four-month production plan. The demand for motors is shown in Table 3.4.

Production planning at Osgoode Motors must consider four factors:

1. The desirability of producing the same number of each motor each month. This simplifies planning and the scheduling of workers and machines.

2. The necessity to keep down inventory carrying, or holding, costs. This suggests producing in each month only what is needed in that month.

TABLE 3.4	MODEL	JANUARY	FEBRUARY	MARCH	APRIL
Four-Month Order Schedule for Electrical Motors	GM3A	800	700	1000	1100
	GM3B	1000	1200	1400	1400

3. Warehouse limitations that cannot be exceeded without great additional storage costs.

4. The company's no-layoff policy, which has been effective in preventing a unionization of the shop. This suggests a minimum production capacity that should be used each month.

Although these four factors often conflict, Osgoode has found that LP is an effective tool in setting up a production schedule that will minimize total costs of per unit production and monthly holding.

Double-subscripted variables can be used here to develop the LP model. We let

$$P_{A,i} = \text{number of model GM3A motors produced in month } i$$
$$(i = 1, 2, 3, 4 \text{ for January–April})$$

$$P_{B,i} = \text{number of model GM3B motors produced in month } i$$

Production costs are currently \$10 per GM3A motor produced and \$6 per GM3B unit. However, a labour agreement going into effect on March 1 will raise each figure by 10%. We can write the part of the objective function that deals with production cost as

$$\text{Cost of production} = \$10P_{A1} + \$10P_{A2} + \$11P_{A3} + \$11P_{A4} + \$6P_{B1}$$
$$+ \$6P_{B2} + \$6.60P_{B3} + \$6.60P_{B4}$$

To include the inventory carrying costs in the model, we can introduce a second variable. Let

$$I_{A,i} = \text{level of on-hand inventory for GM3A motors at end of month } i$$
$$(i = 1, 2, 3, 4)$$

$$I_{B,i} = \text{level of on-hand inventory for GM3B motors at end of month } i$$

Each GM3A motor held in stock costs \$0.18 per month, and each GM3B held in stock costs \$0.13 per month. Osgoode's accountants allow monthly ending inventories as an acceptable approximation to the average inventory levels during the month. So the carrying cost part of the LP objective function is

$$\text{Cost of carrying inventory} = \$0.18I_{A1} + \$0.18I_{A2} + \$0.18I_{A3} + \$0.18I_{A4}$$
$$+ \$0.13I_{B1} + \$0.13I_{B2} + \$0.13I_{B3} + \$0.13I_{B4}$$

The total objective function becomes

$$\text{Minimize total costs} = 10P_{A1} + 10P_{A2} + 11P_{A3} + 11P_{A4} + 6P_{B1} + 6P_{B2}$$
$$+ 6.6P_{B3} + 6.6P_{B4} + 0.18I_{A1} + 0.18I_{A2} + 0.18I_{A3} + 0.18I_{A4}$$
$$+ 0.13I_{B1} + 0.13I_{B2} + 0.13I_{B3} + 0.13I_{B4}$$

In setting up the constraints, we must recognize the relationship between last month's ending inventory, the current month's production, and the sales to Mixwell this month. The inventory at the end of a month is

$$\begin{pmatrix} \text{Inventory} \\ \text{at the} \\ \text{end of} \\ \text{this month} \end{pmatrix} = \begin{pmatrix} \text{Inventory} \\ \text{at the} \\ \text{end of} \\ \text{last month} \end{pmatrix} + \begin{pmatrix} \text{Current} \\ \text{month's} \\ \text{production} \end{pmatrix} - \begin{pmatrix} \text{Sales} \\ \text{to Mixwell} \\ \text{this month} \end{pmatrix}$$

Suppose that Osgoode is starting the new four-month production cycle with a change in design specifications that left no old motors in stock on January 1. Then, recalling that January's demand for GM3As is 800 and for GM3Bs is 1000, we can write

$$I_{A1} = 0 + P_{A1} - 800$$

$$I_{B1} = 0 + P_{B1} - 1000$$

Double-subscripted variables are often used in LP. Osgoode Motors is more easily formulated with this approach.

Inventory constraints set the relationship between closing inventory this month, closing inventory last month, this month's production, and sales this month.

Transposing all unknown variables to the left of the equal sign and multiplying all terms by –1, these January constraints can be rewritten as

$$P_{A1} - I_{A1} = 800$$

$$P_{B1} - I_{B1} = 1000$$

The constraints on demand in February, March, and April follow:

$$
\begin{aligned}
P_{A2} + I_{A1} - I_{A2} &= 700 &&\text{February GM3A demand}\\
P_{B2} + I_{B1} - I_{B2} &= 1200 &&\text{February GM3B demand}\\
P_{A3} + I_{A2} - I_{A3} &= 1000 &&\text{March GM3A demand}\\
P_{B3} + I_{B2} - I_{B3} &= 1400 &&\text{March GM3B demand}\\
P_{A4} + I_{A3} - I_{A4} &= 1100 &&\text{April GM3A demand}\\
P_{B4} + I_{B3} - I_{B4} &= 1400 &&\text{April GM3B demand}
\end{aligned}
$$

If Osgoode also wants to have on hand an additional 450 GM3As and 300 GM3Bs at the end of April, we add the constraints

$$I_{A4} = 450$$

$$I_{B4} = 300$$

The constraints discussed address demand; they do not, however, consider warehouse space or labour requirements. First, we note that the storage area for Osgoode Motors can hold a maximum of 3300 motors of either type (they are similar in size) at any one time. Then

$$I_{A1} + I_{B1} \leq 3300$$

$$I_{A2} + I_{B2} \leq 3300$$

$$I_{A3} + I_{B3} \leq 3300$$

$$I_{A4} + I_{B4} \leq 3300$$

Second, we return to the issue of employment. So that no worker is ever laid off, Osgoode has a base employment level of 2240 labour hours per month. In a busy period, though, the company can bring two retired skilled employees on board to increase capacity to 2560 hours per month. Each GM3A motor produced requires 1.3 hours of labour, and each GM3B takes a worker 0.9 hours to assemble.

Employment constraints are set for each month.

$$
\begin{aligned}
1.3PA_1 + 0.9PB_1 &\geq 2240 &&\text{(January minimum worker hours/month)}\\
1.3PA_1 + 0.9PB_1 &\leq 2560 &&\text{(January maximum labour available/month)}\\
1.3PA_2 + 0.9PB_2 &\geq 2240 &&\text{(February labour minimum)}\\
1.3PA_2 + 0.9PB_2 &\leq 2560 &&\text{(February labour maximum)}\\
1.3PA_3 + 0.9PB_3 &\geq 2240 &&\text{(March labour minimum)}\\
1.3PA_3 + 0.9PB_3 &\leq 2560 &&\text{(March labour maximum)}\\
1.3PA_4 + 0.9PB_4 &\geq 2240 &&\text{(April labour minimum)}\\
1.3PA_4 + 0.9PB_4 &\leq 2560 &&\text{(April labour maximum)}\\
\text{All variables} &\geq 0
\end{aligned}
$$

There are several ways of setting up the Osgoode Motors problem in Excel. The setup shown in Screenshot 3.9A on the next page follows the same logic we have used in all problems so far; that is, all parameters associated with a specific decision variable are modeled in the same column. The solution, summarized in Table 3.5 on the next page, indicates that the four-month total cost is $76 301.61.

For such multiperiod problems, it may often be more convenient to group all the variables for a given month in the same column. Screenshot 3.9B on page 108 shows an alternative model for the Osgoode Motors problem. Note that in this model, the only decision variables are the

File: 3-9.xls

SCREENSHOT 3.9A   Excel Layout and Solver Entries for Osgoode Motors

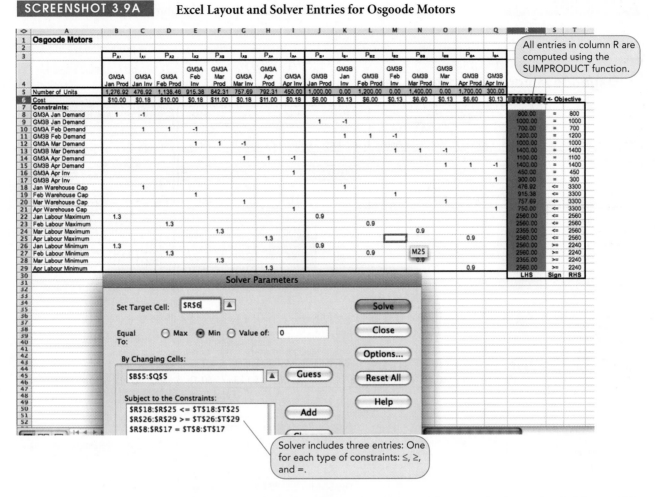

All entries in column R are computed using the SUMPRODUCT function.

Solver includes three entries: One for each type of constraints: ≤, ≥, and =.

Ending inventory is not set as a decision variable in this alternative Excel layout for the Osgoode Motors problem.

production variables. The inventory variables are no longer explicitly stated as decision variables (Changing Cells in Solver). Rather, they are calculated as simple byproducts of the other parameters in the problem. That is, using the standard inventory constraints, the ending inventory each month is calculated as follows:

$$
\begin{pmatrix} \text{Inventory} \\ \text{at the} \\ \text{end of} \\ \text{this month} \end{pmatrix} = \begin{pmatrix} \text{Inventory} \\ \text{at the} \\ \text{end of} \\ \text{last month} \end{pmatrix} + \begin{pmatrix} \text{Current} \\ \text{month's} \\ \text{production} \end{pmatrix} - \begin{pmatrix} \text{Sales} \\ \text{to Mixwell} \\ \text{this month} \end{pmatrix}
$$

$$
\text{Row 8} = \text{Row 5} + \text{Row 6} - \text{Row 7}
$$

TABLE 3.5

Solution to Osgoode Motors Problem

PRODUCTION SCHEDULE	JANUARY	FEBRUARY	MARCH	APRIL
Units of GM3A produced	1277	1138	842	792
Units of GM3B produced	1000	1200	1400	1700
Inventory of GM3A carried	477	915	758	450
Inventory of GM3B carried	0	0	0	300
Labour hours required	2560	2560	2355	2560

SCREENSHOT 3.9B   **Alternate Excel Layout and Solver Entries for Osgoode Motors**

Begin inventory in February = Ending inventory in January

Only decision variables are the production quantities.

	A	B	C	D	E	F	G	H	I	J	K	L
1	**Osgoode Motors (Alternate Model)**											
2												
3		P_{A1}	P_{A2}	P_{A3}	P_{A4}	P_{B1}	P_{B2}	P_{B3}	P_{B4}			
4		GM3A January	GM3A February	GM3A March	GM3A April	GM3B January	GM3B February	GM3B March	GM3B April			
5	Begin Inventory	0	476.9	915.38	757.6923	0	0	0	0			
6	Production	1,276.92	1,138.46	842.31	792.31	1,000.00	1,200.00	1,400.00	1,700.00			
7	Demand	800	700	1000	1100	1000	1200	1400	1400			
8	Ending Inventory	476.92	915.38	757.69	450.00	0.00	0.00	0.00	300.00			
9												
10		Total inv	Sign	Cap		Labour	Needed	Min (>=)	Max (<=)			
11	Jan Warehouse	476.9	<=	3300		Jan	2560.0	2240	2560			
12	Feb Warehouse	915.4	<=	3300		Feb	2,560.0	2240	2560			
13	Mar Warehouse	757.7	<=	3300		Mar	2,355.0	2240	2560			
14	Apr Warehouse	750.0	<=	3300		Apr	2,560.0	2240	2560			
15												
16		Have	Sign	Need								
17	GM3A Apr Inv	450	=	450								
18	GM3B Apr Inv	300	=	300								
19												
20	Prod Cost	$10.00	$10.00	$11.00	$11.00	$6.00	$6.00	$6.60	$6.60	$75,794.62		
21	Inv Cost	$0.18	$0.18	$0.18	$0.18	$0.13	$0.13	$0.13	$0.13	$507.00		
22									Total Cost =	$76,301.62		

Solver Parameters

Set Target Cell: $J$22

Equal To: ○ Max ⦿ Min

By Changing Cells:

$B$6:$I$6

Subject to the Constraints:

$B$11:$B$14 <= $D$11:$D$14
$B$17:$B$18 = $D$17:$D$18
$B$8:$I$8 >= 0
$G$11:$G$14 <= $I$11:$I$14
$G$11:$G$14 >= $H$11:$H$14

Ensure ending inventories are ≥0.

Ending inventories are *not* decision variables in this implementation.

Ending inventory = Begin inventory + Production – Demand
Row 8 = Row 5 + Row 6 – Row 7

Total cost is the same as that in Screenshot 3.9A.

The SUMPRODUCT function is used to compute cells J20 and J21. Formula in C20 = SUMPRODUCT (B20:I20, B6:I6) formula in cell C21 = SUMPRODUCT (B21:I21, B8:I8)

Since they are no longer decision variables, however, we do need to add constraints to ensure that the ending inventories have nonnegative values. Depending on individual preferences and expertise, we can design other layouts for setting up and solving this problem using Excel.

The Osgoode Motors example illustrates a relatively simple production planning problem in that there were only two products being considered. The LP model discussed here can, however, be applied successfully to problems with dozens of products and hundreds of constraints.

Sinking Fund

Another excellent example of a multiperiod problem is the sinking fund problem. In this case, an investor or firm seeks to establish an investment portfolio using the lowest possible initial investment that will generate specific amounts of capital at specific time periods in the future.

Consider the example of Marcel Lapierre, who is trying to plan for his daughter Chantal's university expenses. Based on current projections (it is now the start of year 1),

Marcel anticipates that his financial need at the start of each of the following years is as follows:

Year 3	$20 000
Year 4	$22 000
Year 5	$24 000
Year 6	$26 000

Marcel has several investment choices (assume these are tax free if used for education) at the present time, as listed in Table 3.6. Each choice has a fixed known return on investment and a specified maturity date. Assume that each choice is available for investment at the start of every year. Since choices C and D are relatively risky, Marcel wants no more than 20% of his total investment in those two choices at any point in time.

Marcel wants to establish a sinking fund to meet his requirements. Note that at the start of year 1, the entire initial investment is available for investing in the choices. However, in subsequent years, only the amount maturing from a prior investment is available for investment.

Let us first define the following decision variables. Note that in defining these variables, we need to consider only those investments that will mature by the end of year 5, at the latest, since there is no requirement after six years.

$$A_1 = \text{\$ amount invested in choice } A \text{ at the start of year 1}$$

$$B_1 = \text{\$ amount invested in choice } B \text{ at the start of year 1}$$

$$C_1 = \text{\$ amount invested in choice } C \text{ at the start of year 1}$$

$$D_1 = \text{\$ amount invested in choice } D \text{ at the start of year 1}$$

$$A_2 = \text{\$ amount invested in choice } A \text{ at the start of year 2}$$

$$B_2 = \text{\$ amount invested in choice } B \text{ at the start of year 2}$$

$$C_2 = \text{\$ amount invested in choice } C \text{ at the start of year 2}$$

$$D_2 = \text{\$ amount invested in choice } D \text{ at the start of year 2}$$

$$A_3 = \text{\$ amount invested in choice } A \text{ at the start of year 3}$$

$$B_3 = \text{\$ amount invested in choice } B \text{ at the start of year 3}$$

$$C_3 = \text{\$ amount invested in choice } C \text{ at the start of year 3}$$

$$A_4 = \text{\$ amount invested in choice } A \text{ at the start of year 4}$$

$$B_4 = \text{\$ amount invested in choice } B \text{ at the start of year 4}$$

$$A_5 = \text{\$ amount invested in choice } A \text{ at the start of year 5}$$

TABLE 3.6

Investment Choices for Marcel Lapierre

CHOICE	ROI	MATURITY
A	5%	1 year
B	13%	2 years
C	28%	3 years
D	40%	4 years

The objective is to minimize the initial investment and can be expressed as

$$\text{Minimize } A_1 + B_1 + C_1 + D_1$$

As in the multiperiod production scheduling problem, we need to recognize the relationship between the investment decisions made in any given year and the investment decisions made in all prior years. Specifically, we need to ensure that the amount used for investment at the start of a given year is restricted to the amount maturing at the end of the previous year *less* any payments made for Chantal's education that year. This relationship can be modeled as

This equation is analogous to the inventory equations in the production scheduling problem.

Amount invested at start of year i + Amount paid for education at start of year i
$$= \text{Amounts maturing at the end of year} (i - 1)$$

At the start of year 2, the total amount maturing is $1.05A_1$ (investment in choice A in year 1 plus 5% interest). The constraint at the start of year 2 can therefore be written as

$$A_2 + B_2 + C_2 + D_2 = 1.05A_1 \quad \text{(Year 2 cash flow)}$$

Cash flow constraints   or

$$1.05A_1 - A_2 - B_2 - C_2 - D_2 = 0$$

Constraints at the start of years 3 through 6 are as follows and also include the amounts payable for Chantal's education each year:

$$A_3 + B_3 + C_3 + 20\,000 = 1.13B_1 + 1.05A_2 \qquad \text{(Year 3 cash flow)}$$

or

$$1.13B_1 + 1.05A_2 - A_3 - B_3 - C_3 = 20\,000$$

$$A_4 + B_4 + 22\,000 = 1.28C_1 + 1.13B_2 + 1.05A_3 \qquad \text{(Year 4 cash flow)}$$

or

$$1.28C_1 + 1.13B_2 + 1.05A_3 - A_4 - B_4 = 22\,000$$

$$A_5 + 24\,000 = 1.4D_1 + 1.28C_2 + 1.13B_3 + 1.05A_4 \qquad \text{(Year 5 cash flow)}$$

or

$$1.4D_1 + 1.28C_2 + 1.13B_3 + 1.05A_4 - A_5 = 24\,000$$

$$26\,000 = 1.4D_2 + 1.28C_3 + 1.13B_4 + 1.05A_5 \qquad \text{(Year 6 cash flow)}$$

or

$$1.4D_2 + 1.28C_3 + 1.13B_4 + 1.05A_5 = 26\,000$$

These five constraints address the cash flow issues. However, they do not account for Marcel's risk preference with regard to investments in choices C and D in any given year. To satisfy these requirements, we need to ensure that total investment in choices C and D in any year is no more than 20% of the total investment in *all* choices that year. In keeping track of these investments, it is important to also account for investments in *prior* years that may have still not matured. At the start of year 1, this constraint can be written as

$$C_1 + D_1 \leq 0.2(A_1 + B_1 + C_1 + D_1)$$

Risk preference constraints   or

$$0.8(C_1 + D_1) - 0.2(A_1 + B_1) \leq 0 \qquad \text{(Year 1 risk)}$$

In writing this constraint at the start of year 2, we must take into account the fact that investments B_1, C_1, and D_1 have still not matured. Therefore,

$$C_1 + D_1 + C_2 + D_2 \leq 0.2(B_1 + C_1 + D_1 + A_2 + B_2 + C_2 + D_2)$$

or

$$0.8(C_1 + D_1 + C_2 + D_2) - 0.2(B_1 + A_2 + B_2) \leq 0 \qquad \text{(Year 2 risk)}$$

Constraints at the start of years 3 through 5 are as follows. Note that there is no constraint necessary at the start of year 6 since there are no investments that year.

$$C_1 + D_1 + C_2 + D_2 + C_3 \leq 0.2(C_1 + D_1 + B_2 + C_2 + D_2 + A_3 + B_3 + C_3)$$

or

$$0.8(C_1 + D_1 + C_2 + D_2 + C_3) - 0.2(B_2 + A_3 + B_3) \leq 0 \quad \text{(Year 3 risk)}$$

$$D_1 + C_2 + D_2 + C_3 \leq 0.2(D_1 + C_2 + D_2 + B_3 + C_3 + A_4 + B_4)$$

or

$$0.8(D_1 + C_2 + D_2 + C_3) - 0.2(B_3 + A_4 + B_4) \leq 0 \qquad \text{(Year 4 risk)}$$

$$D_2 + C_3 \leq 0.2(D_2 + C_3 + B_4 + A_5)$$

or

$$0.8(D_2 + C_3) - 0.2(B_4 + A_5) \leq 0 \qquad\qquad \text{(Year 5 risk)}$$

All variables ≥ 0

File: 3-10.xls

Screenshot 3.10 shows the Excel layout and Solver entries for this model. As with the production scheduling problem, there are several ways in which this model could have been structured, depending on the preference and expertise of the analyst.

SCREENSHOT 3.10   **Excel Layout and Solver Entries for Marcel Lapierre's Sinking Fund**

> Decision variables are arranged on a yearly basis.

	A	B	C	D	E	F	G	H	I	J	K	L	M	N	O	P	Q	R
1	**Marcel Lapierre's Sinking Fund**																	
2																		
3		A_1	B_1	C_1	D_1	A_2	B_2	C_2	D_2	A_3	B_3	C_3	A_4	B_4	A_5			
4		Inv A Year 1	Inv B Year 1	Inv C Year 1	Inv D Year 1	Inv A Year 2	Year 2	Year 2	Year 2	Inv A Year 3	Inv B Year 3	Year 3	Inv A Year 4	Inv B Year 4	Inv A Year 5			
5	$ Invested	0.00	61,064.11	3,804.66	8,445.95	0.00	0.00	0.00	0.00	38,227.50	10,774.93	0.00	0.00	23,008.85	0.00			
6	Objective Coefficient	1	1	1	1											$73,314.71	<- Objective	
7	Constraints:																	
8	Year 2 Investments	1.05				-1	-1	-1	-1							0.00	=	0
9	Year 3 Investments		1.13			1.05				-1	-1	-1				20000.00	=	20000
10	Year 4 Investments			1.28			1.13			1.05			-1	-1		22000.00	=	22000
11	Year 5 Investments				1.40			1.28			1.13		1.05		-1	24000.00	=	24000
12	Year 6 Investments								1.40				1.28		1.13	1.05	26000.00	=	26000
13	Year 1 Risk	-0.2	-0.2	0.8	0.8											-2412.33	<=	0
14	Year 2 Risk		-0.2	0.8	0.8	-0.2	-0.2	0.8	0.8							-2412.33	<=	0
15	Year 3 Risk			0.8	0.8		-0.2	0.8	0.8	-0.2	-0.2	0.8				0.00	<=	0
16	Year 4 Risk				0.8			0.8	0.8		-0.2	0.8	-0.2	-0.2		0.00	<=	0
17	Year 5 Risk								0.8			0.8		-0.2	-0.2	-4601.77	<=	0
18																LHS	Sign	RHS

> All constraints have been algebraically modified to bring all variables to the LHS.

> These are the cash requirements each year.

Solver Parameters

Set Target Cell: $P$6

Equal To: ○ Max ● Min ○ Value of: 0

By Changing Cells:

...6:$O$5

Subject to the Constraints:

...$13:$P$17 <= $R$13:$R$17
$P$8:$P$12 = $R$8:$R$12

[Solve] [Close] [Guess] [Options] [Add]

The optimal solution requires Marcel to invest a total of $73 314.71 at the start of year 1, putting $61 064.11 in choice *B*, $3804.66 in choice *C*, and $8445.95 in choice *D*. There is no money maturing for investment at the start of year 2. At the start of year 3, using the maturing amounts, Marcel should pay off $20 000 for Chantal's education, invest $38 227.50 in choice *A*, and invest $10 774.93 in choice *B*. At the start of year 4, Marcel should use the maturing amounts to pay off $22 000 for Chantal's education and invest $23 008.85 in choice *B*. The investments in place at this time will generate $24 000 at the start of year 5 and $26 000 at the start of year 6, meeting Marcel's requirements in those years.

SUMMARY

This chapter continues the discussion of LP models. To show ways of formulating and solving problems from a variety of disciplines, we examine applications from marketing, manufacturing, employee scheduling, finance, transportation, ingredient blending, and multiperiod planning. We also illustrate how to set up and solve all these models using Excel's Solver add-in.

⫸ SELF-TEST

- Before taking the self-test, refer back to the learning objectives at the beginning of the chapter and the notes in the margins.
- Use the key at the back of the book to correct your answers.
- Restudy pages that correspond to any questions that you answered incorrectly or material you feel uncertain about.

1. LP can be used to select effective media mixes, allocate fixed or limited budgets across media, and maximize audience exposure.
   a. True
   b. False

2. Blending problems arise when one must decide which of two or more ingredients is to be chosen to produce a product.
   a. True
   b. False

3. The only objective functions that are allowed for LP problems are maximizing profits or minimizing costs.
   a. True
   b. False

4. When setting up LP models on Excel, you are always required to manipulate constraints so that all variables appear on the left-hand side.
   a. True   b. False

5. Using LP to maximize audience exposure in an advertising campaign is an example of the type of LP application known as
   a. marketing research.
   b. media selection.
   c. portfolio assessment.
   d. media budgeting.
   e. all of the above.

6. Which of the following *does not* represent a factor a manager might consider when employing LP for production scheduling?
   a. labour capacity
   b. space limitations
   c. product demand
   d. risk assessment
   e. inventory costs

7. Labour planning is a type of LP problem that
   a. is used to address staffing needs over a specific time period.
   b. is useful when there is flexibility in assigning workers to jobs requiring interchangeable talents.
   c. is frequently used by large banks.
   d. might be used to determine teller assignments in banks.
   e. is all of the above.

8. When applying LP to diet problems, the objective function is usually designed to
   a. maximize profits from blends of nutrients.
   b. maximize ingredient blends.
   c. minimize production losses.
   d. maximize the number of products to be produced.
   e. minimize the costs of nutrient blends.

9. The diet problem is
   a. also called the feed mix problem in agriculture.
   b. a special case of the ingredient mix problem.

c. a special case of the blending problem.
d. all of the above.

10. Determining the most efficient allocation of people, machines, equipment, and so on is characteristic of the LP problem type known as
   a. production scheduling.
   b. labour planning.
   c. assignment.
   d. blending.
   e. none of the above.

11. The selection of specific investments from among a wide variety of alternatives is the type of LP problem known as
   a. the product mix problem.
   b. the investment banker problem.

c. the portfolio selection problem.
d. the Wall Street problem.
e. none of the above.

12. A type of LP problem that is used in marketing is called
   a. the 4P problem.
   b. the Madison Avenue problem.
   c. the marketing research problem.
   d. all of the above.

13. An LP problem in which decisions made in one period affect decisions made in future periods is typically called
   a. a sequential problem.
   b. a multiperiod problem.
   c. a periodic problem.
   d. none of the above.

PROBLEMS

3-1 **(Product mix)**) Belle Cuisine Kitchen Renovations, located in Quebec, manufactures custom designed kitchen cabinets in oak or maple. Manufacturing requires each type of cabinet to go through three processes: carpentry, staining, and French polishing. The table below shows production times required for each type of cabinet, available labour hours per day for each of the three processes, and profit per cabinet. The manufacturing plant operates five days a week. Belle Cuisine has a contract with a home renovation firm in Ontario to supply a minimum of 300 of each type of cabinet per week. The company wants to determine a production schedule to maximize weekly profit.

(a) Formulate as an LP problem.
(b) Solve using Excel.

3-2 **(Investment decision)** The Turner-Laberge Brokerage firm has just been instructed by one of its clients to invest $250 000 for her, money obtained recently through the sale of land holdings in British Columbia. The client has a good deal of trust in the investment house, but she also has her own ideas about the distribution of the funds being invested. She requests that the firm select whatever stocks and bonds it believes are well rated but within the following guidelines:

1. At least 20% of the investment should be in a self-directed RRSP account with only Canadian content.
2. At least 40% of the investment should be placed in a combination of U.S. electronics firms, aerospace firms, and pharmaceutical companies.

3. No more than 50% of the amount invested in a self-directed RRSP should be in precious metals.

   Subject to these restraints, the client's goal is to maximize projected return on investments. The analysts at Turner-Laberge, aware of these guidelines, prepare a list of high-quality stocks and bonds and their corresponding rates of return.

INVESTMENT	PROJECTED RATE OF RETURN (%)
Canadian RRSP	5.3
Thompson Electronics, Inc. (USA)	6.8
United Aerospace Corp. (USA)	4.9
Palmer Pharmaceuticals (USA)	8.4
Alberta Gold Mines (Canada)	11.8

(a) Formulate this portfolio selection problem using LP.
(b) Solve this problem using Excel.

3-3 **(Security agent scheduling)** John Powell, chief of airport security at a large Canadian airport, is responsible for scheduling security agents around the clock. Powell has divided the day into six 4-hour periods: midnight to 4:00 A.M., 4:00 A.M. to 8:00 A.M., etc. Security agents work 8-hour shifts. Passenger traffic in the airport is determined by domestic and international flight schedules, and Powell

Table for Problem 3-1

TYPE OF WOOD	CARPENTRY (HOURS/CABINET)	STAINING (HOURS/CABINET)	FRENCH POLISHING (HOURS/CABINET)	PROFIT/ CABINET
Oak	3	1.5	0.75	$19.50
Maple	2	1.0	0.75	$21.75
Available Hours	**360**	**200**	**125**	

has decided that the minimum number of security agents that he needs on duty during the different 4-hour shifts is as shown in the table:

SHIFT	TIME	MINIMUM NUMBER OF SECURITY AGENTS REQUIRED
1	Midnight – 4:00 A.M.	6
2	4:00 A.M. – 8:00 A.M.	10
3	8:00 A.M. – noon	24
4	Noon – 4:00 P.M.	24
5	4:00 P.M. – 8:00 P.M.	16
6	8:00 P.M. to midnight	12

Since Powell has been requested to keep the security budget at a minimum, he needs to minimize the number of security agents who work in the airport in a day. In making up a daily roster of security agents, Powell has to specify the starting time for each agent, therefore he has to decide how many agents should start their 8-hour shift at the beginning of each 4-hour time block.

(a) Formulate the security agent scheduling problem as a linear program.

(b) Solve using Excel.

3-4 *(Animal feed mix)* The Cheval Blanc Stable feeds and houses the horses used to pull tourist-filled carriages (known as *calèches* in Quebec) through the cobblestoned streets of Quebec's historic Old City. The stable owner recognizes the need to set a nutritious diet for the horses in his care. At the same time, he would like to keep the overall daily cost of feed to a minimum.

The feed mixes available for the horses' diet are an oat product, a highly enriched grain, and a mineral product. Each of these mixes contains a certain amount of five ingredients needed daily to keep the average horse healthy. The table below shows these minimum requirements, the units of each ingredient per kilogram of feed mix, and the costs for the three mixes.

In addition, the stable owner is aware that an overfed horse is a sluggish worker. Consequently, he determines that 3 kilograms of feed per day is the most that any horse needs to function properly.

(a) Formulate this problem as a linear program.

(b) Solve for the optimal daily mix of the three feeds.

(c) How many kilograms of food will a horse receive daily?

3-5 *(Media selection)* The advertising director for Manitoba Paint and Supply, a chain of four retail stores in Winnipeg, is considering two media possibilities. One plan is for a series of half-page ads in the local Sunday newspaper; the other is for advertising time on the local CTV affiliate. The stores are expanding their lines of do-it-yourself tools, and the advertising director is interested in an exposure level of at least 90% within the city's neighbourhoods and 60% in suburban areas.

The TV viewing time under consideration has an exposure rating per spot of 6% in city homes and 3% in the suburbs. The Sunday newspaper has corresponding exposure rates of 4% and 3% per ad. The cost of a half-page advertisement in the newspaper is $925; a television spot costs $1250.

Manitoba Paint and Supply would like to select the least costly advertising strategy that would meet desired exposure levels.

(a) Formulate as an LP model.

(b) Solve the problem using Excel.

3-6 *(Acquiring equipment)* Fleish Meat Company, a national supplier of vacuum-packed sliced meat products, needs 100 new meat slicing machines. Machines are heavily used and need to be replaced every two years. Machines can be purchased for $8000 each or leased for $5000 per year. At the end of two years, machines have no salvage value. Fleish has budgeted $200 000 to lease and/or buy new machines. If extra cash is needed, Fleish can borrow up to half a million dollars at a rate of 8% per year. Fleish's agreement with the bank requires the company to repay the amount borrowed, plus any interest accrued, at the end of each year. Each machine will earn $5500 per year, so that $550 000 will be available at the end of each year. Earnings from the first year can be applied to lease costs and repayment of debt at the beginning of the second year.

(a) Formulate an LP model that will help Fleish Meat Company to minimize the cost of acquiring 100 machines for a two-year period.

Table for Problem 3-4

DIET REQUIREMENT (INGREDIENTS)	OAT PRODUCT (UNITS/kg)	ENRICHED GRAIN (UNITS/kg)	MINERAL PRODUCT (UNITS/kg)	MINIMUM DAILY REQUIREMENT
A	2	3	1	3
B	0.5	1	0.5	1
C	3	5	6	4.5
D	1	1.5	2	4
E	0.5	0.5	1.5	2.5
Cost/kg	$0.36	$0.56	$0.68	

(b) Solve the problem. How many machines should be bought? Leased? How much cash should Fleish borrow at the beginning of each year?

3-7 (*Ingredient mix*) Paddy O'Sullivan's new Irish Pub is scheduled to have its grand opening in Saskatoon on March 17th, St. Patrick's Day. Paddy decides to have a private reception on March 16th. Attendance will be by invitation only and Paddy has invited friends and business colleagues, in addition to local radio and TV personalities. Complimentary drinks will be served at the reception. Paddy instructs his bartenders to fill shot glasses with his four new cocktail innovations: The Irish Slugger, The Dublin Delight, The Tipperary Tippler, and The Belfast Blaster. The ingredients for these cocktails are Irish Whiskey, Irish Cream Liqueur, Crème de Menthe, and Coffee Cream Liqueur. Shot glasses hold 45 millilitres (approximately 1.5 ounces or 1 jigger) of liquor. The composition of the four cocktails is shown in the table below.

Paddy has set aside ten 750-millilitre bottles each of Irish Cream Liqueur, Crème de Menthe, and Coffee Cream Liqueur, and six 1-litre bottles of Irish Whiskey. His objective is to make the largest possible number of the four cocktails in advance.

(a) Formulate as an LP problem.

(b) Solve using Excel.

INGREDIENT	IRISH SLUGGER	DUBLIN DELIGHT	TIPPERARY TIPPLER	BELFAST BLASTER
Irish Whiskey		30 mL	10 mL	10 mL
Irish Cream Liqueur	15 mL	10 mL	20 mL	
Crème de Menthe	15 mL	5 mL		25 mL
Coffee Cream Liqueur	15 mL		15 mL	10 mL

3-8 (*Ingredient mix revisited*) Paddy O'Sullivan's wife, Siobhan, points out that it will look funny having a different number of each of the four types of drinks.
(a) Formulate as an LP problem, adding the constraints that there should be equal numbers of each type of cocktail.
(b) Solve using Excel.

3-9 (*Pricing and marketing strategy*) The Atlantic Steel Corporation, based in Sydney, Nova Scotia, specializes in manufacturing thin metal sheets 1.2 metres × 2.4 metres × 1 millimetre. Atlantic Steel has set itself the goal of being the leading supplier of these sheets in Canada. Atlantic Steel forecasts demand for sheet metal as a function of several variables: dollars spent on advertising in trade magazines, dollars spent on travelling for sales personnel, dollars spent on employee overtime, and the percentage markup taken above the cost of manufacturing a steel sheet. Estimates obtained from the sales department indicate that Atlantic Steel will sell nine sheets for every dollar spent on advertising in trade magazines, 11 sheets for every dollar spent on travelling, and 12 sheets for every dollar spent on employee overtime. Because demand is highly sensitive to price, Atlantic Steel realizes that it will sustain a significant sales loss for every percentage point that it charges above manufacturing costs. Best estimates of this loss, based on economic analysis and historical evidence, are that demand will decrease by 65 000 sheets of metal for every one point increase in markup above manufacturing costs.

Atlantic Steel budgets $250 000 for advertising in trade magazines, travel, and overtime for the next year. It decides to spend at least $30 000 on advertising, and notes that the amount spent on overtime should not exceed twice the amount spent on travel. In order to remain competitive, Atlantic must keep its markup in the range of 20% to 35%.

(a) Formulate an LP model to determine how much Atlantic Steel should spend on each of the four variables, with the goal of selling the largest possible number of steel sheets.
(b) Solve using Excel.

3-10 (*College meal selection*) Kathy Moriyama, campus dietician for a small college, is responsible for formulating a nutritious meal plan for students. For an evening meal, she feels that the following five meal-content requirements should be met: (1) between 900 and 1500 calories; (2) at least 4 milligrams of iron; (3) no more than 50 grams of fat; (4) at least 26 grams of protein; and (5) no more than 50 grams of carbohydrates. On a particular day, Moriyama's food stock includes seven items that can be prepared and served for supper to meet these requirements. The cost per kilogram for each food item and its contribution to each of the five nutritional requirements are given in the table for this problem (shown on page 116).

What combination and amounts of food items will provide the nutrition Moriyama requires at the least total food cost?
(a) Formulate as an LP problem.
(b) What is the cost per meal?
(c) Is this a well-balanced diet?

Table for Problem 3-10

FOOD ITEM	CALORIES/ kg	IRON (mg/kg)	FAT (g/kg)	PROTEIN (g/kg)	CARBOHYDRATES (g/kg)	COST/kg ($)
	TABLE OF FOOD VALUES* AND COSTS					
Milk	590	0.4	32	32	44	1.20
Ground meat	2432	0.4	192	162	0	4.70
Chicken	788	8.6	18	148	0	2.30
Fish	716	6.4	1.0	166	0	4.50
Beans	256	6.4	1.6	14	56	1.16
Spinach	236	28.2	2.8	28	38	2.34
Potatoes	558	4.4	1.0	16	126	0.66

Source: adapted from C. F. Church and H. N. Church. *Bowes and Church's Food Values of Portions Commonly Used*, 12/e. Philadelphia: J.B. Lippincott, 1975.

Table for Problem 3-11

	REGULAR EXTERNAL DVD	DELUXE EXTERNAL DVD	1 GB FLASH MEMORY CARD	30 GB EXTERNAL HD	60 GB EXTERNAL HD	2 GB MEMORY STICK
Dept. 1	10	12	4	10	12	5
Dept. 2	6	6	5	7	9	4
Dept. 3	3	3	4	4	5	2

3-11 *(High-tech product mix)* Alta Electronics Incorporated specializes in external memory expansion devices for PCs. Alta manufactures the following six peripheral devices for PCs in its Calgary plant: regular external DVD writers, deluxe external DVD writers, 1 GB flash memory cards, 30 GB external hard drives, 60 GB external hard drives, and 2 GB USB memory sticks. Each of these technical products requires time, in minutes, to be processed in three departments (covering assembly, testing etc.), as shown in the table above.

The first two departments are available 120 hours per week. The third department is only available for 100 hours each week. Since the demand for all six external storage devices is very large, Alta Electronics believes that it can sell as many units of each product as it can manufacture. The table that follows summarizes the revenue and material cost for each product:

DEVICE	REVENUE PER UNIT SOLD ($)	MATERIAL COST PER UNIT ($)
Regular external DVD writer	200	35
Deluxe external DVD writer	240	45
1 GB flash memory card	80	7
30 GB external HD	180	45
60 GB external HD	230	48
2 GB memory stick	90	6

In addition, variable labour costs are $15 per hour for department 1, $12 per hour for department 2, and $18 per hour for department 3. Alta also has the following production requirements based on existing standing weekly orders:

- At least 43 external hard drives must be produced each week
- At least 20 units of each of the six products must be produced each week.

Alta Electronics wants to maximize its profits.

(a) Formulate this problem as an LP model.
(b) Solve the problem using Excel, specifying the best weekly product mix and the maximum weekly profit.

3-12 *(Agricultural planning)* Three prairie farmers, Boyarchuk, Jorgensen, and Paisley, have decided to form a co-operative for the crop growing aspect of their farming business so that they can share resources such as expensive harvesting equipment, limited water supplies for irrigation, etc. The table below shows the amount of arable land each farmer owns and the amount of water allocated by a provincial water authority to each farmer for irrigation.

FARMER	USABLE LAND (HECTARES)	WATER ALLOCATION (MILLION LITRES)
Boyarchuk	40	60
Jorgensen	60	80
Paisley	30	50

Table for Problem 3-12

CROP	MAXIMUM QUOTA (HECTARES)	WATER CONSUMPTION (MILLION LITRES/HECTARE)	NET PROFIT (DOLLARS/HECTARE)
Maize	60	2.9	$4120
Corn	50	2.1	$3650
Wheat	33	2.4	$3300

The farmers have considered several crops that are suited for the region and have decided to grow the following three crops: maize, corn, and wheat. These crops yield different expected net profits per hectare and consume different amounts of water. In addition, provincial agricultural recommendations set maximum quotas for the total area that can be devoted to each of these crops by the farmers' co-operative. The relevant information is shown in the table above.

The agreement worked out between Boyarchuk, Jorgensen, and Paisley stipulates that each farmer will use at least 60% of his available land for planting crops. The remaining 40% may be used for other farm activities such as grazing cattle and sheep, but this lies outside the farmers' agreement. Also, to meet local demand they have agreed that at least 6 hectares of wheat must be planted in total.

In order to formulate the problem as an LP, the decision variables will be the number of acres of each type of crop to be planted by each farmer. The following table shows the decision variables for each crop–farmer combination:

CROP	BOYARCHUK	FARMER JORGENSEN	PAISLEY
Maize	MB	MJ	MP
Corn	CB	CJ	CP
Wheat	WB	WJ	WP

MB = Number of hectares of maize planted by Boyarchuk; CJ = Number of hectares of corn planted by Jorgensen; and so on.

(a) Formulate as an LP.
(b) Solve using Excel.
(c) How many hectares of each crop should be planted?
(d) What percentage of net profit does each farmer obtain? Is this fair?

3-13 *(Material blending)* Thunder Bay Automobile Construction Inc. has just received a contract to construct steel body frames for automobiles that are to be assembled at a Canadian plant for a major Japanese auto manufacturer. The Japanese company has strict quality control standards for all its component subcontractors and has informed Thunder Bay that each frame must have the following steel content:

MATERIAL	MINIMUM PERCENT	MAXIMUM PERCENT
Manganese	2.10	3.10
Silicon	4.30	6.30
Carbon	1.05	2.05

Thunder Bay mixes batches of eight different available materials to produce one tonne of steel used in the body frames. The table at the bottom of the page shows details of these materials.

Table for Problem 3-13

MATERIAL AVAILABLE	MANGANESE (%)	SILICON (%)	CARBON (%)	AVAILABLE (kg)	COST/kg
Alloy 1	70.0	15.0	3.0	No limit	$0.24
Alloy 2	55.0	30.0	1.0	150	0.26
Alloy 3	12.0	26.0	0	No limit	0.30
Iron 1	1.0	10.0	3.0	No limit	0.18
Iron 2	5.0	2.5	0	No limit	0.14
Carbide 1	0	24.0	18.0	25	0.20
Carbide 2	0	25.0	20.0	100	0.24
Carbide 3	0	23.0	25.0	50	0.18

Thunder Bay wants to know how much of each of the eight materials to blend into a one-tonne load of steel so that they meet all requirements while minimizing cost.

(a) Formulate as an LP problem.
(b) Solve using Excel.

3-14 (**Blending coffee**) The Great Canadian Coffee Company imports coffee beans and is attempting to create a coffee blend that will maximize profit and appeal to Canadian tastes. Two major characteristics of coffee are acidity and body. Consumer studies have indicated that Canadians prefer a coffee blend that is not overly acidic and that can be characterized as full-bodied. The company packages its coffee blends in 150 gram vacuum-sealed bags and sells 10 000 bags a day. Each bag produces $1.20 sales revenue. The four types of coffee bean that the company imports for blending have the following characteristics:

COFFEE BEAN	COST PER kg	ACIDITY COEFFICIENT	BODY COEFFICIENT	DAILY AVAILABILITY (kg)
Brazilian	$4.60	7	4	4000
Colombian	$4.40	2	6	5000
Jamaican	$3.80	6	3	3000
Hawaiian	$3.60	3	5	4000

The company has decided that a Canadian blend should have an average acidity coefficient that is not more than 5 and an average body coefficient that is at least 4. Also, each 150 gram bag should contain at most 30% Jamaican coffee and at least 20% Colombian coffee.

(a) Formulate the Great Canadian Coffee Company's blending problem as a linear program.
(b) Solve the problem using Excel. How many grams of each type of coffee bean should be mixed in a 150 gram bag?

3-15 (**Purchasing school buses**) A Saskatchewan school district is considering purchasing three types of school buses: large buses, small buses, and minivans. Large buses can seat 60 students and cost $160 000 each. Small buses seat 30 students and cost $110 000, while minivans can seat eight students and cost $75 000. The board has authorized a total budget of $1 million for purchasing buses. There are 12 school bus drivers available. A study of the school district's transportation needs for different types of events has shown that they must purchase at least one large bus, at least two small buses, and at least four minivans. The maintenance department can

service 20 minivans at any time, and has noted that servicing a small bus is equivalent in labour-hours and parts to servicing two minivans. Similarly, servicing one large bus would be equivalent to servicing four minivans. Based on school enrollments, the school district has to be able to transport 212 students daily.

(a) Formulate a linear program to help the school board decide how many of each type of bus to purchase.
(b) Solve using Excel.

3-16 (**Venture capital**) Four recent MBA graduates from a leading Canadian business school have formed a partnership in a venture capital enterprise that they have decided to name the Canfund Group (they like this name because of the two possible interpretations of the "Can" in Canfund—they are proudly Canadian and they "Can Fund" your project!). The group is considering six projects that they might fund this year. The table at the bottom of the page shows the expected net profits for each of the projects, as well as the expenditures (cash outflows) required for each of the next three years to fund the projects.

Canfund has the following projected cash availabilities for the next three years: $500 000 for the first year, $350 000 for the second year, and $400 000 for the third year. Canfund has been offered first choice for funding each of the projects. It is possible to adopt a fraction of a project, in which case the cash outflows and net profits accrue in the same proportion. The partners must determine to what extent they should participate in each of the projects in order to maximize the total return.

(a) Formulate as a linear program.
(b) Solve using Excel.

3-17 (**Purchasing equipment**) The FlyCan airline serves both regional and cross-country flights within Canada. FlyCan has been authorized by the board of directors to purchase new airplanes to fly long-range, medium-range, and short-range routes. After lengthy negotiations with two of the major aircraft manufacturers, Boring and Airflus, FlyCan has decided to buy the B949 jumbo jets for its long-range service at $210 million each. For medium-range flights, it has chosen the A656 aircraft at a cost of $143 million each. Finally, the company has selected the B343 short-range planes at a cost of $56 million each. The board of directors has authorized a maximum commitment of $5 billion for these purchases. It is estimated that the net annual profit after subtracting capital recovery costs will be $3 800 000 for each B949, $3 400 000 per A656, and $2 800 000 for each short-range B343 plane.

Table for Problem 3-16

	PROJECT 1	PROJECT 2	PROJECT 3	PROJECT 4	PROJECT 5	PROJECT 6
Net Profits	$700 000	$1 200 000	$350 000	$450 000	$800 000	$1 200 000
Cash Out: Year 1	250 000	400 000	0	160 000	40 000	0
Cash Out: Year 2	110 000	120 000	100 000	0	0	445 000
Cash Out: Year 3	95 000	65 000	85 000	100 000	0	300 000

FlyCan has an aggressive recruitment and training program that will ensure that enough trained flight crews will be available to fly up to 30 new airplanes. If only B343s were being serviced, the maintenance facilities would be able to handle a total of 40 aircraft. Likewise, it could handle a total of 32 A656s or 24 B949s.

FlyCan has determined it will need at least 20 aircraft in total, and no less than five of each type of aircraft. Management wishes to know how many planes of each type should be purchased in order to maximize profit.

(a) Formulate the aircraft purchase problem as a linear program.

(b) Solve using Excel.

3-18 (*Inventory management*) NB Campers Inc. manufactures small camper trailers. John Dunphy, president of NB Campers, has forecast demand for the four quarters of 2009 as follows:

QUARTER	DEMAND
1	35
2	50
3	75
4	30

Quarter 1= January, February, March; Quarter 2=April, May, June; and so on.

At the beginning of the first quarter, NB Campers has an inventory of 10 campers. Dunphy has to decide how many campers to manufacture during each quarter. It costs $4500 to manufacture a camper, and NB Campers can produce a maximum of 60 campers per quarter. The company's production capabilities are such that any camper manufactured during a quarter can be used to meet demand for that quarter. Any campers manufactured but not sold during a quarter will incur a one time inventory cost of $200. Assume that the inventory holding cost for the 10 campers in inventory at the begining of the first quarter has already been accounted for in the previous year.

NB Campers Inc. has to decide how many campers to produce during each quarter and how many to hold in inventory at the end of each quarter in order to minimize the combined annual cost of manufacturing and holding inventory.

(a) Formulate the problem as a linear program

(b) Solve using Excel

3-19 (*Multi-period investment strategy*) Bert Humphries has left his home in a small town in rural Manitoba and moved to Toronto to enroll in a four-year undergraduate program in economics. Bert is planning an investment strategy for the four-year period, with the goal of having the largest possible amount of cash on hand when he graduates. Bert has some revenue from a combination of an RESP (registered education savings plan) fund that his parents opened for him when he was a baby, scholarship funds, and a small inheritance he recently received from his grandmother. His estimate of revenues and expenses over the four years is shown in the following table. Bert has $5000 in cash at the beginning of the first year.

YEAR	REVENUES	EXPENSES
2009–2010	$30 000	$10 000
2010–2011	$40 000	$25 000
2011–2012	$25 000	$25 000
2012–2013	$15 000	$12 500

Any money left over at the end of a year can be invested in guaranteed investment certificates (GICs) for one year at an annual interest rate of 2.9%, for two years at 3.0%, for three years at 3.1%, or for four years at 3.4%. Bert uses the following rule for each of the four years:

Money Invested + Expenses Paid ≤

Revenues + Money Earned from Investment

(a) Formulate a linear program to determine an investment strategy that will maximize the value of Bert's GICs at the end of the fourth year. (*Hint*: Bert can have up to four GICs coming due at the end of the fourth year: a four-year GIC invested at the beginning of Year 1, a three-year GIC invested at the beginning of Year 2, a two-year GIC invested at the beginning of Year 3, and a one-year GIC invested at the beginning of Year 4. It is the sum of these values that Bert wants to maximize, as he plans to cash in all of his GICs and travel the world for a year between graduation and starting his career.)

(b) Solve using Excel.

3-20 (*Blending gasoline*) A small Alberta refinery blends three types of refined petroleum to produce two commercial gasoline products: automobile gasoline and aviation gasoline (also known as AvGas). The petroleum products used for blending the two gasolines have the following characteristics:

PETROLEUM TYPE	OCTANE RATING	SULFUR CONTENT (PARTS PER MILLION)
A	87	490
B	95	440
C	102	400

Octane rating is a measure of the quality of a gasoline—the higher the octane rating, the better the performance of the engine. Clearly, aviation fuel will require a higher octane rating than automobile fuel. Sulfur is one of the leading contributors to air pollution. Recent guidelines require sulfur content of fuels to be less than 500 parts per million.

The following table shows the required characteristics of the two blended gasolines:

FINAL PRODUCT	MINIMUM OCTANE RATING	MAXIMUM SULFUR CONTENT
Aviation Fuel	100	430
Auto Fuel	89	470

For the next three months the refinery has 30 000 bbl of petroleum A available, 100 000 bbl of petroleum B, and

70 000 bbl of petroleum C. (A barrel of oil, denoted bbl, is equivalent to 159 litres.) The refinery can sell as much automobile fuel as it blends, but the maximum demand for aviation fuel is 20 000 bbl, since AvGas is only sold to owners of private jets at a small municipal airport.

The estimated average selling price of automobile gas at the pump is expected to be $0.85 per litre, and aviation fuel can be sold at $1.40 a litre.

(a) Formulate a linear program to maximize revenue from the sales of auto and aviation gasoline over the next three months.

(b) Solve using Excel.

(c) Specify the octane rating and the sulfur content of aviation gasoline and automobile gasoline.

(Hint: When petroleum types are blended, the resulting gasoline mixture has an octane rating and a sulfur content in proportion to the volume of each petroleum type within the mix. For example, if a blend was formulated by mixing 1000 barrels of petroleum A, 1200 barrels of petroleum B, and 800 barrels of petroleum C, the resulting gasoline would have an octane rating of

$$\frac{1000(87) + 1200(95) + 800(102)}{1000 + 1200 + 800} = 94.2$$

and a sulfur content of

$$\frac{1000(490) + 1200(440) + 800(400)}{1000 + 1200 + 800} = 446$$

⊪➡ CASE STUDY 3.1

Dofasco Fuel Management

The works manager at Dominion Foundries and Steel (DOFASCO) was faced with rapidly increasing market prices for fuel oil and natural gas. Anticipating that similar price increases were likely to continue for the foreseeable future, the works manager wanted to be certain that the steel works was making the best use of its energy dollars, and in particular, that the fuels produced as by-products from plant operations were being efficiently utilized.

THE COMPANY

DOFASCO, founded in 1912, was an important steel producer that manufactured a variety of flat rolled steel products and castings. The company began as a foundry operation that supplied castings for the rail car manufacturing sector, but by the mid-1970s had grown into a fully integrated steelmaking operation with over 10 000 employees. The company produced over three million ingot tons of steel, and had annual sales of $621 million.

Major production facilities located at its 700-acre plant included six coke oven batteries, four blast furnaces, two steelmaking shops, and a hot strip mill as well as cold rolling and associated finishing lines. DOFASCO's product line included hot rolled sheet and strip—for automotive frames, wheels and miscellaneous stampings as well as construction and agricultural applications; cold rolled sheet and strip—for auto parts, appliances, metal containers, mechanical tubing and agricultural equipment; tin plate chromium-coated steels—for food and beverage cans, crown, caps and aerosol containers; galvanized steels—for building and road construction, appliances, and automotive uses; electrical steels—for transformers and motors; prepainted steel products—for building cladding, auto parts and miscellaneous end uses; and steel castings—for railway components, gears, valves and other industrial uses.

ENERGY SOURCES

Fuel was produced within the plant from the blast furnaces and coke ovens. The blast furnaces produced 15 500 cubic feet (CF) of blast furnace gas (BFG) during production of each ton of iron. BFG had a low heat content (only 90 BTU per CF) but since production was forecast at 3.3 million tons of iron, BFG represented a major energy source for DOFASCO. Further, since BFG was an essential by-product of blast furnace operation, the only cost associated with using BFG as a fuel gas was the cost of maintaining the BFG lines and necessary equipment. This cost was estimated at $5.00 per million CF used.

Coke oven gas (COG) produced during coking by the coke ovens, had a much higher BTU content (540 BTU per CF) than BFG, and each ton of coke produced was accompanied by the production of 12 000 CF of COG. Coke production was forecast at 1.3 million tons. The maintenance cost of the COG lines was estimated at $45.00 per million CF used.

The fuel gas produced internally was augmented by natural gas and fuel oil purchased at market prices. Commercial fuel oil was currently available at $40 per thousand pounds and natural gas at $2200 per million CF, although these prices were expected to increase dramatically in the future. A thousand pounds of fuel oil had a heat content of about 18.75 million BTU, while natural gas produced 1000 BTU per CF. Maintenance costs for the natural gas lines were estimated at $0.10 per million CF and for the fuel oil lines at $8.00 per thousand pounds used.

ENERGY REQUIREMENTS

Production of steel was an energy-intensive process, consuming large quantities of electricity, coal, and fuel gas. There was considerable flexibility in how the demands for fuel gas could be met from the available supplies.

The coke ovens, annealing, finishing operations, and foundry were major users of fuel gases. Each of these plants required gas of a certain heat content (measured by BTU value), which could be made by combining different fuels. There were, however, restrictions on the amounts of some fuels which could be used to make up the BTUs necessary to produce a ton of steel by each process, which resulted from the physical characteristics of the process. Table 3.7 summarizes the fuel gas requirements and restrictions for the eight major user plants.

Coke ovens had somewhat different, but strict, requirements. There were three types of fuel used by the coke ovens: 1. Primary fuel (BFG) providing 1.6 million BTU per ton,

2. "Sweetened" gas, a mixture of BFG and COG averaging 100 BTU per CF, providing 0.37 million BTU per ton, 3. "Enriched" gas, a mixture of BFG and COG averaging 250 BTU per CF, and providing 0.23 million BTU per ton.

The above three fuels, in combination, met the fuel requirement of 2.2 million BTU per ton of coke produced.

DISTRIBUTION

Although the actual flow of gas at the plant was complex and conditions changed from hour to hour, the works manager decided to consider, for the purpose of long-run analysis, that the distribution of fuel gases in the steel works was limited only by the requirements of the producer and user plants. If the analysis demonstrated that fuel costs could be reduced by improved allocation, then the necessary changes in equipment and operating rules could be implemented to bring this about.

The works manager requested the manufacturing controls department to determine the most efficient pattern for fuel use within the plant.

DISCUSSION QUESTION

What pattern of fuel use would you recommend?

TABLE 3.7

Uses of Fuel Gas

ch03_ivey_7A98EO25.xls

USER PLANT	FUEL GASES CURRENTLY USED	FUEL GASES THAT COULD BE USED	REQUIREMENTS FOR FUEL (MILLION BTU/TON)	PRODUCTION FORECAST(THOUSAND TONS/MONTH)	MAXIMUM QUANTITIES (MILLION CF/MONTH)
Soaking Pits	NG, COG, OIL	NG, BFG, COG, OIL	1.16	275	2,147 (NG), 510 (COG)
Batch Anneal	COG	NG, BFG, COG	1.02	52	166 (COG)
Galvanizing Lines	NG, COG	NG, BFG, COG	1.16	45	45(COG), 56.8 (NG)
Coreplate Line	NG	NG, BFG, COG	0.54	2.6	17.4 (NG)
Specialty Steels	NG	NG	0.57	7	
Foundry	COG	NG, BFG, COG	12.34	2.8	1080 (COG)
Normalizing Lines	NG	NG, BFG, COG	1.15	10.8	9 (NG)
Coke Ovens	BFG, COG	BFG, COG	Primary Fuel 1.6; "Sweetened" Gas 0.37; "Enriched" Gas 0.23	108.3	

NG—Natural Gas   BFG—Blast Furnace Gas   COG—Coke Oven Gas   OIL—Fuel Oil

⟩ CASE STUDY 3.2

Canadian Military Electronics: Part I

Canadian Military Electronics Inc. (CME) supplies the air force with four electronic items: cockpit display units, flight simulators, Doppler wind profilers, and aviation radar units. Table 3.8 shows the model number and selling price of each type of unit produced by CME and also the fixed and variable manufacturing costs as well as the number of hours of labour required to produce each item.

CME's CEO, General James Dyment (ret'd), has called a meeting of his senior staff. He announces, "I have heard from my contacts in Ottawa that over the next two years the air force will be expanding peacekeeping operations overseas and that they will be purchasing 15 cockpit displays, 8 flight simulators, 12 Doppler wind profilers, and 20 aviation radar units. Before I bid for the contract I want to be sure how many units of each of our four major products we can produce within our current production capacity." Production manager Marc A. Gagnon asks, "How much money is available for production?" Dyment replies, "Our CFO tells me that in our present financial position we can spend up to $10 million for manufacturing." Gagnon points out that because of the high fixed manufacturing costs, it is not worth producing an item unless the company produces at least five units of that item. Dyment assures him that the contract will certainly require that each of the four items will be produced and he asks Marc to include the five-item minimum in his production plans. "What other manufacturing constraints do we have?" Dyment asks. Marc says, "Because of the sharing of resources among the manufacturing divisions, cockpit displays and aviation radar units cannot account for more than 50% of CME's total production. Also, the CDU-75X and the AR-3000F are made by the same production crew and the total available time for production by that crew during the production period is 50 000 hours. The team producing the FS-232A has 32 000 hours of production time available, and the DWP-4 production crew can plan for a maximum of 36 000 hours." "OK," Jim Dyment replies, "I will need a report on our optimum production plan—how many units of each product can we produce within our existing resources, and what would our expected profit be? Can you get me that information?" Peng Li, head of the Management Science division at CME, speaks up and says, "Leave the problem with me—I will construct a linear programming model and I will report back to you after the weekend with a recommendation regarding the optimal product mix that will maximize our profit."

Marc Gagnon speaks up to say, "Peng—keep in mind that I will need more than just the information about how many units of each product to manufacture. I am concerned about the estimates of available time by the production crews. Remember that the CDU-75X and the AR-3000F are produced by a crew that has a maximum availability of 50 000 hours. It would be important to know if we will need to utilize all of the available time—I have other jobs that the crew can work on if they have some free time. Also, how about the available time for producing the FS-232A and the DWP-4, do we have any unused hours there? Can you check that out for me?" Peng Li assures Marc that he will be able to include an analysis of the time constraints in his report.

James Dyment says, "Peng, please also let me know what percentage of our profit will be generated by each of the four products—I'm curious about which of the four will be our biggest profit maker for this project. I will expect you to report back to us with your recommendations at our meeting this time next week. I have a meeting with some top brass in Ottawa later in the week, and I need to be able to tell them how many units of each of the four products we can supply."

Canadian Military Electronics: Part II

James Dyment is not happy with the solution obtained when the LP problem of part I is solved. He calls his executive to a meeting and, after exchanging pleasantries, he says, "Peng, I have read your report and I have some issues with your recommendations. It seems to me that we are losing an opportunity to

TABLE 3.8

Selling Price and Expenses for CME

UNIT	SELLING PRICE	FIXED MANUFACTURING COST	VARIABLE COST PER UNIT PRODUCED	PRODUCTION HOURS PER UNIT
CDU-75X cockpit display	$ 650 000	$100 000	$120 000	2400
FS-232A Flight Simulator	$1 500 000	$240 000	$300 000	4000
DWP-4 Doppler Wind Profiler	$ 760 000	$130 000	$210 000	3600
AR-3000F Aviation Radar Unit	$ 745 000	$195 000	$190 000	2800

make a lot more profit. Furthermore, I am not sure the military decision makers will be pleased if we tell them that we cannot fully supply the number of units of each product that they are planning to purchase. Remember: they have indicated that they are hoping to purchase 15 cockpit displays, 8 flight simulators, 12 Doppler wind profilers, and 20 aviation radar units. The optimal decision that Peng has produced based on our previous conversation falls far short of those specifications."

Marc Gagnon interjects, "Jim, that is the best we can do because our decision is based on time and budget constraints. Without relaxing those constraints we simply cannot produce anymore units than Peng has recommended."

Dyment says, "Okay—then let's rethink the problem. I want to analyze it again but this time we will insist on exactly meeting the military's projected demand for each of the four items. In effect, let's act as if we have an unlimited budget and unlimited manpower to manufacture the four items. Peng, run the problem again without any time or budget constraints, and report back telling me how much extra money we would need for manufacturing and how many extra hours of production time we will need. As I recall from our last meeting, we have three work crews—one for the FS-232A, one for the DWP-4, and a combined crew for the CDU-75X and the AR-3000F. I need to know how many extra hours each crew will need. For the moment, assume that fixed and variable production costs will remain unchanged. If there is an increase in these costs we will deal with that later. All I need to know for now is how much more money and how many extra hours of labour we will require. Once we have these figures we can decide if we can meet the extra hours by hiring the work crews for overtime or if we will have to hire new technicians. If we need a lot more money, I will go to the shareholders and find a way to raise it. That's my job—you just have to let me know what I need to ask for. Please get to work on this right away as we are really pushing the deadlines."

Marc Gagnon interjects, "You may remember that I had previously stipulated that cockpit displays and aviation radar units cannot account for more than 50% of CME's total production. Under these new conditions that Jim is suggesting, that constraint becomes irrelevant. Also, since we are now setting the goal of exactly meeting the military's requirements, we can drop the five-item minimum for each item."

"Good point," Peng Li replies, "I will get on it right away."

BIBLIOGRAPHY

Bermon, Stuart, and Sarah Jean Hood. "Capacity Optimization Planning System (CAPS)," *Interfaces* 29, 5 (September 1999): 31–50.

Desrosiers, Jacques et al. "Air Transat Uses ALTITUDE to Manage its Aircraft Routing, Crew Pairing, and Work Assignment" *Interfaces* 30 (March–April, 2000): 41–53.

Eliman, A. A., M. Girgis, and S. Kotob. "A Solution to Post-Crash Debt Entanglements in Kuwait's al-Manakh Stock Market," *Interfaces* 27, 1 (January–February 1997): 89–106.

Ferris, M. C., and A. B. Philpott. "On the Performance of Karmarkar's Algorithm," *Journal of the Operational Research Society,* 39 (March 1988): 257–270.

Fletcher, L. Russell, Henry Alden, Scott P. Holmen, Dean P. Angelides, and Matthew J. Etzenhouser. "Long-Term Forest Ecosystem Planning at Pacific Lumber," *Interfaces* 29, 1 (January 1999): 90–111.

Gass, S. I. *An Illustrated Guide to Linear Programming.* New York: Dover Publications, Inc., 1990.

Gautier, Antoine, Bernard F. Lamond, Daniel Pare, and François Rouleau. "The Quebec Ministry of Natural Resources Uses Linear Programming to Understand the Wood-Fiber Market," *Interfaces* 30, 6 (November 2000): 32–48.

Greenberg, H. J. "How to Analyze the Results of Linear Programs—Part 1: Preliminaries." *Interfaces* 23, 4 (July–August 1993): 56–68.

_____. "How to Analyze the Results of Linear Programs—Part 3: Infeasibility Diagnosis," *Interfaces* 23, 6 (November–December 1993): 120–139.

Leach, Howard. "Optimizing the Resources for Several Mills/Products," Presented to the Canadian Woodlands Forum Workshop, "Optimizing Softwood Log Quality," (May 23–24, 2001). Fredericton, N.B., Canada.

Lyon, Peter, R. John Milne, Robert Orzell, and Robert Rice. "Matching Assets with Demand in Supply-Chain Management at IBM Microelectronics," *Interfaces* 31, 1 (January 2001): 108–124.

Orden, A. "LP from the '40s to the '90s," *Interfaces* 23, 5 (September–October 1993): 2–12.

Quinn, P., B. Andrews, and H. Parsons. "Allocating Telecommunications Resources at L. L. Bean, Inc.," *Interfaces* 21, 1 (January–February 1991): 75–91.

Saltzman, M. J. "Survey: Mixed Integer Programming," *OR/MS Today* 21, 2 (April 1994): 42–51.

Schindler, S., and T. Semmel. "Station Staffing at Pan American World Airways," *Interfaces* 23, 3 (May–June 1993): 91–98.

Sexton, T. R., S. Sleeper, and R. E. Taggart, Jr. "Improving Pupil Transportation in North Carolina," *Interfaces* 24, 1 (January–February 1994): 87–104.

Zappe, C., W. Webster, and I. Horowitz. "Using Linear Programming to Determine Post-Facto Consistency in Performance Evaluations of Major League Baseball Players," *Interfaces* 23, 6 (November–December 1993): 107–119.

CHAPTER 4

Linear Programming Sensitivity Analysis

LEARNING OBJECTIVES

After completing this chapter, students will be able to

1. Understand, using graphs, the impact of changes in objective function coefficients, right-hand-side values, and constraint coefficients on the optimal solution of an LP problem.

2. Generate answer and sensitivity reports using Excel's Solver.

3. Interpret all parameters of these reports for maximization and minimization problems.

4. Analyze the impact of simultaneous changes in input data values using the 100% rule.

5. Analyze the impact of the addition of a new variable using the pricing-out strategy.

CHAPTER OUTLINE

4.1 Introduction

4.2 Sensitivity Analysis Using Graphs

4.3 Sensitivity Analysis Using Solver Reports

4.4 Sensitivity Analysis for a Larger Maximization Example

4.5 Analyzing Simultaneous Changes Using the 100% Rule

4.6 Pricing Out New Variables

4.7 Sensitivity Analysis for a Minimization Example

Summary • Glossary • Solved Problem • Self-Test • Discussion Questions and Problems • Case Study: Red Brand Canners • Case Study: Vytec Corporation • Case Study: Airy Dairy • Bibliography

Using Shadow Prices to Estimate the Cost of Forest Fires in Canada

Natural Resources Canada reports that, on average, about 8500 forest fires are reported each year in Canada, burning an area of 2.5 million hectares. The area burned varies significantly from year to year. For example, 0.3 million hectares were burned in 1978 while 7.5 million hectares were lost to forest fires in 1989. By comparison, the area harvested each year is about 1 million hectares. About 60% of forest fires are caused by humans. Lightning is another major cause of forest fires.

During the 1998 fire season in Alberta, almost 1700 fires burned more than 726 000 hectares of forest, and the provincial government spent $242 million on forest protection, primarily the cost of fighting forest fires. Because of the severity of the losses, the Alberta Forest Protection Advisory Committee commissioned consulting firm KPMG to study the fire season and to make recommendations to improve the efficiency of forest protection in Alberta.

Source: PhotoDisc

The management plans for many forest management areas are developed with the aid of LP-based forest activity scheduling models. A standard output of these models is the marginal contribution of each hectare of each forest type to the management objective specified for the forest. These marginal contributions are known as shadow prices. These shadow prices can be viewed as the cost of losing a hectare of a forest type to wildfire.

Shadow prices provide an appraisal of the value of the area destroyed by a fire and consequently help the appropriate agencies to decide on the budget required to help prevent and control forest fires in Canada.

Sources: G. W. Armstrong and S. G. Cumming. "Shadow Prices as Estimates of the Cost of Forest Fires," Working Paper #2002-3 of the Sustainable Forest Management Network (SFM), University of Alberta (May 2002); Natural Resources Canada: http://atlas.nrcan.gc.ca/site/english/maps/environment/naturalhazards/forest_fires/1

4.1   INTRODUCTION

We have solved LP models under deterministic assumptions.

Optimal solutions to LP problems have thus far been found under what are called *deterministic* assumptions. This means that we assume complete certainty in the data and relationships of a problem—namely, prices are fixed, resources' availabilities are known, production time needed to make a unit is exactly set, and so on. That is, we assume that all the coefficients (constants) in the objective function and each of the constraints are fixed and do not change. But in most real-world situations, conditions are dynamic and changing. This could mean, for example, that just as we determine the optimal solution to an LP model that has the profit contribution for a given product set at $10 per unit, we find out that the profit contribution has changed to $9 per unit. What does this change mean for our solution? Is it no longer optimal?

Managers are often interested in studying the impact of changes in the values of input parameters.

In practice, such changes to input data values typically occur for two reasons. First, the value may have been estimated incorrectly. For example, a firm may realize that it has overestimated the selling price by $1, resulting in an incorrect profit contribution of $10 per unit, rather than $9 per unit. Or it may determine during a production run that it has only 175 pumps in inventory, rather than 200, as specified in the LP model. Second, management is often interested in getting quick answers to a series of what-if questions. For example, what if the profit contribution of a product decreases by 10%? What if less money is available for advertising? What if workers can each stay one hour longer every day at 1.5-times pay to provide increased production capacity? What if new technology will allow a product to be wired in one-third the time it used to take?

Why Do We Need to Study Sensitivity Analysis?

Sensitivity analysis, also known as **postoptimality analysis**, is a procedure that allows us to answer questions such as those posed above, using the current optimal solution itself, without having to resolve the LP model each time. Before we discuss this topic in more detail, let us first address a question that may arise commonly: Why do we need to study sensitivity analysis when we can use the computer to make the necessary changes to the model and quickly solve it again? The answer is as follows.

If the change in an input data value is certain, the easiest approach is to change it in the formulation and resolve the model.

If, in fact, we know that a change in an input data value is definite (for example, we know *with certainty* that the profit contribution has decreased from $10 to $9 per unit), the easiest and logical course of action is to do just what the question suggests. That is, we should simply change the input data value in the formulation and solve the model again. Given the ease with which most real-world models can be solved using computers today, this approach should not be too difficult or time-consuming. Clearly, this same approach can be used even if we are making *definite* changes to more than one input data value at the same time.

In contrast, what if changes in input data values are just hypothetical, such as in the various what-if scenarios listed earlier? For example, assume that we are just considering lowering the selling price of a product but have not yet decided to what level it should be lowered. If we are considering 10 different selling price values, changing the input data value and resolving the LP model for every proposed value results in 10 separate models. If we expand this argument to consider 10 selling price levels each for two different products, we now have 100 ($= 10 \times 10$) LP models to solve. Clearly, this approach (i.e., changing and resolving the LP model) quickly becomes impractical when we have many input data values in a model and we are considering what-if multiple changes in each of their values.

Sensitivity analysis involves examining how sensitive the optimal solution is to changes in profits, resources, or other input parameters.

In such situations, the preferred approach is to formulate and solve a *single* LP model with a given set of input data values. However, after solving this model, we conduct a sensitivity analysis of the optimal solution to see just how *sensitive* it is to changes in each of these input data values. That is, for each input data value, we attempt

DECISION MODELING IN ACTION
The Right Stuff at NASA

There are many areas at NASA where management science tools such as LP have been successfully applied. With the culture of the U.S. space program changing because of an increasing pressure to develop missions under rigid schedule and budget constraints, NASA has begun to work in an environment of faster-better-cheaper (FBC). After the recent highly publicized Mars failure, NASA now addresses the issue of scarce resources with a technique called *sensitivity analysis* and a measure of marginal costs called the *shadow price.*

For example, at the margin, money is sometimes spent on tests that are not justified by the value of information. In other cases, more funds would yield risk-reduction benefits that would justify the costs and greatly improve the scientific benefit of a space mission. The landing of *Mars Pathfinder* was designed to operate for one month but lasted longer than anticipated. The shadow prices of the LP resource constraints in such a case provide valuable insights into the cost–benefit tradeoff.

When NASA looks at a project that is critical to the success of new missions, the costs of losing the project will include marginal values of the delays and loss of data incurred by these future missions. LP doesn't just provide optimal solutions; it provides the ability to conduct sensitivity analysis on these solutions as well.

Source: M. E. Pate-Cornell and R. L. Dillon. "The Right Stuff," *OR/MS Today* (February 2000): 36–39. Copyright © 2000. Reprinted with permission.

to determine a *range of values* within which the current optimal solution will remain optimal. For example, if the current selling price for a product is $10 per unit, we identify the extent to which this value can change (both on the higher side and on the lower side) without affecting the optimality of the current solution. We can obtain this information, as we shall see, from the current solution itself, without resolving the LP model each time.

Excel's Solver can be used to generate sensitivity reports.

As we did previously with LP formulations and solutions, we first study LP sensitivity analysis using a two-variable product mix problem. We recognize here again that we are unlikely to encounter two-variable problems in real-world situations. Nevertheless, a big advantage of studying such models is that we can demonstrate the concepts of sensitivity analysis using a graphical approach. This experience will be invaluable in helping understand the various issues in sensitivity analysis even for larger problems. For these larger problems, because we cannot view them graphically, we will rely on Excel's Solver to generate sensitivity analysis reports. We discuss three separate Solver Sensitivity Reports in this chapter: (1) a report for the two-variable product mix problem that we also first analyze graphically, (2) a report for a larger problem (i.e., more than two variables) with a maximization objective function, and (3) a report for a larger problem with a minimization objective function. The two larger problems allow us to illustrate fully the various types of information we can obtain by using sensitivity analysis.

We will first study the impact of only one change at a time.

We will initially study sensitivity analysis by varying only one input data value at a time. Later, we will expand our discussion to include simultaneous changes in several input data values.

4.2   SENSITIVITY ANALYSIS USING GRAPHS

To analyze LP sensitivity analysis by using graphs, let us revisit the Flair Furniture problem that we first used in Chapter 2 to introduce LP formulation and solution. Our motivation for using the same problem here is that you are hopefully already familiar with that problem and its graphical solution. Nevertheless, you might want to briefly review Sections 2.3 and 2.4 in Chapter 2 before proceeding further.

Recall that the Flair Furniture Company problem involved two products: tables and chairs. The constraints dealt with the hours available in the carpentry and painting departments, production limits on chairs, and the minimum production level on tables. If we let

T denote the number of tables to make and C denote the number of chairs to make, we can formulate the following LP problem to determine the best product mix:

$$\text{Maximize profit} = \$7T + \$5C$$

subject to the constraints

$3T + 4C \leq$	2400	(carpentry time)
$2T + 1C \leq$	1000	(painting time)
$C \leq$	450	(maximum chairs allowed)
$T \geq$	100	(minimum tables required)
$T, C \geq$	0	(nonnegativity)

The solution to this problem is illustrated graphically in Figure 4.1 (which is the same as Figure 2.6 in Chapter 2). Recall from Chapter 2 that we can use the level profit lines method to identify the optimal corner point solution. (The level profit line for a profit value of $2800 is shown in Figure 4.1.) It is easy to see that Flair's optimal solution is at corner point ④. At this corner point, the optimal solution is to produce 320 tables and 360 chairs, for a profit of $4040.

Types of Sensitivity Analysis

In the preceding LP formulation, note that there are three types of input parameter values:

1. **Objective Function Coefficient (OFC).** The OFCs are the coefficients for the decision variables in the objective function (such as the $7 and $5 for T and C, respectively, in Flair's model). In many business-oriented LP models, OFCs typically represent unit profits or costs, and they are measured in monetary units such as dollars, euros, and rupees.

   Are OFCs likely to have any uncertainty in their values? Clearly, the answer is yes because in many real-world situations, selling and cost prices are seldom likely to be static or fixed. For this reason, we will study how the optimal solution may be affected by changes in OFC values.

FIGURE 4.1

Optimal Corner Point Solution for Flair Furniture

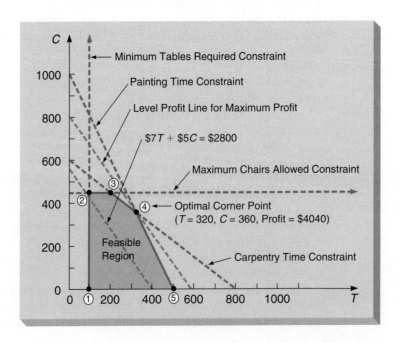

2. **Right-Hand-Side (RHS) Value** *of a Constraint.* The RHS values are constants, such as the 2400 and 1000 in Flair's model, that typically appear on the RHS of a constraint (i.e., to the right of the equality or inequality sign). For ≤ constraints, they typically represent the amount available of a resource, and for ≥ constraints, they typically represent the minimum level of satisfaction needed.

   Are these types of input data subject to uncertainty in practice? Here again, the answer is a clear yes. In many practical situations, companies may find that their resource availability has changed due to, for example, miscounted inventory, broken-down machines, absent labour, etc. For this reason, we will study how the optimal solution may be affected by changes in RHS values.

3. *Constraint Coefficient.* The constraint coefficients are the coefficients for the decision variables in a model's constraints (such as the 3 and 4 in the carpentry constraint in Flair's model). In many problems, these represent design issues with regard to the decision variables. For example, needing three hours of carpentry per table is a product design issue that has probably been specified by design engineers.

   Although we could think of specific situations where these types of input parameters could also be subject to uncertainty in their values, such changes are less likely here than in OFC and RHS values. For this reason, we do not usually study the impact of changes in constraint coefficient values on the optimal solution.

Most computer-based LP software packages, including Excel's Solver, provide sensitivity reports only for analyzing the effect of changes in OFC and RHS values.

Impact of Changes in an Objective Function Coefficient

We examine changes in OFCs first.

When the value of an OFC changes, the feasible solution region remains the same (because it depends only on the constraints). That is, we have the same set of corner points, and their locations do not change. All that changes is the slope of the level profit (or cost) line.

   Let us consider the impact of changes in the profit contribution of tables (T). First, what if the demand for tables becomes so high that the profit contribution can be raised from $7 to $8 per table? Is corner point ④ still the optimal solution? The answer is definitely yes, as shown in Figure 4.2. In this case, the slope of the level profit line accentuates

FIGURE 4.2

Small Changes in Profit Contribution of Tables

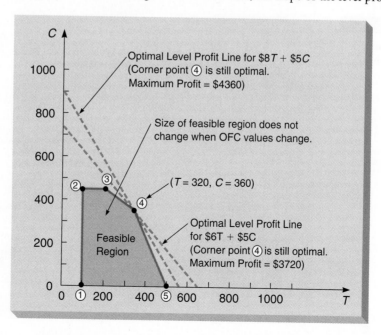

the optimality of the solution at corner point ④. However, even though the decision variable values did not change, the new optimal objective function value (i.e., the profit) does change and is now $4360 (= $8 × 320 + $5 × 360).

In a similar fashion, let us analyze what happens if the demand for tables forces us to reduce the profit contribution from $7 to $6 per table. Here again, we see from the level profit line in Figure 4.2 that corner point ④ continues to remain the optimal solution, and the production plan does not change. The optimal profit, however, is now only $3720 (= $6 × 320 + $5 × 360).

On the other hand, what if a table's profit contribution can be raised all the way to $11 per table? In such a case, the level profit line, shown in Figure 4.3, indicates that the optimal solution is now at corner point ⑤, instead of at corner point ④. The new solution is to make 500 tables and 0 chairs, for a profit of $5500. That is, tables are now so profitable compared to chairs that we should devote all our resources to making only tables.

Likewise, what if a table's profit contribution was highly overestimated and should only have been $3 per table? In this case also, the slope of the level profit line changes enough to cause a new corner point ③ to become optimal (as shown in Figure 4.3). That is, tables have now become relatively unattractive compared to chairs, and so we will make fewer tables and more chairs. In fact, the only reason we even make any tables in this case is because we are explicitly constrained in the problem to make at least 100 tables, and from making more than 450 chairs. At corner point ③, the solution is to make 200 tables and 450 chairs, for a profit of $2850 (= $3 × 200 + $5 × 450).

From the preceding discussion regarding the OFC for a table, it is apparent that there is a range of possible values for this OFC for which the *current* optimal corner point solution remains optimal. Any change in the OFC value beyond this range (either on the higher end or the lower end) causes a *new* corner point to become the optimal solution. Clearly, we can repeat the same discussion with regard to the OFC for chairs.

It is algebraically possible to use the graphical solution procedure to determine the allowable range for each OFC within which the current optimal solution remains optimal.

If the OFC changes too much, a new corner point could become optimal.

There is a range for each OFC over which the current solution remains optimal.

FIGURE 4.3

Larger Changes in Profit Contribution of Tables

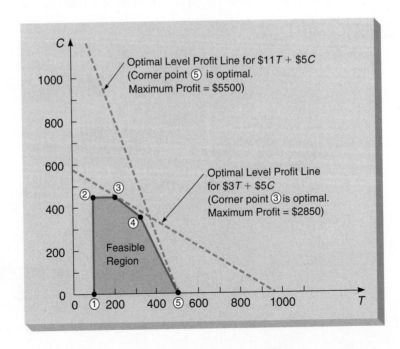

However, we use the information provided in Solver's Sensitivity Report to discuss this issue further in the next section.

Changes in OFC values do not affect the size of the feasible region.

Again, whenever changes occur in OFC values, the feasible region of the problem (which depends only on the constraints) does not change. Therefore, there is no change in the physical location of each corner point. To summarize, the only two things that can occur due to a change in an OFC are: (1) if the current optimal corner point continues to remain optimal, the decision variable values do not change, even though the objective function value may change; and (2) if the current corner point is no longer optimal, the values of the decision variables change, as does the objective function value.

Impact of Changes in a Constraint's Right-Hand-Side Value

Changes in RHS values could affect the size of the feasible region.

Unlike changes in OFC values, a change in the RHS value of a nonredundant constraint results in a change in the size of the feasible region.[1] Hence, one or more corner points may physically shift to new locations. Recall from Chapter 2 that at the optimal solution, constraints can either be binding or nonbinding. Binding constraints intersect at the optimal corner point and are, hence, exactly satisfied at the optimal solution. Nonbinding constraints have a nonzero slack (for ≤ constraints) or surplus (for ≥ constraints) value at the optimal solution. Let us analyze impacts of changes in RHS values for binding and nonbinding constraints separately.

Impact of Change in RHS Value of a Binding Constraint   From Figure 4.1, we know that the two binding constraints in Flair's problem are the carpentry and painting hours. Let us analyze, for example, potential changes in the painting hours available. Flair currently projects an availability of 1000 hours, all of which will be needed by the current production plan.

Let us first analyze the impact if this value is increased. What happens if, for example, the painting time availability can be increased by 300 hours (to 1300 hours) by adding an extra painter? Figure 4.4 shows the revised graph for Flair's problem under this scenario.

FIGURE 4.4

Increase in Availability of Painting Hours to 1300 Hours

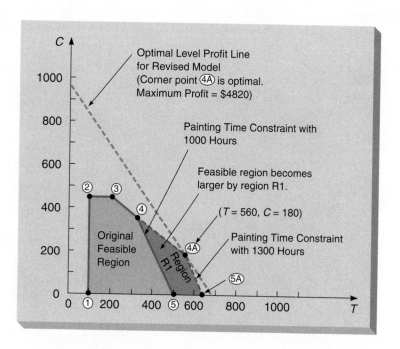

---

[1] Recall from Section 2.7 in Chapter 2 that a *redundant* constraint does not affect the feasible region in any way.

The location of the optimal corner point changes if the RHS of a binding constraint changes.

The first point to note is that because the painting constraint is a binding ≤ constraint, any increase in its RHS value causes the feasible region to become larger, as shown by the region marked R1 in Figure 4.4. As a consequence of this increase in the size of the feasible region, the locations of corner points ④ and ⑤ shift to new locations—④A and ⑤A, respectively. However, the level profit lines approach (shown in Figure 4.4) indicates that the intersection of the carpentry and painting constraints (i.e., corner point ④A) is still the optimal solution. That is, the "same" corner point (in the sense that the same two constraints intersect at this point) is still optimal. But it now has a new location and, hence, there are new values for T, C, and profit. The values at corner point ④A can be computed to be $T = 560$ and $C = 180$, for a profit of $4820. This implies that if Flair is able to obtain an additional 300 hours of painting time, it can increase profit by $780 (from $4040 to $4820) by revising the production plan. This profit increase of $780 for 300 additional hours of painting time translates to a profit increase of $2.60 per additional hour of painting time.

The feasible region becomes smaller if the RHS value of a binding ≤ constraint is decreased.

Next, let us analyze the impact if the painting time availability is decreased. What happens if, for example, this value is only 900 hours instead of 1000 hours? The revised graph, shown in Figure 4.5, indicates that this decrease in the RHS value of a binding ≤ constraint shrinks the size of the feasible region (as shown by the region marked R2 in Figure 4.5). Here again, the locations of corner points ④ and ⑤ have shifted to new locations, ④B and ⑤B, respectively. However, as before, the level profit lines approach indicates that the "same" corner point (i.e., intersection of the carpentry and painting constraints, point ④B) is still optimal. The values of the decision variables and the resulting profit at corner point ④B can be computed to be $T = 240$ and $C = 420$, for a profit of $3780. That is, the loss of 100 hours of painting time causes Flair to lose $260 in profit (from $4040 to $3780). This translates to a decrease in profit of $2.60 per hour of painting time lost.

The shadow price is the change in objective function value for a one-unit increase in a constraint's RHS value.

Observe that the profit increases by $2.60 per each additional hour of painting time gained, and it decreases by the *same* $2.60 per each hour of painting time lost from the current level. This value, known as the **shadow price**, is an important concept in LP models. The shadow price of a constraint can be defined as the change in the optimal objective function value for a one-unit increase in the RHS value of that constraint. In the

---

FIGURE 4.5

Decrease in Availability of Painting Hours to 900 Hours

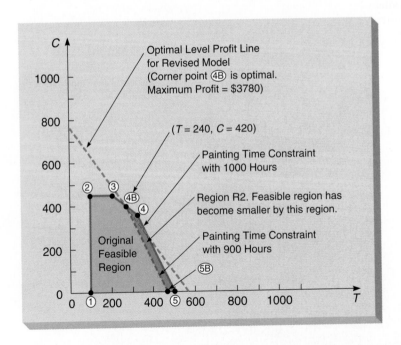

case of painting time, the shadow price is $2.60; this implies that each hour of painting time (with respect to the current availability) affects Flair's profit by $2.60. Because painting time is a binding ≤ constraint, each additional hour obtained increases profit by $2.60, while each hour lost decreases profit by $2.60.

Is this shadow price of $2.60 valid for any level of change in the painting time availability? That is, for example, can Flair keep obtaining additional painting time and expect its profit to keep increasing endlessly by $2.60 for each hour obtained? Clearly, this cannot be true, and we illustrate the reason for this in the following section.

Validity Range for the Shadow Price   Consider, for example, what happens if Flair can increase the painting time availability even further, to 1700 hours. Under this scenario, as shown in Figure 4.6, the feasible region increases by the region marked R3. However, due to the presence of the nonnegativity constraint $C \geq 0$, the corner point defined by the intersection of the carpentry and painting constraints is no longer feasible. In fact, the painting constraint has now become a redundant constraint. Obviously, in such a case, the optimal solution has shifted to a new corner point. The level profit lines approach indicates that the optimal solution is now at corner point ⑤Ⓒ ($T = 800$, $C = 0$, profit = $5600). Note that this translates to a profit increase of $1560 (= $5600 − $4040) for 700 additional hours, or $2.23 per hour, which is different from the shadow price of $2.60. That is, the shadow price of $2.60 is not valid for an increase of 700 hours in the painting time availability.

What happens if the painting time availability is decreased all the way down to 700 hours? Here again, as shown in Figure 4.7, the intersection point of the carpentry and painting constraints is no longer even feasible. The carpentry constraint is now redundant, and the optimal solution has switched to a new corner point given by corner point ③Ⓐ ($T = 125$, $C = 450$, profit = $3125). This translates to a profit decrease of $915 (= $4040 − $3125) for a decrease of 300 hours, or $3.05 per hour, which is again different from the shadow price of $2.60. That is, the shadow price of $2.60 is not valid for a decrease of 300 hours in the painting time availability.

The shadow price is valid only for a certain range of change in a constraint's RHS value.

Increasing the RHS of a ≤ constraint endlessly will eventually make it a redundant constraint.

Decreasing the RHS of a ≤ constraint endlessly will eventually make some other constraint a redundant constraint.

FIGURE 4.6

Increase in Availability of Painting Hours to 1700 Hours

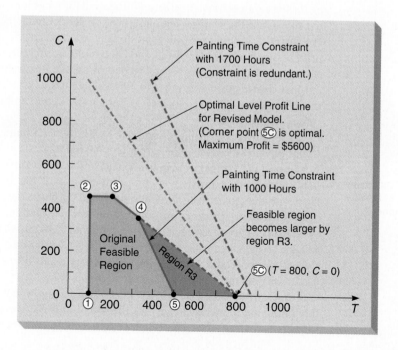

Decrease in Availability of Painting Hours to 700 Hours

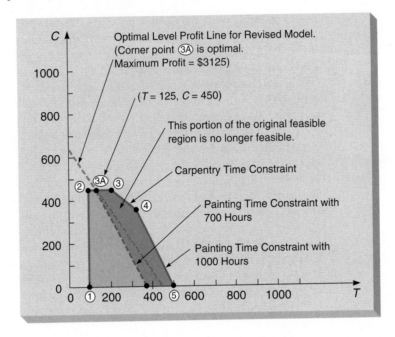

There is a range of values for each RHS for which the current corner points exist.

The preceding discussion based on Figures 4.4 to 4.7 shows that for a certain range of change in the RHS value of a binding constraint, the "same" corner point will continue to remain optimal. That is, the constraints that are currently binding at the optimal solution will continue to remain the binding constraints. The location of this optimal corner point will, however, change, depending on the change in the RHS value. In fact, it turns out that as long as this corner point exists in the feasible region, it will continue to remain optimal. In Flair's case, this means that the corner point where the carpentry and painting constraints intersect will remain the optimal solution *as long as it exists in the feasible region*. Also, the shadow price of $2.60 measures the impact on profit for a unit change in painting time availability as long as this corner point continues to exist in the feasible region. Once this RHS value changes to such an extent that the current binding constraints no longer intersect in the feasible region, the shadow price of $2.60 is no longer valid and changes to a different value. It is algebraically possible to use the graphical solution to determine the RHS range within which the current optimal corner point continues to exist, albeit at a new location. We will, however, use the information provided in Solver's Sensitivity Report to further discuss this issue in a subsequent section.

A similar analysis can be conducted with the RHS value for the other binding constraint in Flair's example—the carpentry constraint.

Increasing the RHS value of a nonbinding ≤ constraint does not affect the optimality of the current solution.

Impact of Changes in RHS Value of a Nonbinding Constraint   Let us now consider a nonbinding constraint such as the production limit on chairs ($C \le 450$). As shown in Figure 4.8, the gap between corner point ④ and the chairs constraint represents the amount of slack in this nonbinding constraint. At the present solution, the slack is 90 ($= 450 - 360$). What happens now if the marketing department allows more chairs to be produced (i.e., the 450 limit is increased)? As we can see in Figure 4.8, such a change only serves to increase the slack in this constraint and does not affect the optimality of corner point ④ in any way. How far can we raise the 450 limit? Clearly, the answer is infinity.

Now consider the case where the marketing department wants to make this production limit even more restrictive (i.e., the 450 limit is decreased). As long as we are permitted to make at least 360 chairs, Figure 4.8 indicates that corner point ④ is feasible and still

FIGURE 4.8

Change in RHS Value of a Nonbinding Constraint

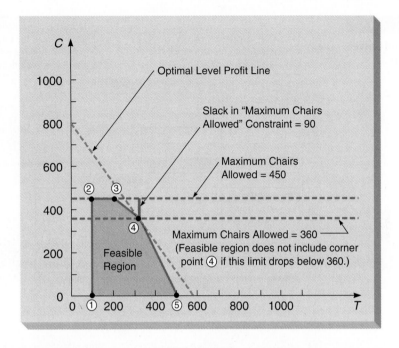

The RHS value of a nonbinding ≤ constraint can be decreased up to its slack without affecting the optimality of the current solution.

optimal. That is, as long as the change in the RHS value for the chairs constraint is within the slack of 90 units, the current optimal corner point continues to exist and remains optimal. However, if the chairs production limit is reduced below 360, corner point ④ is no longer feasible, and a new corner point becomes optimal. A similar analysis can be conducted with the other nonbinding constraint in the model (i.e., $T \geq 100$).

The preceding discussion illustrates that for nonbinding constraints, the allowable change limit on one side is infinity. On the opposite side, the allowable change limit equals the slack (or surplus).

4.3 SENSITIVITY ANALYSIS USING SOLVER REPORTS

Maximize $\$7T + \$5C$
subject to
$$3T + 4C \leq 2400$$
$$2T + 1C \leq 1000$$
$$C \leq 450$$
$$T \geq 100$$
$$T, C \geq 0$$

File: 4-1.xls, sheet: 4-1A

Let us consider Flair Furniture's LP model again (for your convenience, the formulation is shown in the margin note). Screenshot 4.1A shows the Excel layout and Solver entries for this model. Recall that we saw the same information in Chapter 2. Cells B5 and C5 are the **CHANGING CELLS** that denote the optimal quantities of tables and chairs to make, respectively. Cell D6 is the **TARGET CELL** (profit), and cells D8 to D11 contain the formulas for the left-hand-sides (LHS) of each of the four constraints.

Excel Notes

- The CD-ROM that accompanies this textbook contains the Excel file for each problem in the examples discussed here. The relevant file name is shown in the margin next to each example.
- In each of our Excel layouts, for clarity, Changing Cells are shaded yellow, the Target Cell is shaded green, and cells denoting LHS formulas of constraints are shaded blue. If the RHS of a constraint also includes a formula, that cell is also shaded blue.
- Also, to make the equivalence of the *written* formulation and the Excel layout clear, our Excel layouts show the decision variable names used in the written formulation of the model. Note that these names have no role in using Solver to solve the model.

Excel Layout and Solver Entries for Flair Furniture

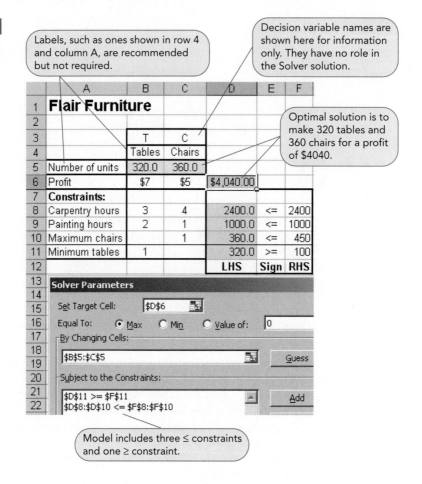

Labels, such as ones shown in row 4 and column A, are recommended but not required.

Decision variable names are shown here for information only. They have no role in the Solver solution.

Optimal solution is to make 320 tables and 360 chairs for a profit of $4040.

Model includes three ≤ constraints and one ≥ constraint.

We must check the Assume Linear Model option to obtain LP sensitivity reports.

The desired Solver reports must be selected in order for them to be created.

We are analyzing only one change at a time.

Solver Reports

Before solving the LP model, we need to ensure that the **ASSUME LINEAR MODEL** box has been checked in the **SOLVER OPTIONS** window (see Screenshot 4.1B). If this box is not checked, Solver does not solve the model as a linear program, and the resulting Sensitivity Report will look very different from the report we discuss here. Also, recall that we check the **ASSUME NON-NEGATIVE** option to enforce the nonnegativity constraints.

When Solver finds the optimal solution for a problem, the **SOLVER RESULTS** window provides options to obtain three reports: **ANSWER, SENSITIVITY,** and **LIMITS.** Note that to obtain the desired reports, we must select them *before* we click OK. In our case, we select the *Answer Report* and the *Sensitivity Report* and then click OK (see Screenshot 4.1B). The *Limits Report* is relatively less useful, and we therefore do not discuss it here.

We have already discussed the **Answer Report** extensively in Section 2.8 of Chapter 2 (see page 58) and urge you to read that section again at this time. Recall that this report provides essentially the same information as the original Excel layout (such as in Screenshot 4.1A), but in a more descriptive manner.

We now turn our attention to the information in the Sensitivity Report. Before we do so, it is important to note once again that while using the information in this report to answer what-if questions, we assume that we are considering a change to only a *single* input data value. Later, in Section 4.5, we will expand our discussion to include simultaneous changes in several input data values.

SCREENSHOT 4.1B   **Solver Options and Solver Results Windows**

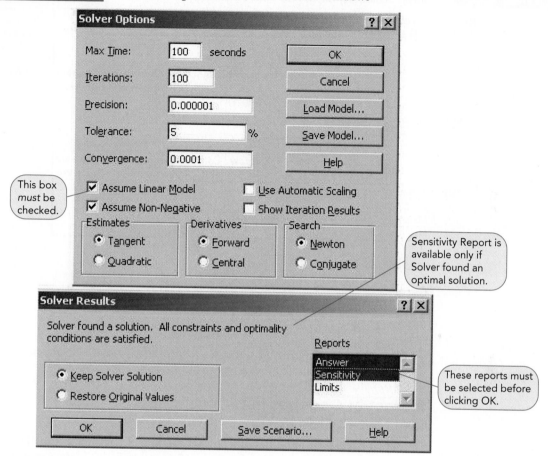

Sensitivity Report

The Sensitivity Report has two parts: Adjustable Cells and Constraints.

File: 4-1.xls, sheet: 4-1C

The Sensitivity Report for the Flair Furniture example is shown in Screenshot 4.1C. We have added grid lines to this report to make it clearer and have also formatted all values to display a consistent number of decimal points. The Sensitivity Report has two distinct components: (1) a table titled **ADJUSTABLE CELLS** and (2) a table titled **CONSTRAINTS.** These tables permit us to answer several what-if questions regarding the problem solution.

Excel Note

Solver does a rather poor job of formatting the Sensitivity Report. There is no consistency in the number of decimal points shown. While some values are displayed with no decimal points, others are displayed with many decimal points. This could sometimes cause a value such as 0.35 to be displayed (and erroneously interpreted) as 0. For this reason, we urge you to format the Sensitivity Report as needed to display a consistent number of decimal points.

The Adjustable Cells table presents information regarding the impact of changes to the OFCs (i.e., unit profits of $7 and $5) on the optimal solution. The Constraints table presents information related to the impact of changes in constraint RHS values (such as the 2400 and 1000 availabilities in carpentry and painting times, respectively) on the optimal

SCREENSHOT 4.1C   **Solver Sensitivity Report for Flair Furniture**

Two components of the sensitivity report

The shadow prices are valid for this range of change in the RHS values.

Microsoft Excel 10.0 Sensitivity Report
Worksheet: [4-1.xls]Flair Furniture

Adjustable Cells

Cell	Name	Final Value	Reduced Cost	Objective Coefficient	Allowable Increase	Allowable Decrease
$B$5	Number of units Tables	320.00	0.00	7.00	3.00	3.25
$C$5	Number of units Chairs	360.00	0.00	5.00	4.33	1.50

Constraints

Cell	Name	Final Value	Shadow Price	Constraint R.H. Side	Allowable Increase	Allowable Decrease
$D$8	Carpentry hours	2400.00	0.60	2400.00	225.00	900.00
$D$9	Painting hours	1000.00	2.60	1000.00	600.00	150.00
$D$10	Maximum chairs	360.00	0.00	450.00	1E+30	90.00
$D$11	Minimum tables	320.00	0.00	100.00	220.00	1E+30

Each additional hour of painting time will increase profit by $2.60.

The shadow price for a nonbinding constraint is zero.

Solver's way of showing infinity

solution. Although different LP software packages may format and present these tables differently, the programs all provide essentially the same information.

Impact of Changes in a Constraint's Right-Hand-Side Value

Let us first discuss the impact on the optimal solution of a change in the RHS value of a constraint. As with the graph-based analysis earlier, we study this issue separately for binding and nonbinding constraints.

Impact of Changes in RHS Value of a Binding Constraint   Recall from the graph-based analysis in Section 4.2 that if the RHS value of a binding constraint changes, the size of the feasible region also changes. If the change causes the feasible region to *increase* in size, the optimal objective function value could potentially improve. In contrast, if the change causes the feasible region to *decrease* in size, the optimal objective function value could potentially worsen. The magnitude of this change in the objective function value is given by the shadow price of the constraint, provided that the RHS change is within a certain range. In Solver's Sensitivity Report, this information is shown in the Constraints table in Screenshot 4.1C.

If the size of the feasible region increases, the optimal objective function value could improve.

Recall from Section 4.2 that the shadow price can be defined as the change in the optimal objective function value for a one-unit increase in the RHS value of a constraint. In Screenshot 4.1C, the entry labelled **SHADOW PRICE** for the painting constraint shows a value of $2.60. This means that for each *additional* hour of painting time that Flair can obtain, its total profit changes by $2.60. What is the direction of this change? In this specific case, the change is an increase in profit because the additional painting time causes the feasible region to become larger and, hence, the solution to improve.

The shadow price is the change in objective function value for a one-unit increase in a constraint's RHS value.

Validity Range for the Shadow Price   For what level of increase in the RHS value of the painting constraint is the shadow price of $2.60 valid? Once again, recall from our discussion in Section 4.2 that there is a specific range of possible values for the RHS value of a binding constraint for which the current optimal corner point (i.e., the intersection point of the current binding constraints) exists, even if its actual location has changed. Increasing or decreasing the RHS value beyond this range causes this corner point to be no longer feasible and causes a new corner point to become the optimal solution.

The shadow price is valid only as long as the change in the RHS is within the Allowable Increase and Allowable Decrease values.

The information to compute the upper and lower limits of this range is given by the entries labelled **Allowable Increase** and **Allowable Decrease** in the Sensitivity Report. In Flair's case, these values show that the shadow price of $2.60 for painting time availability is valid for an increase of up to 600 hours from the current value and a decrease of up to 150 hours. That is, the painting time available can range from a low of 850 (= 1000 − 150) to a high of 1600 (= 1000 + 600) for the shadow price of $2.60 to be valid. Note that the *allowable decrease* value implies that for each hour of painting time that Flair loses (up to 150 hours), its profit decreases by $2.60. Likewise, the *allowable increase* value implies that for each hour of painting time that Flair gains (up to 600 hours), its profit increases by $2.60.

The preceding discussion implies that if Flair can obtain an additional 300 hours of painting time, its profit will increase by 300 × $2.60 = $780, to $4820. In contrast, if it loses 100 hours of painting time, its profit will decrease by 100 × $2.60 = $260, to $3780. If the painting time availability increases by more than 600 hours (for example, increases by 700 hours, to 1700 hours) or decreases by more than 150 hours (for example, decreases by 300 hours, to 700 hours) the current corner point is no longer feasible, and the solution has switched to a new corner point. Recall that we made these same observations earlier graphically using Figures 4.4 to 4.7.

For carpentry time, the shadow price is $0.60, with a validity range of 1500 (= 2400 − 900) to 2625 (= 2400 + 225) hours. This means for every hour of carpentry time in this range, Flair's profit changes by $0.60.

Impact of Changes in RHS Value of a Nonbinding Constraint   We note that Flair is planning to make only 360 chairs even though it is allowed to make as many as 450. Clearly, Flair's solution would not be affected in any way if we increased this production limit. Therefore, the shadow price for the chairs limit constraint is zero.

The shadow price of a nonbinding constraint is zero.

Solver displays infinity as 1E +30.

In Screenshot 4.1C, the allowable increase for this RHS value is shown to be infinity (displayed as **1E + 30** in Solver). This is logical because any addition to the chair production limit will only cause the slack in this constraint to increase and will have no impact on profit. In contrast, once we decrease this limit by 90 chairs (our current slack), this constraint also becomes binding. Any further reduction in this limit will clearly have an adverse effect on profit. This is revealed by the value of 90 for the allowable decrease in the RHS of the chairs limit constraint. To evaluate the new optimal solution if the production limit decreases by more than 90 chairs from its current value, the problem would have to be solved again.

In a similar fashion, we note that Flair is planning to make 320 tables even though it is required to make only 100. Clearly, Flair's solution would not be affected in any way if we decreased this requirement from 100. This is indicated by the infinity in the Allowable Decrease column for this RHS. The current optimal solution will also not be affected as long as the increase in this RHS value is below 220. However, if Flair increases the RHS by more than 220 (and specifies that more than 320 tables must be made), the current optimal solution is no longer valid, and the model must be resolved to find the new solution.

Impact of Changes in an Objective Function Coefficient

Let us now focus on the information provided in the table titled Adjustable Cells. For your convenience, we repeat that part of Screenshot 4.1C here as Screenshot 4.1D. Each row in the Adjustable Cells table contains information regarding a decision variable in the model.

SCREENSHOT 4.1D

**Partial Solver
Sensitivity Report
for Flair Furniture**

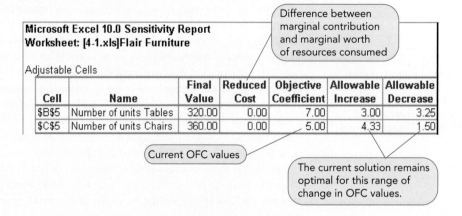

Microsoft Excel 10.0 Sensitivity Report
Worksheet: [4-1.xls]Flair Furniture

Difference between marginal contribution and marginal worth of resources consumed

Adjustable Cells

Cell	Name	Final Value	Reduced Cost	Objective Coefficient	Allowable Increase	Allowable Decrease
$B$5	Number of units Tables	320.00	0.00	7.00	3.00	3.25
$C$5	Number of units Chairs	360.00	0.00	5.00	4.33	1.50

Current OFC values

The current solution remains optimal for this range of change in OFC values.

Allowable Ranges for OFCs   In Figure 4.2, repeated here as Figure 4.9, we saw that as the unit profit contribution of either product changes, the slope of the isoprofit line changes. The size of the feasible region, however, remains the same. That is, the locations of the corner points do not change.

In the case of tables, as the unit profit increases from the current value of $7, the slope of the profit line in Figure 4.9 changes in a manner that makes corner point ④ an even more attractive optimal point. On the other hand, as the unit profit decreases, the slope of the profit line changes in a manner that makes corner point ③ become more and more attractive. At some point, the unit profit of tables is so low as to make corner point ③ the optimal solution.

There is an allowable decrease and an allowable increase for each OFC over which the current optimal solution remains optimal.

The limits to which the profit coefficient of tables can be changed without affecting the optimality of the current solution (corner point ④) are revealed by the values in the *Allowable Increase* and *Allowable Decrease* columns of the Sensitivity Report in Screenshot 4.1D. In the case of tables, their profit contribution per table can range anywhere from a low of $3.75 (= $7 − $3.25) to a high of $10 (= $7 + $3), and the current production plan

FIGURE 4.9

**Changes in Profit
Contribution of Tables**

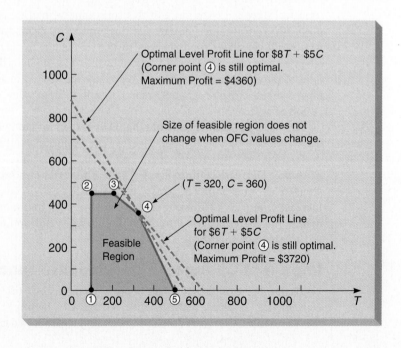

($T = 320$, $C = 360$) will continue to remain optimal. The total profit will, of course, change, depending on the actual profit contribution per table. For example, if the profit contribution is $6 per table, the total profit is $3720 (= $6 × 320 + $5 × 360). This is the same result we saw earlier in Figure 4.2. Any profit contribution below $3.75 or over $10 per table will result in a different corner point solution being optimal.

For chairs, the profit contribution per chair can range anywhere from a low of $3.50 (= $5 − $1.50) to a high of $9.33 (= $5 + $4.33), and the current production plan will continue to remain optimal. Here again, the total profit will depend on the actual profit contribution per chair. For example, if the profit contribution is $8 per chair, the total profit is $5120 (= $7 × 320 + $8 × 360). Any profit contribution below $3.50 or over $9.33 per chair will result in a different corner point solution being optimal.

Reduced Cost The **Reduced Cost** values in Screenshot 4.1D show the difference between the marginal contribution of a decision variable to the objective function value (profit, in Flair's example) and the marginal worth of the resources it would consume if produced. A property of LP models is that if a variable has a non-zero value at optimality, its marginal contribution to the objective function value will equal the marginal worth of the resources it consumes. For instance, each table we produce uses 3 hours of carpentry time, uses 2 hours of painting time, counts 1 unit toward the 100-unit minimum tables requirement, and counts 0 units toward the 450-unit maximum chairs limit. Based on the preceding discussion of the shadow price, the marginal worth of these resources can be calculated as

> Reduced cost is the difference between the marginal contribution of a variable and the marginal worth of the resources it uses.

$$= 3 \times \text{shadow price of carpentry constraint} +$$
$$2 \times \text{shadow price of painting constraint} +$$
$$1 \times \text{shadow price of minimum tables required constraint} +$$
$$0 \times \text{shadow price of maximum chairs allowed constraint}$$
$$= 3 \times \$0.6 + 2 \times \$2.6 + 1 \times \$0 + 0 \times \$0$$
$$= \$7$$

Note that this is equal to the profit contribution per table. The same calculation will hold for chairs also. The profit contribution per chair is $5, and the marginal worth of the resources it consumes is calculated as

$$= 4 \times \text{shadow price of carpentry constraint} +$$
$$1 \times \text{shadow price of painting constraint} +$$
$$0 \times \text{shadow price of minimum tables required constraint} +$$
$$1 \times \text{shadow price of maximum chairs allowed constraint}$$
$$= 4 \times \$0.6 + 1 \times \$2.6 + 0 \times \$0 + 1 \times \$0$$
$$= \$5$$

There is an alternate interpretation for the reduced cost that is relevant especially for decision variables with zero values in the current optimal solution. Because both variables in the Flair example had nonzero values at optimality, this interpretation was not relevant here. We will, however, see this alternate interpretation in the larger example we consider next.

4.4 SENSITIVITY ANALYSIS FOR A LARGER MAXIMIZATION EXAMPLE

Now that we have explained some of the basic concepts in sensitivity analysis, let us consider a larger production mix example that will allow us to discuss some further issues.

Anderson Electronics Example

A larger product mix example.

Anderson Electronics is considering the production of four potential products: VCRs, stereos, TVs, and DVD players. For the sake of this example, let us assume that the input for all products can be viewed in terms of just three resources: electronic components, nonelectronic components, and assembly time. The composition of the four products in terms of these three inputs is shown in Table 4.1, along with the unit selling prices of the products.

Electronic components can be obtained at $7 per unit; nonelectronic components can be obtained at $5 per unit; assembly time costs $10 per hour. Each resource is available in limited quantities, as shown in Table 4.1.

By subtracting the total cost of making a product from its unit selling price, the profit contribution of each product can be easily calculated. For example, the profit contribution of each VCR is $29 (= selling price of $70 less the total cost of $3 \times $7 + $2 \times $5 + $1 \times 10). Using similar calculations, see if you can confirm that the profit contribution of each stereo is $32, each TV is $72, and each DVD player is $54.

Let V, S, T, and D denote the number of VCRs, stereos, TVs, and DVD players to make, respectively. We can then formulate the LP model for this problem as follows:

$$\text{Maximize } \$29V + \$32S + \$72T + \$54D \text{ (Profit)}$$

subject to

$$3V + 4S + 4T + 3D \leq 4700 \quad \text{(electronic components)}$$
$$2V + 2S + 4T + 3D \leq 4500 \quad \text{(nonelectronic components)}$$
$$V + S + 3T + 2D \leq 2500 \quad \text{(assembly time in hours)}$$
$$V, S, T, D \geq 0$$

File: 4-2.xls

Screenshots 4.2A, 4.2B, and 4.2C on the next two pages show the Excel layout and Solver entries, Answer Report, and Sensitivity Report, respectively, for Anderson's problem. The results show that Anderson should make 380 stereos, 1060 DVD players, and no VCRs or TVs, for a total profit of $69 400.

Some Questions We Want Answered

We now ask and answer several questions that will allow us to understand the shadow price, reduced costs, and allowable range information in Anderson Electronics' sensitivity report. Each question is independent of the other questions and assumes that only the change mentioned in that question is being considered.

Q: What is the impact on profit of a change in the supply of nonelectronic components?

Nonelectronic components are a nonbinding constraint.

A: The slack values in the Answer Report (Screenshot 4.2B) indicate that of the potential supply of 4500 units of nonelectronic components, only 3940 units are used, leaving

TABLE 4.1

Data for Anderson Electronics Example

	VCR	STEREO	TV	DVD	SUPPLY
Electronic components	3	4	4	3	4700
Nonelectronic components	2	2	4	3	4500
Assembly time (hours)	1	1	3	2	2500
Selling price (per unit)	$70	$80	$150	$110	

SCREENSHOT 4.2A   **Excel Layout and Solver Entries for Anderson Electronics**

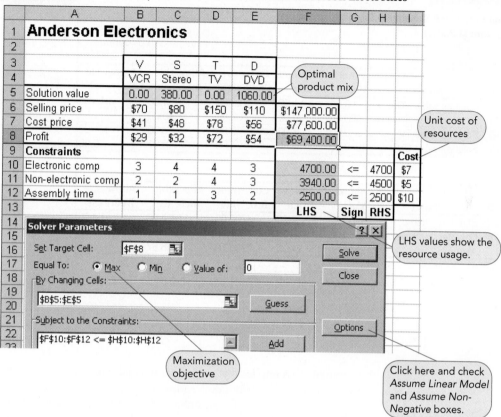

SCREENSHOT 4.2B   **Solver Answer Report for Anderson Electronics**

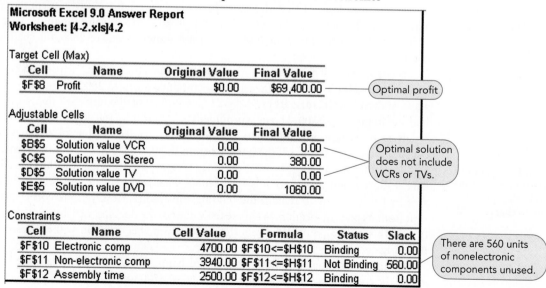

SCREENSHOT 4.2C   Solver Sensitivity Report for Anderson Electronics

Microsoft Excel 9.0 Sensitivity Report
Worksheet: [4-2.xls]4.2

For changes to OFC values in this range, the current solution remains optimal.

Adjustable Cells

Cell	Name	Final Value	Reduced Cost	Objective Coefficient	Allowable Increase	Allowable Decrease
$B$5	Solution value VCR	0.00	-1.00	29.00	1.00	1E+30
$C$5	Solution value Stereo	380.00	0.00	32.00	40.00	1.67
$D$5	Solution value TV	0.00	-8.00	72.00	8.00	1E+30
$E$5	Solution value DVD	1060.00	0.00	54.00	10.00	5.00

The allowable decrease is infinity since the product is not attractive even at current OFC value.

Constraints

Cell	Name	Final Value	Shadow Price	Constraint R.H. Side	Allowable Increase	Allowable Decrease
$F$10	Electronic comp	4700.00	2.00	4700.00	2800.00	950.00
$F$11	Non-electronic comp	3940.00	0.00	4500.00	1E+30	560.00
$F$12	Assembly time	2500.00	24.00	2500.00	466.67	1325.00

Since nonelectronic components are nonbinding, the shadow price is zero.

The allowable increase is infinity since there are already 560 units of slack.

560 units unused. This implies that additional nonelectronic components are of no value to Anderson in terms of contribution to profit; that is, the shadow price is zero.

This shadow price is valid for an unlimited (infinite) increase in the supply of non-electronic components. Further, Anderson could give up as much as 560 units of these components with no impact on profit. These values are shown in the Allowable Increase and Allowable Decrease columns in Screenshot 4.2C, respectively, for the supply of non-electronic components.

Q: What would the impact on profit be if we could increase the supply of electronic components by 400 units (to a total of 5100 units)?

A: We first look at the Allowable Increase column for electronic components in Screenshot 4.2C to verify whether the current shadow price is valid for an increase of 400 units in this resource. Since the increase column shows a value of 2800, the shadow price is valid.

Electronic components are a binding constraint.

Next, we look at the shadow price for electronic components, which is $2 per unit. That is, each additional unit of electronic components (up to 2800 additional units) will allow Anderson to increase its profit by $2. The impact of 400 units will therefore be a net increase in profit by $800. The new profit will be $70 200 (= $69 400 + $800).

It is important to remember that whenever the RHS value of a nonredundant constraint changes, the size of the feasible region changes. Hence, some of the corner points shift locations. In the current situation, since the proposed change is within the allowable change, the current corner point is still optimal. That is, the constraints that are binding at present will continue to remain the binding constraints. However, the corner point will shift from its present location. What are the values of the decision variables at the new location of this corner point? We cannot usually answer this question without resolving the model again.

Change in the RHS value of a binding constraint causes the coordinates of the optimal corner point to change.

Q: In the previous question, what would happen if we could increase the supply of electronic components by 4000 units (to a total of 8700 units)?

Changes beyond the
allowable increase or
decrease cannot be analyzed
using the current report.

A: From Screenshot 4.2C, we see that the shadow price of $2 per unit is valid only up to 2800 additional units. This means that the first 2800 units will cause the total profit to increase by $5600 (= $2 × 2800). However, the impact of the last 1200 units (assuming we are forced to accept all or nothing of the 4000 units) cannot be analyzed using the current report. The problem would have to be resolved using Solver to measure its impact.

It is important to note that the fact the potential additional supply (4000) of electronic components is beyond the allowable increase value (2800) does *not* mean Anderson's management should not implement this change. It just means that the total impact of the change cannot be evaluated from the *current* sensitivity report in Screenshot 4.2C.

Q: Refer back to the question about getting an additional 400 units of electronic components. What would happen if the supplier of these 400 units wants $8 per unit (rather than the current cost of $7 per unit)?

We must correct the shadow
price for any premium that
we pay.

A: We know that the shadow price of $2 for electronic components represents the increase in total profit from each additional unit of this resource. This value is net after the cost of this additional unit has been taken into account. That is, it is actually beneficial for Anderson to pay a premium of up to $2 per additional unit of electronic components. In the current situation, getting 400 additional units of electronic components would cost Anderson $8 per unit. This represents a premium of $1 per unit over the current rate of $7 per unit. However, it would still be beneficial to get these units, since each additional unit would increase the total profit by $1 (= shadow price of $2, less the premium of $1). The total profit would therefore increase by $400, to a new value of $69 600.

This adjusted value of $1 represents the actual increase in profit and can be referred to as the *adjusted shadow price.*

Q: Assume we have an opportunity to get 250 additional hours of assembly time. However, this time will cost us time and a half (i.e., $15 per hour, rather than the current $10 per hour). Should we take it?

We must calculate the
adjusted shadow price here.

A: From Screenshot 4.2C, the shadow price of $24 per hour of assembly time is valid for an increase of up to 466.67 hours. This shadow price, however, assumes the additional time costs only $10 per hour. The $5 per hour premium paid on the additional time therefore results in an increase of only $19 (= $24 − $5) per each additional hour of assembly time obtained.

The net impact on profit of the additional 250 hours of assembly time is an increase of $4750 (= 250 × $19). Anderson should definitely accept this opportunity.

Q: If we force the production of VCRs, what would be the impact on total profit? Alternatively, how profitable must VCRs become before Anderson should consider producing them?

The impact of forcing
VCRs is shown by the
reduced cost.

A: VCRs are currently not being produced, since they are not profitable enough. The reduced cost of −$1 for VCRs (shown in Screenshot 4.2C) implies that the net impact of producing a VCR will be to decrease total profit by $1 (to $69 399). You may recall from our discussion in Section 4.3 that the reduced cost of VCRs shows the difference between their marginal contribution to Anderson's total profit and the marginal worth of resources they would consume if produced. As an exercise, see if you can verify that these values are $29 and $30, respectively.

However, if Anderson can find a way of increasing the selling price of VCRs by $1 (to $71 per unit), VCRs would then become attractive. This information is also seen from the $1 in the Allowable Increase column for the OFC for VCRs.

Q: Assume that there is some uncertainty in the price for DVD players. For what range of prices will the current production be optimal? If DVD players sold for $106, what would be Anderson's new total profit?

Even though the production
values do not change, the
total profit will decrease.

A: DVD players currently sell for $110, yielding a profit of $54 per unit. The allowable ranges for the OFC of DVD players in Screenshot 4.2C shows that this value can increase by up to $10 (to $64; selling price of $120) or decrease by up to $5 (to $49; selling price of $105) for the current production plan to remain optimal.

If DVD players actually sold for $106, the profit per unit would drop to $50. The current values of the decision variables would remain optimal. However, the new total profit would decrease by $4240 (= $4 per DVD player for 1060 DVD players) to $65 160.

Alternate Optimal Solutions

Is the optimal solution identified in Screenshot 4.2A for Anderson Electronics (380 stereos and 1060 DVD players, for a total profit of $69 400) unique? Are there alternate production mixes that will also yield a profit of $69 400?

Recall that in Chapter 2 (Section 2.7) we showed a graphical example of a situation in which a problem with only two variables had alternate optimal solutions (also referred to as multiple optimal solutions). How can we detect a similar condition from the Solver output for problems involving more than two variables?

Zeros in the Allowable Increase or Allowable Decrease columns for OFC values may indicate alternate optimal solutions.

In most cases, when the Allowable Increase or Allowable Decrease column for the OFC of a variable has a value of zero in the *Adjustable Cells* table, this indicates the presence of alternate optimal solutions. In Anderson's problem, we see from Screenshot 4.2C that this is not the case.

Note also from Screenshot 4.2C that the reduced costs for both products currently not being produced in the optimal solution (VCRs and TVs) are nonzero. This indicates that if Anderson is forced to produce either of these products, the net impact will be a reduction in total profit (as discussed earlier). That is, there is no solution possible involving products other than stereos and DVD players that will yield a profit as high as the current solution ($69 400). The current optimal solution is therefore, unique.

In Solved Problem 4-1 at the end of this chapter, we discuss how Solver's sensitivity report can be used to detect the presence of alternate optimal solutions for a problem. We also discuss how Solver can be used to identify these alternate optimal solutions.

4.5   ANALYZING SIMULTANEOUS CHANGES USING THE 100% RULE

Until now, we have analyzed the impact of a change in just a single parameter value on the optimal solution. That is, when we are studying the impact of one item of the input data (OFC or RHS value), we assume that all other input data in the model stay constant at their current values. What happens when there are *simultaneous* changes in more than one OFC value or more than one RHS value? Is it possible to analyze the impact of such simultaneous changes on the optimal solution with the information provided in the sensitivity report?

The answer is yes, albeit only under a specific condition, as discussed in the following section. It is important to note that the condition is valid for analyzing simultaneous changes in *either* OFC values *or* RHS values, but not for a mixture of the two types of input data.

Simultaneous Changes in Constraint RHS Values

Consider a situation in which Anderson Electronics realizes that its available number of electronic components is actually only 4200 and, *at the same time*, finds that it has an opportunity to obtain an additional 200 hours of assembly time. What is the impact of these *simultaneous* changes on the optimal solution? To answer this question, we first use a condition called the **100% rule**. This condition can be stated as follows:

The 100% rule can be used to check if simultaneous changes in RHS or OFC values can be analyzed using the current sensitivity report.

$$\sum_{changes} \frac{\text{Change}}{\text{Allowable change}} \leq 1$$

That is, we compute the ratio of each proposed change in a parameter's value to the maximum allowable change in its value, as given in the sensitivity report. The sum of these ratios must not exceed 1 (or 100%) to ensure that the information given in the current sensitivity report is valid. If the sum of the ratios does exceed 1, the current information may still be valid; we just cannot guarantee its validity. However, if the ratio does not exceed 1, the information is definitely valid.

To verify this rule for the proposed change in Anderson's problem, consider each change in turn. First, there is a decrease of 500 units (i.e., from 4700 to 4200) in the number of electronic components. From the sensitivity report (see Screenshot 4.2C), the allowable decrease in this RHS value is 950. The ratio is therefore

$$\frac{500}{950} = 0.5263$$

Next, there is an increase of 200 hours (from 2500 to 2700) in the assembly time available. From the sensitivity report, the allowable increase for this RHS value is 466.67. This ratio is, therefore,

$$\frac{200}{466.67} = 0.4285$$

The sum of these ratios is

$$\text{Sum of ratios} = 0.5263 + 0.4285 = 0.9548 < 1$$

If the sum of ratios does not exceed 1, the information in the sensitivity report is valid.

Since this sum does not exceed 1, the information provided in the sensitivity report is valid to analyze the impact of these changes. First, the decrease of 500 units in electronic component availability reduces the size of the feasible region and will therefore cause profit to decrease. The magnitude of this decrease is $1000 (= 500 units of electronic components, at a shadow price of $2 per unit).

In contrast, the additional 200 hours of assembly time will result in a larger feasible region and a net increase in profit of $4800 (= 200 hours of assembly time, at a shadow price of $24 per hour). The net impact of these simultaneous changes is therefore an increase in profit of $3800 (= $4800 − $1000).

Simultaneous Changes in OFC Values

The 100% rule can also be used to analyze simultaneous changes in OFC values in a similar manner. For example, what is the impact on the optimal solution if Anderson decides to drop the selling price of DVD players by $3 per unit but, at the same time, increase the selling price of stereos by $8 per unit?

Once again, we calculate the appropriate ratios to verify the 100% rule. For the current solution to remain optimal, the allowable decrease in the OFC for DVD players is $5, while the allowable increase in the OFC for stereos is $40. The sum of ratios is therefore

$$\text{Sum of ratios} = \$3/\$5 + \$8/\$40 = 0.80 < 1$$

Since the sum of ratios does not exceed 1, the current production plan is still optimal. The $3 decrease in profit per DVD player causes total profit to decrease by $3180 (= $3 × 1060). However, the $8 increase in the unit profit of each stereo results in an increase of $3040 (= $8 × 380) in total profit. The net impact is, therefore, a decrease in profit of only $140 to a new value of $69 260.

4.6   PRICING OUT NEW VARIABLES

Pricing out analyzes the impact of adding a new variable to the existing LP model.

The information given in the sensitivity report can also be used to study the impact of the introduction of new decision variables (products, in the Anderson example) in the model. For example, if Anderson's problem is solved again with a new product also included in the model, will we recommend that the new product be made? Or will we recommend that we do not make the new product and continue making the same products (i.e., stereos and DVD players) Anderson is making now?

Anderson's Proposed New Product

Suppose Anderson Electronics wants to introduce a new product, a home theatre system (HTS), to take advantage of the hot market for that product. The design department estimates that each HTS will require five units of electronic components, four units of nonelectronic components, and four hours of assembly time. The marketing department estimates that it can sell each HTS for $175.

The question now is whether the HTS will be a profitable product for Anderson to produce. That is, is it worthwhile to divert resources from Anderson's existing products to make this new product? Alternatively, we could pose the question as this: What is the minimum price at which Anderson would need to sell each HTS in order to make it a viable product?

The answer to such questions involves a procedure called **pricing out**. Assume that Anderson decides to make a single HTS. Note that the resources required to make this player (five units of electronic components, four units of nonelectronic components, and four hours of assembly time) will no longer be available to meet Anderson's existing production plan (380 stereos and 1060 DVD players for a total profit of $69 400).

Checking the Validity of the 100% Rule   Clearly, the loss of these resources is going to reduce the profit that Anderson could have made from its existing products. Using the shadow prices of these resources, we can calculate the exact impact of the loss of these resources. However, we must first use the 100% rule to check if the shadow prices are valid by calculating the ratio of the reduction in each resource's availability to the allowable decrease for that resource (given in Screenshot 4.2C). The resulting calculation is as follows:

$$\text{Sum of ratios} = \frac{5}{950} + \frac{4}{560} + \frac{4}{1325} = 0.015 < 1$$

We first calculate the worth of the resources that would be consumed by the new product, if produced.

Required Profit Contribution of Each HTS   Since the total ratio is less than 1, the shadow prices are valid to calculate the impact on profit of using these resources to produce an HTS, rather than the existing products. We can determine this impact as

$$
\begin{aligned}
&= 5 \times \text{shadow price of electronic components} \\
&\quad + 4 \times \text{shadow price of nonelectronic components} \\
&\quad + 4 \times \text{shadow price of assembly time} \\
&= 5 \times \$2 + 4 \times \$0 + 4 \times \$24 \\
&= \$106
\end{aligned}
$$

Hence, in order for the HTS to be a viable product, the profit contribution of each HTS has to at least make up this shortfall in profit. That is, the OFC for the HTS must be at least $106 in order for the optimal solution to have a nonzero value for HTS. Otherwise, the optimal solution for Anderson's model with a decision variable for the HTS included will be the same as for the current one, with the HTS having a value of zero.

We then calculate the actual cost of making the new product, if produced.

The actual cost of the resources used to make one HTS unit can be calculated as

$$
\begin{aligned}
&= 5 \times \text{unit price of electronic components} \\
&\quad + 4 \times \text{unit price of nonelectronic components} \\
&\quad + 4 \times \text{unit price of assembly time} \\
&= 5 \times \$7 + 4 \times \$5 + 4 \times \$10 \\
&= \$95
\end{aligned}
$$

Finding the Minimum Selling Price of Each HTS Unit   To find out whether it is worthwhile diverting resources from their current use to make HTS units, we need one more calculation. We must find the minimum selling price for HTS units. This is calculated as the sum of the cost of making an HTS unit and the marginal worth of resources diverted from existing products. In Anderson's case, this works out to $201 (= $106 + $95). Since Anderson's marketing department estimates it can sell each HTS unit for only $175, this product will not be profitable for Anderson to produce.

What will happen if Anderson *does* include HTS as a variable in its model and solve the expanded formulation again? In this case, from the discussion so far, we can say that the optimal solution will once again recommend producing 380 stereos and 1060 DVDs for a total profit of $69 400. The HTS will have a final value of zero (just as the VCR and TV do in the current solution). What will be the reduced cost of HTS in this revised solution? We have calculated that the minimum selling price required for the HTS to be a viable product is $201, while the actual selling price is only $175. Therefore, the reduced cost will be $26, indicating that each HTS unit produced will cause Anderson's profit to decrease by $26.

To verify our conclusions, let us revise the LP model for Anderson Electronics to include the new product, the HTS. The Excel layout and Solver entries for this revised model are shown in Screenshot 4.3A. The sensitivity report for this model is shown in Screenshot 4.3B.

The results show that it continues to be optimal for Anderson to produce 380 stereos and 1060 DVD players, for a total profit of $69 400. Further, the magnitude of the reduced cost for the HTS is $26 (as we had already calculated).

File: 4-3.xls

SCREENSHOT 4.3A   **Revised Excel Layout and Solver Entries for Anderson Electronics**

The revised model includes the HTS.

Selling price is $175 per HTS.

	A	B	C	D	E	F	G	H	I	J
1	**Anderson Electronics (Revised)**									
2										
3		V	S	T	T	H				
4		VCR	Stereo	TV	DVD	HTS				
5	Solution value	0.00	380.00	0.00	1060.00	0.00				
6	Selling price	$70	$80	$150	$110	$175	$147,000.00			
7	Cost price	$41	$48	$78	$56	$95	$77,600.00			
8	Profit	$29	$32	$72	$54	$80	$69,400.00			
9	**Constraints**									Cost
10	Electronic comp	3	4	4	3	5	4700.00	<=	4700	$7
11	Non-electronic comp	2	2	4	3	4	3940.00	<=	4500	$5
12	Assembly time	1	1	3	2	4	2500.00	<=	2500	$10
13							LHS	Sign	RHS	

Solver Parameters   ? ✕

Se_t Target Cell: $G$8

Equal To: ⦿ Max   ○ Mi_n   ○ _Value of: 0

By Changing Cells:

$B$5:$F$5   _Guess_

Su_bject to the Constraints:

$G$10:$G$12 <= $I$10:$I$12   Add

Solve

Close

Options

There are five decision variables in the model.

SCREENSHOT 4.3B   **Revised Solver Sensitivity Report for Anderson Electronics**

Microsoft Excel 9.0 Sensitivity Report
Worksheet: [4-3.xls]4.3

Note that this is the same product mix as in Screenshot 4.2C.

Adjustable Cells

Cell	Name	Final Value	Reduced Cost	Objective Coefficient	Allowable Increase	Allowable Decrease
$B$5	Solution value VCR	0.00	-1.00	29.00	1.00	1E+30
$C$5	Solution value Stereo	380.00	0.00	32.00	40.00	1.67
$D$5	Solution value TV	0.00	-8.00	72.00	8.00	1E+30
$E$5	Solution value DVD	1060.00	0.00	54.00	10.00	5.00
$F$5	Solution value HTS	0.00	-26.00	80.00	26.00	1E+30

The HTS is not included in the optimal product mix.

The reduced cost for the HTS is $26.

Constraints

Cell	Name	Final Value	Shadow Price	Constraint R.H. Side	Allowable Increase	Allowable Decrease
$G$10	Electronic comp	4700.00	2.00	4700.00	2800.00	950.00
$G$11	Non-electronic comp	3940.00	0.00	4500.00	1E+30	560.00
$G$12	Assembly time	2500.00	24.00	2500.00	466.67	1325.00

Note that these are the same shadow prices as in Screenshot 4.2C.

SENSITIVITY ANALYSIS FOR A MINIMIZATION EXAMPLE

Minimization problems will typically involve some $\geq$ constraints.

So far, we have analyzed maximization examples in which all constraints have been of the $\leq$ type. The analysis is similar for problems with minimization objectives and constraints of the $\geq$ type. However, we need to be aware that when a solution improves in a minimization problem, the objective value actually decreases rather than increases. We illustrate this with an example.

Burn-Off Diet Drink Example

Burn-Off, a manufacturer of diet drinks, is planning to introduce a miracle drink that will magically burn the fat away. The drink is made up of four "mystery" ingredients (which we will call ingredients A, B, C, and D). The dosage calls for a person to consume at least three 355 mL doses per day (i.e., at least 1065 mL, or 1.065 L per day).

Each of the four ingredients contains different levels of three chemical compounds (which we will call chemicals X, Y, and Z). Health regulations mandate that the dosage consumed per day should contain minimum prescribed levels of chemicals X and Y, and not exceed maximum prescribed levels for the third chemical, Z.

The composition of the four ingredients in terms of the chemical compounds (units per litre) is shown in Table 4.2 on the next page, along with the unit cost prices of the ingredients. Burn-Off wants to find the optimal way to mix the ingredients to create the drink, at minimum cost per daily dose.

To formulate this problem, let A, B, C, and D denote the number of litres of ingredients A, B, C, and D to use, respectively. The problem can then be formulated as follows:

Minimize $1.33A + 2.33B + 2.00C + 1.00D$ (daily dose cost in dollars)

subject to

$$A + B + C + D \geq 1.065 \quad \text{(daily dose requirement)}$$
$$100A + 132B + 265C + 330D \geq 280 \quad \text{(chemical X requirement)}$$

TABLE 4.2	Data for Diet Drink Example				
	INGREDIENT A	INGREDIENT B	INGREDIENT C	INGREDIENT D	REQUIREMENT
Chemical X	100	132	265	330	At least 280 units
Chemical Y	165	100	200	200	At least 200 units
Chemical Z	330	835	670	1340	At most 1050 units
Cost per litre	$1.33	$2.33	$2.00	$1.00	

$$165A + 100B + 200C + 200D \geq 200 \quad \text{(chemical Y requirement)}$$
$$330A + 835B + 670C + 1340D \leq 1050 \quad \text{(chemical Z max limit)}$$
$$A, B, C, D \geq 0$$

File: 4-4.xls

Burn-Off's Excel Solution

Screenshots 4.4A, 4.4B, and 4.4C on the next two pages show the Excel layout and Solver entries, Answer Report, and Sensitivity Report, respectively, for Burn-Off's problem. The Solver output shows that the optimal solution is to use 264 mL of ingredient A, 165 mL of ingredient C, and 636 mL of ingredient D to make the diet drink. No ingredient B is used. The total cost per daily dosage is $1.32.

The answer report (Screenshot 4.4B) details the same information but also shows that the constraint for chemical Y is nonbinding. Although the minimum requirement is only 200 units of chemical Y, the final drink actually provides 203.76 units of this chemical. The extra 3.76 units denote the level of oversatisfaction of this requirement. You may recall from Chapter 2 that we refer to this quantity as **surplus**, even though the Solver report always titles this value **slack**. The difference between the LHS and RHS values of a $\geq$ constraint is called surplus.

SCREENSHOT 4.4A   **Excel Layout and Solver Entries for Burn-Off Diet Drink**

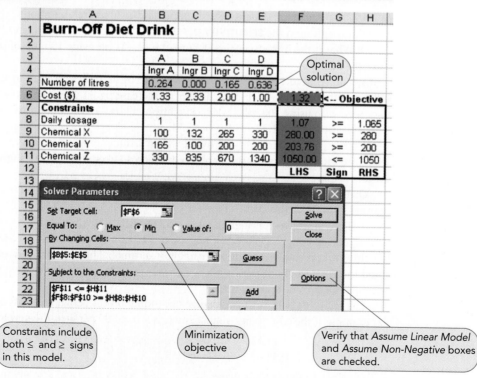

Excel Answer Report for Burn-Off Diet Drink

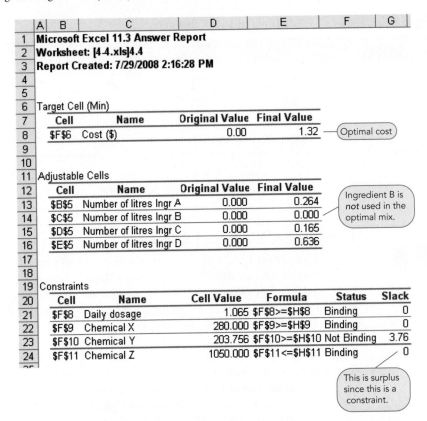

Microsoft Excel 11.3 Answer Report
Worksheet: [4-4.xls]4.4
Report Created: 7/29/2008 2:16:28 PM

Target Cell (Min)

Cell	Name	Original Value	Final Value
$F$6	Cost ($)	0.00	1.32

— Optimal cost

Adjustable Cells

Cell	Name	Original Value	Final Value
$B$5	Number of litres Ingr A	0.000	0.264
$C$5	Number of litres Ingr B	0.000	0.000
$D$5	Number of litres Ingr C	0.000	0.165
$E$5	Number of litres Ingr D	0.000	0.636

Ingredient B is *not* used in the optimal mix.

Constraints

Cell	Name	Cell Value	Formula	Status	Slack
$F$8	Daily dosage	1.065	$F$8>=$H$8	Binding	0
$F$9	Chemical X	280.000	$F$9>=$H$9	Binding	0
$F$10	Chemical Y	203.756	$F$10>=$H$10	Not Binding	3.76
$F$11	Chemical Z	1050.000	$F$11<=$H$11	Binding	0

This is surplus since this is a constraint.

Answering Sensitivity Analysis Questions for Burn-Off

As with the Anderson Electronics example, we use several questions to interpret the information given in the **SENSITIVITY REPORT** (Screenshot 4.4C) for Burn-Off.

Q: What is the impact on cost if Burn-Off insists on using 100 mL of ingredient B to make the drink?

A: The reduced cost indicates that each litre of ingredient B used to make the drink will cause the total cost per daily dosage to increase by $1.905. Therefore the extra cost associated with using 100 mL (1/10th of a litre) will be $0.1905 or approximately 19 cents. The new cost will be $1.32 + $0.19 = $1.51.

Alternatively, if Burn-Off can find a way of reducing ingredient B's cost per litre by at least $1.91 (to 42 cents or less), then it becomes cost-effective to use this ingredient to make the diet drink.

Q: There is some uncertainty in the cost of ingredient C. How sensitive is the current optimal solution to this cost?

A: The current cost of ingredient C is $2 per litre. The range for the cost coefficient of this ingredient shows an allowable increase of $4.29 and an allowable decrease of $0.78, for the current corner point solution to remain optimal. The cost per litre of ingredient C could therefore fluctuate between $1.22 (= $2 − $0.78) and $6.29 (= $2 + $4.29) without affecting the current optimal mix.

The total cost will, however, change depending on the actual unit cost of ingredient C. For example, if the cost of ingredient C increases to $4.00 per litre, the new total cost will be

$$= \$1.32 + (\$2.00 \text{ extra per litre} \times 0.165 \text{ litres of C})$$
$$= \$1.32 + \$0.33 = \$1.65$$

Q: What do the shadow prices for chemical X and chemical Z imply in this problem?

SCREENSHOT 4.4C   **Solver Sensitivity Report for Burn-Off Diet Drink**

	A B	C	D	E	F	G	H
1	**Microsoft Excel 11.3 Sensitivity Report**						
2	**Worksheet: [4-4.xls]4.4**						
3	**Report Created: 7/29/2008 2:16:29 PM**						
4							
5							
6	Adjustable Cells						
7			**Final**	**Reduced**	**Objective**	**Allowable**	**Allowable**
8	**Cell**	**Name**	**Value**	**Cost**	**Coefficient**	**Increase**	**Decrease**
9	$B$5	Number of litres A	0.264	0.000	1.33	1.18	0.80
10	$C$5	Number of litres B	0.000	1.905	2.33	1E+30	1.91
11	$D$5	Number of litres C	0.165	0.000	2	4.29	0.78
12	$E$5	Number of litres D	0.636	0.000	1	1.26	1E+30
13							
14	Constraints						
15			**Final**	**Shadow**	**Constraint**	**Allowable**	**Allowable**
16	**Cell**	**Name**	**Value**	**Price**	**R.H. Side**	**Increase**	**Decrease**
17	$F$8	Daily dosage	1.065	1.216	1.065	0.58	0.03
18	$F$9	Chemical X	280.00	0.009	280	34.87	14.17
19	$F$10	Chemical Y	203.76	0.000	200	3.76	1E+30
20	$F$11	Chemical Z	1050.00	-0.002	1050	63.34	341.03

Reduced cost shows increase in total cost if ingredient B is used.

Infinity

Shadow price shows decrease in total cost if chemical Z's limit is increased.

A: The shadow price for chemical X is $0.009. Since the constraint for chemical X is a ≥ constraint, an increase by one unit in the RHS (from 280 to 281) makes the problem solution even more restrictive. That is, the feasible region becomes smaller. The optimal objective function value could, therefore, worsen. The shadow price indicates that for each additional unit of chemical X required to be present in the drink, the overall cost will increase by $0.009 or approximately 1 cent. This value is valid for an increase of up to 34.866 units and a decrease by 14.168 units in the requirement for chemical X.

In contrast, the constraint for chemical Z is a ≤ constraint. An increase in the RHS of the constraint (from 1050 to 1051) will cause the feasible region to become bigger. Hence, the optimal objective function value could possibly improve. The negative value of the shadow price for this constraint indicates that each unit increase in the maximum limit allowed for chemical Z will cause total cost to decrease by $0.002. This value is valid for an increase of up to 63.341 units. Likewise, the total cost will *increase* by 0.002 cents for each unit *decrease* in the maximum limit allowed for chemical Z. This is valid for a decrease of up to 341.035 units in the maximum limit for chemical Z.

Q: Burn-Off can decrease the minimum requirement for chemical X by 5 units (from 280 to 275) provided the maximum limit allowed for chemical Z is reduced to 1000 units (that is, reduced by 50 units). Is this trade-off cost effective for Burn-Off to implement?

A: Since we are dealing with simultaneous changes in RHS values, we first verify whether the 100% rule is satisfied. To do so, we take the ratio of each proposed change to its maximum allowable change. The calculations are

$$\text{Sum of ratios} = \frac{5}{14.168} + \frac{5}{341.035} = 0.4995 < 1$$

A negative value for the shadow price implies that cost will decrease if the RHS value increases.

Analyzing simultaneous changes requires the use of the 100% rule.

Since the sum of ratios does not exceed 1, we can use the shadow price information in the sensitivity report (Screenshot 4.4C). The reduction of five units in the requirement for chemical X will cause the feasible region to increase in size. The total cost will therefore improve (i.e., go down) by $0.045 (= 5 units, at a shadow price of $0.009 per unit).

In contrast, the reduction of 50 units in the maximum allowable limit for chemical Z makes the feasible region shrink in size. The total cost will therefore be adversely affected (i.e., go up) by $0.10 (= 50 units, at a shadow price of $0.002 cents per unit).

The net impact of this trade-off is therefore an increase in total cost of 5.5 cents (= $0.10 − $0.045). The new cost will be $1.375, or $1.38 to the nearest cent. Clearly, this trade-off is not cost effective from Burn-Off's perspective and should be rejected.

SUMMARY

In this chapter we present the important concept of sensitivity analysis. Sometimes referred to as postoptimality analysis, sensitivity analysis is used by management to answer a series of what-if questions about inputs to an LP model. It also tests just how sensitive the optimal solution is to changes in (1) profit or cost coefficients and (2) constraint RHS values.

We first explore sensitivity analysis graphically (for problems with only two decision variables). We then discuss how to interpret information in the Answer and Sensitivity Reports generated by Solver. We also discuss how the information in these reports can be used to analyze simultaneous changes in model parameter values and determine the potential impact of a new variable in the model.

GLOSSARY

Allowable Decrease. (1) For an objective function coefficient: The maximum amount by which the OFC of a decision variable can decrease for the current optimal solution to remain optimal. (2) For the right-hand side of a constraint: the maximum amount by which the RHS value of a constraint can decrease for the shadow price to be valid.

Allowable Increase. (1) For an objective function coefficient: The maximum amount by which the OFC of a decision variable can increase for the current optimal solution to remain optimal. (2) For the right-hand side of a constraint: The maximum amount by which the RHS value of a constraint can increase for the shadow price to be valid.

Answer Report. A report created by Solver when it solves an LP model. This report presents the optimal solution in a detailed manner.

Objective Function Coefficient (OFC). The coefficient for a decision variable in the objective function. Typically, this refers to unit profit or unit cost.

100% Rule. A rule used to verify the validity of the information in the sensitivity report when dealing with simultaneous changes to more than one RHS value or more than one OFC value. The rule states that the sum of these ratios of proposed changes in parameters' values to the maximum allowable change in these values, as given in the sensitivity report, must not exceed 1 (or 100%) to ensure that the information given in the current sensitivity report is valid.

Pricing Out. A procedure by which the shadow price information in the sensitivity report can be used to gauge the impact of the addition of a new variable in the LP model.

Reduced Cost. The difference between the marginal contribution to the objective function value from the inclusion of a decision variable and the marginal worth of the resources it consumes. In the case of a decision variable that has an optimal value of zero, it is also the minimum amount by which the OFC of that variable should change before it would have a nonzero optimal value.

Right-Hand-Side (RHS) Value. The amount of resource available (for a ≤ constraint) or the minimum requirement of some criterion (for a ≥ constraint). Typically expressed as a constant for sensitivity analysis.

Sensitivity Analysis or Postoptimality Analysis. The study of how sensitive an optimal solution is to model assumptions and to data changes.

Shadow Price. The magnitude of the change in the objective function value for a unit increase in the RHS of a constraint.

Slack. The difference between the RHS and the left-hand side (LHS) of a ≤ constraint. Typically represents the unused resource.

Surplus. The difference between the LHS and the RHS of a ≥ constraint. Typically represents the level of oversatisfaction of a requirement.

SOLVED PROBLEM

Solved Problem 4-1

Let us revisit the Atlantic Bank of Canada example in Chapter 3 (Section 3.4 on page 91). We will use the sensitivity report for this example to illustrate the detection of alternative optimal solutions for an LP problem and the manner in which Excel can be used to identify those alternative optimal solutions. Please reread that example. We repeat just the formulation portion as follows.

For the example, let

$$F = \text{full-time tellers}$$

$$P_1 = \text{part-timers starting at 9 A.M. (leaving at 1 P.M.)}$$

$$P_2 = \text{part-timers starting at 10 A.M. (leaving at 2 P.M.)}$$

$$P_3 = \text{part-timers starting at 11 A.M. (leaving at 3 P.M.)}$$

$$P_4 = \text{part-timers starting at noon (leaving at 4 P.M.)}$$

$$P_5 = \text{part-timers starting at 1 P.M. (leaving at 5 P.M.)}$$

Objective function:

$$\text{Minimize total daily personnel cost} = \$160F + \$42(P_1 + P_2 + P_3 + P_4 + P_5)$$

Constraints:

For each hour, the available labour hours must be at least equal to the required labour hours.

$$
\begin{array}{lll}
F + P_1 & \geq 10 & \text{(9 A.M.–10 A.M. needs)} \\
F + P_1 + P_2 & \geq 12 & \text{(10 A.M.–11 A.M. needs)} \\
\tfrac{1}{2}F + P_1 + P_2 + P_3 & \geq 14 & \text{(11 A.M.–noon needs)} \\
\tfrac{1}{2}F + P_1 + P_2 + P_3 + P_4 & \geq 16 & \text{(noon–1 P.M. needs)} \\
F + P_2 + P_3 + P_4 + P_5 & \geq 18 & \text{(1 P.M.–2 P.M. needs)} \\
F + P_3 + P_4 + P_5 & \geq 17 & \text{(2 P.M.–3 P.M. needs)} \\
F + P_4 + P_5 & \geq 15 & \text{(3 P.M.–4 P.M. needs)} \\
F + P_5 & \geq 10 & \text{(4 P.M.–5 P.M. needs)}
\end{array}
$$

Only 12 full-time tellers are available, so

$$F \leq 12$$

Part-time worker hours cannot exceed 50% of total hours required each day, which is the sum of the tellers needed each hour.

$$4(P_1 + P_2 + P_3 + P_4 + P_5) \leq 0.50(10 + 12 + 14 + 16 + 18 + 17 + 15 + 10)$$

or

$$4P_1 + 4P_2 + 4P_3 + 4P_4 + 4P_5 \leq 56$$

$$F, P_1, P_2, P_3, P_4, P_5 \geq 0$$

Solution

File: 4-5.xls

The Excel implementation and Solver entries for this model are shown in Screenshot 4.5A. The Sensitivity Report is shown in Screenshot 4.5B on page 157.

Screenshot 4.5A reveals that the optimal solution is to employ 10 full-time tellers, seven part-time tellers at 10 A.M., two part-time tellers at 11 A.M., and five part-time tellers at noon, for a total cost of $724 per day.

In Screenshot 4.5B, the shadow price of –4.333 for the part-time limit of 56 hours (row 17) indicates that each additional hour (over the 56-hour limit) that part-timers are allowed to work will allow the bank to reduce costs by $4.333. This shadow price is valid for a limit of 60 more hours

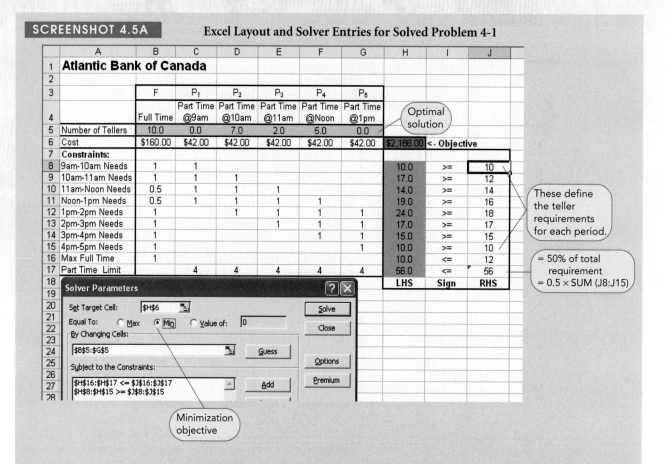

SCREENSHOT 4.5A   **Excel Layout and Solver Entries for Solved Problem 4-1**

(i.e., up to 116 hours). Note that the shadow price is fractional, since we are allowing the solution to include fractional values for the decision variables.

Examining the allowable increase and allowable decrease values for the OFCs, we see several zeros in these columns. This indicates that there are alternate optimal solutions to this problem.

Likewise, consider the reduced cost for variables P_1 and P_5. These are zero, even though these variables have values of zero (their lower limit). This implies that, for example, it is possible to force P_1 (or P_5) to have a nonzero value at optimality and not affect the total cost in any way. This is another indication of the presence of alternate optimal solutions to this problem.

We can force Excel to identify these alternate optimal solutions.

How can we identify these optimal solutions? Sometimes, simply rearranging the order in which the constraints are included in Solver makes Excel identify an alternate optimal solution. There are, however, a couple of ways of *forcing* Excel to identify these alternate optimal solutions. One way would be to include the current objective function as a constraint, as follows:

$$50F + 16(P_1 + P_2 + P_3 + P_4 + P_5) = 2188$$

Then, the new objective for the problem would be the maximization of the relevant variable (P_1 or P_5). That is,

$$\text{Max } P_1 \text{ (or } P_5)$$

An alternate approach is to add a constraint forcing the relevant variable (P_1 or P_5 in this case) to be nonzero. In many cases, even a constraint such as $P_1 \geq 0.001$ will suffice.

SCREENSHOT 4.5B   **Solver Sensitivity Report for Solved Problem 4-1**

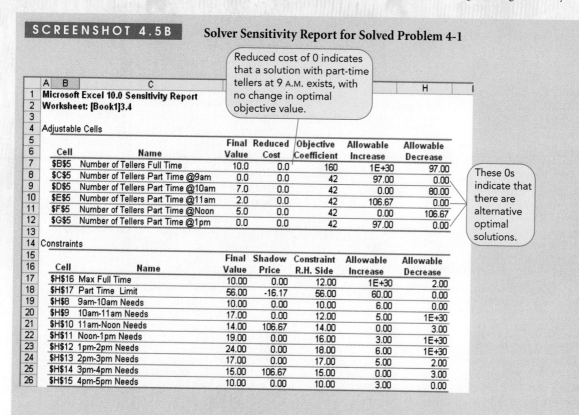

> Reduced cost of 0 indicates that a solution with part-time tellers at 9 A.M. exists, with no change in optimal objective value.

> These 0s indicate that there are alternative optimal solutions.

Microsoft Excel 10.0 Sensitivity Report
Worksheet: [Book1]3.4

Adjustable Cells

Cell	Name	Final Value	Reduced Cost	Objective Coefficient	Allowable Increase	Allowable Decrease
$B$5	Number of Tellers Full Time	10.0	0.0	160	1E+30	97.00
$C$5	Number of Tellers Part Time @9am	0.0	0.0	42	97.00	0.00
$D$5	Number of Tellers Part Time @10am	7.0	0.0	42	0.00	80.00
$E$5	Number of Tellers Part Time @11am	2.0	0.0	42	106.67	0.00
$F$5	Number of Tellers Part Time @Noon	5.0	0.0	42	0.00	106.67
$G$5	Number of Tellers Part Time @1pm	0.0	0.0	42	97.00	0.00

Constraints

Cell	Name	Final Value	Shadow Price	Constraint R.H. Side	Allowable Increase	Allowable Decrease
$H$16	Max Full Time	10.00	0.00	12.00	1E+30	2.00
$H$17	Part Time Limit	56.00	-16.17	56.00	60.00	0.00
$H$8	9am-10am Needs	10.00	0.00	10.00	6.00	0.00
$H$9	10am-11am Needs	17.00	0.00	12.00	5.00	1E+30
$H$10	11am-Noon Needs	14.00	106.67	14.00	0.00	3.00
$H$11	Noon-1pm Needs	19.00	0.00	16.00	3.00	1E+30
$H$12	1pm-2pm Needs	24.00	0.00	18.00	6.00	1E+30
$H$13	2pm-3pm Needs	17.00	0.00	17.00	5.00	2.00
$H$14	3pm-4pm Needs	15.00	106.67	15.00	0.00	3.00
$H$15	4pm-5pm Needs	10.00	0.00	10.00	3.00	0.00

By using either of these changes, we can identify alternate solutions for Atlantic Bank as follows. The cost of both these employment policies is also $724.

1. 10 full-time tellers, 6 part-time tellers at 9 A.M., 1 part-time teller at 10 A.M., 2 part-time tellers at 11 A.M., and 5 part-time tellers at noon.
2. 10 full-time tellers, 7 tellers at 10 A.M., 2 part-time tellers at 11 A.M., 4 part-time tellers at noon, and 1 part-time teller at 1 P.M.

⟶ SELF-TEST

- Before taking the self-test, refer back to the learning objectives at the beginning of the chapter, the notes in the margins, and the glossary at the end of the chapter.
- Use the key at the back of the book to correct your answers.
- Restudy pages that correspond to any questions that you answered incorrectly or material you feel uncertain about.

1. The measure that shows the change in the optimal objective function value for a unit increase in a constraint RHS value is the
    a. shadow price.
    b. reduced cost.
    c. allowable increase.
    d. allowable decrease.

2. The measure that compares the marginal contribution of a variable with the marginal worth of the resources it consumes is the
    a. shadow price.
    b. reduced cost.
    c. allowable increase.
    d. allowable decrease.

3. For a nonbinding constraint, the shadow price will always equal zero.
   a. True
   b. False

4. The measure that shows the change in the optimal objective function value if a product that is not currently produced is forced to be produced is the
   a. shadow price.
   b. reduced cost.
   c. allowable increase.
   d. allowable decrease.

5. For a constraint, the Allowable Increase column in the sensitivity report shows
   a. the allowable increase in the objective value.
   b. the allowable increase in the RHS value of the constraint for which the current optimal corner point remains optimal.
   c. the allowable increase in the shadow price.

6. When analyzing simultaneous changes in parameter values, we need to first verify the 100% rule.
   a. True
   b. False

7. If the 100% rule is violated, the information in the sensitivity report is always invalid.
   a. True
   b. False

8. If the RHS value of a ≥ constraint increases, the optimal value of a maximization objective function can *never*
   a. increase.
   b. decrease.
   c. stay the same.

9. If we wish to increase a constraint RHS value beyond the allowable increase value shown in the sensitivity report, this means
   a. there will no longer be a feasible solution for the problem.
   b. the problem needs to be solved again to get a new sensitivity report.

c. such a change should never be made.
d. the shadow price in the report is still valid.

10. The pricing out procedure allows us to
    a. analyze the impact of changes in the selling price of existing products.
    b. analyze the impact of changes in the cost of resources.
    c. analyze the impact of the introduction of a new variable.
    d. analyze simultaneous changes in parameter values.

11. Sensitivity reports can be used to detect the presence of alternate optimal solutions.
    a. True
    b. False

12. The reduced cost of a variable that has a value of zero in the current optimal solution will always be nonzero.
    a. True
    b. False

13. If the RHS value of a ≤ constraint decreases, the optimal value of a maximization objective function can *never*
    a. increase.
    b. decrease.
    c. stay the same.

14. *Surplus* refers to the
    a. LHS value of a ≥ constraint.
    b. difference between the LHS and RHS values of a ≥ constraint.
    c. difference between the LHS and RHS values of a ≤ constraint.
    d. RHS value of a ≥ constraint.

15. If the objective function coefficient of a variable changes within its allowable range,
    a. the current variable values and the objective value remain the same.
    b. the current variable values remain the same, but the objective value changes.
    c. the current variable values and the objective value change.

DISCUSSION QUESTIONS AND PROBLEMS

Discussion Questions

4-1 Discuss the role of sensitivity analysis in LP. Under what circumstances is it needed, and under what circumstances is it not needed?

4-2 Is sensitivity analysis a concept applied to LP only, or should it also be used when analyzing results derived from other techniques (e.g., break-even analysis)? Provide examples to prove your point.

4-3 Explain how a change in resource availability can affect the optimal solution of a problem.

4-4 Explain how a change in an objective function coefficient can affect the optimal solution of a problem.

4-5 Are simultaneous changes in input data values logical? Provide examples to prove your point.

4-6 Explain the 100% rule and its role in analyzing the impact of simultaneous changes in model input data values.

4-7 How can a firm benefit from using the pricing out procedure?

4-8 How do we detect the presence of alternate optimal solutions from a Solver Sensitivity Report?

4-9 Why would a firm find information regarding the shadow price of a resource useful?

Problems

4-10 We used a graphical approach to solve the following LP model in Problem 2-14:

$$\text{Maximize profit} = \$1X + \$1Y$$

subject to

$$2X + Y \leq 100$$

$$X + 2Y \leq 100$$

$$X, Y \geq 0$$

Now use the graphical solution to answer the following questions. Each question is independent of the others.

(a) If a technical breakthrough occurred that raised the profit per unit of X to $3, would this affect the optimal corner point? Would it change the optimal objective value?

(b) If the technical breakthrough raised the profit per unit of X to only $1.25, would this affect the optimal corner point? Would it change the optimal objective value?

(c) If the second constraint were changed from $X + 2Y \leq 100$ to $X + 4Y \leq 100$, what effect would this have on the optimal corner point and profit? (Use the profit function $1X + $1Y.)

4-11 We used a graphical approach to solve the following LP model in Problem 2-15:

$$\text{Maximize profit} = \$3X + \$2Y$$

subject to

$$2X + 1Y \leq 150$$

$$2X + 3Y \leq 300$$

$$X, Y \geq 0$$

Now use the graphical solution to answer the following questions. Each question is independent of the others.

(a) Does the optimal solution change if the profit per unit of X changes to $4.50? What about the optimal profit?

(b) What happens if the profit function changes to $3X + 3Y?

4-12 We used a graphical approach to solve the following LP model in Problem 2-16:

$$\text{Maximize profit} = \$4X + \$6Y$$

subject to

$$1X + 2Y \leq 8$$

$$6X + 4Y \leq 24$$

$$X, Y \geq 0$$

Now use the graphical solution to answer the following questions. Each question is independent of the others.

(a) If the first constraint is altered to $X + 3Y \leq 8$, does the feasible region or optimal solution change? If so, how?

(b) If the second constraint is altered to $6X + 4Y \leq 36$, does the feasible region or optimal solution change? If so, how?

4-13 We used a graphical approach to solve the following LP model in Problem 2-18:

$$\text{Maximize profit} = \$5X + \$3Y$$

subject to

$$5X + 2Y \leq 40$$

$$3X + 6Y \leq 48$$

$$X \leq 7$$

$$2X - Y \geq 3$$

$$X, Y \geq 0$$

Now use the graphical solution to answer the following questions. Each question is independent of the others.

(a) If a technical breakthrough raises the profit per unit of Y to $5, would this affect the optimal corner point? Does it change the optimal objective value?

(b) If the profit per unit of X decreases to only $1.50, how would this affect the optimal corner point and profit?

(c) If the first constraint changes to $5X + 2Y \leq 42$, how would this affect the optimal corner point and profit?

4-14 We used a graphical approach to solve the following LP model in Problem 2-19:

$$\text{Minimize cost} = \$1X + \$2Y$$

subject to

$$X + 3Y \geq 90$$

$$8X + 2Y \geq 160$$

$$3X + 2Y \geq 120$$

$$Y \leq 70$$

$$X, Y \geq 0$$

Now use the graphical solution to answer the following questions. Each question is independent of the others.

(a) Does the optimal solution change if the cost per unit of Y increases to $4? What about the optimal cost?

(b) If the first constraint changes to $X + 3Y \geq 100$, does the optimal solution change? If so, how?

(c) If the fourth constraint changes to $Y \leq 50$, does the optimal solution change? If so, how?

4-15 We used a graphical approach to solve the following LP model in Problem 2-20:

$$\text{Minimize cost} = \$4X + \$7Y$$

subject to

$$3X + 7Y \geq 231$$

$$10X + 2Y \geq 200$$

$$2Y \geq 45$$

$$2X \leq 75$$

$$X, Y \geq 0$$

Now use the graphical solution to answer the following questions. Each question is independent of the others.

(a) Does the optimal solution change if the cost per unit of X decreases to $2? What about the optimal cost?

(b) If the first constraint changes to $3X + 7Y \geq 250$, does the optimal solution change? If so, how?

(c) If the third constraint changes to $2Y \geq 55$, does the optimal solution change? If so, how?

4-16 Consider the Kitchener Electronics media selection example discussed in Section 3.2 of Chapter 3. Use the Sensitivity Report for this LP model (shown in Screenshot 4.6) to answer the following questions. Each question is independent of the others.

(a) What would be the impact if management approved spending $200 more on radio advertising each week?

(b) Would it help Kitchener if it could get out of the contractual agreement to place at least five radio spots each week?

SCREENSHOT 4.6   Solver Sensitivity Report for Problem 4-16

	A B	C	D	E	F	G	H
1	Microsoft Excel 10.0 Sensitivity Report						
2	Worksheet: [Book2]Sheet1						
3							
4	Adjustable Cells						
5			Final	Reduced	Objective	Allowable	Allowable
6	Cell	Name	Value	Cost	Coefficient	Increase	Decrease
7	$B$5	Number of Units TV spots	1.97	0.00	5000.00	1620.69	5000.00
8	$C$5	Number of Units Newspaper ads	5.00	0.00	8500.00	1E+30	2718.75
9	$D$5	Number of Units Prime-time radio spots	6.21	0.00	2400.00	1E+30	263.16
10	$E$5	Number of Units Afternoon radio spots	0.00	-344.83	2800.00	344.83	1E+30
11							
12	Constraints						
13			Final	Shadow	Constraint	Allowable	Allowable
14	Cell	Name	Value	Price	R.H. Side	Increase	Decrease
15	$F$14	Min Radio Spots	6.21	0.00	5.00	1.21	1E+30
16	$F$8	Max TV	1.97	0.00	12.00	1E+30	10.03
17	$F$9	Max Newspaper	5.00	2718.75	5.00	1.70	5.00
18	$F$10	Max Prime-Time Radio	6.21	0.00	25.00	1E+30	18.79
19	$F$11	Max Afternoon Radio	0.00	0.00	20.00	1E+30	20.00
20	$F$12	Budget	$8,000.00	$6.25	8000.00	8025.00	1575.00
21	$F$13	Max Radio $	$1,800.00	$2.03	1800.00	1575.00	350.00
22							

(c) The radio station manager agrees to run the afternoon radio spots during some of the more popular programs. He thinks this will increase the audience reached per ad to 3100. Will this change the optimal solution? Why or why not?

(d) There is some uncertainty in the audience reached per TV spot. For what range of values for this OFC will the current solution remain optimal?

4-17 Consider the CMR marketing research example discussed in Section 3.2 of Chapter 3. Use the Sensitivity Report for this LP model (shown in Screenshot 4.7) to answer the following questions. Each question is independent of the others.

(a) What is the maximum unit cost that will make it worthwhile to include persons 30 years of age or younger who live in a large city in the survey?

(b) What is the impact if CMR wants to increase the sample size to 3000?

(c) What is the impact if CMR insists on including people 31–50 years of age who do not live in a large city?

(d) What is the impact if we can reduce the minimum required number of respondents aged 30 or younger to 900, provided we raise the number of respondents 31–50 years of age to 650?

4-18 Consider the Perky Puppy Pet Food diet problem example discussed in Section 3.7 of Chapter 3. Use the Sensitivity Report for this LP model (shown in Screenshot 4.8) to answer the following questions. Each question is independent of the others.

(a) What is the impact if the daily allowance for zinc is increased to 1.02 mg?

(b) If the price of Food A increases by $0.05 per kilogram and the price of Food B decreases by $0.10 per

kilogram, what are the new optimal solution and optimal total cost?

(c) What is the impact if there is an increase of 1% in the daily allowance for zinc and a simultaneous increase in the daily allowance of vitamin D to 325 units?

4-19 Consider Cheval Blanc Stable's animal feed problem first presented in Chapter 3 as Problem 3-4 . Use Solver to create the Answer and Sensitivity Reports for this LP problem. Now answer the following questions using these reports. Each question is independent of the others.

(a) If the price of grain decreases by $0.01 per kilo, will the optimal solution change?

(b) Which constraints are binding? Interpret the shadow price for the binding constraints.

(c) What would happen to the total cost if the price of the mineral product decreased by 20% from its current value?

(d) For what price range of oats is the current solution optimal?

4-20 Consider Kathy Moriyama's diet problem first presented in Chapter 3 as Problem 3-10. Use Solver to create the Answer and Sensitivity reports for this LP problem. Now answer the following questions using these reports. Each question is independent of the others.

(a) Interpret the shadow prices for the carbohydrate and iron constraints.

(b) What would happen to total cost if Kathy insisted on using milk in her diet?

(c) What is the maximum price for beans that would make it a cost-effective item for inclusion in the college diet?

(d) Is the solution to this problem a unique optimal solution? Justify your answer.

SCREENSHOT 4.7   **Solver Sensitivity Report for Problem 4-17**

Microsoft Excel 10.0 Sensitivity Report
Worksheet: [Book3]Sheet1

Adjustable Cells

Cell	Name	Final Value	Reduced Cost	Objective Coefficient	Allowable Increase	Allowable Decrease
$B$5	Number of Households <= 30 and large	0.00	0.60	7.5	1E+30	0.6
$C$5	Number of Households 31 - 50 and large	600.00	0.00	6.8	0.45	0.82
$D$5	Number of Households >= 51 and large	140.00	0.00	5.5	0.6	29.9
$E$5	Number of Households <= 30 and not large	1000.00	0.00	6.9	0.6	0.92
$F$5	Number of Households 31 - 50 and not large	0.00	0.45	7.25	1E+30	0.45
$G$5	Number of Households >= 51and not large	560.00	0.00	6.1	1.025	0.6

Constraints

Cell	Name	Final Value	Shadow Price	Constraint R.H. Side	Allowable Increase	Allowable Decrease
$H$12	>= 51 in Large	0.00	-0.60	0	560	140
$H$8	Total Households	2300.00	5.98	2300	1E+30	700
$H$9	<= 30 Households	1000.00	0.92	1000	700	1000
$H$10	31-50 Households	600.00	0.82	600	700	493.75
$H$11	Large Cities	395.00	0.00	0	395	1E+30

4-21 Consider Alta Electronics' product mix problem, first presented in Chapter 3 as Problem 3-11. Use Solver to create Answer and Sensitivity Reports for this LP problem. Now answer the following questions using these reports. Each question is independent of the others.

(a) How is Alta's optimal solution affected if the cost of material for the 60 GB external drives is increased by 50%?

(b) A new employee at Alta Electronics is assigned to work for 10 hours in department 2. How will this affect profit?

(c) The minimum production quantity for 30 GB hard drives is decreased from the current minimum of 20 units to a minimum of 10 units. How will this affect profit?

(d) Alta Electronics has the opportunity to increase the number of hours in department 1 by 10 hours in exchange for a decrease in the number of hours in department 2 of 50 hours. Is this deal worthwhile? Explain your answer.

4-22 Consider the following LP problem, in which X and Y denote the number of units of products X and Y to produce, respectively.

Maximize profit = $4X + 5Y$

subject to

$X + 2Y \le 10$ (Labour available in hours)
$6X + 6Y \le 36$ (Material available in kilograms)

SCREENSHOT 4.8

Solver Sensitivity Report for Problem 4-18

Microsoft Excel 10.0 Sensitivity Report
Worksheet: [Book4]Sheet1

Adjustable Cells

Cell	Name	Final Value	Reduced Cost	Objective Coefficient	Allowable Increase	Allowable Decrease
$B$5	Number of grams Food A	111.67	0.000	0.00080	0.001150	0.0000342
$C$5	Number of grams Food B	31.67	0.000	0.00075	0.000038	1E+30
$D$5	Number of grams Food C	106.67	0.000	0.00090	0.000325	0.0001438

Constraints

Cell	Name	Final Value	Shadow Price	Constraint R.H. Side	Allowable Increase	Allowable Decrease
$E$12	Total Mix	250.00	0.00020	250.00	26.4613	4.2449
$E$8	Vitamin A	261.67	0.00000	250.00	11.6667	1E+30
$E$9	Vitamin D	300.00	0.00038	300.00	13.5714	40.0000
$E$10	Iron	46.19	0.00000	12.00	34.1933	1E+30
$E$11	Zinc	1.00	0.04333	1.00	0.0279	0.0438

$8X + 4Y \leq 40$ (Storage available in square metres)

$X, Y \geq 0$

The Excel Answer and Sensitivity Reports for this problem are shown in Screenshot 4.9. Calculate and explain what happens to the optimal solution for each of the following situations. Each question is independent of the other questions.

(a) You acquire 2 additional kilograms of material.
(b) You acquire 1.5 additional hours of labour.
(c) You give up 1 hour of labour and get 1.5 kilograms of material.
(d) The profit contributions for both products X and Y are changed to $4.75 each.
(e) You decide to introduce a new product that has a profit contribution of $2. Each unit of this product will use 1 hour of labour, 1 kilogram of material, and 2 square metres of storage space.

4-23 The Good-to-Go Suitcase Company makes three styles of suitcase: (1) Standard, (2) Deluxe, and (3) Luxury. Each suitcase goes through four production stages: (1) cutting and colouring, (2) assembly, (3) finishing, and (4) quality and packaging. The total numbers of hours available in each of these departments are 630, 600, 708, and 135, respectively.

Each Standard suitcase requires 0.7 hours of cutting and colouring, 0.5 hours of assembly, 1 hour of finishing, and 0.1 hours of quality and packaging. The corresponding numbers for each Deluxe suitcase are 1 hour, 0.83 hours, 0.67 hours, and 0.25 hours, respectively. Likewise, the corresponding numbers for each Luxury suitcase are 1 hour, 0.67 hours, 0.9 hours, and 0.4 hours, respectively.

The sales revenues for each type of suitcase are as follows: Standard $36.05, Deluxe $39.50, and Luxury $43.30.

The material costs are: Standard $6.25, Deluxe $7.50, and Luxury $8.50. The hourly cost of labour is $10 for cutting and colouring, $6 for assembly, $9 for finishing, and $8 for quality assurance and packaging.

The Excel layout and LP Sensitivity Report of Good-to-Go's problem are shown in Screenshots 4.10A and 4.10B, respectively. Each of the following questions is independent of the others:

(a) What is the optimal production plan? Which of the resources are scarce?
(b) Suppose Good-to-Go is considering including a polishing process, the cost of which would be added directly to the price. Each Standard suitcase would require 10 minutes of time in this treatment, each Deluxe suitcase would need 15 minutes, and each Luxury suitcase would need 20 minutes. Would the current production plan change as a result of this additional process if 170 hours of polishing time were available? Explain your answer.
(c) Now consider the addition of a waterproofing process where each Standard suitcase would use 1 hour of time in the process, each Deluxe suitcase would use 1.5 hours, and each Luxury suitcase would use 1.75 hours. Would this change the production plan if 900 hours were available? Why or why not? (Source: Professors Mark and Judith McKnew, Clemson University.)

4-24 Suppose Good-to-Go (Problem 4-23) is considering the possible introduction of two new products to its line of suitcases: the Compact model (for teenagers) and the Kiddo model (for children). Market research suggests that Good-to-Go can sell the Compact model for no more than $30, whereas the Kiddo model would go for as much

Solver Sensitivity Report for Problem 4-22

Microsoft Excel 11.0 Sensitivity Report
Problem 4-22

Cell	Name	Final Value	Reduced Cost	Objective Coefficient	Allowable Increase	Allowable Decrease
$B$5	X	2.00	0.00	4.00	1.00	1.50
$C$5	Y	4.00	0.00	5.00	3.00	1.00

Constraints

Cell	Name	Final Value	Shadow Price	Constraint R.H. Side	Allowable Increase	Allowable Decrease
$D$7	Labour	10.00	1.00	10.00	2.00	2.00
$D$8	Material	36.00	0.50	36.00	4.00	6.00
$D$9	Storage	32.00	0.00	40.00	1E+30	8.00

SCREENSHOT 4.10A

Excel Layout for
Problem 4-23: Good-to-
Go Suitcase Company

	A	B	C	D	E	F	G	H
1	**Good-to-Go Suitcase Company**							
2								
3		Standard	Deluxe	Luxury				
4	Solution value	540	252	0				
5	Selling price per unit	$36.05	$39.50	$43.30	$29,421.00			
6	Material cost per unit	$6.25	$7.50	$8.50	$5,265.00			
7	Labour cost per unit	$19.80	$23.00	$25.30	$16,488.00			
8	Profit	$10.00	$9.00	$9.50	$7,668.00	<-- Objective		
9	Constraints							Cost
10	Cutting & Colouring	0.70	1.00	1.00	630.00	<=	630	$10
11	Assembly	0.50	0.83	0.67	480.00	<=	600	$6
12	Finishing	1.00	0.67	0.90	708.00	<=	708	$9
13	Quality & Packaging	0.10	0.25	0.40	117.00	<=	135	$8
14					LHS	Sign	RHS	
15								

as $37.50 to specialty toy stores. The amount of labour and the cost of raw materials for each possible new product are as follows:

COST CATEGORY	COMPACT	KIDDO
Cutting and colouring (h)	0.50	1.20
Assembly (h)	0.75	0.75
Finishing (h)	0.75	0.50
Quality and packaging (h)	0.20	0.20
Raw materials ($)	$5.00	$4.50

Use a pricing out strategy to check whether either model would be economically attractive to make.

4-25 The Strollers-to-Go Company makes lightweight umbrella-type strollers for three different groups of children. The TiniTote is designed specifically for newborns who require extra neck support. The ToddleTote is for toddlers up to 30 pounds. Finally, the company also produces a heavy-duty model called TubbyTote, which is designed to carry children up to 60 pounds. The stroller company is in the process of determining its production for each of the three types of strollers for the upcoming planning period.

The marketing department has forecast the following maximum demand for each of the strollers during the planning period: TiniTote 180, TubbyTote 70, and

SCREENSHOT 4.10B   Solver Sensitivity Report for Problem 4-23: Good-to-Go Suitcase Company

	A B	C	D	E	F	G	H
1	Microsoft Excel 10.0 Sensitivity Report						
2	Problem P4-23 Good-to-Go Suitcase Company						
3							
4	Adjustable Cells						
5			Final	Reduced	Objective	Allowable	Allowable
6	Cell	Name	Value	Cost	Coefficient	Increase	Decrease
7	$B$4	Solution value Standard	540	0	10	3.50	2.56
8	$C$4	Solution value Deluxe	252	0	9	5.29	1.61
9	$D$4	Solution value Luxury	0	-1.12	9.5	1.12	1E+30
10							
11	Constraints						
12			Final	Shadow	Constraint	Allowable	Allowable
13	Cell	Name	Value	Price	R.H. Side	Increase	Decrease
14	$E$10	Cutting & Colouring	630.00	4.38	630	52.36	134.40
15	$E$11	Assembly	480.00	0.00	600	1E+30	120.00
16	$E$12	Finishing	708.00	6.94	708	192.00	128.00
17	$E$13	Quality & Packaging	117.00	0.00	135	1E+30	18.00

ToddleTote 160. Strollers-to-Go sells TiniTotes for $63.75, TubbyTotes for $82.50, and ToddleTotes for $66.00. As a matter of policy, it wants to produce no less than 50% of the forecast demand for each product. It also wants to keep production of ToddleTotes to a maximum of 40% of total stroller production.

The production department has estimated that the material costs for TiniTote, TubbyTote, and ToddleTote strollers will be $4, $6, and $5.50 per unit, respectively. The strollers are processed through fabrication, sewing, and assembly workstations. The metal and plastic frames are made in the fabrication station. The fabric seats are cut and stitched together in the sewing station. Finally, the frames are put together with the seats in the assembly station. In the upcoming planning period, there will be 620 hours available in fabrication, where the direct labour cost is $8.25 per hour. The sewing station has 500 hours available, and the direct labour cost is $8.50 per hour. The assembly station has 480 hours available, and the direct labour cost is $8.75 per hour.

The standard processing rate for TiniTotes is 3 hours in fabrication, 2 hours in sewing, and 1 hour in assembly. TubbyTotes require 4 hours in fabrication, 1 hour in sewing and 3 hours in assembly, whereas ToddleTotes require 2 hours in each station.

The Excel layout and LP Sensitivity Report for Strollers-to-Go's problem are shown in Screenshots 4.11A and 4.11B on page 165, respectively. Each of the following questions is independent of the other.

(a) How many strollers of each type should Strollers-to-Go make? What is the profit? Which constraints are binding?

(b) How much labour time is being used in the fabrication, sewing, and assembly areas?

(c) How much would Strollers-to-Go be willing to pay for an additional hour of fabrication time? For an additional hour of sewing time?

(d) Is Strollers-to-Go producing any product at its maximum sales level? Is it producing any product at its minimum level? (Source: Professors Mark and Judith McKnew, Clemson University.)

4-26 Consider the Strollers-to-Go production problem (Problem 4-25).

(a) Over what range of costs could the TiniTote materials vary and the current production plan remain optimal? (*Hint*: How are material costs reflected in the problem formulation?)

(b) Suppose that Strollers-to-Go decided to polish each stroller prior to shipping. The process is fast and would require 10, 15, and 12 minutes, respectively, for TiniTote, TubbyTote, and ToddleTote strollers. Would this change the current production plan if 48 hours of polishing time were available?

4-27 Consider the Strollers-to-Go production problem (Problem 4-25).

(a) Suppose that Strollers-to-Go could purchase additional fabrication time at a cost of $10.50 per hour. Should it be interested? Why or why not? What is the most that it would be willing to pay for an additional hour of fabrication time?

(b) Further suppose that it could only purchase fabrication time in multiples of 40 hour bundles. How many should it be willing to purchase then?

4-28 Suppose that Strollers-to-Go (Problem 4-25) is considering the production of TwinTotes for those families that were doubly blessed. Each TwinTote would require $5.75 in materials, 3.5 hours of fabrication time, 1.75 hours of sewing time, and only 1.5 hours to assemble. Would this product be economically attractive to manufacture if the sales price was $72.00? Why or why not?

4-29 The Classic Furniture Company is trying to determine the optimal quantities to make of six possible products—tables and chairs made of oak, cherry, and pine. The products are to be made using the following resources: labour hours and three types of wood. Minimum production requirements are as follows: at least 3 each of oak and cherry tables, at least 10 each of oak and cherry chairs, and at least 5 pine chairs.

The Excel layout and LP Sensitivity Report for Classic Furniture's problem are shown in Screenshots 4.12A and 4.12B, respectively. The OFCs in the screenshots refer to unit profit per item. Answer the following questions, each of which is independent of the others.

(a) What is the profit represented by the objective function, and what is the production plan?

(b) Which constraints are binding?

(c) What is the range over which the unit profit for oak chairs can change without changing the production plan?

(d) What is the range over which the amount of available oak could range without changing the combination of binding constraints?

(e) Does this Sensitivity Report indicate the presence of multiple optimal solutions? How do you know?

(f) After production is over, how many pounds of cherry wood will be left over?

(g) According to this report, how many more chairs were made than were required?

4-30 Consider the Classic Furniture product mix problem (Problem 4-29). For each of the following situations, what would be the impact on the production plan and profit? If it is possible to compute the new profit or production plan, please do so.

(a) Unit profit for oak tables increased to $83.

(b) Unit profit for pine chairs decreased by $15.

(c) Unit profit for pine tables increased by $15.

(d) Unit profit for cherry tables increased to $95.

(e) Company was required to make at least 20 pine chairs.

(f) Company was required to make no more than 55 cherry chairs.

4-31 Consider the Classic Furniture product mix problem (Problem 4-29). For each of the following situations, what would be the impact on the production plan and profit? If it is possible to compute the new profit or production plan, please do so.

(a) Number of labour hours expanded to 1240.

(b) Amount of cherry wood increased to 4000.

(c) Number of labour hours decreased to 900.

(d) Company did not have a minimum requirement for oak chairs.

SCREENSHOT 4.11A

Excel Layout for
Problem 4-25: Strollers-
to-Go Company

	A	B	C	D	E	F	G	H
1	**Strollers-to-Go Company**							
2								
3		TiniTote	TubbyTote	ToddleTote				
4	Solution value	100	35	90				
5	Selling price per unit	$63.75	$82.50	$66.00	$15,202.50			
6	Material cost per unit	$4.00	$6.00	$5.50	$1,105.00			
7	Labour cost per unit	$50.50	$67.75	$51.00	$12,011.25			
8	Profit	$9.25	$8.75	$9.50	$2,086.25	<- Objective		
9	Constraints							Cost
10	Fabrication	3.0	4.0	2.0	620.00	<=	620	$8.25
11	Sewing	2.0	1.0	2.0	415.00	<=	500	$8.50
12	Assembly	1.0	3.0	2.0	385.00	<=	480	$8.75
13	TiniTote demand	1.0			100.00	<=	180	
14	TubbyTote demand		1.0		35.00	<=	70	
15	ToddleTote demand			1.0	90.00	<=	160	
16	ToddleTote max prod	-0.4	-0.4	0.6	0.00	<=	0	
17	TiniTote min prod	1.0			100.00	>=	90	
18	TubbyTote min prod		1.0		35.00	>=	35	
19	ToddleTote min prod			1.0	90.00	>=	80	
20					LHS	Sign	RHS	

SCREENSHOT 4.11B   Solver Sensitivity Report for Problem 4-25: Strollers-to-Go Company

Adjustable Cells

Cell	Name	Final Value	Reduced Cost	Objective Coefficient	Allowable Increase	Allowable Decrease
$B$4	Solution value TiniTote	100	0	9.25	5	3.33
$C$4	Solution value TubbyTote	35	0	8.75	4.10	1E+30
$D$4	Solution value ToddleTote	90	0	9.5	1E+30	3.33

Constraints

Cell	Name	Final Value	Shadow Price	Constraint R.H. Side	Allowable Increase	Allowable Decrease
$E$10	Fabrication	620.00	3.60	620.00	110.5	43.33
$E$11	Sewing	415.00	0.00	500.00	1E+30	85.00
$E$12	Assembly	385.00	0.00	480.00	1E+30	95.00
$E$13	TiniTote demand	100.00	0.00	180.00	1E+30	80.00
$E$14	TubbyTote demand	35.00	0.00	70.00	1E+30	35.00
$E$15	ToddleTote demand	90.00	0.00	160.00	1E+30	70.00
$E$16	ToddleTote max prod	0.00	3.85	0.00	13	8.67
$E$17	TiniTote min prod	100.00	0.00	90.00	10	1E+30
$E$18	TubbyTote min prod	35.00	-4.10	35.00	8.13	35.00
$E$19	ToddleTote min prod	90.00	0.00	80.00	10	1E+30

Microsoft Excel 10.0 Sensitivity Report
Problem 4-25. Strollers-to-Go Company

SCREENSHOT 4.12A

Excel Layout for
Problem 4-29: Classic
Furniture

◇	A	B	C	D	E	F	G	H	I	J
1	**Classic Furniture Company**									
2										
3		Oak tables	Oak chairs	Cherry tables	Cherry chairs	Pine tables	Pine chairs			
4	Nuber of units	3	51.67	3	85.56	42.26	33.08			
5	Profit	$75	$35	$90	$60	$45	$20	$10,000.00		
6	**Constraints**									
7	Labour hours	7.5	3.5	9.0	6.0	4.5	2.0	1000	<=	1000
8	Oak (pounds)	200	30					2150	<=	2150
9	Cherry (pounds)			240	36			3800	<=	3800
10	Pine (pounds)					180	27	8500	<=	8500
11	Min oak tables	1						3	>=	3
12	Min cherry tables			1				3	>=	3
13	Min oak chairs		1					51.67	>=	10
14	Min cherry chairs				1			85.56	>=	10
15	Min pine chairs						1	33.08	>=	5
16								LHS	Sign	RHS

SCREENSHOT 4.12B   Solver Sensitivity Report for Problem 4-29: Classic Furniture

	A B	C	D	E	F	G	H
1	Microsoft Excel 11.3 Sensitivity Report						
2	Problem 4-29. Classic Furniture Company						
5	Adjustable Cells						
6			Final	Reduced	Objective	Allowable	Allowable
7	Cell	Name	Value	Cost	Coefficient	Increase	Decrease
8	$B$4	Number of units Oak tables	3.00	0	75	0.00	1E+30
9	$C$4	Number of units Oak chairs	51.67	0	35	1E+30	0.00
10	$D$4	Number of units Cherry tables	3.00	0	90	0.00	1E+30
11	$E$4	Number of units Cherry chairs	85.56	0	60	1E+30	0.00
12	$F$4	Number of units Pine tables	42.26	0	45	88.33	0.00
13	$G$4	Number of units Pine chairs	33.08	0	20	0.00	13.25
15	Constraints						
16			Final	Shadow	Constraint	Allowable	Allowable
17	Cell	Name	Value	Price	R.H. Side	Increase	Decrease
18	$H$7	Labour hours	1000.00	10.00	1000.00	373.30	37.21
19	$H$8	Oak (pounds)	2150.00	0.00	2150.00	318.93	1250.00
20	$H$9	Cherry (pounds)	3800.00	0.00	3800.00	223.25	2239.78
21	$H$10	Pine (pounds)	8500.00	0.00	8500.00	1488.33	5039.50
22	$H$11	Min oak tables	3.00	0.00	3.00	6.25	2.35
23	$H$12	Min cherry tables	3.00	0.00	3.00	11.33	1.20
24	$H$13	Min oak chairs	51.67	0.00	10.00	41.67	1E+30
25	$H$14	Min cherry chairs	85.56	0.00	10.00	75.56	1E+30
26	$H$15	Min pine chairs	33.08	0.00	5.00	28.08	1E+30

4-32 Consider the Classic Furniture product mix problem (Problem 4-29). For each of the following situations, what would be the impact on the production plan and profit? If it is possible to compute the new profit or production plan, please do so.

(a) OFCs for oak tables and cherry tables each decreased by $15.

(b) OFCs for oak tables and oak chairs were reversed.

(c) OFCs for pine tables and pine chairs were reversed.

(d) OFC$_{Pine Table}$ increased by $20, while at the same time OFC$_{Pine Chair}$ decreased by $10.

(e) Unit profit for all three types of chairs increased by $6 each.

4-33 Consider the Classic Furniture product mix problem (Problem 4-29). In answering each of the following questions, be as specific as possible. If it is possible to compute a new profit or production plan, please do so.

(a) A part-time employee who works 25 hours per week decides to quit his job. How would this affect the profit and production plan?

(b) Classic has been approached by the factory next door, CabinetsRUs, which has a shortage of both labour and oak. CabinetsRUs proposes to take one full-time employee (who works 35 hours) plus 1200 pounds of oak. It has offered $880 as compensation. Should Classic make this trade?

(c) Classic is considering adding a new product, a cherry armoire. The armoire would consume 450 pounds of cherry wood and take 15 hours of labour. Cherry wood costs $6 per pound, and labour costs $12 per hour. The armoire would sell for $3000. Should this product be made?

(d) What would happen to the solution if a constraint were added to make sure that for every table made, at least two matching chairs were made?

4-34 The Tiger Catering Company is trying to determine the most economical combination of sandwiches to make for a tennis club. The club has asked Tiger to provide 70 sandwiches in a variety that includes tuna, tuna and cheese, ham, ham and cheese, and cheese. The club has specified a minimum of 10 each of tuna and ham, and 12 each of tuna/cheese and ham/cheese. Tiger makes the sandwiches, using the following resources: bread, tuna, ham, cheese, mayonnaise, mustard, lettuce, tomato, packaging material, and labour hours.

The Excel Layout and LP Sensitivity Report for Tiger's problem are shown in Screenshots 4.13A and 4.13B, respectively. The OFCs in the screenshots refer to unit cost per item. Answer the following questions, each of which is independent of the others.

(a) What is the cost represented by the objective function, and what is the sandwich-making plan?

(b) Which constraints are binding?

(c) What is the range over which the cost for cheese sandwiches could vary without changing the production plan?

(d) What is the range over which the quantity of tuna could vary without changing the combination of binding constraints?

(e) Does this Sensitivity Report indicate the presence of multiple optimal solutions? How do you know?

(f) After the sandwiches are made, how many labour hours remain?

4-35 Consider the Tiger Catering problem (Problem 4-34). For each of the following situations, what would be the impact on the sandwich-making plan and total cost? If it is possible to compute the new cost or sandwich-making plan, please do so.

(a) Unit cost for tuna sandwiches increased by $0.50.

(b) Unit cost for tuna and cheese sandwiches decreased to $2.00.

(c) Unit cost for ham sandwiches increased to $3.75.

(d) Unit cost for ham and cheese sandwiches decreased by $0.60.

(e) Club did not want any more than 14 ham sandwiches.

(f) Unit cost for cheese sandwiches increased to $2.15.

4-36 Consider the Tiger Catering problem (Problem 4-34). For each of the following situations, what would be the impact on the sandwich-making plan and total cost? If it is possible to compute the new cost or sandwich-making plan, please do so.

(a) Quantity of tuna available decreased to 3600 grams.

(b) Quantity of bread available increases to 150 slices.

(c) Quantity of ham available decreases to 2000 grams.

(d) Tiger is required to deliver a minimum of 65 sandwiches.

SCREENSHOT 4.13A   **Excel Layout for Problem 4-34: Tiger Catering**

	A	B	C	D	E	F	G	H	I
1	**Tiger Catering Company**								
2									
3		Tuna	Tuna/Cheese	Ham	Ham/Cheese	Cheese			
4	Number to make	10	30	10	12	8			
5	Cost	$2.42	$2.12	$3.35	$3.02	$2.05	$173.94		
6	Constraints								
7	Bread (slices)	2	2	2	2	2	140	<=	140
8	Tuna (g)	110	80				3500	<=	4000
9	Ham (g)			110	80		2060	<=	3000
10	Cheese (g)		30		30	120	2220	<=	3000
11	Mayo (g)	35	25	14	14	14	1520	<=	2000
12	Mustard (g)			5	5		110	<=	250
13	Lettuce (g)	7	7	7	7	7	490	<=	500
14	Tomato (g)	14	14	14	14	14	980	<=	1000
15	Package (unit)	1	1	1	1	1	70	<=	70
16	Labour (hours)	0.08	0.08	0.08	0.08	0.08	5.6	<=	10
17	Min total	1	1	1	1	1	70	>=	70
18	Min Tuna	1					10	>=	10
19	Min Tuna/Ch		1				30	>=	30
20	Min Ham			1			10	>=	10
21	Min Ham/Ch				1		12	>=	12
22							LHS	Sign	RHS

SCREENSHOT 4.13B

Solver Sensitivity Report for Problem 4-34: Tiger Catering

Microsoft Excel 10.0 Sensitivity Report
Problem 4-34 Tiger Catering Company

Adjustable Cells

Cell	Name	Final Value	Reduced Cost	Objective Coefficient	Allowable Increase	Allowable Decrease
$B$4	Number to make Tuna	10.00	0.00	2.42	1E+30	0.37
$C$4	Number to make Tuna/Cheese	30.00	0.00	2.12	1E+30	0.07
$D$4	Number to make Ham	10.00	0.00	3.35	1E+30	1.30
$E$4	Number to make Ham/Cheese	12.00	0.00	3.02	1E+30	0.97
$F$4	Number to make Cheese	8.00	0.00	2.05	0.07	2.05

Constraints

Cell	Name	Final Value	Shadow Price	Constraint R.H. Side	Allowable Increase	Allowable Decrease
$G$17	Min total	70.00	2.05	70.00	0.00	8.00
$G$18	Min Tuna	10.00	0.37	10.00	4.55	6.50
$G$19	Min Tuna/Ch	30.00	0.07	30.00	6.25	8.67
$G$20	Min Ham	10.00	1.30	10.00	8.00	6.50
$G$21	Min Ham/Ch	12.00	0.97	12.00	8.00	8.67
$G$7	Bread (slices)	140.00	0.00	140.00	1E+30	0.00
$G$8	Tuna (g)	3500.00	0.00	4000.00	1E+30	500.00
$G$9	Ham (g)	2060.00	0.00	3000.00	1E+30	940.00
$G$10	Cheese (g)	2220.00	0.00	3000.00	1E+30	780.00
$G$11	Mayo (g)	1520.00	0.00	2000.00	1E+30	480.00
$G$12	Mustard (g)	110.00	0.00	250.00	1E+30	140.00
$G$13	Lettuce (g)	490.00	0.00	500.00	1E+30	10.00
$G$14	Tomato (g)	980.00	0.00	1000.00	1E+30	20.00
$G$15	Package (unit)	70.00	0.00	70.00	1E+30	0.00
$G$16	Labour (hours)	5.60	0.00	10.00	1E+30	4.40

(e) Tiger is required to deliver a minimum of 16 ham sandwiches.

4-37 Consider the Tiger Catering problem (Problem 4-34). For each of the following situations, what would be the impact on the sandwich-making plan and total cost? If it is possible to compute the new cost or sandwich-making plan, please do so.

(a) Cost of ham sandwiches and cost of ham and cheese sandwiches each decreased by $0.35.

(b) Cost of both ham and cheese sandwiches and cheese sandwiches increased by $0.05.

(c) Cost of tuna decreased by $0.001 per gram. (*Hint:* Note that tuna sandwiches use 110 grams of tuna and tuna/cheese sandwiches use 80 grams of tuna.)

(d) Availability of tuna decreases by 400 grams and availability of cheese increases by 250 grams.

(e) A 250 gram jar of mustard is sent by mistake, instead of a 250 gram jar of mayonnaise. (*Hint:* This would decrease the available quantity of mayonnaise by 250 grams and increase the quantity of mustard by 250 grams.)

4-38 Consider the Tiger Catering problem (Problem 4-34). In answering each of the following problems, be as specific as possible. If it is possible to compute a new cost or sandwich-making plan, please do so.

(a) An additional kilogram of tuna can be purchased for $5.00. Should this tuna be purchased? Explain your answer.

(b) The tennis club is willing to accept fewer ham sandwiches. How many ham sandwiches would Tiger try to substitute with other types before it would not be able to predict its new total cost?

(c) The tennis club wants to include a dill pickle slice with each sandwich containing tuna or ham. If Tiger finds an average of 18 pickle slices in a 500 gram jar, how many jars should be included with the club's order?

⇒ CASE STUDY 4.1

Red Brand Canners

Red Brand Canners is a classic case in sensitivity analysis. Originally developed at Leland Stanford Junior University in 1965, the case has been reproduced in several textbooks and remains a popular and insightful illustration of sensitivity analysis in LP We include it here both for its pedagogical value and its historical interest.

On Monday, September 13, 1965, Mitchell Gordon, vice president of operations, asked the controller, the sales manager, and the production manager to meet with him to discuss the amount of tomato products to pack that season. The tomato crop, which had been purchased at planting, was beginning to arrive at the cannery, and packing operations would have to be started by the following Monday. Red

Brand Canners is a medium-sized company that cans and distributes a variety of fruit and vegetable products under private brands in the western states.

William Cooper, the controller, and Charles Myers, the sales manager, were the first to arrive in Gordon's office. Dan Tucker, the production manager, came in a few minutes later and said that he had picked up Produce Inspection's latest estimate of the quality of the incoming tomatoes. According to the report, about 20% of the crop was grade A quality, and the remaining portion of the 3-million-pound crop was grade B.

Gordon asked Myers about the demand for tomato products for the coming year. Myers replied that they could sell all of the whole canned tomatoes they could produce. The expected demand for tomato juice and tomato paste, on the other hand, was limited. The sales manager then passed around the latest demand forecast, which is shown in Table 4.3. He reminded the group that the selling prices had been set in light of the long-term marketing strategy of the company and that the potential sales had been forecast at these prices. Bill Cooper, after looking at Myers's estimates of demand, said that it looked as if the company "should do quite well [on the tomato crop] this year." With the new accounting system that had been set up, he had been able to compute the contribution for each product, and according to his analysis the incremental profit on whole tomatoes was greater than the incremental profit on any other tomato product. In May, after Red Brand had signed contracts agreeing to purchase the grower's production at an average delivered price of 6 cents per pound, Cooper had computed the tomato products' contributions (see Table 4.4).

Dan Tucker brought to Cooper's attention that although there was ample production capacity, it was impossible to produce all whole tomatoes because too small a portion of the tomato crop was "grade A" quality. Red Brand used a numerical scale to record the quality of both raw produce and prepared products. This scale ran from 0 to 10, the higher number representing better quality. According to this scale, grade A tomatoes averaged nine points per pound and grade B tomatoes averaged five points per pound. Tucker noted that the minimum average input quality was eight points per pound for canned whole tomatoes and six points

per pound for juice. Paste could be made entirely from grade B tomatoes. This meant that whole-tomato production was limited to 800 000 pounds.

Gordon stated that this was not a real limitation. He had been solicited recently to purchase 80 000 pounds of grade A tomatoes at $8\frac{1}{2}$ cents per pound and at that time had turned down the offer. He felt, however, that the tomatoes were still available.

Myers, who had been doing some calculations, said that although he agreed that the company "should do quite well this year," it would not be by canning whole tomatoes. It seemed to him that the tomato cost should be allocated on the basis of quality and quantity rather than by quantity only, as Cooper had done. Therefore, he had recomputed the marginal profit on this basis (see Table 4.5) and from his results had concluded that Red Brand should use 2 million pounds of the grade B tomatoes for paste, and the remaining 400 000 pounds of grade B tomatoes and all of the grade A tomatoes for juice. If the demand expectations were realized, a contribution of $48 000 would be made on this year's tomato crop.

DISCUSSION QUESTIONS

1. Structure this problem verbally, including a written description of the constraints and the objective function. What are the decision variables?
2. Develop a mathematical formulation of the LP model for Red Brand's problem.
3. Solve the LP model using Excel and discuss the results. Use the Answer and Sensitivity Reports for Red Brand's LP model to answer the following questions. Each question is independent of the others.
4. Which constraints are binding?
5. Should Gordon reconsider the offer of 80 000 pounds of grade A tomatoes at $8\frac{1}{2}$ cents per pound? If so, what is its impact on profit?
6. Gordon thinks that Myers, the sales manager, may be underestimating the demand of all tomato products by as much as 5% each. If Gordon is right, what would be the impact on the optimal profit?
7. Red Brand Canners' sister concern, Red Label Ketchup Company, has an excess of grade B tomatoes but is severely short of grade A tomatoes. Joan Yu, vice president

TABLE 4.3	PRODUCT	SELLING PRICE PER CASE ($)	DEMAND FORECAST (CASES)
Demand Forecasts			
	24—2½ whole tomatoes	4.00	800 000
	24—2½ choice peach halves	5.40	10 000
	24—2½ peach nectar	4.60	5 000
	24—2½ tomato juice	4.50	50 000
	24—2½ cooking apples	4.90	15 000
	24—2½ tomato paste	3.80	80 000

TABLE 4.4	Product Item Profitability					
PRODUCT	24—2½ WHOLE TOMATOES	24—2½ CHOICE PEACH HALVES	24—2½ PEACH JUICE	24—2½ TOMATO JUICE	24—2½ COOKING APPLES	24—2½ TOMATO PASTE
Selling price	$4.00	$5.40	$4.60	$4.50	$4.90	$3.80
Variable cost						
Direct labour	1.18	1.40	1.27	1.32	0.70	0.54
Variable overhead	0.24	0.32	0.23	0.36	0.22	0.26
Variable selling	0.40	0.30	0.40	0.85	0.28	0.38
Packaging material	0.70	0.56	0.60	0.65	0.70	0.77
Fruit*	1.08	1.80	1.70	1.20	0.90	1.50
Total variable costs	3.60	4.38	4.20	4.38	2.80	3.45
Contribution	0.40	1.02	0.40	0.12	1.10	0.35
Less allocated overhead	0.28	0.70	0.52	0.21	0.75	0.23
Net profit	$0.12	$0.32	$(0.12)	$(0.09)	$0.35	$0.12

*Product usage is as follows:

Product	Pounds per Case
Whole tomatoes	18
Peach halves	18
Peach nectar	17
Tomato juice	20
Cooking apples	27
Tomato paste	25

Z = cost per pound of grade A tomatoes in cents

Y = cost per pound of grade B tomatoes in cents

$$(600\ 000\ \text{lb} \times Z) + (2\ 400\ 000\ \text{lb} \times Y) = (3\ 000\ 000\ \text{lb} \times 6) \quad (1)$$

$$\frac{Z}{9} = \frac{Y}{5} \quad (2)$$

implies Z = 9.32 cents per pound

Y = 5.18 cents per pound

TABLE 4.5				
Marginal Analysis of Tomato Products	PRODUCT	CANNED WHOLE TOMATOES	TOMATO JUICE	TOMATO PASTE
	Selling price	$4.00	$4.50	$3.80
	Variable cost (excluding tomato cost)	2.52	3.18	1.95
		$1.48	$1.32	$1.85
	Tomato cost	1.49	1.24	1.30
	Marginal profit	($0.01)	$0.08	$0.55

of operations at Red Label, called Gordon this morning with an offer to make the following trade: 100 000 pounds of grade A tomatoes to Red Label in exchange for 200 000 pounds of grade B tomatoes to Red Brand. Should Gordon accept the trade? Why or why not?

Source: "Red Brand Canners," revised with permission of Stanford University, Graduate School of Business, Copyright © 1969 and 1977 by the Board of Trustees of the Leland Stanford Junior University.

⇒ CASE STUDY 4.2

Vytec Corporation: Warehouse Layout Planning

During one of his customary walks through Vytec's warehouse, Operations Analyst James Van Brenk noticed a high-demand product at the far end of the warehouse. It appeared that high-demand products should be stored in locations with easy access to the shipping docks. Since Van Brenk was responsible for problem identification, analysis and solution implementation, this appeared to be a simple problem with an easy solution.

His first reaction was to move the product closer to the main shipping docks, reducing the time and distance required to retrieve the product for shipping. Doing so, however, would displace another product that should also be near the docks. Further research into the problem revealed many other issues. The problem was not as simple as it first appeared.

VYTEC CORPORATION

Vytec Corporation (Vytec, www.vytec.com), a subsidiary of Owens Corning, first opened for business in 1962 as Anden Holdings in London, Ontario, and expanded rapidly to serve markets in Canada, the United States, Australia, New Zealand and Europe. Vytec emerged as a leading manufacturer of top quality, innovative, vinyl siding products, joining Owens Corning (well-known for its "Pink Panther" and "Pink Insulation") in 1997.

Vytec designed, formulated, engineered, and manufactured its own line of products for home remodellers, builders, and homeowners worldwide. The company manufactured more than 50 different variations ("profiles") of siding, soffit, and accessories. Siding was installed on exterior walls, soffit on overhangs, and accessories were used to finish corners and fill around windows and doors. Each profile was typically available in 15 colours, creating a catalogue of more than 750 stock keeping units (SKUs).

THE MANUFACTURING PROCESS

Vinyl siding was manufactured from vinyl resin, which was combined with additives and modifiers to create different properties of the final product, including colour, flexibility, ultravio-

let (UV) resistance, and numerous other attributes. After the raw materials were mixed, the resulting compound was heated and extruded through a die into one of the profiles and then cut to length.

The finished product was packaged in corrugated cardboard cartons. The average carton held 20 pieces of 3.85 metre (12 foot) long vinyl siding. Cartons were then placed on stackable steel racks or "beds."

THE FINISHED GOODS WAREHOUSE

Production Hold

The beds could hold between 32 and 60 cartons of siding, depending on the particular product and size of the carton. Once full, the beds were immediately conveyed to the "Production Hold" area. This area bordered both the extrusion area and the finished goods warehouse. Forklifts driven by warehouse personnel emptied the hold area arbitrarily several times per day by transferring product, one bed at a time, to its appropriate location in the warehouse.

Warehouse

The finished goods warehouse occupied more than 200 000 square feet. It had been built in many phases over the years, as warehouse requirements increased. Some expansions had incorporated surrounding buildings into the warehouse creating a floor space that was a labyrinth of walls and aisles.

The warehouse was arranged into 15 different locations, each holding 15 different product groups of siding and soffit. Accessories were kept at an offsite warehouse and shipped daily to the finished goods warehouse as orders required.

Shipping

Product was shipped in one of two ways: "from the docks" or "palletized." Each method used different areas, loaded product differently, and utilized different shipping methods.

The majority of products were shipped from the docks. At the docks, several hundred cartons were loaded onto a covered trailer by five warehouse workers per truck. At times these

Richard Ivey School of Business
The University of Western Ontario

James Van Brenk prepared this case under the supervision of Professor Peter C. Bell solely to provide material for class discussion. The authors do not intend to illustrate either effective or ineffective handling of a managerial situation. The authors may have disguised certain names and other identifying information to protect confidentiality. Ivey Management Services prohibits any form of reproduction, storage or transmittal without its written permission. This material is not covered under authorization from CanCopy or any reproduction rights organization. To order copies or request permission to reproduce materials, contact Ivey Publishing, Ivey Management Services, c/o Richard Ivey School of Business, The University of Western Ontario, London, Ontario, Canada, N6A 3K7; phone (519) 661-3208; fax (519) 661-3882; e-mail cases@ivey.uwo.ca. Copyright © 2003, Ivey Management Services; Version: (A) 2003-05-21

workers waited for the forklift to return with more product to load. When the customer received the shipment, they also unloaded the product by hand.

Some customers either did not have the proper docks or preferred to unload using a forklift. For these customers, product was crated. This was done in the palletizing area of the warehouse. A wooden crate was manufactured and filled with an average of 20 cartons. Eighteen crates were then loaded on a flatbed trailer for delivery to the customer. When the customer received the shipment, it was unloaded by forklift.

Product Location

There were 15 storage locations, each holding a different product line. Some products required more area than others because of high product demand, or a broad range of colour offerings in that particular line. Over time, the storage locations evolved to reflect physical expansion as well as product line changes. New warehouse space was quickly filled with products, and any alterations in product lines were stored in any available spaces. Some effort was made to keep a few perceived high-demand products closest to the docks. Current product location in the warehouse had, therefore, developed through an incremental rather than a planned approach.

PLANNING A NEW WAREHOUSE LAYOUT

Van Brenk collected two sets of data: warehouse information and product flow information (see Table 4.6).

Locations, identified by the product they held, were measured (in feet) by their distance to the hold area, the docks, and palletizing. The capacity of each location was measured by the number of beds it could hold. Since products were not always fully stocked and locations could also expand slightly into aisles if required, it was estimated that any location could be over capacity by 25 per cent. This meant that a product in an area capable of holding 125 beds could fit into a location meant for 100 beds. Additionally, two more locations could be freed up for storage if it was deemed beneficial: one was in the palletizing area, the other in the maintenance area.

To determine product movement, production and shipping statistics were collected. Production reports provided information on product mix and volume, from which the number of trips from the hold area to individual locations could be determined for a typical two-week period.

Shipping data were gathered by collecting two weeks of orders from three months of data. Two Mondays were selected at random, two Tuesdays, etc. This was done to mirror the weekly activity while also attempting to smooth any abnormal weeks.

The number of trips to different locations was calculated from the last three months' orders using heuristics given by the forklift drivers. It was felt that the past three months were representative of annual activity. In all cases, the number of trips included round trips.

TABLE 4.6

Warehouse and Product Data

ch04_ivey_7B03E013.xls

PRODUCT	AREA	BED CAPACITY	DISTANCE TO HOLD AREA	DISTANCE TO DOCK	DISTANCE TO PALLETIZING	NUMBER OF TRIPS HOLD AREA	NUMBER OF TRIPS DOCK	NUMBER OF TRIPS PALLETIZING
BVIII	A	40	128	59	351	74	70	—
6.5" Nantucket	O	42	396	458	781	16	5	3
Proside White D4.5, DLD4.5	B	48	262	90	536	13	116	12
UVS	G	60	377	249	113	17	29	10
Prestige D4.5	L	90	618	553	876	56	199	—
Board and Batten	M	90	718	653	976	47	108	17
Shurlock	K	96	663	598	921	28	11	—
Vytec T3.0	N	105	716	651	974	66	112	—
Cedar Glen	F	108	411	362	79	57	90	33
Nantucket D5	C	131	324	191	598	83	201	—
Eminence	I	160	138	200	523	103	83	39
Vertical/Soffitt	D	195	141	90	304	103	161	22
Wellington Square DLD	J	214	258	306	629	177	324	11
Proside	E	225	266	144	392	118	387	41
Prestige D5DL, DLD4.5	H	248	99	120	523	205	370	58
OTHER AREAS AVAILABLE								
Palletizing Available	P	60	377	249	113			
Maintenance Available	Q	42	269	331	654			

IMPROVING THE LAYOUT OF THE WAREHOUSE

Van Brenk's hopes for a simple solution had long since vanished. The traditional strategy of locating the most popular products nearest to the shipping docks was simple; however, Van Brenk sensed that it was suboptimal. He was eager to determine a better layout for the warehouse that would reduce fuel costs, travel time, and labour costs, and was confident that he could find some improvements. What he was less sure about was whether the improved system would be worth the additional effort every time there was a change in demand or product mix.

He would know more and be able to make a better decision after analyzing some of the information he had gathered.

DISCUSSION QUESTION

Do you think it would be worth implementing a new layout? If so, what would you suggest?

⇒ CASE STUDY 4.3

Airy Dairy: Part I

Jones Family Farm of British Columbia has a herd of 150 milk cows. At any given time 120 of the cows are actively producing milk. The herd consists entirely of Holsteins, the breed that comprises about 95% of milk-producing cows in Canada. Average daily milk production is 27 litres per cow.

Two enterprising young MBA graduates, Bruno and Mario, who are looking for a business opportunity, establish Airy Dairy, a local dairy that, initially, will process raw milk and resell it in 1-litre containers. They have signed an exclusive contract with Jones Family Farm to purchase all their raw milk at a price of $72 per hectolitre. (1 hectolitre (hL) = 100 litres)

Raw milk is 3.5% cream and can be processed (by pasteurization, etc.) to produce whole milk (3.5% cream), reduced fat milk (2% cream), and skim milk (a negligible trace of cream). Each hectolitre of whole milk will contain 3.5 litres of cream and 96.5 litres of skim milk. Similarly, a hectolitre of 2% milk will contain 2 litres of cream and 98 litres of skim milk.

Airy Dairy has surveyed local area merchants and found that it can sell whole milk in 1-litre containers at $1.10 per litre, 2% milk at $1.05 per litre, and skim milk at $0.95 per litre. After separating the milk from the cream for the production of skim milk and 2% milk, the dairy will have residual unused cream that it can sell at $2.00 per litre.

Bruno and Mario have already decided that all the available raw milk purchased from the Jones Family Farm will be processed every day. They now have to decide how many 1-litre containers of each type of milk, including cream, to package in order to maximize daily profit.

A survey of local demand for milk reveals that the dairy should produce at least 400 litres each of whole milk and 2% milk, and at least 200 litres of skim milk daily. However the amount of 2% milk should not exceed 500 litres daily. Production and demand constraints also require that the amount of 2% milk produced should not exceed twice the quantity of whole milk. Also, the amount of skim milk produced should be equivalent to at least two-thirds of the amount of 2% milk.

QUESTIONS FOR AIRY DAIRY: PART I

1. Formulate an LP model to determine the optimal production quantities for the various products. *Hint:* Define the following decision variables.

   X_W = the number of litres of whole milk to produce

   X_R = the number of litres of reduced fat (2%) milk to produce

   X_S = the number of litres of skim milk to produce

   X_C = the number of litres of cream to produce

2. Specify the optimal solution. How many 1-litre containers of each type of milk should Airy Dairy produce daily? How many 1-litre containers of cream should be produced? What is the dairy's maximum daily revenue? What is the daily profit after subtracting the cost of purchasing the raw milk from the Jones farm?

3. If one of the milk-producing cows at Jones Farm cannot produce milk for several days, how will this affect Airy Dairy's profit for each day that the cow is not producing milk?

4. If the minimum 2% milk requirement is increased by 20%, determine the profit.

5. The selling price for skim milk goes up by $0.10. How will this affect the optimal solution? What is the new value of profit?

6. The minimum requirement for skim milk is 200 litres. How will a change in this lower limit affect profit? Specify the change in profit per unit in the right-hand side of the constraint, and also the range within which this change in profit is valid. Explain your conclusion in your own words.

7. What percentage of total daily revenue can be attributed to either 2% or skim milk?

8. A neighbouring farm that specializes in the production of butter uses all its cream to manufacture butter but has a surplus of skim milk. It offers to sell 400 litres of skim milk to Airy Dairy at $0.90 a litre. Should Airy Dairy accept this offer? How would revenue be affected?

PRODUCT	QUANTITY	WHOLE MILK	2% MILK	SKIM MILK	CREAM
Cheddar Cheese	500 grams	5 litres			
Fat-Free Cottage Cheese	500 grams			3 litres	
Yogurt	500 millilitres		0.5 litre		
Butter	250 grams				0.25 litres

Airy Dairy: Part II

Mario and Bruno have decided to expand the line of dairy products produced by Airy Dairy. They are planning to add

- Cheddar cheese – 500 gram vacuum packed slabs
- Fat-free cottage cheese – 500 gram containers
- Yogurt – 500 mL containers
- Butter – 250 gram slabs

The table above shows the quantities of the different milk products that are required to produce the four items.

Bruno and Mario have estimated that they can sell the cheddar cheese for $4.50 per slab, the cottage cheese for $3.25 per container, the yogurt for $2.50 per container, and the butter for $2.75 per slab. Initial conservative estimates indicate that demand is at least 100 units of each item. However, local demand suggests that no more than 1000 containers of yogurt should be produced.

A final production constraint requires that at least 20% of available skim milk should be used in the production of cheese products. All constraints specified in Airy Dairy: Part I are still in effect.

QUESTIONS FOR AIRY DAIRY: PART II

1. Formulate an LP model for Airy Dairy with the goal of maximizing revenue from the original milk products (whole milk, 2% milk, skim milk, and cream), in addition to the four new products listed in the table above.

2. Specify the optimal solution. How many units of each product should be produced? What is the dairy's maximum daily revenue?

3. What percentage of the total maximum revenue is contributed by the four new products: cheddar cheese, cottage cheese, yogurt, and butter?

4. Cottage cheese is currently in the optimal solution. At what selling price would you first consider reducing the amount of cottage cheese in the solution? If the selling price of cottage cheese drops to the point where it is no longer desirable to include it in the optimal product mix, would you continue to produce cottage cheese? If so, how much would you produce?

5. In the optimal solution, no cream is to be sold. Provide an explanation for this result. If Mario and Bruno decide to ignore this optimal decision and to produce some cream, specify the impact this decision will have on the optimal solution. Be as specific as possible.

6. If the minimum requirement for 2% milk is decreased by 25%, how will this affect daily revenue?

7. One of the constraints requires that at least 20% of skim milk should be used in the production of cheese products. By how much is the goal exceeded in the optimal solution?

8. The maximum yogurt constraint requires the production of at most 1000 containers of yogurt for local demand. If Mario and Bruno learn of a neighbouring community that will purchase an unlimited quantity of yogurt at $2.50 per container, use the sensitivity output from Solver to determine how many containers of yogurt should be produced, and specify the resulting revenue.

BIBLIOGRAPHY

Bermon, Stuart, and Sarah Jean Hood. "Capacity Optimization Planning System (CAPS)," *Interfaces* 29, 5 (September 1999): 31–50.

Desrosiers, Jacques et al. "Air Transat Uses ALTITUDE to Manage its Aircraft Routing, Crew Pairing, and Work Assignment" *Interfaces* 30 (March–April, 2000): 41–53.

Eliman, A. A., M. Girgis, and S. Kotob. "A Solution to Post-Crash Debt Entanglements in Kuwait's al-Manakh Stock Market," *Interfaces* 27, 1 (January–February 1997): 89–106.

Ferris, M. C., and A. B. Philpott. "On the Performance of Karmarkar's Algorithm," *Journal of the Operational Research Society,* 39 (March 1988): 257–270.

Fletcher, L. Russell, Henry Alden, Scott P. Holmen, Dean P. Angelides, and Matthew J. Etzenhouser. "Long-Term Forest Ecosystem Planning at Pacific Lumber," *Interfaces* 29, 1 (January 1999): 90–111.

Gass, S. I. *An Illustrated Guide to Linear Programming.* New York: Dover Publications, Inc., 1990.

Gautier, Antoine, Bernard F. Lamond, Daniel Pare, and François Rouleau. "The Quebec Ministry of Natural Resources Uses Linear Programming to Understand the Wood-Fiber Market," *Interfaces* 30, 6 (November 2000): 32–48.

Greenberg, H. J. "How to Analyze the Results of Linear Programs—Part 1: Preliminaries." *Interfaces* 23, 4 (July–August 1993): 56–68.

_____. "How to Analyze the Results of Linear Programs—Part 3: Infeasibility Diagnosis," *Interfaces* 23, 6 (November–December 1993): 120–139.

Leach, Howard. "Optimizing the Resources for Several Mills/Products," Presented to the Canadian Woodlands Forum Workshop, "Optimizing Softwood Log Quality," (May 23–24, 2001). Fredericton, N.B., Canada.

Lyon, Peter, R. John Milne, Robert Orzell, and Robert Rice. "Matching Assets with Demand in Supply-Chain Management at IBM Microelectronics," *Interfaces* 31, 1 (January 2001): 108–124.

Orden, A. "LP from the '40s to the '90s," *Interfaces* 23, 5 (September–October 1993): 2–12.

Quinn, P., B. Andrews, and H. Parsons. "Allocating Telecommunications Resources at L. L. Bean, Inc.," *Interfaces* 21, 1 (January–February 1991): 75–91.

Saltzman, M. J. "Survey: Mixed Integer Programming," *OR/MS Today* 21, 2 (April 1994): 42–51.

Schindler, S., and T. Semmel. "Station Staffing at Pan American World Airways," *Interfaces* 23, 3 (May–June 1993): 91–98.

Sexton, T. R., S. Sleeper, and R. E. Taggart, Jr. "Improving Pupil Transportation in North Carolina," *Interfaces* 24, 1 (January–February 1994): 87–104.

Zappe, C., W. Webster, and I. Horowitz. "Using Linear Programming to Determine Post-Facto Consistency in Performance Evaluations of Major League Baseball Players," *Interfaces* 23, 6 (November–December 1993): 107–119.

CHAPTER 5

Transportation, Assignment, and Network Models

LEARNING OBJECTIVES

After completing this chapter, students will be able to

1. Structure special LP network flow models.

2. Set up and solve transportation models, using Excel's Solver to determine the minimum-cost shipping routes in a network.

3. Extend the basic transportation model to include transshipment points.

4. Set up and solve facility location and other application problems as transportation models.

5. Set up and solve maximal-flow network models using Excel's Solver.

6. Set up and solve shortest-path network models, using Excel's Solver.

7. Connect all points of a network while minimizing total distance, using the minimal-spanning tree model.

CHAPTER OUTLINE

5.1 Introduction

5.2 Characteristics of Network Flow Problems

5.3 Transportation Model

5.4 Facility Location Analysis

5.5 Transshipment Model

5.6 Assignment Model

5.7 Maximal-Flow Model

5.8 Shortest-Path Model

5.9 Minimal-Spanning Tree Model

Summary • Glossary • Key Equation • Solved Problems • Self-Test • Discussion Questions and Problems • Case Study: Ste-Agathe Wood Store • Case Study: Custom Vans of Canada, Inc. • Case Study: Bonnie Bagels • Bibliography

Assigning Telephone Operators at New Brunswick Telephone Company

Scheduling telephone operators to time shifts is a complex problem that must include a number of criteria. In assigning operators to shifts, New Brunswick Telephone Company (NBTel) set the objective of ensuring that all shifts would be covered, while satisfying employee choices for shifts as best as possible.

Although traditional models for solving a shift assignment problem (SAP) focus primarily on minimizing the cost of scheduling employees, the issue of satisfying the individual requirements of full-time employees is often neglected. However, NBTel is contractually obligated to satisfy individual employee requests for shift choice whenever possible.

In attempting to meet personal requests, there is a danger that some unpopular shifts, for example, overnight, weekend, or holiday shifts, would be hard to staff. Therefore, it was necessary to formulate an assignment model that would simultaneously provide adequate coverage of all time periods while at the same time minimizing staff dissatisfaction.

An assignment decision model called SSAH (Specialized Shift Assignment Heuristic) was developed. Various constraints such as employee skills, seniority, and availability are incorporated in the model. An employee satisfaction index was constructed, with a value of zero indicating perfect satisfaction. The larger the index, the higher the degree of dissatisfaction experienced by an operator.

When the SSAH model was implemented, employees welcomed its ability to handle requests for weekends off, and management was pleased because SSAH removed a source of employee discontent and provided staff with the ability to explore the effects of taking a specific day off or changing shift requirements.

Source: PhotoDisc Green

A manager at NBTel wrote "After a fair trial period, the staff have voted to adopt the system and so replace the very cumbersome and arbitrary manual process we have used for many years."

G.M. Thompson. "Assigning Telephone Operators to Shifts at New Brunswick Telephone Company," *Interfaces* 27, 4 (July–August 1997): 1–11.

Assignment models, such as the one used by the New Brunswick Telephone Company, are examples of special LP models, called **network flow models. Networks** consist of **nodes** (or points) and **arcs** (or lines) that connect the nodes together. Roadways, telephone systems, and city-wide water systems are all examples of networks. In this chapter, we examine six different network flow models: (1) transportation, (2) transshipment, (3) assignment, (4) maximal flow, (5) shortest path, and (6) minimal spanning tree.

Transportation Model

Transportation problems deal with distribution of goods from supply points to demand points at minimum cost.

The transportation problem deals with the distribution of goods from several points of supply (called **origins** or **sources**) to a number of points of demand (called **destinations** or **sinks**). Usually, we have a given capacity of goods at each source and a given requirement for the goods at each destination. The most common objective of the transportation problem is to schedule shipments from sources to destinations so that total production and transportation costs are minimized. Occasionally, transportation models can have a maximization objective (e.g., maximize total profit of shipping goods from sources to destinations).

Transportation models can also be used when a firm is trying to decide where to locate a new facility. Before opening a new warehouse, factory, or office, it is good practice to consider a number of alternative sites. The choice of facility location should consider, among other factors, minimizing total production and transportation costs for the entire system.

Transshipment Model

In transshipment problems, some points can have shipments that arrive as well as leave.

In the basic transportation problem, shipments either leave a supply point or arrive at a demand point. An extension of the transportation problem is called the **transshipment problem**, in which a point can have shipments that arrive as well as leave. An example would be a warehouse at which shipments arrive from factories and then leave for retail outlets. It may be possible for a firm to achieve cost savings (economies of scale) by consolidating shipments from several factories at the warehouse and then sending them together to retail outlets. This type of approach is the basis for the **hub-and-spoke** system of transportation employed by most major North American airlines. For example, most travel on Air Canada from western Canada to eastern Canada (or vice versa) involves a connection through Air Canada's hub in Toronto.

Assignment Model

The assignment problem seeks to find the optimal one-to-one assignment of people to projects, jobs to machines, and so on.

The **assignment problem** refers to the class of LP problems that involve determining the most efficient assignment of people to projects, salespeople to territories, contracts to bidders, jobs to machines, and so on. The typical objective is to minimize total cost or total time of performing the tasks at hand, although a maximization objective is also possible. An important characteristic of assignment problems is that each job or worker can be assigned to one machine or project, and vice versa.

Maximal-Flow Model

The maximal-flow problem finds the maximum flow possible through a network.

Consider a network with a specific starting point (called the *origin*) and a specific ending point (called the *destination*). The arcs in the network have capacities that limit the amounts of flow that can occur on them. These capacities can be different for different arcs. The **maximal-flow problem** finds the maximum flow that can occur from the origin to the destination through this network. This model can be used to determine, for example, the maximum number of vehicles (cars, trucks, and so forth) that can go through a network of roads from one location to another.

Shortest-Path Model

The shortest-path problem finds the shortest route from an origin to a destination.

Consider a network with a specified origin and a specified destination. The arcs in the network are such that there are many paths available to go from the origin to the destination. The **shortest-path problem** finds the shortest path or route through this network from the origin to the destination. For example, this model can be used to find the shortest distance and route from one city to another through a network of roads. The *length* of each arc can be a function of distance, travel time, travel cost, or any other measure.

Minimal-Spanning Tree Model

The minimal-spanning tree problem connects all nodes in a network while minimizing total distance.

The **minimal-spanning tree model** determines the path through the network that connects all the points. The most common objective is to minimize the total distance of all arcs used in the path. For example, when the points represent houses in a subdivision, the minimal-spanning tree model can be used to connect all of the houses to electrical power, water systems, and so on, in a way that minimizes the total distance or length of power lines or water pipes.

All of the examples used to describe the various network models in this chapter are small and simple, compared with real problems, to make it easier for you to understand the models. In many cases, these smaller network problems can be solved by inspection or intuition. For larger problems, however, finding a solution can be very difficult and requires the use of computer-based modeling approaches.

5.2 CHARACTERISTICS OF NETWORK FLOW PROBLEMS

A node is a specific point or location in a network.

An arc connects two nodes to each other.

Figure 5.1 shows a network that has five nodes and 10 arcs. Each of the circles (numbered 1 to 5) in the figure is called a node. A node can be defined as the location of a specific point on the network. An arc can be defined as the line that connects two nodes to each other. For example, the nodes could represent cities on a road network, and the arcs could represent roads connecting these cities.

As shown in Figure 5.1, it is not necessary for an arc to exist between every pair of nodes in a network. A network that does have arcs between all pairs of nodes is called a *fully connected* network. Arcs can be either unidirectional (meaning flow can occur only in one direction, as in a one-way road) or bidirectional (meaning that flow can occur in either direction). From a modeling perspective, it is convenient to represent a bidirectional arc with a pair of unidirectional arcs with opposite flow directions. This concept is illustrated in Figure 5.1 by the pairs of arcs between nodes 1 and 3, nodes 3 and 5, and nodes 2 and 4. Flows between all other pairs of nodes in Figure 5.1 are unidirectional.

Arcs can be one way or two way.

Nodes can be sources, destinations, or transshipment points.

Nodes can be classified as sources, destinations, or **transshipment points**. A source node (or supply point) denotes a location, such as a factory, that creates goods. A destination node (or demand point) denotes a location, such as a retail outlet, that consumes goods. A transshipment node denotes a location through which goods pass on their way to and from other locations.

FIGURE 5.1

Example of a Network

Note: Nodes are circles; arcs are lines.

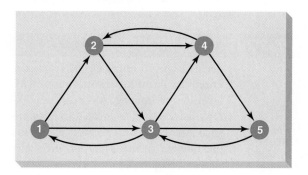

In many practical networks, the same node can be a combination of a source, destination, and transshipment point. For example, in the case of Air Canada, Toronto's Pearson Airport is a source node for those people originating from Toronto, a destination node for those people terminating in Toronto, and a transshipment node for those people connecting through Toronto.

Why are transportation models (and other network flow models) a special case of LP problems? There are several reasons:

1. In all network models, the decision variables represent the amount of flows (or shipments) that occur on the unidirectional arcs in the network. For example, the LP model for the network shown in Figure 5.1 will have 10 decision variables representing the flows on the 10 unidirectional arcs.

2. Second, there will be a *flow balance* constraint written for each node in the network. These flow balance constraints calculate the **net flow** at each node (i.e., the difference between the total flow on all arcs entering a node and the total flow on all arcs leaving the node).

$$\text{Net flow} = \text{Total flow } in \text{ to node} - \text{Total flow } out \text{ of node} \qquad (5\text{-}1)$$

> The net flow at a node is the difference between the total flow in to the node and the total flow out of the node.

At source nodes, the total flow *out* of the node will exceed the total flow *in* to the node, since goods are created at the node. Hence, the net flow is a negative quantity and represents the amount of goods (flow) created at the source node.

Conversely, at destination nodes, total flow *out* of the node will be less than the total flow *in* to the node, since goods are consumed at the node. The net flow is therefore a *positive* quantity and represents the amount of goods (flow) consumed at the destination node.

At pure transshipment nodes, goods are neither created nor consumed. The total flow *out* of such a node equals the total flow *in* to the node, and the net flow is therefore zero.

3. The constraint coefficients (i.e., the coefficients in front of decision variables in a constraint) for all flow balance constraints and most other problem-specific constraints in network models equal either 0 or 1. That is, if a decision variable exists in a constraint in a network model, its constraint coefficient is usually 1. This special trait allows network flow models to be solved very quickly using specialized algorithms. However, we use Solver in the same manner as in Chapters 2 and 3 to solve these models here.

4. If all supplies at the source nodes and all demands at the destination nodes are whole numbers (i.e., integer values), the solution to the LP model will automatically result in integer values for the decision variables, even without specifying the integer condition. This property is especially useful in modeling the assignment and shortest-path models later in this chapter.

> If all supplies and demands are integers, all flows in a network will also be integer values.

5.3   TRANSPORTATION MODEL

Let us begin to illustrate the **transportation model** with an example dealing with the Executive Furniture Corporation. This company manufactures office desks at three locations: Winnipeg, Montreal, and Halifax. The firm distributes the desks through regional warehouses located in Edmonton, Toronto, and Ottawa (see Figure 5.2 on page 182). An estimate of the monthly production capacity at each factory and an estimate of the number of desks that are needed each month at each of the three warehouses is shown in Figure 5.3.

> Our goal is to select the shipping routes and units to be shipped to minimize total transportation cost.

MODELING IN THE REAL WORLD

AT&T Solves Network Problems

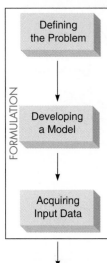

FORMULATION

Defining
the Problem

↓

Developing
a Model

↓

Acquiring
Input Data

SOLUTION

Developing
a Solution

↓

Testing the
Solution

INTERPRETATION

Analyzing
the Results
and Conducting
a Sensitivity
Analysis

↓

Implementing
the Results

Serving more than 80 million customers in North America and requiring more than 40 thousand miles (65 thousand kilometres) of cable, AT&T's fibre-optic network is the largest in the industry. Handling about 80 billion calls each year, AT&T defined maintaining network reliability, while maximizing network flow and minimizing network resources, as one of its most important problems.

AT&T developed several comprehensive models to analyze reliability issues. These models investigated two important aspects of network reliability: (1) preventing failures and (2) responding quickly when failures occur. The models included real-time network routing (RTNR), fast automatic restoration (FASTAR), and synchronous optical network (SONET).

More than 10 months were spent on collecting a vast amount of data for the models.

The solution used a network model to find the best way to route voice and data traffic so as to minimize the number of message failures and network resources required. Because of the large size of the problem, a solution was generated for each set of possible traffic demand and failure possibilities.

AT&T performed testing by comparing the solutions obtained by the new model's approach with the solutions obtained by older planning tools. Improvement expectations of 5% to 10% were established. The company also used computer simulation to test the solution over varying conditions.

To analyze the results, AT&T had to reverse the aggregation steps performed during data collection. Once the disaggregation process was completed, AT&T was able to determine the best routing approach through the vast network. The analysis of the results included an investigation of embedded capacity and spare capacity provided by the solution.

When implemented, the new approach was able to reduce network resources by more than 30% while maintaining high network reliability. During the study, 99.98% of all calls were successfully completed on the first attempt. The successful implementation also resulted in ideas for changes and improvements, including a full optimization approach that could identify unused capacity and place it into operation.

Source: K. Ambs et al. "Optimizing Restoration Capacity at the AT&T Network," *Interfaces* (January–February 2000): 26–44.

FIGURE 5.2   **Geographical Locations of Executive Furniture's Factories and Warehouses**

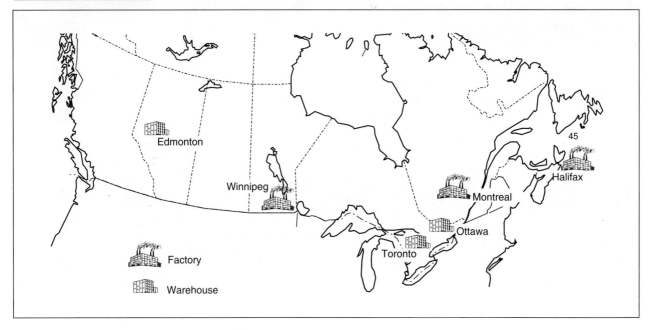

The firm has found that production costs per desk are identical at each factory, and hence the only relevant costs are those of shipping from each source to each destination. These costs, shown in Table 5.1 on page 183, are assumed to be constant regardless of the volume shipped.[1] The transportation problem can now be described as *how to select the shipping routes to be used and the number of desks shipped on each route so as to minimize total transportation cost.* This, of course, must be done while observing the restrictions regarding factory capacities and warehouse requirements.

We see in Figure 5.3 that the total factory supply available is exactly equal to the total warehouse demand. When this situation of equal demand and supply occurs (something that is rather unusual in real life) a **balanced problem** is said to exist. Later in this section we look at how to deal with unbalanced problems, namely, those in which total destination requirements are greater than or less than total origin capacities.

> Balanced supply and demand occurs when total supply equals total demand.

FIGURE 5.3

Network Model for Executive Furniture's Transportation Problem

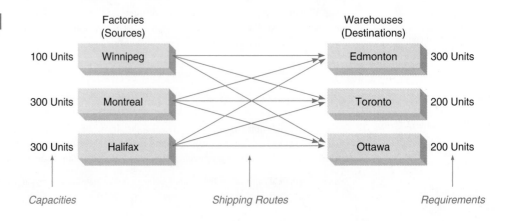

---

[1] The other assumptions that held for LP problems (see Chapter 2) are still applicable to transportation problems.

TABLE 5.1			

Transportation Costs per Desk for Executive Furniture Corporation

FROM \ TO	EDMONTON	TORONTO	OTTAWA
Winnipeg	$5	$4	$3
Montreal	3	2	1
Halifax	9	7	5

LP Model of Executive Furniture's Transportation Model

Since there are three factories (Winnipeg, Montreal, and Halifax) and three warehouses (Edmonton, Toronto, and Ottawa), there are nine potential shipping routes. We therefore need nine decision variables to define the number of units that would be shipped from each source (factory) to each destination (warehouse). In general, the number of decision variables in the basic transportation problem is the product of the number of sources times the number of destinations.

Recall (from Section 5.2) that in the transportation model (as well as in other network flow models), decision variables denote the flow between two nodes in the network. Therefore, it is convenient to represent these flows using double-subscripted decision variables. We let the first subscript represent the source (or origin) and the second subscript represent the destination of the flow. Hence, for the Executive Furniture problem, let

It is convenient to express all network flows using double-subscripted variables.

$$X_{ij} = \text{number of desks shipped from factory } i \text{ to warehouse } j$$

where

$$i = \text{W (for Winnipeg), M (for Montreal), or H (for Halifax)}$$

$$j = \text{E (for Edmonton), T (for Toronto), or O (for Ottawa)}$$

Objective Function   The objective function for this problem seeks to minimize the total transportation cost and can be expressed as

$$\text{Minimize total shipping costs} = 5X_{WE} + 4X_{WT} + 3X_{WO} + 3X_{ME} + 2X_{MT} + 1X_{MO} + 9X_{HE} + 7X_{HT} + 5X_{HO}$$

Constraints   As discussed earlier, we need to write *flow balance* constraints for each node in the network. Since the Executive Furniture example is a balanced problem, we know that all desks will be shipped from the factories and all demand will be satisfied at the warehouses. The number of desks shipped from each factory will therefore be equal to the number of desks available, and the number of desks received at each warehouse will be equal to the number of desks required.

We write a flow balance constraint for each node in the network.

Supply Constraints   At all factories, the total flow *in* is zero since there are no arcs coming into the node. The net flow at the Winnipeg factory (for example) can therefore be expressed as

We write a supply constraint for each factory.

$$\text{Net Flow at Winnipeg} = (\text{Total flow } in) - (\text{Total flow } out) = (0) - (X_{WE} + X_{WT} + X_{WO})$$

This net flow is equal to the total number of desks available (supply) at Winnipeg. Recall (from Section 5.2) that supply is written as a negative quantity in network flow balance constraints. Therefore,

Supplies are written as negative quantities.

$$\text{Net flow at Winnipeg} = -X_{WE} - X_{WT} - X_{WO} = -100 \quad \text{(Winnipeg capacity)}$$

Likewise, the flow balance constraints at the other factories can be expressed as

$$-X_{ME} - X_{MT} - X_{MO} = -300 \qquad \text{(Montreal capacity)}$$
$$-X_{HE} - X_{HT} - X_{HO} = -300 \qquad \text{(Halifax capacity)}$$

The preceding three constraints are known as *supply constraints*. If we wish, we can multiply each constraint by -1 and rewrite as

$$X_{WE} + X_{WT} + X_{WO} = 100 \qquad \text{(Winnipeg capacity)}$$
$$X_{ME} + X_{MT} + X_{MO} = 300 \qquad \text{(Montreal capacity)}$$
$$X_{HE} + X_{HT} + X_{HO} = 300 \qquad \text{(Halifax capacity)}$$

We write a demand constraint for each warehouse.

Demand Constraints   Now, let us model the constraints (referred to as the *demand constraints*) that represent the warehouse requirements. At all warehouses, the total flow *out* is zero since there are no arcs leaving from the node. The net flow at the Edmonton warehouse, for example, can therefore be expressed as

$$\text{Net flow at Edmonton} = (\text{Total flow } in) - (\text{Total flow } out) = (X_{WE} + X_{ME} + X_{HE}) - (0)$$

Net flow at a demand point is written as a positive number.

This net flow is equal to the total number of desks required (demand) at Edmonton. Recall (from Section 5.2) that the net flow at a destination node is expressed as a positive number. Therefore,

$$\text{Net flow at Edmonton} = X_{WE} + X_{ME} + X_{HE} = 300 \qquad \text{(Edmonton demand)}$$

Likewise, the flow balance constraints at the other warehouses can be expressed as

$$X_{WT} + X_{MT} + X_{HT} = 200 \qquad \text{(Toronto demand)}$$
$$X_{WO} + X_{MO} + X_{HO} = 200 \qquad \text{(Ottawa demand)}$$

In general, the number of constraints in the basic transportation problem will be the sum of the number of sources and the number of destinations. There could, however, be other problem-specific constraints that restrict shipments in individual routes. For example, if we wish to ensure that no more than 100 desks are shipped from Montreal to Ottawa, an additional constraint in the model will be $X_{MO} \leq 100$.

Solving the Transportation Model Using Excel

File: 5-1.xls

Screenshot 5.1 shows the Excel setup and Solver entries for Executive Furniture's transportation problem. The supply constraints have been modeled here with negative values for supplies (i.e., the supply constraints have not been multiplied through by -1). The Excel layout in Screenshot 5.1 follows the same logic as in Chapter 3. This means that (1) each decision variable is modeled in a separate column of the worksheet and (2) the objective function and left-hand-side (LHS) formulas for all constraints are computed using Excel's SUMPRODUCT function.

Excel Notes

■ The CD-ROM that accompanies this textbook contains the Excel file for each example problem discussed here. The relevant file name is shown in the margin next to each example.

■ In each of our Excel layouts, for clarity, Changing Cells are shaded yellow, the Target Cell is shaded green, and cells containing the LHS formula for each constraint are shaded blue.

The optimum solution for Executive Furniture Corporation is to ship 100 desks from Winnipeg to Edmonton, 200 desks from Montreal to Toronto, 100 desks from Montreal to Ottawa, 200 desks from Halifax to Edmonton, and 100 desks from Halifax to Ottawa. The total shipping cost is $3900. Observe that since all supplies and demands were integer-valued, all shipments turned out to be integer-valued as well.

SCREENSHOT 5.1   **Excel Layout and Solver Entries for Executive Furniture—Transportation**

	A	B	C	D	E	F	G	H	I	J	K	L	M
1	**Executive Furniture (Transportation)**												
2													
3		X_{WE}	X_{WT}	X_{WO}	X_{ME}	X_{MT}	X_{MO}	X_{HE}	X_{HT}	X_{HO}			
4		Win to Edm	Win to Toro	Win to Otta	Mont to Edm	Mont to Toro	Mont to Otta	Hali to Edm	Hali to Toro	Hali to Otta			
5	Number of desks shipped	100.0	0.0	0.0	0.0	200.0	100.0	200.0	0.0	100.0			
6	Cost	$5.00	$4.00	$3.00	$8.00	$4.00	$3.00	$9.00	$7.00	$5.00	$3,900.00	<-- Objective	
7	**Constraints:**												
8	Winnipeg supply	-1	-1	-1							-100.0	=	-100
9	Montreal supply				-1	-1	-1				-300.0	=	-300
10	Halifax supply							-1	-1	-1	-300.0	=	-300
11	Edmonton demand	1			1			1			300.0	=	300
12	Toronto demand		1			1			1		200.0	=	200
13	Ottawa demand			1			1			1	200.0	=	200
14											LHS	Sign	RHS

Decision variable names are shown here for information purposes only.

Supplies are shown as negative numbers.

All entries in column K are computed using the SUMPRODUCT function.

Solver Parameters

Set Target Cell: $K$6

Equal To: ○ Max ● Min ○ Value of: 0

By Changing Cells:

$B$5:$J$5

Subject to the Constraints:

$K$8:$K$13 = $M$8:$M$13

Solve

Close

Options...

Guess

Reset All

Help

Add

All constraints are = since the problem is balanced.

Alternate Excel Layout for the Model

The alternative Excel layout for network flow models uses a "tabular" form to model the flows.

File: 5-2.xls

For many network models, the number of arcs (and hence, decision variables) could be quite large. Modeling the problem in Excel using the layout used in Screenshot 5.1 can therefore become quite cumbersome. For this reason, it may be more convenient to model network flow models in Excel in such a way that decision variables are in a *tabular* form, with rows (for example) denoting sources and columns denoting destinations. The formula view of the alternate Excel layout for Executive Furniture's transportation model is shown in Screenshot 5.2A, with the optimal solution shown in Screenshot 5.2B (both on the next page). By adding the row (or column) entries, we can easily calculate the appropriate total flows *out* and total flows *in* at each node. It is then possible to model a flow balance constraint for each node by calculating each net flow as the difference between the total flow in to the node and the total flow out of the node.

For example, the net flow at Winnipeg (cell H5) is computed as (0 − E4), where cell E4 is the sum of cells B4:D4. This net flow is set equal to −100 since the supply at Winnipeg is 100. Likewise, the net flow at Edmonton (cell H8) is computed as (B7 − 0), where cell B7 is the sum of cells B4:B6. This net flow is set equal to +300, since the demand at Edmonton is 300.

Note that the optimal solution resulting from this alternative layout, shown in Screenshot 5.2B, is the same as the one shown in Screenshot 5.1.

SCREENSHOT 5.2A   **Formula View of Alternate Excel Layout for Executive Furniture—Transportation**

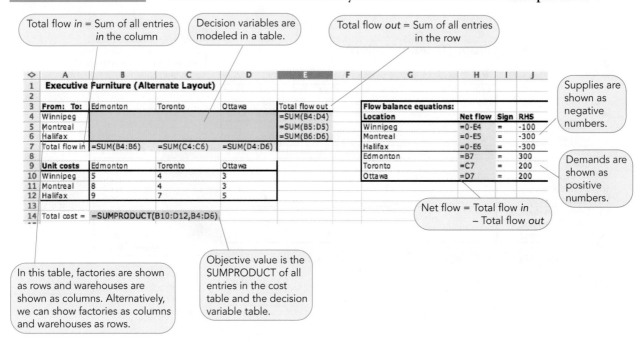

Total flow *in* = Sum of all entries *in* the column

Decision variables are modeled in a table.

Total flow *out* = Sum of all entries *in* the row

Supplies are shown as negative numbers.

Demands are shown as positive numbers.

Net flow = Total flow *in* − Total flow *out*

In this table, factories are shown as rows and warehouses are shown as columns. Alternatively, we can show factories as columns and warehouses as rows.

Objective value is the SUMPRODUCT of all entries in the cost table and the decision variable table.

SCREENSHOT 5.2B   **Solver Entries for Alternate Layout of Executive Furniture—Transportation**

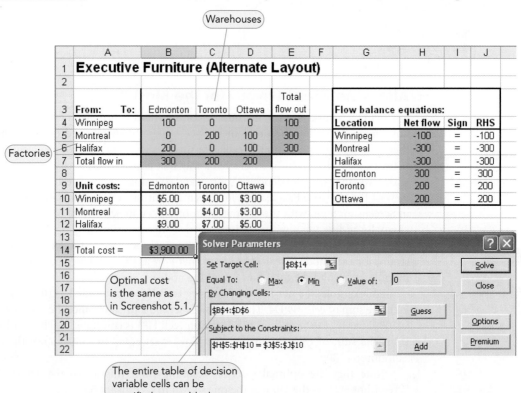

Warehouses

Factories

Optimal cost is the same as in Screenshot 5.1.

The entire table of decision variable cells can be specified as one block.

Unbalanced Transportation Problems

In the Executive Furniture example, the total supply from the three factories equals the total requirements at the three warehouses. All supply and demand constraints could therefore be specified as equalities (i.e., using the "=" sign). But what if the total supply exceeds the total requirement, or vice versa? In these cases, we have an **unbalanced problem**, and the supply or demand constraints need to be modified accordingly.

There are two possible scenarios: (1) total supply exceeds the total requirement and (2) total supply is less than the total requirement.

The problem is unbalanced if the total supply does not equal the total demand.

Total Supply Exceeds the Total Requirement   If total supply exceeds the total requirement, all requirements will be fully satisfied at the destinations, but some of the items at one or more sources will not need to be shipped out. That is, they will remain at the sources. To allow for this possibility, the total flow *out* of each supply node should be permitted to be smaller than the supply at that node. The total flow *in* to the demand nodes will, however, continue to be written with "=" signs.

For example, assume the supply and demand values in the Executive Furniture problem are altered so that the total supply at the three factories exceeds the total demand at the three warehouses. Consider the supply at the Winnipeg factory. The total flow out of Winnipeg (i.e., $X_{WE} + X_{WT} + X_{WO}$) should now be permitted to be smaller than the total supply (i.e., 100). Hence, the constraint would need to be written as

$$X_{WE} + X_{WT} + X_{WO} \leq 100$$

If total supply exceeds total demand, the supply constraints are written as inequalities.

In keeping with our convention of writing flows *out* of nodes with negative constraint coefficients, and expressing the supply at the node as a negative number, we multiply this expression through by −1 and rewrite the supply constraint for Winnipeg as

$$-X_{WE} - X_{WT} - X_{WO} \geq -100 \qquad \text{(Winnipeg capacity)}$$

Likewise, the supply constraints at the Montreal and Halifax factories would need to be revised as

$$-X_{ME} - X_{MT} - X_{MO} \geq -300 \qquad \text{(Montreal capacity)}$$
$$-X_{HE} - X_{HT} - X_{HO} \geq -300 \qquad \text{(Halifax capacity)}$$

Total Supply Less Than the Total Requirement   When total supply is less than total requirement, all items at the sources will be shipped out, but requirements at one or more destinations will remain unsatisfied. To allow for this possibility, the total flow *in* at demand nodes should be permitted to be smaller than the requirement at those nodes. The total flow *out* of supply nodes will, however, continue to be written with "=" signs.

If total demand exceeds total supply, the demand constraints are written as inequalities.

For example, assume the supply and demand values in the Executive Furniture problem are altered so that the total supply at the three factories is now *less* than the total demand at the three warehouses. Consider the demand at the Edmonton warehouse. The total flow *in* to Edmonton (i.e., $X_{WE} + X_{ME} + X_{HE}$) should now be permitted to be smaller than the total demand (i.e., 300). In keeping with our convention of writing flows *in* to nodes with positive constraint coefficients and expressing the demand at the node as a positive number, the demand constraint for this warehouse should therefore be written as

$$X_{WE} + X_{ME} + X_{HE} \leq 300 \qquad \text{(Edmonton demand)}$$

Likewise, the demand constraints at the Toronto and Ottawa warehouses would need to be written as

$$X_{WT} + X_{MT} + X_{HT} \leq 200 \qquad \text{(Toronto demand)}$$
$$X_{WO} + X_{MO} + X_{HO} \leq 200 \qquad \text{(Ottawa demand)}$$

DECISION MODELING IN ACTION
Warehousing in Canada

Metro Canada Logistics (MCL) is a leading third-party provider of warehousing, transportation, and customized supply chain solutions in Canada, managing over 7 million square feet of premium warehouse space across Canada, including locations in Montreal, Toronto, Calgary, and Vancouver.

MCL provides a comprehensive package of services that includes warehousing, transportation, inventory management, and freight optimization and consolidation. With 700 employees, MCL manages 35 facilities, and its clients include grocery, consumer, and industrial-products companies. About 45% of MCL's revenues come from the paper and newsprint industries, where the company's client list includes major Canadian businesses such as Abitibi-Consolidated, Uniboard Canada Inc., and Kruger Inc.

In 2002, MCL opened a huge 650 000-square-foot, $35-million logistics centre in Concord, Ontario. Containers are transferred onto trucks at this transportation hub located inside a Canadian National Railway yard. This greatly expedites the delivery of shipments to customers in the Toronto area.

A major key to the company's success is the introduction of value-added services in computer operations, such as inventory and transportation management and optimization. Company president and sole owner Hanif Nanji has made a point of hiring people who are well educated, including engineering and information-technology professionals. For a typical outsourcing job, MCL's engineers visit the company, study its supply chain, determine its needs, and plot the optimal warehouse locations. These can vary depending on the type and frequency of traffic, and preferred shipping methods—ship, truck, train, or a combination of these methods.

MCL is a successful, innovative company serving Canada's business community in providing logistical services in transportation modeling.

Sources: http://www.metrocanlogistics.com; Peter Diekmeyer, "Value-added storage: Metro Canada Logistics manages warehouses and helps its clients move the goods in them," *The Gazette* (Montreal) January 26, 2002, final edition, p. I.6.

More Than One Optimal Solution

> It is quite common for transportation models to have alternate optimal solutions.

Just as with regular LP problems, it is possible (and, in fact, quite common) for a transportation problem to have multiple optimal solutions. Practically speaking, multiple optimal solutions provide management with greater flexibility in selecting and using resources. Chapter 4 (Section 4.4) indicates that if the allowable increase or allowable decrease for the objective coefficient of a variable has a value of zero (in the Adjustable Cells table of the LP Sensitivity Report), this usually indicates the presence of alternate optimal solutions. In Solved Problem 4-1, we saw how Solver can be used to identify alternate optimal solutions.

5.4   FACILITY LOCATION ANALYSIS

The transportation model has proven to be especially useful in **facility location analysis**: helping firms decide where to locate a new factory or warehouse. Since a new location has major financial implications for a firm, several alternative locations must usually be considered and evaluated. Even though a firm may consider a wide variety of subjective factors, including quality of labour supply, presence of labour unions, community attitude, utilities, and recreational and educational facilities, a final decision also involves minimizing total production and shipping costs. This means that each alternative facility location should be analyzed within the framework of one overall distribution system. The new location that will yield the minimum cost for the entire system should be the one recommended. Let us consider the case of the Hardgrave Machine Company.

> The transportation model can help an organization decide where to locate a new facility within an overall distribution system.

Locating a New Factory for Hardgrave Machine Company

The Hardgrave Machine Company produces computer components at its plants in Cranbrooke, Kingston, and Prince George. These plants have not been able to keep up with demand for orders at Hardgrave's four warehouses in Charlotteville, Hamilton, Nanaimo, and Regina. As a result, the firm has decided to build a new plant to expand its productive

TABLE 5.2						

Hardgrave's Demand and Supply Data

WAREHOUSE	MONTHLY DEMAND (UNITS)		PRODUCTION PLANT	MONTHLY SUPPLY	COST TO PRODUCE ONE UNIT ($)
Charlotteville	10 000		Cranbrooke	15 000	48
Hamilton	12 000		Kingston	6 000	50
Nanaimo	15 000		Prince George	14 000	52
Regina	9 000			35 000	
	46 000				

Supply needed from new plant = 46 000 − 35 000 = 11 000 units per month

ESTIMATED PRODUCTION COST PER UNIT AT PROPOSED PLANTS	
Sudbury	$53
Abbotsford	49

capacity. To facilitate air transportation, all of Hardgrave's plants and warehouses are located close to Level II airports, which have regularly scheduled flights but handle fewer than 1 million passengers per year. The two sites being considered are Sudbury, Ontario, and Abbotsford, B.C. Both cities are attractive in terms of labour supply, municipal services, and ease of factory financing.

Table 5.2 above presents the production costs and monthly supplies at each of the three existing plants, monthly demands at each of the four warehouses, and estimated production costs at the two proposed plants. Transportation costs from each plant to each warehouse are summarized in Table 5.3.

The important question now facing Hardgrave is which of the new locations, in combination with the existing plants and warehouses, will yield the lowest cost for the firm. Note that the cost of each individual plant-to-warehouse route is found by adding the shipping costs (in the body of Table 5.3) to the respective unit production costs (from Table 5.2). For example, the total production plus shipping cost of one computer component from Cranbrooke to Charlotteville is $73 (= $25 for shipping plus $48 for production).

To determine which new plant (Sudbury or Abbotsford) yields the lowest total systemwide cost, we solve two transportation problems: one for each of the two possible combinations.

Screenshots 5.3A and 5.3B on the next page show the resulting optimum solutions with the total cost for each of the two locations. The layout followed in both models is

We solve two transportation problems to find the new plant with the lowest system cost.

TABLE 5.3					

Hardgrave's Shipping Costs

FROM \ TO	CHARLOTTEVILLE	HAMILTON	NANAIMO	REGINA
Cranbrooke	$25	$55	$40	$60
Kingston	35	30	50	40
Prince George	36	45	26	66
Sudbury	60	38	65	27
Abbotsford	35	30	41	50

SCREENSHOT 5.3A   **Excel Layout and Solver Entries for Hardgrave Machine's Facility Location Problem with a New Facility in Sudbury**

The model includes a new plant at Sudbury.

Proposed capacity of Sudbury plant

	A	B	C	D	E	F	G	H	I	J	K
1	**Facility Location (Sudbury)**										
2											
3	From: To:	Charlottetown	Hamilton	Nanaimo	Regina	Total flow out		Flow balance equations:			
4	Cranbrooke	10000	4000	1000	0	15000		Location	Net flow	Sign	RHS
5	Kingston	0	6000	0	0	6000		Cranbrooke	-15000	=	-15000
6	Prince George	0	0	14000	0	14000		Kingston	-6000	=	-6000
7	Sudbury	0	2000	0	9000	11000		Prince George	-14000	=	-14000
8	Total flow in	10000	12000	15000	9000			Sudbury	-11000	=	-11000
9								Charlottetown	10000	=	10000
10	Unit costs:	Charlottetown	Hamilton	Nanaimo	Regina			Hamilton	12000	=	12000
11	Cranbrooke	$73	$103	$88	$108			Nanaimo	15000	=	15000
12	Kingston	$85	$80	$100	$90			Regina	9000	=	9000
13	Prince George	$88	$97	$78	$118						
14	Sudbury	$113	$91	$118	$80						
15											
16	Total cost =	$3,704,000									

Optimal cost

Solver Parameters

Set Target Cell: $B$16

Equal To: ○ Max ⊙ Min ○ Value of: 0

By Changing Cells:
$B$4:$E$7

Subject to the Constraints:
$I$5:$I$12 = $K$5:$K$12

SCREENSHOT 5.3B   **Excel Layout and Solver Entries for Hardgrave Machine's Facility Location Problem with a New Facility in Abbotsford**

The model includes a new plant at Abbotsford.

Proposed capacity of plant at Abbotsford.

	A	B	C	D	E	F	G	H	I	J	K
1	**Facility Location (Abbotsford)**										
2											
3	From: To:	Charlottetown	Hamilton	Nanaimo	Regina	Total flow out		Flow balance equations:			
4	Cranbrooke	10000	0	1000	4000	15000		Location	Net flow	Sign	RHS
5	Kingston	0	1000	0	5000	6000		Cranbrooke	-15000	=	-15000
6	Prince George	0	0	14000	0	14000		Kingston	-6000	=	-6000
7	Abbotsford	0	11000	0	0	11000		Prince George	-14000	=	-14000
8	Total flow in	10000	12000	15000	9000			Abbotsford	-11000	=	-11000
9								Charlottetown	10000	=	10000
10	Unit costs:	Charlottetown	Hamilton	Nanaimo	Regina			Hamilton	12000	=	12000
11	Cranbrooke	$73	$103	$88	$108			Nanaimo	15000	=	15000
12	Kingston	$85	$80	$100	$90			Regina	9000	=	9000
13	Prince George	$88	$97	$78	$118						
14	Abbotsford	$84	$79	$90	$99						
15											
16	Total cost =	$3,741,000									

Optimal cost

Solver Parameters

Set Target Cell: $B$16

Equal To: ○ Max ⊙ Min ○ Value of: 0

By Changing Cells:
$B$4:$E$7

Subject to the Constraints:
$I$5:$I$12 = $K$5:$K$12

File: 5-3.xls

similar to the one shown in Screenshot 5.2A for the Executive Furniture problem. From these solutions, it appears that Sudbury should be selected as the new plant site. Its total cost of $3 704 000 is less than the $3 741 000 cost at Abbotsford.

5.5 TRANSSHIPMENT MODEL

Transshipment problems include nodes that can have shipments arrive as well as leave.

In the basic transportation problem, shipments either flow *out* of nodes (sources) or flow *in* to nodes (destinations). That is, it is possible to explicitly distinguish between source nodes and destination nodes for flows. In the more general form of the transportation problem, called the transshipment problem, flows can occur both out of and into the same node in three ways:

1. If the total flow in to a node is less than the total flow out from the node, the node then represents a net creator of goods, that is, a supply point. The flow balance equation will therefore have a negative right-hand-side (RHS) value.

2. However, if the total flow in to a node exceeds the total flow out from the node, the node then represents a net consumer of goods, that is, a demand point. The flow balance equation will therefore have a positive RHS value.

3. Finally, if the total flow in to a node is equal to the total flow out from the node, the node then represents a pure transshipment point. The flow balance equation will therefore have a zero RHS value.

Executive Furniture Corporation Example—Revisited

To study the transshipment problem, let us consider a modified version of the Executive Furniture Corporation example from Section 5.3. As before, we have factories at Winnipeg, Montreal, and Halifax, and warehouses at Edmonton, Ottawa, and Toronto. Recall that the supply at each factory and demand at each warehouse were shown in Figure 5.3 on page 182.

Now assume that due to a special contract with a Montreal-based shipping company, it is possible for Executive Furniture to ship desks from its Montreal factory to its three warehouses at very low unit shipping costs. These unit costs are so attractive that Executive is considering shipping all the desks produced at its other two factories (Winnipeg and Halifax) to Montreal, and then using this new shipping company to move desks from Montreal to all its warehouses.

The revised unit shipping costs are shown in Table 5.4. Note that the Montreal factory now shows up both in the "From" and "To" entries since it is possible for this factory to receive desks from other factories and then ship them out to the warehouses. There are

TABLE 5.4				
Revised Transportation Costs per Desk for Executive Furniture Corporation				

TO FROM	EDMONTON	TORONTO	OTTAWA	MONTREAL
Winnipeg	$5	$4	$3	$2
Montreal	3	2	1	—
Halifax	9	7	5	3

therefore two additional shipping routes available: Winnipeg to Montreal, and Halifax to Montreal.

These data are used in the transshipment model.

LP Model for Executive Furniture's Transshipment Problem

The LP model for this problem follows the same logic and structure as the model for Executive Furniture's transportation problem (see Section 5.3). However, we now have two *additional* decision variables for the two new shipping routes. We define these as follows:

$$X_{WM} = \text{number of desks shipped from Winnipeg to Montreal}$$
$$X_{HM} = \text{number of desks shipped from Halifax to Montreal}$$

Objective Function   The objective function for this transshipment problem, including the two additional decision variables and using the unit costs shown in Table 5.4, can be written as follows:

$$\text{Minimize total shipping costs} = 5X_{WE} + 4X_{WT} + 3X_{WO} + 2X_{WM} + 3X_{ME} + 2X_{MT} + 1X_{MO}$$
$$+ 9X_{HE} + 7X_{HT} + 5X_{HO} + 3X_{HM}$$

Constraints   Once again, we need to write flow balance constraints for each node in the network. Let us first consider the net flows at the Winnipeg and Halifax factories. After taking into account the desks shipped from either of these locations to the Montreal factory (rather than directly to the warehouses), the relevant flow balance equations can be written as

$$(0) - (X_{WE} + X_{WT} + X_{WO} + X_{WM}) = -100 \quad \text{(Winnipeg capacity)}$$
$$(0) - (X_{HE} + X_{HT} + X_{HO} + X_{HM}) = -300 \quad \text{(Halifax capacity)}$$

As usual, supplies have been expressed as negative numbers in the RHS. Now, let us model the flow equation at Montreal.

$$\text{Net flow at Montreal} = (\text{Total flow } in) - (\text{Total flow } out)$$
$$= (X_{WM} + X_{HM}) - (X_{ME} + X_{MT} + X_{MO})$$

This net flow is equal to the total number of desks produced, namely, the supply, at Montreal (which would also appear as a negative number in the flow balance constraint). Therefore,

$$\text{Net flow at Montreal} = (X_{WM} + X_{HM}) - (X_{ME} + X_{MT} + X_{MO}) = -300$$

There is no change in the demand constraints that represent the warehouse requirements. So, as discussed in Section 5.2, they are

$$X_{WE} + X_{ME} + X_{HE} = 300 \quad \text{(Edmonton demand)}$$
$$X_{WT} + X_{MT} + X_{HT} = 200 \quad \text{(Toronto demand)}$$
$$X_{WO} + X_{MO} + X_{HO} = 200 \quad \text{(Ottawa demand)}$$

File: 5.4.xls

Excel Solution   Screenshot 5.4, which uses the tabular layout for representing the network flows, shows the Excel layout and Solver entries for Executive Furniture's transshipment problem. Note that the net flow at Montreal (cell I6) is calculated as (E7−F5), where cell E7 is the total flow coming into the Montreal factory, and cell F5 represents the total flow out of Montreal. The difference of 300 is the supply of desks created at the Montreal factory.

In the revised solution, which now has a total transportation cost of $2600, Executive should ship the 300 desks made at Halifax to Montreal and then ship the consolidated load to the warehouses. It continues, though, to be cost beneficial to ship desks made at the Winnipeg factory directly to a warehouse.

SCREENSHOT 5.4   **Excel Layout and Solver Entries for Executive Furniture's Transshipment Problem**

These 300 desks are shipped from the Halifax factory to the Montreal factory.

	A	B	C	D	E	F	G	H	I	J	K
1	**Executive Furniture (Transshipment)**										
2											
3	From: To:	Edmonton	Toronto	Ottawa	Montreal	Total flow out		**Flow balance equations:**			
4	Winnipeg	0	0	100	0	100		**Location**	**Net flow**	**Sign**	**RHS**
5	Montreal	300	200	100	0	600		Winnipeg	-100	=	-100
6	Halifax	0	0	0	300	300		Montreal	-300	=	-300
7	Total flow in	300	200	200	300			Halifax	-300	=	-300
8								Edmonton	300	=	300
9	**Unit costs:**	Edmonton	Toronto	Ottawa	Montreal			Toronto	200	=	200
10	Winnipeg	$5.00	$4.00	$3.00	$2.00			Ottawa	200	=	200
11	Montreal	$3.00	$2.00	$1.00	$0.00						
12	Halifax	$9.00	$7.00	$5.00	$3.00						
13											
14	Total cost =	$2,600.00									
15											
16	=SUMPRODUCT (B4:E6, B10:E12)										

Solver Parameters

Set Target Cell: $B$14

Equal To: ○ Max ● Min ○ Value of: 0

By Changing Cells: $B$4:$E$6

Subject to the Constraints: $I$5:$I$10 = $K$5:$K$10

Total flow into Montreal includes shipments from other two factories.

Montreal is now included as a destination.

5.6   ASSIGNMENT MODEL

The next model we study is the assignment model. Each assignment model has associated with it a table, or matrix. Generally, the rows denote the people or objects we wish to assign, and the columns denote the tasks or jobs we want them assigned to. The numbers in the table are the costs (or benefits) associated with each particular assignment.

Fix-It Shop Example

The goal is to assign projects to people (one project to one person) so that the total costs are minimized.

As an illustration of the assignment model, let us consider the case of the Fix-It Shop, which has just received three new rush projects to repair: (1) a radio, (2) a toaster oven, and (3) a coffee table. Three workers, each with different talents and abilities, are available to do the jobs. The Fix-It Shop owner estimates what it will cost in wages to assign each of the workers to each of the three projects. The costs, which are shown in Table 5.5, differ because the owner believes that each worker will differ in speed and skill on these quite varied jobs.

TABLE 5.5

Estimated Project Repair Costs for the Fix-It Shop Assignment Problem

PERSON	PROJECT 1	2	3
Adams	$11	$14	$ 6
Brown	8	10	11
Cooper	9	12	7

The owner's objective is to assign the three projects to the workers in a way that will result in the lowest total cost to the shop. Note that the assignment of people to projects must be on a one-to-one basis; each project must be assigned to one worker only, and vice versa. If the number of rows in an assignment model is equal to the number of columns (such as in the Fix-It example), we refer to this problem as a *balanced* assignment model.

One way to solve (small) problems is to enumerate all possible outcomes.

Because the Fix-It Shop problem only consists of three workers and three projects, one easy way to find the best solution is to list all possible assignments and their respective costs. For example, if Adams is assigned to project 1, Brown to project 2, and Cooper to project 3, the total cost will be $11 + $10 + $7 = $28. Table 5.6 summarizes all six assignment options. The table also shows that the least-cost solution would be to assign Cooper to project 1, Brown to project 2, and Adams to project 3, at a total cost of $25.

Obtaining solutions by enumeration works well for small problems but quickly becomes inefficient as assignment problems become larger. For example, a problem involving the assignment of eight workers and eight tasks, which actually is not that large in a real-world situation, yields 8! ($= 8 \times 7 \times 6 \times 5 \times 4 \times 3 \times 2 \times 1$) or 40 320 possible solutions! Since it would clearly be impractical to individually examine so many alternatives, a more efficient solution approach is needed.

Solving Assignment Models

All supplies and demands in an assignment model equal one unit.

A straightforward approach to solving assignment problems is to model them as LP problems in the same manner as transportation problems. To do so for the Fix-It Shop problem, let us view each worker as a source node in a network with a supply of 1 unit. Likewise, let us view each project as a destination node in a network with a demand of 1 unit. The arcs connecting the source nodes to the destination nodes represent the possible assignment of a source (worker) to a destination (project). The network model is illustrated in Figure 5.4.

We see that this model looks identical to a transportation problem with three sources and three destinations. But here, all supplies and demands are equal to 1 unit each. The objective is to find the least-cost solution for using the 1-unit supplies at the source nodes to satisfy the 1-unit demands at the destination nodes. However, we need to also ensure that each worker *uniquely* gets assigned to just one project, and vice versa. That is, the *entire* supply of 1 unit at a source node (worker) should flow to the same destination node (project), indicating the assignment of a worker to a project. How do we ensure this? The answer lies in the special property of network models stated earlier. When all the supplies and demands in a network model are whole numbers (as in this case), it turns out that the resulting solution will automatically have integer-valued flows on the arcs.

The special integer flow property of network models automatically ensures unique assignments.

Consider the "flow" out of the source node for Adams in the Fix-It Shop problem. The three arcs (to projects 1, 2, and 3) denote the assignment of Adams to these projects. Due to the integer property of the resulting network flows, the only possible solutions will have a flow of 1 on one of the three arcs, and a flow of 0 on the other two arcs. This is the

TABLE 5.6					
Summary of Fix-It Shop Assignment Alternatives and Costs	PROJECT ASSIGNMENT				
	1	2	3	LABOUR COSTS($)	TOTAL COSTS ($)
	Adams	Brown	Cooper	11 + 10 + 7 =	28
	Adams	Cooper	Brown	11 + 12 + 11 =	34
	Brown	Adams	Cooper	8 + 14 + 7 =	29
	Brown	Cooper	Adams	8 + 12 + 6 =	26
	Cooper	Adams	Brown	9 + 14 + 11 =	34
	Cooper	Brown	Adams	9 + 10 + 6 =	25

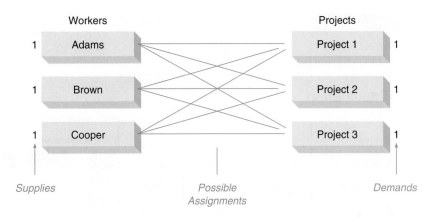

FIGURE 5.4

Network Model for Fix-It's Assignment Problem

only way in which a total flow of 1 (equal to the "supply" at the node representing Adams) can flow on these arcs and have integer values. The arc that has a flow of 1 in the optimal solution will indicate the project to which Adams should be assigned. Likewise, arcs that have flows of 1 originating from the other two source nodes will show the optimal assignments for those two workers.

Even without our constraining it to be so, the solution to the assignment model yields a solution in which the optimal values of the decision variables are either 1 (indicating the assignment of a worker to a project) or 0 (indicating that the worker should not be assigned to the project). In fact, there are several situations in which such decision variables, known as *binary* or 0–1 variables, must have values of zero or one in the formulation itself. We study these types of problems in more detail in Chapter 6.

LP Model for Fix-It Shop's Assignment Problem

We now develop the LP model for Fix-It Shop's problem. Let

X_{ij} = "Flow" on arc from node denoting worker i to node denoting project j. The solution value will equal 1 if worker i is assigned to project j and will equal 0 otherwise.

where

i = A (for Adams), B (for Brown), or C (for Cooper)

j = 1 (for project 1), 2 (for project 2), or 3 (for project 3)

Objective Function   The objective is to minimize the total cost of assignment and is expressed as

$$\text{Minimize total assignment costs} = 11X_{A1} + 14X_{A2} + 6X_{A3} + 8X_{B1}$$
$$+ 10X_{B2} + 11X_{B3} + 9X_{C1} + 12X_{C2} + 7X_{C3}$$

Constraints   As in the transportation model, we have supply constraints at each of the three source nodes (workers) and demand constraints at each of the three destination nodes (projects). Using the standard convention we have adopted for all flow balance equations, these can be written as

$$
\begin{aligned}
-X_{A1} - X_{A2} - X_{A3} &= -1 \quad \text{(Adams availability)} \\
-X_{B1} - X_{B2} - X_{B3} &= -1 \quad \text{(Brown availability)} \\
-X_{C1} - X_{C2} - X_{C3} &= -1 \quad \text{(Cooper availability)} \\
X_{A1} + X_{B1} + X_{C1} &= 1 \quad \text{(Project 1 requirement)}
\end{aligned}
$$

File: 5-5.xls

SCREENSHOT 5.5   **Excel Layout and Solver Entries for Fix-It Shop's Assignment Problem**

Note that the solution has all integer values.

	A	B	C	D	E	F	G	H	I	J
1	**Fix-It Shop**									
2										
3	**From: To:**	Project 1	Project 2	Project 3	Total flow out		**Flow balance equations:**			
4	Adams	0.0	0.0	1.0	1		**Node**	**Net flow**	**Sign**	**RHS**
5	Brown	0.0	1.0	0.0	1		Adams	-1	=	-1
6	Cooper	1.0	0.0	0.0	1		Brown	-1	=	-1
7	Total flow in	1	1	1			Cooper	-1	=	-1
8							Project 1	1	=	1
9	**Unit costs:**	Project 1	Project 2	Project 3			Project 2	1	=	1
10	Adams	$11.00	$14.00	$6.00			Project 3	1	=	1
11	Brown	$8.00	$10.00	$11.00						
12	Cooper	$9.00	$12.00	$7.00						
13										
14	Total cost =	$25.00								
15										
16		=SUMPRODUCT								
17		(B4:D6, B10:D12)								
18										
19										

Workers have supply of 1 unit each.

Projects have demand of 1 unit each.

Solver Parameters

Set Target Cell: $B$14

Equal To: ○ Max   ● Min   ○ Value of: 0

By Changing Cells:

$B$4:$D$6

Subject to the Constraints:

$H$5:$H$10 = $J$5:$J$10

$$X_{A2} + X_{B2} + X_{C2} = 1 \qquad \text{(Project 2 requirement)}$$
$$X_{A3} + X_{B3} + X_{C3} = 1 \qquad \text{(Project 3 requirement)}$$

Assignment models can sometimes involve a maximization objective.

Excel Solution   Screenshot 5.5 above shows the Excel layout and Solver entries for Fix-It Shop's assignment problem. The optimal solution identified by the model indicates that Adams should be assigned to project 3, Brown to project 2, and Cooper to project 1, for a total cost of $25.

Solving Maximization Assignment Models   The model discussed here can be very easily modified to solve *maximization* assignment problems, in which the objective coefficients represent profits or benefits rather than costs. The only change needed would be in the statement of the objective function (which would be set to maximize instead of minimize).

Unbalanced Assignment Problems   In the Fix-It Shop example, the total number of workers equalled the total number of projects. All supply and demand constraints could therefore be specified as equalities (i.e., using the "=" sign). What if the number of workers exceeds the number of projects, or vice versa? In these cases, we have *unbalanced* assignment models and, just as in the case of unbalanced transportation models, the supply or demand constraints need to be modified accordingly. For example, if the number of workers exceeds the number of projects, the supply constraints would become inequalities and the demand constraints would remain equality constraints. In contrast, if the number of projects exceeds the number of workers, the supply constraints would remain equality constraints and the demand constraints would become inequalities.

5.7   MAXIMAL-FLOW MODEL

The maximal-flow model finds the most material that can flow through a network.

The maximal-flow model allows us to determine the maximum amount of a material that can flow through a network. It has been used, for example, to find the maximum number of automobiles that can flow through a highway road system.

DECISION MODELING IN ACTION
Scheduling Home Care Services in British Columbia

John DeHart and Ken Sim each left Ontario for British Columbia, hoping to make a mark in the growing health care business. By coincidence, they each turned to the same business consultant, who brought the two together. The result is Nurse Next Door, an in-home care provider that continues to grow each year. Nurse Next Door offers professional in-home health care, independent living support services, and palliative care services. About 97% of their clients are either elderly or the children of aged parents.

When DeHart and Sim launched Nurse Next Door Professional Homecare Services in 2001, what they had in mind was a new business that would be the proving ground for an eventual franchise operation that would span North America and maybe even reach well beyond. The pair became so good at creating best practices that they were invited to join the Massachusetts Institute of Technology's Birth of Giants program, whose members represent the 60 best entrepreneurs in high-growth industries around the world.

"Scheduling is one of the biggest challenges you face in an operation like this," Ken Sim says. "We knew from the start that if this was to succeed as a franchise operation, we would have to develop ways to make it as simple and smooth-running as possible for potential franchisees. That meant we would have

to be responsible for scheduling, who goes where for what hours, what they were to do, and whom they were going to do it for."

To ensure a smooth operation, the duo created a call centre, staffed around-the-clock, that handles all scheduling for the original company, the three new franchises now in the process of recruiting their own staff, and any new franchises yet to come.

Mathematical modeling techniques are being developed to address the problems associated with home care (HC) delivery. In a paper titled "A Home Care Scheduling Model for Human Resources," Borsani et al describe LP models (including mixed integer,[1] assignment, and scheduling models) that have been tested with two Italian HC providers. Results showed good improvement in performance during the testing phase. Specific outcome measures that showed improvement include quality of service, patient satisfaction, and improved central planning.

[1]We discuss mixed integer programming in Chapter 6.

Sources: *National Post*, Don Mills, ON: June 4, 2007, p. FP.8; V. Borsani, A. Matta, G. Beschi, and F. Sommaruga. "A Home Care Scheduling Model for Human Resources." http://ieeexplore.ieee.org/iel5/4114390/4114391/04114475.pdf

Road Network in Cornwall, PEI

Cornwall, a small town in PEI, is in the process of developing a road system for the downtown area. Bill Driscoll, a city planner, would like to determine the maximum number of cars that can flow through the town from west to east. The road network is shown in Figure 5.5 on the next page, where the arcs represent the roads.

Traffic can flow in both directions.

The numbers by the nodes indicate the maximum number of cars (in hundreds of cars per hour) that can flow (or travel) *from* the various nodes. For example, the number 3 by node 1 (on the road from node 1 to node 2) indicates that 300 cars per hour can travel from node 1 to node 2. Likewise, the numbers 1, 1, and 2 by node 2 indicate that 100, 100, and 200 cars can travel per hour on the roads from node 2 to nodes 1, 4, and 6, respectively. Note that traffic can flow in both directions down a road. A zero (0) means no flow in that direction, or a one-way road.

Unlike the transportation and assignment models, in which there are multiple source nodes and multiple destination nodes, the typical maximal flow model has a single starting node (source) and a single ending node (destination).

LP Model for Cornwall Road System's Maximal-Flow Problem

We replace each two-way road (arc) with a pair of one-way roads.

To model this problem as an LP problem, we first replace each two-way (bidirectional) road in the network with two one-way (unidirectional) roads with flows in opposite directions. Note that some of the unidirectional roads (e.g., the road from node 4 to node 1, the

FIGURE 5.5

Road Network for Cornwall

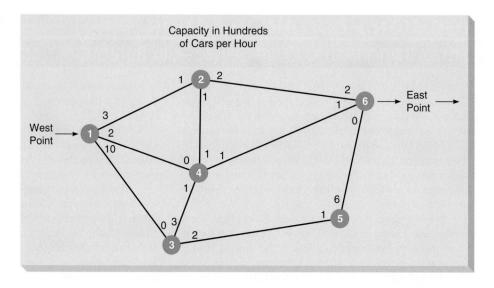

Capacity in Hundreds of Cars per Hour

road from node 6 to node 5) are not needed, since the maximum flow permissible in that direction is zero (i.e., it is a one-way road). The revised network for Cornwall therefore has 15 unidirectional roads (i.e., roads $1 \to 2$, $1 \to 3$, $1 \to 4$, $2 \to 1$, $2 \to 4$, $2 \to 6$, $3 \to 4$, $3 \to 5$, $4 \to 2$, $4 \to 3$, $4 \to 6$, $5 \to 3$, $5 \to 6$, $6 \to 2$, and $6 \to 4$).

There is a decision variable associated with each arc in the network.

As with the transportation and assignment models, the presence of 15 unidirectional arcs in the network implies that there are 15 decision variables in the model—one for each arc (road) in the network. Let

$$X_{ij} = \text{Number of cars that flow (or travel) per hour on road from node } i \text{ to node } j$$

where

$$i = 1, \ 2, \ 3, \ 4, \ 5, \ \text{or } 6 \ (\text{only roads that actually exist are defined})$$

$$j = 1, \ 2, \ 3, \ 4, \ 5, \ \text{or } 6 \ (\text{only roads that actually exist are defined})$$

We need to determine the maximum number of cars that can originate at node 1 and terminate at node 6. Hence, node 1 is the source node in this model and node 6 is the destination node. All other nodes (nodes 2 to 5) are transshipment nodes, where flows of cars neither start nor end. However, unlike the transportation and assignment models, there is neither a known quantity of "supply" of cars available at node 1, nor a known quantity of "demand" for cars required at node 6. For this reason, we need to slightly modify the network to set up and solve the maximal flow model using LP.

We add a one-way dummy road (arc) from the destination node to the source node.

The modification consists of creating a unidirectional *dummy* arc (road) going *from* the destination node (node 6) *to* the source node (node 1). We call this a dummy arc since the arc (road) really does not exist in the network and has been created only for modeling purposes. The capacity of this dummy arc is set at infinity (or any artificially high number, such as 1000 for the Cornwall problem). The modified network is shown in Figure 5.6.

Objective Function   Let us consider the objective function first. The objective is to maximize the total number of cars flowing into node 6. Assume there is an unknown number of cars flowing on the dummy road from node 6 to node 1. However, since there is no "supply" at node 6 (i.e., no cars are "created" at node 6), the entire number of cars flowing out of node 6 (on road $6 \to 1$) must consist of cars that flowed into node 6. Likewise, since there is no "demand" at node 1 (i.e., no cars are "consumed" at node 1), the entire number

FIGURE 5.6

Modified Road Network for Cornwall

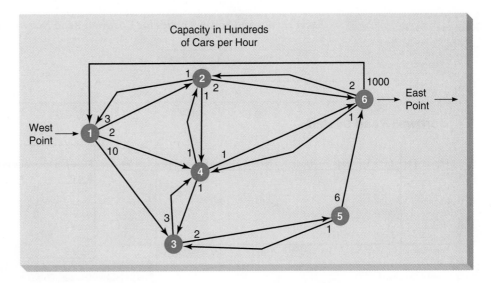

of cars on road $6 \to 1$ must consist of cars that originally flowed out of node 1 (to nodes 2, 3, and 4).

These two issues imply that if we maximize the number of cars flowing on the dummy road $6 \to 1$, this is equivalent to maximizing the total number of cars flowing out of node 1 as well as the total number of cars flowing into node 6. The objective for the Cornwall problem can therefore be written as

The objective is to maximize the flow on the dummy arc.

$$\text{Maximize } X_{61}$$

Constraints   Since all nodes in the network are transshipment nodes with no supplies or demands, the flow balance equations need to ensure that the net flow (i.e., number of cars) at each node is zero. Hence,

All net flows are zero.

$$
\begin{aligned}
(X_{61} + X_{21}) - (X_{12} + X_{13} + X_{14}) &= 0 && \text{(net flow at node 1)} \\
(X_{12} + X_{42} + X_{62}) - (X_{21} + X_{24} + X_{26}) &= 0 && \text{(net flow at node 2)} \\
(X_{13} + X_{43} + X_{53}) - (X_{34} + X_{35}) &= 0 && \text{(net flow at node 3)} \\
(X_{14} + X_{24} + X_{34} + X_{64}) - (X_{42} + X_{43} + X_{46}) &= 0 && \text{(net flow at node 4)} \\
(X_{35}) - (X_{53} + X_{56}) &= 0 && \text{(net flow at node 5)} \\
(X_{26} + X_{46} + X_{56}) - (X_{61} + X_{62} + X_{64}) &= 0 && \text{(net flow at node 6)}
\end{aligned}
$$

Capacity constraints limit the flows on the arcs.

Finally, we have capacity constraints on the maximum number of cars that can flow on each road. These are written as

$X_{12} \leq 3$	$X_{13} \leq 10$	$X_{14} \leq 2$
$X_{21} \leq 1$	$X_{24} \leq 1$	$X_{26} \leq 2$
$X_{34} \leq 3$	$X_{35} \leq 2$	
$X_{42} \leq 1$	$X_{43} \leq 1$	$X_{46} \leq 1$
$X_{53} \leq 1$	$X_{56} \leq 6$	
$X_{61} \leq 1000$	$X_{62} \leq 2$	$X_{64} \leq 1$

File: 5-6.xls

Excel Solution   Screenshot 5.6 on the next page shows the Excel layout and Solver entries for Cornwall's maximal-flow problem. To be consistent with earlier models, flows on arcs have been modeled here using a tabular layout (cells B4:G9). As noted earlier, a big advantage of the tabular layout is that it greatly simplifies the calculations of the total flows in and total flows out of each node in the network.

SCREENSHOT 5.6   **Excel Layout and Solver Entries for Cornwall Road Network's Maximal-Flow Problem**

All values are in 100s of cars per hour.

Only the shaded cells represent roads that actually exist.

RHS = 0 since all nodes are transshipment nodes.

Table shows road capacities.

Road capacity constraints

Changing Cells that are not contiguous are entered with commas separating them.

=B9

Capacity of dummy road from node 6 to node 1 is set to an artificially high value.

Cornwall Road System

	Node 1	Node 2	Node 3	Node 4	Node 5	Node 6	Total flow out
From: To:							
Node 1		2.0	2.0	1.0			5.0
Node 2	0.0			0.0		2.0	2.0
Node 3	0.0			0.0	2.0		2.0
Node 4	0.0	0.0	0.0			1.0	1.0
Node 5			0.0			2.0	2.0
Node 6	5.0	0.0		0.0	0.0		5.0
Total flow in	5.0	2.0	2.0	1.0	2.0	5.0	

Flow balance equations:

Node	Net flow	Sign	RHS
Node 1	0	=	0
Node 2	0	=	0
Node 3	0	=	0
Node 4	0	=	0
Node 5	0	=	0
Node 6	0	=	0

Flow capacity:

From: To:	Node 1	Node 2	Node 3	Node 4	Node 5	Node 6
Node 1		3	10	2		
Node 2	1			1		2
Node 3	0			3	2	
Node 4	0	1	1			1
Node 5			1			6
Node 6	1000	2		1	0	

Maximal flow =	5.0

Solver Parameters

Set Target Cell: [$B$21]

Equal To: ⊙ Max   ○ Min   ○ Value of:

By Changing Cells:

[$B$5:$B$7,$B$9,$C$4,$C$7,$C$9,$D$4,$D$7:]

Subject to the Constraints:

$B$4:$G$9 <= $B$14:$G$19
$K$5:$K$10 = $M$5:$M$10

Entries for nonadjacent cells are separated by commas in Solver.

However, since arcs do not exist from every node to every other node in the network, the decision variables in this model refer only to selected entries in the table. These entries have been shaded yellow in Screenshot 5.6.

How do we handle this situation in Solver? There are several simple ways of doing this. First, rather than specify the entire table (cells B4:G9) as the Changing Cells in Solver, we simply enter the shaded cells, as shown in the Changing Cells windows in Screenshot 5.6. Note that we separate entries for nonadjacent cells by commas.

Although this approach is easy, it could be cumbersome, especially if there are too many decision variables in the model. The second (and easier) approach is to specify the entire table (cells B4:G9) as the Changing Cells in Solver. Then, for all roads that do not exist (e.g., road 1 → 5, road 2 → 3), we simply set the flow capacity on these roads to 0 (modeled in cells B14:G19 in Screenshot 5.6). To illustrate, we enter 0 in cell F14 to prevent a nonzero flow of cars on road 1 → 5 (which does not exist). Solved Problem 5-3 at the end of this chapter shows an example of this approach.

Arc capacities of 0 will prevent flows on arcs.

Alternatively, we can design an Excel layout for this problem without using the tabular layout for the arc flows. That is, we can use 16 contiguous cells to represent the 16 arc flows for the Cornwall problem. Although this approach creates Changing Cells in Solver only for those arcs that actually exist, computing the total flow in and total flow out at different nodes could be cumbersome. In any case, we encourage you to try different Excel layouts for yourself and pick the one you find most convenient.

DECISION MODELING IN ACTION
Simulating Future Traffic Flows in Victoria, B.C.

The Capital Regional District (CRD) is a local government administrative district encompassing the southern tip of Vancouver Island and the southern Gulf Islands. CRD headquarters is in the City of Victoria. The total land area of the CRD is 2341.11 square kilometres. Within two years, a computer model that is being upgraded at CRD will simulate future traffic flows and will allow Greater Victoria politicians to see the impact that a development such as building a new high-rise will have on local traffic.

"It's a move that's overdue, especially in the CRD where there's been no serious attempt to link land use with transportation," said Councillor Vic Derman of the District of Saanich. Mr Derman is chairman of the CRD's TravelChoices committee.

The CRD is spending about $500 000 over the next 18 months to update a computer transportation model it has owned since 1993. About $60 000 of that is to buy new software and licences for the CRD, B.C. Transit, and member municipalities and to update it. The balance is to buy data

such as special runs of census data. The system will allow for traffic testing on several levels, Derman said, ranging from the immediate impact on a local intersection to municipal-wide or regional effects.

"Travel demand is a result of thousands of individuals making decisions on how, where, and when to travel," said Tracy Corbett, CRD senior manager of regional planning. Those decisions are based on a variety of factors ranging from age and income, to household composition, and reasons and modes of travel.

The system is data hungry and has to be fed to be effective, said Corbett. Everything from census data to traffic counts, occupancy counts, car ownership rates, and bus service availability to land-use patterns is plugged in. The new software is visual and will allow politicians to see the impacts of their decisions prior to making them, she said.

Sources: Wikipedia Encyclopedia; *Times-Colonist*. Victoria, B.C.: October 13, 2007, p. A.2.

The solution shows that 500 cars (recall that all numbers are in hundreds of cars) can flow through the town from west to east. The values of the decision variables indicate the actual car flow on each road. Total flow out (column H) and total flow in (row 10) at each node are also shown. For example, the total flow out of node 1 is 500 cars, split as 200 cars on $1 \rightarrow 2$, 200 cars on $1 \rightarrow 3$, and 100 cars on $1 \rightarrow 4$.

5.8 SHORTEST-PATH MODEL

The shortest-path model finds the path with the minimum distance through a network.

The shortest-path model finds how a person or item can travel from one location to another through a network while minimizing the total distance travelled, time taken, or some other measure. In other words, it finds the shortest path or route from an origin to a series of destinations.

Ray Design, Inc. Example

Every day, Ray Design, Inc. must transport beds, chairs, and other furniture items from the factory to the warehouse. This involves going through several cities (nodes). Ray would like to find the path with the shortest distance, in kilometres. The road network is shown in Figure 5.7 on the next page.

The shortest-path problem has a unique starting node and a unique ending node.

The shortest-path model is another example of a network problem that has a unique starting node (source) and a unique terminating node (destination). If we assume that there is a supply of 1 unit at node 1 (plant) and a demand of 1 unit at node 6 (warehouse), the shortest path model for the Ray Design example is identical to a transshipment problem with a single source node (node 1), a single destination node (node 6), and 4 transshipment nodes (node 2 through node 5).

All flows in a shortest-path problem will equal one unit.

Since the supply and demand both equal 1 unit, which is a whole number, the solution to the problem will have integer-valued flows on all arcs. Hence, the supply of 1 unit at

FIGURE 5.7

**Roads from Ray's Plant
to Warehouse**

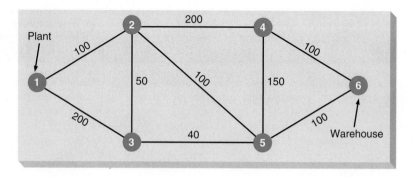

node 1 will flow in its entirety on either road 1 → 2 or road 1 → 3. Further, since the net flow is zero at each of the transshipment nodes (cities), a flow of 1 unit on an incoming arc (road) at any of these cities automatically has to result in a flow of 1 unit on an outgoing road from that city.

LP Model for Ray Design, Inc.'s Shortest-Path Problem

Since all nine arcs (roads) in the network are bidirectional, we first replace each one by a pair of unidirectional roads. There are, therefore, 18 decision variables in the model. As usual, let

X_{ij} = "Flow" on the road from node i to node j. The solution value will equal 1 if travel occurs on the road from node i to node j and will equal 0 otherwise.

where

$i = 1, 2, 3, 4, 5,$ or 6 (only roads that actually exist are defined)

$j = 1, 2, 3, 4, 5,$ or 6 (only roads that actually exist are defined)

Objective Function   The objective is to minimize the distance between node 1 and node 6 and can be expressed as

$$\text{Minimize } 100\,X_{12} + 200\,X_{13} + 100\,X_{21} + 50\,X_{23} + 200\,X_{24} + 100\,X_{25}$$
$$+\ 200\,X_{31} + 50\,X_{32} + 40\,X_{35} + 200\,X_{42} + 150\,X_{45} + 100\,X_{46}$$
$$+\ 100\,X_{52} + 40\,X_{53} + 150\,X_{54} + 100\,X_{56} + 100\,X_{64} + 100\,X_{65}$$

The optimal value for each variable will be 0 or 1 depending on whether travel occurs on that road. So the objective function is the sum of road distances on which travel (flow) actually occurs.

Constraints   We write the flow balance constraints at each node as follows:

$$(X_{21} + X_{31}) - (X_{12} + X_{13}) = -1 \quad \text{(Supply of 1 unit at node 1)}$$
$$(X_{12} + X_{32} + X_{42} + X_{52}) - (X_{21} + X_{23} + X_{24} + X_{25}) = 0 \quad \text{(Transshipment at node 2)}$$
$$(X_{13} + X_{23} + X_{53}) - (X_{31} + X_{32} + X_{35}) = 0 \quad \text{(Transshipment at node 3)}$$
$$(X_{24} + X_{54} + X_{64}) - (X_{42} + X_{45} + X_{46}) = 0 \quad \text{(Transshipment at node 4)}$$
$$(X_{25} + X_{35} + X_{45} + X_{65}) - (X_{52} + X_{53} + X_{54} + X_{56}) = 0 \quad \text{(Transshipment at node 5)}$$
$$(X_{46} + X_{56}) - (X_{64} + X_{65}) = 1 \quad \text{(Demand of 1 unit at node 6)}$$

File: 5-7.xls

Excel Solution   Screenshot 5.7 shows the Excel layout and Solver entries for Ray Design, Inc.'s shortest-path problem. Once again, we use the tabular layout to represent arc flows. However, as with the maximal-flow problem, certain arcs do not exist and need to be excluded when specifying entries for the Changing Cells in Solver. This can be achieved by separating noncontiguous cell entries by commas (as shown in Screenshot 5.7).

SCREENSHOT 5.7   **Excel Layout and Solver Entries for Ray Design, Inc.'s Shortest-Path Problem**

> Only the shaded cells represent roads that actually exist.

	A	B	C	D	E	F	G	H	I	J	K	L	M
1	**Ray Design, Inc.**												
2													
3	**From: To:**	Node 1	Node 2	Node 3	Node 4	Node 5	Node 6	Total flow out		**Flow balance equations:**			
4	Node 1		1.0	0.0				1.0		**Node**	**Net flow**	**Sign**	**RHS**
5	Node 2	0.0		1.0	0.0	0.0		1.0		Node 1	-1	=	-1
6	Node 3	0.0	0.0			1.0		1.0		Node 2	0	=	0
7	Node 4		0.0			0.0	0.0	0.0		Node 3	0	=	0
8	Node 5		0.0	0.0	0.0		1.0	1.0		Node 4	0	=	0
9	Node 6			0.0	0.0			0.0		Node 5	0	=	0
10	Total flow in	0.0	1.0	1.0	0.0	1.0	1.0			Node 6	1	=	1
11													
12	**Distances:**												
13	**From: To:**	Node 1	Node 2	Node 3	Node 4	Node 5	Node 6						
14	Node 1		100	200									
15	Node 2	100		50	200	100							
16	Node 3	200	50			40							
17	Node 4		200			150	100						
18	Node 5		100	40	150		100						
19	Node 6				100	100							
20													
21	Shorest distance =	290.0											

> Supply of one unit at node 1.

> Demand of one unit at node 6.

Solver Parameters

Set Target Cell: [$B$21]

Equal To: ○ Max ◉ Min ○ Value of:

By Changing Cells:

[$B$5:$B$6,$C$4,$C$6:$C$8,$D$4:$D$5,$D$8,]

Subject to the Constraints:

[$K$5:$K$10 = $M$5:$M$10]

> Noncontiguous cell entries are separated by commas.

> =SUMPRODUCT (B4:G9, B14:G19)

Arcs with large (infinite) distances will have zero flows.

Alternatively, the entire table (cells B4:G9) can be specified as the Changing Cells in Solver. However, to prevent items from flowing on roads that do not exist (e.g., $1 \rightarrow 4$, $1 \rightarrow 5$), the distance of these roads can be set to infinity (or a very large number) in the corresponding cells in B14:G19. For example, we would enter a distance of infinity for road $1 \rightarrow 4$ in cell E14. Since the objective is to minimize total distance, no travel will occur on these roads due to their high cost.

The solution shows that the shortest distance from the plant to the warehouse is 290 kilometres and involves travel through cities 2, 3, and 5.

5.9 MINIMAL-SPANNING TREE MODEL

The minimal-spanning tree model connects nodes at a minimum total distance.

The *minimal-spanning tree model* can be used to connect all the nodes of a network to one another while minimizing the total distance of all the arcs used for this connection. It has been applied, for example, by telephone companies to connect a number of phones (nodes) together while minimizing the total length of telephone cable (arcs).

Lauderdale Construction Company Example

Let us consider the Lauderdale Construction Company, which is currently developing a luxurious housing project on a lakefront in Northern Ontario. Melvin Lauderdale, owner and president of Lauderdale Construction, must determine the least expensive way to provide water and power to each house. The network of houses is shown in Figure 5.8 on the next page.

As seen in Figure 5.8, there are eight houses on the waterfront. The distances between houses (in hundreds of metres) are shown on the network. For example, the

DECISION MODELING IN ACTION
Spanning Tree Analysis of a Telecommunications Network

Network models have been used to solve a variety of problems for many different companies. In telecommunications, there is always a need to connect computer systems and devices together in an efficient and effective manner. Digital Equipment Corporation (DEC) for example, was concerned about how computer systems and devices were connected to a local area network (LAN) using a technology called Ethernet. The DEC net routing department was responsible for this and other network and telecommunications solutions.

Because of a number of technical difficulties, it was important to have an effective way to transport packets of information throughout the LAN. The solution was to use a spanning tree algorithm. The success of this approach can be seen in a poem written by one of the developers:

"I think I shall never see a graph more lovely than a tree.

A tree whose critical property is loop-free connectivity.

A tree that must be sure to span, so packets can reach every LAN.

First the route must be selected, by ID it is elected.

Least-cost paths from the root are traced.

In the tree these paths are placed.

A mesh is made for folks by me, then bridges find a spanning tree."

Source: Radia Perlman et al. "Spanning the LAN," *Data Communications* (October 21, 1997): 68.

distance between houses 1 and 2 is 300 metres (shown by the 3 on the arc connecting houses 1 and 2). Now, we can use the minimal-spanning tree model to determine the minimum total length (of water pipes or power cables) needed to connect all the houses.

Unlike the other network flow models studied so far in this chapter, the minimal-spanning tree problem is difficult to formulate as an LP problem using the typical flow balance equations. However, the minimal-spanning tree model is very easy to solve by hand using a simple solution procedure. The procedure is outlined as follows:

There are four steps in the solution procedure for minimal-spanning tree problems.

FIGURE 5.8

Network for Lauderdale Construction

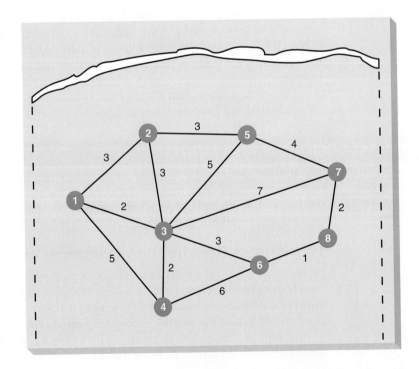

There are four steps in the
solution procedure for
minimal-spanning tree
problems.
Step 1: We select node 1.
Step 2: We connect node 1 to
node 3.
Step 3: We connect the next
nearest node (node 4).
Step 4: We repeat Step 3 until
all nodes are connected.

Steps for Solving the Minimal-Spanning Tree Model

1. Begin by selecting any node in the network.
2. Connect this node to its nearest node.
3. Considering all the connected nodes, find the nearest *unconnected* node, and connect it. If there is a tie and two or more unconnected nodes are equally near, select one arbitrarily. A tie suggests there may be more than one optimal solution.
4. Repeat the third step until all the nodes are connected.

We can now solve the network in Figure 5.8 for Melvin Lauderdale. We start by arbitrarily selecting any node (house). Let's say we select house 1. Since house 3 is the nearest one to house 1 at a distance of 2 (200 metres), we connect these two houses. That is, we select arc 1 → 3 for inclusion in the spanning tree. This is shown in Figure 5.9.

Next, considering connected houses 1 and 3, we look for the unconnected house that is closest to either house. This turns out to be house 4, which is 200 metres from house 3. We connect houses 3 and 4 by selecting arc 3 → 4 (see Figure 5.10(a) on the next page).

We continue, looking for the nearest unconnected house to houses 1, 3, and 4. This is house 2 or house 6, both at a distance of 300 metres from house 3. We arbitrarily pick house 2 and connect it to house 3 by selecting arc 3 → 2 (see Figure 5.10(b) on the next page).

We continue the process. There is another tie for the next iteration with a minimum distance of 300 metres (house 2 to house 5, and house 3 to house 6). Note that we do not consider house 1 to house 2 with a distance of 300 metres at this iteration since both houses are already connected. We arbitrarily select house 5 and connect it to house 2 by selecting arc 2 → 5 (see Figure 5.11(a) on the next page). The next nearest house is house 6, and we connect it to house 3 by selecting arc 3 → 6 (see Figure 5.11(b) on the next page).

At this stage, we have only two unconnected houses left. House 8 is the nearest one to house 6 with a distance of 100 metres, and we connect it using arc 6 → 8 (see Figure 5.12(a) on the next page). Then the remaining house (house 7) is connected to house 8 using arc 8 → 7 (see Figure 5.12(b) on the next page).

FIGURE 5.9

First Iteration for Lauderdale Construction

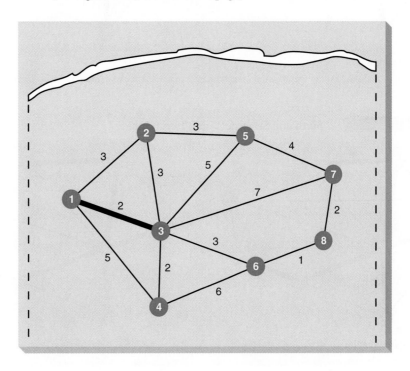

FIGURE 5.10 Second and Third Iterations

(*a*) Second Iteration (*b*) Third Iteration

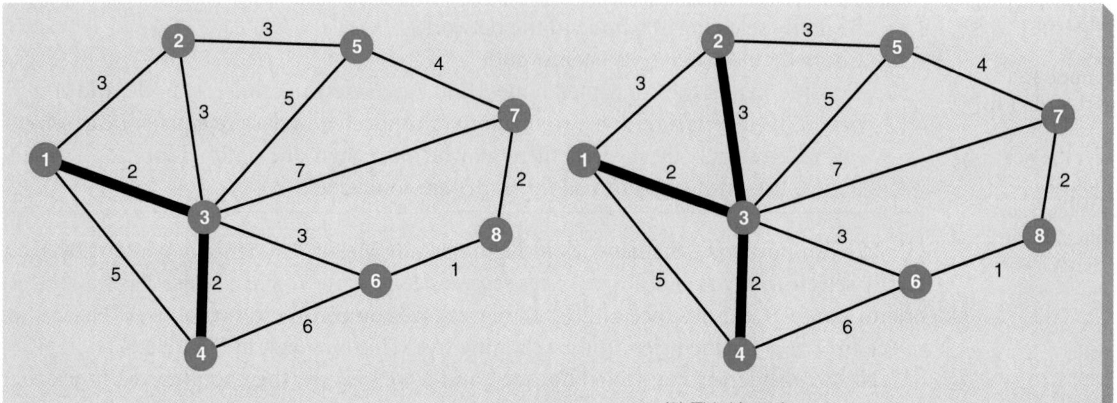

FIGURE 5.11 Fourth and Fifth Iterations

(*a*) Fourth Iteration (*b*) Fifth Iteration

FIGURE 5.12 Sixth and Seventh (Final) Iterations

(*a*) Sixth Iteration (*b*) Seventh Iteration

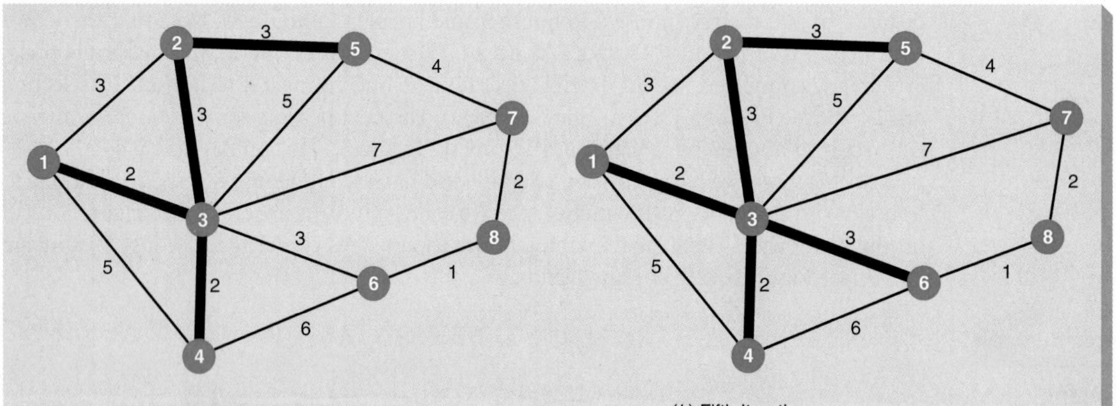

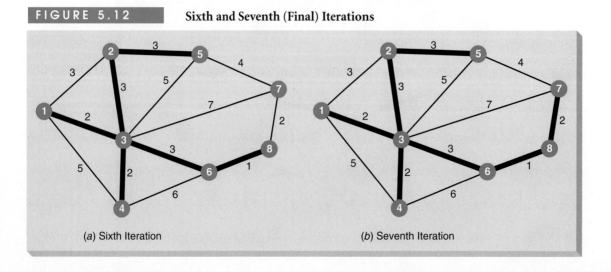

Since there are no more unconnected houses, Figure 5.12(b) shows the final solution. Houses 1, 2, 4, and 6 are all connected to house 3. House 2 is connected to house 5. House 6 is connected to house 8, and house 8 is connected to house 7. The total distance is 1600 metres.

SUMMARY

This chapter presents six important network flow models. First, we discuss the transportation model, which deals with the distribution of goods from several supply points to a number of demand points. We then extend this discussion to the transshipment model, which includes points that permit goods to both flow in and flow out of them. Next, we discuss the assignment model, which deals with determining the most efficient assignment of issues such as people to projects.

The fourth model covered is the maximal-flow model, which finds the maximum flow of any quantity or substance that can go through a network. This is followed by a discussion of the shortest-path model, which finds the shortest path through a network. Finally, we introduce the minimal-spanning tree model, which determines the path through the network that connects all of the nodes while minimizing total distance.

GLOSSARY

Arc. The line or path between two nodes in a network.

Assignment Problem. A specific class of LP problems that involves determining the most efficient assignment of people to projects, salespeople to territories, contracts to bidders, jobs to machines, and so on.

Balanced Problem. The condition under which total demand (at all destinations) is equal to total supply (at all sources).

Destination or **Sink.** A demand location in a transportation problem.

Facility Location Analysis. An application of the transportation model to help a firm decide where to locate a new factory, warehouse, or other facility.

Hub-and-spoke. A transportation system in which travel from one area to another is routed through a central point, or *hub*.

Maximal-Flow Problem. A problem that finds the maximum flow of any quantity or substance through a network.

Minimal-Spanning Tree Model. Determines the path through the network that connects all of the nodes while minimizing total distance.

Net Flow. The difference between the total flow in to a node and the total flow out of the node.

Network. A series of connections, such as transportation or telecommunications, between a number of *nodes*, or points.

Network Flow Model. A special type of LP model, used for problems such as transportation and assignment, that deals with *arcs* (paths) connecting a number of *nodes*, or points.

Node. A specific point or location in a network.

Shortest-Path Problem. A problem that determines the shortest path or route through a network.

Source or **Origin.** An origin or supply location in a transportation problem.

Transportation Model. A specific case of LP involving scheduling shipments from sources to destinations so that total shipping costs are minimized.

Transshipment Point. A point in a network that is both a source and a destination; flows go both in and out.

Transshipment Problem. An extension of the transportation problem in which some points have flows both in to and out of them.

Unbalanced Problem. A situation in which total demand is not equal to total supply.

KEY EQUATION

(5-1) Net flow = Total flow in to node − Total flow out of node
Flow balance constraint written for each node in the network.

SOLVED PROBLEMS

Solved Problem 5-1

Jorge daSilva, president of Hardrock Concrete Company, has plants in three locations and is currently working on three major construction projects, located at different sites. The shipping cost per truckload of concrete, plant capacities, and project requirements are provided in the accompanying table.

FROM \ TO	PROJECT A	PROJECT B	PROJECT C	PLANT CAPACITIES
Plant 1	$10	$ 4	$11	70
Plant 2	$12	$ 5	$ 8	50
Plant 3	$ 9	$ 7	$ 6	30
Project Requirements	40	50	60	150

Set up and solve Hardrock's problem as a transportation model.

File: 5-8.xls

Solution

There are three sources (plants 1, 2, and 3) and three destinations (projects A, B, and C). Hence, there are nine decision variables. The Excel layout and solution is shown in Screenshot 5.8. The optimal solution costs $1040 and involves shipping truckloads of concrete as follows: 20 truckloads from plant 1 to project A, 50 truckloads from plant 1 to project B, 50 truckloads from plant 2 to project C, 20 truckloads from plant 3 to project A, and 10 truckloads from plant 3 to project C.

SCREENSHOT 5.8 **Excel Layout and Solver Entries for Hardrock Concrete Company's Transportation Problem**

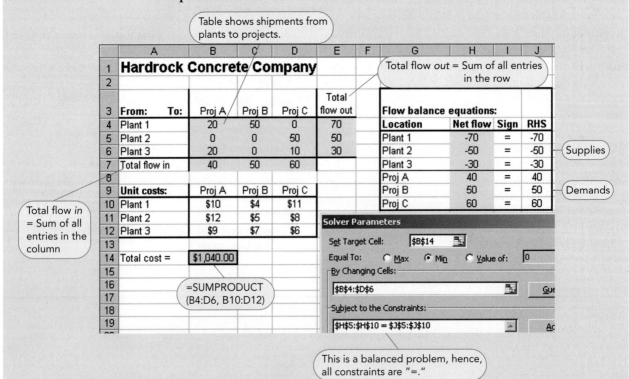

Solved Problem 5-2

Pearson Canada, a publisher headquartered in Toronto, wants to assign three recently hired university graduates, Jones, Smith, and Wilson, to regional sales districts in Ottawa, Edmonton, and Vancouver. But the firm also has an opening in Toronto and would send one of the three there if it were more economical than a move to Ottawa, Edmonton, or Vancouver. It will cost $1000 to relocate Jones to Toronto, $800 to relocate Smith there, and $1500 to move Wilson. What is the optimal assignment of personnel to offices?

HIRE \ OFFICE	OTTAWA	EDMONTON	VANCOUVER
Jones	$800	$1100	$1200
Smith	$500	$1600	$1300
Wilson	$500	$1000	$2300

Solution

Since this is an unbalanced assignment problem with three supply points (hirees) and four demand points (offices), note that the demand constraints should be expressed as inequalities (that is, they should have ≤ signs).

The Excel layout and solution for Pearson Canada's assignment problem is shown in Screenshot 5.9. The optimal solution is to assign Wilson to Ottawa, Smith to Toronto, and Jones to Edmonton. Nobody is assigned to Vancouver. The total cost is $2400.

File: 5-9.xls

SCREENSHOT 5.9

Excel Layout and Solver Entries for Pearson Canada's Assignment Problem

> Optimal solution has no one assigned to Vancouver.

	A	B	C	D	E	F	G	H	I	J	K
1	**Pearson Canada**										
2											
3	Hiree: Office:	Ottawa	Edmonton	Vancouver	Toronto	Total flow out		Flow balance equations:			
4	Jones	0.0	1.0	0.0	0.0	1		Node	Net flow	Sign	RHS
5	Smith	0.0	0.0	0.0	1.0	1		Jones	-1	=	-1
6	Wilson	1.0	0.0	0.0	0.0	1		Smith	-1	=	-1
7	Total flow in	1	1	0	1			Wilson	-1	=	-1
8								Ottawa	1	<=	1
9	Unit costs:	Ottawa	Edmonton	Vancouver	Toronto			Edmonton	0	<=	1
10	Jones	$800	$1,100	$1,200	$1,000			Vancouver	1	<=	1
11	Smith	$500	$1,600	$1,300	$800			Toronto	1	<=	1
12	Wilson	$500	$1,000	$2,300	$1,500						
13											
14	Total cost =	$2,400									
15											
16											
17											
18											
19											
20											
21											
22											
23											
24											
25											
26											
27											

> Demand flow balance constraints are ≤ since number of locations exceeds number of hirees.

Solver Parameters

Set Target Cell: $B$14

Equal To: ○ Max ● Min ○ Value of: 0

By Changing Cells:

$B$4:$E$6

Subject to the Constraints:

$I$5:$I$7 = $K$5:$K$7
$I$8:$I$11 <= $K$8:$K$11

Solved Problem 5-3

OiloCan, an oil refinery located in Northern Alberta, is designing a new plant to produce diesel fuel. Figure 5.13 shows the network of the main processing centres along with the existing rate of flow (in thousands of litres of fuel). The management at OiloCan would like to determine the maximum amount of fuel that can flow through the plant, from node 1 to node 7.

Solution

Node 1 is the source node and node 7 is the destination node. As described in Section 5.7, we introduce a dummy arc from node 7 to node 1 (see Figure 5.14). The capacity of this arc is set at a large number (say, 1000).

The Excel layout and solution for this problem is shown in Screenshot 5.10. Unlike our earlier example in Screenshot 5.6, the entire table (cells B4:H10) has been specified as the Changing Cells in Solver. However, the capacity of all arcs that do not exist (shown by the non-yellow cells in B4:H10) has been set to zero to prevent any fuel flows on these pipes (arcs).

The optimal solution shows that it is possible to have 10 000 litres flow from node 1 to node 7 using the existing network.

File: 5-10.xls

FIGURE 5.13

Network for OiloCan

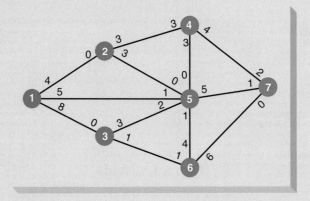

FIGURE 5.14

Modified Network for Solved Problem 5-3

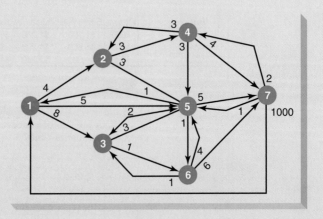

SCREENSHOT 5.10 **Excel Layout and Solver Entries for OiloCan's Maximal-Flow Problem**

	A	B	C	D	E	F	G	H	I	J	K	L	M	N
1	**OiloCan**													
2					*Table shows the flow between nodes.*		*Only the shaded cells denote pipes that actually exist.*							
3	From: To:	Node 1	Node 2	Node 3	Node 4	Node 5	Node 6	Node 7	Total flow out		**Flow balance equations:**			
4	Node 1	0.0	4.0	1.0	0.0	5.0	0.0	0.0	10.0		Node	Net flow	Sign	RHS
5	Node 2	0.0	0.0	0.0	3.0	1.0	0.0	0.0	4.0		Node 1	0	=	0
6	Node 3	0.0	0.0	0.0	0.0	0.0	1.0	0.0	1.0		Node 2	0	=	0
7	Node 4	0.0	0.0	0.0	0.0	0.0	0.0	3.0	3.0		Node 3	0	=	0
8	Node 5	0.0	0.0	0.0	0.0	0.0	1.0	5.0	6.0		Node 4	0	=	0
9	Node 6	0.0	0.0	0.0	0.0	0.0	0.0	2.0	2.0		Node 5	0	=	0
10	Node 7	10.0	0.0	0.0	0.0	0.0	0.0	0.0	10.0		Node 6	0	=	0
11	Total flow in	10.0	4.0	1.0	3.0	6.0	2.0	10.0			Node 7	0	=	0
12														
13	**Flow capacity:**													
14	From: To:	Node 1	Node 2	Node 3	Node 4	Node 5	Node 6	Node 7						
15	Node 1	0	4	8	0	5	0	0						
16	Node 2	0	0	0	3	3	0	0						
17	Node 3	0	0	0	0	3	1	0						
18	Node 4	0	3	0	0	3	0	4						
19	Node 5	1	0	2	0	0	1	5						
20	Node 6	0	0	1	0	4	0	6						
21	Node 7	1000	0	0	2	1	0	0						
22														
23	Maximal flow =	10.0												
24														

Solver Parameters

Set Target Cell: $B$23

Equal To: ● Max ○ Min ○ Value of:

By Changing Cells:
$B$4:$H$10

Subject to the Constraints:
$B$4:$H$10 <= $B$15:$H$21
$L$5:$L$11 = $N$5:$N$11

This is the capacity of dummy pipe from node 7 to node 1.

Capacities of pipes that do not exist are set to zero.

All cells in the table (B4:H10) are specified as Changing Cells. No flow occurs on pipes that do not exist since their capacities are zero.

Solved Problem 5-4

The network of Figure 5.15 on the next page shows highways and cities to the east of Russett Hill. Numbers on the arcs represent distances between cities in kilometres. Safeheads Inc., a bicycle helmet manufacturer in Russett Hill, must transport its helmets to a distributor based in Haleford. To do this, the company must go through several cities. Safeheads would like to find the shortest way to get from Russett Hill to Haleford. What do you recommend?

Solution

We associate a supply of 1 unit at Russett Hill (node 1) and a demand of 1 unit at Haleford (node 16). The Excel layout and solution for this problem are shown in Screenshot 5.11 on the next page. As we saw earlier in Screenshot 5.7, the Changing Cell entries in Solver include only those cells that represent actual arcs (shown by the yellow shaded cells in B4:G19). Note that it is not possible to denote the entire table as Changing Cells in this example since the number of decision variables will be 256 (= 16 × 16). This exceeds the maximum permissible size of 200 decision variables for the standard version of Solver.

The optimal solution shows that the shortest distance from Russett Hill to Haleford is 460 kilometres and involves travel through nodes 3, 7, 11, and 14.

File: 5-11.xls

FIGURE 5.15

Network for Safeheads Inc.

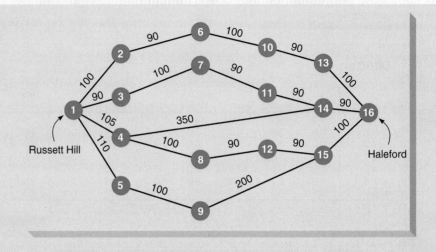

SCREENSHOT 5.11

Excel Layout and Solver Entries for Safeheads Inc.'s Shortest-Path Problem

Shaded cells denote routes that actually exist.

Table shows the flows between cities.

	A	B	C	D	E	F	G	H	I	J	K	L	M	N	O	P	Q	R	S	T	U	V	W
1	**Safeheads**																						
2																							
3	**From: To**	Nd1	Nd2	Nd3	Nd4	Nd5	Nd6	Nd7	Nd8	Nd9	Nd10	Nd11	Nd12	Nd13	Nd14	Nd15	Nd16	Flow out		Flow balance equations:			
4	Nd1		0.0	1.0	0.0	0.0												1.0		Node	Net flow	Sign	RHS
5	Nd2	0.0					0.0											0.0		Nd1	-1	=	-1
6	Nd3	0.0						1.0										1.0		Nd2	0	=	0
7	Nd4	0.0							0.0				0.0					0.0		Nd3	0	=	0
8	Nd5	0.0								0.0								0.0		Nd4	0	=	0
9	Nd6		0.0								0.0							0.0		Nd5	0	=	0
10	Nd7			0.0								1.0						1.0		Nd6	0	=	0
11	Nd8				0.0								0.0					0.0		Nd7	0	=	0
12	Nd9				0.0													0.0		Nd8	0	=	0
13	Nd10					0.0								0.0				0.0		Nd9	0	=	0
14	Nd11						0.0								1.0			1.0		Nd10	0	=	0
15	Nd12							0.0								0.0		0.0		Nd11	0	=	0
16	Nd13								0.0								0.0	0.0		Nd12	0	=	0
17	Nd14				0.0					0.0							1.0	1.0		Nd13	0	=	0
18	Nd15							0.0			0.0						0.0	0.0		Nd14	0	=	0
19	Nd16												0.0	0.0	0.0			0.0		Nd15	0	=	0
20	Total flow in	0.0	0.0	1.0	0.0	0.0	0.0	1.0	0.0	0.0	0.0	1.0	0.0	0.0	1.0	0.0	1.0			Nd16	1	=	1
21																							
22	**Distances:**																						
23	**From: To**	Nd1	Nd2	Nd3	Nd4	Nd5	Nd6	Nd7	Nd8	Nd9	Nd10	Nd11	Nd12	Nd13	Nd14	Nd15	Nd16						
24	Nd1		100	90	105	110																	
25	Nd2	100					90																
26	Nd3	90						100															
27	Nd4	105							100				350										
28	Nd5	110								100													
29	Nd6		30								100												
30	Nd7			100								90											
31	Nd8				100								90										
32	Nd9				100											200							
33	Nd10					100								90									
34	Nd11						30								90								
35	Nd12							30								30							
36	Nd13								30								100						
37	Nd14				350					30							30						
38	Nd15							200			30						100						
39	Nd16												100	30	100								
40																							
41	Shortest distance =	460																					

Solver Parameters

Set Target Cell: $B$41

Equal To: ○ Max ⦿ Min ○ Value of:

By Changing Cells:

$B$5:$B$8,$C$4,$C$9,$D$4,$D$10,$E$4,$E$1

Subject to the Constraints:

$U$5:$U$20 = $W$5:$W$20

This is the supply of one unit at node 1.

This is the demand of one unit at node 16.

Changing cells not in adjacent cells are separated by commas.

Solved Problem 5-5

Fred and Martha Wilder, owners of the F&M horse-breeding ranch in Alberta, are planning to install a complete water system connecting all the various stables and barns. The locations of the facilities and the distances between them are given in the network shown in Figure 5.16. The Wilders must determine the least expensive way to provide water to each facility. What do you recommend?

FIGURE 5.16

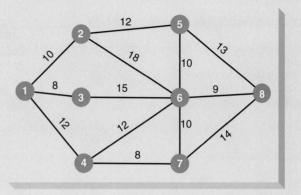

Solution

This is a typical minimum-spanning tree problem that can be solved by hand. We begin by selecting node 1 and connecting it to the nearest node, which is node 3. Nodes 1 and 2 are the next to be connected, followed by nodes 1 and 4. Now we connect node 4 to node 7 and node 7 to node 6. At this point, the only remaining points to be connected are node 6 to node 8 and node 6 to node 5. The final solution can be seen in Figure 5.17.

FIGURE 5.17

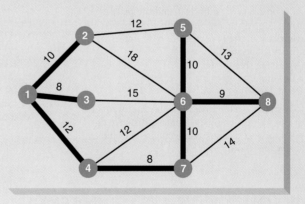

SELF-TEST

- Before taking the self-test, refer back to the learning objectives at the beginning of the chapter, the notes in the margins, and the glossary at the end of the chapter.
- Use the key at the back of the book to correct your answers.
- Restudy pages that correspond to any questions that you answered incorrectly or material you feel uncertain about.

1. Which model is used to connect all points of a network together while minimizing the distance between them?
   a. maximal flow
   b. minimal flow
   c. minimal-spanning tree
   d. shortest route
   e. longest span

2. The first step in solving the minimal-spanning tree model is to select
   a. the node with the greatest distance between it and any other node.
   b. the node with the least distance between it and any other node.
   c. the node that is closest to the origin.
   d. any arc that connects two nodes.
   e. any node.

3. Which model involves finding the nearest node to the origin?
   a. maximal flow
   b. minimal flow
   c. maximal-spanning tree
   d. minimal-spanning tree
   e. shortest route

4. The fire chief was not satisfied with the amount of water put on the warehouse fire by pumper 3. With two hydrant connections and a number of different (known) hose capacities due to leakage and repairs, the chief could determine the best combination by several uses of the
   a. minimal-spanning tree model.
   b. maximal-flow model.
   c. shortest-route model.

5. The fire chief is on a very tight budget, and the price of gasoline has just gone up again. She wants to minimize the distance travelled by all the fire trucks to each fire hydrant in case of a fire call. She should use the
   a. minimal-spanning tree model.
   b. maximal-flow model.
   c. shortest-route model.

6. Tearing up city streets is expensive. The fire chief wants to convince the city council, using the smallest-distance figures, to put in a new water main connecting eight vital spots downtown. She should use the
   a. minimal-spanning tree model.
   b. maximal-flow model.
   c. shortest-route model.

7. The Enfield Company is very concerned about shipping costs when moving its products from its various factories to its regional warehouses. To minimize these costs, it should use the
   a. transportation model.
   b. assignment model.
   c. shortest-path model.
   d. maximal-flow model.

8. A student project has four tasks and is to be done by a group of four students. Which model is appropriate to use when deciding which student should be responsible for which task?
   a. the transportation model
   b. the assignment model
   c. the shortest-path model
   d. the maximal-flow model

9. _____ is a model that is used to find how a person or item can travel from one location to another while minimizing the total distance travelled.

10. The model that allows us to determine the maximum amount of a material that can flow through a network is called _____.

11. The _____ model can be used to connect all the points of a network together while minimizing the distance between them.

12. A point or node that has shipments arrive as well as leave is called a
    a. supply node.
    b. demand node.
    c. transshipment node.
    d. dummy node.

13. The net flow at each node is calculated as
    a. total flow in − total flow out.
    b. total flow in + total flow out.
    c. total flow in.
    d. total flow out.

DISCUSSION QUESTIONS AND PROBLEMS

Discussion Questions

5-1 Is the transportation model an example of decision making under certainty or decision making under uncertainty? Why?

5-2 What is a balanced transportation problem? Describe the approach you would use to solve an unbalanced problem.

5-3 What is the enumeration approach to solving assignment problems? Is it a practical way to solve a 5 row × 5 column problem? A 7 × 7 problem? Why?

5-4 What is the minimal-spanning tree model? What types of problems can be solved using this type of model?

5-5 Give several examples of problems that can be solved using the maximal-flow model.

5-6 Describe a problem that can be solved by the shortest-route model.

5-7 What is a flow balance constraint? How is it implemented at each node in a network model?

5-8 How can we manipulate a maximal-flow network model in order to set it up as a linear program?

5-9 Why might it be more convenient to set up network models in Excel using a "tabular" form?

5-10 How can we manipulate a maximal-flow network model

in order to specify all arcs between each pair of nodes (i.e., the entire table) as the Changing Cells in Solver?

5-11 How can we manipulate a shortest-path network model in order to specify all arcs between each pair of nodes (i.e., the entire table) as the Changing Cells in Solver?

Problems

5-12 The superintendent of schools in a district is responsible for assigning students to the three high schools in the district. He recognizes the need to bus a certain number of students, because some areas of the district are beyond walking distance to a school. The superintendent partitions the district into five geographic sectors as he attempts to establish a plan that will minimize the total number of student kilometres travelled by bus. He also recognizes that if a student happens to live in a certain sector and is assigned to the high school in that sector, there is no need to bus that student because he or she can walk to school. The three schools are located in sectors, B, C, and E.

The table for this problem (at the bottom of the page) reflects the number of high-school-aged students living in each sector and the distance in kilometres from each sector to each school.

Each high school has a capacity of 900 students. Set up the objective function and constraints of this problem using LP so that the total number of student kilometres travelled by bus is minimized. Then solve the problem.

5-13 Marc Simard's construction firm currently has three projects under way in various towns in Quebec. Each requires a specific supply of gravel. Three gravel pits are available in Quebec to provide for Simard's needs, but shipping costs differ from location to location. The following table summarizes the problem Simard faces.

TO / FROM	JOB 1	JOB 2	JOB 3	TONNAGE ALLOWANCE
Kamouraska pit	$9	$8	$7	1500
Chicoutimi pit	7	11	6	1750
Maniwaki pit	4	3	12	2750
Job requirements (tonnes)	2000	3000	1000	6000

(a) Determine Simard's optimal shipping quantities so as to minimize total transportation costs.

(b) Examining the map, Simard recognizes that jobs 1 and 2 are very near Maniwaki. Rather than shipping gravel directly from the Kamouraska and Chicoutimi pits to these job sites, Simard wonders if it would be better for him to consolidate shipping at Maniwaki. Given the excellent roads between major cities in Quebec, he believes he can ship gravel between Chicoutimi and Maniwaki and between Kamouraska and Maniwaki for as little as $2 per tonne. Set up and solve Simard's problem now with this new information.

5-14 The Caledonia Lines Railway Company specializes in transporting coal. On Friday, April 13, Caledonia had empty cars at the following towns in the quantities indicated:

TOWN	SUPPLY OF CARS
Truro	35
New Bedford	60
Glace Bay	25

By Monday, April 16, the following towns will need coal cars as follows:

TOWN	DEMAND FOR CARS
Coal Valley	30
Coaltown	45
Coal Junction	25
Coalsburg	20

Using a railway city-to-city distance chart, the dispatcher constructs a table showing distances, in kilometres, for the preceding towns. The result is shown at the top of the next page.

Minimizing total distance over which cars are moved to new locations, compute the best shipment of coal cars.

Table for Problem 5-12

SECTOR	DISTANCE TO SCHOOL — SCHOOL IN SECTOR B	SCHOOL IN SECTOR C	SCHOOL IN SECTOR E	NUMBER OF STUDENTS
A	5	8	6	700
B	0	4	12	500
C	4	0	7	100
D	7	2	5	800
E	12	7	0	400
				2500

Table for Problem 5-14

FROM \ TO	COAL VALLEY	COALTOWN	COAL JUNCTION	COALSBURG
Truro	50	30	60	70
New Bedford	20	80	10	90
Glace Bay	100	40	80	30

5-15 The B. Hall Real Estate Investment Corporation has identified four small apartment buildings in which it would like to invest. Mrs. Hall has approached three loan companies regarding financing. Because Hall has been a good client in the past and has maintained a high credit rating in the community, each loan company is willing to consider providing all or part of the mortgage loan needed on each property. Each loan officer has set differing interest rates on each property (rates are affected by the neighbourhood of the apartment building, condition of the property, and desire by the individual loan company to finance various-size buildings), *and* each loan company has placed a maximum credit ceiling on how much it will lend Hall in total. This information is summarized in the table for this problem (shown at the bottom of the page).

Each apartment building is equally attractive as an investment to Hall, so she has decided to purchase all buildings possible at the lowest total payment of interest. From which loan company should she borrow to purchase which buildings? More than one loan company can finance the same property.

5-16 The J. Mehta Company's production manager is planning for a series of one-month production periods for stainless steel sinks. The demand for the next four months is as follows:

MONTH	DEMAND FOR STAINLESS STEEL SINKS
1	120
2	160
3	240
4	100

The Mehta firm can normally produce 100 stainless steel sinks in a month. This is done during regular production hours at a cost of $100 per sink. If demand in any one month cannot be satisfied by regular production, the production manager has three other choices: (1) he can produce up to 50 more sinks per month in overtime but at a cost of $130 per sink; (2) he can purchase a limited number of sinks from a friendly competitor for resale (the maximum number of outside purchases over the four-month period is 450 sinks, at a cost of $150 each); or (3) he can fill the demand from his on-hand inventory. The inventory carrying cost is $10 per sink per month. Back orders are not permitted. Inventory on hand at the beginning of month 1 is 40 sinks. Set up and solve this "production smoothing" problem as a transportation problem to minimize cost.

5-17 Ashley's Auto Top Carriers currently maintains plants in Yellowknife and Truro that supply major distribution centres in Halifax and Victoria. Because of an expanding demand, Ashley's has decided to open a third plant and has narrowed the choice to one of two cities—Saskatoon or Quebec City. The pertinent production and distribution costs, as well as the plant capacities and distribution demands, are shown in the table for this problem on page 217. Which of the new possible plants should be opened?

5-18 Michael Chang, vice president for operations of HHN, Inc., a manufacturer of cabinets for telephone switches, is constrained from meeting the five-year forecast by limited capacity at the existing three plants. These three plants are in Waterloo, Pusan, and Bogota. You, as his able assistant, have been told that because of existing capacity constraints and the expanding world market for HHN cabinets, a new plant is to be added to the existing three plants. The real estate department has advised Mr. Chang that two sites seem particularly good because of a stable political situation and tolerable exchange rate: Dublin, Ireland, and Fontainebleau, France. Mr. Chang suggests that you should be able to take the data in the table for this problem on page 217 and determine where the fourth plant should be located on the basis of production costs and transportation costs.

5-19 Don Levine Corporation is considering adding an additional plant to its three existing facilities in Sarnia, Hamilton, and Sherbrooke. Both Toronto and Mississauga are being considered. Evaluating only the transportation costs per unit as shown in the tables on page 217, which site is best?

Table for Problem 5-15

SAVINGS AND LOAN COMPANY	PROPERTY (INTEREST RATES) (%)				MAXIMUM CREDIT LINE ($)
	ALBERT ST.	BANKS ST.	COLLINS AVE.	DRURY LANE	
Ontario Loan	8	8	10	11	80 000
Oshawa Mutual	9	10	12	10	100 000
Cobourg Savings	9	11	10	9	120 000
Loan required to purchase building	$60 000	$40 000	$130 000	$70 000	

Table for Problem 5-17

FROM PLANTS	TO DISTRIBUTION CENTRES		HALIFAX	VICTORIA	NORMAL PRODUCTION	UNIT PRODUCTION COST ($)
Yellowknife			$8	$5	600	6
Truro			$4	$7	900	5
Saskatoon			$5	$6	500	4 (anticipated)
Quebec City			$4	$6	500	3 (anticipated)
Forecast Demand			800	1200	2000	

Existing plants → Yellowknife, Truro

Proposed locations → Saskatoon, Quebec City

Indicates distribution cost (shipping, handling, storage) will be $6 per carrier if sent from Quebec City to Victoria

Table for Problem 5-18

MARKET AREA	PLANT LOCATION				
	WATERLOO	PUSAN	BOGOTA	FONTAINEBLEAU	DUBLIN
Canada					
Demand 4000					
Production cost	$50	$30	$40	$50	$45
Transportation cost	10	25	20	25	25
South America					
Demand 5000					
Production cost	50	30	40	50	45
Transportation cost	20	25	10	30	30
Pacific Rim					
Demand 10 000					
Production cost	50	30	40	50	45
Transportation cost	25	10	25	40	40
Europe					
Demand 5000					
Production cost	50	30	40	50	45
Transportation cost	25	40	30	10	20
Capacity	8000	2000	5000	9000	9000

Tables for Problem 5-19

TO	FROM EXISTING PLANTS			
	SARNIA	HAMILTON	SHERBROOKE	DEMAND
Kitchener	$20	$17	$21	250
London	25	27	20	200
Windsor	22	25	22	350
Capacity	300	200	150	

TO	FROM PROPOSED PLANTS	
	TORONTO	MISSISSAUGA
Kitchener	$29	$27
London	30	28
Windsor	30	31
Capacity	150	150

5-20 Satish Iyer, vice president of operations at Don Levine Corporation (see Problem 5-19), recognizes that unit shipping costs from either of the proposed plants are very high. The reason is that all long-haul carriers in either city already have contracts with other companies. Satish feels confident, however, that he can find short-haul carriers who will ship his product from the proposed plant in Toronto to Sarnia for only $6 per unit and to Hamilton for only $5 per unit. Set up and solve Don Levine's problem now with this new information.

5-21 In a job shop operation, four jobs can be performed on any of four machines. The hours required for each job on each machine are presented in the following table. The plant supervisor would like to assign jobs so that total time is minimized. Use the assignment model to find the best solution.

| JOB | MACHINE | | | |
	W	X	Y	Z
A12	10	14	16	13
A15	12	13	15	12
B2	9	12	12	11
B9	14	16	18	16

5-22 The Bonville School boys' hockey team is scheduled to play against four rival teams in the Montreal area: Laval, Ahuntsic, Pierrefonds, and Candiac. The coach, Marc Gagnon, has to schedule his four goalies for appropriate games. Because the games are being played in less than a week, and the goalies are not permitted by school policy to play in more than one game per week, Gagnon must assign a different goalie for each game.

Gagnon, knowing the strengths and weaknesses of his own goalies and also of the opposing teams, estimates the probability of winning each of the four games with each of the four goalies as follows:

| GOALIE | OPPONENT | | | |
	LAVAL	AHUNTSIC	PIERREFONDS	CANDIAC
André	0.60	0.80	0.50	0.40
Brian	0.70	0.40	0.80	0.30
Charlie	0.90	0.80	0.70	0.80
Dominique	0.50	0.30	0.40	0.20

Which goalie should Coach Gagnon assign to each game to provide the highest winning probability (i.e., the sum of the probabilities of winning each game) for the Bonville School boys' hockey team?

(a) Formulate this problem using LP.

(b) Solve the problem.

5-23 The hospital administrator at St. Charles General must appoint head nurses to four newly established departments: urology, cardiology, orthopedics, and obstetrics. In anticipation of this staffing problem, she had hired four nurses: Hawkins, Condriac, Bardot, and Hoolihan.

Believing in the decision modeling approach to problem solving, the administrator has interviewed each nurse, considered his or her background, personality, and talents, and developed a cost scale ranging from 0 to 100 to be used in the assignment. A 0 for Nurse Bardot being assigned to the cardiology unit implies that she would be perfectly suited to that task. A value close to 100, conversely, would imply that she is not at all suited to head that unit. The accompanying table gives the complete set of cost figures that the hospital administrator felt represented all possible assignments. Which nurse should be assigned to which unit?

| NURSE | DEPARTMENT | | | |
	UROLOGY	CARDIOLOGY	ORTHOPEDICS	OBSTETRICS
Hawkins	28	18	15	75
Condriac	32	48	23	38
Bardot	51	36	24	36
Hoolihan	25	38	55	12

5-24 The Orange Top Cab Company has a taxi waiting at each of four cab stands in Medicine Hat, Alberta. Four customers have called and requested service. The distances, in kilometres, from the waiting taxis to the customers are given in the table. Find the optimal assignment of taxis to customers so as to minimize total driving distances to the customers.

| CAB SITE | CUSTOMER | | | |
	A	B	C	D
Stand 1	7	3	4	8
Stand 2	5	4	6	5
Stand 3	6	7	9	6
Stand 4	8	6	7	4

5-25 The Burlington Police Department has five detective squads available for assignment to five open crime cases. The chief of detectives wishes to assign the squads so that the total time to conclude the cases is minimized. The estimated number of days, based on past performance, for each squad to complete each case is as follows:

| SQUAD | CASE | | | | |
	A	B	C	D	E
1	14	7	3	7	27
2	20	7	12	6	30
3	10	3	4	5	21
4	8	12	7	12	21
5	13	25	24	26	8

Each squad is composed of different types of specialists and, as noted, whereas one squad may be very effective in certain types of cases, it may be almost useless in others. Solve the problem by using the assignment method.

5-26 Roscoe Davis, chairman of a college's business department, has decided to use decision modeling to assign professors to courses next semester. As a criterion for judging who should teach each course, Professor Davis reviews the past two years' teaching evaluations (which were filled out by students). Since each of the four professors taught each of the four courses at one time or another during the two-year period, Davis is able to record a course rating for each instructor. These ratings are shown in the table. Find the best assignment of professors to courses to maximize the overall teaching ratings.

	COURSE			
PROFESSOR	STATISTICS	MANAGEMENT	FINANCE	ECONOMICS
Andersen	90	65	95	40
Mandarano	70	60	80	75
Manji	85	40	80	60
McKinney	55	80	65	55

5-27 Bechtold Construction is in the process of installing power lines to a large housing development. Steve Bechtold wants to minimize the total length of wire used, which will minimize his costs. The housing development is shown as a network in Figure 5.18. Each house has been numbered, and the distances between houses are given in hundreds of metres. What do you recommend?

5-28 The city of New Berlin is considering making several of its streets one way. What is the maximum number of cars per hour that can travel from east to west? The network is shown in Figure 5.19.

5-29 Transworld Moving has been hired to move the office furniture and equipment of Cohen Properties to its new headquarters. What route do you recommend? The network of roads is shown in Figure 5.20 on the next page.

5-30 The director of security wants to connect security video cameras to the main control site from five potential trouble locations. Ordinarily, cable would simply be run from each location to the main control site. However, because the environment is potentially explosive, the cable must be run in a special conduit that is continually air-purged. This conduit is very expensive but large enough to handle five cables (the maximum that might be needed). Use the minimal-spanning tree model to find a minimum-distance route for the conduit between the locations noted in Figure 5.21 on the next page. (Note that it makes no difference which one is the main control site.)

FIGURE 5.18

Network for Problem 5-27

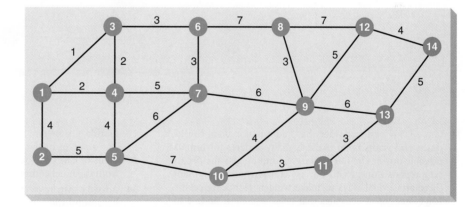

FIGURE 5.19

Network for Problem 5-28

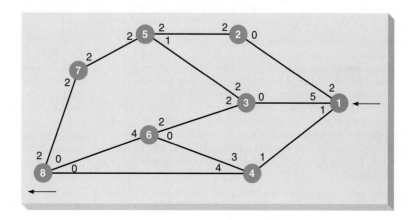

FIGURE 5.20

**Network for
Problem 5-29**

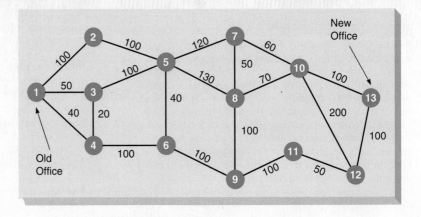

FIGURE 5.21

**Network for
Problem 5-30**

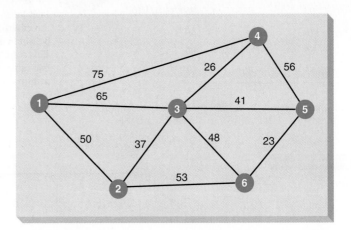

5-31 One of our best customers has had a major plant break-down and wants us to make as many widgets for him as possible during the next few days, until he gets the necessary repairs done. With our general-purpose equipment there are several ways to make widgets (ignoring costs). Any sequence of activities that takes one from node 1 to node 6 in Figure 5.22 on page 221 will produce a widget. How many widgets can we produce per day? Quantities given are number of widgets per day.

5-32 Transworld Moving, like other moving companies, closely follows the impact of road construction to make sure that its routes remain the most efficient. Unfortunately, there has been unexpected road construction due to a lack of planning for road repair around the town of Lethbridge, represented by node 9 in the network. (See Figure 5.20.) All roads leading to node 9, except the road from node 9 to node 11, can no longer be travelled. Does this have any impact on the route that should be used to ship the office furniture and equipment of Cohen Properties to its new headquarters?

5-33 The road system around the hotel complex on International Drive (node 1) to Disney World (node 11) in Orlando,

Florida, is shown in the network of Figure 5.23 on page 221. The numbers by the nodes represent the traffic flow in hundreds of cars per hour. What is the maximum flow of cars from the hotel complex to Disney World?

5-34 A road construction project would increase the road capacity around the outside roads from International Drive to Disney World by 200 cars per hour (see Problem 5-33). The two paths affected would be $1 \rightarrow 2 \rightarrow 6 \rightarrow 9 \rightarrow 11$ and $1 \rightarrow 5 \rightarrow 8 \rightarrow 10 \rightarrow 11$. What impact would this have on the total flow of cars? Would the total flow of cars increase by 400 cars per hour?

5-35 Solve the maximal-flow problem presented in the network shown in Figure 5.24. The numbers in the network represent thousands of litres per hour as they flow through a chemical processing plant.

5-36 Two terminals in the chemical processing plant, represented by nodes 6 and 7, require emergency repair (see Problem 5-35). No material can flow into or out of these nodes. What impact does this have on the capacity of the network?

5-37 Solve the shortest-route problem presented in the network of Figure 5.25 (on page 222), going from node 1 to node 16.

FIGURE 5.22

**Network for
Problem 5-31**

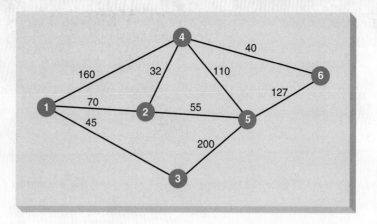

All numbers represent kilometres between towns in the Laurentian Mountains.

5-38 Due to bad weather, the roads represented by nodes 7 and 8 have been closed (see Problem 5-37). No traffic can get onto or off of these roads. Describe the impact (if any) that this will have on the shortest route through this network.

5-39 Grey Construction would like to determine the least expensive way of connecting cable TV in the houses it is

building. It has identified 11 possible branches or routes that could be used to connect the houses. The cost in hundreds of dollars and the branches are summarized in the table for this problem (on page 222). What is the least expensive way to run cable to the houses?

5-40 Solve the minimal-spanning tree problem in the network shown in Figure 5.26 on page 222. Assume that the numbers in the network represent distances in hundreds of metres.

FIGURE 5.23

**Network for
Problem 5-33**

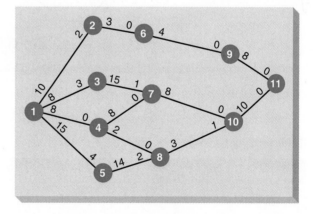

FIGURE 5.24

**Network for
Problem 5-35**

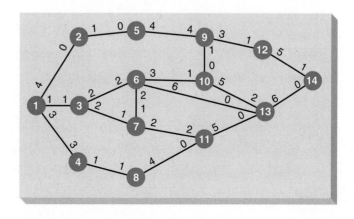

FIGURE 5.25

Network for
Problem 5-37

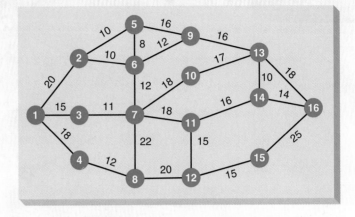

FIGURE 5.26

Network for
Problem 5-40

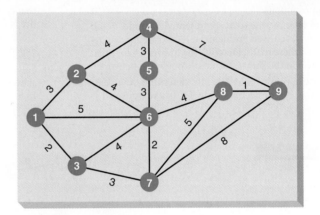

Table for Problem 5-39

BRANCH	START NODE	END NODE	COST (HUNDREDS OF DOLLARS)
Branch 1	1	2	5
Branch 2	1	3	6
Branch 3	1	4	6
Branch 4	1	5	5
Branch 5	2	6	7
Branch 6	3	7	5
Branch 7	4	7	7
Branch 8	5	8	4
Branch 9	6	7	1
Branch 10	7	9	6
Branch 11	8	9	2

CASE STUDY 5.1

Ste-Agathe Wood Store

In 2001, Marcel Brun started the Ste-Agathe Wood Store to manufacture his trademark Marcel Brun tables. Each table is carefully constructed by hand, using the highest-quality Quebec oak. Marcel Brun tables can support more than 250 kilograms, and since the start of the Ste-Agathe Wood Store, not one table has been returned because of faulty workmanship or structural problems. In addition to being rugged, each table is beautifully finished using a urethane varnish that Marcel developed over 20 years of working with wood-finishing materials.

The manufacturing process consists of four steps: preparation, assembly, finishing, and packaging. Each step is performed by one person. In addition to overseeing the entire operation, Marcel does all of the finishing. Jean Leblanc performs the preparation step, which involves cutting and forming the basic components of the tables. Geneviève Fournier is in charge of the assembly, and Pierre Gagnon performs the packaging.

Although each person is responsible for only one step in the manufacturing process, everyone can perform any one of the steps. It is Marcel's policy that occasionally everyone should complete several tables on his or her own without any assistance. A small competition is used to see who can complete an entire table in the least amount of time. Marcel maintains

average total and intermediate completion times. The data are shown in Figure 5.27.

It takes Pierre longer than the other employees to construct a Marcel Brun table. In addition to being slower than the other employees, Pierre is also unhappy about his current responsibility for packaging, which leaves him idle most of the day. His first preference is finishing, and his second preference is preparation.

In addition to quality, Marcel is concerned with costs and efficiency. When one of the employees misses a day, it causes major scheduling problems. In some cases, Marcel assigns another employee overtime to complete the necessary work. At other times, Marcel simply waits until the employee returns to work to complete his or her step in the manufacturing process. Both solutions cause problems. Overtime is expensive, and waiting causes delays and sometimes stops the entire manufacturing process.

To overcome some of these problems, Renée Laberge was hired. Renée's major duties are to perform miscellaneous jobs and to help out if one of the employees is absent. Marcel has given Renée training in all phases of the manufacturing process, and he is pleased with the speed at which she has been able to learn how to completely assemble Marcel Brun tables. Renée's total and intermediate completion times are given in Figure 5.28.

FIGURE 5.27

Manufacturing Time in Minutes

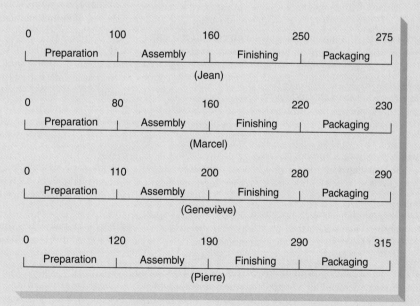

FIGURE 5.28

Renée's Completion Times in Minutes

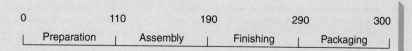

DISCUSSION QUESTIONS

1. What is the fastest way to manufacture Marcel Brun tables using the original crew? How many could be made per day?
2. Would production rates and quantities change significantly if Marcel allowed Renée to perform one of the four functions and made one of the original crew the backup person?

3. What is the fastest time to manufacture a table with the original crew if Pierre is moved to either preparation or finishing?
4. Whoever performs the packaging function is severely underutilized. Can you find a better way of utilizing the four- or five-person crew than either giving each a single job or allowing each to manufacture an entire table? How many tables could be manufactured per day with this scheme?

⇒ CASE STUDY 5.2

Custom Vans of Canada, Inc.

Custom Vans of Canada, Inc. specializes in converting standard vans into campers. Depending on the amount of work and customizing to be done, the customizing could cost anywhere from less than $1000 to more than $5000. In less than four years, Tony Rizzo was able to expand his small operation in London, Ontario, to other major outlets in Toronto, Calgary, Vancouver, and Halifax.

Innovation was the major factor in Tony's success in converting a small van shop into one of the largest and most profitable custom van operations in Canada. Tony seemed to have a special ability to design and develop unique features and devices that were always in high demand by van owners. An example was Shower-Rific, which was developed by Tony only six months after Custom Vans was started. These small showers were completely self-contained, and they could be placed in almost any type of van and in a number of different locations within a van. Shower-Rific was made of fibreglass and contained towel racks, built-in soap and shampoo holders, and a unique plastic door. Each Shower-Rific took seven litres of fibreglass resin and three hours of labour to manufacture.

Most of the Shower-Rifics were manufactured in London in the same warehouse where Custom Vans, Inc., was founded. The manufacturing plant in London could produce 300 Shower-Rifics in a month, but this capacity never seemed to be enough. Custom Van shops in all locations were complaining about not getting enough Shower-Rifics, and because Vancouver was farther away from London than were the other locations, Tony was always inclined to ship Shower-Rifics to the other locations before Vancouver. This infuriated the manager of Custom Vans at Vancouver, and after many heated discussions, Tony decided to start another manufacturing plant for Shower-Rifics at Fredericton, New Brunswick. The manufacturing plant at Fredericton could produce 150 Shower-Rifics per month.

The manufacturing plant at Fredericton was still not able to meet current demand for Shower-Rifics, and Tony knew that the demand for his unique camper shower would grow rapidly in the next year. After consulting with his lawyer and banker, Tony concluded that he should open two new manufacturing plants as soon as possible. Each plant would have the same capacity as the Fredericton manufacturing plant. An initial investigation into possible manufacturing locations was made, and Tony decided that the two new plants should be located in Halifax, Nova Scotia; Ottawa, Ontario; or Regina, Saskatchewan. Tony knew that selecting the best location for the

two new manufacturing plants would be difficult. Transportation costs and demands for the various locations should be important considerations.

The Toronto shop was managed by Bill Burch. This Custom Van shop was one of the first established by Tony, and it continued to outperform the other locations. The manufacturing plant in London was supplying 200 Shower-Rifics each month, although Bill knew that the demand for the showers in Toronto was 300 units. The transportation cost per unit from London was $10, and although the transportation cost from Fredericton was double that amount, Bill was always pleading with Tony to get an additional 50 units from the Fredericton manufacturer. The two additional manufacturing plants would certainly be able to supply Bill with the additional 100 showers he needed. The transportation costs would, of course, vary, depending on which two locations Tony picked. The transportation cost per shower would be $30 from Halifax, $5 from Ottawa, and $10 from Regina.

Wilma Jackson, manager of the Custom Van shop in Calgary, was the most upset about not getting an adequate supply of showers. She had a demand for 100 units, and at the present time, she was getting only half of this demand from the Fredericton manufacturing plant. She could not understand why Tony didn't ship her all 100 units from London. The transportation cost per unit from London was only $20, while the transportation cost from Fredericton was $30. Wilma was hoping that Tony would select Regina for one of the manufacturing locations. She would be able to get all of the showers needed, and the transportation cost per unit would only be $5. If not Regina, a new plant in Ottawa would be able to supply her total needs, but the transportation cost per unit would be twice as much as it would be from Regina. Because the transportation cost per unit from Halifax would be $40, Wilma speculated that even if Halifax became one of the new plants, she would not be getting any units from Halifax.

Custom Vans, Inc. of Vancouver was managed by Tom Chen. He was getting 100 showers from the London plant. Demand was 150 units. Tom faced the highest transportation costs of all locations. The transportation cost from London was $40 per unit. It would cost $10 more if showers were sent from the Fredericton location. Tom was hoping that Halifax would not be one of the new plants, as the transportation cost would be $60 per unit. Ottawa and Regina would have a cost of $30 and $25, respectively, to ship one shower to Vancouver.

The Halifax shop's position was similar to Calgary's—only getting half of the demand each month. The 100 units that

Halifax did receive came directly from the Fredericton plant. The transportation cost was only $15 per unit from Fredericton, whereas it was $25 from London. Seamus Murphy, manager of Custom Vans, Inc. of Halifax, placed the probability of having one of the new plants in Halifax fairly high. The factory would be located across town, and the transportation cost would be only $5 per unit. He could get 150 showers from the new plant in Halifax and the other 50 showers from Fredericton. Even if Halifax was not selected, the other two locations were not intolerable. Ottawa had a transportation cost per unit of $35, and Regina had a transportation cost of $40.

Tony pondered the dilemma of locating the two new plants for several weeks before deciding to call a meeting of all the managers of the van shops. The decision was complicated, but the objective was clear—to minimize total costs. The meeting was held in London, and everyone was present except Wilma.

Tony: Thank you for coming. As you know, I have decided to open up two new plants at Ottawa, Regina, or Halifax. The two locations, of course, will change our shipping practices, and I sincerely hope that they will supply you with the Shower-Rifics that you have been wanting. I know you could have sold more units, and I want you to know that I am sorry for this situation.

Seamus: Tony, I have given this situation a lot of consideration, and I feel strongly that at least one of the new plants should be located in Halifax. As you know, I am now getting only half of the showers that I need. My brother, Liam, is very interested in running the plant, and I know he would do a good job.

Tom: Seamus, I am sure that Liam could do a good job, and I know how difficult it has been since the recent layoffs by the auto industry. Nevertheless, we should be considering total costs and not personalities. I believe that the new plants should be located in Regina and Ottawa. I am farther away from the other plants than any other shop, and these locations would significantly reduce transportation costs.

Seamus: That may be true, but there are other factors. Halifax has one of the largest suppliers of fibreglass, and I have checked prices. A new plant in Halifax would be able to purchase fibreglass resin for $2 per litre less than any of the other existing or proposed plants.

Tom: At Regina, we have an excellent labour force. This is due primarily to the large number of students attending the University of Regina. These students are hard workers, and they will work for $1 less per hour than the other locations that we are considering.

Bill: Calm down, you two. It is obvious that we will not be able to satisfy everyone in locating the new plants. Therefore, I would like to suggest that we vote on the two best locations.

Tony: I don't think that voting would be a good idea. Wilma was not able to attend, and we should be looking at all of these factors together in some type of logical fashion.

DISCUSSION QUESTION

Where would you locate the two new plants?

⇒ CASE STUDY 5.3

Bonnie Bagels

Sean McAlister and Sally-Ann Rafferty have recently joined forces to open a new bagel factory, called Bonnie Bagels, in their home town in Newfoundland. Rafferty takes care of the bagel production, while McAlister delivers the freshly baked bagels to local coffee shops, supermarkets, and convenience stores. Because of zoning and pollution regulations regarding the use of wood-fired ovens in the municipality, the bakery is located outside the town limits. Consequently, McAlister's biggest problem is battling the morning traffic to deliver the bagels to one of their major customers, Murphy's Café, which is located some distance away from the factory. Murphy has expressed dissatisfaction a couple of times when the morning delivery has been late, and he has threatened to take his business elsewhere if McAlister and Rafferty cannot guarantee that they will deliver the order by the time he opens at 7:00 A.M.

Having tried several routes to get from the factory to Murphy's Café, McAlister is not sure which is the best route and, in particular, he has not decided whether it is better to go on the highway or stick to city streets. McAlister decided to buy a GPS system to help navigate the route between the factory and Murphy's. When he started to use the GPS, he noticed that there are different choices for planning the route. Since the most important criterion is not to be late with the delivery, he chose the "Fastest Time" option.

The factory is located at the corner of Ontario Street and Commonwealth Avenue (see Figure 5.29). High Street also intersects Ontario and Commonwealth at the factory. Twenty minutes due north of the factory on Ontario Street is the Cartier Freeway, the major east–west highway running through the town.

Ontario Street intersects the Cartier Freeway at Exit 135. It takes five minutes driving east on the Cartier to reach exit 136. This exit connects the Cartier with High Street and Clarke Avenue. Ten minutes east on the Cartier is Exit 137. This exit connects the Cartier with Rose Street and Pearson Avenue.

From the factory, it takes 20 minutes on High Street, which goes in a northeast direction, to reach Trudeau Street. It takes another 20 minutes on High Street to reach the Cartier Freeway at Exit 136.

It takes 30 minutes on Commonwealth Avenue to reach Trudeau Street from the factory. Commonwealth Avenue travel east and slightly north.

Trudeau Street runs east and west. From High Street, it takes 15 minutes to get to Clarke Avenue. Commonwealth Avenue also comes into this intersection. From this intersection, it takes an additional 20 minutes on Trudeau Street to get to Rose Street, and another 15 minutes to get to Pearson Avenue.

From Exit 136 on Clarke Avenue it takes 5 minutes to get to Trudeau Street. Clarke Avenue continues to Rose Street, requiring 25 minutes. Clarke Avenue then goes directly to Murphy's Café.

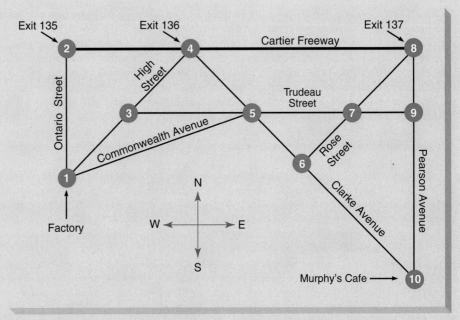

FIGURE 5.29

Street Map for Bonnie Bagels Case

Note: This map is not drawn to scale. Distances shown on the map do not reflect the actual driving times betwen locations.

From Rose Street, it takes 40 minutes to get to Murphy's on Clarke Avenue

At Exit 137, Rose Street travels southwest. It takes 20 minutes to intersect with Trudeau Street, and another 20 minutes to get to Clarke Avenue. From Exit 137, Pearson Avenue goes due south. It takes 10 minutes to get to Trudeau Street and another 15 minutes to get to Murphy's

DISCUSSION QUESTION

Sean McAlister programs his new GPS system to drive from the factory to Murphy's Café. He selects the "Fastest Time" option. Which route should the GPS select to minimize travel time? At what time should Sean leave the bakery if he wants to arrive at Murphy's 10 minutes before opening time?

BIBLIOGRAPHY

Ambs, K. et al. "Optimizing Restoration Capacity at the AT&T Network," *Interfaces* (January–February 2000): 26–44.

Anbil, R., E. Gelman, B. Patty, and R. Tanga. "Recent Advances in Crew-Pairing Optimization at American Airlines," *Interfaces* 21, 1 (January–February 1991): 62–74.

Bentley, Jon. "Faster And Faster And Faster Yet, " *UNIX Review* (June 1997): 59.

Cipra, Barry. "Taking Hard Problems to the Limit: Mathematics," *Science* (March 14, 1997): 15–70.

Current, J. "The Minimum-Covering/Shortest Path Problem," *Decision Sciences* 19 (Summer 1988): 490–503.

Domich, P. D., K. L. Hoffman, R. H. F. Jackson, and M. A. McClain. "Locating Tax Facilities: A Graphics-Based Microcomputer Optimization Model." *Management Science* 37 (August 1991): 960–979.

Glassey, C. Roger, and Michael Mizrach. "A Decision Support System for Assigning Classes to Rooms," *Interfaces* 16, 5 (September–October 1986): 92–100.

LeBlanc, Larry J., Dale Randels, Jr., and T. K. Swann. "Heery International's Spreadsheet Optimization Model for Assigning Managers to Construction Projects," *Interfaces* 30, 6 (November 2000): 95–106.

Onal, Hayri et al. "Two Formulations of the Vehicle Routing Problem," *The Logistics and Transportation Review* (June 1996): 117–130.

Perlman, Radia et al. "Spanning the LAN," *Data Communications* (October 21, 1997): 68.

Sancho, N. G. F. "On the Maximum Expected Flow in a Network," *Journal of Operational Research Society* 39 (May 1988): 481–485.

William, Carlton et al. "Solving the Traveling-Salesman Problem with Time Windows Using Tabu Search," *IIE Transactions* (August 1996): 617–629.

Williams, Martyn. "When Does the Shortest Route Between Tokyo and Singapore Include a Stop in New York?" *Data Communications* (December 19, 1997): 45.

CHAPTER 6

Integer Programming Models

LEARNING OBJECTIVES

After completing this chapter, students will be able to

1. Formulate integer programming (IP) models.
2. Set up and solve IP models using Excel's Solver.
3. Understand the difference between general integer and binary integer variables.
4. Understand the use of binary integer variables in formulating problems involving fixed (or setup) costs.
5. Understand the use of the branch-and-bound method in determining solutions to integer programming problems.

CHAPTER OUTLINE

6.1 Introduction
6.2 Models with General Integer Variables
6.3 Solving IP Problems: Branch-and-Bound
6.4 Models with Binary Variables
6.5 Mixed Integer Models: Fixed-Charge Problems

Summary • Glossary • Key Equation • Solved Problems • Self-Test • Discussion Questions and Problems • Case Study: St. Lawrence River Bridge • Case Study: Jackpine Mall • Bibliography

Scheduling Employees in Quebec's Liquor Stores with Integer Programming

The Société des Alcools du Québec (SAQ), a public corporation of the Province of Quebec, is one of the largest retail networks in Quebec, handling commerce of all alcoholic beverages in the province. With 379 retail branches, 303 agencies, and 9200 store outlets, the SAQ handles 29 million transactions per year, offers more than 5299 products, and provides liquor permits to 14 000 hotels, bars, discotheques, and restaurants.

Every week, the SAQ has to schedule more than 3000 employees. Until 2002, it handled this process manually, incurring estimated expenses of $1 300 000. Professor Bernard Gendron of the University of Montreal developed a solution engine that implements an integer programming (IP) model using the proprietary software CPLEX.

Source: CP Photo/Robert Dall

CPLEX Optimization, Inc. was founded in 1988 with the mission of providing the highest-performance optimizers for LP. CPLEX was the first commercial LP optimizer developed in C programming language. The name CPLEX comes from the combination of the letter C for the programming language and the word "simplex" for the simplex method for LP.

The IP problem was to generate a weekly schedule per employee subject to several constraints, including the length of the employee day (no more than 10 hours) with a maximum of 38 hours over the whole week; a union agreement specifying that the schedule be generated a day at a time, starting from the end of the week (Saturday) and going backward until Sunday: this rule is called the backward-assignment rule; a union objective to maximize the number of hours the employee works each day by taking into account the shifts to be assigned and the availabilities the employee expresses; and a mandatory one-hour lunch break.

The rationale behind the backward-assignment rule is to push the days off toward the beginning of the week (Sunday and Monday) and ideally to grant the most senior employees an additional day off (Tuesday). This rule was inflexible, because the solution method had to strictly adhere to all union agreement rules.

Typically, the store managers enter data for the coming week on Wednesday nights, and the SAQ sends schedules to the employees on Thursdays, or on Friday mornings. Three employees dedicate part of their time to the project: a computer analyst maintains the database and interface system and updates the CPLEX versions; an employee from the human resources department and a representative of the union ensure that schedules respect all rules of the union agreement and answer the store managers' and the employees' questions about the schedules the system produces.

In the stores, the system has greatly simplified the work of the managers and union representatives by eliminating paperwork, by simplifying the management of data, and overall by reducing the time dedicated to scheduling. In addition, the system interprets the union agreement rules in a uniform way in all stores across the province, which has eliminated many of the complaints union representatives made prior to its implementation.

The project has contributed in many ways to increasing the SAQ's efficiency by reducing its scheduling costs and improving its management of human resources. By replacing manual scheduling, the automated process saves an estimated $750 000 or more annually (about 80% of the total prior salary expenses). In addition, because the program produces accurate schedules that respect all the rules of the union agreement, employees make very few complaints; this reduction in complaints translates into annual savings estimated at about $250 000 (90% of the total prior expenses related to employees' complaints). Overall, the SAQ estimates that the automated scheduling program saves over $1 000 000 annually. Because developing the new scheduling system (over 2.5 years) cost around $1 300 000, the payback period is less than two years.

Sources: Bernard Gendron. "Scheduling Employees in Quebec's Liquor Stores with Integer Programming" *Interfaces* 35, 5(September–October 2005): 402–410; http://www.ilog.com/products/cplex/news/history.cfm; http://www.cognos.com/news/releases/2001/1221_1.html

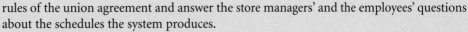

6.1   INTRODUCTION

Earlier chapters focus on the LP category of mathematical programming models. One of the characteristics of an LP model is that decision variables may have fractional values.

This chapter presents an important class of mathematical models that allows us to require that the decision variable assume integer values. The new model—**integer programming (IP)**—is introduced here and then discussed in detail in the remainder of Chapter 6.

Integer Programming Models

Although fractional values such as $X = 0.33$ and $Y = 109.4$ may be valid for decision variables in many problems, there are a large number of business problems that can be solved only if variables have *integer* values. For example, when a railway decides how many cars to put on a given train, it cannot decide to attach 30.38 cars; it must attach 30, 31, or some other integer.

In Section 6.2, we present general integer variables and in Section 6.3 we present the branch-and-bound method for solving general IP problems. In Section 6.4 we introduce models with binary variables. **General integer variables** are variables that can take on any nonnegative integer value that satisfies all the constraints in a model (e.g., 5 submarines, 8 employees, 20 insurance policies). **Binary variables**, also called **0-1 variables** or **zero-one variables**, are a special type of integer variable that can only take on either of two values: 0 or 1. We present how problems involving both of these types of integer variables can be formulated and solved using Excel's Solver. In Section 6.5 we introduce fixed-charge problems, which require either linear or general integer variables to model variable costs, as well as binary variables to model one-time fixed charges. We also introduce the Big-M method, a technique commonly used to formulate constraints that assigns the appropriate value (0 or 1) to a binary integer variable.

> Integer programming is the extension of LP that solves problems requiring integer solutions.

> General integer variables can take on any nonnegative integer value.

> Binary variables must equal either 0 or 1.

IP problems can be classified into four types:

1. *Pure IP problems:* problems in which all decision variables must have integer solutions.

2. **Mixed IP problems**: problems in which some, but not all, decision variables must have integer solutions. The noninteger variables can have fractional optimal values.

3. *Pure binary (or 0–1) IP problems:* problems in which all decision variables must have solution values of either 0 or 1.

4. *Mixed binary IP problems:* problems in which some decision variables are binary and other decision variables are either general integer or continuous valued.

| 6.2 | **MODELS WITH GENERAL INTEGER VARIABLES** |

Models with general integer variables are similar to LP models—except that variables must be integer-valued.

A model with general integer variables (which we call an *IP model*) has an objective function and constraints identical to that of LP models. There is no real difference in the basic procedure for formulating an IP model and an LP model.

The only additional requirement in an IP model is that one or more of the decision variables have to take on integer values in the optimal solution. The actual value of this integer variable is, however, limited only by the constraints in the model. That is, values such as 0, 1, 2, 3, and so on are perfectly valid for these variables as long as these values satisfy all constraints in the model.

Let us look at a simple example of an IP problem and see how to formulate it. We then demonstrate how this model can be set up and solved using Excel's Solver.

Lightwell Chandelier Company

The Lightwell Chandelier Company of British Columbia produces two expensive products that are popular with renovators of historic old homes: ornate chandeliers and old-fashioned ceiling fans. Both chandeliers and ceiling fans require a two-step production process involving wiring and assembly time. It takes about two hours to wire each chandelier and three hours to wire a ceiling fan. Final assembly of each chandelier and fan requires six and five hours, respectively. Only 12 hours of wiring time and 30 hours of assembly time are available during the production period. If each chandelier produced nets the firm $600 in profit and each fan nets $700, Lightwell's production mix decision can be formulated using LP as follows:

$$\text{Maximize profit} = \$600C + \$700F$$

subject to

$$
\begin{aligned}
2C + 3F &\leq 12 &&\text{(wiring hours)} \\
6C + 5F &\leq 30 &&\text{(assembly hours)} \\
C, F &\geq 0
\end{aligned}
$$

where

$$
\begin{aligned}
C &= \text{number of chandeliers produced} \\
F &= \text{number of ceiling fans produced}
\end{aligned}
$$

With only two decision variables and two constraints to consider, Lightwell's production planner, John Takemitsu, decided to employ the graphical LP approach to generate the optimal solution. The shaded region in Figure 6.1 shows the feasible region for the LP problem. The optimal corner point solution turned out to be $C = 3.75$ chandeliers and $F = 1.5$ ceiling fans, for a profit of $3300 during the production period.

Rounding is one way to reach integer solution values, but it often does not yield the best solution.

Since Lightwell could not produce and sell a fraction of a product, John recognized that he was dealing with an IP problem. It seemed to John that the simplest approach was to round the optimal fractional LP solutions for C and F to integer values. Figure 6.1 shows all possible

Graph for the Lightwell Chandelier Problem

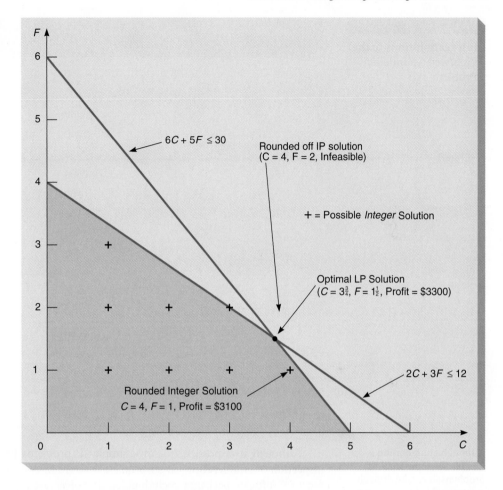

integer solutions for this problem. Unfortunately, rounding can produce two problems. First, the new integer solution may not be in the feasible region and is, hence, not a practical answer. For example, assume we round the LP solution to $C = 4$ chandeliers and $F = 2$ ceiling fans. As we can see from Figure 6.1, this solution is not feasible. Second, even if we round to a feasible integer solution such as $C = 4$ and $F = 1$, it may not be the optimal feasible IP solution.

Table 6.1 on the next page lists the entire set of integer-valued solutions for the Lightwell Chandelier problem. By inspecting the right-hand column, we see that the optimal integer solution is $C = 3$ chandeliers, $F = 2$ ceiling fans, for a total profit = $3200. The rounded solution of $C = 4$ and $F = 1$ yields a profit of only $3100.

We note that the optimal solution $C = 3$ and $F = 2$ is not even a corner point (i.e., a point at which two or more constraints intersect) in the LP feasible region. In fact, unlike LP problems, in which the optimal solution is always a corner point of the feasible region, the optimal solution in an IP model need not be a corner point. As we will discuss subsequently, this is what makes it difficult to solve IP models in practice.

We also note that the integer restriction results in an objective value that is no better (and usually, is worse) than the optimal LP solution. The logic behind this occurrence is quite simple. The feasible region for the original LP problem includes *all* IP solution points, in addition to several LP solution points. That is, the optimal IP solution will always be a feasible solution for the LP problem, but *not vice versa*. We call the LP equivalent of an IP problem (i.e., the IP model with the integer requirement deleted) the relaxed problem. As a rule, the IP solution can never produce a better objective value than its LP relaxed problem. At best, the two solutions can be equal (if the optimal LP solution turns out to be integer-valued).

An IP solution can never be better than the LP solution to the same problem.

TABLE 6.1	CHANDELIERS (C)	CEILING FANS (F)	PROFIT ($600C + $700F)	
Integer Solutions to the Lightwell Chandelier Problem	0	0	$ 0	
	1	0	600	
	2	0	1200	
	3	0	1800	
	4	0	2400	
	5	0	3000	
	0	1	700	
	1	1	1300	
	2	1	1900	
	3	1	2500	
	4	1	3100	← *Solution if rounding is used*
	0	2	1400	
	1	2	2000	
	2	2	2600	
	3	2	3200	← *Optimal solution to integer programming problem 1*
	0	3	2100	
	1	3	2700	
	0	4	2800	

Although enumeration is feasible for some small IP problems, it can be difficult or impossible for large ones.

Although it is possible to solve simple IP problems like Lightwell Chandelier's by inspection or enumeration, larger problems cannot be solved in this manner. Fortunately, most LP software packages, including Excel's Solver, are capable of handling models with integer variables.

Using Solver to Solve Models with General Integer Variables

We can set up Lightwell Chandelier's problem on Excel in exactly the same manner as we have done for several LP examples in Chapters 2 through 4. For clarity, we once again use the same Excel layout here as in those chapters; that is, all parameters (solution value, objective coefficients, and constraint coefficients) associated with a decision variable are modeled in the same column. The objective function and each constraint in the model are shown on separate rows of the worksheet.

Excel Notes

■ The CD-ROM that accompanies this textbook contains the Excel file for each example problem discussed here. The relevant file name is shown in the margin next to each example.

■ In each of the Excel layouts, for clarity, Changing Cells are shaded yellow, the Target Cell is shaded green, and cells containing the left-hand side (LHS) formula for each constraint are shaded blue.

■ Also, to make the equivalence of the written formulation and the Excel layout clear, the Excel layouts show the decision variable names used in the written formulation of the model. Note that these names have no role in using Solver to solve the model.

MODELING IN THE REAL WORLD
Scheduling Emergency Room Physicians

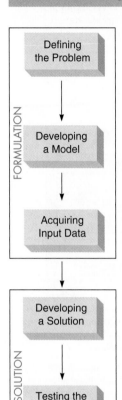

To run a hospital emergency room efficiently, administrators must plan for the best use of ER physicians' time.

The researchers showed how to modify a hospital's existing scheduling rules to produce better schedules and reduce the time needed to build them. One of the models defines binary integer decision variables as follows:

$$X_{ijk} = \begin{cases} 1 \text{ if shift type } i \text{ is assigned to physician } k \text{ on day } j \\ 0 \text{ otherwise} \end{cases}$$

To get a good understanding of ER scheduling, researchers interviewed physicians from six hospitals in greater Montreal. ERs in these hospitals employ from 3 to 16 full-time physicians and up to 17 part-time physicians. Many scheduling criteria and personal preferences, such as not working overnight shifts or weekends, have to be included as constraints in the model.

Solutions were generated for different hospitals by applying a binary variable model and incorporating the constraints specific to each institution.

A schedule was developed for ER physicians at the Jewish General Hospital (JGH), which has one of the busiest ERs in Quebec. Physicians at the hospital were generally pleased with the results.

ER physicians provided feedback on the scheduling rules in order to adjust the algorithm's system of weighting preferences. The algorithm was adjusted to take individual physicians' preferences into consideration.

Both physicians and the scheduler are pleased with the new schedules.

Source: M. C. Carter and S. D. Lapierre. "Scheduling Emergency Room Physicians," *Health Care Management Science* 4, (2001): 347–360.

File: 6-1.xls

The Excel layout for Lightwell Chandelier's problem is shown in Screenshot 6.1 on the next page. As usual, we specify the Target Cell (objective function), Changing Cells (decision variables), and constraint LHS and RHS cell references in the Solver Parameters window.

Excel Layout and Solver Entries for Lightwell Chandelier General Integer Programming Problem

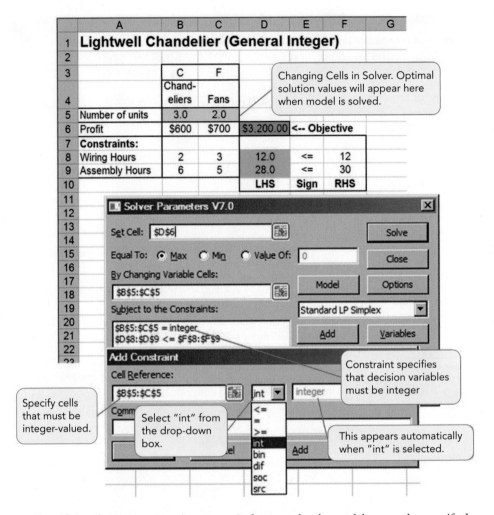

Integer requirement is specified as an additional constraint in Solver.

Specifying the Integer Requirement   Before we solve the model, we need to specify the integer value requirement for the two decision variables. To enforce this, we use the Add option to include a new constraint. In the LHS entry for the new constraint (see Screenshot 6.1), we enter the cell reference for a decision variable that must be integer-valued. If there are several decision variables in the model that must be integer-valued, and these are in contiguous cells (i.e., next to each other), we can enter the entire block of cell references in the LHS entry. For Lightwell's problem, we enter B5:C5 in this box, which denotes the number of chandeliers and fans to make, respectively.

The "int" option is used in Solver to specify general integer variables

Next we click on the drop-down box in the Add Constraint window. Recall that, in Premium Solver, this box has eight options: "<=", ">=", "=", "int" (for integer), "bin" (for binary), "dif" (for alldifferent), "soc" (for second order cone), and "src" (for rotated second order cone). Of these, we have so far used only the first three. We now click on the option "int." The word "integer" is displayed automatically in the box for the RHS entry. This indicates to Solver that all variables specified in the LHS box must be integer-valued in the optimal solution.

Solving the IP Model We are now ready to solve the IP model. To do so, we verify that the "Standard LP Simplex" is selected in the dropdown box in the Solver main window (in Premium Solver) or Assume Linear option is enabled in the Solver Option window (in Standard Solver). In either case, we have to verify that the Assume Non-Negative option is enabled in the Solver Options window and then click Solve. The result, shown in Screenshot 6.1 (three chandeliers and two fans, for a profit of $3200), is identified as the optimal solution.

For small problems like Lightwell Chandelier, and even for problems of slightly larger size, Solver will find the IP solution very quickly. However, the time and computational effort required to solve IP problems grows rapidly with problem size. We now briefly discuss the reason for this phenomenon.

How Solver Solves IP Models

As shown in Figure 6.1, the optimal solution to an IP model need not be at a corner point of the feasible region. Unfortunately, the simplex method evaluates only corner points as candidates for the optimal solution. In order to use the simplex method to identify an integer-valued optimal point that may *not* be a corner point, we employ a procedure called the **branch-and-bound (B&B) method**. This method is used by most software packages, including Solver, to solve IP models.

Before we proceed to demonstrate the B&B procedure in Section 6.3, we will first provide a brief description of how it works. Essentially, the B&B procedure uses a "divide and conquer" strategy. Rather than trying to search for the optimal IP solution over the entire feasible region at one time, the B&B procedure splits the feasible region progressively into smaller and smaller subregions. This is accomplished by eliminating noninteger solutions of the original LP problem. Thus, if the optimal solution includes the value $X = 3.6$, we create two subproblems, one requiring that $X \leq 3$ and the other requiring that $X \geq 4$. We then solve the two resulting LP problems. In this way we eliminate all noninteger values of X between 3 and 4. This process is repeated for each subproblem until solutions are found that contain only integer values for the decision variables. Clearly, the best IP solution over all subregions will be the optimal IP solution over the entire feasible region.

In creating each subregion, the B&B procedure makes a corner point of the new region have integer values (at least for one of the variables in the model). This procedure is called *branching*.

Finding the optimal solution for each subregion involves the solution of an LP model. Hence, in order to solve a single IP model, we may have to solve several LP models. This process of repeatedly creating subproblems to remove noninteger values of the decision variables (branching) and using the resultant optimal values of the objective function to create upper and lower bounds on the value of the objective function (bounding) eventually converges to an optimal integer-valued solution. Clearly, the branch-and-bound process can become computationally quite burdensome, depending on the number of subregions that need to be created for an IP model. Stopping rules used to efficiently stop the search process for different subregions will be described in Section 6.3.

Solver Options

Now let us return to Solver's treatment of IP problems. In addition to the Assume Linear Model and Assume Non-Negative options, the Solver Options window includes several other options. These are shown in Screenshot 6.2A for the standard Solver, and in Screenshot 6.2B for Premium Solver for Education (both on the next page). We have not concerned ourselves about these options so far, since the default values are adequate to solve most, if not all, LP models considered here. However, for IP models, two of the options deserve additional attention.

Maximum Time Allowed   The **MAX TIME** option is set to a default value of 100 seconds. As the number of integer-valued decision variables increases in an IP model, this time limit can be easily exceeded and may need to be extended. In practice, however, it is a good idea to keep the limit at its default value and run the problem. Solver will warn you when the limit is reached and give you the opportunity to allow more time for an IP problem to solve.

Tolerance of the Optimal Solution   The **TOLERANCE** option is set at a default value of 5%, shown as 0.05 in Standard Solver in Screenshot 6.2A (the default value in the Premium Solver being 0.0005). Note that to see this option in Premium Solver for Education, we must

(margin notes)

Solver uses the branch-and-bound procedure to solve IP problems.

Solving a single IP problem can involve solving several LP problems.

The maximum time allowed could become an issue for large IP problems.

Reducing the tolerance will yield a more accurate IP solution—but could take more time.

Options for Integer Programming Problems in Standard Version of Solver

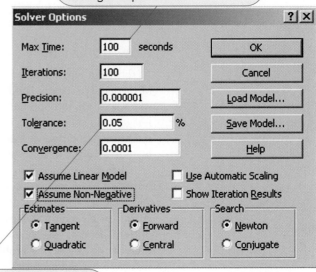

This limit may need to be increased for larger IP problems.

Tolerance specifies how close to the optimal solution the identified IP solution must be in order for Solver to stop.

Options for Integer Programming Problems in Premium Solver for Education

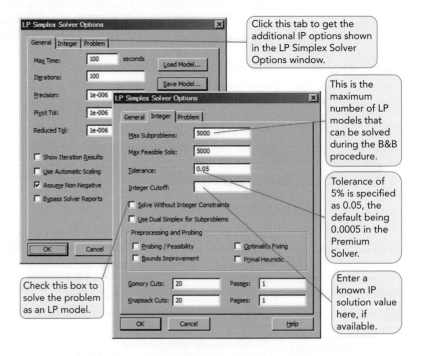

Click this tab to get the additional IP options shown in the LP Simplex Solver Options window.

This is the maximum number of LP models that can be solved during the B&B procedure.

Tolerance of 5% is specified as 0.05, the default being 0.0005 in the Premium Solver.

Check this box to solve the problem as an LP model.

Enter a known IP solution value here, if available.

click on the **INTEGER TAB** in the LP Simplex Solver Options window. A tolerance value of 5% implies that we are willing to accept an IP solution that is within 5% of the true optimal IP solution value. When Solver finds a solution within the allowable tolerance, it stops and presents this as the final solution. In Premium Solver for Education, this is explicitly indicated by the message "Solver found an integer solution within tolerance." If we wish to find the *true* optimal solution, we must set the tolerance to 0%. However, in practice, this may increase the solution time significantly.

Additional options are available in Premium Solver for Education.

Other Options Premium Solver for Education has some additional options for IP models (see Screenshot 6.2B). The default value of 5000 for the **MAX SUBPROBLEMS** and **MAX FEASIBLE SOLS** options should be sufficient for most models.

If we already know an integer-valued solution to the model, we can enter that objective value in the **INTEGER CUTOFF** box. This will prevent Solver from wasting time searching for IP solutions that are worse than the cutoff solution. For example, suppose we know that a feasible integer solution with an objective value of 100 exists for a maximization IP problem. In this case, it is clearly not necessary for the B&B procedure to search for solutions in subregions in which even the best noninteger solution has an objective value of less than 100.

Finally, checking the **SOLVE WITHOUT INTEGER CONSTRAINTS** box causes Solver to ignore the integer constraints while solving the model. As discussed earlier, the optimal objective value of an IP model will always be *worse* than that for the corresponding LP model (i.e., lower profit for a maximization problem and higher cost for a minimization problem). Hence, this option allows us to quickly get an idea about the best IP solution that we can find for the problem.

6.3 SOLVING IP PROBLEMS: BRANCH-AND-BOUND

Let us consider the following simple example to illustrate the branch-and-bound (B&B) methodology. Lee-Anne Maracle and Rebecca General have a home-based business called SpiritWood, which produces unusual hand-made furniture using thin branches of local trees, bent and stained to play up the natural quality of the wood. Their best-selling items are loveseats, one type made from poplar and one type from willow. The poplar sells for $600 and the willow for $500. Because of the different qualities of the wood, the poplar requires five hours for construction and six hours for sanding, staining, and varnishing; the willow requires eight hours for construction and five hours for sanding, staining, and varnishing. Only Lee-Anne has mastered the technique of construction; Rebecca does all the sanding, staining, and varnishing. The partners have agreed to limit their hours per week so that the business doesn't take over their whole lives. Lee-Anne, who has young children, is willing to work a maximum of 40 hours per week; Rebecca, whose children are older, is willing to work 48 hours per week.

The IP formulation is as follows:

$$\text{Maximize sales revenue } R = \$600P + \$500W$$

subject to

$$5P + 8W \leq 40 \quad \text{(construction hours)}$$

$$8P + 6W \leq 48 \quad \text{(sanding and finishing hours)}$$

$$P, W \geq 0 \text{ and integer}$$

where

$$P = \text{number of poplar loveseats produced}$$

$$W = \text{number of willow loveseats produced}$$

The *relaxed problem* (i.e., the LP problem without the integer constraints), has the optimal solution $P = 4.24$, $W = 2.35$, and sales revenue $R = \$3719$. The solution is shown in Figure 6.2 on the next page.

We can find an integer-valued solution by rounding both P and W to the nearest integer so that $P = 4$, $W = 2$, and $R = \$3400$. While this solution is feasible, it is not clear whether this integer-valued solution is optimal. This solution is indicated in Figure 6.2.

FIGURE 6.2

Graph for SpiritWood

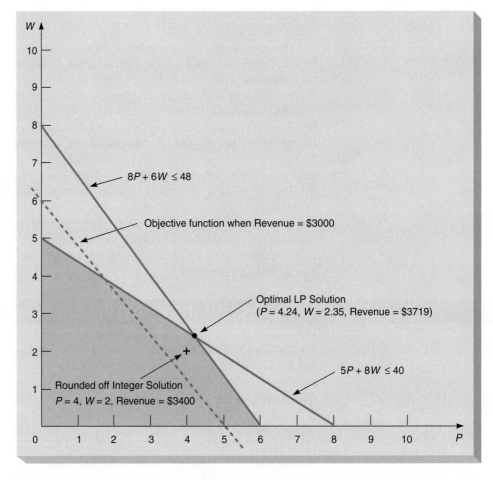

As described in Section 6.2, we now implement a strategy of "divide and conquer" as we seek new solutions, always forcing one of the variables to assume an integer value. This is accomplished by eliminating the fractional part of the noninteger value of one of the decision variables. In the SpiritWood example we select, arbitrarily, the value $P = 4.24$ and eliminate all possibilities between 4 and 5. That is, we allow 4 as a possible value of P, and we allow 5 as a possible value, but we *eliminate everything greater than 4 or less than 5.* In mathematical terms, we impose the restriction $P \leq 4$ or $P \geq 5$. (*Note:* We could just as easily have started with the value $W = 2.35$ and imposed the conditions $W \leq 2$ or $W \geq 3$.)

We have now created two new LP problems as follows:

Subproblem 1

Maximize $R = \$600P + \$500W$

subject to

$$5P + 8W \leq 40$$

$$8P + 6W \leq 48$$

$$P \leq 4$$

$$P, W \geq 0$$

Subproblem 2

Maximize $R = \$600P + \$500W$

subject to

$$5P + 8W \leq 40$$

$$8P + 6W \leq 48$$

$$P \geq 5$$

$$P, W \geq 0$$

The LP problems, labelled Subproblem 1 and Subproblem 2 are shown in Figure 6.3. Observe that all values between the vertical lines $P = 4$ and $P = 5$ have been removed from the original feasible region, leaving two disconnected feasible regions, one on or to the left

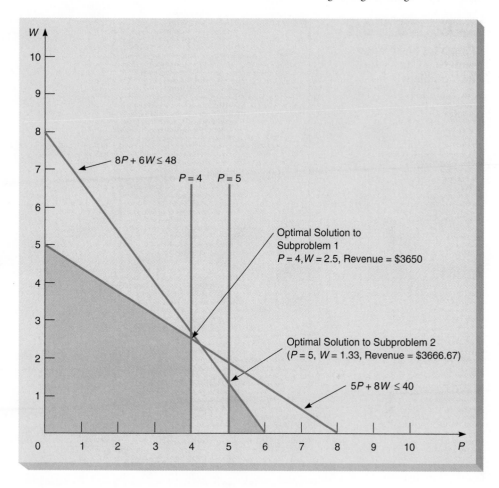

FIGURE 6.3

Graph for SpiritWood with New Constraints $P \le 4$ and $P \ge 5$

of the line $P = 4$ and the other on or to the right of the line $P = 5$. It can easily be seen that by moving the objective function line outward from the origin, the optimal solution to Subproblem 1 is at the corner point defined by the two straight lines $P = 4$ and $5P + 8W = 40$. Elementary algebra yields the solution $P = 4$, $W = 2.5$, and $R = \$3650$. This solution accomplishes the goal of forcing P to be the integer value 4.

The solution to Subproblem 2 is seen to be at the intersection of the lines $P = 5$ and $8P + 6W = 48$, yielding the result $P = 5$, $W = 1.33$, and $R = \$3666.67$. Once again we have a solution in which one of the variables, P, has an integer value.

This process of *branching*, in which one LP problem gives rise to two new subproblems, is now continued until eventually we arrive at a solution in which both variables are integer-valued.

We observe that the solution to the original LP problem has an optimal objective function value of \$3719. Each time we branch, we are reducing the size of the feasible region by imposing a new constraint, and therefore the optimal solution of a subproblem cannot exceed the optimal value of the problem that generates it. Thus, we can assert that an upper bound to the solution of the IP problem is \$3719. Since Subproblem 1 has an optimal solution of \$3650 and Subproblem 2 has an optimal solution of \$3666.67, it follows that as we continue to branch, subsequent optimal solutions cannot exceed the larger of these two values. Therefore, we have now established an upper bound of \$3666.67.

Figure 6.4 on the next page indicates the branching operations from Subproblems 1 and 2.

Referring to the region to the left of the vertical line $P = 4$ in Figure 6.3, we add the two new constraints $W \le 2$ and $W \ge 3$.

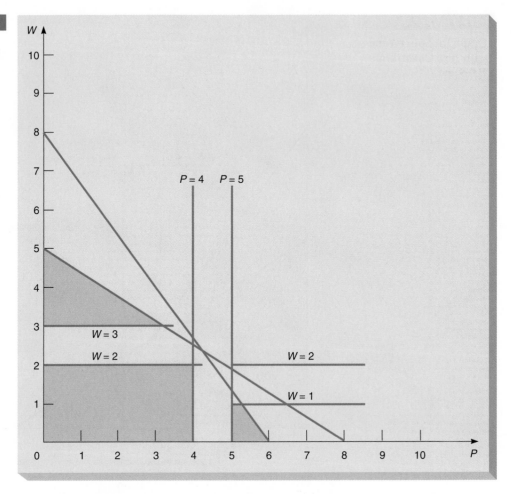

FIGURE 6.4

Graph for SpiritWood with New Constraint on Variable W

This branching operation creates new subproblems, enumerated below.

The Branch $W \leq 2$ The rectangular region bounded on the right by $P = 4$ and above by $W = 2$ results in the integer-valued solution $P = 4$, $W = 2$, $R = \$3400$. This is the solution we obtained earlier by simply rounding the two values to the nearest integers. We were already aware of this integer solution, but we still do not know if it is the optimal solution. Since both decision variables are integers, there will be no further branches below this solution. This illustrates the first stopping rule in the B&B method: stop branching when all decision variables are integer-valued.

The Branch $W \geq 3$ The triangular feasible region bounded below by the horizontal line $W = 3$ and bounded above by the line $5P + 8W = 40$ yields the optimal corner point solution $P = 3.2$, $W = 3$, $R = \$3420$. Notice that in this solution W has been forced to be the integer value 3, but P, an integer in the previous LP model, has reverted to a noninteger value.

Referring now to the region to the right of the vertical line $P = 5$, we observe a small triangular region bounded above by the straight line $8P + 6W = 48$ and below by the horizontal axis. Since the optimal corner point solution for this region is $P = 5$ and $W = 1.33$, we must eliminate all values of W greater than 1 and less than 2.

The Branch $W \leq 1$ When we add the constraint $W \leq 1$, we find the optimal corner point solution is at the intersection of the line $8P + 6W = 48$ and $W = 1$, yielding the result $P = 5.25$, $W = 1$, $R = \$3650$.

The Branch $W \geq 2$ When we impose the restriction W ≥ 2 we have an infeasible LP formulation. We see that the solution cannot simultaneously be bounded by the triangular region lying below the line $8P + 6W = 48$ and also on or above the horizontal line $W = 2$. Clearly, there can be no further branches. This illustrates the second stopping rule: stop branching when the LP model is infeasible.

Stopping Rules in the B&B Method

We have already seen two reasons for stopping the branching procedure—we stop when we have already reached an integer-valued solution, and also when the LP becomes infeasible. There is one other reason for stopping, namely when we have already achieved an integer-valued solution with an objective function value that is better than the value of the current solution. Recall that whenever we branch, the value of the objective function in the new LP is not as good as the value of the solution from which we have done the branching. We will call this the *inferior solution* reason for stopping.

In summary, stop branching when:

1. The current solution is integer-valued.

2. There is no feasible solution to the current LP problem.

3. In a *maximization problem,* the objective function value for the current LP is less than or equal to the best integer-valued solution found so far.

4. In a *minimization problem,* the objective function value for the current LP is greater than or equal to the best integer-valued solution found so far.

For SpiritWood, Figure 6.5 on the next page shows the original LP problem and all of its subproblems, found by repeatedly branching until the optimal integer-valued solution is found at $P = 6$, $W = 0$, $R = \$3600$.

We see that the optimal integer-valued solution is $P = 6$, $W = 0$, and Revenue = $3600. Note that this solution is superior to the solution $P = 4$, $W = 2$ obtained by rounding, since it had an objective function value of only $3400. It is important to note that in this case the optimal integer-valued solution at $P = 6$, $W = 0$ is not even close to the optimal noninteger corner point solution of the relaxed problem at $P = 4.24$, $W = 2$.

Setting Upper and Lower Bounds

Now that we have seen how to create and solve the LP problems for each of the branches, we must add upper and lower bounds to the B&B diagram. When the lower and upper bounds coincide, we will have found the optimal integer-valued solution. For a maximization problem we have already seen that the solution to the relaxed LP problem is an upper bound for the optimal value to the IP problem. As we branch from the relaxed problem to the next level, we observe that the maximum objective function value to the problems at that level forms a new upper bound. If there are any integer-valued solutions at that level, the maximum objective function value for these solutions is a lower bound, because once we have found an integer-valued solution, any solution with a lesser value cannot be optimal. This process is continued for each level of the B&B diagram. We summarize the bounding rules below.

For a maximization problem:

- The solution of the relaxed LP problem is the first upper bound for the IP problem.
- At any level of the branches, the maximum LP solution is an upper bound.
- At any level of the branches, the maximum IP solution is a lower bound.

FIGURE 6.5   **Relaxed LP Problem and All Subproblems**

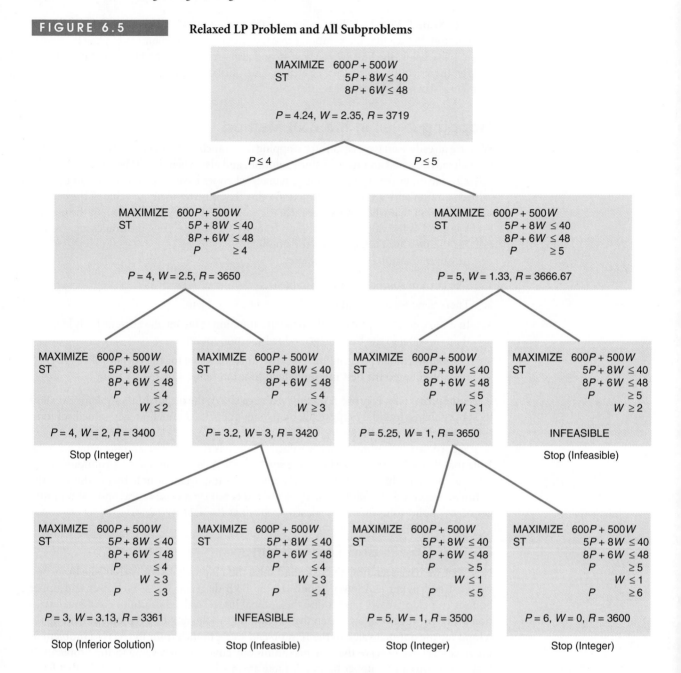

For a minimization problem:

- The solution of the relaxed LP problem is the first lower bound for the IP problem.
- At any level of the branches, the minimum LP solution is a lower bound.
- At any level of the branches, the minimum IP solution is an upper bound.

Figure 6.6 illustrates the branch-and-bound diagram for the SpiritWood problem.

In conclusion, we see that it is possible to obtain optimal integer-valued solutions using the B&B method. However, it is clear that the computational effort involved is much more onerous than for an LP problem without the integer constraints. In this simple example with only two variables and two constraints, it is necessary to attempt to solve 11 LP

FIGURE 6.6   **Branch-and-Bound Diagram for SpiritWood**

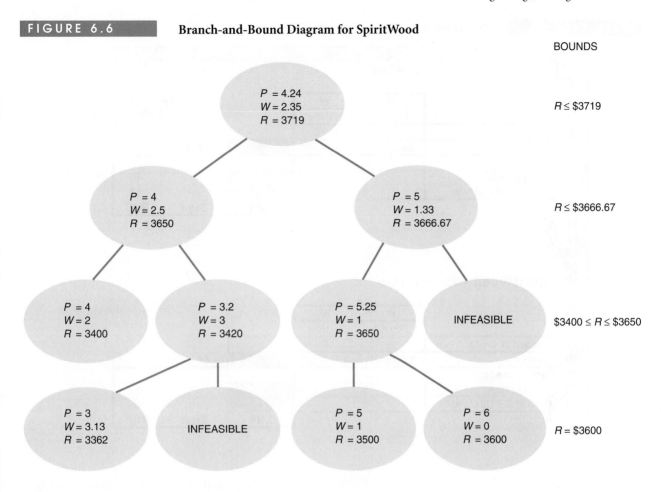

problems in order to find the optimal IP solution. For larger problems involving many variables and constraints, the search for the optimal IP solution may not be realistic, hence the Solver options for limiting the length of the search. The extra time spent searching for an optimal integer-valued solution may not be justified if the incremental improvement in the objective function value is small.

Screenshot 6.3 on the next page shows optimal solutions to both the LP problem and the IP problem.

File: 6-3.xls

6.4   MODELS WITH BINARY VARIABLES

Binary variables are restricted to values of 0 or 1.

As discussed earlier, binary variables are restricted to values of 0 or 1. Recall that the assignment model and shortest-path model in Chapter 5 both involve variables that ultimately take on values of either 0 or 1 at optimality. However, in both of those models, we did not have to explicitly specify that the variables were binary. The integer property of network-flow models, along with the supply and demand values of one unit each, automatically ensured that the optimal solution had values of 0 or 1.

In contrast, we now examine a model in which we will explicitly specify that the variables are binary. Binary variables are a powerful modeling tool and are applicable whenever we want to model a decision between exactly two choices. Typical examples include decisions such as introducing a new product (introduce it or not), building a new facility (build it or not), selecting a team (select a specific individual or not), and investing in projects (invest in a specific project or not).

SCREENSHOT 6.3   Solver Solution to SpiritWood Problem

	A	B	C	D	E	F
1	SpiritWood – LP Solution					
2						
3		P	W			
4		Poplar	Willow			
5	Number of Units	4.24	2.35			
6	Revenue	$600.00	$500.00	$3,717.65	<- Objective	
7	Constraints:					
8	Construction	5	8	40	<=	40
9	Sanding & Finishing	8	6	48	<=	48
10				LHS	Sign	RHS
11						
12						
13						
14						
15	SpiritWood – IP Solution					
16						
17		P	W			
18		Poplar	Willow			
19	Number of Units	6	0			
20	Revenue	$600.00	$500.00	$3,600.00	<- Objective	
21	Constraints:					
22	Construction	5	8	30	<=	40
23	Sanding & Finishing	8	6	48	<=	48
24				LHS	Sign	RHS

LP solution to relaxed problem.

Optimal solution to IP problem.

When we are faced with a decision that has exactly two choices, we associate a binary variable with it. With one of the two choices, we associate a value of 1 for the binary variable. A value of 0 for the binary variable is then associated with the other choice. Now, we write the objective function and constraints in a manner that is consistent with this definition of the binary variable.

Hi-tech Portfolio Selection

Let us consider a simple example to illustrate the use of binary variables. Richard Richman wants to make a selection of possible hi-tech stocks that he is interested in adding to his portfolio. He has made the following specifications:

■ At least two Alberta hi-tech firms must be in the portfolio

■ No more than one investment can be made in foreign (i.e., non-Canadian) companies

■ Exactly one of the two Quebec companies must be included

■ If British Telecom stock is included in the portfolio, then Alberta Telecom must also be included in the portfolio.

Richard has up to $3 million available for investments. Table 6.2 describes the various companies that Richard Richman is considering. The objective is to maximize annual return on investment, subject to the various constraints.

Note that the decision with regard to each company has to be one of two choices. That is, Richman either buys shares in the hi-tech company or he does not buy the company's shares. To formulate this problem, let us therefore associate a binary variable with each of the seven hi-tech companies. For each company i, we define the binary variable as follows:

$$X_i = \begin{cases} 1 \text{ if a large block of shares in company } i \text{ is purchased} \\ 0 \text{ if a large block of shares in company } i \text{ is } not \text{ purchased} \end{cases}$$

where

i = AT (Alberta Telecom), B (British Telecom), D (Dutch Electronics), C (Calgary Hi-Tec), AC (Alberta Computers), Q (Quebec Electronics), or M (Montreal Tech)

We now need to express the objective function and constraints in a manner that is consistent with the previous definition of the binary variables. The objective function can be written as

$$\text{Maximize return on investment} = \$50\,X_{AT} + \$80\,X_B + \$90\,X_D \\ + \$120\,X_C + \$110\,X_{AC} + \$40\,X_Q + \$75\,X_M$$

All costs and revenues are in thousands of dollars. In the previous expression, if X_{AT} has an optimal value of 1 (implying we buy a block of shares in Alberta Telecom), this would contribute \$50 000 to the total return. In contrast, if X_{AT} has an optimal value of 0 (implying we do *not* buy shares in this company), this would contribute \$0 to the total return.

Next, we model the constraints. The constraint regarding the \$3 million investment limit can be expressed in a similar manner to that of the objective function. That is,

$$\$480X_{AT} + \$540X_B + \$680X_D + \$1000X_C + \$700X_{AC} + \$510X_Q + \$900X_M \leq \$3000$$

Again, all figures are in thousands of dollars.

Depending on whether the optimal value of a binary variable is 0 or 1, the corresponding investment cost will be calculated in the LHS of the previous expression. The other constraints in the problems are special ones that exploit the binary nature of these variables. These types of constraints are what make the use of binary variables a powerful modeling tool. We discuss these special constraints in the following sections.

k **out of** *n* **Variables**   The requirement that at least two Alberta hi-tech firms must be in the portfolio is an example of a "k out of n variables" constraint. There are three (i.e., $n = 3$)

Binary variables can be used to write different types of constraints.

Selecting k out of n choices

TABLE 6.2

Hi-tech Investment Opportunities

Here is an example of stock portfolio analysis with 0–1 programming

COMPANY NAME	EXPECTED ANNUAL RETURN ($1000s)	COST FOR BLOCK OF SHARES ($1000s)
Alberta Telecom	50	480
British Telecom	80	540
Dutch Electronics	90	680
Calgary Hi-Tec (Alberta)	120	1000
Alberta Computers	110	700
Quebec Electronics	40	510
Montreal Tech (Quebec)	75	900

Alberta hi-tech firms (X_{AT}, X_C, and X_{AC}), of which at least two (i.e., $k = 2$) must be selected. We can model this constraint as

$$X_{AT} + X_C + X_{AC} \geq 2$$

Avoiding incompatible selections

Mutually Exclusive Variables   The condition that no more than one investment can be made in foreign companies is an example of a *mutually exclusive* constraint. Note that the inclusion of one foreign company (British Telecom or Dutch Electronics) means that the other must be excluded. We can model this constraint as

$$X_B + X_D \leq 1$$

The condition regarding the Quebec companies (exactly one of the two Quebec companies must be included) is also an example of having mutually exclusive variables. The sign of this constraint is, however, an equality rather than an inequality since Richman *must* include a Quebec stock in the portfolio. That is,

$$X_Q + X_M = 1$$

Enforcing dependencies

If–Then (or Linked) Variables   The condition that if British Telecom stock is included in the portfolio, then Alberta Telecom stock must also be included in the portfolio, is an example of an *if-then* constraint. We can model this relationship as

$$X_B \leq X_{AT}$$

or

$$X_B - X_{AT} \leq 0$$

Note that if X_B equals 0 (i.e., British Telecom is not included in the portfolio), this constraint allows X_{AT} to equal either 0 or 1. However, if X_B equals 1, then X_{AT} must also equal 1.

The relationship discussed here is a one-way linkage in that Alberta Telecom must be included if British Telecom is included, but not vice versa. If the relationship is two-way (i.e., either include both or include neither), we must then rewrite the constraint as

$$X_B = X_{AT}$$

or

$$X_B - X_{AT} = 0$$

Solution to the Hi-tech Portfolio 0-1 Model

The complete formulation of Richman's Hi-tech portfolio selection problem is as follows:

Maximize return = $\$50X_{AT} + \$80X_B + \$90X_D + \$120X_C + \$110X_{AC} + \$40X_Q + \$75X_M$

subject to

$$
\begin{aligned}
\$480X_{AT} + \$540X_B + \$680X_D + \$1000X_C & \\
+ \$700X_{AC} + \$510X_Q + \$900X_M \leq \$3000 \quad & \text{(investment limit)} \\
X_{AT} + X_C + X_{AC} \geq 2 \quad & \text{(Alberta)} \\
X_B + X_D \leq 1 \quad & \text{(foreign companies)} \\
X_Q + X_M = 1 \quad & \text{(Quebec)} \\
X_B - X_{AT} \leq 0 \quad & \text{(British Telecom and Alberta Telecom)} \\
\text{All } X_i \in (0, 1) \quad &
\end{aligned}
$$

The Excel layout and Solver entries for Richman's 0–1 problem are shown in Screenshot 6.4. The specification of the Target Cell, Changing Cells, and constraint LHS and RHS cell references in the Solver Parameters window is similar to that used for LP and general IP models.

SCREENSHOT 6.4   **Excel Layout and Solver Entries for Hi-tech Portfolio Selection Binary Integer Programming Problem**

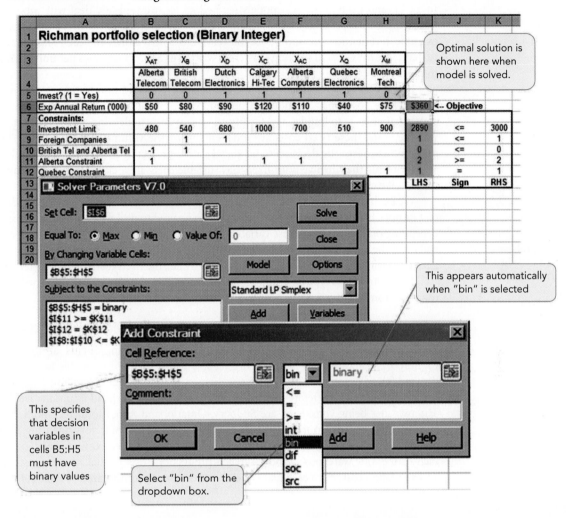

Specifying the Binary Requirement

File: 6-4.xls

To specify the binary requirement for all variables, we again use the **ADD** option to include a new constraint. In the LHS entry for the new constraint (see Screenshot 6.4), we enter the cell reference for a decision variable that must be binary-valued. If there are several decision variables that must be binary-valued, we can enter the entire cell range, provided these variables are in contiguous cells. For Richman's problem, we enter B5:H5 in this box, corresponding to X_{AT} through X_M, respectively.

We then click on the drop-down box in the **ADD CONSTRAINT** window and click on the choice **BIN**. The word "Binary" automatically is displayed in the box for the RHS entry. This indicates to Solver that all variables specified in the LHS box are binary variables.

Screenshot 6.4 shows that the optimal solution is for Richman to invest in Dutch Electronics (X_D), Calgary Hi-Tec (X_C), Alberta Computers (X_{AC}), and Quebec Electronics (X_Q). The expected return is $360 000, since the $360 in cell I6 is in units of $1000.

6.5   MIXED INTEGER MODELS: FIXED-CHARGE PROBLEMS

In all LP and general integer models studied so far, we typically deal with situations in which the total cost is directly proportional to the magnitude of the decision variable. For example, if X denotes the number of toasters we will be making, and each toaster costs $10 to make, the total cost of making toasters is written as $10X$. Such costs per unit are referred to as *variable* costs.

In many situations, however, there are fixed costs in addition to the per unit variable costs. These costs may include the costs to set up machines for the production run, construction costs to build a new facility, or design costs to develop a new product. Unlike variable costs, these fixed costs are independent of the volume of production. They are incurred whenever the decision to go ahead with a project or production run is taken.

Problems that involve both fixed and variable costs are a classic example of mixed IP models. We call such problems **fixed-charge problems**.

We use binary variables to model the fixed cost issue (e.g., whether we will incur the setup cost or not). Either linear or integer variables can be used to deal with the variable costs issue, depending on the nature of these variables. In formulating the model, we need to ensure that whenever the decision variable associated with the variable cost is nonzero, the binary variable associated with the fixed cost takes on a value of 1 (i.e., the fixed cost is also incurred).

Fixed-charge problems include fixed costs in addition to variable costs.

To illustrate this type of situation, let us reintroduce the Hardgrave Machine Company example from Section 5.4 of Chapter 5.

Locating a New Factory for Hardgrave Machine Company

The Hardgrave Machine Company produces computer components at its plants in Cranbrooke, Kingston, and Prince George. These plants have not been able to keep up with demand for orders at Hardgrave's four warehouses in Charlotteville, Hamilton, Nanaimo, and Regina. The firm has therefore decided to build a new plant to expand its productive capacity. The two sites being considered are Sudbury, Ontario, and Abbotsford, B.C. Both cities are attractive in terms of labour supply, municipal services, and ease of factory financing. Table 6.3 presents the production costs and capacities for each of the three existing plants, demand at each of the four warehouses, and estimated production costs for the new proposed plants. Transportation costs from each plant to each warehouse are summarized in Table 6.4.

TABLE 6.3 **Hardgrave's Demand and Supply Data**	WAREHOUSE	MONTHLY DEMAND (UNITS)	PRODUCTION PLANT	MONTHLY SUPPLY	COST TO PRODUCE ONE UNIT ($)
	Charlotteville	10 000	Cranbrooke	15 000	48
	Hamilton	12 000	Kingston	6 000	50
	Nanaimo	15 000	Prince George	14 000	52
	Regina	9 000		35 000	
		46 000			

Supply needed from new plant = 46 000 − 35 000 = 11 000 units per month

We use regular variables (continuous-valued or general integer) to model the shipping quantities.

ESTIMATED PRODUCTION COST PER UNIT AT PROPOSED PLANTS	
Sudbury	$53
Abbotsford	$49

<table>
<tr><td colspan="2" rowspan="2">TABLE 6.4</td></tr>
</table>

TABLE 6.4

Hardgrave's Shipping Costs

FROM \ TO	CHARLOTTEVILLE	HAMILTON	NANAIMO	REGINA
Cranbrooke	$25	$55	$40	$60
Kingston	35	30	50	40
Prince George	36	45	26	66
Sudbury	60	38	65	27
Abbotsford	35	30	41	50

Hardgrave estimates that the monthly fixed cost of operating the proposed facility in Sudbury would be $400 000. The Abbotsford plant would be somewhat lower due to the lower cost of living at that location. Hardgrave therefore estimates that the monthly fixed cost of operating the proposed facility in Abbotsford would be $325 000. Note that the fixed costs at *existing* plants need not be considered here since they will be incurred regardless of which new plant Hardgrave decides to open—that is, they are *sunk costs.*

Sunk costs are not considered in the optimization model.

As in Chapter 5, the question facing Hardgrave is this: Which of the new locations will yield the lowest cost in combination with the existing plants and warehouses? Note that the unit cost of shipping from each plant to each warehouse is found by adding the shipping costs (Table 6.4) to the corresponding production costs (Table 6.3). In addition, the solution needs to consider the monthly fixed costs of operating the new facility.

Recall that we handled this problem in Section 5.4 by setting up and solving two separate transportation models (one for each of the two new locations). In what follows, we show how we can use binary variables to model Hardgrave's problem as a single mixed, binary integer programming model.

Decision Variables There are two types of decisions to be made in this problem. The first involves deciding which of the new locations (Sudbury or Abbotsford) to select for the new plant. The second involves trying to decide the shipment quantities from each plant (including the new plant) to each of the warehouses.

We use binary variables to model the opening of a plant.

To model the first decision, we associate a binary variable with each of the two locations. Let

$$Y_S = \begin{cases} 1 \text{ if Sudbury is selected for the new plant} \\ 0 \text{ otherwise} \end{cases}$$

$$Y_A = \begin{cases} 1 \text{ if Abbotsford is selected for the new plant} \\ 0 \text{ otherwise} \end{cases}$$

To model the shipping quantities, we once again use double-subscripted variables, as discussed in Chapter 5. Note that there will be 20 decision variables (= 5 plants × 4 warehouses) denoting the shipping quantities (one variable for each possible shipping route). Let

$$X_{ij} = \text{Number of units shipped from plant } i \text{ to warehouse } j$$

where

i = C (Cranbrooke), K (Kingston), P (Prince George), S (Sudbury), or A (Abbotsford)

j = C (Charlotteville), H (Hamilton), N (Nanaimo), or R (Regina)

Objective Function   Let us first model the objective function. We want to minimize the total cost of producing and shipping the components and the monthly fixed costs of maintaining the new facility. This can be written as

$$
\begin{aligned}
\text{Minimize total costs} = \ & \$73X_{CC} + \$103X_{CH} + \$88X_{CN} + \$108X_{CR} \\
& + \$85X_{KC} + \$80X_{KH} + \$100X_{KN} + \$90X_{KR} \\
& + \$88X_{PC} + \$97X_{PH} + \$78X_{PN} + \$118X_{PR} \\
& + \$113X_{SC} + \$91X_{SH} + \$118X_{SN} + \$80X_{SR} \\
& + \$84X_{AC} + \$79X_{AH} + \$90X_{AN} + \$99X_{AR} \\
& + \$400\ 000Y_{S} + \$325\ 000Y_{A}
\end{aligned}
$$

The last two terms in the expression for the objective function represent the fixed costs. Note that these costs will be incurred only if the plant is built at the location (i.e., the variable Y_i has a value of 1).

Constraints   We need to write flow balance constraints at each of the plants and warehouses. Recall that at each node, the flow balance constraint ensures that

$$\text{Net flow = Total flow } in \text{ to node} - \text{Total flow } out \text{ of node} \qquad (6\text{-}1)$$

At source nodes, the net flow is a negative quantity and represents the amount of goods (flow) created at the source node. In contrast, at destination nodes, the net flow is a positive quantity, and represents the amount of goods (flow) consumed at the source node.

The flow balance constraints at the existing plants (Cranbrooke, Kingston, and Prince George) are straightforward and can be written as

$$
\begin{aligned}
(0) - (X_{CC} + X_{CH} + X_{CN} + X_{CR}) &= -15\ 000 & \text{(Cranbrooke supply)} \\
(0) - (X_{KC} + X_{KH} + X_{KN} + X_{KR}) &= -6000 & \text{(Kingston supply)} \\
(0) - (X_{PC} + X_{PH} + X_{PN} + X_{PR}) &= -14\ 000 & \text{(Prince George supply)}
\end{aligned}
$$

However, when writing the flow balance constraint for a new plant (Sudbury or Abbotsford), we need to ensure that a supply is available at that plant *only* if it is actually built. For example, the supply at Sudbury is 11 000 units if the new plant is built there and 0 otherwise. We can model this as follows:

$$
\begin{aligned}
(0) - (X_{SC} + X_{SH} + X_{SN} + X_{SR}) &= -11\ 000Y_{S} & \text{(Sudbury supply)} \\
(0) - (X_{AC} + X_{AH} + X_{AN} + X_{AR}) &= -11\ 000Y_{A} & \text{(Abbotsford supply)}
\end{aligned}
$$

Note that if Sudbury is selected for the new plant, Y_S would equal 1. Hence, a supply of 11 000 would be available there. In contrast, if Sudbury is not selected for the new plant, Y_S would equal 0. Hence, the supply in the flow balance constraint would become 0; that is, all flows from Sudbury would have to equal 0. The flow balance constraint for Abbotsford works in a similar manner.

The flow balance constraints at the four existing warehouses (Charlotteville, Hamilton, Nanaimo, and Regina) can be written as

$$
\begin{aligned}
X_{CC} + X_{KC} + X_{PC} + X_{SC} + X_{AC} &= 10\ 000 & \text{(Charlotteville demand)} \\
X_{CH} + X_{KH} + X_{PH} + X_{SH} + X_{AH} &= 12\ 000 & \text{(Hamilton demand)} \\
X_{CN} + X_{KN} + X_{PN} + X_{SN} + X_{AN} &= 15\ 000 & \text{(Nanaimo demand)} \\
X_{CR} + X_{KR} + X_{PR} + X_{SR} + X_{AR} &= 9000 & \text{(Regina demand)}
\end{aligned}
$$

Only one of the two sites can be selected.

Finally, we need to ensure that exactly one of the two sites is selected for the new plant. This is another example of the mutually exclusive variables discussed in Section 6.4. We can express this as

$$Y_S + Y_A = 1$$

The formula view of the Excel layout for Hardgrave's fixed-charge problem is shown in Screenshot 6.5A. The Solver entries and optimal solution are shown in Screenshot 6.5B.

SCREENSHOT 6.5A   **Formula View of Excel Layout for Hardgrave Machine Company's Mixed Integer Programming Problem**

Sum of entries in rows 4–8 gives the total flow *in*.

Sum of entries in columns B–E gives the total flow *out*.

Hardgrave Machine Company (Mixed Integer)

	A	B	C	D	E	F	G	H	I	J	K
3	From: To:	Charlotteville	Hamilton	Nanaimo	Regina	Total flow out		Flow balance equations:			
4	Cranbrooke					=SUM(B4:E4)		Location	Net flow	Sign	RHS
5	Kingston					=SUM(B5:E5)		Cranbrooke	=0-F4	=	-15000
6	Prince George					=SUM(B6:E6)		Kingston	=0-F5	=	-6000
7	Abbotsford					=SUM(B7:E7)		Prince George	=0-F6	=	-14000
8	Sudbury					=SUM(B8:E8)		Abbotsford	=0-F7	=	=-11000*B19
9	Total flow in	=SUM(B4:B8)	=SUM(C4:C8)	=SUM(D4:D8)	=SUM(E4:E8)			Sudbury	=0-F8	=	=-11000*C19
10								Charlotteville	=B9	=	10000
11	Unit costs:	Charlotteville	Hamilton	Nanaimo	Regina			Hamilton	=C9	=	12000
12	Cranbrooke	73	103	88	108			Nanaimo	=D9	=	15000
13	Kingston	85	80	100	90			Regina	=E9	=	9000
14	Prince George	88	97	78	118						
15	Abbotsford	84	79	90	99			# of new plants	=B19+C19	=	1
16	Sudbury	113	91	118	80						
17											
18		Abbotsford	Sudbury								
19	Build? (1 = Yes)										
20	Fixed Cost	325000	400000								
21											
22	Shipping cost =	=SUMPRODUCT(B4:E8,B12:E16)									
23	Fixed Cost =	=SUMPRODUCT(B19:C19,B20:C20)									
24	Total Cost =	=B22+B23									

This specifies that only one of the two sites must be selected.

RHS = –11 000 if site is selected, = 0 if site is not selected.

Solver will place the solution values in these shaded cells.

Total cost is the sum of shipping cost and fixed cost.

SCREENSHOT 6.5B   **Solver Entries and Solution for Hardgrave Machine Company's Mixed Integer Programming Problem**

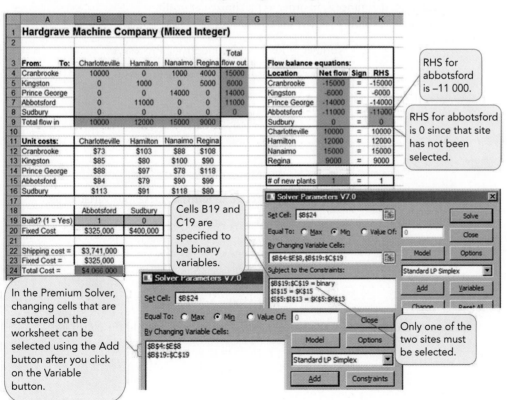

RHS for abbotsford is –11 000.

RHS for abbotsford is 0 since that site has not been selected.

Cells B19 and C19 are specified to be binary variables.

In the Premium Solver, changing cells that are scattered on the worksheet can be selected using the Add button after you click on the Variable button.

Only one of the two sites must be selected.

File: 6-5.xls

Total cost includes fixed costs and shipping costs.

Referring back to Section 5.4, we see that the cost of shipping would be $3 704 000 if the new plant were built in Sudbury. The cost of shipping would be $3 741 000 if the new plant were built at Abbotsford. With the fixed costs included, these costs would be

Sudbury:　$3 704 000 + $400 000 = $4 104 000
Abbotsford: $3 741 000 + $325 000 = $4 066 000

That is, Hardgrave should select Abbotsford as the site for the new plant. Screenshot 6.5B shows this solution. Note that the shipping quantities in this solution are the same as those obtained in Section 5.4 for the solution with the Abbotsford plant (as we saw in Screenshot 5.3B on page 190).

The Big-M Method

When using binary variables to model fixed costs we will need a way to ensure that the appropriate cost is incurred, i.e., we need to be able to force the computer to "switch on" a binary variable associated with a fixed cost. This may be accomplished by using the **Big-M method**. We illustrate this method with the following example.

A production manager has to make a decision regarding which of two processes to use to assemble a particular electronic device. Process A will require 5 hours of labour, 13 transistors, and 27 diodes. Process B will require 8 hours of labour, 21 transistors, and 12 diodes. An analysis of revenues and production costs indicates that regardless of the production process chosen, each device produced will yield a net profit of $240. Weekly availabilities are 400 person-hours of labour, 2000 transistors, and 1500 diodes. There is a one-time fixed cost for setting up the production processes, which amounts to $1200 for Process A and $900 for Process B. We wish to formulate a mixed integer programming problem to help the manufacturer decide which process to use, and how many units to produce using that process, in order to maximize net profit.

Decision Variables　There are two integer variables:

$$X_A = \text{Number of items to produce using Process A}$$

$$X_B = \text{Number of items to produce using Process B}$$

We also define two binary variables:

$$Y_A = \begin{cases} 1 \text{ if Process A is used} \\ 0 \text{ if Process A is not used} \end{cases}$$

$$Y_B = \begin{cases} 1 \text{ if Process B is used} \\ 0 \text{ if Process B is not used} \end{cases}$$

The objective function may now be expressed in terms of these four variables as:

$$\text{Maximize net profit} = \$240X_A + \$240X_B - \$1200Y_A - \$900Y_B$$

The resource-based constraints are

$$5X_A + 8X_B \leq 400 \qquad \text{(hours of labour)}$$
$$13X_A + 21X_B \leq 2000 \qquad \text{(transistors)}$$
$$27X_A + 12X_B \leq 1500 \qquad \text{(diodes)}$$

Since one and only one of the two processes is to be used, we add the constraint:

$$Y_A + Y_B = 1$$

Finally, we need to add a constraint to ensure that if Process A is not employed then $Y_A = 0$ (i.e., the fixed cost of $1200 will not be charged) and if Process A is used then $Y_A = 1$ (i.e., the fixed cost of $1200 will be charged). We will need a similar constraint for Process B. For Process A, the following constraint will achieve the desired goal:

$$X_A - MY_A \leq 0, \text{ where } M \text{ is a "big number."}$$

The reason that this constraint works may be explained as follows:

The constraint $X_A - MY_A \leq 0$, may be written in the form $Y_A \geq \frac{1}{M} X_A$.

This shows us that whenever $X_A > 0$ (i.e., Process A is used to produce some units), then Y_A, being a binary variable and greater than 0, must equal 1. Thus we see that the cost for Process A, namely $1200, will be subtracted from the value of the objective function.

Why does M have to be a big number? Since Y_A can only equal 0 or 1, it follows that $(1/M)X_A$ has to be a number less than 1. Therefore M has to be large to ensure that $(1/M)X_A$ is small. Furthermore, we do not want to limit our production of items using Process A any more than is already necessary as a result of the resource-based constraints. For example, if $M = 10$ and $Y_A = 1$ (i.e., Process A is used) the constraint $X_A - MY_A \leq 0$ implies that $X_A \leq 10$. It would hardly be worthwhile using Process A if we were limited to producing 10 units! Therefore M has to be a big number to ensure that we do not place any unnecessary upper limit on the number of units to produce using Process A. In practice we can let M equal the largest number that appears on the right-hand side of any of the constraints. In our example we will add the two constraints:

$$X_A - MY_A \leq 0$$

$$X_B - MY_B \leq 0$$

And we will let $M = 2000$.

The complete formulation will now appear as:

$$\text{Maximize net profit} = \$240X_A + \$240X_B - \$1200Y_A - \$900Y_B$$

subject to

$$5X_A + 8X_B \leq 400 \quad \text{(hours of labour)}$$

$$13X_A + 21X_B \leq 2000 \quad \text{(transistors)}$$

$$27X_A + 12X_B \leq 1500 \quad \text{(diodes)}$$

$$Y_A + Y_B = 1 \quad \text{(only one process can be used)}$$

$$X_A - 2000Y_A \leq 0$$

$$X_B - 2000Y_B \leq 0$$

where X_A, X_B are integer variables and Y_A, Y_B are binary variables.

Screenshot 6.6 shows the Excel layout and the Solver entries for this fixed cost problem.

We see that the optimal solution is to use Process A to produce 55 units ($X_A = 55$). Notice that $Y_A = 1$, so that the fixed cost of starting up Process A is subtracted from revenues.

File: 6-6.xls

SCREENSHOT 6.6

Excel Layout and Solver Entries for Fixed Cost Problem

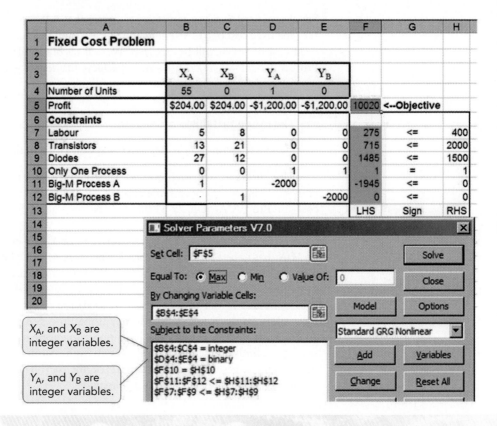

X_A, and X_B are integer variables.

Y_A, and Y_B are integer variables.

SUMMARY

This chapter deals with integer programming (IP), that is, LP problems that cannot have fractional answers. There are three types of IP problems: (1) pure or all-integer programs, (2) mixed programs, in which some solution variables need not be integers, and (3) binary, or 0–1, problems, in which some or all variables have values of either 0 or 1. We illustrate how all these models can be set up on Excel and solved using Solver.

We also discuss the branch-and-bound (B&B) method of solution and demonstrate how this technique can be used to solve simple problems with two decision variables by constructing a B&B diagram. Exploration of the B&B method gives us a deeper insight into the complexity of finding integer-valued solutions to LP problems, and provides an appreciation of the difficulties of finding optimal integer-valued solutions to large-scale problems, even with the help of an optimizer such as the Solver.

Finally, we introduce the Big-M method and show how it can be used to help solve problems involving fixed costs.

GLOSSARY

Big-M Method. A technique used to assign values of 0 or 1 to a binary integer variable as appropriate.

Binary Variables. Integer variables that can only take on either of two values: 0 or 1. Also called *0–1 variables*.

Branch-and-Bound (B&B) Method. An algorithm used by Solver to solve IP problems. It divides the set of feasible solutions into subregions that are examined systematically.

Fixed-Charge Problem. A problem in which there is a fixed cost in addition to variable costs. Fixed costs need to be modeled using binary (0–1) variables.

General Integer Variables. Decision variables that are required to be integer-valued. The actual value of these variables is restricted only by the constraints in the problem.

Integer Programming (IP). A mathematical programming technique that produces integer solutions to LP problems.

Mixed IP Problems. Problems in which some decision variables must have integer values (either general integer or binary) and other decision variable can have fractional values.

Zero–One Variables. Decision variables that are required to have integer values of either 0 or 1. Also called *binary variables*.

KEY EQUATION

(6-1) Net flow = Total flow *in* to node − Total flow *out* of node

Flow balance constraint written for each node in network-flow problems.

SOLVED PROBLEMS

Solved Problem 6-1

Consider the 0–1 IP problem that follows:

$$\text{Maximize } 50X_1 + 45X_2 + 48X_3$$

subject to

$$19X_1 + 27X_2 + 34X_3 \leq 80$$
$$22X_1 + 13X_2 + 12X_3 \leq 40$$
$$X_1, X_2, X_3 \text{ must be either 0 or 1}$$

Now reformulate this problem with additional constraints so that no more than two of the three variables can take on a value equal to 1 in the solution. Further, make sure that if $X_1 = 1$, then $X_2 = 1$ also, and vice versa. Then solve the new problem using Excel.

Solution

We need two new constraints to handle the reformulated problem:

$$X_1 + X_2 + X_3 \leq 2$$

and

$$X_1 - X_2 = 0$$

The Excel layout and Solver entries for this problem are shown in Screenshot 6.7. The optimal solution is $X_1 = 1$, $X_2 = 1$, $X_3 = 0$, with an objective value of 95.

SCREENSHOT 6.7   **Excel Layout and Solver Entries for Solved Problem 6-1**

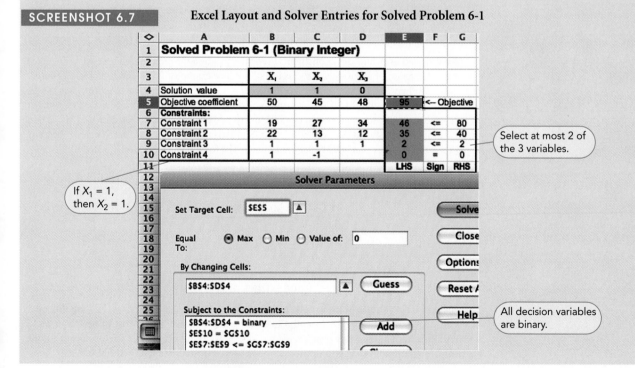

Solved Problem 6-2

The Atlantic Textile Company can use any of three different processes for weaving its hallmark Nova Scotia tartan fabric. Each process has a variable cost per square metre for weaving the fabric. Due to recent advances in weaving machine technology, there is also a fixed setup cost for the weaving machine used by each process. Table 6.5 shows the setup cost, variable production cost, and production for each of the three processes.

TABLE 6.5

PROCESS COST	SETUP COST	PRODUCTION $/m^2$	MAXIMUM DAILY CAPACITY (m^2)
1	$ 500	$0.17	30 000
2	800	0.14	35 000
3	1200	0.12	45 000

The company wants to minimize the total cost of production, subject to the constraint that it has to produce 50 000 square metres of the fabric daily to meet demand.

Solution

We define the decision variables X_j = the number of square metres to produce using Process j, where $j = 1, 2, 3$ and

$$Y_j = \begin{cases} 1 \text{ if Process } j \text{ is used} \\ 0 \text{ if Process } j \text{ is not used} \end{cases} \quad \text{for } j = 1, 2, 3$$

The objective function can now be written as

$$\text{Minimize cost} = 0.17X_1 + 0.14X_2 + 0.12X_3 + 500Y_1 + 800Y_2 + 1200Y_3$$

subject to

$$X_1 + X_2 + X_3 = 50\ 000 \text{ m}^2$$
$$X_1 \leq 30\ 000 \text{ m}^2$$
$$X_2 \leq 35\ 000 \text{ m}^2$$
$$X_3 \leq 45\ 000 \text{ m}^2$$

We also need to include extra constraints to ensure that the appropriate setup cost will be incurred whenever production of a particular process is initiated. For example, if production Process 1 is used, so that $X_1 > 0$, then $Y_1 = 1$ and the setup cost of $500 is added to the objective function. This can be accomplished by using the Big-M method and including constraints of the form $X_j - MY_j \leq 0$, for $j = 1, 2, 3$. However, we note that we can combine the two constraints $X_1 \leq 30\ 000$ and $X_1 - MY_1 \leq 0$ to obtain the single constraint $X_1 - 30\ 000Y_1 \leq 0$. Similarly, the constraints for X_2 and X_3 become $X_2 - 35\ 000Y_2 \leq 0$ and $X_3 - 45\ 000Y_3 \leq 0$, respectively. The formulation now takes the form:

$$\text{Minimize cost} = 0.17X_1 + 0.14X_2 + 0.12X_3 + 500Y_1 + 800\ Y_2 + 1200Y_3$$

subject to

$$X_1 + X_2 + X_3 = 50\ 000 \text{ m}^2$$
$$X_1 - 30\ 000\ Y_1 \leq 0$$
$$X_2 - 35\ 000\ Y_2 \leq 0$$
$$X_3 - 45\ 000\ Y_3 \leq 0$$

where

$$X_i \text{ are } \geq 0 \text{ and integer, } Y_i \text{ are binary.}$$

The optimal solution, shown in Screenshot 6.8, is to produce 5000 m^2 of fabric using Process 1 (at a cost of 5000 × $0.17 = $850) and 45 000 m^2 using Process 3 (at a cost of 45000 × $0.12 = $5 400). In addition, Process 1 incurs a setup cost of $500 and Process 3 has a setup cost of $1200. Therefore, the minimum total cost of production is $850 + $5400 + $500 + $1200 = $7950.

SCREENSHOT 6.8

Excel Layout and Solver Entries for Solved Problem 6-2

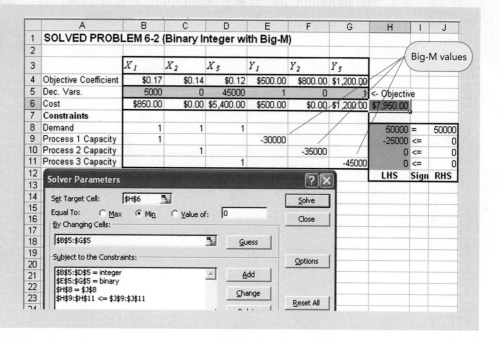

	A	B	C	D	E	F	G	H	I	J
1	SOLVED PROBLEM 6-2 (Binary Integer with Big-M)									
2										
3		X_1	X_2	X_3	Y_1	Y_2	Y_3			
4	Objective Coefficient	$0.17	$0.14	$0.12	$500.00	$800.00	$1,200.00			
5	Dec. Vars.	5000	0	45000	1	0	1	<- Objective		
6	Cost	$850.00	$0.00	$5,400.00	$500.00	$0.00	$1,200.00	$7,950.00		
7	Constraints									
8	Demand	1	1	1				50000	=	50000
9	Process 1 Capacity	1		-30000				-25000	<=	0
10	Process 2 Capacity		1		-35000			0	<=	0
11	Process 3 Capacity			1		-45000		0	<=	0
12								LHS	Sign	RHS

Big-M values

Solver Parameters [?][X]

Set Target Cell: $H$6

Equal To: ○ Max   ● Min   ○ Value of: 0

By Changing Cells:

$B$5:$G$5

Subject to the Constraints:

$B$5:$D$5 = integer
$E$5:$G$5 = binary
$H$8 = $J$8
$H$9:$H$11 <= $J$9:$J$11

Solve
Close
Guess
Options
Add
Change
Reset All

SELF-TEST

- Before taking the self-test, refer back to the learning objectives at the beginning of the chapter, the notes in the margins, and the glossary at the end of the chapter.
- Use the key at the back of the book to correct your answers.
- Restudy pages that correspond to any questions that you answered incorrectly or material you feel uncertain about.

1. If all of the decision variables require integer solutions, the problem is a
   a. pure IP type of problem.
   b. simplex method type of problem.
   c. mixed IP type of problem.
   d. mixed binary type of problem.

2. The fixed-charge problem is an example of a
   a. programming problem.
   b. general integer problem.
   c. mixed IP problem.
   d. pure IP problem.

3. In a mixed IP problem
   a. some integers must be even and others must be odd.
   b. some decision variables must require integer results only and some variables must allow for continuous results.
   c. some decision variables must be 0–1 variables.

4. The branch-and-bound method is used by Solver to solve
   a. LP problems.
   b. binary programming problems.
   c. fixed-charge problems.
   d. IP problems.

5. A model containing a linear objective function and linear constraints and requiring that some but not all of the decision variables take on an integer value in the final solution is called a
   a. pure IP problem.
   b. mixed IP problem.
   c. mixed binary IP problem.
   d. pure LP problem.

6. An IP solution can never produce a greater profit than the LP solution to the same problem.
   a. True
   b. False

7. In a pure IP problem, the B&B method will find an optimal solution when the upper and lower bounds are equal.
   a. True
   b. False

8. In general, it requires less effort to find integer-valued solutions than noninteger solutions because there are fewer integer-valued solutions in the feasible region.
   a. True
   b. False

9. In order to find integer-valued solutions using Excel's Solver, it is necessary to add a constraint specifying which variables are integers.
   a. True
   b. False

10. If X_A is a binary variable that is equal to 1 if Product A is produced, and X_B is a binary variable that is equal to 1 if Product B is produced, then the constraint that Product B can be produced only if Product A is produced is given by
    a. $X_A + X_B = 1$
    b. $X_A + X_B \geq 0$
    c. $X_A - X_B = -1$
    d. $X_A - X_B \geq 0$

11. The 0–1 integer programming problem
    a. requires that the decision variables have values of 0 or 1.
    b. requires that the constraints all have RHS values of 0 or 1.
    c. requires that the decision variables have coefficients of 0 or 1.
    d. includes the transportation type of problem.

12. If X_A is a binary variable that is equal to 1 if Product A is produced, and X_B is a binary variable that is equal to 1 if Product B is produced, then the constraint that either Product A or Product B can be produced, but they cannot both be produced, is given by
    a. $X_A + X_B = 1$
    b. $X_A + X_B \leq 1$
    c. $X_A - X_B = 1$
    d. $X_A - X_B \geq 0$

13. If a programming problem has integer values for all of the decision variables but a noninteger value for the objective function, then it is not an example of a pure IP problem.
    a. True
    b. False

DISCUSSION QUESTIONS AND PROBLEMS

Discussion Questions

6-1 Compare the similarities and differences of linear, integer, and binary programming.

6-2 Provide your own examples of five applications of IP.

6-3 What is the difference between the three types of IP problems? Which do you think is most common, and why?

6-4 Explain in your own words the rationale behind the Big-M method.

6-5 Provide two examples of mixed IP models.

6-6 Specify the three stopping rules in the B&B method.

6-7 Explain in your own words how the lower and upper bounds are established in a B&B diagram.

6-8 A manufacturer produces four different electronic components. To produce any one of the components requires the manufacturer to prepare an assembly station at a one-time cost of $2000. In addition, each component has a variable cost per unit of production; the variable costs are $12, $14, $17, and $21 for the four components, respectively. Define decision variables and formulate an objective function to minimize the manufacturer's cost of production.

6-9 Explain in your own words why IP problems are more difficult to solve than LP problems.

Problems

6-10 Student Enterprises sells two sizes of wall posters: a large 1 m by 1.2 m poster and a smaller 0.5 m by 1 m poster. The profit earned from the sale of each large poster is $3; each smaller poster earns $2. Because the firm is operated by an entrepreneurial student at the University of Alberta with limited time available, the following weekly constraints apply: (1) up to three large posters can be sold, (2) up to five smaller posters can be sold, (3) up to 10 hours can be spent on posters during the week, with each large poster requiring two hours of work and each small one taking one hour. With the semester almost over, the student does not want to leave any unfinished posters behind. Find, using Excel, the integer solution that will maximize her profit.

6-11 An airline owns an aging fleet of Boeing 727 jet airplanes. It is considering a major purchase of up to 17 new Boeing model 787 and 797 jets. The decision must take into account numerous cost and capability factors including the following: the airline can finance up to $400 million in purchases; (2) each Boeing 787 will cost $35 million, and each Boeing 797 will cost $22 million; (3) at least one-third of the planes purchased should be of the longer-range 787; (4) the annual maintenance budget is to be no more than $8 million; (5) the annual maintenance cost is estimated at $800 000 for each 787 and $500 000 for each 797; and (6) each 787 can carry 125 000 passengers per year, and each 797 can carry 81 000 passengers per year. Formulate this as an IP problem to maximize the annual passenger-carrying capability. What category of IP problem is this? Solve using Excel.

6-12 Quebec Homes Inc. specializes in building moderately priced homes in various Montreal neighbourhoods. The company's president, Pierre O'Sullivan, has identified eight potential locations to construct new single-family dwellings, but he cannot put up homes on all the sites because he has only $300 000 to invest in all projects. The accompanying table shows the cost of constructing homes in each area and the expected profit to be made from the sale of each home. Note that the home-building costs differ considerably due to lot costs, site preparation, and differences in the models to be built. Note also that a fraction of a home cannot be built.

LOCATION	COST OF BUILDING AT THIS SITE ($)	EXPECTED PROFIT ($)
Beaconsfield	60 000	5 000
Brossard	50 000	6 000
Pierrefonds	82 000	10 000
Westmount	103 000	12 000
Anjou	50 000	8 000
Chomedey	41 000	3 000
St. Laurent	80 000	9 000
Côte St. Luc	69 000	10 000

(a) Formulate Quebec Homes' problem using 0–1 IP.
(b) Solve with Excel.

6-13 Stockbroker Mary Bloom has made the following recommendations to a client:

TYPE OF INVESTMENT	COST ($)	EXPECTED RETURN ($)
B.C. Bonds	500	50
Quebec City Bonds	1000	100
Saskatchewan Electricity	350	30
New Brunswick Gas	490	45
PEI Electric	700	65
Canada Paint Co.	270	20
Northern Hotels Co.	800	90
Nunavut Art Co.	400	35

The client agrees to this list but provides several conditions: (1) no more than $3000 can be invested, (2) the money is to be spread among at least five investments, (3) no more than one type of bond can be purchased, and (4) at least two utility stocks and at least two regular stocks must be purchased. Formulate this as a 0–1 IP problem for Ms. Bloom to maximize expected return. Solve using Excel.

6-14 The following IP problem has been developed to help an Ontario Savings and Loan company decide where, out of 10 possible sites, to locate four new branch offices:

Maximize expected returns = $120X_1 + 100X_2 + 110X_3 + 140X_4 + 155X_5 + 128X_6 + 145X_7 + 190X_8 + 170X_9 + 150X_{10}$

subject to

$20X_1 + 30X_2 + 20X_3 + 25X_4 + 30X_5 + 30X_6 + 25X_7 + 20X_8 + 25X_9 + 30X_{10} \le 110$

$15X_1 + 5X_2 + 20X_3 + 20X_4 + 5X_5 + 5X_6 + 10X_7 + 20X_8 + 5X_9 + 20X_{10} \le 50$

$X_2 + X_6 + X_7 + X_9 + X_{10} \le 3$

$X_2 + X_3 + X_5 + X_8 + X_9 \ge 2$

$X_1 + X_3 + X_{10} \ge 1$

$X_1 + X_2 + X_3 + X_4 + X_5 + X_6 + X_7 + X_8 + X_9 + X_{10} \ge 4$

All $X_1 = 0$ or 1

where X_i represents Hamilton, Oshawa, Windsor, Toronto, Mississauga, Ottawa, Peterborough, Kingston, Thunder Bay, London for i equals 1 to 10, respectively.

(a) Where should the four new sites be located, and what will be the expected return?
(b) If at least one new branch *must* be opened in Oshawa or Windsor, will this change the answers? Add the new constraint and rerun.
(c) The expected return at Kingston was overestimated. The correct value is $160 000 per year (i.e., 160). Using the original assumptions (i.e., ignoring (b)), does your answer to part (a) change?

6-15 A manufacturer produces four items and uses three resources with limited availabilities in the manufacturing process. The following technology table shows the profit per unit of each of the four items as well as the rate at which each product depletes the available resources.

	PRODUCT 1	PRODUCT 2	PRODUCT 3	PRODUCT 4	
Profit/unit	12	15	17	20	
Constraints					Availability
Resource 1	7	5	6	3	90
Resource 2	5	4	5	8	100
Resource 3	4	7	3	12	110

(a) Use the Excel Solver to find the optimal solution of the LP problem.
(b) Use the Excel Solver to find the optimal solution of the general IP problem.
(c) Comment on the difference between the relaxed LP solution and the optimal integer solution. Would it be possible to find the optimal IP solution by rounding?
(d) Use the Premium Solver for Education and select the option *Show Iteration Results*. How many LP problems and subproblems does the Solver have to run in order to arrive at the optimal integer-valued solution?

6-16 An aircraft purchasing agent for a provincial airline is considering purchasing three possible types of aircraft. Model A20 is a 20-seat plane used for very short local trips, the B35 is a 35-seater and is used for slightly longer trips serving mid-sized communities. Finally, the C70 seats 70 passengers and is primarily used on the route serving the two largest towns within the provincial area served by the airline. The total budget for buying aircraft is $150 million. Each model A20 costs $3.3 million, each B35 costs $5 million, and each C70 aircraft costs $6.9 million. The airline has 30 flight crews available to staff the aircraft. The other constraint the airline is concerned about is maintenance. It takes four hours to service a model A20 or a model B35 aircraft, while the larger model C70 takes seven hours to service. Under the airline's current maintenance operation there are 60 hours available. Estimated profit after recovery of capital expenditures is estimated to be $400 000 for each A20, $515 000 for each B35, and $750 000 for each C70.

(a) Formulate an LP model

(b) Solve the model using the Excel solver.

(c) Compare the solutions with and without integer constraints.

6-17 A manufacturer, deciding on a production schedule, is limited by the available units of three different raw materials. The availabilities and product profitabilities are given in the table below:

	PRODUCT 1	PRODUCT 2	PRODUCT 3	PRODUCT 4	AVAIL- ABILITY
Material 1	7	3	4	5	2000
Material 2	6	12	11	9	3000
Material 3	8	9	7	4	1500
Profit/Unit	$30	$60	$20	$40	

The fixed start-up costs associated with producing each of the four products are $1000, $1500, $2000, and $1250, respectively.

Formulate a mixed integer model and solve using Excel Solver.

6-18 Marketing Concepts is a telemarketing company that needs the following numbers of employees on the phones during the upcoming week: Monday 23, Tuesday 16, Wednesday 21, Thursday 17, Friday 20, Saturday 12, and Sunday 15. Each employee is entitled to 2 consecutive days off per week. How many telemarketers need to be scheduled each day of the week to begin their five-day work week? The objective is to minimize the total number of employees needed to fulfill the daily requirements.

(a) Solve as an IP model.

(b) Additional information is now available for Marketing Concepts. Daily pay from Monday through Friday is $90, pay for Saturday is $110, and Sunday workers earn $125. In addition, up to four people can be hired who will work Friday, Saturday, and Sunday. Their pay for this three-day week is $250. The new objective is to minimize total weekly labour costs. Revise the IP model and solve it.

6-19 The Beacon Company is a large manufacturer of automotive supplies. The company has decided to spend $35 million next year to expand its manufacturing and warehouse facilities. Each warehouse will cost $3.5 million and will contribute $17 000 per month toward profitability. Each plant will cost $5.5 million and will contribute $36 000 per month toward profitability. Management does not want to build more than seven warehouses or four plants next year. How many plants and warehouses should be constructed to maximize profitability?

6-20 Formulate and solve an IP model that will decide how to make change for $22.98, based on the availability of coins and bills shown in the following table.

The objective should be to minimize the total number of bills and coins used to make the change.

DENOMINATION	AVAILABILITY
$10 bill	1
$5 bill	4
$1 bill	1
Quarter ($0.25)	8
Dime ($0.10)	1
Nickel ($0.05)	5
Penny ($0.01)	6

6-21 Peters Financial needs to develop an investment portfolio for Mrs. Charles from the following list of possible investments:

INVESTMENT	COST ($)	EXPECTED RETURN ($)
A	5 000	500
B	8 000	640
C	3 500	390
D	10 000	700
E	8 500	750
F	12 000	1 000
G	4 000	300

Mrs. Charles has a total of $30 000 to invest. The following conditions must be met: (1) If investment F is chosen, then investment G must also be part of the portfolio, (2) at least four investments should be chosen, and (3) of investments A and B, exactly one must be included. What stocks should be included in Mrs. Charles's portfolio?

6-22 A truck with the capacity to load 2 000 cubic feet of cargo is available to transport items selected from the following table:

ITEM	VALUE ($)	VOLUME (CUBIC FEET)
A	1 900	700
B	1 500	600
C	1 200	450
D	800	400
E	1 700	650
F	1 000	350
G	1 400	600

If selected, an item must be shipped in its entirety (i.e., partial shipments are not allowed). Of items B, C, and D, at least two items must be selected. If item B is selected, then item G cannot be selected. Which items should be selected to maximize the value of the shipment?

6-23 Allied Products has six R&D projects that are potential candidates for selection during the upcoming fiscal year. The table at the top of page 261 provides the expected net present value (NPV) and capital requirements over the next five years for each project.

The table also indicates the planned budget expenditures for the entire R&D program during each of the next five years. Which projects should be selected?

6-24 TransCan Airlines needs to decide which cities that it currently operates from will be designated as a hub. The candidate cities are shown in the table below, along with the distances, in kilometres, between them.

Each hub will serve other cities within a 2000 kilometre radius. TransCan would like to identify the minimum number of hubs required to cover all eight cities and also identify the cities that are covered by each hub.

Table for Problem 6-23

PROJECT	NPV (IN THOUSANDS)	CAPITAL REQUIRED (IN THOUSANDS)				
		YEAR 1	YEAR 2	YEAR 3	YEAR 4	YEAR 5
1	$182	$80	$25	$22	$18	$10
2	167	95	40	5	10	35
3	114	58	17	14	12	12
4	98	32	24	10	6	7
5	250	115	25	25	10	0
6	130	48	20	12	32	40
R&D Budget		$225	$80	$60	$50	$50

Table for Problem 6-24

	HALIFAX	QUEBEC	TORONTO	WINNIPEG	SASKATOON	EDMONTON	VANCOUVER	VICTORIA
Halifax	—	1000	1800	3560	4500	5000	6050	6150
Quebec		—	800	2675	3500	4050	5075	5275
Toronto			—	2100	2925	3450	4500	4600
Winnipeg				—	825	1350	2225	2325
Saskatoon					—	525	1675	1800
Edmonton						—	1250	1350
Vancouver							—	100

6-25 The borough of North York has six communities that need to be served by fire stations. The number of minutes it takes to travel between the communities is shown in the following table:

	A	B	C	D	E	F
A	—	10	6	9	10	4
B		—	3	3	4	6
C			—	5	5	3
D				—	6	5
E					—	8

The borough would like to establish the minimum number of fire stations so that each community can be responded to in five minutes or less. How many stations will be needed, and what communities will each station serve?

6-26 Manitoba Distributors Inc. needs to decide on the location of two new warehouses. The candidate sites are Kelowna, Calgary, Mississauga, and Fredericton. The following table provides the monthly capacities and the monthly fixed costs for operating warehouses at each potential site:

WAREHOUSE	MONTHLY CAPACITY (UNITS)	MONTHLY FIXED COST ($)
Kelowna	250	1000
Calgary	260	800
Mississauga	280	1200
Fredericton	270	700

The warehouses will need to ship to three marketing areas: A, B, and C. Monthly requirements are 400 units for Area A,

300 units for Area B, and 360 units for Area C. The following table shows the cost to ship one unit between each location and destination:

WAREHOUSE	AREA A	AREA B	AREA C
Kelowna	$4	$7	$9
Calgary	6	3	11
Mississauga	5	6	5
Fredericton	8	10	2

In addition, the following conditions must be met by the final decision: (1) A warehouse must be opened in either Kelowna or Fredericton, possibly both, and (2) if a warehouse is opened in Calgary, then one must also be opened in Mississauga. Which two sites should be selected for the new warehouses to minimize the total fixed and shipping costs?

6-27 Furniture Unlimited has the capability to manufacture desks, cabinets, and chairs. In order to manufacture these products, it must rent the appropriate equipment at a weekly cost of $2000 for the desks, $2500 for the cabinets, and $1500 for the chairs. The labour and material requirements for each product are shown in the following table, along with the selling price and variable cost to manufacture:

	LABOUR HOURS	LUMBER (SQ. FT.)	SALES PRICE($)	VARIABLE COSTS($)
Desks	3	10	110	82
Cabinets	4	12	135	97
Chairs	2	5	50	32

There are 2500 labour hours and 4000 square feet of lumber available each week. Determine the product mix that maximizes weekly profit.

6-28 PH Publishing needs to decide what textbooks to publish from the following table:

	DEMAND	FIXED COST	VARIABLE COST	SELLING PRICE
Book 1	5000	$15 000	$30	$52
Book 2	7000	18 000	20	45
Book 3	9000	12 000	19	40
Book 4	6000	10 000	20	34
Book 5	8000	21 000	28	60

For each book, the maximum demand, fixed cost of publishing, variable cost, and selling price are provided. PH only has the capacity to publish a total of 20 000 books. Which books should be selected, and how many of each should be published?

6-29 Consider the following IP problem:

$$\text{Maximize profit} = 8X_1 + 10X_2$$

subject to

$$4X_1 + 3X_2 \leq 24$$

$$X_1 + 2X_2 \leq 10$$

where

$$X_1, X_2 \geq 0 \text{ and integer}$$

(a) Find the optimal integer-valued solution using the branch-and-bound method.

(b) Verify the solution found in part (a) using the Excel Solver.

6-30 Consider the following IP problem:

$$\text{Minimize cost} = 40X_1 + 50X_2$$

subject to

$$3X_1 + 6X_2 \geq 18$$

$$10X_1 + 8X_2 \geq 20$$

$$8X_1 + 2X_2 \geq 16$$

$$7X_1 + 6X_2 \leq 42$$

where

$$X_1, X_2 \geq 0 \text{ and integer}$$

(a) Find the optimal integer-valued solution using the B&B method.

(b) Verify the solution found in part (a) using the Excel Solver.

⇉ CASE STUDY 6.1

St. Lawrence River Bridge

An expanding suburban area on the South Shore of the St. Lawrence River serves as a garden suburb for Montreal. The river makes it difficult for people living in the South Shore community to commute to jobs in and around the city and to take advantage of the shopping and cultural attractions that the city has to offer. Similarly, the river is an impediment to Montreal inhabitants who must cross the St. Lawrence to gain access to the Eastern Townships of Quebec and the major highways leading to New York State and Vermont. An existing bridge over the St. Lawrence

River that serves the area was built prior to World War II and was grossly inadequate to handle the existing traffic, much less the increased traffic that would accompany the forecasted growth in the area. The Canadian government has agreed to fund a major portion of the cost of a new bridge over the St. Lawrence River, and the Province of Quebec will supply the rest of the needed monies for the project.

Progress in construction of the bridge has been in accordance with what was anticipated at the start of construction. Transport Québec, which will have operational jurisdiction over the bridge, has concluded that the bridge is likely to be open at the beginning of next summer, as scheduled. Provincial authorities have decided that they will need to charge tolls for motorists using the bridge as a means of paying for the high cost of construction. A personnel task force has been established to recruit, train, and schedule the workers needed to operate the toll facility.

The personnel task force is well aware of the budgetary problems facing the province. Its members have taken as part of their mandate the requirement that personnel costs be kept as low as possible. One particular area of concern is the number of tollbooth operators that will be needed. The bridge is scheduling three shifts of operators: shift A from midnight to 8 A.M., shift B from 8 A.M. to 4 P.M., and shift C from 4 P.M. to midnight. Recently, the provincial employees' union negotiated a contract with the province that requires that all tollbooth operators be permanent, full-time employees. In addition, all operators must work a five-on, two-off schedule on the same shift. Thus, for example, a worker could be assigned to work Tuesday, Wednesday, Thursday, Friday, and Saturday on shift A, followed by Sunday and Monday off. An employee could not be scheduled to work, say, Tuesday on shift A followed by Wednesday, Thursday, Friday, and Saturday on shift B or on any other mixture of shifts during a five-day block. The employees will choose their assignments in order of seniority.

The task force has received projections of traffic flow on the bridge by day and hour. These projections are based on extrapolations of existing traffic patterns—the pattern of commuting, shopping, and highway traffic currently experienced, with growth projections factored in. Standards data from other toll facilities have allowed the task force to convert these traffic flows into tollbooth operator requirements, that is, the minimum number of operators required per shift, per day, to handle the anticipated traffic load. These tollbooth operator requirements are summarized in the following table:

Minimum Number of Tollbooth Operators Required per Shift

SHIFT	SUN.	MON.	TUE.	WED.	THU.	FRI.	SAT.
A	8	13	12	12	13	13	15
B	10	10	10	10	10	13	15
C	15	13	13	12	12	13	8

The numbers in the table include one or two extra operators per shift to fill in for operators who call in sick and to provide relief for operators on their scheduled breaks. Note that each of the eight operators needed for shift A on Sunday, for example, could have come from any of the A shifts scheduled to begin on Wednesday, Thursday, Friday, Saturday, or Sunday.

DISCUSSION QUESTIONS

1. Determine the minimum number of tollbooth operators that must be hired to meet the requirements expressed in the table.
2. The union had indicated that it might lift its opposition to the mixing of shifts in a five-day block in exchange for additional compensation and benefits. By how much could the numbers of toll operators required be reduced if this is done?

Source: Adapted from B. Render, R. M. Stair, and I. Greenberg. *Cases and Readings in Management Science*, 2/e. 1990, pp. 55–56. Reprinted by permission of Prentice Hall, Upper Saddle River, New Jersey.

⭢ CASE STUDY 6.2

Jackpine Mall

Jane Rodney, president of the Rodney Development Company, was trying to decide what types of stores to include in her new shopping centre at Jackpine Mall. She had already contracted for a supermarket, a drugstore, and a few other stores that she considered essential. However, she had available an additional 4800 square metres of floor space yet to allocate. She drew up a list of the 15 types of stores she might consider (see Table 6.6), including the floor space required by each. Rodney did not think she would have any trouble finding occupants for any type of store.

The lease agreements Rodney used in her developments included two types of payment. The store had to pay a certain annual rent, depending on the size and type of store. In addition, Rodney would receive a small percentage of the store's sales if the sales exceeded a specified minimum amount. The amount of annual rent from each store is shown in the third column of the table. To estimate the profitability of each type of store, Rodney

calculated the present value of all future rent and sales percentage payments. These are given in the fourth column. Rodney wants to achieve the highest total *present value* over the set of stores she selects. However, she could not simply pick those stores with the highest present values, for there were several restrictions. The first, of course, was that she has available only 4800 square metres.

In addition, a condition on the financing of the project required that the total annual rent should be at least as much as the annual fixed costs (taxes, management fees, debt service, and so forth). These annual costs were $130 000 for this part of the project. Finally, the total funds available for construction of this part of the project were $700 000, and each type of store required different construction costs depending on the size and type of store (fifth column in the table).

In addition, Rodney had certain requirements in terms of the mix of stores that she considered best. She wanted at least one store from each of the clothing, hard goods, and miscellaneous groups, and at least two from the restaurant category. She wanted no more than two from the clothing group. Furthermore, she felt the number of stores in the miscellaneous group should not exceed the total number of stores in the clothing and hard goods groups combined.

DISCUSSION QUESTION

Which tenants should be selected for the mall?

Source: Adapted from H. Bierman, C. P. Bonini, and W. H. Hausman. *Quantitative Analysis*, 7/e. (Homewood, IL: Richard D. Irwin, Inc. 1986), pp. 467–468.

TABLE 6.6

Characteristics of Possible Leases, Jackpine Mall Shopping Centre

TYPE OF STORE	SIZE OF STORE (1000s OF SQ METRES)	ANNUAL RENT ($1000s)	PRESENT VALUE ($1000s)	CONSTRUCTION COST ($1000s)
Clothing				
1. Men's	0.3	$4.4	$28.1	$24.6
2. Women's	0.5	6.1	34.6	32.0
3. Variety (both)	.65	8.3	50.0	41.4
Restaurants				
4. Fancy restaurant	1.1	24.0	162.0	124.4
5. Lunchroom	0.6	19.5	77.8	64.8
6. Cocktail lounge	0.7	20.7	100.4	79.8
7. Candy and ice cream shop	0.4	7.7	45.2	38.6
Hard goods				
8. Hardware store	0.8	19.4	80.2	66.8
9. Cutlery and variety	0.5	11.7	51.4	45.1
10. Luggage and leather	0.7	15.2	62.5	54.3
Miscellaneous				
11. Travel agency	0.2	3.9	18.0	15.0
12. Tobacco shop	0.2	3.2	11.6	13.4
13. Camera store	0.3	11.3	50.4	42.0
14. Toys	0.7	16.0	73.6	63.7
15. Beauty parlour	0.3	9.6	51.2	40.0

BIBLIOGRAPHY

Arntzen, Bruce C. et al. "Global Supply Chain Management at Digital Equipment Corporation," *Interfaces* 25, 1 (January–February 1995): 69–93.

Bertsimas, Dimitris, C. Darnell, and R. Soucy. "Portfolio Construction Through Mixed-Integer Programming at Grantham, Mayo, Van Otterloo and Company," *Interfaces* 29, 1 (January 1999): 49–66.

Bohl, Alan H. "Computer Aided Formulation of Silicon Defoamers for the Paper Industry," *Interfaces* 24, 5 (September–October 1994): 41–48.

Charnes, A., and W. W. Cooper. *Management Models and Industrial Applications of Linear Programming.* New York: Wiley, 1961.

Kuby, Michael et al. "Planning China's Coal and Electricity Delivery System," *Interfaces* 25, 1 (January–February 1995): 41–68.

Render, B., R. M. Stair, and M. Hanna. *Quantitative Analysis for Management*, 8/e. Upper Saddle River, NJ: Prentice Hall, 2003.

Stowe, J. D. "An Integer Programming Solution for the Optimal Credit Investigation/Credit Granting Sequence," *Financial Management* 14 (Summer 1985): 66–76.

Wang, Hongbo. "A Branch and Bound Approach for Sequencing Expansion Projects," *Production and Operations Management* 4, 1 (Winter 1995): 57–75.

CHAPTER 7

Multicriteria and Nonlinear Programming Models

LEARNING OBJECTIVES

After completing this chapter, students will be able to

1. Formulate and solve problems involving multiple criteria using the analytic hierarchy process.
2. Formulate goal programming problems and solve them using Excel's Solver.
3. Formulate nonlinear programming problems and solve them using Excel's Solver.

CHAPTER OUTLINE

7.1 Introduction

7.2 The Analytic Hierarchy Process

7.3 Goal Programming Models

7.4 Nonlinear Programming Models

Summary • Glossary • Solved Problems • Self-Test • Discussion Questions and Problems • Case Study: Schank Marketing Research • Case Study: The Whom Should We Hire Case • Bibliography

Goal Programming at Toronto's Mount Sinai Hospital

Allocation of resources in hospitals is an important factor in controlling costs under Canada's medicare system. In Ontario, 32.5% of public funds are spent in the health care sector. When the surgical division in Toronto's Mount Sinai Hospital was presented with a planned 18% reduction in hospital funding over a three-year period, the unit turned to a goal programming model as a means of implementing this objective.

The traditional LP objective of maximizing income may not be suitable in the not-for-profit public hospital environment, and instead the goal of achieving a predetermined level of income may be more appropriate. Since Ontario hospitals may choose their own mix and volume of medical cases, a goal programming model will attempt to select a case mix that will meet multiple goals that may include (1) producing revenue sufficient to recover fixed and variable costs, (2) ensuring that physicians attain a satisfactory level of income, (3) allocating case time in operating rooms, and (4) allocating enough beds to accommodate patient needs.

When applied to the surgical division of Mount Sinai Hospital, model results show that the economic goals of both the hospital administration and the medical staff could be achieved by modifying the case

Source: CP Photo/Kevin Frayer

mix or physician practice, while achieving budget reductions in the 5% to 11% range. Allocation of operating room time was shown to be one of the major determinants in developing a solution satisfactory to both management and physicians.

J. T. Blake and M. W. Carter. "A goal programming approach to strategic resource allocation in acute care hospitals," *European Journal of Operations Research* 140 (2002): 541–561.

7.1   INTRODUCTION

This chapter presents a selection of important mathematical models that allow us to extend our ability to solve a wider variety of problems by specifying multiple goals (analytic hierarchy process, goal programming) and relaxing the linearity assumption to solve problems that have nonlinear object functions and constraints (nonlinear programming).

Analytic Hierarchy Process Models

The **analytic hierarchy process (AHP)**, developed by Thomas Saaty at the Wharton School of Business, is a method for solving problems involving multiple criteria. The underlying principle is to rank decision alternatives and choose the one that best satisfies the decision maker's multiple objectives. Each of the criteria is ranked according to the decision maker's preferences.

The process first lays out a hierarchy of the decision model with three different levels. The highest level specifies the overall goal; the middle level lists criteria (or factors); and the lowest level shows the decision alternatives.

The decision maker must establish priorities for the criteria in terms of the overall goal and also determine the priorities for each of the decision alternatives in terms of each of the criteria.

Output ranks the overall preference for each decision and produces a mathematically derived score for each alternative, with the highest score indicating the best decision. AHP will be discussed in detail in Section 7.2.

Goal Programming Models

Organizations usually have more than one objective. Goal programming permits more than one objective.

A major limitation of LP is that it forces the decision maker to state one objective only. But what if a business has several objectives? Management may indeed want to maximize profit, but it might also want to maximize market share, maintain full employment, and minimize costs. Many of these goals can be conflicting and difficult to quantify. For example, a province may want to build a nuclear power plant. Its objectives may be to maximize power generated, reliability, and safety, and to minimize the cost of operating the system and the environmental effects on the community. *Goal programming* is an extension to LP that can permit multiple objectives such as these. We discuss goal programming in detail in Section 7.3.

Nonlinear Programming Models

Linear programming can, of course, be applied only to cases in which the objective function and all constraints are linear expressions. Yet in many situations this may not be the case. For example, consider a price curve that relates the unit price of a product to the number of units made. As more units are made, the price per unit may decrease in a nonlinear fashion. Hence, if X and Y denote the number of units of two products to make, the objective function could be

$$\text{Maximize profit} = 25X - 0.4X^2 + 30Y - 0.5Y^2$$

Nonlinear programming is used when objectives or constraints are nonlinear.

Because of the squared terms, this is a nonlinear objective function. In a similar manner, we could have one or more nonlinear constraints in the model. We discuss nonlinear programming models in detail in Section 7.4.

7.2 THE ANALYTIC HIERARCHY PROCESS

The analytic hierarchy process (AHP) is a technique for solving decision problems involving several different criteria. Priorities have to be established (1) for each decision alternative relative to each criterion and (2) for each criterion relative to the overall goal.

Criteria are prioritized by assigning pairwise rankings on a 9-point scale.

AHP employs **pairwise comparisons** of decision alternatives for each criterion. Experienced researchers have developed a scale that assigns values from 1 to 9 to designate the decision maker's preferences. The scale is shown in Table 7.1 on page 269.

To illustrate AHP, consider the decision problem confronting Danny Smith. Danny is trying to decide which university to attend to pursue an undergraduate business degree. He wants to attend a university away from his home in Manitoba and he has narrowed his choice down to three Canadian universities, one in Montreal, one in Toronto, and the third in Vancouver. Danny has decided the most important factors in his decision

MODELING IN THE REAL WORLD

AHP Helps Canadian Municipal Governments

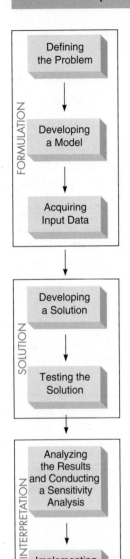

Since mid-1999, the annual capital budget of Ontario municipalities has been approximately $4 billion. Municipal governments have to prioritize capital projects necessary to expand and maintain the municipal infrastructure for an increasing population.

The analytic hierarchy process (AHP) was selected because of its ability to encompass both quantitative and qualitative aspects of the decision-making process. Five factors (criteria) considered in the model are health and safety, financial impact, asset maintenance/replacement, growth-related needs, and service enhancement.

Questionnaires were mailed to a random sample of 484 Canadian municipal governments. A total of 106 completed questionnaires were returned. Respondents included city mayors, chief financial officers, treasurers, and administrators. City mayors and directors of finance were asked to respond to a series of questions to assess their rankings of the five factors in the model.

Using pairwise comparisons of the decision alternatives (allocation of funds to capital projects) for each of the decision criteria, as well as a ranking of the criteria, the model produces a solution that encompasses the input data.

Solutions produced by the AHP model are compared with solutions obtained by other methods such as discounted cash flow analysis.

The AHP methodology can accommodate multiple decision makers and several levels of hierarchy with a large number of criteria. AHP improves on other models because pairwise comparisons guarantee greater consistency of response data and allow greater democratization of the decision process.

The resources of the municipal governments can be allocated more effectively among the many capital projects that they have to fund. It is anticipated that the AHP model will be increasingly adopted by decision makers in Canadian municipal governments.

Source: Y-C Lilian Chan. "Use of Capital Budgeting Techniques and an Analytic Approach to Capital Investment Decisions in Canadian Municipal Governments." *Public Budgeting & Finance* 24, 2 (2004): 40–58.

are cost (tuition and living expenses), quality of education (as determined by published rankings in an academic journal on a 20-point scale), location (Montreal, Toronto, Vancouver), and quality of student residences (as reported to Danny by friends who have attended the different universities). Table 7.2 shows the value of each criterion for each decision alternative (university).

TABLE 7.1

Pairwise Comparison Scale for AHP

PREFERENCE VALUE	NUMERICAL RANKING
Equally preferred	1
Equally to moderately preferred	2
Moderately preferred	3
Moderately to strongly preferred	4
Strongly preferred	5
Strongly to very strongly preferred	6
Very strongly preferred	7
Very strongly to extremely preferred	8
Extremely preferred	9

Before we discuss the ranking of the four criteria for each university, we will develop a graphical representation of the hierarchy in terms of the overall goal, the criteria, and the decision alternatives (Figure 7.1 on page 270). The highest level of the hierarchy indicates that the overall goal is to select the best university, the second level specifies the four criteria (cost, education, location, and residence), and the third (lowest) level shows the decision alternatives.

The next stage in the AHP process is for Danny to specify his preferences for each of the three universities based on each of the criteria. We illustrate by considering the cost criterion. Since Danny has a limited budget to pay for his education, he will generally prefer less expensive universities over more expensive ones. For example, if he believes that the cost of university C (the cheapest) is very strongly preferred to the cost of university A (the most expensive), he should use a value of 7. He also needs to identify his preference between university A and university B, and he decides that university B is moderately to strongly preferred to university A, corresponding to a numerical ranking of 4. Finally, Danny says that the cost of university C is moderately preferred to the cost of university B, for a ranking of 3.

The information obtained so far can be presented in a partial **pairwise comparison matrix** (PCM) for each of the three universities with regard to the cost criterion.

The pairwise comparison matrix shows the preference ratings assigned to the decision alternatives for a criterion.

	COST		
	UNIVERSITY A	UNIVERSITY B	UNIVERSITY C
	4		
	7	3	

TABLE 7.2

Value of Each Decision Criterion for Each University

	UNIVERSITY A	UNIVERSITY B	UNIVERSITY C
Cost	$28 400	$24 300	$19 600
Education	18	16	15
Location	Toronto	Montreal	Vancouver
Residence	Comfortable	Fair	Luxury

FIGURE 7.1

Hierarchy for the
University Selection
Problem

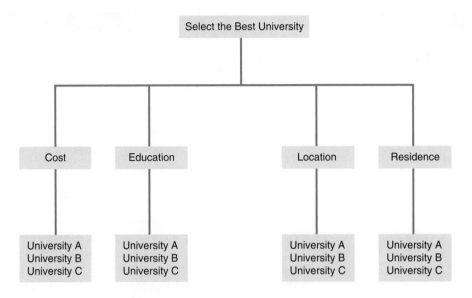

It is still necessary to determine the ratings for university A compared with university B, university A with university C, and university B with university C. Interpreting the numerical rating of 4 for university B over university A as meaning that B is four times as preferable as university A, it follows that university A must be $\frac{1}{4}$ as preferable as university B. In other words, the preference of university A when compared with university B is simply the reciprocal of the preference of university B compared with university A. Applying this reasoning to the other missing values in the pairwise comparison table, and identifying that when we compare a decision criterion with itself the preference rating must be 1, we obtain the complete matrix.

	COST		
	UNIVERSITY A	UNIVERSITY B	UNIVERSITY C
University A	1	$\frac{1}{4}$	$\frac{1}{7}$
University B	4	1	$\frac{1}{3}$
University C	7	3	1

Synthesis Is the Process of Prioritizing Decision Alternatives

The next step in the AHP process is called synthesis. This determines the priority of each of the decision alternatives for each criterion. We will illustrate how to establish the relative priorities for each of the three universities in terms of the cost criterion. The underlying vector algebra is beyond the scope of this text, but a good approximation to the results of synthesization can be obtained by the following three-step procedure.

1. Compute the column totals for the pairwise comparison matrix.
2. Divide each value in the matrix by its column total. The resulting array is called the *normalized pairwise comparison matrix.*
3. Compute the average values of each row in the normalized matrix.

The three-step procedure is applied to the three decision alternatives (choices of university) for the cost criterion.

1. Compute column totals (Table 7.3). Note that the entries in the pairwise comparison matrix have been converted to decimal form.

2. Normalize the pairwise comparison matrix (Table 7.4). Observe that in this normalized pairwise comparison matrix, each column now has a sum of 1.

3. Average the values in each row (Table 7.5). Observe that the three row averages sum to 1 (subject to rounding error).

The three row averages show Danny Smith's priorities for the three universities with respect to the cost criterion. We can summarize the result of the synthesis for the cost criterion in a **priority vector**:

$$\begin{bmatrix} A & 0.080 \\ B & 0.265 \\ C & 0.656 \end{bmatrix}$$

The priority vector indicates that, based on cost, Danny's preference for university A is 0.080, for university B is 0.265, and for university C is 0.656. Therefore for this criterion,

TABLE 7.3

Computed Totals for the Completed Pairwise Comparison Matrix for Cost

	COST		
	UNIVERSITY A	UNIVERSITY B	UNIVERSITY C
University A	1	0.250	0.143
University B	4	1	0.333
University C	7	3	1
Column Totals	12	4.250	1.476

TABLE 7.4

Normalized Pairwise Comparison Matrix for Cost

	COST		
	UNIVERSITY A	UNIVERSITY B	UNIVERSITY C
University A	0.083	0.059	0.097
University B	0.333	0.235	0.226
University C	0.583	0.706	0.677
Column Totals	1	1	1

TABLE 7.5

Averaged Values for a Pairwise Comparison Matrix for Cost

	COST			
	UNIVERSITY A	UNIVERSITY B	UNIVERSITY C	ROW AVERAGE
University A	0.083	0.059	0.097	**0.080**
University B	0.333	0.235	0.226	**0.265**
University C	0.583	0.706	0.677	**0.656**
				1.001

Danny's most preferred university is university C (with a priority of 0.656). The second choice is university B (priority 0.265), and university A is the third choice (priority 0.080).

Danny now turns his attention to creating the pairwise comparison matrix for each of the other three criteria and decides on the preferences shown in Table 7.6.

Applying the synthesis algorithm to each of these pairwise comparison matrices, and including the results already obtained for cost, we obtain the following priority vectors:

$$
\begin{array}{cccc}
\text{Cost} & \text{Education} & \text{Location} & \text{Residence} \\
\begin{bmatrix} 0.080 \\ 0.265 \\ 0.656 \end{bmatrix} &
\begin{bmatrix} 0.727 \\ 0.182 \\ 0.091 \end{bmatrix} &
\begin{bmatrix} 0.103 \\ 0.216 \\ 0.681 \end{bmatrix} &
\begin{bmatrix} 0.272 \\ 0.608 \\ 0.120 \end{bmatrix}
\end{array}
$$

Summarizing the results obtained so far, we see that with regard to cost, Danny prefers university C, followed by university B and, in last place, university A. For quality of education, Danny's first choice is university A, his second choice is university B, and his third choice is university C. Based on location, Danny prefers university C, then university B, and, in last place, university A. Finally, based on quality of residence, he prefers university B, then university A, and in last place university C.

Poor Danny is getting confused, since each criterion seems to provide a different ranking of the three universities. Obviously, he needs a way to take all four decision criteria into consideration.

Before proceeding to calculate the overall prioritized rankings, Danny needs to ensure that he has been consistent in assigning preference scores in the pairwise comparison matrices for each criterion. When making many comparisons, it is not easy to be completely consistent. For example, if on a particular criterion Danny claims that his preference for university A over university B is *equal to moderate* (rating 2) and his preference for university B over university C is *moderate to strong* (rating 4), then to be consistent his

TABLE 7.6	EDUCATION		
Pairwise Comparison Matrices for Education, Location, and Residence	A	B	C
A	1.000	4.000	8.000
B	0.250	1.000	2.000
C	0.125	0.500	1.000

	LOCATION		
	A	B	C
A	1.000	0.500	0.143
B	2.000	1.000	0.333
C	7.000	3.000	1.000

	RESIDENCE		
	A	B	C
A	1.000	0.333	3.000
B	3.000	1.000	4.000
C	0.333	0.250	1.000

preference for university A over university C should be *very strong to extreme* (rating 8). To summarize, he is saying that his preference for university A is twice his preference for university B and his preference for university B is four times his preference for university C, so that his preference for university A should be $2 \times 4 = 8$ times his preference for university C. However, it is not at all unlikely in this situation that Danny would assign a value other than 8 to his rating of university A over university C. A certain amount of inconsistency is to be expected and is acceptable. The AHP model requires the decision maker to compute a consistency ratio (CR) that can determine whether the degree of inconsistency in a particular pairwise comparison matrix is acceptable. A CR value of 0.10 or less in a matrix indicates reasonable consistency.

Consistency ensures that pairwise comparison matrices do not contain contradictions.

The following five-step procedure will be used to compute the consistency ratio for the university selection problem with respect to the cost criterion.

Step 1. Compute a *weighted sum vector*. This is accomplished by multiplying each value in the priority matrix by the entries in the corresponding column of the pairwise comparison matrix and then adding the resulting values. For the university selection example the priority matrix and the pairwise comparison matrix based on the cost criterion are as follows:

$$\begin{bmatrix} 0.080 \\ 0.265 \\ 0.656 \end{bmatrix} \text{ and } \begin{bmatrix} 1 & \frac{1}{4} & \frac{1}{7} \\ 4 & 1 & \frac{1}{3} \\ 7 & 3 & 1 \end{bmatrix}$$

The calculation of the weighted sum vector is shown below:

$$0.080 \begin{bmatrix} 1 \\ 4 \\ 7 \end{bmatrix} + 0.265 \begin{bmatrix} \frac{1}{4} \\ 1 \\ 3 \end{bmatrix} + 0.656 \begin{bmatrix} \frac{1}{7} \\ \frac{1}{3} \\ 1 \end{bmatrix} = \begin{bmatrix} 0.080 \\ 0.320 \\ 0.560 \end{bmatrix} + \begin{bmatrix} 0.066 \\ 0.265 \\ 0.795 \end{bmatrix} + \begin{bmatrix} 0.094 \\ 0.219 \\ 0.656 \end{bmatrix} = \begin{matrix} \text{Weighted} \\ \text{Sum} \\ \text{Vector} \\ \begin{bmatrix} 0.240 \\ 0.804 \\ 2.011 \end{bmatrix} \end{matrix}$$

Step 2. Divide the values in the weighted sum vector by the corresponding priority values:

$$\frac{0.240}{0.080} = 3.000$$

$$\frac{0.804}{0.265} = 3.034$$

$$\frac{2.011}{0.656} = 3.066$$

Step 3. Calculate λ, the average of the values obtained in step 2:

$$\lambda = \frac{3.000 + 3.034 + 3.066}{3} = 3.033$$

Step 4. The consistency index (CI) is defined as $\frac{\lambda - n}{n - 1}$, where n is the number of decision alternatives being compared. In the university selection example, $\lambda = 3.033$ and $n = 3$ so that

$$\text{CI} = \frac{3.033 - 3}{3 - 1} = 0.0165$$

TABLE 7.7		
	n	RI
	3	0.58
	4	0.90
	5	1.12
	6	1.24
	7	1.32
	8	1.41

Values of the Random Index RI

Step 5. The fifth and final step consists of computing the consistency ratio defined as $CR = \dfrac{CI}{RI}$, where the random index (RI) is obtained from Table 7.7 above and represents the consistency index of a randomly generated pairwise comparison matrix. The RI value is a function of the number of decision alternatives n. The CR for the cost criterion in the university selection example is

$$CR = \frac{0.0165}{0.58} = 0.028$$

Since the CR value is less than the threshold limit of 0.10, we conclude that Danny's ratings of the three universities for the cost criterion are consistent.

Applying the five-step procedure to the other criteria, we find the following CRs:

CRITERION	CR
Cost	0.028
Education	0.000
Location	0.002
Residence	0.064

Since all four CRs are less than 0.10, we conclude that Danny's rankings of the criteria are consistent. In particular, note that the CR value for education is 0. This is expected because when we examine the pairwise comparison matrix for education we observe that Danny's preference for A is four times his preference for B, and his preference for B is two times his preference for C. Therefore, it follows that his preference for A should be $4 \times 2 = 8$ times his preference for C. Since that is the value entered in the pairwise comparison matrix, we see that Danny is completely consistent in his statements of preferences based on the education criterion, hence the CR is 0.

In order to develop an overall weighted ranking taking all four decision criteria into consideration, Danny must also specify how important he believes each criterion is in relation to each of the other criteria. This is accomplished by generating a pairwise comparison matrix for the four criteria. Danny's pairwise rankings of the criteria are shown in Table 7.8.

Applying the three-step synthesis procedure to compute the priorities for the four criteria yields the following results:

PRIORITIES	
Cost	0.336
Education	0.396
Location	0.122
Residence	0.145

TABLE 7.8

Pairwise Comparison Matrix for the Four Criteria

CRITERION	COST	EDUCATION	LOCATION	RESIDENCE
Cost	1	1	2	3
Education	1	1	3	4
Location	$\frac{1}{2}$	$\frac{1}{3}$	1	$\frac{1}{2}$
Residence	$\frac{1}{3}$	$\frac{1}{4}$	2	1

This table shows us that education is the highest priority (0.396), cost the second highest (0.336), residence the third (0.145), and location the least important (0.122). Clearly Danny has decided that education and cost are considerably more important than location and residence.

Finally, we must use all the information obtained so far to develop an overall priority ranking of the three universities. In effect this consists of computing a weighted average: we calculate the product of the priority for each criterion times the priority of the decision alternative (university) for that criterion, then sum the resulting products to get a prioritized ranking for each decision.

For clarity we reproduce the priority matrix for the four criteria in Table 7.9, along with the priority ranking of the criteria themselves:

The prioritized rankings are now computed using the values in Table 7.9 as follows:

For university A: $0.336(0.080) + 0.396(0.727) + 0.122(0.103) + 0.145(0.272) = 0.367$

For university B: $0.336(0.265) + 0.396(0.182) + 0.122(0.216) + 0.145(0.608) = 0.276$

For university C: $0.336(0.656) + 0.396(0.091) + 0.122(0.681) + 0.145(0.120) = 0.357$

We conclude that the analytic hierarchy process has produced the following rankings of the decision alternatives:

DECISION	PRIORITY
University A	0.367
University B	0.276
University C	0.357

Based on the AHP ratings, Danny should select university A. Danny's pairwise comparisons of the rankings have clearly indicated that quality of education is his top priority, hence the AHP analysis recommends that he attend university A. It is important to keep in mind that AHP does not *make the decision* for Danny, but it does provide him with a recommendation based on his expressed priorities. If, for example, Danny finds that he just cannot raise sufficient funds to attend university A, which is the most expensive, he will have to reconsider his options.

TABLE 7.9

Criterion Priorities Alongside University Priorities by Criterion

CRITERION PRIORITIES		UNIVERSITY	PRIORITIES BY CRITERION			
			COST	EDUCATION	LOCATION	RESIDENCE
Cost	0.336	University A	0.080	0.727	0.103	0.272
Education	0.396	University B	0.265	0.182	0.216	0.608
Location	0.122	University C	0.656	0.091	0.681	0.120
Residence	0.145					

7.3   GOAL PROGRAMMING MODELS

Firms usually have more than one objective.

In today's business environment, profit maximization or cost minimization are not always a firm's only objectives. Often, maximizing total profit is just one of several objectives, including such contradictory objectives as maximizing market share, maintaining full employment, protecting the environment, minimizing noise levels in the neighbourhood, and meeting numerous other noneconomic targets.

Goal progamming permits multiple objectives.

Mathematical programming techniques such as LP and IP have the shortcoming that their objective function is measured in one dimension only. It's not possible for LP models to have multiple objectives unless they are all measured in the same units (such as dollars), a highly unusual situation. An important technique that has been developed to supplement LP is called **goal programming (GP)**.

While LP tries to *optimize*, GP *satisfices*—that is, comes as close as possible to reaching goals.

How do LP/IP and GP models differ? In LP/IP models, we try to find the best possible value for a single objective. That is, the aim is to *optimize* a single measure. In GP models, on the other hand, we first set a goal (or desired target) for each objective. In most decision modeling situations, some of these goals may be achievable only at the expense of other goals. We therefore establish a hierarchy or rank of importance among these goals so that lower-ranked goals are given less prominence than higher-ranked goals. Based on this hierarchy, GP then attempts to reach a "satisfactory" level for each goal. That is, GP tries to **satisfice** the multiple objectives (i.e., to come as close as possible to their respective goals) rather than to optimize them. Nobel laureate Herbert A. Simon of Carnegie-Mellon University states that modern managers may not be able to optimize but may instead have to satisfice to reach goals.

The objective function is the main difference between GP and LP.

In GP we want to minimize deviational variables, which are the only terms in the objective function.

How does GP satisfice the goals? Instead of trying to maximize or minimize the objective function directly, as in LP/IP, with GP we try to minimize *deviations* between the specified goals and what we can actually achieve for the multiple objective functions within the given constraints. Deviations can be either positive or negative, depending on whether we overachieve or underachieve a specific goal. These deviations are not only real decision variables in the GP model, but they are also the only terms in the objective function. The objective is to minimize some function of these **deviational variables**.

HISTORY   A BRIEF HISTORY OF GOAL PROGRAMMING

Goal programming (GP) was first introduced in 1955 in a paper entitled "Optimal Estimation of Executive Compensation by Linear Programming," by A. Charnes, W. W. Cooper, and R. Ferguson. Although GP techniques were introduced in that paper, the actual name *goal programming* first appeared in the text *Management Models and Industrial Applications of Linear Programming* by Charnes and Cooper, published by John Wiley and Sons in 1961.

International conferences on multi-objective programming and goal programming (MOP/GP) have been offered since 1994 and provide a forum in which academics and practitioners can meet and learn about recent developments. Participants at these conferences, whose common interest is multi-objective analysis, are from various disciplines such as optimization, operational research, mathematical programming, and multi-criteria decision aid.

The GP model was popularized with applications introduced by various researchers (e.g., Lee, Clayton, Ignizio) in the 1970s. Successful GP applications include management of the reservoir watershed, management of solid wastes, accounting and financial resources management, marketing and quality control, human resources management, production, and transportation and facility location analysis.

Today, GP continues to be an active and productive area of research for solving practical problems in a wide range of disciplines.

Sources: A. Charnes, W. W. Cooper, and R. Ferguson. "Optimal estimation of executive compensation by linear programming," *Management Science* 1 (1955): 138–151; B. Aouni and O. Kettani. "Goal programming model: A glorious history and a promising future," *European Journal of Operational Research* 133, 2 (1 January 2001): 225–231.

DECISION MODELING IN ACTION
The Use of Goal Programming for TB Drug Allocation in Manila

Allocation of resources is critical when applied to the health industry. It is a matter of life and death when neither the right supply nor the correct quantity is available to meet patient demand. This was the case faced by the Manila (Philippines) Health Centre, whose drug supply to patients afflicted with Category 1 tuberculosis (TB) was not being efficiently allocated to its 45 regional health centres. When the TB drug supply does not reach patients on time, the disease becomes worse and can result in death. Only 74% of TB patients were being cured in Manila, 11% short of the 85% target cure rate set by the government. Unlike other diseases, TB can be treated only with four medicines and cannot be cured by alternative drugs.

Researchers at the Mapka Institute of Technology set out to create a model, using GP, to optimize the allocation of resources for TB treatment while considering supply constraints. The objective function of the model was to meet the target cure rate of 85% (which is the equivalent of minimizing the underachievement in the allocation of anti-TB drugs to the 45 centres). Four goal constraints considered the interrelationships among variables in the distribution system. Goal 1 was to satisfy the medication requirement (a six-month regimen) for each patient. Goal 2 was to supply each health centre with the proper allocation. Goal 3 was to satisfy the cure rate of 85%. Goal 4 was to satisfy the drug requirements of each health centre.

The GP model successfully dealt with all these goals and raised the TB cure rate to 88%, a 13% improvement in drug allocation over the previous distribution approach. This means that 335 lives per year were saved through this thoughtful use of GP.

Source: G. J. C. Esmeria. "An Application of Goal Programming in the Allocation of Anti-TB Drugs in Rural Health Centers in the Philippines," *Proceedings of the 12th Annual Conference of the Production and Operations Management Society* (March 2001), Orlando, FL.

Goal Programming Example: Wilson Doors Company

To illustrate the formulation of a GP problem, let us consider the product mix problem faced by the Wilson Doors Company. The company manufactures three styles of doors—exterior, interior, and commercial. Each door requires a certain amount of steel and two separate production steps: forming and assembly. Table 7.10 shows the material requirement, forming and assembly times, and selling price per unit of each product, along with the monthly availability of all resources.

Formulating and Solving the LP Model   Let us denote E = number of exterior doors to make, I = number of interior doors to make, and C = number of commercial doors to make. If Wilson's management had just a single objective (i.e., to maximize total sales), the LP formulation for the problem would be written as

$$\text{Maximize total sales} = \$70E + \$110I + \$110C$$

subject to the constraints

$$4E + 3I + 7C \leq 9000 \qquad \text{(steel usage)}$$
$$2E + 4I + 3C \leq 6000 \qquad \text{(forming time)}$$
$$2E + 3I + 4C \leq 5200 \qquad \text{(assembly time)}$$
$$E,\ I,\ C \geq 0$$

TABLE 7.10		EXTERIOR	INTERIOR	COMMERCIAL	AVAILABILITY
Data for Wilson Doors	Steel (kilograms/door)	4	3	7	9000 kilograms
	Forming (hours/door)	2	4	3	6000 hours
	Assembly (hours/door)	2	3	4	5200 hours
	Selling price/door	$70	$110	$110	

File: 7-1.xls, sheet: 7-1 LP

The optimal LP solution turns out to be $E = 1400$, $I = 800$, and $C = 0$, for total sales of $186 000. At this stage, you should be able to easily verify this yourself. However, for your convenience, this LP solution is included in the Excel file 7-1.xls on the CD-ROM that accompanies this textbook; see the worksheet named 7-1 LP.

Specifying the Goals   Now suppose that Wilson is not happy with this LP solution because it generates no sales from commercial doors. In contrast, exterior doors generate $98 000 (= $70 × 1400) and interior doors generate $88 000 (= $110 × 800) in sales. This would imply that while the sales agents for exterior and interior doors get sales bonuses this month, the sales agent for commercial doors gets nothing. To alleviate this situation, Wilson would prefer that each type of door contribute a certain level of sales. Wilson is, however, not willing to compromise too much on the *total* sales. Further, it does not want to be unduly unfair to the sales agents for exterior and interior doors by taking away too much of their sales potential (and hence, their sales bonus). Considering all issues, suppose Wilson sets the following goals:

Goal 1: Achieve total sales of at least $180 000

Goal 2: Achieve exterior doors sales of at least $70 000

Goal 3: Achieve interior doors sales of at least $60 000

Goal 4: Achieve commercial doors sales of at least $35 000

Goals look similar to constraints except that goals may remain unsatisfied in the final solution.

Notice that these goals look somewhat similar to constraints. However, there is a key difference. Constraints are restrictions that *must* be satisfied by the solution. Goals, on the other hand, are specifications that we would *like* to satisfy. However, it is acceptable to leave one or more goals unsatisfied in the final solution if it is impossible to satisfy them (because of other, possibly conflicting, goals and constraints in the model). We now have a GP problem in which we want to find the product mix that achieves these four goals as much as possible, given the production resource constraints.

We must first define two deviation variables for each goal in a GP problem.

Formulating the GP Model   To formulate any problem as a GP problem, we must first define two deviation variables for each goal. These two deviation variables represent, respectively, the extent to which a goal is underachieved or overachieved. Because there are four goals in Wilson's problem, we define eight deviation variables, as follows:

d_T^- = amount by which the total sales goal is underachieved

d_T^+ = amount by which the total sales goal is overachieved

d_E^- = amount by which the exterior doors sales goal is underachieved

d_E^+ = amount by which the exterior doors sales goal is overachieved

d_I^- = amount by which the interior doors sales goal is underachieved

d_I^+ = amount by which the interior doors sales goal is overachieved

d_C^- = amount by which the commercial doors sales goal is underachieved

d_C^+ = amount by which the commercial doors sales goal is overachieved

Using these deviation variables, we express the four goals mathematically as follows:

We use the deviation variables to express goals as equations.

$$70E + 110I + 110C + d_T^- - d_T^+ = 180\,000 \qquad \text{(total sales goal)}$$
$$70E + d_E^- - d_E^+ = 70\,000 \qquad \text{(exterior doors sales goal)}$$
$$110I + d_I^- - d_I^+ = 60\,000 \qquad \text{(interior doors sales goal)}$$
$$110C + d_C^- - d_C^+ = 35\,000 \qquad \text{(commercial doors sales goal)}$$

The first equation states that the total sales (i.e., $70E + \$110I + \$110C$) plus any underachievement of total sales minus any overachievement of total sales has to equal the goal of $180\ 000$. For example, the LP solution ($E = 1400$, $I = 800$, and $C = 0$) yields total sales of $\$186\ 000$. Because this exceeds the goal of $\$180\ 000$ by $\$6000$, d_T^+ would equal $\$6000$, and d_T^- would equal $\$0$. Note that it is not possible for both d_T^+ and d_T^- to be nonzero at the same time because it is not logical for a goal to be both underachieved and overachieved at the same time. The second, third, and fourth equations specify a similar issue with regard to sales from exterior, interior, and commercial doors, respectively.

> **We are concerned only about minimizing the underachievement of goals here.**

Because all four of Wilson's goals specify that their targets should be *at least* met, we want to minimize only the level of underachievement in each goal. That is, we are not concerned if any or all goals are overachieved. With this background information, we can now formulate Wilson's problem as a single GP model, as follows:

$$\text{Minimize total underachievement of goals} = d_T^- + d_E^- + d_I^- + d_C^-$$

subject to the constraints

$$
\begin{array}{ll}
70E + 110I + 110C + d_T^- - d_T^+ = 180\ 000 & \text{(total sales goal)} \\
70E + d_E^- - d_E^+ = 70\ 000 & \text{(exterior doors sales goal)} \\
110I + d_I^- - d_I^+ = 60\ 000 & \text{(interior doors sales goal)} \\
110C + d_C^- - d_C^+ = 35\ 000 & \text{(commercial doors sales goal)} \\
4E + 3I + 7C \leq 9000 & \text{(steel usage)} \\
2E + 4I + 3C \leq 6000 & \text{(forming time)} \\
2E + 3I + 4C \leq 5200 & \text{(assembly time)}
\end{array}
$$

$$E,\ I,\ C,\ d_T^-, d_T^+, d_E^-, d_E^+, d_I^-, d_I^+, d_C^-, d_C^+ \geq 0$$

> **Deviation variables are 0 if a goal is fully satisfied.**

If Wilson was just interested in *exactly* achieving all four goals, how would the objective function change? In that case, we would specify it to minimize the total underachievement and overachievement (i.e., the sum of all eight deviation variables). This, of course, is probably not a reasonable objective in practice because Wilson is not likely to be upset with an overachievement of any of its sales goals.

In general, once all the goals have been defined in a GP problem, management should analyze each goal to see if they wish to include only one or both of the deviation variables for that goal in the minimization objective function. In some cases, the goals could even be one-sided in that it is not even feasible for one of the deviation variables to be nonzero. For example, if Wilson specifies that the $\$180\ 000$ target for total sales is an absolute minimum (i.e., it cannot be violated), the underachievement deviation variable d_T^- can be completely eliminated from the GP model.

> **There are approaches to solve GP models: using (1) weighted goals and (2) ranked goals.**

Now that we have formulated Wilson's GP model with the four goals, how do we solve it? Two approaches are commonly used in practice: (1) using **weighted goals** and (2) using **ranked** (or prioritized) **goals.** Let us now discuss each of these approaches.

Solving Goal Programming Models with Weighted Goals

> **Weights can be used to distinguish between different goals.**

As currently formulated, Wilson's GP model assumes that all four goals are equally important to its managers. That is, because the objective function is just the sum of the four deviation variables (d_T^-, d_E^-, d_I^-, and d_C^-), a unit underachievement in the total sales goal(d_T^-) has the same impact on the objective function value as a unit underachievement in any of the other three sales goals (d_E^-, d_I^-, or d_C^-). If that is indeed the case in Wilson's problem, we can simply solve the model as currently formulated. However, as noted earlier, it is common in practice for managers to rank different goals in some hierarchical fashion.

Formulating the Weighted GP Model Suppose Wilson specifies that the total sales goal is five times as important as each of the other three sales goals. To include this specification in the weighted goal approach for solving GP models, we assign numeric weights to each deviation variable in the objective function. These weights serve as the objective coefficients for the deviation variables. The magnitude of the weight assigned to a specific deviation variable would depend on the relative importance of that goal. In Wilson's case, because minimizing d_T^- is five times as important as minimizing d_E^-, d_I^-, or d_C^-, we could assign the following weights to the four goals:

Goal 1: Achieve total sales of at least $180 000	Weight = 5
Goal 2: Achieve exterior doors sales of at least $70 000	Weight = 1
Goal 3: Achieve interior doors sales of at least $60 000	Weight = 1
Goal 4: Achieve commercial doors sales of at least $35 000	Weight = 1

With this information, we can now write the objective function with weighted goals for Wilson's model as

$$\text{Minimize total } weighted \text{ underachievement of goals} = 5d_T^- + d_E^- + d_I^- + d_C^-$$

In the weighted goals approach, the problem reduces to an LP model with a single objective function.

File: 7-1.xls, sheet: 7-1A

The constraints are as listed earlier for the model. The problem now reduces to an LP model with a single objective function. Setting up this model on Excel and solving it by using Solver therefore become rather straightforward tasks.

Solving the Weighted GP Model The Excel layout and Solver entries for Wilson's problem with weighted goals are shown in Screenshot 7.1A. Note that the model includes 11 decision variables (3 product variables associated with the three types of doors and 8 deviation variables associated with the four goals). The results also show the extent to which each goal has been achieved (shown in cells P8:P11).

Interpreting the Results The optimal weighted GP solution is for Wilson to produce 1000 exterior doors, 800 interior doors, and 200 commercial doors. This results in total revenue of $180 000, which exactly satisfies that goal (i.e., d_T^+ and d_T^- are both equal to 0). Regarding the goals for the different types of doors, the exterior doors sales goal is also exactly satisfied, while the interior doors sales goal is overachieved by $28 000. In contrast, sales from commercial doors are only $22 000 (= $110 × 200), which underachieves the goal of $35 000 by $13 000. Wilson should, however, be willing to accept this result because it is more concerned about the total sales goal (and hence, assigned it a larger weight) than with the commercial doors sales goal. That is, in trying to satisfy Wilson's *stronger* desire to generate at least $180 000 in total sales, the weighted GP solution continues to leave the commercial doors sales goal underachieved to a certain extent.

The weighted goals approach has two major drawbacks.

Drawbacks of the Weighted Goals Approach Although the weighted goals approach is rather easy to use, it suffers from two major drawbacks. First, it is appropriate to use only if all the goals (and hence, the deviation variables) are being measured in the same units (such as dollars). This is indeed the case in Wilson's problem, where all four goals are measured in dollars. However, what happens if different goals are measured in different units? For example, the first goal could be about sales (measured in dollars), and the second goal could be about steel usage (measured in kilograms). In such cases, it is very difficult to assign appropriate weights because different deviation variables in the same objective function are measured in different units.

It is not always easy to assign suitable weights for the different deviation variables.

Second, even if all goals are measured in the same units, it is not always easy to assign suitable weights for the different deviation variables. For example, in Wilson's problem, how does management decide that the total sales goal is exactly five times as important

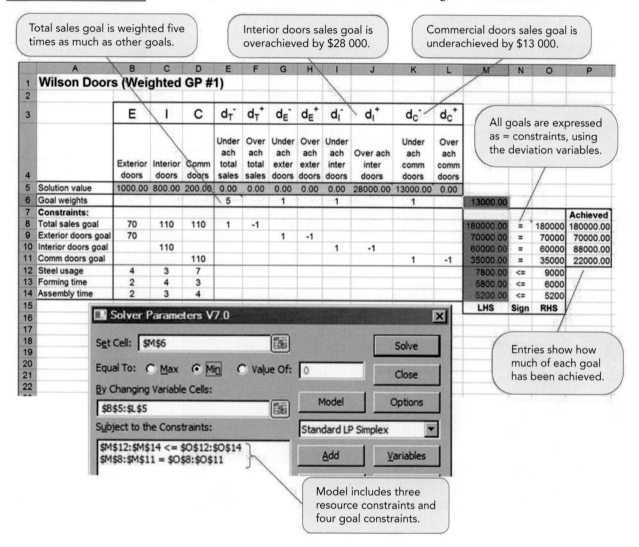

SCREENSHOT 7.1A   **Excel Layout and Solver Entries for Wilson Doors—Weighted Goals Solution 1**

Total sales goal is weighted five times as much as other goals.

Interior doors sales goal is overachieved by $28 000.

Commercial doors sales goal is underachieved by $13 000.

All goals are expressed as = constraints, using the deviation variables.

Entries show how much of each goal has been achieved.

Model includes three resource constraints and four goal constraints.

File: 7-1.xls, sheet: 7-1B

as the other three goals? What if it is only 2.5 times as important? Clearly, this would affect the choice of weights, which, in turn, could affect the optimal solution.

In fact, as shown in Screenshot 7.1B, if we assign a weight of only 2.5 (instead of 5) to the total sales goal in Wilson's weighted GP model and continue to assign a weight of 1 to each of the other three goals, the optimal solution changes completely. Interestingly, the total sales goal, which Wilson has specified as the most important goal, now turns out to be the only goal that is underachieved (by $4333.33). The exterior and commercial doors sales goals are fully satisfied, while the interior doors sales goal is actually overachieved by $10 666.67. This clearly illustrates the importance of properly selecting weights.

By the way, the LP solution shown in Screenshot 7.1B has fractional solution values for interior and commercial doors. Wilson can fix this either by solving the problem as a general IP model or by rounding off the fractional values appropriately. For your convenience, the IP solution (obtained by constraining variables E, I, and C to be integer valued in Solver) for this problem is included in the Excel file 7-1.xls on the CD-ROM that accompanies this textbook; see the worksheet named 7-1B IP. The total sales goal turns out to be underachieved by $4290 in the IP solution.

SCREENSHOT 7.1B   **Excel Layout and Solver Entries for Wilson Doors—Weighted Goals Solution 2**

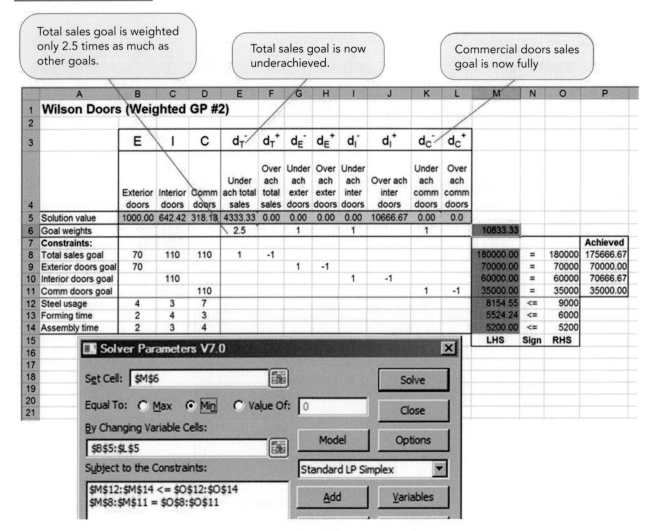

Total sales goal is weighted only 2.5 times as much as other goals.

Total sales goal is now underachieved.

Commercial doors sales goal is now fully

We use ranks when it is difficult to assign weights for deviation variables.

To overcome these two drawbacks with the weighted GP approach, we examine an alternate approach—the ranked, or prioritized, goals approach—for solving GP problems.

Solving Goal Programming Models with Ranked Goals

Lower-ranked goals are considered only after higher-ranked goals are met.

In the ranked goals approach to solving GP models, we assign ranks (or priorities), rather than weights, to goals. The idea is that goals can be ranked based on their importance to management. Lower-ranked goals are considered only after higher-ranked goals are met. Note that it is possible to assign the same rank to two or more goals.

Let us discuss this approach by revisiting Wilson Doors Company's problem. Recall that Wilson's management has currently specified the following four goals:

Goal 1: Achieve total sales of at least $180 000

Goal 2: Achieve exterior doors sales of at least $70 000

Goal 3: Achieve interior doors sales of at least $60 000

Goal 4: Achieve commercial doors sales of at least $35 000

Because in the ranked goals approach we are no longer restricted to measuring all goals in the same units, let us expand Wilson's problem by adding another goal. Suppose Wilson plans to switch to a different type of steel for the next production period. Management would therefore like to ensure that the production plan this period uses up as much of the current availability of steel (9000 kilograms) as possible. This is formally stated in the following goal:

Goal 5: Achieve steel usage of as close to 9000 kilograms as possible

Wilson's management has examined these five goals and has decided to rank them in decreasing order of rank, as follows:

Rank R_1: Goal 1

Rank R_2: Goal 5

Rank R_3: Goals 2, 3, and 4

This means, in effect, that meeting the total sales goal is much more important than meeting the steel usage goal which, in turn, is much more important than meeting the sales goals for each of the three types of doors. If we wish, we can further distinguish among goals within the same rank by assigning appropriate weights. For example, we can assign appropriate weights to any of the three goals with rank R_3 (i.e., goals 2, 3, and 4) to make that goal more important than the other two.

Formulating the Ranked GP Model   In addition to the eight deviation variables that we have already defined earlier (i.e., d_T^-, d_T^+, d_E^-, d_E^+, d_I^-, d_I^+, d_C^-, and d_C^+), we define a ninth deviation variable, as follows:

$$d_S^- = \text{amount by which the steel usage goal is underachieved}$$

Note that we do not have to define a deviation variable for overachievement of steel usage (i.e., d_S^+) because steel is a resource constraint. That is, steel usage can never exceed 9000 kilograms. Also, unlike the eight deviation variables associated with the four sales goals, which are measured in dollars, the deviation variable d_S^- is measured in kilograms.

Using the deviation variable d_S^-, we can express the steel usage goal mathematically, as follows, just as we expressed the other four goals:

$$4E + 3I + 7C + d_S^- = 9000 \qquad \text{(steel usage goal)}$$

Based on the specified ranking of goals (recall that goals with rank R_1 are the most important, goals with rank R_2 are the next most important, then R_3, and so on), Wilson's ranked GP problem can be stated as

$$\text{Minimize ranked deviations} = R_1(d_T^-) + R_2(d_S^-) + R_3(d_E^- + d_I^- + d_C^-)$$

subject to the constraints

$$
\begin{aligned}
70E + 110I + 110C + d_T^- - d_T^+ &= 180\,000 & &\text{(total sales goal)} \\
4E + 3I + 7C + d_S^- &= 9\,000 & &\text{(steel usage goal)} \\
70E + d_E^- - d_E^+ &= 70\,000 & &\text{(exterior doors sales goal)} \\
110I + d_I^- - d_I^+ &= 60\,000 & &\text{(interior doors sales goal)} \\
110C + d_C^- - d_C^+ &= 35\,000 & &\text{(commercial doors sales goal)} \\
2E + 4I + 3C &\leq 6000 & &\text{(forming time)} \\
2E + 3I + 4C &\leq 5200 & &\text{(assembly time)}
\end{aligned}
$$

$$E,\ I,\ C,\ d_T^-, d_T^+, d_S^-, d_E^-, d_E^+, d_I^-, d_I^+, d_C^-, d_C^+ \geq 0 \qquad \text{(nonnegativity)}$$

Note that within each rank, the objective function in this model includes only the under-achievement deviation variable because all four sales goals specify that the goals should be "at least" met, and the steel usage goal can never be overachieved.

Solving a model with ranked goals requires us to solve a series of LP models.

Rank R_1 goals are considered first.

File: 7-2.xls, sheet: 7-2A

Rank R_2 goals are considered next. Optimal values of rank R_1 goals are explicitly specified in the model.

Solving the Rank R_1 GP Model and Interpreting the Results   To find the optimal solution for a GP model with ranked goals, we need to set up and solve a series of LP models. In the first of these LP models, we consider only the highest ranked (rank R_1) goals and ignore all other goals (ranks R_2 and R_3). The objective function then includes only the deviation variable with rank R_1. In Wilson's problem, the objective of the first LP model is

$$\text{Minimize rank } R_1 \text{ deviation} = d_T^-$$

Solving this LP model using Solver is a rather simple task, and Screenshot 7.2A shows the relevant information. The results show that it is possible to fully achieve the rank R_1 goal (that is, the total sales goal can be fully satisfied and the optimal value of d_T^- is 0). However, at the present time, the steel usage goal is underachieved by 1200 kilograms, the interior doors sales goal is overachieved by \$28 000, and the commercial doors sales goal is underachieved by \$13 000.

Solving the Rank R_2 GP Model and Interpreting the Results   Now that we have optimally solved the model with the rank R_1 goal, we consider all goals with the next-highest rank (R_2) in the second LP model. In Wilson's problem, this is the steel usage goal. However, in setting up this LP model, we explicitly specify the optimal value of the total sales goal from the rank R_1 model. To do so, we set the value of the relevant deviation variable (i.e., d_T^-) to its optimal value of 0 in the LP model.

SCREENSHOT 7.2A   **Excel Layout and Solver Entries for Wilson Doors—Rank R_1 Goals Only**

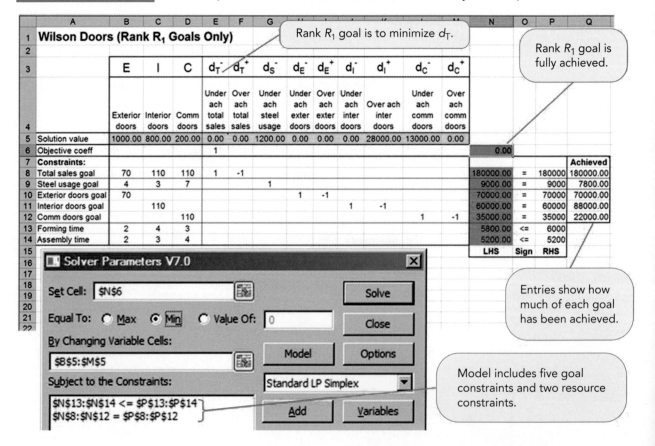

For Wilson's second LP model, the objective function and *additional* constraint are as follows:

$$\text{Minimize rank } R_2 \text{ deviation} = d_S^-$$

and

$$d_T^- = 0 \qquad \text{(optimal value of rank } R_1 \text{ goal)}$$

File: 7-2.xls, sheet: 7-2B

Screenshot 7.2B shows the Excel layout and Solver entries for this LP model. The results show that it is possible to fully achieve the rank R_2 goal also. That is, it is possible to reduce the value of the deviation variable d_S^- also to 0, while maintaining the value of the rank R_1 deviation variable d_T^- at its optimal value of 0. In fact, the total sales goal is now overachieved by $4333.33, and the exterior doors sales goal is overachieved by $63 000.

However, this emphasis on reducing the value of d_S^- results in the value of d_C^- ballooning up from $13 000 in the rank R_1 solution (Screenshot 7.2A) to $35 000 in the rank R_2 solution (Screenshot 7.2B). This implies that the commercial doors sales goal is fully unsatisfied and that no commercial doors should be made. Likewise, the interior doors sales goal is also underachieved by $8666.67. While this solution may seem unfair to the sales agents for interior and commercial doors, it is still perfectly logical because Wilson has ranked the steel usage goal higher than the sales goals for all three door types.

The LP solution shown in Screenshot 7.2B has a fractional solution value for interior doors. Interestingly, the IP solution for this problem (which is included in the Excel file 7-2.xls on the CD-ROM that accompanies this textbook; see the worksheet named 7-2B IP) is

SCREENSHOT 7.2B   **Excel Layout and Solver Entries for Wilson Doors—Rank R_2 Goals Only**

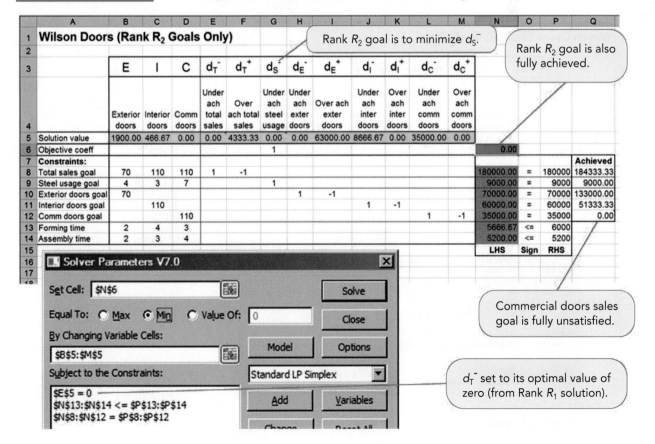

considerably different from the LP solution in Screenshot 7.2B. The steel usage goal is still fully satisfied. However, while overachievements d_T^+ and d_E^+ and underachievement d_C^- all decrease from their corresponding LP solution values, underachievement d_T^- increases from \$8666.67 to \$13 580. That is, the IP solution pulls three of the four goals closer to their target while moving one farther away from its target, when compared to the LP solution.

R_3 goals are now considered. Optimal values of rank R_1 and R_2 goals are explicitly specified in the model.

Solving the Rank R_3 GP Model and Interpreting the Results   Now that the goals with ranks R_1 and R_2 have been optimized, we now consider all goals with the next-highest rank (R_3) in the third LP model. As before, in setting up this model, we explicitly specify the optimal values of the rank R_1 and R_2 goals obtained from the first two LP models.

For Wilson's third LP model, the objective function and *additional* constraints are as follows:

$$\text{Minimize rank } R_3 \text{ deviation} = d_E^- + d_I^- + d_C^-$$

and

$$d_T^- = 0 \qquad \text{(optimal value of rank } R_1 \text{ goal)}$$

$$d_S^- = 0 \qquad \text{(optimal value of rank } R_2 \text{ goal)}$$

File: 7-2.xls, sheet: 7-2C

Screenshot 7.2C shows the Excel layout and Solver entries for this LP model. The results show that after fully optimizing the rank R_1 and R_2 goals, the best we can do is to

SCREENSHOT 7.2C   **Excel Layout and Solver Entries for Wilson Doors—Rank R_3 Goals Only**

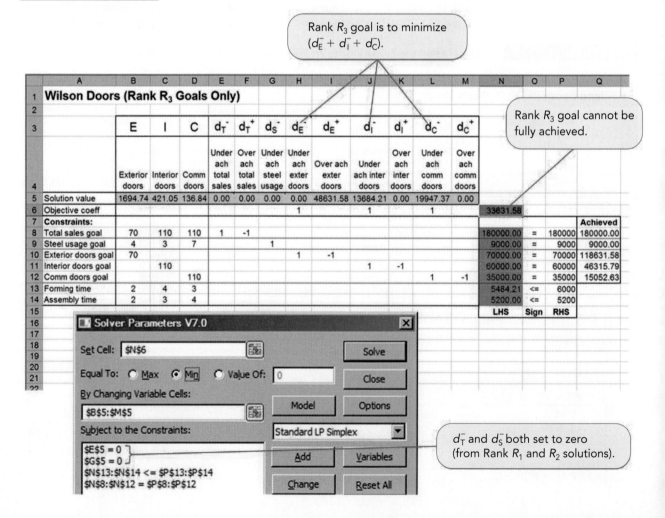

DECISION MODELING IN ACTION

Goal Programming Model for Vehicle Park Management in Quebec

Institutions in government and industry often have to manage large fleets of vehicles and other equipment. In 1995 the Ministère des Transports du Québec (MTQ) created a new agency, the Centre de gestion de l'équipement roulant (CGER), which was assigned the responsibility for managing the Ministry's vehicle park. The park is used for the storage and maintenance of vehicles and equipment required for maintaining the provincial roads. The equipment in the park consisted of 1450 light vehicles, 650 trucks, 1000 motorized pieces of equipment, and almost 5000 other pieces of equipment.

For each piece of equipment in the park, management has to decide whether to sell the item, repair it, or replace it. Analysts working on the problem observed that there were

multiple objectives to be optimized. Two of the most important, and conflicting, objectives for the CGER are reducing costs and providing adequate customer service (the customers are the 53 service centres operated by the MTQ). The analysts concluded that GP was an appropriate model.

The CGER set the goals of reducing the fleet by 20% while at the same time meeting customer requirements, renovating equipment, and respecting the budgetary constraints.

The GP model produced useful results and provided insight into budgetary thresholds necessary for the successful operation of the vehicle park.

Source: H. Goghrod, J-M. Martle, and B. Aouni. "Vehicle park management through the goal programming model." *INFOR* 41, 1 (Feb. 2003): 93–104.

achieve a total underachievement of $33 631.58 in the rank R_3 goals. In the final solution, the total sales goal is exactly satisfied while the exterior doors sales goal is overachieved by $48 631.58. In contrast, the interior doors and commercial doors sales goals are underachieved by $13 684.21 and $19 947.37, respectively.

As with the second LP model, this solution too has fractional values for the production variables. The IP solution for this problem (which is included in the Excel file 7-2.xls on the CD-ROM that accompanies this textbook; see the worksheet named 7-2C IP) turns out to be the same as the IP solution we obtained for the rank R_2 model. That is, if we solve Wilson's problem as IP models, the rank R_3 model is not able to improve on the solution obtained in the rank R_2 model.

7.4   NONLINEAR PROGRAMMING MODELS

In many real-world problems, the objective function and/or one or more constraints may be nonlinear.

LP, IP, and GP all assume that a problem's objective function and constraints are linear. That means that they cannot contain nonlinear terms such as X^3, $1/X$, $\log X$, or $5XY$. Yet, in many real-world situations, the objective function and/or one or more constraints may be nonlinear. Here are two simple examples:

■ We have assumed in all models so far that the profit contribution per unit of a product is fixed, irrespective of how many units we make of the product. That is, if Y denotes the number of units made of a specific product and the product has a profit contribution of $6 per unit, the total profit is 6Y$, for *all* values of Y. However, it is likely that the unit profit contribution of a product decreases as its supply (i.e., number of units made) increases. Suppose this relationship turns out to be

$$\text{Profit contribution per unit} = \$6 - \$0.02Y$$

Then, the total profit from this product is given by the following nonlinear expression:

$$\text{Total profit} = (\$6 - \$0.02Y) \times Y = \$6Y - \$0.02Y^2$$

■ Likewise, we have assumed in all models so far that the relationship between resource usage and production level is linear. For example, if each patient requires 5 minutes of nursing time and there are P patients, the total time needed is $5P$ minutes, for all values of P. This term would be included in the LHS of the nursing time constraint. However, it is quite possible that the efficiency of nurses decreases as the patient load increases. Suppose the time required per patient is actually $(5 + 0.25P)$. That is, the time per patient increases as the number of patients increases. The term to be included in the nursing time constraint's LHS would now be $(5 + 0.25P) \times P = (5P + 0.25P^2)$, which would make the constraint nonlinear.

In such situations, the resulting model is called a **nonlinear programming (NLP)** model. By definition, an NLP model has a nonlinear objective function, or at least one nonlinear constraint, or both. In this section, we examine NLP models and also illustrate how Excel's Solver can often be used to solve these models. In practice, NLP models are difficult to solve and should be used with a lot of caution. Let us first examine the reason for this difficulty.

Why Are NLP Models Difficult to Solve?

In every LP, IP, and GP model, the objective function and all constraints are linear. This implies, for example, that with two variables, each equation in the model corresponds to a straight line. In contrast, as shown in Figure 7.2, a nonlinear expression in two variables is a curve. Depending on the extent of nonlinearity in the expression, the curve could be quite pronounced in that it could have many twists and turns.

The optimal solution to an NLP model need not be at a corner point of the feasible region.

You may recall from Chapter 2 that a feature of all LP models is that an optimal solution always occurs at a corner point (i.e., point where two or more linear constraints intersect). Software packages (including Solver) exploit this feature to find optimal solutions quickly even for large linear models. Unfortunately, if one or more constraints are nonlinear, an optimal solution need not be at a corner point of the feasible region. Further, as you can see from Figure 7.2, if the objective function itself is nonlinear (as in the equation of an ellipse or a sphere), it is not even easy to visualize at which feasible point the solution is optimized. This is one major reason

FIGURE 7.2

Model with Nonlinear Constraints and a Nonlinear Objective Function

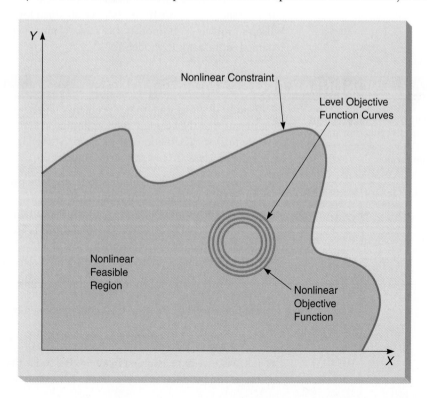

why many NLP models are so difficult to solve in practice. As you can well imagine, this issue becomes even more difficult for NLP models that involve more decision variables.

Local versus Global Optimal Solutions   A second reason for the difficulty in solving NLP models is the concept of local versus global optimal solutions. Perhaps a simple analogy will help you understand this concept. A local optimal solution is like the peak of a specific mountain in a mountain range. The global optimal solution, in contrast, is the peak of the highest mountain in that range. If you are on a specific mountain, it is likely that you can easily see the peak of that mountain—and possibly even find your way to it. However, unless you are able to see all the mountains in the entire range from your current location, you have no way of knowing if the peak of your specific mountain is just a local peak or whether it is the global peak.

Figure 7.3 illustrates this phenomenon with respect to NLP models. For the linear objective function shown in the figure, point Ⓐ is a local optimal solution, whereas point Ⓑ is a global optimal solution. The difficulty with all NLP solution procedures (including the procedure available in Solver) is that depending on where the procedure starts the search process, it could terminate the search at either a global or a local optimal solution. For example, if the procedure starts at point Ⓓ, the search process could in fact lead it to the global optimal solution, point Ⓑ, first. In contrast, if it starts at point Ⓒ, the search process could find the local optimal solution, point Ⓐ, first. Because there are no better solutions in the immediate vicinity of point Ⓐ, the procedure will erroneously terminate and yield point Ⓐ as the optimal solution.

Unfortunately, there is no precise way of knowing where to start the search process for a given NLP problem. Hence, it is usually a good idea to try different starting solutions for NLP models. Hopefully, at least one of them will result in the global optimal solution. Some of the more advanced NLP software packages include procedures to try to prevent the search process from terminating at local optimal solutions. However, these are beyond the scope of this textbook.

As a first example of optimizing a nonlinear function, consider the case of the ABC Furniture Company's production of end tables. The company has found that the relationship

An NLP model can have both local and global optimal solutions.

There is no precise way to know where to start the solution search process for an NLP model.

FIGURE 7.3

Local versus Global Optimal Solutions in an NLP Model

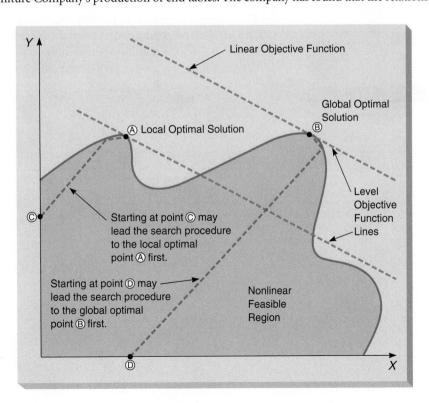

between price p and sales volume (demand) X is given by $X = 2000 - 40p$. This linear relationship shows that as the price p increases, the sales volume X will decrease. If the fixed cost of production is $1000 and the variable cost is $2 per unit then the profit is given by

$$\text{Profit } P = XP - (1000 + 2X) = (2000 - 40p)p - 1000 - 2(2000 - 40p)$$
$$= -40p^2 + 2080p - 5000$$

Using elementary calculus, we compute the derivative

$$\frac{dP}{dp} = -80p + 2080.$$

Setting the derivative equal to zero, we find a maximum when

$$-80p + 2080 = 0$$

so that $p = \$26$.

Since $X = 2000 - 40p$, it follows that when $p = 26$, $X = 2000 - 40(26) = 960$ and maximum profit is given by $P = -40(26)^2 + 2080(26) - 5000 = \$22\,040$.

To summarize: the optimal solution is to produce 960 end tables and sell them at $26 each for a maximum profit of $22 040.

The graph of the profit as a function of price is shown in Figure 7.4.

This is an example of unconstrained optimization, and we see that it can be solved by a simple application of calculus.

Let us see how the Excel Solver can be used to solve this problem. Screenshot 7.3A on page 291 shows the Excel spreadsheet and the solver screen. Cell B5 is the only Changing Cell (the variable p). Cell C5 contains the sales volume formula $X = 2000 - 40p$ and cell D5 contains the profit formula $P = Xp - (1000 + 2X)$. Since this is an example of unconstrained optimization, there are no constraints specified in the Solver's Constraints area. Before clicking on Solve, it is necessary to make sure that "*Standard GRG Nonlinear*" is selected in the dropdown box of the Solver main window (Screenshot 7.3A) and the options Assume Non-Negative box is checked in the GRG Nonlinear Solver Option window (Figure 7.5).

Clicking on *Solve* produces the results shown in Screenshot 7.3B on page 292. Note that cells B5, C5, and D5 contain the optimal solution $p = \$26$, $X = 960$, and Profit $= \$22\,040$.

The Excel formulas are shown in Screenshot 7.3C on page 292.

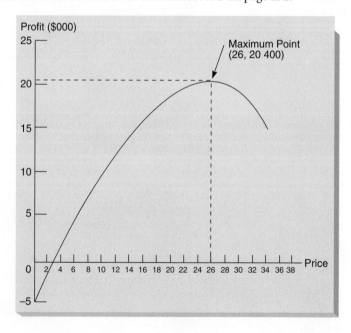

FIGURE 7.4

Profit as a Function of Price

SCREENSHOT 7.3A

Excel Layout and Solver Entries for Profit Maximization Problem

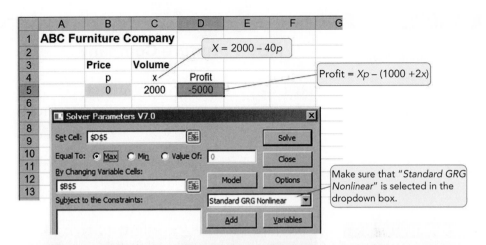

FIGURE 7.5

Solver Options Screen Showing Selections for a Nonlinear Optimization Problem

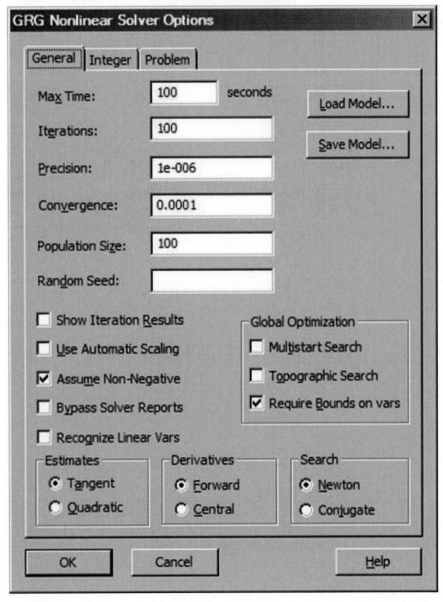

Solver Solution to Profit Maximization Problem

	A	B	C	D	E	F
1	**ABC Furniture Company**					
2						
3		**Price**	**Volume**			
4		p	x	Profit		
5		0	2000	-5000		
6						
7						
8						

Formula View of Solver Solution to Profit Maximization Problem

	A	B	C	D
1	**ABC Furniture Company**			
2				
3		Price	Volume	
4		p	x	Profit
5			=2000-40*B5	=B5*C5-(1000+2*C5)
6				
7				
8				

We see from this example that the Solver can find solutions when the quantity to be optimized is nonlinear. The Solver is a powerful optimizer that can accommodate both linear and nonlinear functions.

It is generally understood that mathematical programming problems involve constraints. In the above example we simply find the maximum value of the nonlinear (quadratic) function without imposing any constraints. As can be seen from Figure 7.4, the maximum value is found by determining the stationary points of the function—that is, the points at which the derivative is zero.

Suppose the ABC Furniture Company realizes that the consumer would not tolerate a price over \$36; that is, the constraint $p \leq 36$ is imposed on the problem. Will this constraint affect the optimal solution? Figure 7.6 shows the original with the new constraint $p \leq 36$. The shaded area now shows that the region of feasible solutions lies on or to the left of the vertical line $p = 36$. However, the point (26, 22 040) lies inside this region, so that the optimal solution is not affected by the constraint.

File: 7-3.xls

However, if new information indicates that the price should not exceed \$22, then the profit–price relationship is as shown in Figure 7.7 on page 293.

Now we see that the feasible region is bounded on the right by the vertical line $p = 22$. Since the stationary point (26, 22 040) is now excluded from the feasible region, the new optimal solution is at the boundary point (22, 21 400).

This example helps to explain why NLP is more complicated than LP is. In LP we know that there is an optimal solution at a corner point of the feasible region, and we have the simplex algorithm that can perform a search of corner points and is guaranteed to converge to an optimal corner point solution. In NLP, on the other hand, the optimal value of a nonlinear function may be found in the interior of the feasible region, as in the case when the constraint $p \leq 36$ is added to the problem, or at a boundary point, as when the constraint is $p \leq 22$.

FIGURE 7.6

Profit vs. Price with Constraint Price ≤ 36

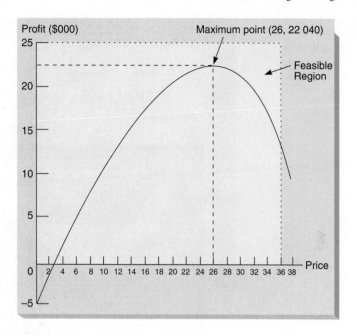

Screenshot 7.4A shows the Solver setup for the problem:

$$\text{Maximize } P = -40p^2 + 2080p - 5000$$
$$\text{subject to } p \le 22$$

where

$$p \ge 0.$$

File: 7-4.xls

Screenshot 7.4B shows the optimal solution is $p = \$22$, $X = 1120$, and Profit = $21\ 400$. Screenshot 7.4C shows the same formulas as in Screenshot 7.3C with the additional formula in cell B7 showing that the value of p is less than or equal to 22.

FIGURE 7.7

Profit vs. Price with Constraint Price ≤ 22

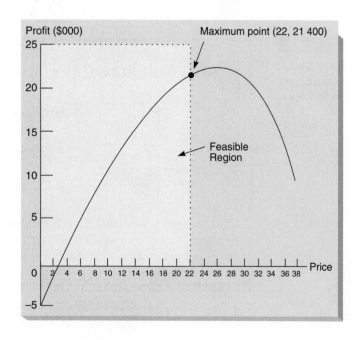

SCREENSHOT 7.4A

SCREENSHOT 7.4A

Excel Layout and Solver
Entries for Constrained
Maximization Problem

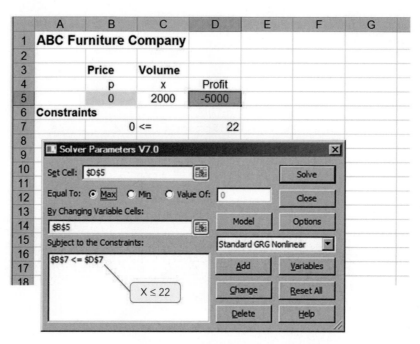

SCREENSHOT 7.4B

Solver Solution
to Constrained
Maximization Problem

	A	B	C	D	E
1	ABC Furniture Company				
2					
3		Price	Volume		
4		p	x	Profit	
5		22	1120	21400	
6	Constraints				
7			22 <=	22	

SCREENSHOT 7.4C

Formula View of Solver
Solution to Constrained
Maximization Problem

	A	B	C	D
1	ABC Furniture Company			
2				
3		Price	Volume	
4		p	x	Profit
5		22	=2000-40*B5	=B5*C5-(1000+2*C5)
6	Constraints			
7		=B5	<=	22

This example shows that Excel Solver can be used to solve NLP problems. In the remainder of this section, we examine three categories of NLP problems and illustrate how Excel's Solver can often be used to solve such problems.

File: 7-5.xls

Nonlinear Objective Function and Linear Constraints

The Great Western Appliance Company sells two models of toaster ovens, the Microtoaster and the Self-Clean Toaster Oven. Let M and T denote the numbers of microtoasters and toaster ovens produced, respectively. The firm earns a profit of $28 for each microtoaster, regardless of the number sold. Profits for the self-clean model, however, increase as more units are sold because of fixed overhead. Profit on this model can be expressed as $21T + 0.25T^2$. Hence the firm's objective function is nonlinear:

$$\text{Maximize profit} = 28M + 21T + 0.25T^2$$

Great Western's profit is subject to the following two linear constraints on production capacity and sales time available.

$$M + T \leq 1000 \quad \text{(units of production capacity)}$$
$$0.5M + 0.4T \leq 500 \quad \text{(hours of sales time available)}$$
$$M, T \geq 0$$

When an objective function contains squared terms (such as $0.25T^2$) and the problem's constraints are linear, it is called a **quadratic programming** problem. A number of useful problems in the field of portfolio selection fall into this category. Quadratic programs can be solved by a modified version of the simplex method. Although such work is outside the scope of this textbook, it can be found in sources listed in the Bibliography.

Using Excel's Solver Screenshot 7.5A shows the formula view of the Excel layout used for Great Western's NLP model.

There are only two decision variables (M and T) in the model. These are denoted by cells B5 and C5, respectively, in Screenshot 7.5A. However, the objective function has a third nonlinear term involving T^2. We can include this term in our Excel layout in several different ways. For example, we can directly type the formula for the objective function in the Target Cell (E9); that is, the formula in cell E9 can be written as

$$= 28*B5+21*C5+0.25*C5^2$$

However, if we wish to be consistent with the Excel layouts we have used in our discussions so far, we can implement this model as follows. We create an entry for every linear or nonlinear term involving M and T that exists in the model. In Great Western's case, we need entries for M, T, and T^2. We have created entries for these variable terms in cells B8, C8, and D8, respectively. The formulas for these cells are

$$= B5 \quad \text{(entry for } M \text{ in cell B8)}$$
$$= C5 \quad \text{(entry for } T \text{ in cell C8)}$$
$$= C5^2 \quad \text{(entry for } T^2 \text{ in cell D8)}$$

Quadratic programming contains squared terms in the objective function.

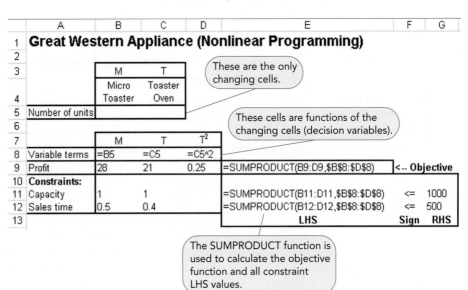

Solver Entries and Solution for Great Western Appliance's NLP Problem

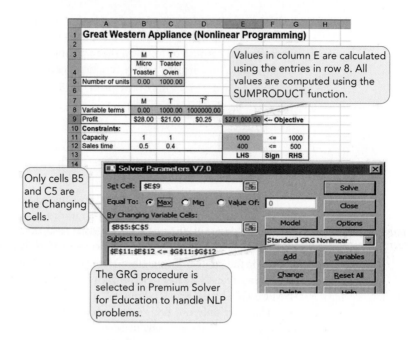

SUMPRODUCT function is again used to calculate all constraint LHS values and the objective function value.

The layout for this model now looks similar to all other Excel layouts we have used so far. Hence, we can use the SUMPRODUCT function to model the objective function as well as the constraint left-hand-side (LHS) values. Note, however, that only cells B5 and C5 are the Changing Cells in Solver. The entries in row 8 are simply calculated from the final values in cells B5 and C5.

Screenshot 7.5B shows the Solver entries and solution for Great Western's problem. The optimal solution is to make 1000 toaster ovens and no microtoasters, for a total profit of $271 000.

Assume Linear Model must *not* be checked in Solver.

Screenshot 7.5B also shows the options in the standard Solver for solving an NLP problem. Note that the Assume Linear Model box is not checked. This is important, since the presence of the T^2 term means the model cannot be solved as an LP model (i.e., using the simplex method). For most problems, we can leave all other options at their default values.

The options window in Premium Solver for Education is slightly different, and we illustrate its use in the next example.

Both Nonlinear Objective Function and Nonlinear Constraints

An example in which the objective and constraints are both nonlinear.

Pressed for operating funds, a rural hospital wants to maximize its revenue from federal and provincial payments for patients hospitalized under medicare. The annual revenue depends on the number of medical patients admitted (M) and the number of surgical patients admitted (S). The nonlinear objective function for the hospital is

$$\text{Maximize profit (in \$1000)} = \$13M + \$6MS + \$5S + \$1/S$$

The hospital identifies three constraints, two of which are also nonlinear, that affect operations:

File: 7-6.xls

$$2M^2 + 4S \leq 90 \qquad \text{(nursing capacity, in thousands of labour-days)}$$
$$M + S^3 \leq 75 \qquad \text{(X-ray capacity, in thousands)}$$
$$8M - 2S \leq 61 \qquad \text{(materials budget required, in thousands of \$)}$$
$$M, S \geq 0$$

To set up the hospital's problem on Excel and solve it using Solver, we follow the same logic we used in Great Western's problem. Screenshot 7.6 shows the Excel layout and Solver entries for the hospital's problem. Here again, only cells B5 and C5 are decision variables (i.e., Changing Cells in Solver). In row 8, we have created entries for all terms in the model that are functions of these two decision variables. The relevant formulas are

$$= B5 \quad \text{(entry for } M \text{ in cell B8)}$$
$$= C5 \quad \text{(entry for } S \text{ in cell C8)}$$
$$= B5*C5 \quad \text{(entry for } MS \text{ in cell D8)}$$
$$= 1/C5 \quad \text{(entry for } 1/S \text{ in cell E8)}$$
$$= B5\wedge2 \quad \text{(entry for } M^2 \text{ in cell F8)}$$
$$= C5\wedge3 \quad \text{(entry for } S^3 \text{ in cell G8)}$$

The rest of the Excel layout is similar to all other layouts we have created so far. To solve this example, however, we have used Premium Solver for Education rather than the standard Solver. Unlike the standard Solver, in which we had to make sure the Assume Linear Model box was not checked, specifying an NLP model is slightly different here.

Recall from our discussion of LP models that we have always selected Standard Simplex LP as the program Solver should use to solve the model. For NLP models, we should select **STANDARD GRG NONLINEAR** as the program to use. Screenshot 7.6 shows this selection in the Solver Parameters window.

The optimal solution for the hospital is to admit 6066 medical patients and 4100 surgical patients (note that all values are given in thousands). The total revenue obtained is $248 850.

Linear Objective Function and Nonlinear Constraints

Thermolock Gaskets produces massive rubber washers and gaskets like the type used to seal joints on the NASA space shuttles. To do so, it combines two ingredients, rubber (R) and

File: 7-7.xls

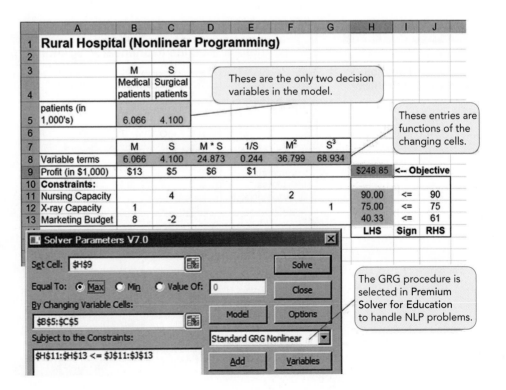

oil (O). The cost of the industrial quality rubber used is $5 per litre and the cost of the high-viscosity oil is $7 per litre. Two of the three constraints Thermolock faces are nonlinear. The firm's objective function and constraints are

$$\text{Minimize costs} = \$5R + \$7O$$

subject to

$$
\begin{aligned}
3R + 0.25R^2 + 4O + 0.3O^2 &\geq 125 &&\text{(hardness constraint)}\\
13R + R^3 &\geq 80 &&\text{(tensile strength constraint)}\\
0.7R + O &\geq 17 &&\text{(elasticity constraint)}\\
R, O &\geq 0
\end{aligned}
$$

The Excel layout and Solver entries for Thermolock's problem are shown in Screenshot 7.7. As before, row 8 has entries for all linear and nonlinear terms involving the decision variables in the model. We have used Premium Solver for Education here also to solve the model. Screenshot 7.7 shows that the optimal solution is to use 3.325 litres of rubber and 14.672 litres of oil, at a total cost of $119.33.

Computational Procedures for Nonlinear Programming Problems

We cannot always find an optimal solution to NLP problems.

We have used Solver to find optimal solutions to all three NLP examples considered in this section. There is, however, no guarantee that computational procedures to solve NLP problems will yield an optimal solution in a finite number of steps. Moreover, there is no general method for solving all NLP problems. NLP problems are inherently harder to solve than LP problems.

SCREENSHOT 7.7

Excel Layout and Solver Entries for Thermolock Gaskets' NLP Problems

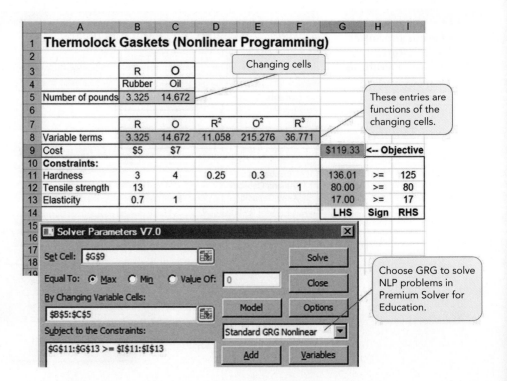

Classical optimization techniques based on calculus can handle some special cases— usually simpler types of problems. Solver uses the **generalized reduced gradient (GRG) method**, sometimes called the *steepest ascent (or descent)* method. This is an iterative *procedure* that moves from one feasible solution to the next in improving the value of the objective function. As demonstrated in our discussion, the GRG method can handle problems with both nonlinear constraints and objective function.

But perhaps the best way to deal with NLPs is to try to reduce them into a form that is linear or almost linear. One such approach, called **separable programming**, deals with a class of problems in which the objective and constraints are approximated by linear functions. In this way, the powerful procedures (such as the simplex algorithm) for solving LP problems can again be applied.

In general, however, work in the area of NLP is the least charted and most difficult of all the decision models.

SUMMARY

This chapter addresses three special types of problems. The first, analytic hierarchy process (AHP), examines multicriteria decision problems in which the decision maker has to assign pairwise preferences to each decision alternative for each of the criteria. Rankings also have to be applied to the criteria themselves. In a process called synthesization, the AHP methodology produces a best decision taking all criteria into account. Computational methods illustrated in the text generate good approximations to the overall prioritized rankings of the decision alternatives.

The second model for solving problems involving multiple criteria is goal programming (GP). This extension of LP allows problems to have multiple objective functions, each with its own goal. We show how to model such problems using weighted goals as well as ranked goals. In either case, we use Excel's Solver to obtain optimal solutions.

Finally, we introduce the advanced topic of nonlinear programming (NLP)as a special mathematical programming problem. Excel's Solver can be a useful tool in solving simple NLP models.

GLOSSARY

Analytic Hierarchy Process (AHP). A decision model for selecting the best among several alternative decisions based on prioritized rankings of a selection of decision criteria.

Deviational Variables. The difference, or deviation, between a set goal and the actual achievement; the only terms in the objective function of a goal programming problem, which seeks to minimize these deviations.

Generalized Reduced Gradient (GRG) Method. An iterative procedure used by Solver to solve NLP problems that moves from one feasible solution to the next in improving the value of the objective function.

Goal Programming (GP). A mathematical programming technique that permits decision makers to set and prioritize multiple objective functions.

Nonlinear Programming (NLP). A category of mathematical programming techniques that allow the objective function and/or constraints to be nonlinear.

Pairwise Comparison. A ranking on a nine-point scale of preferences for two decision alternatives for a given criterion.

Pairwise Comparison Matrix. A table showing all pairwise comparisons for the decision alternatives based on a decision criterion.

Priority Vector. A vector ranking decision alternatives based on a decision criterion.

Quadratic Programming. A category of programming involving squared terms in the objective function and linear constraints.

Ranked Goals. An approach in which one ranks goals based on their relative importance to the decision maker. Lower-order goals are considered only after higher-order goals have been optimized. Also known as *prioritized goals*.

Satisficing. The process of coming as close as possible to reaching a set of objectives.

Separable Programming. An approach to NLP problems in which the objective and constraints are approximated by linear functions.

Weighted Goals. An approach in which one assigns weights to deviational variables based on their relative importance to the decision maker.

SOLVED PROBLEMS

Solved Problem 7-1

A recruiter, Molly Malone, in the human resources department of a large multinational company with headquarters in Toronto, has short-listed three candidates for a position in the finance department—Broussard, Jones, and Wong. To assist in making a final choice, the recruiter has listed the following characteristics for the candidates: level of education, years of prior experience, and competence in French. The results are summarized in the table below.

	BROUSSARD	JONES	WONG
Education	MBA	B.Com.	Ph.D.
Experience	8	10	7
French	Fluent	Fair	Weak

Molly has constructed the following pairwise comparison matrices for the three candidates based on each of the decision criteria. For convenience we will call Jean Broussard candidate A, William Jones candidate B, and Jennifer Wong candidate C.

Use the AHP to help Molly decide on the best candidate.

Solution

The first step is to ask Molly to construct pairwise comparison matrices for the three decision criteria.

EDUCATION	A	B	C
A	1	3	2
B	$1/3$	1	$1/2$
C	$1/2$	2	1

EXPERIENCE	A	B	C
A	1	$1/4$	2
B	4	1	7
C	$1/2$	$1/7$	1

FRENCH	A	B	C
A	1	6	9
B	$1/6$	1	4
C	$1/9$	$1/4$	1

In addition, Molly has prioritized the criteria by the following pairwise comparisons:

CRITERIA	Education	Experience	French
Education	1	$1/2$	3
Experience	2	1	5
French	$1/3$	$1/5$	1

The next step is to generate the normalized matrices for each of the above pairwise comparison matrices and to compute the row averages (relative priorities) for each of the criteria. This process is called synthesis.

NORMALIZED MATRIX: EDUCATION			
	A	B	C	Row Avg.
A	0.545	0.500	0.571	**0.539**
B	0.182	0.167	0.143	**0.164**
C	0.273	0.333	0.286	**0.297**
				1.000

NORMALIZED MATRIX: EXPERIENCE			
	A	B	C	Row Avg.
A	0.182	0.179	0.200	**0.187**
B	0.727	0.718	0.700	**0.715**
C	0.091	0.103	0.100	**0.098**
				1.000

NORMALIZED MATRIX: FRENCH			
	A	B	C	Row Avg.
A	0.783	0.828	0.643	**0.751**
B	0.130	0.138	0.286	**0.185**
C	0.087	0.034	0.071	**0.064**
				1.000

Summarizing the row averages yields the following matrix of preferences for the three criteria:

CRITERIA			
Candidate	Education	Experience	French
A	0.539	0.187	0.751
B	0.164	0.715	0.185
C	0.297	0.098	0.064

We now apply the same process of synthesis to the pairwise comparison matrix for the criteria.

CRITERIA			
	Education	Experience	French	Row Avg.
Education	0.300	0.294	0.333	**0.309**
Experience	0.600	0.588	0.556	**0.581**
French	0.100	0.118	0.111	**0.110**
				1.000

We see that the preference vector for the criteria is

$$\begin{matrix} \text{Education} \\ \text{Experience} \\ \text{French} \end{matrix} \begin{bmatrix} 0.309 \\ 0.581 \\ 0.110 \end{bmatrix}$$

Finally, we compute the overall ranking of the decisions based on the preference matrix and the preference vector, which we reproduce below for convenience:

$$\begin{bmatrix} 0.309 \\ 0.581 \\ 0.110 \end{bmatrix} \quad \begin{bmatrix} 0.539 \\ 0.164 \\ 0.297 \end{bmatrix} \begin{bmatrix} 0.187 \\ 0.715 \\ 0.098 \end{bmatrix} \begin{bmatrix} 0.751 \\ 0.185 \\ 0.064 \end{bmatrix}$$

The priorities for the three candidates are now calculated from the two matrices as follows:

Candidate A: $0.309(0.539) + 0.581(0.187) + 0.110(0.751) = 0.358$
Candidate B: $0.309(0.164) + 0.581(0.715) + 0.110(0.185) = 0.486$
Candidate C: $0.309(0.297) + 0.581(0.098) + 0.110(0.064) = 0.156$

The AHP rankings of the three candidates are summarized as follows:

CANDIDATE	PRIORITY
Broussard	0.358
Jones	0.487
Wong	0.156

We conclude that Molly Malone should offer the job to William Jones. Molly's strong emphasis on experience leads her to hire Jones, who is the most experienced of the three applicants.

Solved Problem 7-2

Recall the Lightwell Chandelier Company integer programming problem introduced in Section 6.2. Its LP formulation is

$$\text{Maximize profit} = \$600C + \$700F$$

subject to

$$2C + 3F \le 12 \quad \text{(wiring hours)}$$
$$6C + 5F \le 30 \quad \text{(assembly hours)}$$
$$C, F \ge 0$$

where

$$C = \text{number of chandeliers produced}$$
$$F = \text{number of ceiling fans produced}$$

Reformulate Lightwell Chandelier as a GP model with the following goals:
Priority 1: Produce at least 4 chandeliers and 3 ceiling fans.
Priority 2: Limit overtime in the assembly department to 10 hours and in the wiring department to 6 hours.
Priority 3: Maximize profit.

Solution

The GP problem can be formulated as follows:

$$\text{Minimize} = P_1(d_1^- + d_2^-) + P_2(d_3^+ + d_4^+) + P_3(d_5^-)$$

subject to

$$\left.\begin{array}{l} C + d_1^- - d_1^+ = 4 \\ F + d_2^- - d_2^+ = 3 \end{array}\right\} \text{Priority 1}$$

$$\left.\begin{array}{l} 2C + 3F + d_3^- - d_3^+ = 18 \\ 6C + 5F + d_4^- - d_4^+ = 40 \end{array}\right\} \text{Priority 2}$$

$$600C + 700F + d_5^- - d_5^+ = 99\ 999\} \text{Priority 3}$$

$$C, F, \text{all } d_i \ge 0$$

The target of 99 999 for the priority 3 goal constraint represents an unrealistically high profit. It is just a mathematical trick to use as a target so that we can get as close as possible to the maximum profit.

Note that with regard to the first goal, we must minimize only the underachievement deviational variables d_1^- and d_2^-. Likewise, for the priority 2 goal, we must minimize only the overachievement deviational variables d_3^+ and d_4^+. Finally, for the priority 3 goal, we must minimize only the underachievement deviational variable d_5^-.

Screenshots 7.8A, 7.8B, and 7.8C show the Excel layout and Solver entries for this problem when each goal is considered in order of its priority. In each case, optimal values of the deviational variables for a higher-order goal are explicitly specified while solving the problem for a lower-order goal. For example, while solving the problem with the priority 2 goal (Screenshot 7.8B), the optimal values of the priority 1 deviational variables (namely $d_1^- = 0$ and $d_2^- = 0$) from Screenshot 7.8A are explicitly specified.

The optimal solution shown in Screenshot 7.8A considers only the priority 1 goals and does not attempt to restrict overtime in assembly and wiring. The solution therefore uses a large amount of overtime (note values for d_3^+ and d_4^+ in Screenshot 7.8A).

However, when we now solve the priority 2 goal problem in Screenshot 7.8B, the solution minimizes the use of excessive overtime. As a consequence, the deviational variable for underachieving profit (d_5^-) now has a large value (due to the artificially large value of 99 999 we used as the target).

When we now try to minimize this deviational variable in the next problem (Screenshot 7.8C), we obtain the overall optimal solution for this GP problem. The optimal solution is $C = 4$, $F = 3.2$, $d_1^- = 0$, $d_2^- = 0$, $d_3^+ = 0$, $d_4^+ = 0$, and $d_5^- = 95\,359$. In effect, this means that the maximum profit we can get while achieving our higher-order goals is only \$4640 (= \$600 × 4.00 + \$700 × 3.20).

File: 7-8.xls

Excel Layout and Solver Entries for Solved Problem 7-2 Considering Only Priority P_1 Goals

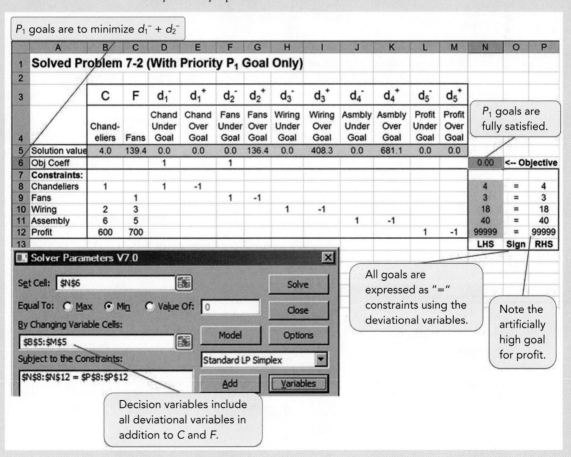

P_1 goals are to minimize $d_1^- + d_2^-$

	A	B	C	D	E	F	G	H	I	J	K	L	M	N	O	P
			C	F	d_1^-	d_1^+	d_2^-	d_2^+	d_3^-	d_3^+	d_4^-	d_4^+	d_5^-	d_5^+		
1	**Solved Problem 7-2 (With Priority P_1 Goal Only)**															
2																
3																
4			Chand-eliers	Fans	Chand Under Goal	Chand Over Goal	Fans Under Goal	Fans Over Goal	Wiring Under Goal	Wiring Over Goal	Asmbly Under Goal	Asmbly Over Goal	Profit Under Goal	Profit Over Goal	P_1 goals are fully satisfied.	
5	Solution value	4.0	139.4	0.0	0.0	0.0	136.4	0.0	408.3	0.0	681.1	0.0	0.0			
6	Obj Coeff			1		1								0.00	<-- Objective	
7	Constraints:															
8	Chandeliers	1		1	-1									4	=	4
9	Fans		1			1	-1							3	=	3
10	Wiring	2	3					1	-1					18	=	18
11	Assembly	6	5							1	-1			40	=	40
12	Profit	600	700									1	-1	99999	=	99999
13														LHS	Sign	RHS

Solver Parameters V7.0

Set Cell: $N$6

Equal To: ○ Max ● Min ○ Value Of: 0

By Changing Variable Cells:
$B$5:$M$5

Subject to the Constraints:
$N$8:$N$12 = $P$8:$P$12

Standard LP Simplex

Solve
Close
Model
Options
Add
Variables

Decision variables include all deviational variables in addition to C and F.

All goals are expressed as "=" constraints using the deviational variables.

Note the artificially high goal for profit.

SCREENSHOT 7.8B   **Excel Layout and Solver Entries for Solved Problem 7-2 Considering Only Priority P_2 Goals**

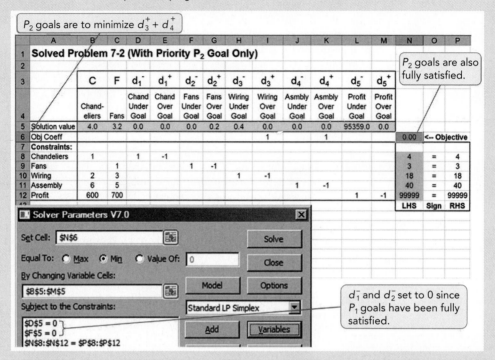

P_2 goals are to minimize $d_3^+ + d_4^+$

P_2 goals are also fully satisfied.

d_1^- and d_2^- set to 0 since P_1 goals have been fully satisfied.

SCREENSHOT 7.8C   **Excel Layout and Solver Entries for Solved Problem 7-2 Considering Only Priority P_3 Goals**

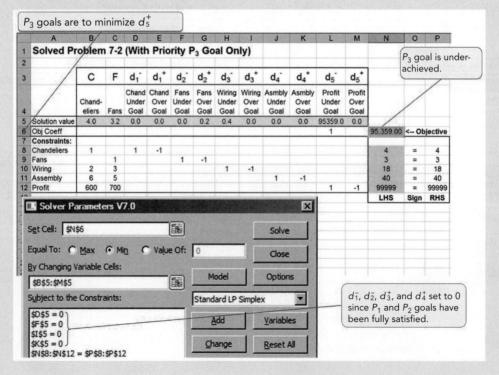

P_3 goals are to minimize d_5^+

P_3 goal is under-achieved.

d_1^-, d_2^-, d_3^+, and d_4^+ set to 0 since P_1 and P_2 goals have been fully satisfied.

⯈ SELF-TEST

- ■ Before taking the self-test, refer back to the learning objectives at the beginning of the chapter, the notes in the margins, and the glossary at the end of the chapter.
- ■ Use the key at the back of the book to correct your answers.
- ■ Restudy pages that correspond to any questions that you answered incorrectly or material you feel uncertain about.

1. If a decision maker wants to choose a best solution based on a prioritization of decision alternatives with respect to a selection of decision criteria, the appropriate model is
   a. goal programming with ranked goals.
   b. goal programming with weighted goals.
   c. nonlinear programming.
   d. analytic hierarchy process.

2. The pairwise comparison matrix is used in
   a. a goal programming problem with weighted goals.
   b. an analysis herarchy process problem.
   c. a nonlinear programming problem.
   d. a goal programming problem with prioritized goals.

3. In a goal programming problem
   a. deviational variables can be positive or negative.
   b. only deviational variables appear in the objective function
   c. all goals are equally important.

4. The main object of a goal programming model is to
   a. optimize.
   b. satisfice.
   c. maximize.
   d. minimize.

5. A quadratic programming model contains a squared term in
   a. the objective function.
   b. a constraint.
   c. both the objective function and a constraint.

6. In a goal programming problem using prioritized goals, the problem cannot be reduced to a simple linear programming problem.
   a. True
   b. False

7. In goal programming, if all the goals are achieved, the value of the objective function will always be zero.
   a. True
   b. False

8. The quantities that are maximized in a goal programming problem are termed *deviational variables*.
   a. True
   b. False

9. Nobel laureate Herbert A. Simon of Carnegie-Mellon University says that modern managers should always optimize, not satisfice.
   a. True
   b. False

10. The weighted goal approach to setting up and solving a goal programming problem reduces it to a simple LP problem.
    a. True
    b. False

11. In a goal programming model, when lower-order goals are only to be considered after higher-order goals are achieved, which type of goals are required in the formulation?
    a. deviational goals
    b. weighted goals
    c. ranked goals
    d. multiple goals

12. Goal programming
    a. requires only that you know whether the goal is direct profit maximization or cost minimization.
    b. allows you to have multiple goals, with or without priorities.
    c. is an algorithm with the goal of a quicker solution to a pure integer programming problem.
    d. is an algorithm with the goal of a quicker solution to a mixed IP problem.

13. Nonlinear programming includes problems
    a. in which the objective function is linear but some constraints are not linear.
    b. in which the constraints are linear but the objective function is not linear.
    c. in which both the objective function and all of the constraints are not linear.
    d. solvable by quadratic programming.
    e. in which all of the above occur.

DISCUSSION QUESTIONS AND PROBLEMS

Discussion Questions

7-1 Compare the similarities and differences of AHP and GP.

7-2 Provide your own examples of two applications of AHP.

7-3 What is the difference between the two types of GP problems? Provide one example of each.

7-4 What is meant by *satisficing*, and why is the term often used in conjunction with GP?

7-5 What are deviational variables? How do they differ from decision variables in traditional LP problems?

7-6 If you were the president of the university you are attending and were employing GP to assist in decision making, what might your goals be? What kinds of constraints would you include in your model?

7-7 What does it mean to rank goals in GP? How does this affect the problem's solution?

7-8 Provide your own examples of problems where (a) the objective is nonlinear and (b) one or more constraints are nonlinear.

7-9 Explain in your own words the relationship between GP problems and LP models.

7-10 Explain the difference between assigning weights to goals and ranking goals.

7-11 What does the term *quadratic programming* mean?

7-12 Which of the following are NLP problems, and why?

(a) Maximize profit = $3X_1 + 5X_2 + 99X_3$

subject to $X_1 \geq 10$
$X_1 \leq 5$
$X_3 \geq 18$

(b) Minimize cost = $25X_1 + 30X_2 + 8X_1X_2$

subject to $X_1 \geq 8$
$X_1 + X_2 \geq 12$
$0.0005X_1 - X_2 = 11$

(c) Minimize $Z = P_1d_1^- + P_2d_2^+ + P_3d_3^+$

subject to $X_1 + X_2 + d_1^- - d_1^+ = 300$
$X_2 + d_2^- - d_2^+ = 200$
$X_1 + d_3^- - d_3^+ = 100$

(d) Maximize profit = $3X_1 + 4X_2$

subject to $X_1^2 - 5X_2 \geq 8$
$3X_1 + 4X_2 \geq 12$

(e) Minimize cost = $18X_1 + 5X_2 + X_2^2$

subject to $4X_1 - 3X_2 \geq 8$
$X_1 + X_2 \geq 18$

Are any of these quadratic programming problems?

Problems

7-13 The Teaching Awards Committee at a technical college in Manitoba has to give the award to one of three professors who have been nominated by a group of faculty members and students. In order to help make the decision the committee plans to use AHP. Evaluations are based on three criteria—classroom performance (CLASS), publications in journals on pedagogy (RESEARCH), and participation in the college's tutoring centre (TUTOR). The committee's pairwise comparisons of the three nominees on each of the three criteria have resulted in the following pairwise comparison matrix. The nominees are Professors Armstrong, Benson, and Chowdhury (A, B, and C, respectively).

CLASS			
	A	B	C
A	1	2	3
B	$\frac{1}{2}$	1	2
C	$\frac{1}{3}$	$\frac{1}{2}$	1

RESEARCH			
	A	B	C
A	1	3	$\frac{1}{2}$
B	$\frac{1}{3}$	1	$\frac{1}{3}$
C	2	3	1

TUTOR			
	A	B	C
A	1	$\frac{1}{4}$	$\frac{1}{3}$
B	4	1	2
C	3	$\frac{1}{2}$	1

CRITERIA			
	Class	Research	Tutor
Class	1	3	5
Research	$\frac{1}{3}$	1	2
Tutor	$\frac{1}{5}$	$\frac{1}{2}$	1

Determine a priority ranking for the three nominees and recommend a winner for the award.

7-14 Mario Mellita has decided to evaluate three criteria in trying to decide which model car to buy—price, safety, and comfort. He has narrowed his choice to one of three models: A, B, and C. His pairwise rankings of the three features for each model are summarized as:

PRICE			
	A	B	C
A	1	$\frac{1}{4}$	3
B	4	1	6
C	$\frac{1}{3}$	$\frac{1}{6}$	1

SAFETY			
	A	B	C
A	1	$\frac{1}{2}$	3
B	2	1	7
C	$\frac{1}{3}$	$\frac{1}{7}$	1

COMFORT			
	A	B	C
A	1	$\frac{1}{4}$	$\frac{1}{6}$
B	4	1	$\frac{1}{3}$
C	6	3	1

CRITERIA			
	Price	Safety	Comfort
Price	1	$\frac{1}{7}$	$\frac{1}{4}$
Safety	7	1	2
Comfort	4	$\frac{1}{2}$	1

Verify that the pairwise comparison matrices above are consistent, and advise Mario about the best car to buy to satisfy his criteria.

7-15 Shelley Kelly has recently received a small inheritance and has decided to invest in one of three mutual funds recommended by her Bay Street financial advisor: A, B, or C. Shelley's criteria are (1) expected return (based on historical data), (2) risk, and (3) fees charged by the fund manager. Shelley has established the following pairwise comparison matrices for the three criteria for each fund, and also for the criteria themselves.

RETURN			
	A	B	C
A	1	$\frac{1}{4}$	3
B	4	1	5
C	$\frac{1}{3}$	$\frac{1}{5}$	1

RISK			
	A	B	C
A	1	2	$\frac{1}{3}$
B	$\frac{1}{2}$	1	$\frac{1}{4}$
C	3	4	1

FEES			
	A	B	C
A	1	$\frac{1}{2}$	$\frac{1}{4}$
B	2	1	$\frac{1}{3}$
C	4	3	1

CRITERIA			
	Return	Risk	Fees
Return	1	4	6
Risk	$\frac{1}{4}$	1	2
Fees	$\frac{1}{6}$	$\frac{1}{2}$	1

(a) Was Shelley consistent in assigning pairwise rankings?
(b) Use AHP to compute the weighted average score for each fund.
(c) Which fund should Shelley invest in?

7-16 The Canadian Suit Company is planning to open a new factory in Alberta, British Columbia, or Quebec, labelled A, B, and Q, respectively. The company's decision criteria are (1) taxes (provincial sales tax, income tax, etc.), (2) labour costs, and (3) transportation facilities. Canadian Suit has constructed the following pairwise comparison matrices for the three criteria for each province, and also for the three criteria.

TAXES			
	A	B	Q
A	1	$\frac{1}{2}$	2
B	2	1	3
Q	$\frac{1}{2}$	$\frac{1}{3}$	1

LABOUR			
	A	B	Q
A	1	2	$\frac{1}{2}$
B	$\frac{1}{2}$	1	$\frac{1}{3}$
Q	2	3	1

TRANSPORT			
	A	B	Q
A	1	$\frac{1}{4}$	$\frac{1}{6}$
B	4	1	$\frac{1}{3}$
Q	6	3	1

CRITERIA			
	Taxes	Labour	Transport
Taxes	1	3	7
Labour	$\frac{1}{3}$	1	3
Transport	$\frac{1}{7}$	$\frac{1}{3}$	1

(a) Was the Canadian Suit Company consistent in assigning pairwise rankings?
(b) Use AHP to compute the weighted average score for each province.
(c) Which is the best province for the new factory?

7-17 The Victoria Book Club recommends a Readers' Choice Award every year. Books are judged on four criteria: plot, suspense, pace, and humour. The club's awards committee has ranked the four priorities as follows:

	Plot	Suspense	Pace	Humour
Plot	1	$\frac{1}{4}$	$\frac{1}{2}$	3
Suspense	4	1	3	7
Pace	2	$\frac{1}{3}$	1	4
Humour	$\frac{1}{3}$	$\frac{1}{7}$	$\frac{1}{4}$	1

Three books are being considered for the Readers' Choice Award. Call the books A, B, and C. The committee has ranked the books in the following pairwise comparison matrices for each of the four criteria.

PLOT			
	A	B	C
A	1	$\frac{1}{4}$	$\frac{1}{5}$
B	4	1	$\frac{1}{2}$
C	5	2	1

SUSPENSE			
	A	B	C
A	1	4	5
B	$\frac{1}{4}$	1	$\frac{1}{2}$
C	$\frac{1}{5}$	2	1

PACE			
	A	B	C
A	1	$\frac{1}{2}$	8
B	2	1	6
C	$\frac{1}{8}$	$\frac{1}{6}$	1

HUMOUR			
	A	B	C
A	1	$\frac{1}{3}$	4
B	3	1	7
C	$\frac{1}{4}$	$\frac{1}{7}$	1

(a) Was the awards committee consistent in assigning pairwise rankings?
(b) Use AHP to compute the preference vector for the books.
(c) Which book should get the award?

7-18 Geraldine Shawhan is president of Shawhan File Works, a firm that manufactures two types of metal file cabinets. The demand for her two-drawer model is up to 600 cabinets per week; demand for a three-drawer cabinet is limited to 400 per week. Shawhan File Works has a weekly operating capacity of 1300 hours, with the two-drawer cabinet taking 1 hour to produce and the three-drawer cabinet requiring 2 hours. Each two-drawer model sold yields a $10 profit, and the profit for the large model is $15. Shawhan has listed the following goals in rank order:

Rank 1: Attain a profit as close to $11 000 as possible each week.

Rank 2: Avoid underutilization of the firm's production capacity.

Rank 3: Sell as many two and three-drawer cabinets as the demand indicates.

Set this up as a GP problem.

7-19 Solve Problem 7-18 using Excel. Are any goals unachieved in this solution? Explain.

7-20 Harris Segal, marketing director for Upper Canada Power Corporation, is about to begin an advertising campaign promoting energy conservation. In trying to budget between television and newspaper advertisements, he sets the following goals and assigns the weights shown.

1. The total advertising budget of $120 000 should not be exceeded. Weight = 100
2. There should be a mix of TV and newspaper ads, with at least 10 TV spots (costing $5000 each) and at least 20 newspaper ads (costing $2000 each). Weight = 75 each
3. The total number of people to read or hear the advertisements should be at least 9 million. Weight = 40 per 100 000 people.

Each television spot reaches approximately 300 000 people. A newspaper advertisement is read by about 150 000 people. Formulate Segal's goal programming problem to find out how many of each type of ad to place. Solve using Excel. How many people, in total, will read or hear the advertisements?

7-21 Reconsider Harris Segal's problem (see Problem 7-20). Recall that each TV ad costs $5000, while each newspaper ad costs $2000. Also, each TV ad reaches approximately 300 000 people, and a newspaper ad is read by approximately 150 000 people. Instead of the weights used in Problem 7-20, Segal has set the following goals, in the rank order specified below:

Rank 1: The total advertising budget of $120 000 should not be exceeded.

Rank 2: There should be at least 10 TV ads and at least 20 newspaper ads.

Rank 3: The total number of people reached by the ads should be at least 9 million.

Set up and solve Segal's GP problem using the ranked goals approach. How many of each type of ad should Segal place?

7-22 Hilliard Electronics produces specially coded computer chips for laser surgery in 64MB, 256MB, and 512MB sizes. A 64MB chip requires 8 hours of labour, a 256MB chip requires 13 hours, and a 512MB chip requires 16 hours. Hilliard's monthly production capacity is 1200 hours. Mr. Blank, the firm's sales manager, estimates that the maximum monthly sales of the 64MB, 256MB, and 512MB chips are 40, 50, and 60, respectively. The company has the following goals (ranked in order from most important to least important):

Rank 1: Fill an order from the best customer for 30 64MB chips and 35 256MB chips.

Rank 2: Provide sufficient chips to at least equal the sales estimates set by Mr. Blank.

Rank 3: Avoid underutilization of the production capacity.

Formulate this problem using GP. Solve using Excel.

7-23 An Ontario manufacturer produces two products: speaker telephones (X_1) and pushbutton telephones (X_2). The following GP model has been formulated to find the number of each to produce each day to meet this firm's goals:

$$R_1 d_1^- + R_2 d_2^- + R_3 d_3^+ + R_4 d_1^+$$

subject to

$$2X_1 + 4X_2 + d_1^- - d_1^+ = 80$$

$$8X_1 + 10X_2 + d_2^- - d_2^+ = 320$$

$$8X_1 + 6X_2 + d_3^- - d_3^+ = 240$$

$$\text{all } X_i, d_i \geq 0$$

Solve this problem using Excel.

7-24 Major Campbell is concerned about how the 20 officers taking his officer training course spend their precious time while in his charge. Major Campbell recognizes that there are 168 hours per week and thinks that his students have been using them rather inefficiently. Campbell lets

X_1 = number of hours of sleep needed per week

X_2 = number of personal hours (eating, personal hygiene, handling laundry, and so on)

X_3 = number of hours of class and studying

X_4 = number of hours of social time off base (dating, sports, family visits, and so on)

He thinks that students should study 30 hours a week to have time to absorb material. This is his most important goal. Campbell feels that students need at most 7 hours' sleep per night on average, and that this goal is number 2. He believes that goal number 3 is to provide at least 20 hours per week of social time.

(a) Formulate this as a GP problem.
(b) Solve this problem using Excel.

7-25 White & Becker Tools (W&B) requires 2000 electric motors next month for its product line of weed trimmers. Each motor is composed of three components: a coil, a shaft, and housing. W&B has the capability to produce these components or purchase them from an outside vendor. The costs of producing them and purchasing them are shown in the following table:

COMPONENT	PRODUCTION COST PER UNIT	PURCHASE COST PER UNIT
Coil	$2.50	$3.90
Shaft	$1.75	$2.95
Housing	$1.25	$2.00

The components that are produced by W&B must pass through three departments: fabrication, molding, and inspection. The number of hours each component requires in each department and the total number of hours available next month in each department are shown in the following table:

DEPARTMENT	COIL (HRS.)	SHAFT (HRS.)	HOUSING (HRS.)	AVAILABILITY (HRS.)
Fabrication	0.5	0.2	0.6	2500
Molding	0.4	0.7	0.3	2500
Inspection	0.2	0.3	0.4	1600

In order to determine the number of components that will be produced and the number that will be purchased, W&B has set the following goals, in rank order:

Rank 1: The total costs to produce and purchase components next month should not exceed $13 000.

Rank 2: Idle time in the fabrication department should be minimized.

Rank 3: At least 200 coils should be purchased from the vendor next month.

Determine the number of components produced and purchased next month according to these ranked goals.

7-26 Kent County has plans to develop several new recreational facilities that must be completed within the $3.5 million budget. A survey of county residents has resulted in information about the type of facilities that county residents would like to see built, described in the following table:

FACILITY	COST PER FACILITY	ACRES PER FACILITY	USAGE IN PEOPLE PER MONTH	ANNUAL MAINTENANCE
Basketball courts	$300 000	3	700	$3000
Baseball fields	250 000	5	1000	6000
Playgrounds	75 000	2	800	3000
Soccer fields	175 000	3	1200	7000

More specifically, this table provides the cost to construct and maintain each facility, the acres each facility will require, and the average monthly usage of each facility. The county has decided that at least 15 facilities will be built and has set aside 55 acres to be used for construction.

The county has also established the following list of ranked goals:

Rank 1: The county would like to spend the entire budget.

Rank 2: The county would like to build enough facilities so that 15 000 people or more each month can use them.

Rank 3: The county wants to avoid using more than the 55 acres that have been set aside for the project.

Rank 4: The county would like to avoid spending more than $80 000 per year on maintenance costs for the new facilities.

How many of each type of facility should be constructed?

7-27 John Parson earns $35 000 a year and has $6000 to invest in a portfolio. His investment alternatives and their expected returns are shown in the following table:

INVESTMENT	DESCRIPTION	EXPECTED RETURN
A	RRSP (retirement)	6.5%
B	Employer's retirement plan	15.8%
C	Deferred income (retirement)	18.0%
D	Unity mutual fund	11.9%
E	Liberty mutual fund	9.5%
F	Money market	4.8%

John's investment goals are as follows and can be ranked according to the weights shown in parentheses:

Goal 1: (25) Invest all funds available.

Goal 2: (20) Maximize the total annual return in dollars, with a target of $1200.

Goal 3: (15) Avoid investing less than 3% of salary in employer's retirement plan.

Goal 4: (15) Avoid investing less than 10% of the total investment in the money market.

Goal 5: (10) Avoid investing more than 25% of the total investment for retirement plans.

Goal 6: (10) Avoid investing less than 50% of the total investment to non-retirement plans.

Goal 7: (5) Avoid investing more than 50% of the total investment in mutual funds.

Which investments should be included in John's portfolio?

7-28 We need to make a fruit salad that contains at least 6500 units of vitamin A and 1800 units of vitamin C. Data on five available fruits are shown in the following table:

FRUIT TYPE	VITAMIN A (UNITS/kg)	VITAMIN C (UNITS/kg)	COST PER kg	MAX kg AVAILABLE
Apple	660	72	$2.98	No limit
Banana	734	82	0.98	5.5
Grape	906	36	3.38	4
Pear	182	36	1.98	No limit
Strawberry	244	508	5.98	7

It is estimated that at least 12 kilograms of fruit salad will be necessary, but no more than 16 kilograms. The following goals (in rank order) need to be considered for the mix:

Rank 1: The salad should cost no more than $40.

Rank 2: At least 2.5 kilograms of bananas should be in the salad.

Rank 3: At most 1 kilogram of pears should be in the salad.

How many kilograms of each type of fruit should be included in the salad?

7-29 Consider the following NLP problem.

$$\text{Maximize } 20X_1 + 40X_2 + 31X_3$$

subject to

$$X_1 + X_2 + X_3 \le 15$$
$$X_1^2 + X_2^2 \le 49$$
$$2X_1 + X_3^3 \le 53$$
$$X_1, X_2, X_3 \le 0$$

(a) Set up and solve the model using Solver. Use a starting value of zero for all decision variables.

(b) Is the solution obtained a local optimal or global optimal solution? How do you know?

7-30 Consider the following NLP problem.

$$\text{Maximize } 4X_1 + 2X_2 - 3X_3 + 2X_1X_2 + 8X_3^3$$

subject to

$$2X_1 + 4X_2 + 3X_3 \ge 29$$
$$3X_1 + X_2 \ge 14$$
$$X_1 + X_2 + X_3 \le 10$$
$$X_1, X_2, X_3 \ge 0$$

(a) Set up and solve the model using Solver. Use a starting value of zero for all decision variables.

(b) Is the solution obtained a local optimal or global optimal solution? How do you know?

7-31 Hinkel Rotary Engine, Ltd. produces four- and six-cylinder models of automobile engines. The firm's profit for each four-cylinder engine sold during its quarterly production cycle is $1800 − $50X_1$, where X_1 is the number sold. Hinkel makes $2400 − $70X_2$ for each of the larger engines sold, with X_2 equal to the number of six-cylinder engines sold. There are 5000 hours of production time available during each production cycle. A four-cylinder engine requires 100 hours of production time, whereas a six-cylinder engine takes 130 hours to manufacture. Formulate this production problem for Hinkel. Solve using Excel. Use several different starting values for the decision variables to try to identify a global optimal solution.

7-32 SnowSport of Quebec produces two models of snowmobiles, the XJ6 and the XJ8. In any given production-planning week, SnowSport has 40 hours available in its final testing bay. Each XJ6 requires 1 hour to test and each XJ8 takes 2 hours. The revenue (in $1000s) for the firm is nonlinear and is stated as (no. of XJ6s)(4 − 0.1 no. of XJ6s) + (no. of XJ8s)(5 − 0.2 no. of XJ8s). Formulate this problem and solve using Excel. Use several different starting values for the decision variables to try to identify a global optimal solution.

7-33 Susan Jones would like her investment portfolio to be selected from a combination of three stocks—Alpha, Beta, and Gamma. Let variables A, B, and G denote the percentages of the portfolio devoted to Alpha, Beta, and Gamma, respectively. Susan's objective is to minimize the variance of the portfolio's return, given by the following function:

$$3A^2 + 2B^2 + 2G^2 + 2AB - 1.1AG - 0.7BG$$

The expected returns for Alpha, Beta, and Gamma are 15%, 11%, and 9%, respectively. Susan wants the expected return for the total portfolio to be at least 10%. No individual stock can constitute more than 70% of the portfolio. Formulate this portfolio selection problem and solve using Excel. Use several different starting values for the decision variables to try to identify a global optimal solution.

7-34 Ashworth Industries would like to make a price and production decision on two of its products. Define Q_A and Q_B as the quantities of products A and B to produce and P_A and P_B as the prices for products A and B. The weekly quantities of A and B that are sold are functions of the price, according to the following expressions:

$$Q_A = 5500 - 200P_A$$
$$Q_B = 4500 - 225P_B$$

The variable costs per unit of A and B are $18 and $12, respectively. The weekly production capacities for A and B are 275 and 350 units, respectively. Each unit of A requires 1 hour of labour, while each unit of B requires 2 hours. There are 700 hours of labour available each week. What quantities and prices of products A and B will maximize weekly profit? (*Hint*: Set up the objective function in terms of profit per unit multiplied by the number of units produced for both products.) Use several different starting values for the decision variables to try to identify a global optimal solution.

⇒ CASE STUDY 7.1

Schank Marketing Research

Schank Marketing Research has just signed contracts to conduct studies for four clients. At present, three project managers are free for assignment to the tasks. Although all are capable of handling any of the assignments, the times and costs to complete the studies depend on the experience and knowledge of each manager. Using his judgment, John Schank, the president, has established a cost for each possible assignment. These costs, which are really the salaries each manager would draw on each task, are summarized in the table below.

Schank is very hesitant about neglecting Bombardier, which has been an important customer in the past. (Bombardier has employed the firm to study the public's attitude to new midsize jet aircraft that are being used for domestic flights in Canada.) In addition, Schank has promised to try to provide Ed Ruth a salary of at least $3000 on his next assignment. From previous contracts, Schank also knows that Linda Gardener does not get along well with the management at Air Canada, so he hopes to avoid assigning her to that company. Finally, as Nortel is also an old and valued client, Schank feels that it is twice as important to assign a project manager immediately to Nortel's task as it is to provide one to CN, a brand-new client. Schank wants to minimize the total costs of all projects while considering each of these goals. He feels that all of these goals are important, but if he had to rank them, he would put his concern about Bombardier first, his worry about Linda Gardener second, his need to keep Nortel happy third, his promise to Ed Ruth fourth, and his concern about minimizing all costs last.

Each project manager can handle only one new client.

		CLIENT		
PROJECT MANAGAER	NORTEL	BOMBARDIER	CN	AIR CANADA
Linda Gardener	$3200	$3000	$2800	$2900
Ed Ruth	2700	3200	3000	3100
Jim Polanski	1900	2100	3300	2100

DISCUSSION QUESTIONS

1. If Schank were not concerned about noncost goals, how would he formulate this problem so that it could be solved quantitatively?

2. Develop a formulation that will incorporate all five objectives.
3. Solve using Excel.

⇒ CASE STUDY 7.2

The Whom Should We Hire Case

E. S. Rosenbloom, I. H. Asper School of Business

There are many decision problems where expected value is not an appropriate way to decide. Often we have to choose between alternatives where there are conflicting attributes. An alternative that is very good on one attribute may be quite mediocre on some other attribute. AHP can often be used for such problems.

The I. H. Asper School of Business has four candidates for a tenure track assistant professor position in the department of business administration. Responsibilities for professors are covered in the collective agreement between the University of Manitoba and the University of Manitoba Faculty Association.

The responsibilities mentioned in the collective agreement are teaching, research and scholarly activities, university service, and community service. Weightings can and do vary from department to department.

The I. H. Asper School of Business has a B.Comm. (Hons) program, two MBA programs (evening and MBA Manitoba), and a Ph.D. program. The advertisement for the job says that the department wants somebody who is both an excellent teacher and an excellent researcher. The advertisement says a Ph.D. or equivalent is expected.

The hiring committee has the following information about the candidates.

John Jones was born in 1962. He has a 1983 B.Comm. (Hons) from U. of Manitoba, a 1985 MBA from Bowling Green, and a 2003 Ph.D. from the business school at Utah State University. He taught for a number of years at a community college. Jones is currently teaching at the University of North Dakota where he is an assistant professor. He is a Canadian citizen.

Interviews with him seemed to go well. Members of the hiring committee thought he was a decent guy with a good sense of humour. However, a couple of members of the committee thought he was an intellectual lightweight. Each interview was about 30 minutes long.

Jones has provided his teaching ratings. On a 1–5 scale (5 being the highest) he averages 4.1, which is well above average. Reference letters from academics indicate that he is very good teaching introductory courses but not so good teaching advanced courses. One reference letter indicates that he would not have confidence in Jones supervising Ph.D. students. There are letters from students that state that Jones is one of the best teachers they ever had.

Jones has one refereed publication. It is in a good journal. The article seems easy to understand. Jones has authored an introductory textbook. Reference letters indicate that Jones's research potential is good. The reference letters are not from well-established academics.

Jones has done a considerable amount of university service. He has served on tenure, promotion, and departmental committees. Reference letters indicate that he has performed very well on these committees. There is a letter from a former student thanking Jones for the advice he gave her on course selection.

Interviews with Jones indicate that although he would like to concentrate on introductory courses, he is eager to do more research.

Sharon Smith was born in 1977. She has a 1998 BA from Harvard and a 2003 Ph.D. from the business school at Stanford. Smith is currently teaching at U.B.C. where she is a visiting assistant professor. She is a landed immigrant in Canada.

Smith was interviewed by the hiring committee. Some members of the committee said she was one of the most brilliant people they had ever met. However, other members of the committee thought she was quite arrogant. The interviews lasted 30 minutes.

Smith has provided her teaching ratings. On a 1–5 scale (5 being the highest) she averages 2.9. Reference letters indicate that she is a very good though demanding teacher. In particular, the reference letters stress her ability to teach advanced courses and work with Ph.D. students.

Smith has seven refereed publications. One is in a very good journal, three are in good journals and three are in less prestigious journals. The articles are quite theoretical and somewhat difficult for a non-expert to understand. The reference letters indicate that she will be an outstanding researcher. The letters are from some of the most famous researchers at Stanford, Wharton, and Chicago. She was recently awarded a $20 000 research grant from SSHRC.

In terms of service, Smith is an associate editor of a journal.

She has refereed a number of papers. In interviews she has indicated that she would prefer fulfilling her service commitment with editorial responsibilities rather than serving on university committees.

Interviews with Smith indicate that she is very committed to her research. She said her teaching preferences would be advanced courses and the supervision of Ph.D. students.

Bob Brauler was born in 1943. He has a 1964 BA from the University of Toronto, a 1966 MBA from the University of Western Ontario, and a 1970 Ph.D. from the University of Chicago. From 1970 to 2002 he was a member with the faculty of management at the University of Toronto. Brauler was promoted to full professor in 1980. He was dismissed by the University of Toronto in 2002 for gross misconduct after assaulting a dean of the University of Toronto. He has been unable to find academic employment since that incident. He is a Canadian citizen.

Brauler has taught undergraduate, MBA, and Ph.D. students. His teaching ratings on a scale of 1–5 average 3.8, which is above average. He has supervised six successful Ph.D. students. All of these Ph.D. students have gone on to successful careers in either academia or consulting.

Brauler has 32 refereed articles published. Most of his work has appeared in top journals. Some of his work is very well known and most academics agree that he has made a significant contribution to his discipline. In addition, he has a one–year $500 000 research grant from SSHRC. Since the University of Manitoba charges a 20% overhead charge on research grants, in effect Brauler would be subsidizing his own salary for the first year. Since Brauler has a record of obtaining research grants, there is certainly a reasonable probability that he would receive future grants. However, one of the administrators at the University of Toronto was critical of Brauler's research. Some of Brauler's research was very critical of management practices at leading Canadian companies. The result was that these same companies were not terribly supportive of U of T's faculty of management while Brauler was a tenured member there.

In terms of service, Brauler had been the editor for a number of years of one of the more prestigious journals in his discipline.

Discussions with former colleagues at the University of Toronto were somewhat negative. Although agreeing that he was a good teacher and a gifted researcher, his former colleagues used terms such as "incredibly conceited" and "arrogant bastard." However, his colleagues felt that the physical confrontation with the dean was an aberration and that the university had overreacted in dismissing him. Although in general his teaching ratings were above average, administrators at the University of Toronto stated that there had been two complaints by students. The student complaints concerned his arrogant behaviour. In interviews with the search committee, Brauler explained his dismissal by stating that he had suffered through emotional problems caused by the break-up of his sixth marriage. He wanted to return to academia, even as an assistant professor. He felt that with counselling and medication his past problems were behind him. Brauler did not display any of his past emotional problems in the interview. Everybody on the hiring committee was impressed by his breadth of knowledge in his discipline. However, several members of the search committee felt Brauler was quite conceited.

Tom Thompson was born in 1966. He has a 1987 B.Comm. (Hons) from the University of Manitoba and a 1993 MBA from Harvard. He is a Canadian citizen.

Thompson has been a very successful businessman in Winnipeg. Since 1995 he has been teaching the occasional course for the I. H. Asper School of Business at the University of Manitoba. He has taught at both the undergraduate and MBA level.

Thompson's average teaching rating of 4.3 (on a 1–5 scale) is well above average in the faculty. Students are particularly impressed by his contacts in the Winnipeg business community. Almost all students agree that his lectures are very practical.

Unlike the other candidates, Thompson is well known by the students, faculty, and administrators of the I. H. Asper School of Business. He is well liked. Some members of the hiring committee have argued that Thompson's close contacts with the Winnipeg business community are very beneficial to the faculty and hence should be considered an important community

service. In particular, Thompson is likely to convince a number of Manitoba businesses to sponsor students in both MBA programs.

Thompson has told the hiring committee that he is no longer interested in teaching on a sessional basis. If he is appointed to the position of assistant professor, Thompson plans to sell his business interests but continue to do consulting. Thompson has no research record. Thompson has also told the hiring committee that he has no intention of obtaining a Ph.D. This was a concern for some members of the hiring committee. Since this was a tenure track position, if Thompson were hired he would have to come up for tenure in six years. Even with outstanding teaching and service, he might not get tenure without a Ph.D. and a research record. (Not getting tenure means being terminated.)

Some members of the hiring committee argue that Thompson should not be considered since he does not have a Ph.D. However, other members of the search committee argue that Thompson's practical and current business experience is in effect equivalent to a Ph.D.

The hiring committee is split with two votes for each candidate. They have decided to have this class decide. Remember, the candidate who will be hired may be with the faculty for the next 30 years and could have an impact on the quality of education in the I. H. Asper School of Business. What is your recommendation on who should be hired? Why?

BIBLIOGRAPHY

Arntzen, Bruce C. et al. "Global Supply Chain Management at Digital Equipment Corporation," *Interfaces* 25, 1 (January–February 1995): 69–93.

Bohl, Alan H. "Computer Aided Formulation of Silicon Defoamers for the Paper Industry," *Interfaces* 24, 5 (September–October 1994): 41–48.

Ignizio, J. P. *Goal Programming and Extensions*. Lexington, MA: D.C. Heath and Company, 1976.

Kuby, Michael et al. "Planning China's Coal and Electricity Delivery System," *Interfaces* 25, 1 (January–February 1995): 41–68.

Montgomery, D., and E. Del Castillo. "A Nonlinear Programming Response to the Dual Response Problem," *Journal of Quality*

Technology 25, 3 (1993): 199–204.

Render, B., R. M. Stair, and M. Hanna. *Quantitative Analysis for Management*, 8/e. Upper Saddle River, NJ: Prentice Hall, 2003.

Taylor, B. W. "An Integer Nonlinear Goal Programming Model for the Deployment of State Highway Patrol Units," *Management Science* 31, 11 (November 1985): 1335–1347.

Varberg, D., and E. J. Purcell, *Calculus*, 6th ed. Prentice Hall, Englewood Cliffs, NJ. 1992.

Zangwill, W. I. *Nonlinear Programming: A Unified Approach*. Upper Saddle River, NJ: Prentice Hall, 1969.

CHAPTER 8

Project Management

LEARNING OBJECTIVES

After completing this chapter, students will be able to

1. Understand how to plan, monitor, and control projects using PERT/CPM.

2. Determine earliest start, earliest finish, latest start, latest finish, and slack times for each activity.

3. Understand the impact of variability in activity times.

4. Develop load charts to plan, monitor, and control the use of various resources during the project.

5. Use LP to find the least cost solution to reduce total project time, and solve these LP models using Excel's Solver.

6. Understand the important role of software such as Microsoft Project in project management.

CHAPTER OUTLINE

8.1 Introduction

8.2 Project Networks

8.3 Determining the Project Schedule

8.4 Using Linear Programming to Identify the Critical Path

8.5 Variability in Activity Times

8.6 Managing Project Costs and Other Resources

8.7 Project Crashing

8.8 Using Microsoft Project to Manage Projects

Summary • Glossary • Key Equations • Solved Problems • Self-Test • Discussion Questions and Problems • Case Study: Haygood Brothers Construction Company • Case Study: Family Planning Research Center of Nigeria • Bibliography

Project Management Helps Casino Resort Development in Niagara Falls

On August 26, 2003, the Ontario Lottery and Gaming Corporation (OLGC), accompanied by local members of Parliament and the Mayor of Niagara Falls, announced the new casino in Niagara Falls, to be called Niagara Fallsview Casino Resort, with a scheduled opening date of Spring 2004. It was reported that the resort would "create an additional 2500 direct jobs, and many thousands of additional indirect jobs." The $1 billion resort features a 30-storey, five-star hotel and a casino with 3000 slot machines and150 gaming tables.

The Falls Management Co. used project management techniques to help keep the large-scale project on track. During the peak building period two new floors were added to the hotel tower every 10 days. A myriad of activities had to be undertaken in the course of the development of the resort. Although the tower was only eight storeys high, teams of workers started to install ventilation ducts in the ceilings of the hotel's lower floors. Meanwhile, six huge water chillers were installed in the basement of the hotel and pipes were in the process of being installed. Workers had already begun construction of the one-storey penthouse that sits on top of the casino area, holding its air-conditioner and ventilation systems.

Source: CP Photo/Dennis Cahill

With so many tasks occurring simultaneously, and with others waiting to be started after the completion of activities on which they depended, it was of paramount importance to ensure that activities be completed according to schedule. Given the size of the project, one of the biggest challenges facing management was to ensure that there would be no delay in starting a task on schedule. Therefore all of the tasks that had to be completed prior to the start of a new task were completed according to a strict timeline. Critical Path Method (CPM) is the management term for planning how each phase of the project dovetailed with the next.

As Falls Management Co. president Jim Dougan said, " Good communication has kept one of Canada's biggest construction projects moving smoothly, on schedule, and on budget."

Corey Larocque. "New casino taking shape: Steel work, hotel tower most visible signs of progress at site," *Niagara Falls Review* (August 26, 2002): A1.

8.1   INTRODUCTION

Every organization at one time or another will take on a large and complex project. As noted in the preceding application, the project management team at Falls Management Co. had to carefully monitor start and finish times for a huge number of activities in the Niagara Fallsview Resort Project. Likewise, when Microsoft Corporation set out to develop Windows Vista, a program costing hundreds of millions of dollars that had hundreds of programmers working on millions of lines of code, immense stakes rode on the project being delivered on time. Other examples of large companies that undertake expensive projects include the Bombardier Company, which designs and manufactures planes and trains, as well as recreational products, and SNC-Lavalin, one of the world's leading engineering-construction firms, which has been involved in the development of all four phases of the complex Vancouver SkyTrain System. Companies in almost every industry worry about how to manage large-scale, complicated projects effectively.

> **Project management techniques can be used to manage large, complex projects.**

Scheduling large projects is a difficult challenge to most managers, especially when the stakes are high. Millions of dollars in cost overruns have been wasted due to poor project planning. Unnecessary delays have occurred due to poor scheduling, and companies have gone bankrupt due to poor controls. How can such problems be solved? The answers lie in a popular decision modeling approach known as **project management**.

Phases in Project Management

A **project** can be defined as a series of related tasks (or activities) directed toward a major well-defined output. A project can consist of thousands of specific activities, each with its own set of requirements of time, money, and other resources such as labour, raw materials, and machinery. Regardless of the scope and nature of the project, the management of large projects involves three phases, discussed in the following sections (see Figure 8.1). Each phase addresses specific questions regarding the project.

> **There are three phases in managing large projects.**

> **Project planning is the first phase.**

Project Planning   Project planning is the first phase and involves goal setting, defining the project, and team organization. Specific questions that are considered in this phase include the following:

1. What is the goal or objective of the project?
2. What various activities (or tasks) constitute the project?
3. How are these activities linked? That is, what are the precedence relationships between the activities?
4. What time is required for each activity?
5. What other resources (e.g., labour, raw materials, machinery) are required for each activity?

> **Project scheduling is the second phase.**

Project Scheduling   The second phase involves developing a time schedule for each activity and assigning people, money, and supplies to specific activities. The questions addressed in this phase should be considered soon after the project has been planned but *before* it is actually started. These questions include the following:

1. When will the entire project be completed?
2. What is the schedule (start and finish time) for each activity?
3. What are the critical activities in the project? That is, what activities will delay the entire project if they are late?
4. What are the noncritical activities in the project? That is, what activities can run late without delaying the completion time of the entire project?
5. By how much can a noncritical activity be delayed without affecting the completion time of the entire project?

6. Considering variability in activity times, what is the probability that the project will be completed by the deadline?

One popular project scheduling approach is a **Gantt chart**. Gantt charts are low-cost means of helping managers make sure that (1) all activities are planned for, (2) their order

Gantt charts are useful for project scheduling.

FIGURE 8.1

Project Planning, Scheduling, and Controlling

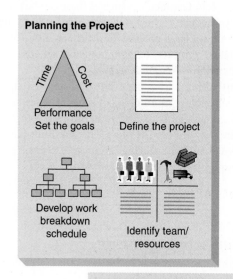

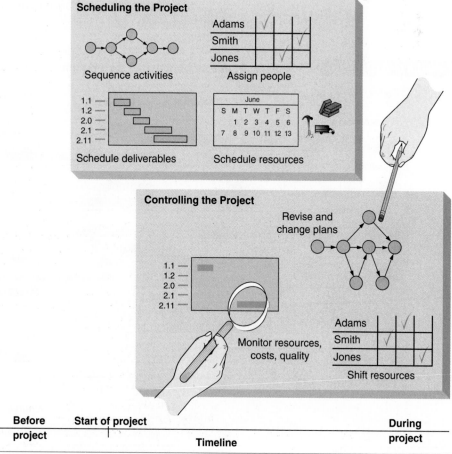

Source: J. Heizer and B. Render. *Operations Management*, 6/e. Upper Saddle River, NJ: Prentice Hall, 2001.

of performance is accounted for, (3) the activity time schedules are recorded, and (4) the overall project time is developed. Gantt charts are easy to construct and understand, and permit managers to plan and track the progress of each activity. For example, Figure 8.2 shows the Gantt chart for a routine servicing of a Delta jetliner during a 60-minute layover. Horizontal bars are drawn for each project activity along a timeline.

For large projects, Gantt charts are used mainly to provide project summaries.

On simple projects, Gantt charts such as these can be used alone. Gantt charts, though, do not adequately illustrate the interrelationships between the activities and the resources. For this reason, on most large projects Gantt charts are used mainly to provide summaries of a project's status. Projects are planned and scheduled using other network-based approaches discussed in subsequent sections.

Project Controlling   Like the control of any management system, the control of large projects involves close monitoring of schedules, resources, and budgets. Control also means using a feedback loop to revise the project plan and having the ability to shift resources to where they are needed most. The questions addressed in this phase should be considered at regular intervals during the project to ensure that it meets all time and cost schedules. These questions include the following:

Projects must be monitored and controlled at regular intervals. Project controlling is the third phase.

1.   At any particular date or time, is the project on schedule, behind schedule, or ahead of schedule?

2.   At any particular date or time, is the money spent on the project equal to, less than, or greater than the budgeted amount?

3.   Are there enough resources available to finish the project on time?

4.   If the project is to be finished in a shorter amount of time, what is the best way to accomplish this at the least cost?

FIGURE 8.2   Gantt Chart of Service Activities for a Commercial Aircraft During a 60-Minute Layover

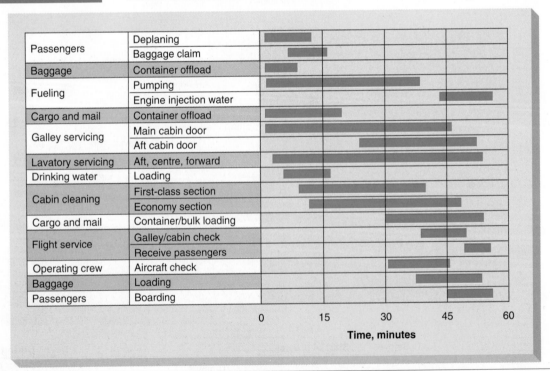

Source: J. Heizer and B. Render. *Operations Management*, 6/e. Upper Saddle River, NJ: Prentice Hall, 2001.

In this chapter, we investigate how project management techniques can be used to answer all these questions.

Use of Software Packages in Project Management

Software packages automate many of the routine calculations in project management.

In recent times, managing large and complex projects has become considerably easier due to the availability and capabilities of specialized project management software packages. These programs typically have simple interfaces for entering the project data, and they automate many of the routine calculations required for effective project management. In addition, they are capable of efficiently presenting the status of a project using comprehensive graphs and tables. Some of these programs are Primavera (by Primavera Systems, Inc.), Microsoft Project (by Microsoft Corp.), MacProject (by Apple Computer Corp.), Pertmaster (by Primavera Systems, Inc.), Turboproject (by OfficeWork Software), and Prochain Project Management (by Prochain Solutions, Inc.)

These programs produce a broad variety of reports, including (1) detailed cost breakdowns for each task, (2) total program labour curves, (3) cost distribution tables, (4) functional cost and hour summaries, (5) raw material expenditure forecasts, (6) variance reports, (7) time analysis reports, and (8) work status reports.

Although it is possible to set up spreadsheets to perform many of the routine calculations that are involved, Excel is not the ideal choice for such tasks. So, in this chapter, we illustrate how Microsoft Project 2000 can be used for planning, scheduling, and monitoring projects.

There are, however, some issues that Microsoft Project does not handle. One such issue is question 4 posed in the section "Project Controlling" (How can we reduce a project's completion time at minimum cost?). We can best answer this question by setting up and solving the problem as a linear programming (LP) model. For this question, we describe using Excel's Solver to solve the LP model.

8.2   PROJECT NETWORKS

As noted previously, once the project mission or goal has been clearly specified, we need to deal with *project planning*. That is, we need to identify the **activities** that constitute the project, the precedence relationships among these activities, and the time and other resources required for each activity.

Identifying Activities

A project can be subdivided into several activities.

Almost any large project can be subdivided into a series of smaller activities or tasks. Identifying the activities involved in a project and the precedence relationships among them is the responsibility of the project team. In subdividing a project into various activities, however, the project team must be careful to ensure the following:

- Each activity has clearly identifiable starting and ending points. In other words, we should be able to recognize when an activity has started and when it has ended. For example, if the project goal is to build a house, an activity may be to lay the foundation. It is possible to clearly recognize when we start this activity and when we finish this activity.
- Each activity is clearly distinguishable from every other activity. That is, we should be able to associate every action we take and every dollar we spend with a specific (and unique) activity. For example, while building a house, we will be able to recognize which actions and expenses are associated with laying the foundation.

The number of activities in a project will depend on the nature and scope of the project. It will also depend on the level of detail with which the project manager wants to monitor and control the project. In a typical project, each activity may be a project of its own.

An activity in a project may be a project of its own.

That is, a project may actually be a master project in turn consisting of several miniprojects. In practice, it is convenient to develop a work breakdown structure to identify the activities in a project.

MODELING IN THE REAL WORLD

PERT Helps Change the Face of British Airways

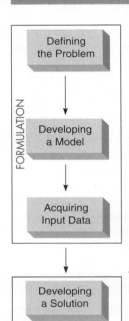

FORMULATION

- Defining the Problem
- Developing a Model
- Acquiring Input Data

SOLUTION

- Developing a Solution
- Testing the Solution

INTERPRETATION

- Analyzing the Results and Conducting a Sensitivity Analysis
- Implementing the Results

British Airways (BA) wanted to rejuvenate its image using international design consultants to help develop a new identity. The "makeover" was to be completed in all areas of BA's public image as quickly as possible.

Using a computerized project management package, Pertmaster, a BA team constructed a PERT model of all tasks involved.

Data were collected from each department involved. Printers were asked to develop time estimates for new company stationery, tickets, timetables, and baggage tags; clothing suppliers for uniforms; and Boeing Corp. for all the tasks involved in remaking the inside and outside of BA's jets.

All the data were entered into Pertmaster for a schedule and critical path.

The resulting schedule did not please BA management. Boeing could not prepare a huge 747 in time for a December 4 gala launch date. Uniform designs were also going to delay the entire project.

An analysis of the earliest possible date that all items for a refurbished airplane could be ready (new paint, upholstery, carpets, trim, and so on) revealed that there were just sufficient materials to totally convert a smaller Boeing 737 that was available in the Seattle plant. Critical path analysis also showed that uniforms—the work of British designer Roland Klein—would have to be launched six months later in a separate ceremony.

The smaller 737 was outfitted just in time for a brilliant light show in an auditorium specially built in a Heathrow Airport hangar. Ground vehicles were also prepared in time.

Source: *Industrial Management and Data Systems* (March–April 1986): 6–7.

Work Breakdown Structure   A **work breakdown structure** (WBS) defines the project by dividing it into its major subcomponents, which are then subdivided into more detailed subcomponents, and so on. Gross requirements for people, supplies, and equipment are also estimated in this planning phase. The work breakdown structure typically decreases in size from top to bottom and is indented like this:

Level
1   Project
2   Major tasks in the project
3   Subtasks in major tasks
4   Activities to be completed

This hierarchical framework can be illustrated with the development of Microsoft's operating system, Windows Vista. As we see in Figure 8.3, the project, creating a new operating system, is labelled 1.0. The first step is to identify the major tasks in the project (level 2). Two examples would be development of graphic user interfaces (GUIs) (1.1) and creating compatibility with previous versions of Windows (1.2). The major subtasks for 1.2 are creating a team to handle compatibility with Windows XP (1.21), another for Windows 2000 (1.22), and another with Windows 98 (1.23). Then each major subtask is broken down into level-4 activities that need to be done, such as importing files created in Windows XP (1.231). There are usually many level-4 activities.

Identifying Activity Times and Other Resources

Once the activities have been identified, the time required and other resources (e.g., money, labour, raw materials) for each activity are determined. In practice, identifying these input data is a complicated task involving a fair amount of expertise and competence on the project leader's part. For example, many individuals will automatically present inflated time estimates, especially if their job is on the line if they fail to complete the activity on time. The project leader has to be able to recognize such inaccuracies and adjust estimates accordingly.

Project Management Techniques: PERT and CPM

When the questions in the project planning phase have been addressed, we move on to the project scheduling phase. The **program evaluation and review technique (PERT)** and the **critical path method (CPM)** are two popular decision modeling procedures that help managers answer the questions in this phase, even for large and complex projects. They were developed because there was a critical need for a better way to manage projects (see the History box).

Although some people still view PERT and CPM as separate techniques and refer to them by their original names, the two are similar in their basic approach. The growing practice, therefore, is to refer to PERT and CPM simply as *project management* techniques.

A work breakdown structure details the activities in a project.

Activity times need to be estimated.

PERT and CPM are two popular project management techniques.

FIGURE 8.3

Work Breakdown Structure

Level	Level ID Number	Activity
1	1.0	Develop/launch Windows Vista Operating System
2	1.1	Development of GUIs
2	1.2	Ensure compatibility with earlier Windows versions
3	1.21	Compatibility with Windows XP
3	1.22	Compatibility with Windows 2000
3	1.23	Compatibility with Windows 98
4	1.231	Ability to import files

Source: Adapted from J. Heizer and B. Render. *Operations Management*, 8/e. Upper Saddle River, NJ: Prentice Hall, 2006.

HISTORY   How PERT and CPM Started

Managers have been planning, scheduling, monitoring, and controlling large-scale projects for hundreds of years, but it has only been in the past 50 years that decision modeling techniques have been applied to major projects. One of the earliest techniques was the *Gantt chart*. This type of chart shows the start and finish times of one or more activities, as shown in the accompanying chart.

In 1958, the Special Projects Office of the U.S. Navy developed the program evaluation and review technique (PERT) to plan and control the Polaris missile program. This project involved the coordination of thousands of contractors. Today, PERT is still used to monitor countless government contract schedules. At about the same time (1957), the critical path method (CPM) was developed by J. E. Kelly of Remington Rand and M. R. Walker of Du Pont. Originally, CPM was used to assist in the building and maintenance of chemical plants at Du Pont.

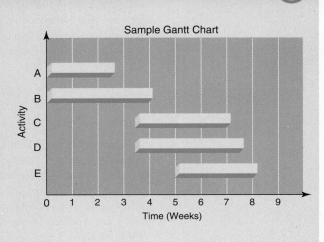

PERT versus CPM   The primary difference between PERT and CPM is in the way the time needed for each activity in the project is estimated. In PERT, each activity has three time estimates, which are combined to determine the expected activity completion time and its variance. PERT is considered a *probabilistic* technique; it allows us to find the probability that the entire project will be completed by a specific due date.

In contrast, CPM uses a *deterministic* approach. It estimates the completion time of each activity using just a single time estimate. This estimate, called the *normal* or *standard time*, is the time we estimate it will take under typical conditions to complete the activity. In some cases, CPM also associates a second time estimate with each activity. This estimate, called the *crash time*, is the shortest time it would take to finish an activity if additional funds and resources were allocated to the activity.

> PERT is a probabilistic technique, whereas CPM is a deterministic technique.

As noted previously, identifying these time estimates is a complicated task in most real-world projects. In our discussions in this chapter, however, we will assume that the time estimates (single time estimates in CPM and three time estimates in PERT) are available for each activity.

Project Management Example: General Foundry, Inc.

General Foundry, Inc., a metal works plant in Ontario, has long been trying to avoid the expense of installing air pollution control equipment. The local environmental protection group has recently given the foundry 16 weeks to install a complex air filter system on its main smokestack. General Foundry has been warned that it may be forced to close unless the device is installed in the allotted period. Lester Harky, the managing partner, wants to make sure that installation of the filtering system progresses smoothly and on time.

General Foundry has identified the eight activities that need to be performed in order for the project to be completed. When the project begins, two activities can be simultaneously started: building the internal components for the device (activity A) and the modifications necessary for the floor and roof (activity B). The construction of the collection stack (activity C) can begin when the internal components are completed. Pouring the concrete floor and installing the frame (activity D) can start as soon as the internal components are completed and the roof and floor have been modified.

After the collection stack has been constructed, two activities can begin: building the high-temperature burner (activity E) and installing the pollution control system (activity F).

The air pollution device can be installed (activity G) after the concrete floor has been poured, the frame has been installed, and the high-temperature burner has been built. Finally, after the control system and pollution device have been installed, the system can be inspected and tested (activity H).

All these activities and precedence relationships seem rather confusing and complex when they are described in text, as we just did. It is therefore convenient to list all the activity information in a table, as shown in Table 8.1. We see in the table that activity A is listed as an **immediate predecessor** of activity C. Likewise, both activities D and E must be performed prior to starting activity G.

It is enough to list only the immediate predecessors for each activity.

Note that it is enough to list just the *immediate predecessors* for each activity. For example, in Table 8.1, since activity A precedes activity C and activity C precedes activity E, the fact that activity A precedes activity E is implicit. This relationship need not be explicitly shown in the activity precedence relationships.

Networks consist of nodes that are connected by arcs.

When there are many activities in a project with fairly complicated precedence relationships, it is difficult for an individual to comprehend the complexity of the project from just the tabular information. In such cases, a visual representation of the project, using a **project network**, is convenient and useful. A project network is a diagram of all the activities in a project and the precedence relationships among them. We now illustrate how to construct a project network for General Foundry, Inc.

Drawing the Project Network

Two types of project networks—AON and AOA.

There are two approaches to drawing a project network: **activity on node (AON) network**, and **activity on arc (AOA) network**. Although both approaches are popular, many of the project management software packages, including Microsoft Project 2000, use AON networks. For this reason, although we illustrate both types of project networks next, we focus on AON networks in all our subsequent discussions in this chapter.

Nodes denote activities in an AON network.

Activity on Node (AON) Network   Recall from the discussion in Chapter 5 that a network consists of nodes (or points) and arcs (or lines) that connect the nodes together. In an AON approach, we denote each activity by a node. The arcs represent the precedence relationships between the activities.

Arcs denote precedence relationships.

In the General Foundry example, there are two activities (A and B) that do not have any predecessors. We draw separate nodes for each of these activities, as shown in Figure 8.4 on the next page. Although not required, it is usually convenient to have a unique starting activity for a project. We have therefore included a **dummy activity** called Start in Figure 8.4. This dummy activity does not really exist and takes up zero time and resources. Activity Start is an immediate predecessor for both activities A and B, and serves as the unique starting activity for the entire project.

TABLE 8.1			
Activities and Their Immediate Predecessors for General Foundry	ACTIVITY	DESCRIPTION	IMMEDIATE PREDECESSORS
	A	Build internal components	—
	B	Modify roof and floor	—
	C	Construct collection stack	A
	D	Pour concrete and install frame	A, B
	E	Build high-temperature burner	C
	F	Install pollution control system	C
	G	Install air pollution device	D, E
	H	Inspect and test	F, G

FIGURE 8.4

Beginning AON Network for General Foundry

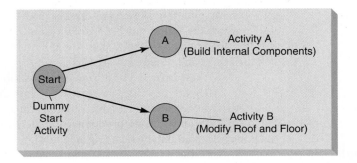

We now show the precedence relationships using arcs (shown as the arrow symbols: →). For example, an arrow from activity Start to activity A indicates that Start is a predecessor for activity A. In a similar fashion, we draw an arrow from Start to B.

Next, we add a new node for activity C. Since activity A precedes activity C, we draw an arc from node A to node C (see Figure 8.5). Likewise, we first draw a node to represent activity D. Then, since activities A and B both precede activity D, we draw arcs from A to D, and B to D (see Figure 8.5).

We proceed in this fashion, adding a separate node for each activity and a separate arc for each precedence relationship that exists. The complete AON project network for the General Foundry project example is shown in Figure 8.6.

Drawing a project network properly takes some time and experience. When we first draw a project network, it is not unusual that we place our nodes (activities) in the network in such a fashion that the arcs (precedence relationships) are not simple straight lines. The arcs might intersect each other or even face in opposite directions. For example, if we had switched the location of the nodes for activities E and F in Figure 8.6, the arcs from F to H and E to G would have intersected. Although such a project network is perfectly valid, it is good practice to have a well-drawn network. One rule that we especially recommend is to place the nodes in such a fashion that all arrows point in the same direction. To achieve this, we suggest that you first get a rough draft version of the network, making sure all the relationships are shown. Then you can redraw the network to make appropriate changes in the location of the nodes.

It is convenient, but not required, to have unique starting and ending activities in a project.

As with the unique starting node, it is convenient to have the project network finish with a unique ending node. In the General Foundry example, it turns out that a unique activity H is the last activity in the project. We therefore automatically have a unique ending node.

In situations in which a project has multiple ending activities, we include a dummy ending activity. This is an activity that does not exist and takes up zero time or resources.

This dummy activity has all the multiple ending activities in the project as immediate predecessors. We illustrate this type of situation in Solved Problem 8-1 at the end of this chapter.

FIGURE 8.5

Intermediate AON Network for General Foundry

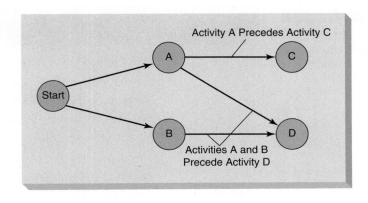

FIGURE 8.6   **Complete AON Network for General Foundry**

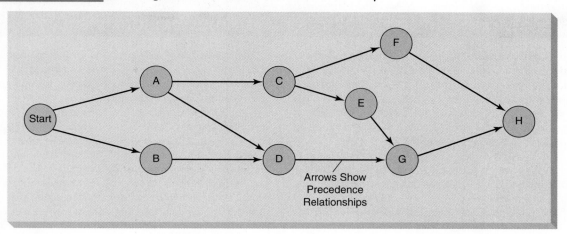

In AOA networks, arcs denote activities. Nodes denote events.

Activity on Arc (AOA) Network   In an AOA project network, we represent activities by arcs (shown as arrow symbols: →). A node represents an **event**, which marks the start or completion time of an activity. We usually identify an event (node) by a number. The complete AOA project network for General Foundry's problem, shown in Figure 8.7, is drawn as discussed in the following paragraphs.

Activity A starts at event 1 and ends at event 2. Likewise, activity B starts at event 1 and ends at event 3. Activity C, whose only immediate predecessor is activity A, starts at node 2 and ends at node 4. Activity D, however, has two predecessors (i.e., A and B). Hence, we need both activities A and B to end at event 3, so that activity D can start at that event. However, we cannot have multiple activities with common starting and ending nodes in an AOA network. To overcome this difficulty, in such cases, we may need to add a dummy arc (activity) to enforce the precedence relationship. The dummy activity, shown in Figure 8.7 as a dashed line, is inserted between events 2 and 3 to make the diagram reflect the precedence between A and D. Remember that the dummy activity does not really exist in the project and takes up zero time.

Dummy activities may be needed in AOA networks to show all precedence relationships.

FIGURE 8.7   **Complete AOA Network (with Dummy Activities) for General Foundry**

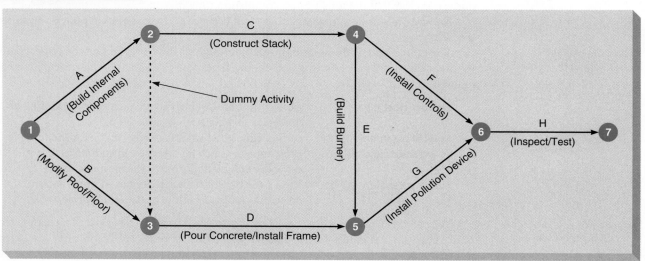

DECISION MODELING IN ACTION
Project Management at Norigen Communications Inc.

Norigen Communications Inc. is a privately held Canadian integrated telecommunications provider that offers a range of communication services to businesses across Canada. In the course of a year it grew rapidly from 15 to 500 employees and made several strategic acquisitions. Headquartered in Toronto, Norigen offers services in Toronto, Montreal, Calgary, Vancouver, Edmonton, Ottawa, and Hamilton.

Allan McNeely, Norigen's director of program management, attributes the company's ability to handle its incredible rate of growth to the use of project management techniques, which helped to keep the company on track.

"The powerful thing about what we're doing here at Norigen is the way we're set up," says McNeely. "We have a formal program management office where we handle not only all of our projects, but we also handle the processes... Project Management gets into every aspect of the business—it's absolutely full spectrum."

McNeely directs a team of nine project managers who implement projects within different departments. Projects that involve several departments are called programs and are supervised by a program manager.

An important criterion for hiring managers is their skill in both the art and science of project management. "Science" refers to the quantitative problem solving skills (finance, computer expertise, construction of Gantt charts), while "art" encompasses communications and business skills.

McNeely hires project coordinators based largely on their proven ability to implement project management techniques. Once they join the organization, they can learn the necessary skills on the job and eventually assume the responsibility of project managers.

Source: Computing Canada (October 13, 2000), Vol. 26. No. 21.

The remainder of the AOA project network for General Foundry's example is quite simple to draw and should be self-explanatory.

8.3   DETERMINING THE PROJECT SCHEDULE

Look back to Figure 8.6 for a moment to see General Foundry's completed AON project network. Once this project network has been drawn to show all the activities and their precedence relationships, the next step is to determine the project schedule. That is, we need to identify the planned starting and ending time for each activity.

Critical path analysis helps determine the project schedule.

Let us assume General Foundry estimates the time required for each activity, in weeks, as shown in Table 8.2. The table indicates that the total time for all eight of General Foundry's activities is 25 weeks. However, since several activities can take place simultaneously, it is clear that the total project completion time may be much less than 25 weeks.

To find out just how long the project will take, we perform a **critical path analysis** for the network.

The critical path is the longest path in the network.

The critical path is the *longest* time path through the network. To find the critical path, we calculate two distinct starting and ending times for each activity. These are defined as follows:

Earliest start time (EST) = earliest time at which an activity can start, assuming all predecessors have been completed

Earliest finish time (EFT) = earliest time at which an activity can be finished

Latest start time (LST) = latest time at which an activity can start so as to not delay the completion time of the entire project

Latest finish time (LFT) = latest time by which an activity has to finish so as to not delay the completion time of the entire project

We use a two-pass procedure to find the project schedule.

We use a two-pass process, consisting of a forward pass and a backward pass, to determine these time schedules for each activity. The earliest times (EST and EFT) are determined during the **forward pass**. The latest times (LST and LFT) are determined during the **backward pass**.

	TABLE 8.2		

Time Estimates for General Foundry

ACTIVITY	DESCRIPTION	TIME (WEEKS)
A	Build internal components	2
B	Modify roof and floor	3
C	Construct collection stack	2
D	Pour concrete and install frame	4
E	Build high-temperature burner	4
F	Install pollution control system	3
G	Install air pollution device	5
H	Inspect and test	2
	Total time (Weeks)	25

Forward Pass

The *forward pass* identifies all the earliest times.

To clearly show the activity schedules on the project network, we use the notation shown in Figure 8.8. The EST of an activity is shown in the top left corner of the node denoting that activity. The EFT is shown in the top right corner. The latest times, LST and LFT, are shown in the bottom left and bottom right corners, respectively.

Earliest Start Time Rule   Before an activity can start, *all* its immediate predecessors must be finished.

All predecessor activities must be completed before an activity can begin.

- If an activity has only a single immediate predecessor, its EST equals the EFT of the predecessor.
- If an activity has multiple immediate predecessors, its EST is the maximum of all EFT values of its predecessors. That is,

$$EST = \text{Maximum \{EFT of all immediate predecessors\}} \qquad (8\text{-}1)$$

Earliest Finish Time Rule   The earliest finish time (EFT) of an activity is the sum of its earliest start time (EST) and its activity time. That is,

$$EFT = EST + \text{Activity time} \qquad (8\text{-}2)$$

	FIGURE 8.8	

Notation Used in Nodes for Forward and Backward Pass

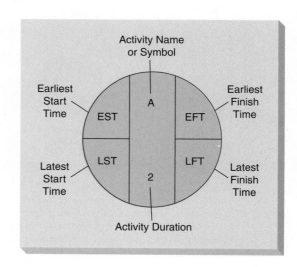

Figure 8.9 shows the complete project network for General Foundry's project, along with the EST and EFT values for all activities. In what follows, we describe how these values have been calculated.

EFT = EST + activity time

Since activity Start has no predecessors, we begin by setting its EST to 0. That is, activity Start can begin at the *end* of week 0, which is the same as the beginning of week 1.[1] If activity Start has an EST of 0, its EFT is also 0, since its activity time is 0.

Next, we consider activities A and B, both of which have only Start as an immediate predecessor. Using the earliest start time rule, the EST for both activities A and B equals zero, which is the EFT of activity Start. Now, using the earliest finish time rule, the EFT for A is 2 (= 0 + 2), and the EFT for B is 3 (= 0 + 3).

Since activity A precedes activity C, the EST of C equals the EFT of A (= 2). The EFT of C is therefore 4 (= 2 + 2).

EST of an activity = maximum EFT of all predecessor activities

We now come to activity D. Both activities A and B are immediate predecessors for B. Whereas A has an EFT of 2, activity B has an EFT of 3. Using the earliest finish time rule, we compute the EST of activity D as follows:

$$\text{EST of D} = \text{Max}(\text{EFT of A, EFT of B}) = \text{Max}(2, 3) = 3$$

FIGURE 8.9   **Earliest Start and Earliest Finish Times for General Foundry**

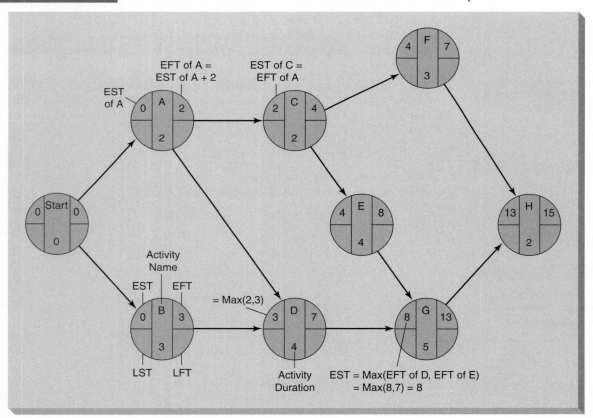

---

[1] In writing all earliest and latest times, we need to be consistent. For example, if we specify that the EST value of activity *i* is week 4, do we mean the *beginning* of week 4 or the *end* of week 4? Note that if the value refers to the *beginning* of week 4, it means that week 4 is also available for performing activity *i*. In our discussions, *all* earliest and latest time values correspond to the *end* of a period. That is, if we specify that the EST of activity *i* is week 4, it means that activity *i* starts work only at the beginning of week 5.

The EFT of D equals 7 (= 3 + 4). Next, both activities E and F have activity C as their only immediate predecessor. Therefore, the EST for both E and F equals 4 (= EFT of C). The EFT of E is 8 (= 4 + 4), and the EFT of F is 7 (= 4 + 3).

Activity G has both activities D and E as predecessors. Using the earliest start time rule, its EST is therefore the maximum of the EFT of D and the EFT of E. Hence, the EST of activity G equals 8 (= maximum of 7 and 8), and its EFT equals 13 (= 8 + 5).

Finally, we come to activity H. Since it also has two predecessors, F and G, the EST of H is the maximum EFT of these two activities. That is, the EST of H equals 13 (= maximum of 13 and 7). This implies that the EFT of H is 15 (= 13 + 2). Since H is the last activity in the project, this also implies that the earliest time in which the entire project can be completed is 15 weeks.

Although the forward pass allows us to determine the earliest project completion time, it does not identify the critical path. In order to identify this path, we need to now conduct the backward pass to determine the LST and LFT values for all activities.

Backward Pass

The backward pass finds all latest times.

Just as the forward pass began with the first activity in the project, the backward pass begins with the last activity in the project. For each activity, we first determine its LFT value, followed by its LST value. The following two rules are used in this process.

Latest Finish Time Rule This rule is again based on the fact that before an activity can start, all its immediate predecessors must be finished.

- If an activity is an immediate predecessor for just a single activity, its LFT equals the LST of the activity that immediately follows it.
- If an activity is an immediate predecessor to more than one activity, its LFT is the minimum of all LST values of all activities that immediately follow it. That is,

$$\text{LFT} = \text{Minimum\{LST of all immediate followers\}} \qquad (8\text{-}3)$$

Latest Start Time Rule The latest start time (LST) of an activity is the difference of its latest finish time (LFT) and its activity time. That is,

$$\text{LST} = \text{LFT} - \text{Activity time} \qquad (8\text{-}4)$$

Figure 8.10 on the next page shows the complete project network for General Foundry's project, along with LST and LFT values for all activities. In what follows, we analyze how these values were calculated.

LST = LFT – Activity time

We begin by assigning an LFT value of 15 weeks for activity H. That is, we specify that the latest finish time for the entire project is the same as its earliest finish time. Using the latest start time rule, the LST of activity H is equal to 13 (= 15 − 2).

Since activity H is the lone succeeding activity for both activities F and G, the LFT for both F and G equals 13. This implies that the LST of G is 8 (= 13 − 5), and the LST of F is 10 (= 13 − 3).

Proceeding in this fashion, the LFT of E is 8 (= LST of G), and its LST is 4 (= 8 − 4). Likewise, the LFT of D is 8 (= LST of G), and its LST is 4 (= 8 − 4).

We now consider activity C, which is an immediate predecessor to two activities: E and F. Using the latest finish time rule, we compute the LFT of activity C as follows:

LFT of an activity = minimum LST of all activities that follow

$$\text{LFT of C} = \text{Min(LST of E, LST of F)} = \text{Min(4, 10)} = 4$$

The LST of C is computed as 2 (= 4 − 2). Next, we compute the LFT of B as 4 (= LST of D), and its LST as 1 (= 4 − 3).

We now consider activity A. We compute its LFT as 2 (= minimum of LST of C and LST of D). Hence, the LST of activity A is 0 (= 2 − 2). Finally, both the LFT and LST of activity Start are equal to 0.

FIGURE 8.10   **Latest Start and Latest Finish Times for General Foundry**

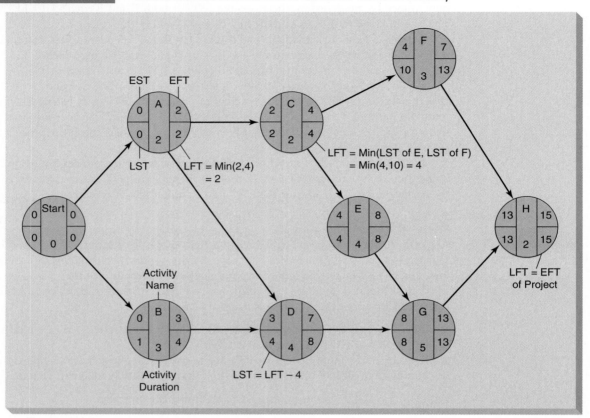

Calculating Slack Time and Identifying the Critical Path(s)

After we have computed the earliest and latest times for all activities, it is a simple matter to find the amount of **slack time**, or free time, that each activity has. Slack is the length of time an activity can be delayed without delaying the entire project. Mathematically,

$$\text{Slack} = \text{LST} - \text{EST} \quad \text{or} \quad \text{Slack} = \text{LFT} - \text{EFT} \tag{8-5}$$

Slack time is free time for an activity.

Table 8.3 summarizes the EST, EFT, LST, LFT, and slack time for all of General Foundry's activities. Activity B, for example, has 1 week of slack time since its LST is 1 and its EST is 0 (alternatively, its LFT is 4 and its EFT is 3). This means that activity B can be delayed by up to one week, and the whole project can still finish in 15 weeks.

Critical activities have no slack time.

Conversely, activities A, C, E, G, and H have *no* slack time. This means that none of them can be delayed without delaying the entire project. If Harky wants to reduce the total project time, he will have to reduce the length of one of these activities.

Critical path is the longest path through the network.

These activities are called *critical activities* and are said to be on the **critical path**. The critical path is a continuous path through the project network that

- starts at the first activity in the project (Start in our example)
- terminates at the last activity in the project (H in our example)
- includes only critical activities (i.e., activities with no slack time)

		EARLIEST START, EST	EARLIEST FINISH, EFT	LATEST START, EST	LATEST FINISH, EFT	SLACK, LST − EST	ON CRITICAL PATH?
TABLE 8.3	ACTIVITY						
General Foundry's Schedule and Slack Times	A	0	2	0	2	0	Yes
	B	0	3	1	4	1	No
	C	2	4	2	4	0	Yes
	D	3	7	4	8	1	No
	E	4	8	4	8	0	Yes
	F	4	7	10	13	6	No
	G	8	13	8	13	0	Yes
	H	13	15	13	15	0	Yes

General Foundry's critical path, Start-A-C-E-G-H, is shown in network form in Figure 8.11. The total project completion time of 15 weeks corresponds to the longest path in the network.

A project can have multiple critical paths.

Multiple Critical Paths In General Foundry's case, there was just a single critical path. Can a project have multiple critical paths? The answer is yes. For example, what if the time required for activity B had been estimated as 4 weeks, instead of 3 weeks? Due to this

FIGURE 8.11 **Critical Path and Slack Times for General Foundry**

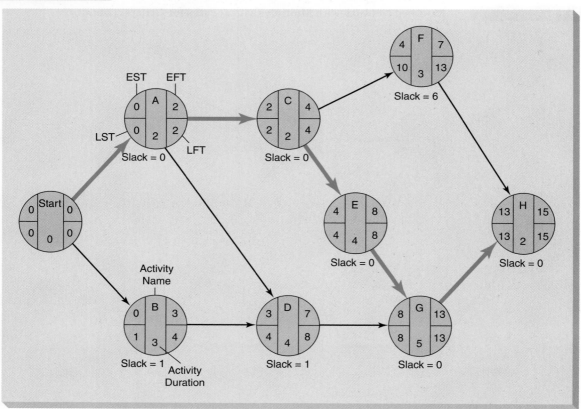

change, the earliest and latest times for activities B and D would have to be revised, as shown in Figure 8.12.

Note that in addition to the original critical path (Start-A-C-E-G-H), there is now a second critical path (Start-B-D-G-H). Delaying an activity on either critical path will delay the completion of the entire project.

Total Slack Time versus Free Slack Time

Let us now refer back to our original project network in Figure 8.11. Consider activities B and D, which have slacks of 1 week each. Does it mean that we can delay *each* activity by 1 week, and still complete the project in 15 weeks? The answer is no, as discussed next.

Let's assume that activity B is delayed by 1 week. It has used up its slack of 1 week and now has an EFT of 4. This implies that activity D now has an EST of 4 and an EFT of 8. Note that these are also its LST and LFT values, respectively. That is, activity D also has no slack time now. Essentially, the slack of 1 week that activities B and D had was *shared* between them. Delaying either activity by 1 week causes not only that activity, but also the other activity, to lose its slack. This type of a slack time is referred to as *total slack*. Typically, when two or more noncritical activities appear successively in a path, they share total slack.

> Total slack time is shared among more than one activity.

In contrast, consider the slack time of 6 weeks in activity F. Delaying this activity decreases only its slack time and does not affect the slack time of any other activity. This type of slack time is referred to as *free slack*. Typically, if a noncritical activity has critical activities on either side of it in a path, its slack time is free slack.

> Free slack time is associated with a single activity.

FIGURE 8.12 **Modified Network with Multiple Critical Paths for General Foundry**

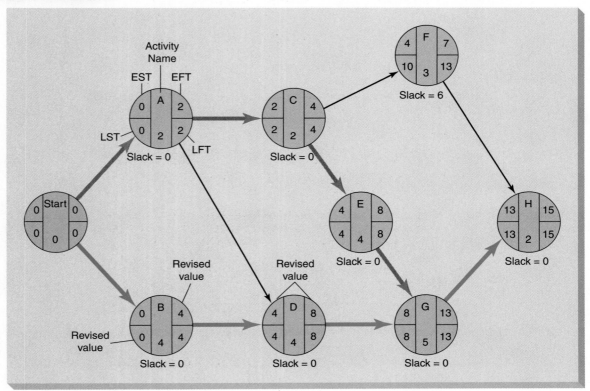

We can also use an approach based on linear programming (LP) to determine the earliest and latest times for each activity in a project network. To do so, we solve two LP problems: the first to identify the earliest times and the second to identify the latest times. The only input data required are the activity precedence information (see Figure 8.11) and the activity times. Let us use the General Foundry example to illustrate the LP models.

Linear Programming Model to Determine the Earliest Times

The decision variables are the start times.

As with all the LP models we formulated in Chapters 2–5, we begin by defining the decision variables. For each activity, i, we define E_i as its EST. Since there are eight activities in General Foundry's project, there are eight decision variables in the LP model.

Minimization objective

Next, we formulate the objective function. Since we are interested in finding the EST for each activity, the objective of the LP model here is to *minimize* the sum of all E_i values. That is,

$$\text{Minimize } E_A + E_B + E_C + E_D + E_E + E_F + E_G + E_H$$

Finally, we formulate the constraints. The only constraints in this LP model are those that enforce the precedence relationships between activities (shown in the project network in Figure 8.11). We write one constraint for each precedence relationship (i.e., arc) in the network.

Constraints enforce the precedence relationships.

Consider, for example, the precedence relationship between activities A and C. Activity A starts at E_A, and its duration is 2 weeks. Therefore, activity A finishes at time $(E_A + 2)$. This implies that the earliest start time of activity C (i.e., E_C) can be *no earlier* than $(E_A + 2)$. We can express this mathematically as

$$E_C \geq E_A + 2 \qquad (\text{precedence A} \rightarrow \text{C})$$

In a similar fashion, we can express all other activity precedence relationships as follows

$$
\begin{aligned}
E_D &\geq E_A + 2 &&(\text{precedence A} \rightarrow \text{D}) \\
E_D &\geq E_B + 3 &&(\text{precedence B} \rightarrow \text{D}) \\
E_E &\geq E_C + 2 &&(\text{precedence C} \rightarrow \text{E}) \\
E_F &\geq E_C + 2 &&(\text{precedence C} \rightarrow \text{F}) \\
E_G &\geq E_D + 4 &&(\text{precedence D} \rightarrow \text{G}) \\
E_G &\geq E_E + 4 &&(\text{precedence E} \rightarrow \text{G}) \\
E_H &\geq E_F + 3 &&(\text{precedence F} \rightarrow \text{H}) \\
E_H &\geq E_G + 5 &&(\text{precedence G} \rightarrow \text{H}) \\
\text{All } E_i &\geq 0 &&(\text{nonnegativity})
\end{aligned}
$$

Excel Solution Screenshot 8.1A on the next page shows the formula view of the Excel layout for General Foundry's LP model to determine EST values. This layout follows the same structure and logic we have used in earlier chapters for all LP models. That is, we have modeled all parameters (solution value, objective coefficients, and constraint coefficients) associated with a decision variable in a separate column of the worksheet. We have then computed the objective function and left-hand-side (LHS) formulas for all constraints using Excel's SUMPRODUCT function. Finally, we have algebraically modified each constraint so that all variables are in the LHS of the equation. For example, the precedence relationship between activities A and C has been modified as $[E_C - E_A \geq 2]$.

File: 8-1.xls

Solver entries are Target Cell, Changing Cells, and constraints.

The Solver entries and solution for this LP model are shown in Screenshot 8.1B on the next page. As expected, the EST values for all activities (shown in cells B5:I5)

Excel Layout to Compute General Foundry's Earliest Starting Times Using Linear Programming

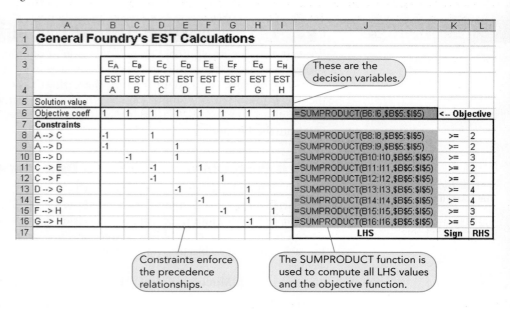

	A	B	C	D	E	F	G	H	I	J	K	L
1	**General Foundry's EST Calculations**											
2												
3		E_A	E_B	E_C	E_D	E_E	E_F	E_G	E_H			
4		EST A	EST B	EST C	EST D	EST E	EST F	EST G	EST H			
5	Solution value											
6	Objective coeff	1	1	1	1	1	1	1	1	=SUMPRODUCT(B6:I6,$B$5:$I$5)	<-- Objective	
7	Constraints											
8	A --> C	-1		1						=SUMPRODUCT(B8:I8,$B$5:$I$5)	>=	2
9	A --> D	-1			1					=SUMPRODUCT(B9:I9,$B$5:$I$5)	>=	2
10	B --> D		-1		1					=SUMPRODUCT(B10:I10,$B$5:$I$5)	>=	3
11	C --> E			-1		1				=SUMPRODUCT(B11:I11,$B$5:$I$5)	>=	2
12	C --> F			-1			1			=SUMPRODUCT(B12:I12,$B$5:$I$5)	>=	2
13	D --> G				-1			1		=SUMPRODUCT(B13:I13,$B$5:$I$5)	>=	4
14	E --> G					-1		1		=SUMPRODUCT(B14:I14,$B$5:$I$5)	>=	4
15	F --> H						-1		1	=SUMPRODUCT(B15:I15,$B$5:$I$5)	>=	3
16	G --> H							-1	1	=SUMPRODUCT(B16:I16,$B$5:$I$5)	>=	5
17										LHS	Sign	RHS

These are the decision variables.

Constraints enforce the precedence relationships.

The SUMPRODUCT function is used to compute all LHS values and the objective function.

are the same obtained earlier using the two-pass procedure. The EST value of 13 weeks for activity H implies the entire project has an earliest completion time of 15 (= 13 + 2) weeks.

Solver Entries to Compute General Foundry's Earliest Starting Times Using Linear Programming

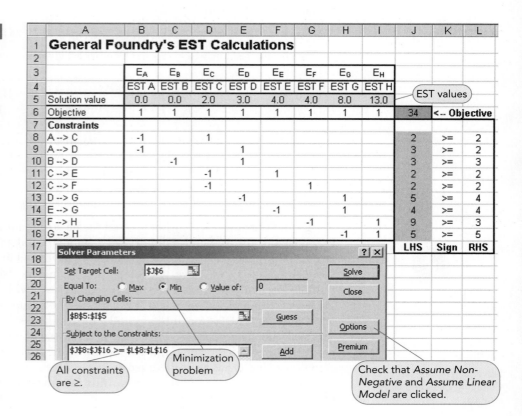

	A	B	C	D	E	F	G	H	I	J	K	L
1	**General Foundry's EST Calculations**											
2												
3		E_A	E_B	E_C	E_D	E_E	E_F	E_G	E_H			
4		EST A	EST B	EST C	EST D	EST E	EST F	EST G	EST H			
5	Solution value	0.0	0.0	2.0	3.0	4.0	4.0	8.0	13.0			
6	Objective	1	1	1	1	1	1	1	1	34	<-- Objective	
7	Constraints											
8	A --> C	-1		1						2	>=	2
9	A --> D	-1			1					3	>=	2
10	B --> D		-1		1					3	>=	3
11	C --> E			-1		1				2	>=	2
12	C --> F			-1			1			2	>=	2
13	D --> G				-1			1		5	>=	4
14	E --> G					-1		1		4	>=	4
15	F --> H						-1		1	9	>=	3
16	G --> H							-1	1	5	>=	5
17										LHS	Sign	RHS

EST values

Solver Parameters

Set Target Cell: $J$6

Equal To: ○ Max ● Min ○ Value of: 0

By Changing Cells:

$B$5:$I$5 | Guess

Subject to the Constraints:

$J$8:$J$16 >= $L$8:$L$16 | Add

Solve | Close | Options | Premium

All constraints are ≥.

Minimization problem

Check that *Assume Non-Negative* and *Assume Linear Model* are clicked.

Excel Notes

- The CD-ROM that accompanies this textbook contains the Excel file for each example problem discussed here. The relevant file name is shown in the margin next to each example.
- In each of our Excel layouts, for clarity, Changing Cells are shaded yellow, the Target Cell is shaded green, and cells containing the left-hand-side (LHS) formula for each constraint are shaded blue. Although these colours are not apparent in the screen captures shown in the textbook, they are seen in the Excel files in your CD-ROM.
- Also, to make the equivalence of the written formulation and the Excel layout clear, our Excel layouts show the decision variable names used in the written formulation of the model. Note that these names have no role in using Solver to solve the model.

Linear Programming Model to Determine the Latest Times

Maximization objective function

We need to constrain the project completion time.

For each activity i, we define decision variable L_i as its LST. In this LP model, the objective is to *maximize* the sum of all activity start times since we want to find the *latest* start times. However, we need to ensure that the entire project finishes at its earliest completion time (i.e., in 15 weeks, as computed in Screenshot 8.1B). Hence, in addition to the constraints defining the activity precedence relationships, we also constrain the finish time of the *last activity* in the project. In General Foundry's case, we know that the last activity is H. Hence, we set the latest finish time of activity H to 15 weeks.

The complete LP model can be written as

$$\text{Maximize } L_A + L_B + L_C + L_D + L_E + L_F + L_G + L_H$$

subject to

$$
\begin{array}{ll}
L_C \geq L_A + 2 & (\text{precedence A} \rightarrow \text{C}) \\
L_D \geq L_A + 2 & (\text{precedence A} \rightarrow \text{D}) \\
L_D \geq L_B + 3 & (\text{precedence B} \rightarrow \text{D}) \\
L_E \geq L_C + 2 & (\text{precedence C} \rightarrow \text{E}) \\
L_F \geq L_C + 2 & (\text{precedence C} \rightarrow \text{F}) \\
L_G \geq L_D + 4 & (\text{precedence D} \rightarrow \text{G}) \\
L_G \geq L_E + 4 & (\text{precedence E} \rightarrow \text{G}) \\
L_H \geq L_F + 3 & (\text{precedence F} \rightarrow \text{H}) \\
L_H \geq L_G + 5 & (\text{precedence G} \rightarrow \text{H}) \\
L_H + 2 = 15 & (\text{latest finish time of H}) \\
\text{All } L_i \geq 0 & (\text{nonnegativity})
\end{array}
$$

File: 8-2.xls

Excel Solution Screenshot 8.2 on the next page shows the Excel layout and Solver entries for this LP model. In this model also, we have algebraically modified each constraint so that all variables are in the LHS.

Here again, as expected, the LST values for all activities (shown in cells B5:I5 in Screenshot 8.2) are the same obtained earlier using the two-pass procedure.

8.5 VARIABILITY IN ACTIVITY TIMES

Activity times are subject to variability.

In identifying all earliest and latest times so far, and the associated critical path(s), we have adopted the CPM approach of assuming that all activity times are known and fixed constants. That is, there is no variability in activity times. However, in practice, it is likely that activity completion times vary depending on various factors.

SCREENSHOT 8.2 **Excel Layout and Solver Entries to Compute General Foundry's Latest Starting Times Using Linear Programming**

	A	B	C	D	E	F	G	H	I	J	K	L
1	**General Foundry's LST Calculations**											
2												
3		L_A	L_B	L_C	L_D	L_E	L_F	L_G	L_H			
4		LST A	LST B	LST C	LST D	LST E	LST F	LST G	LST H		LST values	
5	Solution value	0.0	1.0	2.0	4.0	4.0	10.0	8.0	13.0			
6	Objective coeff	1	1	1	1	1	1	1	1	42	<-- Objective	
7	**Constraints**											
8	A --> C	-1		1							2	>=	2
9	A --> D	-1			1						4	>=	2
10	B --> D		-1		1						3	>=	3
11	C --> E			-1		1					2	>=	2
12	C --> F			-1			1				8	>=	2
13	D --> G				-1			1			4	>=	4
14	E --> G					-1		1			4	>=	4
15	F --> H						-1		1		3	>=	3
16	G --> H							-1	1		5	>=	5
17	Project Finish								1		13	=	13
18											LHS	Sign	RHS

(Solver Parameters dialog box)

Solver Parameters   ? ✕

Set Target Cell: `$J$6`

Equal To: ⦿ Max ○ Min ○ Value of: 0

By Changing Cells:

`$B$5:$I$5`

Subject to the Constraints:

`$J$17 = $L$17`
`$J$8:$J$16 >= $L$8:$L$16`

[Solve] [Close] [Guess] [Options] [Premium] [Add]

Annotations:
- LST values
- Activity H must start at week 13 so that project can finish by week 15.
- Check ≥ 0 and linear model.
- Precedence constraints
- Maximization problem

For example, building internal components (activity A) for General Foundry is estimated to finish in 2 weeks. Clearly, factors such as late arrival of raw materials, absence of key personnel, and so on, could delay this activity. Suppose activity A actually ends up taking 3 weeks. Since A is on the critical path, the entire project will now be delayed by 1 week to 16 weeks. If we had anticipated completion of this project in 15 weeks, we would obviously miss our deadline.

The preceding discussion implies that we cannot ignore the impact of variability in activity times when deciding the schedule for a project. In general, there are three approaches that we can use to analyze the impact of variability in activity times on the completion time of the project:

There are three approaches to studying the impact of variability in activity times.

■ The first approach is to provide for variability by building in "buffers" to activity times. For example, if we know based on past experience that a specific activity has exceeded its time estimate by 20% on several occasions, we can build in a 20% time buffer for this activity by inflating its time estimate by 20%. There are, of course, a few obvious drawbacks to this approach. For example, if every activity has inflated time estimates due to these buffers, the entire project duration will be artificially large. Incidentally, practising project managers will tell you that providing time buffers is not practical because the people concerned with the activity will just proceed more slowly than planned on the activity because they know that the buffer exists (i.e., the duration will stretch to fit the allotted time).

DECISION MODELING IN ACTION
Project Management and Software Development

Although computers have revolutionized how companies conduct business and have allowed some organizations to achieve a long-term competitive advantage in the marketplace, the software that controls these computers is often more expensive than intended and takes longer to develop than expected. In some cases, large software projects are never fully completed. The London Stock Exchange, for example, had an ambitious software project called TAURUS that was intended to improve computer operations at the exchange. The TAURUS project, which cost hundreds of millions of dollars, was never completed. After numerous delays and cost overruns, the project was finally halted. The FLORIDA system, an ambitious software development project for the Department of Health and Rehabilitative Services for the state of Florida, was also delayed, cost more than expected, and didn't operate as

everyone had hoped. Although not all software development projects are delayed or over budget, it has been estimated that more than half of all software projects cost more than 189% of their original projections.

To control large software projects, many companies are now using project management techniques. Ryder Systems, Inc.; American Express Financial Advisors; and United Airlines have all created project management departments for their software and information systems projects. These departments have the authority to monitor large software projects and make changes to deadlines, budgets, and resources used to complete software development efforts.

Source: Julia King. "Tough Love Reins in IS Projects," *Computerworld* (June 19, 1995): 1–2.

■ The second approach, known as PERT analysis, employs a probability-based analysis of the project completion time. A primary advantage of this approach is that it is fairly easy to understand and implement. However, the drawback is that we have to make certain assumptions regarding the probability distributions of activity times. We discuss this approach in detail in this section.

■ The third approach uses computer simulation, the topic of Chapter 11. This approach, while typically being the most difficult approach from an implementation point of view, is also likely to be the most comprehensive in terms of its capabilities and analysis. We illustrate this approach for a project management problem in Solved Problem 11-4 at the end of Chapter 11.

PERT Analysis

PERT uses three time estimates for each activity.

Recall that in our study so far, we have estimated the duration for each activity by using a single time estimate (such as two weeks for activity A in General Foundry's project). In practice, such durations may be difficult to estimate for many activities. For example, think about the difficulty you would have if someone asked you to estimate exactly how long your next assignment in this course will take to complete (remember, your estimate must be guaranteed to be sufficient and should not include any unnecessary buffers). To correct for this difficulty, in PERT analysis we base the duration of each activity on three separate time estimates:

Optimistic time (a)   =   time an activity will take if everything goes as planned. In estimating this value, there should be only a small probability (say, 1/100) that the activity time will be ≤ *a*.

Pessimistic time (b)   =   time an activity will take assuming very unfavourable conditions. In estimating this value, there should also be only a small probability that the activity time will be ≥ *b*.

Most likely time (m)   =   most realistic estimate of the time required to complete an activity.

When using PERT, you must often assume that **activity time estimates** follow the **beta probability distribution** (see Figure 8.13 on the next page). This continuous distribution

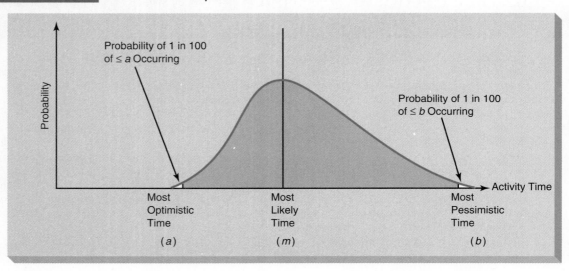

FIGURE 8.13   **Beta Probability Distribution with Three Time Estimates**

The beta probability distribution is often used to describe activity times.

has been found to be very appropriate, in many cases, for determining the expected value and variance for activity completion times.

To find the **expected activity time**, t, the beta distribution weights the three time estimates as follows:

$$t = (a + 4m + b)/6 \qquad (8\text{-}6)$$

That is, the **most likely time (m)** is given four times the weight of the **optimistic time (a)** and **pessimistic time (b)**. The time estimate t, computed using Equation 8-6 for each activity, is used in the project network to compute all earliest and latest times.

To compute the *dispersion* or **variance of activity completion time**, we use the formula:[2]

$$\text{Variance} = [(b - a)/6]^2 \qquad (8\text{-}7)$$

The standard deviation of activity completion time is the square root of the variance. Hence,

$$\text{Standard deviation} = \sqrt{\text{Variance}} = (b - a)/6 \qquad (8\text{-}8)$$

Let us assume that Lester Harky has estimated the optimistic, most likely, and pessimistic times for each activity in General Foundry's project, as shown in columns C, D, and E, respectively, in Screenshot 8.3. Using these estimates in Equations 8.6 through 8.8, we compute the expected time, variance, and standard deviation for each activity. These values are shown in columns F, G, and H, respectively. Note that expected times shown in column F in Screenshot 8.3 are, in fact, the activity times we used in our earlier computation and identification of the critical path.

File: 8-3.xls

Probability of Project Completion

The critical path analysis helped us determine that General Foundry's expected project completion time is 15 weeks. Lester Harky knows, however, that there is significant variation in the time estimates for several activities. Variation in activities that are on the

---

[2] This formula is based on the statistical concept that from one end of the beta distribution to the other is 6 standard deviations (± 3 standard deviations from the mean). Since $(b - a)$ is 6 standard deviations, the variance is $[(b - a)/6]^2$.

SCREENSHOT 8.3   **Excel Layout to Compute General Foundry's Expected Times and Variances**

Column G =
$$\left(\frac{\text{Column E} - \text{Column C}}{6}\right)^2$$

	A	B	C	D	E	F	G	H
1	**Time Estimates (in Weeks) for General Foundry**							
2								
3	Activity	Description	Optimistic time (a)	Most likely time (m)	Pessimistic time (b)	Expected time	Variance	Standard deviation
4	A	Build internal components	1	2	3	2.0	0.11	0.33
5	B	Modify roof and floor	2	3	4	3.0	0.11	0.33
6	C	Construct collection stack	1	2	3	2.0	0.11	0.33
7	D	Pour concrete and install frame	2	4	6	4.0	0.44	0.67
8	E	Build high-temperature burner	1	4	7	4.0	1.00	1.00
9	F	Install pollution control system	1	2	9	3.0	1.78	1.33
10	G	Install air pollution device	3	4	11	5.0	1.78	1.33
11	H	Inspect and test	1	2	3	2.0	0.11	0.33

Three time estimates for each activity

Column F =
$$\frac{\text{Column C} + 4 \times \text{Column D} + \text{Column E}}{6}$$

=SQRT (column G)

critical path can affect the overall project completion time—possibly delaying it. This is one occurrence that worries Harky considerably.

PERT uses the variance of critical path activities to help determine the variance of the overall project. Project variance is computed by summing variances of critical activities:

We compute the project variance by summing variances of only those activities on the critical path.

$$\text{Project variance} = \Sigma \text{ (Variances of activities on critical path)} \qquad (8\text{-}9)$$

From Screenshot 8.3 we know that the variance of activity A is 0.11, variance of activity C is 0.11, variance of activity E is 1.00, variance of activity G is 1.78, and variance of activity H is 0.11. Hence, the total project variance and project standard deviation may be computed as

$$\text{Project variance } (\sigma_p^2) = 0.11 + 0.11 + 1.00 + 1.78 + 0.11 = 3.11$$

which implies

$$\text{Project standard deviation } (\sigma_p) = \sqrt{\text{Project variance}} = \sqrt{3.11} = 1.76$$

How can this information be used to help answer questions regarding the probability of finishing the project on time? PERT makes two more assumptions: (1) total project completion times follow a normal probability distribution and (2) activity times are statistically independent. With these assumptions, the bell-shaped normal curve shown in Figure 8.14 on the next page can be used to represent project completion dates. This normal curve implies that there is a 50% chance the project completion time will be less than 15 weeks and a 50% chance that it will exceed 15 weeks.

For Harky to find the probability that his project will be finished on or before the 16-week deadline, he needs to determine the appropriate area under the normal curve. The standard normal equation can be applied as follows:

$$Z = (\text{Due date} - \text{Expected date of completion})/\sigma_p \qquad (8\text{-}10)$$

$$= (16 \text{ weeks} - 15 \text{ weeks})/1.76 \text{ weeks} = 0.57$$

where Z is the number of standard deviations the due date or target date lies from the mean or expected date.

FIGURE 8.14

**Probability Distribution
for Project Completion
Times**

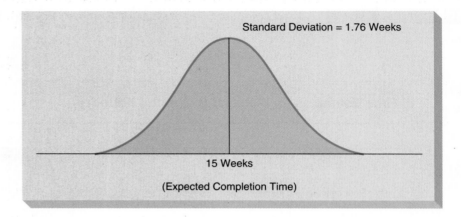

*Computing the probability
of project completion.*

Referring to the Normal Table in Appendix C, we find a probability of 0.7157. Thus, there is a 71.6% chance that the pollution control equipment can be put in place in 16 weeks or less. This is shown in Figure 8.15.

Determining Project Completion Time for a Given Confidence Level

Lester Harky is extremely worried that there is only a 71.6% chance that the pollution control equipment can be put in place in 16 weeks or less. He thinks that it may be possible for him to plead with the environmental group for more time. However, before he approaches the group, he wants to arm himself with sufficient information about the project. Specifically, he wants to find the deadline by which he has a 99% chance of completing the project. He hopes to use his analysis to convince the group to agree to this extended deadline.

Clearly, this due date would be greater than 16 weeks. However, what is the exact value of this new due date? To answer this question, we again use the assumption that General Foundry's project completion time follows a normal probability distribution with a mean of 15 weeks and a standard deviation of 1.76 weeks.

For Harky to find the due date under which the project has a 99% chance of completion, he needs to determine the Z value corresponding to 99%, as shown in Figure 8.16.

*Computing the due date for
a given probability.*

Referring again to the Normal Table in Appendix C, we identify a Z value of 2.33 as being closest to the probability of 0.99. That is, Harky's due date should be 2.33 standard

FIGURE 8.15

**Probability of General
Foundry Meeting the
16-Week Deadline**

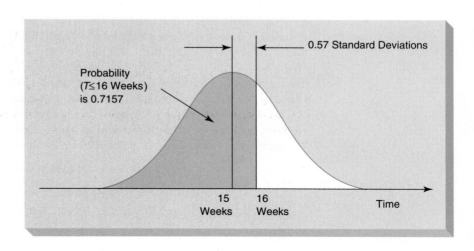

FIGURE 8.16

Z-Value for 99% Probability of Project Completion

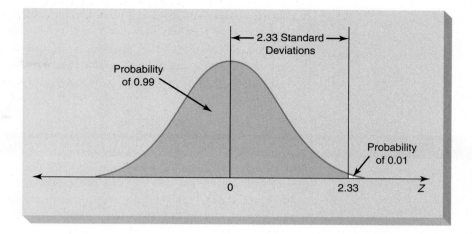

FIGURE 8.16

Z-Value for 99% Probability of Project Completion

deviations above the mean project completion time. Starting with the standard normal equation (see Equation 8-10), we can solve for the due date and rewrite the equation as

$$\text{Due date} = \text{Expected completion time} + Z \times \sigma_p \qquad (8\text{-}11)$$

$$= 15 + 2.33 \times 1.76 = 19.1 \text{ weeks}$$

Hence, if Harky can get the environmental group to agree to give him a new deadline of 19.1 weeks (or more), he can be 99% sure of finishing the project on time.

Variability in Completion Time of Noncritical Paths

In our discussion so far, we focus exclusively on the variability in the completion times of activities on the critical path. This seems logical since these activities are, by definition, the more important activities in a project network. However, when there is variability in activity times, it is important that we also investigate the variability in the completion times of activities on *noncritical* paths.

Consider, for example, activity D in General Foundry's project. Recall from Table 8.3 that this is a noncritical activity, with a slack time of 1 week. We have therefore not considered the variability in D's time in computing the probabilities of project completion times. We observe, however, that D has a variance of 0.44 (see Screenshot 8.3). In fact, the pessimistic completion time for D is 6 weeks. This means that if D ends up taking its pessimistic time to finish, the project will not finish in 15 weeks, even though D is not a critical activity.

For this reason, in determining probabilities of project completion times, we need to pay attention not only to the critical path(s), but also to noncritical paths, especially those with relatively large variances. If a noncritical path has a high probability of being completed late, it can sometimes evolve into a critical path.

Noncritical paths with large variances should also be closely monitored.

What Project Management Has Provided So Far

Project management techniques have thus far been able to provide Lester Harky with several valuable pieces of management information:

1. The project's expected completion date is 15 weeks.

2. There is a 71.6% chance that the equipment will be in place within the 16-week deadline. PERT analysis can easily find the probability of finishing by any date Harky is interested in.

3. Five activities (A, C, E, G, and H) are on the critical path. If any one of these is delayed for any reason, the entire project will be delayed.

4. Three activities (B, D, F) are not critical but have some slack time built in. This means that Harky can delay these activities, if needed.

5. A detailed schedule of activity starting and ending dates has been made available (see Table 8.3).

8.6   MANAGING PROJECT COSTS AND OTHER RESOURCES

The techniques discussed so far are very good for planning, scheduling, and monitoring a project with respect to time. We have not, however, considered another very important factor—project *cost*. In this section, we begin by investigating how costs can be planned and scheduled. Then we see how costs can be monitored and controlled.

Planning and Scheduling Project Costs: Budgeting Process

The budgeting process determines the budget per period of the project.

The overall approach in the budgeting process of a project is to determine how much is to be spent every week or month. This is accomplished as follows.

Three Steps of the Budgeting Process

1. Identify all costs associated with each of the activities. Then add these costs together to get one estimated cost or budget for each activity. When dealing with a large project, several activities may be combined into larger **work packages**. A work package is simply a logical collection of activities. Since the General Foundry project is quite small, each activity can be a work package.

2. Convert the budgeted cost per activity into a cost per time period. To do this, assume that the cost of completing any activity is spent at a linear rate over time. Thus, if the budgeted cost for a given activity is $48 000 and the activity's expected time is four weeks, the budgeted cost per week is $12 000 (= $48 000/4 weeks).

3. Using the earliest and latest start times, find out how much money should be spent during each week or month to finish the project by the due date.

Budgeting for General Foundry   Let us apply this budgeting process to the General Foundry problem. Lester Harky has carefully computed the costs associated with each of his eight activities. He has also divided the total budget for each activity by the activity's expected time to determine the weekly budget for the activity. The budget for activity A, for example, is $22 000 (see Table 8.4). Since its expected time (t) is 2 weeks, $11 000 is spent each week to complete the activity. Table 8.4 also provides two pieces of data we found earlier: the EST and LST for each activity.

Looking at the total of the budgeted activity costs, we see that the entire project will cost $308 000. Finding the weekly budget will help Harky determine how the project is progressing on a week-to-week basis.

Weekly budgeting using EST values.

The weekly budget for the project is developed from the data in Table 8.4. The EST for activity A is 0. Since A takes 2 weeks to complete, its weekly budget of $11 000 should be spent in weeks 1 and 2. For activity B, the EST is 0, the expected completion time is 3 weeks, and the budgeted cost per week is $10 000. Hence, $10 000 should be spent for activity B in each of weeks 1, 2, and 3. Using the EST, we can find the exact weeks during which the budget for each activity should be spent. These weekly amounts can be summed for all

TABLE 8.4	ACTIVITY	EARLIEST START TIME, EST	LATEST START TIME, LST	EXPECTED TIME, t	TOTAL BUDGETED COST ($)	BUDGETED COST PER WEEK ($)
Activity Cost for General Foundry	A	0	0	2	22 000	11 000
	B	0	1	3	30 000	10 000
	C	2	2	2	26 000	13 000
	D	3	4	4	48 000	12 000
	E	4	4	4	56 000	14 000
	F	4	10	3	30 000	10 000
	G	8	8	5	80 000	16 000
	H	13	13	2	16 000	8 000
					Total 308 000	

activities to arrive at the weekly budget for the entire project. For example, a total of $21 000 each should be spent during weeks 1 and 2. These weekly totals can then be added to determine the total amount that should be spent to date (total to date). All these computations are shown in Table 8.5.

Those activities along the critical path must spend their budgets at the times shown in Table 8.5. The activities that are *not* on the critical path, however, can be started at a later date. This concept is embodied in the LST for each activity. Thus, if LST values are used, another budget can be obtained. This budget will delay the expenditure of funds until the last possible moment. The procedures for computing the budget when LST is used are the same as when EST is used. The results of the new computations are shown in Table 8.6.

Compare the budgets given in Tables 8.5 and 8.6. The amount that should be spent to date (total to date) for the budget in Table 8.5 reveals the earliest possible time that funds can be expended. In contrast, the budget in Table 8.6 uses fewer financial resources

TABLE 8.5   **Budgeted Cost (in Thousands of Dollars) for General Foundry, Using Earliest Start Times**

	WEEK															TOTAL
ACTIVITY	1	2	3	4	5	6	7	8	9	10	11	12	13	14	15	
A	11	11														22
B	10	10	10													30
C			13	13												26
D				12	12	12	12									48
E					14	14	14	14								56
F					10	10	10									30
G									16	16	16	16	16			80
H														8	8	16
																308
Total per week	21	21	23	25	36	36	36	14	16	16	16	16	16	8	8	
Total to date	21	42	65	90	126	162	198	212	228	244	260	276	292	300	308	

| TABLE 8.6 | | | | | | | | | | | | | | | Budgeted Cost (in Thousands of Dollars) for General Foundry, Using Latest Start Times |

ACTIVITY	1	2	3	4	5	6	7	8	9	10	11	12	13	14	15	TOTAL
A	11	11														22
B		10	10	10												30
C			13	13												26
D					12	12	12	12								48
E					14	14	14	14								56
F											10	10	10			30
G									16	16	16	16	16			80
H														8	8	16
																308
Total per week	11	21	23	23	26	26	26	26	16	16	26	26	26	8	8	
Total to date	11	32	55	78	104	130	156	182	198	214	240	266	292	300	308	

The two tables form the feasible budget ranges.

in the first few weeks since it was prepared using LST values. That is, the budget in Table 8.6 shows the latest possible time that funds can be expended and still finish the project on time. Therefore, Lester Harky can use any budget between these feasible ranges and still complete the air pollution project on time. These two tables form feasible budget ranges.

This concept is illustrated in Figure 8.17, which plots the total-to-date budgets for EST and LST.

Monitoring and Controlling Project Costs

Costs must be tracked to see if the project is on budget.

Budgets like the ones shown in Figure 8.17 are normally developed before the project is started. Then, once the project is underway, funds expended should be monitored and controlled to ensure that the project is progressing on schedule and that cost overruns are kept to a minimum. The status of the entire project should be checked periodically.

Lester Harky wants to know how his air pollution project is going. It is now the end of the sixth week of the 15-week project. Activities A, B, and C have been fully completed. These activities incurred costs of $20 000, $36 000, and $26 000, respectively. Activity D is only 10% complete, and so far the cost expended on it has been $6000. Activity E is 20% complete, with an incurred cost of $20 000. Activity F is 20% complete, with an incurred cost of $4000. Activities G and H have not been started. Is the air pollution project on schedule? What is the value of work completed? Are there any cost overruns?

Compute value of work completed for each activity.

One way to measure the value of the work completed (or the cost-to-date) for an activity is to multiply its total budgeted cost times the percentage of completion for that activity.[3] That is,

$$\text{Value of work completed} = \text{Percent of work completed} \times \text{Total activity budget} \quad \textbf{(8-12)}$$

To determine the cost difference (i.e., the amount of overrun or underrun) for an activity, the value of work completed is subtracted from the actual cost. Hence,

$$\text{Cost difference} = \text{Actual cost} - \text{Value of work completed} \quad \textbf{(8-13)}$$

---

[3] The percentage of completion for each activity can be measured in many ways. For example, we might use the ratio of labour hours expended to total labour hours estimated.

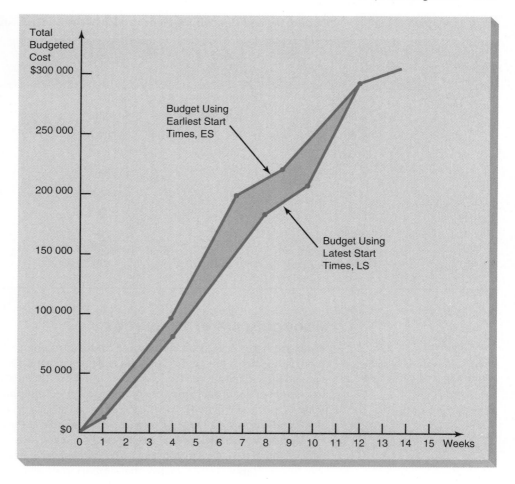

FIGURE 8.17

Budget Ranges for General Foundry

If a cost difference is negative, it implies there is a cost underrun. In contrast, if the number is positive, there has been a cost overrun.

Table 8.7 summarizes this information for General Foundry's project. The second column shows the total budgeted cost (from Table 8.4), and the third column contains the percent of completion for each activity. Using these data and the actual cost expended for each activity, we can compute the value of work completed and the cost difference for every activity.

Compute cost underruns and overruns.

Activity D, for example, has a value of work completed of $4800 (= $48 000 × 10%). The actual cost is $6000, implying there is a cost overrun of $1200. The cost difference for all activities can be added to determine the total project overrun or underrun. In General Foundry's case, we can see from Table 8.7 that there is a $12 000 cost overrun at the end of the sixth week. The total value of work completed so far is only $100 000, and the actual cost of the project to date is $112 000.

How do these costs compare with the budgeted costs for week 6? If Harky had decided to use the budget for ESTs (see Table 8.5), we can see that $162 000 should have been spent.

Thus, the project is behind schedule and there are cost overruns. Harky needs to move faster on this project to finish on time. He must also control future costs carefully to try to eliminate the current cost overrun of $12 000. To monitor and control costs, the budgeted amount, the value of work completed, and the actual costs should be computed periodically.

TABLE 8.7			Monitoring and Controlling Budgeted Costs for General Foundry		
ACTIVITY	TOTAL BUDGETED COST ($)	PERCENT OF COMPLETION	VALUE OF WORK COMPLETED ($)	ACTUAL COST ($)	ACTIVITY DIFFERENCE ($)
A	22 000	100	22 000	20 000	−2 000
B	30 000	100	30 000	36 000	6 000
C	26 000	100	26 000	26 000	0
D	48 000	10	4 800	6 000	1 200
E	56 000	20	11 200	20 000	8 800
F	30 000	20	6 000	4 000	−2 000
G	80 000	0	0	0	0
H	16 000	0	0	0	0
Total			100 000	112 000	12 000

Overrun

Managing Other Resources

Other resources can also be planned for and monitored.

So far, we have focused on monitoring and controlling costs. Although costs are clearly important, other resources (e.g., labour, machinery, materials) may also need to be carefully planned for and monitored for a project to finish on schedule. For example, activity E (build high-temperature burner) may need some specialized equipment. Likewise, installing the air pollution device (activity G) may need a specialist. Managers must be aware of such requirements and ensure that the right resources are available at the right time.

Just as we constructed a weekly budget using activity schedules and costs (see Tables 8.5 and 8.6), we can construct weekly requirement charts for any resource. Assume that Lester Harky has estimated the support staff requirement for each of the eight

DECISION MODELING IN ACTION
Costing Projects at Nortel

Many companies, including Nortel, a large telecommunications company, are benefiting from project management. With more than 20 000 active projects worth a total of more than $2 billion, effectively managing projects at Nortel has been challenging. Getting the needed input data, including times and costs, can be difficult.

Like most companies, Nortel used standard accounting practices to monitor and control costs. This typically involves allocating costs to each department. Most projects, however, span multiple departments. This can make it very difficult to get timely cost information. Project managers often get project cost data later than they wanted. Because the cost data are allocated to departments, the data are often not detailed enough to help manage projects and get an accurate picture of true project costs.

To get more accurate cost data for project management, Nortel adopted an activity-based costing (ABC) method

often used in manufacturing operations. In addition to standard cost data, each project activity was coded with a project identification number and a regional researched development location number. This greatly improved the ability of project managers to control costs. Because some of the month-end costing processes were simplified, the approach also lowered project costs in most cases. Project managers also were able to get more detailed costing information. Because the cost data were coded for each project, getting timely feedback was also possible. In this case, getting good input data reduced project costs, reduced the time needed to get critical project feedback, and made project management more accurate.

Source: Chris Dorey. "The ABCs of R&D at Nortel," *CMA Magazine* (March 1998): 19–22.

TABLE 8.8			

Support Staff Requirement for General Foundry

ACTIVITY	DESCRIPTION	SUPPORT STAFF NEEDED PER WEEK
A	Build internal components	4
B	Modify roof and floor	5
C	Construct collection stack	6
D	Pour concrete and install frame	4
E	Build high-temperature burner	3
F	Install pollution control system	4
G	Install air pollution device	7
H	Inspect and test	2

activities in the project, as shown in Table 8.8 above. For example, during each week that activity A is in progress, Harky needs four support staffers to be available.

Table 8.9 shows the weekly support staff needed for General Foundry's project using EST values. A graph that plots the total resource (such as labour) needed per period (*y*-axis) versus time (*x*-axis) is called a *resource-loading chart*.

8.7 PROJECT CRASHING

While managing a project, it is not uncommon for a project manager to be faced with either (or both) of the following situations: (1) the project is behind schedule and (2) the scheduled project completion time has been moved forward. In either situation, some or all of the remaining activities need to be speeded up in order to finish the project by the desired due date. The process by which we shorten the duration of a project in the cheapest manner possible is called project **crashing**.

Reducing a project's duration is called crashing.

As mentioned earlier, CPM is a deterministic technique in which each activity has two sets of time. The first is the *normal* or *standard* time that we used in our computation of

TABLE 8.9																	

Support Staff Required for General Foundry Using Earliest Start Times

	WEEK																
ACTIVITY	1	2	3	4	5	6	7	8	9	10	11	12	13	14	15		TOTAL
A	4	4															8
B	5	5	5														15
C			6	6													12
D				4	4	4	4										16
E					3	3	3	3									12
F					4	4	4										12
G									7	7	7	7	7				35
H														2	2		4
																	114
Total per week	9	9	11	10	11	11	11	3	7	7	7	7	7	2	2		
Total to date	9	18	29	39	50	61	72	75	82	89	96	103	110	112	114		

Crash time is the shortest duration of an activity.

earliest and latest times. Associated with this normal time is the *normal cost* of the activity, which we used in Section 8.6 to schedule and monitor the cost of the project.

The second time is the **crash time**, which is defined as the shortest duration required to complete an activity. Associated with this crash time is the **crash cost** of the activity. Usually, we can shorten an activity by adding extra resources (e.g., equipment, people). Hence, it is logical for the crash cost of an activity to be higher than its normal cost.

The amount by which an activity can be shortened (i.e., the difference between its normal time and crash time) depends on the activity in question. We may not be able to shorten some activities at all. For example, if a casting needs to be heat-treated in the furnace for 48 hours, adding more resources does not help shorten the time. In contrast, we may be able to shorten some activities significantly (e.g., frame a house in three days instead of 10 days by using three times as many workers).

We want to find the cheapest way of crashing a project to the desired due date.

Likewise, the cost of crashing (or shortening) an activity depends on the nature of the activity. Managers are usually interested in speeding up a project at the least additional cost. Hence, in choosing which activities to crash, and by how much, we need to ensure the following:

- the amount by which an activity is crashed is, in fact, permissible
- taken together, the shortened activity durations will enable us to finish the project by the due date
- the total cost of crashing is as small as possible

In what follows, we first illustrate how to crash a small project using simple calculations that can be performed by hand. Then, we describe an LP-based approach that can be used to determine the optimal crashing scheme for projects of any size.

Crashing General Foundry's Project (Hand Calculations)

Suppose that General Foundry has been given only 13 weeks (instead of 16 weeks) to install the new pollution control equipment or face a court-ordered shutdown. As you recall, the length of Lester Harky's critical path was 15 weeks. Which activities should Harky crash, and by how much, in order to meet this 13-week due date? Naturally, Harky is interested in speeding up the project by two weeks at the least additional cost.

Crashing a project using hand calculations involves four steps, as follows.

Four Steps of Project Crashing

1. Compute the crash cost per week (or other time period) for all activities in the network. If crash costs are assumed to be linear over time, the following formula can be used:

$$\text{Crash cost per period} = \frac{(\text{Crash cost} - \text{Normal cost})}{(\text{Normal time} - \text{Crash time})} \qquad (8\text{-}14)$$

2. Using the current activity times, find the critical path(s) in the project network. Identify the critical activities.

3. If there is only one critical path, then select the activity on this critical path that (a) can still be crashed and (b) has the smallest crash cost per period. Crash this activity by one period.

   If there is more than one critical path, then select one activity from each critical path such that (a) each selected activity can still be crashed and (b) the total crash cost per period of *all* selected activities is the smallest. Crash each activity by one period. Note that the same activity may be common to more than one critical path.

4. Update all activity times. If the desired due date has been reached, stop. If not, return to Step 2.

TABLE 8.10

Normal and Crash Data for General Foundry

ACTIVITY	TIME (WEEKS) NORMAL	TIME (WEEKS) CRASH	COST ($) NORMAL	COST ($) CRASH	CRASH COST PER WEEK ($)	CRITICAL PATH?
A	2	1	22 000	22 750	750	Yes
B	3	1	30 000	34 000	2 000	No
C	2	1	26 000	27 000	1 000	Yes
D	4	3	48 000	49 000	1 000	No
E	4	2	56 000	58 000	1 000	Yes
F	3	2	30 000	30 500	500	No
G	5	2	80 000	84 500	1 500	Yes
H	2	1	16 000	19 000	3 000	Yes

General Foundry's normal and crash times, and normal and crash costs, are shown in Table 8.10 above. Note, for example, that activity B's normal time is three weeks (the estimate used in computing the critical path), and its crash time is one week. This means that activity B can be shortened by up to two weeks if extra resources are provided. The cost of these additional resources is $4000 (= difference between the crash cost of $34 000 and the normal cost of $30 000). If we assume that the crashing cost is linear over time (i.e., the cost is the same each week), activity B's crash cost per week is $2000 (= $4000/2).

This calculation is shown in Figure 8.18. Crash costs for all other activities can be computed in a similar fashion.

Steps 2, 3, and 4 can now be applied to reduce General Foundry's project completion time at a minimum cost. For your convenience, we show the project network for General Foundry again in Figure 8.19 on page 351.

The current critical path (using normal times) is Start-A-C-E-G-H, in which Start is just a dummy starting activity. Of these critical activities, activity A has the lowest

FIGURE 8.18

Crash and Normal Times and Costs for Activity B

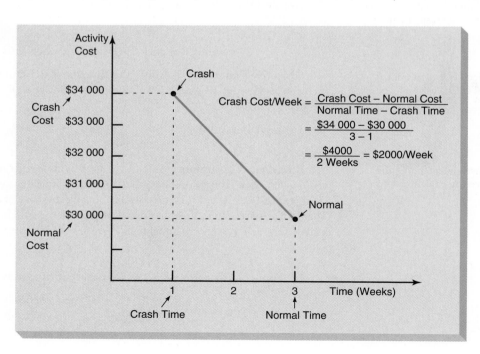

crash cost per week of $750. Harky should therefore crash activity A by one week to reduce the project completion time to 14 weeks. The cost is an additional $750. Note that activity A cannot be crashed any further since it has reached its crash limit of one week.

There are now two critical paths.

At this stage, the original path Start-A-C-E-G-H remains critical, with a completion time of 14 weeks. However, a new path Start-B-D-G-H is also critical now, with a completion time of 14 weeks. Hence, any further crashing must be done to both critical paths.

On each of these critical paths, we need to identify one activity that can still be crashed. We also want the total cost of crashing an activity on each path to be the smallest. We might be tempted to simply pick the activities with the smallest crash cost per period in each path. If we do this, we would select activity C from the first path and activity D from the second path. The total crash cost would then be $2000 (= $1000 + $1000).

Crashing activities common to more than one critical path may be cheaper.

But we spot that activity G is common to both paths. That is, by crashing activity G, we will simultaneously reduce the completion time of both paths. Even though the $1500 crash cost for activity G is higher than that for activities C and D, we would still prefer crashing G since the total cost is now only $1500 (compared with $2000 if we crash C and D).

Hence, to crash the project down to 13 weeks, Lester Harky should crash activity A by one week, and activity G by one week. The total additional cost is $2250 (= $750 + $1500).

Crashing General Foundry's Project Using Linear Programming

Although the preceding crashing procedure is simple for projects involving just a few activities, we can see how it can become extremely cumbersome to use for larger projects. Let us instead examine an LP-based approach that can be applied to projects of any size.

The data needed for General Foundry's LP model are the normal and crash time and cost data (see Table 8.10), and the activity precedence information (see Figure 8.19). We develop the model as follows.

Decision variables are start times and crash amounts.

Decision Variables   For each activity i, we define the following two decision variables:

$$T_i = \text{time at which activity } i \text{ starts}$$

$$C_i = \text{number of periods (weeks) by which activity } i \text{ is crashed}$$

Objective is to minimize total crash cost.

Objective Function   The objective function is to minimize the total cost of crashing the project down to 13 weeks. Using the crash cost per week, computed in Table 8.10, we can express this as

$$\text{Minimize crash cost} = \$750C_A + \$2000C_B + \$1000C_C + \$1000C_D + \$1000C_E$$
$$+ \$500C_F + \$1500C_G + \$3000C_H$$

Constraints defining the precedence relationships

Precedence Constraints   As in the LP models discussed earlier to determine the EST and LST values, these constraints describe the activity precedence relationships in the project (see Figure 8.19). The only difference is that now the duration of activity i can be reduced by C_i. That is, if activity A starts at T_A, it finishes at $(T_A + 2 - C_A)$. This implies that the start time of activity C (i.e., T_C) can be *no earlier* than $(T_A + 2 - C_A)$. We can express this mathematically as

$$T_C \geq T_A + 2 - C_A \text{ (precedence A} \rightarrow \text{C)}$$

In a similar fashion, we can express all other activity precedence relationships as follows:

$$T_D \geq T_A + 2 - C_A \text{ (precedence A} \rightarrow \text{D)}$$
$$T_D \geq T_B + 3 - C_B \text{ (precedence B} \rightarrow \text{D)}$$
$$T_E \geq T_C + 2 - C_C \text{ (precedence C} \rightarrow \text{E)}$$

FIGURE 8.19   **Critical Path and Slack Times for General Foundry**

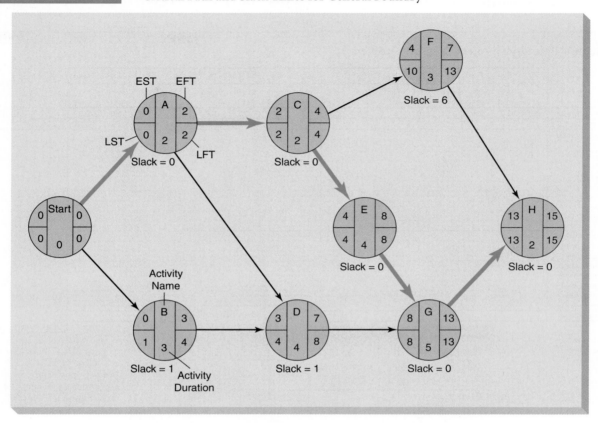

$$T_F \geq T_C + 2 - C_C \text{ (precedence C} \rightarrow \text{F)}$$
$$T_G \geq T_D + 4 - C_D \text{ (precedence D} \rightarrow \text{G)}$$
$$T_G \geq T_E + 4 - C_E \text{ (precedence E} \rightarrow \text{G)}$$
$$T_H \geq T_F + 3 - C_F \text{ (precedence F} \rightarrow \text{H)}$$
$$T_H \geq T_G + 5 - C_G \text{ (precedence G} \rightarrow \text{H)}$$
$$\text{All } T_i \text{ and } C_i \geq 0 \text{ (nonnegativity)}$$

Each activity can be crashed only by a finite amount.

Crash Time Limit Constraints   This set of constraints restricts the amount by which each activity can be crashed. Using the crash time limits given in Table 8.10, we can write these constraints as

$$C_A \leq 1 \quad C_B \leq 2 \quad C_C \leq 1$$
$$C_D \leq 1 \quad C_E \leq 2 \quad C_F \leq 1$$
$$C_G \leq 3 \quad C_H \leq 1$$

Constraint regarding project due date

Project Completion Constraint   Finally, we specify that the project must be completed in 13 weeks or less. Activity H, the last activity in the project, starts at time T_H. The normal time for H is two weeks, and C_H denotes the number of weeks by which its duration can be crashed. Hence, the actual duration of activity H is $(2 - C_H)$ and its completion time is $(T_H + 2 - C_H)$. We write this constraint as

$$T_H + 2 - C_H \leq 13$$

SCREENSHOT 8.4   **Excel Layout and Solver Entries for General Foundry's Crashing Problem**

Activity start times. *Crash values.* *Total crash cost.*

General Foundry's Project Crashing Problem

	T_A Start Act A	T_B Start Act B	T_C Start Act C	T_D Start Act D	T_E Start Act E	T_F Start Act F	T_G Start Act G	T_H Start Act H	C_A Crash Act A	C_B Crash Act B	C_C Crash Act C	C_D Crash Act D	C_E Crash Act E	C_F Crash Act F	C_G Crash Act G	C_H Crash Act H	LHS	Sign	RHS
Solution value	0.0	0.0	1.0	3.0	3.0	8.0	7.0	11.0	1.0	0.0	0.0	0.0	0.0	0.0	1.0	0.0			
Crash Cost									\$750	\$2,000	\$1,000	\$1,000	\$1,000	\$500	\$1,500	\$3,000	\$2,250		
Constraints																			
A --> C	-1		1						1								2	>=	2
A --> D	-1			1					1								4	>=	2
B --> D		-1		1						1							3	>=	3
C --> E			-1		1						1						2	>=	2
C --> F			-1			1					1						7	>=	2
D --> G				-1			1					1					4	>=	4
E --> G					-1		1						1				4	>=	4
F --> H						-1		1						1			3	>=	3
G --> H							-1	1							1		5	>=	5
Crash Limit A									1								1	<=	1
Crash Limit B										1							0	<=	2
Crash Limit C											1						0	<=	1
Crash Limit D												1					0	<=	1
Crash Limit E													1				0	<=	2
Crash Limit F														1			0	<=	1
Crash Limit G															1		1	<=	3
Crash Limit H																1	0	<=	1
Project Finish								1								-1	11	<=	11

Minimization objective.

The SUMPRODUCT function is used to compute all values in column R.

Solver Parameters   [? X]

- Set Target Cell: $R$6
- Equal To: ○ Max   ● Min   ○ Value of: 0
- By Changing Cells: $B$5:$Q$5   [Guess]
- Subject to the Constraints:
  $R$17:$R$25 <= $T$17:$T$25
  $R$8:$R$16 >= $T$8:$T$16   [Add]

[Solve] [Close] [Options] [Premium]

Precedence constraints.

Crash limit constraints and project deadline constraint.

Check ≥ 0 and linear model.

File: 8-4.xls

Excel Solution   Screenshot 8.4 above shows the Excel layout and Solver entries for General Foundry's project crashing LP model. As usual, we have algebraically modified each constraint so that all variables are on the LHS.

The results show that the General Foundry project can be crashed to 13 weeks at a cost of \$2250 (cell R6). To do so, activities A (cell J5) and G (cell P5) should be crashed by one week each. As expected, this is the same as the result we obtained earlier using hand calculations. Cells B5:I5 show the revised starting times for activities A through H, respectively.

8.8   USING MICROSOFT PROJECT TO MANAGE PROJECTS

The analyses discussed so far are effective for managing small projects. However, for managing large complex projects, specialized project management software is preferred. In this section, we provide a brief introduction to a popular example of such specialized software, Microsoft Project.

In this brief overview, we will not describe the full capabilities of this program but simply illustrate how it can be used to perform basic calculations in managing projects. We leave it to you to explore the advanced capabilities and functions of Microsoft Project (or any other project management software) in greater detail, either on your own or as part of an elective course in project management.

Microsoft Project is extremely useful in drawing project networks (Section 8.2), identifying the project schedule (Section 8.3), and managing project costs and other resources (Section 8.6). It does not, however, perform PERT probability calculations (Section 8.5), or have an LP-based procedure built in for project crashing (Section 8.7).

Creating a Project Schedule Using Microsoft Project

Let us consider the General Foundry project again. Recall from Section 8.2 that this project has eight activities. The first step is to define the activities and their precedence relationships. To do so, we start Microsoft Project and click **FILE|NEW** to open a blank project. We can now enter the project start date in the summary information that is first presented (see Screenshot 8.5A). Note that dates are referred to by actual calendar dates rather than as day 0, day 1, and so on. For example, the starting date for the General Foundry project was June 27, 2005, as shown in Screenshot 8.5A. Microsoft Project automatically updates the project finish date once we have entered all the project information. In Screenshot 8.5A the current date was specified as August 8, 2005 (8/8/05), and Microsoft Project estimated a finish date of Friday, October 7, 2005 (10/7/05).

Entering Activity Information   After entering the summary information, we now use the window shown in Screenshot 8.5B (on the next page) to enter all activity information. For each activity (or task, as Microsoft Project calls it), we enter its name and duration. Microsoft Project identifies tasks by numbers (e.g., 1, 2) rather than letters. Hence, for convenience, we have shown both the letter (e.g., A, B) and the description of the activity in the **TASK NAME** column in Screenshot 8.5B. By default, the duration is measured in days.

Microsoft Project is useful for project scheduling and control.

File: 8-5.mpp

First, we define a new project.

Project Summary Information in Microsoft Project

SCREENSHOT 8.5B   **Activity Entry in Microsoft Project for General Foundry**

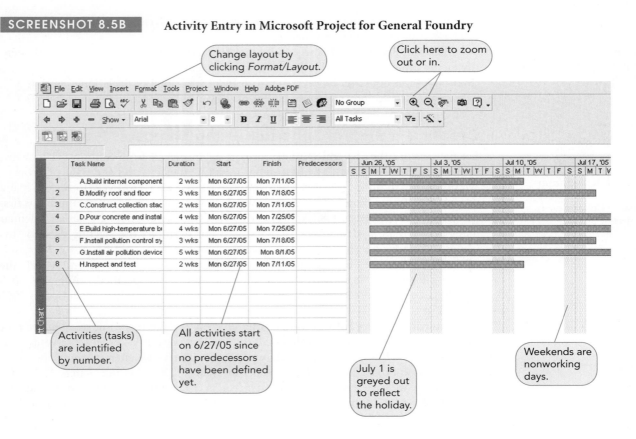

Next, we enter the activity information.

Durations

Activity	Time in Weeks
A	2
B	3
C	2
D	4
E	4
F	3
G	5
H	2

The schedule automatically takes nonworking days into account.

To specify weeks, we include the letter "*w*" after the duration of each activity. For example, we enter the duration of activity A as 2*w*.

As we enter the activities and durations, the software automatically inserts start and finish dates. Note that all activities have the same start date (i.e., 6/27/05) since we have not yet defined the precedence relationships. Also, as shown in Screenshot 8.5B, if the **GANTT CHART** option is selected in the **VIEW** menu, a horizontal bar corresponding to the duration of each activity appears on the right pane of the window.

Observe that Saturdays and Sundays are automatically greyed out in the Gantt chart to reflect the fact that these are nonworking days. In most project management software, we can link the entire project to a master calendar (or alternatively, link each activity to its own specific calendar). Additional nonworking days can be defined using these calendars. For example, we have used **TOOLS|CHANGE WORKING TIME** to specify July 1, 2005 (Canada Day), as a nonworking day in Screenshot 8.5B. This automatically extends all activity completion times by one day. Since activity A starts on Monday, June 27, 2005, and takes two weeks (i.e., 10 working days), its finish time is now Monday, July 11, 2005 (rather than Friday, July 8, 2005).

Defining Precedence Relationships   The next step is to define precedence relationships (or links) between these activities. There are two ways of specifying these links. The first is to enter the relevant activity numbers (e.g., 1, 2) in the **PREDECESSOR** column, as shown in Screenshot 8.5C for activities C and D. The other approach uses the Link icon. For example, to specify the precedence relationship between activities C and E, we click activity C first, hold down the Ctrl key, and then click activity E. We then click the **LINK** icon, as shown in Screenshot 8.5C. As soon as we define a link, the bars in the Gantt chart

SCREENSHOT 8.5C   **Defining Links between Activities in Microsoft Project**

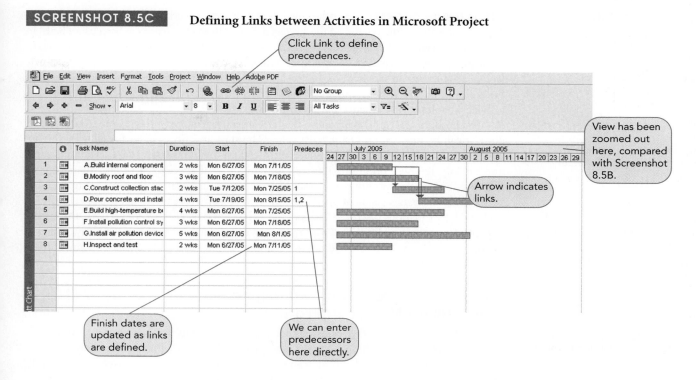

are automatically repositioned to reflect the new start and finish times for the linked activities. Further, the link itself is shown as an arrow extending from the predecessor activity.

Viewing the Project Schedule   When all links have been defined, the complete project schedule can be viewed as a Gantt chart, as shown in Screenshot 8.5D. We can also select

SCREENSHOT 8.5D   **Gantt Chart in Microsoft Project for General Foundry**

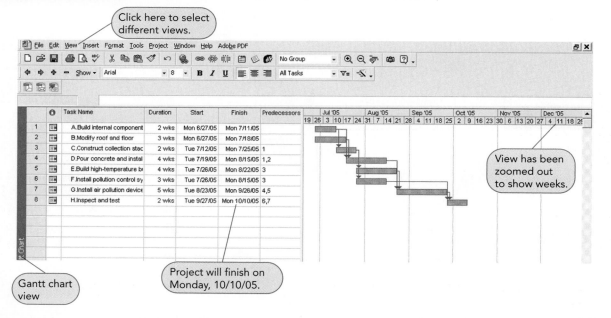

Precedences

Activity	Predecessors
A	—
B	—
C	A
D	A, B
E	C
F	C
G	D, E
H	F, G

The project can be viewed either as a Gantt chart or as a network.

VIEW|NETWORK DIAGRAM to view the schedule as a project network (shown in Screenshot 8.5E). The critical path is shown in red on the screen (shown with thicker arrows in Screenshot 8.5E) in the network diagram. We can click on any of the activities in the project network to view details of the activities. Likewise, we can easily add or remove activities and/or links from the project network. Each time we do so, Microsoft Project automatically updates all start dates, finish dates, and the critical path(s). If desired, we can manually change the layout of the network (e.g., reposition activities) by changing the options in Format|Layout.

Screenshots 8.5D and 8.5E show that if General Foundry's project starts on June 27, 2005, it can be finished on October 10, 2005. The start and finish dates for all activities are also clearly identified. This schedule takes into account the nonworking days on all weekends, and on July 1. These programs illustrate how the use of specialized project management software can greatly simplify the scheduling procedures discussed in Sections 8.2 to 8.4.

PERT Analysis   As mentioned previously, Microsoft Project does not perform the PERT probability calculations discussed in Section 8.5. However, by clicking **VIEW|TOOLBARS|PERT ANALYSIS**, we can get Microsoft Project to allow us to enter optimistic, most likely, and pessimistic times for each activity. We can then choose to view Gantt charts based on any of these three times for each activity.

Tracking Progress and Managing Costs Using Microsoft Project

The biggest benefit of using software is to track a project.

Perhaps the biggest advantage of using specialized software to manage projects is that project managers can track the progress of the project. Microsoft Project has many features available to track individual activities in terms of time, cost, resource usage, and so on. In this section, we first illustrate how we can track the progress of a project in terms of time. We then introduce project costs so that we can compute cost overruns or underruns (as we did in Table 8.7).

Tracking the Time Status of a Project   An easy way to track the time progress of tasks is to enter the percentage of work completed for each task. One way to do so is to double-click

File: 8-6.mpp

Project Network in Microsoft Project for General Foundry

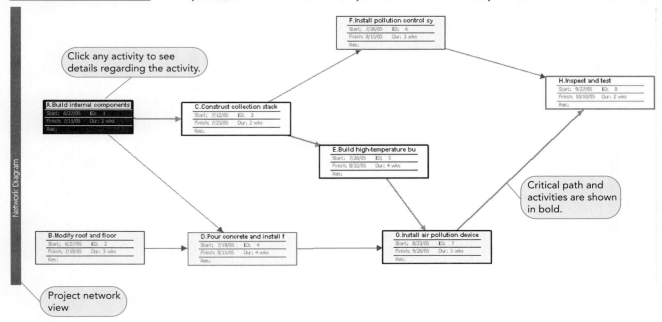

Revisited Percent Completed

Activity	Completed
A	100
B	100
C	100
D	10
E	20
F	20
G	0
H	0

Defining costs for each activity

on any activity in the Task Name column, shown in Screenshot 8.5D. A window, like the one shown in Screenshot 8.6A, is displayed. Let us now enter the percent of work completed for each task (as we did earlier in Table 8.7). For example, Screenshot 8.6A shows that activity A is 100% complete. We enter the percentage completed for all other activities in a similar fashion.

As shown in Screenshot 8.6B, the Gantt chart immediately reflects this updated information by drawing a thick line within each activity's bar. The length of this line is proportional to the percent of that activity's work that has been completed.

How do we know if we are on schedule? Let us assume today is Monday, August 8, 2005 (i.e., the end of the sixth week in the project schedule).[4] Notice that there is a vertical line shown on the Gantt chart corresponding to today's date. Microsoft Project will automatically move this line to correspond with the current date. If the project is on schedule, we should see all bars to the *left* of today's line indicate that they have been completed. For example, Screenshot 8.6B (on the next page) shows that activities A, B, and C are on schedule. In contrast, activities D, E, and F appear to be behind schedule. These activities need to be investigated further to determine the reason for the delay. This type of easy visual information is what makes such software so useful in practice for project management.

Tracking the Cost Status of a Project   Just as we tracked a project's progress with regard to time, we can track its current status with regard to the budget. There are several ways to define the cost of an activity. If the total cost consists of both fixed and variable costs, we need to define the resources used in the project, the unit costs of these resources, and the level of usage for each resource by each activity. We can even specify how resources should be charged to an activity (e.g., prorated basis, full billing upon completion). Microsoft Project uses this information to first calculate the variable cost of each activity, based on its level of resource usage, and then add this amount to the fixed costs to find the total cost for each activity.

In the case of General Foundry's project, since we do not have separate fixed and variable costs available, an easier way to enter activity costs is to click **VIEW|TABLE|COST**. The window shown in Screenshot 8.6C (on the next page) is displayed. We enter the costs (see Table 8.7) in the **FIXED COST** column. Microsoft Project automatically shows these values in the **TOTAL COST**

Updating Activity Progress in Microsoft Project

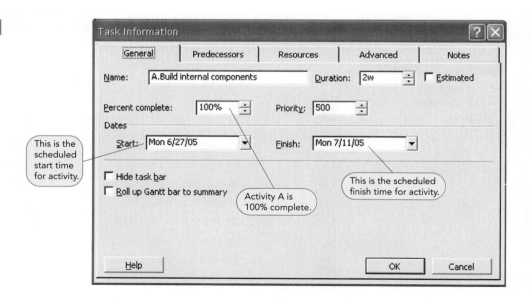

[4] Remember that the nonworking day on July 1 has moved all schedules by one day. Therefore, activities end on Mondays rather than on Fridays.

SCREENSHOT 8.6B   **Tracking Project Progress in Microsoft Project**

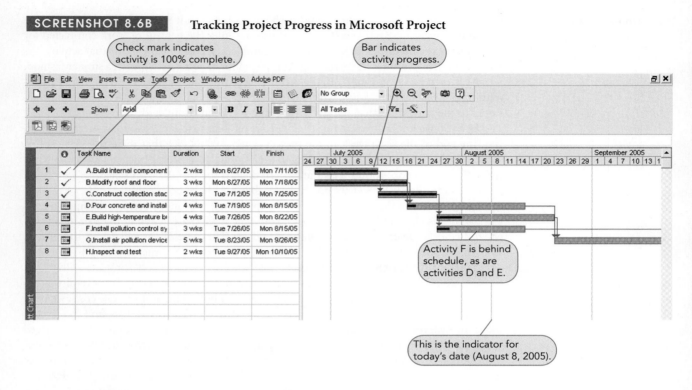

Check mark indicates activity is 100% complete.

Bar indicates activity progress.

Activity F is behind schedule, as are activities D and E.

This is the indicator for today's date (August 8, 2005).

column. We can now use these total costs to establish a **BASELINE COST** (or budgeted cost) by clicking **TOOLS|TRACKING|SAVE BASELINE**. This information is also shown in Screenshot 8.6C.

Once we have entered this cost information, how do we compare our current expenses with the budget? To do so, we first need to turn off the automatic calculation option in Microsoft Project by clicking **TOOLS|OPTIONS|CALCULATION** and unchecking the box labelled "Actual costs are always calculated by Microsoft Project." Note that if we

SCREENSHOT 8.6C

Entering Cost Information in Microsoft Project

Establish Baseline by clicking **Tools|Tracking| Save Baseline.**

	Task Name	Fixed Cost	Fixed Cost Accrual	Total Cost	Baseline
1	A.Build internal c	$22,000.00	Prorated	$22,000.00	$22,000.00
2	B.Modify roof an	$30,000.00	Prorated	$30,000.00	$30,000.00
3	C.Construct colle	$26,000.00	Prorated	$26,000.00	$26,000.00
4	D.Pour concrete	$48,000.00	Prorated	$48,000.00	$48,000.00
5	E.Build high-temp	$56,000.00	Prorated	$56,000.00	$56,000.00
6	F.Install pollution	$30,000.00	Prorated	$30,000.00	$30,000.00
7	G.Install air pollul	$80,000.00	Prorated	$80,000.00	$80,000.00
8	H.Inspect and te:	$16,000.00	Prorated	$16,000.00	$16,000.00

In this case, we have entered the activity costs as fixed costs.

Total cost = Fixed cost, since no variable costs have been defined.

SCREENSHOT 8.6D   **Checking Budget Status in Microsoft Project**

Budgeted costs

	Task Name	Fixed Cost	Fixed Cost Accrual	Total Cost	Baseline	Variance	Actual	Remaining
1	A.Build internal component	$22,000.00	Prorated	$20,000.00	$22,000.00	($2,000.00)	$20,000.00	$0.00
2	B.Modify roof and floor	$30,000.00	Prorated	$36,000.00	$30,000.00	$6,000.00	$36,000.00	$0.00
3	C.Construct collection stac	$26,000.00	Prorated	$26,000.00	$26,000.00	$0.00	$26,000.00	$0.00
4	D.Pour concrete and instal	$48,000.00	Prorated	$49,200.00	$48,000.00	$1,200.00	$6,000.00	$43,200.00
5	E.Build high-temperature b	$56,000.00	Prorated	$64,800.00	$56,000.00	$8,800.00	$20,000.00	$44,800.00
6	F.Install pollution control sy	$30,000.00	Prorated	$28,000.00	$30,000.00	($2,000.00)	$4,000.00	$24,000.00
7	G.Install air pollution device	$80,000.00	Prorated	$80,000.00	$80,000.00	$0.00	$0.00	$80,000.00
8	H.Inspect and test	$16,000.00	Prorated	$16,000.00	$16,000.00	$0.00	$0.00	$16,000.00

Total cost values are changed to reflect variances.

Cost overruns and underruns. (Negative values indicate underruns.)

Current expenses. You must turn off automatic calculations in order to enter information here.

Revisited Actual Expenses

Activity	Expense
A	$20 000
B	36 000
C	26 000
D	6 000
E	20 000
F	4 000
G	0
H	0

Computing variances in activity budgets

do not turn off this option, Microsoft Project assumes that all activities are always working as per the budget.

We now enter the actual costs (from Table 8.7) in the column titled **ACTUAL**, as shown in Screenshot 8.6D above. The Variance column shows the budget overrun or underrun associated with each activity.

This software (and other specialized project management software) has several other features and capabilities that we have not discussed here. For example, we can associate individual resources with specific activities and establish a separate calendar for each resource. The time schedule of the activity will then be determined based not only on its duration and predecessors, but also on the resource calendars. Likewise, we can track each resource and identify possible conflicts (e.g., the same resource being required by two different activities at the same time). We encourage you to try these procedures on your own to understand the full capabilities of specialized project management software.

SUMMARY

This chapter presents the fundamentals of project management techniques. We discuss two techniques, PERT and CPM, both of which are excellent for controlling large and complex projects.

We first show how to express projects using project networks. Using a two-pass procedure, we can then identify the project schedule and the critical path(s). PERT is probabilistic and allows three time estimates for each activity, which are used to compute the project's expected completion time and variance. We show how to use these parameters to find the probability that the project will be completed by a given date.

We discuss how project management techniques can also be used to plan, schedule, monitor, and control project costs. Using these techniques, we show how to determine whether the project is on schedule at any point in time and whether there are cost overruns or underruns.

Next, we discuss how to crash projects by reducing their completion time through additional resource expenditures. We also illustrate how LP can be used to find the least-cost approach to crashing large projects.

Finally, we provide a brief introduction to Microsoft Project, one of several popular project management software packages currently used.

GLOSSARY

Activity. A job or task that consumes time and is a key subpart of the total project.

Activity on Arc (AOA) Network. A project network in which arcs denote activities and nodes denote events.

Activity on Node (AON) Network. A project network in which nodes denote activities and arcs denote precedence relationships.

Activity Time Estimate. Estimated completion time of an activity.

Backward Pass. A procedure that moves from the end of the network to the beginning of the network. It is used in determining an activity's LFT and LST.

Beta Probability Distribution. Probability distribution that is often used in PERT to compute expected activity completion times and variances.

Crash Cost. The cost of completing a project in a time shorter than originally planned; usually higher than the normal cost.

Crash Time. A shortened time required to complete an activity.

Crashing. The process of reducing the total time that it takes to complete a project by expending additional funds.

Critical Path. The series of activities that have zero slack. It is the longest time path through the network. A delay for any activity that is on the critical path will delay the completion of the entire project.

Critical Path Analysis. An analysis that determines the total project completion time, the critical path for the project, slack, EST, EFT, LST, and LFT for every activity.

Critical Path Method (CPM). A deterministic network technique that is similar to PERT but uses only one time estimate. Used for monitoring budgets and crashing projects.

Dummy Activity. A fictitious activity that consumes no time and is inserted into an AOA project network to display the proper precedence relationships between activities.

Earliest Finish Time (EFT). The earliest time that an activity can be finished without violation of precedence requirements.

Earliest Start Time (EST). The earliest time that an activity can start without violation of precedence requirements.

Event. A point in time that marks the beginning or end of an activity. Used in AOA networks.

Expected Activity Time. The average time that it should take to complete an activity. Expected time = $(a + 4m + b)/6$.

Forward Pass. A procedure that moves from the beginning of a network to the end of the network. It is used in determining an activity's EST and EFT.

Gantt Chart. An alternative to project networks for showing a project schedule; a Gantt chart consists of bars drawn along a timeline.

Immediate Predecessor. An activity that must be completed before another activity can be started.

Latest Finish Time (LFT). The latest time that an activity can be finished without delaying the entire project.

Latest Start Time (LST). The latest time that an activity can be started without delaying the entire project.

Most Likely Time (m). The time that you would expect it would take to complete the activity. Used in PERT.

Optimistic Time (a). The shortest time that could be required to complete the activity. Used in PERT.

Pessimistic Time (b). The longest time that could be required to complete the activity. Used in PERT.

Program Evaluation and Review Technique (PERT). A network technique that allows three time estimates for each activity in a project.

Project. A series of related tasks (or activities) directed toward a major well-defined output.

Project Management. A set of techniques for scheduling and budgeting projects, especially large projects, and controlling costs and timelines.

Project Network. A graphical display of a project that shows activities and precedence relationships.

Slack Time. The amount of time that an activity can be delayed without delaying the entire project. Slack is equal to the LST minus the EST, or the LFT minus the EFT.

Variance of Activity Completion Time. A measure of dispersion of the activity completion time. Variance = $[(b - a)/6]^2$.

Work Breakdown Structure. The process of defining a project by dividing it into its major subcomponents, which are then further subdivided.

Work Package. A logical grouping of activities that can be considered as a whole in estimating project costs.

KEY EQUATIONS

(8-1) EST = Maximum {EFT value of all immediate predecessors}

Earliest start time.

(8-2) EFT = EST + Activity time

Earliest finish time.

(8-3) LFT = Minimum {LST value of all immediate followers}

Latest finish time.

(8-4) LST = LFT − Activity time

Latest start time.

(8-5) Slack = LST− EST or Slack = LFT − EFT

Slack time in an activity.

(8-6) $t = (a + 4m + b)/6$

Expected activity completion time.

(8-7) Variance $= [(b - a)/6]^2$

Activity variance.

(8-8) Standard deviation $= \sqrt{\text{Variance}} = (b - a)/6$

Activity standard deviation.

(8-9) Project variance $= \Sigma$ (Variances of activities on critical path)

(8-10) $Z = $ (Due date $-$ Expected date of completion)$/\sigma_p$

Number of standard deviations the target date lies from the expected date, using the normal distribution.

(8-11) Due date $=$ Expected completion time $+ Z \times \sigma_p$

Determine due date for given completion probability.

(8-12) Value of work completed $=$ Percent of work completed $\times$ Total activity budget)

(8-13) Cost difference $=$ Actual cost $-$ Value of work completed

(8-14) Crash cost per period $= \dfrac{(\text{Crash cost} - \text{Normal cost})}{(\text{Normal time} - \text{Crash time})}$

The cost of reducing an activity completion time per time period.

SOLVED PROBLEMS

Solved Problem 8-1

To complete the wing assembly for an experimental aircraft, Scott DeWitte has laid out the seven major activities involved. These activities have been labelled A through G in the following table, which also shows their estimated completion times (in weeks) and immediate predecessors. Determine the expected time and variance for each activity.

ACTIVITY	a	m	b	IMMEDIATE PREDECESSORS
A	1	2	3	—
B	2	3	4	—
C	4	5	6	A
D	8	9	10	B
E	2	5	8	C, D
F	4	5	6	D
G	1	2	3	E

Solution

Expected times and variances can be computed using the formulas presented in the chapter. The results are summarized in the following table:

ACTIVITY	EXPECTED TIME (IN WEEKS)	VARIANCE
A	2	$\frac{1}{9}$
B	3	$\frac{1}{9}$
C	5	$\frac{1}{9}$
D	9	$\frac{1}{9}$
E	5	1
F	5	$\frac{1}{9}$
G	2	$\frac{1}{9}$

Solved Problem 8-2

Referring to Solved Problem 8-1, now Scott would like to determine the critical path for the entire wing assembly project as well as the expected completion time for the total project. In addition, he would like to determine the earliest and latest start and finish times for all activities.

Solution

The AON network for Scott DeWitte's project is shown in Figure 8.20. Note that this project has multiple activities (A and B) with no immediate predecessors, and multiple activities (F and G) with no successors. Hence, in addition to a dummy unique starting activity (Start), we have included a dummy unique finishing activity (End) for the project.

Figure 8.20 shows the earliest and latest times for all activities. The results are also summarized in the table below.

ACTIVITY	ACTIVITY TIME				
	EST	EFT	LST	LFT	SLACK
A	0	2	5	7	5
B	0	3	0	3	0
C	2	7	7	12	5
D	3	12	3	12	0
E	12	17	12	17	0
F	12	17	14	19	2
G	17	19	17	19	0

FIGURE 8.20   **Critical Path for Solved Problem 8-2**

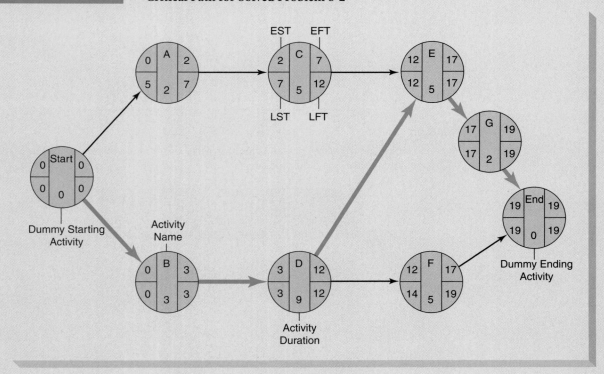

Expected project length = 19 weeks

Variance of the critical path = 1.333

Standard deviation of the critical path = 1.155 weeks

The activities along the critical path are B, D, E, and G. These activities have zero slack, as shown in the table.

⟫ SELF-TEST

- Before taking the self-test, refer back to the learning objectives at the beginning of the chapter, the notes in the margins, and the glossary at the end of the chapter.
- Use the key at the back of the book to correct your answers.
- Restudy pages that correspond to any questions that you answered incorrectly or material you feel uncertain about.

1. Network models such as PERT and CPM are used to
   a. manage complex projects.
   b. save time.
   c. save money.
   d. do all of the above.
   e. do none of the above.

2. PERT is an acronym for
   a. practical evaluation and research technique.
   b. program evaluation and review technique.
   c. performance elevation and restoration time.
   d. promotion effectiveness and retail trial.
   e. none of the above.

3. In PERT, if the pessimistic time was 14 weeks, the optimistic time was 8 weeks, and the most likely time was 11 weeks,
   a. the variance would be 1 week.
   b. the variance would be 11 weeks.
   c. the expected time would be 6 weeks.
   d. the expected time would be $5\frac{1}{2}$ weeks.
   e. there is not enough information.
   f. none of the above is correct.

4. The critical path is
   a. the least-slack path.
   b. the longest time path through the network.
   c. that series of activities whose delay is most likely to delay the entire project.
   d. one or more paths through a network whose last activity's EFT is the largest for any activity in the project.
   e. all of the above.
   f. none of the above.

5. In PERT, the time estimate b represents
   a. the optimistic time.
   b. the most likely time.
   c. the pessimistic time.
   d. the expected time.
   e. none of the above.

6. In PERT, slack time equals
   a. EST + t.
   b. LST − EST.
   c. zero.

   d. EFT − EST.
   e. none of the above.

7. The standard deviation for the PERT project is approximately
   a. the square root of the sum of the variances along the critical path.
   b. the sum of the critical path activity standard deviations.
   c. the square root of the sum of the variances of the project activities.
   d. all of the above.
   e. none of the above.

8. The crash cost per week
   a. is the difference in costs divided by the difference in times (crash and normal).
   b. is considered to be linear in the range between normal and crash.
   c. needs to be determined so that the smallest values on the critical path may be considered for time reduction first.
   d. is all of the above.

9. _____ activities are ones that will delay the entire project if they are late or delayed.

10. PERT can use three estimates for activity time. These three estimates are _____, _____, and _____.

11. The probability distribution often used by PERT to describe activity times is the
    a. normal distribution.
    b. exponential distribution.
    c. beta distribution.
    d. uniform distribution.

12. PERT and CPM differ in that
    a. PERT uses dummy activities and CPM does not.
    b. PERT uses three time estimates and CPM uses single-time estimates.
    c. PERT does not allow us to monitor costs and CPM does.
    d. PERT uses AOA networks and CPM uses AON networks.

13. PERT assumes that the completion time of a project follows a(n)
    a. normal distribution.
    b. exponential distribution.

c. beta distribution.
d. uniform distribution.

14. If an activity with free slack time of two weeks is delayed by one week,
    a. the project will be delayed by one week.
    b. the slack time of all activities that follow this activity is reduced by one week.

c. no other activity in the project is affected.
d. the probability of completing the project on time decreases.

15. An AON project network *must* have a unique starting activity (node) and a unique ending activity (node).
    a. True
    b. False

DISCUSSION QUESTIONS AND PROBLEMS

Discussion Questions

8-1 What are some of the questions that can be answered with project management?

8-2 What are the major differences between PERT and CPM?

8-3 What is an activity? What is an immediate predecessor?

8-4 Describe how expected activity times and variances can be computed in a PERT analysis.

8-5 Briefly discuss what is meant by critical path analysis. What are critical path activities, and why are they important?

8-6 What are the earliest activity start time and latest activity start time? How are they computed?

8-7 Describe the meaning of slack and discuss how it can be determined.

8-8 How can we determine the probability that a project will be completed by a certain date? What assumptions are made in this computation?

8-9 Briefly describe how project budgets can be monitored.

8-10 What is crashing, and how is it done by hand?

8-11 Why is LP useful in project crashing?

Problems

8-12 Sid Davidson is the personnel director of Babson and Willcount, a company that specializes in consulting and research. Sid is considering a leadership training program for the firm's middle-level managers. Sid has listed a number of activities that must be completed before the program could be conducted. The activities and immediate predecessors appear in the following table:

ACTIVITY	IMMEDIATE PREDECESSORS
A	—
B	—
C	—
D	B
E	A, D
F	C
G	E, F

Develop a network for this problem.

8-13 Sid Davidson has determined the activity times of the leadership training program, as shown in the following table:

ACTIVITY	TIME (DAYS)
A	2
B	5
C	1
D	10
E	3
F	6
G	8
	35

Determine the EST, EFT, LST, LFT, and slack for each activity. Also determine the total project completion time and the critical path(s).

8-14 Terry Anderson is responsible for planning a local political campaign. A variety of activities need to be coordinated in order to be prepared for the upcoming election date. The following table describes the relationships between these activities that need to be completed, as well as estimated times:

ACTIVITY	IMMEDIATE PREDECESSORS	TIME (WEEKS)
A	—	3
B	—	5
C	A	7
D	A	5
E	B, C	4
F	B	6
G	D, E	2
H	F	3

(a) Develop a project network for this problem.
(b) Determine the EST, EFT, LST, LFT, and slack for each activity. Also determine the total project completion time and the critical path(s).

8-15 Monohan Machinery specializes in developing weed-harvesting equipment that is used to clear small lakes of weeds. George Monohan, president of Monohan Machinery, is convinced that harvesting weeds is far better than using chemicals to kill them. Chemicals cause pollution, and the weeds seem to grow faster after chemicals have been used. George is contemplating the construction of a machine that would harvest weeds on narrow rivers and waterways. The activities that are necessary to build one of these experimental weed-harvesting machines are listed in the following table, along with their immediate predecessors and estimated durations:

ACTIVITY	IMMEDIATE PREDECESSORS	TIME (DAYS)
A	—	6
B	—	5
C	A	3
D	A	2
E	B	4
F	B	6
G	C, E	10
H	D, F	7

(a) Develop a project network for this problem.
(b) Determine the EST, EFT, LST, LFT, and slack for each activity. Also determine the total project completion time and the critical path(s).

8-16 The Johnstone Advertising Agency is developing a TV advertising campaign for a new client. The following table describes the relationships between the activities that need to be completed:

ACTIVITY	IMMEDIATE PREDECESSORS	TIME (DAYS)
A	—	4
B	A	6
C	B	12
D	B	11
E	D	9
F	D	8
G	D	10
H	C	5
I	C	7
J	E, F, G	4
K	H, I	9

(a) Develop a project network for this problem.
(b) Determine the EST, EFT, LST, LFT, and slack for each activity. Also determine the total project completion time and the critical path(s).

8-17 Tim Smith is responsible for planning an installation of a computer system. The following table describes the relationships between the activities that need to be completed:

ACTIVITY	IMMEDIATE PREDECESSORS	TIME (DAYS)
A	—	5
B	A	6
C	A	2
D	A	9
E	B	9
F	C, D	3
G	D	7
H	D	4
I	E, F, G	6
J	H	5

(a) Develop a project network for this problem.
(b) Determine the EST, EFT, LST, LFT, and slack for each activity. Also determine the total project completion time and the critical path(s).

8-18 Zuckerman Wiring and Electric is a company that installs wiring and electrical fixtures in residential construction. John Zuckerman has been concerned with the amount of time that it takes to complete wiring jobs. Some of his workers are very unreliable. A list of activities and their optimistic, pessimistic, and most likely completion times in days are given in the following table:

ACTIVITY	DAYS			IMMEDIATE PREDECESSORS
	a	m	b	
A	3	6	8	—
B	2	4	4	—
C	1	2	3	—
D	6	7	8	C
E	2	4	6	B, D
F	6	10	14	A, E
G	1	2	4	A, E
H	3	6	9	F
I	10	11	12	G
J	14	16	20	C
K	2	8	10	H, I

Determine the expected completion time and variance for each activity.

8-19 John Zuckerman would like to determine the total project completion time and the critical path for installing electrical wiring and equipment in residential houses.

(See Problem 8-18 for details.) In addition, determine EST, EFT, LST, LFT, and slack for each activity.

8-20 What is the probability that Zuckerman will finish the project described in Problems 8-18 and 8-19 in 40 days or less?

8-21 A plant engineering group needs to set up an assembly line to produce a new product. The following table describes the relationships between the activities that need to be completed for this product to be manufactured:

ACTIVITY	DAYS a	m	b	IMMEDIATE PREDECESSORS
A	3	6	8	—
B	5	8	10	A
C	5	6	8	A
D	1	2	4	B, C
E	7	11	17	D
F	7	9	12	D
G	6	8	9	D
H	3	4	7	F, G
I	3	5	7	E, F, H

(a) Develop a project network for this problem.
(b) Determine the expected duration and variance for each activity.
(c) Determine the EST, EFT, LST, LFT, and slack for each activity. Also determine the total project completion time and the critical path(s).
(d) Determine the probability that the project will be completed in less than 34 days.
(e) Determine the probability that the project will take more than 29 days.

8-22 Ali Marwani, director of personnel of Management Resources, Inc., is in the process of designing a program that its customers can use in the job-finding process. Some of the activities include preparing résumés, writing letters, making appointments to see prospective employers, researching companies and industries, and so on. Some of the information on the activities is shown in the following table.

(a) Construct a network for this problem.
(b) Determine the expected times and variances for each activity.
(c) Determine EST, EFT, LST, LFT, and slack for each activity.
(d) Determine the critical path and project completion time.
(e) Determine the probability that the project will be finished in 70 days.
(f) Determine the probability that the project will be finished in 80 days.
(g) Determine the probability that the project will need at least 75 days.

Table for Problem 8-22

ACTIVITY	DAYS a	m	b	IMMEDIATE PREDECESSORS
A	8	10	12	—
B	6	7	9	—
C	3	3	4	—
D	10	20	30	A
E	6	7	8	C
F	9	10	11	B, D, E
G	6	7	10	B, D, E
H	14	15	16	F
I	10	11	13	F
J	6	7	8	G, H
K	4	7	8	I, J
L	1	2	4	G, H

8-23 Laura Thompson needs to plan and manage a local construction project. The following table describes the relationships between the activities that need to be completed:

ACTIVITY	DAYS a	m	b	IMMEDIATE PREDECESSORS
A	4	8	13	—
B	4	10	15	A
C	7	14	20	B
D	9	16	19	B
E	6	9	11	B
F	2	4	5	D, E
G	4	7	11	C, F
H	3	5	9	G
I	2	3	4	G, H

(a) Determine the expected times and variances for each activity.
(b) Construct a project network for this problem.
(c) Determine the EST, EFT, LST, LFT, and slack for each activity. Also determine the critical path and project completion time.
(d) What is the probability that the project will be finished in less than 57 days?
(e) What is the probability that the project will need at least 50 days?

8-24 David Sikersky is responsible for developing a supervisory training program for his organization. The following table describes the relationships between the activities that need to be completed.

(a) Determine the expected times and variances for each activity.
(b) Construct a project network for this problem.

(c) Determine the EST, EFT, LST, LFT, and slack for each activity. Also determine the critical path and project completion time.

(d) What is the probability that the project will be finished in less than 49 days?

(e) What is the probability that the project will need at least 54 days?

Table for Problem 8-24

ACTIVITY	DAYS			IMMEDIATE PREDECESSORS
	a	m	b	
A	3	7	13	—
B	5	10	17	—
C	3	5	8	A, B
D	5	12	14	C
E	2	5	9	C
F	2	5	15	E
G	5	8	12	F
H	6	10	12	D
I	3	4	8	F, H
J	4	7	10	G, I

8-25 Ed Rose was able to determine that the expected project completion time for the construction of a pleasure yacht is 21 months, and the project variance is 4. What is the probability that the project will

(a) need at least 17 months?
(b) be completed in 20 months?
(c) need at least 23 months?
(d) be completed in 25 months?

8-26 Laporte Brothers Construction Company of Quebec has determined that the expected completion time for its most popular model home follows the normal probability distribution with a mean of 25 weeks and a standard deviation of 4 weeks.

(a) What is the probability that the next home will be completed within 30 weeks?
(b) What is the probability that the next home will be completed within 22 weeks?
(c) Find the number of weeks within which Laporte Brothers is 99% sure the next home will be completed.
(d) Find the number of weeks within which Laporte Brothers is 85% sure the next home will be completed.

8-27 Fred Ridgeway has been given the responsibility of managing a training and development program. He knows the EST and LST (both in months), and the total costs for each activity. This information is given in the table in the next column.

(a) Using ESTs, determine Fred's total monthly budget.
(b) Using LSTs, determine Fred's total monthly budget.

8-28 Fred Ridgeway's project (see Problem 8-27) has progressed over the past several months, and it is now the end of month 16. Fred would like to know the current status of the project with regard to schedule and budget by developing an appropriate table. The relevant data are shown in the table in the next column.

Table for Problem 8-27

ACTIVITY	EST	LST	T	TOTAL COST($)
A	0	0	6	10 000
B	1	4	2	14 000
C	3	3	7	5 000
D	4	9	3	6 000
E	6	6	10	14 000
F	14	15	11	13 000
G	12	18	2	4 000
H	14	14	11	6 000
I	18	21	6	18 000
J	18	19	4	12 000
K	22	22	14	10 000
L	22	23	8	16 000
M	18	24	6	18 000

Table for Problem 8-28

ACTIVITY	PERCENTAGE COMPLETED	ACTUAL COST($)
A	100	13 000
B	100	12 000
C	100	6 000
D	100	6 000
E	80	12 000
F	13	1 000
G	100	4 500
H	20	500

Assume that activities not shown in the table have not yet started and have incurred no cost to date. All activities follow their earliest time schedules.

8-29 Susan Clark needs to coordinate the opening of a new office for her company in Calgary. The activity time and relationships for this project, as well as the total budgeted cost for each activity, are shown in the following table:

ACTIVITY	IMMEDIATE PREDECESSORS	TIME (WEEKS)	TOTAL COST
A	—	2	1400
B	A	3	4800
C	A	4	4000
D	B, C	2	2800
E	C	3	2400
F	D, E	3	1500

(a) Develop a weekly budget for this project using the earliest start times.

(b) Develop a weekly budget for this project using the latest start times.

8-30 Susan Clark's project (see Problem 8-29) has progressed over the past several weeks, and it is now the end of week eight. Susan would like to know the current status of the project with regard to schedule and budget by developing an appropriate table. Assume that all activities follow their earliest time schedules. The relevant data are shown in the following table:

ACTIVITY	PERCENTAGE COMPLETED	ACTUAL ($) COST
A	100	1500
B	100	4500
C	100	4000
D	70	2800
E	70	2000
F	0	0

8-31 The General Foundry air pollution project discussed in the chapter has progressed over the past several weeks and it is now the end of week eight. Lester Harky would like to know the value of the work completed, the amount of any cost overruns or underruns for the project, and the extent to which the project is ahead of schedule or behind schedule by developing a table like Table 8.7 (see page 346). The revised cost figures appear in the following table:

ACTIVITY	PERCENT OF COMPLETION	ACTUAL COST ($)
A	100	20 000
B	100	36 000
C	100	26 000
D	100	44 000
E	50	25 000
F	60	15 000
G	10	5 000
H	10	1 000

8-32 General Foundry's project crashing data were shown in Table 8.10 on page 349. Crash this project by hand to 11 weeks. What are the final times for each activity after crashing?

8-33 Bowman Builders manufactures steel storage sheds for commercial use. Joe Bowman, president of Bowman Builders, is contemplating producing sheds for home use. The activities necessary to build an experimental model and related data are given in the table in the next column. Set up and solve an LP model using Excel to crash this project to 10 weeks.

8-34 The table in the next column describes the various activities of a construction project in a chemical plant.

Set up and solve an LP model using Excel to crash this project to 23 days. What is the total crashing cost?

Table for Problem 8-33

ACTIVITY	IMMEDIATE PREDECES-SORS	NORMAL TIME (WEEKS)	NORMAL COST ($)	CRASH TIME (WEEKS)	CRASH COST ($)
A	—	3	1000	2	1600
B	—	2	2000	1	2700
C	—	1	300	1	300
D	A	7	1300	3	1600
E	B	6	850	3	1000
F	C	2	4000	1	5000
G	D, E	4	1500	2	2000

Table for Problem 8-34

ACTIVITY	IMMEDIATE PREDECES-SORS	NORMAL TIME (DAYS)	NORMAL COST ($)	CRASH TIME (DAYS)	CRASH COST ($)
A	—	4	2000	2	2600
B	A	6	3500	5	4300
C	A	8	3300	6	3900
D	B	5	1200	4	1800
E	C, D	3	1700	2	2200
F	E	7	2200	5	3600
G	E	5	900	4	1550
H	F, G	4	1200	3	1700

8-35 A new order filling system needs to be installed as soon as possible. The following activities need to be completed in the order shown in the table below. Also provided is the cost information to reduce the normal activity times.

ACTIVITY	IMMEDIATE PREDECES-SORS	NORMAL TIME (DAYS)	NORMAL COST ($)	CRASH TIME (DAYS)	CRASH COST ($)
A	—	7	2000	5	3500
B	A	10	3000	8	4700
C	A	8	3400	7	3700
D	C	6	1600	4	2600
E	C	7	1900	4	4000
F	D, E	5	1200	3	2800
G	B, C	11	8200	8	10900
H	F, G	4	2600	3	3800

Set up and solve an LP model using Excel to crash this project to 25 days. What is the total crashing cost?

8-36 Software Development Specialists (SDS) is involved with developing software for customers in the banking industry. SDS breaks a large programming project into teams that perform the necessary steps. Team A is responsible for going from general systems design all the way through to actual systems testing. This involves 18 separate activities. Team B is then responsible for the final installation.

To determine cost and time factors, optimistic, most likely, and pessimistic time estimates have been made for all of the 18 activities involved for team A. The first step that this team performs is general systems design. The optimistic, most likely, and pessimistic times are 3 weeks, 4 weeks, and 5 weeks. Following this, a number of activities can begin. Activity 2 is involved with procedures design. Optimistic, most likely, and pessimistic times for completing this activity are 4, 5, and 7 weeks. Activity 3 is developing detailed report designs. Optimistic, most likely, and pessimistic time estimates are 6, 8, and 9 weeks. Activity 4, detailed forms design, has optimistic, most likely, and pessimistic time estimates of 2, 3, and 5 weeks.

Activities 5 and 6 involve writing detailed program specifications and developing file specifications. The three time estimates for activity 5 are 6, 7, and 9 weeks, and the three time estimates for activity 6 are 3, 4, and 5 weeks. Activity 7 involves specifying system test data. Before this is done, activity 6, involving file specifications, must be completed. The time estimates for activity 7 are 2, 4, and 5 weeks. Activity 8 involves reviewing forms. Before activity 8 can be conducted, detailed forms design must be completed. The time estimates for activity 8 are 3, 4, and 6 weeks. The next activity, activity 9, is reviewing the detailed report design. This requires that the detailed report design, activity 3, be completed first. The time estimates for activity 9 are 1, 2, and 4 weeks.

Activity 10 involves reviewing procedures design. Time estimates are 1, 3, and 4 weeks. Of course, procedures design must be done before activity 10 can be started. Activity 11 involves the system design checkpoint review. A number of activities must be completed before this is done. These activities include reviewing the forms, reviewing the detailed report design, reviewing the procedures design, writing detailed program specs, and specifying system test data. The optimistic, most likely, and pessimistic time estimates for activity 11 are 3, 4, and 6 weeks. Performing program logic design is activity 12. This can be started only after the system design checkpoint review is completed. The time estimates for activity 12 are 4, 6, and 7 weeks.

Activity 13, coding the programs, is done only after the program logic design is completed. The time estimates for this activity are 6, 8, and 10 weeks. Activity 14 is involved in developing test programs. Activity 13 is the immediate predecessor. Time estimates for activity 14 are 3, 4, and 6 weeks. Developing a system test plan is activity 15. A number of activities must be completed before activity 15 can be started. These activities include specifying system test data, writing detailed program specifications, and reviewing procedure designs, the detailed report design, and forms. The time estimates for activity 15 are 3, 4, and 5 weeks.

Activity 16, creating system test data, has time estimates of 2, 4, and 6 weeks. Activity 15 must be done before activity 16 can be started. Activity 17 is reviewing program test results. The immediate predecessor to activity 17 is to test the programs (activity 14). The three time estimates for activity 17 are 2, 3, and 4 weeks. The final activity is conducting system tests. This is activity 18. Before activity 18 can be started, activities 16 and 17 must be complete. The three time estimates for conducting these system tests are 3, 5, and 6 weeks. How long will it take for team A to complete its programming assignment?

8-37 Bender Construction Co. is involved in constructing municipal buildings and other structures that are used primarily by city and state municipalities. This requires developing legal documents, drafting feasibility studies, obtaining bond ratings, and so forth. Recently, Bender was given a request to submit a proposal for the construction of a municipal building. The first step is to develop legal documents and to perform all steps necessary before the construction contract is signed. This requires more than 20 separate activities that must be completed. These activities, their immediate predecessors, and optimistic (a), most likely (m), and pessimistic (b) time estimates are given in the table on page 370.

Determine the total project completion time for this preliminary step, the critical path, and slack time for all activities involved.

8-38 Getting a degree from a college or university can be a long and difficult task. Certain courses must be completed before other courses may be taken. Develop a network diagram in which every activity is a particular course that you must take for your degree program. The immediate predecessors will be course prerequisites. Don't forget to include all university, college, and departmental course requirements. Then try to group these courses into semesters or quarters for your particular school. How long do you think it will take you to graduate? Which courses, if not taken in the proper sequence, could delay your graduation?

8-39 Dream Team Productions is in the final design phases of its new film, *Killer Worms*, to be released next summer. Market Wise, the firm hired to coordinate the release of *Killer Worms* toys, has identified 16 activities to be completed before the release of the film. These activities, their immediate predecessors, and optimistic (a), most likely (m), and pessimistic (b) time estimates are given in the following table:

ACTIVITY	IMMEDIATE PREDECESSORS	WEEKS REQUIRED		
		a	m	b
A	—	1	2	4
B	—	3	3.5	4
C	—	10	12	13
D	—	4	5	7
E	—	2	4	5
F	A	6	7	8
G	B	2	4	5.5
H	C	5	7.7	9
I	C	9.9	10	12
J	C	2	4	5
K	D	2	4	6
L	E	2	4	6
M	F, G, H	5	6	6.5
N	J, K, L	1	1.1	2
O	I, M	5	7	8
P	N	5	7	9

(a) How many weeks in advance of the film release should Market Wise start its marketing campaign? What are the critical paths?

(b) If activities I and J were not necessary, what impact would this have on the critical path and the number of weeks needed to complete the marketing campaign?

8-40 Sager Products has been in the business of manufacturing and marketing toys for toddlers for the past two decades. Jim Sager, president of the firm, is considering the development of a new manufacturing line to allow it to produce high-quality plastic toys at reasonable prices. The development process is long and complex. Jim estimates that there are five phases involved and multiple activities for each phase.

Phase 1 of the development process involves the completion of four activities. These activities have no immediate predecessors. Activity A has an optimistic completion time of 2 weeks, a probable completion time of 3 weeks, and a pessimistic completion time of 4 weeks. Activity B has estimated completion times of 5, 6, and 8 weeks; these represent optimistic, probable, and pessimistic time estimates. Similarly, activity C has estimated completion times of 1 week, 1 week, and 2 weeks; and activity D has expected completion times of 8 weeks, 9 weeks, and 11 weeks.

Phase 2 involves six separate activities. Activity E has activity A as an immediate predecessor. Time estimates are 1 week, 1 week, and 4 weeks. Activity F and activity G both have activity B as their immediate predecessor. For activity F, the time estimates are 3 weeks, 3 weeks, and 4 weeks. For activity G, the time estimates are 1 week, 2 weeks, and 2 weeks. The only immediate predecessor for activity H is activity C. Time estimates for activity H are 5 weeks, 5 weeks, and 6 weeks. Activity D must be performed before activity I and activity J can be started. Activity I has estimated completion times of 9 weeks, 10 weeks, and 11

Table for Problem 8-37

ACTIVITY	WEEKS REQUIRED a	m	b	DESCRIPTION OF ACTIVITY	IMMEDIATE PREDECESSORS
1	1	4	5	Draft legal documents	—
2	2	3	4	Prepare financial statements	—
3	3	4	5	Draft history	—
4	7	8	9	Draft demand portion of feasibility study	—
5	4	4	5	Review and approve legal documents	1
6	1	2	4	Review and approve history	3
7	4	5	6	Review feasibility study	4
8	1	2	4	Draft final financial portion of feasibility study	7
9	3	4	4	Draft facts relevant to the bond transaction	5
10	1	1	2	Review and approve financial statements	2
11	18	20	26	Receive firm price of project	—
12	1	2	3	Review and complete financial portion of feasibility study	8
13	1	1	2	Complete draft statement	6, 9, 10, 11, 12
14	0.10	0.14	0.16	Send all materials to bond rating services	13
15	0.20	0.30	0.40	Print statement and distribute it to all interested parties	14
16	1	1	2	Make presentation to bond rating services	14
17	1	2	3	Receive bond rating	16
18	3	5	7	Market bonds	15, 17
19	0.10	0.10	0.20	Execute purchase contract	18
20	0.10	0.14	0.16	Authorize and complete final statement	19
21	2	3	6	Purchase contract	19
22	0.10	0.10	0.20	Make bond proceeds available	20
23	0	0.20	0.20	Sign construction contract	21, 22

weeks. Activity J has estimated completion times of 1 week, 2 weeks, and 2 weeks.

Phase 3 is the most difficult and complex of the entire development project. It also consists of six separate activities. Activity K has three time estimates of 2 weeks, 2 weeks, and 3 weeks. The immediate predecessor for this activity is activity E. The immediate predecessor for activity L is activity F. The time estimates for activity L are 3 weeks, 4 weeks, and 6 weeks. Activity M has 2 weeks, 2 weeks, and 4 weeks for the optimistic, probable, and pessimistic time estimates. The immediate predecessor for activity M is activity G. Activities N and O both have activity I as their immediate predecessor. Activity N has 8 weeks, 9 weeks, and 11 weeks for its three time estimates. Activity O has 1 week, 1 week, and 3 weeks as its time estimates. Finally, activity P has time estimates of 4 weeks, 4 weeks, and 8 weeks. Activity J is the only immediate predecessor.

Phase 4 involves five activities. Activity Q requires activity K to be completed before it can be started. The three time estimates for activity Q are 6 weeks, 6 weeks, and 7 weeks. Activity R requires that both activity L and activity M be completed first. The three time estimates for activity R are 1 week, 2 weeks, and 4 weeks. Activity S requires activity N to be completed first. Its time estimates are 6 weeks, 6 weeks, and 7 weeks. Activity T requires that activity O be completed. The time estimates for activity T are 3 weeks, 3 weeks, and 4 weeks. The final activity for phase 4 is activity U. The time estimates for this activity are 1 week, 2 weeks, and 3 weeks. Activity P must be completed before activity U can be started.

Phase 5 is the final phase of the development project. It consists of only two activities. Activity V requires that activity Q and activity R be completed before it can be started. Time estimates for this activity are 9 weeks, 10 weeks, and 11 weeks. Activity W is the final activity of the

process. It requires three activities to be completed before it can be started: activities S, T, and U. The estimated completion times for activity W are 2 weeks, 4 weeks, and 5 weeks.

(a) Given this information, determine the expected completion time for the entire process. Also determine which activities are along the critical path.
(b) Jim hopes that the total project will take less than 40 weeks. Is this likely to occur?
(c) Jim has just determined that activities D and I have already been completed and that no additional work is required on these activities. What is the impact of this change on the activities along the critical path?

8-41 (*Project scheduling with LP*) Kitchener Construction Company (KCC) must complete its current office building renovation as quickly as possible. The first portion of the project consists of six activities, some of which must be finished before others are started. The activities, their precedences, and their estimated times are shown in the following table:

ACTIVITY		PRECEDENCE	TIME (DAYS)
Prepare financing options	(A)	—	2
Prepare preliminary sketches	(B)	—	3
Outline specifications	(C)	—	1
Prepare drawings	(D)	A	4
Write specifications	(E)	C and D	5
Run off prints	(F)	B	1

Let X_i represent the earliest completion of an activity where i = A, B, C, D, E, F. Formulate and solve KCC's problem as a linear program.

➠ CASE STUDY 8.1

Haygood Brothers Construction Company

George and Harry Haygood are building contractors who specialize in the construction of private home dwellings, storage warehouses, and small businesses (less than 7000 square metres of floor space). Both George and Harry entered a carpenter union's apprenticeship program in the early 1990s and, upon completion of the apprenticeship, became skilled craftsmen in 1996. Before going into business for themselves, they worked for several local building contractors.

Typically, the Haygood Brothers submit competitive bids for the construction of proposed dwellings. Whenever their bids are accepted, various aspects of the construction (e.g., electrical wiring, plumbing, brick laying, painting) are subcontracted. George and Harry, however, perform all carpentry work. In

addition, they plan and schedule all construction operations, frequently arrange interim financing, and supervise all construction activities.

The philosophy under which the Haygood Brothers have always operated can be simply stated: "Time is money." Delays in construction increase the costs of interim financing and postpone the initiation of their building projects. Consequently, they deal with all bottlenecks promptly and avoid all delays whenever possible. To minimize the time consumed in a construction project, the Haygood Brothers use PERT.

First, all construction activities and events are itemized and properly arranged (in parallel and sequential combinations) in a network. Then time estimates for each activity are made, the expected time for completing each activity is determined, and the critical (longest) path is calculated. Finally, earliest times, latest times, and slack values are computed. Having made these calculations, George and Harry can place their resources in the critical areas to minimize the time of completing the project.

The following are the activities that constitute an upcoming project (home dwelling) of the Haygood Brothers:

1. Arrange financing (A)
2. Let subcontracts (B)
3. Set and pour foundations (C)
4. Plumbing (D)
5. Framing (E)
6. Roofing (F)
7. Electrical wiring (G)
8. Installation of windows and doors (H)
9. Ductwork and insulation (including heating and cooling units) (I)
10. Sheetrock, paneling, and paper hanging (J)
11. Installation of cabinets (K)
12. Bricking (L)
13. Outside trim (M)
14. Inside trim (including fixtures) (N)
15. Painting (O)
16. Flooring (P)

The immediate predecessors and optimistic (*a*), most likely (*m*), and pessimistic (*b*) time estimates are shown in Table 8.11.

DISCUSSION QUESTIONS

1. What is the time length of the critical path? What is the significance of the critical path?
2. Compute the amount of time that the completion of each activity can be delayed without affecting the overall project.

3. The project was begun August 1. What is the probability that the project can be completed by September 30? (Note: Scheduled completion time = 60 days.)

Source: *Professor Jerry Kinard, Western Carolina University.*

TABLE 8.11

Haygood Brothers Construction Co.

ACTIVITY	IMMEDIATE PREDECESSORS	DAYS		
		a	*m*	*b*
A	—	4	5	6
B	A	2	5	8
C	B	5	7	9
D	B	4	5	6
E	C	2	4	6
F	E	3	5	9
G	E	4	5	6
H	E	3	4	7
I	E	5	7	9
J	D, I	10	11	12
K	F, G, H, J	4	6	8
L	F, G, H, J	7	8	9
M	L	4	5	10
N	K	5	7	9
O	N	5	6	7
P	M, O	2	3	4

⏵ CASE STUDY 8.2

Family Planning Research Center of Nigeria

Dr. Adinombe Watage, deputy director of the Family Planning Research Center in Nigeria's Over-The-River Province, was assigned the task of organizing and training five teams of field workers to perform educational and outreach activities as part of a large project to demonstrate acceptance of a new method of birth control. These workers already have training in family planning education but must receive specific training regarding the new method of contraception. Two types of materials must also be prepared: (1) those for use in training the workers and (2) those for distribution in the field. Training faculty must be brought in and arrangements made for transportation and accommodations for the participants.

Dr. Watage first called a meeting of this office staff. Together they identified the activities that must be carried out, their necessary sequences, and the time that they would require. Their results are displayed in Table 8.12.

Louis Odaga, the chief clerk, noted that the project had to be completed in 60 days. Whipping out his solar-powered calculator, he added up the time needed. It came to 94 days. "An impossible task, then," he noted. "No," Dr. Watage replied, "some of these tasks can go forward in parallel."

"Be careful, though," warned Mr. Oglagadu, the chief nurse, "there aren't that many of us to go around. There are only 10 of us in this office."

"I can check whether we have enough heads and hands once I have tentatively scheduled the activities," Dr. Watage

TABLE 8.12 — Family Planning Research Center Activities

ACTIVITY	MUST FOLLOW	TIME (DAYS)	STAFFING NEEDED
A. Identify faculty and their schedules	—	5	2
B. Arrange transport to base	—	7	3
C. Identify and collect training materials	—	5	2
D. Arrange accommodations	A	3	1
E. Identify team	A	7	4
F. Bring in team	B, E	2	1
G. Transport faculty to base	A, B	3	2
H. Print program material	C	10	6
I. Have program materials delivered	H	7	3
J. Conduct training program	D, F, G, I	15	0
K. Perform fieldwork training	J	30	0

TABLE 8.13 — Family Planning Research Center Costs

ACTIVITY	NORMAL TIME	NORMAL COST ($)	MINIMUM TIME	MINIMUM COST ($)	AVERAGE COST PER DAY SAVED ($)
A. Identify faculty	5	400	2	700	100
B. Arrange transport	7	1 000	4	1 450	150
C. Identify materials	5	400	3	500	50
D. Make accommodations	3	2 500	1	3 000	250
E. Identify team	7	400	4	850	150
F. Bring team in	2	1 000	1	2 000	1 000
G. Transport faculty	3	1 500	2	2 000	500
H. Print materials	10	3 000	5	4 000	200
I. Deliver materials	7	200	2	600	80
J. Train team	15	5 000	10	7 000	400
K. Do fieldwork	30	10 000	20	14 000	400

responded. "If the schedule is too tight, I have permission from the Pathminder Foundation to spend some funds to speed it up, just so long as I can prove that it can be done at the least cost necessary. Can you help me prove that? Here are the costs for the activities with the elapsed time that we planned and the costs and times if we shorten them to an absolute minimum." Those data are given in Table 8.13 above.

DISCUSSION QUESTIONS

1. Some of the tasks in this project can be done in parallel. Prepare a diagram showing the required network of tasks and define the critical path. What is the length of the project without crashing?
2. At this point, can the project be done given the personnel constraint of 10 persons?
3. If the critical path is longer than 60 days, what is the least amount that Dr. Watage can spend and still achieve this schedule objective? How can he prove to Pathminder Foundation that this is the minimum-cost alternative?

Source: Professor Curtis P. McLaughlin, Kenan-Flagler Business School, University of North Carolina at Chapel Hill.

BIBLIOGRAPHY

Angus, R. B., N. R. Gunderson, and T. P. Cullinano. *Planning, Performing, and Controlling Projects*, 3/e. Upper Saddle River, NJ: Prentice Hall, 2000.

Charoenngam, C., and A.S., Khazi. "Cost/Schedule Information System," *Cost Engineering 3*, 9 (September 1997): 29–35.

Dorey, C. "The ABCs of R&D at Nortel," *CMA Magazine* (March 1998): 19–22.

Ghattas, R. G., and S. L. McKee. *Practical Project Management*. Upper Saddle River, NJ: Prentice Hall, 2001.

Graham, R. et al. "Creating an Environment for Successful Projects," *Research Technology Management* (February 1998): 60.

Kolisch, R. "Resource Allocation Capabilities of Commercial Project Management Software Packages," *Interfaces* 29, 4 (July 1999): 19–31.

Mantel, S. J., J. R. Meredith, S. M. Shafer, and M. M. Sutton. *Project Management in Practice*. New York: Wiley, 2000.

Meredith, J. R., and S. J. Mantel. *Project Management: A Managerial Approach*, 4/e. New York: Wiley, 1999.

Murch, R. *Project Management: Best Practices for IT Professionals*. Upper Saddle River, NJ: Prentice Hall, 2001.

Roe, J. "Bringing Discipline to Project Management," *Harvard Business Review* (April 1998): 153–159.

Sander, W. "The Projects Manager's Guide," *Quality Progress* (January 1998): 109.

Sivathanu, P. "Enhanced PERT for Program Analysis, Control, and Evaluation," *International Journal of Project Management* (February 1993): 39–43.

CHAPTER 9

Decision Analysis

LEARNING OBJECTIVES

After completing this chapter, students will be able to:

1. List the steps of the decision-making process and describe the different types of decision-making environments.

2. Make decisions under uncertainty and under risk.

3. Use Excel to set up and solve problems involving decision tables.

4. Develop accurate and useful decision trees.

5. Use TreePlan to set up and analyze decision tree problems with Excel.

6. Revise probability estimates using Bayesian analysis.

7. Understand the importance and use of utility theory in decision making.

CHAPTER OUTLINE

9.1 Introduction

9.2 The Five Steps in Decision Analysis

9.3 Types of Decision-Making Environments

9.4 Decision Making under Uncertainty

9.5 Decision Making under Risk

9.6 Decision Trees

9.7 Using TreePlan to Solve Decision Tree Problems with Excel

9.8 Decision Trees for Multistage Decision-Making Problems

9.9 Estimating Probability Values Using Bayesian Analysis

9.10 Utility Theory

Summary • Glossary • Key Equations • Solved Problems • Self-Test • Discussion Questions and Problems • Case Study: Ski Right • Case Study: Blake Electronics • Case Study: Jupiter Corporation • Bibliography

Decision Theory Helps Develop Cost-Effective Strategies for Treating Dyspepsia

Dyspepsia, better known to the lay person as heartburn, is a common medical condition that affects people in their everyday lives. There are a variety of different treatment options for patients who suffer from heartburn, and treatment protocols differ with regard to alleviation of symptoms, invasiveness of the procedure, and cost of treatment. A study conducted in collaboration with the Department of Gastroenterology at Montreal's McGill University was intended to find cost-effective strategies for treating dyspepsia in patients who present with symptoms such as heartburn or stomach pain.

Commenting on the use of decision theory in the management of medical treatment, one of the principal researchers, Ralph Crott, said, "There are five to seven management strategies a doctor could start with." In the research study on the treatment of dyspepsia, the "decision tree" technique was used. This technique allows doctors to track the treatment decisions made for patients and to assess the outcomes over a period of one year following their initial visit.

The decision tree model is ideal for comparing different strategies based on cost and effectiveness. In order to evaluate different options it was necessary to specify data reflecting the probabilities of the different outcomes, as well as the costs of procedures and treatments.

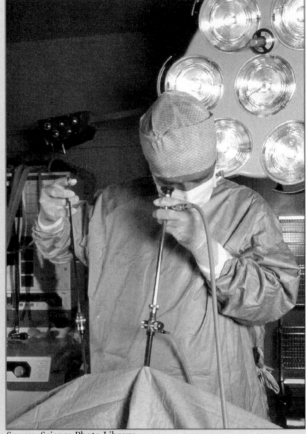

Source: Science Photo Library

Medical decision making involves trade-offs between the use of medical tests such as endoscopy for heartburn patients and less expensive alternatives. As Ralph Crott explained "It's a costly and invasive procedure. You want to do that only when really necessary . . . it is typical for medical decisions to involve such tradeoffs . . . For decision makers, that's the whole problem."

Under the Canadian medicare system, the government, as the sole provider of health care in Canada, has to make decisions about the efficacy of treatment protocols and whether it is willing to pay for these procedures.

N. Makris, A. Barkun, R. Crott, and C. A. Fallone. "Cost-Effectiveness of Alternative Approaches in the Management of Dyspepsia," *International Journal of Technology Assessment in Health Care* 19, 3 (2003): 446–464.

9.1   INTRODUCTION

Decision analysis is an analytic and systematic way to tackle problems.

To a great extent, the successes or failures that a person experiences in life depend on the decisions that he or she makes. The development of DOS, followed by Windows and other software, has made Bill Gates a very wealthy person. In contrast, the person who designed the flawed tires at Firestone (which caused so many accidents with Ford Explorers in the late 1990s) is probably not working there anymore. Why and how did these people make their respective decisions? A single decision can make the difference between a successful career and an unsuccessful one. *Decision analysis* is an analytic and systematic approach to the study of decision making. In this chapter, we present the decision models that are useful in helping managers make the best possible decisions.

A good decision is based on logic.

What makes the difference between good and bad decisions? In most practical situations, managers have to make decisions without knowing for sure which events will occur in the future. In such cases, a good decision can be defined as one that is based on logic, considers all possible decision alternatives, examines all available information about the future, and applies the decision modeling approach described in this chapter. Occasionally, due to the uncertainty of future events, a good decision could result in an unfavourable outcome. But if a decision is made properly, it is still a good decision.

A bad decision does not consider all alternatives.

In contrast, a bad decision is one that is not based on logic, does not use all available information, does not consider all alternatives, and does not employ appropriate decision modeling techniques. If you make a bad decision but are lucky enough that a favourable outcome occurs, you have still made a bad decision. Although occasionally good decisions yield bad results, in the long run, using decision analysis will result in successful outcomes.

9.2   THE FIVE STEPS IN DECISION ANALYSIS

Whether you are deciding about signing up for next semester's classes, buying a new computer, or building a multimillion-dollar factory, the steps in making a good decision are basically the same:

Five Steps of Decision Making

1. Clearly define the problem at hand.
2. List *all* possible decision alternatives.
3. Identify the possible future outcomes for each decision alternative.
4. Identify the payoff (usually profit or cost) for each combination of alternatives and outcomes.
5. Select one of the decision analysis modeling techniques discussed in this chapter. Apply the decision model and make your decision.

Thompson Lumber Company Example

We use the case of Thompson Lumber Company as an example to illustrate the use of the five decision analysis steps. John Thompson is the founder and president of Thompson Lumber Company, a profitable firm located in Kamloops, B.C.

The first step is to define the problem.

Step 1   John identifies his decision-making problem as follows: whether to expand his business by manufacturing and marketing a new product, backyard storage sheds.

The second step is to list alternatives.

Step 2   Generate the complete list of decision alternatives available to the decision maker. In decision analysis, a decision alternative is defined as a course of action that is available to the decision maker. There is no limit to the number of decision alternatives that a problem can have. The decision maker has total control over which decision alternative he or she chooses and must choose exactly one of the alternatives listed in the problem.

In Thompson Lumber's case, let us assume that John decides that his alternatives are as follows: (1) build a large plant to manufacture the storage sheds, (2) build a small plant to manufacture the storage sheds, or (3) build no plant at all (i.e., not develop the new product line and keep his business at its current size).

One of the biggest mistakes that decision makers make in practice is to leave out important decision alternatives. For example, suppose John had left out the alternative to build no plant at all. It could well turn out that based on all the issues in the decision-making problem, the best decision for him would have been to not expand his business. However, by not including that alternative among his choices, John would have been unable to select that decision. In general, it is important to remember that while a particular decision alternative may sometimes appear to be inappropriate on the surface, it may turn out to be an excellent choice when all issues in the problem are considered.

The third step is to identify possible outcomes.

Step 3   Identify all possible future **outcomes** for each decision alternative. In decision analysis, outcomes are also known as *states of nature*. There is no limit to the number of outcomes that can be listed for a decision alternative, and each alternative can have its own unique set of outcomes. Exactly one of the listed outcomes will occur for a specific decision alternative. However, the decision maker has little or no control over which outcome will occur.

In Thompson Lumber's case, suppose John determines that all three of his decision alternatives have the same three possible outcomes: (1) demand for the sheds will be high, (2) demand for the sheds will be moderate, or (3) demand for the sheds will be low.

As with decision alternatives, a common mistake in practice is to forget about some of the possible outcomes. Optimistic decision makers may tend to ignore bad outcomes under the mistaken assumption that they will not happen, whereas pessimistic managers may discount a favorable outcome. If we don't consider all possibilities, we will not make a logical decision, and the results may be undesirable.

The fourth step is to list payoffs.

Step 4   Define the measurable output resulting from each possible combination of decision alternative and outcome. That is, we need to identify the output that will result if we choose a specific decision alternative, and a particular outcome then occurs. In decision analysis, we call these outputs **payoffs**, regardless of whether they denote profit or cost. Payoffs can also be nonmonetary (e.g., number of units sold, number of workers needed).

In Thompson Lumber's case, let us assume that John wants to use net profits to measure his payoffs. He has already evaluated the potential profits associated with the various combinations of alternatives and outcomes, as follows:

- If John decides to build a large plant, he thinks that with high demand for sheds, the result would be a net profit of $200 000 to his firm. The net profit would, however, be only $100 000 if demand were moderate. If demand were low, there would actually be a net loss of $120 000. Payoffs are also called **conditional values** because, for example, John receiving a profit of $200 000 is conditional upon both his building a large factory and having high demand.

- If he builds a small plant, the results would be a net profit of $90 000 if there were high demand for sheds, a net profit of $50 000 if there were moderate demand, and a net loss of $20 000 if there were low demand.

- Finally, doing nothing would result in $0 payoff in any demand scenario.

TABLE 9.1

Payoff Table for
Thompson Lumber

| | OUTCOMES | | |
ALTERNATIVES	HIGH DEMAND	MODERATE DEMAND	LOW DEMAND
Build large plant	$200 000	$100 000	−$120 000
Build small plant	90 000	50 000	−20 000
No plant	0	0	0

During the fourth step, the decision maker can construct decision or payoff tables.

The easiest way to present payoff values is by constructing a *payoff table*, or **decision table**. A payoff table for John's conditional profit values is shown in Table 9.1 above. All the decision alternatives are listed down the left side of this table, and all the possible outcomes are listed across the top. The body of the table contains the actual payoffs (profits, in this case).

The last step is to select and apply a decision analysis model.

Step 5   Select a decision analysis model and apply it to the data to help make the decision. The types of decision models available for selection depend on the environment in which we are operating and the amount of uncertainty and risk involved. The model specifies the criteria to be used in choosing the best decision alternative.

9.3   TYPES OF DECISION-MAKING ENVIRONMENTS

The types of decisions people make depend on how much knowledge or information they have about the problem scenario. There are three decision-making environments, as described in the following sections.

The consequence of every alternative is known in decision making under certainty.

Type 1: Decision Making Under Certainty   In the environment of **decision making under certainty**, decision makers know for sure (i.e., with certainty) the payoff for every decision alternative. Typically, this means that there is only one outcome for each alternative. Naturally, decision makers will select the alternative that will result in the best payoff. The mathematical programming approaches covered in Chapters 2–6 are all examples of decision modeling techniques suited for decision making under certainty.

Let's see how decision making under certainty could affect Thompson Lumber's problem. In this environment, we assume that John knows exactly what will happen in the future. For example, if he knows with certainty that demand for storage sheds will be high, what should he do? Looking at John's conditional profit values in Table 9.1, it is clear in this case that he should build the large plant, which has the highest profit, $200 000.

In real-world cases, however, few managers would be fortunate enough to have complete information and knowledge about the outcomes under consideration. In most situations, managers would either have no information at all about the outcomes, or, at best, have probabilistic information about future outcomes. These are the second and third types of decision-making environments.

Probabilities are not known in decision making under uncertainty.

Type 2: Decision Making Under Uncertainty   In **decision making under uncertainty**, decision makers have no information at all about the various outcomes. That is, they do not know the likelihood (or probability) that a specific outcome will occur. For example, it is impossible to predict the probability that the Liberal Party will control Parliament 25 years from now. Likewise, it may be impossible in some cases to assess the probability that a new product or undertaking will be successful.

There are several decision models available to handle decision-making problems under uncertainty. These are explained in Section 9.4.

➠MODELING IN THE REAL WORLD
Using Decision Tree Analysis on R&D Projects

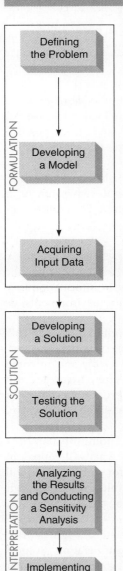

The Canadian subsidiary of ICI discovered a new unpatentable process for anthraquinone (AQ) to reduce paper mill pollution. The company had to decide whether to invest funds in research and development (R&D) for the new process.

A traditional decision tree model was used. Instead of expected monetary values, the model used expected net present value, which converts future monetary flows into today's dollars.

ICI collected both probability and monetary values. The probability data included the probability of a technical success, the probability of a significant market for the new process, and the probability of a commercial success.

The solution was obtained using decision tree analysis like the analyses performed in this chapter.

ICI tested the solution by analyzing various risks of the process, including whether the new process could be developed, the market for the new process, the accuracy of the conditional probabilities in the decision tree, and various expenses and monetary flows.

The estimated net present value from decision tree analysis was $3.2 million. If the new project was successful, the net present value could be as high as $25 million.

The decision tree analysis moved this R&D project forward. As a result, it was decided to investigate the process further. After field testing, however, difficulty with pulp mills resulted in the project being cancelled.

Source: Sidney Hess. "Swinging on the Branch of a Tree: Project Selection Applications," *Interfaces* 23, 6 (November–December 1993): 5–12.

Probabilities are known in decision making under risk.

Type 3: Decision Making Under Risk   In **decision making under risk**, decision makers have some knowledge regarding the probability of occurrence of each outcome. The probability could be a precise measure (e.g., the probability of being dealt an ace from a deck of cards is exactly $\frac{1}{13}$) or an estimate (e.g., the probability that it will rain tomorrow is 0.40). Regardless of how the probabilities are determined, in decision making under risk, decision makers attempt to identify the alternative that optimizes their *expected* payoff.

DECISION MODELING IN ACTION

Decision Analysis Helps Allocate Health Care Funds in the United Kingdom

Individuals and companies have often used decision-making techniques to help them invest or allocate funds to various projects. In some cases, decision-making techniques can be used to determine how millions of dollars are to be spent. This same type of analysis can also be used on a larger scale for countries or governments. This was the case in the allocation of health care funds for the United Kingdom.

Over the years, the United States has debated the possible implementation of a comprehensive national health care program. Although this does not seem likely for the United States in the near future, other countries, such as the United Kingdom and Canada, have been using some form of national health care system for decades. For the United Kingdom, the question is not whether to have a national health care system, but how funds from such a system are to be allocated.

The United Kingdom's National Health service (NHS) is funded through general tax revenues. The funds are dispersed to about 105 different local health authorities. The annual funding for the NHS is approximately $35 billion. With such a large sum of national funds going to such an important area,

the decision-making process to justly allocate funds can be difficult indeed.

Starting in the 1970s, a formula, based partly on a standardized mortality ratio, was developed to distribute health funds to the local authorities. This formula, however, failed to take into account social deprivation and general health care needs. As a result, the NHS decided to seek a better way to allocate health care dollars to the local authorities.

A team from York University spent about 4 months developing the original allocation model and another 14 months refining the decision-making model. Using decision analysis, the team identified a set of key variables to explain health care needs and usage in the United Kingdom. This resulted in modifications to the decision-making approach regarding health care funds. Many believe that the new model will more fairly and justly allocate the United Kingdom's important national health care funds to those who truly need the assistance.

Source: Nancy Bistritz. "RX for UK Healthcare Woes," *OR/MS Today* (April 1997): 18. Copyright © 1997. Reprinted with permission.

Decision analysis models for business problems in this environment typically employ one of two criteria: (1) maximization of expected monetary value or (2) minimization of expected opportunity loss. We study models using both criteria for decision making under risk in Section 9.5.

9.4   DECISION MAKING UNDER UNCERTAINTY

As noted previously, an environment of decision making under uncertainty exists when a manager cannot assess the probabilities of the different outcomes with confidence, or when virtually no probability data are available. In this section, we discuss the following five different decision-making criteria to handle such situations:

Probabilities of outcomes are not known.

1. Maximax
2. Maximin
3. Criterion of realism
4. Equally likely
5. Minimax regret

In discussing these criteria here, we assume that all payoffs represent profits. That is, we prefer higher payoffs to smaller ones. If the payoffs represent costs (i.e., we prefer smaller payoffs to higher ones), some of the criteria would need to be used differently. To avoid this confusion, an easy option is to convert costs in a payoff table to profits by multiplying all cost values by −1. This way, we can apply the criteria as discussed here for all problems, regardless of whether the payoffs represent profits or costs.

The first four criteria can be computed directly from the decision (payoff) table, whereas the minimax regret criterion requires use of the opportunity loss table (which we

TABLE 9.2	OUTCOMES			
Thompson Lumber's Maximax Decision				
ALTERNATIVES	HIGH DEMAND	MODERATE DEMAND	LOW DEMAND	MAXIMUM FOR ALTERNATIVE
Build large plant	$200 000	$100 000	−$120 000	$200 000 → Maximax
Build small plant	90 000	50 000	−20 000	90 000
No plant	0	0	0	0

compute subsequently). Let us look at each of the five criteria and apply them to the Thompson Lumber example. Remember that the decision-making environment assumes that John has no probability information about the three outcomes—high demand, moderate demand, and low demand for storage sheds.

Maximax Criterion

Maximax is an optimistic approach.

The **maximax** criterion selects the decision alternative that *maxi*mizes the *maxi*mum payoff over all alternatives. We first locate the maximum payoff for each alternative and then select the alternative with the highest value among these maximum payoffs. Because this criterion takes an extremely rosy view of the future and locates the alternative with the overall highest possible payoff, it is also called the *optimistic* criterion.

In Table 9.2 above we see that John's maximax choice is the first alternative, build large plant. The $200 000 payoff is the maximum of the maximum payoffs (i.e., $200 000, $90 000, and $0) for each decision alternative.

Maximin Criterion

Maximin is a pessimistic approach.

The exact opposite of the maximax criterion is the **maximin** criterion, which takes an extremely conservative view of the future. For this reason, it is also called the *pessimistic* criterion. The maximin criterion finds the alternative that *maxi*mizes the *min*imum payoff over all decision alternatives. We first locate the minimum payoff for each alternative and then select the alternative with the highest value among those minimum payoffs.

John's maximin choice, no plant, is shown in Table 9.3. The $0 payoff is the maximum of the minimum payoffs (i.e., −$120 000, −$20 000, and $0) for each alternative.

Criterion of Realism (Hurwicz)

The criterion of realism uses the weighted average approach.

Decision makers are seldom extreme optimists or extreme pessimists. Because most tend to be somewhere in between the two extremes, the *criterion of realism* (or *Hurwicz*) decision criterion offers a compromise between optimistic and pessimistic decisions. In this criterion, we use a parameter called the **coefficient of realism** to measure the decision maker's level of optimism regarding the future. This coefficient, denoted by α, has a value between 0 and 1. An α value of 0 implies that the decision maker is totally pessimistic about

TABLE 9.3	OUTCOMES			
Thompson Lumber's Maximin Decision				
ALTERNATIVES	HIGH DEMAND	MODERATE DEMAND	LOW DEMAND	MINIMUM FOR ALTERNATIVE
Build large plant	$200 000	$100 000	−$120 000	−$120 000
Build small plant	90 000	50 000	−20 000	−20 000
No plant	0	0	0	0 → Maximin

TABLE 9.4

Thompson Lumber's Criterion of Realism Decision ($\alpha = 0.45$)

	OUTCOMES			
ALTERNATIVES	HIGH DEMAND	MODERATE DEMAND	LOW DEMAND	WT. AVG. ($\alpha = 0.45$) FOR ALTERNATIVE
Build large plant	$200 000	$100 000	−$120 000	$24 000
Build small plant	90 000	50 000	−20 000	29 500 → Realism
No plant	0	0	0	0

the future, while an α value of 1 implies that the decision maker is totally optimistic about the future. The advantage of this approach is that it allows the decision maker to build in personal feelings about relative optimism and pessimism. The formula is as follows:

$$\text{Realism payoff for alternative} = \alpha \times \text{Maximum payoff for alternative}$$
$$+ (1-\alpha) \times \text{Minimum payoff for alternative} \qquad \text{(9-1)}$$

Because the realism payoff is just a weighted average for the maximum and minimum payoffs (where α is the weight), this criterion is also called the *weighted average* criterion.

Suppose we identify John Thompson's coefficient of realism to be $\alpha = 0.45$. That is, John is a slightly pessimistic person (note that $\alpha = 0.5$ implies a strictly neutral person). Under this situation, his best decision would be to build a small plant. As shown in Table 9.4 above, this alternative has the highest realism payoff, at $29 500 [= 0.45 \times \$90\,000 + 0.55 \times (-\$20\,000)]$.

Equally Likely (Laplace) Criterion

The equally likely criterion selects the highest average alternative.

The **equally likely** (or *Laplace*) criterion finds the decision alternative that has the highest average payoff. We first calculate the average payoff for each alternative and then pick the alternative with the maximum average payoff. Note that the Laplace approach essentially assumes that each outcome is equally likely to occur.

The equally likely choice for Thompson Lumber is the first alternative, build a large plant. This strategy, as shown in Table 9.5, has a maximum average payoff of $60 000 over all alternatives.

Minimax Regret Criterion

Minimax regret is based on opportunity loss.

The final decision criterion that we discuss is based on **opportunity loss**, also called *regret*. Opportunity loss is defined as the difference between the optimal payoff and the actual payoff received. In other words, it's the amount lost by *not* picking the best alternative. **Minimax regret** finds the alternative that *mini*mizes the *max*imum opportunity loss within each alternative.

To use this criterion, we need to first develop the opportunity loss table. This is done by determining the opportunity loss of not choosing the best alternative for each outcome. To do so, we subtract each payoff for a specific outcome from the *best* payoff for that outcome. For example, the best payoff with high demand in Thompson Lumber's payoff table

TABLE 9.5

Thompson Lumber's Equally Likely Decision

	OUTCOMES			
ALTERNATIVES	HIGH DEMAND	MODERATE DEMAND	LOW DEMAND	AVERAGE FOR ALTERNATIVE
Build large plant	$200 000	$100 000	−$120 000	$60 000 → Equally likely
Build small plant	90 000	50 000	−20 000	40 000
No plant	0	0	0	0

TABLE 9.6   **Opportunity Loss Table for Thompson Lumber**

	OUTCOMES		
ALTERNATIVES	HIGH DEMAND	MODERATE DEMAND	LOW DEMAND
Build large plant	$200 000 − $200 000 = $ 0	$100 000 − $100 000 = $ 0	$0 − (−$120 000) = $120 000
Build small plant	200 000 − 90 000 = 110 000	100 000 − 50 000 = 50 000	0 − (−20 000) = 20 000
No plant	200 000 − 0 = 200 000	100 000 − 0 = 100 000	0 − 0 = 0

File: 9-1.xls

Excel worksheets can be created to solve decision-making problems under uncertainty.

is $200 000 (corresponding to building a large plant). Hence, we subtract all payoffs for that outcome (i.e., in that column) from $200 000. Likewise, the best payoffs with moderate demand and low demand are $100 000 and $0, respectively. We therefore subtract all payoffs in the second column from $100 000 and all payoffs in the third column from $0. Table 9.6 above illustrates these computations and shows John's complete opportunity loss table.

Once the opportunity loss table has been constructed, we first locate the maximum opportunity loss (regret) for each alternative. We then pick the alternative with the smallest value among these maximum regrets. As shown in Table 9.7, John's minimax regret choice is the second alternative, build a small plant. The regret of $110 000 is the minimum of the maximum regrets (i.e., $120 000, $110 000, and $200 000) over all three alternatives.

Using Excel to Solve Decision-Making Problems under Uncertainty

As just demonstrated in the Thompson Lumber example, calculations for the different criteria in decision making under uncertainty are fairly straightforward. In most cases, we can perform these calculations quickly even by hand. However, if we wish, we can easily construct Excel spreadsheets to calculate these results for us. Screenshot 9.1A shows the relevant formulas for the different decision criteria in the Thompson Lumber example. The results are shown in Screenshot 9.1B.

Excel Notes

- The CD-ROM that accompanies this textbook contains the Excel file for each sample problem discussed here. The relevant file name is shown in the margin next to each example.
- For clarity, our Excel layouts in this chapter are colour coded as follows:
  - *Input cells*, where we enter the problem data, are shaded yellow.
  - *Output cells*, where the results are shown, are shaded green.

  Although these colours are not apparent in the screenshots shown in the textbook, they are seen in the Excel files on the CD-ROM.

TABLE 9.7

Thompson Lumber's Minimax Regret Decision

	OUTCOMES			
ALTERNATIVES	HIGH DEMAND	MODERATE DEMAND	LOW DEMAND	MAXIMUM FOR ALTERNATIVE
Build large plant	$ 0	$ 0	$120 000	$120 000
Build small plant	110 000	50 000	20 000	110 000 → Minimax
No plant	200 000	100 000	0	200 000

SCREENSHOT 9.1A   Formula View of Excel Layout for Thompson Lumber:
Decision Making under Uncertainty

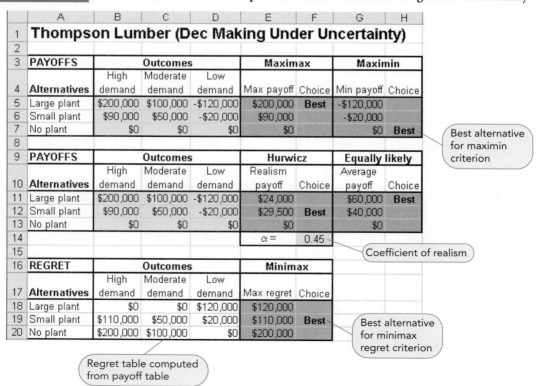

Identifies maximum payoff.

IF function is used to identify the best alternative.

Identifies minimum payoff.

	A	B	C	D	E	F	G	H
1	Thompson Lumber (Dec Making Under Uncertainty)							
2								
3	PAYOFFS		Outcomes		Maximax		Maximin	
4	Alternatives	High demand	Moderate demand	Low demand	Max payoff	Choice	Min payoff	Choice
5	Large plant	200000	100000	-120000	=MAX(B5:D5)	=IF(E5=MAX(E$5:E$7),"Best","")	=MIN(B5:D5)	=IF(G5=MAX(G$5:0
6	Small plant	90000	50000	-20000	=MAX(B6:D6)	=IF(E6=MAX(E$5:E$7),"Best","")	=MIN(B6:D6)	=IF(G6=MAX(G$5:0
7	No plant	0	0	0	=MAX(B7:D7)	=IF(E7=MAX(E$5:E$7),"Best","")	=MIN(B7:D7)	=IF(G7=MAX(G$5:0
8								
9	PAYOFFS		Outcomes		Hurwicz		Equally likely	
10	Alternatives	Good market	Fair market	Poor market	Realism payoff	Choice	Average payoff	Choice
11	Large plant	200000	100000	-120000	=F$14*MAX(B11:D11)+(1-F$14)*MIN(B11:D11)	=IF(E11=MAX(E$11:E$13),"Best","")	=AVERAGE(B11:D11)	=IF(G11=MAX(G$11:
12	Small plant	90000	50000	-20000	=F$14*MAX(B12:D12)+(1-F$14)*MIN(B12:D12)	=IF(E12=MAX(E$11:E$13),"Best","")	=AVERAGE(B12:D12)	=IF(G12=MAX(G$11:
13	No plant	0	0	0	=F$14*MAX(B13:D13)+(1-F$14)*MIN(B13:D13)	=IF(E13=MAX(E$11:E$13),"Best","")	=AVERAGE(B13:D13)	=IF(G13=MAX(G$11:
14					α =	0.45		
15								
16	REGRET		Outcomes		Minimax			
17	Alternatives	High demand	Moderate demand	Low demand	Max regret	Choice		
18	Large plant	=MAX(B$5:B$7)-B5	=MAX(C$5:C$7)-C5	=MAX(D$5:D$7)-D5	=MAX(B18:D18)	=IF(E18=MIN(E$18:E$20),"Best","")		
19	Small plant	=MAX(B$5:B$7)-B6	=MAX(C$5:C$7)-C6	=MAX(D$5:D$7)-D6	=MAX(B19:D19)	=IF(E19=MIN(E$18:E$20),"Best","")		
20	No plant	=MAX(B$5:B$7)-B7	=MAX(C$5:C$7)-C7	=MAX(D$5:D$7)-D7	=MAX(B20:D20)	=IF(E20=MIN(E$18:E$20),"Best","")		

AVERAGE function is used to calculate equally likely payoffs.

Formula to calculate regret values

Identifies maximum regret.

= α × Maximum payoff
+ (1–α) × Minimum payoff

SCREENSHOT 9.1B   Excel Solution for Thompson Lumber: Decision Making under Uncertainty

	A	B	C	D	E	F	G	H
1	Thompson Lumber (Dec Making Under Uncertainty)							
2								
3	PAYOFFS		Outcomes		Maximax		Maximin	
4	Alternatives	High demand	Moderate demand	Low demand	Max payoff	Choice	Min payoff	Choice
5	Large plant	$200,000	$100,000	-$120,000	$200,000	Best	-$120,000	
6	Small plant	$90,000	$50,000	-$20,000	$90,000		-$20,000	
7	No plant	$0	$0	$0	$0		$0	Best
8								
9	PAYOFFS		Outcomes		Hurwicz		Equally likely	
10	Alternatives	High demand	Moderate demand	Low demand	Realism payoff	Choice	Average payoff	Choice
11	Large plant	$200,000	$100,000	-$120,000	$24,000		$60,000	Best
12	Small plant	$90,000	$50,000	-$20,000	$29,500	Best	$40,000	
13	No plant	$0	$0	$0	$0		$0	
14					α =	0.45		
15								
16	REGRET		Outcomes		Minimax			
17	Alternatives	High demand	Moderate demand	Low demand	Max regret	Choice		
18	Large plant	$0	$0	$120,000	$120,000			
19	Small plant	$110,000	$50,000	$20,000	$110,000	Best		
20	No plant	$200,000	$100,000	$0	$200,000			

Best alternative for maximin criterion

Coefficient of realism

Best alternative for minimax regret criterion

Regret table computed from payoff table

Note that the number of decision alternatives and the number of outcomes would vary from problem to problem. The formulas shown in Screenshot 9.1A can, however, easily be modified to accommodate any changes in these parameters.

9.5   DECISION MAKING UNDER RISK

In many real-world situations, it is common for the decision maker to have some idea about the probabilities of occurrence of the different outcomes. These probabilities may be based on the decision maker's personal opinions about future events or on data obtained from market surveys, expert opinions, and so on. As noted previously, when the probability of occurrence of each outcome can be assessed, the problem environment is called *decision making under risk*.

In this section we consider one of the most popular methods of making decisions under risk: selecting the alternative with the highest expected monetary value. We also look at the concepts of expected opportunity loss and expected value of perfect information.

Expected Monetary Value

EMV is the weighted average of possible payoffs for each alternative.

Given a decision table with payoffs and probability assessments, we can determine the **expected monetary value (EMV)** for each alternative. The EMV for an alternative is computed as the *weighted average* of all possible payoffs for that alternative, where the weights are the probabilities of the different outcomes. That is,

$$
\begin{aligned}
\text{EMV (Alternative } i) = \ & \text{Payoff of first outcome} \\
& \times \text{Probability of first outcome} \\
& + \text{Payoff of second outcome} \\
& \times \text{Probability of second outcome} \\
& + \ldots + \text{Payoff of last outcome} \\
& \times \text{Probability of last outcome}
\end{aligned}
\tag{9-2}
$$

In Thompson Lumber's case, let us assume that John has used his knowledge of the storage shed industry to specify that the probabilities of high demand, moderate demand, and low demand are 0.3, 0.5, and 0.2, respectively. Under this scenario, which alternative would give him the greatest EMV? To determine this, we compute the EMV for each alternative, as shown in Table 9.8. The largest EMV, $86 000, results from the first alternative, build a large plant.

TABLE 9.8

Thompson Lumber's EMV Decision

| | OUTCOMES | | | |
ALTERNATIVES	HIGH DEMAND	MODERATE DEMAND	LOW DEMAND	EMV FOR ALTERNATIVE
Build large plant	$200 000	$100 000	−$120 000	$200 000 × 0.3 + $100 000 × 0.5 + (−$120 000) × 0.2 = $86 000
Build small plant	$ 90 000	$ 50 000	−$ 20 000	$90 000 × 0.3 + $50 000 × 0.5 + (−$20 000) × 0.2 = $48 000
No plant	$ 0	$ 0	$ 0	$0 × 0.3 + $0 × 0.5 + $0 × 0.2 = $ 0
Probabilities	0.3	0.5	0.2	

Observe that the EMV represents the long-run *average* payoff, while the *actual* payoff from a decision will be one of the payoffs listed in the decision table. That is, the EMV of $86 000 does not mean that John will actually realize a profit of $86 000 if he builds a large plant. Nevertheless, the EMV is widely used as an acceptable criterion to compare decision alternatives in many business decisions because companies make similar decisions on a repeated basis over time.

Expected Opportunity Loss

An alternative approach in decision making under risk is to minimize **expected opportunity loss (EOL)**. Recall from Section 9.4 that opportunity loss, also called regret, refers to the difference between the optimal payoff and the actual payoff received. The EOL for an alternative is computed as the weighted average of all possible regrets for that alternative, where the weights are the probabilities of the different outcomes. That is,

$$
\begin{aligned}
\text{EOL (Alternative } i) = \ &\text{Regret of first outcome} \\
&\times \text{Probability of first outcome} \\
&+ \text{Regret of second outcome} \\
&\times \text{Probability of second outcome} \\
&+ \ldots + \text{Regret of last outcome} \\
&\times \text{Probability of last outcome}
\end{aligned}
\tag{9-3}
$$

The EOL values for Thompson Lumber's problem are computed as shown in Table 9.9. Using minimum EOL as the decision criterion, the best decision would be the first alternative, build a large plant, with an EOL of $24 000. It is important to note that the minimum EOL will *always* result in the same decision alternative as the maximum EMV.

Expected Value of Perfect Information

John Thompson has now been approached by Scientific Marketing, Inc., a market research firm, with a proposal to help him make the right decision regarding the size of the new plant. Scientific claims that its analysis will tell John with *certainty* whether the demand for storage sheds will be high, moderate, or low. In other words, it will change John's problem environment from one of decision making under risk to one of decision making under certainty. Obviously, this information could prevent John from making an expensive mistake. Scientific would charge $30 000 for the information. What should John do? Should he hire Scientific to do the marketing study? Is the information worth $30 000? If not, what is it worth?

We call the type of information offered by Scientific *perfect information* because it is certain (i.e., it is never wrong). Although such perfect information is almost never available in practice, determining its value can be very useful because it places an upper bound on

EOL is the cost of not picking the best solution.

The EOL will always result in the same decision as the maximum EMV.

EVPI places an upper bound on what to pay for any information.

TABLE 9.9

Thompson Lumber's EOL Decision

	OUTCOMES			
ALTERNATIVES	HIGH DEMAND	MODERATE DEMAND	LOW DEMAND	EOL FOR ALTERNATIVE
Build large plant	$ 0	$ 0	$120 000	$0 × 0.3 + $0 × 0.5 + $120 000 × 0.2 = $24 000
Build small plant	$110 000	$ 50 000	$ 20 000	$110 000 × 0.3 + $50 000 × 0.5 + $20 000 × 0.2 = $62 000
No plant	$200 000	$100 000	$ 0	$200 000 × 0.3 + $100 000 × 0.5 + $0 × 0.2 = $110 000
Probabilities	0.3	0.5	0.2	

what we should be willing to spend on *any* information. In what follows, we therefore investigate two related issues: the **expected value with perfect information (EVwPI)** and the **expected value of perfect information (EVPI)**.

The EVwPI is the expected payoff if we have perfect information *before* a decision has to be made. Clearly, if we knew for sure that a particular outcome was going to occur, we would choose the alternative that yielded the best payoff for that outcome. Unfortunately, until we get this information we don't know for sure which outcome is going to occur. Hence, to calculate the EVwPI value, we choose the best payoff for each outcome and multiply it by the probability of occurrence of that outcome. That is,

$$
\begin{aligned}
\text{EVwPI} = \ & \text{Best payoff of first outcome} \\
& \times \text{Probability of first outcome} \\
& + \text{Best payoff for second outcome} \\
& \times \text{Probability of second outcome} \\
& + \ldots + \text{Best payoff of last outcome} \\
& \times \text{Probability of last outcome}
\end{aligned}
\tag{9-4}
$$

We then compute the EVPI as the EVwPI minus the expected value *without* information, namely, the maximum EMV. That is,

EVPI is the expected value with perfect information minus the maximum EMV.

$$
\text{EVPI} = \text{EVwPI} - \text{Maximum EMV}
\tag{9-5}
$$

By referring back to Table 9.8, we can calculate the EVPI for John as follows:

1. The best payoff for the outcome high demand is $200 000, associated with building a large plant. The best payoff for moderate demand is $100 000, again associated with building a large plant. Finally, the best payoff for low demand is $0, associated with not building a plant. Hence,

    $$\text{EVwPI} = \$200\ 000 \times 0.3 + \$100\ 000 \times 0.5 + \$0 \times 0.50 = \$110\ 000$$

    That is, if we had perfect information, we would expect an *average* payoff of $110 000 if the decision could be repeated many times.

2. Recall from Table 9.8 that the maximum EMV, or the expected value *without* information, is $86 000. Hence,

    $$\text{EVPI} = \text{EVwPI} - \text{Maximum EMV} = \$110\ 000 - \$86\ 000 = \$24\ 000$$

    Thus, the most John should pay for perfect information is $24 000. Because Scientific Marketing wants $30 000 for its analysis, John should reject the offer. It is important to note that the following relationship always holds: EVPI = Minimum EOL. Referring back to Thompson Lumber's example, we see that EVPI = Minimum EOL = $24 000.

EVPI = Minimum EOL

File: 9-2.xls

Using Excel to Solve Decision-Making Problems under Risk

Just as with decision making under uncertainty, calculations for finding the EMV, EOL, EVwPI, and EVPI in decision making under risk are also fairly straightforward. In most small cases, we can perform these calculations quickly even by hand. However, if we wish, we can once again easily construct Excel spreadsheets to calculate these values for us. Screenshot 9.2A shows the relevant formulas to solve the Thompson Lumber example. The results are shown in Screenshot 9.2B.

As with Screenshot 9.1A, note that the number of decision alternatives and number of outcomes would vary from problem to problem. The formulas shown in Screenshot 9.2A can, however, be easily modified to accommodate any changes in these parameters.

SCREENSHOT 9.2A   **Formula View of Excel Layout for Thompson Lumber: Decision Making under Risk**

This is the best payoff for each outcome, used in calculating regret values and EVwPI.

IF function is used to identify the best alternative.

	A	B	C	D	E	F
1	**Thompson Lumber (Dec Making Under Risk)**					
2						
3	**PAYOFFS**		**Outcomes**		**Maximize EMV**	
4	**Alternatives**	High demand	Moderate demand	Low demand	EMV	Choice
5	Large plant	200000	100000	-120000	=SUMPRODUCT(B5:D5,B$8:D$8)	=IF(E5=MAX(E$5:E$7),"Best","")
6	Small plant	90000	50000	-20000	=SUMPRODUCT(B6:D6,B$8:D$8)	=IF(E6=MAX(E$5:E$7),"Best","")
7	No plant	0	0	0	=SUMPRODUCT(B7:D7,B$8:D$8)	=IF(E7=MAX(E$5:E$7),"Best","")
8	Probability	0.3	0.5	0.2		
9						
10	Best outcome	=MAX(B5:B7)	=MAX(C5:C7)	=MAX(D5:D7)		
11						
12	Expected Value WITH Perfect Information (EVwPI) =					=SUMPRODUCT(B10:D10,B8:D8)
13	Best Expected Monetary Value (EMV) =					=MAX(E5:E7)
14	Expected Value OF Perfect Information (EVPI) =					=F12-F13
15						
16	**REGRET**		**Outcomes**		**Minimize EOL**	
17	**Alternatives**	High demand	Moderate demand	Low demand	EOL	Choice
18	Large plant	=MAX(B$5:B$7)-B5	=MAX(C$5:C$7)-C5	=MAX(D$5:D$7)-D5	=SUMPRODUCT(B18:D18,B$21:D$21)	=IF(E18=MIN(E$18:E$20),"Best","")
19	Small plant	=MAX(B$5:B$7)-B6	=MAX(C$5:C$7)-C6	=MAX(D$5:D$7)-D6	=SUMPRODUCT(B19:D19,B$21:D$21)	=IF(E19=MIN(E$18:E$20),"Best","")
20	No plant	=MAX(B$5:B$7)-B7	=MAX(C$5:C$7)-C7	=MAX(D$5:D$7)-D7	=SUMPRODUCT(B20:D20,B$21:D$21)	=IF(E20=MIN(E$18:E$20),"Best","")
21	Probability	0.3	0.5	0.2		

Best EMV

SUMPRODUCT function is used to compute EMV and EOL values for each alternative.

EVPI is the difference between EVwPI and best EMV

SCREENSHOT 9.2B   **Excel Solution for Thompson Lumber: Decision Making under Risk**

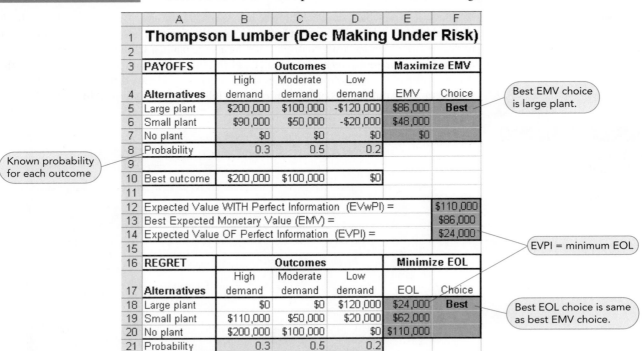

	A	B	C	D	E	F
1	**Thompson Lumber (Dec Making Under Risk)**					
2						
3	**PAYOFFS**		**Outcomes**		**Maximize EMV**	
4	**Alternatives**	High demand	Moderate demand	Low demand	EMV	Choice
5	Large plant	$200,000	$100,000	-$120,000	$86,000	**Best**
6	Small plant	$90,000	$50,000	-$20,000	$48,000	
7	No plant	$0	$0	$0	$0	
8	Probability	0.3	0.5	0.2		
9						
10	Best outcome	$200,000	$100,000	$0		
11						
12	Expected Value WITH Perfect Information (EVwPI) =					$110,000
13	Best Expected Monetary Value (EMV) =					$86,000
14	Expected Value OF Perfect Information (EVPI) =					$24,000
15						
16	**REGRET**		**Outcomes**		**Minimize EOL**	
17	**Alternatives**	High demand	Moderate demand	Low demand	EOL	Choice
18	Large plant	$0	$0	$120,000	$24,000	**Best**
19	Small plant	$110,000	$50,000	$20,000	$62,000	
20	No plant	$200,000	$100,000	$0	$110,000	
21	Probability	0.3	0.5	0.2		

Best EMV choice is large plant.

Known probability for each outcome

EVPI = minimum EOL

Best EOL choice is same as best EMV choice.

HISTORY   The Origin of Decision Analysis

Professor Ronald Howard of Stanford University defined the decision analysis discipline in 1965. Since then he has played a major role in research and education in the field, and he has applied decision analysis techniques in such diverse areas as the isolation of nuclear waste, technological risk, and biotechnological investment. In 1986 he received the Operations Research Society of America's Frank P. Ramsey Medal for Distinguished Contributions in

Decision Analysis. Dr. Howard continues to teach Decision Analysis at Stanford where he is a professor in the Management Science and Engineering (MS&E) Department and professor of Management Science in the Graduate School of Business.

Source: http://www.sdg.com/home.nsf/sdg/AboutSDG–StaffBios–RonaldHoward

9.6   DECISION TREES

Any problem that can be presented in a decision table can also be graphically illustrated in a *decision tree*. A decision tree consists of nodes (or points) and arcs (or lines), just like a network. (You may recall that we studied several network models in Chapter 5.) We illustrate the construction and use of decision trees using the Thompson Lumber example.

Decision trees contain decision nodes and outcome nodes.

A decision tree presents the decision alternatives and outcomes in a sequential manner. All decision trees are similar in that they contain *decision nodes* and *outcome nodes*. These nodes are represented using the following symbols:

□ = A *decision* node. Arcs (lines) originating from a decision node denote all decision alternatives available to the decision maker at that node. Of these, the decision maker must select only one alternative.

○ = An *outcome* node. Arcs (lines) originating from an outcome node denote all outcomes that could occur at that node. Of these, only one outcome will actually occur.

A decision tree usually begins with a decision node.

Although it is possible for a decision tree to begin with an outcome node, most trees begin with a decision node. In Thompson Lumber's case, this decision node indicates that John has to decide among his three alternatives: building a large plant, a small plant, or no plant. Each alternative is represented by an arc originating from this decision node. Once John makes this decision, one of three possible outcomes (high demand, moderate demand, or low demand) will occur. The simple decision tree to represent John's decision is shown in Figure 9.1.

FIGURE 9.1

Decision Tree for Thompson Lumber

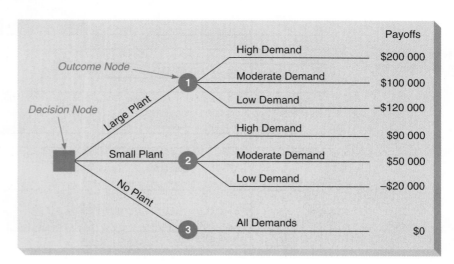

Observe that all alternatives available to John are shown as arcs originating from a decision node (□). Likewise, at each outcome node (○), all possible outcomes that could occur if John chooses that decision alternative are shown as arcs. The payoffs resulting from each alternative and outcome combination are shown at the end of each relevant path in the tree. For example, if John chooses to build a large plant and demand turns out to be high, the resulting payoff is $200 000.

Folding Back a Decision Tree

We fold back a decision tree to identify the best decision.

The process by which a decision tree is analyzed to identify the optimal decision is referred to as *folding back* the decision tree. We start with the payoffs (i.e., the right extreme of the tree) and work our way back to the first decision node. In folding back the decision tree, we use the following two rules:

■ At each outcome node, we compute the expected payoff, using the probabilities of all possible outcomes at that node and the payoffs associated with those outcomes.
■ At each decision node, we select the alternative that yields the better expected payoff. If the expected payoffs represent profits, we select the alternative with the largest value. In contrast, if the expected payoffs represent costs, we select the alternative with the smallest value.

The EMV is calculated at each outcome node.

The complete decision tree for Thompson Lumber is presented in Figure 9.2. For convenience, the probability of each outcome is shown in parentheses next to each outcome. The EMV at each outcome node is then calculated and placed by that node. The EMV at node 1 (if John decides to build a large plant) is $86 000, while the EMV at node 2 (if John decides to build a small plant) is $48 000. Building no plant has, of course, an EMV of $0.

At this stage, the decision tree for Thompson Lumber has been folded back to just the first decision node and the three alternatives (arcs) originating from it. That is, all outcome nodes and the outcomes from these nodes have been examined and collapsed into the EMVs. The reduced decision tree for Thompson Lumber is shown in Figure 9.3.

The best alternative is selected at a decision node.

Using the rule stated earlier for decision nodes, we now select the alternative with the highest EMV. In this case, it corresponds to the alternative to build a large plant. The resulting EMV is $86 000.

FIGURE 9.2

Completed Decision Tree for Thompson Lumber

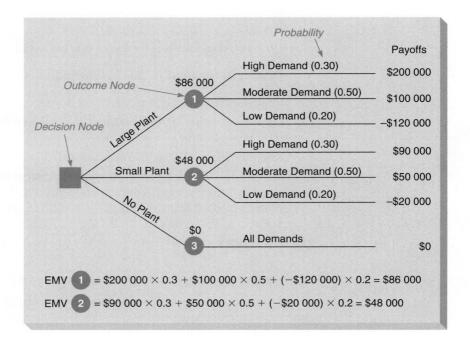

EMV ① = $200 000 × 0.3 + $100 000 × 0.5 + (−$120 000) × 0.2 = $86 000

EMV ② = $90 000 × 0.3 + $50 000 × 0.5 + (−$20 000) × 0.2 = $48 000

FIGURE 9.3

Reduced Decision Tree for Thompson Lumber

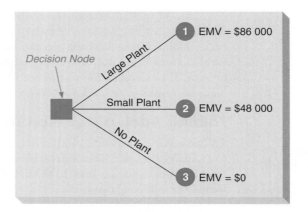

9.7   USING TREEPLAN TO SOLVE DECISION TREE PROBLEMS WITH EXCEL

TreePlan is an Excel add-in for solving decision tree problems.

We can use TreePlan, an add-in for Excel, to set up and solve decision tree problems. The TreePlan program consists of a single Excel add-in file, Treeplan.xla, which can be found on the CD-ROM that accompanies this textbook. You can either run this program directly from the CD-ROM or copy it to your hard disk and run it from there.

Loading TreePlan

To load and enable TreePlan in Excel, you can use either of the two approaches described in the following sections.

There are two ways of loading TreePlan in Excel.

Loading Manually   Each time you run Excel, you can load TreePlan manually, as follows:

1. Open Excel. **CLICK FILE|OPEN** and use the browse window to find the *Treeplan.xla* file (either on your hard disk or on the CD-ROM).
2. Open the file. Note that you will not see anything new on your Excel spreadsheet at this time.
3. Click **TOOLS** in Excel's main menu. You will see an option called **DECISION TREE**.

Loading Automatically   You have to load automatically only once, as follows:

1. Copy the *Treeplan.xla* file to your hard drive.
2. Open Excel. Click **TOOLS|ADD-INS**. Then click **BROWSE** and use the window to locate the *Treeplan.xla* file.
3. Select the file by clicking it. Then click **OK**.
4. You will see an option named **TREEPLAN DECISION TREE ADD-IN** in the Add-In list. Make sure the box next to this option is checked. Click **OK**. *Note:* To subsequently prevent TreePlan from loading automatically, click **TOOLS|ADD-INS** and uncheck the box next to this option.
5. Click **TOOLS** in Excel's main menu. You will see an option called **DECISION TREE**.

Creating a Decision Tree Using TreePlan

Once you have installed and loaded TreePlan, you can use the following six steps to set up and solve a decision tree problem: (1) start TreePlan; (2) start a new tree; (3) add nodes and branches; (4) change titles, probabilities, and payoffs; (5) identify the best decision; and (6) make minor formatting changes. On the next several pages, we illustrate these six steps using the Thompson Lumber problem. Recall that we saw the complete decision tree for this problem in Figure 9.2.

Step 1: Start TreePlan   Start Excel and open a blank worksheet. Place the cursor in any blank cell (say, cell A1). Select **TOOLS|DECISION TREE** from Excel's main menu. *Note:* If you don't see Decision Tree as a choice in the Tools menu, you have to install TreePlan, as discussed in the preceding section.

Step 2: Start a New Tree   Select **NEW TREE**. As shown in Screenshot 9.3A, this creates an initial decision tree with a single decision node (in cell B5, if the cursor was placed in cell A1). Two alternatives (named Decision 1 and Decision 2, respectively) are automatically created at this node.

Step 3: Add Nodes and Branches   We now modify the basic decision tree in Screenshot 9.3A to reflect our full decision problem. To do so, we use TreePlan menus. To bring up a TreePlan menu, we either select **TOOLS|DECISION TREE** or press the Control (Ctrl), Shift, and T keys at the same time. The TreePlan menu that is displayed each time depends on the location of the cursor when we bring up the menu, as follows:

- If the cursor is at a node in the tree (such as cell B5 in Screenshot 9.3A), the menu shown in Screenshot 9.3B(a) is displayed.
- If the cursor is at a terminal point in the tree (such as cells F3 and F8 in Screenshot 9.3A), the menu shown in Screenshot 9.3B(b) is displayed.
- If the cursor is at any other location in the spreadsheet, the menu shown in Screenshot 9.3B(c) is displayed.

For the Thompson Lumber example, we begin by placing the cursor in cell B5 and bringing up the menu in Screenshot 9.3B(a). We then select Add Branch and click OK to get the third decision branch (named Decision 3).

Next, we move the cursor to the end of the branch for Decision 1 (i.e., to cell F3 in Screenshot 9.3A) and bring up the menu in Screenshot 9.3B(b). We first select **CHANGE TO EVENT NODE**. (Note that TreePlan refers to outcome nodes as event nodes.) Then we select

Select **TOOLS|DECISION TREE** in Excel to start TreePlan.

File: 9-3.xls, sheet: 9-3A

The TreePlan menu that appears depends on the location of the cursor.

TreePlan refers to outcome nodes as event nodes.

Initial Decision Tree from TreePlan

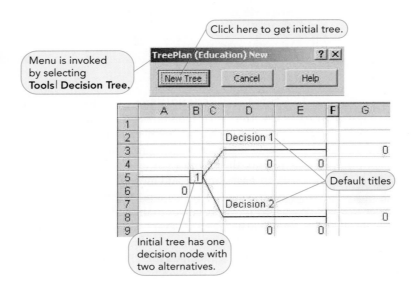

SCREENSHOT 9.3B   **TreePlan Menus**

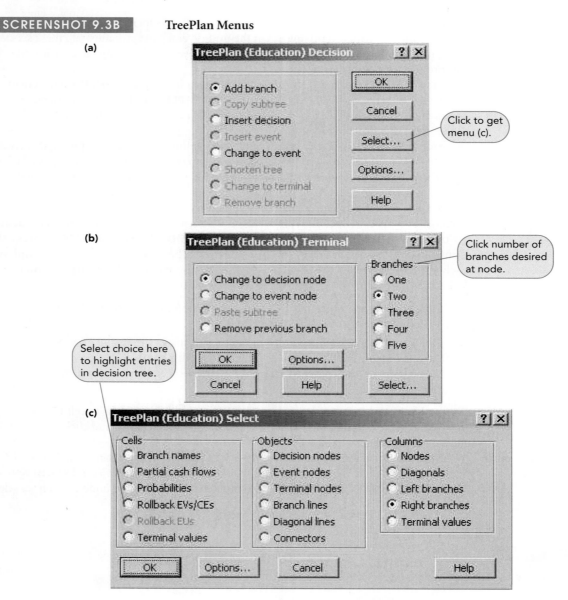

(a)

(b)

(c)

THREE under **BRANCHES** to add three outcome arcs to this outcome node. When we click **OK**, TreePlan creates three arcs, named Event 4, Event 5, and Event 6, respectively. Because these are outcomes, we need to associate probability values with the events. TreePlan automatically assigns equal probability values by default. In this case, because there are three events, the default value assigned is ⅓ (shown as 0.33333).

Each time we add more decision alternatives or outcomes to a decision tree, TreePlan automatically repositions the tree on the Excel worksheet to make it fit better. We next move the cursor to the end of the branch for Decision 2 and repeat the preceding step to create Event 7, Event 8, and Event 9. The structure of the decision tree, shown in Screenshot 9.3C, is now similar to the tree in Figure 9.2.

Step 4: Change Titles, Probabilities, and Payoffs   We can change the default titles for all arcs in the decision tree to reflect the Thompson Lumber example. For example, we can

File: 9-3.xls, sheet: 9-3C

Titles can be changed in TreePlan, if desired.

SCREENSHOT 9.3C   **Complete Decision Tree Using TreePlan for Thompson Lumber**

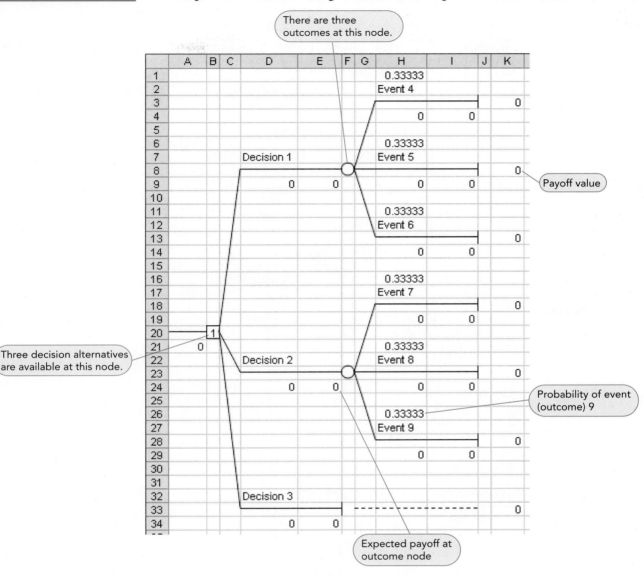

replace Decision 1 (in cell D7 of Screenshot 9.3C) with Large plant. Likewise, we can replace Event 4 (in cell H2 of Screenshot 9.3C) with High demand. The changes are shown in Screenshot 9.3D on page 396.

Next, we change the default probability values on the event arcs to the correct values. Finally, we enter the payoffs. TreePlan allows us to enter these values in two ways:

There are two ways of entering payoffs in TreePlan.

File: 9-3.xls, sheet: 9-3D

■ We can directly enter the payoffs at the end of each path in the decision tree. That is, we can enter the appropriate payoff values in cells K3, K8, K13, K18, K23, K28, and K33 (see Screenshot 9.3D).

■ We can allow TreePlan to compute the payoffs. Each time we create an arc (decision alternative or outcome) in TreePlan, it assigns a default payoff of zero to that branch. We can edit these payoffs (or costs) for all alternatives and outcomes. For example, we leave cell D9 at $0 (default value) because there is no cost specified for building

SCREENSHOT 9.3D **Solved Decision Tree Using TreePlan for Thompson Lumber**

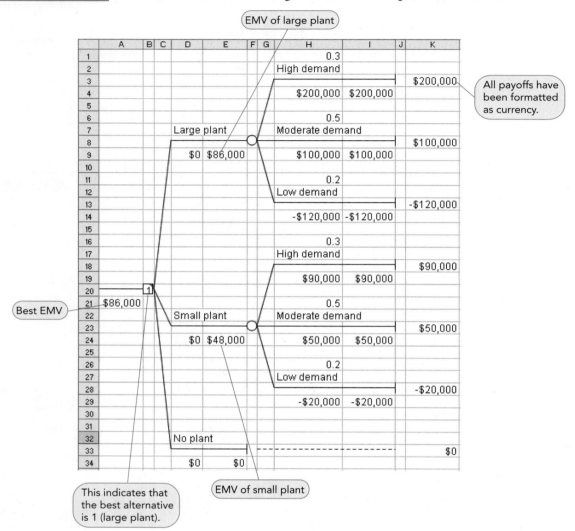

a large plant. However, we change the entry in cell H4 to $200 000 to reflect the pay-off if demand turns out to be high. TreePlan adds these two entries (in cells D9 and H4) automatically and reports it as the payoff in cell K3. We can do likewise for all other payoffs in John's tree.

TreePlan writes formulas in the appropriate cells as the tree is created.

Step 5: Identify the Best Decision TreePlan automatically writes formulas into the appropriate cells as the tree is created and structured. For example, TreePlan writes the following formula in cell E9 (which computes the EMV of building a large plant) of Screenshot 9.3D:

=IF(ABS(1-SUM(H1, H6, H11))<=0.00001, SUM(H1*14, H6*19, H11*I14), NA())

The ABS part of the formula verifies that the sum of probabilities of all outcomes at a given outcome node equals 1. The second part (SUM) computes the EMV using the appropriate payoffs and probability values. The EMVs are shown next to the outcome nodes. For example, cell E9 shows an EMV of $86 000 for the large plant.

DECISION MODELING IN ACTION
Decision Analysis Helps Solve Airport Ground Delay Problems

One of the most frustrating aspects of air travel is rushing to the airport only to find out that your flight has been delayed. Often triggered by what is called the Ground-Delay Program (GDP), the Federal Aviation Administration (FAA) keeps flights from departing when the air traffic or weather at the destination is unfavourable.

Decisions involving GDP are classic problems in decision analysis. At the heart of such a problem, there are two decision alternatives: allow the flight to depart or do not allow the flight to depart. In choosing from these alternatives, the decision maker has to consider several unknown future outcomes, such as the weather, expected air traffic, and a variety of other factors that could develop at the destination. These factors could delay or prevent a flight from landing safely.

The original GDP system was administered by the FAA. The FAA monitored existing imbalances between demand and capacity at given airports to determine whether a ground delay was warranted and justified at other airports that fed into it. Some experts, however, claimed that the FAA lacked current and accurate information. In some cases, the FAA relied on the published airline schedules, which were subject to change and inaccuracies. This resulted in the inefficient use of arrival resources and unnecessary ground delays at some airports. To overcome some of these problems, a decision analysis model was developed.

Using decision analysis models can improve not only information flow but also performance. Before the initiative, 51% of flights left on time. After it, 66% left on time. In addition to conserving fuel and improving utilization of arrival resources, these types of initiatives can save travellers a tremendous amount of frustration and lost time.

Source: K. Chang, et al. "Enhancements to the FAA Ground-Delay Program Under Collaborative Decision Making," *Interfaces* (January–February 2001): 57–76.

Once all expected values have been computed, TreePlan then selects the optimal decision alternative at each decision node. The selection is indicated within that node. For example, the 1 in the decision node in cell B20 indicates that the first alternative (i.e., large plant) is the best choice for Thompson Lumber. The best EMV of $86 000 is shown next to this decision node (in cell A21).

If the payoffs denote costs, we can click Options in any of the TreePlan menus (see Screenshot 9.3B) to change the selection criterion from maximizing profits to minimizing costs. In this case, TreePlan will select the decision alternative with the smallest expected costs.

Step 6: Make Minor Formatting Changes   If desired, we can add titles, format payoffs to be shown as dollar values, change the number of decimals shown, and make other cosmetic changes to the tree, as shown in Screenshot 9.3D. Appendix A illustrates how to make such formatting changes in Excel.

9.8   DECISION TREES FOR MULTISTAGE DECISION-MAKING PROBLEMS

The Thompson Lumber problem discussed so far is a single-stage problem. That is, John has to choose a decision alternative, which is followed by an outcome. Depending on the alternative chosen and the outcome that occurs, John gets a payoff, and the problem ends there.

Multistage decision problems involve a sequence of decision alternatives and outcomes.

In many cases, however, the decision-making scenario is a multistage problem. In such cases, the decision maker must evaluate and make a set of **sequential decisions** up front (i.e., before the first decision is implemented). However, the decisions are actually implemented in a sequential manner, as follows. The problem usually begins with the decision maker implementing his or her initial decision. This is followed by an outcome. Depending on the initial decision and the outcome that occurs after it, the decision maker next implements his or her next decision. The alternatives for this follow-up decision may be different for different outcomes of the earlier decision. This decision, in turn, is followed by an outcome. The set of outcomes for this decision may be different from the set of outcomes for the earlier decision. This sequence could continue several more times, and the final payoff is a function of the sequence of decisions made and the outcomes that occurred at each stage of the problem.

At one or more stages in a problem, it is possible for a specific decision to have no outcomes following it. In such cases, the decision maker is immediately faced with the next decision. Likewise, at one or more stages in the problem, it is possible to have one outcome occur directly after another outcome without the decision maker facing a decision in between the two.

For multistage scenarios, decision tables are no longer convenient, and we are forced to analyze these problems using decision trees. Although we can, in theory, extend multistage scenarios to a sequence of as many decisions and outcomes as we wish, we will limit our discussion here to problems involving just two stages. To facilitate this discussion, let us consider an expanded version of the Thompson Lumber problem.

A Multistage Decision-Making Problem for Thompson Lumber

Before deciding about building a new plant, let's suppose John Thompson has been approached by Smart Services, another market research firm. Smart will charge John $4000 to conduct a market survey. The results of the survey will indicate either positive or negative market conditions for storage sheds. What should John do?

John recognizes that Smart's market survey will not provide him with *perfect* information, but it may help him get a better feel for the outcomes nevertheless. The type of information obtained here is referred to either as *sample* information or *imperfect* information.

Recall from Section 9.5 that we calculated John's EVPI as $24 000. That is, if the results of the market survey are going to be 100% accurate, John should be willing to pay up to $24 000 for the survey. Because Smart's survey will cost significantly less (only $4000), it is at least worth considering further. However, given that it yields only imperfect information, how much is it actually worth? We determine this by extending the decision tree analysis for Thompson Lumber to include Smart's market survey.

Expanded Decision Tree for Thompson Lumber

John's new decision tree is represented in Figure 9.4. Let's take a careful look at this more complex tree. Note that all possible alternatives and outcomes are included in their logical sequence. This is one of the strengths of using decision trees in making decisions. The user is forced to examine all possible outcomes, including unfavourable ones. He or she is also forced to make decisions in a logical, sequential manner.

Examining the tree, we see that John's first decision point is whether to conduct Smart's market survey. If he chooses not to do the survey (i.e., the upper part of the tree), he is immediately faced with his second decision node: whether to build a large plant, a small plant, or no plant. The possible outcomes for each of these alternatives are high demand (0.3 probability), moderate demand (0.5 probability), and low demand (0.2 probability). The payoffs for each of the possible consequences are listed along the right side of the tree. As a matter of fact, this portion of John's tree in Figure 9.4 is identical to the simpler decision tree shown in Figure 9.2. Can you see why this is so?

The lower portion of Figure 9.4 reflects the decision to conduct the market survey. This decision has two possible outcomes—positive survey result or negative survey result—each with a specific probability. For now, let us assume that John knows these probabilities to be as follows: probability of 0.57 that the survey will indicate positive market conditions for storage sheds, and probability of 0.43 that the survey will indicate negative market conditions. An explanation of how these probabilities can be calculated in real-world situations is the topic of Section 9.9.

It is possible for one outcome (or alternative) to directly follow another outcome (or alternative).

Multistage decision problems are analyzed using decision trees.

EVPI is an upper bound on the cost of a survey.

All outcomes and alternatives must be considered.

FIGURE 9.4   **Expanded Decision Tree with Payoffs and Probabilities for Thompson Lumber**

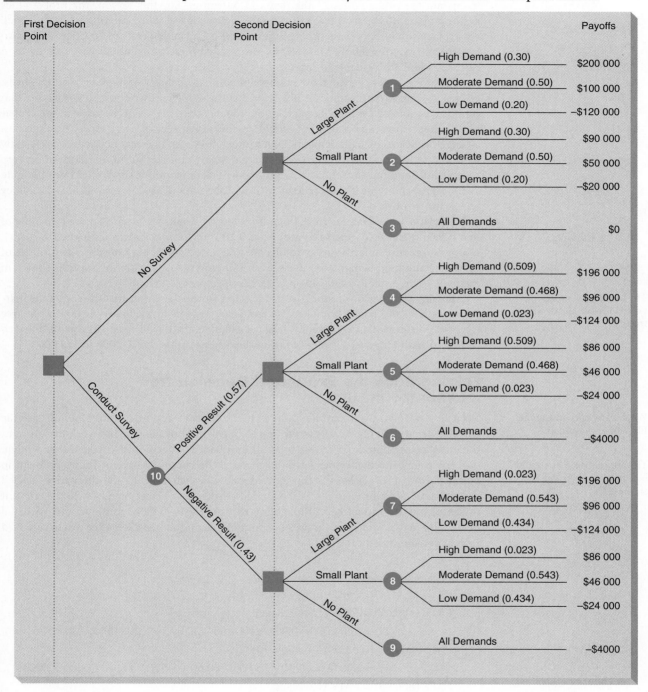

First Decision Point
Second Decision Point
Payoffs

No Survey

Conduct Survey

Positive Result (0.57)

Negative Result (0.43)

10

Large Plant — 1
- High Demand (0.30) — $200 000
- Moderate Demand (0.50) — $100 000
- Low Demand (0.20) — −$120 000

Small Plant — 2
- High Demand (0.30) — $90 000
- Moderate Demand (0.50) — $50 000
- Low Demand (0.20) — −$20 000

No Plant — 3
- All Demands — $0

Large Plant — 4
- High Demand (0.509) — $196 000
- Moderate Demand (0.468) — $96 000
- Low Demand (0.023) — −$124 000

Small Plant — 5
- High Demand (0.509) — $86 000
- Moderate Demand (0.468) — $46 000
- Low Demand (0.023) — −$24 000

No Plant — 6
- All Demands — −$4000

Large Plant — 7
- High Demand (0.023) — $196 000
- Moderate Demand (0.543) — $96 000
- Low Demand (0.434) — −$124 000

Small Plant — 8
- High Demand (0.023) — $86 000
- Moderate Demand (0.543) — $46 000
- Low Demand (0.434) — −$24 000

No Plant — 9
- All Demands — −$4000

Most of the probabilities are conditional probabilities.

Regardless of which survey outcome occurs, John is now faced with his next decision. Although the decision alternatives at this point could be different for different survey outcomes, let us assume in John's case that for both survey outcomes he has the same three alternatives: whether to build a large plant, a small plant, or no plant. Each alternative has the same three outcomes as before: high demand, moderate demand, and low demand.

The key difference, however, is that the survey outcome (positive or negative) allows John to update the probabilities of the demand outcomes. For this reason, the probabilities shown in parentheses for these outcomes in Figure 9.4 are called *conditional probabilities*. An explanation of how these probabilities can be calculated in real-world situations is also presented in Section 9.9. For now, let us assume that these probabilities have already been calculated and are available to John.

From Figure 9.4, we note, for example, that the probability of high demand for sheds, given a positive survey result, is 0.509. Note that this is higher than the 0.30 probability that John had estimated for high demand before the market survey. This increase in the probability is not surprising because you would, of course, expect a positive survey result to be a stronger indicator of high demand. Don't forget, however, that any market research study is subject to error. Therefore, it is possible that Smart's market survey didn't result in very reliable information. In fact, as shown in Figure 9.4, demand for sheds could be moderate (with a probability of 0.468) or low (with a probability of 0.023), even if Smart's survey results are positive.

Likewise, we note in Figure 9.4 that if the survey results are negative, the probability of low demand for sheds increases from the 0.20 that John originally estimated to 0.434. However, because Smart's survey results are not perfect, there are nonzero probabilities of moderate and high demand for sheds, even if the survey results are negative. As shown in Figure 9.4, these values are 0.543 and 0.023, respectively.

The cost of the survey has to be included in the decision tree.

Finally, when we look to the payoff values in Figure 9.4, we note that the cost of the market survey ($4000) has to be subtracted from every payoff in the lower portion of the tree (i.e., the portion with the survey). Thus, for example, the payoff for a large plant followed by high demand for sheds is reduced from the original value of $200 000 to $196 000.

Folding Back the Expanded Decision Tree for Thompson Lumber

We start by computing the EMV of each branch.

With all probabilities and payoffs specified in the decision tree, we can start folding back the tree. We begin with the payoffs at the end (or right side) of the tree and work back toward the initial decision node. When we finish, the sequence of decisions to make will be known.

The alternative that should be chosen is indicated by slashes (//).

For your convenience, we have summarized the computations for John's problem in Figure 9.5. A pair of slashes (//) through a decision branch indicates the alternative selected at a decision node. In Figure 9.5, all expected payoffs have been noted next to the relevant nodes on the decision tree. Although we explain each of these computations in detail below, you may find it easier to do all computations on the tree itself after you have solved several decision tree problems.

1.   If the market survey is *not* conducted,

$$\text{EMV (node 1)} = \text{EMV (Large plant)}$$
$$= \$200\ 000 \times 0.30 + \$100\ 000 \times 0.50 + (-\$120\ 000) \times 0.20 = \$86\ 000)$$
$$\text{EMV (node 2)} = \text{EMV (Small plant)}$$
$$= \$90\ 000 \times 0.30 + \$50\ 000 \times 0.50 + (-\$20\ 000) \times 0.20 = \$48\ 000$$
$$\text{EMV (node 3)} = \text{EMV (No plant)}$$
$$= \$0$$

Thus, if the market survey is not conducted, John should build a large plant, for an expected payoff of $86 000. As expected, this is the same result we saw earlier in Figure 9.2.

FIGURE 9.5   **Thompson Lumber's Expanded Decision Tree, with EMVs Shown**

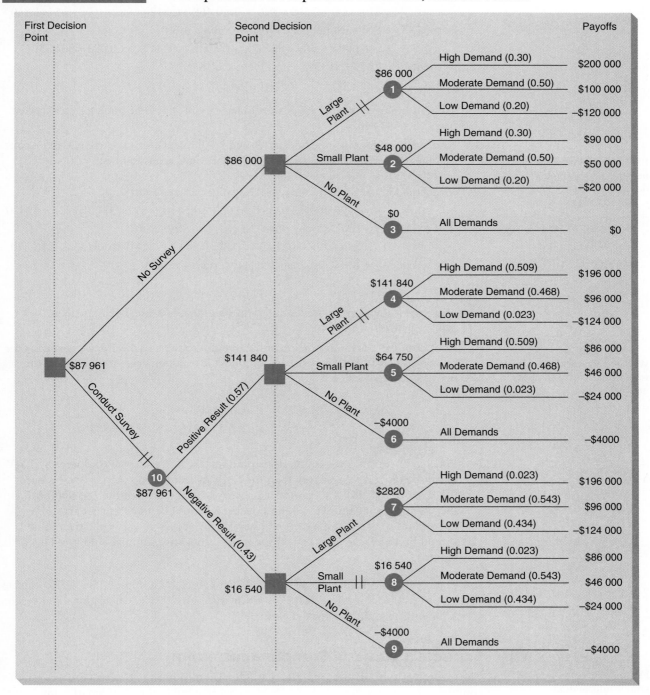

EMV calculations for a positive survey result are done first.

2. Now let us examine the portion of the tree where the market survey is conducted. Working backward from the payoffs, we first consider outcome nodes 4, 5, and 6. All calculations at these nodes are conditional on a positive survey result. The calculations are as follows:

$$\text{EMV (node 4)} = \text{EMV (Large plant | Positive survey result)}$$
$$= \$196\ 000 \times 0.509 + \$96\ 000 \times 0.468 + (-\$124\ 000) \times 0.023 = \$141\ 840$$

$$\text{EMV (node 5)} = \text{EMV (Small plant | Positive survey result)}$$
$$= \$86\ 000 \times 0.509 + \$46\ 000 \times 0.468 + (-\$24\ 000) \times 0.023 = \$64\ 750$$

$$\text{EMV (node 6)} = \text{EMV (No plant | Positive survey result)}$$
$$= -\$4000$$

Thus, if the survey results are positive, a large plant should be built, for an expected payoff of $141 840.

3.   Next, we consider outcome nodes 7, 8, and 9. All calculations at these nodes are conditional on a negative survey result. The calculations are as follows:

EMV calculations for a negative survey result are done next.

$$\text{EMV (node 7)} = \text{EMV (Large plant | Negative survey result)}$$
$$= \$196\ 000 \times 0.023 + \$96\ 000 \times 0.543 + (-\$124\ 000) \times 0.434 = \$2820$$

$$\text{EMV (node 8)} = \text{EMV (Small plant | Negative survey result)}$$
$$= \$86\ 000 \times 0.023 + \$46\ 000 \times 0.543 + (-\$24\ 000) \times 0.434 = \$16\ 540$$

$$\text{EMV (node 9)} = \text{EMV (No plant | Negative survey result)}$$
$$= -\$4000$$

Thus, given a negative survey result, John should build a small plant, with an expected payoff of $16 540.

4.   Continuing on the lower portion of the tree and moving backward, we next consider outcome node 10. At this node, we compute the expected value if we conduct the market survey, as follows:

We continue working backward to the origin, computing EMV values.

$$\text{EMV (node 10)} = \text{EMV (Conduct survey)}$$
$$= \$141\ 840 \times 0.57 + \$16\ 540 \times 0.43 = \$87\ 961$$

5.   Finally, we consider the initial decision node. At this node, we compare the EMV of not conducting the survey with the EMV of conducting the survey. Because the EMV of $87 961 if we conduct the survey is higher than the $86 000 EMV if the survey is not conducted, John's decision should be to accept Smart's offer to conduct a survey and await the result. If the survey result is positive, John should build a large plant; but if the result is negative, John should build a small plant.

As a practice exercise, see if you can use TreePlan to develop Thompson Lumber's complete decision tree, including the Smart Services market survey. The calculations and results should be similar to those shown in Figure 9.5.

Expected Value of Sample Information

EVSI measures the value of sample information.

The preceding computations indicate that John Thompson should accept Smart's offer to conduct a survey at a cost of $4000. However, what should John do if Smart wants $6000 for the survey? In this case, the EMV if the survey is conducted will be only $85 961. (Can you see why this is so?) Because this is less than the $86 000 EMV without the survey, John should reject the survey and build a large plant right away.

We can perhaps pose an alternate question here: What is the actual value of Smart's survey information? An effective way of measuring the value of a market survey (which is typically imperfect information) is to compute the **expected value of sample information (EVSI)**, as follows:

$$EVSI = \text{EMV of best decision } with \text{ sample information,} assuming\ no\ cost\ to\ get\ it$$
$$- \text{EMV of best decision } without \text{ any information} \qquad (9\text{-}6)$$

In John's case, the EMV without any information (i.e., if the survey is not conducted) is $86 000. In contrast, if the survey is conducted, the EMV becomes $91 961 (remember that we need to add the $4000 survey cost to the EMV value at node 10 in Figure 9.5 because we are assuming that there is no survey cost here). Thus,

$$EVSI = \$91\,961 - \$86\,000 = \$5961$$

This means that John could have paid up to $5961 for this *specific* market survey and still come out ahead. Because Smart charges only $4000, it is indeed worthwhile. In contrast, if Smart charges $6000, it is not worthwhile.

Comparing EVSI to EVPI may provide a good measure of the relative value of the current survey.

We address an interesting question at this point: If the cost of a proposed survey is less than its EVSI, does it mean we should immediately accept it? Although we recommended this decision in John's example, the answer to this question in many real-world settings could be *no*. The reason is as follows. Suppose John could approach *several* different market survey firms for help. Because each survey is different in terms of how imperfect its information is, each survey has its own EVSI. In John's example, the survey offered by Smart Services has an EVSI of only $5961, much less than the EVPI of $24 000. Although paying $4000 to get $5961 worth of information may seem to be a good idea, the better question for John to ask could be whether there is some *other* survey available that perhaps costs more than $4000 but yields considerably more than $5961 worth of information. In this regard, a measure that may be useful to compute is the **efficiency of sample information**, as follows:

$$\text{Efficiency of sample information} = EVSI/EVPI \qquad (9\text{-}7)$$

In the case of the current survey, the efficiency is $5961 / $24 000 = 0.2484, or 24.84%. That is, the survey offered by Smart is only 24.84% as good as the best possible information. As noted earlier, if John can find a survey that is more efficient, it may be worthwhile to consider it, even if it costs more than the Smart Services survey.

9.9   ESTIMATING PROBABILITY VALUES USING BAYESIAN ANALYSIS

Bayes' theorem allows decision makers to revise probability values.

In discussing Thompson Lumber's multistage decision problem (see Figure 9.5), we assumed that the following event and conditional probabilities were available to John with regard to the survey offered by Smart Services:

P(Positive survey result)	$= P(PS)$	$= 0.570$
P(Negative survey result)	$= P(NS)$	$= 0.430$
P(High demand I Positive survey result)	$= P(HD\,|\,PS)$	$= 0.509$
P(Moderate demand I Positive survey result)	$= P(MD\,|\,PS)$	$= 0.468$
P(Low demand I Positive survey result)	$= P(LD\,|\,PS)$	$= 0.023$
P(High demand I Negative survey result)	$= P(HD\,|\,NS)$	$= 0.023$
P(Moderate demand I Negative survey result)	$= P(MD\,|\,NS)$	$= 0.543$
P(Low demand I Negative survey result)	$= P(LD\,|\,NS)$	$= 0.434$

In practice, as illustrated in this section, John would have computed these probabilities using Bayes' theorem on data regarding Smart Services' performance on past surveys.

Bayes' theorem allows decision makers to incorporate additional information (such as past performance) to revise their probability estimates of various outcomes. Before continuing further, you may wish to review Bayes' theorem in Appendix B.

Calculating Revised Probabilities

In order to evaluate the reliability of the survey, John asks Smart Services to provide him with information regarding its performance on past surveys. Specifically, he wants to know how many similar surveys the company has conducted in the past, what it predicted each time, and what the actual result turned out to be eventually in each case. Let's assume that Smart has data on 75 past surveys that it has conducted. These data are summarized in Table 9.10.

Table 9.10 reveals, for example, that in 29 of 30 past cases where a product's demand subsequently turned out to be high, Smart's surveys had predicted positive market conditions. That is, the probability of positive survey results, given high demand, $P(PS|HD)$, is 0.967. Likewise, in 7 of 15 past cases where a product's demand subsequently turned out to be moderate, Smart's surveys had predicted negative market conditions. That is, the probability of negative survey results, given moderate demand, $P(NS|MD)$, is 0.467. How does John use this information to gauge the accuracy of Smart's survey in his specific case?

Recall that without any market survey information, John's current probability estimates of high, moderate, and low demand are $P(HD) = 0.30$, $P(MD) = 0.50$, and $P(LD) = 0.30$, respectively. These are referred to as *prior* probabilities. Based on the survey performance information in Table 9.10, we compute John's revised, or *posterior*, probabilities—namely, $P(HD|PS)$, $P(MD|PS)$, $P(LD|PS)$, $P(HD|NS)$, $P(MD|NS)$, and $P(LD|NS)$. This computation, using the formula for Bayes' theorem (see Equation B-7 on page 639 of Appendix A), proceeds as follows:

$$P(HD|PS) = \frac{P(PS \text{ and } HD)}{P(PS)} = \frac{P(PS|HD) \times P(HD)}{P(PS)}$$
$$= \frac{P(PS|HD) \times P(HD)}{P(PS|HD) \times P(HD) + P(PS|MD) \times P(MD) + P(PS|LD) \times P(LD)}$$
$$= \frac{0.967 \times 0.30}{0.967 \times 0.30 + 0.533 \times 0.50 + 0.067 \times 0.20} = \frac{0.290}{0.570} = 0.509$$

The other five revised probabilities (i.e., $P(MD|PS)$, $P(LD|PS)$, etc.) can also be computed in a similar manner. However, as you can see, Bayes' formula is rather cumbersome and somewhat difficult to follow intuitively. For this reason, it is perhaps easier in practice to compute these revised probabilities by using a probability table. We show these calculations in Table 9.11 for the case where the survey result is positive, and in Table 9.12 for the case where the survey result is negative.

The calculations in Table 9.11 are as follows. For any outcome, such as high demand (HD), we know the conditional probability, $P(PS|HD)$, and the prior probability, $P(HD)$. Using Equation B-6 on page 637 of Appendix A, we can compute the joint probability, $P(PS$

Prior probabilities are estimates before the market survey.

Revised probabilities are determined using the prior probabilities and the market survey information.

We can calculate conditional probabilities using a probability table.

TABLE 9.10		SURVEY RESULT WAS	
Reliability of Smart Services' Survey in Predicting Actual Outcomes	**WHEN ACTUAL OUTCOME WAS**	POSITIVE (PS)	NEGATIVE (NS)
	High demand (**HD**)	$P(PS | HD) = 29/30 = 0.967$	$P(NS | HD) = 1/30 = 0.033$
	Moderate demand (**MD**)	$P(PS | MD) = 8/15 = 0.533$	$P(NS | MD) = 7/15 = 0.467$
	Low demand (**LD**)	$P(PS | LD) = 2/30 = 0.067$	$P(NS | LD) = 28/30 = 0.933$

TABLE 9.11

Probability Revisions, Given a Positive Survey Result (PS)

OUTCOME	CONDITIONAL PROB. $P(\text{PS} \mid \text{OUTCOME})$	PRIOR PROB.		JOINT PROB.	REVISED PROB. $P(\text{OUTCOME} \mid \text{PS})$
High Demand (**HD**)	0.967	× 0.30	=	0.290	0.290 / 0.57 = 0.509
Moderate Demand (**MD**)	0.533	× 0.50	=	0.267	0.267 / 0.57 = 0.468
Low Demand (**LD**)	0.067	× 0.20	=	0.013	0.013 / 0.57 = 0.023
	$P(\textbf{PS}) = P(\text{Positive Survey}) =$			0.570	1.000

TABLE 9.12

Probability Revisions, Given a Negative Survey Result (NS)

OUTCOME	CONDITIONAL PROB. $P(\text{NS} \mid \text{OUTCOME})$	PRIOR PROB.		JOINT PROB.	REVISED PROB. $P(\text{OUTCOME} \mid \text{NS})$
High Demand (**HD**)	0.033	× 0.30	=	0.010	0.010 / 0.43 = 0.023
Moderate Demand (**MD**)	0.467	× 0.50	=	0.233	0.233 / 0.43 = 0.543
Low Demand (**LD**)	0.933	× 0.20	=	0.187	0.187 / 0.43 = 0.434
	$P(\textbf{NS}) = P(\text{Negative Survey}) =$			0.430	1.000

and HD), as the product of the conditional and prior probabilities. After we repeat this computation for the other two outcomes (moderate demand and low demand), we add the three joint probabilities—$P(\text{PS and HD}) + P(\text{PS and MD}) + P(\text{PS and LD})$—to determine $P(\text{PS})$. Observe that this computation is the same as that in the denominator of the Bayes' theorem formula. After we have computed $P(\text{PS})$, we can use Equation B-5 on page 636 of Appendix A to compute the revised probabilities $P(\text{HD} \mid \text{PS})$, $P(\text{MD} \mid \text{PS})$, and $P(\text{LD} \mid \text{PS})$. Table 9.12 shows similar calculations when the survey result is negative. As you can see, the probabilities obtained here are the same ones we used earlier in Figure 9.5 on page 401.

Potential Problems in Using Survey Results

In using past performance to gauge the reliability of a survey's results, we typically base our probabilities only on those cases in which a decision to take some course of action is

DECISION MODELING IN ACTION
Using Utility and Decision Trees in Hip Replacement

Should you or a family member undergo a somewhat dangerous surgery for an illness, or is it better to manage the illness medically by using drugs? Should a health care firm put a new drug on its list of approved medicines? What medical procedures should the government reimburse? Individuals and institutions face medical treatment decision problems from a variety of perspectives. For example, the decision an individual patient faces is driven by the medical treatment that best describes the patient's attitudes about risk (utility) and quality of life over the rest of his or her life.

One common application of utility theory decision tree modeling in medicine is total hip replacement surgery for patients with severe arthritis of the hip. More than 120 000 hip replacements are performed per year in North America. Although this surgery is mostly successful, the treatment decision for an individual patient can be difficult. Although surgery offers the potential of increased quality of life, it also carries the risk of death.

A decision tree analysis helps define all the time-sequenced outcomes that can occur in dealing with arthritis of the hip. Conservative management by medicine is a surgical alternative, but the disease is degenerative, and a worsening condition is inevitable. A successful surgery, which restores full function, is likely, but uncertainty exists even then. First, infection can cause the new prosthetic hip to fail. Or the new hip may fail over time due to breakage or malfunction. Both cases require a revision surgery, whose risks are greater than the first surgery. Decision trees and utility theory help patients first assess their personal risk levels and then allow them to compute life expectancy based on sex and race.

Source: G. Hazen, J. Pellissier, and J. Sounderpandian. "Stochastic Tree Models in Medical Decision Making," *Interfaces* (July–August 1998): 64–80.

actually made. For example, we can observe demand only in those cases where the product was actually introduced after the survey was conducted. Unfortunately, there is no way to collect information about the demand in those situations in which the decision after the survey was to not introduce the product. This implies that conditional probability information is not quite always as accurate as we would like it to be. Nevertheless, calculating conditional probabilities helps to refine the decision-making process and, in general, to make better decisions. For this reason, the use of Bayesian analysis in revising prior probabilities is very popular in practice.

9.10 UTILITY THEORY

EMV is not always the best criterion to use to make decisions.

So far we have used monetary values to make decisions in all our examples. In practice, however, using money to measure the value of a decision could sometimes lead to bad decisions. The reason for this is that different people value money differently at different times. For example, having $100 in your pocket may mean a lot to you today, when you are a student, but may be relatively unimportant in a few years, when you are a wealthy businessperson. This implies that while you may be unwilling to bet $100 on a risky project today, you may be more than willing to do so in a few years. Unfortunately, when we use monetary values to make decisions, we do not account for these perceptions of risk in our model.

Here's another example to drive home this point. Assume that you are the holder of a lottery ticket. In a few moments, a fair coin will be flipped. If it comes up tails, you win $100 000. If it comes up heads, you win nothing. Now suppose a wealthy person offers you $35 000 for your ticket before the coin is flipped. What should you do? According to a decision based on monetary values, as shown in the decision tree in Figure 9.6, you should reject the offer and hold on to your ticket because the EMV of $50 000 is greater than the offer of $35 000. In reality, what would *you* do? It is likely that many people would take the guaranteed $35 000 in exchange for a risky shot at $100 000 (in fact, many would probably be willing to settle for a lot less than $35 000). Of course, just how low a specific individual would go is a matter of personal preference because, as noted earlier, different people value money differently. This example, however, illustrates how basing a decision on EMV may not be appropriate.

One way to get around this problem and incorporate a person's attitudes toward risk in the model is through **utility theory**. In the next section we explore first how to measure a person's utility function and then how to use utility measures in decision making.

FIGURE 9.6

Decision Tree for a Lottery Ticket

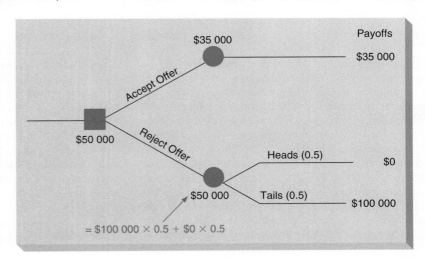

Measuring Utility and Constructing a Utility Curve

Utility function converts a person's value for money and attitudes toward risk into a dimensionless number between 0 and 1.

Using a utility function is a way of converting a person's value for money and attitudes toward risk into a dimensionless number between 0 and 1. There are three important issues to note at this stage, as follows:

- Each person has his or her own utility function. It is therefore critical in any problem to determine the utility function for the decision maker in that problem.
- A person's utility function could change over time as his or her economic and other conditions change. Recall the earlier example about how important $100 is to you today as opposed to how important it may be to you in a few years. A person's utility function should therefore be updated periodically.
- A person may have different utility functions for different magnitudes of money. For example, most people tend to be very willing to take risks when the monetary amounts involved are small. (After all, we're all willing to buy a $1 lottery ticket, even when we know very well that we're unlikely to win anything.) However, the same people tend to be unwilling to take risks with larger monetary amounts. (Would you be willing to buy a $1000 lottery ticket even if the potential top prize was $1 billion?) This implies that we should consider a person's utility function only over the relevant range of monetary values involved in the specific problem at hand.

Let us use an example to study how we can determine a person's utility function.

We assign the worst payoff a utility of 0 and the best payoff a utility of 1.

Gina de Marco's Utility Function   Gina de Marco would like to construct a utility function to reveal her preference for monetary amounts between $0 and $50 000. We start assessing Gina's utility function by assigning a utility value of 0 to the worst payoff and a utility value of 1 to the best payoff. That is, $U(\$0) = 0$ and $U(\$50\ 000) = 1$. Monetary values between these two payoffs will have utility values between 0 and 1. To determine these utilities, we begin by posing the following gamble to Gina, as outlined in Figure 9.7:

> You have a 50% chance at getting $0 and a 50% chance at getting $50 000. That is, the EMV of this gamble is $25 000. What is the minimum guaranteed amount that you will accept in order to walk away from this gamble? In other words, what is the minimum amount that will make you indifferent between alternative 1 (gamble between $0 and $50 000) and alternative 2 (obtain this amount for sure).

The answer to this question may vary from person to person, and it is called the **certainty equivalent** between the two payoff values ($0 and $50 000, in this case). Let's suppose Gina is willing to settle for $15 000. (Some of you may have settled for less, while others may

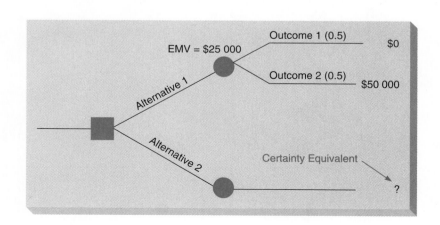

Certainty equivalent is the minimum guaranteed amount you are willing to accept to avoid the risk associated with a gamble.

have wanted more.) That is, Gina is willing to accept a guaranteed payoff of $15 000 to avoid the risk associated with a potential payoff of $50 000. The implication is that from a utility perspective (i.e., with respect to Gina's attitudes toward risk and value for money), the expected value between $0 and $50 000 is only $15 000, and not the $25 000 we calculated in Figure 9.7. In other words, $U(\$15\ 000) = U(\$0) \times 0.5 + U(\$50\ 000) \times 0.5 = 0 \times 0.5 + 1 \times 0.5 = 0.5$ for Gina.

We repeat the gamble in Figure 9.7, except that the two monetary amounts presented to Gina in the gamble are $15 000 and $50 000. The EMV is $32 500. Let's suppose Gina is willing to settle for a certainty equivalent of $27 000. This implies that for Gina, $U(\$27\ 000) = U(\$15\ 000) \times 0.5 + U(\$50\ 000) \times 0.5 = 0.5 \times 0.5 + 1 \times 0.5 = 0.75$.

We repeat the gamble in Figure 9.7 again, this time with monetary amounts of $0 and $15 000. The EMV is $7500. Let's suppose Gina is willing to settle for a certainty equivalent of $6000. This implies that for Gina, $U(\$6000) = U(\$0) \times 0.5 + U(\$15\ 000) \times 0.5 = 0 \times 0.5 + 0.5 \times 0.5 = 0.25$.

A utility curve plots utility values versus monetary values.

At this stage, we know the monetary values associated with utilities of 0, 0.25, 0.5, 0.75, and 1 for Gina. If necessary, we can continue this process several more times to find additional utility points. For example, we could present the gamble between $27 000 (with a utility of 0.75) and $50 000 (with a utility of 1) to determine the monetary value associated with a utility of 0.875 ($= 0.75 \times 0.5 + 1 \times 0.5$). However, the five assessments shown here are usually enough to get an idea of Gina's feelings toward risk. Perhaps the easiest way to view Gina's utility function is to construct a **utility curve** that plots utility values (*y*-axis) versus monetary values (*x*-axis). This is shown in Figure 9.8. In the figure, the assessed utility points of $0, $6000, $15 000, $27 000, and $50 000 are obtained from the preceding discussion, while the rest of the curve is eyeballed in. As noted earlier, it is usually enough to know five points on the curve in order to get a reasonable approximation.

Gina's utility curve is typical of a risk avoider. A **risk avoider** is a decision maker who gets less utility or pleasure from a greater risk and tends to avoid situations in which high

FIGURE 9.8   **Utility Curve for Gina de Marco**

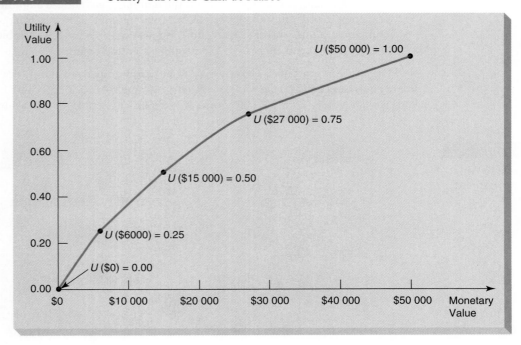

losses might occur. As monetary value increases on her utility curve, the utility increases at a slower rate. Another way to characterize a person's attitude toward risk is to compute the risk premium, defined as

$$\text{Risk premium} = \text{EMV of gamble} - \text{Certainty equivalent} \qquad (9\text{-}8)$$

Risk premium is the EMV that a person is willing to give up in order to avoid the risk associated with a gamble.

The **risk premium** represents the monetary amount that a decision maker is willing to give up in order to avoid the risk associated with a gamble. For example, Gina's risk premium in the first gamble between $0 and $50 000 is computed as $25 000 − $15 000 = $10 000. That is, Gina is willing to give up $10 000 to avoid the uncertainty associated with a gamble. Likewise, she is willing to give up $5500 (= $32 500 − $27 000) to avoid the risk of gambling between $15 000 and $50 000.

Clearly, a person who is more averse to risk will be willing to give up an even larger amount to avoid the uncertainty. In contrast, a person who is a risk seeker will insist on getting a certainty equivalent that is greater than the EMV in order to walk away from a gamble. Such a person will therefore have a negative risk premium. Finally, a person who is risk neutral will always specify a certainty equivalent that is exactly equal to the EMV. Based on the preceding discussion, we can now define the following three preferences for risk:

- Risk avoider or risk-averse person: Risk premium > 0
- Risk indifferent or risk-neutral person: Risk premium = 0
- Risk seeker or risk-prone person: Risk premium < 0

A risk neutral person has a utility curve that is a straight line.

Figure 9.9 illustrates the utility curves for all three risk preferences. As shown in the figure, a person who is a **risk seeker** has an opposite-shaped utility curve to that of a risk avoider. This type of decision maker gets more utility from a greater risk and a higher potential payoff. As monetary value increases on his or her utility curve, the utility increases at an increasing rate. A person who is **risk neutral** has a utility curve that is a straight line.

The shape of a person's utility curve depends on the specific decision being considered, the person's psychological frame of mind, and how the person feels about the future. As noted earlier, it may well be that a person has one utility curve for some situations and a

FIGURE 9.9

Utility Curves for Different Risk Preferences

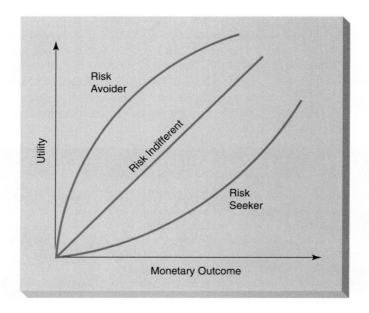

completely different curve for others. In practice, most people are likely to be risk seekers when the monetary amounts involved are small (recall the earlier comment about buying a $1 lottery ticket) but tend to become risk avoiders as the monetary amounts increase. The exact monetary amount at which a specific individual switches from being a risk seeker to a risk avoider is, of course, a matter of personal preference.

Exponential Utility Function   If a person is a risk avoider, it is possible to use curve-fitting techniques to fit an equation to the utility curve. This makes it convenient to determine the person's utility for any monetary value within the appropriate range. Looking at the utility curve in Figure 9.9 for a risk avoider, it is apparent that the curve can be approximated by an exponential function. The equation would be as follows:

$$U(X) = 1 - e^{-X/R}$$

where e is the exponential constant (equal to 2.7182), X represents the monetary value, and R is a parameter that controls the shape of the person's utility curve. As R increases, the utility curve becomes flatter (corresponding to a decision maker who is less risk averse).

Utility as a Decision-Making Criterion

Utility values replace monetary values.

Once we have determined a decision maker's utility curve, how do we use it in making decisions? We construct the decision tree and make all prior and revised probability estimates and computations as before. However, instead of using monetary values as payoffs, we now replace all monetary payoffs with the appropriate utility values. We then fold back the decision tree, using the criterion of maximizing expected utility values. Let's look at an example.

Mark Simkin has an opportunity to invest in a new business venture. If the venture is a big success, Mark will make a profit of $40 000. If the venture is a moderate success, Mark will make a profit of $10 000. If the venture fails, Mark will lose his investment of $30 000. Mark estimates the venture's chances as 20% for big success, 30% for moderate success, and 50% for failure. Should Mark invest in the venture?

Mark's alternatives are displayed in the tree shown in Figure 9.10. Using monetary values, the EMV at node 1 is $40 000 × 0.2 + $10 000 × 0.3 + (−$30 000) × 0.5 = −$4000. Because this is smaller than the EMV of $0 at node 2, Mark should turn down the venture and invest his money elsewhere.

Now let's view the same problem from a utility perspective. Using the procedure outlined earlier, Mark is able to construct a utility curve showing his preference for monetary amounts between $40 000 and –$30 000 (the best and worst payoffs in his problem). This curve, shown in Figure 9.11, indicates that within this monetary range Mark is a risk seeker (i.e., a gambler).

Mark's objective is to maximize expected utility.

From Figure 9.11, we note the following utility values for Mark: $U(-\$30\ 000) = 0$, $U(\$0) = 0.15$, $U(\$10\ 000) = 0.30$, and $U(\$40\ 000) = 1$. Substituting these values in the decision tree in Figure 9.10 in place of the monetary values, we fold back the tree to maximize Mark's expected utility. The computations are shown in Figure 9.12.

HISTORY   The Beginning of Marginal Utility

The first published statement of any sort of theory of marginal utility was by Daniel Bernoulli, in "*Specimen theoriae novae de mensura sortis.*" This paper appeared in 1738. In 1728, Gabriel Cramer had produced fundamentally the same theory in a private letter. Each had sought to resolve a classic lottery problem, called the St. Petersburg paradox, and had concluded that the marginal desirability of money decreased as it was accu-

mulated. Bernoulli postulated that the natural logarithm would make a suitable utility function, while Cramer suggested the square root. We note that both the logarithmic and square root functions exhibit the characteristic profile of the risk avoider.

Source: http://en.wikipedia.org/wiki/Marginal_utility

FIGURE 9.10

Decision Tree Using
EMV for Mark Simkin

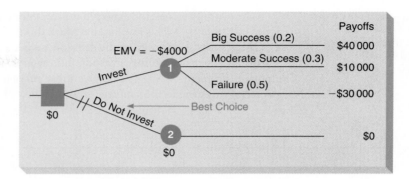

FIGURE 9.10

Decision Tree Using
EMV for Mark Simkin

FIGURE 9.11   Utility Curve for Mark Simkin

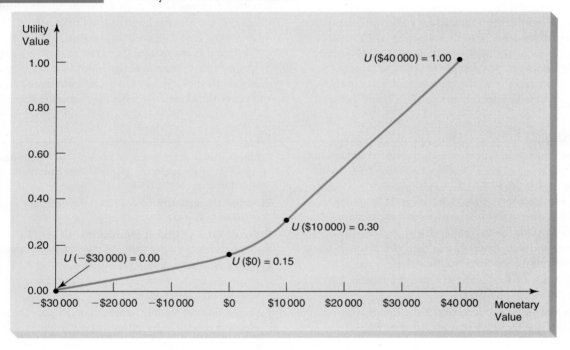

FIGURE 9.12

Decision Tree Using
Utility Values for
Mark Simkin

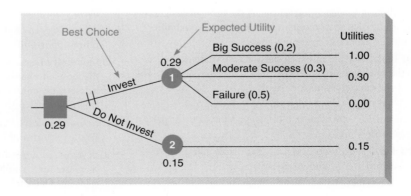

Using expected utility may lead to a decision that is different from the one suggested by EMV.

Using utility values, the expected utility at node 1 is 0.29, which is greater than the utility of 0.15 at node 2. This implies that Mark should invest his money in the venture. As you can see, this is the opposite of the decision suggested if EMV had been used, and it clearly illustrates how using utilities instead of monetary values may lead to different decisions in the same problem. In Mark's case, the utility curve indicates that he is a risk seeker, and the choice of investing in the venture certainly reflects his preference for risk.

SUMMARY

This chapter introduces the topic of decision analysis, which is an analytic and systematic approach to studying decision making. We first indicate the steps involved in making decisions in three different environments: (1) decision making under certainty, (2) decision making under uncertainty, and (3) decision making under risk. For decision problems under uncertainty, we identify the best alternatives, using criteria such as maximax, maximin, criterion of realism, equally likely, and minimax regret. For decision problems under risk, we discuss the computation and use of the expected monetary value (EMV), expected opportunity loss (EOL), and expected

value of perfect information (EVPI). We also illustrate the use of Excel to solve decision analysis problems.

Decision trees are used for larger decision problems in which decisions must be made in sequence. In this case, we compute the expected value of sample information (EVSI). Bayesian analysis is used to revise or update probability values. We also discuss how decision trees can be set up and solved using TreePlan, an Excel add-in.

When it is inappropriate to use monetary values, utility theory can be used to assign a utility value to each decision payoff. In such cases, we compute expected utilities and select the alternative with the highest utility value.

GLOSSARY

Certainty Equivalent. The minimum guaranteed amount one is willing to accept to avoid the risk associated with a gamble.

Coefficient of Realism (α). A number from 0 to 1 such that when α is close to 1, the decision criterion is optimistic, and when α is close to zero, the decision criterion is pessimistic.

Conditional Value, or Payoff. A consequence or payoff, normally expressed in a monetary value, which occurs as a result of a particular alternative and outcome.

Decision Alternative. A course of action or a strategy that can be chosen by a decision maker.

Decision Making Under Certainty. A decision-making environment in which the future outcomes are known.

Decision Making Under Risk. A decision-making environment in which several outcomes can occur as a result of a decision or alternative. Probabilities of the outcomes are known.

Decision Making Under Uncertainty. A decision-making environment in which several outcomes can occur. Probabilities of these outcomes, however, are not known.

Decision Table. A table in which decision alternatives are listed down the rows and outcomes are listed across the columns. The body of the table contains the payoffs.

Efficiency of Sample Information. A ratio of the expected value of sample information and the expected value of perfect information.

Equally Likely. A decision criterion that places an equal weight on all outcomes. Also known as Laplace.

Expected Monetary Value (EMV). The average or expected monetary outcome of a decision if it can be repeated many

times. This is determined by multiplying the monetary outcomes by their respective probabilities. The results are then added to arrive at the EMV.

Expected Opportunity Loss (EOL). The average or expected regret of a decision.

Expected Value of Perfect Information (EVPI). The average or expected value of information if it is completely accurate.

Expected Value with Perfect Information (EVwPI). The average or expected value of the decision if the decision maker knew what would happen ahead of time.

Expected Value of Sample Information (EVSI). The average or expected value of imperfect or survey information.

Maximax. An optimistic decision-making criterion. This is the alternative with the highest possible return.

Maximin. A pessimistic decision-making criterion that maximizes the minimum outcome. It is the best of the worst possible outcomes.

Minimax Regret. A decision criterion that minimizes the maximum opportunity loss.

Opportunity Loss. The amount you would lose by not picking the best alternative. For any outcome, this is the difference between the consequences of any alternative and the best possible alternative. Also called *regret*.

Outcome. An occurrence over which the decision maker has little or no control. Also known as a state of nature.

Risk Avoider. A person who avoids risk. As the monetary value increases on the utility curve, the utility increases at a decreasing rate. This decision maker gets less utility for a greater risk and higher potential returns.

Risk Neutral. A person who is indifferent toward risk. The utility curve for a risk-neutral person is a straight line.

Risk Premium. The monetary amount that a person is willing to give up in order to avoid the risk associated with a gamble.

Risk Seeker. A person who seeks risk. As the monetary value increases on the utility curve, the utility increases at an increasing rate. This decision maker gets more pleasure for a greater risk and higher potential returns.

Sequential Decisions. Decisions in which the outcome of one decision influences other decisions.

Utility Curve. A graph or curve that illustrates the relationship between utility and monetary values. When this curve has been constructed, utility values from the curve can be used in the decision-making process.

Utility Theory. A theory that allows decision makers to incorporate their risk preference and other factors into the decision making process.

KEY EQUATIONS

(9-1) Criterion of realism = α × Maximum payoff for an alternative + $(1 - \alpha)$ × Minimum payoff for an alternative

Computes the payoffs for the coefficient of realism criterion.

(9-2) EMV (Alternative i) = Payoff of first outcome × Probability of first outcome + Payoff of second outcome × Probability of second outcome + ... + Payoff of last outcome × Probability of last outcome

Computes the expected monetary value.

(9-3) EOL (Alternative i) = Regret of first outcome × Probability of first outcome + Regret of second outcome × Probability of second outcome + ... + Regret of last outcome × Probability of last outcome

Computes the expected opportunity loss.

(9-4) EVwPI = Best payoff for first outcome × Probability of first outcome + Best payoff for second outcome × Probability of second outcome + ... + Best payoff for last outcome × Probability of last outcome

Computes the expected value with perfect information.

(9-5) EVPI = EVwPI − Maximum EMV

Computes the expected value of perfect information.

(9-6) Expected value of sample information (EVSI)

$$EVSI = \begin{bmatrix} \text{Expected value of best} \\ \text{decision } with \text{ sample} \\ \text{information, assuming} \\ \text{no cost to gather it} \end{bmatrix} - \begin{bmatrix} \text{Expected value} \\ \text{of best decision} \\ without \text{ sample} \\ \text{information} \end{bmatrix}$$

(9-7) Efficiency of sample information = EVSI/EVPI

Computes the efficiency of the sample information.

(9-8) Risk premium = EMV of gamble − Certainty equivalent

Computes the risk premium.

SOLVED PROBLEMS

Solved Problem 9-1

Cal Bender and Becky Trinh are undergraduates in business school. In an attempt to make extra money, Cal and Becky have decided to look into the possibility of starting a small company that would provide word-processing services to students who need term papers or other reports prepared in a professional manner. They have identified three strategies. Strategy 1 is to invest in a fairly expensive computer system with a high-quality laser printer. In a good market, they should be able to obtain a net profit of $10 000 over the next two years. If the market is bad, they could lose $8000. Strategy 2 is to purchase a cheaper system. With a good market, they could get a return during the next two years of $8000. With a bad market, they could incur a loss of $4000. Their final strategy, strategy 3, is to do nothing. Cal is basically a risk taker, whereas Becky tries to avoid risk.

(a) Which decision criterion should Cal use? What would Cal's decision be?
(b) Which decision criterion should Becky use? What decision would Becky make?
(c) If Cal and Becky were indifferent to risk, which decision criterion should they use? What would be the decision?

Solution

The problem is one of decision making under uncertainty. To answer the specific questions, it is helpful to construct a decision table showing the alternatives, outcomes, and payoffs, as follows on the next page:

ALTERNATIVE	GOOD MARKET	BAD MARKET
Expensive system	$10 000	−$8 000
Cheaper system	8 000	−4 000
Do nothing	0	0

(a) Cal should use the maximax, or optimistic, decision criterion. The maximum payoffs for the three alternatives are $10 000, $8000, and $0, respectively. Hence, Cal should select the expensive system.
(b) Becky should use the maximin, or pessimistic, decision criterion. The minimum payoffs for the three alternatives are −$8000, −$4000, and $0, respectively. Hence, Becky should choose to do nothing.
(c) If Cal and Becky are indifferent to risk, they should use the equally likely criterion. The average payoffs for the three alternatives are $1000, $2000, and $0, respectively. Hence, their decision would be to select the cheaper system.

Solved Problem 9-2

Maria Rojas is considering the possibility of opening a small dress shop on a busy street a few blocks from the university. She has located a good mall that attracts students. Her options are to open a small shop, a medium-sized shop, or no shop at all. The market for a dress shop can be good, average, or bad. The probabilities for these three possibilities are 0.2 for a good market, 0.5 for an average market, and 0.3 for a bad market. The net profit or loss for the medium-sized and small shops for the various market conditions are given in the following table. Opening no shop at all yields no loss and no gain. What do you recommend?

ALTERNATIVE	GOOD MARKET ($)	AVERAGE MARKET ($)	BAD MARKET ($)
Small shop	75 000	25 000	−40 000
Medium-sized shop	100 000	35 000	−60 000
No shop	0	0	0

Solution

The problem can be solved by developing a payoff table that contains all alternatives, outcomes, and probability values. The EMV for each alternative is also computed. See the following table:

	OUTCOMES			
ALTERNATIVE	GOOD MARKET ($)	AVERAGE MARKET ($)	BAD MARKET ($)	EMV ($)
Small shop	75 000	25 000	−40 000	15 500
Medium-sized shop	100 000	35 000	−60 000	19 500
No shop	0	0	0	0
Probabilities	0.20	0.50	0.30	

$$\text{EMV(small shop)} = (0.2)(\$75\ 000) + (0.5)(\$25\ 000) + (0.3)(-\$40\ 000) = \$15\ 500$$

$$\text{EMV(medium-sized shop)} = (0.2)(\$100\ 000) + (0.5)(\$35\ 000) + (0.3)(-\$60\ 000) = \$19\ 500$$

$$\text{EMV(no shop)} = (0.2)(\$0) + (0.5)(\$0) + (0.3)(\$0) = \$0$$

As can be seen, the best decision is to build the medium-sized shop. The EMV for this alternative is $19 500.

Solved Problem 9-3

Monica Britt has enjoyed sailing small boats since she was seven years old, when her mother started sailing with her. Today Monica is considering the possibility of starting a company to produce small sailboats for the recreational market. Unlike other mass-produced sailboats, however, these boats will be made specifically for children between the ages of 10 and 15. The boats will be of the highest quality and extremely stable, and the sail size will be reduced to prevent problems with capsizing.

Because of the expense involved in developing the initial molds and acquiring the necessary equipment to produce fibreglass sailboats for young children, Monica has decided to conduct a pilot study to make sure that the market for the sailboats will be adequate. She estimates that the pilot study will cost her $10 000. Furthermore, the pilot study can be either successful or not successful. Her basic decisions are to build a large manufacturing facility, a small manufacturing facility, or no facility at all. With a favourable market, Monica can expect to make $90 000 from the large facility or $60 000 from the smaller facility. If the market is unfavourable, however, Monica estimates that she would lose $30 000 with a large facility, whereas she would lose only $20 000 with the small facility. Monica estimates that the probability of a favourable market, given a successful pilot study result, is 0.8. The probability of an unfavourable market, given an unsuccessful pilot study result, is estimated to be 0.9. Monica feels that there is a 50–50 chance that the pilot study will be successful. Of course, Monica could bypass the pilot study and simply make the decision as to whether to build a large plant, a small plant, or no facility at all. Without doing any testing in a pilot study, she estimates that the probability of a successful market is 0.6. What do you recommend?

Solution

The decision tree for Monica's problem is shown in Figure 9.13 on page 416. The tree shows all alternatives, outcomes, probability values, and payoffs.

For your convenience, the decision tree in Figure 9.13 also shows all EMVs. The expected value computations at the various nodes are as follows:

$$\text{EMV (node 1)} = \$60\ 000 \times 0.6 + (-\$20\ 000) \times 0.4 = \$28\ 000$$

$$\text{EMV (node 2)} = \$90\ 000 \times 0.6 + (-\$30\ 000) \times 0.4 = \$42\ 000$$

$$\text{EMV (node 3)} = \$0$$

$$\text{EMV (node 4)} = \$50\ 000 \times 0.8 + (-\$30\ 000) \times 0.2 = \$34\ 000$$

$$\text{EMV (node 5)} = \$80\ 000 \times 0.8 + (-\$40\ 000) \times 0.2 = \$56\ 000$$

$$\text{EMV (node 6)} = -\$10\ 000$$

$$\text{EMV (node 7)} = \$50\ 000 \times 0.1 + (-\$30\ 000) \times 0.9 = -\$22\ 000$$

$$\text{EMV (node 8)} = \$80\ 000 \times 0.1 + (-\$40\ 000) \times 0.9 = -\$28\ 000$$

$$\text{EMV (node 9)} = -\$10\ 000$$

$$\text{EMV (node 10)} = \$56\ 000 \times 0.5 + (-\$10\ 000) \times 0.5 = \$23\ 000$$

Monica's optimal solution is to *not* conduct the pilot study and construct the large plant directly. The EMV of this decision is $42 000.

Solved Problem 9-4

Developing a small driving range for golfers of all abilities has long been a desire of John Jenkins. John, however, believes that the chance of a successful driving range is only about 40%. A friend of John's has suggested that he conduct a survey in the community to get a better feel for the demand for such a facility. There is a 0.9 probability that the research will be favourable if the driving range facility will be successful. Furthermore, it is estimated that there is a 0.8 probability that the marketing research will be unfavourable if indeed the facility will be unsuccessful. John would like to determine the chances of a successful driving range, given a favourable result from the marketing survey.

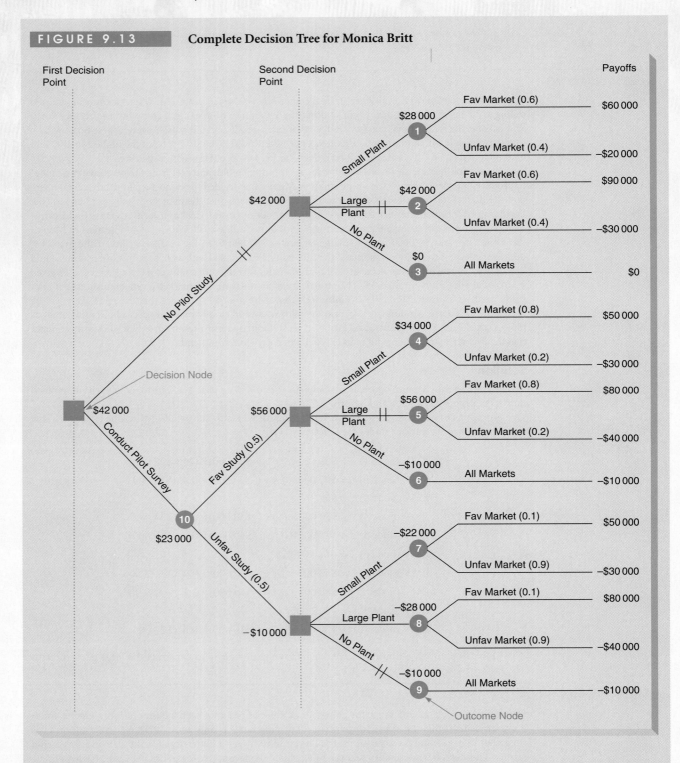

FIGURE 9.13   **Complete Decision Tree for Monica Britt**

Solution

This problem requires the use of Bayes' theorem. Before we start to solve the problem, we will define the following terms:

$$P(SF) = \text{probability of successful driving range facility}$$

$$P(UF) = \text{probability of unsuccessful driving range facility}$$

$$P(RF|SF) = \text{probability that the research will be favourable, given a successful driving range facility}$$

$$P(RU|SF) = \text{probability that the research will be unfavourable, given a successful driving range facility}$$

$$P(RU|UF) = \text{probability that the research will be unfavourable, given an unsuccessful driving range facility}$$

$$P(RF|UF) = \text{probability that the research will be favourable, given an unsuccessful driving range facility}$$

Now, we can summarize what we know:

$$P(SF) = 0.4$$
$$P(RF|SF) = 0.9$$
$$P(RU|UF) = 0.8$$

From this information we can compute three additional probabilities that we need to solve the problem:

$$P(UF) = 1 - P(SF) = 1 - 0.4 = 0.6$$
$$P(RU|SF) = 1 - P(RF|SF) = 1 - 0.9 = 0.1$$
$$P(RF|UF) = 1 - P(RU|UF) = 1 - 0.8 = 0.2$$

Now we can put these values into Bayes' theorem to compute the desired probability, as shown in the following table:

OUTCOMES	CONDITIONAL PROBABILITY		PRIOR PROBABILITY		JOINT PROBABILITY	POSTERIOR PROBABILITY
Favourable market	0.9	×	0.4	=	0.36	0.36 / 0.48 = 0.75
Unfavourable market	0.2	×	0.6	=	0.12	0.12 / 0.48 = 0.25
					0.48	

The probability of a successful driving range, given a favourable research result, is 0.36/0.48, or 0.75.

⟫ SELF-TEST

- Before taking the self-test, refer back to the learning objectives at the beginning of the chapter, the notes in the margins, and the glossary at the end of the chapter.
- Use the key at the back of the book to correct your answers.
- Restudy pages that correspond to any questions that you answered incorrectly or material you feel uncertain about.

1. Which of the following is not a type of decision making?
   a. decision making under chance
   b. decision making under risk
   c. decision making under certainty
   d. decision making under uncertainty

2. A payoff table
   a. lists states of nature on one axis and alternatives on the other axis.
   b. is also called a decision table.
   c. is a matrix (table) of conditional values.
   d. is all of the above.

3. Which of these models is valid under conditions of uncertainty?
   a. maximax
   b. maximin
   c. equally likely
   d. minimax regret
   e. all of the above

4. Probabilities are needed under
   a. conditions of certainty.
   b. conditions of risk.
   c. conditions of uncertainty.
   d. both a and c.

5. The minimum EOL is
   a. the minimum expected opportunity loss.
   b. the minimum regret.
   c. equivalent to the EVPI.
   d. the alternative to select.
   e. all of the above.

6. The sum of the products of the probabilities of mutually exclusive and exhaustive states of nature and the conditional values of those same states of nature is called the
   a. EOL.
   b. EMV.
   c. EVPI.

7. EVPI is
   a. the expected value with perfect information.
   b. equal to maximum EOL.
   c. equal to expected value with perfect information minus maximum EMV.

8. An α value is needed to indicate the decision maker's optimism when using the
   a. maximax.
   b. equally likely.

   c. criterion of realism.
   d. minimax regret.

9. The decision model that utilizes the opportunity loss table is the
   a. maximax.
   b. maximin.
   c. equally likely.
   d. criterion of realism.
   e. minimax regret.

10. In calculating the expected monetary value on decision trees
    a. all probabilities and payoffs should be specified first.
    b. you begin at the right-hand side of each route and travel backward.
    c. the EMV at each decision node should be the highest of the choices from the succeeding branches.
    d. you assume a constantly increasing utility for constantly increasing amounts of money.
    e. all of the above are correct.

11. Constantly increasing utility for constantly increasing amounts of money
    a. is an attribute of a person who is risk indifferent.
    b. would eliminate your desire to gamble and also your desire to buy life insurance.
    c. is a fundamental assumption to EMV analysis.
    d. is all of the above.
    e. is none of the above.

12. A utility curve
    a. can be used in the decision-making process.
    b. shows utility increasing at an increasing rate when the monetary value increases for a risk seeker.
    c. shows utility increasing at a decreasing rate when the monetary value increases for a risk avoider.
    d. is all of the above.

13. _____ are typically used when a sequence of decisions needs to be made.

14. The revised probabilities computed using Bayesian analysis are called _____.

15. In utility theory, _____ is used to determine utility values for various decision outcomes.

DISCUSSION QUESTIONS AND PROBLEMS

Discussion Questions

9-1 Give an example of a good decision that you made that resulted in a bad outcome. Also give an example of a bad decision that you made that had a good outcome. Why was each decision good or bad?

9-2 Describe what is involved in the decision process.

9-3 What is an alternative? What is an outcome or a state of nature?

9-4 Discuss the differences between decision making under certainty, decision making under risk, and decision making under uncertainty.

9-5 State the meanings of EMV and EVPI.

9-6 Under what conditions is a decision tree preferable to a decision table?

9-7 What is the difference between prior and posterior probabilities?

9-8 What is the purpose of Bayesian analysis? Describe how you would use Bayesian analysis in the decision-making process.

9-9 What is the purpose of utility theory?

9-10 Briefly discuss how a utility function can be assessed. What is a standard gamble, and how is it used in determining utility values?

9-11 How is a utility curve used in selecting the best decision for a particular problem?

9-12 What is a risk seeker? What is a risk avoider? How does the utility curve for these types of decision makers differ?

Problems

9-13 Kenneth Brown is the principal owner of Brown Oil, Inc. After quitting his university teaching job, Ken has been able to increase his annual salary by a factor of over 100. At the present time, Ken is forced to consider purchasing some more equipment for Brown Oil because of competition. His alternatives are shown in the following table:

EQUIPMENT	FAVOURABLE MARKET ($)	UNFAVOURABLE MARKET ($)
Sub 100	300 000	−200 000
Oiler J	250 000	−100 000
Texan	75 000	−18 000

For example, if Ken purchases a Sub 100 and there is a favourable market, he will realize a profit of $300 000. On the other hand, if the market is unfavourable, Ken will suffer a loss of $200 000. But Ken has always been a very optimistic decision maker.

(a) What type of decision is Ken facing?
(b) What decision criterion should he use?
(c) Which alternative is best?

9-14 Although Ken Brown (discussed in Problem 9-13) is the principal owner of Brown Oil, his brother Ryan is credited with making the company a financial success. Ryan is vice president of finance. Ryan attributes his success to his pessimistic attitude about business and the oil industry. Given the information from Problem 9-13, it is likely that Ryan will arrive at a different decision. What decision criterion should Ryan use, and what alternative will he select?

9-15 *The Lubricant* is an expensive oil newsletter to which many oil giants subscribe, including Brown Oil. In the last issue, the letter described how the demand for oil products would be extremely high. Apparently, the North American consumer will continue to use oil products even if the price of these products doubles. Indeed, one of the articles in *The Lubricant* states that the chance of a favourable market for oil products was 70%, whereas the

chance of an unfavourable market was only 30%. Ken would like to use these probabilities in determining the best decision. (See Problem 9-13 for details.)

(a) What decision model should be used?
(b) What is the optimal decision?

9-16 Janet Kim, president of Kim Manufacturing, Inc., is considering whether to build more manufacturing plants in Manitoba. Her decision is summarized in the following table:

ALTERNATIVES	FAVOURABLE MARKET ($)	UNFAVOURABLE MARKET ($)
Build a large plant	400 000	−300 000
Build a small plant	80 000	−10 000
Don't build	0	0
Probabilities	0.4	0.6

(a) Construct an opportunity loss table.
(b) Determine EOL and the best strategy.
(c) What is the expected value of perfect information?

9-17 Bob's Bike Shop is considering three options for its facility next year. Bob can expand his current shop, move to a larger facility, or make no change. With a good market, the annual payoff would be $56 000 if he expands, $70 000 if he moves, and $30 000 if he does nothing. With an average market, his payoffs will be $21 000, $35 000, and $10 000, respectively. With a poor market, his payoff will be −$29 000, −$45 000, and $5000, respectively.

(a) Which option should Bob choose if he uses the maximax criterion?
(b) Which option should Bob choose if he uses the maximin criterion?
(c) Which option should Bob choose if he uses the equally likely criterion?
(d) Which option should Bob choose if he uses the criterion of realism with $\alpha = 0.6$?
(e) Which option should Bob choose if he uses the minimax regret criterion?

9-18 Bob (see Problem 9-17) has gathered some additional information. The probabilities of good, average, and poor markets are 0.25, 0.45, and 0.3, respectively.

(a) Using EMVs, which option should Bob choose? What is the maximum EMV?
(b) Using EOL, which option should Bob choose? What is the minimum EOL?
(c) Compute the EVPI and show that it is the same as the minimum EOL.

9-19 Debbie Gibson is considering three investment options for a small inheritance that she has just received— stocks, bonds, and money market. The return on her investment will depend on the performance of the economy, which can be strong, average, or weak. The returns for each possible combination are shown in the following table:

| | ECONOMIC PERFORMANCE | | |
INVESTMENT	STRONG	AVERAGE	WEAK
Stocks	12%	6%	−10%
Bonds	7%	4%	1%
Money market	4%	3%	2%

Assume that Debbie will choose only one of the investment options.

(a) Which investment should Debbie choose if she uses the maximax criterion?
(b) Which investment should Debbie choose if she uses the maximin criterion?
(c) Which investment should Debbie choose if she uses the equally likely criterion?
(d) Which investment should Debbie choose if she uses the criterion of realism with α = 0.5?
(e) Which investment should Debbie choose if she uses the minimax regret criterion?

9-20 After reading about economic predictions, Debbie Gibson (see Problem 9-19) has assigned the probability that the economy will be strong, average, and weak at 0.2, 0.35, and 0.45, respectively.

(a) Using EMVs, which option should Debbie choose? What is the maximum EMV?
(b) Using EOL, which option should Debbie choose? What is the minimum EOL?
(c) Compute the EVPI and show that it is the same as the minimum EOL.

9-21 Mary Pierce is the manager of a home supply store in Grande Isle, a relatively new community in Newfoundland. Mary is trying to decide whether to add a large extension onto the existing store, to add a small extension, or to leave the store at its current capacity with no extension. If the population continues to grow, Mary estimates that a large extension would increase store profit by $150 000, and a small extension would increase profit by $60 000. If the population of Grande Isle does not grow, the store would suffer a loss of $85 000 if the large extension were added, and a loss of $45 000 if the small extension were added. Unfortunately, Mary does not have any projections about the future population of Grande Isle.

(a) What type of decision problem is Mary confronting?
(b) Construct a decision table for Mary' problem.
(c) Using the equally likely criterion, determine the best alternative.
(d) If Mary is feeling optimistic about the potential for population growth in Grande Isle, what is her optimal decision?

9-22 Mary Pierce's boss, Liam Smith, is not convinced that Mary has made the best decision. As a realist, he suggests that Mary should reconsider the problem using a coefficient of realism of 0.75. What is the best alternative using this decision criterion?

9-23 Jeff Park sells newspapers on Sunday mornings in an area surrounded by three busy churches. Assume that Jeff's demand can either be for 100, 200, or 300 newspapers, depending on traffic and weather. Jeff has the option to order 100, 200, or 300 newspapers from his supplier. Jeff pays $1.25 for each newspaper he orders and sells each for $2.00.

(a) How many papers should Jeff order if he chooses the maximax criterion?
(b) How many papers should Jeff order if he chooses the maximin criterion?
(c) How many papers should Jeff order if he chooses the equally likely criterion?
(d) How many papers should Jeff order if he chooses the criterion of realism with α = 0.4?
(e) How many papers should Jeff order if he chooses the minimax regret criterion?

9-24 Jeff Park (see Problem 9-23) has done some research and discovered that the probabilities for demands of 100, 200, and 300 newspapers are 0.4, 0.35, and 0.25, respectively.

(a) Using EMVs, how many papers should Jeff order?
(b) Using EOL, how many papers should Jeff order?
(c) Compute Jeff's EVwPI and EVPI.

9-25 Waldo Books needs to decide how many copies of a new hardcover release to purchase for its shelves. The store has assumed that demand will be 50, 100, 150, or 200 copies next month, and it needs to decide whether to order 50, 100, 150, or 200 books for this period. Each book costs Waldo $20 and can be sold for $30. Waldo can sell any unsold books back to the supplier for $4.

(a) Which option should Waldo choose if it uses the maximax criterion?
(b) Which option should Waldo choose if it uses the maximin criterion?
(c) Which option should Waldo choose if it uses the equally likely criterion?
(d) Which option should Waldo choose if it uses the criterion of realism with α = 0.7?
(e) Which option should Waldo choose if it uses the minimax regret criterion?

9-26 After researching the market, Waldo Books (see Problem 9-25) has concluded that the probabilities of selling 50, 100, 150, and 200 books next month are 0.2, 0.35, 0.25, and 0.2, respectively.

(a) Using EMVs, how many books should Waldo order?
(b) Using EOL, how many books should Waldo order?
(c) Compute Waldo's EVwPI and EVPI.

9-27 Megley Cheese Company is a small manufacturer of several different cheese products. One of the products is a cheese spread that is sold to retail outlets. Jason Megley must decide how many cases of cheese spread to manufacture each month. The probability that the demand will be six cases is 0.1, seven cases is 0.3, eight cases is 0.5, and nine cases is 0.1. The cost of every case is $45, and the price that Jason gets for each case is $95. Unfortunately, any cases not sold by the end of the month are of no value, due to spoilage. How many cases of cheese should Jason manufacture each month?

9-28 Even though independent gasoline stations have been having a difficult time, Susan Solomon has been thinking about starting her own independent gasoline station. Susan's problem is to decide how large her station should be. The annual returns will depend both on the size of her station and on a number of marketing factors related to the oil industry and demand for gasoline. After a careful analysis, Susan developed the following table:

SIZE OF FIRST STATION	GOOD MARKET ($)	FAIR MARKET ($)	POOR MARKET ($)
Small	50 000	20 000	−10 000
Medium	80 000	30 000	−20 000
Large	100 000	30 000	−40 000
Very large	300 000	25 000	−160 000

For example, if Susan constructs a small station and the market is good, she will realize a profit of $50 000.

(a) What is the maximax decision?
(b) What is the maximin decision?
(c) What is the equally likely decision?
(d) What is the criterion of realism decision? Use an α value of 0.8.
(e) Develop an opportunity loss table.
(f) What is the minimax regret decision?

9-29 Chantal Poirier has three major routes to take to work in Montreal. She can take Rue Ste. Catherine the entire way, she can take several back streets to work, or she can use the Decarie Expressway. The traffic patterns are, however, very complex. Under good conditions, Rue Ste. Catherine is the fastest route. When Ste. Catherine is congested, one of the other routes is usually preferable. Over the past two months, Chantal has tried each route several times under different traffic conditions. This information is summarized in minutes of travel time to work in the table below:

	NO TRAFFIC CONGESTION (MINUTES)	MILD TRAFFIC CONGESTION (MINUTES)	SEVERE TRAFFIC CONGESTION (MINUTES)
Rue Ste. Catherine	15	30	45
Back roads	20	25	35
Expressway	30	30	30

In the past 60 days, Chantal encountered severe traffic congestion 10 days and mild traffic congestion 20 days. Assume that the past 60 days are typical of traffic conditions.

(a) Develop a decision table for this decision.
(b) Which route should Chantal take?
(c) Chantal has learned that a new Montreal radio station would tell her the exact traffic conditions before she started to work each morning. How much time in minutes on the average would Chantal save by listening to the radio station?

9-30 A group of radiologists is considering opening a private imaging centre, offering imaging services such as ultrasounds, CT scans, and MRIs. If the provincial government liberalizes access to private services, the radiologists estimate that they would realize a net profit of $100 000 in the first year of operation. However, if the government restricts access, their estimated loss in the first year would be $40 000. Of course, they do not have to proceed at all, in which case there would be neither profit nor loss. In the absence of any solid evidence on which way the government is leaning, the best guess the radiologists can make is that there is a 50% chance the government will liberalize access and a 50% chance that it will restrict access. Construct a decision tree to help analyze this problem. What would you recommend the radiologists do?

9-31 The radiologists in Problem 9-30 have been approached by a professor of public health who offers to perform an analysis of government health care decisions for a fee of $5000. The professor's area of expertise is in predicting government decisions on public health issues. He provides one of two opinions—positive or negative—and he claims that based on his previous consulting experience he can make the following probabilistic statements:

- The probability that the government will liberalize access given that he issues a positive report is 0.82.
- The probability that the government will restrict access given that he issues a positive report is 0.18.
- The probability that the government will liberalize access given that he issues a negative report is 0.11.
- The probability that the government will restrict access given that he issues a negative report is 0.89.
- The probability that he issues a positive report is 0.55.
- The probability that he issues a negative report is 0.45.

(a) Expand the decision tree of Problem 9-30 to reflect the new options now available with the professor's report. What should the radiologists do now?
(b) If the professor announces that he is going to increase his consulting fee, what is the maximum amount that the radiologists should be willing to pay?
(c) What is the efficiency of the professor's report?

9-32 In Problem 9-31, you helped a group of radiologists analyze a decision using EMV as the decision criterion. This group has already assessed its utility for money:
$U(−\$45\ 000) = 0$, $U(−\$40\ 000) = 0.1$, $U(−\$5000) = 0.7$, $U(\$0) = 0.9$, $U(\$95\ 000) = 0.99$, and $U(\$100\ 000) = 1$.

(a) Are the radiologists risk seekers or risk avoiders? Justify your answer.
(b) Use expected utility as the decision criterion and determine the best decision for the radiologists (including the option to use the professor's report).

9-33 Jerry Young is thinking about opening a bicycle shop in his hometown. Jerry loves to take his own bike on 80-kilometre trips with his friends, but he believes that any small business should be started only if there is a good chance of making a profit. Jerry can open a small shop, a large shop, or no shop at all. Because there will be a five-year lease on the building that Jerry is thinking about using, he wants to make sure that he makes the correct decision.

Jerry has done some analysis about the profitability of the bicycle shop. If Jerry builds the large bicycle shop, he will earn $60 000 if the market is good, but he will lose $40 000 if the market is bad. The small shop will return a $30 000 profit in a good market and a $10 000 loss in an bad market. At the present time, he believes that there is a 59% chance that the market will be good.

Jerry also has the option of hiring his old marketing professor for $5000 to conduct a marketing research study. If the study is conducted, the results could be either favourable or unfavourable. It is estimated that there is a 0.6 probability that the survey will be favourable. Furthermore, there is a 0.9 probability that the market will be good, given a favourable outcome from the study. However, the marketing professor has warned Jerry that there is only a probability of 0.12 of a good market if the marketing research results are not favourable.

(a) Develop a decision tree for Jerry and help him decide what he should do.
(b) How much is the marketing professor's information worth? What is the efficiency of this information?

9-34 Kuality Komponents buys on–off switches from two suppliers. The quality of the switches from the suppliers is as follows:

PERCENTAGE DEFECTIVE	PROBABILITY FOR SUPPLIER A	PROBABILITY FOR SUPPLIER B
1	0.70	0.30
3	0.20	0.40
5	0.10	0.30

For example, the probability of getting a batch of switches that are 1% defective from supplier A is 0.70. Because Kuality Komponents orders 10 000 switches per order, this would mean that there is a 0.7 probability of getting 100 defective switches out of the 10 000 switches if supplier A is used to fill the order. A defective switch can be repaired for 50 cents. Although the quality of supplier B is lower, it will sell an order of 10 000 switches for $37 less than supplier A.

(a) Develop a decision tree to help Kuality Komponents decide which supplier it should use.
(b) For how much less would supplier B have to sell an order of 10 000 switches than supplier A for Kuality Komponents to be indifferent between the two suppliers?

9-35 You have been hired by the No Flight Golf Company, and your first task is to decide whether to market a new golf ball utilizing breakthrough technology and, if so, determine the price. The payoff of your decision will be affected by whether your competitor will market similar balls and the price of its golf balls after you go to market. The cost to market the golf balls is $80 000, and the probability that your competitor will enter the market is 0.75. The following table describes the payoffs of each pricing combination, assuming that No Flight will have competition:

	COMPETITOR'S PRICE		
OUR PRICE	HIGH ($)	MEDIUM ($)	LOW ($)
High	400 000	250 000	25 000
Medium	475 000	325 000	175 000
Low	350 000	250 000	125 000

If No Flight sets its price high, the probability that the competition will set its price high, medium, and low is 0.3, 0.55, and 0.15, respectively. If No Flight sets its price medium, the probability that the competition will set its price high, medium, and low is 0.2, 0.7, and 0.1, respectively. Finally, if No Flight sets its price low, the probability that the competition will set its price high, medium, and low is 0.15, 0.25, and 0.6, respectively.

If No Flight has no competition for its new golf balls, its expected payoff for setting the price high, medium, and low is $600 000, $500 000, and $400 000, respectively, excluding marketing costs. Do you recommend marketing the new golf balls? If so, what is your pricing recommendation?

9-36 After observing the heavy snow that his town received the previous winter, Ajay Patel, an enterprising student, plans to offer a snow-clearing service in his neighbourhood this winter. If he invests in a new heavy-duty blower, Ajay forecasts a profit of $700 if snowfall this winter is heavy, a profit of $200 if it is moderate, and a loss of $900 if it is light. As per the current weather forecasts, the probabilities of heavy, moderate, and light snowfall this winter are 0.4, 0.3, and 0.3, respectively.

Rather than purchase a new blower, Ajay could get his father's blower repaired and just accept smaller jobs. Under this option, Ajay estimates a profit of $350 for a heavy snowfall, a profit of $100 for a moderate snowfall, and a loss of $150 for a light snowfall. Ajay, of course, has the option of choosing neither of these options.

The local weather expert, Samantha Adams, is Ajay's good friend. For $50, she is willing to run sophisticated weather models on her computer and tell Ajay whether she expects this winter to be unseasonably cold. For the sake of solving this problem, assume that the following information is available. There is a 45% chance that Samantha will predict this winter to be unseasonably cold. If she does say this, the probabilities of heavy, moderate, and light snowfall are revised to 0.7, 0.25, and 0.05, respectively. On the other hand, if she predicts that this winter will not be unseasonably cold, these probabilities are revised to 0.15, 0.33, and 0.52, respectively

Draw the decision tree for the situation faced by Ajay. Fold back the tree and determine the strategy you would recommend he follow. What is the efficiency of Samantha's information?

9-37 Oscar Weng is planning to raise funds to pay for a scouting trip by running a concession stand during tomorrow's high school soccer game. Oscar needs to decide whether to rent a large insulated thermos from the local rental store and sell cocoa at the game, or to rent a large refrigerated container and sell lemonade. Unfortunately, Oscar does not have the resources to rent both items. Sales depend on whether it is sunny or rainy during the game. If the weather is sunny, Oscar will make a profit of $60 from lemonade but only $20 from cocoa. If, however, it is rainy, Oscar will make a profit of $80 from cocoa but only break even if he brings lemonade. Based on the local newspaper's prediction, Oscar thinks there is a 60% chance of it being sunny tomorrow.

Oscar's friend Susan is a budding meteorologist who claims she can predict the weather more accurately than the newspaper. For only $4, she offers to study the weather and tell him if there is a "good chance" or "bad chance" of it being sunny tomorrow. Assume that the following data are available about the accuracy of Susan's information:

- The probability that she will say "good chance" is 0.7.
- If she says "good chance," then there is a 0.83 probability that it will actually be sunny tomorrow.
- If she says "bad chance," then there is only a 0.25 probability that it will actually be sunny tomorrow.

(a) Draw the complete decision tree for Oscar's problem and fold it back to help him decide what he should do.
(b) How much is Susan's information actually worth?

9-38 Rob Johnson is a product manager for Diamond Chemical. The firm is considering whether to launch a new product line that will require building a new facility. The technology required to produce the new product is yet untested. If Rob decides to build the new facility and the process is successful, Diamond Chemical will realize a profit of $650 000. If the process does not succeed, the company will lose $800 000. Rob estimates that there is a 0.6 probability that the process will succeed.

Rob can also decide to build a pilot plant for $50 000 to test the new process before deciding to build the full-scale facility. If the pilot plant succeeds, Rob feels the chance of the full-scale facility succeeding is 85%. If the pilot plant fails, Rob feels the chance of the full-scale facility succeeding is only 20%. The probability that the pilot plant will succeed is estimated at 0.6. Structure this problem with a decision tree and advise Rob what to do.

9-39 Rob Johnson (see Problem 9-38) has some revised information concerning the accuracy of the pilot plant probabilities. According to his new information, the probability that the pilot plant will be successful, given that the full-scale facility will work, is 0.8. The probability that the pilot plant will fail, given that the full-scale facility will fail, is 0.85. Calculate the posterior probabilities and reevaluate the decision tree from Problem 9-38. Does this new information affect Diamond Chemical's original decision?

9-40 Your regular tennis partner has made a friendly wager with you. The two of you will play out one point in which you can serve. The loser pays the winner $100. If your first serve is not in play, you get a second serve. If your second serve is not in play, you lose the point. You have two kinds of serves: a hard one and a soft one. You know that your hard serve is in play 60% of the time and, when it is in play, you win the point 70% of the time. You put your soft serve in play 85% of the time and, when it is in play, you win the point 25% of the time. Should you accept the wager? If so, should you use your hard or soft serve?

9-41 You are reconsidering your analysis of the tennis wager between you and your partner (see Problem 9-40) and have decided to incorporate utility theory into the decision making process. The following table describes your utility values for various payoffs:

MONETARY VALUE ($)	UTILITY
−100	0.00
−50	0.50
0	0.80
50	0.95
100	1.00

(a) Redo Problem 9-40 using this information.
(b) How can you best describe your attitude toward risk? Justify your answer.

9-42 Shamrock Oil owns a parcel of land that has the potential to be an underground oil field. It will cost $500 000 to drill for oil. If oil does exist on the land, Shamrock will realize a payoff of $4 000 000 (not including drilling costs). With current information, Shamrock estimates that there is a 0.2 probability that oil is present on the site. Shamrock also has the option of selling the land as is for $400 000, without further information about the likelihood of oil being present. A third option is to perform geological tests at the site, which would cost $100 000. There is a 30% chance that the test results will be positive, after which Shamrock can sell the land for $650 000 or drill the land, with a 0.65 probability that oil exists. If the test results are negative, Shamrock can sell the land for $50 000 or drill the land, with a 0.05 probability that oil exists. Using a decision tree, recommend a course of action for Shamrock Oil.

9-43 Shamrock Oil (see Problem 9-42) has some revised information concerning the accuracy of the geological test probabilities. According to this new information, the probability that the test will be positive, given that oil is present in the ground, is 0.85. The probability that the test will be negative, given that oil is not present, is 0.75. Calculate the posterior probabilities and reevaluate the decision tree from Problem 9-42. Does this new information affect Shamrock Oil's original decision?

9-44 Shamrock Oil (see Problem 9-42) has decided to rely on utility theory to assist in the decision concerning the oil field. The following table describes its utility function; all monetary values are in thousands of dollars:

MONETARY VALUE ($)	UTILITY
−600	0.00
−500	0.03
−50	0.10
400	0.15
550	0.17
3400	0.90
3500	1.00

(a) Redo Problem 9-42 using this information.

(b) How can you best describe Shamrock Oil's attitude toward risk? Justify your answer.

9-45 Jim Sellers is thinking about producing a new type of electric razor for men. If the market is good, he would get a return of $100 000, but if the market for this new type of razor is poor, he would lose $60 000. Because Ron Bush is a close friend of Jim Sellers, Jim is considering the possibility of using Bush Marketing Research to gather additional information about the market for the razor. Ron has suggested two options to Jim. The first alternative is a sophisticated questionnaire that would be administered to a test market. It will cost $5000. The second alternative is to run a pilot study. This would involve producing a limited number of the new razors and trying to sell them in two cities that are typical of American cities. The pilot study is more accurate but is also more expensive. It will cost $20 000. Ron has suggested that it would be a good idea for Jim to conduct either the questionnaire or the pilot before making the decision concerning whether to produce the new razor. But Jim is not sure if the value of either option is worth the cost.

For the sake of solving this problem, assume that Jim has the following probability estimates available: the probability of a successful market without performing the questionnaire or pilot study is 0.5, the probability of a successful market given a positive questionnaire result is 0.78, the probability of a successful market given a negative questionnaire result is 0.27, the probability of a successful market given a positive pilot study result is 0.89, and the probability of a successful market given a negative pilot study result is 0.18. Further, the probability of a positive questionnaire result is 0.45 and the probability of a positive pilot study result is also 0.45.

(a) Draw the decision tree for this problem and identify the best decision for Jim.

(b) What is the value of the questionnaire's information? What is its efficiency?

(c) What is the value of the pilot study's information? What is its efficiency?

9-46 Jim Sellers (see Problem 9-45) has been able to estimate his utility for a number of different values, and he would like to use these utility values in making his decision. The utility values are $U(-\$80\ 000) = 0$, $U(-\$65\ 000) = 0.5$, $U(-\$60\ 000) = 0.55$, $U(-\$20\ 000) = 0.7$, $U(-\$5000) = 0.8$, $U(\$0) = 0.81$, $U(\$80\ 000) = 0.9$, $U(\$95\ 000) = 0.95$, and $U(\$100\ 000) = 1$.

(a) Solve Problem 9-45(a) again using utility values.

(b) Is Jim a risk avoider or risk seeker? Justify your answer.

9-47 Jason Scott has applied for a mortgage to purchase a house, and he will go to settlement in two months. His loan can be locked in now at the current market interest rate of 7% and a cost of $1000. He also has the option of waiting one month and locking in the rate available at that time at a cost of $500. Finally, he can choose to accept the market rate available at settlement in two months at no cost. Assume that interest rates will either

increase by 0.5% (0.3 probability), remain unchanged (0.5 probability), or decrease by 0.5% (0.2 probability) at the end of one month.

Rates can also increase, remain unchanged, or decrease by another 0.5% at the end of the second month. If rates increase after one month, the probability that they will increase, remain unchanged, and decrease at the end of the second month is 0.5, 0.25, and 0.25, respectively. If rates remain unchanged after one month, the probability that they will increase, remain unchanged, and decrease at the end of the second month is 0.25, 0.5, and 0.25, respectively. If rates decrease after one month, the probability that they will increase, remain unchanged, and decrease at the end of the second month is 0.25, 0.25, and 0.5, respectively.

Assuming that Jason will stay in the house for 5 years, each 0.5% increase in the interest rate of his mortgage will cost him $2400. Each 0.5% decrease in the rate will likewise save him $2400. What strategy would you recommend?

9-48 Jason Scott (see Problem 9-47) has decided to incorporate utility theory into his decision with his mortgage application. The following table describes Jason's utility function:

MONETARY VALUE ($)	UTILITY
−4800	0.00
−2900	0.10
−2400	0.12
−1000	0.15
−500	0.19
0	0.21
1900	0.26
2400	0.30
4800	1.00

(a) How can you best describe Jason's attitude toward risk? Justify your answer.

(b) Will the use of utilities affect Jason's original decision in Problem 9-47?

9-49 Sue Reynolds has to decide whether she should get information (at a cost of $20 000) to invest in a retail store. If she gets the information, there is a 0.6 probability that it will be favourable. If the information is favourable, there is a 0.9 probability that the store will be a success. If the information is not favourable, the probability of a successful store is only 0.2. Without any information, Sue estimates that the probability of a successful store will be 0.6. A successful store will give a return of $100 000. If the store is built but is not successful, Sue will see a loss of $80 000. Of course, she could always decide not to build the retail store.

(a) What do you recommend?

(b) How much is the information worth? What is its efficiency?

9-50 Replace all monetary values in Sue Reynolds' problem (see Problem 9-49) with the following utilities:

MONETARY VALUE ($)	UTILITY
100 000	1.00
80 000	0.40
0	0.20
−20 000	0.10
−80 000	0.05
−100 000	0.00

(a) What do you recommend based on expected utility?
(b) Is Sue a risk seeker or a risk avoider? Justify your answer.

9-51 Before market research was done, Peter Martin believed that there was a 50–50 chance that his food store would be a success. The research team determined that there was a 0.8 probability that the market research would be favourable, given a successful food store. Moreover, there was a 0.7 probability that the market research would be unfavourable, given an unsuccessful food store. This information is based on past experience.

(a) If the market research is favourable, what is Peter's revised probability of a successful food store?
(b) If the market research is unfavourable, what is Peter's revised probability of a successful food store?

9-52 A market research company has approached you about the possibility of using its services to help you decide whether to launch a new product. According to its customer portfolio, it has correctly predicted a favourable market for its clients' products 14 out of the last 16 times. It has also correctly predicted an unfavourable market for its clients' products 9 out of 11 times. Without this research company's help, you have estimated the probability of a favourable market at 0.55. Calculate the posterior probabilities, using the track record of the research firm.

9-53 Lathum Consulting is an econometrics research firm that predicts the direction of the gross national product (GNP) during the next quarter. More specifically, it forecasts whether the GNP will grow, hold steady, or decline. The following table describes Lathum's track record from past predictions by displaying the probabilities of its predictions, given the actual outcome:

| | GNP PREDICTION | | |
ACTUAL GNP	GROWTH	STEADY	DECLINE
Growth	0.75	0.08	0.05
Steady	0.18	0.80	0.12
Decline	0.07	0.12	0.83

For example, the chance that Lathum will predict that the GNP will grow when it actually is steady is 18%. Your company is considering a contract with Lathum Consulting to assist in predicting the direction of next quarter's GNP. Prior to enlisting Lathum's services, you have assessed the probability of the GNP growing, holding steady, and declining at 0.3, 0.45, and 0.25, respectively. Calculate the posterior probabilities, using the services of Lathum Consulting.

9-54 The Klean Corporation is involved with waste management. During the past 10 years it has become one of the largest waste disposal companies in Eastern Canada, serving primarily Quebec and Ontario. Chris Klean, president of the company, is considering the possibility of establishing a waste treatment plant in British Columbia. From past experience. Chris believes that a small plant in Southern B.C. would yield a $500 000 profit regardless of the market for the facility. The success of a medium-sized waste treatment plant would depend on the market. With a low demand for waste treatment, Chris expects a $200 000 return. A medium demand would yield a $700 000 return in Chris's estimation, and a high demand would return $800 000. Although a large facility is much riskier, the potential return is much greater. With a high demand for waste treatment in B.C., the large facility should return a million dollars. With a medium demand, the large facility should return $400 000. Chris estimates that the large facility would be a big loser if there is a low demand for waste treatment. He estimates that he would lose approximately $200 000 with a large treatment facility if demand was indeed low. Looking at the economic conditions for the southern part of the province of British Columbia and using his experience in the field, Chris estimates that the probability of a low demand for treatment plants is 0.15. The probability for a medium-demand facility is approximately 0.40, and the probability of a high demand for a waste treatment facility is 0.45.

Because of the large potential investment and the possibility of a loss, Chris has decided to hire a market research team that is based in Kelowna, B.C. This team will perform a survey to get a better feeling for the probability of a low, medium, or high demand for a waste treatment facility. The cost of the survey is $50 000. To help Chris determine whether to go ahead with the survey, the marketing research firm has provided Chris with the following information:

P (survey results | possible outcomes)

| | SURVEY RESULTS | | |
POSSIBLE OUTCOME	LOW SURVEY RESULTS	MEDIUM SURVEY RESULTS	HIGH SURVEY RESULTS
Low demand	0.7	0.2	0.1
Medium demand	0.4	0.5	0.1
High demand	0.1	0.3	0.6

As you see, the survey could result in three possible outcomes. Low survey results mean that a low demand is likely. In a similar fashion, medium survey results or high survey results would mean a medium or a high demand, respectively. What should Chris do?

9-55 In the past few years, the traffic problems in Bill Kelly's hometown in Nova Scotia have become more serious. Now, Main Street is congested about half the time. The normal travel time to work for Bill is only 15 minutes when Main Street is used and there is no congestion. With congestion, however, it takes Bill 40 minutes to get to work. If Bill decides to take the expressway, it will take 30 minutes regardless of the traffic conditions. Bill's utility for travel time is: $U(15 \text{ minutes}) = 0.9$, $U(30 \text{ minutes}) = 0.7$, and $U(40 \text{ minutes}) = 0.2$.

(a) Which route will minimize Bill's expected travel time?
(b) Which route will maximize Bill's utility?
(c) When it comes to travel time, is Bill a risk seeker or a risk avoider?

⫸ CASE STUDY 9.1

Ski Right

After retiring as a family doctor, Marc Marks became an avid downhill skier on the steep slopes of the Rocky Mountains in Banff, Alberta. As an amateur inventor, Marc was always looking for something new. After a series of recent highly publicized skiing accidents, Marc believed he could use his creative mind to make skiing safer and his bank account larger. He knew that many deaths on the slopes were caused by head injuries. Although ski helmets have been on the market for some time, most skiers considered them boring and basically ugly. As a physician, Marc knew that some type of new ski helmet was the answer.

Marc's biggest challenge was to invent a helmet that was attractive, safe, and fun to wear. Multiple colours, using the latest fashion design, would be a must. After years of skiing, Marc knew that many skiers believe that how you look on the slopes is more important than how you ski. His helmets would have to look good and fit in with current fashion trends. But attractive helmets were not enough. Marc had to make the helmets fun and useful. The name of the new ski helmet, Ski Right, was sure to be a winner. If Marc could come up with a good idea, he believed that there was a 20% chance that the market for the Ski Right helmet would be excellent. The chance of a good market should be 40%. Marc also knew that the market for his helmet could be only average (30% chance) or even poor (10% chance).

The idea of how to make ski helmets fun and useful came to Marc on a gondola ride to the top of a mountain. A busy executive on the gondola ride was on his cell phone trying to complete a complicated merger. When the executive got off the gondola, he dropped the phone and it was crushed by the gondola mechanism. Marc decided that his new ski helmet would have a built-in cell phone and an AM/FM Stereo radio. All of the electronics could be operated by a control pad worn on a skier's arm or leg.

Marc decided to try a small pilot project for Ski Right. He enjoyed being retired and didn't want a failure to cause him to go back to work. After some research, Marc found Progressive Products (PP). The company was willing to be a partner in developing the Ski Right and sharing any profits. If the market was excellent, Marc would net $5000. With a good market, Marc would net $2000. An average market would result in a loss of $2000, and a poor market would mean Marc would be out $5000.

Another option for Marc was to have Lester Barnes (LB), a company with experience in making bicycle helmets, manufacture the new ski helmets. Progressive would then take the helmets made by Lester Barnes and do the rest. Marc had a greater risk. He estimated that he could lose $10 000 in a poor market or $4000 in an average market. A good market for Ski Right would result in a $6000 profit for Marc, and an excellent market would mean a $12 000 profit.

A third option for Marc was to use True Radio (TR), an Ontario-based radio manufacturing company. True Radio had extensive experience in making portable radios. Lester Barnes could make the helmets, and Progressive Products could do the rest. Again, Marc would be taking on greater risk. A poor market would mean a $15 000 loss, and an average market would mean a $10 000 loss. A good market would result in a net profit of $7000 for Marc. An excellent market would return $13 000.

Marc could also have Celestial Cellular (CC) develop the cell phones. Thus, another option was to have Celestial make the phones and have Progressive do the rest of the production and distribution. Because the cell phone was the most expensive component of the helmet, Marc could lose $30 000 in a poor market. He could lose $20 000 in an average market. If the market was good or excellent, Marc would see a net profit of $10 000 or $30 000, respectively.

Marc's final option was to forget about Progressive Products entirely. He could use Lester Barnes to make the helmets, Celestial Cellular to make the phones, and True Radio to make the AM/FM stereo radios. Marc could then hire some friends to assemble everything and market the finished Ski Right helmets. With this final alternative, Marc could realize a net profit of $55 000 in an excellent market. Even if the market was just good, Marc would net $20 000. An average market, however, would mean a loss of $35 000. If the market was poor, Marc would lose $60 000.

DISCUSSION QUESTIONS

1. What do you recommend?
2. What is the opportunity loss for this problem?
3. Compute the expected value of perfect information.
4. Was Marc completely logical in how he approached this decision problem?

⇒ CASE STUDY 9.2

Blake Electronics

In 1969, Steve Blake founded Blake Electronics in Hamilton, Ontario, to manufacture resistors, capacitors, inductors, and other electronic components. During his military career, Steve was a radio operator, and it was during this time that he became proficient at repairing radios and other communications equipment. Steve viewed his four-year experience in the armed forces, including his overseas postings on peacekeeping missions, as a valuable training period that gave him the confidence and the initiative to start his own electronics firm.

Over the years, Steve kept the business relatively unchanged. By 1980, total annual sales were in excess of $2 million. In 1984, Steve's son, Sean, joined the company after finishing high school and two years of courses in electronics at the local community college. Sean was always aggressive in high school athletics, and he became even more aggressive as general sales manager of Blake Electronics. This aggressiveness bothered Steve, who was more conservative. Sean would make deals to supply companies with electronic components before he bothered to find out if Blake Electronics had the ability or capacity to produce the components. On several occasions this behaviour caused the company some embarrassing moments when Blake Electronics was unable to produce the electronic components for companies with which Sean had made deals.

In 1988, Sean started to go after government contracts for electronic components. By 1990, total annual sales had increased to more than $10 million, and the number of employees exceeded 200. Many of these employees were electronic specialists and graduates of electrical engineering programs from top colleges and universities. But Sean's tendency to stretch Blake Electronics to contracts continued as well, and by 1997, Blake Electronics had a reputation with government agencies as a company that could not deliver what it promised. Almost overnight, government contracts stopped, and Blake Electronics was left with an idle workforce and unused manufacturing equipment. This high overhead started to melt away profits, and in 1999, Blake Electronics was faced with the possibility of sustaining a loss for the first time in its history.

In 2001, Steve decided to look at the possibility of manufacturing electronic components for home use. Although this was a totally new market for Blake Electronics, Steve was convinced that this was the only way to keep Blake Electronics from dipping into the red. The research team at Blake Electronics was given the task of developing new electronic devices for home use. The first idea from the research team was the Master Control Centre. The basic components for this system are shown in Figure 9.14.

The heart of the system is the master control box. This unit, which would have a retail price of $250, has two rows of five buttons. Each button controls one light or appliance and can be set as either a switch or a rheostat. When set as a switch, a light finger touch on the button turns a light or appliance either on or off. When set as a rheostat, a finger touching the

FIGURE 9.14   **Master Control Centre**

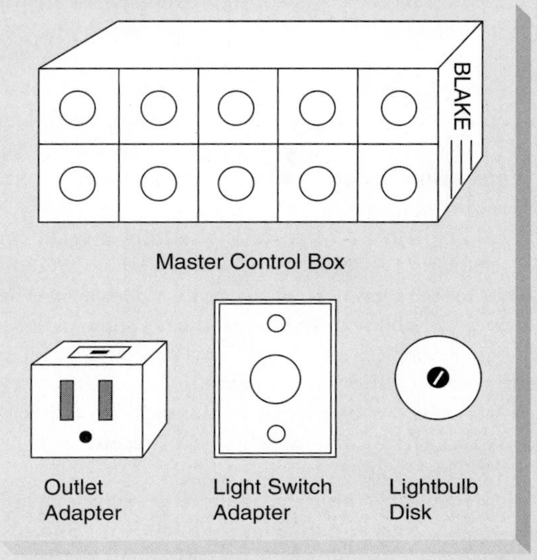

Master Control Box

Outlet Adapter   Light Switch Adapter   Lightbulb Disk

button controls the intensity of the light. Leaving your finger on the button makes the light go through a complete cycle ranging from off to bright and back to off again.

To allow for maximum flexibility, each master control box is powered by two D-sized batteries that can last up to a year, depending on usage. In addition, the research team has developed three versions of the master control box—versions A, B, and C. If a family wants to control more than 10 lights or appliances, another master control box can be purchased.

The light bulb disk, which would have a retail price of $2.50, is controlled by the master control box and is used to control the intensity of any light. A different disk is available for each button position for all three master control boxes. When the light bulb disk is inserted between the light bulb and the socket, the appropriate button on the master control box can completely control the intensity of the light. If a standard light switch is used, it must be on at all times for the master control box to work.

One disadvantage of using a standard light switch is that only the master control box can be used to control a particular light. To avoid this problem, the research team developed a special light switch adapter that would sell for $15. When this device is installed either the master control box or the light switch adapter can be used to control the light.

When used to control appliances other than lights, the master control box must be used in conjunction with one or more outlet adapters. The adapters are plugged into a standard wall outlet, and the appliance is then plugged into the adapter. Each outlet adapter has a switch on top that allows the appliance to be controlled from the master control box or the outlet adapter. The price of each outlet adapter would be $25.

The research team estimated that it would cost $500 000 to develop the equipment and procedures needed to manufacture the master control box and accessories. If successful, this venture could increase sales by approximately $2 million. But would the master control boxes be a successful venture? With the research team estimating a 60% chance of success, Steve had serious doubts about trying to market the master control boxes, even though he liked the basic idea. Because of his reservations, Steve decided to send requests for proposals (RFPs) for additional marketing research to 30 marketing research companies in southern Ontario.

The first RFP to come back was from a small company called Marketing Associates, Inc. (MAI), which would charge $100 000 for the survey. According to its proposal, MAI has been in business for about three years and has conducted about 100 marketing research projects. MAI's major strengths appeared to be individual attention to each account, experienced staff, and fast work. Steve was particularly interested in one part of the proposal, which revealed MAI's success record with previous accounts. This is shown in Table 9.13.

The only other proposal to be returned was by a branch office of I&K, a large marketing research firm. The cost for a complete survey would be $300 000. Although the proposal did not contain the same success record as MAI, the proposal from I&K did contain some interesting information. The chance of getting a positive survey result, given a successful venture, was

TABLE 9.13

Success Figures for MAI

| OUTCOME | SURVEY RESULTS | | |
	FAVOURABLE	UNFAVOURABLE	TOTAL
Successful venture	35	20	55
Unsuccessful venture	15	30	45

90%. However, the chance of getting a negative survey result, given an unsuccessful venture, was 80%. Thus, it appeared to Steve that I&K would be able to predict the success or failure of the master control boxes with a great amount of certainty.

Steve pondered the situation. Unfortunately, both marketing research teams gave different types of information in their proposals. Steve concluded that there would be no way that the two proposals could be compared unless he got additional information from I&K. Furthermore, Steve wasn't sure what he would do with the information, and if it would be worth the expense of hiring one of the marketing research firms.

DISCUSSION QUESTIONS

1. Does Steve need additional information from I&K?
2. What would you recommend?

CASE STUDY 9.3

Jupiter Corporation

Jupiter Corporation has developed a new car, the Sunburst, that will significantly decrease fuel consumption by combining alternative fuels with advanced solar energy technology. Jupiter has to make a decision regarding the construction of a production facility. Depending on anticipated demand, Jupiter will build a regular plant or build a megaplant, or it may decide to scrap the project and not build at all.

The estimated costs to build a regular plant are $22 million, plus $12 million for the promotion and advertising campaign to promote the Sunburst. Preliminary R&D costs for the Sunburst total $14 million. In this case, Jupiter has estimated that one of four events will occur as shown in the following table. Revenues are projected over a five-year planning horizon.

LEVEL OF SALES DEMAND	SALES REVENUE WITH REGULAR PLANT ($ MILLIONS)
Excellent	194
Good	144
Moderate	116
Poor	18

In the event that a megaplant is constructed, the following revenues are projected for the different levels of demand:

LEVEL OF SALES DEMAND	SALES REVENUE WITH MEGA PLANT ($ MILLIONS)
Excellent	264
Good	194
Moderate	109
Poor	4

In this case, construction costs are estimated at $48 million, and a very aggressive advertising campaign would be undertaken at a cost of $22 million. Once again, revenues would be reduced by the R&D costs. If Jupiter decides to scrap the project, it will incur a loss of the R&D costs of $14 million regardless of the level of demand.

Based on this information, Jupiter wants to construct a payoff table to help make a decision. Payoffs are to be profit after subtracting R&D, construction, and advertising costs.

In the absence of information on the probabilities of the different levels of demand, the company wants to know what decision to make under conditions of uncertainty. Therefore, the first task is to recommend decisions based on several decision criteria (maximin, maximax, minimax opportunity loss, etc.). For each decision, identify the type of decision maker who would be attracted to the decision.

Meanwhile, the following table, showing preliminary estimates of the probabilities of the four levels of demand for the Sunburst, has been obtained from the company statisticians:

DEMAND	EXCELLENT	GOOD	MODERATE	POOR
Probability	0.35	0.40	0.15	0.10

Using these probabilities, Jupiter wants to determine the optimal decision using risk-based decision criteria. In particular, management wants to know the maximum amount that they should be willing to pay for new information.

Juanita Alvarez, CFO of Jupiter, points out that it is possible to submit a proposal for funding the Sunburst to a government agency. Based on historical evidence and consultation with a statistician, Juanita estimates a 60% probability that they will get the government grant. She has also been able to ascertain, by retroactively applying data mining procedures to government grant data, that in similar ventures in the past, a government grant has been awarded in 80% of cases with excellent sales, 60% with good sales, 20% with moderate sales, and 10% with poor sales. Juanita wonders whether it is worthwhile applying for the grant. She estimates that the cost of applying, including the cost of professional consultation to complete the application documents, legal fees for filing documents, etc., will be $600 000.

To pursue this possibility, Juanita wants someone in the company to prepare a decision tree and solve it in order to recommend a strategy to Jupiter. In particular, Jupiter needs to know if it is worth paying the fee for applying for the grant. A complete analysis of the decision tree, using profit as payoff, is to be conducted.

Walter Opatu, a VP at Jupiter, is not convinced that the optimal strategy using profit as the payoff is reliable. He suggests that the analysis is not complete unless the company's utility for money is used to assess the outcomes. Walter is assigned the task of drawing a utility curve for Jupiter. He decides to establish utilities in the range –$100 million to $200 million, assigning a utility of 0 to –$100 million and a utility of 1 to $200 million. After careful analysis Walter comes up with the following table of utilities:

DOLLAR VALUE ($ MILLIONS)	UTILITY
–100	0.00
–50	0.40
0	0.58
50	0.71
100	0.82
150	0.91
200	1.00

Based on this utility function, a utility curve is drawn and Jupiter's decision problem is reanalyzed.

DISCUSSION QUESTIONS

1. Construct a payoff table and conduct a comprehensive analysis, with and without probabilities. Determine the expected value of perfect information.
2. Construct a decision tree and recommend an optimal strategy to Jupiter based on profit. Determine the expected value of sample information and interpret it in the context of this problem.
3. Comment on Jupiter's attitude to risk. Determine the optimal decision strategy based on Jupiter's utility for money.

BIBLIOGRAPHY

Ahlbrecht, M., and M. Weber. "An Empirical Study on Intertemporal Decision Making under Risk," *Management Science* (June 1997): 813–826.

Bistritz, Nancy. "Rx for UK Healthcare Woes," *OR/MS Today* (April 1997): 18.

Borison, Adam. "Oglethorpe Power Corporation Decides about Investing in a Major Transmission System," *Interfaces* 25, 2 (March 1995): 25–36.

Brown, R. "Do Managers Find Decision Theory Useful?" *Harvard Business Review* (May–June 1970): 78–89.

Brown, R. V. "The State of the Art of Decision Analysis: A Personal Perspective," *Interfaces* 22, 6 (November–December 1992): 5–14.

Derfler, Frank. "Use These Decision Trees and Our Questionnaire to Find the Best Way to Reduce Your Total Cost of Ownership," *PC Magazine* (May 5, 1998): 231.

Hammond, J. S., R. L. Kenney, and H. Raiffa. "The Hidden Traps in Decision Making," *Harvard Business Review* (September–October 1998): 47–60.

Jbuedj, Coden. "Decision Making Under Conditions of Uncertainty: A Wakeup Call for the Financial Planning Profession," *Journal of Financial Planning* (October 1997): 84.

Lane, M. S., A. H. Mansour, and J. L. Harpell. "Operations Research Techniques: A Longitudinal Update 1973–1988," *Interfaces* 23, 2 (March–April 1993): 63–68.

Lev, B. "Airline Operations Research," *Interfaces* 20, 3 (May–June 1990): 100–102.

Makris, N. A. Barkun et al. "Cost-Effectiveness of Alternative Approaches in the Management of Dyspepsia," *International Journal of Technology Assessment in Health Care* 19, 3 (2003): 446–464.

McDonald, John. "Decision Trees Clarify Novel Technology Applications," *Oil and Gas Journal* (February 24, 1997): 69–74.

Miller, Craig. "A Systematic Approach to Tax Controversy Management," *Tax Executive* (May 15, 1998): 231–233.

Perdue, Robert K., William J. McAllister, Peter V. King, and Bruce G. Berkey. "Valuation of R and D Projects Using Options Pricing and Decision Analysis Models," *Interfaces* 29, 6 (November 1999): 57–74.

Raiffa, H. *Decision Analysis.* Reading, MA: Addison-Wesley Publishing Co., Inc., 1968.

Schlaifer, R. *Analysis of Decisions under Uncertainty.* New York: McGraw-Hill Book Company, 1969.

Stafira, S., G. Parnell, and J. Moore. "A Methodology for Evaluating Military Systems in a Counterproliferation Role," *Management Science* (October 1997): 1420–1430.

Stone, Lawrence D. "Search for the SS *Central America*: Mathematical Treasure Hunting," *Interfaces* 21, 1 (January–February 1992): 32–54.

Strait, Scott. "Decision Analysis Approach to Competitive Situations with a Pure Infinite Regress," *Decision Sciences* (September 1994): 853–864.

Sullivan, Gerald, and Kenneth Fordyce. "IBM Burlington's Logistics Management System," *Interfaces* 20, 1 (January–February 1990): 43–64.

CHAPTER 10

Queuing Models

LEARNING OBJECTIVES

After completing this chapter, students will be able to

1. Discuss the trade-off curves for cost of waiting time and cost of service.
2. Understand the three parts of a queuing system: the arrival population, the queue itself, and the service facility.
3. Describe the basic queuing system configurations.
4. Understand the assumptions of the common queuing models dealt with in this chapter.
5. Use Excel to analyze a variety of operating characteristics of queuing systems.
6. Understand more complex queuing systems.

CHAPTER OUTLINE

10.1 Introduction
10.2 Queuing System Costs
10.3 Characteristics of a Queuing System
10.4 Single-Server Queuing System with Poisson Arrivals and Exponential Service Times (M/M/1 Model)
10.5 Multiple-Server Queuing System with Poisson Arrivals and Exponential Service Times (M/M/s Model)
10.6 Single-Server Queuing System with Poisson Arrivals and Constant Service Times (M/D/1 Model)
10.7 Single-Server Queuing System with Poisson Arrivals and General Service Times (M/G/1 Model)
10.8 Multiple-Server Queuing System with Poisson Arrivals, Exponential Service Times, and Finite Population Size (M/M/s/∞/N Model)
10.9 More Complex Queuing Systems

Summary • Glossary • Key Equations • Solved Problems • Self-Test • Discussion Questions and Problems • Case Study: Winnipeg Ambulance Problem • Case Study: Winter Park Hotel • Bibliography

Queuing Theory Improves Waiting Times at The Bay

For the 1999 Christmas season, The Bay implemented a new "Express" format for giving Christmas shoppers fast access to cashiers. The central idea behind the plan was to revamp each floor in the style of a racetrack, with cashiers located in an island in the middle of the floor. By reducing the time required to stand in line waiting for a cashier, it was hoped that customer frustration resulting from long lineups would be alleviated.

Stopwatches and surveillance cameras were employed to monitor lineups of shoppers at the checkout counters. Instead of the traditional approach of forming a separate queue for each cashier, each floor had only two lineups, one for each pool of five to six cashiers. The weekend before Christmas—the busiest two-day period of the year—was selected to test the system.

The system was tested at two Bay stores—one in Toronto's Centerpoint Mall, where customers waited an average of two minutes to reach a cashier. The longest time clocked during the two days was four minutes. The other store at the Erin Mills Town Centre in Mississauga had a slightly longer time, with an average of 2.5 minutes and a maximum of 5.8 minutes.

Source: James Leynse/Corbis/Magma Photo

A shopper at the Centerpoint store noted that it was much faster than before and that it seemed like The Bay finally realized that its customers were too busy for long waiting times while shopping.

Using pooled cashiers to serve a common lineup is, by definition, quicker and more fair. It eliminates the risk of getting stuck behind the customer from hell trying to exchange something without a receipt or paying with a cheque but not having enough identification.

The experiment applies a queuing theory model to the problem of customer congestion.

Based on the success of the new format, The Bay was considering converting 15 to 20 stores to the Express format over the following year.

10.1 INTRODUCTION

The study of **queues**,[1] also called **waiting lines**, is one of the oldest and most widely used decision modeling techniques. Queues are an everyday occurrence, affecting people shopping for groceries, buying gasoline, making a bank deposit, or waiting on the telephone for the first available airline reservation person to answer. Queues can also take the form of machines waiting to be repaired, prisoners to be processed in the Kingston penitentiary, or airplanes lined up on a runway for permission to take off.

A primary goal of queuing analysis is finding the best level of service for an organization.

Most queuing problems are centred on the question of finding the ideal level of services that a firm should provide. Supermarkets must decide how many cash register checkout positions should be opened. Gasoline stations must decide how many pumps should be available. Manufacturing plants must determine the optimal number of mechanics to have on duty each shift to repair machines that break down. Banks must decide how many teller windows to keep open to serve customers during various hours of the day. In most cases, this level of service is an option over which management has control. An extra teller, for example, can be borrowed from another chore or can be hired and trained quickly if demand warrants it. This may not always be the case, though. A plant may not be able to locate or hire skilled mechanics to repair sophisticated electronic machinery.

In this chapter, we discuss how analytical models of queues can help managers evaluate the cost effectiveness of service systems. We begin with a look at queuing system costs. Then, we describe the characteristics of queues and the underlying mathematical assumptions used to develop queuing decision models. Next, we discuss several different queuing systems and provide examples of how they are analyzed and used. Although we show the equations needed to compute the operating performance characteristics of these queuing systems, we use Excel worksheets (included on your CD-ROM) to actually calculate these values in each case. Finally, we briefly discuss more complex queuing models and how these can be analyzed in practical situations.

More sophisticated models exist to handle variations of basic assumptions, but when even these do not apply, we can turn to computer simulation, which is the topic of Chapter 11.

Many real-world queuing systems can, however, be so complex that they cannot be modeled analytically at all. When this happens, decision modelers usually turn to the second approach—computer simulation—to analyze the performance of these systems. We discuss simulation in Chapter 11 and also illustrate how this technique can be used to analyze queuing systems.

10.2 QUEUING SYSTEM COSTS

As noted earlier, a primary goal of queuing analysis is to find the best level of service that a firm should provide. In deciding this ideal level of service, managers have to deal with two types of costs:

1. *Cost of providing the service.* This is also known as the *service cost*. Examples of this type of cost include wages paid to servers, the cost of buying an extra machine, and the cost of constructing a new teller window at a bank. As a firm increases the size

HISTORY   How Queuing Models Began

Queuing theory had its beginning in the research work of a Danish engineer named A. K. Erlang. In 1909 Erlang experimented with fluctuating demand in telephone traffic. Eight years later he published a report addressing the delays in automatic dialling equipment. At the end of World War II, Erlang's early work was extended to more general problems and to business applications of waiting lines.

---

[1] The word *queue* is pronounced like the letter Q, that is, "kew."

of its staff and provides added service facilities, the result could be excellent customer service with seldom more than one or two customers in a queue. While customers may be happy with the quick response, the cost of providing this service can, however, become very expensive.

2. *Cost of* not *providing the service.* This is also known as the *waiting cost* and is typically the cost of customer dissatisfaction. If a facility has just a minimum number of checkout lines, pumps, or teller windows open, the service cost is kept low, but customers may end up with long waiting times in the queue. How many times would you return to a large department store that had only one cash register open every time you shopped? As the average length of the queue increases and poor service results, customers and goodwill may be lost.

Most managers recognize the trade-off that must take place between the cost of providing good service and the cost of customer waiting time. They want queues that are short enough so that customers don't become unhappy and either storm out without buying or buy but never return. But they are willing to allow some waiting in line if this wait is balanced by a significant savings in service costs.

One means of evaluating a service facility is thus to look at a total expected cost, a concept illustrated in Figure 10.1. Total expected cost is the sum of expected waiting costs and expected costs of providing service.

Service costs are seen to increase as a firm attempts to raise its level of service. For example, if three teams of stevedores, instead of two, are employed to unload a cargo ship, service costs are increased by the additional price of wages. As service improves in speed, however, the cost of time spent waiting in lines decreases. This waiting cost may reflect lost productivity of workers while their tools or machines are awaiting repairs or may simply be an estimate of the costs of customers lost because of poor service and long queues.

Nova Scotia Shipping Company Example   As an illustration of a queuing system, let's look at the case of the Nova Scotia Shipping Company. Nova Scotia Shipping runs a huge docking facility located near the Port of Halifax. Approximately five ships arrive to unload their cargoes during every 12-hour work shift. Each hour that a ship sits idle in line waiting to be unloaded costs the firm a great deal of money, about $1000 per hour. From experience, management estimates that if one team of stevedores is on duty to handle the unloading work, each ship will wait an average of seven hours to be unloaded. If two teams are working, the average waiting time drops to four hours; for three teams, it is three hours;

Managers must deal with the trade-off between the cost of providing good service and the cost of customer waiting time. The latter may be hard to quantify.

Total expected cost is the sum of service plus waiting costs.

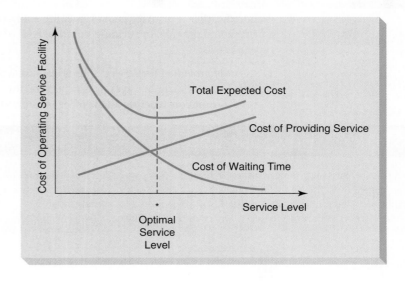

FIGURE 10.1

Queuing Costs and Service Levels

MODELING IN THE REAL WORLD

Hospital Overcrowding in Canada

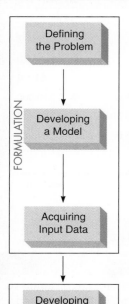

Defining
the Problem

FORMULATION

Developing
a Model

Acquiring
Input Data

Developing
a Solution

SOLUTION

Testing the
Solution

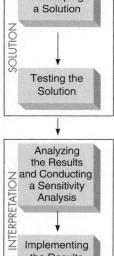

INTERPRETATION

Analyzing
the Results
and Conducting
a Sensitivity
Analysis

Implementing
the Results

The Report on Emergency Department Utilization and Overcrowding in the Hospitals of Greater Vancouver, published by the B.C. Ministry of Health in 1992, showed that a congestion problem affected all the hospitals in the Lower Mainland. Similar findings have been documented in other provinces.

A computerized queuing model of hospital bed use successfully predicted the number of beds needed at one of the affected B.C. hospitals, the Royal Columbian. The model determined a mathematical relationship between the number of available beds and the number of patients in the emergency room, and demonstrated that significant congestion began to occur whenever hospital occupancy exceeded 92% capacity.

Data were gathered from an inter-hospital computer system. The data indicated that "one of the major causes of emergency department overcrowding was the unavailability of medical beds" and that "current policies that result in closure of hospital beds appear to be ill advised . . . having the effect of shifting the patient burden from in-patient wards to the emergency department."

A committee made up of senior representatives of the ambulance service and the heads of the major hospital emergency departments in the Lower Mainland issued its final report in June 1998. The report unanimously endorsed the computerized queuing model and made a number of recommendations, including an urgent need to increase long-term care beds, psychiatric beds, and intensive care beds.

The queuing model allows for the analysis of the number of patients waiting for hospital beds, as well as the expected waiting times in the emergency room and the waiting period for transfer to beds for patients admitted to the hospital.

The Romanow Commission on the Future of Health Care in Canada released a report in November 2002 recommending sweeping changes to Canada's medicare system, including the development of a national homecare strategy. The implementation of such a strategy would affect the parameters of the queuing model.

Canada's medicare system continues to change in response to external stimuli, so that implementation is monitored continuously as the system itself evolves.

Sources: L. Vertesi, 'Emergency Overload's Legacy of Neglect," *The Vancouver Sun* (December 16, 1999), p. A19; "Romanow Report Proposes Sweeping Changes to Medicare," (November 2 8, 2002) Health Canada, http://www.hc-sc.gc.ca/english/care/romanow/hcc0403.html

and for four teams of stevedores, only two hours. But each additional team of stevedores is also an expensive proposition, due to union contracts.

The goal is to find the service level that minimizes total expected cost.

Nova Scotia's superintendent would like to determine the optimal number of teams of stevedores to have on duty each shift. The objective is to minimize total expected costs. This analysis is summarized in Table 10.1 on page 436. To minimize the sum of service costs and waiting costs, the firm makes the decision to employ two teams of stevedores each shift.

TABLE 10.1   **Nova Scotia Shipping Company Waiting Line Cost Analysis**

	NUMBER OF TEAMS OF STEVEDORES WORKING			
	1	**2**	**3**	**4**
(a) Average number of ships arriving per shift	5	5	5	5
(b) Average time each ship waits to be unloaded (hours)	7	4	3	2
(c) Total ship hours lost per shift $(a \times b)$	35	20	15	10
(d) Estimated cost per hour of idle ship time	$1000	$1000	$1000	$1000
(e) Value of ship's lost time or waiting cost $(c \times d)$	$35 000	$20 000	$15 000	$10 000
(f) Stevedore team salary,* or service cost	$6 000	$12 000	$18 000	$24 000
(g) Total expected cost $(e + f)$	$41 000	($32 000)	$33 000	$34 000

→ Optimal cost

*Stevedore team salaries are computed as the number of people in a typical team (assumed to be 50), times the number of hours each person works per day (12 hours), times an hourly salary of $10 per hour. If two teams are employed, the rate is just doubled.

10.3   CHARACTERISTICS OF A QUEUING SYSTEM

In this section we look at the three parts of a queuing system: (1) the arrivals or inputs to the system (referred to as the **arrival population** or **calling population**), (2) the queue or the waiting line itself, and (3) the service facility. These three components have certain characteristics that we must examine before we can develop mathematical **queuing models**.

Arrival Characteristics

The input source that generates arrivals or customers for the service system has major characteristics. It is important to consider (1) the *size* of the arrival population, (2) the *pattern* of arrivals (or the *arrival distribution*) at the queuing system, and (3) the *behaviour* of the arrivals.

Unlimited (or infinite) populations are assumed for most queuing models.

Size of the Arrival Population   Population sizes are considered to be either **infinite (unlimited)** or **finite (limited)**. When the number of customers or arrivals on hand at any given moment is just a small portion of potential arrivals, the arrival population is considered unlimited. For practical purposes, examples of unlimited populations include cars arriving at a highway tollbooth, shoppers arriving at a supermarket, or students arriving to register for classes at a large university. Most queuing models assume such an infinite arrival population. When this is not the case, modeling becomes much more complex. An example of a finite population is a shop with only eight machines that might break down and require service.

Analytical queuing models typically use the average arrival rate.

Arrival Distribution   Arrivals can be characterized either by an average *arrival rate* or by an average *arrival time*. Because both measures occur commonly in practice, it is important to distinguish between the two. An average arrival rate denotes the average number of arrivals in a given interval of time. Examples include two customers per hour, four trucks per minute, two potholes per kilometre of road, and five typing errors per printed page. In contrast, an average arrival time denotes the average time between successive arrivals. Examples include 30 minutes between customers, 0.25 minutes between trucks, 0.5 kilometres between potholes, and 0.2 pages between typing errors. It is important to remember that for analytical queuing models, we typically use the average arrival *rate*.

Arrivals are random when they are independent of one another and cannot be predicted exactly.

Customers can arrive at a service facility either according to some known constant schedule (e.g., one patient every 15 minutes or one student for advising every half hour), or they can arrive in a random manner. Arrivals are considered random when they are independent of one another and their occurrence cannot be predicted exactly.

It turns out that in many real-world queuing problems, even when arrivals are random, the actual number of arrivals per unit of time can be estimated by using a probability distribution known as the **Poisson distribution**. The Poisson distribution is applicable whenever the following assumptions are satisfied: (1) The average arrival rate over a given interval of time is known, (2) this average rate is the same for all equal-sized intervals, (3) the actual number of arrivals in one interval has no bearing on the actual number of arrivals in another interval, and (4) there cannot be more than one arrival in an interval as the size of the interval approaches zero. For a given average arrival rate, a discrete Poisson distribution can be established by using the following formula[2]:

The Poisson distribution is used in many queuing models to represent arrival patterns.

$$P(X) = \frac{e^{-\lambda}\lambda^X}{X!} \quad \text{for } X = 0, 1, 2, \ldots \tag{10-1}$$

where

X = number of arrivals per unit of time (e.g., hour)

$P(X)$ = probability of exactly X arrivals

λ = average arrival *rate* (i.e., average number of arrivals per unit of time)

e = 2.7183 (known as the exponential constant)

These values are easy to compute with the help of a calculator or Excel. Figure 10.2 illustrates the shape of the Poisson distribution for $\lambda = 2$ and $\lambda = 4$. This means that if the average arrival rate is $\lambda = 2$ customers per hour, the probability of 0 customers arriving in any random hour is 0.1353, the probability of 1 customer is 0.2707, 2 customers is 0.2707, 3 customers is 0.1804, 4 customers is 0.0902, and so on. The chance that 9 or more will arrive in any hour is virtually zero.

FIGURE 10.2   **Two Examples of the Poisson Distribution for Arrival Times**

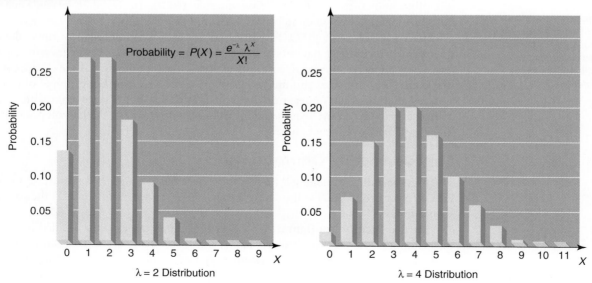

$\lambda = 2$ Distribution

$\lambda = 4$ Distribution

---

[2] The term X!, called X factorial, is defined as $(X)(X - 1)(X - 2) \ldots (3)(2)(1)$. For example, $5! = (5)(4)(3)(2)(1) = 120$. By definition, $0! = 1$.

All the analytical models discussed in this chapter assume Poisson arrivals. However, in practice, arrivals in queuing systems need not always be Poisson and could follow other probability distributions. The use of statistical goodness of fit tests to identify these distributions and analytical queuing models to analyze such systems are topics discussed in more advanced texts. Of course, as we will discuss in Chapter 11, we can also analyze such queuing systems by using computer simulation.

Behaviour of the Arrivals   Most queuing models assume that an arriving customer is a patient customer. Patient customers are people or machines that wait in the queue until they are served and do not switch between lines. Unfortunately, life and decision models are complicated by the fact that people have been known to balk or renege. **Balking** refers to customers who refuse to join a queue because it is too long to suit their needs or interests. **Reneging** customers are those who enter the queue but then become impatient and leave without completing their transaction. Actually, both of these situations just serve to accentuate the need for queuing models. How many times have you seen a shopper with a basket full of groceries, including perishables such as milk, frozen food, or meats, simply abandon the shopping cart before checking out because the queue was too long? This expensive occurrence for the store makes managers acutely aware of the importance of service-level decisions.

> Balking refers to customers who do not join a queue. Reneging customers join a queue, but leave before being served.

Queue Characteristics

The queue itself is the second component of a queuing system. A queue may be considered limited or unlimited. A **limited queue length** (or **finite queue length**) occurs when the queue cannot increase beyond a certain length due to physical or other restrictions. For example, the queue at a bank's drive-up window may be limited by space available to 10 cars. Or the number of people waiting for service in an airline's phone reservation system may be limited to 30 because there are only 30 telephone lines available. In contrast, an **unlimited queue length** or **infinite queue length** occurs when there is no such restriction, as in the case of the tollbooth serving arriving automobiles. In all the analytic queuing models we discuss in this chapter we assume that queue lengths are *unlimited*.

> The models in this chapter assume unlimited queue length.

A second waiting line characteristic deals with **queue discipline**. This refers to the rule by which customers in the line are to receive service. Most systems use a queue discipline known as the *first-in, first-out* rule **(FIFO)**. However, in places such as a hospital emergency room or an express checkout line at a supermarket, various assigned priorities may preempt FIFO. Patients who are critically injured will move ahead in treatment priority over patients with broken fingers or noses. Shoppers with eight or fewer items may be allowed to enter the express checkout queue but are then treated as first come, first served. Computer programming runs are another example of queuing systems that operate under priority scheduling. In many large companies, when computer-produced paycheques are due out on a specific date, the payroll program has highest priority over other runs.[3]

> Most queuing models use the first-in, first-out rule. This is obviously not appropriate in all service systems, especially those dealing with emergencies.

Service Facility Characteristics

The third part of any queuing system is the service facility itself. It is important to examine two basic properties: (1) the configuration of the service facility and (2) the pattern of service times.

Service Facility Configurations   Service facilities are usually classified in terms of their number of servers (or channels), and number of phases (or service stops) that must be made. A **single-server queuing system** is typified by the drive-in bank that has only one

---

[3] The term FIFS (*first in, first served*) is often used in place of FIFO. Another discipline, LIFS (*last in, first served*), is common when material is stacked or piled and the items on top are used first.

open teller, or by a drive-through fast-food restaurant. If, however, the bank had several tellers on duty and each customer waited in one common line for the first available teller, we would have a **multiple-server queuing system** at work. Many banks today are multiple-server service systems, as are most post offices and many airline ticket counters.

A **single-phase system** is one in which the customer receives service from only one station and then exits the system. A fast-food restaurant in which the person who takes your order also brings you the food and takes your money is a single-phase system. So is a driver's licence licensing agency in which the person taking your application also grades your test and collects the licence fee. But if a fast-food restaurant requires you to place your order at one station, pay at a second, and pick up the food at a third service stop, it becomes a **multiphase system**. Similarly, if the driver's licence agency is large or busy, you will probably have to wait in line to complete the application (the first service stop), then queue again to have the test graded (the second service stop), and finally go to a third service counter to pay the fee. To help you relate the concepts of channels and phases, Figure 10.3 on page 440 presents four possible service facility configurations.

Service Time Distribution

Service patterns are like arrival patterns in that they can be either constant or random. If the service time is constant, it takes the same amount of time to take care of each customer. This is the case, for example, in a machine-performed service operation such as an automatic car wash. More often, however, service times are randomly distributed. Even in many such cases, it turns out we can assume that random service times are described by the **exponential probability distribution**.

The Poisson and exponential probability distributions are directly related to each other. If the number of arrivals follows a Poisson distribution, it turns out that the time between successive arrivals follows an exponential distribution. Processes that follow these distributions are commonly referred to as *Markovian* processes.

Just as we did with arrivals, we need to distinguish here between service rate and service time. While the service rate denotes the number of units served in a given interval of time, the service time denotes the length of time taken to actually perform the service. Although the exponential distribution estimates the probability of service times, the parameter used in this computation is the average service rate. For any given service rate, such as two customers per hour, or four trucks per minute, an exponential distribution can be established using the formula:

$$P(t) = e^{-\mu t} \quad \text{for } t \geq 0 \tag{10-2}$$

where

t = service time

$P(t)$ = probability that service times will be greater than t

μ = average service rate (i.e., average number of customers served per unit of time)

$e \approx 2.7183$ (exponential constant)

Figure 10.4 on page 441 illustrates that if service times follow an exponential distribution, the probability of any very long service time is low. For example, when the average service *rate* is 3 customers per hour (i.e., the average service *time* is 20 minutes per customer), seldom if ever will a customer require more than 1.5 hours (= 90 minutes). Likewise, if the average service rate is one customer per hour (i.e., $\mu = 1$), the probability of the customer spending more than 3 hours (= 180 minutes) in service is quite low.

The number of service channels in a queuing system is the number of servers.

Single-phase means the customer receives service at only one station before leaving the system.

Multiphase implies two or more stops before leaving the system.

Service times often follow the exponential distribution.

FIGURE 10.3   **Four Basic Queuing System Configurations**

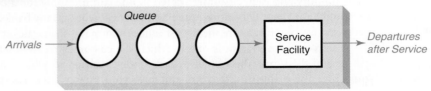

Single-Server, Single-Phase System

Single-Server, Multiphase System

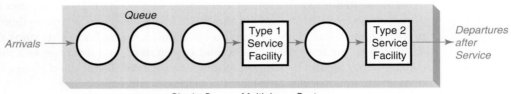

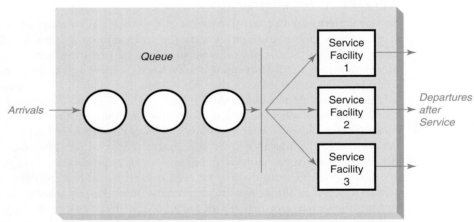

Multiple-Server, Single-Phase System

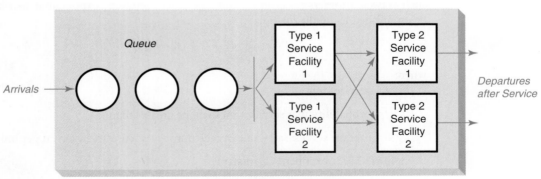

Multiple-Server, Multiphase System

It is important to confirm that the queuing assumptions of Poisson arrivals and exponential services are valid before applying the model.

The exponential distribution is important to the process of building mathematical queuing models, because many of the models' theoretical underpinnings are based on the assumption of Poisson arrivals and exponential services. Before they are applied, however, the decision modeler can and should observe, collect, and plot service time data to determine if they fit the exponential distribution.

FIGURE 10.4   **Two Examples of the Exponential Distribution for Service Times**

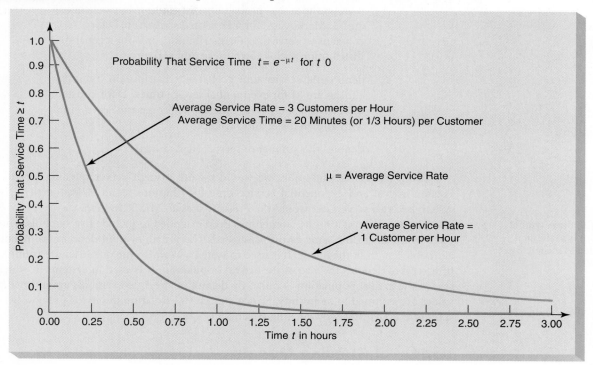

Measuring the Queue's Performance

Queuing models can help a manager obtain many performance measures (also known as operating characteristics) of a waiting line system. We list here some of the measures commonly used in practice. For each performance measure, we also list the standard notation that is used.

Here is a listing of the key operating characteristics of a queuing system.

- ρ = **Utilization factor** of the system (i.e., probability that all servers are busy)
- L_q = Average length (i.e., number of customers) of the queue
- L = Average number of customers in the system (i.e., the number in the queue plus the number being served)
- W_q = Average time that each customer spends in the queue
- W = Average time that each customer spends in the system (i.e., time spent waiting plus time spent being served)
- P_0 = Probability that there are no customers in the system (i.e., the probability that the service facility will be idle)
- P_n = Probability that there are exactly n customers in the system

Kendall's Notation for Queuing Systems

Kendall's notation is used to classify queuing systems.

In queuing theory we commonly use a three-symbol notation, known as Kendall's notation, to classify the wide variety of queuing models that are possible in practice. The three-symbol notation is as follows:

$$A/B/s$$

where

A   denotes the arrival probability distribution. Typical choices are M (Markovian) for a Poisson distribution, D for a constant or deterministic distribution, or G for a general distribution with known mean and variance.

B   denotes the service time probability distribution. Typical choices are M for exponential service times, D for constant or deterministic service times, or G for general service times with known mean and variance.

s   denotes the number of servers (or channels)

Using the Kendall notation, we would denote a single-server queuing system with Poisson arrival and exponential service time distributions as an **M/M/1** system. If this system had two servers, we would then classify it as an M/M/2 system.

Kendall's three-symbol notation is sometimes extended to include five symbols.

The Kendall notation has sometimes been extended to include five symbols. The first three symbols are the same as just discussed. The fourth symbol denotes the maximum allowable length of the queue. It is used in systems in which the queue length is finite. The fifth symbol denotes the size of the arrival population. It is used in systems in which the size of the arrival population is finite. By default, if these two symbols are omitted, their values are assumed to be infinity. Hence, the M/M/1 notation discussed previously corresponds to an M/M/1/∞/∞ queuing system.

Variety of Queuing Models

We study five commonly used queuing models.

Although a wide variety of queuing models can be applied in practice, we introduce you in this chapter to five of the most widely used models. These are outlined in Table 10.2 and examples of each follow in the next few sections. More complex models are described in

TABLE 10.2   Queuing Models Described in This Chapter

NAME (KENDALL'S NOTATION IN PARENTHESES)	EXAMPLE	NUMBER OF SERVERS	NUMBER OF PHASES	ARRIVAL RATE PATTERN	SERVICE TIME PATTERN	POPULATION SIZE	QUEUE DISCIPLINE
Simple system (M/M/1)	Information counter at department store	Single	Single	Poisson	Exponential	Unlimited	FIFO
Multiple-server (M/M/s)	Airline ticket counter	Multiple	Single	Poisson	Exponential	Unlimited	FIFO
Constant service (M/D/1)	Automated car wash	Single	Single	Poisson	Constant	Unlimited	FIFO
General service (M/G/1)	Auto repair shop	Single	Single	Poisson	General	Unlimited	FIFO
Limited population (M/M/s/∞/N)	Shop with only a dozen machines that might break	Multiple	Single	Poisson	Exponential	Limited	FIFO

queuing theory textbooks[4] or can be developed through the use of computer simulation (which is the focus of Chapter 11). Note that all five queuing models listed in Table 10.2 have five characteristics in common. They all assume the following:

1. Arrivals that follow the Poisson probability distribution.
2. FIFO queue discipline.
3. A single-phase service facility.
4. Infinite queue length. That is, the fourth symbol in Kendall's notation is ∞.
5. Service systems that operate under steady, ongoing conditions. This means that both arrival rates and service rates remain stable during the analysis.

10.4 SINGLE-SERVER QUEUING SYSTEM WITH POISSON ARRIVALS AND EXPONENTIAL SERVICE TIMES (M/M/1 MODEL)

In this section we present a decision model to determine the operating characteristics of an M/M/1 queuing system. After these numeric measures have been computed, we then add in cost data and begin to make decisions that balance desirable service levels with waiting line costs.

Assumptions of the M/M/1 Queuing Model

The single-server, single-phase model we consider here is one of the most widely used and simplest queuing models. It assumes that seven conditions exist:

These seven assumptions must be met if the single-server, single-phase model is to be applied.

1. Arrivals are served on a FIFO basis.
2. Every arrival waits to be served regardless of the length of the line; that is, there is no balking or reneging.
3. Arrivals are independent of preceding arrivals, but the average number of arrivals (the arrival rate) does not change over time.
4. Arrivals are described by a Poisson probability distribution and come from an infinite or very large population.
5. Service times also vary from one customer to the next and are independent of one another, but their average rate is known.
6. Service times occur according to the exponential probability distribution.
7. The average service rate is greater than the average arrival rate; that is, $\mu > \lambda$. If this condition does not hold (and $\mu \leq \lambda$), the queue length will grow indefinitely since the service facility does not have the capacity to handle the arriving customers (on average).

When these seven conditions are met, we can develop equations that define the system's operating characteristics. The mathematics used to derive each equation is rather complex and outside the scope of this textbook, so we will just present the resulting equations here.

We use Excel templates to calculate operating characteristics for our queuing models.

Although we could calculate the operating characteristic equations for *all* the queuing systems discussed in this chapter by hand, it can be quite cumbersome to do so. An easier approach is to develop Excel worksheets for these formulas and use them for all calculations. This allows us to focus on what is really important for managers, the interpretation and use of the results of queuing models. Therefore, we adopt this approach in our discussions in this chapter.

---

[4] See, for example, B. D. Bunday. *An Introduction to Queuing Theory.* New York: Halsted Press, 1996; or C. H. Ng. *Queuing Modeling Fundamentals.* New York: Wiley, 1996.

DECISION MODELING IN ACTION
Inefficient Queuing Systems Cause Dissatisfaction in Canada

The need for decision models to improve queuing systems in Canada is highlighted by a recent poll that indicates a high level of discontent among Canadians with the amount of time spent waiting in queues. Not only is there significant consumer dissatisfaction, but there is also a serious impact on business as a result of potential customers leaving and taking their business elsewhere.

On April 26, 2007, Canada NewsWire published the results of an Ipsos Reid/NCR poll on Canadian attitudes to time spent waiting in queues. More than 60% of those surveyed reported that they wasted between 30 minutes and 4 hours in queues in a typical week. Eighty-four percent of respondents agree, "Canadians are becoming less patient about lining up." Comparison with a similar question posed to consumers in Europe and Australia showed that Canadians' dissatisfaction about queuing is the highest, followed by respondents in France (82%), Australia (81%), Spain (80%), Italy (77%), Germany (76%), and the United Kingdom (66%).

Dissatisfaction in the queue may have a harmful impact on business: three-quarters of Canadians surveyed said that they have left a line because of the wait time, and 45% said they vowed never to return. When asked what would remedy the queuing problem, 92% replied, "employing more staff," while 82% suggested, "offering self-service technology." Specific suggestions include the use of ATMs (automated teller machines) and the internet. In Ontario and Alberta, retail self-checkout proved to be a popular response.

Worst offenders in the "bad queue" lineup are airport check-in, waiting at the bank, and registering a car or renewing a driver's licence. From a human-interest perspective, there may be some unexpected, positive social benefits. Thirteen percent of Canadians in the survey said that they had "gotten a date" while waiting in line and, in particular, 39% of Quebecers made the same claim.

Source: Canada NewsWire. "When It Comes to Lining Up, Canadian Consumers Can't Take It Anymore," April 26, 2007; http://www.newswire.ca/en/releases/archive/April2007/26/c9795.html

Operating Characteristic Equations for an M/M/1 Queuing System

We let

λ and μ must be defined for the same time period.

λ = average number of arrivals per time period (e.g., per hour)

μ = average number of people or items served per time period

It is very important that we define both λ and μ for the same time period. That is, if λ denotes the number of units arriving per hour, then μ must denote the number of units served per hour. As noted earlier, it is necessary for the average service rate to be greater than the average arrival rate (i.e., $\mu > \lambda$). The operating characteristic equations for the M/M/1 queuing system are as follows:

These seven queuing equations for the single-server, single-phase model describe the important operating characteristics of the service system.

1. Average server utilization in the system:
$$\rho = \lambda/\mu \tag{10-3}$$

2. Average number of customers or units waiting in line for service:
$$L_q = \frac{\lambda^2}{\mu(\mu - \lambda)} \tag{10-4}$$

3. Average number of customers or units in the system:
$$L = L_q + \lambda/\mu \tag{10-5}$$

4. Average time a customer or unit spends waiting in line for service:
$$W_q = L_q/\lambda = \frac{\lambda}{\mu(\mu - \lambda)} \tag{10-6}$$

5. Average time a customer or unit spends in the system (namely, in the queue or being served):

$$W = W_q + 1/\mu \tag{10-7}$$

6. Probability that there are zero customers or units in the system:

$$P_0 = 1 - \lambda/\mu \tag{10-8}$$

7. Probability that there are n customers or units in the system:

$$P_n = (\lambda/\mu)^n P_0 \tag{10-9}$$

Arnold's Muffler Shop Example

We now apply these formulas to the queuing problem faced by Arnold's Muffler Shop in Peterborough. Arnold's mechanic, Reid Blank, is able to install new mufflers at an average rate of 3 per hour, or about 1 every 20 minutes. Customers needing this service arrive at the shop on the average of 2 per hour. Larry Arnold, the shop owner, studied queuing models in an MBA program and feels that all seven of the conditions for a single-server queuing model are met. He proceeds to calculate the numerical values of the operating characteristics of his queuing system.

Using ExcelModules for Queuing Model Computations

When we run the ExcelModules program, we see a menu option titled **EXCELMODULES** in the main menu bar of Excel. We click on **EXCELMODULES**, and then click on **QUEUING MODELS**. The choices shown in Screenshot 10.1A are displayed. From these choices, we select the appropriate queuing model.

Excel Note

■ The CD-ROM that accompanies this textbook contains a set of Excel worksheets, bundled together in a software package called ExcelModules. The procedure for installing and running this program, as well as a brief description of its contents, is given in Appendix A.

■ The CD-ROM also contains the Excel file for each example problem discussed here. The relevant file name is shown in the margin next to each example.

■ For clarity, all worksheets for queuing models in ExcelModules are colour-coded as follows:

   ■ *input cells*, where we enter the problem data, are shaded yellow.
   ■ *output cells*, where the results are shown, are shaded green.

■ Although these colours are not apparent in the screen captures shown in the textbook, they are seen in the Excel files in your CD-ROM.

When *any* of the queuing models is selected in ExcelModules, we are first presented with an option to specify a title for the problem (see Screenshot 10.1B on the next page). The default title is Problem Title.

ExcelModules Solution for Arnold Muffler Shop's Case   The M/M/1 queuing model has been included in ExcelModules as a special case of the **M/M/s** model with $s = 1$. Hence, to analyze Arnold's problem using ExcelModules, we first select the choice labelled **EXPONENTIAL SERVICE TIMES** (M/M/s) as shown in Screenshot 10.1A. When we click **OK**

SCREENSHOT 10.1A　　**Queuing Models Submenu in ExcelModules**

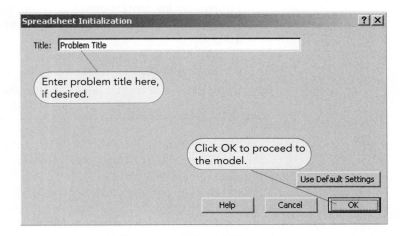

ExcelModules is seen in Excel's main menu bar when the program is running.

Queuing Models submenu in ExcelModules

ExcelModules options; see Appendix A for details.

Main menu in ExcelModules

To analyze M/M/1 systems, we use the M/M/s worksheet in ExcelModules and set s = 1.

File: 10-2.xls

Important: The total service rate must exceed the arrival rate.

after entering the problem title, we get the screen shown in Screenshot 10.2A on the next page. Each queuing worksheet in ExcelModules includes one or more messages specific to that model. It is important to note and follow the messages. For example, the M/M/s worksheet includes the following two messages:

1. Both λ and μ must be RATES and use the same time unit. For example, given a service time such as 10 minutes per customer, convert it to a service rate such as 6 per hour.

2. The total service rate (rate $\times$ servers) must be greater than the arrival rate.

If the total service rate ($\mu \times s$) does *not* exceed the arrival rate (λ), the worksheet will automatically print an error message in row 16. This message is seen in Screenshot 10.2A, since the values of λ, μ, and number of servers (s) have not been input yet and have defaulted to zero values.

In Larry Arnold's case, the arrival rate (λ) is 2 cars per hour. The service rate (μ) is 3 mufflers per hour. We therefore enter these values in cells B9 and B10, respectively, as shown in Screenshot 10.2B on page 448. The number of servers (cell B11) equals 1 here since there is only one mechanic.

SCREENSHOT 10.1B

Input Window for Optional Problem Title

Spreadsheet Initialization

Title: Problem Title

Enter problem title here, if desired.

Click OK to proceed to the model.

Use Default Settings

Help　　Cancel　　OK

SCREENSHOT 10.2A   **M/M/s Worksheet in ExcelModules**

Default title

Queuing model being used

Important messages to be followed

	A	B	C	D	E	F
1	**Problem Title**					
2	**Queuing Model**	**M/M/s (Exponential Service Times)**				
3						
4	1. Both λ and μ must be RATES, and use the same time unit. For example, given a service time such as 10 minutes					
5	per customer, convert it to a service rate such as 6 per hour.					
6	2. The total service rate (rate x servers) must be greater than the arrival rate.					
7						
8	Input Data			Operating Characteristics		
9	Arrival rate (λ)			Average server utilization (ρ)	#VALUE!	
10	Service rate (μ)			Average number of customers in the queue (L_q)	#N/A	
11	Number of servers (s)			Average number of customers in the system (L)	#N/A	
12				Average waiting time in the queue (W_q)	#N/A	
13				Average time in the system (W)	#N/A	
14				Probability (% of time) system is empty (P_0)	#N/A	
15						
16	ERROR. The total service rate (rate x servers) must be greater than the arrival rate.					
17						
18	Probabilities					
19	Number of Units	Probability	Cumulative Probability			
20	0	#N/A	#N/A			
21	1	#VALUE!	#N/A			
22	2	#VALUE!	#N/A			
23	3	#VALUE!	#N/A			
24	4	#VALUE!	#N/A			
25	5	#VALUE!	#N/A			
36	16	#VALUE!	#N/A			
37	17	#VALUE!	#N/A			
38	18	#VALUE!	#N/A			
39	19	#VALUE!	#N/A			
40	20	#VALUE!	#N/A			

Input values

Output values

This message is displayed only when total service rate is not greater than the arrival rate.

Hidden rows; see CD-ROM for full file.

Table shows probabilities of 0 through 20 units in the system.

Excel Notes

■ The worksheets in ExcelModules contain formulas to compute the operating characteristics for different queuing models. The default values of zero for input data such as λ and μ cause the results of these formulas to initially appear as #N/A, #VALUE!, or #DIV/0! (see Screenshot 10.2A). However, as soon as we enter valid values for these input data, the worksheets will display the formula results.

■ Once ExcelModules has been used to create an Excel worksheet for a particular queuing model (such as M/M/s), the resulting worksheet can be used to compute the operating characteristics with several different input parameter values. For example, we can enter different input values in cells B9:B11 of Screenshot 10.2A and compute the resulting operating characteristic values without having to create a *new* M/M/s worksheet each time.

The worksheet now displays the operating characteristics of this queuing system in cells E9:E14. In addition, the worksheet computes the probability that there are exactly *n* customers in the system, for *n* = 0 through 20. Cumulative probabilities (i.e., the probability that there are *n* or fewer customers) are also calculated. These values are shown in cells A19:C40.

Results for Arnold's Muffler Shop problem

The results show that there are, on average, 2 cars in the system (i.e., L = 2), and each car spends an average of one hour in the system (i.e., W = 1 hour). The corresponding values for the waiting line alone (not including the server) are L_q = 1.33 cars, and W_q = 0.667 hours (or 40 minutes). The mechanic (server) is busy 67% of the time

SCREENSHOT 10.2B   **Operating Characteristics with $\mu = 3$ for Arnold's Muffler Shop M/M/1 Queuing System**

	A	B	C	D	E	F
1	**Arnold's Muffler Shop**					
2	Queuing Model	M/M/s (Exponential Service Times)				
3						
4	1. Both λ and μ must be RATES, and use the same time unit. For example, given a service time such as 10 minutes					
5	per customer, convert it to a service rate such as 6 per hour.					
6	2. The total service rate (rate x servers) must be greater than the arrival rate.					
7						
8	Input Data			Operating Characteristics		
9	Arrival rate (λ)	2		Average server utilization (ρ)	0.6667	
10	Service rate (μ)	3		Average number of customers in the queue (L_q)	1.3333	
11	Number of servers (s)	1		Average number of customers in the system (L)	2.0000	
12				Average waiting time in the queue (W_q)	0.6667	
13				Average time in the system (W)	1.0000	
14				Probability (% of time) system is empty (P_0)	0.3333	
15						
16						
17						
18	**Probabilities**					
19	Number of Units	Probability	Cumulative Probability			
20	0	0.3333	0.3333			
21	1	0.2222	0.5556			
22	2	0.1481	0.7037			
23	3	0.0988	0.8025			
24	4	0.0658	0.8683			
25	5	0.0439	0.9122			
36	16	0.0005	0.9990			
37	17	0.0003	0.9993			
38	18	0.0002	0.9995			
39	19	0.0002	0.9997			
40	20	0.0001	0.9998			

(i.e., the utilization factor $\rho = 0.67$). Since there is only one mechanic, this implies that an arriving car has a 33% chance of not having to wait ($P_0 = 0.33$).

Introducing Costs into the Model   Now that the operating characteristics of the queuing system have been computed, Arnold decides to do an economic analysis of their impact. The queuing model was valuable in predicting potential waiting times, queue lengths, idle times, and so on. But it did not identify optimal decisions or consider cost factors. As stated earlier, the solution to a queuing problem may require a manager to make a trade-off between the increased cost of providing better service and the decreased waiting costs derived from providing that service.

Arnold estimates that the cost of customer waiting time, in terms of customer dissatisfaction and lost goodwill, is $10 per hour spent in his shop. Observe that this time includes the time a customer's car is waiting in the queue for service as well as the time when the car is actually being serviced. The only cost of providing service that Arnold can identify is the salary of Reid Blank, the mechanic, who is paid $12 per hour.

The total cost, defined as the sum of the waiting cost and the service cost, is calculated as follows:

$$\text{Total cost} = C_w \times L + C_s \times s \qquad (10\text{-}10)$$

where

$$C_w = \text{customer waiting cost per unit time period}$$

$$L = \text{average number of customers in the system}$$

Conducting an economic analysis is the next step. It permits cost factors to be included.

Customer waiting time is often considered the most important factor.

$$C_s = \text{cost of providing service per server per unit time period}$$

$$s = \text{number of servers in the queuing system}$$

In Arnold's case, $C_w = \$10$ per hour, $L = 2$ (see Screenshot 10.2B), $C_s = \$12$ per hour, and $s = 1$ (since there is only one mechanic). Hence, Arnold computes his total cost as $(\$10)(2) + (\$12)(1) = \$32$ per hour.

Increasing the Service Rate

Now comes a decision. Arnold finds out through the muffler business grapevine that the Rusty Muffler, a crosstown competitor, employs a mechanic named Danny Smith who can efficiently install new mufflers at the rate of 4 per hour. Larry Arnold contacts Smith and inquires as to his interest in switching employers. Smith says that he would consider leaving the Rusty Muffler but only if he were paid $15 per hour. Arnold, being a crafty businessman, decides that it may be worthwhile to fire Blank and replace him with the speedier but more expensive Smith.

He first recomputes all the operating characteristics using a new service rate (μ) of 4 mufflers per hour. The arrival rate (λ) remains at 2 cars per hour. The revised characteristic values if Smith is employed are shown in Screenshot 10.2C.

It is quite evident that Smith's higher speed (4 mufflers per hour compared with Blank's 3 mufflers per hour) will result in considerably shorter queues and waiting times. For example, a customer would now spend an average of 0.5 hours in the system (i.e., $W = 0.5$) and 0.25 hours waiting in the queue ($W_q = 0.25$) as opposed to 1 hour in the system and 0.67 hours in the queue with Blank as the mechanic. The average number of customers in the system (L) decreases from 2 units to 1 unit.

SCREENSHOT 10.2C   **Revised Operating Characteristics with $\mu = 4$ for Arnold's Muffler Shop M/M/1 Queuing System**

	A	B	C	D	E	F
1	**Arnold's Muffler Shop**					
2	Queuing Model	**M/M/s (Exponential Service Times)**				
3						
4	1. Both λ and μ must be RATES, and use the same time unit. For example, given a service time such as 10 minutes					
5	per customer, convert it to a service rate such as 6 per hour.					
6	2. The total service rate (rate x servers) must be greater than the arrival rate.					
7						
8	Input Data			Operating Characteristics		
9	Arrival rate (λ)	2		Average server utilization (ρ)	0.5000	
10	Service rate (μ)	4		Average number of customers in the queue (L_q)	0.5000	
11	Number of servers (s)	1		Average number of customers in the system (L)	1.0000	
12				Average waiting time in the queue (W_q)	0.2500	
13		New service rate		Average time in the system (W)	0.5000	
14				Probability (% of time) system is empty (P_0)	0.5000	
15						0.25 hours =
16				= 30 minutes		15 minutes
17						
18	Probabilities					
19	Number of Units	Probability	Cumulative Probability			
20	0	0.5000	0.5000			
21	1	0.2500	0.7500			
22	2	0.1250	0.8750			
23	3	0.0625	0.9375			
24	4	0.0313	0.9688			
25	5	0.0156	0.9844			
36	16	0.0000	1.0000			
37	17	0.0000	1.0000			
38	18	0.0000	1.0000			
39	19	0.0000	1.0000			
40	20	0.0000	1.0000			

Arnold revises his economic analysis with the new information. The revised values are $C_w = \$10$ per hour, $L = 1$ (see Screenshot 10.2C), $C_s = \$15$ per hour, and $s = 1$ (since there is still only one mechanic). Hence, Arnold's revised total cost with Smith as the mechanic is $(\$10)(1) + (\$15)(1) = \$25$ per hour. Since total cost with Blank as the mechanic was $32 per hour, Arnold may very well decide to hire Smith and reduce costs by $7 per hour (or $56 per 8-hour day).

10.5 MULTIPLE-SERVER QUEUING SYSTEM WITH POISSON ARRIVALS AND EXPONENTIAL SERVICE TIMES (M/M/s MODEL)

The next logical step is to look at a multiple-server queuing system, in which two or more servers are available to handle arriving customers. Let us still assume that customers awaiting service form one single line and then proceed to the first available server. An example of such a multiple-server, single-phase waiting line is found in many banks or post offices today. A common line is formed, and the customer at the head of the line proceeds to the first free teller or clerk. (Refer back to Figure 10.3 for a typical multiple-server configuration.)

The multiple-server system presented here again assumes that arrivals follow a Poisson probability distribution and that service times are distributed exponentially. Service is first come, first served, and all servers are assumed to perform at the same rate. Other assumptions listed earlier for the single-server model apply as well.

The multiple-server model also assumes Poisson arrivals and exponential services.

Operating Characteristic Equations for an M/M/s Queuing System

We let

λ = average number of arrivals per time period (e.g., per hour)

μ = average number of customers served per time period *per server*

s = number of servers

DECISION MODELING IN ACTION
Using Queuing Models in a Hospital Eye Clinic

The hospital outpatient eye clinic at the United Kingdom's Royal Preston Hospital is not unlike clinics at hospitals throughout the world: It is regularly overbooked, overrun, and has excessive patient waiting times. Even though its Patient Charter states no one should wait to be seen for more than 30 minutes past their appointment time, patients, on average, waited more than 50 minutes.

Many problems in hospital clinics can be explained as a vicious circle of events: (1) appointments staff overbook every clinic session because of the large patient volume; (2) this means patients wait in long queues; (3) doctors are overburdened; and (4) when a doctor is ill, the staff spends much time cancelling and rescheduling appointments.

To break out of this cycle, the clinic at Royal Preston needed to reduce patient waiting times. This was done by applying computer-driven queuing models and attempting to reduce the patient time variability. The hospital used queuing software to specifically address the 30-minute statistic in the

Patient Charter. Researchers assumed that (1) each patient arrived on time, (2) the service distribution was known from past history, (3) 12% of patients missed their appointments, and (4) one-third of the patients queued for a second consultation.

Making a list of 13 recommendations (many nonquantitative) to the clinic, researchers returned two years later to find that most of their suggestions were followed (or at least seriously attempted), yet performance of the clinic had shown no dramatic improvement. Patient waiting times were still quite long, the clinic was still overbooked, and appointments sometimes had to be cancelled. The conclusion: Even though models can often help *understand* a problem, some problems, like those in the outpatient clinic, are messy and hard to fix.

Source: J. C. Bennett and D. J. Worthington. "An Example of a Good but Partially Successful OR Engagement: Improving Outpatient Clinic Operations," *Interfaces* (September–October 1998): 56–69.

As with the M/M/1 system, it is very important that we define both λ and μ for the *same time period*. It is also important to note that the service rate μ is defined *per server*. That is, if there are 2 servers and each server is capable of handling 3 customers per hour, μ is defined as 3 per hour, *not* 6 per hour ($= 2 \times 3$). Finally, as noted earlier, it is necessary for the average total service rate to be greater than the average arrival rate (that is, $s\mu > \lambda$).

The operating characteristic equations for the M/M/s queuing system are as follows:

1. Average server utilization in the system:

$$\rho = \lambda/(s\mu) \tag{10-11}$$

2. Probability that there are zero customers or units in the system:

$$P_0 = \frac{1}{\left[\sum_{k=0}^{s-1} \frac{1}{k!} \left(\frac{\lambda}{\mu} \right)^k \right] + \frac{1}{s!} \left(\frac{\lambda}{\mu} \right)^s \frac{s\mu}{(s\mu - \lambda)}} \tag{10-12}$$

3. Average number of customers or units waiting in line for service:

$$L_q = \frac{(\lambda/\mu)^s \lambda\mu}{(s-1)!\,(s\mu - \lambda)^2} P_0 \tag{10-13}$$

4. Average number of customers or units in the system:

$$L = L_q + \lambda/\mu \tag{10-14}$$

5. Average time a customer or unit spends waiting in line for service:

$$W_q = L_q/\lambda \tag{10-15}$$

6. Average time a customer or unit spends in the system:

$$W = W_q + 1/\mu \tag{10-16}$$

7. Probability that there are n customers or units in the system:

$$P_n = \frac{(\lambda/\mu)^n}{n!} P_0 \quad \text{for } n \le s \tag{10-17}$$

$$P_n = \frac{(\lambda/\mu)^n}{s!\, s^{(n-s)}} P_0 \quad \text{for } n > s \tag{10-18}$$

These equations are more complex than the ones used in the single-server model. Yet they are used in exactly the same fashion and provide the same type of information as the simpler M/M/1 model.

Arnold's Muffler Shop Revisited

For an application of the multiple-server queuing model, let us return to the Arnold's Muffler Shop problem. Earlier, Larry Arnold examined two options. He could retain his current mechanic, Reid Blank, at a total system cost of $32 per hour; or he could fire Blank and hire a slightly more expensive but faster worker named Danny Smith. With Smith on board, system costs could be reduced to $25 per hour.

A third option is now explored. Arnold finds that at minimal after-tax cost he can open a second garage bay in which mufflers can be installed. Instead of firing his first mechanic, Blank, he would hire a second worker. The new mechanic would be expected to install mufflers at the same rate as Blank ($\mu = 3$ per hour). Customers, who would still arrive at

The muffler shop considers opening a second muffler service channel that operates at the same speed as the first one.

File: 10-3.xls

In the M/M/s model, the service rate μ is per server.

Dramatically lower waiting time results from opening the second service bay.

the rate of $\lambda = 2$ per hour, would wait in a single line until one of the two mechanics becomes available. To find out how this option compares with the old single-server queuing system, Arnold computes the operating characteristics for the M/M/2 system.

ExcelModules Solution for Arnold's Muffler Shop with Two Mechanics Once again, we select the choice titled **EXPONENTIAL SERVICE TIMES** (M/M/s) in the Queuing Model's submenu (see Screenshot 10.1A) of ExcelModules. After entering the optional title, we enter the input data as shown in Screenshot 10.3. For Arnold's problem, observe that the arrival rate (λ) is 2 cars per hour. The service rate (μ) is 3 mufflers per hour *per mechanic*. We enter these values in cells B9 and B10, respectively, as shown in Screenshot 10.3. The number of servers (cell B11) is 2 since there are now two mechanics.

The worksheet now displays the operating characteristics of this queuing system in cells E9:E14. Probabilities of having a specific number of units in the system are shown in cells A19:C40. Arnold first compares these results with the earlier results. The information is summarized in Table 10.3 on the next page. The increased service from opening a second bay has a dramatic effect on almost all results. In particular, time spent waiting in line (W_q) drops from 40 minutes with one mechanic (Blank) to 15 minutes, with Smith down to only 2.5 minutes! Similarly, the average number of cars in the system (L) falls to 0.75.[5] But does this mean that a second bay should be opened?

SCREENSHOT 10.3   **Revised Operating Characteristics for Arnold's Muffler Shop M/M/2 Queuing System**

> M/M/s with s = 2 is the M/M/2 model.

	A	B	C	D	E	F
1	**Arnold's Muffler Shop**					
2	Queuing Model	M/M/s (Exponential Service Times)				
3						
4	1. Both λ and μ must be RATES, and use the same time unit. For example, given a service time such as 10 minutes					
5	per customer, convert it to a service rate such as 6 per hour.					
6	2. The total service rate (rate x servers) must be greater than the arrival rate.					
7						
8	Input Data			Operating Characteristics		
9	Arrival rate (λ)	2		Average server utilization (ρ)	0.3333	
10	Service rate (μ)	3		Average number of customers in the queue (L_q)	0.0833	
11	Number of servers (s)	2		Average number of customers in the system (L)	0.7500	
12				Average waiting time in the queue (W_q)	0.0417	
13				Average time in the system (W)	0.3750	
14				Probability (% of time) system is empty (P_0)	0.5000	
15						
16						
17						
18	Probabilities					
19	Number of Units	Probability	Cumulative Probability			
20	0	0.5000	0.5000			
21	1	0.3333	0.8333			
22	2	0.1111	0.9444			
23	3	0.0370	0.9815			
24	4	0.0123	0.9938			
25	5	0.0041	0.9979			
36	16	0.0000	1.0000			
37	17	0.0000	1.0000			
38	18	0.0000	1.0000			
39	19	0.0000	1.0000			
40	20	0.0000	1.0000			

> Servers are busy only 33.3% of the time.

> Two mechanics on duty

> Equal service rate for both mechanics. Rate shown is *per mechanic.*

> 0.0417 hours = 2.5 minutes

> Hidden rows; see CD-ROM for full file.

---

[5] Note that adding a second mechanic cuts queue waiting time and length by more than half; that is, the relationship between number of servers and queue characteristics is *nonlinear.* This is because of the random arrival and service processes. When there is only one mechanic and two customers arrive within a minute of each other, the second will have a long wait. The fact that the mechanic may have been idle for 30 minutes before they both arrived does not change the average waiting time. Thus, single-server models often have high wait times relative to multiple-server models.

TABLE 10.3	Effect of Service Level on Arnold's Operating Characteristics		
	LEVEL OF SERVICE		
OPERATING CHARACTERISTIC	ONE MECHANIC (REID BLANK) $\mu = 3$	TWO MECHANICS $\mu = 3$ FOR EACH	ONE FAST MECHANIC (DANNY SMITH) $\mu = 4$
Probability that the system is empty (P_0)	0.33	0.50	0.50
Average number of cars in the system (L)	2 cars	0.75 cars	1 car
Average time spent in the system (W)	60 minutes	22.5 minutes	30 minutes
Average number of cars in the queue (L_q)	1.33 cars	0.083 cars	0.50 cars
Average time spent in the queue (W_q)	40 minutes	2.5 minutes	15 minutes

Cost Analysis of the Queuing System

Economic analysis with two bays

To complete his economic analysis of the M/M/2 queuing system, Arnold assumes that the second mechanic would be paid the same as the current one, Blank, namely, $12 per hour. The relevant values are C_w = $10 per hour, L = 0.75 (see Screenshot 10.3), C_s = $12 per hour, and s = 2 (since there are two mechanics). The total cost is, therefore, ($10)(0.75) + ($12)(2) = $31.50 per hour.

As you recall, total cost with just Blank as mechanic was found to be $32 per hour. Cost with just Smith was $25 per hour. Although opening a second bay would be likely to have a positive effect on customer goodwill and hence lower the cost of waiting time (i.e., lower C_w), it means an increase in the total cost of providing service. Look back to Figure 10.1 and you will see that such trade-offs are the basis of queuing theory. Arnold's decision is to replace his present worker with the speedier Smith and not to open a second service bay.

10.6 SINGLE-SERVER QUEUING SYSTEM WITH POISSON ARRIVALS AND CONSTANT SERVICE TIMES (M/D/1 MODEL)

Constant service rates speed the process compared to exponentially distributed service times with the same value of μ.

When customers or equipment are processed according to a fixed cycle, as in the case of an automatic car wash or an amusement park ride, constant service rates are appropriate. Because constant rates are certain, the values for L_q, W_q, L, and W are always less than they would be in the models discussed previously, which have variable service times. As a matter of fact, both the average queue length and the average waiting time in the queue are *halved* with the constant service rate model.

Operating Characteristic Equations for an M/D/1 Queuing System

We let

λ = average number of arrivals per time period (e.g., per hour)

μ = constant number of people or items served per time period

The operating characteristic equations follow.

1. Average server utilization in the system:

$$\rho = \lambda/\mu$$

(10-19)

2. Average number of customers or units waiting in line for service:

$$L_q = \frac{\lambda^2}{2\mu(\mu - \lambda)} \qquad (10\text{-}20)$$

3. Average number of customers or units in the system:

$$L = L_q + \lambda/\mu \qquad (10\text{-}21)$$

4. Average time a customer or unit spends waiting in line for service:

$$W_q = L_q/\lambda = \frac{\lambda}{2\mu(\mu - \lambda)} \qquad (10\text{-}22)$$

5. Average time a customer or unit spends in the system (namely, in the queue or being served):

$$W = W_q + 1/\mu \qquad (10\text{-}23)$$

6. Probability that there are zero customers or units in the system:

$$P_0 = 1 - \lambda/\mu \qquad (10\text{-}24)$$

Garcia-Golding Recycling, Inc.

Garcia-Golding Recycling, Inc. collects and compacts aluminum cans and glass bottles in Southern B.C. Their truck drivers, who arrive to unload these materials for recycling, currently wait an average of 15 minutes before emptying their loads. The cost of the driver and truck time wasted while in queue is valued at $60 per hour. A new automated compactor can be purchased that will process truckloads at a constant rate of 12 trucks per hour (i.e., 5 minutes per truck). Trucks arrive according to a Poisson distribution at an average rate of 8 per hour. If the new compactor is put in use, its cost will be amortized at a rate of $3 per truck unloaded. Should Garcia-Golding purchase the new compactor?

File: 10-4.xls

ExcelModules Solution for Garcia-Golding's Problem   We select the choice titled **CONSTANT SERVICE TIMES (M/D/1)** in the Queuing Models submenu (see Screenshot 10.1A) of ExcelModules. After entering the optional title, we enter the input data as shown in the screen in Screenshot 10.4. For Garcia-Golding's problem, the arrival rate (λ) is 8 trucks per hour. The constant service rate (μ) is 12 trucks per hour. We enter these values

Operating Characteristics for Garcia-Golding Recycling M/D/1 Queuing System

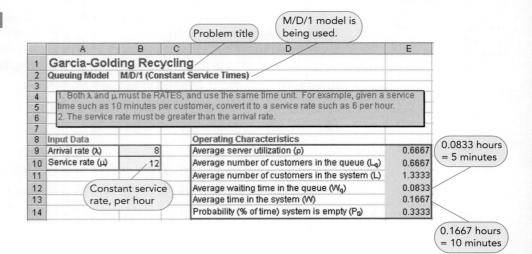

in cells B9 and B10, respectively. The worksheet now displays the operating characteristics of this queuing system in cells E9:E14.

Cost Analysis of the Queuing System

The *current* system makes drivers wait an average of 15 minutes before emptying their trucks. The waiting cost per trip is

$$\text{Current waiting cost per trip} = 0.25 \text{ hours waiting} \times \$60/\text{hour}$$
$$= \$15 \text{ per trip}$$

As seen in Screenshot 10.4, the average waiting time in the queue (W_q) with the new automated compactor is only 0.0833 hours, or 5 minutes. Therefore, the revised waiting cost per trip is

$$\text{Revised waiting cost per trip} = 0.0833 \text{ hours waiting} \times \$60/\text{hour}$$
$$= \$5 \text{ per trip}$$

$$\text{Savings with new equipment} = \$15 - \$5 = \$10 \text{ per trip}$$

$$\text{Amortized cost of equipment} = \$3 \text{ per trip}$$

$$\text{Hence, net savings} = \$10 - \$3 = \$7 \text{ per trip}$$

Garcia-Golding should therefore purchase the new compactor.

10.7 SINGLE-SERVER QUEUING SYSTEM WITH POISSON ARRIVALS AND GENERAL SERVICE TIMES (M/G/1 MODEL)

So far, we have studied systems in which service times are either exponentially distributed or constant. In many cases, however, service times could follow some **arbitrary distribution** with a mean μ and a standard deviation σ. In such cases, we refer to the model as a *general service time model*. Real-world examples of general service times include (1) time required to service vehicles at an auto repair shop (e.g., an oil change service) and (2) time required by a store clerk to complete a sales transaction.

General service time models assume arbitrary distributions for service times.

The single-server system presented here assumes that arrivals follow a Poisson probability distribution. As in earlier models, we also assume (1) service is first come, first served, (2) there is no balking or reneging, and (3) the average service rate is greater than the average arrival rate.

Operating Characteristic Equations for an M/G/1 Queuing System

We let

λ = average number of arrivals per time period (e.g., per hour)

μ = average number of people or items served per time period

σ = standard deviation of service time

The operating characteristic equations follow.

1. Average server utilization in the system:
$$\rho = \lambda/\mu \tag{10-25}$$

2. Average number of customers or units waiting in line for service:
$$L_q = \frac{\lambda^2\sigma^2 + (\lambda/\mu)^2}{2[1 - (\lambda/\mu)]} \tag{10-26}$$

3. Average number of customers or units in the system:
$$L = L_q + \lambda/\mu \tag{10-27}$$

4. Average time a customer or unit spends waiting in line for service:
$$W_q = L_q/\lambda \tag{10-28}$$

5. Average time a customer or unit spends in the system:
$$W = W_q + 1/\mu \tag{10-29}$$

6. Probability that there are zero customers or units in the system:
$$P_0 = 1 - \lambda/\mu \tag{10-30}$$

Meetings with Professor Crino

Example of a general service time model

Professor Michael Crino advises all Honours students at Central College. During the preregistration period, students meet with Professor Crino to decide courses for the following semester and to discuss any other issues they may be concerned about. Rather than have students set up specific appointments to see him, Professor Crino prefers setting aside two hours each day during the preregistration period and having students drop in informally. This approach, he believes, makes students feel more at ease with him.

Based on his experience, Professor Crino thinks that students arrive at an average rate of 1 every 12 minutes (or 5 per hour) to see him. He also thinks the Poisson distribution is appropriate to model the arrival process. Advising meetings last an average of 10 minutes; that is, Professor Crino's service rate is 6 per hour. However, since some students have concerns that they wish to discuss with Professor Crino, the length of these meetings varies. Professor Crino estimates that the standard deviation of the service time (i.e., the meeting length) is 5 minutes.

File: 10-5.xls

ExcelModules Solution for Professor Crino's Problem   We select the choice titled **GENERAL SERVICE TIMES (M/G/1)** in the Queuing Models submenu (see Screenshot 10.1A) of ExcelModules. After entering the optional title, we enter the input data in the screen shown in Screenshot 10.5A. For Professor Crino's problem, the mean arrival rate (λ) is 5 students per hour. The mean service rate (μ) is 6 students per hour. Observe that μ must exceed λ, and both must be for the same time period (per hour, in this case). The standard deviation (σ) of the service time is 5 minutes. However, since λ and μ are expressed per hour, we also express σ in hours and write it as 0.0833 hours (= 5 minutes).

SCREENSHOT 10.5A   **Operating Characteristics for Professor Crino's Problem M/G/1 Queuing System**

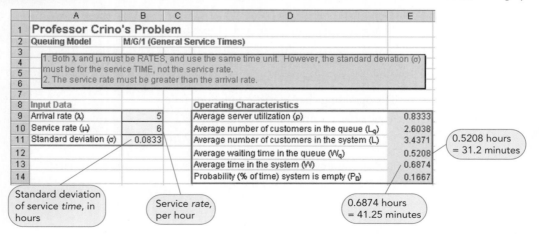

λ and μ are rates and must be for the same time unit. The standard deviation, σ, must also be for this same time unit.

We enter the values λ, μ, and σ in cells B9, B10, and B11, respectively, as shown in Screenshot 10.5A. The worksheet now displays the operating characteristics of this queuing system in cells E9:E14.

The results indicate that, on average, Professor Crino is busy during 83.3% of his advising period. There are 2.60 students waiting to see him on average, and each student waits an average of 0.52 hours (or approximately 31 minutes).

Using Excel's Goal Seek to Identify Required Model Parameters

Looking at the results in Screenshot 10.5A, Professor Crino decides that making students wait an average of 31 minutes is unacceptable. Ideally, he would like to speed these meetings up so that students wait no more than 15 minutes (or 0.25 hours) on average. He realizes that he has little control over the standard deviation of the service time. However, by insisting that students come prepared for these meetings (e.g., with a good idea of which courses they want to take), Professor Crino thinks he can decrease the average meeting length. The question is this: What average meeting length will enable Professor Crino to meet his goal of a 15-minute average waiting time?

Excel's Goal Seek procedure allows us to find the required value of a queue parameter to achieve a stated goal.

One way to solve this problem is to plug in different values for the service rate μ in cell B10 of Screenshot 10.5A and keep track of the W_q value in cell E12 until it drops below 0.25. An alternative, and preferred, approach is to use a procedure in Excel called **Goal Seek** to automate the search process for the value of μ. Assume we designate a cell as the Changing Cell in a spreadsheet model. Also assume a different cell (which we designate as the Target Cell) is a function of the value in the Changing Cell. That is, the Target Cell contains a formula that involves the Changing Cell. The Goal Seek procedure allows us to try to find the value in the Changing Cell that will make the Target Cell achieve a specified value.

In our model, the Changing Cell is the service rate μ (cell B10). The Target Cell is the average waiting time W_q (cell E12). We want the Target Cell to achieve a value of 15 minutes (which we specify as 0.25 hours since μ and λ are per hour). After bringing up the General Service Times (M/G/1) worksheet in ExcelModules (see Screenshot 10.5A), we invoke the Goal Seek procedure by clicking **TOOLS|GOAL SEEK** in Excel's main menu bar. The window shown in Screenshot 10.5B is now displayed.

We specify cell E12 as the target, set its value to 0.25, and identify cell B10 as the Changing Cell. When we click OK, we get the windows shown in Screenshot 10.5C. The results indicate that if Professor Crino can increase his service rate to 6.92 students per hour, the average waiting time drops to around 15 minutes. That is, Professor Crino needs to reduce his average meeting length to approximately 8.67 minutes (= 6.92 students per 60 minutes).

We can use Goal Seek in any of the queuing models discussed here to determine the value of an input parameter (e.g., μ or λ) that would make an operating characteristic reach a desired value. For example, we could have used it in the M/M/1 worksheet (Section 10.4) to find the value of μ that would allow Arnold to offer his customers a guarantee of having to wait no more than 5 minutes (or 0.0833 hours). The answer turns out to be 6 mufflers per hour. See if you can verify this using Goal Seek and the Exponential Service Times (M/M/s) worksheet in ExcelModules.

SCREENSHOT 10.5B

Goal Seek Input Window in Excel

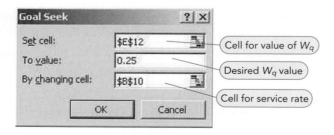

Goal Seek Status Window and Revised Operating Characteristics for Professor Crino's Problem: M/G/1 Queuing System

	A	B	C	D	E
1	**Professor Crino's Problem**				
2	Queuing Model	M/G/1 (General Service Times)			
3-6	1. Both λ and μ must be RATES, and use the same time unit. However, the standard deviation (σ) must be for the service TIME, not the service rate. 2. The service rate must be greater than the arrival rate.				
7					
8	Input Data			Operating Characteristics	
9	Arrival rate (λ)	5		Average server utilization (ρ)	0.7226
10	Service rate (μ)	6.9199		Average number of customers in the queue (L_q)	1.2535
11	Standard deviation (σ)	0.0833		Average number of customers in the system (L)	1.9760
12				Average waiting time in the queue (W_q)	0.2507
13				Average time in the system (W)	0.3952
14				Probability (% of time) system is empty (P_0)	0.2774

Goal of 15 minutes (= 0.25 hours)

Goal Seek Status

Goal Seeking with Cell E12 found a solution.

Target value: 0.25
Current value: 0.2507

[OK] [Cancel] [Step] [Pause]

Goal Seek message indicating whether desired goal was achieved

Service rate required to achieve goal of 6.92 students per hour ⟹ 1 student every 8.67 minutes

10.8 MULTIPLE-SERVER QUEUING SYSTEM WITH POISSON ARRIVALS, EXPONENTIAL SERVICE TIMES, AND FINITE POPULATION SIZE (M/M/S/∞/N MODEL)

When there is a limited population of potential customers for a service facility, we need to consider a different queuing model. This model would be used, for example, if we were considering equipment repairs in a factory that has five machines, if we were in charge of maintenance for a fleet of 10 commuter airplanes, or if we ran a hospital ward that has 20 beds. The limited population model permits any number of servers to be considered.

In the finite population model, the arrival rate is dependent on the length of the queue.

The reason this model differs from the earlier queuing models is that there is now a dependent relationship between the length of the queue and the arrival rate. To illustrate this situation, assume your factory has five machines. If all five are broken and awaiting repair, the arrival rate drops to zero. In general, as the waiting time becomes longer in a limited population queuing system, the arrival rate of customers drops lower.

In this section, we describe a finite arrival population model that has the following assumptions:

1. There are *s* servers with *identical* service time distributions.

2. The population of units seeking service is finite, of size N.[6]

Arrival rate λ is per customer or unit.

3. The arrival distribution of *each customer* in the population follows a Poisson distribution, with a mean rate of λ.

---

[6] Although there is no definite number that we can use to divide finite from infinite arrival populations, the general rule is this: if the number in the queue is a significant proportion of the arrival population, we should use a finite queuing model.

4. Service times are exponentially distributed, with a mean rate of μ.
5. Both λ and μ are specified for the same time period.
6. Customers are served on a first-come, first-served basis.

Operating Characteristic Equations for the Finite Population Queuing System

We let

λ = average number of arrivals per time period (e.g., per hour)

μ = average number of people or items served per time period

s = number of servers

N = size of the population

The operating characteristic equations follow.

1. Probability that there are zero customers or units in the system:

$$P_0 = \frac{1}{\displaystyle\sum_{n=0}^{s-1} \frac{N!}{(N-n)!\,n!}\left(\frac{\lambda}{\mu}\right)^n + \sum_{n=s}^{N} \frac{N!}{(N-n)!\,s!\,s^{n-s}}\left(\frac{\lambda}{\mu}\right)^n} \tag{10-31}$$

2. Probability that there are exactly n customers in the system:

$$P_n = \frac{N!}{(N-n)!\,n!}\left(\frac{\lambda}{\mu}\right)^n P_0, \qquad \text{if } 0 \leq n \leq s \tag{10-32}$$

$$P_n = \frac{N!}{(N-n)!\,s!\,s^{n-s}}\left(\frac{\lambda}{\mu}\right)^n P_0, \quad \text{if } s < n \leq N \tag{10-33}$$

$$P_n = 0, \qquad\qquad\qquad \text{if } n > N \tag{10-34}$$

3. Average number of customers or units in line waiting for service:

$$L_q = \sum_{n=s}^{N} (n-s)P_n \tag{10-35}$$

4. Average number of customers or units in the system:

$$L = \sum_{n=0}^{s-1} nP_n + L_q + s\left(1 - \sum_{n=0}^{s-1} P_n\right) \tag{10-36}$$

5. Average time a customer or unit spends in the queue waiting for service:

$$W_q = \frac{L_q}{\lambda(N-L)} \tag{10-37}$$

6. Average time a customer or unit spends in the system:

$$W = \frac{L}{\lambda(N-L)} \tag{10-38}$$

Government Agency Example

Example of a finite population model.

File: 10-6.xls

A government agency located in Ottawa uses five high-speed printers to print all documents. Past records indicate that each of these printers needs repair after about 20 hours of use. Breakdowns have been found to be Poisson-distributed. The one technician on duty can repair a printer in an average of two hours, following an exponential distribution.

ExcelModules Solution for Government Agency Problem We select the choice titled Finite Population Model (Multiple Servers) in the Queuing Models submenu (see Screenshot 10.1A) of ExcelModules. After entering the optional title, we get the screen shown in Screenshot 10.6A. For the government agency's problem, the arrival rate (λ) for *each printer* is $1/20 = 0.05$ per hour. The mean service rate (μ) is 1 every two hours, or 0.50 printers per hour. As before, both μ and λ are expressed for the same time period (per hour, in this case). The number of servers (s) is 1, since there is only one technician on duty. Finally, the population size (N) is 5, since there are five printers at the government agency.

We enter the values of λ, μ, s, and N in cells B9, B10, B11, and B12, respectively, as shown in Screenshot 10.6A. The worksheet now displays the operating characteristics of this queuing system in cells E9:E15. Probability values (P_n) are shown in cells A18:C50.

SCREENSHOT 10.6A   **Operating Characteristics for the Government Agency's Problem: M/M/1 Queuing System with Finite Population**

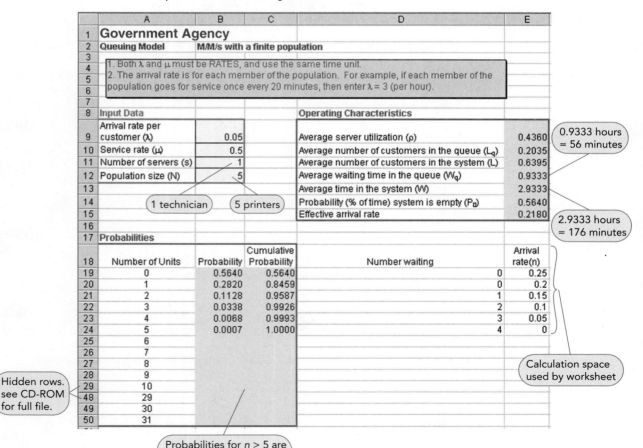

Cost Analysis of the Queuing System

The results indicate that there are 0.64 printers on average in the system. If printer down-time is estimated at $120 per hour, and the technician is paid $25 per hour, we can compute the total cost per hour as

$$\text{Total cost} = \text{average number of printers down} \times \text{cost of downtime hour}$$
$$+ \text{cost of technician hour}$$

$$= (0.64)(\$120) + \$25 = \$101.80 \text{ per hour}$$

The office manager is willing to consider hiring a second printer technician provided it is cost-effective. To check this, we compute the agency queue's operating characteristics again. However, the number of servers this time (cell B11) is 2. The results are shown in Screenshot 10.6B.

Screenshot 10.6B indicates that there are now only 0.46 printers on average in the system. We can compute the revised total cost per hour as

$$\text{Total cost} = \text{average number of printers down} \times \text{cost of downtime hour}$$
$$+ \text{cost of technician hour} \times \text{number of technicians}$$

$$= (0.46)(\$120) + (\$25)(2) = \$105.20 \text{ per hour}$$

Since the total cost is higher in this case ($105.20 versus $101.80 per hour), the office manager should not hire a second technician.

SCREENSHOT 10.6B **Revised Operating Characteristics for the Government Agency's Problem: M/M/2 Queuing System with Finite Population**

	A	B	C	D	E
1	**Government Agency**				
2	**Queuing Model**	**M/M/s with a finite population**			
3					
4	1. Both λ and μ must be RATES, and use the same time unit.				
5	2. The arrival rate is for each member of the population. For example, if each member of the				
6	population goes for service once every 20 minutes, then enter λ = 3 (per hour).				
7					
8	**Input Data**			**Operating Characteristics**	
9	Arrival rate per customer (λ)	0.05		Average server utilization (ρ)	0.2268
10	Service rate (μ)	0.5		Average number of customers in the queue (L_q)	0.0113
11	Number of servers (s)	2		Average number of customers in the system (L)	0.4648
12	Population size (N)	5		Average waiting time in the queue (W_q)	0.0497
13				Average time in the system (W)	2.0497
14		2 technicians		Probability (% of time) system is empty (P_0)	0.6186
15				Effective arrival rate	0.2268
16					
17	**Probabilities**				
18	Number of Units	Probability	Cumulative Probability	Number waiting	Arrival rate(n)
19	0	0.6186	0.6186	0	0.25
20	1	0.3093	0.9279	0	0.2
21	2	0.0619	0.9897	0	0.15
22	3	0.0093	0.9990	1	0.1
23	4	0.0009	1.0000	2	0.05
24	5	0.0000	1.0000	3	0
25	6				
26	7				
27	8				
28	9				
29	10				
48	29				
49	30				
50	31				

L drops to 0.46 with two technicians.

System is empty 62% of the time—that is, no printers are broken.

Calculation space used by worksheet

Hidden rows; see CD-ROM for full file.

10.9 MORE COMPLEX QUEUING SYSTEMS

Many queuing systems that occur in real-world situations have characteristics like those of Arnold's Muffler Shop, Garcia-Golding Recycling, Inc., Professor Crino's advising meetings, or the government agency examples. This is true when the situation calls for issues such as (1) single or multiple servers, (2) Poisson arrivals, (3) exponential, constant, or arbitrary service times, (4) a finite or an infinite arrival population, (5) no balking or reneging, and (6) first-in, first-out service.

Often, however, variations are present in an analysis. Arrival times, for example, may not be Poisson-distributed. A college registration system in which fourth-year students have first choice of courses and hours over all other students is an example of a first-come, first-served model with a preemptive priority queue discipline. A physical examination for military recruits is an example of a multiphase system—one that differs from the single-phase models discussed in this chapter. Recruits first line up to have blood drawn at one station, then wait to take an eye exam at the next station, talk to a psychiatrist at the third, and are examined by a doctor for medical problems at the fourth. At each phase, the recruits must enter another queue and wait their turn.

More sophisticated models exist to handle variations of basic assumptions, but when even these do not apply we can turn to computer simulation, the topic of Chapter 11.

Analytical models to handle these cases have been developed by operations researchers. The mathematical expressions for the operating characteristics are somewhat more complex than the ones covered in this chapter.[7] Many real-world queuing applications are, in fact, too complex to be modeled analytically at all. When this happens, decision modelers usually turn to computer simulation, the topic of Chapter 11.

SUMMARY

Queuing systems are an important part of the business world. This chapter describes several common queuing situations and presents decision models for analyzing systems that follow certain assumptions: (1) the queuing system involves just a single phase of service; (2) arrivals are Poisson-distributed; (3) arrivals are treated on a first-in, first-out basis and do not balk or renege; (4) service times follow the exponential distribution or an arbitrary distribution, or are constant; and (5) the average service rate is faster than the average arrival rate.

The models illustrated in this chapter are for single-server, single-phase and multiple-server, single-phase problems. We show how to compute a series of operating characteristics in each case using Excel worksheets and then study total expected costs. Total cost is the sum of the cost of providing service plus the cost of waiting time.

Key operating characteristics for a system are (1) utilization rate, (2) percent idle time, (3) average time spent waiting in the system and in the queue, (4) average number of customers in the system and in the queue, and (5) probabilities of various numbers of customers in the system.

We emphasize that a variety of queuing situations exist that do not meet all of the assumptions of the traditional models. In these cases, we need to use more complex mathematical models or turn to computer simulation. The application of simulation to problems of inventory control, queuing systems, and other decision modeling situations will be discussed in Chapter 11.

GLOSSARY

Arbitrary Distribution. A probability distribution that is sometimes used to describe random service times in a queuing system.

Arrival Population or Calling Population. The population from which arrivals at the queuing system come.

Balk. To refuse to join the waiting line.

Exponential Probability Distribution. A probability distribution that is often used to describe random service times in a queuing system.

---

[7] Often, the qualitative results of queuing models are as useful as the quantitative results. Results show that it is inherently more efficient to pool resources, use central dispatching, and provide single multiple-server systems rather than multiple single-server systems.

FIFO. Denotes first in, first out. A queue discipline in which the customers are served in the strict order of arrival.

Goal Seek. A procedure in Excel that can be used to identify the value of a queuing system parameter required to achieve a desired value of an operating characteristic.

Limited or Finite Population. A case in which the number of customers in the system is a significant proportion of the calling population.

Limited Queue Length or Finite Queue Length. A waiting line that cannot increase beyond a specific size.

M/D/1. Kendall's notation for the constant service time model.

M/G/1. Kendall's notation for the arbitrary service time model.

M/M/1. Kendall's notation for the single-server model with Poisson arrivals and exponential service times.

M/M/s. Kendall's notation for the multiple-server queuing model (with *s* servers), Poisson arrivals, and exponential service times.

Multiphase System. A system in which service is received from more than one station, one after the other.

Multiple-Server Queuing System. A system that has more than one service facility, all fed by the same single queue.

Operating Characteristics. Descriptive characteristics of a queuing system, including the average number of customers in a line and in the system, the average waiting times in a line and in the system, and percent idle time.

Poisson Distribution. A probability distribution that is often used to describe random arrivals in a queue.

Queue or Waiting Line. One or more customers or units waiting to be served.

Queue Discipline. The rule by which customers in a line receive service.

Queuing Model. A mathematical model that studies the performance of waiting lines or queues.

Renege. To enter a queue but then leave before being served.

Service Cost. The cost of providing a particular level of service.

Single-Phase System. A queuing system in which service is received at only one station.

Single-Server Queuing System. A system with one service facility fed by one queue. Servers are also referred to as *channels*.

Unlimited or Infinite Population. A calling population that is very large relative to the number of customers currently in the system.

Unlimited Queue Length or Infinite Queue Length. A queue that can increase to an infinite size.

Utilization Factor (ρ). The proportion of time that the service facility is in use.

Waiting Cost. The cost to the firm of having customers or units waiting in line to be served.

KEY EQUATIONS

λ = average number of arrivals per time period (e.g., per hour)

μ = average number of people or items served per time period

(10-1) $P(X) = \dfrac{(e^{-\lambda} \lambda^x)}{X!}$ for $X = 0, 1, 2, \ldots$

Poisson probability distribution used in describing arrivals.

(10-2) $P(t) = e^{-\mu t}$ for $t \geq 0$

Exponential probability distribution used in describing service times.

Equations 10-3 through 10-9 describe the operating characteristics in a single-server queuing system that has Poisson arrivals and exponential service times.

(10-3) $\rho = \lambda/\mu$

Average server utilization in the system.

(10-4) $L_q = \dfrac{\lambda^2}{\mu(\mu - \lambda)}$

Average number of customers or units waiting in line for service.

(10-5) $L = L_q + \lambda/\mu$

The average number of customers or units in the system.

(10-6) $W_q = L_q/\lambda = \dfrac{\lambda}{\mu(\mu - \lambda)}$

Average time a customer or unit spends waiting in line for service.

(10-7) $W = W_q + 1/\mu$

Average time a customer or unit spends in the system.

(10-8) $P_0 = 1 - \lambda/\mu$

The probability that there are zero customers or units in the system.

(10-9) $P_n = (\lambda/\mu)^n \, P_0$

The probability that there are *n* customers or units in the system.

(10-10) Total cost = $C_w \times L + C_s \times s$

Total cost is the sum of waiting cost and service cost.

Equations 10-11 through 10-18 describe the operating characteristics in a multiple-server queuing system that has Poisson arrivals and exponential service times.

(10-11) $\rho = \lambda/(s\mu)$

Average server utilization in the system.

(10-12) $$P_0 = \dfrac{1}{\left[\displaystyle\sum_{k=0}^{s-1} \dfrac{1}{k!}\left(\dfrac{\lambda}{\mu}\right)^k\right] + \dfrac{1}{s!}\left(\dfrac{\lambda}{\mu}\right)^s \dfrac{s\mu}{(s\mu - \lambda)}}$$

Probability that there are zero customers or units in the system.

(10-13) $L_q = \dfrac{(\lambda/\mu)^s \lambda\mu}{(s-1)!(s\mu - \lambda)^2} P_0$

Average number of customers or units waiting in line for service.

(10-14) $L = L_q + \lambda/\mu$

The average number of customers or units in the system.

(10-15) $W_q = L_q/\lambda$

Average time a customer or unit spends waiting in line for service.

(10-16) $W = W_q + 1/\mu$

Average time a customer or unit spends in the system.

(10-17) $P_n = \dfrac{(\lambda/\mu)^n}{n!} P_0 \quad$ for $n \le s$

(10-18) $P_n = \dfrac{(\lambda/\mu)^n}{s!s^{(n-s)}} P_0 \quad$ for $n > s$

Probability that there are n customers or units in the system.

Equations 10-19 through 10-24 describe the operating characteristics in a multiple-server queuing system that has Poisson arrivals and constant service times.

(10-19) $\rho = \lambda/\mu$

Average server utilization in the system.

(10-20) $L_q = \dfrac{\lambda^2}{2\mu(\mu - \lambda)}$

Average number of customers or units waiting in line for service.

(10-21) $L = L_q + \lambda/\mu$

Average number of customers or units in the system.

(10-22) $W_q = L_q/\lambda = \dfrac{\lambda}{2\mu(\mu - \lambda)}$

Average time a customer or unit spends waiting in line for service.

(10-23) $W = W_q + 1/\mu$

Average time a customer or unit spends in the system.

(10-24) $P_0 = 1 - \lambda/\mu$

Probability that there are zero customers or units in the system.

Equations 10-25 through 10-30 describe the operating characteristics in a single-server queuing system that has Poisson arrivals and general service times.

(10-25) $\rho = \lambda/\mu$

Average server utilization in the system.

(10-26) $L_q = \dfrac{\lambda^2\sigma^2 + (\lambda/\mu)^2}{2[1 - (\lambda/\mu)]}$

Average number of customers or units waiting in line for service.

(10-27) $L = L_q + \lambda/\mu$

Average number of customers or units in the system.

(10-28) $W_q = L_q/\lambda$

Average time a customer or unit spends waiting in line for service.

(10-29) $W = W_q + 1/\mu$

Average time a customer or unit spends in the system.

(10-30) $P_0 = 1 - \lambda/\mu$

Probability that there are zero customers or units in the system.

Equations 10-31 through 10-38 describe the operating characteristics in a multiple-server queuing system that has Poisson arrivals, exponential service times, and a finite population of size N.

(10-31) $$P_0 = \dfrac{1}{\displaystyle\sum_{n=0}^{s-1} \dfrac{N!}{(N-n)!n!}\left(\dfrac{\lambda}{\mu}\right)^n + \sum_{n=s}^{N} \dfrac{N!}{(N-n)!s!s^{n-s}}\left(\dfrac{\lambda}{\mu}\right)^n}$$

Probability that there are zero customers or units in the system.

(10-32) $P_n = \dfrac{N!}{(N-n)!n!}\left(\dfrac{\lambda}{\mu}\right)^n P_0, \qquad$ if $0 \le n \le s$

(10-33) $P_n = \dfrac{N!}{(N-n)!s!s^{n-s}}\left(\dfrac{\lambda}{\mu}\right)^n P_0, \quad$ if $s < n \le N$

(10-34) $P_n = 0, \quad$ if $n > N$

Probability that there are exactly n customers in the system.

(10-35) $L_q = \displaystyle\sum_{n=s}^{N} (n-s)P_n$

Average number of customers or units waiting in line for service.

(10-36) $L = \displaystyle\sum_{n=0}^{s-1} nP_n + L_q + s\left(1 - \sum_{n=0}^{s-1} P_n\right)$

Average number of customers or units in the system.

(10-37) $W_q = \dfrac{L_q}{\lambda(N-L)}$

Average time a customer or unit spends waiting in line for service.

(10-38) $W = \dfrac{L}{\lambda(N-L)}$

Average time a customer or unit spends in the system.

SOLVED PROBLEMS

Solved Problem 10-1

The Maitland Furniture store gets an average of 50 customers per shift. The manager of Maitland wants to calculate whether she should hire one, two, three, or four salespeople. She has determined that average waiting times will be seven minutes with one salesperson, four minutes with two salespeople, three minutes with three salespeople, and two minutes with four salespeople. She has estimated the cost per minute that customers wait at $1. The cost per salesperson per shift (including fringe benefits) is $70.

How many salespeople should be hired?

Solution

The manager's calculations are as follows:

		NUMBER OF SALESPEOPLE			
		1	2	3	4
(a)	Average number of customers per shift	50	50	50	50
(b)	Average waiting time per customer (minutes)	7	4	3	2
(c)	Total waiting time per shift (a × b) (minutes)	350	200	150	100
(d)	Cost per minute of waiting time (estimated)	$1.00	$1.00	$1.00	$1.00
(e)	Value of lost time (c × d) per shift	$ 350	$ 200	$ 150	$ 100
(f)	Salary cost per shift	$ 70	$ 140	$ 210	$ 280
(g)	Total cost per shift	$ 420	$340	$360	$380

Because the minimum total cost per shift relates to two salespeople, the manager's optimum strategy is to hire two salespeople.

Solved Problem 10-2

Marty Martin owns and manages a hot dog and soft drink store near a campus. Although Marty can service 30 customers per hour on the average (μ), he only gets 20 customers per hour (λ). Because Marty could wait on 50% more customers than actually visit his store, it doesn't make sense to him that he should have any waiting lines.

Marty hires you to examine the situation and to determine some characteristics of his queue. After looking into the problem, you make the seven assumptions listed in Section 10.4. What are your findings?

File: 10-7.xls

Solution

For this problem, we use the Exponential Service Times (M/M/s) queuing worksheet in ExcelModules. The arrival rate (λ) is 20 customers per hour, service rate (μ) is 30 customers per hour, and there is one server. We enter these values in cells B9, B10, and B11, respectively, as shown in Screenshot 10.7 on the next page.

The operating characteristics of this queuing system are displayed in cells E9:E14. The probabilities that there are exactly n customers in the system, for $n = 0$ through 20, are shown in cells A19:C40.

Solved Problem 10-3

Refer to Solved Problem 10-2. Marty agreed that these figures seemed to represent his approximate business situation. You are quite surprised at the length of the lines and elicit from him an estimated value of the customer's waiting time (in the queue, not being waited on) at 10 cents per minute. During the 12 hours that he is open he gets $(12 \times 20) = 240$ customers. The average customer is in a queue 4 minutes, so the total customer waiting time is $(240 \times 4 \text{ minutes}) = 960$ minutes. The

SCREENSHOT 10.7   Operating Characteristics for Solved Problem 10-2: M/M/1 Queuing System

	A	B	C	D	E	F
1	Solved Problem 10-2					
2	Queuing Model	M/M/s (Exponential Service Times)		M/M/s with s = 1		
3						
4	1. Both λ and μ must be RATES, and use the same time unit. For example, given a service time such as 10 minutes					
5	per customer, convert it to a service rate such as 6 per hour.					
6	2. The total service rate (rate x servers) must be greater than the arrival rate.					
7						
8	Input Data			Operating Characteristics		
9	Arrival rate (λ)	20		Average server utilization (ρ)	0.6667	0.0667 hours = 4 minutes
10	Service rate (μ)	30		Average number of customers in the queue (Lq)	1.3333	
11	Number of servers (s)	1		Average number of customers in the system (L)	2.0000	
12				Average waiting time in the queue (Wq)	0.0667	
13		1 server		Average time in the system (W)	0.1000	
14				Probability (% of time) system is empty (P0)	0.3333	
15						
16						= 6 minutes
17						
18	Probabilities					
19	Number of Units	Probability	Cumulative Probability			
20	0	0.3333	0.3333			
21	1	0.2222	0.5556			
22	2	0.1481	0.7037			
23	3	0.0988	0.8025			
24	4	0.0658	0.8683			
25	5	0.0439	0.9122			
36	16	0.0005	0.9990			
37	17	0.0003	0.9993			
38	18	0.0002	0.9995			
39	19	0.0002	0.9997			
40	20	0.0001	0.9998			

Hidden rows; see CD-ROM for full file.

value of 960 minutes is ($0.10)(960 minutes) = $96. You tell Marty that not only is 10 cents per minute quite conservative, but he could probably save most of that $96 of customer ill will if he hired another salesclerk. After much haggling, Marty agrees to provide you with all the hot dogs you can eat during a week-long period in exchange for your analysis of the results of having two clerks wait on the customers.

Assuming that Marty hires one additional salesclerk whose service rate equals Marty's rate, complete the analysis.

Solution

File: 10-8.xls

We once again use the Exponential Service Times (M/M/s) queuing worksheet in ExcelModules. The arrival rate (λ) is 20 customers per hour and the service rate (μ) is 30 customers per hour. There are, however, two servers now. We enter these values in cells B9, B10, and B11, respectively, as shown in Screenshot 10.8.

The operating characteristics of this queuing system are displayed in cells E9:E14. The probabilities that there are exactly *n* customers in the system, for *n* = 0 through 20, are shown in cells A19:C40.

You now have 240 customers × 0.0042 hours = 1 hour total customer waiting time per day. The total cost of one hour of customer waiting time is 60 minute × $0.10 per minute = $6.

You are ready to point out to Marty that the hiring of one additional clerk will save $96 − $6 = $90 of customer ill will per 12-hour shift. Marty responds that the hiring should also reduce the number of people who look at the line and leave as well as those who get tired of waiting in line and leave. You tell Marty that you are ready for two chili dogs, extra hot.

SCREENSHOT 10.8   **Operating Characteristics for Solved Problem 10-3: M/M/2 Queuing System**

	A	B	C	D	E	F
1	**Solved Problem 10-3**					
2	Queuing Model	M/M/s (Exponential Service Times)				
3						
4	1. Both λ and μ must be RATES, and use the same time unit. For example, given a service time such as 10 minutes					
5	per customer, convert it to a service rate such as 6 per hour.					
6	2. The total service rate (rate x servers) must be greater than the arrival rate.					
7						
8	Input Data			Operating Characteristics		
9	Arrival rate (λ)	20		Average server utilization (ρ)	0.3333	
10	Service rate (μ)	30		Average number of customers in the queue (Lq)	0.0833	
11	Number of servers (s)	2		Average number of customers in the system (L)	0.7500	
12				Average waiting time in the queue (Wq)	0.0042	
13		*2 servers*		Average time in the system (W)	0.0375	
14				Probability (% of time) system is empty (P₀)	0.5000	
15						
16						
17						
18	Probabilities					
19	Number of Units	Probability	Cumulative Probability			
20	0	0.5000	0.5000			
21	1	0.3333	0.8333			
22	2	0.1111	0.9444			
23	3	0.0370	0.9815			
24	4	0.0123	0.9938			
25	5	0.0041	0.9979			
36	16	0.0000	1.0000			
37	17	0.0000	1.0000			
38	18	0.0000	1.0000			
39	19	0.0000	1.0000			
40	20	0.0000	1.0000			

Wq drops from 0.0667 hours to 0.0042 hours (= 0.25 minutes) with two servers.

Hidden rows; see CD-ROM for full file.

⇒ SELF-TEST

■ Before taking the self-test, refer back to the learning objectives at the beginning of the chapter, the notes in the margins, and the glossary at the end of the chapter.

■ Use the key at the back of the book to correct your answers.

■ Restudy pages that correspond to any questions that you answered incorrectly or material you feel uncertain about.

1. Most systems use the queue discipline known as the first-in, first-out rule.
   a. True   b. False

2. Before using exponential distributions to build queuing models, the decision analyst should determine if the service-time data fit the distribution.
   a. True   b. False

3. In a multiserver single-phase queuing system, the arrival will pass through at least two different service facilities.
   a. True   b. False

4. Which of the following is *not* an assumption in common queuing mathematical models?
   a. Arrivals come from an infinite or very large population.
   b. Arrivals are Poisson-distributed.
   c. Arrivals are treated on a first-in, first-out basis and do not balk or renege.
   d. Service times follow the exponential distribution.
   e. The average arrival rate is faster than the average service rate.

5. Which of the following is *not* a key operating characteristic for a queuing system?
   a. utilization rate
   b. percent idle time
   c. average time spent waiting in the system and in the queue
   d. average number of customers in the system and in the queue
   e. none of the above

6. Three parts of a queuing system are
   a. the inputs, the queue, and the service facility.
   b. the arrival population, the queue, and the service facility.
   c. the arrival population, the waiting line, and the service facility.
   d. all of the above.

7. The utilization factor for a system is defined as
   a. the mean number of people served divided by the mean number of arrivals per time period.
   b. the average time a customer spends waiting in a queue.
   c. the proportion of the time the service facilities are in use.
   d. the percent idle time.
   e. none of the above.

8. If everything else remains constant, including the mean arrival rate and service rate, except that the service time becomes constant instead of exponential,
   a. the average queue length will be halved.
   b. the average waiting time will be doubled.
   c. the average queue length will increase.
   d. none of the above will occur.

9. A queuing system with one server, Poisson arrivals, and arbitrary service times is denoted by the following Kendall's notation:
   a. M/M/1
   b. M/G/1
   c. G/G/1
   d. M/D/1

10. The case in which a customer joins a queue but then leaves before being served is called
    a. balking.
    b. reneging.
    c. first in, first out.
    d. finite queue length.

11. The total cost of a queuing system is typically calculated as the
    a. waiting cost.
    b. service cost.
    c. sum of waiting cost and service cost.
    d. difference of the waiting cost and service cost.

12. In the standard queuing model, we assume that the queue discipline is _____.

13. The service *time* in the basic queuing model is assumed to be _____.

14. When managers find standard queuing formulas inadequate or the mathematics unsolvable, they often resort to _____ to obtain their solutions.

15. In the basic queuing model, the number of arrivals is assumed to be _____.

DISCUSSION QUESTIONS AND PROBLEMS

Discussion Questions

10-1 What is the queuing problem? What are the components in a queuing system?

10-2 What are the assumptions underlying common queuing models?

10-3 Describe the important operating characteristics of a queuing system.

10-4 Why must the service rate be greater than the arrival rate in a single-server queuing system?

10-5 Briefly describe three situations in which the FIFO discipline rule is not applicable in queuing analysis.

10-6 Provide examples of four situations in which there is a limited, or finite, waiting line.

10-7 What are the components of the following systems? Draw and explain the configuration of each.
   (a) Barbershop
   (b) Car wash
   (c) Laundromat
   (d) Small grocery store

10-8 Do doctors' offices generally have random arrival rates for patients? Are service times random? Under what circumstances might service times be constant?

10-9 Do you think the Poisson distribution, which assumes independent arrivals, is a good estimation of arrival rates in the following queuing systems? Defend your position in each case.
   (a) Cafeteria in your school
   (b) Barbershop
   (c) Hardware store
   (d) Dentist's office
   (e) College class
   (f) Movie theatre

Problems

10-10 The Sell-Rite Discount Department Store has approximately 300 customers shopping in its store between 9 A.M. and 5 P.M. on Saturdays. In deciding how many cash registers to keep open each Saturday, Sell-Rite's manager considers two factors: customer waiting time (and the associated waiting cost) and the service costs of employing additional checkout clerks. Checkout clerks are paid an average of $8 per hour. When only one is on duty, the waiting time per customer is about 10 minutes (or $\frac{1}{6}$ of an hour); when two clerks are on duty, the average checkout time is 6 minutes per person; 4 minutes when three clerks are working; and 3 minutes when four clerks are on duty.

Sell-Rite's management has conducted customer satisfaction surveys and has been able to estimate that the store suffers approximately $10 in lost sales and goodwill for every *hour* of customer time spent waiting in checkout lines. Using the information provided, determine the optimal number of clerks to have on duty each Saturday to minimize the store's total expected cost.

10-11 The Rockwell Electronics Corporation retains a service crew to repair machine breakdowns that occur on an average of $\lambda = 3$ per day (approximately Poisson in nature). The crew can service an average of $\mu = 8$ machines per day, with a repair time distribution that resembles the exponential distribution.

(a) What is the utilization rate of this service system?

(b) What is the average downtime for a machine that is broken?

(c) How many machines are waiting to be serviced at any given time?

(d) What is the probability that more than one machine is in the system? What is the probability that more than two are broken and waiting to be repaired or being serviced? More than three? More than four?

10-12 From historical data, Harry's Car Wash estimates that dirty cars arrive at the rate of 10 per hour all day Saturday. With a crew working the wash line, Harry figures that cars can be cleaned at the rate of one every five minutes. One car at a time is cleaned in this example of a single-server waiting line.

Assuming Poisson arrivals and exponential service times, find the

(a) average number of cars in line.

(b) average time a car waits before it is washed.

(c) average time a car spends in the service system.

(d) utilization rate of the car wash.

(e) probability that no cars are in the system.

10-13 Mary Manley manages a large Toronto movie theatre complex called Cinema I, II, III, and IV. Each of the four auditoriums plays a different film; the schedule is set so that starting times are staggered to avoid the large crowds that would occur if all four movies started at the same time. The theatre has a single ticket booth and a cashier who can maintain an average service rate of 280 movie patrons per hour. Service times are assumed to follow an exponential distribution. Arrivals on a typically active day are Poisson-distributed and average 210 per hour.

To determine the efficiency of the current ticket operation, Mary wishes to examine several queue operating characteristics.

(a) Find the average number of moviegoers waiting in line to purchase a ticket.

(b) What percentage of the time is the cashier busy?

(c) What is the average time that a customer spends in the system?

(d) What is the average time spent waiting in line to get to the ticket window?

(e) What is the probability that there are more than two people in the system? More than three people? More than four?

10-14 A computer processes jobs on a first-come, first-served basis in a time-sharing environment. The jobs have Poisson arrival rates with an average of six minutes between arrivals. The objective in processing these jobs is that they spend no more than eight minutes on average in the system. How fast does the computer have to process jobs on average to meet this objective?

10-15 A university cafeteria line in the student centre is a self-serve facility in which students select the food items they want and then form a single line to pay the cashier. Students arrive at a rate of about four per minute according to a Poisson distribution. The single cashier ringing up

sales takes about 12 seconds per customer, following an exponential distribution.

(a) What is the probability that there are more than two students in the system? More than three students? More than four?

(b) What is the probability that the system is empty?

(c) How long will the average student have to wait before reaching the cashier?

(d) What is the expected number of students in the queue?

(e) What is the average number in the system?

(f) If a second cashier is added (who works at the same pace), how will the operating characteristics computed in parts (b), (c), (d), and (e) change? Assume that customers wait in a single line and go to the first available cashier.

10-16 The wheat harvesting season in the Canadian prairies is short, and most farmers deliver their truckloads of wheat to a giant central storage bin within a two-week span. Because of this, wheat-filled trucks waiting to unload and return to the fields have been known to back up for a block at the receiving bin. The central bin is owned cooperatively, and it is to every farmer's benefit to make the unloading/storage process as efficient as possible. The cost of grain deterioration caused by unloading delays and the cost of truck rental and idle driver time are significant concerns to the cooperative members. Although farmers have difficulty quantifying crop damage, it is easy to assign a waiting and unloading cost for truck and driver of $18 per hour. The storage bin is open and operated 16 hours per day, 7 days per week, during the harvest season and is capable of unloading 35 trucks per hour according to an exponential distribution. Full trucks arrive all day long (during the hours the bin is open) at a rate of about 30 per hour, following a Poisson pattern.

To help the cooperative get a handle on the problem of lost time while trucks are waiting in line or unloading at the bin, find the

(a) average number of trucks in the unloading system.

(b) average time per truck in the system.

(c) utilization rate for the bin area.

(d) probability that there are more than three trucks in the system at any given time.

(e) total daily cost to the farmers of having their trucks tied up in the unloading process.

(f) The cooperative, as mentioned, uses the storage bin only two weeks per year. Farmers estimate that enlarging the bin would cut unloading costs by 50% next year. It will cost $9000 to do so during the off-season. Would it be worth the cooperative's while to enlarge the storage area?

10-17 Ashley's Department Store in Regina maintains a successful catalogue sales department in which a clerk takes orders by telephone. If the clerk is occupied on one line, incoming phone calls to the catalogue department are answered automatically by a recording machine and asked to wait. As soon as the clerk is free, the party that has waited the longest is transferred and answered first. Calls come in at a rate of about 12 per hour. The clerk is capable of taking an order in an average of four minutes. Calls tend to follow a Poisson distribution, and service times tend to be exponential. The clerk is paid $10 per hour, but because of lost goodwill and sales, Ashley's loses about $50 per hour of customer time spent waiting for the clerk to take an order.

(a) What is the average time that catalogue customers must wait before their calls are transferred to the order clerk?

(b) What is the average number of callers waiting to place an order?

(c) Ashley is considering adding a second clerk to take calls. The store would pay that person the same $10 per hour. Should it hire another clerk? Explain.

10-18 Sal's Barbershop is a popular haircutting and styling salon near the campus of the University of New Brunswick. Four barbers work full-time and spend an average of 15 minutes on each customer. Customers arrive all day long at an average rate of 12 per hour. When they enter, they take a number to wait for the first available barber. Arrivals tend to follow the Poisson distribution, and service times are exponentially distributed.

(a) What is the probability that the shop is empty?

(b) What is the average number of customers in the barbershop?

(c) What is the average time spent in the shop?

(d) What is the average time that a customer spends waiting to be called to the barber chair?

(e) What is the average number waiting to be served?

(f) What is the shop's utilization factor?

(g) Sal's is thinking of adding a fifth barber. How will this affect the utilization rate?

10-19 Sal (see Problem 10-18) is considering changing the queuing characteristics of his shop. Instead of selecting a number for the first available barber, a customer will be able to select which barber he or she prefers upon arrival. Assuming that this selection does not change while the customer is waiting for his or her barber to become available and that the requests for each of the four barbers are evenly distributed, answer the following:

(a) What is the average number of customers in the barber shop?

(b) What is the average time spent in the shop?

(c) What is the average time a customer spends waiting to be called to a chair?

(d) What is the average number of customers waiting to be served?

(e) Explain why the results from Problems 10-18 and 10-19 differ.

10-20 The medical director of an urgent-care clinic faces a problem of providing treatment for patients who arrive at different rates during the day. There are four doctors available to treat patients when needed. If not needed, they can be assigned to other responsibilities (e.g., lab tests, reports, X-ray diagnoses) or else rescheduled to work at other hours.

It is important to provide quick and responsive treatment, and the medical director feels that, on average, patients should not have to sit in the waiting area for more than five minutes before being seen by a doctor. Patients are treated on a first-come, first-served basis and see the first available doctor after waiting in the queue. The arrival pattern for a typical day is as follows:

TIME	ARRIVAL RATE (PATIENTS/HOUR)
9 A.M.–3 P.M.	6
3 P.M.–8 P.M.	4
8 P.M.–midnight	12

These arrivals follow a Poisson distribution, and treatment times, 12 minutes on the average, follow the exponential pattern.

How many doctors should be on duty during each period to maintain the level of patient care expected?

10-21 George Foster is responsible for the warehouse operation for a local discount department store chain. The warehouse has only one unloading dock that is currently operated by a single three-person crew. Trucks arrive according to the Poisson distribution, with an average rate of five per hour. The average time for one of the crews to unload a truck is nine minutes, which tends to follow the exponential distribution. George has estimated the cost of operating a truck at $40 per hour. George pays each person of the unloading crew $11 per hour. The unloading dock operates eight hours each day. George is considering the economic feasibility of adding a second three-person crew to the unloading operation. George estimates that adding this second crew will reduce the average unloading time to six minutes per truck. This will still be an M/M/1 system because only one truck can be unloaded at any given time. Should George add the second crew?

10-22 Juhn and Sons Wholesale Fruit Distributors employ one worker whose job it is to load fruit on outgoing company trucks. Trucks arrive at the loading gate at an average of 24 per day, or three per hour, according to a Poisson distribution. The worker loads them at a rate of four per hour, following approximately the exponential distribution in service times.

Determine the operating characteristics of this loading gate problem. What is the probability that there will be more than three trucks either being loaded or waiting? Discuss the result of your queuing model computation.

10-23 Juhn believes that adding a second fruit loader will substantially improve the firm's efficiency. He estimates that a two-person crew, still acting like a single-server system at the loading gates, will double the loading rate from four trucks per hour to eight trucks per hour. Analyze the effect on the queue of such a change and compare the results with those found in Problem 10-22.

10-24 Truck drivers working for Juhn and Sons (see Problems 10-22 and 10-23) are paid a salary of $20 per hour on average. Fruit loaders receive about $12 per hour. Truck drivers waiting in the queue or at the loading gate are drawing a salary but are productively idle and unable to generate revenue during that time. What would be the *hourly* cost savings to the firm associated with employing two loaders instead of one?

10-25 Juhn and Sons Wholesale Fruit Distributors (of Problem 10-22) are considering building a second platform or gate to speed the process of loading their fruit trucks. This, they think, will be even more efficient than simply hiring another loader to help out the first platform (as in Problem 10-23).

Assume that the single workers at each platform will be able to load four trucks per hour each and that trucks will continue to arrive at the rate of three per hour. Then apply the preceding equations to find the waiting line's new operating conditions. Is this new approach more cost effective than the other two considered?

10-26 Recreational boats arrive at a single gasoline pump located at the dock at Trident Marina at an average rate of 10 per hour on Saturday mornings. The fill-up time for a boat is normally distributed, with an average of five minutes and a standard deviation of 1.5 minutes. Assume that the arrival rate follows the Poisson distribution.

   (a) What is the probability that the pump is vacant?
   (b) On average, how long does a boat wait before the pump is available?
   (c) How many boats, on average, are waiting for the pump?

10-27 Canadian Brew is a chain of drive-through coffee outlets where customers arrive, on average, every five minutes. Management has a goal that customers will be able to complete their transaction, on average, in six minutes with a single server. Assume that this system can be described as an M/M/1 configuration. What is the average service time that is necessary to meet this goal?

10-28 A chemical plant stores spare parts for maintenance in a large warehouse. Throughout the working day, maintenance personnel go to the warehouse to pick up supplies needed for their jobs. The warehouse receives a request for supplies, on average, every two minutes. The average request requires 1.7 minutes to fill. Maintenance employees are paid $20 per hour, and warehouse employees are paid $12 per hour. The warehouse is open eight hours each day. Assuming that this system follows the M/M/s requirements, what is the optimal number of warehouse employees to hire?

10-29 A toll booth for a bridge crossing Halifax Harbour in Nova Scotia experiences an average arrival rate of nine cars per minute and follows the Poisson distribution. The average car requires 12 seconds for the toll collection, and this process follows the exponential distribution. The goal of the bridge authority is to schedule enough collection lanes so that the average delay for each car is less than 20 seconds. How many collection lanes are necessary?

10-30 Customers arrive at an automated coffee vending machine at a rate of four per minute, following a Poisson distribution. The coffee machine dispenses a cup of coffee at a constant rate of 10 seconds.

   (a) What is the average number of people waiting in line?
   (b) What is the average number in the system?
   (c) How long does the average person wait in line before receiving service?

10-31 Customers arrive at Rao's Insurance Agency at an average rate of one per hour. Arrivals can be assumed to follow the Poisson distribution. Anand Rao, the insurance agent, estimates that he spends an average of 30 minutes with each customer. The standard deviation of service time is 15 minutes, and the service time distribution is arbitrary. Calculate the operating characteristics of the queuing system at Rao's agency. What is the probability that an arriving customer will have to wait for service?

10-32 Refer again to Rao's agency in Problem 10-31. If Rao wants to ensure that his customers wait an average of around 10 minutes, what should be his mean service time? Assume the standard deviation of service time remains at 15 minutes.

10-33 Chuck's convenience store has only one gas pump. Cars pull up to the pump at the rate of one car every eight minutes. Depending on the speed at which the customer works, the pumping time varies. Chuck estimates that the pump is occupied for an average of five minutes, with a standard deviation of one minute. Calculate Chuck's operating characteristics. Comment on the values obtained. What, if anything, would you recommend Chuck change?

10-34 Quebec Online Inc. operates several internet kiosks in Montreal. Customers can access the web at these kiosks, paying $2 for 30 minutes or a fraction thereof. The kiosks are typically open for 10 hours each day and are always full.

   Due to the rough usage these PCs receive, they break down frequently. Quebec Online has a central repair facility to fix these PCs. PCs arrive at the facility at an average rate of 0.9 per day. Repair times take an average of one day, with a standard deviation of 0.5 day.

   Calculate the operating characteristics of this queuing system. How much is it worth to Quebec Online to increase the average service rate to 1.25 PCs per day?

10-35 One mechanic services five drilling machines for a steel plate manufacturer. Machines break down an average of once every six working days, and breakdowns tend to follow a Poisson distribution. The mechanic can handle an average of one repair job per day. Repairs follow an exponential distribution.

   (a) How many machines are waiting for service, on average?
   (b) How many are currently being served?
   (c) How many drills are in running order, on average?
   (d) What is the average waiting time in the queue?
   (e) What is the average wait in the system?

10-36 A technician monitors a group of five computers that run an automated manufacturing facility. It takes an average of 15 minutes (exponentially distributed) to adjust a computer that develops a problem. The computers run for an average of 85 minutes (Poisson-distributed) without requiring adjustments. What is the

   (a) average number of computers waiting for adjustment?
   (b) average number of computers not in working order?
   (c) probability the system is empty?
   (d) average time in the queue?
   (e) average time in the system?

10-37 The Johnson Manufacturing Company operates six identical machines that are serviced by a single technician when they break down. Breakdowns occur according to the Poisson distribution and average 0.03 breakdowns per machine operating hour. Average repair time for a machine is five hours and follows the exponential distribution.

   (a) What percentage of the technician's time is spent repairing machines?
   (b) On average, how long is a machine out of service because of a breakdown?

(c) On average, how many machines are out of service?

(d) Johnson wants to investigate the economic feasibility of adding a second technician. Each technician costs the company $18 per hour. Each hour of machine downtime costs $120. Should a second technician be added?

10-38 A subway station has six turnstiles, each of which can be controlled by the station manager to be used for either entrance or exit control—but never for both. The manager must decide at different times of the day just how many turnstiles to use for entering passengers and how many to be set up to allow exiting passengers.

Passengers enter the station at a rate of about 84 per minute between the hours of 7 and 9 A.M. Passengers exiting trains at the stop reach the exit turnstile area at a rate of about 48 per minute during the same morning rush hours. Each turnstile can allow an average of 30 passengers per minute to enter or exit. Arrival and service times have been thought to follow Poisson and exponential distributions, respectively. Assume riders form a common queue at both entry and exit turnstile areas and proceed to the first empty turnstile.

The station manager does not want the average passenger at his station to have to wait in a turnstile line for more than six seconds, nor does he want more than eight people in any queue at any average time.

(a) How many turnstiles should be opened in each direction every morning?

(b) Discuss the assumptions underlying the solution of this problem, using queuing theory.

10-39 The help desk for a small business college is staffed by a single employee who handles requests on a first-come, first-served basis. Requests for help have been observed at an average rate of five per hour and follow the Poisson distribution. The times to service the requests have an average of seven minutes, with a standard deviation of two and a half minutes, and follow the normal probability distribution.

(a) What is the probability that a student will have to wait for service?

(b) On average, how many students will be waiting for service?

(c) How long is the average wait for service?

10-40 County General Hospital's cardiac care unit (CCU) has seven beds, which are virtually always occupied by patients who have just undergone heart surgery. Two registered nurses are on duty at the CCU in each of the three eight-hour shifts. On average, a patient requires a nurse's attention every 66 minutes. The arrival rate follows a Poisson distribution. A nurse will spend an average of 19 minutes (exponentially distributed) assisting a patient and updating medical records regarding the care provided.

(a) What percentage of the nurses' time is spent responding to these requests?

(b) What is the average time a patient spends waiting for one of the nurses to arrive at bedside?

(c) What is the average number of patients waiting for a nurse to arrive?

(d) What is the probability that a patient will not have to wait for a nurse to arrive?

⇒ CASE STUDY 10.1

Winnipeg Ambulance Problem

Winnipeg has 20 ambulances available for emergency service. The busiest part of the day is between 4:00 P.M. and 12:00 A.M. During this period there is an average of 36 calls per hour. The average seems fairly constant during this period; however the calls are completely random and there can be a great deal of variability in the number of calls in a given hour.

It takes an average of 20 minutes for an ambulance to respond to an emergency call and then be available for a future call. However, the actual time to respond and then be available for a future call can vary considerably. Sometimes it takes two minutes, other times it can take as much as 60 minutes.

If all ambulances are busy, Emergency Response must dispatch a different kind of vehicle to respond to a medical emergency (police car, fire truck, taxi, transit bus). Of course, this is considered undesirable. Approximately 1% of all calls that require ambulances have a nonambulance response.

Because of budget cuts, there is a proposal to reduce the number of available ambulances to 18.

Alderman Billy Budgetcuts supports this proposal. Alderman Budgetcuts has stated that reducing the number of ambulances by 10% (from 20 to 18) will mean the number of nonambulance responses will go up by 10% from 1% to 1.1%, which is insignificant. Besides, Alderman Budgetcuts has said, "An average of 20 minutes a response means an ambulance can handle three emergencies an hour and 18 ambulances can handle 54 emergencies per hour. Since we have only 36 calls per hour, there should never be a nonambulance response. The reason for these nonambulance responses is the laziness and inefficiency of the unionized ambulance employees."

Alderman Barry Bleedingheart is opposed to this proposal. He argues that reducing the number of ambulances by 10% will reduce the percentage of ambulance responses by 10% (i.e., from 99% to 89%). That is unacceptable. Since poor people tend to have more physical problems than the middle class, Alderman Bleedingheart believes this is part of a right-wing attack on the poor of Winnipeg.

DISCUSSION QUESTION

Whose analysis is correct?

Source: Professor E. S. Rosenbloom, I. H. Asper School of Business, University of Manitoba.

⟾ CASE STUDY 10.2

Winter Park Hotel

Donna Papakis, manager of the Winter Park Hotel, a popular hotel in Toronto's bustling business area, is considering how to restructure the front desk to reach an optimum level of staff efficiency and guest service. At present, the hotel has five clerks on duty, each with a separate waiting line, during the peak check-in time of 3 P.M. to 5 P.M. Observation of arrivals during this time shows that an average of 90 guests arrive each hour (although there is no upward limit on the number that could arrive at any given time). It takes an average of three minutes for the front-desk clerk to register each guest.

Ms. Papakis is considering three plans for improving guest service by reducing the length of time guests spend waiting in line. The first proposal would designate one employee as a quick-service clerk for guests registering under corporate accounts, a market segment that fills about 30% of all occupied rooms. Because corporate guests are preregistered, their registration takes just two minutes. With these guests separated from the rest of the clientele, the average time for registering a typical guest would climb to 3.4 minutes. Under plan 1, noncorporate guests would choose any of the remaining four lines.

The second plan is to implement a single-line system. All guests could form a single waiting line to be served by whichever of five clerks became available. This option would require sufficient lobby space for what could be a substantial queue.

The third proposal is to install an automatic machine for check-ins. Customers with reservations would insert a credit card for identification, and the machine would find the customer's reservation and print out a reservation slip. The customer could then proceed directly to his or her assigned room without having to see one of the clerks. The automated machine would provide approximately the same service rate as would a clerk. Given that initial use of this technology might be minimal, Donna Papakis estimated that 20% of customers, primarily frequent guests, would be willing to use the machine. Ms. Papakis would set up a single queue for customers who prefer human check-in clerks. This would be served by the five clerks, although Papakis is hopeful that the machine will allow a reduction to four.

DISCUSSION QUESTIONS

1. Determine the average amount of time that a guest spends checking in. How would this change under each of the stated options?
2. Which option do you recommend?

BIBLIOGRAPHY

Cooper, R. B. *Introduction to Queuing Theory*, 2/e. New York: Elsevier–North Holland, 1980.

Grassmann, Winfried, K. "Finding the Right Number of Servers in Real-World Queuing Systems," *Interfaces* 18, 2 (March–April 1988): 94–104.

Haksever, C., B. Render, and R. Russell. *Service Management and Operations*, 2/e. Upper Saddle River, NJ: Prentice Hall, 2000.

Ho, C., and H. Lau. "Minimizing Total Cost in Scheduling Outpatient Appointments," *Management Science* 38, 12 (December 1992): 17–50.

Kaplan, Edward H. "A Public Housing Queue with Reneging and Task-Specific Servers," *Decision Sciences* 19 (1988): 383–391.

Katz, K., B. Larson, and R. Larson. "Prescription for the Waiting-in-Line Blues," *Sloan Management Review* (Winter 1991): 44–53.

Mandelbaum, A., and M. I. Reiman. "On Pooling Queuing Networks," *Management Science* 44, 7 (July 1998): 971–981.

Prabhu, N. U. *Foundations of Queuing Theory*. Klewer Academic Publishers, 1997.

Quinn, Phil, Bruce Andrews, and Henry Parsons. "Allocating Telecommunications Resources at L.L. Bean, Inc.," *Interfaces* 21, 1 (January–February 1991): 75–91.

Solomon, S. *Simulation of Waiting Lines*. Upper Saddle River, NJ: Prentice Hall, 1983.

Swersey, Arthur J. et al. "Improving Fire Department Productivity," *Interfaces* 23, 1 (January–February 1993): 109–129.

Whitt, W. "Predicting Queuing Delays," *Management Science* 45, 6 (June 1999): 870–888.

Worthington, D. J. "Queuing Models for Hospital Waiting Lists," *Journal of the Operational Research Society* 38, 5 (May 1987): 413–422.

CHAPTER 11

Simulation Modeling

LEARNING OBJECTIVES

After completing this chapter, students will be able to

1. Understand the basic steps of conducting a simulation.
2. Explain the advantages and disadvantages of simulation.
3. Tackle a wide variety of problems by simulation.
4. Set up and solve simulation models using Excel's standard functions.
5. Use the Oracle Crystal Ball add-in for Excel to solve simulation models.
6. Explain other types of simulation models.

CHAPTER OUTLINE

11.1 Introduction

11.2 Monte Carlo Simulation

11.3 Role of Computers in Simulation

11.4 Simulation Model to Compute Expected Profit

11.5 Simulation Model of an Inventory Problem

11.6 Simulation Model of a Queuing Problem

11.7 Simulation Model of a Revenue Management Problem

11.8 Simulation Model of an Inventory Problem Using Oracle Crystal Ball

11.9 Simulation Model of a Revenue Management Problem Using Oracle Crystal Ball

11.10 Other Types of Simulation Models

Summary • Glossary • Solved Problems • Self-Test • Discussion Questions and Problems • Case Study: OntAir Airlines • Case Study: Smyth Transport Company • Case Study: Muskoka Land Development • Bibliography

Modeling Pollution in Lake Ontario

Water quality management in the rivers and lakes of Canada is a matter of concern for government agencies and, indeed, for every citizen. Levels of pollutants in Lake Ontario and its aquatic life have been studied and modeled using Monte Carlo simulation techniques. A model has been developed for estimating concentrations of a major class of pollutants (hydrophobic organic chemicals or HOCs) in fish and aquatic plants based on the concentrations of these compounds in the water. For example, in order to monitor pollution levels in fish, it is necessary to be able to estimate the concentration in the water of chemicals that can be absorbed via the gills.

A model for predicting the bioaccumulation of HOCs in the "aquatic food-webs" of Lake Ontario has been developed, and model confidence is determined by Monte Carlo simulation. The ability to forecast the quantity of chemical pollutants in the lake water, as well as the mechanism by which pollutants enter the aquatic food chain, is a valuable tool for the management of contamination on the level of an ecosystem.

Source: Layne Kennedy/Corbis/Magma Photo

Simulation models have also been used to classify specific diseases of fish (infectious pancreatic necrosis virus, or IPNV, and *Aeromonas salmonicida* or *A. salmonicida*) and their prevalence in Ontario fish hatcheries. Monte Carlo techniques have been used to estimate the probability of correctly classifying the status (presence or absence) of IPNV and *A. salmonicida* in commercial fish farms and natural habitats in Ontario. This is significant since false negatives (i.e., believing that a site is free of disease when in fact it is infected) can lead to shipping contaminated fish to a site previously free of the pathogen, while a false positive may result in unnecessarily destroying the fish in a healthy farm.

F. Gobas. "A model for predicting the bioaccumulation of hydrophobic organic chemicals in aquatic food-webs: Application to Lake Ontario," *Ecological Modelling* 69 (1993): 1–17; N. N. Bruneau et al., "Hatchery-level predictive values for infectious pancreatic necrosis virus and *Aeromonas salmonicida* in Ontario, Canada," *Preventive Veterinary Medicine 48* (2001): 129–141.

11.1 INTRODUCTION

We are all aware to some extent of the importance of simulation models in our world. Boeing Corporation and Airbus Industries, for example, commonly build **simulation** models of their proposed jet aircraft and then test the aerodynamic properties of the models. Your local emergency measures organization may carry out rescue and evacuation practices as it simulates the natural disaster conditions of a hurricane or tornado. Armed forces simulate enemy attacks and defence strategies in war games played on a computer. Business students take courses that use management games to simulate realistic competitive business situations. And thousands of organizations such as Nortel Networks develop simulation models to assist in making decisions involving their supply chain, inventory control, maintenance scheduling, plant layout, investments, and sales forecasting. Simulation is one of the most widely used decision modeling tools. Various surveys of the largest U.S. corporations reveal that more than half use simulation in corporate planning.

Simulation sounds as if it may be the solution to all management problems. This is, unfortunately, by no means true. Yet we think you may find it one of the most flexible and fascinating of the decision modeling techniques in your studies. Let's begin our discussion of simulation with a simple definition.

What Is Simulation?

Simulate means to duplicate the features of a real system. The idea is to imitate a real-world situation with a mathematical model that does not affect operations.

To *simulate* is to try to duplicate the features, appearance, and characteristics of a real system. In this chapter we show how to simulate a business or management system by building a *mathematical model* that comes as close as possible to representing the reality of the system. We won't build any *physical* models, as might be used in airplane wind tunnel simulation tests. But just as physical model airplanes are tested and modified under experimental conditions, our mathematical models need to be experimented with to estimate the effects of various actions. The idea behind simulation is to imitate a real-world situation mathematically, then to study its properties and operating characteristics, and finally, to draw conclusions and make action decisions based on the results of the simulation. In this way, the real-life system is not touched until the advantages and disadvantages of what may be a major policy decision are first measured on the system's model.

To use simulation, a manager should (1) define a problem, (2) introduce the variables associated with the problem, (3) construct a numerical model, (4) set up possible courses of action for testing, (5) run the experiment, (6) consider the results (possibly deciding to modify the model or change data inputs), and (7) decide what course of action to take. These steps are illustrated in Figure 11.1.

The problems tackled by simulation can range from very simple to extremely complex, from bank teller lines to an analysis of the Canadian economy. Although very small simulations can be conducted by hand, effective use of this technique requires some automated means of calculation, namely, a computer. Even large-scale models, simulating perhaps years of business decisions, can be handled in a reasonable amount of time by computer. Though simulation is one of the oldest decision modeling tools (see the History box), it was not until the introduction of computers in the mid-1940s and early 1950s that it became a practical means of solving management and military problems.

We begin this chapter with a presentation of the advantages and disadvantages of simulation. We then explain the Monte Carlo method and present several sample simulations. We also briefly discuss other simulation models.

For each simulation model, we show how Excel can be used to set up and solve the problem. We discuss two approaches. In the first approach, we show how Excel's standard built-in functions can be used for simulation. This approach is adequate for many applications and is especially useful if you are operating in a computer environment where the

FIGURE 11.1

Process of Simulation

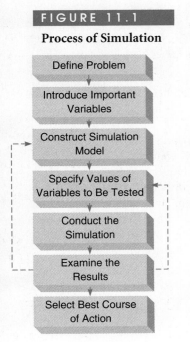

HISTORY   Simulation

The history of simulation goes back 5000 years to Chinese war games, called *weich'i*, and continues through 1780, when the Prussians used the games to help train their army. Since then, all major military powers have used war games to test military strategies under simulated environments.

From military or operational gaming, a new concept, *Monte Carlo simulation*, was developed as a decision modeling technique by the great mathematician John von Neumann during World War II. Working with neutrons at the Los Alamos Scientific Laboratory, von Neumann used simulation to solve physics problems that were too complex or expensive to analyze by hand or by physical model. The random nature

of the neutrons suggested the use of a roulette wheel in dealing with probabilities. Because of the gaming nature, von Neumann called it the Monte Carlo model of studying laws of chance.

With the advent and common use of business computers in the 1950s, simulation grew as a management tool. Specialized computer languages were developed in the 1960s (GPSS and SIMSCRIPT) to handle large-scale problems more effectively. In the 1980s, prewritten simulation programs to handle situations ranging from queuing to inventory were developed. They have such names as ProModel, Xcell, SLAM, Witness, and MAP/1.

installation of additional software is not preferred or possible. There are, however, several add-ins available that make setting up and solving simulation models on Excel even easier. Therefore, in our second approach, we illustrate the use of one of the more powerful Excel add-ins for simulation, Oracle Crystal Ball. Access to the student version of this package (valid for 140 days from date of installation) is included on your CD-ROM.

Advantages and Disadvantages of Simulation

Simulation is a tool that has become widely accepted by managers for several reasons:

The advantages of simulation make it one of the most widely used decision modeling techniques in the corporate world.

1. It is relatively straightforward and flexible. Properly implemented, a simulation model can be made flexible enough to easily accommodate several changes to the problem scenario.

2. It can be used to analyze large and complex real-world situations that cannot be solved by conventional decision models. For example, it may not be possible to build and solve a purely mathematical model of a city government system that incorporates important economic, social, environmental, and political factors. But simulation has been used successfully to model urban systems, hospitals, educational systems, national and state economies, and even world food systems.

3. Simulation allows what-if types of questions. With a simulation model, a manager can try out several policy decisions within a matter of minutes.

4. Simulations do not interfere with the real-world system. It may be too disruptive, for example, to experiment with new policies or ideas in a hospital, school, or manufacturing plant. With simulation, experiments are done with the model, not on the system itself.

5. Simulation allows us to study the interactive effects of individual components or variables to determine which ones are important. In any given problem scenario, not all inputs are equally important. We can use simulation to selectively vary each input (or combination of inputs) to identify the ones that most affect the results.

6. "Time compression" is possible with simulation. The effect of ordering, advertising, or other policies over many months or years can be obtained by a computer simulation model in a short time.

7. Simulation allows for the inclusion of real-world complications that most decision models cannot permit. For example, some of the queuing models discussed in Chapter 10 require exponential or Poisson distributions; the PERT analysis covered

in Chapter 8 requires normal distributions. But simulation can use any probability distribution that the user defines (see Appendix B for more information on probability distributions).

The main disadvantages of simulation are as follows:

1. Good simulation models can be very expensive. It is often a long, complicated process to develop a model. A corporate planning model, for example, can take months or even years to develop.

2. Simulation does not generate optimal solutions to problems, as do other decision modeling techniques, such as linear programming or integer programming. It is a trial-and-error approach that can produce different solutions in repeated runs.

3. Managers must generate all of the conditions and constraints for solutions that they want to examine. The simulation model does not produce answers by itself.

4. Each simulation model is unique. Its solutions and inferences are not usually transferable to other problems.

11.2   MONTE CARLO SIMULATION

The Monte Carlo method can be used with variables that are probabilistic.

When a system contains elements that exhibit chance in their behaviour, the *Monte Carlo* method of simulation may be applied. The basis of **Monte Carlo simulation** is experimentation on the chance (or *probabilistic*) elements through random sampling. The technique breaks down into the following simple steps. This section examines each of these steps in turn.

Steps of Monte Carlo Simulation

1. Set up a probability distribution for each variable in the model that is subject to chance.
2. Using random numbers, simulate values from the probability distribution for each variable in Step 1.
3. Repeat the process for a series of *replications* or *trials*.

Step 1. Establish a Probability Distribution for Each Variable

Variables we may want to simulate abound in business problems because very little in life is certain.

The basic idea in Monte Carlo simulation is to generate values for the variables in the model being studied. There are many variables in real-world systems that are probabilistic in nature and that we might want to simulate. A few of these variables are as follows:

■ Product demand
■ Lead time for orders to arrive
■ Time between machine breakdowns
■ Time between arrivals at a service facility
■ Service time
■ Time to complete a project activity
■ Number of employees absent from work each day
■ Stock market performance

MODELING IN THE REAL WORLD
Air Canada Check-in Simulation

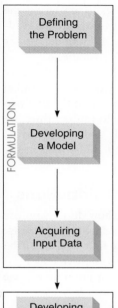

FORMULATION

- Defining the Problem
- Developing a Model
- Acquiring Input Data

SOLUTION

- Developing a Solution
- Testing the Solution

INTERPRETATION

- Analyzing the Results and Conducting a Sensitivity Analysis
- Implementing the Results

Air Canada is the 10th largest commercial airline in the world. It has grown to provide its clients with 150 flight destinations, offering 690 scheduled flights daily and transporting 23 million scheduled and charter customers annually. Scheduling check-in agents is an important factor in maximizing revenue and reducing customer waiting times.

After the events of September 11, 2001, new check-in procedures and increased security measures resulted in increased queue length and waiting times for passengers.

A decision support system (DSS) was developed from a descriptive resource simulation of Air Canada's check-in process. The simulation software package Arena 3.0 (Rockwell Software, Sewickley, PA) was used for the simulation. The model was to be prescriptive and would need to reflect significant changes as a result of 9-11. It was intended to generate a proposed staff roster that would help Air Canada meet its internal standards for any given flight schedule.

Extensive data collection was needed as Air Canada did not have the required historical data. Passenger arrivals on Fridays at the Calgary International Airport were investigated. Specifically, data needed to be collected with respect to arrival rates and services times. Friday was selected for observation because it is typically the busiest day of the week, encompasses a variety of passenger types (business and pleasure) and has a large number of Air Canada departures to multiple locations.

A simulation created in Arena 3.0 modeled Air Canada's typical Friday check-in process at Calgary International Airport. Since the passenger arrival pattern was dependent on flight schedule, destination, and time before departure, a simulation model was preferred over an analytical queuing theory model, as it gave more flexibility in modeling the probability distribution of arrivals.

Recommendations were made in the areas of staff scheduling, improved signage, and process improvements to alleviate service time delays. Air Canada continues to monitor the system and further studies are being considered to collect a larger data set and to expand the scope of the project.

What-if analysis was employed to see what kind of impact seemingly minor changes to the flight schedule had on waiting times. Moving a flight 30 minutes earlier or later, changing the load factors or even changing the plane size could materially affect waiting times. Air Canada could use this model to make changes to flight schedules and hence reduce waiting times, especially during seasonal holidays when waiting times are generally the longest.

The model assists the Air Canada management team in determining the level of staff needed at the check-in counters. Decisions on hiring, layoffs, and work hours are affected, and passengers are affected since the staffing level determines how long they wait in line. Both Air Canada and the project team considered the study a success. Work is already underway to build upon this DSS to provide solutions for other areas within Air Canada.

Source: Kar-Li Chong, Manvir Grewal, Judy Loo, and Sherry L Oh. "A Simulation-Enabled DSS for Allocating Check-In Agents," *INFOR* 41, 3 (August 2003): 259.

To establish a probability distribution for a variable, we often assume that historical behaviour is a good indicator of future outcomes.

There are several ways in which we can establish a *probability distribution* for a given variable. One common approach is to examine the historical outcomes of that variable. Then, we can compute the probability of each possible outcome of the variable by dividing the frequency of each observation by the total number of observations. Alternatively, we can use statistical goodness-of-fit tests to identify a commonly known probability distribution (e.g., normal, uniform, exponential, Poisson, binomial) that best characterizes the behaviour of the variable. In practice, there are hundreds of probability distributions available to characterize the behaviour of the various variables in a simulation model. In our study here, however, we will examine only a few of these probability distributions.

Harry's Auto Shop Example   To illustrate how to establish a probability distribution for a variable, let us consider, for example, the monthly demand for radial tires at Harry's Auto Shop over the past 60 months. The data are shown in the first two columns of Table 11.1. If we assume that past demand rates will hold in the future, we can convert these data to a probability distribution for tire demand. To do so, we divide each demand frequency by the total number of months, 60. This is illustrated in the third column of Table 11.1.

Step 2: Simulate Values from the Probability Distributions

Once we have established the probability distribution for a variable, how do we simulate random values from this distribution? As we shall see shortly, the procedure to do so varies, based on the type of probability distribution. In this section, let us see how we can use the probability distribution identified in Table 11.1 to simulate Harry's tire demand for a *specific* month in the future. Note that in simulating the demand for any given month, we need to ensure the following:

■ The actual monthly demand value is 300, 320, 340, 360, 380, or 400.

■ There is a 5% chance that the monthly demand is 300, 10% chance that it is 320, 20% chance that it is 340, 30% chance that it is 360, 25% chance that it is 380, and 10% chance that it is 400.

Probabilities reflect long-term behavior.

These probability values, however, reflect only the long-term behaviour. That is, if we simulate tire demand for many months (several hundred, or, better yet, several thousand), the demand will be 300 for exactly 5% of the months, 320 for exactly 10% of the months, and so on. Based on our knowledge of probability distributions, we can also use these probability values to compute Harry's expected value (or average) of monthly demand, as follows:

$$\text{Expected monthly demand} = \Sigma_i (i \text{ demand value}) \times (Probability \text{ of } i \text{ demand value})$$

$$= 300 \times 0.05 + 320 \times 0.10 + 340 \times 0.20$$
$$+ 360 \times 0.30 + 380 \times 0.25 + 400 \times 0.10$$

$$= 358 \text{ tires}$$

TABLE 11.1		

Historical Monthly Demand for Radial Tires at Harry's Auto Shop

DEMAND	FREQUENCY	PROBABILITY
300	3	3/60 = 0.05
320	6	6/60 = 0.10
340	12	12/60 = 0.20
360	18	18/60 = 0.30
380	15	15/60 = 0.25
400	6	6/60 = 0.10

Simulated results can differ from analytical results in a short simulation.

In the short term, however, the occurrence of demand may be quite different from these probability values. For example, if we simulate demand for just five months, it is entirely possible (and logical) for the demand to be 320 tires per month for *all* five months. The average demand for these five months would then be 320 tires per month, which is quite different from the expected value of 358 tires per month we just calculated. Hence, what we need is a procedure that will achieve the following objectives:

- Generate, in the *short term*, random demand values that do not exhibit any specific pattern. The expected value need not necessarily equal 358 tires per month.

- Generate, in the *long term*, random demand values that conform exactly to the required probability distribution. The expected value must equal 358 tires per month.

In simulation, we achieve these objectives by using a concept called random numbers.

There are several ways to pick random numbers—using a computer, a table, a roulette wheel, and so on.

Random Numbers   A **random number** is a number that has been selected through a totally random process. For example, assume that we want to generate a series of random numbers from a set consisting of 100 integer valued numbers: 0, 1, 2, . . . , 97, 98, 99. There are several ways to do so. One simple way would be as follows:

1. Mark each of 100 identical balls with a unique number between 0 and 99. Put all the balls in a large bowl and mix thoroughly.

2. Select *one* ball from the bowl. Write down the number.

3. Replace the ball in the bowl and mix again. Go back to step 2.

Instead of balls in a bowl, we could have accomplished this task by using the spin of a roulette wheel with 100 slots, or by using tables of random digits that are commonly available.[1] Also, as we shall see shortly, it turns out that most computer software packages (including Excel) and many handheld calculators have built-in procedures for generating an endless set of random numbers.

Cumulative probabilities are found by summing all the previous probabilities up to the current demand.

Using Random Numbers to Simulate Demand in Harry's Auto Shop   How do we use random numbers to simulate Harry's tire demand? We begin by converting the probability distribution in Table 11.1 to a *cumulative probability* distribution. As shown in Table 11.2, the cumulative probability for each demand value is the sum of the probability of that demand and all demands *less than* that demand value. For example, the cumulative probability for a demand of 340 tires is the sum of the probabilities for 300, 320, or 340 tires. Obviously, the cumulative probability for a demand of 400 tires (the maximum demand) is 1.

TABLE 11.2

Cumulative Probabilities for Radial Tires at Harry's Auto Shop

DEMAND	PROBABILITY	CUMULATIVE PROBABILITY
300	0.05	0.05
320	0.10	0.05 + 0.10 = 0.15
340	0.20	0.15 + 0.20 = 0.35
360	0.30	0.35 + 0.30 = 0.65
380	0.25	0.65 + 0.25 = 0.90
400	0.10	0.90 + 0.10 = 1.00

[1] See, for example, *A Million Random Digits with 100,000 Normal Deviates*. New York: The Free Press, 1955, p. 7.

Random Number Intervals for Radial Tires at Harry's Auto Shop

DEMAND	PROBABILITY	CUMULATIVE PROBABILITY	RANDOM NUMBER INTERVAL
300	0.05	0.05	0 to 4
320	0.10	0.15	5 to 14
340	0.20	0.35	15 to 34
360	0.30	0.65	35 to 64
380	0.25	0.90	65 to 89
400	0.10	1.00	90 to 99

We create a random number interval for each value of the variable. The specific numbers assigned to an interval are not relevant as long as the right proportion of unique numbers is assigned to the interval.

Consider the set of 100 integer-valued numbers ranging from 0 to 99. We now use the cumulative probabilities computed in Table 11.2 to create *random number intervals* by assigning these 100 numbers to represent the different possible demand values. Because there is a 5% probability that demand is 300 tires, we assign 5% of the numbers (i.e., five of the 100 numbers between 0 and 99) to denote this demand value. For example, we could assign the first five numbers possible (i.e., 0, 1, 2, 3, and 4) to denote a demand of 300 tires. Every time the random number drawn is one of these five numbers, the implication is that the simulated demand that month is 300 tires. Likewise, because there is a 10% chance that demand is 320 tires, we could let the next 10 numbers (i.e., 5 to 14) represent that demand—and so on for the other demand values. The complete random number intervals for the Harry's Auto Shop problem are shown in Table 11.3 above. It is important to note that the specific random numbers assigned to denote a demand value are not relevant, as long as the assignment is unique and includes the right proportion of numbers. That is, for example, we can use any set of five random numbers between 0 and 99 to denote a demand value of 300 tires, as long as these numbers are not assigned to denote any other demand level.

We simulate values by comparing the random numbers against the random number intervals.

To simulate demand using the random number intervals, we need to generate random numbers between 0 and 99. Suppose we use a computer for this purpose (we will see how to do so shortly). Assume that the first random number generated is 52. Because this is between 35 and 64, it implies that the simulated demand in month 1 is 360 tires. Now assume that the second random number generated is 6. Because this is between 5 and 14, it implies that the simulated demand in month 2 is 320 tires. The procedure continues in this fashion.

Step 3: Repeat the Process for a Series of Replications

A simulation process must be repeated numerous times to get meaningful results.

As noted earlier, although the long-term average demand is 358 tires per month in Harry's example, it is likely that we will get different average values from a short-term simulation of just a few months. It would be very risky to draw any hard and fast conclusion regarding any simulation model from just a few simulation replications. We need to run the model for several thousand replications (also referred to as *runs*, or *trials*) in order to gather meaningful results.

11.3 ROLE OF COMPUTERS IN SIMULATION

Although it is possible to simulate small examples such as the Harry's Auto Shop problem by hand, it is easier and much more convenient to conduct most simulation exercises using a computer. Three of the primary reasons for this follow:

Software packages have built-in procedures for simulating from several different probability distributions.

1. It is quite cumbersome to use hand-based random number generation procedures for even common probability distributions, such as the normal, uniform, and exponential distributions. As noted earlier, most computer software packages (including Excel) have built-in procedures for generation of random numbers. It is quite easy to simulate values from many probability distributions by using a software package's random number generator.

2. In order for the simulation results to be valid and useful, it is necessary to replicate the process hundreds (or even thousands) of times. Doing this by hand is laborious and time-consuming. In contrast, it is possible to simulate thousands of replications for a model in just a matter of seconds by using most software packages.

Software packages allow us to easily replicate a model and keep track of several output measures.

3. During the simulation process, depending on the complexity and scope of the model, we may need to manipulate many input parameters and keep track of several output measures. Here again, doing so by hand could become very cumbersome. Software packages, on the other hand, can be used to easily change multiple input values and track as many output measures as required in any simulation model.

Types of Simulation Software Packages

Three types of software packages are available to help set up and run simulation models on computers, as discussed in the following sections.

The use of simulation has been broadened by the availability of computing technology.

General-Purpose Programming Languages   These include standard programming languages such as Visual Basic, C++, and FORTRAN. The main advantage of these languages is that an experienced programmer can use them to develop simulation models for many diverse situations. The big disadvantage, however, is that a program written for a simulation model is specific to that model and is not easily portable. That is, a simulation model developed for one problem or situation may not be easily transferable to a different situation.

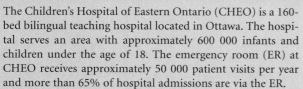

DECISION MODELING IN ACTION

Simulating Emergency Room Wait Times at the Children's Hospital of Eastern Ontario

The Children's Hospital of Eastern Ontario (CHEO) is a 160-bed bilingual teaching hospital located in Ottawa. The hospital serves an area with approximately 600 000 infants and children under the age of 18. The emergency room (ER) at CHEO receives approximately 50 000 patient visits per year and more than 65% of hospital admissions are via the ER.

When a problem arose with regard to the length of the waiting times for patients with less serious problems, with 20% of patients waiting for more than two hours, the hospital administration sought a solution that would satisfy the four constituent groups that were affected by the delays: physicians, nurses, administrators, and patients.

A simulation study was undertaken to investigate the major causes of the long waits and to suggest improvements to the existing system. The factors that were considered most likely to be causing the delays were (1) shortages of scarce resources, (2) the inability of the system to return to normal after emergency cases, and (3) the queuing system currently in operation in the ER.

The results of the simulation indicated that patients' waiting times are primarily caused by the availability of ER physicians and the amount of time that attending physicians have to devote to educating medical residents. Based on the recommendations of the study, the hospital's administration implemented a fast-track facility in the ER at peak periods and added a walk-in clinic that reduces the number of arrivals at the ER. It has also increased the number of physician hours in the emergency room.

Source: J. T. Blake, M. W. Carter, and S. Richardson. "An Analysis of Emergency Room Wait Time Issues via Computer Simulation," *Journal of the Canadian Operational Research Society* 34, 4 (1996): 263–273.

Special-purpose simulation
languages have several
advantages over general-
purpose languages.

Special-Purpose Simulation Languages and Programs   These include languages such as GPSS/H, Simscript II.5, and Visual SLAM, and programs such as Extend, MicroSaint, BuildSim, AweSim, ProModel, and Xcell. Using such special-purpose languages and programs has three advantages compared with using general-purpose languages: (1) They require less programming time for large simulations, (2) they are usually more efficient and easier to check for errors, and (3) they have built-in procedures to automate many of the tasks in simulation modeling. However, because of the significant learning curve associated with these languages, they are typically likely to be most useful to experienced modelers dealing with extremely complex simulation models.

We focus on building
simulation models using
Excel in this chapter.

Spreadsheet Models   The built-in ability to generate random numbers and use them to select values from several probability distributions makes spreadsheets excellent tools for conducting simple simulations. Spreadsheets are also very powerful for quickly tabulating results and presenting them using graphs. In keeping with the focus of this textbook, we therefore use Excel (and an Excel add-in, Oracle Crystal Ball) in the remainder of this chapter to develop several simulation models.

Random Generation from Some Common Probability Distributions Using Excel

In the following pages, we discuss how we can use Excel's built-in functions to generate random values from six commonly used probability distributions in simulation models: (1) continuous uniform, (2) discrete uniform, (3) normal, (4) exponential, (5) discrete general with two outcomes, and (6) discrete general with more than two outcomes.

Excel's RAND function
generates random numbers.

Generating Random Numbers in Excel   Excel uses the **RAND** function to generate random numbers. The format for using this function is

$$=\text{RAND}()$$

Note that the = sign before the RAND function implies that the cell entry is a formula. Also, there is no argument within the parentheses; that is, the left parenthesis is immediately followed by the right parenthesis.

If we enter =RAND() in any cell of a spreadsheet, it will return a random value between 0 and 1 (actually, between 0 and 0.9999 . . .) *each time you press the calculate key* (i.e., the F9 key). The RAND function can be used either by itself in a cell or as part of a formula. For example, to generate a random number between 0 and 4.9999 . . . , the appropriate formula to use would simply be

Uniform distributions can be
either discrete or continuous.

Continuous Uniform Distribution   A variable follows a continuous uniform distribution between a lower limit a and an upper limit b if all values between a and b, including fractional values, are equally likely. To simulate a variable that follows this distribution, we use the following formula:

$$=a + (b - a)*\text{RAND}()$$

For example, if $a = 3$ and $b = 9$, we know that $(9 - 3)*\text{RAND}()$ will generate a random value between 0 and 5.9999. . . . If we add this to 3, we will get a random value between 3 and 8.999 . . . (which, for all practical purposes, is 9).

There are two ways of
simulating from a discrete
uniform distribution.

Discrete Uniform Distribution   If all values between a and b are equally likely, but the variable is allowed to take on only integer values between a and b (inclusive), we refer to this as a discrete uniform distribution. To generate values randomly from this distribution, there are two different approaches we can use in Excel. First, we can extend the preceding formula for continuous uniform distributions by including Excel's INT function. The resulting formula is

$$=\text{INT}(a + (b - a + 1)*\text{RAND}())$$

Note that we need to add 1 to the $(b - a)$ term in this formula because the INT function always rounds down (that is, it just drops the fractional part from the value).

Alternatively, if the Analysis ToolPak add-in is installed and enabled in Excel (see Section B.6 in Appendix A for details), Excel has a built-in function called **RANDBETWEEN** that we can use to generate random values from discrete uniform distributions between a and b. The format for this function is

$$=\text{RANDBETWEEN}(a,b)$$

So, for example, if we want to generate random integers between 0 and 99 (as we did in the Harry's Auto Shop example earlier), we can use either of these two Excel formulas:

$$=\text{INT}(100*\text{RAND}()) \quad \text{or} \quad =\text{RANDBETWEEN}(0, 99)$$

Excel's NORMINV function can be used to simulate from a normal distribution.

Normal Distribution   The normal distribution is probably one of the most commonly used distributions in simulation models. The normal distribution is always identified by two parameters: mean μ and standard deviation σ (or variance σ^2). To simulate a random value from a normal distribution with mean μ and standard deviation σ, we use the **NORMINV** function in Excel as follows:

$$=\text{NORMINV}(\text{RAND}(), \mu, \sigma)$$

For example, the formula $=\text{NORMINV}(\text{RAND}(),30,5)$ will generate a random value from a normal distribution with a mean of 30 and a standard deviation of 5. If we repeat this process several thousand times, 50% of the values will be below 30 and 50% will be above 30, 68.26% will be between 25 and 35 (= mean ± 1 standard deviation), and so on. Note that a normally distributed random value will include fractions because the normal distribution is a continuous distribution. If we need to convert normally distributed random values to integers, we can do so by using Excel's ROUND function as follows:

$$=\text{ROUND}(\text{NORMINV}(\text{RAND}(), \mu, \sigma), 0)$$

The argument of 0 in the ROUND function specifies that we want to round-off fractional values to the nearest number with zero decimal points (i.e., integer). In this case, fractional values of 0.5 and above are rounded up, while fractional values below 0.5 are rounded down.

In some situations, we may need to truncate the value generated from a normal distribution. For example, if we randomly generate demand values from a normal distribution with a mean of 10 and a standard deviation of 4, it is possible that the generated value is sometimes negative. Because demand cannot be negative, we may need to truncate the generated demand by setting any negative value to zero. A simple way of doing so is to use Excel's MAX function, as follows:

$$=\text{MAX}(0, \text{NORMINV}(\text{RAND}(), 10, 4))$$

Excel's LN function can be used to simulate from an exponential distribution.

Exponential Distribution   The exponential distribution is commonly used to model arrival and service times in queuing systems (you may recall that we saw a few examples of this in Chapter 9). The exponential distribution can be described by a single parameter, μ, which describes the average *rate* of occurrences. (Alternatively, $1/\mu$ describes the mean time between successive occurrences.) To simulate a random value from an exponential distribution with average rate μ, we use the following formula in Excel:

$$=-(1/\mu)*LN(RAND())$$

where LN in the formula refers to the natural logarithmic function. For example, if the average service rate in a queuing system is 10 customers per hour, the service *time* (in hours) for a specific customer may be randomly generated by using the following formula:

$$=-(1/10)*LN(RAND())$$

Excel's IF function can be used to select from two possible outcomes.

Discrete General Distribution with Two Outcomes   If the outcomes of a probability distribution are discrete but the probabilities of the various outcomes are *not* the same, we refer to this as a **discrete general distribution** (as opposed to a discrete uniform distribution, where all outcomes have the same probability).

Let us first consider a discrete general distribution with only two outcomes. Suppose we want to randomly select individuals from a population where there are 55% males and 45% females. This implies that in the long term, our selected group will have exactly 55% males and 45% females. However, in the short term, any combination of males and females is possible and logical. To simulate these random draws in Excel, we can use the IF function as follows:

$$=IF(RAND()<0.55, \text{"Male"}, \text{"Female"})$$

Note that the quotes are needed in the IF function because Male and Female are both text characters. If we use numeric codes (e.g., 1 = Male, 2 = Female) instead of text characters, the formula is then

$$=IF(RAND()<0.55, 1, 2)$$

Random numbers can actually be assigned in many different ways, as long as they represent the correct proportion of the outcomes.

Because RAND() has a 55% chance of returning a value between 0 and 0.55 (which implies it has a 45% chance of returning a value between 0.55 and 0.999 . . .), the preceding formula is logical. Note that we could have set up the IF function such that *any* 55% of values between 0 and 1 denotes male and the other 45% denotes female. For example, we could have expressed the formula as follows:

$$=IF(RAND()< 0.45, \text{"Female"}, \text{"Male"})$$

If we replicate the simulation enough times, the male-to-female split will be the same (i.e., 55% male and 45% female), regardless of how the IF function is set up.

Distribution of Tire Demand

Demand	Probability
300	0.05
320	0.10
340	0.20
360	0.30
380	0.25
400	0.10

Discrete General Distribution with More Than Two Outcomes   Let us now consider a discrete general distribution with more than two outcomes by revisiting the Harry's Auto Shop example. (Table 11.1 is repeated in the margin for your convenience.) The demand for tires is one of six values: 300, 320, 340, 360, 380, or 400. However, unlike with the discrete uniform distribution, in this case the probability of demand for each value is not the same.

We want to use Excel to simulate demands randomly from this distribution, just as we did manually in Table 11.3 (on page 482) using random number intervals. To do so, a more experienced Excel user could use a *nested* IF function (i.e., IF function within IF function). However, it is probably more convenient to use Excel's LOOKUP, VLOOKUP, or HLOOKUP functions to randomly select values from this type of probability distribution. In our discussion here, we illustrate the use of the **LOOKUP** function.

Excel Notes

- The CD-ROM that accompanies this textbook contains the Excel file for each sample problem discussed here. The relevant file name is shown in the margin next to each example.
- For clarity, our simulation worksheets are colour coded as follows:
  - *Input cells*, where we enter known data, are shaded yellow.
  - *Simulation cells*, which show simulated values, are shaded blue.
  - *Output cells*, where the results are shown, are shaded green.

  Although these colours are not apparent in the screenshots shown in this textbook, they are seen in the Excel files on the CD-ROM.
- When you open any of the Excel files for the examples in this chapter, depending on whether the Calculation option is set to Automatic, Excel may automatically recalculate all random numbers in the model. This, in turn, may cause all simulated values in the worksheet to change. Hence, the values you see in the Excel file may not be the same as those shown in the screenshots included in the textbook.
- *Tip:* After creating a simulation model, if you wish to save your results in such a way that the values do *not* change each time you open the Excel file, you can set the Calculation option in Excel to Manual. Alternatively, you can use the Paste Values feature in Excel (see Appendix A for details). You can copy the cells showing the results and use Paste Values to save your answers as values rather than as formulas. Remember, however, that any cell overwritten in this manner will no longer contain the formula.

File: 11-1.xls, sheet: 11-1A

Excel's LOOKUP function can be used to simulate from a discrete general distribution.

File: 11-1.xls, sheet: 11-1B

We use random number intervals in this simulation.

The first range in the LOOKUP function must contain the lower limits of the random number intervals.

Screenshot 11.1A shows the Excel layout showing the formulas for setting up a LOOKUP function. We begin by arranging all the demand values in a column (say, column A). Titles, like the ones shown in row 1, are optional. We then list the probability of each demand in another column (say, column B). In Screenshot 11.1A, we have shown the demand values in cells A2:A7 and the corresponding probabilities in cells B2:B7.

Just as we did in Table 11.3, we now create the *random number intervals*. The only difference is that instead of using two-digit random numbers from 0 to 99, we use continuous-valued random numbers from 0 to 0.9999. The formulas to compute the random number intervals for Harry's example are shown in cells C2:D7 of Screenshot 11.1A. The actual values are shown in Screenshot 11.1B. Notice that the lower-limit numbers in cells C2:C7 are identical to the ones we developed in Table 11.3. The upper-limit numbers are slightly different because we used discrete random numbers in Table 11.3 and we are using continuous random numbers here. Although we have shown the random number intervals in columns that are adjacent to the demand and probability values here, these could be in any location of the spreadsheet.

The format for the LOOKUP function is

$$=LOOKUP(RAND(),C2:C7, A2: A7)$$

The first cell range in the LOOKUP function must contain the *lower limits* of the random number intervals (i.e., cells C2:C7). Excel takes the value generated by the RAND() function and proceeds down this column to identify the entry where the RAND() value exceeds the lower limit. It then moves to the other range specified in the LOOKUP function

SCREENSHOT 11.1A

**Excel Layout and
Formulas for a
LOOKUP Function**

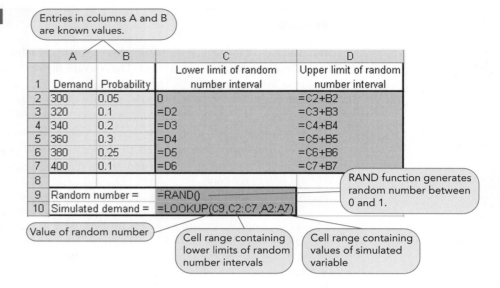

Entries in columns A and B are known values.

	A	B	C	D
			Lower limit of random number interval	Upper limit of random number interval
1	Demand	Probability		
2	300	0.05	0	=C2+B2
3	320	0.1	=D2	=C3+B3
4	340	0.2	=D3	=C4+B4
5	360	0.3	=D4	=C5+B5
6	380	0.25	=D5	=C6+B6
7	400	0.1	=D6	=C7+B7
8				
9	Random number =		=RAND()	
10	Simulated demand =		=LOOKUP(C9,C2:C7,A2:A7)	

RAND function generates random number between 0 and 1.

Value of random number

Cell range containing lower limits of random number intervals

Cell range containing values of simulated variable

SCREENSHOT 11.1B

**Simulation Using a
LOOKUP Function**

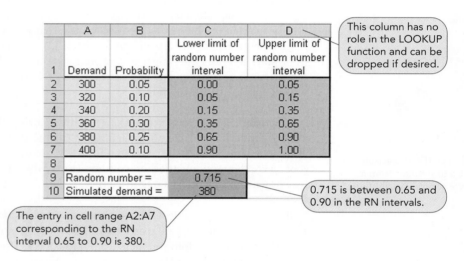

	A	B	C	D
			Lower limit of random number interval	Upper limit of random number interval
1	Demand	Probability		
2	300	0.05	0.00	0.05
3	320	0.10	0.05	0.15
4	340	0.20	0.15	0.35
5	360	0.30	0.35	0.65
6	380	0.25	0.65	0.90
7	400	0.10	0.90	1.00
8				
9	Random number =		0.715	
10	Simulated demand =		380	

This column has no role in the LOOKUP function and can be dropped if desired.

0.715 is between 0.65 and 0.90 in the RN intervals.

The entry in cell range A2:A7 corresponding to the RN interval 0.65 to 0.90 is 380.

(i.e., cells A2:A7) and selects the corresponding entry shown there. In our case, this range has the demand value that we wish to simulate.[2]

The values of this simulation are shown in Screenshot 11.1B. Let's suppose the random number generated is 0.715 (shown in cell C9). Using the preceding logic, the LOOKUP function compares this number to the entries in the cell range C2:C7. Having recognized that 0.715 exceeds the fifth entry (0.65) in the range but not the sixth (0.90), it returns the fifth entry in the cell range A2:A7. This is cell A6 (also shown in cell A10), which corresponds to a demand value of 380 tires.[3]

---

[2] Note that the upper limit of the random number interval (cells D2:D7) played no role in the LOOKUP function. In fact, it is not necessary to even show this column, and we can safely delete it. However, we have included these entries in all our models here to make it easier to understand the use of the LOOKUP function.

[3] In this example, we have shown the value of the random number separately in cell C9 and used this number in the formula in cell C10. Note that the RAND() function could have been directly embedded in the LOOKUP formula itself. Except for the simulation model discussed in Section 11.4, we do not show the random number values separately in our models.

TABLE 11.4	TO SIMULATE	USE BUILT-IN EXCEL FORMULA
Simulation from Various Probability Distributions Using Excel's Built-in Formulas	Random number	=RAND()
	Continuous uniform distribution Between a and b	$=a + (b - a)*\text{RAND}()$
	Discrete uniform distribution Between a and b	$=\text{INT}(a + (b - a + 1)*\text{RAND}())$ or $=\text{RANDBETWEEN}(a,b)$
	Normal distribution Mean = μ; Standard deviation = σ	$=\text{NORMINV}(\text{RAND}(),\mu,\sigma)$
	Exponential distribution Mean rate = μ	$=-(1/\mu)*\text{LN}(\text{RAND}())$
	Discrete general distribution **Two outcomes only:** A and B Probability of outcome $A = p$	$=\text{IF}(\text{RAND}()<p, A, B)$
	Discrete general distribution **More than two outcomes:** *Range1* = Cell range containing lower limits of the random number intervals *Range2* = Cell range containing the variable values	$=\text{LOOKUP}(\text{RAND}(), Range1, Range2)$

Summary of some of Excel's built-in functions used in simulation.

For your convenience, Table 11.4 above presents a summary of the Excel formulas we have presented so far for simulating random values from various probability distributions. In the following sections, we describe four simulation models that use these formulas for their implementation.

11.4 SIMULATION MODEL TO COMPUTE EXPECTED PROFIT

Let us set up the Harry's Auto Shop example as our first simulation model. Recall from Table 11.1 that Harry's monthly demand of tires is 300, 320, 340, 360, 380, or 400, with specific probabilities for each value. Now let us assume that the following additional information is known regarding Harry's operating environment:

Table 11.1 Revisited

Demand	Probability
300	0.05
320	0.10
340	0.20
360	0.30
380	0.25
400	0.10

Demand, selling price, and profit margin are all probabilistic.

- Depending on competitors' prices and other market conditions, Harry estimates that his average selling price per tire each month follows a discrete uniform distribution between $60 and $80 (in increments of $1).

- Harry's variable cost per tire also varies each month, depending on material costs and other market conditions. This causes Harry's average profit margin per tire (calculated as a percentage of the selling price) to vary each month. Using past data, Harry estimates that his profit margin per tire follows a continuous uniform distribution between 20% and 30% of the selling price.

- Harry estimates that his fixed cost of stocking and selling tires is $2000 per month.

Using this information, let us simulate and calculate Harry's *average profit* per month from the sale of auto tires.

Setting Up the Model

The first issue to understand in any simulation model is what we mean by one replication of the model.

In any simulation model, the first issue we need to understand is what we mean by one **replication** of the model. In Harry's case, each replication corresponds to simulating one month of tire sales. That is, we will set up the model to simulate one month of tire sales at

Harry's Auto Shop and then run the model repeatedly for as many replications as desired. The logic of Harry's simulation process is presented in Figure 11.2. Such **flow diagrams**, or **flowcharts**, are very useful in understanding the logical sequence of events in simulation models, especially in complex problem scenarios.

File: 11-2.xls, sheet: 11-2A

Let us now translate the flowchart in Figure 11.2 into a simulation model, using Excel. Screenshot 11.2A shows the formula view of the Excel layout for Harry's model. All titles, like the ones shown in rows 1 and 3, are optional. For a given replication, the spreadsheet is organized as follows:

- Cell A4 generates the random number used to simulate the demand that month. For this model alone, we show the actual value of the random number used to simulate each variable value.

- The random number in cell A4 is used in a LOOKUP function to simulate the monthly demand in cell B4. The data (demands, probabilities, and random number intervals) of the LOOKUP function are shown in cells I4:L9.

- In cell C4, we simulate the average selling price per tire by using the RANDBETWEEN function (with $a = 60$ and $b = 80$). The formula is =RANDBETWEEN(60,80).

- Cell D4 generates the random number used to simulate the average profit margin per tire.

- The random number in cell D4 is used in cell E4 to simulate the average profit margin per tire. For this, we use the continuous uniform distribution formula, with $a = 0.2$ and $b = 0.3$. The formula is =0.2+(0.3−0.2)*D4.

- Cell F4 shows the fixed cost, equal to $2000 per month.

- Using these simulated values, Harry's monthly profit is calculated in cell G4 as

$$\text{Profit} = (\text{Demand for tires}) \times (\text{Average selling price per tire})$$
$$\times (\text{Average profit margin per tire}) - (\text{Monthly fixed cost})$$

That is, the formula in cell G4 is =B4*C4*E4−F4.

Screenshot 11.2B shows the result for a single replication of Harry's simulation model. This result indicates that Harry will earn a profit of $4125.52 per month. It is important to remember, however, that each randomly simulated value only represents

FIGURE 11.2

**Flowchart for Harry's
Auto Shop Simulation
Model**

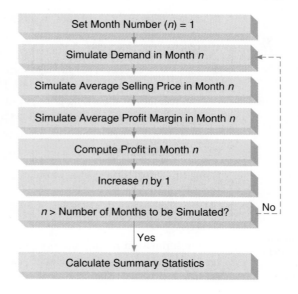

SCREENSHOT 11.2A   **Excel Layout and Formulas for Harry's Auto Shop**

RANDBETWEEN function used to simulate from a discrete uniform distribution

Continuous uniform distribution between 0.2 and 0.3

	A	B	C	D	E	F	G	H	I	J	K	L
1	Harry's Auto Shop											
2										Demand Distribution		
3	RN 1	Demand	Selling price	RN 2	Profit margin	Fixed cost	Profit		Demand	Proba-bility	RN intvl lower limit	RN intvl upper limit
4	=RAND()	=LOOKUP(A4,$K$4:$K$9,$I$4:$I$9)	=RANDBETWEEN(60,80)	=RAND()	=0.2+(0.3-0.2)*D4	2000	=B4*C4*E4-F4		300	0.05	0	=K4+J4
5									320	0.1	=L4	=K5+J5
6									340	0.2	=L5	=K6+J6
7									360	0.3	=L6	=K7+J7
8									380	0.25	=L7	=K8+J8
9									400	0.1	=L8	=K9+J9

LOOKUP function used to simulate from a discrete general distribution

Random number, used in column E to simulate profit margin

Random number, used in column B to simulate demand

Parameters for the LOOKUP function in column B

File: 11-2.xls, sheet: 11-2B

We need to replicate a simulation model at least a few thousand times to get consistent summary results.

something that *could* occur. As such, there is no guarantee that the specific values simulated in Screenshot 11.2B will actually occur. Due to the presence of random numbers, these simulated values will change each time the model is replicated (i.e., they will change each time the F9 key is pressed in Excel). Hence, it would be incorrect to estimate Harry's profit based on just one replication (month).

To calculate Harry's *average* monthly profit, we need to replicate the simulation model several thousand times. However, in order to keep the computation times reasonable (especially in a classroom setting) and to keep the size of the resulting Excel files relatively small, we illustrate only 200 replications in most of our models in this chapter. We then compute summary statistics just from these 200 replications. It is important to note that 200 replications are not enough for a simulation model to yield consistent summary results. That is, an average based on just 200 replications, for example, will be different each time we run the simulation model. Therefore, in practice, we should replicate a model as many times as convenient.

SCREENSHOT 11.2B   **Results for the Simulation Model of Harry's Auto Shop**

Profit for current replication

	A	B	C	D	E	F	G	H	I	J	K	L
1	Harry's Auto Shop											
2	Calculations set to Manual. Press F9 to recalculate.								Demand Distribution			
3	RN 1	Demand	Selling price	RN 2	Profit margin	Fixed cost	Profit		Demand	Proba-bility	RN intvl lower limit	RN intvl upper limit
4	0.001	300	$72.00	0.836	28.36%	$2,000	$4,125.52		300	0.05	0.00	0.05
5									320	0.10	0.05	0.15
6									340	0.20	0.15	0.35
7									360	0.30	0.35	0.65
8									380	0.25	0.65	0.90
9									400	0.10	0.90	1.00

RN of 0.001 is between 0.00 and 0.05, implying a demand of 300.

RN of 0.836 implies profit margin is 28.36%.

Replication by Copying the Model

If the simulation model is very compact, we can perform replications by simply copying the model several times.

In simulation models where each replication consists of just a single row of computations in Excel (such as in Harry's model), an easy way to perform 200 replications is to copy all formulas and values in that row to 199 other rows. For example, we can copy cells A4:G4 in Screenshot 11.2B to cells A5:G203. (*Note:* For your convenience, a worksheet illustrating this way of replicating Harry's model is included in the Excel file 11-2.xls on the CD-ROM that accompanies this textbook; see the sheet named 11-2B1.) Due to the use of random numbers in the formulas, the values of the simulated variables will be different in each replication. Hence, each of the 200 entries computed in cells G4:G203, which represents the monthly profit that *could* result in a given month, will be different. Once we have simulated these 200 monthly profit values, we can compute the average monthly profit by using the following Excel formula =AVERAGE(G4:G203).

Replicating a model by copying it multiple times could make the Excel file very large.

A clear drawback of this approach for replicating a simulation model is that it could make the resulting Excel file quite large and unwieldy. In fact, for models where each replication consists of computations spanning several rows in Excel (as we will see shortly), it is impractical to even consider copying the entire model 200 or more times. For this reason, we next illustrate a different approach—one that replicates a model multiple times without requiring us to copy the entire model each time.

Replication Using a Data Table

Using Data Table in Excel is a convenient way of replicating a large model several times.

For replicating a simulation model, we can use an Excel procedure called **Data Table**. The primary use of this procedure in Excel is to plug in different values for a variable in a formula and compute the result each time. For example, if the formula is $(2a + 5)$, we can set up a Data Table to plug in several values for the variable a and report the result of the formula each time. In a simulation model, however, we don't really have a "variable" and a "formula" to use in Data Table. So, as explained next, we make Data Table plug in multiple values for a dummy variable in a dummy formula (both of which have nothing to do with the simulation model) and report the "result" each time. The key here is that each time Data Table computes the formula's result, it automatically updates all calculations on the Excel sheet (i.e., it activates the F9 key). As a consequence, all random numbers in the simulation model change, and the result is a new replication of the model, with new values for all simulated entries.

We illustrate the use of Data Table to replicate Harry's simulation model 200 times in Screenshot 11.2C. Here again, we have chosen 200 replications just for convenience. The procedure is as follows:

This is how we set up Data Table.

1. We first use 200 cells in an empty column in the spreadsheet to represent the 200 values of the *dummy* variable. If we wish, we can leave these cells blank because they have no real role to play in the simulation model. However, as we have done in cells N4:N203 in Screenshot 11.2C, it is convenient to fill these cells with numbers from 1 to 200, to indicate we are performing 200 replications. If we wish, we can title this column *Replication* or *Run* (as shown in cell N3). *Note:* A convenient way to enter a series of numbers in Excel is to click **EDIT│FILL│SERIES**.

2. In the cell adjacent to the *first* cell in the range N4:N203 (i.e., in cell O4), we specify the cell reference for the output measure we want replicated 200 times. In Harry's model, this corresponds to cell G4, the monthly profit value. Hence, the formula in cell O4 would be =G4. We can title this column *Profit* if we wish (as shown in cell O3). We leave cells O5:O203 blank. Data Table will fill in these cells automatically when we run it.

3. We now use the mouse or keyboard to select the range N4:O203 (i.e., both columns). *After* selecting this range, we choose **DATA│TABLE**. The window titled **TABLE**, shown in Screenshot 11.2C, is now displayed.

SCREENSHOT 11.2C   **Data Table for Harry's Auto Shop**

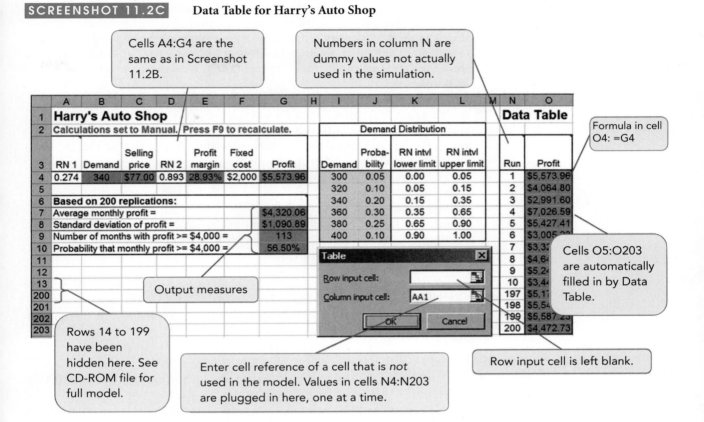

Cells A4:G4 are the same as in Screenshot 11.2B.

Numbers in column N are dummy values not actually used in the simulation.

Formula in cell O4: =G4

Cells O5:O203 are automatically filled in by Data Table.

Rows 14 to 199 have been hidden here. See CD-ROM file for full model.

Output measures

Enter cell reference of a cell that is *not* used in the model. Values in cells N4:N203 are plugged in here, one at a time.

Row input cell is left blank.

4. Because our Data Table is arranged in columns, we leave the Row input cell box blank. We then select any arbitrary cell that has nothing to do with the simulation model and enter this cell reference in the Column input cell box. It is important to make sure this selected cell (AA1, in Screenshot 11.2C) has no role to play in the simulation model. In effect, we are telling Data Table that cell AA1 contains our *dummy* formula.

5. Finally, we click **OK** to run Data Table. The procedure now takes the 200 entries in cells N4:N203, plugs them one at a time in cell AA1, and reports the value of cell G4 each time in cells O4:O203. As noted earlier, even though the variable values in cells N4:N203 and the formula in cell AA1 are dummies, Excel generates new random numbers for each replication of the model. The simulated results in cells O4:O203 are therefore different for each replication.

Excel Notes

- All entries in a simulation model, including columns in Data Table, can be formatted in any manner desired. For example, the profit value can be formatted to display as currency.

- It is usually a good idea to change the Calculation option in Excel to Manual or Automatic except tables (**TOOLS|OPTION|CALCULATION**) when using Data Table. Otherwise, Excel will recalculate the entire Data Table each time we make *any* change in the spreadsheet. Depending on the size of the simulation model and the table, this could be time-consuming.

■ For the same reason, it is a good idea to set up each simulation model in a separate Excel file, rather than in a different sheet of the same file.

■ If we change the Calculation option to manual, remember that Excel will recalculate values only when we press the F9 key. Likewise, Data Table will initially show the same result value for every replication. We need to press F9 to get the final values.

■ Once we have set up and run Data Table, we cannot edit parts of it (if we try to change any entry in the Data Table, Excel will return the message "Cannot change part of a table.") To edit a Data Table, we select all cells that were automatically filled in by the Data Table procedure (e.g., cells O5:O203 in Screenshot 11.2C) and delete those cells. Now we make any changes we wish to the table (such as changing the number of replications) and run the Data Table procedure again.

■ Although Data Table shows the value of the final output measure for each replication, the simulation model itself does not show details (e.g., monthly demand, selling price) for these replications. If we want to see complete details for each replication, we need to copy the entire model as many times as desired.

Analyzing the Results

Cells O4 to O203 show the monthly profit for 200 replications (months). We can now calculate the following statistics:

Cell G7:   =AVERAGE(O4:O203)   Average monthly profit = $4320.06
Cell G8:   =STDEV(O4:O203)   Standard deviation of monthly profit = $1090.89

Note: Values in your file will be different if you recalculate the model because the random numbers will change, and we are using only 200 replications.

Excel's Descriptive Statistics procedure can also be used to compute summary statistics.

Alternatively, if the Analysis ToolPak add-in is installed and enabled, we can use Excel's Descriptive Statistics procedure to compute these and other statistics, such as confidence intervals. We invoke this procedure by clicking **TOOLS|DATA ANALYSIS|DESCRIPTIVE STATISTICS**. The window shown in Screenshot 11.2D(a) appears. We enter the information as shown and press **OK**. The summary statistics shown in Screenshot 11.2D(b) are then displayed. The results indicate, for example, that the 95% confidence interval for the average monthly profit would extend from $4167.95 to $4472.17 (= $4320.06 ± $152.11).

The simulation results can be used to compute several performance measures.

We can also calculate several other measures of performance. For example, suppose Harry estimates that in order for tire sales to be financially viable, he needs to get a monthly profit of at least $4000 from tires. What is the probability that Harry will get this amount of profit? To answer this question, we first need to count the number of months (of the 200 months) in which Harry's profit exceeds $4000. We can use Excel's COUNTIF function to do this, as shown in cell G9 of Screenshot 11.2C. The relevant formula is

Cell G9:   =COUNTIF(O4:O203,">=4000")   Number of months with profit ≥ $4000 = 113

Then, we divide this count by 200 to get the probability value (shown in cell G10). Screenshot 11.2C shows that Harry has a 56.5% chance of getting a monthly profit in excess of $4000. Here again, the values will be different if you recalculate the model because the random numbers will change, and we are using only 200 replications.

Descriptive Statistics for Harry's Auto Shop

Click **Tools|Data Analysis|
Descriptive Statistics** to
get this window.

Cells containing input data.
We can enter more than
one variable here.

(a)

Indicates input
data are arranged
in columns.

Descriptive Statistics   ? X

Input
Input Range: $O$3:$O$203
Grouped By: ⊙ Columns
                        ○ Rows
☑ Labels in first row

Output options
○ Output Range:
⊙ New Worksheet Ply: Summary
○ New Workbook
☑ Summary statistics
☑ Confidence Level for Mean: 95   %
☐ Kth Largest: 1
☐ Kth Smallest: 1

OK
Cancel
Help

(b)   Average monthly profit

	A	B
1	Profit	
2	Mean	4320.06
3	Standard Error	77.14
4	Median	4231.10
5	Mode	#N/A
6	Standard Deviation	1090.89
7	Sample Variance	1190034.08
8	Kurtosis	-0.34
9	Skewness	0.39
10	Range	5037.99
11	Minimum	2142.59
12	Maximum	7180.58
13	Sum	864012.98
14	Count	200
15	Confidence Level(95.0%)	152.11

Summary results

95% confidence interval for
mean is 4320.06 ± 152.11.

Now suppose Harry decides that if his profit from tire sales is below $3000 per month, he will stop selling tires. Using an approach similar to the one discussed here, see if you can calculate the probability of this event.

11.5   SIMULATION MODEL OF AN INVENTORY PROBLEM

Questions in inventory problems include (1) how much to order and (2) when to order.

There are two main questions in most inventory problems: (1) how much to order and (2) when to order. Under specific assumptions, it is possible to develop precise analytical models to answer these questions.[4]

In many real-world inventory situations, though, several inventory parameters are random variables. For example, the demand for an item could be random, implying that the rate at which its inventory is depleted is uncertain. Likewise, the time between when we place an order for an item with our supplier and when we receive it (known as the *lead time*) could be random. This implies that we may run out of inventory for the item before we receive the next consignment, causing a *stockout*.

Although it may be possible for us to express the behaviour of parameters such as demand and lead time by using probability distributions, developing analytical models becomes extremely difficult. In such situations, the best means to answer the kind of inventory questions noted here is simulation.

Simulation is useful when demand and lead time are probabilistic.

In Solved Problem 11-1 at the end of this chapter, we simulate a fairly simple inventory problem in which only the demand is random. In the following pages, we illustrate a more comprehensive inventory problem in which both the demand and lead time are random variables.

[4] We discuss some of these models in Chapter 12.

DECISION MODELING IN ACTION
Simulating Volkswagen's Supply Chain

Volkswagen (VW) of America imports, markets, and distributes Volkswagens and Audis in the United States from its parent company in Germany. As part of a reengineering effort, VW developed a computer simulation model, using ProModel software, to analyze how to save money in its huge supply chain.

Since the early 1900s, vehicle distribution in the United States has followed the system introduced by Ford Motor. This structure, in which manufacturers view auto dealers as their primary customers, is so old that its original performance intentions are rarely examined. Dealers and auto manufacturers are loosely coupled, with each managing its own inventory costs. Like other manufacturers, VW encourages dealers to carry as much stock as possible but understands that having too much inventory could force a dealer out of business. Dealers recognize the threatening inventory costs but know that if they don't purchase enough cars, VW may restrict supply or appoint additional dealers. The average VW dealer sells 30 cars per month and stocks fewer than 100 in inventory.

To better the chances of a customer getting his or her first choice of car, to be able to deliver that car in 48 hours, and to be able to reduce total system (dealers and VW) costs for transportation, financing, and storage, VW considered a new strategy: pooling vehicles in regional depots. Rather than opening these centres and observing how well the concept worked, VW focused on simulating the flow of cars from plants to dealers. The model showed that there would be significant savings by opening its distribution centres. VW managers also learned that supply-chain performance must be viewed from the system level.

Source: N. Karabakal, A. Gunal, and W. Ritchie. "Supply-Chain Analysis at Volkswagen of America," *Interfaces* (July–August 2000): 46–55.

Simkin's Hardware Store

Simkin's Hardware Store sells the Ace model electric drill. Daily demand for the drill is relatively low but subject to some variability. Over the past 300 days, Barry Simkin has observed the demand frequency shown in column 2 of Table 11.5. He converts this historical frequency into a probability distribution for the variable daily demand (column 3).

Lead time is the time between order placement and order receipt.

When Simkin places an order to replenish his inventory of drills, the time between when he places an order and when it is received (i.e., the lead time) is a probabilistic variable. Based on the past 100 orders, Simkin has found that lead time follows a discrete uniform distribution between one and three days. He currently has seven Ace electric drills in stock, and there are no orders due.

Simkin wants to identify the order quantity, Q, and reorder point, R, that will help him reduce his total monthly costs. The *order quantity* is the fixed size of each order that is placed. The *reorder point* specifies the inventory level at which an order is triggered. That is, if the inventory level at the end of a day is at or below the reorder point, an order is placed. The total cost includes the following three components:

There are three components of the total cost.

■ A fixed order cost that is incurred each time an order is placed

■ A holding cost for each drill held in inventory from one period to the next

■ A stockout cost for each drill that is not available to satisfy demand

TABLE 11.5	DEMAND	FREQUENCY	PROBABILITY
Distribution of Daily Demand for Ace Electric Drills	0	15	15/300 = 0.05
	1	30	30/300 = 0.10
	2	60	60/300 = 0.20
	3	120	120/300 = 0.40
	4	45	45/300 = 0.15
	5	30	30/300 = 0.10

Simkin estimates that the fixed cost of placing an order with his Ace drill supplier is $20. The cost of holding a drill in stock is $0.02 per drill per day. Each time Simkin is unable to satisfy a demand (i.e., he has a stockout), the customer buys the drill elsewhere, and Simkin loses the sale. He estimates that the cost of a stockout is $8 per drill. Assume that the shop operates 25 days each month on average.

There are two decision variables: order quantity (Q) and reorder point (R).

Note that there are two decision variables (order quantity, Q, and reorder point, R) and two probabilistic components (demand and lead time) in Simkin's inventory problem. Using simulation, we can try different (Q, R) combinations to see which combination yields the lowest total cost. As an illustration, let us first examine a policy that has $Q = 10$ and $R = 5$; that is, each time the inventory at the end of a day drops to 5 or less, we place an order for 10 drills with the supplier.

Setting Up the Model

A replication here corresponds to one month of operations at Simkin's store.

In Simkin's problem, each replication corresponds to tracking the inventory position and orders for electric drills over a month (i.e., 25 days), on a day-by-day basis. Hence, unlike Harry's Auto Shop problem in Section 11.4, where we could model each replication by using just a single row in Excel, Simkin's simulation model will be much larger. If we represent the inventory operations of each day as a single row, the model will consist of 25 rows.

File: 11-3.xls, sheet: 11-3A

The Excel layout for Simkin's problem is shown in Screenshot 11.3A. Wherever necessary, we have shown the Excel formula used in a column.

To run several what-if scenarios using the same model, it is good to make parameter values cell references in all formulas.

In Screenshot 11.3A, all input parameters for the simulation model (e.g., the order quantity, reorder point, lead time range, all unit costs) are shown in separate cells (in column T). All formulas in the model use these cell references, rather than the values directly. This is a good practice to follow, especially if we want to use the simulation model to run several what-if scenarios using different values for these parameters (as we shall see shortly). The model in Screenshot 11.3A is organized as follows:

- Column A shows the day number (1 to 25).

Here is how we simulate the inventory example.

- Column B shows the beginning inventory at the start of a day. On day 1, this equals 7 (given). On all other days, the beginning inventory equals the ending inventory of the previous day. For example, cell B5 = cell G4, cell B6 = cell G5, and so on.

- Column C shows the units received (if any) that day from a prior order. Because there are no outstanding orders on day 1, cell C4 shows a value of 0. The formula for the remaining cells in this column uses Excel's COUNTIF function. In column L (discussed shortly), we simulate the arrival day for each order that is placed. We use the COUNTIF formula to check the number of times the current day number matches the arrival day number. The formula used to calculate the number of units arriving each day is then as follows:

$$\text{Units received} = \text{Number of orders due that day} \times \text{Order size}$$

For example, the formula in cell C5 is

$$=\text{COUNTIF}(\$L\$4:L4,A5)*\$T\$11$$

We use a $ sign to anchor cell references while copying formulas in Excel.

The COUNTIF portion of the formula checks to see how many orders are due for arrival on day 2 (specified by cell A5). This number is then multiplied by the order quantity, Q, specified in cell T11. Note that the use of a $ sign to anchor cell references in this formula allows us to directly copy it to cells C6:C28.

SCREENSHOT 11.3A   Excel Layout and Results for Simkin's Hardware Store

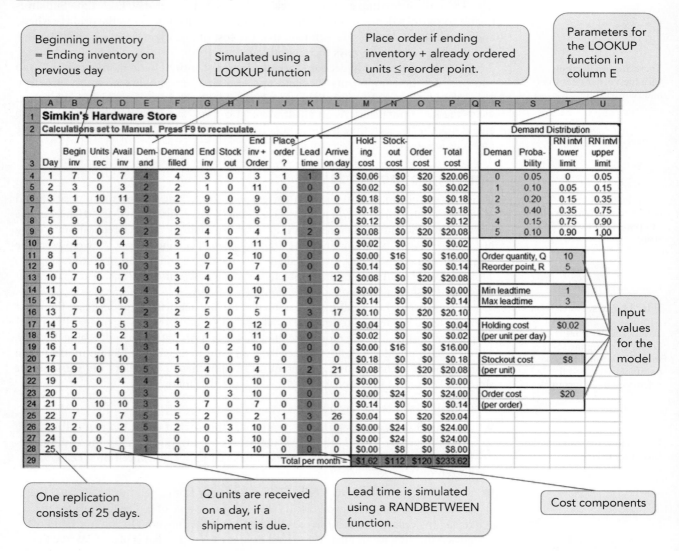

Beginning inventory = Ending inventory on previous day

Simulated using a LOOKUP function

Place order if ending inventory + already ordered units ≤ reorder point.

Parameters for the LOOKUP function in column E

One replication consists of 25 days.

Q units are received on a day, if a shipment is due.

Lead time is simulated using a RANDBETWEEN function.

Cost components

Input values for the model

Simkin's Hardware Store

Calculations set to Manual. Press F9 to recalculate.

Day	Begin inv	Units rec	Avail inv	Dem-and	Demand filled	End inv	Stock out	End inv + Order	Place order?	Lead time	Arrive on day	Holding cost	Stockout cost	Order cost	Total cost
1	7	0	7	4	4	3	0	3	1	1	3	$0.06	$0	$20	$20.06
2	3	0	3	2	2	1	0	11	0	0	0	$0.02	$0	$0	$0.02
3	1	10	11	2	2	9	0	9	0	0	0	$0.18	$0	$0	$0.18
4	9	0	9	0	0	9	0	9	0	0	0	$0.18	$0	$0	$0.18
5	9	0	9	3	3	6	0	6	0	0	0	$0.12	$0	$0	$0.12
6	6	0	6	2	2	4	0	4	1	2	9	$0.08	$0	$20	$20.08
7	4	0	4	3	3	1	0	11	0	0	0	$0.02	$0	$0	$0.02
8	1	0	1	3	1	0	2	10	0	0	0	$0.00	$16	$0	$16.00
9	0	10	10	3	3	7	0	7	0	0	0	$0.14	$0	$0	$0.14
10	7	0	7	3	3	4	0	4	1	1	12	$0.08	$0	$20	$20.08
11	4	0	4	4	4	0	0	10	0	0	0	$0.00	$0	$0	$0.00
12	0	10	10	3	3	7	0	7	0	0	0	$0.14	$0	$0	$0.14
13	7	0	7	2	2	5	0	5	1	3	17	$0.10	$0	$20	$20.10
14	5	0	5	3	3	2	0	12	0	0	0	$0.04	$0	$0	$0.04
15	2	0	2	1	1	1	0	11	0	0	0	$0.02	$0	$0	$0.02
16	1	0	1	3	1	0	2	10	0	0	0	$0.00	$16	$0	$16.00
17	0	10	10	1	1	9	0	9	0	0	0	$0.18	$0	$0	$0.18
18	9	0	9	5	5	4	0	4	1	2	21	$0.08	$0	$20	$20.08
19	4	0	4	4	4	0	0	10	0	0	0	$0.00	$0	$0	$0.00
20	0	0	0	3	0	0	3	10	0	0	0	$0.00	$24	$0	$24.00
21	0	10	10	3	3	7	0	7	0	0	0	$0.14	$0	$0	$0.14
22	7	0	7	5	5	2	0	2	1	3	26	$0.04	$0	$20	$20.04
23	2	0	2	5	2	0	3	10	0	0	0	$0.00	$24	$0	$24.00
24	0	0	0	3	0	0	3	10	0	0	0	$0.00	$24	$0	$24.00
25	0	0	0	1	0	0	1	10	0	0	0	$0.00	$8	$0	$8.00
									Total per month =			$1.62	$112	$120	$233.62

Demand Distribution

Demand	Probability	RN intvl lower limit	RN intvl upper limit
0	0.05	0	0.05
1	0.10	0.05	0.15
2	0.20	0.15	0.35
3	0.40	0.35	0.75
4	0.15	0.75	0.90
5	0.10	0.90	1.00

Order quantity, Q	10
Reorder point, R	5
Min leadtime	1
Max leadtime	3
Holding cost (per unit per day)	$0.02
Stockout cost (per unit)	$8
Order cost (per order)	$20

■ The total *available* inventory each day, shown in column D, is then the sum of the values in columns B and C:

Column D = Column B + Column C

Demand is simulated by using a LOOKUP function.

■ Column E shows the demand each day. These values are simulated from a discrete general probability distribution shown in Table 11.5, using Excel's LOOKUP function. The parameters (demands, probabilities, and random number intervals) of the LOOKUP function are shown in cells R4:U9. Hence, the formula in cells E4:E28 is

=LOOKUP(RAND(),$T$4: $T$9, $R$4: $R$9)

Here again, the use of the $ sign to anchor cell references in the formula allows us to create it in cell E4 and then copy it to cells E5:E28.

■ Column F shows the actual demand filled. If the demand is less than or equal to the available inventory, the entire demand is satisfied. In contrast, if the demand exceeds the available inventory, then only the demand up to the inventory level is satisfied. We can use Excel's MIN function to model this, as follows:

$$\text{Demand satisfied} = \text{MIN(Available inventory, Demand)}$$

Hence, column F = MIN(column D, column E).

If demand is less than available inventory, there is some ending inventory.

■ Column G calculates the ending inventory. If the demand is less than the available inventory, there is some ending inventory. However, if the demand is greater than or equal to the available inventory, the ending inventory is zero. We can use Excel's MAX function to model this, as follows:

$$\text{Ending inventory} = \text{MAX(Available inventory} - \text{Demand, 0)}$$

Hence, column G = MAX(column D − column E, 0).

A stockout occurs when demand exceeds available inventory.

■ We now calculate the stockout (or lost sales) in column H. If the demand exceeds the available inventory, there is a stockout. However, if the demand is less than or equal to the available inventory, there is no stockout. Once again, we can use the MAX function to model this, as follows:

$$\text{Stockout} = \text{MAX(Demand} - \text{Available inventory, 0)}$$

Hence, column H = MAX(column E − column D, 0).

We need to check for outstanding orders before placing a new order.

■ If the ending inventory is at or below the reorder point, an order needs to be placed with the supplier. Before we place an order, however, we need to check whether there are outstanding orders. The reason for this is as follows. If the ending inventory level has already triggered an order on an earlier day, but that order has not yet been received due to the delivery lead time, a duplicate order should not be placed. Hence, in column I, we calculate the *apparent* ending inventory; that is, we add the *actual* ending inventory (shown in column G) and any orders that have already been placed. The logic behind the formula in column I is as follows:

Apparent inventory at end of period $t =$

Apparent inventory at end of period $(t - 1)$

− Demand satisfied in period t + Order size,

if an order was placed at the end of period $(t - 1)$

For example, the formula in cell I5 is

=I4−F5+IF(J4=1,$T$11,0)

■ If the apparent inventory at the end of any day is at or below the reorder point (cell T12), an order is to be placed that day. We denote this event in column J by using an IF function (1 implies place an order, 0 implies don't place an order). For example, the formula in cell J5 is

=IF(I5<=$T$12,1,0)

Lead time is simulated by using a RANDBETWEEN function.

■ If an order is placed, the delivery lead time for this order is simulated in column K by using a RANDBETWEEN function (between 1 and 3). For example, the formula in cell K5 is

=IF(J5=1,RANDBETWEEN($T$14,$T$15),0)

- Finally, in column L, we calculate the arrival day of this order as follows:

$$\text{Arrive on day} = \text{Current day} + \text{Lead time} + 1$$

For example, the formula in cell L5 is

$$=IF(J5=1,A5+K5+1,0)$$

Note that this formula includes +1 because the order is actually placed at the end of the current day (or, equivalently, the start of the next day).

Computation of Costs

Columns M through P show the cost computations for Simkin's inventory model each day of the month. The relevant formulas are as follows:

We compute the costs.

Column M:	Holding cost	$= \$T\$17 \times$ Ending inventory in column G
Column N:	Stockout cost	$= \$T\$20 \times$ Shortage in Column H
Column O:	Order cost	$= \$T\$23$ (if value in Column J $= I$)
Column P:	Total cost	$=$ column M $+$ column N $+$ column O

The totals for each cost component for the entire month are shown in row 29 (cells M29:P29). For instance, the replication in Screenshot 11.3A shows a holding cost of \$1.62 (cell M29), stockout cost of \$112 (cell N29), order cost of \$120 (cell O29), and total cost of \$233.62 (cell P29).

Replication Using Data Table

To compute Simkin's average monthly cost, we need to replicate the model as many times as possible. Each time, due to the presence of random variables, all simulated values in the spreadsheet will change. Hence, the inventory costs will change.

File: 11-3.xls, sheet: 11-3B

We have already seen how we can use Data Table to easily replicate a simulation model multiple times. In Harry's Auto Shop example, we replicated only a single output measure (i.e., monthly profit) by using Data Table (see Screenshot 11.2C). In contrast, suppose we would like to replicate each of the four costs—holding cost, stockout cost, order cost, and total cost—in Simkin's example. It turns out that we can expand the use of Data Table to replicate all four measures at the same time. The procedure, illustrated in Screenshot 11.3B, is as follows:

This is how we set up Data Table to replicate more than one output measure.

1. Here again, we illustrate only 200 replications of the model. We first enter numbers 1 to 200 in cells W4:W203, corresponding to these 200 replications.

2. In cells X4 to AA4 (i.e., adjacent to the *first* cell in the range W4:W203), we specify the cell references for the four output measures we want replicated. Hence, the formula in cell X4 is =M29, in cell Y4 is =N29, in cell Z4 is =O29, and in cell AA4 is =P29. We leave cells X5:AA203 blank. As before, Data Table will fill in these cells when we run it.

3. We now use the mouse or keyboard to select the entire range W4:AA203 (i.e., all five columns). *After* selecting this range, we choose **DATA|TABLE** from Excel's menu.

4. We leave the row input cell box blank and enter some arbitrary cell reference in the column input box. As before, we need to make sure the selected cell (AA1, in this case) is not used anywhere in the simulation model.

5. Finally, we click **OK** to run Data Table. The procedure computes and displays 200 simulated values of the monthly holding, stockout, order, and total costs in columns X, Y, Z, and AA, respectively.

SCREENSHOT 11.3B   Data Table for Simkin's Hardware Store

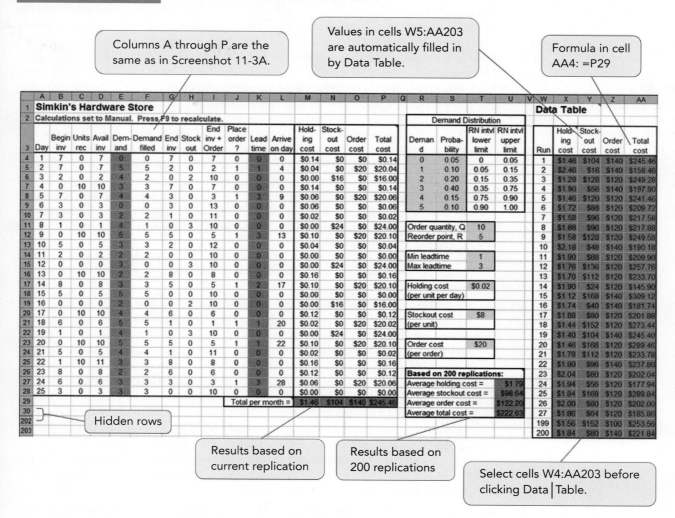

Columns A through P are the same as in Screenshot 11-3A.

Values in cells W5:AA203 are automatically filled in by Data Table.

Formula in cell AA4: =P29

Hidden rows

Results based on current replication

Results based on 200 replications

Select cells W4:AA203 before clicking Data | Table.

Simkin's Hardware Store

Calculations set to Manual. Press F9 to recalculate.

Day	Begin inv	Units rec	Avail inv	Dem-and	Demand filled	End inv	Stock out	End inv + Order	Place order ?	Lead time	Arrive on day	Hold-ing cost	Stock-out cost	Order cost	Total cost
1	7	0	7	0	0	7	0	7	0	0	0	$0.14	$0	$0	$0.14
2	7	0	7	5	5	2	0	2	1	1	4	$0.04	$0	$20	$20.04
3	2	0	2	4	2	0	2	10	0	0	0	$0.00	$16	$0	$16.00
4	0	10	10	3	3	7	0	7	0	0	0	$0.14	$0	$0	$0.14
5	7	0	7	4	4	3	0	3	1	3	9	$0.06	$0	$20	$20.06
6	3	0	3	0	0	3	0	13	0	0	0	$0.06	$0	$0	$0.06
7	3	0	3	2	2	1	0	11	0	0	0	$0.02	$0	$0	$0.02
8	1	0	1	4	1	0	3	10	0	0	0	$0.00	$24	$0	$24.00
9	0	10	10	5	5	5	0	5	1	3	13	$0.10	$0	$20	$20.10
10	5	0	5	3	3	2	0	12	0	0	0	$0.04	$0	$0	$0.04
11	2	0	2	2	2	0	0	10	0	0	0	$0.00	$0	$0	$0.00
12	0	0	0	3	0	0	3	10	0	0	0	$0.00	$24	$0	$24.00
13	0	10	10	2	2	8	0	8	0	0	0	$0.16	$0	$0	$0.16
14	8	0	8	3	3	5	0	5	1	2	17	$0.10	$0	$20	$20.10
15	5	0	5	5	5	0	0	10	0	0	0	$0.00	$0	$0	$0.00
16	0	0	0	2	0	0	2	10	0	0	0	$0.00	$16	$0	$16.00
17	0	10	10	4	4	6	0	6	0	0	0	$0.12	$0	$0	$0.12
18	6	0	6	5	5	1	0	1	1	1	20	$0.02	$0	$20	$20.02
19	1	0	1	4	1	0	3	10	0	0	0	$0.00	$24	$0	$24.00
20	0	10	10	5	5	5	0	5	1	1	22	$0.10	$0	$20	$20.10
21	5	0	5	4	4	1	0	11	0	0	0	$0.02	$0	$0	$0.02
22	1	10	11	3	3	8	0	8	0	0	0	$0.16	$0	$0	$0.16
23	8	0	8	2	2	6	0	6	0	0	0	$0.12	$0	$0	$0.12
24	6	0	6	3	3	3	0	3	1	3	28	$0.06	$0	$20	$20.06
25	3	0	3	3	3	0	0	10	0	0	0	$0.00	$0	$0	$0.00
								Total per month =				$1.46	$104	$140	$245.46

Demand Distribution

Demand	Probability	RN intvl lower limit	RN intvl upper limit
0	0.05	0	0.05
1	0.10	0.05	0.15
2	0.20	0.15	0.35
3	0.40	0.35	0.75
4	0.15	0.75	0.90
5	0.10	0.90	1.00

Order quantity, Q	10
Reorder point, R	5
Min leadtime	1
Max leadtime	3
Holding cost (per unit per day)	$0.02
Stockout cost (per unit)	$8
Order cost (per order)	$20

Based on 200 replications:

Average holding cost =	$1.79
Average stockout cost =	$98.64
Average order cost =	$122.20
Average total cost =	$222.63

Data Table

Run	Hold-ing cost	Stock-out cost	Order cost	Total cost
1	$1.46	$104	$140	$245.46
2	$2.46	$16	$140	$158.46
3	$1.28	$128	$120	$249.28
4	$1.90	$56	$140	$197.90
5	$1.46	$120	$120	$241.46
6	$1.72	$88	$120	$209.72
7	$1.58	$96	$120	$217.58
8	$1.88	$96	$120	$217.88
9	$1.58	$128	$120	$249.58
10	$2.18	$48	$140	$190.18
11	$1.90	$88	$120	$209.90
12	$1.76	$136	$120	$257.76
13	$1.70	$112	$120	$233.70
14	$1.90	$24	$120	$145.90
15	$1.12	$168	$140	$309.12
16	$1.74	$40	$140	$181.74
17	$1.88	$80	$120	$201.88
18	$1.44	$152	$120	$273.44
19	$1.40	$104	$140	$245.40
20	$1.46	$168	$120	$289.46
21	$1.78	$112	$120	$233.78
22	$1.80	$96	$140	$237.80
23	$2.04	$80	$120	$202.04
24	$1.94	$56	$120	$177.94
25	$1.84	$168	$120	$289.84
26	$2.00	$80	$120	$202.00
27	$1.86	$64	$120	$185.86
199	$1.56	$152	$100	$253.56
200	$1.84	$80	$140	$221.84

Analyzing the Results

We can conduct statistical analyses on the replicated values.

We can now use the 200 cost values to conduct statistical analyses, as before. For example, if $Q = 10$ and $R = 5$, Screenshot 11.3B indicates that Simkin's average monthly costs of holding, stockout, and order are $1.79 (cell U27), $98.64 (cell U28), and $122.20 (cell U29), respectively. The average total cost, shown in cell U30, is $222.63.

As an exercise, see if you can set up Data Table to calculate Simkin's average demand fill rate per month. That is, what percentage of monthly demand received does Simkin satisfy on average? *Hint:* The fill rate for each replication is the ratio of demand satisfied (sum of entries in column F) to demand received (sum of entries in column E).

Using Scenario Manager to Include Decisions in a Simulation Model

In simulating Simkin's inventory model so far, we have assumed a fixed order quantity, Q, of 10, and a fixed reorder point, R, of 5. Recall, however, that Simkin's objective was to identify the Q and R values that will help him reduce his total monthly costs. To achieve this objective, suppose Simkin wants to try four different values for Q (i.e., 8, 10, 12, and 14) and two different values for R (i.e., 5 and 8). One approach to run this extended simulation would be to run the model and Data Table (see Screenshot 11.3B) eight times—once for each combination of Q and R values. We could then compare the average total cost (cell U30) in each case to determine which combination of Q and R is best. This approach, of course, could become quite cumbersome, especially if we wanted to vary several different input parameters and try multiple values for each parameter.

We use Scenario Manager when we want to try several values for one or more input parameters in a model.

It turns out that we can use an Excel procedure called Scenario Manager to automatically run a simulation model for several combinations of input parameter values. To do so, we first assume *any* combination of values for the input parameters and set up the complete simulation model (including Data Table) to replicate the desired output measures. After we have done so, we next define multiple scenarios—one for each combination of input parameter values. When we then run Scenario Manager, Excel will automatically run the model and the Data Table replications for each scenario and report the desired results.

We illustrate the construction and use of Scenario Manager by using the simulation model we have already constructed for Simkin (shown in Screenshot 11.3B for $Q = 10$ and $R = 5$). The procedure is as follows:

This is how we set up Scenario Manager.

1. Invoke Scenario Manager by clicking **TOOLS|SCENARIOS**. The window shown in Screenshot 11.3C(a) is displayed.

2. Click **ADD** to create a new scenario. The **EDIT SCENARIO** window shown in Screenshot 11.3C(b) is displayed. In the box titled **SCENARIO NAME**, enter any name of your choice for the scenario. (In Simkin's model, we have used names such as Q8R5, Q8R8, and Q12R5 to make the scenarios self-explanatory.) In the **CHANGING CELLS** box, enter the cell references for the cells whose values you wish to change. In Simkin's model, these would be cells T11 and T12, corresponding to the input parameters Q and R, respectively. If the changing cells are not contiguous in the model, separate the cell references with commas. Next, if desired, enter a comment to describe the scenario. Checking the **PREVENT CHANGES** option protects the scenario from being accidentally edited or deleted, while the **HIDE** option hides the scenario.

    Click **OK** to get the **SCENARIO VALUES** window, as shown in Screenshot 11.3C(c). For each changing cell, enter the appropriate value. For example, for the scenario shown in Screenshot 11.3C(c), the values of Q and R are 12 and 5, respectively.

3. Repeat Step 2 for as many scenarios as desired. In Simkin's model, you define eight scenarios corresponding to the eight combinations of (Q,R) − (8,5), (8,8), (10,5), (10,8), (12,5), (12,8), (14,5), and (14,8). You can also edit or delete a scenario after it has been created (assuming that the **PREVENT CHANGES** option is unchecked).

4. When all scenarios have been defined, click **SUMMARY** to run Scenario Manager. The **SCENARIO SUMMARY** window shown in Screenshot 11.3C(d) appears. In the box titled **RESULT CELLS**, enter the cell references for the output measures you would like Scenario Manager to report for each scenario. In Simkin's model, these would be cells U27:U30, corresponding to the four average cost measures—holding cost, stockout cost, order cost, and total cost (see Screenshot 11.3B). Here again, use commas to separate cell references that are not contiguous.

Scenario Manager's results can be shown either as a Scenario summary table or as a PivotTable.

    The results can be shown either as a Scenario summary table (preferred in most cases) or as a PivotTable report (choose this option if there are many changing cells and scenarios, and if you are comfortable analyzing results using PivotTables).

5. Click **OK**. Scenario Manager runs the simulation model (including Data Table) for each scenario and presents the results in a separate worksheet, as shown in Screenshot 11.3D on page 504 (which has grid lines added to make it clearer).

File: 11-3.xls, sheet: 11-3D

SCREENSHOT 11.3C   **Setting up Scenario Manager in Excel**

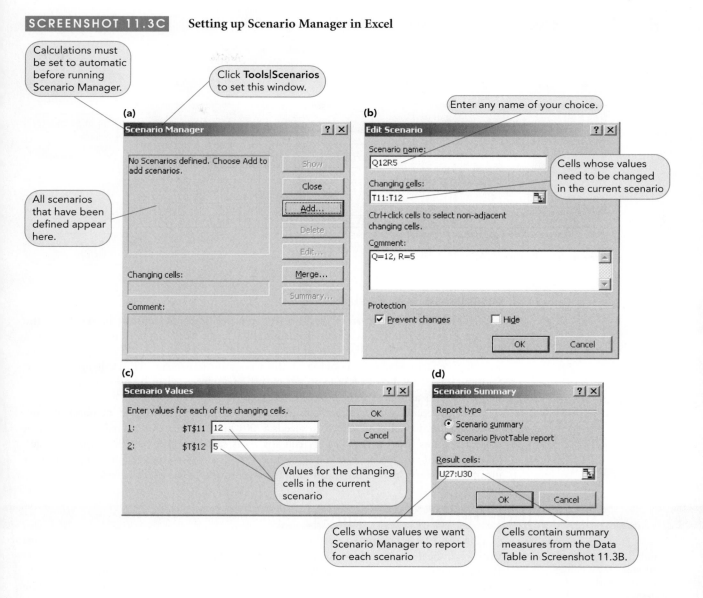

Calculations must be set to automatic before running Scenario Manager.

Click **Tools|Scenarios** to set this window.

Enter any name of your choice.

(a)

All scenarios that have been defined appear here.

Cells whose values need to be changed in the current scenario

(b)

(c)

Values for the changing cells in the current scenario

(d)

Cells whose values we want Scenario Manager to report for each scenario

Cells contain summary measures from the Data Table in Screenshot 11.3B.

Excel Notes

- The Calculation option in Excel must be set to Automatic *before* you run Scenario Manager. If this option is set to Manual, Scenario Manager will report the same summary results for all scenarios.
- The standard version of Excel can accommodate up to 32 changing cells for each scenario.
- Although the number of scenarios allowed in Excel is limited only by your computer's memory, note that Scenario Manager may take a long time to execute if you include too many scenarios, especially if running each scenario involves running Data Table with many replications.

SCREENSHOT 11.3D　　**Scenario Manager Results for Simkin's Hardware Store**

Results for each scenario are presented in a column.

Q=14, R=8 has lowest total cost.

Input parameter values for a scenario

	A	B	C	D	E	F	G	H	I	J	K	L
1												
2		Scenario Summary										
3				Current Values:	Q8R5	Q8R8	Q10R5	Q10R8	Q12R5	Q12R8	Q14R5	Q14R8
5		Changing Cells:										
6			$T$11	10	8	8	10	10	12	12	14	14
7			$T$12	5	5	8	5	8	5	8	5	8
8		Result Cells:										
9			$U$27	$1.77	$1.39	$2.47	$1.79	$2.58	$2.20	$3.05	$2.69	$3.54
10			$U$28	$100.48	$111.64	$44.96	$108.60	$51.20	$91.84	$43.44	$83.08	$40.84
11			$U$29	$121.90	$144.60	$177.10	$121.20	$141.10	$105.90	$119.20	$94.90	$104.80
12			$U$30	$221.89	$261.17	$222.19	$223.28	$194.03	$193.87	$165.45	$174.68	$145.59
13		Notes: Current Values column represents values of Changing Cells at										
14		time Scenario Summary Report was created. Changing Cells for each										
15		scenario are highlighted in grey.										

Output measure values for a scenario

Analyzing the Results

For each combination of order quantity and reorder point, Screenshot 11.3D shows the average monthly holding, stockout, order, and total costs. Note that because all these values are based on only 200 replications of the simulation model, they could change each time we run Scenario Manager. Looking at the values in Screenshot 11.3D, it appears that Simkin's lowest total cost of $145.59 per month is obtained when he uses an order quantity of 14 units and a reorder point of 8 units.

As an exercise, see if you can compute other output measures (e.g., demand fill rate, probability that total monthly cost exceeds $200) in the simulation model. Then, include these measures also in the Results cell for each scenario and run Scenario Manager. Likewise, see if you can analyze the impact on total cost when you vary the values of other input parameters, such as the minimum and maximum delivery lead times.

11.6　SIMULATION MODEL OF A QUEUING PROBLEM

Simulation is an effective technique for modeling many real-world queuing systems that cannot be analyzed analytically.

In Chapter 10, we computed performance measures for several simple queuing systems, using analytical models. However, as noted in that chapter, many real-world queuing systems can be difficult to model analytically. In such cases, we usually turn to simulation to analyze the performance of these systems. To study this issue, in this section we illustrate an example of a queuing model in which both the arrival times of customers and the service times at the facility follow discrete general distributions. Then, in Solved Problem 11-2 at the end of this chapter, we discuss the simulation of another queuing model in which arrival times are exponentially distributed and service times are normally distributed.

Denton Savings Bank

Sanjay Krishnan, manager at the Denton Savings Bank, is attempting to improve customer satisfaction by offering service such that (1) the average customer waiting time does not exceed two minutes and (2) the average queue length is two or fewer customers. The bank gets an average of 150 customers each day. Given the existing situation for service and arrival times, as shown in Table 11.6, does the bank meet Sanjay's criteria?

In discrete-event simulation models, we need to keep track of the passage of time by using a simulation clock.

Note that in simulating this queuing model, we need to keep track of the passage of time to record the specific arrival and departure times of customers. We refer to such

TABLE 11.6

Distribution of Service
Times and Time
between Arrivals at Denton
Savings Bank

SERVICE TIME	PROBABILITY
1	0.25
2	0.20
3	0.40
4	0.15

TIME BETWEEN ARRIVALS	PROBABILITY
0	0.10
1	0.15
2	0.10
3	0.35
4	0.25
5	0.05

models, in which events (e.g., customer arrivals and departures) occur at discrete points in
time, as **discrete-event simulation** models.

Setting Up the Model

File: 11-4.xls

Each replication of this simulation model corresponds to a day's operation at the bank (i.e.,
the arrival and service of 150 customers). The Excel layout for this problem is presented in
Screenshot 11.4. To keep track of the passage of time in this model, we monitor a clock that
starts at zero and continually counts time (in minutes, in Denton's model). Observe that in

SCREENSHOT 11.4   Excel Layout and Results for Denton Savings Bank

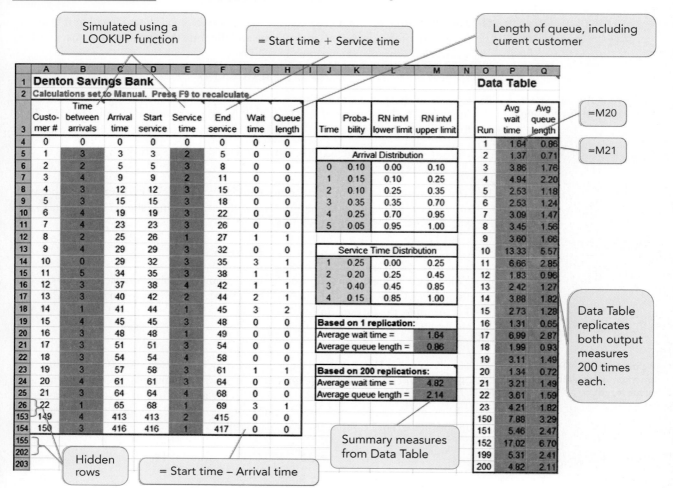

row 4, we have included customer number 0, with zero values for all columns, to *initialize* this simulation clock. This is a good practice in all discrete-event simulation models. Rows 5 through 154 in the spreadsheet are organized as follows:

- Column A lists the customer number (1 through 150).

Time between successive arrivals follows a discrete general distribution.

- Column B shows the time between arrivals of successive customers, simulated using a LOOKUP function. The parameters (i.e., arrival times, probabilities, and random number intervals) for this LOOKUP function are shown in cells J6:M11. The formula in cells B5:B154 is

$$=LOOKUP(RAND(),\$L\$6:\$L\$11,\$J\$6:\$J\$11)$$

  The $ sign in the formula anchors the cell references so that we can create the formula in cell B5 and then copy it to cells B6:B154.

- Column C calculates the actual arrival time of the current customer as the sum of the arrival time of the previous customer and the time between arrivals (simulated in column B). This type of computation is an example of the use of the simulation clock, which records the actual elapsed clock time in a simulation model. For example, the formula in cell C5 is

$$= C4+B5$$

- The actual time at which this customer starts service is calculated in column D as the maximum of the customer's arrival time and the time the previous customer finishes service. For example, the formula in cell D5 is

$$= MAX(C5,F4)$$

Service time also follows a discrete general distribution.

- Column E shows the service time for this customer, simulated using a LOOKUP function. The parameters of this LOOKUP function are shown in cells J14:M17. The formula in cells E5:E154 is

$$=LOOKUP(RAND(),\$L\$14:\$L\$17,\$J\$14:\$J\$17)$$

- The clock time at which this customer ends service is shown in column F as the sum of the start time (shown in column D) and the service time (shown in column E). For example, the formula in cell F5 is

$$= D5+E5$$

- Column G calculates the wait time of this customer as the difference between the customer's start time (shown in column D) and arrival time (shown in column C). For example, the formula in cell G5 is

$$= D5-C5$$

We use Excel's MATCH function to calculate the queue length.

- Finally, column H calculates the queue length by using Excel's MATCH function. The MATCH function is used to determine how many customers (up to the current customer) have start times that are smaller than the arrival time of the current customer. Clearly, all customers (including the current one) who do not meet this criterion are in the queue. For example, the formula in cell H5 is

$$=A5-MATCH(C5,\$D\$5:D5,1)$$

Using the wait times and queue lengths shown in cells G5:H154 for the 150 customers, we can determine the following two performance measures for the bank each day: (1) average wait time per customer (shown in cell M20) and (2) average queue length (shown in cell M21).

Replication Using Data Table

Data Table is used here to replicate both performance measures.

Based on the average wait time and queue length values in cells M20 and M21, respectively, of Screenshot 11.4, it may seem to appear that Denton is meeting both of Sanjay's desired targets. The average wait time is only 1.64 minutes, and there are only 0.86 customers on average in the queue. However, note that these values are based on just one replication and will change each time we recalculate the model. Hence, to determine more precise values for these averages, we now replicate each performance measure 200 times. Screenshot 11.4 shows how we can use Data Table to do so, in columns O through Q. Note that Data Table has been used here to replicate both performance measures at the same time.

Analyzing the Results

Based on the average values computed from 200 replications in Screenshot 11.4, it appears that the system does *not* meet either criterion. The average wait time of 4.82 minutes per customer (cell M24) is more than double Sanjay's desired target of two minutes per customer. The average queue length of 2.14 customers (cell M25) is, however, close to Sanjay's desired target of two customers. Sanjay should, perhaps, focus on initiating training programs to improve the average service rate of his tellers.

11.7 SIMULATION MODEL OF A REVENUE MANAGEMENT PROBLEM

Revenue management problems are popular in the airline and hotel industries.

Another popular application of simulation is in *revenue management* problems, first introduced by the airline and hotel industries as *yield management* problems. This type of problem focuses on trying to identify the most efficient way of using an existing capacity (usually fixed) to manage revenues in situations where customer demand and

DECISION MODELING IN ACTION
Using Simulation at Mexico's Largest Truck Manufacturer

The manufacturing world has gone global. To remain competitive, firms have made strategic and cultural alliances. Mexico is the United States' third-largest trading partner ($27 billion), after Canada and Japan. Trading breakthroughs, such as the North American Economic Community (NAEC), have fundamental implications for industries in the United States and Mexico, including the truck manufacturer Vilpac, which is headquartered in Mexicali, Mexico.

Vilpac developed a comprehensive simulation model for the analysis and design of its manufacturing operation, using SIMNET II (a network-based simulation language on an IBM 3090 supercomputer). The idea was to allow manufacturing engineers to experiment with alternative systems and strategies to seek the best overall factory performance.

The model included 95 machines and 1900 parts, and it performed a wide variety of experiments. SIMNET II was used to study the effects of policies on (1) the flexibility of the factory to adapt to change in the demand and product mix, (2) the factory's responsiveness to customer orders, (3) product quality, and (4) total cost. Benefits of the simulation approach included a 260% increase in production, a 70% decrease in work-in-process, and an increase in market share.

Source: J. P. Nuno, et al. "Mexico's Vilpac Truck Company Uses a CIM Implementation to Become a World Class Manufacturer," *Interfaces* 23, 1 (January–February 1993): 59–75.

behaviour are uncertain.[5] To study this type of problem, in this section let us consider an example in which the owner of a limousine service wants to find the optimal number of reservations she should accept for a trip. Then, in Solved Problem 11-3 at the end of this chapter, we illustrate the simulation of another revenue management problem, involving room reservations at a hotel.

Judith's Airport Limousine Service

Judith McKay is always on the lookout for entrepreneurial opportunities. Living in North Battleford, Saskatchewan, she recognizes that it is approximately 140 kilometres to Saskatoon's John G. Diefenbaker International Airport. Judith estimates that, on average, there are about 45 people from North Battleford (and its vicinity) who need rides to and from the airport each day. To help them, Judith is considering leasing a 10-passenger van and offering a shuttle service between North Battleford and the airport. There would be four trips per day: a morning trip and an evening trip to the airport, and a morning and an evening trip from the airport.

After researching the issue carefully, Judith sets some operating guidelines for her problem and estimates the following parameters for each trip:

- Reservations for a trip can be made up to 12 hours in advance, by paying a nonrefundable $10 deposit. Judith will accept reservations up to her reservation limit (which this simulation model will help her decide).

- The ticket price is $35 per passenger per trip. Passengers with reservations must pay the $25 balance at the start of the trip.

The number of reservations is probabilistic.

- The number of reservations requested each trip follows a discrete uniform distribution between 7 and 14. Judith will, of course, reject a reservation request if she has reached her reservation limit.

The number of show-ups is also probabilistic.

- The probability that a person with a reservation shows up for the trip is 0.80. In other words, 20% of people with reservations do not show up. Anyone who does not show up forfeits the $10 deposit.

- If the number of passengers who show up exceeds 10 (the passenger capacity of the van), alternate arrangements must be made to get these extra people to the airport. This will cost Judith $75 per person. That is, Judith will lose $40 (= $75 − $35) per overbooked person.

Finally, the number of walk-ups is also probabilistic.

- The number of walk-up passengers (i.e., passengers without reservations) for a trip has the following discrete general distribution: probability of zero walk-ups is 0.30, probability of one walk-up is 0.45, and probability of two walk-ups is 0.25. Judith does not anticipate that there will ever be more than two walk-ups per trip.

- Walk-up passengers pay $50 per trip. However, Judith does not have to make alternate arrangements for these passengers if her van is full.

- The total cost per trip (to or from the airport) to Judith is $100. Note that due to the possibility of walk-up passengers on the return trip, Judith has to make a trip to the airport even if she has no passengers on that trip.

Judith wants to find out how many reservations she should accept in order to maximize her average profit per trip. Specifically, she is considering accepting 10, 11, 12, 13, or 14 reservations.

[5] A good description of *yield management* can be found in B. C. Smith, J. F. Leimkuhler, and R. M. Darrow. "Yield Management at American Airlines," *Interfaces* (January 1992), 22, 1, 8–31.

File: 11-5.xls, sheet: 11-5A

Each replication here
corresponds to one trip.

The number of people showing up is simulated using a
nested IF function.

Setting Up the Model

Each replication in Judith's problem corresponds to one trip. The Excel layout for this problem, shown in Screenshot 11.5A, is organized as follows:

- Cell B3 shows the number of reservations accepted for the trip. Note that this is a decision that is specified by Judith. Let us first set up the model assuming that Judith accepts 14 reservations for each trip. Later, we will use Scenario Manager to run this model automatically for all reservation limits (i.e., 10 to 14).

- Cell B4 shows the number of reservations requested for a trip. We simulate this value from a discrete uniform distribution by using the RANDBETWEEN function with parameters $a = 7$ (specified in cell G4) and $b = 14$ (specified in cell G5). The formula in cell B4 is

$$=\text{RANDBETWEEN(G4,G5)}$$

- In cell B5, we set the actual number of reservations accepted by Judith for the trip as the *smaller* of Judith's reservation limit (cell B3) and the number of reservations requested (cell B4). The formula in cell B5 is

$$=\text{MIN(B3,B4)}$$

- Next, we simulate the number of people with reservations who actually show up. To do so, we need to model a separate "yes" (with probability 0.80) or "no" (with

SCREENSHOT 11.5A   **Excel Layout and Results for Judith's Limousine Service**

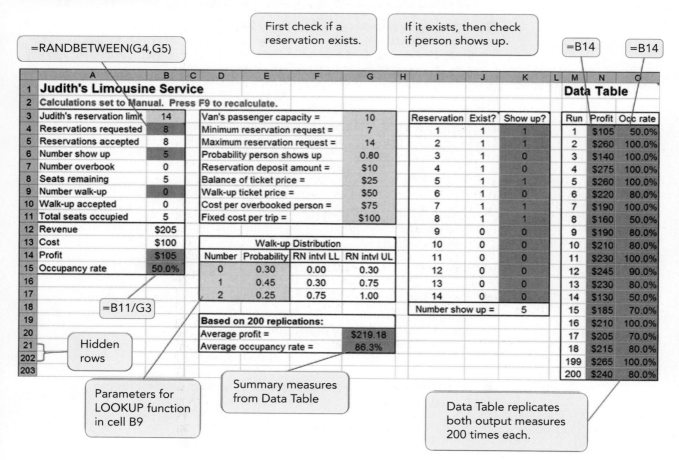

probability 0.20) for each person whose reservation has been accepted. We accomplish this by first listing all 14 *potential* reservations (shown in cells I4:I17). Then, for each person, we first use an IF function to verify whether that reservation exists. For example, the formula in cell J4 is

$$=IF(14<=\$B\$5,1,0)$$

If the result of the IF function in column J is 1 (implying that the reservation exists), we then simulate whether that person actually shows up by using a nested IF function (i.e., IF function within an IF function) in column K. For example, the formula in cell K4 is

$$=IF(J4=1, IF(RAND()<=\$G6,1,0),0)$$

The first part of the IF function checks whether the reservation exists. If it does, the second IF function checks whether the person actually shows up (denoted by 1) or not (denoted by 0). Obviously, if the reservation does not exist, the result is 0, implying that the person did not show up. *Note:* Another way to simulate the result in cell K4 is to use the formula =J4*IF(RAND()<=\$G\$6,1,0). Note that if J4 is 0 (implying that the reservation does not exist), the product will always be 0, regardless of what the IF function returns.

   The values in cells K4:K17 are added in cell K18 to calculate the total number of people who showed up for the trip. This value is also reported in cell B6.

■ If the number of passengers showing up (cell B6) exceeds the van's passenger capacity (specified in cell G3), we have overbooked passengers. Otherwise, we have no overbooked passengers. In cell B7, we calculate the number of overbooked passengers by using the MAX function, as follows:

$$=MAX(B6-G3,0)$$

■ Likewise, if the van capacity exceeds the number of passengers showing up, we have some seats remaining. Otherwise, we are full. In cell B8, we calculate this number as follows:

$$=MAX(G3-B6,0)$$

The number of walk-up passengers is simulated by using a LOOKUP function.

■ Next, in cell B9, we simulate the number of walk-up passengers by using a LOOKUP function. The parameter values for this function are specified in cells D15:G17. The formula in cell B9 is

$$=LOOKUP(RAND(),F15:F17,D15:D17)$$

■ The number of walk-ups who can be accommodated in the van is obviously limited by the seats remaining (cell B8). Hence, in cell B10, we calculate the number of walk-ups accepted by using a MIN function, as follows:

$$=MIN(B8,B9)$$

■ In cell B11, we compute the total number of seats occupied for the trip. The formula is

$$=G3-B8+B10$$

■ The total revenue and cost for the trip are now calculated in cells B12 and B13, respectively, as

$$\text{Revenue} = \$10 \times \text{Reservations accepted} + \$25 \times \text{Number of people who show up} + \$50 \times \text{Walk-ups accepted}$$

$$= \text{G7*B5} + \text{G8*B6} + \text{G9*B10}$$

$$\text{Cost} = \$75 \times \text{Number overbooked} + \$100$$

$$= \text{G10*B7} + \text{G11}$$

■ In cell B14, we calculate the trip profit as (Revenue − Cost).

The load factor defines the percentage of capacity that is occupied.

■ Another performance measure that is popular in many revenue management problems is the percentage of capacity that has been actually utilized. Airlines and hotels refer to this measure as the *load factor*. To illustrate this measure, we compute Judith's occupancy rate for the trip in cell B15 as

$$=\text{B11/G3}$$

Replicating the Model Using Data Table and Scenario Manager

We use Data Table to replicate Judith's model.

The profit of $105 (shown in cell B14) and occupancy rate of 50% (shown in cell B15) in Screenshot 11.5A are based on just one replication of the model. Hence, they should not be used to make any conclusive statements about Judith's problem. To determine more precise values, we now replicate each performance measure 200 times. Columns M through O show how we can use Data Table to do so. The formula in cell N4 is =B14, while the formula in cell O4 is =B15. Cells N5:O203 are left blank and will be automatically filled in by the Data Table procedure when it is run. Based on these 200 replicated values, we calculate the average values of both measures (shown in cells G20 and G21, respectively). With a reservation limit of 14, Screenshot 11.5A indicates that Judith can expect a profit of $219.18 per trip and an occupancy rate of 86.3%.

Next, we use Scenario Manager to try different values for the reservation limit.

Now that we have set up Judith's simulation model and Data Table for a specific reservation limit, we can use Scenario Manager to try different values for this parameter. The procedure is as follows (here again, remember to make sure that calculations are set to Automatic in Excel before running Scenario Manager):

1. Invoke Scenario Manager by clicking **TOOLS|SCENARIOS**.
2. Define five scenarios, corresponding to the five reservation limits that Judith wants to try (i.e., 10 to 14). For each scenario, specify cell B3 as the cell reference in the **CHANGING CELLS** box and enter the appropriate reservation limit in the **SCENARIO VALUES** window.
3. Once all scenarios have been defined, click **SUMMARY**. In the box titled **RESULT CELLS**, specify cells G20 and G21 as the cells to track.
4. Click **OK** to run Scenario Manager. The results appear in a separate worksheet, as shown in Screenshot 11.5B.

File: 11-5.xls, sheet: 11-5B

Analyzing the Results

Comparing the profit values in Screenshot 11.5B, it appears that Judith's best choice would be to accept 12 reservations per trip. (Remember that this result is based on only 200 replications.) The resulting average profit is $230.98 per trip. Not surprisingly, the occupancy rate is highest when Judith accepts 14 reservations, even though the rate does not seem to exceed 90% in any scenario.

Scenario Manager Results for Judith's Limousine Service

Cell showing reservation limit in model

	A	B	C	D	E	F	G	H	I
1									
2		Scenario Summary							
3				Current Values:	R10	R11	R12	R13	R14
5		Changing Cells:							
6		$B$3		14	10	11	12	13	14
7		Result Cells:							
8		$G$20		$224.08	$222.95	$228.20	$230.98	$220.88	$222.20
9		$G$21		86.1%	82.0%	83.8%	85.6%	85.3%	87.6%
10		Notes: Current Values column represents values of Changing Cells at							
11		time Scenario Summary Report was created. Changing Cells for each							
12		scenario are highlighted in grey.							

Profit

Occupancy rate

Values for reservation limit

Limit of 12 yields highest profit here, based on 200 replications.

So far, we have developed four simulation models using only Excel's built-in functions. We have also used Data Table to replicate the output measures in each model and Scenario Manager to automatically try different values for one or more input parameters. Solved Problems 11-1 to 11-3 at the end of this chapter discuss three additional simulation models using only Excel's built-in functions.

There are, however, several add-in programs available that make it even easier to develop and replicate simulation models using Excel. Hence, in the next two sections (and in Solved Problem 11-4 at the end of this chapter, in which we simulate a project management problem), we illustrate the use of one of the more powerful Excel add-ins for simulation, Oracle Crystal Ball.

11.8 SIMULATION MODEL OF AN INVENTORY PROBLEM USING ORACLE CRYSTAL BALL

Oracle Crystal Ball, found on the CD-ROM that accompanies this textbook, is an Excel add-in used for simulation.

Oracle Crystal Ball, an add-in for Excel, is published by Decisioneering, Inc. (For more information, please refer to www.decisioneering.com.) As noted earlier, access to a student version of this package (valid for 140 days from date of installation) is included on the CD-ROM that accompanies this textbook.

Reasons for Using Add-in Programs

From a logic and appearance point of view, a simulation model that is set up in Excel with Oracle Crystal Ball (or any other add-in) will look very similar to one that is set up without an add-in. Hence, any of the simulation models that we have created so far (using only Excel's built-in functions) can also be used with Oracle Crystal Ball. There are, however, three main features that add-ins such as Oracle Crystal Ball offer over Excel's built-in functions and procedures. As we will see shortly, these features are worthwhile enough to make the use of such add-in programs very useful in simulation modeling. The three features that add-ins such as Oracle Crystal Ball offer are as follows:

These three features of add-ins make them useful tools for developing simulation models on spreadsheets.

1. They have built-in functions to simulate not only from the simple probability distributions discussed so far but also from many other distributions that are commonly encountered in practice (e.g., binomial, triangular, lognormal). Further, the formulas

to simulate from these distributions are simple, intuitive, and easy to use. For example, to simulate a random value in Oracle Crystal Ball from a normal distribution with mean μ and standard deviation σ, we use the following formula: =CB.NORMAL(μ,σ). As you can see, this formula is much more intuitive than the formula we used earlier for simulating from a normal distribution: =NORMINV(RAND(),μ,σ).

2. They have built-in procedures that make it very easy to replicate the simulation model several hundred (or even several thousand) times. This means we will not have to set up and use Data Table.

3. They have built-in procedures that make it easy to collect and present information on various output measures. These measures can also be displayed graphically, if desired.

We should note that our intent here is to only provide a brief introduction to Oracle Crystal Ball and not to describe every aspect or capability of this add-in program. Once you have completed this section and the next, however, you should have sufficient knowledge about Oracle Crystal Ball to explore some of its other options and procedures. Many of these are self-explanatory, and we strongly encourage you to try these out on your own.

Simulation of Simkin's Hardware Store Using Oracle Crystal Ball

Here we revisit Simkin's Hardware Store example.

To illustrate the use of Oracle Crystal Ball, let us revisit the inventory problem of Simkin's Hardware Store. Recall from Section 11.5 that Simkin wants to test four different values (8, 10, 12, and 14) for the order quantity, Q, and two different values (5 and 8) for the reorder point, R, to see which combination of values for these two input parameters minimizes his monthly total cost. The total cost includes the following components: holding cost, stockout cost, and order cost. (At this time, we recommend that you refer to Section 11.5 for a quick refresher on this problem and the simulation model we developed for it.)

File: 11-6.xls

The Oracle Crystal Ball menus and toolbar are shown when the program is run.

Starting Oracle Crystal Ball The instructions for installing Oracle Crystal Ball on your PC can be found on this textbook's CD-ROM.[6] Once it is installed, you can start the program (and Excel) by clicking **CRYSTAL BALL** in the Windows **START** menu.

Once Oracle Crystal Ball has been loaded in Excel, you will see the following additional menu options displayed in Excel's main menu bar: **DEFINE, RUN,** and **ANALYZE.**[7] In addition, you will see the Oracle Crystal Ball toolbar, as shown in the top part of Screenshot 11.6A.

As noted earlier, add-ins such as Oracle Crystal Ball include an extensive set of built-in functions to simulate from many probability distributions. For your convenience, Table 11.7 presents a list of some of the functions available in Oracle Crystal Ball to generate random values from some of the distributions commonly used in simulation.[8,9]

---

[6] Basically, you need to run the file named Setup.exe, which is in the Oracle Crystal Ball directory on the CD-ROM. See the Readme.doc file in the same directory for detailed instructions.

[7] Previous versions of Oracle Crystal Ball include slightly different menus and choices within each menu. For example, the items in Excel's main menu bar are titled Cell, Run, CBTools instead of Define, Run, Analyze. Likewise, some of the windows shown in screenshots in this section are formatted slightly differently in previous versions. However, the functionality of the procedures described in this chapter is the same, regardless of which version of Oracle Crystal Ball is used.

[8] You can see a list of all the functions available in Oracle Crystal Ball by clicking f_x in Excel's standard toolbar and selecting Oracle Crystal Ball in the function category.

[9] Instead of using the formulas shown in Table 11.7 to define probability distributions in Oracle Crystal Ball, we could have used the Define|Define Assumption menu option. Using this option opens a graphical template of all the probability distributions available, from which we select the distribution we want. We have, however, chosen to use the formulas here because we find them to be more convenient.

SCREENSHOT 11.6A   **Excel Layout and Results Using Oracle Crystal Ball for Simkin's Hardware Store**

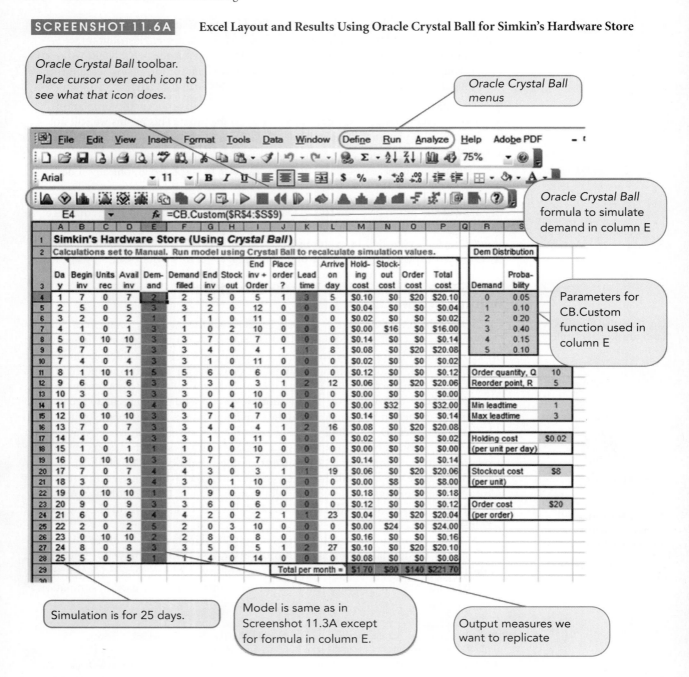

Oracle Crystal Ball toolbar. Place cursor over each icon to see what that icon does.

Oracle Crystal Ball menus

Oracle Crystal Ball formula to simulate demand in column E

Parameters for CB.Custom function used in column E

Simulation is for 25 days.

Model is same as in Screenshot 11.3A except for formula in column E.

Output measures we want to replicate

The model with Oracle Crystal Ball looks very similar to the model that uses only Excel's built-in functions.

Excel Layout Using Oracle Crystal Ball for Simkin's Hardware Store   We begin by setting up Simkin's inventory simulation model for any combination of Q and R values. (Let's use $Q = 10$ and $R = 5$, just as we did in Section 11.5.) Notice that the Excel layout in Screenshot 11.6A is very similar to the one we developed in Section 11.5 for this problem using only Excel's built-in functions (refer to Screenshot 11.3A). In fact, the only change here is in column E, where we simulate the demand each day. Recall that we simulated

TABLE 11.7	TO SIMULATE FROM	CRYSTAL BALL FORMULA
Simulating from Various Probability Distributions Using Oracle Crystal Ball	**Continuous uniform distribution** Between a and b	=CB.Uniform(a,b)
	Discrete uniform distribution Between a and b	=CB.DiscreteUniform(a,b)
	Normal distribution Mean = μ; standard deviation = σ	=CB.Normal(μ,σ)
	Exponential distribution Mean rate = μ	=CB.Exponential(μ)
	Discrete general distribution **Two outcomes only**: A (code 1) and B (code 0) Probability of outcome $A = p$	=CB.YesNo(p)
	Discrete general distribution **Two or more outcomes** $Range$ = Cell range containing variable values (in the first column) and their probabilities (in the second column)	=CB.Custom($Range$)
	Poisson distribution Mean rate = μ	=CB.Poisson(μ)
	Binomial distribution Probability of success = p Number of trials = n	=CB.Binomial(p,n)
	Triangular distribution Minimum value = a Most likely value = b Maximum value = c	=CB.Triangular(a,b,c)

these values in Screenshot 11.3A by using Excel's LOOKUP function. In Screenshot 11.6A, however, we use the CB.Custom function that is available in Oracle Crystal Ball to simulate from discrete general distributions (see Table 11.7 for details). The parameters for this function are shown in cells R4:S9 in Screenshot 11.6A. The formula for the demand in cells E4:E28 is[10]

We use the CB.Custom function to simulate demand here.

$$=\text{CB.Custom(\$R\$4:\$S\$9)}$$

The rest of the formulas in Screenshot 11.6A are the same as in Screenshot 11.3A. Cells M29:P29 show the four total monthly cost measures—holding cost, stockout cost, order cost, and total cost.

Replicating the Model

Once we have set up Simkin's simulation model, we want to replicate it several thousand times and keep track of the cost measures (cells M29:P29) each time. Instead of using Data Table (as we did in Screenshot 11.3B), we replicate the model in Oracle Crystal Ball, using the following two-step procedure (1) define forecasts and (2) run replications.

---

[10] To see the simulated value for a variable change each time the model is recomputed, uncheck the Set cell value to distribution mean box under Define|Cell Preferences. Otherwise, Oracle Crystal Ball will always show the mean of the distribution for the variable.

Defining a Forecast Cell in Oracle Crystal Ball

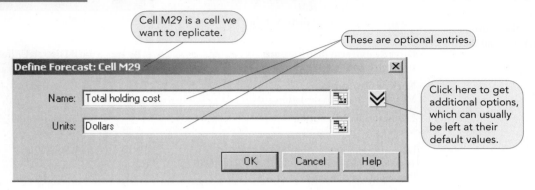

Output measures are called forecasts in Oracle Crystal Ball.

Define Forecasts   First, we define the cells that we want to replicate. This is done as follows:

1. Select cell M29. This cell *must* contain the formula for an output measure (forecast) we want to replicate.

2. Click **DEFINE|DEFINE FORECAST** (or click the **DEFINE FORECAST** icon on the Oracle Crystal Ball toolbar). The window shown in Screenshot 11.6B above is displayed.

3. If desired, specify the name and units of the output measure, as shown in Screenshot 11.6B. Click **OK**.

We can track several forecasts at the same time.

4. Repeat this procedure for the other three output measures (forecasts) in cells N29, O29, and P29.

We can specify a larger number of replications here without worrying about the Excel file becoming too large.

Run Replications   Once all forecasts have been defined, click **RUN|RUN PREFERENCES** (or click the **RUN PREFERENCES** icon on the Oracle Crystal Ball toolbar). The **RUN PREFERENCES** window shown in Screenshot 11.6C is displayed. Specify the number of trials (replications) desired and click **OK**. Note that because Oracle Crystal Ball is not going to

Setting Run Preferences in Oracle Crystal Ball

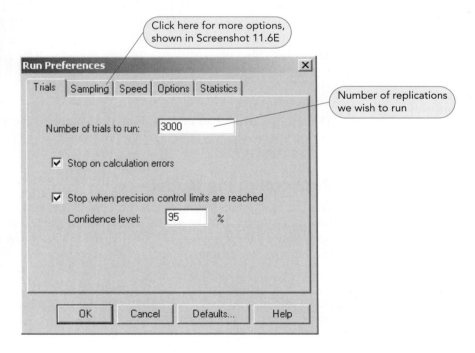

show each replication's cost values in the spreadsheet (unlike Data Table in Section 11.5), we do not have to be concerned about the Excel file getting too large. Hence, we can ask for a much larger number of replications here. For our discussion here, let us simulate the model 3000 times. All other options in the window can be left at their defaults.

The results can be viewed in either graphical or tabular form.

To now run the model, click **RUN|START SIMULATION** (or click the **START SIMULATION** icon on the Oracle Crystal Ball toolbar). Oracle Crystal Ball runs the model for the specified number of replications, keeping track of forecast cells M29:P29 for each replication. When finished, the results of the simulation are presented in a separate window for each output measure. As shown in Screenshot 11.6D for the total cost (cell P29), we can view the results for each output measure either in graphical form or as a summary statistics table. To switch from the graphical view to the table, click **VIEW|STATISTICS** on the menu shown in Screenshot 11.6D.

Screenshot 11.6D indicates that if $Q = 10$ and $R = 5$, Simkin's average monthly total cost is $224.07. Note that this value is a more precise estimate of the average cost than the $222.63 value we computed in Section 11.5 using 200 replications with Data Table. Can you see why?

SCREENSHOT 11.6D   **Graphical and Tabular Results from Oracle Crystal Ball for Simkin's Hardware Store**

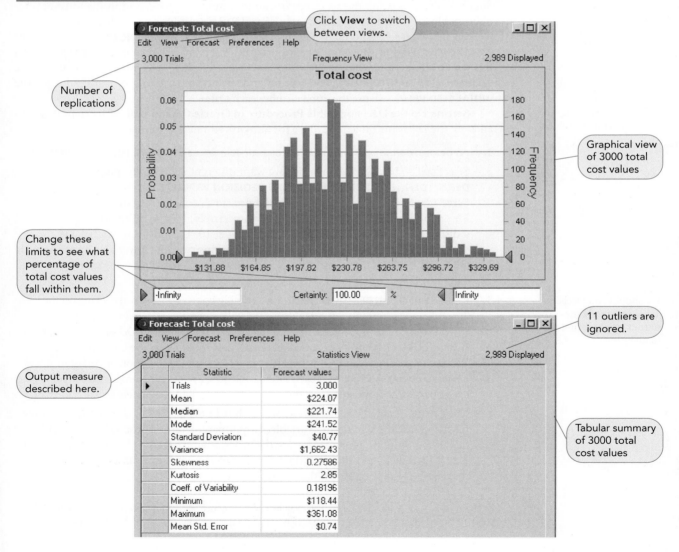

As an exercise, see if you can set up Oracle Crystal Ball to run 3000 replications and compute Simkin's average fill rate per month with $Q = 10$. *Hint:* The answer should be around 82%.

Using Decision Table in Oracle Crystal Ball

The model discussed so far allows us to determine Simkin's average monthly cost for an inventory policy with $Q = 10$, and $R = 5$. However, recall that Simkin wants to test four different values (8, 10, 12, and 14) for Q and two different values (5 and 8) for R to see which combination of values is best for his inventory system. Just as we used Scenario Manager in Section 11.5 to get Excel to try these values of Q and R automatically in the simulation model, we use a procedure called **Decision Table** in Oracle Crystal Ball for this purpose.[11]

We use Decision Table in Oracle Crystal Ball to try several values automatically for an input parameter.

Using the Same Sequence of Random Numbers   Before we describe the Decision Table procedure, we note an important issue. Whenever we run a simulation model multiple times with different values for input parameters, and then compare the results, it is a good idea to run the model using the same series of random numbers. By doing so, we are sure that any observed differences in output measures are due to differences in the input parameter values and not due to the randomness of the simulation process. Although Excel's RAND function does not allow us to fix the sequence of random numbers generated in the examples we discussed in Sections 11.4 to 11.7, Oracle Crystal Ball permits us to do so here. To enable this feature in Oracle Crystal Ball, we first click **RUN|RUN PREFERENCES** to get the **RUN PREFERENCES** window shown in Screenshot 11.6C. We then click the tab titled **SAMPLING** on this window to get the window shown in Screenshot 11.6E. Finally, we check the **USE SAME SEQUENCE OF RANDOM NUMBERS** option and specify any number of our choice for the **INITIAL SEED VALUE** (we use the same number each time).

It is a good idea to use the same series of random numbers each time we run a simulation model with different values for input parameters.

Setting Up the Decision Table Procedure in Oracle Crystal Ball   The steps to set up and run the Decision Table procedure for Simkin's simulation model are as follows:

This is how we set up the Decision Table procedure.

1.   As before, define cells M29:P29 as forecast cells by using **DEFINE|DEFINE FORECAST**.

2.   Select cell T11 (i.e., a cell in which we want different values to be plugged in). Click **DEFINE|DEFINE DECISION**. The **DEFINE DECISION VARIABLE** window shown in Screenshot 11.6F is displayed. Name the decision variable (if desired). Enter the lower and upper bounds (i.e., 8 and 14, respectively) for the order quantity. Specify a discrete step size of 2 to analyze Q values of 8, 10, 12, and 14 only. Click **OK**.

    Repeat this step after selecting cell T12. In this case, the lower and upper bounds are 5 and 8, respectively, and the discrete step size is 3 (because we want to analyze R values of 5 and 8 only).

We should run Decision Table separately for each output measure that we wish to analyze.

3.   Click **RUN|TOOLS|DECISION TABLE**. A welcoming screen appears and clicking on the Target Forecast from the left side menu displays the window shown in Screenshot 11.6G. From the list of defined forecasts, select the forecast that you want Decision Table to track. In Screenshot 11.6G, we have selected the total cost (cell P29) as the target cell. *Note:* Because Decision Table presents detailed results for each combination of deci-sion values, it should be run separately for each forecast. Hence, if we wish to also analyze holding cost, stockout cost, and order cost, we should run Decision Table separately for each forecast.

4.   Click **NEXT**. The window shown in Screenshot 11.6H is displayed. From the window on the left, select all decision variables (input parameters) whose values you wish to vary. In Simkin's model, these are the order quantity (cell T11) and reorder point (cell T12). Click the button marked **>>**. The selected decision variables are now displayed in the window on the right.

---

[11] The professional version of Oracle Crystal Ball includes a product called OptQuest (which we run by clicking Run|OptQuest) that can be used to automatically search for the best combination of decision variable values (within preset bounds) that optimizes a defined output measure.

SCREENSHOT 11.6E   **Using the Same Sequence of Random Numbers in Oracle Crystal Ball**

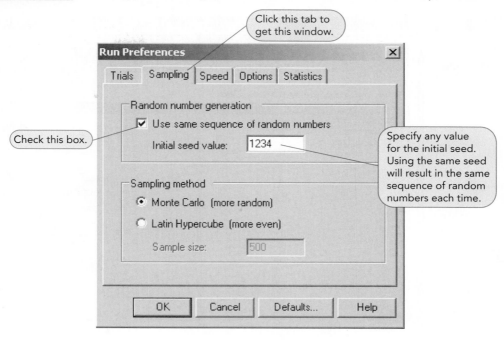

SCREENSHOT 11.6F   **Defining a Decision Variable Cell in Oracle Crystal Ball**

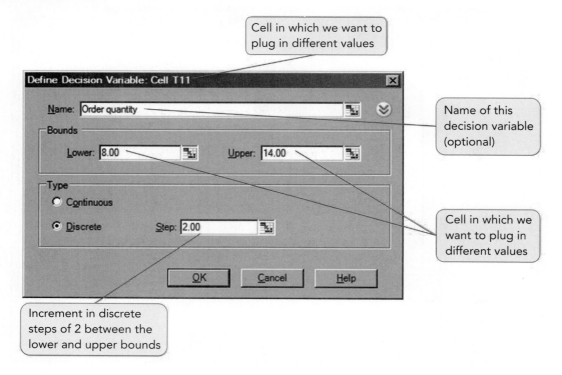

SCREENSHOT 11.6G   Setting Up Decision Table in Oracle Crystal Ball—Step 1 of 3

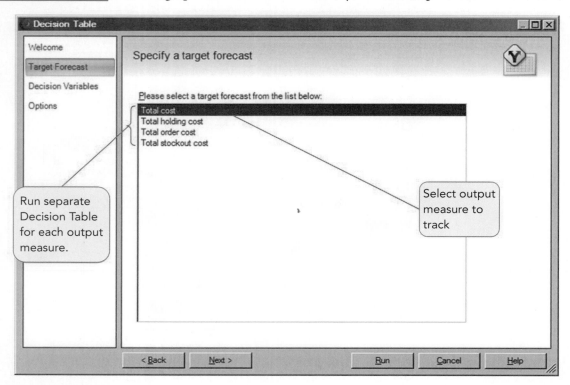

SCREENSHOT 11.6H   Setting Up Decision Table in Oracle Crystal Ball—Step 2 of 3

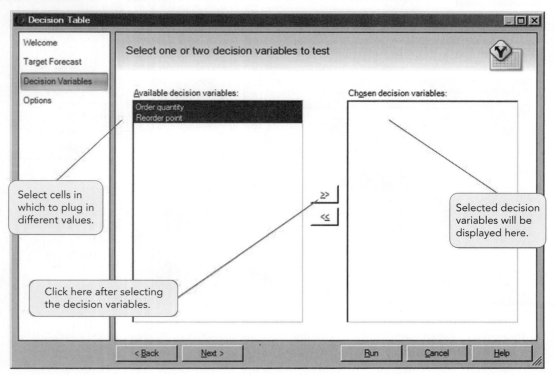

SCREENSHOT 11.6I   **Setting Up Decision Table in Oracle Crystal Ball—Step 3 of 3**

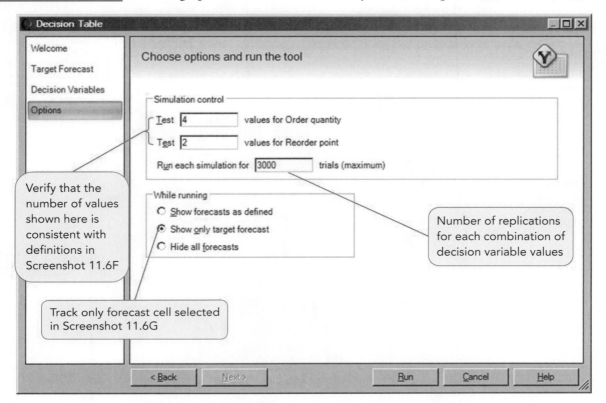

5. Click **NEXT**. The window shown in Screenshot 11.6I is displayed above. Make sure the appropriate number of values are shown for the order quantity (four values) and reorder point (two values). Enter the desired number of replications. Although we have specified 3000 replications in Screenshot 11.6I, it is a good idea to run Decision Table with just a few replications first to verify that everything has been set up properly before running it with a larger number. Click **RUN**.

Decision Table plugs in each value of Q and R in cells T11 and T12 (see Screenshot 11.6A), respectively, and runs 3000 replications in each case. The results, shown in Screenshot 11.6J on page 522, are displayed in a separate workbook. We can click any of these total cost values (cells B2:E3) and select the charts shown (Trend, Overlay, or Forecast) to see details of the simulation for a specific combination of Q and R values. For example, Screenshot 11.6J shows the forecast frequency chart obtained for the total cost in cell D2, which corresponds to a Q value of 12 in cell T11 and an R value of 5 in cell T12.

Comparing the average values in Screenshot 11.6J, it appears that Simkin's best choice, based on 3000 replications, would be to set $Q = 14$ and $R = 8$. The resulting average total cost is $147.98 per month (see cell E3).

11.9 SIMULATION MODEL OF A REVENUE MANAGEMENT PROBLEM USING ORACLE CRYSTAL BALL

We revisit the Judith's Airport Limousine Service example.

In this section, we illustrate the use of Oracle Crystal Ball to simulate the revenue management problem we discussed in Section 11.7. Recall that the problem involves an entrepreneur, Judith McKay, who is trying to decide how many reservations (10, 11, 12, 13, or 14) she should accept per trip for her 10-passenger airport limousine service. (At this time, we

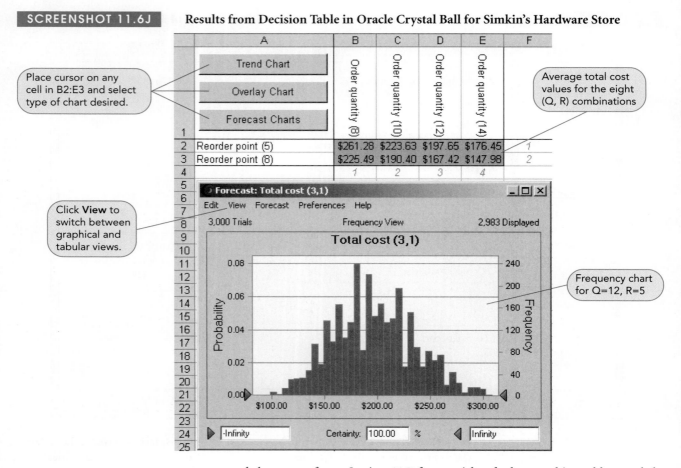

SCREENSHOT 11.6J   **Results from Decision Table in Oracle Crystal Ball for Simkin's Hardware Store**

recommend that you refer to Section 11.7 for a quick refresher on this problem and the simulation model we developed for it.)

Setting Up the Model

We begin by setting up Judith's model for a specific reservation limit (let's use 14, just as we did in Section 11.7). Notice that the Excel layout in Screenshot 11.7A is very similar to the one we developed in Section 11.7 for this problem (refer to Screenshot 11.5A on page 509). The only differences are in the formulas used in cells B6 and B9, as follows:

File: 11-7.xls

The number of people showing up is simulated here using Oracle Crystal Ball's CB.Binomial function.

- Cell B6 simulates the number of passengers with reservations who actually show up for the trip. In Section 11.7, we simulated this using separate nested IF functions for each potential passenger. In Oracle Crystal Ball, however, we can simulate this in a much more straightforward manner by recognizing that the number of people who show up follows a *binomial distribution* with parameters $p = 0.8$ (specified in cell G6) and n = number of reservations accepted (cell B5). Hence, the formula in cell B6 (refer to Table 11.7 on page 515 for details if necessary) is

$$=CB.Binomial(G6,B5)$$

- In cell B9, we simulate the number of walk-up passengers. In Section 11.7, we simulated this by using the LOOKUP function. In Oracle Crystal Ball, however, we can simulate this by using the custom distribution function. The range of values and probabilities has been specified in cells D15:E17 in Screenshot 11.7A. The formula in cell B9 is

$$=CB.Custom(D15:E17)$$

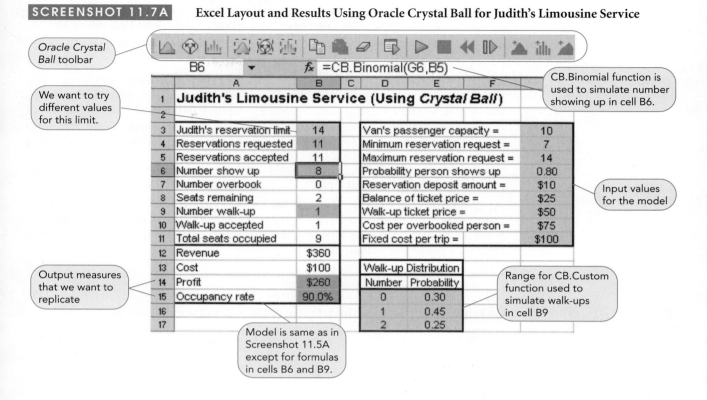

SCREENSHOT 11.7A   Excel Layout and Results Using Oracle Crystal Ball for Judith's Limousine Service

Oracle Crystal Ball toolbar

B6 fx =CB.Binomial(G6,B5)

CB.Binomial function is used to simulate number showing up in cell B6.

We want to try different values for this limit.

Input values for the model

Output measures that we want to replicate

Range for CB.Custom function used to simulate walk-ups in cell B9

Model is same as in Screenshot 11.5A except for formulas in cells B6 and B9.

Judith's Limousine Service (Using *Crystal Ball*)

	A	B		D	E	F
3	Judith's reservation limit	14		Van's passenger capacity =		10
4	Reservations requested	11		Minimum reservation request =		7
5	Reservations accepted	11		Maximum reservation request =		14
6	Number show up	8		Probability person shows up		0.80
7	Number overbook	0		Reservation deposit amount =		$10
8	Seats remaining	2		Balance of ticket price =		$25
9	Number walk-up	1		Walk-up ticket price =		$50
10	Walk-up accepted	1		Cost per overbooked person =		$75
11	Total seats occupied	9		Fixed cost per trip =		$100
12	Revenue	$360				
13	Cost	$100		Walk-up Distribution		
14	Profit	$260		Number	Probability	
15	Occupancy rate	90.0%		0	0.30	
16				1	0.45	
17				2	0.25	

The two desired output measures—profit and occupancy rate—are computed in cells B14 and B15, respectively.

Using Decision Table to Identify the Best Reservation Limit

We use Decision Table to test different values for the reservation limit.

In Judith's problem, we want to try out five different values (10, 11, 12, 13, and 14) for the reservation limit. To do so using Decision Table in Oracle Crystal Ball, we use the following steps, just as we did in Section 11.8 for Simkin's inventory model. Let us run Decision Table to track the profit (cell B14):

1. Specify that Oracle Crystal Ball should use the same sequence of random numbers in each case (refer to Screenshot 11.6E for details).

We define the forecast cells that we want to track.

2. Select cell B14, which contains the formula for the output measure (i.e., profit) that we want to track. Click **DEFINE|DEFINE FORECAST**. If desired, specify the name and units of the output measure in the window that is displayed (refer to Screenshot 11.6B for a sample view of this window). Click **OK**.

We define the input parameter cells that we want to vary automatically.

3. Select cell B3 (the cell in which you want the reservation limit values to be plugged in). Click **DEFINE|DEFINE DECISION**. In the window that is displayed (refer to Screenshot 11.6F for a sample view of this window), enter a lower value of 10 and an upper value of 14. The discrete step size is 1 because we want to study all reservations limits between 10 and 14. Click **OK**.

4. Click **RUN|TOOLS|DECISION TABLE**. Make sure the desired forecast cell (cell B14, in Judith's problem) is shown as the target cell in the window that is displayed. Click **NEXT**.

5. Select the decision variable cell (B3) and click the button marked **>>** in the window that is displayed. Click **NEXT**.

6. In the final window (refer to Screenshot 11.6I for a sample view of this window), make sure the appropriate number of values is shown for cell B3 (five values in Judith's problem). Enter the desired number of replications (such as 3000) for each choice. Click **RUN**.

We can see details for any of the simulation results.

Decision Table plugs in each value (i.e., 10 to 14) of the decision variable (reservation limit) in cell B3 (see Screenshot 11.7A) and runs 3000 replications in each case. The results, shown in Screenshot 11.7B, are displayed in a separate workbook. We can click on any of these profit values (in cells B2:F2) and select the charts shown to see details for that simulation. For example, Screenshot 11.7B shows the tabular summary obtained for the profit when the reservation limit is 11.

Comparing the profit values in Screenshot 11.7B, it appears that based on 3000 replications, Judith's best choice would be to accept 11 reservations per trip. The resulting average profit is $225.91 per trip. Note that this answer is different from, and probably more precise than, the best reservation limit of 12 we identified based on just 200 replications in Screenshot 11.5B. This again illustrates the importance of performing a large number of replications in any simulation model.

SCREENSHOT 11.7B   **Results from Decision Table in Oracle Crystal Ball for Judith's Limousine Service**

Average profit for each reservation limit, based on 3000 replications

Limit of 11 yields highest profit here, based on 3000 replications.

	A	B	C	D	E	F
		Reservation limit (10)	Reservation limit (11)	Reservation limit (12)	Reservation limit (13)	Reservation limit (14)
2		$218.41	$225.91	$224.98	$222.40	$222.00
3		1	2	3	4	5

Forecast: Profit (2)

Edit   View   Forecast   Preferences   Help

3,000 Trials   Statistics View   3,000 Displayed

Statistic	Forecast values
Trials	3,000
Mean	$225.91
Median	$235.00
Mode	$260.00
Standard Deviation	$52.70
Variance	$2,777.12
Skewness	-0.697
Kurtosis	2.94
Coeff. of Variability	0.23328
Minimum	$30.00
Maximum	$310.00
Mean Std. Error	$0.96

Summary table for reservation limit of 11

At this stage, see if you can set up and run Decision Table to track the occupancy rate (cell B15) for all reservation limits.

As noted earlier, our intent here is to provide just a brief introduction to Oracle Crystal Ball. As you navigate the various menus in the package (some of which are discussed here), you may notice several other choices and options. Once again, we encourage you to try out these procedures on your own.

11.10 OTHER TYPES OF SIMULATION MODELS

Simulation models are often broken into three categories. The first, the Monte Carlo method discussed in this chapter, uses the concepts of probability distribution and random numbers to evaluate system responses to various policies. The other two categories are operational gaming and systems simulation. Although in theory the three methods are distinctly different from one another, the growth of computerized simulation has tended to create a common basis in procedures and blur these differences.[12]

Operational Gaming

Operational gaming refers to simulation involving two or more competing players. The best examples are military games and business games. Both allow participants to match their management and decision-making skills in hypothetical situations of conflict.

Business simulation games are popular educational tools in many colleges.

Military games are used worldwide to train a nation's top military officers, to test offensive and defensive strategies, and to examine the effectiveness of equipment and armies. Business games, first developed by the firm Booz, Allen, and Hamilton in the 1950s, are popular with both executives and business students. They provide an opportunity to test business skills and decision-making ability in a competitive environment. The person or team that performs best in the simulated environment is rewarded by knowing that his or her company has been most successful in earning the largest profit, grabbing a high market share, or perhaps increasing the firm's trading value on the stock exchange.

During each period of competition, be it a week, a month, or a quarter, teams respond to market conditions by coding their latest management decisions with respect to inventory, production, financing, investment, marketing, and research. The competitive business environment is simulated using a computer, and a new printout summarizing current market conditions is presented to players. This allows teams to simulate years of operating conditions in a matter of days, weeks, or a semester.

Systems Simulation

Systems simulation is similar to business gaming in that it allows users to test various managerial policies and decisions to evaluate their effect on the operating environment. This variation of simulation models the dynamics of large systems. Such systems are corporate operations,[13] the national economy, a hospital, or a city government system.

---

[12] Theoretically, random numbers are used only in Monte Carlo simulation. However, in some complex gaming or systems simulation problems in which relationships cannot be defined exactly, it may be necessary to use the probability concepts of the Monte Carlo method.

[13] This is sometimes referred to as *industrial dynamics*, a term coined by Jay Forrester. Forrester's goal was to find a way "to show how policies, decisions, structure, and delays are interrelated to influence growth and stability" in industrial systems. See J. W. Forrester. *Industrial Dynamics*. Cambridge, MA: MIT Press, 1961.

FIGURE 11.3

Inputs and Outputs of a Typical Economic System Simulation

Inputs	Model	Outputs
Income Tax Levels →	Econometric Model (in Series of Mathematical Equations)	→ Gross National Product
Corporate Tax Rates →		→ Inflation Rates
Interest Rates →		→ Unemployment Rates
Government Spending →		→ Monetary Supplies
Foreign Trade Policy →		→ Population Growth Rates

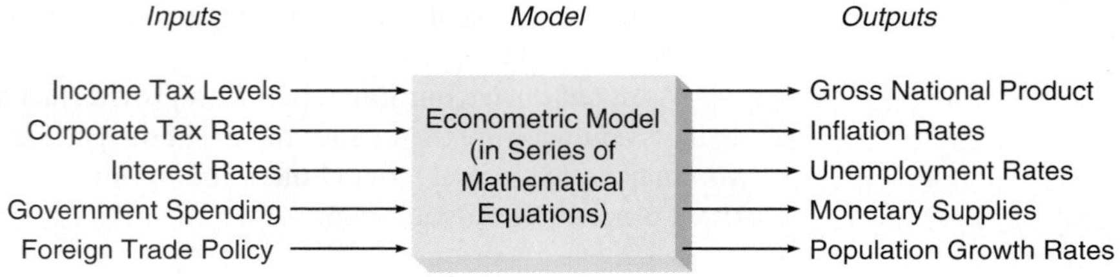

In a corporate operating system, sales, production levels, marketing policies, investments, union contracts, utility rates, financing, and other factors are all related in a series of mathematical equations that are examined through simulation. In a simulation of an urban government, systems simulation could be employed to evaluate the impact of tax increases, capital expenditures for roads and buildings, housing availability, new garbage routes, in-migration and out-migration, locations of new schools or senior citizens centres, birth and death rates, and many more vital issues. Simulations of *economic systems*, often called *econometric* models, are used by government agencies, bankers, and large organizations to predict inflation rates, domestic and foreign money supplies, and unemployment levels. Inputs and outputs of a typical economic system simulation are illustrated in Figure 11.3.

Econometric models are huge simulations involving thousands of regression equations tied together by economic factors. They use what-if questions to test various policies.

The value of systems simulation lies in its allowance of what-if questions to test the effects of various policies. A corporate planning group, for example, can change the value of any input, such as an advertising budget, and examine the impact on sales, market share, or short-term costs. Simulation can also be used to evaluate different research and development projects or to determine long-range planning horizons.

SUMMARY

This chapter discusses the concept and approach of simulation as a problem-solving tool. Simulation involves building a mathematical model that attempts to describe a real-world situation. The model's goal is to incorporate important variables and their interrelationships in such a way that we can study the impact of managerial changes on the total system. The approach has many advantages over other decision modeling techniques and is especially useful when a problem is too complex or difficult to solve by other means.

The Monte Carlo method of simulation uses random numbers to generate random variable values from probability distributions. The simulation procedure is conducted for many time periods to evaluate the long-term impact of each policy value being studied.

We first illustrate how to set up Monte Carlo simulations by using Excel's built-in functions. We also show how Excel's Data Table can be used to run several replications of simulation models and how Scenario Manager can be used to try different values for input parameters. Then, we show how Oracle Crystal Ball, an Excel add-in for simulation, can be used to develop and run simulation models. The major advantages of using add-ins are (1) the availability of easy formulas for many common probability distributions, (2) the ability to quickly set up and run many replications of the model, and (3) the ability to easily collect statistical information on many different output measures.

We conclude this chapter with a brief discussion of operational gaming and systems simulation, two other categories of simulation.

GLOSSARY

Oracle Crystal Ball. An add-in for Excel that simplifies the implementation and solution of simulation models.

Data Table. A procedure in Excel that allows simulation models to be replicated several times.

Decision Table. A feature in Oracle Crystal Ball that is used to automatically try different values for a decision variable in the simulation model.

Discrete-Event Simulation. A simulation model in which we need to keep track of the passage of time by using a simulation clock.

Discrete General Distribution. A distribution in which a variable can take on one of several discrete values, each with its own probability.

Flow Diagram, or Flowchart. A graphical means of presenting the logic of a simulation model. It is a tool that helps in writing a simulation computer program.

LOOKUP. An Excel function that can be used to randomly generate values from discrete general probability distributions.

Monte Carlo Simulation. A simulation that experiments with probabilistic elements of a system by generating random numbers to create values for those elements.

NORMINV. An Excel function that can be used to randomly generate values from normal probability distributions.

Operational Gaming. The use of simulation in competitive situations such as military games and business or management games.

RAND. An Excel function that generates a random number between 0 and 1 each time it is computed.

RANDBETWEEN. An Excel function that can be used to randomly generate values from discrete uniform probability distributions.

Random Number. A number (typically between zero and one in most computer programs) whose value is selected completely at random.

Replication. A single run of a simulation model. Also known as a *run* or *trial*.

Simulation. A technique that involves building a mathematical model to represent a real-world situation. The model is then experimented with to estimate the effects of various actions and decisions.

Systems Simulation. A simulation model that deals with the dynamics of large organizational or governmental systems.

SOLVED PROBLEMS

Solved Problem 11-1

Higgins Plumbing and Heating maintains a supply of eight water heaters in any given week. Owner Jerry Higgins likes the idea of having this large supply on hand to meet customer demand but also recognizes that it is expensive to do so. He examines water heater sales over the past 50 weeks and notes the following data:

WATER HEATER SALES PER WEEK	NUMBER OF WEEKS THIS NUMBER WAS SOLD
4	6
5	5
6	9
7	12
8	8
9	7
10	3

a. Set up a model to simulate Higgins' weekly sales over a two-year (104-week) period and compute the following measures (based on a single replication):

■ Average weekly sales
■ Number of weeks with stockouts over a two-year period

Replicate your model 200 times, using Data Table, to determine (1) the average weekly sales and (2) the probability that Higgins will have more than 20 weeks with stockouts over a two-year period.

b. Use the probability distribution for sales to determine the expected value of sales. Explain any differences between this value and the average value computed using Data Table in part (a).

Solution

The Excel layout to answer all the questions in this problem is presented in Screenshot 11.8. The spreadsheet is organized as follows:

SCREENSHOT 11.8   Excel Layout and Results for Higgins Plumbing and Heating

Parameters for LOOKUP function used to simulate sales

	A	B	C	D	E	F	G	H	I	J	K	L
1	**Higgins Plumbing and Heating**									**Data Table**		
2						Sales Distribution						
3	Week	Sales	Stockout? (1 = Yes)		Sales	Prob-ability	RN intvl lower limit	RN intvl upper limit		Run	Avg sales	Stockout weeks
4	1	8	0		4	0.12	0.00	0.12		1	7.14	24
5	2	8	0		5	0.10	0.12	0.22		2	6.81	21
6	3	4	0		6	0.18	0.22	0.40		3	7.14	23
7	4	9	1		7	0.24	0.40	0.64		4	6.94	22
8	5	6	0		8	0.16	0.64	0.80		5	6.75	21
9	6	7	0		9	0.14	0.80	0.94		6	6.88	23
10	7	8	0		10	0.06	0.94	1.00		7	6.83	21
11	8	7	0							8	7.03	23
12	9	7	0		Supply each week =			8		9	6.84	17
13	10	7	0							10	6.76	23
14	11	9	1		**(a)**					11	6.76	18
15	12	9	1		**Based on 1 replication:**					12	6.76	21
16	13	8	0		Average sales =			7.14		13	6.95	23
17	14	9	1		No. of stockout weeks =			24		14	6.80	16
18	15	8	0							15	6.77	21
19	16	8	0		**Based on 200 replications:**					16	7.12	25
20	17	9	1		Average sales =			6.90		17	6.93	20
21	18	9	1		P(>20 stockout weeks) =			54.5%		18	6.77	22
22	19	7	0							19	7.01	20
23	20	9	1		**(b)**					20	6.65	19
24	21	8	0		Expected sales =			6.88		21	6.95	27
25	22	7	0							22	6.88	20
106	103	7	0							103	6.99	22
107	104	6	0							104	6.92	26
108										105	7.08	21
202										199	6.84	19
203										200	6.94	23

=H16

=H17

Hidden rows

COUNTIF function is used to count number of weeks with >20 stockouts.

Data Table is used to replicate both output measures 200 times each.

File: 11-8.xls

- Column A shows the week number.
- We use a LOOKUP function to simulate the weekly sales in column B. The parameters (random number intervals, sales, and probabilities) for the LOOKUP function are shown in cells E4:H10.
- In column C, we use an IF function to determine the occurrence of a stockout (0 = no stockout, 1 = stockout). For example, the formula in cell C4 is =IF(B4>$H$12,1,0).

a. The average sales over the two-year period is the average of the sales values in cells B4:B107. This value, shown in cell H16 in Screenshot 11.8, is 7.14 units per week. Next, we can add the 104 stockout indicators in cells C4:C107 to determine the number of stockouts over the two-year period. This value, shown in cell H17, is 24 stockout weeks. (Remember that these values will change each time you recalculate the model.)

We now set up Data Table to run 200 replications of the values in cells H16 and H17. Data Table is shown in columns J to L in Screenshot 11.8. From the 200 replicated values in cells K4:K203, we compute the average sales to be 6.90 units per week (shown in cell H20). We then use Excel's COUNTIF function on the 200 replicated values in cells L4:L203 to compute the probability that Higgins will have more than 20 weeks with stockouts over a two-year period. The formula used is =COUNTIF(L4:L203,">20")/200. The value, shown in cell H21, indicates that there is a 54.5% chance that this event will occur.

b. Using expected values, we find the following:

$$\text{Expected heater sales} = 0.12 \times 4 + 0.10 \times 5 + 0.18 \times 6 + 0.24 \times 7$$
$$+ 0.16 \times 8 + 0.14 \times 9 + 0.06 \times 10$$
$$= 6.88 \text{ heaters}$$

We can compute this value by using the following formula:

$$\text{=SUMPRODUCT(E4:E10,F4:F10)}$$

This value is shown in cell H24 in Screenshot 11.8. The simulated average (6.90 in Screenshot 11.8) is based on just 200 replications of the model. Hence, although this value is close to the expected value of 6.88, the two values need not necessarily be the same. With a longer simulation, the two values will become even closer.

Solved Problem 11-2

Norris Medical Clinic is staffed by a single physician who, on average, requires 15 minutes to treat a patient. The distribution of this service time follows a truncated normal distribution with a standard deviation of four minutes and a minimum value of five minutes. Patients arrive at an average rate of 2.5 customers per hour, according to the exponential distribution. Simulate 100 patient arrivals and replicate the model 200 times, using Data Table, to answer the following questions:

a. What percentage of time is the queue empty?
b. How many patients, on average, are in the queue?
c. What is the average wait time per patient in the queue?

File: 11-9.xls

Solution

This is an example of a discrete-event simulation model. The model simulates a queuing system in which arrival times follow an exponential distribution and service times follow a normal distribution. Each replication of the model corresponds to the arrival and service of 100 patients at the clinic. The Excel layout for this problem is presented in Screenshot 11.9. We have included patient number 0, with zero values for all columns, to *initialize* the simulation clock that keeps track of the passage of time. Rows 5 through 104 in the spreadsheet are organized as follows:

- Column A shows the patient number (1 through 100).
- Column B shows the time between arrivals of successive patients, simulated from an exponential distribution by using the LN function. From Table 11.4 on page 489, the Excel formula is =-(1/μ)*LN(RAND()). Note that the average arrival rate, μ, in this case is 2.5 patients per hour. However, because all other times in this problem are counted in minutes, we convert the interarrival time between successive patients to minutes also. The formula in cells B5:B104 is therefore

$$\text{=-60*(1/\$K\$6)*(LN(RAND()))}$$

SCREENSHOT 11.9   **Excel Layout and Results for Norris Medical Clinic**

Simulated using LN function

Simulated using NORMINV function. Set to a minimum of 5 minutes.

=K15   =K16   =K17

	A	B	C	D	E	F	G	H	I	J	K	L	M	N	O	P
1	**Norris Medical Clinic**												**Data Table**			
2																
3	Pati-ent #	Time between arrivals	Arrival time	Start service	Service time	End service	Wait time	Queue length					Run	% empty queue	Avg # patients	Avg wait time
4	0	0.0	0	0	0.0	0	0	0		**Arrival Distribution**			1	0.21	1.90	23.71
5	1	4.0	4.0	4.0	18.0	22.0	0.0	0		**Exponential**			2	0.22	2.32	30.05
6	2	49.6	53.5	53.5	6.2	59.7	0.0	0		Average arrival rate (per hour)	2.5		3	0.46	0.66	5.50
7	3	5.1	58.7	59.7	20.7	80.5	1.1	1					4	0.51	0.87	9.72
8	4	8.0	66.7	80.5	13.8	94.3	13.8	1		**Service Time Distribution**			5	0.41	1.17	13.39
9	5	6.9	73.6	94.3	21.0	115.3	20.7	2		**Normal**			6	0.45	0.72	6.21
10	6	5.0	78.6	115.3	17.1	132.4	36.7	3		Mean service time (minutes)	15		7	0.53	0.65	6.71
11	7	41.7	120.3	132.4	14.6	146.9	12.1	2		Std dev of service time (minutes)	4		8	0.37	0.90	9.55
12	8	8.5	128.8	146.9	15.8	162.8	18.2	2		Minimum service time (minutes)	5		9	0.51	0.70	6.60
13	9	28.7	157.4	162.8	16.4	179.2	5.4	1					10	0.29	1.48	17.16
14	10	12.6	170.0	179.2	16.4	195.6	9.2	1		**Based on 1 replication:**			11	0.34	1.01	11.13
15	11	3.5	173.5	195.6	17.9	213.5	22.1	2		Percent of time the queue is empty =	21.0%		12	0.54	0.53	4.36
16	12	90.5	264.0	264.0	17.8	281.8	0.0	0		Average number of patients in the queue =	1.90		13	0.43	0.95	10.83
17	13	36.2	300.2	300.2	10.4	310.7	0.0	0		Average wait time per patient in the queue =	23.71		14	0.42	1.05	12.79
18	14	2.0	302.2	310.7	16.8	327.5	8.5	1					15	0.30	1.71	20.56
19	15	1.9	304.1	327.5	18.3	345.8	23.4	2		**Based on 200 replications:**			16	0.40	0.90	9.31
20	16	20.9	325.0	345.8	13.5	359.3	20.8	2		Percent of time the queue is empty =	38.7%		17	0.38	1.03	11.20
21	17	1.9	326.9	359.3	13.9	373.3	32.4	3		Average number of patients in the queue =	1.13		18	0.41	0.86	8.82
22	18	19.2	346.1	373.3	18.7	392.0	27.1	2		Average wait time per patient in the queue =	12.66		19	0.38	1.13	12.94
23	19	15.5	361.6	392.0	12.0	404.0	30.3	2					20	0.37	0.88	8.15
24	20	19.7	381.3	404.0	12.2	416.2	22.7	2					21	0.41	1.03	11.35
103	99	24.6	1965.7	2054.4	17.1	2,071.4	88.6	6					100	0.40	1.30	15.94
104	100	1.3	1967.0	2071.4	14.1	2,085.6	104.4	7					101	0.46	0.77	7.55
105													102	0.51	0.85	10.72
106													103	0.37	1.01	10.12
202													199	0.23	2.62	35.11
203													200	0.30	1.49	16.96

Hidden rows

= Start time + Service time

Summary results from Data Table

Data Table is used to replicate all three output measures 200 times each.

- In column C, we calculate the arrival time of the current patient as the sum of the arrival time of the previous patient and the time between arrivals (column B). For example, the formula in cell C5 is

$$=C4+B5$$

- The time this patient actually starts service is calculated in column D as the maximum of the arrival time and the time the previous patient finishes service. For example, the formula in cell D5 is

$$=MAX(C5,F4)$$

- Column E shows the service time for this patient, simulated using a NORMINV function. The parameters of this NORMINV function are shown in cells K10:K11. We use a MAX function to ensure that the minimum service time per patient is five minutes. The formula in cells E5:E104 is

$$=MAX(\$K\$12,NORMINV(RAND(),\$K\$10,\$K\$11))$$

- The time at which this patient ends service is shown in column F as the sum of the start time (shown in column D) and the service time (shown in column E).

- In column G, we calculate the wait time of this patient as the difference between the patient's start time (shown in column D) and arrival time (shown in column C).

■ Finally, in column H, we calculate the queue length, using Excel's MATCH function. For example, the formula in cell H5 is

$$=A5 - MATCH(C5, \$D\$5: D5, 1)$$

Using the 100 wait time and queue length values in cells G5:H104, we determine the following three performance measures for the queuing system each day:

a. Percentage of time the queue
    is empty (cell K15)   = 21%   =COUNTIF(H5:H104,"=0")/100
b. Average number of patients in
    the queue (cell K16)   = 1.90   =AVERAGE(H5:H104)
c. Average wait time per patient
    in the queue (cell K17)   = 23.71 minutes   =AVERAGE(G5:G104)

The values in cells K15:K17 represent results from just one replication of the model. To determine more precise values for these measures, we now replicate all three measures 200 times each. The Data Table procedure to do so is shown in columns M through P in Screenshot 11.9. Based on the 200 replicated values in this Data Table procedure, the queue at the clinic is empty 36.7% of the time, there are 1.13 patients on average in the queue at any time, and each patient in the queue waits for an average of 12.66 minutes.

Solved Problem 11-3

Heartbreak Hotel routinely experiences no-shows (people who make reservations for a room and don't show up) during the peak season when the hotel is always full. No-shows follow the distribution shown in the following table:

NO-SHOWS	PROBABILITY
0	0.10
1	0.13
2	0.31
3	0.16
4	0.21
5	0.09

To reduce the number of vacant rooms, the hotel overbooks three rooms; that is, the hotel accepts three more reservations than the number of rooms available. On a day when the hotel experiences fewer than three no-shows, there are not enough rooms for those who have reservations. The hotel's policy is to send these guests to a competing hotel down the street, at Heartbreak's expense of $125. If the number of no-shows is more than three, the hotel has vacant rooms, resulting in an opportunity cost of $50 per room.

a. Simulate one month (30 days) of operation to calculate the hotel's total monthly cost due to overbooking and opportunity loss. Replicate this cost 200 times to compute the average monthly cost.
b. Heartbreak Hotel would like to determine the most desirable number of rooms to overbook. Of these six choices—0, 1, 2, 3, 4, or 5 rooms—what is your recommendation? Why?

Solution

This is an example of a revenue management problem where the number of no-shows follows a discrete general distribution. Each replication of the simulation model corresponds to 30 days of operations at the hotel. The Excel layout for this model is presented in Screenshot 11.10A. The spreadsheet is organized as follows:

**File: 11-10.xls,
sheet: 11-10A**

SCREENSHOT 11.10A   Excel Layout and Results for Heartbreak Hotel

Parameters for LOOKUP function in column B

Heartbreak Hotel

No-Shows Distribution

Data Table

Day	No-shows	Short rooms	Short cost	Vacant rooms	Vacant cost	Total cost		No-shows	Probability	RN intvl lower limit	RN intvl upper limit		Run	Cost
1	5	0	$0.00	2	$100.00	$100.00		0	0.10	0.00	0.10		1	$140.00
2	4	0	$0.00	1	$50.00	$50.00		1	0.13	0.10	0.23		2	$122.50
3	4	0	$0.00	1	$50.00	$50.00		2	0.31	0.23	0.54		3	$94.17
4	2	1	$125.00	0	$0.00	$125.00		3	0.16	0.54	0.70		4	$140.00
5	1	2	$250.00	0	$0.00	$250.00		4	0.21	0.70	0.91		5	$101.67
6	4	0	$0.00	1	$50.00	$50.00		5	0.09	0.91	1.00		6	$103.33
7	1	2	$250.00	0	$0.00	$250.00							7	$79.17
8	3	0	$0.00	0	$0.00	$0.00		Rooms overbooked	3				8	$135.83
9	2	1	$125.00	0	$0.00	$125.00							9	$104.17
10	2	1	$125.00	0	$0.00	$125.00		Cost per room short	$125				10	$125.00
11	5	0	$0.00	2	$100.00	$100.00		Cost per room vacant	$50				11	$108.33
12	1	2	$250.00	0	$0.00	$250.00							12	$126.67
13	2	1	$125.00	0	$0.00	$125.00		Based on 1 replication:					13	$142.50
14	5	0	$0.00	2	$100.00	$100.00		Average daily cost =	$140.00				14	$137.50
15	2	1	$125.00	0	$0.00	$125.00							15	$115.00
16	3	0	$0.00	0	$0.00	$0.00		Based on 200 replications:					16	$134.17
17	0	3	$375.00	0	$0.00	$375.00		Average daily cost =	$130.35				17	$94.17
18	2	1	$125.00	0	$0.00	$125.00							18	$100.00
19	4	0	$0.00	1	$50.00	$50.00							19	$133.33
20	2	1	$125.00	0	$0.00	$125.00							20	$134.17
21	1	2	$250.00	0	$0.00	$250.00							21	$143.33
22	2	1	$125.00	0	$0.00	$125.00							22	$120.83
23	4	0	$0.00	1	$50.00	$50.00							23	$152.50
24	0	3	$375.00	0	$0.00	$375.00							24	$131.67
25	5	0	$0.00	2	$100.00	$100.00							25	$121.67
26	3	0	$0.00	0	$0.00	$0.00							26	$125.83
27	1	2	$250.00	0	$0.00	$250.00							27	$140.83
28	0	3	$375.00	0	$0.00	$375.00							28	$145.00
29	4	0	$0.00	1	$50.00	$50.00							29	$109.17
30	2	1	$125.00	0	$0.00	$125.00							30	$129.17
													31	$148.33
													199	$141.67
													200	$154.17

=K17

We want to try different values here.

Simulated using LOOKUP function

Total cost is sum of short cost and vacant cost.

- Column A shows the day number (1 through 30).
- In column B, we use a LOOKUP function to simulate the number of no-shows. The parameters for this LOOKUP function are shown in cells I4:L9.
- In column C, we compute the number of short rooms (i.e., rooms that are unavailable for guests) by comparing the number of no-shows with the number of rooms we decide to overbook (shown in cell K11). For example, the formula in cell C4 is

$$=MAX(\$K\$11-B4,0)$$

- Short cost in column D = $K$13 × column C.
- In column E, we compute the number of vacant rooms by once again comparing the number of no-shows with the number of rooms we decide to overbook (shown in cell K11). For example, the formula in cell E4 is

$$=MAX(B4-\$K\$11,0)$$

- Vacant cost in column F = $K$14 × column E.

SCREENSHOT 11.10B	**Scenario Manager Results for Heartbreak Hotel**

Changing Cell is the number of rooms overbooked.

	A	B	C	D	E	F	G	H	I	J
1										
2		**Scenario Summary**								
3				Current Values:	OB0	OB1	OB2	OB3	OB4	OB5
5		**Changing Cells:**								
6		$K$11		3	0	1	2	3	4	5
7		**Result Cells:**								
8		$K$20		$128.42	$125.79	$93.38	$83.55	$128.30	$204.38	$304.69

Notes: Current Values column represents values of Changing Cells at time Scenario Summary Report was created. Changing Cells for each scenario are highlighted in grey.

Result cell is the total cost.

Overbooking two rooms yields the lowest total cost.

Different values we want to try for the number of rooms overbooked

■ Total cost in column G = column D + column E.

a. The average total cost of $140 per day shown in cell K17 is based on only one replication. Hence, to get a more precise estimate of this average, we replicate this measure by using Data Table, as shown in column N and O in Screenshot 11.10A. Based on 200 replications, the average total cost at Heartbreak Hotel appears to be $130.35 per day (shown in cell K20).

b. To determine the number of rooms that Heartbreak Hotel should overbook each day, we set up Scenario Manager to automatically try the six choices—0, 1, 2, 3, 4, and 5. For each scenario, cell K11 is the Changing Cell and cell K20 is the Result Cell. The results of the Scenario Manager procedure, shown in Screenshot 11.10B, indicate that Heartbreak Hotel should overbook two rooms each day. The total cost of $83.55 at this level is the lowest among all scenarios.

File: 11-10.xls, sheet: 11-10B

Solved Problem 11-4

General Foundry, Inc., a metalworks plant in Hamilton, has long been trying to avoid the expense of installing air pollution control equipment. Environment Canada has recently given the foundry 16 weeks to install a complex air filter system on its main smokestack. General Foundry has been warned that it may be forced to close unless the device is installed in the allotted period. John Carter, the managing partner, wants to make sure that installation of the filtering system progresses smoothly and on time. General Foundry has identified the eight activities that need to be performed in order for the project to be completed. For each activity, the following table shows the immediate predecessors and three times estimates—optimistic, most likely, and pessimistic:

ACTIVITY	DESCRIPTION	IMMEDIATE PREDECESSORS	OPTIMISTIC TIME (a)	MOST LIKELY TIME (m)	PESSIMISTIC TIME (b)
A	Build internal components	—	1	2	3
B	Modify roof and floor	—	2	3	4
C	Construct collection stack	A	1	2	3
D	Pour concrete and install frame	A, B	2	4	6
E	Build high-temperature burner	C	1	4	7
F	Install pollution control system	C	1	2	9
G	Install air pollution device	D, E	3	4	11
H	Inspect and test	F, G	1	2	3

File: 11-11.xls

Simulation is a popular technique for analyzing uncertainty in projects.

The actual duration of each activity is assumed to follow a triangular distribution, with the three time estimates shown for that activity.[14] John wants to find the probability that the project will meet Environment Canada's 16-week deadline. Round off all activity times to two decimal places.

Solution

This is an example of analyzing uncertainty in a project management problem. Recall that in Chapter 8, we studied this issue analytically, using probability distributions. In that analysis, we first computed the expected value and variance of the project completion time, assuming that the activity time of each activity followed a beta distribution. We then used a normal distribution to compute various probabilities for the project completion time (see Section 8.4 for details). As noted in that chapter, another popular way to analyze uncertainty in projects is by using simulation. Let us simulate General Foundry's project here.

It is convenient to first express the activities in the project as a project network. We show this in Figure 11.4, where the nodes represent the activities and the arcs represent the precedence relationships between activities.

Before simulating a project, it is convenient to draw the project network.

The Excel layout for this simulation model is presented in Screenshot 11.11. The spreadsheet is organized as follows:

- Columns A through F show the name, description, immediate predecessors, and three time estimates for each activity (activities A through H).

- In column G, we simulate the actual duration of each activity by using Oracle Crystal Ball's CB.Triangular function. We then round this value to two decimal places, using the ROUND function. For example, the formula in cell G4 is

$$=ROUND(CB.Triangular(D4, E4, F4), 2)$$

- In column H, we calculate the actual start time for each activity. In computing this time, we need to ensure that all predecessors for an activity have been completed before that activity can begin. For example, both activities A and B have to finish before activity D can start. Hence, the start

FIGURE 11.4   **Project Network for General Foundry**

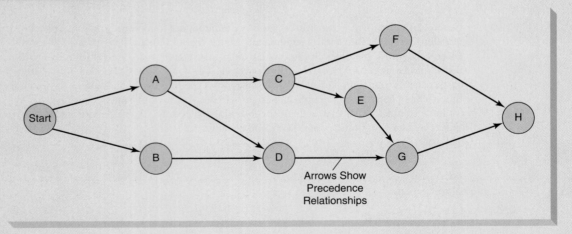

[14] Although we assumed that activity durations followed the beta distribution in Chapter 8, the manner in which Excel (and add-ins such as Oracle Crystal Ball) implements this distribution is different from the three-time estimate approach we used in Chapter 8. In contrast, the triangular distribution, which is also commonly used to model project activity durations, uses the three time estimates. For this reason, we have chosen to model activity durations here by using the triangular distribution.

SCREENSHOT 11.11   **Excel Layout and Results, Using Oracle Crystal Ball, for General Foundry**

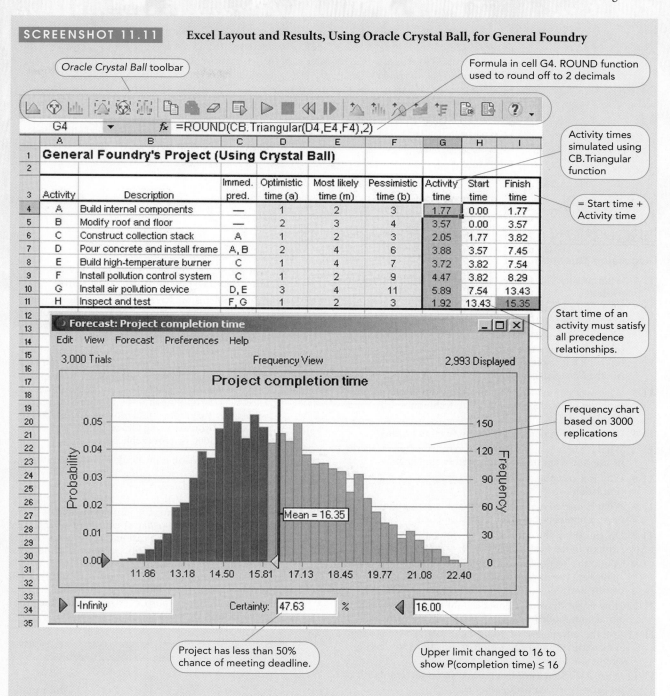

Oracle Crystal Ball toolbar

Formula in cell G4. ROUND function used to round off to 2 decimals

G4   fx =ROUND(CB.Triangular(D4,E4,F4),2)

Activity times simulated using CB.Triangular function

	A	B	C	D	E	F	G	H	I
1	**General Foundry's Project (Using Crystal Ball)**								
2									
3	Activity	Description	Immed. pred.	Optimistic time (a)	Most likely time (m)	Pessimistic time (b)	Activity time	Start time	Finish time
4	A	Build internal components	—	1	2	3	1.77	0.00	1.77
5	B	Modify roof and floor	—	2	3	4	3.57	0.00	3.57
6	C	Construct collection stack	A	1	2	3	2.05	1.77	3.82
7	D	Pour concrete and install frame	A, B	2	4	6	3.88	3.57	7.45
8	E	Build high-temperature burner	C	1	4	7	3.72	3.82	7.54
9	F	Install pollution control system	C	1	2	9	4.47	3.82	8.29
10	G	Install air pollution device	D, E	3	4	11	5.89	7.54	13.43
11	H	Inspect and test	F, G	1	2	3	1.92	13.43	15.35

= Start time + Activity time

Start time of an activity must satisfy all precedence relationships.

Forecast: Project completion time

Edit   View   Forecast   Preferences   Help

3,000 Trials   Frequency View   2,993 Displayed

Project completion time

Mean = 16.35

Probability: 0.05, 0.04, 0.03, 0.02, 0.01, 0.00

Frequency: 150, 120, 90, 60, 30, 0

11.86   13.18   14.50   15.81   17.13   18.45   19.77   21.08   22.40

-Infinity   Certainty: 47.63   %   16.00

Frequency chart based on 3000 replications

Project has less than 50% chance of meeting deadline.

Upper limit changed to 16 to show P(completion time) ≤ 16

time for activity D is set equal to the maximum of the finish times of activities A and B. That is, the formula in cell H7 is

$$=MAX(I4,I5)$$

■ In column I, we compute the finish time of each activity as the sum of the start time of that activity (column H) and the actual duration of that activity (column G).

In General Foundry's project, the project completion time is the completion time of activity H, shown in cell I11. Based on the single replication shown in Screenshot 11.11, it appears that the project will finish in only 15.35 weeks. However, in order to get a more precise value of this output measure, we use Oracle Crystal Ball to replicate the model 3000 times. Cell I11 is defined as the Forecast cell.

The frequency chart obtained from Oracle Crystal Ball is also shown in Screenshot 11.11. Based on this chart, it appears that the average completion time of the project is 16.35 weeks. (To show the mean, click on the graph to get an options window where you can enable this feature.) More importantly for General Foundry, the chart indicates that there is only a 47.63% chance that the project will finish in less than 16 weeks. Based on the results, it appears that John Carter should either try to shorten some of the activity durations or, alternatively, negotiate with Environment Canada for more time.

DISCUSSION QUESTIONS AND PROBLEMS

Discussion Questions

11-1 What are the advantages and limitations of simulation models?

11-2 Why might a manager be forced to use simulation instead of an analytical model in dealing with a problem of
  (a) inventory ordering policy?
  (b) ships docking in a port to unload?
  (c) bank teller service windows?
  (d) the Canadian economy?

11-3 What types of management problems can be solved more easily by using decision modeling techniques other than simulation?

11-4 What are the major steps in the simulation process?

11-5 What is Monte Carlo simulation? What principles underlie its use, and what steps are followed in applying it?

11-6 Why is a computer necessary in conducting a real-world simulation?

11-7 What is operational gaming? What is systems simulation? Give examples of how each may be applied.

11-8 Do you think the application of simulation will increase strongly in the next 10 years? Why or why not?

11-9 Would the average output value in a simulation problem change appreciably if a longer period were simulated? Why or why not?

11-10 How might drawing a flow diagram help in developing a simulation model?

11-11 List the advantages of using an Excel add-in program rather than using Excel's built-in functions to develop a simulation model.

11-12 What does Scenario Manager allow you to accomplish in an Excel-based simulation model?

11-13 Do you think we can use Excel's Solver to solve simulation models? Why or why not?

Problems

Notes

■ Simulation models for all the following problems can be set up by using Excel.

■ Wherever necessary, replications can be done either using Data Table or using Oracle Crystal Ball.

■ In all problems, we have specified the number of replications to use simply as N. Your instructor may specify the actual value of N that he or she wants you to use. If not, we recommend that you try to replicate each simulation model as many times as is convenient. If you are using Data Table, 200 to 300 replications should be appropriate to keep the computation time reasonable and the resulting Excel file relatively small (even though the average values may vary from simulation to simulation). However, if you are using Oracle Crystal Ball, you should try 3000 or more replications.

■ Wherever a decision is involved, you can use either Scenario Manager, or Decision Table if you are using Oracle Crystal Ball.

11-14 Clark Property Management is responsible for the maintenance, rental, and day-to-day operation of several large apartment complexes in the east end of Toronto. George Clark is especially concerned about the cost projections for replacing air conditioner (A/C) compressors. He would like to simulate the number of A/C failures each month. Using data from similar apartment buildings he manages in a Toronto suburb, Clark establishes the probability of failures during a month as follows:

NUMBER OF A/C FAILURES	PROBABILITY
0	0.06
1	0.13
2	0.25
3	0.28
4	0.20
5	0.07
6	0.01

(a) Simulate Clark's monthly A/C failures for a period of three years. Compute the average number of failures per month.

(b) Explain any difference between the simulated average failures and the expected value of failures computed by using the probability distribution.

11-15 Weekly demand for a certain brand of golf ball at The Golf Outlet is normally distributed, with a mean of 35 and a standard deviation of 5. The profit per box is $5.

(a) Simulate one year (52 weeks) of demand and calculate the average weekly profit. Make all demand values integers in your model.

(b) What is the probability that weekly profit will be $200 or more?

11-16 Dan's Electronics sells TVs according to the monthly demand distribution shown in the following table:

DEMAND	PROBABILITY
10	0.03
15	0.07
20	0.09
25	0.12
30	0.20
35	0.18
40	0.21
45	0.08
50	0.02

Simulate 10 years of demand and compare theoretical and simulated results for the following measures:

(a) Average demand

(b) Probability that demand will be less than or equal to 30 TVs

11-17 Vincent Maruggi, a foreign MBA student at a Canadian university, has been having problems balancing his chequebook. His monthly income is derived from a graduate research assistantship; however, he also makes extra money in most months by tutoring undergraduates in their decision modeling course. His chances of various income levels are shown here (assume that this income is received at the beginning of each month):

MONTHLY INCOME ($)	PROBABILITY
750	0.40
800	0.20
850	0.30
900	0.10

Maruggi's expenditures also vary from month to month, and he estimates that they will follow this distribution:

MONTHLY EXPENSES ($)	PROBABILITY
700	0.10
800	0.45
900	0.30
1000	0.15

Maruggi begins his final year with $1000 in his chequing account. Simulate the cash flow for 12 months and identify Maruggi's (a) ending balance at the end of the year and (b) probability that he will have a negative balance in any month. Replicate your model N times and discuss Maruggi's financial picture based on the average values for these two measures.

11-18 Sunrise Bakery has decided to bake 20 loaves of its famous sourdough bread at the beginning of the day. The store has determined that daily demand will follow the distribution shown in the following table:

DAILY DEMAND	PROBABILITY
5	0.08
10	0.12
15	0.25
20	0.20
25	0.20
30	0.15

Each loaf costs Sunrise $1.50 and can be sold for $3. Sunrise can sell any unsold loaves for $0.75 the next day.

(a) Simulate one month (25 days) of operation to calculate the bakery's total monthly profit. Replicate this calculation N times to compute the average total monthly profit.

(b) Sunrise Bakery would like to investigate the profitability of baking 15, 20, 25, or 30 loaves at the start of the day. Which quantity would you recommend? Why?

11-19 Jeff Park sells newspapers on Sunday morning in an area surrounded by three busy churches. Demand for newspapers is distributed as per the following table:

DEMAND	PROBABILITY
50	0.05
75	0.10
100	0.25
125	0.30
150	0.20
175	0.10

Jeff has decided to order 100 papers from his supplier. Jeff pays $1.25 for each paper he orders and sells each paper for $2. Unsold newspapers have no resale value.

(a) Simulate one year (52 Sundays) of operation to calculate Jeff's total yearly profit. Replicate this calculation N times. What is the average yearly profit?

(b) Jeff would like to investigate the profitability of ordering 50, 100, 150, and 175 papers at the start of each Sunday. Which order quantity would you recommend? Why?

11-20 Pierre's Kayak Rentals leases kayaks each day from a supplier and rents them to customers who use them to take trips down the St. Lawrence River. Each day, Pierre leases 30 kayaks from his supplier, at a cost of $14 per kayak. He rents them to his customers for $25 per day. Rental demand follows the normal distribution, with a mean of 30 kayaks and a standard deviation of 6 kayaks. (Make all demands integers in your model.)

(a) Simulate this leasing policy for a month (30 days) of operation to calculate the total monthly profit. Replicate this calculation N times. What is the average monthly profit?

(b) Pierre would like to evaluate the average monthly profit if he leases 25, 30, 35, and 40 kayaks. What is your recommendation? Why?

11-21 The Brennan Aircraft Division of TLN Enterprises operates a large number of computerized plotting machines. For the most part, the plotting devices are used to create line drawings of complex wing airfoils and fuselage part dimensions. The engineers operating the automated plotters are called loft lines engineers.

The computerized plotters consist of a minicomputer system connected to a 4- by 5-foot flat table with a series of ink pens suspended above it. When a sheet of clear plastic or paper is properly placed on the table, the computer directs a series of horizontal and vertical pen movements until the desired figure is drawn.

The plotting machines are highly reliable, with the exception of the four sophisticated ink pens that are built in. The pens constantly clog and jam in a raised or lowered position. When this occurs, the plotter is unusable.

Currently, Brennan Aircraft replaces each pen as it fails. The service manager has, however, proposed replacing all four pens every time one fails. This should cut down the frequency of plotter failures. At present, it takes one hour to replace one pen. All four pens could be replaced in two hours. The total cost of a plotter being unusable is $50 per hour. Each pen costs $8. The breakdown data in the table at the top of the next column are thought to be valid.

(a) For each option (replacing one pen at a time and replacing all four pens at a time), simulate the average total time a plotter would operate before it would have 20 failures. Then compute the total cost per hour for each option to determine which option Brennan Aircraft should use. Use N replications.

HOURS BETWEEN FAILURES (ONE PEN REPLACED)	PROBABILITY	HOURS BETWEEN FAILURES (FOUR PENS REPLACED)	PROBABILITY
10	0.05	70	0.10
20	0.15	100	0.15
30	0.15	110	0.25
40	0.20	120	0.35
50	0.20	130	0.20
60	0.15	140	0.05

(b) Compute the total cost per hour analytically for each option. How do these results compare to the simulation results?

11-22 Margolese Wiring and Electric is a company that installs wiring and electrical fixtures in residential construction. Noah Margolese has been concerned with the amount of time it takes to complete wiring jobs because some of his workers are very unreliable. For each wiring job, a list of activities, their mean duration times, standard deviation of duration times, and immediate predecessors are given in the following table:

ACTIVITY	DAYS		IMMEDIATE PREDECESSORS
	MEAN	STANDARD DEVIATION	
A	5.83	0.83	—
B	3.67	0.33	—
C	2.00	0.33	—
D	7.00	0.33	C
E	4.00	0.67	B, D
F	10.00	1.33	A, E
G	2.17	0.50	A, E
H	6.00	1.00	F
I	11.00	0.33	G
J	16.33	1.00	G
K	7.33	1.33	H, I

Assume that all activity durations follow a normal distribution, with the means and standard deviations shown.

Use simulation to determine the probability that Margolese will finish the project in 40 days or less.

11-23 Dr. Marc Gauthier practises dentistry in Trois-Rivières, Quebec. Gauthier tries hard to schedule appointments so that patients do not have to wait beyond their appointment time. His October 20 schedule is shown in the following table:

PATIENT	SCHEDULED APPOINTMENT	TIME NEEDED (MIN.)
Adams	9:30 A.M.	15
Bernier	9:45 A.M.	20
Coté	10:15 A.M.	15
Dubé	10:30 A.M.	10
Erving	10:45 A.M.	30
Fortin	11:15 A.M.	15
Gagnon	11:30 A.M.	20
Hébert	11:45 A.M.	15

Unfortunately, not every patient arrives exactly on schedule. Also, some examinations take longer than planned, and some take less time than planned. Gauthier's experience dictates the following: 20% of the patients will be 20 minutes early, 10% of the patients will be 10 minutes early, 40% of the patients will be on time, 25% of the patients will be 10 minutes late, and 5% of the patients will be 20 minutes late.

He further estimates that there is a 15% chance that an appointment will take 20% less time than planned, 50% chance it will take exactly the planned time, 25% chance it will take 20% more time than planned, and 10% chance it will take 40% more time than planned.

Dr. Gauthier has to leave at 12:15 P.M. on October 20 to catch a flight to a dental convention in Paris. Assuming that he is ready to start his workday at 9:30 A.M. and that patients are treated in order of their scheduled exam (even if one late patient arrives after an early one), will he be able to make the flight? Comment on this simulation. Use N replications.

11-24 Pelnor Corporation is the nation's largest manufacturer of industrial-size washing machines. A main ingredient in the production process is 8- by 10-foot sheets of stainless steel. The steel is used for both interior washer drums and outer casings. Due to an existing contract, Pelnor must place an order for steel with the Smith-Layton Foundry each week, regardless of on-hand inventory. As per the contract, the foundry can ship either 8500 or 9500 square feet of steel each week, depending on availability. Based on past history, there is a 45% chance that 8500 square feet will arrive and a 55% chance that the larger-size order will arrive. Pelnor's weekly demand for stainless steel is given in the following table:

DEMAND (SQ. FT.)	PROBABILITY
6 000	0.05
7 000	0.15
8 000	0.20
9 000	0.30
10 000	0.20
11 000	0.10

Pelnor has the capacity to store no more than 25 000 square feet of steel at any time. If Pelnor does not have space to store all the steel received in any given week, the excess amount is sent back to the foundry.

(a) Simulate stainless steel order arrivals and use for 52 weeks. (Begin the first week with a starting inventory of 5000 square feet.) If an end-of-week inventory is ever negative, assume that back orders are permitted and fill the demand from the next arriving order.
(b) Should Pelnor add more storage area? If so, how much? If not, comment on the system. Use N replications of your model in (a) to answer these questions.

11-25 Furniture Depot orders a certain brand of mattress from its supplier and sells the mattresses at its retail location. The store currently orders 40 mattresses whenever the inventory level drops to 20. The cost to hold one mattress in inventory for one day is $0.75. The cost to place an order with the supplier is $80, and stockout costs are $150 per mattress. Beginning inventory is 30 mattresses. The daily demand probabilities are shown in the following table:

DAILY DEMAND	PROBABILITY
2	0.08
3	0.14
4	0.20
5	0.26
6	0.22
7	0.10

Lead time is discrete uniformly distributed between two and five days (both inclusive). Simulate this inventory policy for a quarter (90 days) and calculate the total quarterly cost. Also calculate the percentage of stockouts for the quarter. Replicate these calculations N times each to calculate the average values for these measures.

11-26 Consider the Furniture Depot problem described in Problem 11-25.

(a) Furniture Depot would like to evaluate ordering 35, 40, 45, and 50 mattresses when the reorder point of 20 is reached. Based on the average total quarterly cost, which order quantity would you recommend?
(b) Furniture Depot would like to evaluate reorder points of 15, 20, 25, and 30 mattresses, with an order quantity of 40 mattresses. Based on the average total quarterly cost, which reorder point would you recommend?

11-27 Video Works is a retail establishment that sells DVD players to its customers. Video Works orders 30 DVD players from its supplier when its inventory reaches eight units. Daily demand for DVD players is discrete, uniformly distributed between three and six (both inclusive). The lead time from the supplier also varies for each order and is discrete, uniformly distributed between one and three days (both inclusive). The cost to hold one unit in inventory for one day is $0.50. The cost to place an order is $100. Stockout cost per unit is estimated at $40. Initial inventory is 30 units.

Simulate this inventory policy for a quarter (90 days) and calculate the total quarterly cost. Also calculate the percentage of stockouts for the quarter. Replicate these calculations N times each to calculate the average values for these measures.

11-28 Consider the Video Works problem described in Problem 11-27.

   (a) Video Works would like to evaluate ordering 25, 30, 35, and 40 DVD players when the reorder point of eight is reached. Based on the average total quarterly cost, which order quantity would you recommend?

   (b) Video Works would like to evaluate reorder points of 6, 8, and 10 DVD players, with an order quantity of 30 players. Based on the average total cost for the quarter, which reorder point would you recommend?

11-29 The Tire Warehouse (TTW) sells a certain brand tire that has a daily demand which is normally distributed with a mean of 15 tires and a standard deviation of four tires. (Make all demands integers in your model.) TTW replenishes its inventory by ordering 250 tires from the factory whenever its current inventory reaches 40 tires. The lead time (in days) to receive an order from the factory follows the distribution shown in the following table:

LEAD TIME	PROBABILITY
1	0.10
2	0.22
3	0.28
4	0.15
5	0.15
6	0.10

The cost to hold 1 tire in inventory for one day is $0.20. The cost to place an order with the factory is $100. Stockout costs are estimated at $10 per tire. The initial inventory level is 100 tires.

   (a) Simulate six months (180 days) of operation to calculate the total semiannual cost and the percentage of stockouts for the period. Replicate these calculations N times each to calculate the average values for these measures.

   (b) TTW would like to evaluate the economics of ordering 150, 200, 250, 300, and 350 tires, with a reorder point of 40 tires. Based on the average total semiannual cost, which order quantity would you recommend?

   (c) TTW would like to evaluate the economics of ordering 250 tires, with reorder points of 40, 50, 60,

70, and 80 tires. Based on the average total semiannual cost, which reorder point would you recommend?

11-30 ABC Airlines flies a six-passenger commuter flight once a day to Thunder Bay. A nonrefundable one-way fare with a reservation costs $79. The daily demand for this flight is given in the following table, along with the probability distribution of no-shows (a no-show has a reservation but does not arrive at the gate and forfeits the fare):

DEMAND	PROBABILITY	NO-SHOWS	PROBABILITY
5	0.05	0	0.15
6	0.11	1	0.25
7	0.20	2	0.26
8	0.18	3	0.23
9	0.16	4	0.11
10	0.12		
11	0.10		
12	0.08		

ABC currently overbooks three passengers per flight. If there are not enough seats for a passenger at the gate, ABC Airlines refunds his or her fare and also provides a $100 voucher good on any other trip. The fixed cost for each flight is $350, regardless of the number of passengers.

   (a) Set up a simulation model and calculate ABC's profit per flight. Replicate the calculation N times each to calculate the average profit per flight.

   (b) ABC Airlines would like to investigate the profitability of overbooking 0, 1, 2, 3, 4, and 5 passengers. What is your recommendation? Why?

11-31 A large general hospital in Manitoba has an emergency room that is divided into six departments: (1) the initial exam station, to treat minor problems and make diagnoses; (2) an X-ray department; (3) an operating room; (4) a cast-fitting room; (5) an observation room for recovery and general observation before final diagnosis or release; and (6) an out-processing department, where clerks check out patients and arrange for payment or insurance forms. The probabilities that a patient will go from one department to another are presented in the table at the top of page 541.

Simulate the trail followed by 200 emergency room patients. Process one patient at a time, from each one's entry at the initial exam station until he or she leaves through out-processing. Note that a patient can enter the same department more than once. Based on your simulation, what is the probability that a patient enters the X-ray department more than once?

11-32 Management of a New Brunswick bank is concerned about a loss of customers at its main office downtown. One solution that has been proposed is to add one or more drive-through teller windows to make it easier for customers in cars to obtain quick service without parking. Chris Carlson, the bank president, thinks the bank should

Table for Problem 11-31

FROM	TO	PROBABILITY
Initial exam station	X-ray department	0.45
	Operating room	0.15
	Observation room	0.10
	Out-processing clerk	0.30
X-ray department	Operating room	0.10
	Cast-fitting room	0.25
	Observation room	0.35
	Out-processing clerk	0.30
Operating room	Cast-fitting room	0.25
	Observation room	0.70
	Out-processing clerk	0.05
Cast-fitting room	Observation room	0.55
	X-ray department	0.05
	Out-processing clerk	0.40
Observation room	Operating room	0.15
	X-ray department	0.15
	Out-processing clerk	0.70

only risk the cost of installing one drive-through window. He is informed by his staff that the cost (amortized over a 20-year period) of building a drive-through window is $12 000 per year. It also costs $16 000 per year in wages and benefits to staff each new drive-through window.

The director of management analysis, Beth Shader, believes that two factors encourage the immediate construction of two drive-through windows, however. According to a recent article in *Banking Research* magazine, customers who wait in long lines for drive-through service will cost banks an average of $1 per minute in loss of goodwill. Also, adding a second drive-through window will cost an additional $16 000 in staffing, but amortized construction costs can be cut to a total of $20 000 per year if the two drive-through windows are installed together instead of one at a time. To complete her analysis, Shader collected arrival and service rates at a competing downtown bank's drive-through windows for one month. These data are shown in the following table:

TIME BETWEEN ARRIVALS (MIN.)	OCCURRENCES	SERVICE TIME (MIN.)	OCCURRENCES
1	200	1	100
2	250	2	150
3	300	3	350
4	150	4	150
5	100	5	150
		6	100

All times are in minutes.

(a) Simulate a one-hour time period for a system with one drive-through window. Replicate the model N times.

(b) Simulate a one-hour time period for a system with two drive-through windows. Replicate the model N times.

(c) Conduct a cost analysis of the two options. Assume that the bank is open 7 hours per day and 200 days per year.

11-33 Julia DeSouza owns and operates one of the largest Mercedes-Benz auto dealerships in Toronto. In the past 36 months, her sales of this luxury car have ranged from a low of six new cars to a high of 12 new cars, as reflected in the following table:

SALES OF NEW CARS PER MONTH	FREQUENCY
6	3
7	4
8	6
9	12
10	9
11	1
12	1

Julia believes that sales will continue during the next 24 months at about the same historical rates and that delivery lead times will also continue to follow this pace (stated in probability form):

DELIVERY TIME (MOS.)	PROBABILITY
1	0.44
2	0.33
3	0.16
4	0.07

Julia's current policy is to order 14 cars at a time (two full truckloads, with 7 autos on each truck) and to place a new order whenever the stock on hand reaches 12 autos. Beginning inventory is 14 cars. Julia establishes the following relevant costs: (i) The carrying cost per Mercedes per month is $600, (ii) the cost of a lost sale averages $4350, and (iii) the cost of placing an order is $570.

(a) Simulate Julia's inventory policy for the next two years. What is the total monthly cost of this policy? Also, what is the average number of stockouts per month? Use N replications of your model.

(b) Julia wishes to evaluate several different ordering quantities—12, 14, 16, 18, and 20. Based on the total monthly cost, what would you recommend? Why? Set $R = 12$ in each case.

11-34 The Alfredo Fragrance Company produces only one product, a perfume called Hint of Elegance. Hint of Elegance consists of two secret ingredients blended into an exclusive fragrance that is marketed in Zurich. An economic expression referred to as the Cobb–Douglas function describes the production of Hint of Elegance as follows:

$$X = \sqrt{(\text{ingredient 1}) \times (\text{ingredient 2})}$$

where X is the amount of perfume produced. The company operates at a level where ingredient 1 is set daily at 25 units and ingredient 2 at 36 units. Although the price Alfredo pays for ingredient 1 is fixed at $50 per unit, the cost of ingredient 2 and the selling price for the final perfume are both probabilistic. The sales price for Hint of Elegance follows this distribution:

SALES PRICE ($)	PROBABILITY
300	0.2
350	0.5
400	0.3

The cost for ingredient 2 is discrete, uniformly distributed between $35 and $45 (in increments of $1). Simulate the firm's profits for a month (30 days). Use N replications of your model to compute the average monthly profit.

11-35 Janis Miller is considering building a 300-seat theatre in a popular tourist destination. After studying the market, Janis has drawn the following conclusions:

- There will be one show every night.
- The theatre will make a profit of $2 on each occupied seat and suffer a loss of $0.50 on each unoccupied seat.
- The probability that it rains on any given night is 0.30.
- The number of customers on a dry night is normally distributed, with a mean of 275 and a standard deviation of 30.
- The number of customers on a rainy night is normally distributed, with a mean of 250 and a standard deviation of 45.

Set up Janis's problem and simulate total profit for one month (30 days). Make all demands integers in your model. Replicate your model N times and calculate Janis's average monthly profit.

11-36 The owner of Dwayne's Concrete Service notes that the number of jobs each month follows a discrete uniform distribution between 10 and 16. The probability that a specific job will be for a residential driveway is 70%, and the probability that it will be for a commercial project is 30%. Revenues for residential driveways follow a normal distribution, with a mean of $500 and a standard deviation of $50. Commercial projects, although more lucrative, also have larger variability. Dwayne estimates that revenues here follow a normal distribution, with a mean of $1500 and a standard deviation of $400. Set up a simulation model for Dwayne's problem and replicate it N times to calculate the average monthly revenue.

11-37 The Mount Morris Community Association makes annual door-to-door solicitations for funds. Residents of each visited house are asked to contribute either $15 (and receive a free family portrait package) or $25 (and receive two free family portrait packages). An analysis from previous years' solicitations indicates that

- only 80% of the homes visited have the man or woman of the house at home.
- when someone is home, there is only a 40% chance that he or she will make a donation.
- of the people making donations, there is a 50% chance they will contribute $15 and a 45% chance they will contribute $25. Occasionally (5% chance), a person makes a donation in excess of $25. Such distributions follow a discrete uniform distribution between $30 and $50 (in increments of $1).

The association director plans to visit 30 houses tomorrow. Set up a simulation model and replicate it N times to determine the probability that the director will receive more than $250 in donations from these 30 houses.

11-38 A local bank has a single drive-through window with arrival times and service times that follow the distributions from the following table (all times are in minutes):

TIME BETWEEN ARRIVALS (MIN.)	PROBABILITY	SERVICE TIME (MIN.)	PROBABILITY
1	0.15	1	0.15
2	0.24	2	0.35
3	0.27	3	0.22
4	0.22	4	0.28
5	0.12		

Simulate the arrival of 200 customers to compute each of the following measures: (a) average time a customer waits for service, (b) average time a customer is in the system (wait plus service time), and (c) percentage of time the server is busy with customers. Replicate each measure N times to compute the average.

11-39 Ann sells hot dogs at the local softball games. For the upcoming championship game, Ann has to decide how many hot dogs to order (170, 190, or 210), at a cost of $0.25 each. Ann sells hot dogs for $1 each. However, any unsold hot dogs must be thrown away.

If the game is interesting, Ann thinks that fewer people will visit her stand. In such a case, Ann estimates that demand will be normally distributed, with a mean of 140 and a standard deviation of 20. However, if the game is a blowout, she expects more people to visit the stand. Demand in this case will be normally distributed, with a mean of 190 and a standard deviation of 15. Based on her familiarity with the two teams, she estimates that there is only a 40% chance that the game will be a blowout.

Set up a simulation model and replicate it N times for each order size to determine Ann's (a) expected profit and

(b) expected percentage of unsold hot dogs. What do you recommend Ann should do?

11-40 Glace Bay Grocery Store has a single check-out register, with customer arrival distribution shown in the following table (in minutes):

TIME BETWEEN ARRIVALS (MIN.)	PROBABILITY
1	0.18
2	0.20
3	0.22
4	0.25
5	0.15

Service time is discrete uniformly distributed between one and four minutes.

Simulate the arrival of 200 customers to compute each of the following measures: (a) average time a customer waits for service and (b) probability that a customer waits three minutes or longer for service. Replicate each measure N times to compute the average.

11-41 Astro Chemical manufactures chlorine gas by passing electricity through saltwater in a diaphragm cell. The plant has 88 diaphragm cells that operate in parallel. Each cell can produce five tonnes of chlorine gas per day, and each tonne of chlorine gas has a profit contribution of $15. Due to the harsh environment, cell failures occur, causing the cell to be taken offline for maintenance. A cell fails, on average, every 30 hours, according to the exponential probability distribution. Only one cell can be repaired at any given time. Using the current maintenance procedure, the repair time follows a truncated normal probability distribution, with a mean of 21 hours, a standard deviation of six hours, and a minimum value of five hours. A new maintenance procedure is being considered that will require a significant capital investment. If this new procedure is implemented, the repair time will still follow a truncated normal distribution, but the mean time will be 14 hours, the standard deviation will be four hours, and the minimum time will be three hours. Simulate 200 failures to determine the annual savings in downtime with the new method.

11-42 Custom Tee Shirts is planning to print and sell specially designed tee shirts for the upcoming Stanley Cup. The shirts will cost $8 each to produce and can be sold for $21 each until the Stanley Cup. After the Stanley Cup, the price will be reduced to $10 per shirt. The demand at the $21 price is expected to be normally distributed, with a mean of 10 000 shirts and a standard deviation of 2000 shirts. The demand for the $10 price is expected to be normally distributed, with a mean of 4000 shirts and a standard deviation of 800 shirts. Any shirts left over will be discarded. Because of the high setup costs, Custom Tee Shirts is planning on producing one run of 12 000 shirts. Make all demand values integers in your model.

(a) Simulate N setups to calculate the average profit for this quantity of shirts.
(b) Custom Tee Shirts would like to evaluate producing 10 000, 12 000, and 14 000 shirts. Which would you recommend? Why?

11-43 George Foster is responsible for the warehouse operation for a local discount department store chain. The warehouse has only one unloading dock that is currently operated by a single three-person crew. Trucks arrive at an average rate of five per hour and follow the exponential probability distribution. The average time for one of the crews to unload a truck tends to follow a normal distribution, with a mean of nine minutes and standard deviation of three minutes (minimum time is one minute). George has estimated the cost of operating a truck at $40 per hour. George pays each person on the unloading crew $11 per hour. The unloading dock operates eight hours each day. Simulate 100 days of this operation to calculate the total daily cost. Replicate this calculation N times to compute the expected total cost per day of this operation.

11-44 A customer service counter at a local department store is normally staffed by a single employee. The probabilities of arrival times and service times are shown in the following table (all times are in minutes):

TIME BETWEEN ARRIVALS (MIN.)	PROBABILITY	SERVICE TIME (MIN.)	PROBABILITY
1	0.07	1	0.07
2	0.25	2	0.24
3	0.23	3	0.28
4	0.26	4	0.28
5	0.19	5	0.13

Simulate the arrival of 100 customers to compute each of the following measures: (a) average number of customers in line and (b) probability that a customer will have to wait three or more minutes for service to begin. Replicate each measure N times to compute the average.

11-45 A plant engineering group needs to set up an assembly line to produce a new product. The following table describes the relationships between the activities that need to be completed for this product to be manufactured:

ACTIVITY	DAYS a	m	b	IMMEDIATE PREDECESSORS
A	3	6	8	—
B	5	8	10	A
C	5	6	8	A
D	1	2	4	B, C
E	7	11	17	D
F	7	9	12	D
G	6	8	9	D
H	3	4	7	F, G
I	3	5	7	E, F, H

Assume that the actual duration of each activity follows a triangular distribution, with the three time estimates shown for that activity. Round off all activity times to two decimal places.

(a) Use simulation to determine the probability that the project will finish in 37 days or less.
(b) Use simulation to determine the probability that the project will take more than 32 days.

11-46 Gita Margolese, director of personnel of Management Resources, Inc., is in the process of designing a program that its customers can use in the job-finding process. Some of the activities include preparing résumés, writing letters, making appointments to see prospective employers, researching companies and industries, and so on. Information on the activities is shown in the following table:

ACTIVITY	DAYS MEAN	STANDARD DEVIATION	IMMEDIATE PREDECESSORS
A	10.00	0.67	—
B	7.17	0.50	—
C	3.17	0.17	—
D	20.00	3.33	A
E	7.00	0.33	C
F	10.00	0.33	B, D, E
G	7.33	0.67	B, D, E
H	15.00	0.33	F
I	11.17	0.50	F
J	7.00	0.33	G, H
K	6.67	0.67	I, J
L	2.17	0.50	G, H

Assume that all activity durations follow a normal distribution, with the means and standard deviations shown. Round off all activity times to two decimal places.
Use simulation to determine the average project completion time and the probability that the project will take at least 75 days.

11-47 Laura Thompson needs to plan and manage a local construction project. The table at the top of the next column describes the relationships between the activities that need to be completed.
Assume that the actual duration of each activity follows a triangular distribution, with the three time estimates shown for that activity. Round off all activity times to one decimal place. Use simulation to determine the probability that the project will take at least 50 days.

ACTIVITY	DAYS a	m	b	IMMEDIATE PREDECESSORS
A	4	8	13	—
B	4	10	15	A
C	7	14	20	B
D	9	16	19	B
E	6	9	11	B
F	2	4	5	D, E
G	4	7	11	C, F
H	3	5	9	G
I	2	3	4	G, H

11-48 David Stockman is responsible for developing a supervisory training program for his organization. The following table describes the relationships between the activities that need to be completed:

ACTIVITY	DAYS MINIMUM	MAXIMUM	IMMEDIATE PREDECESSORS
A	3	13	—
B	5	17	—
C	3	8	A, B
D	5	14	C
E	2	9	C
F	2	15	E
G	5	12	F
H	6	12	D
I	3	8	F, H
J	4	10	G, I

Assume that the actual duration of each activity follows a discrete uniform distribution between the minimum and maximum times shown for that activity.
Use simulation to determine the probability that the project will be finished in less than 49 days.

11-49 A Saskatchewan grain elevator serves a group of farmers who transport their grain stocks to the elevator by truck. There is one dock available to unload incoming trucks and the unloading crew, consisting of two workers, can unload two trucks per day. Trucks arrive at night after harvesting has been completed and they are ready to be unloaded the following morning. There is a single unloading crew which is paid a full day's wages regardless of the number of trucks that have to be unloaded. The crew is paid $240 per day. There is a penalty of $100 associated with the lost usage of the truck for every day the truck is held over in the dock.
The probability distribution for the number of trucks arriving on a given night is as follows:

NUMBER OF TRUCKS	PROBABILITY
0	0.16
1	0.24
2	0.32
3	0.19
4	0.06
5	0.03

(a) Simulate the truck unloading problem with one unloading crew for a month consisting of 24 working days.

(b) Estimate the monthly cost of unloading the trucks, including the cost of the crew and the penalty associated with trucks that cannot be unloaded on the day of arrival.
(c) Replicate the simulation 20 times and compute the average cost.

11-50 Reconsider the Saskatchewan grain elevator problem (see Problem 11-49). Management is considering hiring extra workers for the crew at an additional cost of $120 a day per worker. If each extra crew member will increase the number of trucks that can be unloaded by one extra truck per day (e.g., with three crew members, three trucks can be unloaded per day) would you recommend hiring extra workers? If so, how many?

⇒ CASE STUDY 11.1

OntAir Airlines

OntAir Airlines was started in 2001 as a short-haul commuter service connecting small Ontario towns. OntAir uses small regional airports and schedules flights from the towns serviced by these airports to Toronto City Centre Airport (convenient for travellers who need to transfer to international flights at Lester B. Pearson International Airport. OntAir also schedules flights between Ontario towns as dictated by consumer demand.

OntAir was started and is managed by Phil Malone and Stan Cuthbert-Jones, both former pilots with now-defunct Canadian Airlines, headquartered in Calgary. After Canadian was taken over by Air Canada in 2000, Phil and Stan decided to go out on their own, and they founded OntAir. The partners acquired a fleet of 12 used prop-jet planes and set up their operations at a small airport in central Ontario.

With business growing rapidly, Phil has turned his attention to OntAir's toll-free reservation system. Between midnight and 6:00 A.M. only one telephone reservations agent is

TABLE 11.9 **Service Time** **Distribution**	TIME TO PROCESS ENQUIRIES (MIN.)	PROBABILITY
	1	0.20
	2	0.19
	3	0.18
	4	0.17
	5	0.13
	6	0.10
	7	0.03

on duty. The time between incoming calls during this period is distributed as shown in Table 11.8. Phil has carefully observed and timed the agent and estimates that the time taken to process passenger information is distributed as shown in Table 11.9.

All customers calling OntAir go on hold and are served in call order unless the reservation agent is available for immediate service. Phil is deciding whether a second agent should go on duty to cope with customer demand. To maintain customer satisfaction, OntAir does not want a customer to hold for more than three to four minutes and also wants to maintain a high operator utilization.

Further, the airline is planning a new TV advertising campaign. As a result, it expects an increase in toll-free line phone inquiries. Based on similar campaigns in the past, the incoming call distribution from midnight to 6:00 A.M. is expected to be as shown in Table 11.10. It is anticipated that the same service time distribution (Table 11.9) will continue to apply.

TABLE 11.8 **Current Incoming** **Call Distribution**	TIME BETWEEN CALLS (MIN.)	PROBABILITY
	1	0.11
	2	0.21
	3	0.22
	4	0.20
	5	0.16
	6	0.10

TABLE 11.10	TIME BETWEEN CALLS (MIN.)	PROBABILITY
Revised Incoming Call Distribution	1	0.22
	2	0.25
	3	0.19
	4	0.15
	5	0.12
	6	0.07

DISCUSSION QUESTIONS

1. What would you advise OntAir to do for the current reservation system based on the original call distribution? Create a simulation model to investigate the scenario. Describe the model carefully and justify the duration of the simulation, assumptions, and measures of performance.
2. What are your recommendations regarding operator utilization and customer satisfaction if the airline proceeds with the advertising campaign?

⟶ CASE STUDY 11.2

Smyth Transport Company

In 2003, Bob Smyth, after receiving an MBA degree with a specialization in entrepreneurship from a leading Canadian university, was looking for a business opportunity. Bob heard that a local business, Halls Manufacturing, with a growing volume of sales was having problems with the transportation of its finished product and had put out tenders for a company to handle its transportation needs. Until now, Halls had been operating its own fleet of trucks and it was proposing that a trucking company buy out the fleet and provide independent trucking service to Halls. Bob saw this as an opportunity and decided to research the situation with a view to starting up his own trucking business.

An immediate problem facing Bob was deciding how many trucks he needed to handle the forecast freight volume. Halls had added trucks to its fleet on an as-needed basis without comprehensive capacity planning. This approach created problems with driver recruitment, truck service and maintenance, and excessive demurrage port fees, because of delays at unloading docks and retention of cargo containers.

Bob forecast that Halls' freight volume should average 160 000 tonnes per month with a standard deviation of 30 000 tonnes. Freight is unloaded on a uniform basis throughout the month. Based on past experience, the amount handled per month is assumed to be normally distributed.

After extensive investigation, Bob concluded that the fleet should be standardized to 12-metre Mercedes 2624 2 × 4 tractor-trailer rigs, which are suitable for carrying two 6-metre containers, one 9-metre container, or one 12-metre container. Cargo capacity is approximately 60 tonnes per rig. Each tractor-trailer unit is estimated to cost $90 000. Moreover, they must meet extreme Canadian climate condition specifications—heavy duty heating units for winter, air-conditioning for summer, and special winter tires. Historical evidence suggests that these Mercedes rigs will operate 96% of the time.

Approximately 25% of the freight handled by these tractor-trailer rigs is in container lengths of 6, 9, and 12 metres. (The balance of the freight—75%—is not containerized.) The 6-metre containers hold approximately 20 tonnes of cargo, the 9-metre containers hold 45 tonnes, and the 12-metre containers hold 60 tonnes of freight. Approximately 60% of the containerized freight is shipped in 12-metre units, 20% is shipped in 9-metre units, and 20% is transported in 6-metre units.

Smyth Transport would pick up freight at the dock and deliver it directly to customers, or warehouse it for later delivery. Based on his study of truck routing and scheduling patterns, Bob concluded that each rig should pick up freight at the dock three times each day.

DISCUSSION QUESTION

How many tractor-trailer rigs should make up the Smyth Transport fleet?

⟶ CASE STUDY 11.3

Muskoka Land Development

Recreational properties are important to many Canadians, and there is a trend for more people to own and enjoy them. In Ontario, one of the prime recreational areas is Muskoka. The 2007 Royal LePage Recreational Property Report states:

As one of the most coveted Canadian recreational destinations, the trendy area of Muskoka boasts over 1000 lakes, stunning waterfalls, granite cliffs, and pine forests. Charming villages and grand lakeside vacation resorts within close proximity to golf courses and historic walking trails define the region. Muskoka is *popular for its affluent properties on Lake Muskoka, Lake Joseph, Lake Rosseau, Lake of Bays, as well as in the Almaguin Highlands and Huntsville. Recreational property prices in Muskoka range from $200 000 to $6 million—attracting a mixture of buyers.*

Located within a comfortable driving distance from Toronto, and providing four-season recreational activities, Muskoka attracts a range of buyers, including young professionals, baby boomers who have acquired inheritances, and affluent business owners interested in higher-end properties.

A group of part-time MBA students is analyzing the opportunity to develop a property in this area. They have heard colleagues speak of the significant profit potential and are now investigating the possibilities. Having identified the steps in a typical development process (see the following list), they are now at steps two and three:

1. Initial concept plan
2. Find suitable land (at an acceptable price)
3. Update concept plan; financial analysis
4. Zoning approval
5. Find financing
6. Subdivision plan
7. Site plan
8. Permits
9. Sales
10. Construction

Site selection started with identification of all Muskoka lakefront properties currently on the market having potential for development. This process identified well over a dozen candidates. Using a scoring model that considered many factors, two particular sites were identified as having the best potential. For analysis purposes, these are identified as site A and site B. While general development plans for each site are similar, there are some differences. Having spent considerable time and effort developing an understanding of the opportunity, the students are now ready to complete a financial analysis of each site.

COMPARISON OF SITES

Site A, comprising some 25 acres, is in a rural setting and currently has a variety of zonings. It is expected that 10% coverage would be allowed (meaning that the ratio of total building space to total land space is 10%). Since this location is out of town, a community centre and restaurant are proposed as part of the development. It is estimated that 55 units could be built, each 2000 square feet in size and sold at $495 000. Construction cost of the units is estimated to be $175 per square foot. The road leading into this site would require considerable upgrading.

Site B is in a popular town. It is smaller, at just over 5 acres. The majority of this site (4.7 acres) is already zoned

resort–commercial. It is expected that 35% coverage would be allowed, resulting in 40 units of 1500 sq ft each. Construction costs would be a bit lower, at an estimated $150 per sq ft. Since this location is deemed more desirable, units would sell at a higher price (estimated to be $545 000 each).

Both developments would include appropriate recreational facilities (a pool and tennis courts), as well as a small marina where each owner would have a slip.

Table 11.11 summarizes expense information, based on development plans for each site. The right-hand column indicates how variable these costs are estimated to be (F = fixed, V1 = ±10%, V2 = ±15%, V3 = ±25%).

The only additional cost is that of a consultant to oversee and manage the project. For a fixed 10% fee (based on estimated costs), the consultant would oversee development of either site. For site A, this fee would include site cleanup, road upgrading, building construction, landscaping, dock/marina, tennis courts, pool, community centre, and restaurant. For site B, this fee would include site cleanup, landscaping, building construction, dock/marina, tennis courts, and pool.

DECISION

With this cost and revenue information in hand, it is time to consider the financial feasibility of both projects. What is the profit potential for each site? Is one site significantly more attractive than the other? If the profit projections are appropriate, the next step will be a cash-flow analysis and preparation of a prospectus for potential investors. There are many remaining steps before the project might be successfully concluded, and there are potential roadblocks that could delay, or entirely block, development. As well, other approaches to ownership (such as time-share or fractional ownership) could be considered. But first, the profit potential of each site must be determined. Recognizing the considerable uncertainty related to the cost estimates, and having recently studied Monte Carlo simulation, the team wants to incorporate this decision analysis technique into its analysis.

QUESTIONS

1. Prepare a pro-forma profit and loss statement for each site. Which, if either, is worth pursuing?
2. Modify your profit and loss statements to consider both best and worst case situations. Does this change your view on proceeding with either development?
3. Perform a Monte Carlo analysis to determine the range of possible profit for each site. Use a uniform distribution for all variable costs. What is your conclusion now?
4. What impact would you expect if you used a normal or triangular distribution to describe cost ranges in your simulation?

TABLE 11.11		SITE A	SITE B	VARIABILITY
Expected Site Expenses and Uncertainty	Construction	$175/sq ft	$150/sq ft	V1
	Land cost	$2 500 000	$5 500 000	F
	Land taxes	100 000	210 000	F
	Rezoning fees	115 000	35 000	V2
	Building permits	333 000	10 000	F
	Site cleanup	100 000	100 000	V3
	Road upgrade	400 000	0	V3
	Landscaping	200 000	200 000	V2
	Dock/marina	195 000	195 000	V2
	Tennis courts	250 000	250 000	V2
	Pool	95 000	95 000	V2
	Community centre	200 000	NA	V2
	Restaurant	500 000	NA	V2
	Sales staff	300 000	300 000	V3
	Advertising & promotion	100 000	100 000	V3

BIBLIOGRAPHY

Abdou, G., and S. P. Dutta. "A Systematic Simulation Approach for the Design of JIT Manufacturing Systems," *Journal of Operations Management* 11, 3 (September 1993): 25–38.

Banks, J., and V. Norman. "Justifying Simulation in Today's Manufacturing Environment," *IIE Solutions* (November 1995): 16–18.

———. "Second Look at Simulation Software," *OR/MS Today* 23, 4 (August 1996): 55–57.

Banks, Jerry, John S. Carson, Barry L. Nelson, and David M. Nicol. *Discrete-Event System Simulation,* 3rd. ed. Upper Saddle River, NJ: Prentice Hall, 2001.

Brennan, J. E., B. L. Golden, and H. K. Rappoport. "Go with the Flow: Improving Red Cross Bloodmobiles Using Simulation Analysis," *Interfaces* 22, 5 (September–October 1992): 1–13.

Buchanan, E., and R. Keeler, "Simulating Health Expenditures under Alternative Insurance Plans," *Management Science* (September 1991): 1069–1088.

Centeno, M. A., E. Lopez, M. A. Lee, M. Carillo, and T. Ogazon. "Challenges of Simulating Hospital Facilities," *Proceedings of the 12th Annual Conference of the Production and Operations Management Society.* Orlando, FL (March 2001).

Evans, J. R., and D. L. Olson. *Introduction to Simulation and Risk Analysis.* Upper Saddle River, NJ: Prentice Hall, 1998.

Fishman, George S. *Monte Carlo: Concepts, Algorithms, and Applications.* Springer-Verlag, New York, 1996.

Grossman, Thomas A., Jr. "Teachers' Forum: Spreadsheet Modeling and Simulation Improves Understanding of Queues," *Interfaces* 29, 3 (May 1999): 88–103.

Hartvigsen, David. *SimQuick: Process Simulation with Excel-Updated Version.* Upper Saddle River, NJ: Prentice Hall, 2001.

Karabakal, N., A. Gunal, and W. Ritchie. "Supply-Chain Analysis at Volkswagen of America," *Interfaces* (July–August 2000): 46–55.

Lev, B. "Simulation of Manufacturing Systems," *Interfaces* 20, 3 (May–June 1990): 99–100.

Pegden, C. D., R. E. Shannon, and R. P. Sadowski. *Introduction to Simulation Using SIMAN,* New York: McGraw-Hill, 1995.

Premachandra, I. M., and Liliana Gonzalez. "A Simulation Model Solved the Problem of Scheduling Drilling Rigs at Clyde Dam," *Interfaces* 26, 2 (March 1996): 80–91.

Samuelson, Douglas A. "Predictive Dialing for Outbound Telephone Call Centers," *Interfaces* 29, 5 (September 1999): 66–81.

Winston, Wayne L. *Simulation Modeling Using @Risk.* Pacific Grove, CA: Duxbury, 2001.

CHAPTER 12

Forecasting Models

LEARNING OBJECTIVES

After completing this chapter, students will be able to

1. Understand and know when to use various types of forecasting models.
2. Compute a variety of forecasting error measures.
3. Understand Delphi and other qualitative forecasting techniques.
4. Compute moving averages, weighted moving averages, and exponential smoothing time-series models.
5. Decompose time-series datas to identify and analyze trends and seasonality.
6. Identify variables and use them in causal simple and multiple linear regression models.
7. Use Excel to analyze a variety of forecasting models.

CHAPTER OUTLINE

12.1 Introduction
12.2 Types of Forecasts
12.3 Qualitative Forecasting Models
12.4 Measuring Forecast Error
12.5 Basic Time-Series Forecasting Models
12.6 Trend and Seasonality in Time-Series Data
12.7 Multiplicative Decomposition of a Time Series
12.8 Causal Forecasting Models: Simple and Multiple Regression

Summary • Glossary • Key Equations • Solved Problems • Self-Test • Discussion Questions and Problems • Case Study: Quantico Computerware • Case Study: Forecasting Ticket Sales at CineBarn • Bibliography

Forecasting at Loblaw

Loblaw Companies Limited, based in Toronto, is one of Canada's largest grocery store chains, with more than 1300 supermarkets. Accurate forecasting of sales is an essential characteristic of Loblaw's operations. Consequently, the company made a decision to use advanced forecasting technology in order to improve its inventory management and customer service.

In a press release on March 16, 2004, Teradata Corporation, a division of the National Cash Register Company (NCR), announced that Loblaw Companies had purchased the Teradata® Demand Chain Management (DCM) 3.1 suite of solutions. This cutting edge parallel processing technology makes Teradata a world leader in data warehousing and forecasting.

The Teradata software would be installed in all Loblaw stores and it would "help Loblaw increase sales and decrease inventory by improving the accuracy of demand forecasting."

Photo courtesy of Dick Hemingway

Loblaw had outgrown its previous forecasting engine, which had run into problems with the increased scale of the company's operations. With Teradata's DCM 3.1 software and access to the Teradata data warehouse, Loblaw would be able to optimize store-replenishment decisions, reduce inventory costs, minimize stockouts, and improve customer-service.

"Leading retailers like Loblaw understand they have to be merchants first and foremost to thrive in today's marketplace. Teradata DCM will assist Loblaw in better predicting the wants and needs of their customers, improving the company's ability to deliver what customers want, when and where they expect it," said Rick Makos, head of Teradata in Canada.

Loblaw anticipates that it will improve its stock levels and be better able to supply customers while controlling inventory costs. With the new forecasting system in place, Loblaw will be able to minimize stocksouts and reduce safety-stock levels.

"Loblaw to Optimize Store Replenishment and Improve Service Levels with Teradata(R) Demand Chain Management Solutions," Canada NewsWire. (Mar 16, 2004).

12.1   INTRODUCTION

Every day, managers make decisions without knowing exactly what will happen in the future. Inventory is ordered, though no one knows what sales will be, new equipment is purchased though no one knows the demand for products, and investments are made though no one knows what profits will be. Managers are always trying to reduce this uncertainty and to make better estimates of what will happen in the future. As shown by the preceding application at Loblaw, accomplishing this is the main purpose of forecasting.

There are many ways to forecast the future. In numerous firms (especially smaller ones), the entire process is subjective, involving seat-of-the-pants methods, intuition, and years of experience. There are also many *quantitative* forecasting models, such as moving averages, exponential smoothing, trend analysis, seasonality analysis, decomposition models, and causal regression analysis.

No single method is superior—whatever works best should be used.

There is seldom a single superior forecasting method. One firm may find regression models effective, another firm may use several quantitative models, and a third may combine both quantitative and subjective techniques. Whatever tool works best for a firm is the one that should be used. In this chapter, we discuss several commonly used forecasting models. For each model, we show the equations needed to compute the forecasts and provide examples of how they are analyzed.

Regardless of the model used, forecasting involves the following eight steps, which provide a systematic way of initiating, designing, and implementing a forecast system.

Eight Steps to Forecasting

1. Determine the use of the forecast—what objective are we trying to attain?
2. Select the items or quantities that are to be forecast.
3. Determine the time horizon of the forecast: Is it 1 to 30 days (short time horizon), one month to one year (medium time horizon), or more than one year (long time horizon)?
4. Select the forecasting model or models.
5. Gather the data needed to make the forecast.
6. Validate the forecasting model.
7. Make the forecast.
8. Implement the results.

When the forecasting model is to be used to generate forecasts regularly over time, data must be collected routinely, and the actual computations must be repeated. In this day of technology and computers, however, forecast calculations are seldom performed by hand. Computers and forecasting software packages greatly simplify these tasks. Numerous statistical programs such as SAS, SPSS, and Minitab are readily available to handle various forecasting models. However, in keeping with the spreadsheet focus of this textbook, we use Excel worksheets (included on your CD-ROM) to calculate the forecast values for each model. Several other spreadsheet-based forecasting software programs (such as Crystal Ball Predictor by Decisioneering, Inc. and StatPro by Palisade Corporation) are also commonly used.

12.2   TYPES OF FORECASTS

The three categories of models are time series, causal, and qualitative.

The forecasting models we consider here can be classified into one of three categories: qualitative, time-series, and causal (see Figure 12.1 on the next page). Although we briefly describe a few qualitative models in Section 12.3, the focus of this chapter is on time-series and causal models.

Forecasting Models Discussed

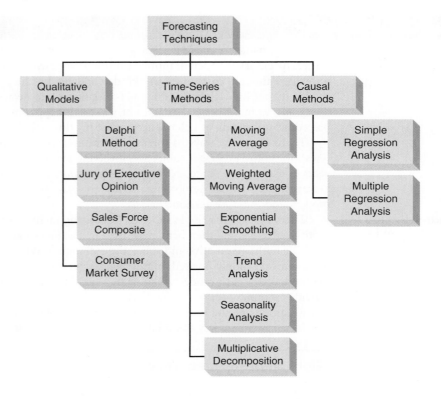

Qualitative Models

Qualitative models incorporate subjective factors.

Qualitative models attempt to incorporate judgmental or subjective factors into the forecasting model. Opinions by experts, individual experiences and judgments, and other subjective factors may be considered. Qualitative models are especially useful when subjective factors are expected to be very important or when accurate quantitative data are difficult to obtain. Qualitative models are also useful for long-term forecasting.

Time-Series Models

Time-series models assume the past is an indication of the future.

Whereas qualitative models rely on judgmental or subjective data, **time-series models** rely on quantitative data. Time-series models attempt to predict the future by using historical data. These models assume that what happens in the future is a function of what has happened in the past. Thus, if we are forecasting weekly sales for lawn mowers, we use the past weekly sales for lawn mowers in making the forecast. The time-series models we examine in this chapter are (1) moving averages, (2) weighted moving averages, (3) exponential smoothing, (4) linear trend analysis, (5) seasonality analysis, and (6) multiplicative decomposition.

Causal Models

Causal models incorporate factors that influence the quantity being forecast.

Causal models also rely on quantitative data. They incorporate the variables or factors that might influence the quantity being forecast. For example, daily sales of a cola drink might depend on the season, the average temperature, the average humidity, whether it is a weekend or a weekday, and so on. Thus, a causal model would attempt to include factors for temperature, humidity, season, day of the week, and so on. Causal models can also include past sales data as time-series models do.

MODELING IN THE REAL WORLD
Improving Demand Forecasting at CN Railways

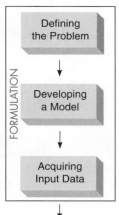

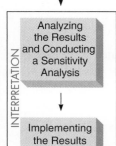

Canadian National Railway Company (CN) has to manage a highly complex transportation system involving tens of thousands of railcars and approximately 1500 locomotives. Duncan Robertson, CN's Director of Revenue, Forecasting and Workload Translation, said, "We did not have a good match between what demand was and how we were using our assets, so we didn't have the ability to forecast revenue."

CN executives chose i2 Demand Planner because of its ability to rapidly generate forecasts based on data input.

CN collected a huge amount of data from customers across North America. "The amount of data we collect is overwhelming," Robertson said. "We found that other solutions could not process all of that data."

Demand Planner processes information from customers, interprets business factors, and generates solutions that can forecast what will occur in the supply chain so that CN can take appropriate action.

With the accurate forecasting provided by Demand Planner, CN has been able to improve its business methods.

Demand Planner has helped CN to identify problems in its business plan and adjust its solution accordingly.

The improved forecasts help CN to use assets more efficiently and save time and money by having the right equipment in the right place when a customer submits a request.

Source: SuccessStory #245. http://planet.i2.com/assets/pdf/CSS_TRN_cnr_css7174.pdf

---

12.3 QUALITATIVE FORECASTING MODELS

Here is a brief overview of four qualitative common forecasting techniques:

Delphi, jury of executive opinion, sales force composite, and consumer market survey are four qualitative or judgmental approaches.

1. **Delphi** method. This iterative group process allows experts, who may be located in different places, to make forecasts. The Delphi process involves three types of participants: decision makers, staff personnel, and respondents. The **decision-making group** usually consists of five to ten experts who will be making the actual forecast. The *staff personnel* assist the decision makers by preparing, distributing, collecting, and summarizing a series of questionnaires and survey results. The *respondents* are a group of people

whose judgments are valued. This group provides inputs to the decision makers before the forecast is made.

2. *Jury of executive opinion.* This method takes the opinions of a small group of high-level managers, often in combination with statistical models, and results in a group estimate of demand.

3. *Sales force composite.* In this approach, each salesperson estimates what sales will be in his or her region; these forecasts are reviewed to ensure that they are realistic and are then combined at the district and national levels to reach an overall forecast.

4. *Consumer market survey.* This method solicits input from customers or potential customers regarding their future purchasing plans. It can help not only in preparing a forecast but also in improving product design and planning for new products.

12.4   MEASURING FORECAST ERROR

The overall accuracy of a forecasting model can be determined by comparing the forecast values with the actual or observed values. If F_t denotes the forecast in period t and A_t denotes the actual value in period t, the **forecast error** (or deviation) is defined as

$$\text{Forecast error} = \text{Actual value} - \text{Forecast value}$$

The forecast error tells us how well the model performed, using past data.

$$= A_t - F_t \tag{12-1}$$

Several measures are commonly used to calculate the overall forecast error. These measures can be used to compare different forecasting models or to monitor forecasting performance. Three of the most popular measures are covered in the following sections.

Mean Absolute Deviation   **Mean absolute deviation (MAD)** is computed as the average of the *absolute* values of the individual forecast errors. That is, if we have forecast and actual values for T periods, the MAD is calculated as

$$\text{MAD} = \sum_{t=1}^{T} \left| \text{forecast error} \right| / T = \sum_{t=1}^{T} \left| A_t - F_t \right| / T \tag{12-2}$$

Mean Squared Error   The **mean squared error (MSE)** is computed as the average of the *squared* values of the individual forecast errors. That is, if we have forecast and actual values for T periods, the MSE is calculated as

$$\text{MSE} = \sum_{t=1}^{T} \left| \text{forecast error} \right|^2 / T = \sum_{t=1}^{T} (A_t - F_t)^2 / T \tag{12-3}$$

MSE accentuates large deviations.

A drawback of MSE is that it tends to accentuate large deviations due to the squared term. For example, if the forecast error for period 1 is twice as large as the error for period 2, the squared error in period 1 is four times as large as that for period 2. Hence, using MSE as the measure of forecast error typically indicates that we prefer to have several smaller deviations rather than even one large deviation.

MAPE expresses the error as a percentage of the actual values.

Mean Absolute Percent Error   A problem with both the MAD and MSE is that their values depend on the magnitude of the item being forecast. If the forecast item is measured in thousands, the MAD and MSE values can be very large. To avoid this problem, we can use the **mean absolute percent error (MAPE)**. This is computed as the average of the absolute difference between the forecast and actual values, expressed as a percentage of the actual values. That is, if we have forecast and actual values for T periods, the MAPE is calculated as

$$\text{MAPE} = 100 \sum_{t=1}^{T} [\left| A_t - F_t \right| / A_t] / T \tag{12-4}$$

The MAPE is perhaps the easiest measure to interpret. For example, a result that the MAPE is 2% is a clear statement that is not dependent on issues such as the magnitude of the input data. For this reason, although we calculate all three measures in our analyses, we focus primarily on the MAPE in our discussions.

12.5   BASIC TIME-SERIES FORECASTING MODELS

A time series is based on a sequence of evenly spaced (e.g., weekly, monthly, quarterly) data points. Examples include weekly sales of Dell personal computers, quarterly earnings reports of Bombardier stock, daily shipments of Energizer batteries, and annual Canadian consumer price indices. Forecasting time-series data implies that future values are predicted *only* from past values. Other variables, no matter how potentially valuable, are ignored.

Components of a Time Series

We can view a long-term time series (i.e., data for more than one year) as being made up of four distinct components. Analyzing a time series means breaking down the data to identify these four components and then projecting them forward. The process of identifying the four components is referred to as *decomposition*. The four components are as follows:

Four components of a time series are trend, seasonality, cycles, and random variations.

1. **Trend**. This is the upward or downward movement of the data over time. For example, prices for many consumer goods exhibit an upward trend over time due to the presence of inflation. Although it is possible for the relationship between time and the data to have any form (linear or nonlinear), we focus only on linear trend relationships in this chapter.

2. **Seasonality**. This is the pattern of demand fluctuations that occurs every year above or below the average demand. That is, the same seasonal pattern repeats itself every year over the time horizon. For example, lawn mower sales are always above average each year in spring and below average in winter.

3. **Cycles**. Whereas seasonality refers to a pattern that occurs each year, cycles are patterns that occur over several years. Cycles are usually tied into the business cycle. For example, the economies of most countries experience cycles of high growth followed by a period of relatively low growth or even recession.

4. **Random variations**. These are "blips" in the data caused by chance and unusual situations. They follow no discernible pattern. For this reason, we cannot use this component to forecast future values.

Figure 12.2 on the next page shows a time series and its components.

There are two general forms of time-series models in statistics. The most widely used is a **multiplicative decomposition model**, which assumes that the forecast value is the product of the four components. It is stated as

Multiplicative decomposition model

$$\text{Forecast} = \text{Trend} \times \text{Seasonality} \times \text{Cycles} \times \text{Random Variations} \qquad (12\text{-}5)$$

We study the multiplicative model in Section 12.7. An **additive decomposition model** that adds the components together to provide an estimate is also available. It is stated as

Additive decomposition model

$$\text{Forecast} = \text{Trend} + \text{Seasonality} + \text{Cycles} + \text{Random Variations} \qquad (12\text{-}6)$$

The additive decomposition model is illustrated in Solved Problem 12-4 at the end of this chapter.

As noted earlier, the random variations follow no discernible pattern. In most real-world models, forecasters assume these variations average out over time. They then concentrate on the seasonal component and a component that is a combination of the trend and cyclical factors.

FIGURE 12.2

FIGURE 12.2

Components of a Time Series (Charted over Four Years)

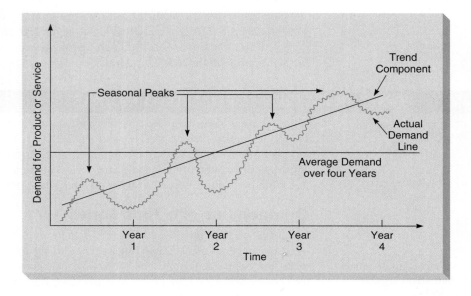

Stationary and Nonstationary Time-Series Data

Stationary data have no trend.

Time-series data are said to be **stationary data** if there is no significant upward or downward movement (or trend) in the data over time. That is, the average value for the time-series data remains constant over the time horizon considered in the model. Stationary time-series data are typically encountered when the time horizon is short term (1–30 days) or medium term (one month to one year). Data for long-term time horizons (one year or greater), tend to exhibit some trend. In such cases, we refer to the data as *nonstationary*.

Nonstationary data exhibit a trend.

In the remainder of this section, we discuss three popular forecasting models used for stationary time-series data: (1) moving averages, (2) weighted moving averages, and (3) exponential smoothing. Although we show the equations needed to compute the forecasts for each model, we use Excel worksheets (included in your CD-ROM) to actually calculate these values.

Moving Averages

Moving averages smooth out variations when forecasting demands are fairly steady.

Moving averages are useful if we can assume the item we are trying to forecast will stay fairly steady over time. We calculate a three-period moving average by summing the actual value of the item for the past three periods and dividing the total by 3. This three-period moving average serves as the forecast for the next period. With each passing period, the most recent period's actual value is added to the sum of the previous two periods' data, and the earliest period is dropped. This tends to smooth out short-term irregularities in the time series.

The moving average for the preceding k periods (where k can be any integer ≥ 2) serves as the forecast for the following period. Mathematically, the k-period moving average can be expressed as

$$k\text{-period moving average} = \sum(\text{Actual value in previous } k \text{ periods})/k \qquad (12\text{-}7)$$

Wallace Garden Supply Example   Monthly sales of storage sheds at Wallace Garden Supply are shown in the middle column of Table 12.1. A three-month moving average is shown in the right-hand column. As discussed next, we can also use the ExcelModules program to calculate these moving averages.

MONTH	ACTUAL SALES	THREE-MONTH MOVING AVERAGES
January	10	
February	12	
March	16	
April	13	$(10 + 12 + 16)/3 = 12.67$
May	17	$(12 + 16 + 13)/3 = 13.67$
June	19	$(16 + 13 + 17)/3 = 15.33$
July	15	$(13 + 17 + 19)/3 = 16.33$
August	20	$(17 + 19 + 15)/3 = 17.00$
September	22	$(19 + 15 + 20)/3 = 18.00$
October	19	$(15 + 20 + 22)/3 = 19.00$
November	21	$(20 + 22 + 19)/3 = 20.33$
December	19	$(22 + 19 + 21)/3 = 20.67$

TABLE 12.1

Three-Month Moving Averages Forecast for Wallace Garden Supply

Using ExcelModules for Forecasting Model Computations

Excel Note

- The CD-ROM that accompanies this textbook contains a set of Excel worksheets, bundled together in a software package called ExcelModules. The procedure for installing and running this program, as well as a brief description of its contents, is given in Appendix A.
- The CD-ROM also contains the Excel file for each example problem discussed here. The relevant file name is shown in the margin next to each example.
- For clarity, all worksheets for forecasting models in ExcelModules are colour-coded as follows:
  - *input cells*, where we enter the problem data, are shaded yellow.
  - *output cells*, showing forecasts and measures of forecast error, are shaded green.
- Although these colours are not apparent in the screen captures shown in the textbook, they are seen in the Excel files on your CD-ROM.

DECISION MODELING IN ACTION
Forecasting Demand for Ketchup

As head of Deloitte's Canadian supply chain, Jim Kilpatrick has devoted his career to helping companies move products efficiently from supplier to consumer. In Kilpatrick's words, the goal of a successful supply chain is to "get the right product in the right place at the right time and at the right cost." A reliable forecast of consumer demand is essential to initiate this process.

One of Jim Kilpatrick's underlying principles in developing a successful supply chain plan is to investigate historical demand patterns, and then use a forecasting model to project future demand, incorporating market trends and other business information into the forecast.

Kilpatrick has recently helped HJ Heinz Company forecast the demand for their famous ketchup. Heinz has large and costly inventories of bottles of ketchup stored in distribution centres around North America, and it is vital to move these stockpiles to their destinations in a timely fashion. Since the demand for ketchup is fairly predictable, Kilpatrick is concentrating on the spikes produced by promotions and other events that affect the market. The ultimate goal is to avoid the extremes of, on the one hand, too much inventory that is bogged down in the distribution centre, and on the other hand, a shortage of ketchup when it is needed.

Source: "Jim Kilpatrick: Why is Heinz ketchup always there when you need it?" *Deloitte & Touche LLP—Canada* (English). http://www.deloitte.com/dtt/employee_profile/0,2302,sid%253D3630%2526cid%253D33463,00.html

When we run the ExcelModules program, we see a menu option titled **EXCELMODULES** in the main menu bar of Excel. We click on **EXCELMODULES**, and then click on **FORECASTING MODELS**. The choices shown in Screenshot 12.1A are displayed. From these choices, we select the appropriate forecasting model.

When *any* of the forecasting models is selected in ExcelModules, we are first presented with a window that allows us to specify several options. Some of these options are common for all models, whereas others are specific to the forecasting model selected. For example, Screenshot 12.1B shows the Options window when we select the **MOVING AVERAGES** forecasting model. The options here include the following:

1. Title of the problem. Default value is *Problem Title*.

2. Number of past periods for which we have data regarding the item (e.g., demand, sales) being forecast. Default value is *3*.

SCREENSHOT 12.1A **Forecasting Models Submenu in ExcelModules**

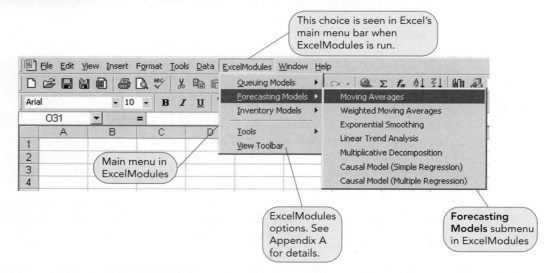

SCREENSHOT 12.1B

Sample Options Window for Forecasting Models in ExcelModules

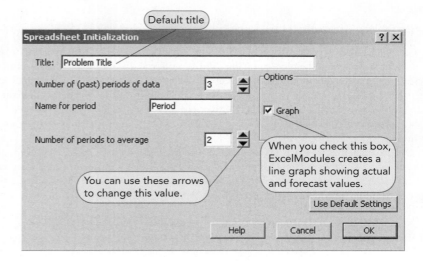

3. Name for the period (e.g., Week, Month). Default value is *Period*.

4. Number of periods to average (i.e., the value of *k* in Equation 12-7). Default value is *2*.

5. Graph. Checking this box results in line graphs of the actual and forecast values.

Using ExcelModules for Moving Averages.   We first show, in Screenshot 12.2A, the options we select for the Wallace Garden Supply example.

When we click OK on this screen, we get the screen shown in Screenshot 12.2B. We now enter the actual shed sales for the 12 months (see Table 12.1) in cells B7:B18.

SCREENSHOT 12.2A

Options Window for Moving Averages Worksheet in ExcelModules

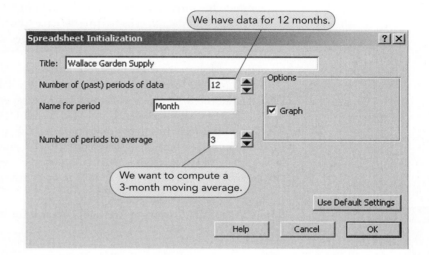

SCREENSHOT 12.2B   **Moving Averages Model for Wallace Garden Supply**

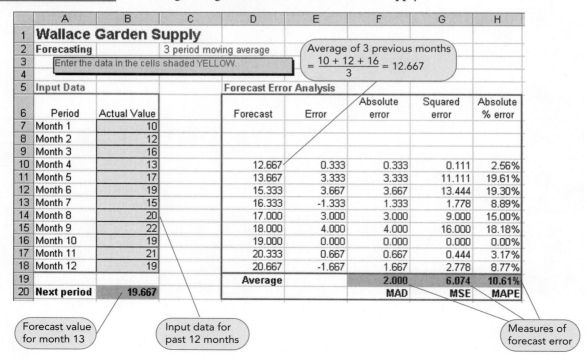

Excel Notes

- The worksheets in ExcelModules contain formulas to compute the forecasts and forecast errors for different forecasting models. The default values of zero for the input data cause the results of these formulas to initially appear as #N/A, #VALUE!, or #DIV/0!. However, as soon as we enter valid values for the input data, the worksheets will display the formula results.
- Once ExcelModules has been used to create the Excel worksheet for a particular forecasting model (such as moving averages), the resulting worksheet can be used to compute the forecasts with several different input data. For example, we can enter different input data in cells B7:B18 of Screenshot 12.2B and compute the results without having to create a new moving averages worksheet each time.

The worksheet now displays the three-month moving averages (shown in cells D10:D18), and the forecast for the next month (i.e., January of the next year), shown in cell B20. In addition, the following measures of forecast error are also calculated and reported: MAD (cell F19), MSE (cell G19), and MAPE (cell H19).

The output indicates that a three-month moving average model results in a MAPE of 10.61%. The forecast for the next period is 19.667 storage sheds. The line graph (if checked in the options in Screenshot 12.2A) is shown in a separate worksheet. We show the graph for the Wallace Garden Supply example in Screenshot 12.2C.

SCREENSHOT 12.2C   **Plot of Three-Period Moving Averages Forecast for Wallace Garden Supply**

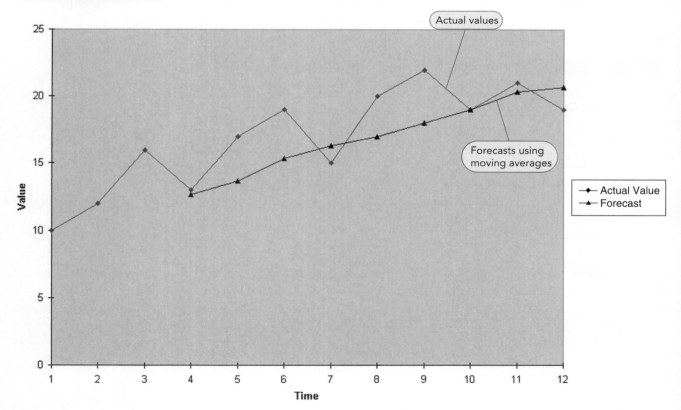

Interpreting Forecast Errors

Forecast error measures permit comparison of different models.

As noted earlier, the measures of forecast error allow us to compare different forecasting models to see which one provides the best forecast. For example, instead of a three-month moving average, we can try a four-month moving average for this example. See if you can repeat the procedure described in Screenshots 12.2A and 12.2B for a four-month moving average. You should see that the MAPE with $k = 4$ is 14.22%. This implies that, at least in this example, the three-month moving average model provides a better forecast than the four-month model. We can try other values for k in a similar fashion.

Weighted Moving Averages

In the regular moving average approach, all the input data are assumed to be equally important. For example, in a three-period model, data for all three previous periods are given equal importance, and a simple average of the three values is computed. In a few cases, however, data for some periods (e.g., recent periods) may be more important than data for other periods (e.g., earlier periods). This is especially true if there is a trend or pattern in the data. In such cases, we can use weights to place more emphasis on some periods and less emphasis on others.

Weights can be used to put more emphasis on recent periods.

The choice of weights is somewhat arbitrary because there is no set formula to determine them. Deciding which weights to use requires some experience and a bit of luck. For example, if the latest period is weighted too heavily, the model might reflect a large unusual change in the forecast value too quickly.

Mathematically, the k-period **weighted moving average**, which serves the forecast for the next period, can be expressed as

$$k\text{-period weighted moving average} = \frac{\sum_{i=1}^{k} (\text{Weight for period } i) \times (\text{Actual value in period } i)}{\sum_{i=1}^{k} (\text{Weights})}$$

(12-8)

Wallace Garden Supply Revisited—Part I   Instead of using a three-month moving average, assume Wallace Garden Supply would like to forecast sales of storage sheds by weighting the past three months as follows:

PERIOD	WEIGHT APPLIED
Last month	3
Two months ago	2
Three months ago	1
Sum of weights	6

The results of the Wallace Garden Supply weighted average forecast using these weights are shown in Table 12.2. Let us now see how we can also use ExcelModules to compute these weighted moving averages.

Using ExcelModules for Weighted Moving Averages   We select the Weighted Moving Averages option from the Forecasting Models submenu in ExcelModules (see Screenshot 12.1A). The window shown in Screenshot 12.3A is displayed. The option entries

File: 12-3.xls

TABLE 12.2	MONTH	ACTUAL SALES	WEIGHTED MOVING AVERAGES
Three-Month Weighted Moving Averages Forecast for Wallace Garden Supply	January	10	
	February	12	
	March	16	
	April	13	$(1 \times 10 + 2 \times 12 + 3 \times 16)/6 = 13.67$
	May	17	$(1 \times 12 + 2 \times 16 + 3 \times 13)/6 = 13.83$
	June	19	$(1 \times 16 + 2 \times 13 + 3 \times 17)/6 = 15.50$
	July	15	$(1 \times 13 + 2 \times 17 + 3 \times 19)/6 = 17.33$
	August	20	$(1 \times 17 + 2 \times 19 + 3 \times 15)/6 = 16.67$
	September	22	$(1 \times 19 + 2 \times 15 + 3 \times 20)/6 = 18.17$
	October	19	$(1 \times 15 + 2 \times 20 + 3 \times 22)/6 = 20.17$
	November	21	$(1 \times 20 + 2 \times 22 + 3 \times 19)/6 = 20.17$
	December	19	$(1 \times 22 + 2 \times 19 + 3 \times 21)/6 = 20.50$

in this window are similar to those for the moving averages (see Screenshot 12.2A). The only additional choice is the box labelled "Weights sum to 1." Although not required (e.g., the sum of weights in the Wallace Garden Supply example is 6), it is common practice to assign weights to various periods such that they sum to 1. Our specific entries for Wallace Garden Supply's problem are shown in Screenshot 12.3A.

Weights usually add up to 1.

When we click OK on this screen, we get the screen shown in Screenshot 12.3B. We now enter the actual shed sales for the 12 months (see Table 12.2) in cells B7:B18 and the weights for the past three months in cells C7:C9.

The worksheet now displays the three-month weighted moving averages (shown in cells E10:E18) and the forecast for the next month (i.e., January of the next year), shown in cell B20. In addition, the following measures of forecast error are also calculated and reported: MAD (cell G19), MSE (cell H19), and MAPE (cell I19). The line graph, if asked for, is shown on a separate worksheet.

In this particular example, you can see that weighting the latest month more heavily actually provides a less accurate forecast. That is, the MAPE value is now 12.20%, compared with a MAPE value of only 10.61% for the three-month simple moving average.

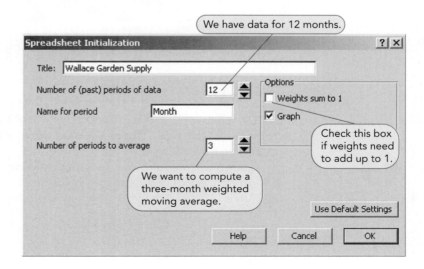

SCREENSHOT 12.3B   Weighted Moving Averages Model for Wallace Garden Supply

	A	B	C	D	E	F	G	H	I
1	**Wallace Garden Supply**								
2	Forecasting		3 period weighted moving average						
3		Enter the data in the cells shaded YELLOW.							
4									
5	Input Data				Forecast Error Analysis				
6	Period	Actual value	Weights		Forecast	Error	Absolute error	Squared error	Absolute % error
7	Month 1	10	1						
8	Month 2	12	2						
9	Month 3	16	3						
10	Month 4	13			13.667	-0.667	0.667	0.444	5.13%
11	Month 5	17			13.833	3.167	3.167	10.028	18.63%
12	Month 6	19			15.500	3.500	3.500	12.250	18.42%
13	Month 7	15			17.333	-2.333	2.333	5.444	15.56%
14	Month 8	20			16.667	3.333	3.333	11.111	16.67%
15	Month 9	22			18.167	3.833	3.833	14.694	17.42%
16	Month 10	19			20.167	-1.167	1.167	1.361	6.14%
17	Month 11	21			20.167	0.833	0.833	0.694	3.97%
18	Month 12	19			20.500	-1.500	1.500	2.250	7.89%
19					**Average**		2.259	6.475	12.20%
20	**Next period**	**19.667**					MAD	MSE	MAPE

Weighted average of the three previous months =
$$\frac{3 \times 16 + 2 \times 12 + 1 \times 10}{6} = 13.667$$

Weights for the three previous months

Measures of forecast error

Using Solver to Determine Optimal Weights   As noted earlier, the choice of weights is somewhat arbitrary because there is no set formula to determine them. However, for a specified value of k (i.e., number of periods to use in computing the weighted moving average), we can use Excel's Solver to find the optimal weights to use in the forecasting model.

Solver can be used to determine the optimal weights.

Recall that we used Solver to solve linear, integer, and nonlinear programming problems in Chapters 2 through 6. Setting up a problem on Solver requires three components:

- *Changing Cells.* These are the cells denoting the decision variables for which we are trying to identify optimal values.
- *Target Cell.* This is the cell containing the formula for the measure we are trying to either maximize or minimize.
- *Constraints.* These are one or more restrictions on the values that the decision variables are allowed to take.

In our case, the decision variables are the weights to be used in computing the weighted moving average. Hence, we specify cells C7:C9 as our Changing Cells. The objective is to minimize some measure of forecast error, such a MAD, MSE, or MAPE. Let us assume we want to minimize the MAPE here. Cell I19 is, therefore, the Target Cell.

If we want to specify that the weights must add up to 1, we must include it as a constraint in the model. The only other constraint is the nonnegativity constraint on the decision variables (weights). Recall that we can easily enforce this constraint by checking the Assume Non-Negative box in Solver's options. It is important to note that the Assume Linear Model option should *not* be checked in solving this problem since the formula for the objective function (MAPE in this case) is *nonlinear*.

The problem is a nonlinear program.

Screenshot 12.3C shows the Solver entries and results for the Wallace Garden Supply problem. For illustration purposes, we have chosen to include the constraint that the sum of weights must equal 1. The formula to model this constraint is shown in Screenshot 12.3C.

SCREENSHOT 12.3C   **Optimal Weights Using Solver for Wallace Garden Supply**

The results indicate that the MAPE decreases to 10.57% when weights of 0.185, 0.593, and 0.222 are associated with the latest period, the period before that, and two periods before that, respectively. Observe that the MSE actually increased from 6.475 in Screenshot 12.3B to 6.952 in Screenshot 12.3C. That is, the weights that minimize the MAPE need not necessarily minimize the MSE value also.

The same weights need not minimize both MAPE and MSE.

Exponential Smoothing

Both moving averages and weighted moving averages are effective in smoothing out sudden fluctuations in the demand pattern in order to provide stable estimates. In fact, increasing the size of k (number of periods averaged) smoothes out fluctuations even better. However, doing so requires us to keep extensive records of past data.

An alternative forecasting approach that is also a type of moving average technique, but requires little record keeping of past data, is called **exponential smoothing**. Let F_t denote the forecast in period t and A_t denote the actual value in period t. The basic exponential smoothing formula is as follows:

Exponential smoothing is also a type of moving average model.

Forecast for period $t + 1$ = Forecast for period t
$\qquad\qquad\qquad$ + α(Actual value in period t − Forecast for period t)

or

$$F_{t+1} = F_t + \alpha(A_t - F_t) \tag{12-9}$$

where α is a weight (called a **smoothing constant**) that has a value from 0 to 1, inclusive. The forecast for a period is equal to the forecast for the previous period, adjusted by a fraction (specified by α) of the forecast error in the previous period. Observe that in Equation 12-9, F_t can be written as

$$F_t = F_{t-1} + \alpha(A_{t-1} - F_{t-1})$$

Likewise, F_{t-1} can be expressed in terms of F_{t-2} and A_{t-2}, and so on. Substituting for F_t, F_{t-1}, F_{t-2}, and so on in Equation 12-9, we can show that

$$F_{t+1} = \alpha A_t + \alpha(1-\alpha)A_{t-1} + \alpha(1-\alpha)^2 A_{t-2} + \alpha(1-\alpha)^3 A_{t-3} + \ldots \tag{12-10}$$

That is, the forecast in period $t+1$ is just a weighted average of the actual values in period t, $t-1$, $t-2$, and so on. Observe that the weight associated with a period's actual value decreases exponentially over time. For this reason, the term *exponential smoothing* is used to describe the technique.

The smoothing constant, α, allows managers to assign weight to recent data.

The actual value of α can be changed to give more weight to recent periods (when α is high), or more weight to past periods (when α is low). For example, when $\alpha = 1$, the forecast in period $t+1$ is equal to the actual value in period t. That is, the entire new forecast is based just on the most recent period. When $\alpha = 0.5$, it can be shown mathematically that the new forecast is based almost entirely on values in just the past three periods. When $\alpha = 0.1$, the forecast places relatively little weight on recent periods and takes many periods of values into account.

Wallace Garden Supply Revisited—Part II   Suppose Wallace Garden Supply would like to forecast sales of storage sheds using an exponential smoothing model. Assume the forecast for sales of storage sheds in January equals the actual sales that month (i.e., 10 sheds). The exponential smoothing forecast calculations are shown in Table 12.3 for $\alpha = 0.1$ and $\alpha = 0.9$. Next, we show how we can use ExcelModules to do these calculations.

TABLE 12.3	MONTH	ACTUAL SALES	FORECAST ($\alpha = 0.1$)	$\alpha = 0.9$
Exponential Smoothing Forecasts for Wallace Garden Supply ($\alpha = 0.1$ and $\alpha = 0.9$)	January	10	10.0	10.0
	February	12	$10.0 + 0.1(10 - 10.0) = 10.0$	10.0
	March	16	$10.0 + 0.1(12 - 10.0) = 10.2$	11.8
	April	13	$10.2 + 0.1(16 - 10.2) = 10.8$	15.6
	May	17	$10.8 + 0.1(13 - 10.8) = 11.0$	13.3
	June	19	$11.0 + 0.1(17 - 11.0) = 11.6$	16.6
	July	15	$11.6 + 0.1(19 - 11.6) = 12.3$	18.8
	August	20	$12.3 + 0.1(15 - 12.3) = 12.6$	15.4
	September	22	$12.6 + 0.1(20 - 12.6) = 13.4$	19.5
	October	19	$13.4 + 0.1(22 - 13.4) = 14.2$	21.7
	November	21	$14.2 + 0.1(19 - 14.2) = 14.7$	19.3
	December	19	$14.7 + 0.1(21 - 14.7) = 15.3$	20.8

SCREENSHOT 12.4A

**Options Window for
Exponential Smoothing
Worksheet in
ExcelModules**

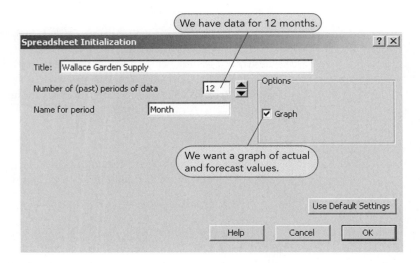

We have data for 12 months.

Spreadsheet Initialization

Title: Wallace Garden Supply

Number of (past) periods of data   12

Name for period   Month

Options

☑ Graph

*We want a graph of actual
and forecast values.*

Use Default Settings

Help   Cancel   OK

File: 12-4.xls

Using ExcelModules for Exponential Smoothing We select the Exponential Smoothing option from the Forecasting Models submenu in ExcelModules (see Screenshot 12.1A). The window shown in Screenshot 12.4A is displayed. The option entries in this window are similar to that for the moving averages (as we saw in Screenshot 12.2A).

When we click OK on this screen, we get the screen shown in Screenshot 12.4B. We now enter the actual shed sales for the 12 months (see Table 12.3) in cells B7:B18 and the value of α in cell B20. We use $\alpha = 0.1$ for this sample computer run. By default, ExcelModules assumes that the forecast for the first period equals the actual sales in that

SCREENSHOT 12.4B   **Exponential Smoothing Model for Wallace Garden Supply
Using a Smoothing Constant of $\alpha = 0.1$**

	A	B	C	D	E	F	G	H
1	**Wallace Garden Supply**							
2	**Forecasting**		Exponential smoothing					
3	Enter the data in the cells shaded YELLOW.							
4								
5	**Input Data**			Forecast Error Analysis				
6	Period	Actual value		Forecast	Error	Absolute error	Squared error	Absolute % error
7	Month 1	10		10.000				
8	Month 2	12		10.000	2.000	2.000	4.000	16.67%
9	Month 3	16		10.200	5.800	5.800	33.640	36.25%
10	Month 4	13		10.780	2.220	2.220	4.928	17.08%
11	Month 5	17		11.002	5.998	5.998	35.976	35.28%
12	Month 6	19		11.602	7.398	7.398	54.733	38.94%
13	Month 7	15		12.342	2.658	2.658	7.067	17.72%
14	Month 8	20		12.607	7.393	7.393	54.650	36.96%
15	Month 9	22		13.347	8.653	8.653	74.879	39.33%
16	Month 10	19		14.212	4.788	4.788	22.925	25.20%
17	Month 11	21		14.691	6.309	6.309	39.806	30.04%
18	Month 12	19		15.322	3.678	3.678	13.529	19.36%
19				**Average**		**5.172**	**31.467**	**28.44%**
20	**Alpha**	0.1				**MAD**	**MSE**	**MAPE**
21								
22	**Next period**	**15.690**						

Assumed forecast for month 1

Value of the smoothing constant

Forecast for month 13

MAPE is 28.44%.

period (i.e., cell D7 = cell B7). In cases where this forecast is a different value, we can just key that entry into cell D7.

The worksheet now displays the exponential smoothing forecasts (shown in cells D7:D18), and the forecast for the next month (i.e., January of the next year), shown in cell B22. In addition, the following measures of forecast error are also calculated and reported: MAD (cell F19), MSE (cell G19), and MAPE (cell H19). The line graph, if asked for, is shown on a separate worksheet.

With $\alpha = 0.1$, the MAPE turns out to be 28.44%. Note that all error values here have been computed using months 2 through 12, compared with earlier cases (see Screenshots 12.2B and 12.3B) where only months 4 through 12 were used.

See if you can repeat the exponential smoothing calculations for $\alpha = 0.9$, and obtain a MAPE of 17.18%.

Using Solver to Determine the Optimal Value of a α   Just as we used Solver to find the optimal weights in the weighted moving average technique, we can use it to find the optimal smoothing constant in the exponential smoothing technique. The lone Changing Cell here is the value of α (cell B20, as shown in Screenshot 12.4C). The Target Cell is the measure of forecast error (i.e., MAD, MSE, or MAPE) that we want to minimize. In Screenshot 12.4C, we have chosen to minimize the MAPE (cell H19). The only constraint (other than the nonnegativity constraint) is that the value of α must be less than or equal to 1.

This nonlinear program has only one constraint.

SCREENSHOT 12.4C   **Optimal Smoothing Constant Using Solver for Wallace Garden Supply**

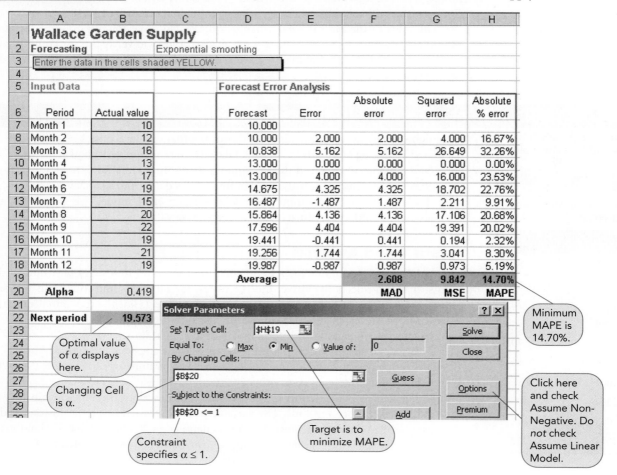

DECISION MODELING IN ACTION
Forecasting Spare Parts at American Airlines

To support the operation of its fleet of more than 400 aircraft, American Airlines maintains a vast inventory of spare repairable (rotatable) aircraft parts. Its PC-based forecasting system, the Rotatables Allocation and Planning System (RAPS), provides demand forecasts for spare parts, helps allocate these parts to airports, and computes the availability of each spare part. With 5000 different kinds of parts, ranging from landing gear to wing flaps to coffeemakers to altimeters, meeting demand for each part at each station can be extremely difficult—and expensive. The average price of a rotatable part is about $5000, with some parts (such as avionics computers) costing well over $500 000 each.

Before developing RAPS, American used only time-series methods to forecast the demand for spare parts. The time-

series approach was slow to respond to even moderate changes in aircraft utilizations, let alone major fleet expansions. RAPS, instead, uses linear regression to establish a relationship between monthly part removals and various functions of monthly flying hours. Correlation coefficients and statistical significance tests are used to find the best regressions, which now take only one hour instead of the days that the old system needed.

The results? Using RAPS, American says that it had a one-time savings of $7 million and recurring annual savings of nearly $1 million.

Source: Mark J. Tedone. "Repairable Part Management," *Interfaces* 19, 4 (July–August 1989): 61–68.

Screenshot 12.4C shows the Solver entries and results for the Wallace Garden Supply problem. The optimal value of α turns out to be 0.419, yielding a MAPE value of 14.70%. Compare this with a MAPE of 28.44% when $\alpha = 0.1$, and a MAPE of 17.18% when $\alpha = 0.9$.

The value of the MSE is 9.842 when $\alpha = 0.419$. However, the minimum value of the MSE is 8.547 and is obtained when $\alpha = 0.646$. (See if you can verify this for yourself using Solver.) That is, the same value of α need not necessarily minimize both the MAPE and MSE measures.

12.6   TREND AND SEASONALITY IN TIME-SERIES DATA

Linear trend analysis fits a straight line to time-series data.

TABLE 12.4

Demand at Midwestern Electric

YEAR	DEMAND
1995	64
1996	68
1997	72
1998	74
1999	79
2000	80
2001	90
2002	105
2003	117
2004	122

Although moving average models smooth out fluctuations in a time series, they are not very good at picking up trends in the data. Likewise, they are not very good at detecting seasonal variations in the data. In this section, we therefore discuss how trend and seasonal variations can be detected and analyzed in time-series data. Here again, although we show the equations needed to compute the forecasts for each model, we use worksheets (included in ExcelModules) to actually calculate these values.

Linear Trend Analysis

The *trend analysis* technique fits a trend equation (or curve) to a series of historical data points. It then projects the curve into the future for medium- and long-term forecasts. Several mathematical trend equations can be developed (e.g., linear, exponential, quadratic equations). However, in this section, we discuss only linear trends. In other words, the mathematical trend equation we develop will be a straight line.

Midwestern Electric Company Example   Let us consider the case of Midwestern Electric Company. The firm's demand for electrical generators over the period 1995–2004 is shown in Table 12.4.

The goal here is to identify a straight line that describes the relationship between demand for generators and time. The variable to be forecasted or predicted (demand, in this case) is called the *dependent variable* and is denoted by Y. The variable used in the prediction (year, in this case) is called the *independent variable*, and is denoted by X.

Scatter Diagram

A scatter diagram helps obtain ideas about a relationship.

File: 12-5.xls

To quickly get an idea whether any relationship exists between two variables, a **scatter diagram** can be plotted on a two-dimensional graph. The independent variable (e.g., time) is usually measured on the horizontal (X) axis, and the dependent variable (e.g., demand) is usually measured on the vertical (Y) axis.

Scatter Diagrams Using Excel Although we can draw a scatter diagram by using ExcelModules (discussed shortly), we can also use Excel's built-in charting capabilities to draw such diagrams. The input data for Midwestern Electric's problem are shown in Screenshot 12.5A. The steps for creating a scatter plot in Excel are as follows:

1. Enter the time period (year) and generator demand data in two columns (preferably adjacent), as shown in Screenshot 12.5A.

2. Start Excel's Chart Wizard either by clicking **INSERT|CHART** or by clicking the Chart Wizard icon on Excel's main menu bar (see Screenshot 12.5A).

3. In the Step 1 of 4 window, select X-Y (Scatter), as shown in Screenshot 12.5A. Click **NEXT**.

SCREENSHOT 12.5A   Using Excel's Chart Wizard to Draw a Scatter Diagram—Step 1 of 4

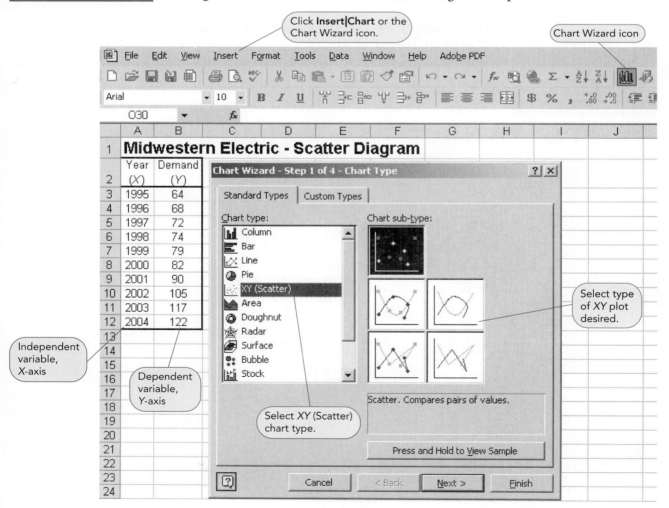

4. In the Step 2 of 4 window, select the appropriate data range (A3:B12, in our case). Click the **COLUMN** box because the data are arranged in columns. Excel automatically puts the variable in the first column on the *X*-axis and the second variable on the *Y*-axis. To swap these (if necessary), click the tab named **SERIES** and make the needed modifications. Add a name for the series, if desired. Click **NEXT**. See Screenshot 12.5B for illustration.

5. In the Step 3 of 4 window, enter titles for the chart, *Y*-axis, and *X*-axis, if desired. Click **NEXT**. See Screenshot 12.5C for illustration.

6. In the Step 4 of 4 window, indicate where you want the chart to be placed (either in a new Excel worksheet or as an object in the same worksheet). Click **FINISH**. See Screenshot 12.5D for illustration.

7. The scatter plot shown in Screenshot 12.5E on page 572 is now displayed. If desired, you can edit the scale and other features of either axis by right-clicking on the axis and selecting the option **FORMAT AXIS**. Also, if you want to display a linear trend line directly on the scatter plot, you can do so by right-clicking any of the data points on the plot and selecting the option **ADD TRENDLINE**.

It appears from the plot in Screenshot 12.5E that it may be reasonable to approximate the relationship between time and demand for generators in Midwestern Electric's problem by using a linear trend line.

Least-Squares Procedure for Developing a Linear Trend Line

A linear trend line between an independent variable (which always denotes time in a trend analysis) and a dependent variable (demand, in Midwestern Electric's example) is

SCREENSHOT 12.5B   **Using Excel's Chart Wizard to Draw a Scatter Diagram—Step 2 of 4**

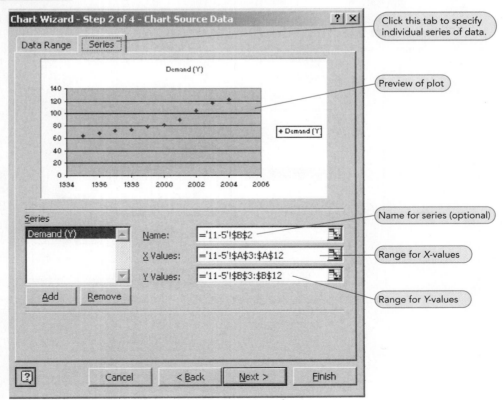

SCREENSHOT 12.5C   **Using Excel's Chart Wizard to Draw a Scatter Diagram—Step 3 of 4**

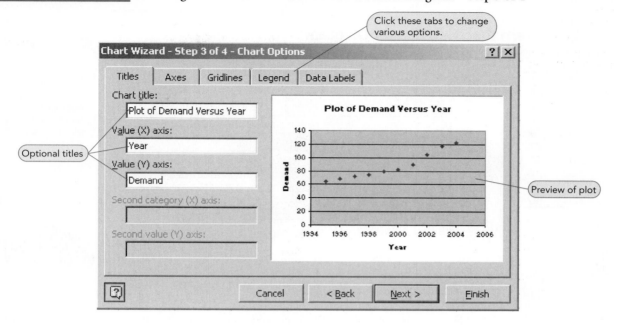

The slope of a linear trend line is the average change in *Y* for a unit increase in the value of time (*X*).

described in terms of its *Y*-intercept (i.e., the *Y*-value at which the line intersects the *Y*-axis) and its slope (i.e., the angle of the line). The slope of a linear trend line can be interpreted as the average change in *Y* for a unit increase in the value of time (*X*). The line can be expressed by using the following equation:

$$\hat{Y} = b_0 + b_1 X \qquad (12\text{-}11)$$

where

$\hat{Y}$ = forecasted average value of the dependent variable (demand) (pronounced "*Y*-hat")

X = value of the independent variable (time)

b_0 = *Y*-intercept of the line, based on the current sample

b_1 = slope of the line, based on the current sample

SCREENSHOT 12.5D

Using Excel's Chart Wizard to Draw a Scatter Diagram—Step 4 of 4

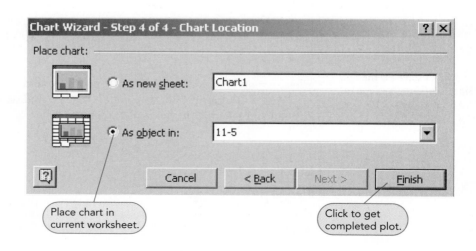

Scatter Diagram for Midwestern Electric

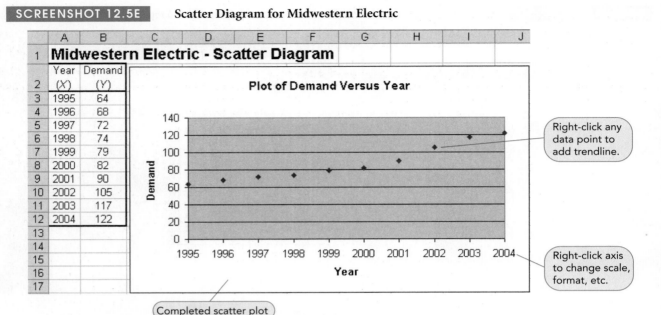

Completed scatter plot

Note that we refer to $\hat{Y}$ as the forecasted *average* value because it is, in fact, the average (or expected value) of a probability distribution of possible values of Y for a given value of X.

To develop a linear trend line between Y and X, there are essentially an infinite number of values that we could assign to b_0 and b_1. Therefore, we cannot determine the best values for b_0 and b_1 either by eyeballing the scatter diagram or by manually trying out different values. Note that we want to find values of b_0 and b_1 that make the forecasted demand (estimated from the trend line) for a specific year as close as possible to the actual demand that year. For example, if we use the linear trend line to forecast demand for 2004, we want the forecast to be as close to 122 as possible. To achieve this objective, we use a precise statistical method known as the **least-squares** procedure. The goal of this procedure is to identify the linear trend line that minimizes the sum of the squares of the vertical differences from the line to each of the actual observations. That is, it minimizes the sum of the squared errors between the forecasted and actual values. Figure 12.3 illustrates the error terms.

Mathematically, we can express the least-squares procedure as follows: Find the values of b_0 and b_1 that minimize the sum of squared errors (SSE), defined as

> The least-squares method finds a straight line that minimizes the sum of the vertical differences from the line to each of the data points.

$$SSE = \sum_{i=1}^{n} (Y_i - \hat{Y}_i)^2 = \sum_{t=1}^{n} [Y_i - (b_0 + b_1 X_i)]^2 \qquad (12\text{-}12)$$

where n = number of observations (10, in Midwestern Electric's example).

We can use calculus to solve Equation 12-12 and develop the following equations to compute the values of b_0 and b_1 and minimize SSE[1]:

> We need to solve for the Y-intercept and the slope to find the equation of the least-squares line.

$$b_1 = \frac{\Sigma XY - n\overline{XY}}{\Sigma X^2 - n\overline{X}^2} \qquad (12\text{-}13)$$

---

[1] Essentially, we take the first derivative of Equation 12-12 with respect to b_0 and b_1, set both equations equal to zero, and solve for b_0 and b_1. See a statistics textbook such as D. F. Groebner, P. W. Shannon, P. C. Fry, and K. D. Smith. *Business Statistics*, 6/e. Upper Saddle River, NJ: Prentice Hall, 2004, for more details.

FIGURE 12.3

Least Squares Method for Finding the Best-Fitting Straight Line

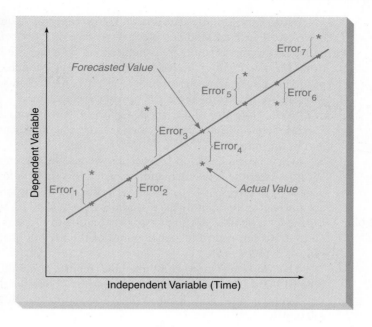

and

$$b_0 = \overline{Y} - b_1 \overline{X}$$

(12-14)

where

$\overline{X}$ = average of the values of the Xs

$\overline{Y}$ = average of the values of the Ys

Even though the formulas for b_0 and b_1 may look somewhat cumbersome, they are fairly easy to use. In fact, most handheld calculators today have built-in functions to compute these values for a given data set. Of course, in keeping with our focus on using spreadsheets in this textbook, we will use Excel for these computations. There are two approaches available in Excel for this purpose:

- *Least-squares procedure using ExcelModules.* We will discuss this approach in the following pages.

- *Least-squares procedure using Excel's Analysis ToolPak add-in.* We will discuss this approach in detail in Section 12.8.

Transforming Time Values   Recall that the independent variable X in linear trend analysis always denotes time. Depending on the manner in which this time is measured, the independent variable can be stated in months, such as January, February, etc., or in years, such as 1995, 1996, etc. (as in Midwestern Electric's example). Hence, in order to facilitate the trend line computations, we may need to transform the time values to a simpler numeric scheme. In the case of Midwestern Electric's data, a convenient way to do so would be to code the year 1995 as $X = 1$, the year 1996 as $X = 2$, and so on.

Using ExcelModules for Linear Trend Analysis   Equations 12-13 and 12-14 have been coded in ExcelModules, along with formulas for computing the usual measures of forecast error. To run these computations, we select the Linear Trend Analysis option from the Forecasting Models submenu in ExcelModules (see Screenshot 12.1A on page 558). The window shown in Screenshot 12.6A is displayed. The option entries in this window are similar to those for moving averages (as we saw in Screenshot 12.2A on page 559). Note that if we check Graph in the options shown in Screenshot 12.2A, ExcelModules will automatically draw a scatter diagram, along with the linear trend line, as part of the output.

When we click OK on this screen, we get the screen shown in Screenshot 12.6B. We now enter the actual demand for generators in 1995 to 2004 (refer to Table 12.4 on page 568) in cells B7:B16 (Y values). The corresponding values for the time periods (X) are automatically input by ExcelModules in cells C7:C16. We also enter the time period for the forecast needed ($X = 11$, corresponding to the year 2005) in cell C21. Finally, if desired, we can enter the actual names of the periods (i.e., the years 1995 to 2004) in cells A7:A16.

The worksheet now computes and reports the values of b_0 and b_1 (shown in cells B18 and B19, respectively, in Screenshot 12.6B) for the least-squares linear trend line between time and demand. In Midwestern Electric's case, the equation of this relationship is

$$\text{Forecasted demand} = 51.267 + 6.552 \times \text{year}$$

Based on this equation, demand forecasts for 1995 through 2004 are displayed in cells E7:E16. The forecast for 2005 (i.e., time $X = 11$) is shown in cell B21 to be 123 generators (rounded). In addition, the following measures of forecast error are also calculated and reported: MAD (cell G17), MSE (cell H17), and MAPE (cell I17).

If specified in the options (see Screenshot 12.6A), ExcelModules shows the scatter diagram between X and Y on a separate worksheet, along with the least-squares linear trend

File: 12-6.xls, sheet: 12-6B

Options Window for Linear Trend Analysis Worksheet in ExcelModules

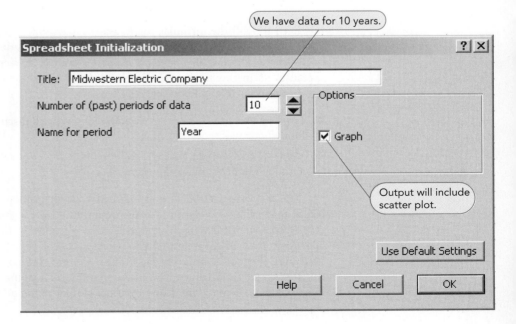

SCREENSHOT 12.6B   **Linear Trend Analysis Model for Midwestern Electric**

	A	B	C	D	E	F	G	H	I
1	**Midwestern Electric Company**								
2	Forecasting		Linear trend analysis						
3	Enter the actual values in cells shaded YELLOW. Enter new time period at the bottom to forecast Y.								
4									
5	Input Data				Forecast Error Analysis				
6	Period	Actual value (or) Y	Period number (or) X		Forecast	Error	Absolute error	Squared error	Absolute % error
7	Year 1995	64	1		57.818	6.182	6.182	38.215	9.66%
8	Year 1996	68	2		64.370	3.630	3.630	13.179	5.34%
9	Year 1997	72	3		70.921	1.079	1.079	1.164	1.50%
10	Year 1998	74	4		77.473	-3.473	3.473	12.060	4.69%
11	Year 1999	79	5		84.024	-5.024	5.024	25.243	6.36%
12	Year 2000	82	6		90.576	-8.576	8.576	73.544	10.46%
13	Year 2001	90	7		97.127	-7.127	7.127	50.798	7.92%
14	Year 2002	105	8		103.679	1.321	1.321	1.746	1.26%
15	Year 2003	117	9		110.230	6.770	6.770	45.829	5.79%
16	Year 2004	122	10		116.782	5.218	5.218	27.229	4.28%
17					Average		4.840	28.901	5.72%
18	Intercept	**51.267**					MAD	MSE	MAPE
19	Slope	**6.552**							
20									
21	Next period	123.333	11						

Forecasts are computed using the trend equation.

Trend equation coefficients

Forecast for 2005

Input value of X = 11 corresponds to year 2005.

Measures of forecast error

File: 12-6.xls, sheet: 12-6C

line. We show this plot in Screenshot 12.6C. We can compare the plot of actual demand values and the trend line to check the validity of the trend line model. In Midwestern Electric's case, the linear trend line seems to approximate the demand values reasonably well. The relatively low MAPE value of 5.72% also supports this conclusion.

Seasonality Analysis

Seasonal variations occur annually.

Time-series forecasting such as that in the example of Midwestern Manufacturing involves looking at the *trend* of data over a series of time observations. Sometimes, however, recurring variations at certain periods (i.e., months) of the year make a *seasonal* adjustment in the time-series forecast necessary. Demand for coal and oil fuel, for example, usually peaks during cold winter months. Demand for golfing equipment or sunscreen may be highest in summer.

Analyzing time-series data in monthly or quarterly terms usually makes it easy to spot seasonal patterns. A seasonal *index*, which can be defined as the ratio of the average value of the item in a season to the overall annual average value, can then be computed for each season.

There are several methods available to compute seasonal indices. One such method, which bases these indices on the *average* value of the item over all periods (e.g., months, quarters), is illustrated in the following example. A different method, which uses a concept called *centred moving average* to compute seasonal indices, is illustrated in Section 12.7.

Eichler Supplies Example   Monthly demands of a brand of telephone answering machines at Eichler Supplies are shown in cells C3:C26 of Screenshot 12.7 on page 577, for the two most recent years.

Plot of Linear Trend Analysis Forecast for Midwestern Electric

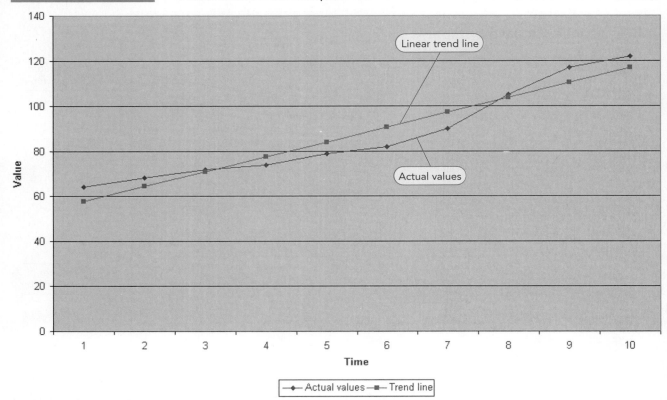

To compute the monthly seasonal indices using the average demand value over the two years, we can create an Excel worksheet as follows:

1. *Column D.* Compute the average monthly demand using all the available data. In Eichler's case, this is calculated by taking the average of the demand values for the 24 months.

2. *Column E.* Compute the seasonal ratio for each month by dividing the actual demand each month by the average demand; that is, column E = column C/column D. For example, the seasonal ratio for January of year 1 is 80/94 = 0.851.

3. *Column F.* Observe that since we have two years of time-series data, we have two seasonal ratios for each month. For example, January has ratios of 0.851 and 1.064, as shown in cells E3 and E15, respectively. We compute the seasonal *index* for January as the average of these two ratios. Hence, the seasonal index for January is equal to (0.851 + 1.064)/2 = 0.957. Similar computations for all 12 months of the year are shown in column F of Screenshot 12.7.

A seasonal index with value below 1 indicates demand is below average that month, and an index with value above 1 indicates demand is above average that month. Using these seasonal indices, we can adjust the monthly demand for any future month appropriately. For example, if we expect the third year's average demand for answering machines to be 100 units per month, we would forecast January's monthly demand as 100 × 0.957 = 96 units, which is below average. Likewise, we would forecast May's monthly demand as 100 × 1.309 = 131 units, which is above average.

SCREENSHOT 12.7

Computation of Seasonal Indices for Eichler Supplies

Average of seasonal ratios for each month

	A	B	C	D	E	F	
1	**Eichler Supplies**						
2	Year	Month	Demand	Average Demand	Ratio	Seasonal Index	
3	1	January	80	94	0.851	0.957	$= \dfrac{0.851 + 1.064}{2}$
4		February	75	94	0.798	0.851	
5		March	80	94	0.851	0.904	
6		April	90	94	0.957	1.064	
7		May	115	94	1.223	1.309	
8		June	110	94	1.170	1.223	
9		July	100	94	1.064	1.117	
10		August	90	94	0.957	1.064	
11		September	85	94	0.904	0.957	
12		October	75	94	0.798	0.851	
13		November	75	94	0.798	0.851	
14		December	80	94	0.851	0.851	
15	2	January	100	94	1.064		
16		February	85	94	0.904		
17		March	90	94	0.957		
18		April	110	94	1.170		
19		May	131	94	1.394		
20		June	120	94	1.277		
21		July	110	94	1.170		
22		August	110	94	1.170		
23		September	95	94	1.011		
24		October	85	94	0.904		
25		November	85	94	0.904		
26		December	80	94	0.851		

Average demand for all 24 months

$\text{Ratio} = \dfrac{\text{Demand}}{\text{Average demand}}$

12.7 MULTIPLICATIVE DECOMPOSITION OF A TIME SERIES

Decomposition breaks down a time series into its components.

Now that we have analyzed both trend and seasonality, we can combine both of these issues to decompose time-series data. Recall from Section 12.5 that a time series comprises four components: trend, seasonality, cycles, and random variations. In this section, we discuss a multiplicative decomposition model that breaks down a time series into two components: (1) a seasonal component and (2) a combination of the trend and cycle component (we refer to this combined component simply as *trend*). In Solved Problem 12-4 at the end of this chapter, we use the same example to illustrate how an additive decomposition model would break down the data. As discussed earlier, it is not possible to discern the random component. The forecast is calculated as the product of the composite trend and seasonality components.

Sawyer Piano House Multiplicative Decomposition Example

Sandy Sawyer's family has been in the piano business for three generations. The Sawyers stock and sell a wide range of pianos, from console pianos to grand pianos. Sandy's father, who currently runs the business, forecasts sales for different types of pianos each year using his experience. Although his forecasts have been reasonably good, Sandy (who has recently completed her undergraduate degree in management) is highly skeptical of such a seat-of-the-pants approach. She feels confident that she can develop a quantitative model that will do a much better job of forecasting piano sales.

To convince her father that she is correct, Sandy decides to develop a model to forecast sales for grand pianos. She hopes to show him how good the model could be in capturing patterns in past sales. For this purpose, she collects sales data for the past five years, broken down by quarters each year. That is, she collects data for the past 20 quarters, as shown in Table 12.5. Since piano sales are seasonal and there has been an upward trend in sales each year, Sandy believes a decomposition model would be appropriate here. More specifically, she decides to use a multiplicative decomposition model.

Although the computations for decomposing a time series using a multiplicative model are fairly simple, we illustrate them using an Excel worksheet included for this purpose in ExcelModules.

Using ExcelModules for Multiplicative Decomposition

File: 12-8.xls

The centred moving average approach helps smooth out fluctuations in the data.

We select the **MULTIPLICATIVE DECOMPOSITION** option from the Forecasting Models submenu in ExcelModules (see Screenshot 12.1A). The window shown in Screenshot 12.8A is displayed. We specify the number of periods for which we have past data (20, in Sandy's example), the name for the period (Quarter, since we have quarterly data), and number of seasons each year (4, in Sandy's example). In addition, we see an option for the procedure to use in computing the seasonal indices.

The option named **AVERAGE ALL DATA** uses the procedure discussed in Section 12.6 to compute the seasonal indices. In Sandy's example, this implies that we would first compute the average sales for all 20 quarters for which we have data. We would then divide the sales each quarter by the average sales to compute that quarter's seasonal ratio. Note that this will yield five ratios for each quarter (one for each year). Finally, we would average the five ratios for each quarter to compute that quarter's seasonal index.

The option named **CENTERED MOVING AVERAGE** uses a slightly more complicated procedure to compute the seasonal indices. Recall from Section 12.5 that moving averages smooth out fluctuations in the time series. Hence, using this option could help us obtain more precise estimates of the seasonal indices. In what follows, we illustrate this procedure for computing seasonal indices, using Sandy's example.

When we click OK on the screen in Screenshot 12.8A, we get the screen shown in Screenshot 12.8B on page 580. We now enter the actual pianos sold during the past 20 quarters (see Table 12.5) in cells B7:B26. The corresponding time periods (i.e., the X-variable values) are automatically specified in cells C7:C26 by the worksheet.

The worksheet now displays the results shown in Screenshot 12.8B. The calculations are as follows:

The seasonal indices are computed first.

1. *Computation of the seasonal indices. Columns D–G.*

    ■ In column D, we first smooth out fluctuations in each quarter's sales data by computing the moving average sales for k quarters, centred on that quarter. Since there are four seasons (quarters) in Sandy's time-series data, we use $k = 4$ here.

TABLE 12.5		2000	2001	2002	2003	2004
Sales of Grand Pianos at Sawyer Piano House	Quarter 1	4	6	10	12	18
	Quarter 2	2	4	3	9	10
	Quarter 3	1	4	5	7	13
	Quarter 4	5	14	16	22	35

SCREENSHOT 12.8A

**Options Window
for Multiplicative
Decomposition
Worksheet in
ExcelModules**

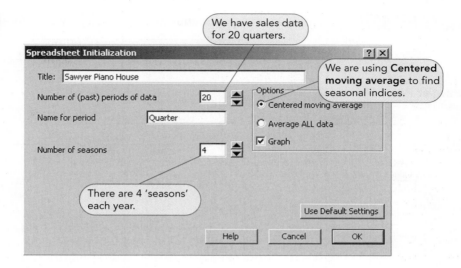

Then, in cell D9 (for example), we compute the average sales for four quarters, where these four quarters are centred on the third quarter of year 1 (i.e., quarter number 3). *Note:* In cases in which k is even (such as here, in which $k = 4$), it is not possible to directly centre k quarters of data on a quarter. We therefore modify the computations as follows (e.g., when $k = 4$):

Centred average for quarter t = [0.5 × Sales in quarter $t - 2$
+ Sales in quarter $t - 1$ + Sales in quarter t
+ Sales in quarter $t + 1$ + 0.5 × Sales in quarter $t + 2$]/4

■ Next, we compute the seasonal ratio for each quarter by dividing the actual sales (column B) in that quarter by its centred average (column D). That is, column E = column B / column D.

■ The seasonal ratios for each quarter (five for each quarter in Sandy's case) are collected in cells B33:E37. The seasonal index for each quarter is computed as the average of all the ratios for that quarter. These seasonal indices are shown in cells B38:E38 and repeated in column F next to the appropriate quarter each year.

The time-series data are then deseasonalized.

■ Finally, in column G, we compute the unseasonalized sales in each quarter as the actual sales (column B) in that quarter divided by the seasonal index (column F) for that quarter. That is, column G = column B / column F.

The linear trend equation is computed.

2. *Computation of the trend equation.* Now that we have the unseasonalized sales data, we can analyze the trend. Since the purpose of the linear trend equation is to minimize the least squares error (as shown in Section 12.6), it is important to remove the seasonal effects from the data before we develop the trend line. Otherwise, the presence of seasonal variations can severely affect the linear trend equation.

Using the unseasonalized sales in column G as the dependent variable (Y) and the time period number in column C as the independent variable (X), we compute the linear trend equation. The resulting Y-intercept (a) and slope (b) for this straight line are shown in cells G28 and G29, respectively. In Sandy's case, the linear trend equation is

Unseasonalized sales forecast $= -0.365 + 1.023 \times$ Quarter number

SCREENSHOT 12.8B   **Multiplicative Decomposition Model for Sawyer Piano House**

$= \dfrac{\text{Actual value}}{\text{Centred moving average}}$ $= \dfrac{\text{Actual value}}{\text{Seasonal index}}$

	A	B	C	D	E	F	G	H	I	J	K	L	M
1	**Sawyer Piano House**												
2	**Forecasting**		Multiplicative decomposition										
3	**4 seasons**		Enter the actual values in the cells shaded YELLOW. Do not change the time period numbers!										
4													
5	**Input Data**			**Seasonal Index Computation**				**Forecast Error analysis**					
6	Period	Actual value (Y)	Time period (X)	Centered average	Seasonal ratio	Seasonal index	Unseasonalized value	Unseasonalized Forecast	Seasonalized Forecast	Error	Absolute error	Squared error	Absolute % error
7	Quarter 1	4	1			1.239	3.227	0.658	0.815	3.185	3.185	10.144	79.62%
8	Quarter 2	2	2			0.596	3.353	1.680	1.002	0.998	0.998	0.996	49.89%
9	Quarter 3	1	3	3.250	0.308	0.485	2.061	2.703	1.311	-0.311	0.311	0.097	31.13%
10	Quarter 4	5	4	3.750	1.333	1.577	3.170	3.725	5.876	-0.876	0.876	0.768	17.53%
11	Quarter 5	6	5	4.375	1.371	1.239	4.841	4.748	5.884	0.116	0.116	0.013	1.93%
12	Quarter 6	4	6	5.875	0.681	0.596	6.706	5.770	3.442	0.558	0.558	0.311	13.95%
13	Quarter 7	4	7	7.500	0.533	0.485	8.244	6.793	3.296	0.704	0.704	0.496	17.60%
14	Quarter 8	14	8	7.875	1.778	1.577	8.875	7.816	12.328	1.672	1.672	2.795	11.94%
15	Quarter 9	10	9	7.875	1.270	1.239	8.069	8.838	10.954	-0.954	0.954	0.910	9.54%
16	Quarter 10	3	10	8.250	0.364	0.596	5.029	9.861	5.882	-2.882	2.882	8.305	96.06%
17	Quarter 11	5	11	8.750	0.571	0.485	10.305	10.883	5.280	-0.280	0.280	0.079	5.61%
18	Quarter 12	16	12	9.750	1.641	1.577	10.143	11.906	18.780	-2.780	2.780	7.730	17.38%
19	Quarter 13	12	13	10.750	1.116	1.239	9.682	12.928	16.023	-4.023	4.023	16.186	33.53%
20	Quarter 14	9	14	11.750	0.766	0.596	15.088	13.951	8.322	0.678	0.678	0.460	7.54%
21	Quarter 15	7	15	13.250	0.528	0.485	14.427	14.973	7.265	-0.265	0.265	0.070	3.78%
22	Quarter 16	22	16	14.125	1.558	1.577	13.947	15.996	25.232	-3.232	3.232	10.447	14.69%
23	Quarter 17	18	17	15.000	1.200	1.239	14.523	17.019	21.093	-3.093	3.093	9.564	17.18%
24	Quarter 18	10	18	17.375	0.576	0.596	16.765	18.041	10.761	-0.761	0.761	0.580	7.61%
25	Quarter 19	13	19			0.485	26.794	19.064	9.249	3.751	3.751	14.067	28.85%
26	Quarter 20	35	20			1.577	22.188	20.086	31.684	3.316	3.316	10.994	9.47%
27									Average		1.722	4.751	23.74%
28						**Intercept**	-0.365				MAD	MSE	MAPE
29						**Slope**	1.023						

Input data for 20 quarters

	A	B	C	D	E
30					
31	**Seasonal Ratios**				
32		Season 1	Season 2	Season 3	Season 4
33				0.308	1.333
34		1.371	0.681	0.533	1.778
35		1.270	0.364	0.571	1.641
36		1.116	0.766	0.528	1.558
37		1.200	0.576		
38	**Average**	1.239	0.596	0.485	1.577
39					
40	**Forecasts for future periods**				
41	Period	Unseasonalized forecast	Seasonal index	Seasonalized forecast	
42	21.000	21.109	1.239	**26.162**	
43	22.000	22.131	0.596	**13.201**	
44	23.000	23.154	0.485	**11.234**	
45	24.000	24.176	1.577	**38.136**	

Regression (trend line) parameters

Measures of forecast error

Seasonal ratios in column E have been collected here.

Seasonal indices, also shown in column F

Forecast using trend equation

Forecasts multiplied by seasonal index

The forecasts are now computed.

3. *Computation of forecast. Columns H and I.*

   ■ In column H, we use the trend equation to compute the unseasonalized forecast for each quarter. For example, for the fourth quarter of year 2 (i.e., quarter number 8), this value is computed in cell H14 as $[-0.365 + 1.023 \times 8] = 7.816$. These values are also computed for the next year (i.e., quarters 21 to 24) in cells B42:B45.

Forecasts are seasonalized.

■   The unseasonalized forecasts are multiplied by the appropriate seasonal indices to get the seasonalized forecast for each quarter in column I. That is, column I = column H × column F. Cells D42:D45 show the seasonal forecasts for quarter numbers 21 to 24.

4.   *Computation of forecast error measures. Columns J through M.* As with all the other forecasting models in ExcelModules discussed so far, we compute the forecast error (i.e., actual value − forecast value) in column J, the absolute error in column K, the squared error in column L, and the absolute percentage error in column M for each quarter. We then use these error values to compute the MAD (cell K27), MSE (cell L27), and MAPE (cell M27) values.

Finally, measures of forecast error are computed.

Using Plots to Check the Validity of the Model   How good is Sandy's multiplicative decomposition model in predicting piano sales? One approach, of course, is to use the measures of forecasting error we have computed as indicators. As discussed earlier, however, these measures are difficult to interpret by themselves and are better suited for purposes of comparing different models. An alternative approach is to draw line plots of the actual and forecast values (columns B and I, respectively, in Screenshot 12.8B) against the quarter number. These line plots are automatically drawn by ExcelModules and presented on a separate worksheet. The graph is shown in Screenshot 12.8C.

Line plots of the actual and forecast values are used to check the validity of the model.

The line plots show that there are a few quarters (e.g., quarters 1, 10, 13, 19, and 20) in which there are sizable errors in the forecast. Overall, however, Sandy's decomposition model seems to do a good job of replicating the pattern of piano sales over the past few years. There is no consistent under- or overforecast seen, and the forecast errors appear to be randomly distributed.

Using this analysis as evidence, Sandy should be able to convince her father that such quantitative forecasting decision models are the way to go in the future!

SCREENSHOT 12.8C   **Plot of Multiplicative Decomposition Forecast for Sawyer Piano House**

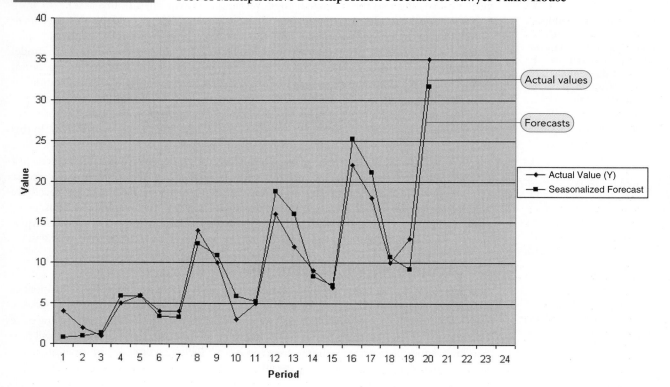

DECISION MODELING IN ACTION
Multiple Regression Modeling at Canada's TransAlta Utilities

TransAlta Utilities (TAU) is a $1.6 billion energy company operating in Canada, New Zealand, Australia, Argentina, and the United States. Headquartered in Alberta, Canada, TAU is Canada's largest publicly owned utility. It serves 340 000 customers in Alberta through 57 customer-service facilities, each of which is staffed by from 5 to 20 customer service linemen. The 270 linemen's jobs are to handle new connections and repairs, and to patrol power lines and check substations. This existing system was not the result of some optimal central planning but was put in place incrementally as the company grew.

With help from the University of Alberta, TAU wanted to develop a causal model to decide how many linemen should be best assigned to each facility. The research team decided to build a multiple regression model with only three independent variables. The hardest part of the task was to select variables that were easy to quantify based on available data. In the

end, the explanatory variables were the number of urban customers, the number of rural customers, and the geographic size of a service area. The implicit assumptions in this model are that the time spent on customers is proportional to the number of customers and the time spent on facilities (line patrol and substation checks) and travel is proportional to the size of the service region. By definition, the unexplained time in the model accounts for time that is not explained by the three variables (e.g., meetings, breaks, unproductive time).

Not only did the results of the model please TAU managers, but the savings of the project (which included optimizing the number of facilities and their locations) is $4 million per year.

Source: E. Erkut, T. Myroon, and K. Strangway. "TransAlta Redesigns its Service-Delivery Network," *Interfaces* (March–April, 2000) 54–69.

12.8   CAUSAL FORECASTING MODELS: SIMPLE AND MULTIPLE REGRESSION

Consider an apparel firm that wishes to forecast the sales of its line of swimwear. It is likely that sales are related to variables such as the selling price, competitors' prices, average daily temperature, whether schools are in session, and advertising budgets. The purpose of a *causal forecasting model* is to develop the best statistical relationship between one or more of these variables and the variable being forecast (swimwear sales, in this case).

In a causal model for the apparel firm, swimwear sales would be the *dependent* (predicted or forecasted) variable, and the variables used to forecast swimwear sales would be *independent* (or predictor) variables. Note that unlike in the linear trend model we studied in Section 12.6, there can be more than one independent variable in a causal model. Further, although time could be an independent variable in a causal model, it does not necessarily need to be one. That is, the data need not be time-series data.

The most common causal model used in practice is **regression analysis**. Several types of regression equations can be developed (e.g., linear, quadratic, cubic, logarithmic). In this section, however, we discuss only linear regression models.

In causal forecasting models, when we try to forecast the dependent variable by using just a single independent variable, the model is called a *simple* regression model. When we use more than one independent variable to forecast the dependent variable, the model is called a *multiple* regression model. We illustrate both types of models in the following sections, using simple examples. As with all models so far in this chapter, although we present a few key equations, we perform the actual calculations by using worksheets provided in ExcelModules.

> The dependent variable is the item we are trying to forecast, and the independent variable is an item (or items) we think might have a causal effect on the dependent variable.

Causal Simple Regression Model

Sue Taylor works for a home appraisal company that is used by several local banks to appraise the price of homes as part of the mortgage approval process. Based on her extensive experience with home appraisals, Sue knows that one factor that has a direct relationship to the selling price of a home is its size. Sue therefore wants to establish a mathematical relationship that will help her forecast the selling price of a home, based on its size. Table 12.6 provides information on the last 12 homes that have been sold in a specific neighbourhood in the city where Sue lives.

		SELLING PRICE	HOME SIZE
TABLE 12.6	**HOME**	**(IN THOUSANDS)**	**(THOUSANDS OF SQ. FT.)**
Home Sales Data for	1	$182.5	2.01
the Simple Regression	2	227.3	2.65
Model	3	251.9	2.43
	4	325.2	2.89
	5	225.1	2.55
	6	315.0	3.00
	7	367.5	3.22
	8	220.8	2.37
	9	266.5	2.91
	10	261.0	2.56
	11	177.5	2.25
	12	235.9	3.41

We can use a scatter diagram to check the relationship.

As a first step toward developing this mathematical relationship, we should draw a scatter diagram that shows selling price and home size. (Refer to Section 12.6 to see how this diagram can be drawn using Excel's Chart Wizard, if necessary.) We will, in fact, draw such a diagram by using ExcelModules shortly. For now, let us proceed under the assumption that the scatter diagram reveals a linear relationship between a home's selling price and its size. That is, the mathematical equation between these variables denotes a straight line.

We use the least-squares procedure here.

Just as we did with linear trend analysis, we use the least-squares procedure here to establish the equation of this straight line. Once again, we let Y represent the dependent variable that we want to forecast (selling price, in this example). But unlike in the trend models, here the independent variable, X, is not time; instead, it is the size of each home. The same basic model discussed in Section 12.6 applies. That is,

$$\hat{Y} = b_0 + b_1 X$$

where

$\hat{Y}$ = forecasted average value of the dependent variable, based on the current sample

X = value of the independent variable

b_0 = Y-intercept of the line, based on the current sample

b_1 = slope of the line, based on the current sample

We determine the Y-intercept (b_0) and slope (b_1) by using the least-squares formulas.

Recall from Section 12.6 that the objective of the least-squares procedure is to determine the values of b_0 and b_1 that minimize the sum of the squared errors between the forecasted ($\hat{Y}$) and actual (Y) values. The formulas to compute these values were given in Equations 12-13 and 12-14 on pages 572 and 573. However, rather than manually using these formulas, we next discuss the following two approaches to using Excel to develop this regression equation, as well as accompanying statistical measures:

We describe two approaches in Excel for regression: using ExcelModules and Analysis ToolPak.

■ *Regression using ExcelModules.* In addition to computing the regression equation, ExcelModules computes the forecast for each observation and the three usual measures of forecast error (i.e., MAD, MSE, and MAPE).

■ *Regression using Excel's Analysis ToolPak add-in.* An advantage of using this procedure is that it provides detailed information regarding the significance of the regression equation.

Causal Simple Regression Using ExcelModules

When we select the Causal Model (Simple Regression) option from the Forecasting Models submenu in ExcelModules (see Screenshot 12.1A), the window shown in Screenshot 12.9A is displayed. The option entries in this window are similar to those for earlier procedures. If we check the Graph option, ExcelModules draws the scatter plot as part of the results, along with the least-squares regression line.

When we click OK on this screen, we get the screen shown in Screenshot 12.9B. We now enter the selling prices (dependent variable, Y) for the 12 homes in cells B7:B18 and the corresponding sizes (independent variable, X) in cells C7:C18.

The worksheet now computes and displays the regression equation. For Sue's problem, the Y-intercept (b_0) is shown in cell B20, and the slope (b_1) is shown in cell B21. The causal simple regression model is

$$\text{Forecasted average selling price} = -8.125 + 97.789 \times \text{Home size}$$

The Y-intercept may not have a practical meaning in many causal models. The slope indicates the average change in Y for a unit increase in X.

Typically, we can interpret the Y-intercept as the forecasted value of the dependent variable when the independent variable has a value of zero. However, in Sue's example, the Y-intercept of -8.125 has no practical meaning because a home with size zero does not exist. Further, because the data set does not include observations with $X = 0$, it would be inappropriate to interpret the Y-intercept at this X-value. On the other hand, the slope of 97.789 implies that the average selling price of a home increases by \$97 789 for every 1000 square foot increase in size. (Remember that the selling price is in thousands of dollars and the sizes are in thousands of square feet.)

In addition to computing the regression equation, ExcelModules plugs the size values for all homes into this equation to compute the forecasted selling price for each home. These forecasts are shown in cells E7:E18. The following measures of forecast error are then calculated and reported: MAD (30.40, in cell G19), MSE (1512.41, in cell H19), and MAPE (11.73%, in cell I19).

Regression Plots   Now that we have identified the equation for the causal simple regression model, how do we determine its validity and accuracy? One way to do so is to use the scatter diagram of selling price versus size. Recall from Section 12.6 that we can

SCREENSHOT 12.9A

Options Window for Causal Model (Simple Regression) Worksheet in ExcelModules

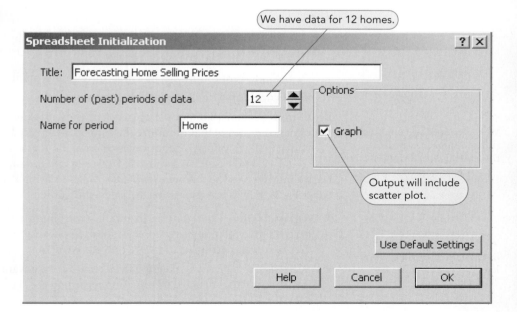

SCREENSHOT 12.9B   **Causal Model (Simple Regression) for Forecasting Home Selling Prices**

	A	B	C	D	E	F	G	H	I
1	**Forecasting Home Selling Prices**								
2	Forecasting		Causal regression analysis						
3	Enter the (Y,X) pairs in cells shaded YELLOW. Enter new value of X at the bottom to forecast Y.								
4									
5	Input Data				Forecast Error Analysis				
6	Period	Dep Variable (or) (Y)	Indep Variable (or) (X)		Forecast	Error	Absolute error	Squared error	Absolute % error
7	Home 1	182.5	2.01		188.431	-5.931	5.931	35.178	3.25%
8	Home 2	227.3	2.65		251.016	-23.716	23.716	562.460	10.43%
9	Home 3	251.9	2.43		229.503	22.397	22.397	501.644	8.89%
10	Home 4	325.2	2.89		274.486	50.714	50.714	2571.944	15.59%
11	Home 5	225.1	2.55		241.237	-16.137	16.137	260.413	7.17%
12	Home 6	315.0	3.00		285.242	29.758	29.758	885.510	9.45%
13	Home 7	367.5	3.22		306.756	60.744	60.744	3689.818	16.53%
14	Home 8	220.8	2.37		223.635	-2.835	2.835	8.039	1.28%
15	Home 9	266.5	2.91		276.441	-9.941	9.941	98.832	3.73%
16	Home 10	261.0	2.56		242.215	18.785	18.785	352.869	7.20%
17	Home 11	177.5	2.25		211.901	-34.401	34.401	1183.396	19.38%
18	Home 12	235.9	3.41		325.336	-89.436	89.436	7998.816	37.91%
19					Average		30.400	1512.410	11.73%
20	Intercept	-8.125					MAD	MSE	MAPE
21	Slope	97.789							
22							SE	42.602	
23	Forecast	295.0	3.10				Correlation	0.702	
24							r-squared	0.493	

Forecasts are computed using the regression equation.

Regression coefficients

Measures of forecast error

Standard error of the regression estimate

Forecasted average selling price for house size of 3100 square feet

49.3% of variability in selling prices is explained by home size.

draw scatter diagrams by using Excel's Chart Wizard. However, ExcelModules automatically provides this chart if specified in the options (see Screenshot 12.9A). The scatter diagram for Sue's example is shown in Screenshot 12.9C, along with the linear regression line, so we can see how well the model fits the data. From this plot, it appears that while there is a reasonable linear relationship between selling price and size, there are sizable differences between the actual values and the fitted line (forecast values) in a few cases.

An alternative way to check the validity and accuracy of the causal model is to draw line plots of the actual and forecasted values (cells B7:B18 and E7:E18, respectively, in Screenshot 12.9B) against the observation number. If the Graph option is checked in Screenshot 12.9A, ExcelModules automatically draws these line plots also (in addition to the scatter diagram) and presents them on a separate worksheet. The line plots for Sue's example, shown in Screenshot 12.9D, indicate that the causal model she has developed does replicate the pattern of selling prices. However, these plots also confirm the presence of a few sizable forecast errors (e.g., homes 4, 7, 11, and 12). Sue may therefore want to consider including other independent variables in her causal model to improve the forecast accuracy.

Standard Error of the Estimate   Another way of measuring the accuracy of the regression estimates is to compute the **standard error of the (regression) estimate**, $S_{Y.X}$, also called the *standard deviation of the regression*. The equation for computing the standard error is

File: 12-9.xls, sheet: 12-9D

The standard error is useful in creating confidence intervals around the regression line.

$$S_{Y.X} = \sqrt{\Sigma(Y_i - \hat{Y}_i)^2 / (n - 2)}$$

(12-15)

SCREENSHOT 12.9C   **Scatter Plot with Regression Line for Forecasting Home Selling Prices**

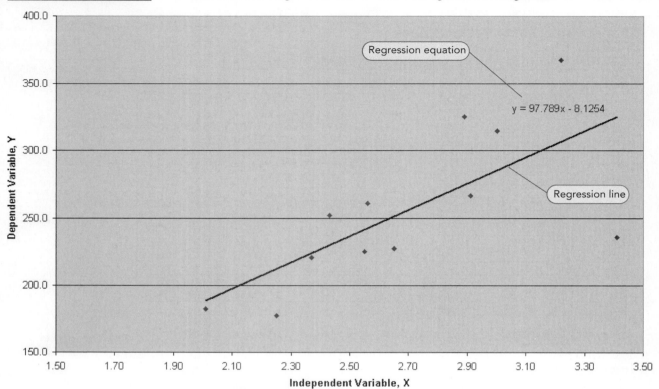

SCREENSHOT 12.9D   **Plot of Causal Model (Simple Regression) Forecast for Forecasting Home Selling Prices**

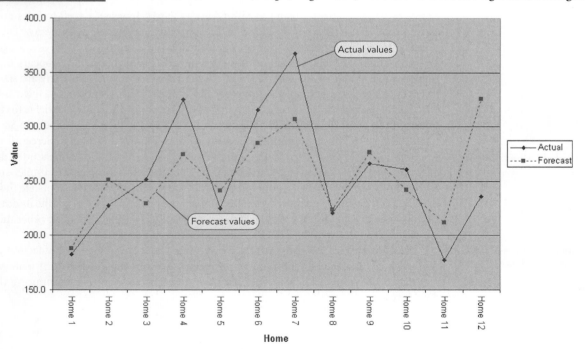

where

Y_i = actual value of the dependent variable for the ith observation

$\hat{Y}_i$ = regression (forecasted) value of the dependent variable for the ith observation

n = number of observations

ExcelModules automatically computes and reports the standard error. The value for Sue's example, shown in cell H22 of Screenshot 12.9B, is 42.602. This implies that the standard deviation of the distribution of home selling prices around the regression line, for a given value of home size, is $42 602. As we will see shortly, the standard error can be used in setting up confidence intervals around the average forecasted values.

> The correlation coefficient helps measure the strength of the linear relationship.

Correlation Coefficient (r)   The regression equation is one way of expressing the nature of the relationship between two variables.[2] The equation shows how one variable relates to the value and changes in another variable. Another way to evaluate the linear relationship between two variables is to compute the **correlation coefficient**. This measure expresses the degree or strength of the linear relationship. It is usually denoted by r and can be any number between and including +1 and −1. Figure 12.4 illustrates what different values of r might look like for different types of relationships between an independent variable X and a dependent variable Y.

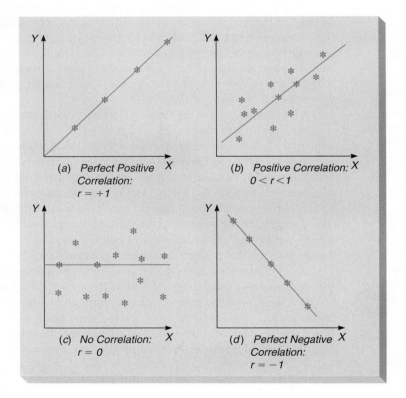

FIGURE 12.4

Four Values of the Correlation Coefficient

(a) Perfect Positive Correlation: $r = +1$

(b) Positive Correlation: $0 < r < 1$

(c) No Correlation: $r = 0$

(d) Perfect Negative Correlation: $r = -1$

---

[2] Regression lines do not always show cause-and-effect relationships. In general, they describe the relationship between the movement of variables.

The rather cumbersome equation for the correlation coefficient r is

$$r = \frac{n\Sigma XY - \Sigma X\Sigma Y}{\sqrt{[n\Sigma X^2 - (\Sigma X)^2][n\Sigma Y^2 - (\Sigma Y)^2]}} \tag{12-16}$$

ExcelModules, however, also calculates and reports the value of the correlation coefficient. Although there is no specific rule to decide when two variables can be deemed to be highly correlated, in general, correlation coefficient magnitudes of 0.6 and greater are indicative of a strong relationship. In Sue's example, therefore, the r-value of 0.702 (shown in cell H23 of Screenshot 12.9B) indicates the presence of a strong positive linear relationship between selling price and home size.

> The coefficient of determination tells us how much of the variability in the dependent variable is explained by the independent variable.

Coefficient of Determination (R^2)   Another measure that is used often to describe the strength of the linear relationship between two variables is the *coefficient of determination.* This is simply the square of the coefficient of correlation and is denoted by R^2. The value of R^2 will always be a positive number in the range $0 \le R^2 \le 1$. The coefficient of determination is defined as the amount of the variability in the dependent variable (Y) that is explained by the regression equation. In Sue's example, the value of R^2 is 0.493 (shown in cell H24 in Screenshot 12.9B), which is just the square of 0.702, the correlation coefficient. This indicates that only 49.3% of the total variation in home selling prices is explained by size, leaving 51.7% unexplained (or explained by other variables). For this reason, as noted earlier, Sue may want to consider including other independent variables in her causal model.

Using the Causal Simple Regression Model   Suppose Sue wants to estimate the average selling price of a home that is 3100 square feet in size. We enter this value in cell C23 in Screenshot 12.9B (note that we should enter 3100 as 3.10). The model forecasts an average selling price of 295.0 (shown in cell B23), or $295 000. This forecast of $295 000 is called a *point estimate* of Y. As noted earlier, the forecasted value (point estimate) is actually the average, or expected value, of a distribution of possible values of home selling prices for a given value of size.

> One weakness of regression is that we need to know the values of the independent variable.

This computation of the forecasted selling price illustrates two potential weaknesses of causal forecasting methods such as regression. First, we see that even after the regression equation has been computed, it is necessary to provide an estimate of the independent variable before forecasting the corresponding value of the dependent variable. This may not be a problem in Sue's example (after all, she can always find out the size of any home for which she wants to forecast the selling price). However, consider a causal model that uses, for example, the unemployment rate to forecast stock market performance. In this case, imagine the difficulty of estimating the unemployment rate in the next period. As you can clearly see, any error in estimating this rate will result in a corresponding error in the forecasted stock market performance, even if the causal model itself is very good.

> A second weakness of regression is that individual values of Y can be quite far from the forecasted average value.

Second, even if we know the value of X for which we want to forecast Y, the regression line forecasts only the *average* value of Y. Depending on the variability of the distribution of Y-values around the regression line (measured by the standard error of the regression estimate, $S_{Y.X}$), the actual value of Y for a given value of X could be quite far from the forecasted average value. Statistically, we can use the following formula to calculate an approximate confidence interval for *all* values of Y for a given value of X:[3]

$$\hat{Y} \pm Z_{\alpha/2} \times S_{Y.X} \qquad \text{(or)} \qquad (b_0 + b_1 X) \pm Z_{\alpha/2} \times S_{Y.X} \tag{12-17}$$

---

[3] We refer to this as an *approximate* formula for the confidence interval because the exact formula varies slightly, depending on the value of X for which the interval is computed. Also, when the sample size is large ($n > 30$), the confidence interval can be computed using normal (Z) tables. However, when the number of observations is small, the t-distribution is appropriate. For details, see any forecasting or statistics textbook, such as J. E. Hanke and A. G. Reitsch. *Business Forecasting,* 7/e. Upper Saddle River, NJ: Prentice Hall, 2003.

where $Z_{\alpha/2}$ is the standard normal value (see Appendix C on page 658) for a confidence level of $(1-\alpha)\%$. For example, an approximate 95% confidence interval for the selling price of *all* homes of size 3100 square feet can be computed to be $295.0 \pm 1.96 \times 42.602 = 211.5$ to 378.5, or \$211 500 to \$378 500. As you can see, this is a fairly broad interval, which is consistent with the fact that the size of a home is able to explain only 49.3% of the variability in its selling price.

Would it be logical to use the causal model developed here to forecast the average selling price of a home of size 5000 square feet? What about a home of size 1400 square feet? We note that the sizes of both these homes are not within the range of sizes for the homes in Sue's data set (see Table 12.6). It is entirely possible, for example, that the relationship between selling price and home size follows a different causal relationship for large homes (i.e., home sizes in excess of 4500 square feet). Hence, we cannot guarantee the validity of the causal model developed here in forecasting the selling prices of these homes.

> A causal model is typically valid only for the range of X values in the data set for which it was developed.

Causal Simple Regression Using Excel's Analysis ToolPak (Data Analysis)

> Excel's Analysis ToolPak add-in includes a procedure for regression.

As noted earlier, Excel's Analysis ToolPak add-in includes a procedure for regression. (See Section A.6 in Appendix A for details on how to install and enable this add-in in Excel.) When enabled, this add-in is called Data Analysis in Excel's menu. To invoke the regression procedure, we click **TOOLS|DATA ANALYSIS** and then select **REGRESSION** from the list of choices, as shown in Screenshot 12.9E(a). The window shown in Screenshot 12.9E(b) is displayed.

Running the Regression Procedure in Data Analysis   We need to specify the cell ranges for the selling prices (Y) and sizes (X), and indicate where we want the output of the regression to be displayed. For example, in Screenshot 12.9E(b), we have specified the Y-range as cells B6:B18 (from the Excel worksheet shown in Screenshot 12.9B) and the X-range as cells C6:C18. We have asked for the output of the regression analysis to be presented in a new worksheet named 12.9F. If we check the box named Labels, the first entry in the cell range for a variable should include the name of that variable. Checking the box named Line Fit Plots will result in a scatter diagram like the one in Screenshot 12.9C.

> Residual plots and the normal probability plot are used to verify the validity of assumptions in a regression model.

All other options (i.e., Residuals, Standardized Residuals, Residual Plots, and Normal Probability Plot) deal with verifying the validity of assumptions made when using the least-squares procedures to develop a regression model. These options are usually more relevant for *explanatory* models, where the intent is to explain the variability in the dependent variable using the independent variable. Although still relevant, they are relatively less important in *predictive* regression models (such as in causal forecasting models), where the objective is mainly to obtain a good forecast of the dependent variable using the independent variable. For this reason, we do not discuss these topics here and refer you to any statistics textbook for a detailed discussion.

Results of the Regression Procedure   When we click OK, Data Analysis runs the regression procedure, and the results shown in Screenshot 12.9F on page 591 are displayed. Just as in the earlier results we obtained using ExcelModules (see Screenshot 12.9B on page 585), the results here too show a Y-intercept of -8.125 (cell B18), a slope of 97.989 (cell B19), a correlation coefficient of 0.702 (cell B5; named Multiple R by Data Analysis), a coefficient of determination R^2 of 0.493 (cell B6), and a standard error of the regression estimate of 42.602 (cell B8). The adjusted R^2 measure in cell B7 is relevant only for multiple regression models, which we will discuss shortly.

File: 12-9.xls, sheet: 12-9F

The table labelled ANOVA details how well the regression equation fits the data. The total sum of squares (SS) value of 35 819.197 (cell C15) is a measure of the total variability in the dependent variable (home selling prices). Of this, 17 670.281 (cell C13) is explained by the regression equation, leaving 18 148.916 unexplained (cell C14, also known as the residual sum of squares). Recall that we defined the R^2 as the percentage of variation in Y that is explained by the regression equation. From the values in the ANOVA table, R^2 can be computed as $17\,670.281 / 35\,819.197 = 0.493$, or 49.3%, which is the same value reported in cell B6.

SCREENSHOT 12.9E   **Simple Regression Using Excel's Analysis ToolPak**

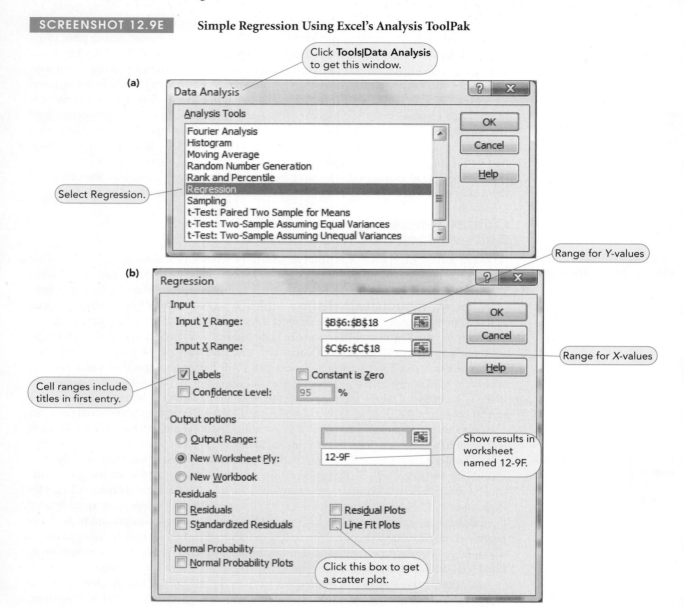

Click **Tools|Data Analysis** to get this window.

(a)

Select Regression.

(b)

Cell ranges include titles in first entry.

Range for Y-values

Range for X-values

Show results in worksheet named 12-9F.

Click this box to get a scatter plot.

Statistical significance tests check whether the regression relationship really exists for the entire population or whether it is just a random occurrence based on the current sample.

Statistical Significance of the Regression Equation   The output from Data Analysis also provides information on the statistical significance of the regression equation. That is, it indicates whether the linear relationship obtained between Y and X is, in fact, a true reflection of the real situation or whether it is just a random occurrence based on this specific data set. Recall from Equation 12-11 that we expressed the regression equation as $\hat{Y} = b_0 + b_1 X$. Note that the two coefficients b_0 and b_1 are sample statistics because they are both estimated based on a specific sample. In Sue's model, for example, b_0 and b_1 have been estimated based on just 12 homes. Now suppose the true population relationship between Y and X (i.e., the relationship if our data set consisted of *all* homes in the population) can be expressed as follows:

$$\mu_{Y|X} = \beta_0 + \beta_1 X \qquad (12\text{-}18)$$

SCREENSHOT 12.9F   **Simple Regression Output from Excel's Analysis ToolPak**

	A	B	C	D	E	F	G
1	**Simple Regression Using Data Analysis**						
2							
3	**SUMMARY OUTPUT**						
4	*Regression Statistics*						
5	Multiple R	0.702					
6	R Square	0.493					
7	Adjusted R Square	0.443					
8	Standard Error	42.602					
9	Observations	12					
10							
11	**ANOVA**						
12		*df*	*SS*	*MS*	*F*	*Signific-ance F*	
13	Regression	1	17670.281	17670.281	9.736	0.011	
14	Residual	10	18148.916	1814.892			
15	Total	11	35819.197				
16							
17		*Coeffi-cients*	*Standard Error*	*t Stat*	*P-value*	*Lower 95%*	*Upper 95%*
18	Intercept	-8.125	85.119	-0.095	0.926	-197.781	181.531
19	Home size ('000 sq ft)	97.789	31.340	3.120	0.011	27.960	167.619

Correlation coefficient

17 670.281 of the total sum of squares of 35 819.197 is explained here.

P-value of 0.011 indicates that regression is significant at the 5% level.

Regression coefficients

95% confidence interval for the population slope

where

$\mu_{Y|X}$ = forecasted average value of Y for a given value of X, based on the entire population

β_0 = Y-intercept of the line, based on the entire population

β_1 = slope of the line, based on the entire population

Does a nonzero value of the slope b_1 based on a specific sample immediately imply that the true population slope β_1 is also nonzero? That is, is the slope between Y and X significantly different from zero, from a statistical perspective? To test this issue, we set up the following null and alternate hypothesis:

$H_0: \beta_1 = 0$ (i.e., the regression between Y and X is not statistically significant)

$H_1: \beta_1 \neq 0$ (i.e., the regression between Y and X is statistically significant)

There are two tests for testing statistical significance in simple regression models: *F*-test and *t*-test.

Using the information provided in the Data Analysis regression output, there are two ways to conduct this hypothesis test: (1) the F-test and (2) the t-test. We refer you to any statistics textbook for the details and rationale behind these tests. In our discussion here, we simply interpret the test results provided in the Data Analysis output.

The result of the F-test is included in the ANOVA table. The computed F-statistic of 9.736, shown in cell E13 in Screenshot 12.9F, is F-distributed with 1 numerator degree of freedom (cell B13) and 10 denominator degrees of freedom (cell B14). The P-value associated with this F-statistic is shown in cell F13 (Data Analysis labels this P-value as Significance F). In Sue's case, the P-value of the test is 0.011, implying that the null hypothesis can be rejected at the 5% significance level but not at the 1% level. Another way of stating this is that we are 98.9% ($= 1 - P$-value) confident that the relationship between Y and X is statistically significant.

The result of the *t*-test is included in the regression coefficients table. The computed *t*-statistic of 3.12, shown in cell D19 in Screenshot 12.9F, is *t*-distributed with 10 degrees of freedom (cell B14). The *P*-value associated with this *t*-statistic is 0.011, shown in cell E19. Note that this is the same *P*-value we obtained in the *F*-test, which leads to the same conclusion as in that test. In fact, in simple regression models, the *P*-value will always be the same for both the *F*-test and the *t*-test. It is therefore not necessary to conduct both tests, although all statistical software packages, including Data Analysis, automatically report the results for both tests.

Significance tests involving the *Y*-intercept are often not relevant and are ignored.

Data Analysis also provides information regarding the statistical significance of the *Y*-intercept. The computed *t*-statistic is shown in cell D18, and the associated *P*-value is shown in cell E18 in Screenshot 12.9F. However, as noted earlier, the *Y*-intercept does not have a practical meaning in many causal regression models. For example, it is meaningless in Sue's model because a home cannot have a size of zero. For this reason, it is quite common for the result of this significance test to be ignored, even though most statistical software packages report it by default.

We can construct intervals of various confidence levels for the population slope.

Confidence Intervals for the Population Slope   In addition to testing for the statistical significance of the slope, we can also compute confidence intervals for the population slope (i.e., β_1). By default, Data Analysis always reports a 95% confidence interval for this parameter (shown in cells F19:G19 in Screenshot 12.9F). The interval implies that while we have obtained a point estimate of 97.989 for the regression slope based on the current sample of 12 homes, we are 95% confident that the true population slope between home selling prices and sizes is somewhere between 27.960 and 167.619. Here again, the interval is fairly broad because the R^2 value of the regression model is only 49.3%.

We can also obtain intervals for other confidence levels by checking the appropriate option (see Screenshot 12.9E) and specifying the desired confidence level. By the way, note that Data Analysis also reports the confidence interval for the *Y*-intercept. However, for the same reasons discussed previously, we typically ignore these types of computations regarding the *Y*-intercept.

Causal Multiple Regression Model

Adding additional independent variables turns a simple regression model into a multiple regression model.

A *multiple regression* model is a practical extension of the simple regression model. It allows us to build a model with more than one independent variable. The general form of the multiple regression equation is

$$\hat{Y} = b_0 + b_1 X_1 + b_2 X_2 + \ldots + b_p X_p \tag{12-19}$$

where

b_0 = *Y*-axis intercept, based on the current sample

b_i = slope of the regression for the *i*th independent variable (X_i), based on the current sample

p = number of independent variables in the model

Calculations in multiple regression are very complex and best left to a computer.

The mathematics of multiple regression becomes quite complex, based on the number of independent variables, and the computations are therefore best left to a computer. As with simple regression, we discuss two approaches here. The first approach uses a worksheet included in ExcelModules, and the second approach uses the regression procedure in Excel's Analysis ToolPak. Next, we illustrate both approaches for causal multiple regression models, using an expanded version of Sue Taylor's home selling price example.

Forecasting Home Selling Prices—Revisited   Sue Taylor is not satisfied with the R^2-value of 0.493 obtained from her causal simple regression model. She thinks she can forecast home selling prices more precisely by including a second independent variable in

HOME	SELLING PRICE (IN THOUSANDS)	HOME SIZE (IN THOUSANDS SQ. FT.)	LAND AREA (ACRES)
1	$182.5	2.01	0.40
2	227.3	2.65	0.60
3	251.9	2.43	0.65
4	325.2	2.89	1.10
5	225.1	2.55	0.75
6	315.0	3.00	1.50
7	367.5	3.22	1.70
8	220.8	2.37	0.45
9	266.5	2.91	0.80
10	261.0	2.56	1.00
11	177.5	2.25	0.50
12	235.9	3.41	0.70

her regression model. In addition to the size of a home, she believes that the area of the land (in acres) would also be a good predictor of selling prices. Sue has updated the information for the 12 homes in her input data, as shown in Table 12.7. What is the effect of including this additional independent variable?

Causal Multiple Regression Using ExcelModules

ExcelModules includes a worksheet for causal forecasting models using multiple regression.

Let us first use ExcelModules to develop a regression model to predict the selling price of a home based both on its size and land area. When we select the Causal Model (Multiple Regression) option from the Forecasting Models submenu in ExcelModules (see Screenshot 12.1A), the window shown in Screenshot 12.10A is displayed. The option entries in this window are similar to those for the simple regression model, with the

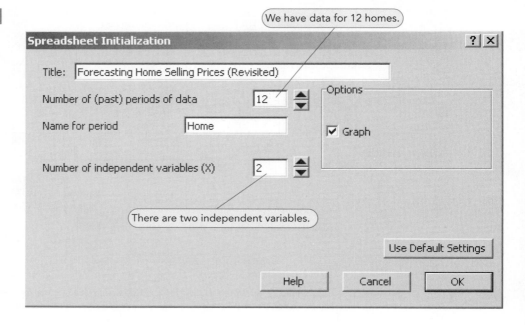

additional choice to specify the number of independent variables. The entries for Sue's example are shown in Screenshot 12.10A.

**File: 12-10.xls,
sheet: 12-10B**

When we click OK on this screen, we get the screen shown in Screenshot 12.10B. We now enter the selling prices (dependent variable, Y) for the past 10 years in cells B8:B19 and the corresponding home sizes (independent variable X_1) and land areas (independent variable X_2) in cells C8:C19 and D8:D19, respectively. Note that the values in cells B3:B19 and C3:C19 are the same as the ones we entered in the simple regression model earlier. Once we have entered all the values, we click the button labelled **REGRESS**.

The worksheet computes the multiple regression equation and displays the results.[4] For Sue's example, the Y-intercept (b_0) is shown in cell B22, and the slopes b_1 for home size and b_2 for land area are shown in cells C23 and D23, respectively. The causal regression model is

$$\text{Forecasted average selling price} = +99.919 + 21.383 \times \text{Home size} + 115.030 \times \text{Land area}$$

SCREENSHOT 12.10B   **Causal Model (Multiple Regression) for Forecasting Home Selling Prices**

Click this button after entering all the input data.

Forecasting Home Selling Prices (Revisited)

Forecasts are computed using the multiple regression equation.

	A	B	C	D	E	F	G	H	I	J
1	**Forecasting Home Selling Prices (Revisited)**									
2	Forecasting		Multiple regression							
3	Regress		Enter the data in the cells shaded YELLOW. Then click the **Regress** button.							
4										
5		Selling price		Home size		Land area				
6	Input Data					Forecast Error Analysis				
7		Y	x 1	x 2		Forecast	Error	Absolute error	Squared error	Absolute % error
8	Home 1	182.5	2.01	0.40		188.912	-6.412	6.412	41.113	3.51%
9	Home 2	227.3	2.65	0.60		225.603	1.697	1.697	2.879	0.75%
10	Home 3	251.9	2.43	0.65		226.650	25.250	25.250	637.540	10.02%
11	Home 4	325.2	2.89	1.10		288.250	36.950	36.950	1365.287	11.36%
12	Home 5	225.1	2.55	0.75		240.719	-15.619	15.619	243.966	6.94%
13	Home 6	315.0	3.00	1.50		336.614	-21.614	21.614	467.178	6.86%
14	Home 7	367.5	3.22	1.70		364.325	3.175	3.175	10.083	0.86%
15	Home 8	220.8	2.37	0.45		202.361	18.439	18.439	339.979	8.35%
16	Home 9	266.5	2.91	0.80		254.169	12.331	12.331	152.055	4.63%
17	Home 10	261.0	2.56	1.00		269.691	-8.691	8.691	75.528	3.33%
18	Home 11	177.5	2.25	0.50		205.547	-28.047	28.047	786.632	15.80%
19	Home 12	235.9	3.41	0.70		253.358	-17.458	17.458	304.771	7.40%
20						Average		16.307	368.918	6.65%
21	Regression Line							MAD	MSE	MAPE
22	Intercept	99.919								
23	Slopes		21.383	115.030				SE	22.179	
24								multiple-r	0.936	
25								r-squared	0.876	

Regression coefficients

Measures of forecast error

87.6% of the variability in selling price is explained by this model.

---

[4] The multiple regression worksheet in ExcelModules uses Excel's Analysis ToolPak add-in to perform the calculations. Hence, this add-in must be installed and enabled for this worksheet to work.

The effect of each independent variable in a multiple regression model is affected by all the other independent variables in the model.

Note the huge difference between the regression coefficients here and the coefficients obtained in the simple regression model between selling price and home size. That is, the addition of the third variable in the model completely changes the regression equation, even though the data remain unchanged for selling price and home size. As it turns out, this is a fairly common occurrence in regression models.

The home size and land area values for the 12 homes in the sample are now plugged in to this regression equation to compute the forecasted selling prices. These forecasts are shown in cells F8:F19. The following measures of forecast error are then calculated and reported: MAD (cell H20), MSE (cell I20), and MAPE (cell J20).

If the Graph option is checked in Screenshot 12.10A, ExcelModules creates line plots of the actual and forecasted values against the observation number, and shows the chart on a separate worksheet. We present the chart for Sue's example in Screenshot 12.10C.

Analyzing the Results   Is this multiple regression model better than the original simple regression model? The R^2 value increases from just 0.493 in the simple regression model to 0.876 with the addition of the second variable, land area. That is, home size and land area together are able to explain 87.6% of the variability in home selling prices. In addition, all three measures of forecast error show sizable drops in magnitude. For example, the MAPE decreases from 11.73% in the simple regression model to just 6.65% in the multiple regression model. Likewise, the MAD decreases from 30.40 in the simple regression model to just 16.307 with the second independent variable.

To further study the effect of adding land area as an independent variable, let us compare the multiple regression model's line plot (shown in Screenshot 12.10C) with the

File: 12-10.xls, sheet: 12-10C

Forecast measures will typically improve in multiple regression models when compared to a simple regression model.

SCREENSHOT 12.10C   **Plot of Causal Model (Multiple Regression) Forecast for Forecasting Home Selling Prices**

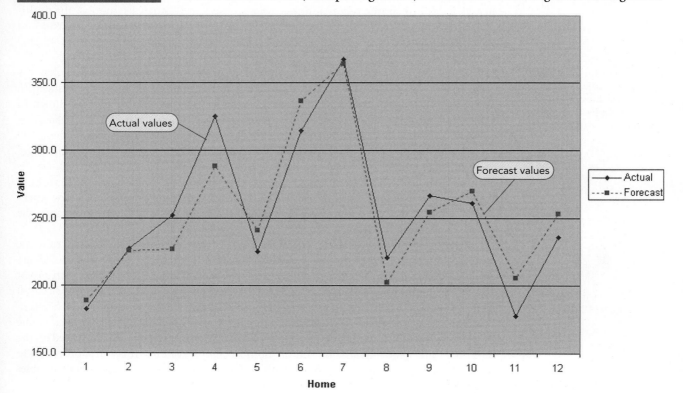

simple regression model's plot (shown in Screenshot 12.9D on page 586). It appears that most of the points in Screenshot 12.10C (especially homes 2, 6, 7, and 12) show a sizable improvement in terms of the forecast error.

All these issues seem to indicate that the addition of the second independent variable does help Sue in being able to forecast home selling prices more accurately. However, as we will see shortly when we study multiple regression analysis using Data Analysis, we need to be cautious in deciding which independent variable to add in a multiple regression model.

Using the Causal Multiple Regression Model   Recall that we used the simple regression model to forecast the average selling price of a 3100 square foot home to be $295 000. Now suppose this home has a land area of 0.90 acres. We can plug these values into the regression equation and compute the revised average selling price as follows: 99.919 + 21.383 × 3.10 + 115.030 × 0.90 = 269.733, or $269 733.

We can use the standard error of the regression esti-mate to construct confidence intervals around the regres-sion line.

As with the simple regression model, we can use this point estimate in conjunction with the standard error of the regression estimate (given in cell I23 in Screenshot 12.10B) to calculate an approximate 95% confidence interval for the selling price of *all* homes of size 3100 square feet and with a land area of 0.9 acres. This confidence interval turns out to be 269.733 ± 1.96 × 22.179 = 226.262 to 313.204, or $226 262 to $313 204. Because the standard error here is smaller than the corresponding value in the simple regression model, the width of this confidence interval is also narrower. However, while the confidence interval computed in the simple regression model was for *all* homes of size 3100 square feet, the interval here is relevant only for those homes that also have a land area of 0.9 acres.

Causal Multiple Regression Using Excel's Analysis ToolPak (Data Analysis)

Just as we did in simple regression, we can also use Excel's Analysis ToolPak for multiple regression. To invoke the procedure, we once again click **TOOLS|DATA ANALYSIS** and select **REGRESSION** from the list of choices. The window shown in Screenshot 12.10D is displayed.

Independent variables must be arranged adjacently in order to use the regression procedure in Data Analysis for multiple regression.

Before we use Data Analysis for multiple regression, we need to ensure that the independent variables in the model are adjacent to each other in an Excel worksheet. In Sue's case, for example, we have entered the selling prices in cells B7:B19, as shown in Screenshot 12.10B, and the two independent variables (home size and land area) in adjacent columns in cells C7:C19 and D7:D19, respectively. We now specify these cell ranges in the appropriate boxes, as shown in Screenshot 12.10D (note that the cell ranges for both independent variables are specified as one entry: C7:D19). The Labels box is checked to indicate that the cell ranges include the name of each variable as the first entry. We then indicate that we want the output of the regression to be displayed in a new work-sheet named 12-10E. The rest of the entries and their implications are the same as in the simple regression procedure.

File: 12-10.xls,
sheet: 12-10E

Results of the Regression Procedure   When we click OK, Data Analysis runs the multiple regression procedure, and the results shown in Screenshot 12.10E on page 598 are displayed. Here again, just as in the earlier results we obtained using ExcelModules (Screenshot 12.10B), the results show a *Y*-intercept of 99.919 (cell B18), a slope of 21.383 for home size (cell B19), a slope of 115.030 for land area (cell B20), a coefficient of determination R^2 of 0.876 (cell B6), and a standard error of the regression estimate of 22.179 (cell B8). The *adjusted* R^2-value in cell B7 is an empirical measure that applies a correction factor to the R^2-value based on the number of independent variables and the number of observations. It is commonly used to compare multiple regression models with different numbers of independent variables

SCREENSHOT 12.10D   **Multiple Regression Using Excel's Analysis ToolPak**

(as opposed to the original R^2-value, which will always be higher for a model with a larger number of independent variables).

Notice that the total SS value of 35 819.197 (in cell C15 of the ANOVA table) is the same value we saw in the simple regression model. Of this, the multiple regression model explains 31 382.185, leaving only 4427.011 unexplained. The R^2-value can therefore be computed as 31 382.185 / 35 819.197 = 0.876, or 87.6%, which is the same value reported in cell B6.

Statistical Significance of the Regression Equation   Just as we did in simple regression, if our data set consists of the entire population of homes, the true population relationship between Y and the two independent variables X_1 and X_2 can be expressed as

$$\mu_{Y|Xs} = \beta_0 + \beta_1 X_1 + \beta_2 X_2 \tag{12-20}$$

where

$\mu_{Y|Xs}$ = forecasted average value of Y for a given values of X_1 and X_2, based on the entire population

β_0 = Y-intercept of the line, based on the entire population

β_1 = slope with respect to X_1, based on the entire population

β_2 = slope with respect to X_2, based on the entire population

Unlike simple regression, where we could test the significance of the regression relationship by using either the F-test or the t-test, in multiple regression these two tests deal with

SCREENSHOT 12.10E   **Multiple Regression Output from Excel's Analysis ToolPak**

	A	B	C	D	E	F	G
1	**Multiple Regression Using Data Analysis**						
2							
3	**SUMMARY OUTPUT**						
4	*Regression Statistics*						
5	Multiple R	0.936					
6	R Square	0.876					
7	Adjusted R Square	0.849					
8	Standard Error	22.179					
9	Observations	12					
10							
11	**ANOVA**						
12		*df*	*SS*	*MS*	*F*	*Significance F*	
13	Regression	2	31392.185	15696.093	31.910	0.000	
14	Residual	9	4427.011	491.890			
15	Total	11	35819.197				
16							
17		*Coefficients*	*Standard Error*	*t Stat*	*P-value*	*Lower 95%*	*Upper 95%*
18	Intercept	99.919	48.807	2.047	0.071	-10.490	210.329
19	(X1) Home size ('000 sq ft)	21.383	21.805	0.981	0.352	-27.944	70.710
20	(X2) Land area (acres)	115.030	21.779	5.282	0.001	65.762	164.297

= 31 392.185 / 35 819.197

Overall model is significant.

95% confidence intervals for population slopes

Regression coefficients

P-value of 0.352 indicates that home size is not significant given presence of land area in the model.

different issues. As before, we refer you to any statistics textbook for the details of these tests, and we only interpret their results in our discussion here.

The F-test tests the overall significance of the model in multiple regression.

In multiple regression, the F-test tests the overall significance of the regression model. That is, the null and alternate hypotheses for this test are as follows:

$H_0: \beta_1 = \beta_2 = 0$ (i.e., the overall regression model is not significant)

H_1: At least one of β_1 and $\beta_2 \neq 0$ (i.e., at least one variable in the model is significant)

In Sue's example, the computed F-statistic for this test is 31.910, as shown in cell E13 in Screenshot 12.10E. This statistic is F-distributed with 2 numerator degrees of freedom (cell B13) and 9 denominator degrees of freedom (cell B14). The P-value associated with this F-statistic, shown in cell F13, is essentially zero, implying that the null hypothesis can be rejected at virtually any level of significance. That is, we can clearly conclude that there is a statistically significant relationship between Y and at least one of the two X variables. It is important to note that this result of the F-test should not be interpreted as an indication that both X variables are significant.

The t-test tests the significance of an individual independent variable in the model, given the presence of all the other independent variables.

The t-test, in contrast, tests the significance of each of the regression slopes, given the presence of all the other independent variables. This previous condition illustrates an important issue about multiple regression: The relationship of each independent variable with the dependent variable in a multiple regression model is affected by all the other independent variables in the model. To illustrate this issue, let us first test the slope for the land area. The null and alternate hypotheses for this test are as follows:

$H_0: \beta_2 = 0$ (i.e., the slope of land area is not significant, given the presence of home size)

$H_1: \beta_2 \neq 0$ (i.e., the slope of land area is significant, given the presence of home size)

The computed t-statistic for this test is 5.282, as shown in cell D20 in Screenshot 12.10E. This statistic is t-distributed with 9 degrees of freedom (cell B14). The P-value associated with this t-statistic, shown in cell E20, is 0.001, implying that there is a statistically significant relationship between Y and X_2 (land area), given the presence of the independent variable X_1 (home size) in the model.

Now let us test the slope for the home size. The null and alternate hypotheses for this test are as follows:

$H_0: \beta_1 = 0$ (i.e., the slope of home size is not significant, given the presence of land area)

$H_1: \beta_1 \neq 0$ (i.e., the slope of home size is significant, given the presence of land area)

Home size is not significant in the model, given the presence of land area.

The computed t-statistic for this test is 0.981, as shown in cell D19 in Screenshot 12.10E. This statistic is also t-distributed with 9 degrees of freedom (cell B14). The P-value for this test, shown in cell E20, is 0.352, implying that there is *no* statistically significant relationship between Y and X_1 (home size), given the presence of the independent variable X_2 (land area) in the model. Are we concluding here that home size is not a relevant variable to predict home selling prices? The answer is an emphatic no. In fact, recall from the simple regression model that we did establish a statistically significant relationship between home selling prices and home size. All we are concluding in the multiple regression model is that home size adds little incremental value to the model when land area has already been included. In other words, when land area has been included in the regression model, we should perhaps not include home size in the model also, and we should possibly look for other independent variables.

Multicollinearity exists when two or more independent variables in a multiple regression model are highly correlated with each other.

Multicollinearity   If home size was a statistically significant predictor in the simple regression model, why did it become nonsignificant when we added land area as a second independent variable? One possible explanation for this could be a phenomenon called *multicollinearity*. This occurs whenever two or more independent variables in a model are highly correlated with each other. When this happens, the relationship between each independent variable and the dependent variable is affected in an unpredictable manner by the presence of the other highly correlated independent variable.

File: 12-10.xls, sheet: 12-10F

How can we detect multicollinearity? We can use a simple correlation analysis to detect highly correlated pairs of independent variables.[5] To invoke the procedure in the Analysis ToolPak add-in, we click **TOOLS│DATA ANALYSIS** and select **CORRELATION** from the list of choices that is presented. The window shown in Screenshot 12.10F(a) is displayed. We enter the cell ranges for all variables, which must be arranged in adjacent columns or rows. (In Sue's example, we have included the cell ranges for Y, X_1, and X_2 from the worksheet shown in

---

[5] Multicollinearity can also exist between more than just a pair of variables. For example, independent variables X_1 and X_2 may together be highly correlated with a third independent variable, X_3. We can detect such situations by using a measure called the variance inflationary factor. We refer you to any statistics textbook for details on this measure and its use.

Correlation Analysis Using Excel's Analysis ToolPak

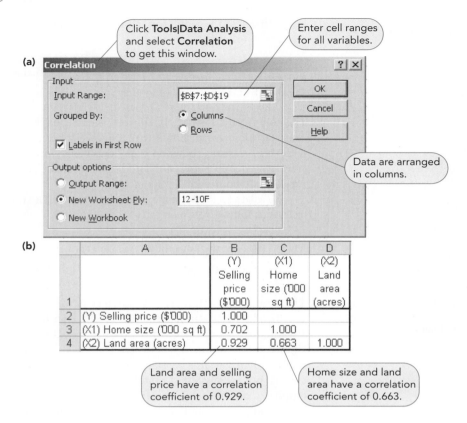

(a)

Click **Tools|Data Analysis** and select **Correlation** to get this window.

Enter cell ranges for all variables.

Data are arranged in columns.

(b)

	A	B	C	D
		(Y) Selling price ($000)	(X1) Home size (000 sq ft)	(X2) Land area (acres)
1				
2	(Y) Selling price ($000)	1.000		
3	(X1) Home size (000 sq ft)	0.702	1.000	
4	(X2) Land area (acres)	0.929	0.663	1.000

Land area and selling price have a correlation coefficient of 0.929.

Home size and land area have a correlation coefficient of 0.663.

We can detect pairwise multicollinearity by using correlation analysis.

Screenshot 12.10B on page 594.) When we now run the procedure, the results shown in Screenshot 12.10F(b) are displayed.

The results indicate that both independent variables are individually highly correlated with the dependent variable. The correlation coefficient between Y and X_1 is 0.702 (cell B3), and it is 0.929 (cell B4) between Y and X_2. This explains why each variable, by itself, is significantly related to Y. However, the results also indicate the X_1 and X_2 are correlated at a level of 0.663 (cell C4). As noted earlier, while there is no clear cut-off to decide when two variables are highly correlated, in general, correlation coefficient magnitudes of 0.6 or greater are indicative of a strong relationship. If two independent variables exhibit this level of relationship, they should not be included in a multiple regression model at the same time. If they are both included, the effect of each independent variable on the other can be unpredictable, as we saw in Sue's example in Screenshot 12.10E.

We can construct various confidence intervals for the population slopes.

Confidence Intervals for the Population Slopes   Just as we did in simple regression, we can compute intervals at various levels of confidence for each population slope (i.e., β_1 and β_2). By default, Data Analysis always reports 95% confidence intervals for both these parameters (shown in cells F19:G19 and F20:G20, respectively, in Screenshot 12.10E). Note that the confidence interval for β_1 extends from a negative value to a positive value (i.e., it spans a value of zero). This is consistent with our earlier finding that the slope of home size is not significantly different from zero, given the presence of land area in the model.

In this model also, the Y-intercept is not relevant for any practical interpretation. (After all, we cannot have a home of size zero with no land area.) For this reason, we ignore the hypothesis test and confidence interval information for the Y-intercept, even though Data Analysis provides that information by default.

SUMMARY

Forecasts are a critical part of a manager's function. Demand forecasts drive the production, capacity, and scheduling systems in a firm and affect the financial, marketing, and personnel planning functions.

This chapter introduces three types of forecasting models: judgmental, time series, and causal. Four qualitative models are discussed for judgmental forecasting: Delphi method, jury of executive opinion, sales force composite, and consumer market survey. We then develop moving averages, weighted moving averages, exponential smoothing, trend projection, seasonality, and multiplicative decomposition models for time-series data. Finally, we

illustrate a popular causal model, regression analysis. In addition, we discuss the use of scatter diagrams and provide an analysis of forecasting accuracy. The forecast measures discussed include mean absolute deviation (MAD), mean squared error (MSE), and mean absolute percent error (MAPE).

As we demonstrate in this chapter, no forecasting method is perfect under all conditions. Even when management has found a satisfactory approach, it must still monitor and control its forecasts to make sure that errors do not get out of hand. Forecasting can be a very challenging but rewarding part of managing.

GLOSSARY

Additive Decomposition Model. A model in which forecast value is the sum of four components: trend, seasonality, cycles, and random variations.

Causal Models. Models that forecast using variables and factors, in addition to time.

Correlation Coefficient. A measure of the strength of the linear relationship between two variables.

Cycle. A pattern that occurs over several years. Cycles are usually tied into the business cycle.

Decision-Making Group. A group of experts in a Delphi technique who are responsible for making the forecast.

Delphi. A judgmental forecasting technique that uses decision makers, staff personnel, and respondents to determine a forecast.

Exponential Smoothing. A forecasting technique that is a combination of the last forecast and the last actual value.

Forecast Error. Difference between the actual and forecast values.

Least Squares. A procedure used in trend projection and regression analysis to minimize the squared distances between the estimated straight line and the actual values.

Mean Absolute Deviation (MAD). The average of the absolute forecast errors.

Mean Absolute Percent Error (MAPE). The average of the absolute forecast errors as a percentage of the actual values.

Mean Squared Error (MSE). The average of the squared forecast errors.

Moving Average. A forecasting technique that averages past values in computing the forecast.

Multiplicative Decomposition Model. A model in which forecast value is the product of the four components: trend, seasonality, cycles, and random variations.

Qualitative Models. Models that forecast using judgments, experience, and qualitative and subjective data.

Random Variations. "Blips" in the data caused by chance and unusual situations. They follow no discernible pattern.

Regression Analysis. A forecasting procedure that uses the least squares approach on one or more independent variables to develop a forecasting model.

Scatter Diagram. A diagram of the variable to be forecast or predicted, plotted against another variable such as time.

Seasonality. The pattern of demand fluctuations above or below the trend line that occurs every year.

Smoothing Constant. A value between 0 and 1 that is used in an exponential smoothing forecast.

Standard Error of the Estimate. A measure of the accuracy of regression estimates.

Stationary Data. Time-series data in which there is no significant upward or downward movement (or trend) over time.

Time-Series Models. Models that forecast using historical data.

Trend. The upward or downward movement of the data over time.

Weighted Moving Average. A moving average forecasting method that places different weights on past values.

KEY EQUATIONS

(12-1) Forecast error $= A_t - F_t$

where A_t = actual value and F_t = forecast value.

(12-2) $\text{MAD} = \sum_{t=1}^{T} \left| \text{forecast error} \right| / T = \sum_{t=1}^{T} \left| A_t - F_t \right| / T$

Equation for computing the mean absolute deviation.

(12-3) $\text{MSE} = \sum_{t=1}^{T} \left| \text{forecast error} \right|^2 / T = \sum_{t=1}^{T} (A_t - F_t)^2 / T$

Equation for computing the mean squared error.

(12-4) $\text{MAPE} = 100 \sum\limits_{t=1}^{T} [|A_t - F_t| / A_t] / T$

Equation for computing the mean absolute percent error.

(12-5) Forecast = Trend × Seasonality × Cycles × Random Variations

Multiplicative decomposition model.

(12-6) Forecast = Trend + Seasonality + Cycles + Random Variations

Additive decomposition model.

(12-7) k-period moving average = Σ(Actual value in previous k periods)/k

Equation for computing a k-period moving average forecast.

(12-8) k-period weighted moving average =

$$\frac{\sum\limits_{i=1}^{k} (\text{Weight for period } i) \times (\text{Actual value in period } i)}{\sum\limits_{i=1}^{k} (\text{Weights})}$$

Equation for computing a k-period weighted moving average forecast.

(12-9) Forecast for period $t + 1$ = Forecast for period t
        $+ \alpha$ (Actual value in period t
        $-$ Forecast for period t)
        or $F_{t+1} = F_t + \alpha(A_t - F_t)$

Equation for computing an exponential smoothing forecast.

(12-10) $F_{t+1} = \alpha A_t + \alpha(1-\alpha)A_{t-1} + \alpha(1-\alpha)^2 A_{t-2}$
         $+ \alpha(1-\alpha)^3 A_{t-3} + \dots$

Expanded equation for an exponential smoothing forecast.

(12-11) $\hat{Y} = b_0 + b_1 X$

Slope of a linear trend line

(12-12) $SSE = \sum\limits_{i=1}^{n} (Y_i - \hat{Y}_i)^2 = \sum\limits_{t=1}^{n} [Y_i - (b_0 + b_1 X_i)]^2$

Least squares procedure

(12-13) $b_1 = \dfrac{\Sigma XY - n\overline{XY}}{\Sigma X^2 - n\overline{X}^2}$

Solving for the Y-intercept

(12-14) $b_0 = \overline{Y} - b_1\overline{X}$

Solving the slope to find the equation of the least-squares line

(12-15) $S_{Y \cdot X} = \sqrt{\Sigma(Y_i - \hat{Y}_i)^2 / (n-2)}$

Standard error equation

(12-16) $r = \dfrac{n\Sigma XY - \Sigma X \Sigma Y}{\sqrt{[n\Sigma X^2 - (\Sigma X)^2][n\Sigma Y^2 - (\Sigma Y)^2]}}$

Correlation Coefficient (r)

(12-17) $\hat{Y} \pm Z_{\alpha/2} \times S_{Y.X}$ (or) $(b_0 + b_1 X) \pm Z_{\alpha/2} \times S_{Y.X}$

Formula to calculate an approximate confidence interval for all values of Y for a given value of X[3]

(12-18) $\mu_{Y|X} = \beta_0 + \beta_1 X$

Statistical significance of the regression equation

(12-19) $\hat{Y} = b_0 + b_1 X_1 + b_2 X_2 + \dots + b_p X_p$

Multiple regression equation

(12-20) $\mu_{Y|Xs} = \beta_0 + \beta_1 X_1 + \beta_2 X_2$

Statistical significance of the regression equation

SOLVED PROBLEMS

Solved Problem 12-1

Demand for outpatient surgery at a small general hospital in rural Manitoba has increased steadily in the past few years, as seen in the following table:

YEAR	OUTPATIENT SURGERIES PERFORMED
1	45
2	50
3	52
4	56
5	58

The director of medical services predicted six years ago that demand in year 1 would be 42 surgeries. Using exponential smoothing with a weight of $\alpha = 0.20$, develop forecasts for years 2 through 6. What is the MAD?

SCREENSHOT 12.11   **Exponential Smoothing Model for Solved Problem 12-1**

	A	B	C	D	E	F	G	H
1	**Solved Problem 12-1**							
2	Forecasting		Exponential smoothing					
3	Enter the data in the cells shaded YELLOW.							
4								
5	Input Data			Forecast Error Analysis			*Given forecast for year 1*	
6	Period	Actual value		Forecast	Error	Absolute error	Squared error	Absolute % error
7	Year 1	45		42.000				
8	Year 2	50		42.600	7.400	7.400	54.760	14.80%
9	Year 3	52		44.080	7.920	7.920	62.726	15.23%
10	Year 4	56		45.664	10.336	10.336	106.833	18.46%
11	Year 5	58		47.731	10.269	10.269	105.448	17.70%
12				Average		8.981	82.442	16.55%
13	Alpha	0.2				MAD	MSE	MAPE
14								
15	Next period	49.785		*Value of the smoothing constant*				

Solution

File: 12-11.xls

To solve this problem, we use the **FORECASTING MODELS|EXPONENTIAL SMOOTHING** choice in ExcelModules. Screenshot 12.11 shows the computations. The input entries are shown in cells B7:B11, and the α value is shown in cell B13.

The MAD is calculated to be 8.98 (cell F12). The rounded-off forecast for year 6 is 50 (cell B15).

Solved Problem 12-2

Room registrations in the Toronto Towers Plaza Hotel have been recorded for the past nine years. Management would like to determine the mathematical trend of guest registration in order to project future occupancy. This estimate would help the hotel determine whether a future expansion will be needed. Given the following time-series data, develop a regression equation relating registrations to time. Then forecast year 11's registrations. Room registrations are in thousands:

Year 1: 17
Year 2: 16
Year 3: 16
Year 4: 21
Year 5: 20
Year 6: 20
Year 7: 23
Year 8: 25
Year 9: 24

Solution

File: 12-12.xls

To solve this problem, we use the **FORECASTING MODELS|LINEAR TREND ANALYSIS** choice in ExcelModules. Screenshot 12.12 on the next page shows the computations. The input entries are shown in cells B7:B15. The period values are automatically entered by ExcelModules in cells C7:C15.

The regression equation is Registrants = 14.556 + 1.133 × Year number. The MAPE is calculated to be 5.88% (cell I16). The projected registration for year 11 is 27 022 guests (cell B20).

Solved Problem 12-3

Quarterly demand for Jaguar XJ8s at a Calgary auto dealership is forecast using the equation

$$\hat{Y} = 10 + 3X$$

where X = quarter number ($X = 1$ is quarter 1 of year 2004, $X = 2$ is quarter 2 of year 2004, and so on), and $\hat{Y}$ = quarterly demand. The demand for luxury sedans is seasonal, and the indices for quarters 1, 2,

SCREENSHOT 12.12   **Trend Analysis Model for Solved Problem 12-2**

	A	B	C	D	E	F	G	H	I
1	**Solved Problem 12-2**								
2	Forecasting		Linear trend analysis						
3	Enter the actual values in cells shaded YELLOW. Enter new time period at the bottom to forecast Y.								
4									
5	Input Data				Forecast Error Analysis				
6	Period	Actual value (or) Y	Period number (or) X		Forecast	Error	Absolute error	Squared error	Absolute % error
7	Year 1	17	1		15.689	1.311	1.311	1.719	7.71%
8	Year 2	16	2		16.822	-0.822	0.822	0.676	5.14%
9	Year 3	16	3		17.956	-1.956	1.956	3.824	12.22%
10	Year 4	21	4		19.089	1.911	1.911	3.652	9.10%
11	Year 5	20	5		20.222	-0.222	0.222	0.049	1.11%
12	Year 6	20	6		21.356	-1.356	1.356	1.838	6.78%
13	Year 7	23	7		22.489	0.511	0.511	0.261	2.22%
14	Year 8	25	8		23.622	1.378	1.378	1.898	5.51%
15	Year 9	24	9		24.756	-0.756	0.756	0.571	3.15%
16					**Average**		1.136	1.610	5.88%
17	Intercept	**14.556**	Regression coefficients				MAD	MSE	MAPE
18	Slope	**1.133**							
19									
20	Next period	27.022	11						

Forecast for next year 11, in thousands

3, and 4 of each year are 0.80, 1.00, 1.30, and 0.90, respectively. Forecast the seasonalized demand for each quarter of year 2006.

Solution

Using the coding scheme for X, quarters 1 to 4 of year 2006 are coded $X = 9$ to 12, respectively. Hence,

$\hat{Y}$ (quarter 9 of year 2006) $= 10 + 3 \times 9 = 37$ Seasonalized forecast $= 37 \times 0.80 = 29.6$

$\hat{Y}$ (quarter 10 of year 2006) $= 10 + 3 \times 10 = 40$ Seasonalized forecast $= 40 \times 1.00 = 40.0$

$\hat{Y}$ (quarter 11 of year 2006) $= 10 + 3 \times 11 = 43$ Seasonalized forecast $= 43 \times 1.30 = 55.9$

$\hat{Y}$ (quarter 12 of year 2006) $= 10 + 3 \times 12 = 46$ Seasonalized forecast $= 40 \times 0.90 = 41.0$

Solved Problem 12-4

In Section 12.7, we helped Sandy Sawyer decompose Sawyer Piano House's time-series data using a multiplicative decomposition model. Repeat the computations now, using an additive decomposition model. For your convenience, the data for this model (showing grand piano sales for the past 20 quarters) are repeated in Table 12.8.

TABLE 12.8

Sales of Grand Pianos at Sawyer Piano House

	2000	2001	2002	2003	2004
Quarter 1	4	6	10	12	18
Quarter 2	2	4	3	9	10
Quarter 3	1	4	5	7	13
Quarter 4	5	14	16	22	35

Solution

Recall from Equation 12-6 that the additive decomposition model can be specified as

$$\text{Forecast} = \text{Trend} + \text{Seasonality} + \text{Cycles} + \text{Random Variations}$$

Although ExcelModules does not include a worksheet for additive decomposition, the worksheet provided for multiplicative decomposition can easily be modified to suit an additive model. We first select the Multiplicative Decomposition option from the Forecasting Models submenu in ExcelModules. Then, as we did in Screenshot 12.8A on page 579, we specify the number of periods for which we have past data (20), the name for the period (Quarter), and the number of seasons each year (4). In addition, we select the Centered Moving Average option to compute seasonal indices. We click OK, and in the resulting screen, we enter the actual number of pianos sold during the past 20 quarters in cells B7:B26. The corresponding time periods (i.e., the *X*-variable values) are automatically specified in cells C7:C26 by the worksheet.

File: 12-13.xls

The worksheet displays the results of the multiplicative decomposition model. We now modify this worksheet as follows to transform it to an additive mode (unless specified here, the computations in a column are the same as in the multiplicative model. The results for the additive model are shown in Screenshot 12.13).

1. *Computation of the seasonal indices, Columns D–G.* We compute the following:

   - In column D we compute the centred moving average sales for each quarter.

   - Next, we compute the seasonal difference for each quarter by *subtracting* from the actual sales (column B) in that quarter its centred average (column D). That is, column E = column B − column D. Note that instead of dividing by the centred moving average (as in a multiplicative model), we subtract it in an additive model.

   - The seasonal differences for each quarter are collected in cells B33:E37, and we compute the seasonal index for each quarter as the average of all the differences for that quarter. These seasonal indices are shown in cells B38:E38 and repeated in column F, next to the appropriate quarters each year. Seasonal index values in an additive model are positive or negative. A positive index indicates that the actual value in that period is above average, while a negative index indicates that the actual value is below average.

We subtract the seasonal indices from the seasonalized data in an additive model.

   - Finally, in column G, we compute the unseasonalized sales in each quarter as the actual sales (column B) in that quarter minus the seasonal index (column F) for that quarter. That is, column G = column B − column F.

2. *Computation of the trend equation.* Using the unseasonalized sales in column G as the dependent variable (*Y*) and the time period number in column C as the independent variable (*X*), we compute the linear trend equation. The resulting *Y*-intercept (*a*) and slope (*b*) for this straight line are shown in cells G28 and G29, respectively. In Sandy's case, the linear trend equation for the additive model is

$$\text{Unseasonalized sales forecast} = 0.149 + 0.959 \times \text{Quarter number}$$

3. *Computation of forecast, columns H and I.* We now calculate the forecast by adding the appropriate seasonal indices to the unseasonalized sales forecasts. Note that instead of multiplying by the seasonal index (as in a multiplicative model), we add it in an additive model. The computations are as follows:

   - In column H, we use the trend equation to compute the unseasonalized forecast for each quarter. For example, for the fourth quarter of year 2 (i.e., quarter 8), this value is computed in cell H14 as $(0.149 + 0.959 \times 8) = 7.821$. These values are also computed for the next year (i.e., quarters 21 to 24, denoting the four quarters in year 2005) in cells B42:B45.

We seasonalize forecasts by adding the appropriate seasonal indices.

   - The appropriate seasonal indices are added to the unseasonalized forecasts to get the seasonalized forecast for each quarter in column I. That is, column I = column H + column F. Cells D42:D45 show the seasonal forecasts for quarters 21 to 24.

SCREENSHOT 12.13   Additive Decomposition Model for Sawyer Piano House

Callouts:
- Additive model
- = Actual value – Centred average
- = Actual value – Seasonal index
- = Unseasonalized forecast + Seasonal index
- These two forecasts must be adjusted to zero.

	A	B	C	D	E	F	G	H	I	J	K	L	M
1	**Sawyer Piano House (Additive Model)**												
2	**Forecasting**		Additive decomposition										
3	4 seasons	Enter the actual values in the cells shaded YELLOW. Do not change the time period numbers!											
4													
5	Input Data				Seasonal Index Computation			Forecast Error analysis					
6	Period	Actual value (Y)	Time period (X)	Centred average	Seasonal difference	Seasonal index	Unseasonalized value	Unseasonalized Forecast	Seasonalized Forecast	Error	Absolute error	Squared error	Absolute % error
7	Quarter 1	4	1			2.000	2.000	1.108	3.108	0.892	0.892	0.796	22.30%
8	Quarter 2	2	2			-4.313	6.313	2.067	-2.245	4.245	4.245	18.024	212.27%
9	Quarter 3	1	3	3.250	-2.250	-3.938	4.938	3.026	-0.911	1.911	1.911	3.654	191.14%
10	Quarter 4	5	4	3.750	1.250	5.375	-0.375	3.985	9.360	-4.360	4.360	19.011	87.20%
11	Quarter 5	6	5	4.375	1.625	2.000	4.000	4.944	6.944	-0.944	0.944	0.891	15.74%
12	Quarter 6	4	6	5.875	-1.875	-4.313	8.313	5.903	1.591	2.409	2.409	5.805	60.23%
13	Quarter 7	4	7	7.500	-3.500	-3.938	7.938	6.862	2.925	1.075	1.075	1.156	26.88%
14	Quarter 8	14	8	7.875	6.125	5.375	8.625	7.821	13.196	0.804	0.804	0.646	5.74%
15	Quarter 9	10	9	7.875	2.125	2.000	8.000	8.780	10.780	-0.780	0.780	0.609	7.80%
16	Quarter 10	3	10	8.250	-5.250	-4.313	7.313	9.739	5.427	-2.427	2.427	5.889	80.89%
17	Quarter 11	5	11	8.750	-3.750	-3.938	8.938	10.698	6.761	-1.761	1.761	3.100	35.22%
18	Quarter 12	16	12	9.750	6.250	5.375	10.625	11.657	17.032	-1.032	1.032	1.066	6.45%
19	Quarter 13	12	13	10.750	1.250	2.000	10.000	12.616	14.616	-2.616	2.616	6.845	21.80%
20	Quarter 14	9	14	11.750	-2.750	-4.313	13.313	13.575	9.263	-0.263	0.263	0.069	2.92%
21	Quarter 15	7	15	13.250	-6.250	-3.938	10.938	14.534	10.597	-3.597	3.597	12.937	51.38%
22	Quarter 16	22	16	14.125	7.875	5.375	16.625	15.493	20.868	1.132	1.132	1.281	5.14%
23	Quarter 17	18	17	15.000	3.000	2.000	16.000	16.452	18.452	-0.452	0.452	0.205	2.51%
24	Quarter 18	10	18	17.375	-7.375	-4.313	14.313	17.411	13.099	-3.099	3.099	9.603	30.99%
25	Quarter 19	13	19			-3.938	16.938	18.370	14.433	-1.433	1.433	2.053	11.02%
26	Quarter 20	35	20			5.375	29.625	19.329	24.704	10.296	10.296	105.998	29.42%
27										Average	2.276	9.982	45.35%
28						Intercept	0.149				MAD	MSE	MAPE
29						Slope	0.959						
30													
31	Seasonal Differences												
32		Season 1	Season 2	Season 3	Season 4								
33				-2.250	1.250								
34		1.625	-1.875	-3.500	6.125								
35		2.125	-5.250	-3.750	6.250								
36		1.250	-2.750	-6.250	7.875								
37		3.000	-7.375										
38	**Average**	2.000	-4.313	-3.938	5.375								
39													
40	Forecasts for Future Periods												
41	Period	Unseasonalized forecast	Seasonal index	Seasonalized forecast									
42	21.000	20.288	2.000	22.288									
43	22.000	21.248	-4.313	16.935									
44	23.000	22.207	-3.938	18.269									
45	24.000	23.166	5.375	28.541									

Annotations:
- Input data for 20 quarters
- Regression (trend line) parameters
- Measures of forecast error
- Seasonal differences in column E have been collected here.
- Seasonal indices, also shown in column F
- Seasonal index added to forecast
- Forecasts using trend line equation

Notice that the seasonal forecasts for quarters 2 and 3, shown in cells I8 and I9, respectively, are negative (because both quarters have negative seasonal indices that exceed their unseasonalized sales forecasts). Clearly, this is illogical in practice, and we should adjust these seasonal forecasts to zero. *Note:* We have not adjusted these values in Screenshot 12.13 to facilitate this discussion.

Finally, we compute measures of forecast error.	4. *Computation of forecast error measures, columns J through M.* We compute the MAD, MSE, and MAPE values in cells K27, L27, and M27, respectively.

The MAPE value of 45.35% in this case is much worse than the MAPE value of 23.74% obtained using the multiplicative model. Sandy may therefore be better off staying with the multiplicative model. If desired, we can ask ExcelModules to also draw line plots of the actual and forecasted values for the additive model. Although this chart is not shown here, it is included in the Excel file 12.13.xls on the CD-ROM that accompanies this textbook.

⟹ SELF-TEST

- ■ Before taking the self-test, refer back to the learning objectives at the beginning of the chapter, the notes in the margins, and the glossary at the end of the chapter.
- ■ Use the key at the back of the book to correct your answers.
- ■ Restudy pages that correspond to any questions that you answered incorrectly or material you feel uncertain about.

1. Qualitative forecasting models include
   a. sales force composite.
   b. Delphi.
   c. consumer market survey.
   d. all of the above.
   e. none of the above.

2. A forecast that projects a company's sales is
   a. an economic forecast.
   b. a technological forecast.
   c. a demand forecast.
   d. none of the above.

3. The method that considers several variables that are related to the variable being predicted is
   a. exponential smoothing.
   b. causal forecasting.
   c. weighted moving average.
   d. all of the above.
   e. none of the above.

4. Exponential smoothing is an example of a causal model.
   a. True   b. False

5. A time-series model incorporates the various factors that might influence the quantity being forecast.
   a. True   b. False

6. In a multiplicative decomposition model, the forecast is calculated as _____.

7. Decomposing a time series refers to breaking down past data into the components of
   a. constants and variations.
   b. trend, seasonality, cycles, and random variations.
   c. strategic, tactical, and operational variations.
   d. long-term, short-term, and medium-term variations.
   e. none of the above.

8. In exponential smoothing, when the smoothing constant is high, more weight is placed on the more recent data.
   a. True   b. False

9. Three popular measures of forecast accuracy are
   a. total error, average error, and mean error.

   b. average error, median error, and maximum error.
   c. median error, minimum error, and maximum absolute error.
   d. mean absolute error, mean squared error, and mean absolute percent error.
   e. none of the above.

10. The value of α that minimizes the MAD in exponential smoothing can be computed in Excel using
    a. Goal Seek.
    b. Solver.
    c. ExcelModules.
    d. the SUMPRODUCT function.

11. Unfortunately, regression analysis can only be used to develop a forecast based on a single independent variable.
    a. True   b. False

12. A fundamental weakness of causal forecasting methods is that we must first forecast the value of the independent variable and *then* apply that value in the forecast of the dependent variable.
    a. True   b. False

13. With regard to a regression-based forecast, the *standard error of the estimate* gives a measure of
    a. the overall accuracy of the forecast.
    b. the time period for which the forecast is valid.
    c. the time required to derive the forecast equation.
    d. the maximum error of the forecast.
    e. none of the above.

14. One method of choosing among various smoothing constants when using exponential smoothing is to evaluate the MAPE for each smoothing constant and choose the smoothing constant that provides the minimum MAPE.
    a. True   b. False

15. No single forecast methodology is appropriate under all conditions.
    a. True   b. False

16. The difference between a *dependent* and an *independent* variable is that _____.

17. Quantitative forecasting methods include
   a. _____,
   b. _____,
   c. _____,
   d. _____,
   e. _____.
18. A time-series variable typically has the four components:
   a. _____
   b. _____
   c. _____
   d. _____

19. Time-series data that show no significant upward or downward movement (or trend) over time are called
   a. immovable.
   b. constant.
   c. stationary.
   d. nonstationary.
20. The main difference between simple and multiple regression is _____.
21. The difference between a *moving average* model and an *exponential smoothing* model is that _____.
22. The purpose of drawing a scatter diagram is to _____.

DISCUSSION QUESTIONS AND PROBLEMS

Discussion Questions

12-1 Briefly describe the steps used to develop a forecasting system.

12-2 What is a time-series forecasting model?

12-3 What is the difference between a causal model and a time-series model?

12-4 What is a qualitative forecasting model, and when is using it appropriate?

12-5 What is the meaning of least squares in a regression model?

12-6 What are some of the problems and drawbacks of the moving average forecasting model?

12-7 What effect does the value of the smoothing constant have on the weight given to the past forecast and the past observed value?

12-8 Briefly describe the Delphi technique.

12-9 What is MAPE, and why is it important in the selection and use of forecasting models?

12-10 Describe how you can use plots to determine whether a forecasting model is valid.

12-11 What is a correlation coefficient? Why is it useful?

12-12 Explain how Solver can be used to identify the optimal weights in the weighted moving average model.

Problems

12-13 Data collected on the yearly demand for 25-kilogram bags of fertilizer at Wallace Garden Supply are in the following table:

YEAR	BAGS (IN THOUSANDS)	YEAR	BAGS (IN THOUSANDS)
1	4	7	7
2	6	8	9
3	4	9	12
4	5	10	14
5	10	11	15
6	8		

(a) Develop two-year, three-year, and four-year moving averages to forecast demand in year 12.
(b) Forecast demand with a three-year weighted moving average in which demand in the most recent year is given a weight of 2 and demands in the other two years are each given a weight of 1.
(c) Forecast demand by using exponential smoothing with a smoothing constant of 0.3. Assume that the forecast for year 1 is 5000 bags to begin the procedure.
(d) Which of the methods analyzed here would you use? Explain your answer.

12-14 Susan Armstrong is a university student who has just completed her third year. The following table summarizes her grade point average (GPA) for each of the past nine semesters:

YEAR	SEMESTER	GPA
First	Fall	2.2
	Winter	2.7
	Summer	2.5
Second	Fall	2.4
	Winter	3.0
	Summer	2.7
Third	Fall	2.5
	Winter	3.6
	Summer	3.2

(a) Forecast Susan's GPA for the fall semester of her fourth year by using a three-period moving average.
(b) Forecast Susan's GPA for the fall semester of her fourth year by using exponential smoothing with $\alpha = 0.3$.
(c) Which of the two methods provides a more accurate forecast? Justify your answer.
(d) If you decide to use a three-period weighted moving average, find the optimal weights that would minimize MAPE. Is this method an improvement over the previous two methods?

12-15 Daily sales volume for Campbell's Convenience Store is shown in the following table:

DAY	SALES ($)	DAY	SALES ($)
1	522	6	556
2	318	7	589
3	508	8	575
4	652	9	606
5	488	10	625

Develop two-day, three-day, and four-day moving averages to forecast the sales for each day. What is the forecast for day 11 in each case?

12-16 Consider the data given in Problem 12-15 for Campbell's Convenience Store.

(a) If the store wants to use exponential smoothing to forecast the sales volume, what is the optimal value of α that would minimize MAPE? What is the forecast for day 11 using this model?
(b) If the store wants to use linear trend analysis to forecast the sales volume, what is the linear equation that best fits the data? What is the forecast for day 11 using this model?
(c) Which of the methods analyzed here and in Problem 12-15 would you use? Explain your answer.

12-17 The following table shows the number of DVD players that Electronic Depot has sold during the past 12 weeks:

WEEK	SALES	WEEK	SALES
1	17	7	19
2	22	8	20
3	25	9	17
4	16	10	25
5	28	11	33
6	23	12	32

Develop two-week, three-week, and four-week moving averages to forecast the sales for each week. What is the forecast for week 13 in each case?

12-18 Consider the data given in Problem 12-17 for DVD player sales at Electronic Depot.

(a) If Electronic Depot decides to forecast sales by using a three-period weighted moving average, what are the optimal weights that minimize MAPE? What would be the week 13 forecast using these weights?
(b) If Electronic Depot decides to forecast sales by using exponential smoothing, what is the optimal value of α that minimizes MAPE? What would be the week 13 forecast using this procedure?
(c) Which of the methods analyzed here and in Problem 12-17 would you use? Explain your answer.

12-19 Sales of Cool-Man air conditioners have grown steadily during the past five years, as shown in the following table:

YEAR	SALES
1	450
2	495
3	518
4	563
5	584

(a) Using exponential smoothing constants of 0.3, 0.6, and 0.9, develop forecasts for years 2 through 6. The sales manager had predicted, before the business started, that year 1's sales would be 410 air conditioners. Which smoothing constant gives the most accurate forecast?
(b) Use a three-year moving average forecasting model to forecast sales of Cool-Man air conditioners.
(c) Using linear trend analysis, develop a forecasting model for the sales of Cool-Man air conditioners.
(d) Which of the methods analyzed here would you use? Explain your answer.

12-20 Highland Automotive wishes to forecast the number of new cars that will be sold next week. The following table summarizes the number of new cars sold during each of the past 12 weeks:

WEEK	NUMBER SOLD	WEEK	NUMBER SOLD
1	20	7	26
2	24	8	24
3	21	9	27
4	25	10	27
5	19	11	25
6	23	12	29

(a) Provide a forecast by using a three-week weighted moving average technique with weights 4, 2, and 1 (4 = most recent).
(b) Forecast sales by using an exponential smoothing model with $\alpha = 0.4$.
(c) Highland would like to forecast sales by using linear trend analysis. What is the linear equation that best fits the data?
(d) Which of the methods analyzed here would you use? Explain your answer.

12-21 The operations manager of a musical instrument distributor feels that demand for bass drums may be related to the number of television appearances by the popular rock group Green Shades during the preceding month. The manager has collected the data shown in the following table:

DEMAND	TV APPEARANCES
3	3
6	4
7	7
5	6
10	8
8	5

(a) Graph these data to see whether a linear equation might describe the relationship between the group's television shows and bass drum sales.

(b) Use the least-squares regression method to derive a forecasting equation.

(c) What is your estimate for bass drum sales if Green Shades performed on TV nine times last month?

12-22 Sales of industrial vacuum cleaners at King's Supply Co. over the past 13 months were as follows:

MONTH	SALES (IN THOUSANDS)	MONTH	SALES (IN THOUSANDS)
January	11	August	14
February	14	September	17
March	16	October	12
April	10	November	14
May	15	December	16
June	17	January	11
July	11		

(a) Using a moving average with three periods, determine the demand for vacuum cleaners for next February.

(b) Using a three-period weighted moving average with weights 3, 2, and 1 (3 = most recent), determine the demand for vacuum cleaners for February.

(c) Evaluate and comment on the accuracy of each of these models.

12-23 Emergency calls to the 911 system in Vancouver for the past 24 weeks are as follows (earliest week is shown first): 50, 35, 25, 40, 45, 35, 20, 30, 35, 20, 15, 40, 55, 35, 25, 55, 55, 40, 35, 60, 75, 50, 40, and 65.

(a) Assuming an initial forecast of 50 calls for week 1, use exponential smoothing with α = 0.1, 0.6, and 0.9 to forecast calls for each week. What is the forecast for the 25th week in each case?

(b) Actual calls during the 25th week were 85. Which smoothing constant provides a superior forecast?

12-24 Passenger distances flown on OntAir Airlines, a commuter firm serving Ontario, are as follows for the past 12 weeks:

WEEK	KILOMETRES (IN THOUSANDS)	WEEK	KILOMETRES (IN THOUSANDS)
1	17	7	20
2	21	8	18
3	19	9	22
4	23	10	20
5	18	11	15
6	16	12	22

(a) Assuming an initial forecast of 17 000 kilometres for week 1, use exponential smoothing with α = 0.2, 0.5, and 0.9 to forecast kilometres for weeks 2 through 12. What is the forecast for week 13 in each case?

(b) Evaluate and comment on the accuracy of each of these models.

12-25 Consulting income at Tanya Smith Associates for the period February–July has been as follows:

MONTH	INCOME (IN THOUSANDS)
February	$70.0
March	68.5
April	64.8
May	71.7
June	71.3
July	72.8

(a) Use exponential smoothing with α = 0.1 and 0.3 to forecast August's income. Assume that the initial forecast for February is $65 000.

(b) Which smoothing constant provides a better forecast? Justify your answer.

(c) Determine the optimal value of α that minimizes MAPE.

12-26 A provincial credit union has been growing steadily since it was established in 1961. Deposits have increased slowly but surely over the years, despite some years when the economy has been sluggish. To help develop a strategic plan, management at the credit union wants to develop a one-year forecast of deposits. Historical data for deposits from the inception of the credit union in 1961 up until 2004 are shown in the table above. The table also shows the provincial GDP for the corresponding years.

(a) Using three forecasting models: (1) exponential smoothing with α= 0.6, (2) trend analysis, and (3) linear regression, discuss which forecasting model fits best for the credit union's strategic plan. Justify why one model should be selected over another.

(b) Examine the data carefully. Can you make a case for excluding a portion of the information? Why? Would that change your choice of model?

12-27 Bus and subway ridership in Toronto during the summer months is believed to be heavily tied to the number of tourists visiting the city. During the past 12 years, the following data have been obtained.

(a) Use trend analysis to forecast ridership in years 13, 14, and 15. How well does the model fit the data?

(b) Plot the relationship between the number of tourists and ridership. Is a linear model reasonable?

(c) Develop a linear regression relationship between the number of tourists and ridership.

(d) What is the expected ridership if 10 million tourists visit the city next year?

YEAR	NUMBER OF TOURISTS (IN MILLIONS)	RIDERSHIP (IN HUNDREDS OF THOUSANDS)
1	7	15
2	2	10
3	6	13
4	4	15
5	14	25
6	15	27
7	16	24
8	12	20
9	14	27
10	20	44
11	15	34
12	7	17

Table for Problem 12-26

YEAR	DEPOSITS (IN MILLIONS)	GDP (IN BILLIONS)	YEAR	DEPOSITS (IN MILLIONS)	GDP (IN BILLIONS)	YEAR	DEPOSITS (IN MILLIONS)	GDP (IN BILLIONS)
1961	$0.25	$0.4	1976	$ 2.3	$1.6	1991	$24.1	$3.9
1962	0.24	0.4	1977	2.8	1.5	1992	25.6	3.8
1963	0.24	0.5	1978	2.8	1.6	1993	30.3	3.8
1964	0.26	0.7	1979	2.7	1.7	1994	36.0	3.7
1965	0.25	0.9	1980	3.9	1.9	1995	31.1	4.1
1966	0.30	1.0	1981	4.9	1.9	1996	31.7	4.1
1967	0.31	1.4	1982	5.3	2.3	1997	38.5	4.0
1968	0.32	1.7	1983	6.2	2.5	1998	47.9	4.5
1969	0.24	1.3	1984	4.1	2.8	1999	49.1	4.6
1970	0.26	1.2	1985	4.5	2.9	2000	55.8	4.5
1971	0.25	1.1	1986	6.1	3.4	2001	70.1	4.6
1972	0.33	0.9	1987	7.7	3.8	2002	70.9	4.6
1973	0.50	1.2	1988	10.1	4.1	2003	79.1	4.7
1974	0.95	1.2	1989	15.2	4.0	2004	94.0	5.0
1975	1.70	1.2	1990	18.1	4.0			

12-28 Kelsey Ross, a Toronto psychologist, specializes in treating patients who are phobic, afraid to leave their homes. The following table indicates how many patients Dr. Ross has seen each year for the past 10 years. It also indicates the crime rate (robberies per 1000 population) in Toronto during each year:

YEAR	NUMBER OF PATIENTS	CRIME RATE
1	36	58.3
2	33	61.6
3	40	73.4
4	41	75.7
5	40	81.1
6	55	89.0
7	60	101.1
8	54	94.8
9	58	103.3
10	61	116.2

Using trend analysis, how many patients do you think Dr. Ross will see in years 11, 12, and 13? How well does the model fit the data?

12-29 Consider the patient data for Dr. Ross given in Problem 12-28.
(a) Plot the relationship between the crime rate and

Dr. Ross's patient load. Is a linear model between these two variables reasonable?
(b) Apply linear regression to study the relationship between the crime rate and Dr. Ross's patient load.
(c) If the crime rate increases to 131.2 in year 11, how many patients will Dr. Ross treat?
(d) If the crime rate drops to 90.6, what is the patient projection?

12-30 In the past two years at Judy Holmes's tire dealership, 200 and 250 radials, respectively, were sold in fall, 300 and 350 radials in winter, 150 and 165 radials in spring, and 285 and 300 radials in summer. With a major expansion planned, Ms. Holmes projects sales next year to increase to 1200 radials. What will the seasonalized demand be each season?

12-31 Management of Davis's Department Store has used time-series extrapolation to forecast retail sales for the next four quarters. The sales estimates are $100 000, $120 000, $140 000, and $160 000 for the respective quarters. Seasonal indices for the four quarters have been found to be 1.30, 0.90, 0.70, and 1.10, respectively. Compute the seasonalized sales forecast for each quarter.

12-32 Liam Smith is thinking about investing in Blue Star Manufacturing Company, which makes central air conditioning units. The company has been in business for over 50 years, and Liam believes it is very stable. Based on his investing knowledge and experience, Liam believes that the dividend paid out by the company is a function of earnings per share (EPS). Using the internet, Liam has been able to find the EPS and dividend per share paid by Blue Star for each of the past 10 years, as shown in the following table:

YEAR	EPS ($)	DIVIDEND PER SHARE ($)
1995	1.59	0.39
1996	0.95	0.24
1997	1.14	0.29
1998	1.19	0.26
1999	0.76	0.15
2000	1.29	0.49
2001	0.97	0.21
2002	1.23	0.37
2003	1.14	0.29
2004	0.82	0.19

(a) Develop a regression model to predict the dividend per share based on EPS.
(b) Identify and interpret the R^2-value.
(c) The EPS next year is projected be $0.33. What is the expected dividend?

12-33 Thirteen students entered the undergraduate business program at Lavalle College two years ago. The table below indicates what their GPAs were after they were in the program for two years and what each student scored on a compulsory mathematics aptitude test (maximum score 800).

(a) Is there a meaningful relationship between GPAs and math aptitude test scores? Justify your answer.
(b) If Noah gets a score of 450 on his mathematics aptitude test, what is his predicted GPA?
(c) If Gita gets a perfect score of 800 on her mathematics aptitude test, what is her predicted GPA? Is it appropriate to use this model to predict Gita's GPA? Why or why not?

STUDENT	MATH	GPA
A	421	2.90
B	377	2.93
C	585	3.00
D	690	3.45
E	608	3.66
F	390	2.88
G	415	2.15
H	481	2.53
I	729	3.22
J	501	1.99
K	613	2.75
L	709	3.90
M	366	1.60

12-34 Waverly Smith is shopping for a used Volkswagen Jetta and feels that there is a relationship between the mileage and market value of the car. The following table provides data on previous car sales from the local area:

CAR	DISTANCE (km)	MARKET VALUE ($)	AGE (YEARS)
1	10 600	16 200	1
2	21 800	16 000	1
3	34 000	12 500	3
4	41 700	11 300	3
5	53 500	14 800	4
6	57 200	12 900	5
7	65 800	11 500	7
8	72 100	9 900	6
9	76 500	8 200	8
10	84 700	9 500	9

(a) Develop a simple regression model to predict the market value of a Volkswagen Jetta based on the distance it has been driven.
(b) What percentage of the market value variation is explained by the distance variable?
(c) Waverly has found a car with 45 700 kilometres. Construct a 95% confidence interval for the market value of this car.

12-35 Waverly Smith (see Problem 12-34) would like to investigate the effect of adding the age of the car (in years) to the regression model. The table in Problem 12-34 includes the ages of the original 10 cars.
(a) Develop a multiple regression model to predict the market value of a Volkswagen Jetta based on its distance driven and age.
(b) What percentage of the selling price variation is explained by this expanded model?
(c) The car that Waverly found with 45 700 kilometres is five years old. What is the revised 95% confidence interval for the market value of this car? Explain why this interval is different from the one in Problem 12-34(c).

12-36 Lake Louise College is a small business school that offers an MBA program. The main entrance criterion for admission to the MBA program is the Graduate Management Admission Test (GMAT) score. The following table provides the GPAs of 12 students who have graduated recently, along with their GMAT scores and ages:

STUDENT	GPA	GMAT	AGE
1	3.70	660	34
2	3.00	580	29
3	3.25	450	24
4	4.00	710	39
5	3.52	550	30
6	2.83	430	27
7	3.80	540	35
8	4.00	590	42
9	3.65	720	24
10	3.47	480	30
11	3.33	520	27
12	3.75	670	28

(a) Develop a simple regression model to predict the GPA of a student based on his or her GMAT score.
(b) Identify and interpret the R^2-value.
(c) A new graduate student has a GMAT score of 600. Construct a 90% confidence interval for this student's predicted GPA.

12-37 Lake Louise College (see Problem 12-36) would like to investigate the effect of adding the age of the student to the regression model. The table in Problem 12-36 includes the ages of the original 12 students.
(a) Develop a multiple regression model to predict the GPA of a student based on his or her GMAT score and age.
(b) Identify and interpret the R^2-value for this expanded regression model.
(c) The new student with a GMAT score of 600 is 29 years old. What is the revised 90% confidence interval for this student's predicted GPA? Explain why this interval is different from the one in Problem 12-36(c).

12-38 Earl's Hardware in Edmonton, Alberta, advertises and sells snow blowers each season. The following table provides the annual demand, level of advertising, in dollars, and snowfall, in centimetres, for the past eight years:

YEAR	DEMAND (UNITS)	ADVERTISING	SNOWFALL (cm)
1	40	$5000	195.6
2	37	4500	149.9
3	25	2800	119.4
4	42	3800	139.7
5	32	4000	134.6
6	29	3400	114.3
7	33	3600	139.7
8	36	3200	121.9

(a) Develop a simple regression model to predict the demand for snow blowers based on the number of advertising dollars spent.
(b) What percentage of the demand variation is explained by the level of advertising?
(c) Next year's advertising budget is $3600. What is the predicted demand for snow blowers?

12-39 Earl's Hardware (see Problem 12-38) would like to investigate the effect of adding annual snowfall to the regression model. The table in Problem 12-38 includes the annual snowfall (in centimetres) for the past eight years.
(a) Develop a multiple regression model to predict the demand for snow blowers based on the advertising budget and the amount of snowfall.
(b) What percentage of the demand variation is explained by this expanded model?

(c) What is the predicted demand for snow blowers if the advertising budget is $3600 and expected snowfall is 152.4 centimetres?

12-40 The Fowler Martial Arts Academy trains young boys and girls in self-defence. Joan Fowler, the owner of the academy, notes that monthly revenue is higher when school is in session but quite low when school is out (because many children are away on vacation or at summer camp). She has researched revenues for the past four years and obtained the following information:

MONTH	2001	2002	2003	2004
January	$54 525	$52 978	$52 066	$51 141
February	58 142	58 145	61 921	62 647
March	18 362	19 756	23 249	23 278
April	25 429	25 975	27 083	26 150
May	22 322	23 720	25 072	27 445
June	14 617	13 376	15 598	16 579
July	15 534	16 609	14 807	18 261
August	15 108	18 359	18 969	18 627
September	15 408	18 124	20 202	22 084
October	53 918	56 279	56 149	56 868
November	83 188	83 298	82 176	84 064
December	72 913	74 194	75 539	76 531

Decompose Joan's data by using a multiplicative model. Use the model to forecast revenues for 2005. Comment on the validity of the model.

12-41 In addition to his day job as an engineer, Charlie Huang runs a small ethnic grocery store in Vancouver. The shop stocks food items from Southeast Asian countries and caters to the large population of people from this region who live in Vancouver and surrounding areas. Charlie wants to develop a quantitative model to forecast sales. His sales data (in thousands) for the past 16 quarters are as follows:

QUARTER	2001	2002	2003	2004
Quarter 1	$48.6	$49.5	$54.7	$57.0
Quarter 2	54.2	56.0	59.9	63.9
Quarter 3	59.8	63.5	65.0	68.6
Quarter 4	79.8	85.5	89.0	94.2

Develop a multiplicative decomposition model for Charlie's sales data. Use the model to forecast revenues for 2005. Comment on the validity of the model.

12-42 The GNP for each quarter of 2001–2004 is shown in the following table:

YEAR	QUARTER	GNP (IN BILLIONS)
2001	1	$ 8 635
	2	8 700
	3	8 802
	4	8 975
2002	1	9 113
	2	9 196
	3	9 334
	4	9 546
2003	1	9 671
	2	9 846
	3	9 893
	4	9 983
2004	1	10 038
	2	10 081
	3	10 109
	4	10 188

(a) Find the optimal value of α that would minimize MAPE for the exponential smoothing model.
(b) What is the linear trend equation that best fits the data? Forecast the GNP for the first quarter of 2005 by using this equation.
(c) Forecast the GNP for the first quarter of 2005 by using a four-period moving average.
(d) Which of these methods is most appropriate to use? Justify your answer.

12-43 Using the data from Problem 12-42, forecast the GNP for each quarter of 2005 by using the multiplicative decomposition model. What is the MAPE value for this model?

12-44 The average price per litre of gasoline in major Canadian cities for each month during a three-year period in the early 2000s when fuel prices soared is shown in the following table:

MONTH	YEAR 1	YEAR 2	YEAR 3
January	$0.972	$1.301	$1.472
February	0.955	1.369	1.484
March	0.991	1.541	1.447
April	1.117	1.506	1.564
May	1.178	1.498	1.729
June	1.148	1.617	1.640
July	1.189	1.593	1.482
August	1.255	1.510	1.427
September	1.280	1.582	1.531
October	1.274	1.559	1.362
November	1.264	1.555	1.263
December	1.298	1.489	1.131

(a) Using exponential smoothing with $\alpha = 0.5$, what is the gasoline price forecast for January of year four?
(b) What is the linear trend equation that best fits the data? Forecast the average gasoline price for January of year four by using this equation.
(c) Which method is more accurate?

12-45 Using the data from Problem 12-44, forecast the average gasoline price for each month in year four by using the multiplicative decomposition model. What is the MAPE value for this model?

12-46 Quarterly sales figures for the Durco Pump Company, in thousands, for the past four years are shown in the following table:

QUARTER	YEAR 1	YEAR 2	YEAR 3	YEAR 4
1	$290	$339	$310	$346
2	327	350	347	330
3	372	325	392	366
4	408	417	425	395

(a) Forecast the demand for the first quarter of year five by using a four-period moving average model.
(b) What is the linear trend equation that best fits the data? Forecast the demand for the first quarter of year five by using this equation.
(c) Which method is more accurate?

12-47 Consider the data from Problem 12-46.
(a) Develop a sales forecast for each quarter in year five by using the multiplicative decomposition model.
(b) Repeat the computations by using an additive decomposition model.
(c) Which decomposition model is more accurate? Explain your answer.

12-48 The following table shows the quarterly demand, in thousands of cases, for a national beer distributor over the past four years:

QUARTER	YEAR 1	YEAR 2	YEAR 3	YEAR 4
1	280	321	419	266
2	485	493	502	510
3	423	515	487	501
4	330	271	468	516

(a) Forecast the demand for the first quarter of year five by using a four-period moving average model.
(b) Forecast the demand for the first quarter of year five by using an exponential smoothing model with $\alpha = 0.3$.
(c) Which method is more accurate?

12-49 Consider the data from Problem 12-48.
(a) Forecast the demand for beer for each quarter in year five by using the multiplicative decomposition model.
(b) Repeat the computations by using an additive decomposition model.
(c) Which decomposition model is more accurate? Explain your answer.

⇒ CASE STUDY 12.1

Quantico Computerware

On January 4, John Markham, the assistant plant manager for Quantico Computerware Ltd., had yet to decide on a production scheduling and inventory management policy for the computer diskettes to be manufactured at the company's new plant in Richmond, British Columbia. Although the company planned to start up the plant on February 7, he had to present his proposal at the management meeting on January 7.

COMPANY BACKGROUND

Quantico, a U.S. company based in Palo Alto, California, manufactured and sold more than 50 products used in the computer industry. Last year, its North American sales had exceeded $150 million. Computer diskettes, including 700 000 boxes exported to Canada, had accounted for a significant portion of this amount. As a result, Quantico saw the Canadian market as a future growth area.

Two years ago, Quantico management realized that the company would have to increase its diskette production capacity. Both political and economic factors led to the decision to build a plant in Canada to supply the Canadian market. Subsequently, the company selected the Richmond, British Columbia, site and built the plant. It had almost finished installing and testing the equipment, key production employees were completing their training in the United States, and everything was on schedule for the February 7 start-up date.

THE CANADIAN MARKET

Sales of computers and computer-related products were booming in Canada. Industry observers expected the high growth rate, particularly in the personal computer market, to continue. The company's records showed that each of Quantico's five diskette models had sold equally well in Canada over the last three years and that there was very little seasonality in diskette demand. However, Quantico was uncertain whether these trends would continue over the long term. With its new Canadian plant, Quantico had forecast first-year sales of 840 000 boxes of diskettes, which the company would sell to distributors. Although the selling price would vary by model from $3.20 to $4.90 per box of 10 diskettes (averaging $4.40), the cost of production would be fairly constant across the product line.

At its previous meeting, the management group had decided to emphasize fast delivery and to avoid any chance of lost sales through stockouts. At the same time, the management group had been aware that the plant could not build up inventory indiscriminately; the accounting department estimated that Quantico's annual inventory carrying costs were 25%. Thus, the management group had instructed Mr. Markham to be certain that his proposal would prevent finished goods stockouts while minimizing costs.

DISKETTE PRODUCTION

The company had invested millions of dollars in highly automated, high-technology equipment for the new plant. Because of variations in the five types of diskettes, operators would have to shut down the line for about 45 minutes so that they could reset the equipment to switch from one type of diskette to another. Each diskette would then go through the same sequence of production steps, at a rate of 6000 diskettes per hour.

The plant would operate from 9:00 A.M. to 5:00 P.M., with one hour (unpaid) off for lunch and breaks, for 250 days per year. Ten production workers were scheduled to start on February 7. Quantico's accountants had advised Mr. Markham that hourly direct labour wages would average $18 per employee for regular time and $27 for overtime. Benefits would amount to 40% of regular pay.

As part of a bulk contract with Quantico's U.S. parent, the company had arranged that all raw material requirements could be delivered to the new plant on short notice. Material costs for diskettes would be $1.77 per box.

Because Quantico's U.S. parent had agreed to continue to supply the Canadian market until the Richmond plant was fully operational, Mr. Markham did not need to worry about building up an initial inventory. Consequently, he could implement the regular production schedule on the start-up date. All that remained was to determine a good schedule—one that would avoid stockouts while keeping costs low. Short runs of each type of diskette would minimize inventory carrying costs, but the costs of set-up time would be very high. Conversely, long runs would reduce set-up costs but create high inventory levels.

As Mr. Markham was about to begin drafting a production schedule, he received a call from Susan Vincze, his counterpart in the marketing department.

"Hi, John. We've looked again at our sales forecasts. You will remember that our earlier projections called for annual volumes of each diskette model of 165 000 to 170 000. I'm afraid we blew it. We based those calculations on overall imports for the past three years. However, during that time, there has been quite a shift in the balance between models.

Source: Professors Ken Bowlby and John Haywood-Farmer prepared this case solely to provide material for class discussion. The authors do not intend to illustrate either effective or ineffective handling of a managerial situation. The authors may have disguised certain names and other identifying information to protect confidentiality.

Even though the three-year totals are about the same for each model, the sales of some have gone up during that period and others down. In particular, sales of the two 5.25-inch models are falling as the more rugged and higher capacity 3.5-inch diskettes replace them. Within the 3.5-inch line, sales of the high density models are rising the fastest. I'll send you a copy of our new forecasts (see Table 12.9). I hope this doesn't screw you up."

After hanging up the phone, Mr. Markham wondered what the new forecasts would look like, if they would affect the schedule, and whether the people in marketing had considered demand variability. He decided to enquire.

"Hi, Susan. I have been thinking about the changes to your forecasts. As you know, although forecasting isn't easy, a lot rests on the results. Do you still think the sales will show no significant daily variation during the year?"

"We're pretty confident about that John. Our import data show no variation at all. We still receive one shipment every three months. I guess sales could still vary though. Let me look into it and get back to you."

Later that day, Ms. Vincze phoned back.

"You were right, John. There *is* some leeway in our projections. Those import stats simply hid the obvious. We have redone the forecasts. A copy to you is in the mail (see Table 12.10). I am confident that these numbers will be OK."

"Sure!" thought Mr. Markham. He decided to draft three schedules to accommodate the changes that he had seen during the past day from equal demand for each model, to demand variation between models, and finally to variation within models. He knew that the forecasts would be a topic of discussion at the management meeting in three days. He thought, "I wonder what tomorrow will bring."

TABLE 12.9

Revised Diskette Sales Forecast Based on Demand Variation between Models (Number of Boxes)

DISKETTE	DAILY DEMAND	ANNUAL DEMAND
Q5A	300	75 000
Q5B	540	135 000
Q3A	720	180 000
Q3B	860	215 000
Q3C	940	235 000
Totals	3360	840 000

TABLE 12.10

Rerevised Diskette Sales Forecast Based on Demand Variation within Models (Number of Boxes)

DISKETTE	DAILY DEMAND	ANNUAL DEMAND
Q5A	200–400	60 000–80 000
Q5B	400–600	105 000–140 000
Q3A	650 –900	170 000–200 000
Q3B	780 –020	200 000–230 000
Q3C	700–980	210 000–240 000
Totals	2730–3900	745 000–890 000

⟫ CASE STUDY 12.2

Forecasting Ticket Sales at CineBarn

The CineBarn is a large cinema complex in Winnipeg. The complex has 18 screens and a total of 4620 seats. Ticket sales vary from day to day but are generally higher on the weekends (Friday and Saturday nights have the highest attendance). Also, children's matinees increase attendance on Sunday. A couple of years ago the CineBarn initiated a half-price policy on Tuesdays to help boost box-office sales on an otherwise slow night.

The CineBarn's co-owner and manager, Eryn Margolese, wants to develop a forecasting model for daily ticket sales at the complex, since this will help her to plan staffing schedules, order quantities for the concessions in the four-level building (there is one concession on each floor), and deal with other aspects of running a large multi-screen movie complex.

Eryn has decided that when the attendance is anticipated to be less than 2500 she will open only two of the four concessions (on the first and third floors), and she will reduce the staff by four persons. The co-owner of the CineBarn, Liam Smith, points out that popular movies usually run simultaneously on two or more screens and recommends that on slow nights those films be shown on only one screen, thereby cutting the staff even further.

In a strategic planning meeting, Liam says, "You know, all of this is highly speculative, we can't make any meaningful decisions until we analyze the data and see what the ticket sales look like on the various days of the week." Eryn nods and replies, "I manage the day-to-day operations of the CineBarn, so we have all the data on file. I will produce a spreadsheet showing attendance for the last month or so and we can use that to develop a plan for the future."

"Great idea," Liam says. "As soon as the spreadsheet is ready send it to me as an attachment. My sister Waverly is a whiz with statistics—I will ask her to run a statistical analysis to detect the weekly pattern of ticket sales."

Eryn asks, "Which statistical analyses would *you* recommend, Liam?" Liam says, "Well, we can try to construct a causal model using regression analysis but we would need to include some explanatory variables—what other data can you include in the spreadsheet?"

| DAY | TICKET SALES | | | | |
	WEEK 1	WEEK 2	WEEK 3	WEEK 4	WEEK 5
Mon	2120	2096	2246	2256	3421
Tues	2870	2768	2872	2879	3041
Wed	2230	2185	2224	2320	2076
Thurs	2459	2543	2446	2654	2580
Fri	3120	3200	3180	3280	3175
Sat	3564	3480	3560	3568	3762
Sun	3342	3312	3427	3342	

| DAY | TEMPERATURE (CELSIUS) | | | | |
	WEEK 1	WEEK 2	WEEK 3	WEEK 4	WEEK 5
Mon	−8	3	2	−6	6
Tues	−2	−1	2	−4	2
Wed	0	−5	1	−7	−3
Thurs	−4	−3	−4	−2	−5
Fri	1	7	3	4	0
Sat	4	10	7	7	6
Sun	5	8	6	5	

Liam and Eryn spend the next half hour brainstorming the problem of which explanatory variables to include in a multiple regression model. After serious consideration, they decide that a useful regression model would involve a variable that differentiates between weekdays (Monday to Thursday) and weekends (Friday, Saturday, Sunday). Therefore, they decide to include the variable

$$X_1 = \begin{cases} 1 \text{ if day = Monday, Tuesday, Wednesday, or Thursday} \\ 0 \text{ if day = Friday, Saturday, or Sunday} \end{cases}$$

The other major factor affecting attendance is climate. In fact, the data were collected during five winter weeks when the temperature was quite variable. Therefore, Eryn includes the average daily temperature in her spreadsheet. The regression analysis will use the two explanatory variables X_1, as defined above, and X_2, average daily temperature.

The tables below show the daily number of ticket sales for the 34 days for which the ticket sales were recorded, and the average daily temperatures for the same period.

"OK," Liam says, "I can run that analysis, but I would like to consult with Waverly to get her take on this." Liam calls Waverly and interrupts her in the middle of a busy schedule. He quickly explains the problem to her and asks if he is on the right track. She replies, "Hmmm, I think I would start with a multiplicative decomposition to try to establish some seasonal indices for the different days of the week—that would help to develop a good forecasting model that explicitly incorporates the daily pattern of ticket sales in the forecast."

"That sounds like a great idea," says Liam, "but I would not have a clue where to begin! Can you be a nice sis and do it for me?" Waverly sighs and says, "OK Liam, but there are two conditions: first, you run the regression model. That's pretty straightforward in Excel. Then we can compare the forecasting error from that model with my multiplicative decomposition model." "What's the second condition?" Liam asks.

Waverly replies, "A year of free passes to the CineBarn."

DISCUSSION QUESTIONS

1. Develop a forecasting model based on Liam's suggestion to use a multiple regression model.
2. Develop a forecasting model based on Waverly's suggestion to use a multiplicative decomposition model.
3. Compare the two models. Which model yields more accurate forecasts for daily ticket sales?
4. For the multiplicative decomposition forecast the next week (seven days) of ticket sales.
5. Assuming that the pattern established in the sample data can be regarded as representative of daily ticket sales, on which days of the week would you recommend that the staff should be reduced by four persons?

BIBLIOGRAPHY

Clements, Dale W., and Richard A. Reid. "Analytical MS/OR Tools Applied to a Plant Closure," *Interfaces* 24, 2 (March–April 1994): 1–43.

De Lurgio, S. A. *Forecasting Principles and Applications.* New York: Irwin-McGraw-Hill, 1998.

Diebold, F. X. *Elements of Forecasting.* Cincinnati: South-Western College Publishing, 1998.

Gardner, E. S. "Exponential Smoothing: The State of the Art," *Journal of Forecasting* 4, 1 (March 1985): 1–28.

Georgoff, D. M., and R. G. Murdick. "Manager's Guide to Forecasting," *Harvard Business Review* 64, 1 (January–February 1986): 110–120.

Hanke, J. E., and A. G. Reitsch. *Business Forecasting,* 6/e. Upper Saddle River, NJ: Prentice Hall, 1998.

Heizer, J., and B. Render. *Operations Management,* 6/e. Upper Saddle River, NJ: Prentice Hall, 2001.

Herbig, P., J. Milewicz, and J. E. Golden. "Forecasting: Who, What, When, and How," *Journal of Business Forecasting* 12, 2 (Summer 1993): 16–22.

Li, X. "An Intelligent Business Forecaster for Strategic Business Planning," *Journal of Forecasting* 18, 3 (May 1999): 181–205.

Murdick, R., and D. M. Georgoff. "Forecasting: A Systems Approach," *Technological Forecasting and Social Change* 44 (1993): 1–16.

Niemera, M. P. *Forecasting Financial and Economic Cycles.* New York: John Wiley & Sons, 1994.

Wilson, J. H., and D. Allison-Koerber. "Combining Subjective and Objective Forecasts Improves Results," *Journal of Business Forecasting* 11, 3 (Fall 1992): 1–10.

Yurkiewicz, J. "Forecasting That Fits," *OR/MS Today* 25, 1 (February 1998): 42–55.

———. "Forecasting 2000," *OR/MS Today* 27, 1 (February 2000): 58–65.

CHAPTER 13

Inventory Control Models

THE CHAPTER IS FOUND ON THE STUDENT
CD-ROM THAT ACCOMPANIES THIS BOOK

APPENDICES

A. Useful Excel Commands and Procedures for Installing ExcelModules

B. Probability Concepts and Applications

C. Areas under the Standard Normal Curve

D. Solutions to Selected Problems

E. Solutions to Self-Tests

APPENDIX A: USEFUL EXCEL COMMANDS AND PROCEDURES FOR INSTALLING EXCELMODULES

A.1 INTRODUCTION

Excel is Microsoft Office's spreadsheet application program. A *spreadsheet* lets you embed hidden formulas that perform calculations on visible data. The main document (or file) used in Excel to store and manipulate data is called a *workbook*. A workbook can consist of a number of worksheets, each of which can be used to list and analyze data. Excel allows you to enter and modify data on several worksheets simultaneously. You can also perform calculations based on data from multiple worksheets and/or workbooks.

This appendix provides a brief overview of some basic Excel commands and procedures. It also discusses how add-ins, such as Solver and Data Analysis, can be installed and enabled in Excel. Finally, it describes the installation and usage procedures for ExcelModules, a software package included in the CD-ROM that accompanies this text. We use ExcelModules to develop and solve decision models for queuing (Chapter 10), forecasting (Chapter 12), and inventory control (Chapter 13).

In addition to the extensive help features built into Excel, there are thousands of online tutorials available to help you learn Excel. Many of these are quite comprehensive in their content. To get a current listing of these online tutorials, simply type in "Excel Tutorial" in the search box of your browser.

A.2 GETTING STARTED

Once Excel has been installed, you can start the program by either clicking **START| PROGRAMS|MICROSOFT EXCEL** (in Microsoft Windows 95 or later) or double-clicking any Excel workbook that already exists in your computer. Depending on how you start Excel, it either opens the existing workbook or automatically creates an empty workbook named **BOOK1**. The number of worksheets in the new workbook is set in the options (click **TOOLS|OPTIONS|GENERAL** to change this number). You can easily add more worksheets (click **INSERT|WORKSHEET**) or remove existing ones (click **EDIT|DELETE|SHEET**). The maximum number of worksheets in a workbook is 255. The sheet tabs at the bottom of each worksheet help you identify and move to each worksheet in your workbook. You can rename any sheet by double-clicking on its tab and typing in the new name.

Organization of a Worksheet

A worksheet consists of columns and rows, as shown in Screenshot A.1. Columns are identified by letters (e.g., A, B, C), and rows are identified by numbers (e.g., 1, 2, 3). Where a row and a column intersect is known as a cell. Each cell has a reference, based on the intersection of the row and column. For example, the cell at the intersection of column B and row 7 is referred to as cell B7 (as shown in Screenshot A.1).

A *cell* is the fundamental storage unit for Excel data, including both values and labels. A *value* is a number or a hidden formula that performs a calculation, and a *label* is a heading or some explanatory text. We can enter different types of entries (e.g., text, numbers, formulas, dates, and times) into cells.

Navigating through a Worksheet

You can navigate through a worksheet using either the mouse or the keys on your keyboard. To select a cell using the mouse, click the cell (e.g., B7, as shown in Screenshot A.1). To move anywhere on a worksheet, you can also use the arrow keys, or the Page Up and Page Down keys, on the keyboard.

SCREENSHOT A.1   **General Layout of an Excel Worksheet**

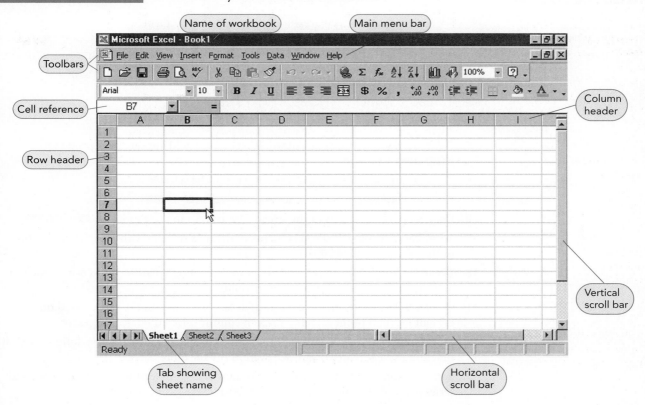

You can also use the **GO TO** menu option to navigate between cells. This option is useful if you want to modify the contents of a cell. To go to a specific cell, click **EDIT|GO TO**. In the **GO TO** dialog box, you can even click the **SPECIAL** button to go to cells with special features. For example, you can choose to go to cells with comments, to blank cells, or to the last cell in the worksheet.

Toolbars

A toolbar consists of icons that provide shortcuts to common tasks. Excel has several toolbars built in for your use. By default, the **STANDARD** and **FORMATTING** toolbars are visible when you open Excel. To view other toolbars (e.g., **DRAWING**, **CHARTS**), click **VIEW|TOOLBARS** and then select the desired toolbar(s). Most of the icons in Excel's toolbars are similar to the ones in other Microsoft Office programs (e.g., PowerPoint, Word). You can customize any toolbar by clicking **VIEW|TOOLBARS|CUSTOMIZE**.

Standard Toolbar   The Standard toolbar, shown in Screenshot A.2 on the next page, includes shortcuts to many common file-related tasks, such as saving or printing.

The following list indicates the tasks associated with some of the icons on this toolbar, along with the corresponding command to use in Excel's main menu bar. To see the specific task associated with an icon, you can move the cursor briefly over that icon to see an on-screen description of that icon (as shown in Screenshot A.2 for the Save icon).

1. *New.* Open a file (**FILE|NEW**).
2. *Open.* Open an existing file (**FILE|OPEN**).
3. *Save.* Save the current file (**FILE|SAVE**).
4. *Print.* Print the current worksheet (**FILE|PRINT**).

SCREENSHOT A.2   **Standard Toolbar in Excel**

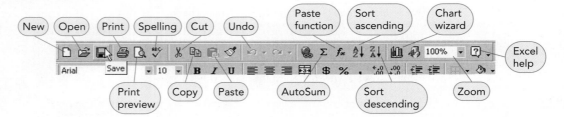

5. *Print Preview.* View the current worksheet as it would appear when printed (**FILE|PRINT PREVIEW**).

6. *Spelling.* Check the spelling of the contents in the selected cells.

7. *Cut.* Cut the contents of the selected set of cells (**EDIT|CUT**).

8. *Copy.* Copy the contents of the selected set of cells to the clipboard (**EDIT|COPY**).

9. *Paste.* Paste the cut or copied contents to the cells starting with the current location of the cursor (**EDIT|PASTE**).

10. *Undo.* Undo the last change made on a worksheet (**EDIT|UNDO**). You can access and undo the last 16 actions that you have done.

11. *AutoSum.* Add the values in a range of cells. (Excel guesses the range based on the current location of the cursor.) You can edit the selected range if necessary.

12. *Paste Function.* Provides a list of functions available in Excel and descriptions of each function (**INSERT|FUNCTION**). See Section A.4 for more details.

13. *Sort Ascending.* Sorts a selected series of numbers from least to greatest or a selected series of words in alphabetical order (**DATA|SORT**).

14. *Sort Descending.* Sorts a selected series of numbers from greatest to least or a selected series of words in reverse alphabetical order (**DATA|SORT**).

15. *Chart Wizard.* Takes you through a step-by-step procedure for creating different types of charts using the data in a workbook (**INSERT|CHART**).

16. *Zoom.* Vary the zoom level of the current worksheet to make cell entries appear larger or smaller (**VIEW|ZOOM**).

17. *Microsoft Excel Help.* Invoke the Office Assistant for help (**HELP|MICROSOFT EXCEL HELP**).

Formatting Toolbar The Formatting toolbar, shown in Screenshot A.3, includes short-cuts to many frequently used formatting operations, such as font sizes and cell alignment.

SCREENSHOT A.3   **Formatting Toolbar in Excel**

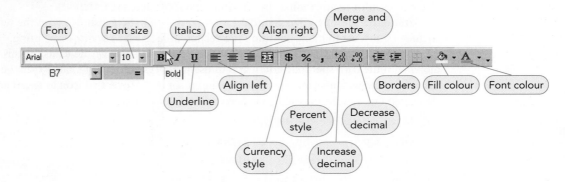

The following list indicates the tasks associated with some of the main icons on this toolbar, along with the corresponding command in Excel's main menu bar. To see the specific task associated with an icon, you can move the cursor briefly over that icon to see an on-screen description of that icon (as shown in Screenshot A.3 for the Bold icon).

1. *Font.* Gives a list of available fonts (**FORMAT|CELLS|FONT**).
2. *Font Size.* Gives a list of available font sizes (**FORMAT|CELLS|FONT**).
3. *Bold.* Toggles the entries in the selected cell between bold and nonbold (**FORMAT|CELLS|FONT**).
4. *Italics.* Toggles the entries in the selected cells between italics and nonitalics (**FORMAT|CELLS|FONT**).
5. *Underline.* Toggles the entries in the selected cells between underlined and nonunderlined (**FORMAT|CELLS|FONT**).
6. *Align Left.* Left justifies the contents of the selected cells.
7. *Center.* Centres the contents of the selected cells.
8. *Align Right.* Right justifies the contents of the selected cells.
9. *Merge and Center.* Select the group of cells you want to merge and centre, and then click the icon. Note that if you merge several cells in a row, only the data in the first cell will be retained. The same is true for columns.
10. *Currency Style.* Converts the numerical values of the selected cells to appear in currency format.
11. *Percent Style.* Converts the numerical values of the selected cell to appear in percentage format.
12. *Increase Decimal.* Increases the number of decimal points shown for the numerical values in the selected cells.
13. *Decrease Decimal.* Decreases the number of decimal points shown for the numerical values in the selected cells.
14. *Borders.* Opens a box that can be used to place different types of borders around the selected cells.
15. *Fill Color.* Fills the selected cells with the selected colour. (Default is no fill.)
16. *Font Color.* Changes the colour of the font to the selected colour. (Default is black.)

Office Assistant

If you are unsure about how to perform any action in Excel (or any other Microsoft Office program), you can use the **OFFICE ASSISTANT** to help you. The Office Assistant can display tips on how to use different Excel features or provide help on the specific task you are performing.

To open the Office Assistant, click the **HELP** icon on the Standard toolbar (or click **HELP|MICROSOFT EXCEL HELP**). The Office Assistant is a cartoon character selected during the installation process. You can change settings for the Office Assistant by clicking the **OPTIONS** button. For example, you can specify that the Office Assistant display tips when you launch an application.

You can use common constructions to query the Office Assistant. For example, you can type, "How do I format a cell?" and click the **SEARCH** button. The Office Assistant then responds with links to various help topics. If none of the suggestions match your query, click **SEE MORE**. When you have located the response that best matches your query, click the item. The help text is then displayed.

To enter data or information in a worksheet, first click on the cell in which you want to enter the data. Then, simply type in the data. You can enter numbers, text, dates, times, or formulas. (These are discussed in Section A.4.) When you are done, hit Enter, and the next cell in the column is automatically selected.

Selecting a Group of Adjacent Cells   Click the first cell to be selected. Hold down the Shift key and click the last cell to be selected. All cells in between these two cells will automatically be selected. Alternatively, after clicking the first cell, hold the left mouse button down and drag until you have selected all the cells you need.

Selecting a Group of Nonadjacent Cells   Left-click the first cell to be selected. Hold down the Ctrl key and click each of the other cells to be selected. Only the cells you clicked will be selected.

Selecting an Entire Row or Column   Click the header (number) of the row that you want to select in its entirety. To select more than one entire row, keep either the Shift or the Ctrl key pressed (as discussed in the preceding item for selecting cells), depending on whether the rows are adjacent or nonadjacent. You can use a similar procedure to select one or more columns in their entirety.

Editing Data   To edit the existing information in a cell, double-click the cell to be edited (or click once on the cell and press the F2 function button on your keyboard). You can now simply type over or modify the contents as desired.

Clearing Data   To clear the data in selected cells, first select the cells that you want to clear. Next, hit the Delete button on your keyboard.

Working with Rows and Columns

There are several operations that you can perform with the rows and columns in a worksheet. Some of these are as follows.

Inserting Rows or Columns   To insert a new row, click on the row header above where you want the new row to be. Then, click **INSERT|ROW**. To insert a column, click on the column header to the left of where you want the new column to be. Then, click **INSERT|COLUMN**. To insert multiple rows or columns, select multiple row or column headers before clicking Insert.

Deleting Rows or Columns   To delete a row or column, select the row(s) or column(s) that you want to delete. Then click **EDIT|DELETE**.

Changing Column Width   To change the width of a column, place the cursor on the right edge of the column header that you want to change. The cursor will change to a plus sign with arrows pointing to the left and right. Click and hold the left mouse button and drag to the desired width. Double-clicking will automatically adjust the column width to the widest entry in the column.

Changing Row Height   To change the height of a row, move the mouse to the bottom edge of the row heading. The cursor will change to a plus sign with arrows on the top and bottom. Click and drag to the new desired height. Double-clicking will automatically adjust the row height to the tallest entry in the row.

Hiding Columns or Rows   To hide a row (or a set of rows), first select the rows to hide. Then, click **FORMAT|ROW|HIDE** (or right-click the mouse and select the Hide option). You can use a similar procedure to hide columns (click **FORMAT|COLUMN|HIDE**).

Unhiding Columns or Rows   To unhide a hidden row (or a set of hidden rows), first select the row before and after the hidden row. Then, click **FORMAT|ROW|UNHIDE** (or right-click the mouse and select the Unhide option). You can use a similar procedure to unhide hidden columns (click **FORMAT|COLUMN|UNHIDE**).

SCREENSHOT A.4

Options for the Paste Special Feature in Excel

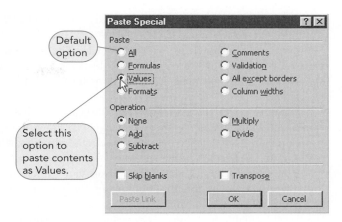

Formatting Worksheets

Once you have created a worksheet, Excel has an extensive set of options you can use to format the appearance of various cells. Some of these options follow.

Changing Appearance of Numbers in Cells   To change the appearance of numbers in cells, first select the cells that you want to format. Then, click on **FORMAT| CELLS|NUMBER** and select the desired format (e.g., currency, numerical, percentage, fraction).

Alignment and Text Control   You can adjust how an entry is positioned within a cell. To do so, select the cells that you want to align and then click **FORMAT|CELLS|ALIGNMENT**. You can now select the desired options (e.g., word wrap, cell orientation).

Paste Special   A useful feature of the paste operation in Excel is the **PASTE SPECIAL** operation. After cutting or copying the content of selected cells, you can invoke this feature by clicking **EDIT|PASTE SPECIAL**. The window shown in Screenshot A.4 is displayed. You can now select any of the choices including the following:

1. *All.* The formulas and formats are pasted in the new locations.

2. *Formulas.* Only the formula is pasted in the new locations (i.e., without the formats). The values in the new cells depend on the cell references in the formulas.

3. *Values.* Only the values of the selected cells are pasted in the new locations (i.e., without the formulas or formats).

4. *Formats.* Only the formats of the selected cells are pasted in the new location.

You can also use the Paste Special feature to perform mathematical operations (e.g., adding the contents of selected cells) before pasting.

A.4   USING FORMULAS AND FUNCTIONS

Formulas allow you to perform calculations on your worksheet data. A formula must start with an "equal to" (=) sign in Excel. To enter a formula, click the cell where you want to enter the formula. Next type an "=" sign, followed by the formula. A formula can consist of mathematical operations involving numbers or cell references that point to cells with numerical values. After typing in a formula, press Enter to perform the calculation. By default, Excel will automatically recalculate the formula if you change any of the input values used in the formula.

Functions are formulas that are already built into Excel. To see the full list of built-in functions in Excel, click **INSERT|FUNCTION** (or the **PASTE FUNCTION** icon on the Standard toolbar shown in Screenshot A.1). The list is shown in Screenshot A.5. You can view subsets of these functions by selecting the category (e.g., **STATISTICAL**, **FINANCIAL**) in the left pane. The functions relevant for that category then appear in the right pane.

When you select a specific function, the syntax for that function is displayed at the bottom of the window. For example, Screenshot A.5 shows the syntax for the SUMPRODUCT function. For more detailed help on the selected function, click the **HELP** button (shown as a "?") in the bottom left of the window.

When using functions in Excel, you can prefix the function with an "=" sign and directly type in the function using the required syntax. Alternatively, you can select the cell in which you want to use a particular function. Then, you can call up the list of available functions (as described previously) and select the desired function. A window that shows the required input entries for the selected function is now displayed to guide you through the creation of the cell entry using the function.

Errors in Using Formulas and Functions

Sometimes, when you use a function or formula, the resulting output indicates an error in your entry. The following is a list of common errors when using formulas or functions, and their possible causes:

1. #DIV/0! indicates that the formula or function involves division by zero.
2. #Name? indicates that the formula or function is not recognized by Excel. This is usually caused by a typographical error.
3. #VALUE indicates that one or more cell references used in a formula or function are invalid.
4. #### indicates that the cell is not wide enough to display the number. This can be easily remedied by increasing the width of the cell.

SCREENSHOT A.5

Functions Available in Excel

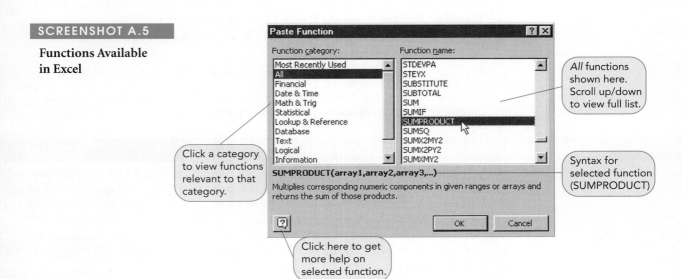

A.5 PRINTING WORKSHEETS

If you wish to print the entire worksheet using the print defaults, you can go directly to the print menu by clicking either **FILE|PRINT** or the **PRINT** icon on the Standard toolbar. Alternatively, you can make modifications to your printed output, as discussed in the following sections.

Setting the Print Area   If you wish to print only a portion of the current worksheet, first select the desired region of cells to print. Then click **PRINT|PRINT AREA|SET PRINT AREA**. You can clear a selected print area by clicking **PRINT|PRINT AREA|CLEAR PRINT AREA**.

Print Preview   Before printing a worksheet, it is a good idea to preview what your printer output would look like. To preview a worksheet, click on **PRINT|PRINT PREVIEW** (or click the **PRINT PREVIEW** icon on the Standard toolbar). Screenshot A.6 shows the options available in the Print Preview window.

Setting Print Margins   To change the print margins, go into **PRINT PREVIEW** and then click **MARGINS**. Position the mouse over the margin handle (i.e., the lines indicating the margins). Click and drag the margins to the desired position. Or click **FILE|PAGE SETUP|MARGINS** and type in the desired margins.

Page Breaks   To insert a page break, first click on the row or column where you want the page break to be. For rows, the break will be above the selected row. For columns, it will be to the left of the selected column. Then, click **INSERT|PAGE BREAK**. To remove an existing page break, first select the rows (or columns) on either side of the page break. Then, click **INSERT|REMOVE PAGE BREAK**.

Centring Data on a Page   To centre data on a page, click **FILE|PAGE SETUP|MARGINS** (or click **SETUP|MARGINS** from within the Print Preview options). Check the boxes corresponding to whether you want the data centred horizontally, vertically, or both.

SCREENSHOT A.6

Options Available in the Print Preview Window

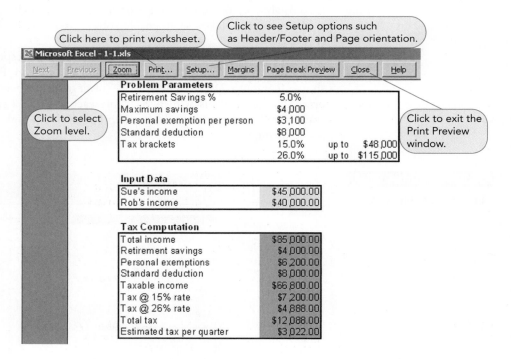

Inserting a Header or Footer   To add a header and/or a footer, click **FILE|PAGE SETUP|HEADER/FOOTER** (or click **SETUP|HEADER/FOOTER** from within the **PRINT PREVIEW** option). To add a header, click on **CUSTOM HEADER**. To add a footer, click on **CUSTOM FOOTER**. When you have selected either option, you get another screen where you can enter the text and format the header or footer.

Printing the Worksheet   After making all adjustments, to print a worksheet you can do one of two things: You can either click **FILE|PRINT** or you can click **PRINT** from within the Print Preview option.

A.6   INSTALLING AND ENABLING EXCEL ADD-INS

Add-ins are special programs that are designed to perform specific tasks in Excel. Although Excel includes several add-ins, we focus here on only two add-ins, **SOLVER** and **DATA ANALYSIS**, that are useful in decision modeling.

Both Solver and Data Analysis are included with all recent versions of Excel. However, if you choose to install Excel using the default options, only Data Analysis is installed during the installation process. To install Solver, you need to change the installation defaults for Excel by clicking on the Excel options during the installation process and then choosing Add-Ins. Make sure the box next to the Solver option is checked. Note that the option to install the **ANALYSIS TOOLPAK** (i.e., Data Analysis) is already checked by default.

Even after these add-ins have been installed, they need to be enabled (or switched on) in order for them to be available in Excel. To check if these add-ins have been enabled, start Excel and click **TOOLS**. If you see Data Analysis and/or Solver as menu options, the add-in has been enabled on that personal computer. However, if you do not see either (or both) add-ins, click **TOOLS|ADD-INS**.

The list of available add-ins is now displayed, as shown in Screenshot A.7. To enable Data Analysis, make sure the boxes next to Analysis ToolPak and Analysis ToolPak—VBA are both checked. Likewise, to enable Solver, make sure the box next to Solver Add-In is checked.

Depending on the boxes you checked, the corresponding add-in should now be shown as an option under the Tools menu in Excel. For example, Screenshot A.8 shows that both Data Analysis and Solver add-ins have been enabled. From here onward, these add-ins will be available each time you start Excel on that personal computer. To access either add-in, simply click **TOOLS** and select the appropriate choice in the menu.

SCREENSHOT A.7

List of Available Add-Ins

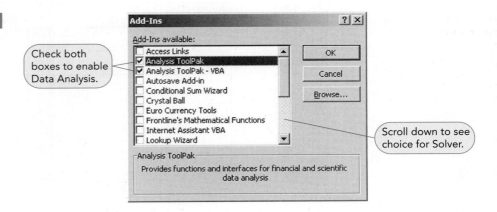

SCREENSHOT A.8

Tools Submenu Showing Enabled Add-Ins

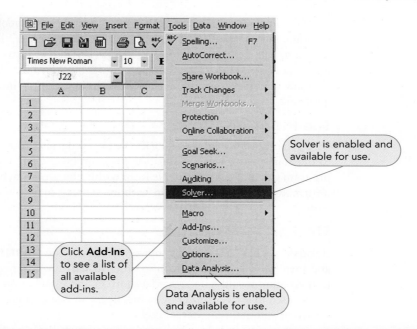

Solver is enabled and available for use.

Click **Add-Ins** to see a list of all available add-ins.

Data Analysis is enabled and available for use.

A.7   INSTALLING AND USING EXCELMODULES

Your CD-ROM includes a customized Excel add-in called **EXCELMODULES**. This program has been designed to help you to better learn and understand decision models in queuing (Chapter 10), forecasting (Chapter 12), and inventory control (Chapter 13). Screenshot A.9 shows the modules available for each topic, as well as the submodules available for forecasting models. Instructions for using each submodule in ExcelModules are provided at appropriate places in Chapters 10, 12, and 13 of this book.

To run ExcelModules on your personal computer, you must have Excel version 5 or better installed. To install ExcelModules, follow these steps:

1. Insert the CD into the CD-ROM drive.
2. Click **START|RUN|BROWSE** in Windows 95/98/Me/2000/XP/Vista.
3. Change to the ExcelModules folder on the CD-ROM.
4. Run the file ExcelModules.exe (by double-clicking the file).
5. Follow the setup instructions on the screen.

SCREENSHOT A.9   **Modules and Forecasting Models Submodules in ExcelModules**

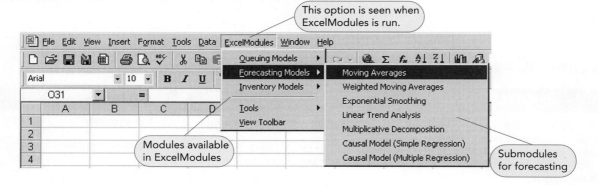

This option is seen when ExcelModules is run.

Modules available in ExcelModules

Submodules for forecasting

Default values have been assigned for most installation parameters in the setup program, but you can change them if you like. For example, the default values are that the program will be installed to a directory on the C: drive named C:\Program Files\ExcelModules and that the program group will be named ExcelModules. Generally speaking, it is only necessary to simply click **NEXT** each time that the installation program asks you a question.

The Program Group

Under Windows 95/98/Me/2000/XP/Vista, a program group with three options is added to the Start menu. You can start the program by clicking the ExcelModules icon in the program group. Help is available from within the program, but if you want to read some information about the program without starting it first, use the **EXCELMODULES HELP** icon.

Starting the Program

If you do not have Excel already open, you can click on **START|PROGRAMS|EXCELMODULES** and then the ExcelModules icon in order to start the program. Alternatively, the installation program would have created a shortcut and placed it on your desktop. This shortcut can be used to start ExcelModules directly by double-clicking on it. When ExcelModules is started, it automatically starts Excel also.

If you already have Excel open, then simply load the file ExcelModules.xla, which is in the directory where the software was installed. (The default is C:\Program Files\ExcelModules if you did not change this at the time of installation.)

It is also possible to install ExcelModules as an add-in. This will load the program each time that you start Excel. To do this, start Excel first. Then, go to **TOOLS|ADD-INS|BROWSE** and select the file named ExcelModules.xla.

ExcelModules serves two purposes in the learning process. First, it can help you solve homework problems. You enter the appropriate data, and the program provides numerical solutions. In addition, ExcelModules allows you to note the Excel formulas used to develop solutions and modify them to deal with a wider variety of problems. This "open" approach allows you to observe, understand, and even change the formulas underlying the Excel calculations, conveying Excel's power as a decision modeling tool.

Technical Support

If you have technical problems with ExcelModules that your instructor cannot answer, send an e-mail message to dsSoftware@prenhall.com. Be sure to include the name of the program (ExcelModules), the version of the program (click **TOOLS|ABOUT** to check the version number), the module in which the problem is occurring, and a detailed explanation of the problem. Attach the data file for which the problem occurs (if appropriate).

APPENDIX B: PROBABILITY CONCEPTS AND APPLICATIONS

B.1   FUNDAMENTAL CONCEPTS

People often misuse the two basic rules of probabilities by making such statements as "I'm 110% sure we're going to win the big game."

There are two basic statements about the mathematics of **probability**:

1. The probability, P, of any event or state of nature occurring is greater than or equal to 0 and less than or equal to 1. That is,

$$0 \le P(\text{event}) \le 1 \qquad \text{(B-1)}$$

A probability of 0 indicates that an event is never expected to occur. A probability of 1 means that an event is always expected to occur.

2. The sum of the simple probabilities for all possible outcomes of an activity must equal 1. Both of these concepts are illustrated in Example 1.

Example 1: Two Laws of Probability   Demand for white latex paint at Yellow Knife Paint and Supply has always been 0, 1, 2, 3, or 4 litres per day. (There are no other possible outcomes and when one occurs, no other can.) Over the past 200 working days, the owner notes the following frequencies of demand:

QUANTITY DEMANDED (LITRES)	NUMBER OF DAYS
0	40
1	80
2	50
3	20
4	10
	Total 200

If this past distribution is a good indicator of future sales, we can find the probability of each possible outcome occurring in the future by converting the data into percentages of the total:

QUANTITY DEMANDED	PROBABILITY
0	0.20 (= 40/200)
1	0.40 (= 80/200)
2	0.25 (= 50/200)
3	0.10 (= 20/200)
4	0.05 (= 10/200)
	Total 1.00 (= 200/200)

Thus, the probability that sales are 2 litres of paint on any given day is $P(2 \text{ litres}) = 0.25 = 25\%$. The probability of any level of sales must be greater than or equal to 0 and less than or equal to 1. Since 0, 1, 2, 3, and 4 litres exhaust all possible events or outcomes, the sum of their probability values must equal 1.

Types of Probability

There are two different ways to determine probability: the **objective approach** and the **subjective approach**.

Objective Probability   Example 1 provides us with an illustration of objective probability assessment. The probability of any paint demand level is the **relative frequency** of occurrence of that demand in a large number of trial observations (200 days in this case). In general:

$$P(\text{event}) = \frac{\text{Number of occurrences of the event}}{\text{Total number of trials or outcomes}}$$

Objective probability can also be set using what is called the **classical or logical approach**. Without performing a series of trials, we can often logically determine what the probabilities of various events should be. For example, the probability of tossing a fair coin once and getting a head is

$$P(\text{head}) = \frac{1}{2} \quad \longleftarrow \textit{number of ways of getting a head}$$
$$\longleftarrow \textit{number of possible outcomes (head or tail)}$$

Similarly, the probability of drawing a spade out of a deck of 52 playing cards can be logically set as

$$P(\text{spade}) = \frac{13}{52} \quad \longleftarrow \textit{number of chances of drawing a spade}$$
$$\longleftarrow \textit{number of possible outcomes}$$
$$= \frac{1}{4} = 0.25 = 25\%$$

Where do probabilities come from? Sometimes they are subjective and based on personal experiences. Other times they are objectively based on logical observations such as the roll of a die. Often, probabilities are derived from historical data.

Subjective Probability   When logic and past history are not appropriate, probability values can be assessed *subjectively*. The accuracy of subjective probabilities depends on the experience and judgment of the person making the estimates. A number of probability values cannot be determined unless the subjective approach is used. What is the probability that the price of gasoline will be more than $4 in the next few years? What is the probability that our economy will be in a severe depression in 2010? What is the probability that you will be president of a major corporation within 20 years?

There are several methods for making subjective probability assessments. Opinion polls can be used to help in determining subjective probabilities for possible election returns and potential political candidates. In some cases, experience and judgment must be used in making subjective assessments of probability values. A production manager, for example, might believe that the probability of manufacturing a new product without a single defect is 0.85. In the Delphi method, a panel of experts is assembled to make their predictions of the future. This approach is discussed in Chapter 12.

B.2   MUTUALLY EXCLUSIVE AND COLLECTIVELY EXHAUSTIVE EVENTS

Events are said to be **mutually exclusive** if only one of the events can occur on any one trial. They are called **collectively exhaustive** if the list of outcomes includes every possible outcome. Many common experiences involve events that have both of these properties. In tossing a coin, for example, the possible outcomes are a head or a tail. Since both of them cannot occur on any one toss, the outcomes head and tail are mutually exclusive. Since obtaining a head and a tail represent every possible outcome, they are also collectively exhaustive.

Example 2: Rolling a Die   Rolling a die is a simple experiment that has six possible outcomes, each listed in the following table with its corresponding probability:

OUTCOME OF ROLL	PROBABILITY
1	$\frac{1}{6}$
2	$\frac{1}{6}$
3	$\frac{1}{6}$
4	$\frac{1}{6}$
5	$\frac{1}{6}$
6	$\frac{1}{6}$
	Total 1

These events are both mutually exclusive (on any roll, only one of the six events can occur) and are also collectively exhaustive (one of them must occur and hence they total in probability to 1).

Example 3: Drawing a Card You are asked to draw one card from a deck of 52 playing cards. Using a logical probability assessment, it is easy to set some of the relationships, such as

$$P(\text{drawing a 7}) = \frac{4}{52} = \frac{1}{13}$$
$$P(\text{drawing a heart}) = \frac{13}{52} = \frac{1}{4}$$

We also see that these events (drawing a 7 and drawing a heart) are *not* mutually exclusive since a 7 of hearts can be drawn. They are also *not* collectively exhaustive since there are other cards in the deck besides 7s and hearts.

You can test your understanding of these concepts by going through the following cases:

DRAWS	MUTUALLY EXCLUSIVE?	COLLECTIVELY EXHAUSTIVE?
1. Draw a spade and a club	Yes	No
2. Draw a face card and a number card	Yes	Yes
3. Draw an ace and a 3	Yes	No
4. Draw a club and a nonclub	Yes	Yes
5. Draw a 5 and a diamond	No	No
6. Draw a red card and a diamond	No	No

This table is especially useful in helping to understand the difference between mutually exclusive and collectively exhaustive.

Adding Mutually Exclusive Events

Often we are interested in whether one event *or* a second event will occur. When these two events are mutually exclusive, the law of addition is simply as follows:

$$P(\text{event } A \text{ or event } B) = P(\text{event } A) + P(\text{event } B)$$

or more briefly,

$$P(A \text{ or } B) = P(A) + P(B) \tag{B-2}$$

For example, we just saw that the events of drawing a spade or drawing a club out of a deck of cards are mutually exclusive. Since $P(\text{spade}) = \frac{13}{52}$ and $P(\text{club}) = \frac{13}{52}$, the probability of drawing either a spade or a club is

$$P(\text{spade or club}) = P(\text{spade}) + P(\text{club})$$
$$= \frac{13}{52} + \frac{13}{52}$$
$$= \frac{26}{52} = \frac{1}{2} = 0.50 = 50\%$$

The Venn diagram in Figure B.1 depicts the probability of the occurrence of mutually exclusive events.

FIGURE B.1

Addition Law for Events that Are Mutually Exclusive

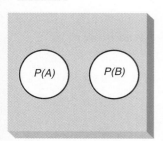

$P(A \text{ or } B) = P(A) + P(B)$

Law of Addition for Events That Are Not Mutually Exclusive

When two events are not mutually exclusive, Equation B-2 must be modified to account for double counting. The correct equation reduces the probability by subtracting the chance of both events occurring together:

$$P(\text{event } A \text{ or event } B) = P(\text{event } A) + P(\text{event } B)$$
$$- P(\text{event } A \text{ and event } B \text{ both occurring})$$

The formula for adding events that are not mutually exclusive is $P(A \text{ or } B) = P(A) + P(B) - P(A \text{ and } B)$. Do you understand why we subtract $P(A \text{ and } B)$?

Addition Law for Events that Are Not Mutually Exclusive

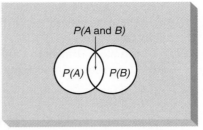

$$P(A \text{ or } B) = P(A) + P(B) - P(A \text{ and } B)$$

This can be expressed in shorter form as

$$P(A \text{ or } B) = P(A) + P(B) - P(A \text{ and } B) \tag{B-3}$$

Figure B.2 illustrates this concept of subtracting the probability of outcomes that are common to both events. When events are mutually exclusive, the area of overlap, called the *intersection*, is 0, as shown in Figure B.1.

Let us consider the events drawing a 5 and drawing a diamond out of the card deck. These events are not mutually exclusive, so Equation B-3 must be applied to compute the probability of either a 5 or a diamond being drawn:

$$
\begin{aligned}
P(\text{five } or \text{ diamond}) &= P(\text{five}) + P(\text{diamond}) \\
&\quad - P(\text{five } and \text{ diamond}) \\
&= \tfrac{4}{52} + \tfrac{13}{52} - \tfrac{1}{52} \\
&= \tfrac{16}{52} = \tfrac{4}{13}
\end{aligned}
$$

B.3 STATISTICALLY INDEPENDENT EVENTS

Events can either be **independent events** or **dependent events**. When they are independent, the occurrence of one event has no effect on the probability of occurrence of the second event. Let us examine four sets of events and determine which are independent:

1. (a) Your education } *Dependent events.*
   (b) Your income level } Can you explain why?

2. (a) Draw a jack of hearts from a full 52-card deck } *Independent events*
   (b) Draw a jack of clubs from a full 52-card deck

3. (a) Chicago Cubs win the National League pennant } *Dependent events*
   (b) Chicago Cubs win the World Series

4. (a) Snow in Santiago, Chile } *Independent events*
   (b) Rain in Tel Aviv, Israel

The three types of probability under both statistical independence and statistical dependence are (1) marginal, (2) joint, and (3) conditional. When events are independent, these three are very easy to compute, as we shall see.

A **marginal (or a simple) probability** is just the probability of an event occurring. For example, if we toss a fair die, the marginal probability of a 2 landing face up is $P(\text{die is a } 2) = \tfrac{1}{6} = 0.167$. Because each separate toss is an independent event (i.e., what we get on the first toss has absolutely no effect on any later tosses), the marginal probability for each possible outcome is $\tfrac{1}{6}$.

A *marginal probability* is the probability of an event occurring.

A *joint probability* is the product of marginal probabilities.

The **joint probability** of two or more independent events occurring is the product of their marginal or simple probabilities. This can be written as

$$P(AB) = P(A) \times P(B) \tag{B-4}$$

where

$P(AB)$ = joint probability or events A and B occurring together, or one after the other

$P(A)$ = marginal probability of event A

$P(B)$ = marginal probability of event B

The probability, for example, of tossing a 6 on the first roll of a die and a 2 on the second roll is

$$P(6 \text{ on first and 2 on second roll})$$
$$= P(\text{tossing a } 6) \times P(\text{tossing a } 2)$$
$$= \frac{1}{6} \times \frac{1}{6} = \frac{1}{36}$$
$$= 0.028$$

A *conditional probability* is the probability of an event occurring given that another event has taken place.

The third type, **conditional probability**, is expressed as $P(B|A)$, or "the probability of event B, given that event A has occurred." Similarly, $P(A|B)$ would mean "the conditional probability of event A, given that event B has taken place." Since events are independent, the occurrence of one in no way affects the outcome of another, $P(A|B) = P(A)$ and $P(B|A) = P(B)$.

Example 4: Probabilities When Events Are Independent   A bucket contains three black balls and seven green balls. We draw a ball from the bucket, replace it, and draw a second ball. We can determine the probability of each of the following events occurring:

1. A black ball is drawn on the first draw.

$$P(B) = 0.30$$

    (*This is a marginal probability.*)

2. Two green balls are drawn.

$$P(GG) = P(G) \times P(G) = (0.7)(0.7) = 0.49$$

    (*This is a joint probability for two independent events.*)

3. A black ball is drawn on the second draw if the first draw is green.

$$P(B \mid G) = P(B) = 0.30$$

    (*This is a conditional probability but equal to the marginal because the two draws are independent events.*)

4. A green ball is drawn on the second draw if the first draw was green.

$$P(G \mid G) = P(G) = 0.70$$

    (*This is a conditional probability as above.*)

B.4   STATISTICALLY DEPENDENT EVENTS

When events are statistically dependent, the occurrence of one event affects the probability of occurrence of some other event. Marginal, conditional, and joint probabilities exist under dependence as they did under independence, but the form of the latter two are changed.

A marginal probability is computed exactly as it was for independent events. Again, the marginal probability of the event A occurring is denoted $P(A)$.

Calculating a conditional probability under dependence is somewhat more involved than it is under independence. The formula for the conditional probability of A, given that event B has taken place, is now stated as

$$P(A \mid B) = \frac{P(AB)}{P(B)} \tag{B-5}$$

The use of this important formula, often referred to as *Bayes' theorem* or *Bayes' law*, is best defined by an example.

Example 5: Probabilities When Events Are Dependent   Assume that we have an urn containing 10 balls of the following descriptions:

4 are white (W) and lettered (L).

2 are white (W) and numbered (N).

3 are yellow (Y) and lettered (L).

1 is yellow (Y) and numbered (N).

You randomly draw a ball from the urn and see that it is yellow. What, then, we may ask, is the probability that the ball is lettered? (See Figure B.3.)

Since there are 10 balls, it is a simple matter to tabulate a series of useful probabilities:

$$P(WL) = \frac{4}{10} = 0.4 \qquad P(YL) = \frac{3}{10} = 0.3$$

$$P(WN) = \frac{2}{10} = 0.2 \qquad P(YN) = \frac{1}{10} = 0.1$$

$$P(W) = \frac{6}{10} = 0.6, \text{ or } P(W) = P(WL) + P(WN) = 0.4 + 0.2 = 0.6$$

$$P(L) = \frac{7}{10} = 0.7, \text{ or } P(L) = P(WL) + P(YL) = 0.4 + 0.3 = 0.7$$

$$P(Y) = \frac{4}{10} = 0.4, \text{ or } P(Y) = P(YL) + P(YN) = 0.3 + 0.1 = 0.4$$

$$P(N) = \frac{3}{10} = 0.3, \text{ or } P(N) = P(WN) + P(YN) = 0.2 + 0.1 = 0.3$$

FIGURE B.3

Dependent Events of Example 5

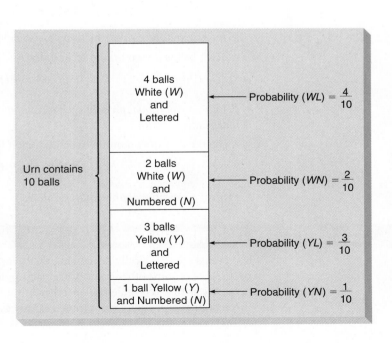

We can now apply Bayes' theorem to calculate the conditional probability that the ball drawn is lettered, given that it is yellow.

$$P(L \mid Y) = \frac{P(YL)}{P(Y)} = \frac{0.3}{0.4} = 0.75$$

This equation shows that we divided the probability of yellow and lettered balls (3 out of 10) by the probability of yellow balls (4 out of 10). There is a 0.75 probability that the yellow ball that you drew is lettered.

Recall that the formula for a joint probability under statistical independence was simply $P(AB) = P(A) \times P(B)$. When events are *dependent*, however, the joint probability is derived from Bayes' conditional formula. Equation B-6 reads "the joint probability of events A and B occurring is equal to the conditional probability of event A, given that B occurred, multiplied by the probability of event B."

$$P(AB) = P(A \mid B) \times P(B) \tag{B-6}$$

We can use this formula to verify the joint probability that $P(YL) = 0.3$, which was obtained by inspection in Example 5, by multiplying $P(L|Y)$ times $P(Y)$:

$$P(YL) = P(L \mid Y) \times P(Y) = (0.75)(0.4) = 0.3$$

Example 6: Joint Probabilities When Events Are Dependent   Your stockbroker informs you that if the stock market reaches the 12 500-point level by January, there is a 70% probability that Tubeless Electronics will go up in value. Your own feeling is that there is only a 40% chance of the market average reaching 12 500 points by January. Can you calculate the probability that *both* the stock market will reach 12 500 points *and* the price of Tubeless Electronics will go up?

Let M represent the event of the stock market reaching the 12 500 level, and let T be the event that Tubeless goes up in value. Then

$$P(MT) = P(T \mid M) \times P(M) = (0.70)(0.40) = 0.28$$

Thus, there is only a 28% chance that *both* events will occur.

B.5   REVISING PROBABILITIES WITH BAYES' THEOREM

Bayes' theorem can also be used to incorporate additional information as it is made available and help create **revised** or **posterior probabilities**. This means that we can take new or recent data and then revise and improve upon our old probability estimates for an event (see Figure B.4). Let us consider the following example.

FIGURE B.4

Using Bayes' Process

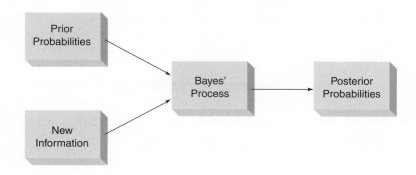

Example 7: Posterior Probabilities   A cup contains two dice identical in appearance. One, however, is fair (unbiased) and the other is loaded (biased). The probability of rolling a 3 on the fair die is $\frac{1}{6}$ or 0.166. The probability of tossing the same number on the loaded die is 0.60.

We have no idea which die is which but select one by chance and toss it. The result is a 3. Given this additional piece of information, can we find the (revised) probability that the die rolled was fair? Can we determine the probability that it was the loaded die that was rolled?

The answer to these questions is yes, and we do so by using the formula for joint probability under statistical dependence and Bayes' theorem. First, we take stock of the information and probabilities available. We know, for example, that since we randomly selected the die to roll, the probability of it being fair or loaded is 0.50:

$$P(\text{fair}) = 0.50 \qquad\qquad P(\text{loaded}) = 0.50$$

We also know that

$$P(3 \mid \text{fair}) = 0.166 \qquad\qquad P(3 \mid \text{loaded}) = 0.60$$

Next, we compute joint probabilities $P(3 \text{ and fair})$ and $P(3 \text{ and loaded})$ using the formula $P(AB) = P(A|B) \times P(B)$:

$$P(3 \text{ and fair}) = P(3 \mid \text{fair}) \times P(\text{fair})$$
$$= (0.166)(0.50) = 0.083$$
$$P(3 \text{ and loaded}) = P(3 \mid \text{loaded}) \times P(\text{loaded})$$
$$= (0.60)(0.50) = 0.300$$

A 3 can occur in combination with the state "fair die" or in combination with the state "loaded die." The sum of their probabilities gives the unconditional or marginal probability of a 3 on the toss, namely, $P(3) = 0.083 + 0.300 = 0.383$.

If a 3 does occur, and if we do not know which die it came from, the probability that the die rolled was the fair one is

$$P(\text{fair} \mid 3) = \frac{P(\text{fair and 3})}{P(3)} = \frac{0.083}{0.383} = 0.22$$

The probability that the die rolled was loaded is

$$P(\text{loaded} \mid 3) = \frac{P(\text{loaded and 3})}{P(3)} = \frac{0.300}{0.383} = 0.78$$

These two conditional probabilities are called the *revised* or *posterior probabilities* for the next roll of the die.

Before the die was rolled in the preceding example, the best we could say was that there was a 50–50 chance that it was fair (0.50 probability) and a 50–50 chance that it was loaded. After one roll of the die, however, we are able to revise our **prior probability** estimates. The new posterior estimate is that there is a 0.78 probability that the die rolled was loaded and only a 0.22 probability that it was not.

General Form of Bayes' Theorem

Another way to compute revised probabilities is with Bayes' theorem.

Revised probabilities can also be computed in a more direct way using a general form for Bayes' theorem. Recall from Equation B-5 that Bayes' law for the conditional probability of event A, given event B, is

$$P(A \mid B) = \frac{P(AB)}{P(B)}$$

However, we can show that

$$P(A \mid B) = \frac{P(B \mid A)P(A)}{P(B \mid A)P(A) + P(B \mid \overline{A})P(\overline{A})} \tag{B-7}$$

where

$\overline{A}$ = the complement of the event A; for example,

if A is the event "fair die," then $\overline{A}$ is "unfair" or "loaded die"

Now let's return to Example 7.

Although it may not be obvious to you at first glance, we used this basic equation to compute the revised probabilities. For example, if we want the probability that the fair die was rolled given the first toss was a 3, namely, $P(\text{fair die} \mid 3 \text{ rolled})$, we can let

event "fair die" replace A in Equation B-7.

event "loaded die" replace $\overline{A}$ in Equation B-7.

event "3 rolled" replace B in Equation B-7.

We can then rewrite Equation B-7 and solve as follows:

$$P(\text{fair die} \mid 3 \text{ rolled}) = \frac{P(3 \mid \text{fair})P(\text{fair})}{P(3 \mid \text{fair})P(\text{fair}) + P(3 \mid \text{loaded})P(\text{loaded})}$$

$$= \frac{(0.166)(0.50)}{(0.166)(0.50) + (0.60)(0.50)}$$

$$= \frac{0.083}{0.383} = 0.22$$

This is the same answer that we computed in Example 7. Can you use this alternative approach to show that $P(\text{loaded die} \mid 3 \text{ rolled}) = 0.78$? Either method is perfectly acceptable, but when we deal with probability revisions in Chapter 9, you may find that Equation B-7 is easier to apply.

B.6   FURTHER PROBABILITY REVISIONS

Although one revision of prior probabilities can provide useful posterior probability estimates, additional information can be gained from performing the experiment a second time. If it is financially worthwhile, a decision maker may even decide to make several more revisions.

Example 8: A Second Probability Revision   Returning to Example 7, we now attempt to obtain further information about the posterior probabilities as to whether the die just rolled is fair or loaded. To do so, let us toss the die a second time. Again, we roll a 3. What are the further revised probabilities?

To answer this question, we proceed as before, with only one exception. The probabilities $P(\text{fair}) = 0.50$ and $P(\text{loaded}) = 0.50$ remain the same, but now we must compute $P(3,3 \mid \text{fair}) = (0.166)(0.166) = 0.027$ and $P(3,3 \mid \text{loaded}) = (0.6)(0.6) = 0.36$. With these joint probabilities of two 3s on successive rolls, given the two types of dice, we can revise the probabilities:

$$P(3,3 \text{ and fair}) = P(3,3 \mid \text{fair}) \times P(\text{fair})$$

$$= (0.027)(0.5) = 0.013$$

$$P(3,3 \text{ and loaded}) = P(3,3 \mid \text{loaded}) \times P(\text{loaded})$$

$$= (0.36)(0.5) = 0.18$$

Thus, the probability of rolling two 3s, a marginal probability, is 0.013 + 0.18 = 0.193, the sum of the two joint probabilities.

$$P(\text{fair} \mid 3,3) = \frac{P(3,3 \text{ and fair})}{P(3,3)}$$

$$= \frac{0.013}{0.193} = 0.067$$

$$P(\text{loaded} \mid 3,3) = \frac{P(3,3 \text{ and loaded})}{P(3,3)}$$

$$= \frac{0.18}{0.193} = 0.933$$

What has this second roll accomplished? Before we rolled the die the first time, we knew only that there was a 0.50 probability that it was either fair or loaded. When the first die was rolled in Example 7, we were able to revise these probabilities:

$$\text{probability the die is fair} = 0.22$$

$$\text{probability the die is loaded} = 0.78$$

Now, after the second roll in Example 8, our refined revisions tell us that

$$\text{probability the die is fair} = 0.067$$

$$\text{probability the die is loaded} = 0.933$$

This type of information can be extremely valuable in business decision making.

B.7   RANDOM VARIABLES

The preceding section discusses various ways of assigning probability values to the outcomes of an experiment. Let us now use this probability information to compute the expected outcome, variance, and standard deviation of the experiment. This can help select the best decision among a number of alternatives.

A **random variable** assigns a real number to every possible outcome or event in an experiment. It is normally represented by a letter such as X or Y. When the outcome itself is numerical or quantitative, the outcome numbers can be the random variable. For example, consider refrigerator sales at an appliance store. The number of refrigerators sold during a given day can be the random variable. Using X to represent this random variable, we can express this relationship as follows:

$$X = \text{number of refrigerators sold during the day}$$

In general, whenever the experiment has quantifiable outcomes, it is beneficial to define these quantitative outcomes as the random variable. Examples are given in Table B.1.

When the outcome itself is not numerical or quantitative, it is necessary to define a random variable that associates each outcome with a unique real number. Examples are given in Table B.2.

There are two types of random variables: **discrete random variables** and **continuous random variables**. Developing probability distributions and making computations based on these distributions depends on the type of random variable.

A random variable is a *discrete random variable* if it can assume only a finite or limited set of values. Which of the random variables in Table B.1 are discrete random variables?

TABLE B.1   **Examples of Random Variables**

EXPERIMENT	OUTCOME	RANDOM VARIABLES	RANGE OF RANDOM VARIABLES
Stock 50 Christmas trees	Number of Christmas trees sold	X = number of Christmas trees sold	$0, 1, 2, \ldots, 50$
Inspect 600 items	Number of acceptable items	Y = number of acceptable items	$0, 1, 2, \ldots, 600$
Send out 5000 sales letters	Number of people responding to the letters	Z = number of people responding to the letters	$0, 1, 2, \ldots, 5000$
Build an apartment building	Percent of building completed after 4 months	R = percent of building completed after 4 months	$0 \leq R \leq 100$
Test the lifetime of a lightbulb (minutes)	Length of time the bulb lasts up to 80 000 minutes	S = time the bulb burns	$0 \leq S \leq 80\,000$

TABLE B.2

Random Variables for Outcomes That Are Not Numbers

EXPERIMENT	OUTCOME	RANDOM VARIABLES	RANGE OF RANDOM VARIABLES
Students respond to a questionnaire	Strongly agree (SA) Agree (A) Neutral (N) Disagree (D) Strongly disagree (SD)	$X = \begin{cases} 5 \text{ if SA} \\ 4 \text{ if A} \\ 3 \text{ if N} \\ 2 \text{ if D} \\ 1 \text{ if SD} \end{cases}$	$1, 2, 3, 4, 5$
One machine is inspected	Defective Not defective	$Y = \begin{cases} 0 \text{ if defective} \\ 1 \text{ if not defective} \end{cases}$	$0, 1$
Consumers respond to how they like a product	Good Average Poor	$Z = \begin{cases} 3 \text{ if good} \\ 2 \text{ if average} \\ 1 \text{ if poor} \end{cases}$	$1, 2, 3$

Try to develop a few more examples of discrete random variables to be sure you understand this concept.

Looking at Table B.1, we can see that stocking 50 Christmas trees, inspecting 600 items, and sending out 5000 letters are all examples of discrete random variables. Each of these random variables can assume only a finite or limited set of values. The number of Christmas trees sold, for example, can only be integer numbers from 0 to 50. There are 51 values that the random variable X can assume in this example.

A *continuous random variable* is a random variable that has an infinite or an unlimited set of values. Are there any examples of continuous random variables in Tables B.1 or B.2? Looking at Table B.1, we can see that testing the lifetime of a lightbulb is an experiment that can be described with a continuous random variable. In this case, the random variable, S, is the time the bulb burns. It can last for 3206 minutes, 6500.7 minutes, 251.726 minutes, or any other value from 0 to 80 000 minutes. In most cases, the range of a continuous random variable is stated as: lower value $\leq S \leq$ upper value, such as $0 \leq S \leq 80\,000$. The random variable R in Table B.1 is also continuous. Can you explain why?

B.8   PROBABILITY DISTRIBUTIONS

Earlier we discussed the probability values of an event. We now explore the properties of **probability distributions**. We see how popular distributions, such as the normal, Poisson, and exponential probability distributions, can save us time and effort. Since selection of the appropriate probability distribution depends partially on whether the random variable is discrete or continuous, we consider each of these types separately.

Probability Distribution of a Discrete Random Variable

When we have a *discrete random variable*, there is a probability value assigned to each event. These values must be from 0 to 1, and they must sum to 1. Let's look at an example.

The 100 students in Pat Shannon's statistics class have just completed the instructor evaluations at the end of the course. Dr. Shannon is particularly interested in student response to the textbook because he is in the process of writing a competing statistics book. One of the questions on the evaluation survey was: "The textbook was well written and helped me acquire the necessary information."

5. Strongly agree
4. Agree
3. Neutral
2. Disagree
1. Strongly disagree

The students' response to this question in the survey is summarized in Table B.3. Also shown is the random variable X and the corresponding probability for each possible outcome. This **discrete probability distribution** was computed using the relative frequency approach presented previously.

The distribution follows the three rules required of all probability distributions: (1) the events are mutually exclusive and collectively exhaustive, (2) the individual probability values are between 0 and 1 inclusive, and (3) the total of the probability values sum to 1.

Although listing the probability distribution as we did in Table B.3 is adequate, it can be difficult to get an idea about characteristics of the distribution. To overcome this problem, the probability values are often presented in graph form. The graph of the distribution in Table B.3 is shown in Figure B.5.

The graph of this probability distribution gives us a picture of its shape. It helps us identify the central tendency of the distribution, called the **expected value**, and the amount of variability or spread of the distribution, called the *variance*.

Expected Value of a Discrete Probability Distribution

Once we have established a probability distribution, the first characteristic that is usually of interest is the *central tendency*, or average of the distribution. The expected value, a measure of central tendency, is computed as a weighted average of the values of the random variable:

The *expected value* of a discrete distribution is a weighted average of the values of the random variable.

$$E(X) = \sum_{i=1}^{n} X_i P(X_i) \tag{B-8}$$

$$= X_1 P(X_1) + X_2 P(X_2) + \ldots + X_n P(X_n)$$

TABLE B.3

Probability Distribution for Textbook Question

OUTCOME	RANDOM VARIABLE (X)	NUMBER RESPONDING	PROBABILITY $P(X)$
Strongly agree	5	10	0.1 = 10/100
Agree	4	20	0.2 = 20/100
Neutral	3	30	0.3 = 30/100
Disagree	2	30	0.3 = 30/100
Strongly disagree	1	10	0.1 = 10/100
		Total 100	1.0 = 100/100

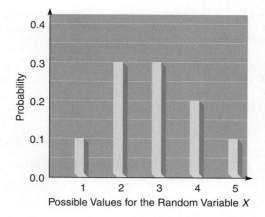

where

$$X_i = \text{random variable's possible values}$$

$$P(X_i) = \text{probability of each of the random variable's possible values}$$

$$\sum_{i=1}^{n} = \text{summation sign indicating we are adding all } n \text{ possible values}$$

$$E(X) = \text{expected value of the random variable}$$

The expected value of any discrete probability distribution can be computed by multiplying each possible value of the random variable, X_i, times the probability, $P(X_i)$, that outcome will occur, and summing the results, Σ. Here is how the expected value can be computed for the textbook question:

$$E(X) = \sum_{i=1}^{5} X_i P(X_i)$$
$$= X_1 P(X_1) + X_2 P(X_2) + X_3 P(X_3)$$
$$\qquad + X_4 P(X_4) + X_5 P(X_5)$$
$$= (5)(0.1) + (4)(0.2) + (3)(0.3)$$
$$\qquad + (2)(0.3) + (1)(0.1)$$
$$= 2.9$$

The expected value of 2.9 implies that the mean response is between disagree (2) and neutral (3), and that the average response is closer to neutral, which is 3. Looking at Figure B.5, this is consistent with the shape of the probability function.

Variance of a Discrete Probability Distribution

In addition to the central tendency of a probability distribution, most people are interested in the variability or the spread of the distribution. If the variability is low, it is much more likely that the outcome of an experiment will be close to the average or expected value. On the other hand, if the variability of the distribution is high, which means that the probability is spread out over the various random variable values, there is less chance that the outcome of an experiment will be close to the expected value.

A probability distribution is often described by its mean and variance. Even if most of the men in class (or in Canada) have heights between 165 cm and 185 cm there is still some small probability of outliers.

The **variance** of a probability distribution is a number that reveals the overall spread or dispersion of the distribution. For a discrete probability distribution, it can be computed using the following equation:

$$\text{Variance} = \sum_{i=1}^{n} [X_i - E(X)]^2 P(X_i) \tag{B-9}$$

where

$$X_i = \text{random variable's possible values}$$

$$E(X) = \text{expected value of the random variable}$$

$$[X_i - E(X)] = \text{difference between each value of the random variable and the expected value}$$

$$P(X_i) = \text{probability of each possible value of the random variable}$$

To compute the variance, each value of the random variable is subtracted from the expected value, squared, and multiplied by the probability of occurrence of that value. The results are then summed to obtain the variance. Here is how this procedure is done for Dr. Shannon's textbook question:

$$\text{Variance} = \sum_{i=1}^{5} [X_i - E(X)]^2 P(X_i)$$

$$\text{Variance} = (5 - 2.9)^2 (0.1) + (4 - 2.9)^2 (0.2) + (3 - 2.9)^2 (0.3) + (2 - 2.9)^2 (0.3)$$
$$+ (1 - 2.9)^2 (0.1)$$

$$= (2.1)^2 (0.1) + (1.1)^2 (0.2) + (0.1)^2 (0.3) + (-0.9)^2 (0.3) + (-1.9)^2 (0.1)$$

$$= 0.441 + 0.242 + 0.003 + 0.243 + 0.361$$

$$= 1.29$$

A related measure of dispersion or spread is the **standard deviation**. This quantity is also used in many computations involved with probability distributions. The standard deviation is just the square root of the variance.

$$\sigma = \sqrt{\text{variance}} \tag{B-10}$$

where

$$\sigma = \text{standard deviation}$$

The standard deviation for the textbook question is

$$\sigma = \sqrt{\text{variance}}$$
$$= \sqrt{1.29} = 1.14$$

Probability Distribution of a Continuous Random Variable

There are many examples of *continuous random variables*. The time it takes to finish a project, the number of litres in a barrel of butter, the high temperature during a given day, the exact length of a given type of lumber, and the weight of a railroad car of coal are all examples of continuous random variables. Since random variables can take on an infinite number of values, the fundamental probability rules for continuous random variables must be modified.

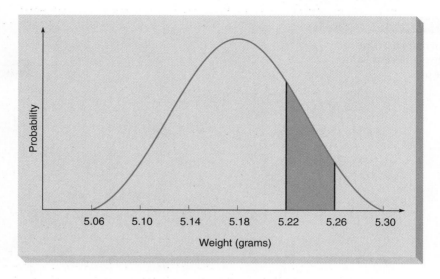

Sample Density Function

As with discrete probability distributions, the sum of the probability values must equal 1. Because there are an infinite number of values of the random variables, however, the probability of each value of the random variable must be 0. If the probability values for the random variable values were greater than 0, the sum would be infinitely large.

With a **continuous probability distribution**, there is a continuous mathematical function that describes the probability distribution. This function is called the **probability density function** or simply the *probability function*. It is usually represented by $f(X)$.

> A probability density function, $f(X)$, is a mathematical way of describing the probability distribution.

We now look at the sketch of a sample density function in Figure B.6. This curve represents the probability density function for the weight of a particular machined part. The weight could vary from 5.06 to 5.30 grams, with weights around 5.18 grams being the most likely. The shaded area represents the probability the weight is between 5.22 and 5.26 grams.

If we wanted to know the probability of a part weighing exactly 5.1300000 grams, for example, we would have to compute the area of a slice of width 0. Of course, this would be 0. This result may seem strange, but if we insist on enough decimal places of accuracy, we are bound to find that the weight differs from 5.1300000 grams *exactly*, be the difference ever so slight.

In this section we investigated the fundamental characteristics and properties of probability distributions in general. In the next three sections we introduce two important continuous distributions—the normal distribution and the exponential distribution—and a useful discrete probability distribution—the Poisson distribution.

B.9   THE NORMAL DISTRIBUTION

> The normal distribution affects a large number of processes in our lives (e.g., filling boxes of cereal with 575 grams of corn flakes). Each normal distribution depends on the mean and standard deviation.

One of the most popular and useful continuous probability distributions is the **normal distribution**. The probability density function of this distribution is given by the rather complex formula

$$f(X) = \frac{1}{\sigma\sqrt{2\pi}}\, e\left[\frac{-\frac{1}{2}\,(X-\mu)^2}{\sigma^2}\right] \tag{B-11}$$

The normal distribution is specified completely when values for the mean, μ, and the standard deviation, σ, are known. Figure B.7 on the next page shows several different normal distributions with the same standard deviation and different means. As shown,

FIGURE B.7

**Normal Distribution
with Different Values
for μ**

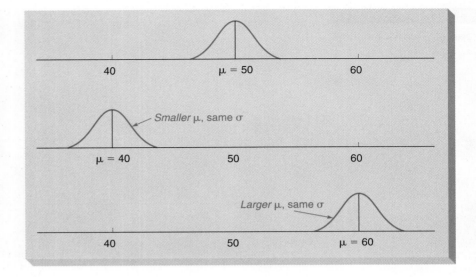

differing values of μ will shift the average or centre of the normal distribution. The overall shape of the distribution remains the same. Conversely, when the standard deviation is varied, the normal curve either flattens out or becomes steeper. This is shown in Figure B.8.

As the standard deviation, σ, becomes smaller, the normal distribution becomes steeper. When the standard deviation becomes larger, the normal distribution has a tendency to flatten out or become broader.

Area under the Normal Curve

Because the normal distribution is symmetrical, its midpoint (and highest point) is at the mean. Values on the X-axis are then measured in terms of how many standard deviations they lie from the mean. Recall that the area under the curve (in a continuous distribution) describes the probability that a random variable has a value in a specified interval. The normal distribution requires mathematical calculations beyond the scope of this book, but tables that provide areas or probabilities are readily available. For example, Figure B.9

FIGURE B.8

**Normal Distribution
with Different Values
for σ**

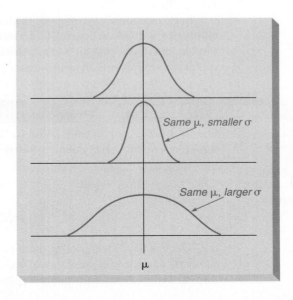

Three Common Areas under Normal Curves

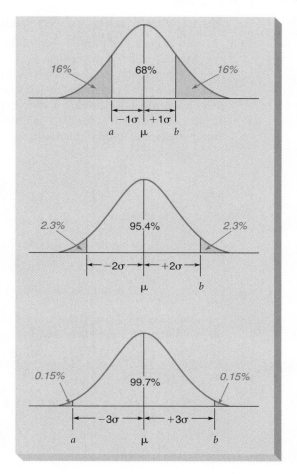

Figure B.9 is very important, and you should comprehend the meanings of ±1, 2, and 3 standard deviation symmetrical areas. Managers often speak of 95% and 99% confidence interval, which roughly refer to ±2 and 3 standard deviation graphs.

95% confidence is actually ±1.96 standard deviations, whereas ±3 standard deviations is actually a 99.7% spread.

illustrates three commonly used relationships that have been derived from standard normal tables (discussed in the next section). The area from point a to point b in the first drawing represents the probability, 68%, that the random variable will be within 1 standard deviation of the mean. In the middle graph, we see that about 95.4% of the area lies within ±2 standard deviations of the mean. The third figure shows that 99.7% lies between ±3σ.

Translating Figure B.9 into an application implies that if the mean IQ in Canada is $\mu = 100$ points and if the standard deviation is $\sigma = 15$ points, we can make the following statements:

1. 68% of the population have IQs between 85 and 115 points (i.e., ±1σ).
2. 95.4% of the people have IQs between 70 and 130 points (±2σ).
3. 99.7% of the population have IQs in the range from 55 to 145 points (±3σ).
4. Only 16% of the people have IQs greater than 115 points (from first graph, the area to the right of +1σ).

Many more interesting remarks could be drawn from these data. Can you tell the probability that a person selected at random has an IQ of less than 70? Greater than 145? Less than 130?

Using the Standard Normal Table

To use a table to find normal probability values, we follow two steps.

Step 1 Convert the normal distribution to what we call a *standard normal distribution*. A standard normal distribution is one that has a mean of 0 and a standard deviation of 1. All normal tables are set up to handle random variables with $\mu = 0$ and $\sigma = 1$. Without a standard normal distribution, a different table would be needed for each pair of μ and σ values. We call the new standard random variable Z. The value for Z for any normal distribution is computed from this equation:

$$Z = \frac{X - \mu}{\sigma} \qquad \text{(B-12)}$$

where

$$X = \text{value of the random variable we want to measure}$$

$$\mu = \text{mean of the distribution}$$

$$\sigma = \text{standard deviation of the distribution}$$

$$Z = \text{number of standard deviations from } X \text{ to the mean, } \mu$$

For example, if $\mu = 100$, $\sigma = 15$, and we are interested in finding the probability that the random variable X is less than 130, we want $P(X < 130)$.

$$Z = \frac{X - \mu}{\sigma} = \frac{130 - 100}{15}$$

$$= \frac{30}{15} = 2 \text{ standard deviations}$$

This means that the point X is 2.0 standard deviations to the right of the mean. This is shown in Figure B.10.

Normal Distribution Showing the Relationship between Z-Values and X-Values

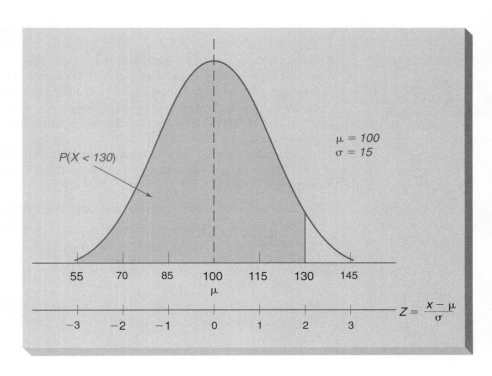

Step 2   Look up the probability from a table of normal curve areas. Appendix C on page 658 is such a table of areas for the standard normal distribution. It is set up to provide the area under the curve to the left of any specified value of Z.

To be sure you understand the concept of symmetry in Appendix C, try to find the probability such as $P(X < 85)$. Note that the standard normal table shows only right-hand-side Z-values.

Let's see how Appendix C can be used. The column of the left lists values of Z, with the second decimal place of Z appearing in the top row. For example, for a value of $Z = 2.00$ as just computed, find 2.0 in the left-hand column and 0.00 in the top row. In the body of the table, we find that the area sought is 0.97725, or 97.7%. Thus,

$$P(X < 130) = P(Z < 2.00) = 97.7\%$$

This suggests that if the mean IQ score is 100, with a standard deviation of 15 points, the probability that a randomly selected person's IQ is less than 130 is 97.7%. By referring back to Figure B.9, we see that this probability could also have been derived from the middle graph. (Note that $1.0 - 0.977 = 0.023 = 2.3\%$, which is the area in the right-hand tail of the curve.)

To feel comfortable with the use of the standard normal probability table, we need to work a few more examples. We now use the Haynes Construction Company as a case in point.

Haynes Construction Company Example

Haynes Construction Company builds primarily three- and four-unit apartment buildings (called triplexes and quadraplexes) for investors, and it is believed that the total construction time in days follows a normal distribution. The mean time to construct a triplex is 100 days, and the standard deviation is 20 days. Recently, the president of Haynes Construction signed a contract to complete a triplex in 125 days. Failure to complete the triplex in 125 days would result in severe penalty fees. What is the probability that Haynes Construction will not be in violation of their construction contract? The normal distribution for the construction of triplexes is shown in Figure B.11.

To compute this probability, we need to find the shaded area under the curve. We begin by computing Z for this problem:

$$Z = \frac{X - \mu}{\sigma}$$

$$= \frac{125 - 100}{20}$$

$$= \frac{25}{20} = 1.25$$

Looking in Appendix C for a Z value of 1.25, we find an area under the curve of 0.89435. (We do this by looking up 1.2 in the left-hand column of the table and then moving to the 0.05 column to find the value of $Z = 1.25$.) Therefore, the probability of not violating the contract is 0.89435, or about an 89% chance.

FIGURE B.11

Normal Distribution for Haynes Construction

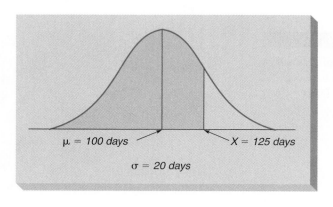

$\mu = 100$ days
$X = 125$ days
$\sigma = 20$ days

**Probability That Haynes
Will Receive the Bonus
by Finishing in 75 Days**

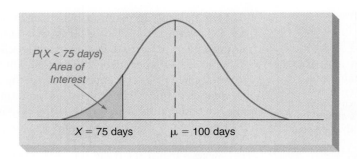

Now let us look at the Haynes problem from another perspective. If the firm finishes this triplex in 75 days or less, it will be awarded a bonus payment of $5000. What is the probability that Haynes will receive the bonus?

Figure B.12 illustrates the probability we are looking for in the shaded area. The first step is again to compute the Z-value:

$$Z = \frac{X - \mu}{\sigma}$$

$$= \frac{75 - 100}{20}$$

$$= \frac{-25}{20} = -1.25$$

This Z-value indicates that 75 days is -1.25 standard deviations to the left of the mean. But the standard normal table is structured to handle only positive Z-values. To solve this problem, we observe that the curve is symmetric. The probability that Haynes will finish in *less than 75 days is equivalent* to the probability that it will finish in *more than 125 days*. In Figure B.11 we found the probability that Haynes will finish in less than 125 days was 0.89435. So the probability it takes more than 125 days is

$$P(X > 125) = 1.0 - P(X < 125)$$

$$= 1.0 - 0.89435 = 0.10565$$

Thus, the probability of completing the triplex in 75 days or less is 0.10565, or about 10%.

One final example: What is the probability that the triplex will take between 110 and 125 days? We see in Figure B.13 that

$$P(110 < X < 125) = P(X < 125) - P(X < 110)$$

**Probability of Haynes'
Completion between
110 and 125 Days**

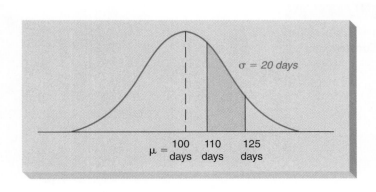

That is, the shaded area in the graph can be computed by finding the probability of completing the building in 125 days or less *minus* the probability of completing it in 110 days or less.

Recall that $P(X < 125$ days$)$ is equal to 0.89435. To find $P(X < 110$ days$)$, we follow the two steps developed earlier:

1. $$Z = \frac{X - \mu}{\sigma} = \frac{110 - 100}{20} = \frac{10}{20}$$

   $= 0.5$ standard deviations

2. From Appendix C, the area for $Z = 0.50$ is 0.69146. So the probability the triplex can be completed in less than 110 days is 0.69146. Finally,

$$P(110 < X < 125) = 0.89435 - 0.69146 = 0.20289$$

The probability that it will take between 110 and 125 days is about 20%.

B.10 THE EXPONENTIAL DISTRIBUTION

The **exponential distribution**, also called the **negative exponential distribution**, is used in dealing with queuing models. The exponential distribution describes the number of customers serviced in a time interval. The exponential distribution is a continuous distribution. Its probability function is given by

$$f(X) = \mu e^{-\mu x} \tag{B-13}$$

where

$X =$ random variable (service times)

$\mu =$ average number of units the service facility can handle in a specific period of time

$e \approx 2.718,$ the base of natural logarithms

The general shape of the exponential distribution is shown in Figure B.14.

FIGURE B.14

Negative Exponential Distribution

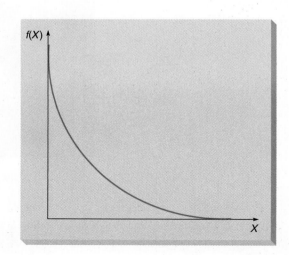

Its expected value and variance can be shown to be

$$\text{Expected value} = \frac{1}{\mu} \qquad \text{(B-14)}$$

$$\text{Variance} = \frac{1}{\mu^2} \qquad \text{(B-15)}$$

B.11   THE POISSON DISTRIBUTION

An important *discrete* probability distribution is the **Poisson distribution**.[1] We examine it because of its key role in complementing the exponential distribution in queuing models in Chapter 10. The distribution describes situations in which customers arrive independently during a certain time interval, and the number of arrivals depends on the length of the time interval. Examples are patients arriving at a health clinic, customers arriving at a bank window, passengers arriving at an airport, and telephone calls going through a central exchange.

The formula for the Poisson distribution is

$$P(X) = \frac{\lambda^x e^{-\lambda}}{X!} \qquad \text{(B-16)}$$

where

$P(X)$ = probability of exactly X arrivals or occurrences

λ = average number of arrivals per unit of time (the mean arrival rate), pronounced "lambda"

e = 2.718, the base of the natural logarithms

X = specific value (0, 1, 2, 3, and so on) of the random variable

FIGURE B.15

Sample Poisson Distribution with $\lambda = 2$

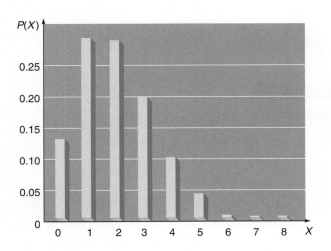

---

[1] This distribution, derived by Simeon Poisson in 1837, is pronounced "pwah-sahn."

The mean and variance of the Poisson distribution are equal and are computed simply as

$$\text{Expected value} = \lambda \qquad \text{(B-17)}$$

$$\text{Variance} = \lambda \qquad \text{(B-18)}$$

A sample distribution for $\lambda = 2$ arrivals is shown in Figure B.15.

GLOSSARY

Bayes' Theorem. A formula that allows us to compute conditional probabilities when dealing with statistically dependent events.

Classical or Logical Approach. An objective way of assessing probabilities based on logic.

Collectively Exhaustive. Including all possible outcomes of an experiment.

Conditional Probability. The probability of one event occurring given that another has taken place.

Continuous Probability Distribution. A probability distribution with a continuous random variable.

Continuous Random Variable. A random variable that can assume an infinite or unlimited set of values.

Dependent Events. The situation in which the occurrence of one event affects the probability of occurrence of some other event.

Discrete Probability Distribution. A probability distribution with a discrete random variable.

Discrete Random Variable. A random variable that can only assume a finite or limited set of values.

Expected Value. The (weighted) average of a probability distribution.

Exponential Distribution or Negative Exponential Distribution. A continuous probability distribution that describes the time between customer arrivals in a queuing situation.

Independent Events. The situation in which the occurrence of one event has no effect on the probability of occurrence of a second event.

Joint Probability. The probability of events occurring together (or one after the other).

Marginal or Simple Probability. The simple probability of an event occurring.

Mutually Exclusive. Describing a situation in which only one event can occur on any given trial or experiment.

Normal Distribution. A continuous bell-shaped distribution that is a function of two parameters, the mean and standard deviation of the distribution.

Objective Approach. A method of determining probability based on relative frequency, historical data, or logic.

Poisson Distribution. A discrete probability distribution used in queuing theory.

Prior Probability. A probability value determined before new or additional information is obtained. It is sometimes called an *a priori* probability estimate.

Probability. A statement about the likelihood of an event occurring. It is expressed as a numerical value from 0 to 1, inclusive.

Probability Density Function. The mathematical function that describes a continuous probability distribution. It is represented by $f(X)$.

Probability Distribution. The set of all possible values of a random variable and their associated probabilities.

Random Variable. A variable that assigns a number to every possible outcome of an experiment.

Relative Frequency Approach. An objective way of determining probabilities based on observing frequencies over a number of trials.

Revised or Posterior Probability. A probability value that results from new or revised information and prior probabilities.

Standard Deviation. The square root of the variance.

Subjective Approach. A method of determining probability values based on experience or judgment.

Variance. A measure of dispersion or spread of the probability distribution.

KEY EQUATIONS

(B-1) $0 \le P(\text{event}) \le 1$

A basic statement of probability.

(B-2) $P(A \text{ or } B) = P(A) + P(B)$

Law of addition for mutually exclusive events.

(B-3) $P(A \text{ or } B) = P(A) + P(B) - P(A \text{ and } B)$

Law of addition for events that are not mutually exclusive.

(B-4) $P(AB) = P(A) \times P(B)$

Joint probability for independent events.

(B-5) $P(A \mid B) = \dfrac{P(AB)}{P(B)}$

Bayes' law for conditional probabilities.

(B-6) $P(AB) = P(A|B) \times P(B)$

Joint probability for dependent events: a restatement of Bayes' law.

(B-7) $P(A|B) = \dfrac{P(B|A)P(A)}{P(B|A)P(A) + P(B|\overline{A})P(\overline{A})}$

A restatement of Bayes' law in general form.

(B-8) $E(X) = \displaystyle\sum_{i=1}^{n} X_i P(X_i)$

Computes the expected value of a discrete probability distribution.

(B-9) $\text{Variance} = \displaystyle\sum_{i=1}^{n} [X_i - E(X)]^2 P(X_i)$

Computes the variance of a discrete probability distribution.

(B-10) $\sigma = \sqrt{\text{variance}}$

Computes the standard deviation from the variance.

(B-11) $f(X) = \dfrac{1}{\sigma\sqrt{2\pi}}\, e^{\left[\dfrac{-\frac{1}{2}(X - \mu)^2}{\sigma^2}\right]}$

The density function for the normal probability distribution.

(B-12) $Z = \dfrac{X - \mu}{\sigma}$

Computes the number of standard deviations, Z, the point X is from the mean μ.

(B-13) $f(X) = \mu e^{-\mu x}$

The exponential distribution.

(B-14) $\text{Expected value} = \dfrac{1}{\mu}$

The expected value of an exponential distribution.

(B-15) $\text{Variance} = \dfrac{1}{\mu^2}$

The variance of an exponential distribution.

(B-16) $P(X) = \dfrac{\lambda^x e^{-\lambda}}{X!}$

The Poisson distribution.

(B-17) $\text{Expected value} = \lambda$

The mean of a Poisson distribution.

(B-18) $\text{Variance} = \lambda$

The variance of a Poisson distribution.

DISCUSSION QUESTIONS AND PROBLEMS

Discussion Questions

B-1   What are the two basic laws of probability?

B-2   What is the meaning of mutually exclusive events? What is meant by collectively exhaustive? Give an example of each.

B-3   Describe the various approaches used in determining probability values.

B-4   Why is the probability of the intersection of two events subtracted in the sum of the probability of two events?

B-5   What is the difference between events that are dependent and events that are independent?

B-6   What is Bayes' theorem, and when can it be used?

B-7   How can probability revisions assist in managerial decision making?

B-8   What is a random variable? What are the various types of random variables?

B-9   What is the difference between a discrete probability distribution and a continuous probability distribution? Give your own example of each.

B-10   What is the expected value, and what does it measure? How is it computed for a discrete probability distribution?

B-11   What is the variance, and what does it measure? How is it computed for a discrete probability distribution?

B-12   Name three business processes that can be described by the normal distribution.

B-13   After evaluating student responses to a question about a case used in class, the instructor constructed the following probability distribution. What kind of probability distribution is it?

RESPONSE	RANDOM VARIABLE, X	PROBABILITY
Excellent	5	0.05
Good	4	0.25
Average	3	0.40
Fair	2	0.15
Poor	1	0.15

Problems

B-14 A student taking Management Science 301 at university will receive one of five possible grades for the course: A, B, C, D, or F. The distribution of grades over the past two years is as follows:

GRADE	NUMBER OF STUDENTS
A	80
B	75
C	90
D	30
F	25
	Total 300

If this past distribution is a good indicator of future grades, what is the probability of a student receiving a C in the course?

B-15 A loonie is flipped twice. Calculate the probability of each of the following occurring.
  (a) A head on the first flip
  (b) A tail on the second flip given that the first toss was a head
  (c) Two tails
  (d) A tail on the first and a head on the second
  (e) A tail on the first and a head on the second or a head on the first and a tail on the second
  (f) At least one head on the two flips

B-16 An urn contains 8 red chips, 10 green chips, and 2 white chips. A chip is drawn and replaced, and then a second chip drawn. What is the probability of
  (a) a white chip on the first draw?
  (b) a white chip on the first draw and a red on the second?
  (c) two green chips being drawn?
  (d) a red chip on the second, given that a white chip was drawn on the first?

B-17 Evertight, a leading manufacturer of quality nails, produces 1-, 2-, 3-, 4-, and 5-inch nails for various uses. In the production process, if there is an overrun or if the nails are slightly defective, they are placed in a common bin. Yesterday, 651 of the 1-inch nails, 243 of the 2-inch nails, 41 of the 3-inch nails, 451 of the 4-inch nails, and 333 of the 5-inch nails were placed in the bin.
  (a) What is the probability of reaching into the bin and getting a 4-inch nail?
  (b) What is the probability of getting a 5-inch nail?
  (c) If a particular application requires a nail that is 3 inches or shorter, what is the probability of getting a nail that will satisfy the requirements of the application?

B-18 Last year, at Northern Manufacturing Company, 200 people had colds during the year. One hundred fifty-five people who did no exercising had colds, whereas the remainder of the people with colds were involved in a weekly exercise program. Half of the 1000 employees were involved in some type of exercise.

  (a) What is the probability that an employee will have a cold next year?
  (b) Given that an employee is involved in an exercise program, what is the probability that he or she will get a cold?
  (c) What is the probability that an employee who is not involved in an exercise program will get a cold next year?
  (d) Are exercising and getting a cold independent events? Explain your answer.

B-19 The Springfield Kings, a professional basketball team, has won 12 of its last 20 games and is expected to continue winning at the same percentage rate. The team's ticket manager is anxious to attract a large crowd to tomorrow's game but believes that depends on how well the Kings perform tonight against the Galveston Comets. He assesses the probability of drawing a large crowd to be 0.90 should the team win tonight. What is the probability that the team wins tonight and that there will be a large crowd at tomorrow's game?

B-20 David Wong teaches two undergraduate statistics courses at Southern Alberta College. The class for Statistics 201 consists of seven second-year students and three third-year students. The more advanced course, Statistics 301, has two second-year students and eight third-year students enrolled. As an example of business sampling technique, Professor Wong randomly selects from the stack of Statistics 201 registration cards the class card of one student, and then places that card back in the stack. If that student was in second year, Wong draws another card from the Statistics 201 stack; if not, he ramdomly draws a card from the Statistics 301 group. Are these two draws independent events? What is the probability of
  (a) a third-year student's name in the first draw?
  (b) a third-year name on the second draw, given that a second-year name was drawn first?
  (c) a third-year name on the second draw, given that a third-year name was drawn first?
  (d) a second-year name on both draws?
  (e) a third-year name on both draws?
  (f) one second-year and one third-year name on the two draws, regardless of order drawn?

B-21 The oasis outpost of Abu Ilan, in the heart of the Negev desert, has a population of 20 Bedouin tribesmen and 20 Farima tribesmen. El Kamin, a nearby oasis, has a population of 32 Bedouins and 8 Farima. A lost Israeli soldier, accidentally separated from his army unit, is wandering through the desert and arrives at the edge of one of the oases. The soldier has no idea which oasis he has found, but the first person he spots at a distance is a Bedouin. What is the probability that he wandered into Abu Ilan? What is the probability that he is in El Kamin?

B-22 The lost Israeli soldier mentioned in Problem B-21 decides to rest for a few minutes before entering the desert oasis he has just found. Closing his eyes, he dozes off for 15 minutes, wakes, and walks toward the centre of the oasis. The first person he spots this time he again recognizes as a Bedouin. What is the posterior probability that he is in El Kamin?

B-23 Ace Machine Works estimates that the probability their lathe tool is properly adjusted is 0.8. When the lathe is properly adjusted, there is a 0.9 probability that the parts produced pass inspection. If the lathe is out of adjustment, however, the probability of a good part being produced is only 0.2. A part randomly chosen is inspected and found to be acceptable. At this point, what is the posterior probability that the lathe tool is properly adjusted?

B-24 The South Street Softball League consists of three teams: Mama's Boys, team 1; the Killers, team 2; and the Machos, team 3. Each team plays the other teams just once during the season. The win–loss record for the past five years is as follows:

WINNER	(1)	(2)	(3)
Mama's Boys (1)	X	3	4
The Killers (2)	2	X	1
The Machos (3)	1	4	X

Each row represents the number of wins over the past five years. Mama's Boys beat the Killers three times, beat the Machos four times, and so on.

(a) What is the probability that the Killers will win every game next year?
(b) What is the probability that the Machos will win at least one game next year?
(c) What is the probability that Mama's Boys will win exactly one game next year?
(d) What is the probability that the Killers will win less than two games next year?

B-25 The schedule for the Killers next year is as follows (refer to Problem B-24):

Game 1: The Machos
Game 2: Mama's Boys

(a) What is the probability that the Killers will win their first game?
(b) What is the probability that the Killers will win their last game?
(c) What is the probability that the Killers will break even—win exactly one game?
(d) What is the probability that the Killers will win every game?
(e) What is the probability that the Killers will lose every game?
(f) Would you want to be the coach of the Killers?

B-26 The Northside Rifle team has two markspersons, Dick and Sally. Dick hits a bull's-eye 90% of the time, and Sally hits a bull's-eye 95% of the time.

(a) What is the probability that either Dick or Sally or both will hit the bull's-eye if each takes one shot?
(b) What is the probability that Dick and Sally will both hit the bull's-eye?
(c) Did you make any assumptions in answering the preceding questions? If you answered yes, do you think that you are justified in making the assumption(s)?

B-27 In a sample of 1000 representing a survey from the entire population, 650 people were from Laketown, and the rest of the people were from River City. Out of the sample, 19 people had some form of cancer. Thirteen of these people were from Laketown.

(a) Are the events of living in Laketown and having some sort of cancer independent?
(b) Which city would you prefer to live in, assuming that your main objective was to avoid having cancer?

B-28 Compute the probability of "loaded die, given that a 3 was rolled," as shown in Example 7, this time using the general form of Bayes' theorem from Equation B-7.

B-29 Which of the following are probability distributions? Why?

(a)

RANDOM VARIABLE X	PROBABILITY
−2	0.1
−1	0.2
0	0.3
1	0.25
2	0.15

(b)

RANDOM VARIABLE Y	PROBABILITY
1	1.1
1.5	0.2
2	0.3
2.5	0.25
3	−1.25

(c)

RANDOM VARIABLE Z	PROBABILITY
1	0.1
2	0.2
3	0.3
4	0.4
5	0.0

B-30 Harrington Health Food stocks five loaves of Nutri-Bread. The probability distribution for the sales of Nutri-Bread is listed in the following table. How many loaves will Harrington sell on average?

NUMBER OF LOAVES SOLD	PROBABILITY
0	0.05
1	0.15
2	0.20
3	0.25
4	0.20
5	0.15

B-31 What are the expected value and variance of the following probability distribution?

RANDOM VARIABLE X	PROBABILITY
1	0.05
2	0.05
3	0.10
4	0.10
5	0.15
6	0.15
7	0.25
8	0.15

B-32 Sales for Fast Kat, a catamaran sailboat, have averaged 250 boats per month over the past five years, with a standard deviation of 25 boats. Assuming that the demand is about the same as past years and follows a normal curve, what is the probability sales will be less than 280 boats?

B-33 Refer to Problem B-32. What is the probability that sales will be more than 265 boats during the next month? What is the probability that sales will be less than 250 boats next month?

B-34 Precision Parts is a job shop that specializes in producing electric motor shafts. The average shaft size for the E300 electric motor is 1 cm, with a standard deviation of 0.20 cm. It is normally distributed. What is the probability that a shaft selected at random will be between 1 and 1.2 cm?

B-35 Refer to Problem B-34. What is the probability that a shaft size will be greater than 1.2 cm? What is the probability that a shaft size will be between 0.96 and 1.08 cm? What is the probability that a shaft size will be under 0.8 cm?

B-36 An industrial oven used to cure sand cores for a factory manufacturing engine blocks for small cars is able to maintain fairly constant temperatures. The temperature range of the oven follows a normal distribution with a mean of 230°C and a standard deviation of 14°C. Leslie Larsen, president of the factory, is concerned about the large number of defective cores that have been produced in the last several months. If the oven gets hotter than 246°C, the core is defective. What is the probability that the oven will cause a core to be defective? What is the probability that the temperature of the oven will range from 238°C to 243°C?

B-37 Steve Goodman, production foreman for the Florida Gold Fruit Company, estimates that the average sale of oranges is 4700 and the standard deviation is 500 oranges. Sales follow a normal distribution.

(a) What is the probability that sales will be greater than 5500 oranges?
(b) What is the probability that sales will be greater than 4500 oranges?
(c) What is the probability that sales will be less than 4900 oranges?
(d) What is the probability that sales will be less than 4300 oranges?

B-38 Susan Williams has been the production manager of Medical Suppliers, Inc., for the past 17 years. Medical Suppliers, Inc. is a producer of bandages and arm slings. During the past five years, the demand for No-Stick bandages has been fairly constant. On the average, sales have been about 87 000 packages of No-Stick. Susan has reason to believe that the distribution of No-Stick follows a normal curve, with a standard deviation of 4000 packages. What is the probability that sales will be less than 81 000 packages?

B-39 Armstrong Faber produces a standard number two pencil called Ultra-Lite. Since Chuck Armstrong started Armstrong Faber, sales had grown steadily. With the increase in the price of wood products, however, Chuck has been forced to increase the price of the Ultra-Lite pencils. As a result, the demand for Ultra-Lite has been fairly stable over the past six years. On the average, Armstrong Faber has sold 457 000 pencils each year. Furthermore, 90% of the time sales have been between 454 000 and 460 000 pencils. It is expected that the sales follow a normal distribution with a mean of 457 000 pencils. Estimate the standard deviation of this distribution. (*Hint:* Work backward from the normal table to find Z. Then apply Equation B-12.)

B-40 Patients arrive at the emergency room of Elmdale Hospital at an average of five per day. The demand for emergency room treatment at Elmdale follows a Poisson distribution.

(a) Compute the probability of exactly 0, 1, 2, 3, 4, and 5 arrivals per day.
(b) What is the sum of these probabilities, and why is the number less than 1?

B-41 Using the data in Problem B-40, determine the probability of more than three visits for emergency room service on any given day.

B-42 Cars arrive at Carla's Muffler shop for repair work at an average of three per hour, following an exponential distribution.

(a) What is the expected time between arrivals?
(b) What is the variance of the time between arrivals?

APPENDIX C: AREAS UNDER THE STANDARD NORMAL CURVE

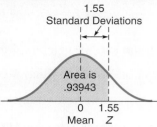

1.55
Standard Deviations

Area is
.93943

0   1.55
Mean Z

Example: To find the area under the normal curve, you must know how many standard deviations that point is to the right of the mean. Then the area under the normal curve can be read directly from the normal table. For example, the total area under the normal curve for a point that is 1.55 standard deviations to the right of the mean is .93943.

Z	.00	.01	.02	.03	.04	.05	.06	.07	.08	.09
0.0	.50000	.50399	.50798	.51197	.51595	.51994	.52392	.52790	.53188	.53586
0.1	.53983	.54380	.54776	.55172	.55567	.55962	.56356	.56749	.57142	.57535
0.2	.57926	.58317	.58706	.59095	.59483	.59871	.60257	.60642	.61026	.61409
0.3	.61791	.62172	.62552	.62930	.63307	.63683	.64058	.64431	.64803	.65173
0.4	.65542	.65910	.66276	.66640	.67003	.67364	.67724	.68082	.68439	.68793
0.5	.69146	.69497	.69847	.70194	.70540	.70884	.71226	.71566	.71904	.72240
0.6	.72575	.72907	.73237	.73536	.73891	.74215	.74537	.74857	.75175	.75490
0.7	.75804	.76115	.76424	.76730	.77035	.77337	.77637	.77935	.78230	.78524
0.8	.78814	.79103	.79389	.79673	.79955	.80234	.80511	.80785	.81057	.81327
0.9	.81594	.81859	.82121	.82381	.82639	.82894	.83147	.83398	.83646	.83891
1.0	.84134	.84375	.84614	.84849	.85083	.85314	.85543	.85769	.85993	.86214
1.1	.86433	.86650	.86864	.87076	.87286	.87493	.87698	.87900	.88100	.88298
1.2	.88493	.88686	.88877	.89065	.89251	.89435	.89617	.89796	.89973	.90147
1.3	.90320	.90490	.90658	.90824	.90988	.91149	.91309	.91466	.91621	.91774
1.4	.91924	.92073	.92220	.92364	.92507	.92647	.92785	.92922	.93056	.93189
1.5	.93319	.93448	.93574	.93699	.93822	.93943	.94062	.94179	.94295	.94408
1.6	.94520	.94630	.94738	.94845	.94950	.95053	.95154	.95254	.95352	.95449
1.7	.95543	.95637	.95728	.95818	.95907	.95994	.96080	.96164	.96246	.96327
1.8	.96407	.96485	.96562	.96638	.96712	.96784	.96856	.96926	.96995	.97062
1.9	.97128	.97193	.97257	.97320	.97381	.97441	.97500	.97558	.97615	.97670
2.0	.97725	.97784	.97831	.97882	.97932	.97982	.98030	.98077	.98124	.98169
2.1	.98214	.98257	.98300	.98341	.98382	.98422	.98461	.98500	.98537	.98574
2.2	.98610	.98645	.98679	.99713	.98745	.98778	.98809	.98840	.98870	.98899
2.3	.98928	.98956	.98983	.99010	.99036	.99061	.99086	.99111	.99134	.99158
2.4	.99180	.99202	.99224	.99245	.99266	.99286	.99305	.99324	.99343	.99361
2.5	.99379	.99396	.99413	.99430	.99446	.99461	.99477	.99492	.99506	.99520
2.6	.99534	.99547	.99560	.99573	.99585	.99598	.99609	.99621	.99632	.99643
2.7	.99653	.99664	.99674	.99683	.99693	.99702	.99711	.99720	.99728	.99736
2.8	.99744	.99752	.99760	.99767	.99774	.99781	.99788	.99795	.99801	.99807
2.9	.99813	.99819	.99825	.99831	.99836	.99841	.99846	.99851	.99856	.99861
3.0	.99865	.99869	.99874	.99878	.99882	.99886	.99899	.99893	.99896	.99900
3.1	.99903	.99906	.99910	.99913	.99916	.99918	.99921	.99924	.99926	.99929
3.2	.99931	.99934	.99936	.99938	.99940	.99942	.99944	.99946	.99948	.99950
3.3	.99952	.99953	.99955	.99957	.99958	.99960	.99961	.99962	.99964	.99965
3.4	.99966	.99968	.99969	.99970	.99971	.99972	.99973	.99974	.99975	.99976
3.5	.99977	.99978	.99978	.99979	.99980	.99981	.99981	.99982	.99983	.99983
3.6	.99984	.99985	.99985	.99986	.99986	.99987	.99987	.99988	.99988	.99989
3.7	.99989	.99990	.99990	.99990	.99991	.99991	.99992	.99992	.99992	.99992
3.8	.99993	.99993	.99993	.99994	.99994	.99994	.99994	.99995	.99995	.99995
3.9	.99995	.99995	.99996	.99996	.99996	.99996	.99996	.99996	.99997	.99997

Source: Reprinted from Robert O. Schlaifer. *Introduction to Statistics for Business Decisions*, published by McGraw-Hill Book Company, 1961, by permission of the copyright holder, the President and Fellows of Harvard College.

APPENDIX D: SOLUTIONS TO SELECTED PROBLEMS

Chapter 1

1-19 (a) 6250 units   (b) 7000 units   (c) $125 000
(d) $140 000   (e) Proposal A   (f) Proposal B

1-20 (a) 12 500 units   (b) $100 000   (c) $350 000

1-22 (a) 25 000 books   (b) $750 000

1-23 (a) 30 000 books   (b) $900 000

1-26 6881 units

Chapter 2

2-14 $X = 33.33$, $Y = 33.33$, Profit = $66.66

2-16 $X = 2$, $Y = 3$, Profit = $26

2-18 $X = 6$, $Y = 5$. Objective = 45

2-22 $X = 7.58$, $Y = 0.47$. Objective = 54.95

2-23 $X = 4.44$, $Y = 4.44$. Objective = 44.44

2-26 Bonds = $145 000, Equities = $105 000,
Return = $21 050

2-27 7 TV spots, 56 newspaper ads, exposure of
1 330 000

2-28 40 air conditioners, 60 fans. Profit = $1900

2-31 25 large sheds, 75 small sheds. Rent = $2750

2-35 NB Telecom = $1358.70, Newfoundland
Fisheries = $1820.65. Investment = $3179.35

Chapter 3

3-1 Produce 60 oak cabinets and 90 maple cabinets per
day. Daily Profit = $3930.

3-3 Solution: $X_1 = 6$, $X_2 = 4$, $X_3 = 20$, $X_4 = 4$, $X_5 = 12$,
$X_6 = 0$. Minimum number of agents = 46

3-5 15 Newspaper ads, 5 TV ads. Minimum
Cost = $20 125

3-7 183 Irish Sluggers, 75 Dublin Delights, 200
Tipperary Tipplers, 175 Belfast Blasters. Maximum
drinks = 633

3-9 Spend $30 000 on advertising, $73 333.33 on
travel, $146 666.67 on overtime, and apply a 20%
markup. Maximum = 2 823 666.67

3-11 Produce 20 regular DVDs, 153 deluxe
DVDs, 1147 1-GB flash drives, 20 30-GB
external hard drives, 23 60-GB external
hard drives, and 20 2-GB memory sticks.
Profit = $120 589.40

3-13 448.315 kilograms of iron 1, $X_5 = 530.337$ kilograms
of iron 2, $X_8 = 21.348$ kilograms of carbide 3.
Cost = $158.79

3-15 $L = 2$ large buses, S = 2 small buses, $M = 4$
minivans. Minimum cost = $820 000

3-17 Purchase 9 long range (B949), 16 medium range
(A656), and 5 short range (B343). Maximum profit
= $102 600 000

Chapter 4

4-10 (a) Solution changes to $X = 50$, $Y = 0$, Profit =
$150   (b) Solution remains at $X = 33.33$,
$Y = 33.33$, Profit changes to $75   (c) Solution
stays at same corner point, but now $X = 42.86$,
$Y = 14.28$, Profit = $57.14

4-12 (a) Solution changes to $X = 2.86$, $Y = 1.71$,
Profit = $21.71   (b) Solution changes to $X = 5$,
$Y = 1.5$, Profit = $29

4-13 (a) Changing the OFC for Y to $5 does not change
the optimal corner point. However, the value of the
objective function increases from $45 to $55.
(b) Changing the unit profit of X to $1.50 makes
the slope of the payoff line parallel to the binding
constraint $3X + 6Y \leq 48$. The problem will now
have multiple optimal solutions.
(c) A two-unit increase to the RHS of the constraint enlarges the feasible region slightly. The
same corner point (i.e., the intersection of the
same two binding constraints) remains optimal,
and the profit increases from $45 to $46.70.

4-18 We use the sensitivity report given in Screenshot 4.8
to answer the following questions.
(a) If the daily allowance for zinc is increased
to 1.02 milligrams, the total cost will increase by
$0.02 \times \$0.043 = \$0.00086$.
(b) Cost of food A increases by $0.05, cost of food
B decreases by $0.10. First we check the 100% rule:
$(0.05/1.15) + (0.10/\infty) < 1$. Therefore, the current
optimal solution remains optimal. The cost of food
A increases by $0.112 \times \$0.05 = \$0.0056$ and the cost
of food B decreases by $0.032 \times \$0.10 = \$0.0032$, for
a net increase of $0.0024.
(c) Check the 100% rule: $(0.01/0.028) + (25/5) > 1$;
therefore we cannot be sure how these simultaneous changes will affect the minimum cost.

4-20 (a) Each additional gram of carbohydrates
allowed in the meal will reduce the meal cost by
$0.007. Each additional milligram of iron
required in the diet will cause the meal cost to
increase by $0.074.
(b) Each kilogram of milk used in the diet will
cause the meal cost to increase by $0.297 (reduced
cost).
(c) Beans currently cost $1.16 per kilogram. The price
of beans would have to decrease by at least $0.522 (to
$0.638) before including them in the meal.
(d) None of the allowable increase and allowable
decrease values for the objective function coefficients is zero. Further, all items that are currently
not in the meal (milk, fish, and beans) have
nonzero reduced costs. The current solution is,
therefore, a unique optimal solution.

4-22 (a) The 2 kilograms will cause profit to increase to
$29.
(b) The 1.5 hours will cause profit to increase to
$29.5.

(c) 100% rule: $(1/2) + (1.5/4) = 0.875 < 1$. The shadow prices are valid. New profit = $27.75. The deal is not worthwhile.

(d) 100% rule: $(0.75/1) + (0.25/1) = 1$. The solution remains optimal. New profit = $28.50.

(e) Decrease in current profit if 1 unit of the new product is produced is $1.50. Profit contribution of new product = $2. Hence, the net profit will increase by $0.50 for each unit produced of the new product.

4-24   Since the Compact model's profit contribution of $7.15 is smaller than the $7.395 value of the resources required, the Compact model is *not* attractive to make. The Kiddo model's profit contribution of $10.40 exceeds the $8.726 cost of resources, therefore the Kiddo model is attractive.

4-26   (a) Assuming labour costs do not change, this implies that material costs can vary between −$1 $(= \$4 - \$5$, rounded to $0) and $7.33 $(= \$4 + \$3.33)$ without affecting the current optimal production mix. Note that a decrease in material cost translates to an increase in the profit contribution, and vice versa.

(b) Given the optimal production plan, we can determine whether or not the new polishing process will have sufficient capacity to support that plan. The constraint (in hours) is: 1/6 (TiniTote) + 1/4 (TubbyTote) + 1/5 (ToddleTote) ≤ 48. Now we substitute the previous optimal production decision: 1/6(100) + 1/4(35) + 1/5(90) = 43.42 ≤ 48. Therefore, there is sufficient capacity in the proposed polishing operation to sustain the optimal production plan.

4-29   (a) The objective function represents the total profit to be made from the sale of all of the tables and chairs. The production plan includes all items in the product list: oak tables and chairs, cherry tables and chairs, and pine tables and chairs.

(b) The binding constraints are: labour, cherry wood, oak wood, pine wood, minimum oak tables, and minimum cherry tables.

(c) The unit profit of oak chairs can be any value between $35 to infinity without changing the production plan.

(d) The amount of oak available can be any value between 900 to 2468.93 pounds without changing the binding constraints.

(e) The report shows evidence of multiple optimal solutions since there are zero values in several entries of the Allowable Increase/Decrease columns for objective coefficients.

(f) The cherry wood will be completely consumed, so there will not be any left.

(g) The total requirement for chairs was 25 (10 each oak and cherry, 5 pine). The total surplus of chairs is 145.31 (41.67 oak, 75.56 cherry, and 28.08 pine).

4-32   (a) First, we check the 100% rule: $(15/\infty) + (15/\infty) \leq 1$. Therefore, the current solution remains optimal. The profit decreases by $(3 + 3) \times \$15 = \$90$.

(b) First, we check the 100% rule: $(40/\infty) + (40/\infty) \leq 1$. Therefore, the current solution remains

optimal. The profit increases by $\$40 \times 51.67 - \$40 \times 3 = \$1946.80$.

(c) These changes would exceed the allowable increase/decrease ranges for these coefficients. Therefore, we cannot evaluate the impact of this change with the current report.

(d) First, we check the 100% rule: $(20/88.33) + (10/13.25) = 0.98 \leq 1$. Therefore, the current production plan remains optimal. The profit increases by $\$20 \times 42.26 - \$10 \times 33.08 = \$514.40$.

(e) An increase of $6 is beyond the allowable increase for the pine chairs' OFC. Therefore, we cannot evaluate the impact of this change with the current report.

4-34   (a) The objective function represents the total cost of making every sandwich ($173.94). The current production plan includes every type of sandwich on the menu.

(b) The binding constraints are: the total number of sandwiches, the minimum number of tuna sandwiches, the minimum number of tuna and cheese sandwiches, the minimum number of ham sandwiches, the minimum number of ham and cheese sandwiches, the bread available, and the packaging material.

(c) The cost of cheese sandwiches can vary between $0 and $2.12.

(d) The quantity of tuna can vary between 3500 grams and infinity.

(e) This report does not show evidence of multiple optima. There are no zero values in the Allowable Increase/Decrease columns, and no items have zeroes in both the Final Value and Reduced Cost columns.

(f) 4.40 hours of labour remain.

4-38   (a) An additional kilogram of tuna would not change the optimal solution (shadow price = 0). This deal is not worthwhile.

(b) The allowable decrease for the constraint on the minimum number of ham sandwiches is 6.5; the allowable decrease on the constraint for the minimum number of ham and cheese sandwiches is 8.67. Tiger can substitute up to the allowable decrease in whole sandwiches (i.e., 6 ham sandwiches and 8 ham and cheese sandwiches and still be able to predict cost.

(c) There are a total of 62 meat sandwiches containing tuna or ham. 62/18 = 3.44. Therefore, Tiger must include 4 jars of pickles.

Chapter 5

5-12   Total distance = 5400 "student kilometres"

5-13   (a) Kamouraksa to Job 1—250 tonnes, Kamouraska to Job 2—250 tonnes, Kamouraska to Job 3—1000 tonnes, Chicoutimi to Job 1—1750 tonnes, Maniwaki to Job 2—2750 tonnes. Minimum Total Cost = $431 750

(b) The formulation should be expanded to include two additional decision variables: Chicoutimi to Maniwaki, and Kamouraska to Maniwaki. The

revised solution (see worksheet "b" in file)
5-13.XLS) is: Kamouraska to Maniwaki—1500
tonnes, Chicoutimi to Job 3—1000 tonnes,
Chicoutimi to Maniwaki—750 tonnes, Maniwaki
to Job 1—2000 tons, Maniwaki to Job 2—3000
tonnes. Total cost $27 500. Marc Simard saves
$4250 by consolidating shipping at Maniwaki.

5-14 Truro-Coaltown = 35, New Bedford-Coal Valley =
30, New Bedford-Coaltown = 5, New Bedford-Coal
Junction = 25, Glace Bay-Coaltown = 5, Glace
Bay-Coalsburg = 20, Total distance = 3100 kilometres

5-17 Cost with Saskatoon = $20 000, Cost with Quebec
City = $19 500. Quebec City should be selected.

5-21 A12 to W, A15 to Z, B2 to Y, B9 to X, Time = 50 hours

5-23 Assign Hawkins to cardiology (18), Condriac to
urology (32), Bardot to orthopedics (24), Hoolihan
to obstetrics (12). Minimum total value on the cost
scale is 86.

5-24 Stand 1 to C, Stand 2 to B, Stand 3 to A, Stand 4 to
D, Total distance = 18 kilometres

5-26 Total rating = 335

5-27 One solution is 1-2, 1-3, 1-4, 3-6, 4-5, 6-7, 7-9, 8-9,
9-12, 9-10, 10-11, 11-13, and 12-14. Total distance
= 4500 metres

5-29 1-3-5-7-10-13, Distance = 430 kilometres

5-34 The impact of the construction project to increase
the road capacity around the outside roads from
international Drive to Disney World would increase
the number of cars per hour to 1700 per hour (17).
The increase is 400 cars per hour as would be
expected.

5-36 The impact of the emergency repair is that nodes 6
and 7 cannot be used. All flow in and out of these
nodes is 0. As a result, the flow from the origin to
the final network node has been reduced to 2000
litres per hour (2).

5-37 Shortest distance is 74. The path is 1-3-7-11-14-16.

5-40 Total length is 21. One solution is 1-2, 1-3, 3-7, 4-5,
5-6, 6-8, 6-7, and 8-9.

Chapter 6

6-10 3 large posters, 4 small posters, Profit = $17

6-12 Build in Brossard, Pierrefonds, Anjou, Chomedey,
and Côte St. Luc, Profit = $37 000

6-13 Invest in BC Bonds, New Brunswick Gas, PEI Electric,
Northern Hotels, and Nunavik Art Company.
Maximum Expected Return = $285

6-15 (a) LP solution: Product 1 = 0, Product 2 = 3.38,
Product 3 = 9.69, Product 4 = 4.65; Maximum
Profit = $311.51

(b) IP Solution: Product 1 = 0, Product 2 = 0,
Product 3 = 12, Product 4 = 5; Maximum
Profit = $304

(c) You cannot find the optimal IP solution by
rounding.

6-17 Formulation:

Max $Z = 30X1 + 60X2 + 20X3 + 40X4 - 1000Y1 - 1500Y2 - 2000Y3 - 1250Y4$ s.t.

$7X1 + 3X2 + 4X3 + 5X4 \leq 2000$

$6X1 + 12X2 + 11X3 + 9X4 \leq 3000$

$8X1 + 9X2 + 7X3 + 4X4 \leq 1500$

$X1 \leq MY1$

$X2 \leq MY2$

$X3 \leq MY3$

$X4 \leq MY4$

where $X1, X2, X3, X4$ are integer
$Y1, Y2, Y3, Y4$ are binary

Solution: $X1 = X2 = X3 = 0, X4 = 333$;
Maximum profit = $12 070

6-19 Build 3 warehouses and 4 plants. Profit = $195 000

6-23 Select Projects 4, 5, and 6. NPV = $478 000

6-27 Make 800 chairs. Profit = $12 900

Chapter 7

7-13 Priority ranking for the three nominees:
Armstrong 0.442, Benson 0.293, Chowdhury 0.266.
Recommend Armstrong for the teaching award.

7-15 Consistency ratios for each of the three criteria are:
Return −0.075, Risk −0.016, Fees 0.016. Also overall
rankings for the three criteria have a consistency
ratio of 0.008. Since all consistency ratios are less
than 1 we conclude that Shelley was consistent in
assigning rankings. The priority rankings of the
three funds are A: 0.223, B: 0.518, and C: 0.260.
Recommend Fund B since it has the highest ranking.

7-17 Consistency ratios for each of the four criteria
are: Plot −0.021, Suspense −0.082, Pace −0.094;
Humour −0.028. Also overall rankings for the
four criteria have a consistency ratio of 0.021.
Since all consistency ratios are less than 1, we
conclude that the Awards Committee was consistent in assigning rankings. The priority rankings
of the three books are A: 0.498, B: 0.291, and
C: 0.211. Book A should get the award since it
has the highest ranking.

7-19 500 two-drawer cabinets, 400 three-drawer cabinets,
and two-drawer sales goal underachieved by 100.

7-23 $X_1 = 15, X_2 = 20$, first 3 priority goals fully satisfied, $d_1^+ = 30$

7-24 (b) $X_1 = 49, X_2 = 69, X_3 = 30, X_4 = 20$. All goals are
fully met. *Note:* To get this solution, we need to
restrict social time to 20 hours.

7-26 We solve 4 LP models that consider the ranked
goals in descending order of rank. Build 6 basketball courts, 4 baseball fields, 7 playgrounds, and 1
soccer field. All goals are fully achieved. Alternate
solutions may exist.

7-30 (a) The optimal solution is: $X_1 = 3.75, X_2 = 2.75$,
and $X_3 = 3.50$. Objective value = 373.63.
(b) This solution appears to be the global optimal
solution.

7-33 Alpha 21%, Beta 33%, Gamma 42%. Minimum
variance = 0.70

Chapter 8

8-13 Critical path: B-D-E-G. Project length = 26 days

8-15 Critical paths: A-C-G and B-E-G. Project length =
19 weeks

8-17 Critical path: A-D-G-I. Project length = 27 days

8-19 Critical path: C-D-E-F-H-K. Project length = 36.33 days

8-25 (a) P(need >= 17 months) = 0.9772
(b) P(need <= 20 months) = 0.3085
(c) P(need >= 23 months) = 0.1587
(d) P(need <= 25 months) = 0.9772

8-28 Value of work completed = $53 090; Actual cost = $55 000; Cost overrun = $1910

8-33 Crash activity D by 4 weeks and activity E by 2 weeks. Total crashing cost = $400

8-39 (a) Critical path: C-H-M-O. Project length = 32.05 weeks
(b) Critical path: C-H-M-O. Project length = 32.05 weeks

Chapter 9

9-14 Maximin criterion: best alternative is Texan. – $18 000

9-18 (a) Max EMV = $19 750. Decision = Move
(b) Min EOL = $15 000. Decision = Move
(c) Min EOL = 15 000 = EVPI

9-21 (a) Uncertainty
(c) Build large extension.
(d) Maximax criterion = build large extension

9-25 (a) Maximax = order 200
(b) Maximin = order 500
(c) Equally Likely = order 100
(d) Criterion of Realism = order 200
(e) Minimax Regret = order 100

9-29 (b) Back roads
(c) Time saved = 3.34 minutes

9-31 (a) Purchase analysis from professor. If the result is positive, construct imaging centre; if result is negative, do not construct.
(b) $11 140
(c) 55.7%

9-35 Market the new golf balls. If competitor enters market, set price Medium. If competitor does not enter market, set the price High. EMV = $325 000

9-41 (a) Accept the wager. Use a hard first serve. If the first serve is out of play, use a hard second serve. Expected utility = 0.588.
(b) You are a risk avoider.

9-45 (a) Conduct the survey. If response is positive, produce razor; if response is negative, do not produce razor. Expected return = $24 160
(b) EVPI = $30 000. EVSI = $9160. Efficiency = 30.53%
(c) EVPI = $30 000. EVSI = $17 080. Efficiency = 56.93%

9-50 (a) Get the information. If it is favourable, build the store; if it is unfavourable, don't build the store. Expected utility = 0.62.
(b) Sue is a risk seeker.

9-55 (a) Expected travel time on Main Street is 27.5 minutes. Main Street has a lower expected travel time.
(b) Expected utility on Main Street = 0.55. Therefore, the expressway maximizes utility.
(c) Bill is a risk avoider.

Chapter 10

10-11 (a) 0.375   (b) 0.2 days or 1.6 hours   (c) 0.225
(d) 0.141, 0.053, 0.020, 0.007

10-12 (a) 4.167 cars   (b) 0.4167 hours   (c) 0.5 hours
(d) 0.8333   (e) 0.1667

10-16 (a) 6 trucks   (b) 12 minutes   (c) 0.857   (d) 0.54
(e) $1728/day   (f) Yes. Savings = $3096

10-20 9 A.M.–3 P.M. shift: 3 doctors; 3 P.M.–8 P.M. shift: 2 doctors; 8 P.M.–midnight: 4 doctors.

10-24 $72 with 1 loader, $36 with 2 loaders, Savings = $36 with 2 loaders

10-25 Do not recommend a second gate.

10-32 Service rate should be 2.64 per hour. Service time should average 22.7 minutes per customer.

10-34 $L = 5.9625$ computers, $W = 6.625$ days. Worth up to $160 per day.

10-39 (a) Probability system is empty = 0.4167. Therefore, the probability of having to wait is 0.5833.
(b) Average number of customers in the queue $(L_q) = 0.4604$ (c) Average waiting time in the queue $(W_q) = 0.0921$ hours, or 5.53 minutes.

Chapter 11

Note: Answers in this chapter will vary based on number of replications used. Answers shown here are based on 200 replications using Data Table. Oracle Crystal Ball can also be used to generate Solutions with a larger number of replications.

11-15 Each replication of the model is for 1 year (52 weeks). The simulation model is then replicated 200 times using Data Table. The results are as follows:

BASED ON 1 REPLICATION		BASED ON 200 REPLICATIONS	
Average profit	$174.90	Average profit	$175.06
Probability (Profit >= $200)	0.1346	Probability (Profit >= $200)	0.1869

11-17 Based on 200 replications using Data Table, Maruggi's average ending balance at the end of the year seems to be positive (around $450). There is only around a 2% chance that Maruggi will have a negative ending balance in a month during the year. This is sufficiently low for us to paint a rather positive picture of his financial health.

11-20 (a) Each replication of the model consists of 1 month (30 days). Based on 200 replications using Data Table, the average monthly profit is around $6375.
(b) We use Scenario Manager to evaluate the impact of each order quantity. Based on 200 replications, the maximum average profit is achieved when Pierre leases 30 kayaks.

11-25 Each replication of the model consists of one quarter (90 days). Based on 200 replications using Data Table, the average quarterly cost is just under $5000, with an average stockout percentage of around 4.32%.

11-30 Each replication of the model consists of 1 flight.
(a) Based on 200 replications using Data Table, the average profit per flight is around $198.
(b) We use Scenario Manager to evaluate the impact of each overbooking quantity. Based on 200 replications, overbooking by zero passengers seems to result in the highest average profit per flight.

11-34 Each replication of the model consists of 1 month (30 days). Based on 200 replications using Data Table, Alfredo's total monthly profit will average around $238 000.

11-39 Each replication of the model consists of one baseball game. We can use Scenario Manager to evaluate the impact of each order size. Based on 200 replications, it appears that Ann should order 170 hotdogs. The expected profit is around $107, and the percentage of unsold hotdogs is around 12%.

11-44 Each replication of the model consists of 100 customers. Based on 200 replications using Data Table, the average number of customers in line (average queue length) is around 2.09. The probability that a customer will have to wait 3 or more minutes is around 0.62.

11-48 Based on 200 replications using Data Table, the average project finish time is around 50.73 days, and probability that the project will finish in ≤ 49 days is around 0.405.

Chapter 12

12-13 $\text{MAPE}_{2\text{-MA}} = 22.57\%$, $\text{MAPE}_{3\text{-MA}} = 22.92\%$, $\text{MAPE}_{4\text{-MA}} = 27.07\%$, $\text{MAPE}_{3\text{-WMA}} = 21.17\%$, $\text{MAPE}_{\text{Exp Sm}} = 25.50\%$. The three-year weighted moving average should be selected because it has the lowest MAPE.

12-17 Week 13 forecasts: 2-period MA = 32.5; 3-period MA = 30.0; 4-period MA = 26.75

12-23 (a) $\text{MAPE}_{0.1} = 40.61\%$, $\text{MAPE}_{0.6} = 38.41\%$, $\text{MAPE}_{0.9} = 38.54\%$. $\text{Forecast}_{0.1} = 47$, $\text{Forecast}_{0.6} = 58$, $\text{Forecast}_{0.9} = 63$.
(b) 0.9

12-31 Seasonalized sales forecast = Trend forecast × seasonal index. Hence the seasonalized forecasts for quarters I to IV are $130 000, $108 000, $98 000, and $176 000 respectively.

12-36 (a) Average GPA = 2.094 + 0.002 × GMAT
(b) $R^2 = 0.439$, which implies 43.9% of the variation in GPA is explained by GMAT scores.
(c) 3.22 to 3.96

12-39 (a) Average Demand = 13.249 + 0.004 × Advertising dollars + 0.104 × Snowfall
(b) $R^2 = 0.461$, which implies 46.1% of the variation in demand is explained by advertising dollars spent and annual snowfall.
(c) The predicted demand for an advertising budget of $3600 and expected snowfall of 152.4 centimetres is 34.01 units.

12-43 We have data for 16 periods, with 4 seasons (quarters) per year. The MAPE for this model is 0.76%. Seasonalized forecasts for the 4 quarters of 2005 are 10 473.877, 10 580.211, 10 657.009, and 10 818.609 respectively.

12-47 (a) Seasonalized forecasts for the 4 quarters of Year 5 are 335.740, 348.626, 372.056, and 426.170 respectively. MAPE = 4.41%
(b) Seasonalized forecasts for the 4 quarters of Year 5 are 335.258, 347.784, 371.059, and 423.335 respectively. MAPE = 4.34%
(c) The additive decomposition model has a slightly lower MAPE.

Appendix B

B-14 0.30

B-16 (a) 0.10   (b) 0.04   (c) 0.25   (d) 0.40

B-18 (a) 0.20   (b) 0.09   (c) 0.31   (d) dependent

B-19 0.54

B-23 0.947

B-28 0.78

B-30 2.85

B-31 $E(X) = 5.45$, Variance = 4.047

B-32 0.8849

B-34 0.3413

B-38 0.0668

B-39 1829.27

B-40 (b) 0.6125

B-41 0.7365

APPENDIX E: SOLUTIONS TO SELF-TESTS

Chapter 1

1. c
2. d
3. b
4. c
5. a
6. a
7. a
8. a
9. b
10. a
11. c
12. Decision modeling
13. Defining the problem
14. schematic model
15. algorithm
16. Decision modeling
17. quantitative analysis, management science
18. probabilities
19. parameter
20. formulation, solution, interpretation

Chapter 2

1. b
2. b
3. a
4. b
5. c
6. d
7. b
8. a
9. b
10. c
11. a
12. b
13. b
14. b
15. a
16. d
17. b

Chapter 3

1. a
2. b
3. b
4. b
5. b
6. d
7. e
8. e
9. d
10. c
11. c
12. c
13. b

Chapter 4

1. a
2. b
3. a
4. b
5. b
6. a
7. b
8. a
9. b
10. c
11. a
12. b
13. a
14. b
15. b

Chapter 5

1. c
2. e

3. e
4. b
5. c
6. a
7. a
8. b
9. shortest path
10. maximal flow
11. minimal-spanning tree
12. c
13. a

Chapter 6

1. a
2. c
3. b
4. d
5. a
6. a
7. a
8. b
9. a
10. d
11. a
12. b
13. b

Chapter 7

1. d
2. b
3. b
4. d
5. a
6. a
7. a
8. b
9. b
10. a
11. c
12. b
13. e

Chapter 8

1. d
2. b
3. a
4. e
5. c
6. b
7. a
8. d
9. critical
10. optimistic, most likely, pessimistic

11. c
12. b
13. a
14. c
15. b

Chapter 9

1. a
2. d
3. e
4. b
5. e
6. b
7. c
8. c
9. e
10. e
11. d
12. d
13. decision trees
14. posterior probabilities
15. standard gamble

Chapter 10

1. a
2. a
3. b
4. e
5. e
6. c
7. c
8. a
9. b
10. b
11. c
12. first come, first served
13. exponentially distributed
14. simulation
15. unlimited

Chapter 11

1. b
2. b
3. a
4. b
5. a
6. b
7. (1) define the problem, (2) introduce the variables associated with the problem, (3) construct a numerical model, (4) set up possible courses of action for testing, (5) run the experiment,

(6) consider the results, and
(7) decide what course of action
to take

8. (1) it is relatively straightforward and flexible, (2) it can be
used to analyze large and complex real-world situations that
cannot be solved by conventional decision models, (3) it
allows what-if types of questions, (4) it does not interfere
with the real-world system,
(5) it allows us to study the
interactive effects of individual
components or variables to
determine which ones are
important, (6) it allows time
compression, and (7) it
allows for the inclusion of real-
world complications that most
decision models cannot permit

9. (1) it can be very expensive,
(2) it does not generate
optimal solutions to problems,
(3) managers must generate
all of the conditions and
constraints for solutions that
they want to examine, and

(4) each simulation model is
unique

10. b
11. d
12. c
13. e
14. c
15. b
16. d
17. b
18. a

Chapter 12

1. d
2. c
3. b
4. b
5. b
6. Trend × Seasonality × Cycles × Random variations
7. b
8. a
9. d
10. b
11. b
12. a
13. a
14. a

15. a
16. independent variable is said to cause variations in the dependent variable
17. (1) moving averages,
(2) weighted moving averages,
(3) exponential smoothing,
(4) linear trend projection,
(5) decomposition
18. (1) trend, (2) seasonality,
(3) cycles, (4) random variations
19. c
20. Simple regression has one independent variable and multiple regression has many independent variables.
21. Exponential smoothing is a weighted moving average model in which all previous values are weighted with a set of exponentially declining weights.
22. Study the shape of the relationship between the dependent and the independent variables.

INDEX

A

accounting data, 17
activities, identification of, 319–321
activity on arc (AOA), 323, 325–326
activity on node (AON), 323–324
activity times
    activity time estimates, 337–338
    beta probability distribution,
        337, 338f
    expected activity time, 338
    identifying, 321
    most likely time (m), 337
    optimistic time (a), 337, 338
    PERT, 337–38
    pessimistic time (b), 337, 338
    project completion, probability
        of, 338–340, 340f
    project completion time, for given
        confidence level, 340–341
    variability in, 335–342
    variance of activity completion
        time, 341
add-ins, reasons for using, 512–513
additive decomposition model, 555
additivity, 28
adjusted shadow price, 145
Air Canada, 95
Air Canada check-in simulation, 479
Air Transat, 43
Alberta Plains Turkey Farm, 43–46,
    60–61
algorithm, 8
algorithmic solution procedures, 64–65
allowable decrease, 139
allowable increase, 139
allowable ranges in objective function
    coefficients, 140–141
alternate optimal solutions, 49–50,
    50f, 146
American Airlines, 29, 568
Analysis ToolPak, 573, 589–592, 596–600
analysts, 9
analytic hierarchy process (AHP)
    consistency, 273
    consistency ratio, 274
    described, 266–267
    illustration of, 267–275
    multiple criteria, 268–270

    pairwise comparisons, 267, 269t, 275t
    pairwise comparisons matrix,
        269, 275
    priorities, 267
    priority matrix, 275, 275t
    priority vector, 271
    recommendations, 275
    synthesis, 270–271
analytic process hierarchy models,
    nature of, 266–267
Anderson Electronics example, 142–146
Answer Report, 57, 59f, 136
arcs, 178
Arnold's Muffler Shop example,
    446–450, 451–453
arrival characteristics, 436–438
arrival distribution, 436–438
arrival population, 436
arrivals, behaviour of, 438
assignment model
    binary variables, 195
    constraints, 195
    described, 178, 193
    Excel solution, 196
    illustration of, 196
    linear programming model,
        195–196
    maximization assignment
        models, 196
    objective function, 195
    solution, 194–195
    unbalanced assignment
        problems, 196
assignment problems, 93, 95
Assume Linear Model, 56, 136
Assume Non-Negative, 56, 136
assumptions, 16–17
AT&T, 65, 181

B

backward pass, 329
balanced problem, 182
balking, 438
basic time-series forecasting models.
    See time-series forecasting models
The Bay, wait times at, 432
Bayesian analysis, 403–406
Bayes' theorem, 636, 637–639
beta probability distribution, 337, 338f

Big-M method, 252–253
binary requirement, 247
binary variables, 195, 229, 243–247
binding constraint, 131
blending problems, 101–103
branch-and-bound (B&B) method
    described, 235
    diagram, 243f
    illustration, 237–241
    inferior solution, 241
    lower bounds, 241–243
    maximization problem, 241
    minimization problem, 242–243
    Solver solution, 243, 244
    stopping rules, 241
    subproblems, creation of, 238–239
    upper bounds, 241–243
branching, 235, 239
break-even analysis spreadsheet
    example, 13–15
break-even point (BEP), 14
break-even point in dollars, 14
British Airways, 320
budgeting process, 342
Burn-off diet drink example, 150–154

C

calling population, 436
Canadian Market Research, 87–89
Canadian National Railway Company
    (CN), 553
Canadian Pacific Railway (CPR), 2–3
Capital Regional District, 201
causal forecasting models
    coefficient of determination, 588
    correlation coefficient, 586
    described, 552
    multiple regression model,
        582, 592–600
    purpose of, 582
    regression analysis, 589–592
    simple regression model, 582–589
    standard error of the estimate,
        585–586, 601
centred moving average, 575, 578
certainty, 28
certainty equivalent, 407
Changing Cells (decision variables),
    52–53, 55–56

Children's Hospital of Eastern Ontario (CHEO), 483
Chile, pollution control, 16
    forests, harvesting, 88
classical approach, 632
coefficient of determination, 588
coefficient of realism, 382–383
collectively exhaustive events, 632, 633
complete enumeration, 8
computers in simulation modeling, 482–489
conditional payoff, 378
conditional probabilities, 635
conditional values, 378
conflicting viewpoints, 16
consistency ratio, 274
constraint coefficients, 129, 180
constraint LHS, 54
constraint RHS, 131–135, 138
constraints, 28, 31–32, 54
    assignment model, 195
    crash time limit constraints, 351
    crashing, 351
    demand constraints, 184
    k out of n variables constraint, 245–246
    linear, 28, 31–32, 288, 293–296
    maximal–flow model, 199
    mixed integer model, 250, 252
    nonlinear, 288, 296–298
    precedence constraints, 325
    precedence relationships, 331, 333
    shortest–path model, 202
    supply constraints, 183–184
    transportation model, 183
    transshipment model, 192
consumer market survey, 554
continuous random variables, 640, 641, 644–645
continuous uniform distribution, 484
controllable variable, 8
corner point method, 40–41, 46
corner point property, 39–40
corner points, 39
Cornwall (PEI) road system, 197–201
correlation coefficient, 586
CPLEX Optimization, Inc., 228
crash cost, 348, 349t
crash time, 322, 348
crash time limit constraints, 351
crashing
    crash cost, 348, 349t
    crash time, 348
    crash time limit constraints, 351
    decision variables, 350
    described, 347

hand calculations, 348–350
    linear programming, 350–352
    objective function, 350
    precedence constraints, 350
    project completion constraint, 351
    Solver solution, 352
    steps of, 348
criterion of realism, 382–383
critical path, 326–329, 330
critical path analysis
    backward pass, 326, 329
    crash time, 348
    described, 326
    earliest finish time (EFT), 326, 327, 328f
    earliest start time (EST), 326, 327, 328f
    forward pass, 326, 327–329
    identification of critical path, 330–332
    latest finish time (LFT), 326, 329, 330f
    latest start time (LST), 326, 329, 330f
    multiple critical paths, 331–332
    slack time, 330–332, 331f
critical path method (CPM), 321–322
cumulative probability distribution, 446, 447t
cycles, 555

D
Dantzig, George D., 26, 84
data
    accounting data, 17
    in decision modeling, 3–4
    garbage in, garbage out (GIGO), 8
    input data, 3–4, 5, 6, 8, 17
    qualitative data, 4
    quantitative data, 4
    validity of, 17
Data Employment Analysis (DEA), 82
Data Table, 492–494, 500–501, 507, 511, 518–521
decision alternative, 378
decision analysts, 16
decision-making environments
    decision making under certainty, 379
    decision making under risk, 380
    decision making under uncertainty, 379, 381–386
decision-making group, 499
decision making under certainty, 379
decision making under risk
    described, 380
    Excel solutions, 388–389
    expected monetary value (EMV), 386–387

expected opportunity loss (EOL), 387
    expected value of perfect information (EVPI), 387–388
    expected value with perfect information (EVwPI), 388
decision making under uncertainty
    coefficient of realism, 382–383
    criterion of realism (Hurwicz criterion), 382–383
    described, 379
    equally likely criterion (Laplace criterion), 383
    Excel solution, 384, 385–386
    maximax criterion, 382
    maximin criterion, 382
    minimax regret criterion, 383–384
decision modeling
    approach, 7f
    data, use of, 3–4
    decision problem, defining the, 6, 16–17
    definitions for, 3
    development of model, 7–8
    formulation, 6–8
    garbage in, garbage out (GIGO), 8
    heuristic approach, 8
    implementation, 7, 18–19
    input data, 4–5, 6, 8, 17
    interpretation step, 9
    introduction, 3
    origin of, 4
    potential development problems, 16–18
    qualitative data, 4
    quantitative data, 4
    real world, in, 9–10
    solution, 8–9, 18
    spreadsheets, role of, 4–5
    steps, 6–9
    types of models, 3
decision models
    break-even analysis spreadsheet example, 13–15
    deterministic models, 3, 5, 26
    mathematical models, 3, 7
    physical models, 3
    probabilistic models, 3, 6
    scale models, 3
    stochastic models, 3
    tax computation, spreadsheet example, 11–13
    textbook models, 17
    types of, 5–6
    understanding the model, 17

decision nodes, 390
decision problem, 6, 16–17
decision table, 379
decision theory
    conditional values, 378
    decision alternative, 378
    described, 390
    five steps of, 377–379
    payoff table, 379
    payoffs, 378
    utility as criterion, 410–412, 411f
decision tree
    creation of, with TreePlan, 392–397
    decision nodes, 390
    described, 390
    expanded example, 398–402
    expected value of sample
        information, 402–403
    folding back, 391
    folding back example, 400–402
    illustration of, 390f
    lottery ticket example, 406
    multistage decision making
        problems, 397
    outcomes, 378
    outcome nodes, 390
    sequential decisions, 397
Decision Tree feature, 318–321
decision variables, 8, 30–31, 33
    Big-M method, 252
    crashing, 350
    critical path, identification of,
        333–335
    mixed integer model, 249
decomposition, 555
defining the problem, 6–7, 16
Dell Corporation, 5
Delphi method, 553–554
Delta Air Lines, 65
Deltart, John, 197
demand constraints, 184
dependent variable, 568, 634
destinations, 178
deterministic approach, 322
deterministic assumptions, 126
deterministic models, 3, 5, 25
deviational variables, 276, 278
diet problems, 43, 100–101
Digital Equipment Corporation, 204
discrete-event simulation models, 505
discrete general distribution with
    more than two outcomes, 486
discrete general distribution with two
    outcomes, 486
discrete probability distribution,
    642–644

discrete random variable, 640, 641,
    642–644
discrete uniform distribution, 484–485
divisibility, 29
dummy activity, 323, 324f
dyspepsia treatment, 376

E
earliest finish time (EFT), 326, 327, 328f
earliest start time (EST), 326, 327, 328
earliest times, determination of,
    328–329, 333–335
econometric models, 526
efficiency of sample information, 403
Eichler Supplies example, 575
emergency room physicians, 233
employee scheduling applications
    (LP models), 91–94
equally likely criterion, event, 383
Erlang, A.K., 433
Excel
    add-ins, 5t, 628–629
    break-even analysis example, 13–15
    Data Table, 492–494, 500–501, 507,
        511, 518–521
    decision making problems under
        risk, 388–389
    decision making problems under
        uncertainty, 384–386
    ExcelModules. See ExcelModules
    formulas and functions, 625–626
    Goal Seek feature, 14
    LOOKUP function, 487–488
    NORMINV, 485
    Oracle Crystal Ball add-in, 5,
        512–515
    Premium Solver for Education, 62
    RAND, 484
    RANDBETWEEN, 490, 499
    random generation from
        probability distributions,
        484–489, 489t
    scatter diagram, 569–570
    Scenario Manager, 501–504, 511
    seasonality analysis, 555, 575–577
    Solver add-in. See Solver add-in
    SUMPRODUCT function, 53–54
    tax computation example, 11–13
    TreePlan add-in, 392–397
    use of, 4–5
ExcelModules, 629–630
    Analysis ToolPak, 573, 589–592,
        596–600
    causal simple regression models,
        584–589
    described, 5

discrete–event models, 505–507
    exponential smoothing,
        552, 564–568
    finite population model, 458–461
    forecasting model computation,
        557–560
    linear trend analysis, 572–573
    M/D/1 queuing model, 454–455
    M/G/1 queuing model, 456–458
    M/M/1 queuing model, 445–450
    M/M/s queuing model, 452
    multiple regression causal models,
        593–596
    multiplicative decomposition,
        555, 578–581
    queuing system models, 504–507
    revenue management problem,
        507–512
    safety stock computation, 577–579
    weighted moving averages, 561–562
Executive Furniture example, 180–187
expected activity time, 338
expected monetary value (EMV),
    386–387
expected opportunity loss (EOL), 387
expected profit, computation of,
    489–495
expected value of perfect information
    (EVPI), 387–388
expected value of sample information,
    402–403
expected value with perfect
    information (EVwPI), 388
exponential distribution, 485–486,
    651–652
exponential probability distribution,
    439–440, 441f
exponential smoothing, 566–567
extreme points, 39
exponential utility function, 410

F
facility location analysis, 188–191
feasible region, 37
feasible solution, 37
Federal Aviation Administration, 397
fibre allocation optimization, 25
FIFO (first–in, first–out), 438
FIFS (first in, first served), 438n
financial applications (LP models),
    94–95
finite population, 436
finite queue length, 438
fish farming, 51
fixed-charge problems, 248–254
    See also mixed integer model

Fix-It-Shop example, 193–196
Flair's Furniture example, 30–42, 51–60
flow balance constraint, 180
flow diagrams, 490
flowcharts, 490
folding back a decision tree, 391, 400–402
forecast error, 561
forecasting models
    causal models, 551, 552
    consumer market survey, 554
    Delphi method, 553–554
    Excel Modules, 557–560
    forecast error, 554–555
    forecast error, measurement of, 554–555
    jury of executive opinion, 554
    line plots, to check validity, 581
    qualitative models, 551, 552, 553–554
    quantitative models, 551
    sales force composite, 554
    steps to forecasting, 551
    time-series models. *See* time-series
    types of forecasts, 551–554
forest fire management, 125
forest industry, 25
Forestal Arauco, 87
formulas and functions, Excel, 625–626
formulation, 6–8, 27
Forrester, Jay, 525*n*
forward pass, 327–329
free slack time, 332
fully connected network, 179

G

Gantt chart, 317–318*f*, 322
garbage in, garbage out (GIGO), 8
Garcia-Golding Recycling, Inc. example, 454–455
general discrete distribution with two outcomes, 486
General Foundry Inc. example, 322–326
Gendron, Bernard, 228
general integer variables
    branch-and-bound (B&B) method, 235
    described, 229
    integer value requirement, 234
    Solver add-in, 232–237
general-purpose programming languages, 483
generalized reduced gradient (GRG) method, 299
generalized reduced gradient (GRG) nonlinear (Premium Solver), 62

goal programming, history of, 276
goal programming models
    described, 267, 276
    deviation variables, 276, 278
    equally important multiple goals, 278–279
    multiple objectives and, 276
    prioritized goals, 282–287
    ranked goals, 282–287
    satisfice, 276
    Solver solution, 284–287
    use of, 277
    weighted goals, 279–282
Goal Seek feature, 14
graphical solution methods
    constraints, representation of, 34–37
    corner point method, 39–40, 42
    corner points, 39
    illustration of, 34–40
    isocost line method, 45–46
    isoprofit line method, 38–39
    minimization linear programming problem, 42–46
    summary, 46
graphs
    constraint coefficients, 129, 180
    objective function coefficients (OFCs), 129–131
    right-hand-side (RHS) value, 129
    and sensitivity analysis, 127–135
    utility curve, 407–410
Ground-Delay Program, 397

H

Hargrave Machine Co. example, 188–191, 248–252
Haynes Construction Co. example, 649–651
heuristic approach, 8
history
    critical path method (CPM), 322
    decision modeling, origin of, 4
    goal programming, 276
    linear programming, origin of, 26
    program evaluation and review technique (PERT), 322
    simulation, 477
HJ Heinz Company, 557
holding cost, 500, 501, 504
Home Care Services (BC), 197
hospital efficiency, 82–83
hospital overcrowding, 435
Howard, Ronald, 390
hub-and-spoke, 178
Hurwicz decision criterion, 382–383

I

If-then constraint, 246
immediate predecessor, 323
implementation, 7, 18–19
independent events, 634–635
independent variable, 568
industrial dynamics, 525*n*
inequality, 28
infeasibility, 47, 48*f*
infeasible solution, 37
inferior solution, 241
infinite population, 436
infinite queue length, 438
ingredient blending applications (LP models), 100–103
ingredient problems, 101–103
input data, 3–4, 5, 8, 17
integer programming (IP) model, 32
    binary variables, 243–247
    branch-and-bound (B&B) method, 235, 237–243
    described, 229–230
    fixed-charge problems, 248–254
    general integer variables, 230–237
    if-then constraint, 246
    illustration, 230–232
    with integer requirement deleted, 231
    integer value requirement, 234
    k out of *n* variables constraint, 245–246
    linked variables, 246
    mixed binary IP problems, 230
    mixed integer models, 248–253
    mixed IP problems, 230
    mutually exclusive constraint, 246
    pure binary IP (or 0 –1) IP problems, 230
    pure IP problem, 230
    Solver add-in, 232–237
    types of problems, 230
integer variable, 229
integer values, 32
interpretation step, 9, 27
inventory control
    irregular supply and demand, 495
    stockouts, 495, 497
    stockout cost, 500, 501, 504
    total cost, 500, 501, 504
inventory problems
    cost computations, 500
    holding cost, 500, 501, 504
    illustration, 496
    Oracle Crystal Ball, 513–521
    order cost, 500, 501, 504
    replication, 500–501
    setting up the model, 497

isocost line method, 43, 45–46
isoprofit line method, 38–39, 46
iterative process, 41

J

Joint probability, 635, 637
JS McMillan Fisheries Ltd., 554
jury of executive opinion, 554

K

k out of *n* variables constraint, 245–246
Kantorovich, Leonid, 26
Karmarkar, N., 26
Karmarkar's algorithm, 65
Kendall's notation, 441–442
Ketchup demand, forecasting, 557
knapsack problems, 100
Kolmogorov, A.N., 26
KORBX, 65

L

labour planning problems, 91–93
Laplace criterion, 383
larger maximization example, and
    sensitivity analysis, 142–147
latest finish time (LFT), 329, 330f
latest start time (LST), 329, 330f
latest start times, determination of,
    335, 336f
Lauderdale Construction Co.
    example, 203–207
lead time, 495
least squares procedure for linear
    regression, 573–575
level lines, 37–41
LHS formula, 54
Lightwell Chandelier Co. example,
    230–237
limited population, 436
limited queue length, 438
linear programming
    applications. *See* linear program-
        ming modeling applications
    crashing, 350–352
    deterministic assumptions, 126
    model. *See* linear programming
        models
    and multiple objectives, 276
    nonnegativity constraints, 28
    origin of, 26
    problems. *See* linear programming
        problems
    resource allocation decisions, 26
    sensitivity analysis. *See* sensitivity
        analysis
    wide use of, 5, 26, 84

linear programming modeling
        applications
    employee scheduling applications,
        91–94
    financial applications, 94–95
    ingredient blending applications,
        100–103
    manufacturing applications, 89–91
    marketing applications, 84–89
    multiperiod applications, 103–112
    packing applications, 96–100
linear programming models. 82. *See
        also* linear programming
    assignment model, 178
    basic assumptions, 28–29
    critical path, identification of,
        333–335
    development of, 27–28
    earliest times, determination
        of, 333–335
    formulation, 27
    guidelines to developing, 32–33
    interpretation, 27
    latest start times, determination
        of, 335, 336f
    maximal-flow model, 178–179
    network flow models. *See* network
        flow models
    properties of, 27–28
    shortest-path model, 202–203
    solution, 27
    transportation model, 178, 180–187
    transshipment model, 178, 192–193
linear programming problems
    algorithmic solution procedures,
        64–65
    alternate optimal solutions,
        49–50, 50f
    constraints, 28, 31–32
    corner point property, 39–40
    decision variables, 30–31
    diet problem, 43
    Excel's Solver, 50–61
    feasible region, 37
    formulation of problem, 30–33
    graphical solutions. *See* graphical
        solution methods
    infeasibility, 47, 48f
    isoprofit line solution, 38–39, 46
    Karmarkar's algorithm, 65
    minimization linear programming
        problem, 42–46
    nonnegativity constraints, 32f
    objective function, 27, 31
    optimal solution, 37–42
    product mix problem, 30–33

redundant constraint, 47, 48f
relaxed problem, 231, 237, 238
simplex method, 64, 69
simultaneous equations method, 40
special situations, 47–50
two-variable problem, graphical
    solution of, 34–42
unbounded, 48–49, 49f
linear trend analysis, 568–577
linked variables, 246
Loblaw Companies Limited, 550
Local vs. global optimal solutions, 289
logical approach, 632
London Stock Exchange, 337
LOOKUP function, 487–488

M

M/D/1 queuing model, 453–455
M/G/1 queuing model, 455–458
M/M/1 queuing models
    assumptions, 443
    costs, introduction of, 448–449
    described, 442t
    ExcelModules solution, 445–448
    operating characteristic equations,
        444–445
    service rate increase, 449–450
M/M/s/∞/N queuing model, 458–461
M/M/s queuing model, 450–453
management science, 4, 13
    See also decision modeling
management support, 19
manufacturing applications
    (LP models), 89–91
marginal probability, 634–635
marginal utility, beginning of, 410
marketing applications (LP models),
    84–89
marketing research problems, 87–89
Markovian processes, 439
mathematical models, 3, 7, 18, 83
mathematical programming, 26
Max Time option, 235
maximal-flow model
    constraints, 199
    described, 178, 196
    Excel solution, 199–201
    illustration of, 197
    linear programming model, 197–201
    objective function, 198–199
maximal-flow problem, 178
maximax criterion, 382
maximin criterion, 382
maximization problems
    assignment models, 196
    branch-and-bound method, 241

larger maximization example, and sensitivity analysis, 142–146
McGill University, 376
mean absolute deviation (MAD), 554
mean absolute percent error (MAPE), 554–555
mean squared error (MSE), 554
media selection problems, 84–86
Metro Canada Logistics, 188
Mexican truck manufacturer, 507
Microsoft Excel. *See* Excel
Microsoft Project
  activity information, entering, 353–354
  budget status, 357
  cost status, tracking, 357–359
  precedence relationships, defining, 354–355
  project scheduling, 353–356
  time status, tracking, 356–357
  viewing project schedule, 355–356
Midwestern Electric Company, 568
minimal-spanning tree model
  described, 179, 203
  illustration, 203–204
  solution, 205–207
  steps for solving, 205
  unconnected node, 205
minimax regret criterion, 383–384
minimization problems
  branch-and-bound method, 242–243
  minimization example, and sensitivity analysis, 150–154
  minimization linear programming problem, 42–46
minimum selling price, 148–149
Ministère des Transports du Québec (MTQ), 287
mixed binary IP problems, 230
mixed integer model
  Big-M method, 252–253
  constraints, 250, 252
  decision variables, 249
  described, 248
  illustration of, 250–252
  objective function, 250
mixed IP problems, 230
models, 3
Monte Carlo simulation
  described, 478
  development of, 477
  probability distribution, establishment of, 478, 480
  replications, 482
  simulation of values, 480–482
  steps of, 478

most likely time (*m*), 317
Mount Sinai Hospital (Toronto), 266
moving averages, 556
multicollinearity, 599
multiperiod applications (LP models), 103–112
multiphase queuing system, 439
multiple regression analysis, 582, 592–600
multiple-server queuing system, 439
multiplicative decomposition, 577–581
multiplicative decomposition model, 555, 577–581
multistage decision making problems, 397–403
municipal governments, 268
mutually exclusive constraint, 246
mutually exclusive events, 632–634

N
NASA, 127
National Health Service (UK), 381
Natural Resources Canada, 125
negative exponential distribution, 651–652
net flow, 180
network flow models
  arcs, 178
  assignment model, 178
  characteristics of network flow problems, 179–180
  constraint coefficients, 180
  described, 178
  flow balance constraint, 180
  maximal-flow model, 178
  minimal-spanning tree model, 179
  nodes, 178
  shortest-path model, 179
  transportation model, 178
  transshipment model, 178
  transshipment points, 179
networks, 179, 179f
New Brunswick Telephone Company (NBTel), 177
new variables, pricing out, 147–150
Niagara Falls casino resort, 315
nodes, 178, 179, 180
noncritical paths, 341
nonlinear objective function
  and linear constraints, 288, 293–296
  and nonlinear constraints, 288, 296–297
  quadratic programming, 295
nonlinear problems
  generalized reduced gradient (GRG) method, 299

nonlinear programming models. *See* nonlinear programming models
separable programming, 299
nonlinear programming models
  complexity of, 288–289
  computational procedures, 298–299
  described, 267, 288
  linear objective function and nonlinear constraints, 298
  local vs. global optimal solutions, 289
  nonlinear objective function and linear constraints, 288, 293–296
  nonlinear objective function and nonlinear constraints, 288, 296–297
  optimizing nonlinear function, 289–291
  Solver solution, 290–293, 294, 295–296, 297–298
  unconstrained optimization, 290
nonnegativity constraints, 28, 32
nonstationary data, 556
Norigen Communication Inc., 326
normal curve, area under, 646–647, 658
normal distribution, 645–651
  area under the normal curve, 646–647, 658
normal time, 322
normalized pairwise comparison matrix, 270
NORMINV, 485
Nortel, 346
Nova Scotia Shipping Company, 434–435
Nurse Next Door, 197

O
objective approach, 631–632
objective function, 27, 31
  assignment model, 195
  crashing, 350
  linear, 286
  maximal-flow model, 198–199
  mixed integer model, 250
  nonlinear, 293, 296
  shortest-path model, 202
  transportation problem, 183
  transshipment model, 192
objective function coefficients (OFCs)
  allowable ranges, 140–141
  change in, 129–131
  impact of changes, 139–141
  Reduced Cost value, 141
  simultaneous changes, 147

objectives, 7
one answer limitation, 18
100% rule, 146–150
Ontario hospitals, 82–83
Ontario Lottery and Gaming
    Corporation, 315
Ontario Ministry of Health, 82
Ontario municipal governments, 268
operating characteristics
    described, 443
    finite population queuing system
        (M/M/s/∞/N model), 459
    M/D/1 queuing model, 453–454
    M/G/1 queuing model, 455–456
    M/M/1 queuing model, 444–445
    M/M/s queuing model, 450–451
operational gaming, 525
operations research, 13
    See also decision modeling
opportunity loss, 383–384
optimal solution, 27, 37–41, 188
optimistic time (*a*), 337
Oracle Crystal Ball add-in
    best reservation limit, 523–525
    Decision Table feature, 518–521
    described, 5, 512–513
    inventory problem simulation,
        513–521
order quantity, 496, 497
origins, 178
outcome node, 390
outcomes, 378
outdated solutions, 17

P

packing applications (LP models)
    knapsack problems, 100
    transportation problems, 100
    truck loading problem, 96–99
pairwise comparisons, 267, 269*t*, 275*t*
pairwise comparisons matrix, 269
parameter, 8
payoff table, 379
payoffs, 378
perfect information, 387–388
PERT. *See* program evaluation and
    review technique (PERT)
pessimistic time (*b*), 337
point estimate, 588
Poisson distribution, 437, 438, 652
pollution control, 16
pollution in Lake Ontario, 475
portfolio selection problems
    if-then constraint, 246
    integer programming (IP) model
        with binary variables, 244–247

k out of *n* variables constraint,
    245–246
    linear programming, 94–95
    linked variables, 246
    mutually exclusive constraint, 246
post-optimality analysis, 9
    See also sensitivity analysis
posterior probabilities, 404
precedence constraints, 333
precedence relationships, 354–355
Premium Solver for Education, 62, 237
pricing out, 147–150
prior probabilities, 404
prioritized goals, 282–287
priority vector, 271
probabilistic models, 3, 6
probabilistic technique, 478
probabilities, 6
probability
    Bayes' theorem, 636, 637–639
    collectively exhaustive events,
        632–633
    concepts, 630–631
    conditional, 635
    joint, 635, 637
    laws of, 631
    marginal (simple), 634–635
    mutually exclusive events, 632, 633
    objective, 631–632
    prior, 637, 638
    random variables, 640–641
    revised/posterior, 637, 638
    revising, 637–640
    statistically dependent events,
        635–637
    statistically independent events,
        634–635
    subjective, 631, 632
    types of, 631–632
probability density function, 645
probability distribution, 588, 641
    of continuous random variables,
        644–645
    of discrete random variables,
        642–644
    standard deviation, 644
probability estimates, 403–405
probability revisions, 639–640
problem, defining, 6–7, 16
product mix problem, 89–90
production scheduling problems,
    103–108
program evaluation and review
    technique (PERT), 320,
    321–322, 337–338
project, 316

project completion constraint, 351
project completion times, 338–341,
    340*f*, 341*f*
project controlling, 318–319
project costs, 348
project management
    activity times, variability in, 335–342
    crashing, 347–352
    critical path method (CPM),
        321–322
    described, 316
    example of, 322–323
    illustration of, 317
    Microsoft Project, 352–359
    phases in, 316–319
    program evaluation and review
        technique (PERT), 320,
        321–322, 337–338
    project completion, 338–341
    project controlling, 318–319
    project costs, 342–346
    project networks, 319–326
    project planning, 316
    project scheduling, 316–318,
        326–327
    resource-loading chart, 347
    resources, management of, 346–347
    results of, 341–342
    software development, 337
    software packages, use of, 319
    techniques, 321–322
project networks, 319–326
project planning
    activities, identification of, 319–321
    activity on arc (AOA), 323, 325–326
    activity on node (AON), 323–324
    activity times, 321
    described, 319
    dummy activity, 323, 324*f*
    event, 325
    free slack time, 332
    immediate predecessor, 323
    multiple critical paths, 331–332
    project networks, 319–326
    total slack time, 332
    work breakdown structure (WBS),
        321, 321*f*
    work packages, 342
project scheduling
    backward pass, 329
    critical path analysis, 326–329
    described, 316–318
    forward pass, 327–329
    Gantt chart, 317, 318*f*
    Microsoft Project, 353–356
    slack time, 330–332

proportionality, 28
pure binary IP (or 0–1)
    IP problems, 230
problems, 230
pure IP problem, 230

Q

quadratic programming, 295
qualitative data, 4
qualitative forecasting models, 552,
    553–554
quantitative analysis. *See* decision
    modeling
quantitative data, 4, 551
queue characteristics, 438
queue discipline, 438
queues, 433
queuing models
    development of, 433
    economic analysis, 453
    M/D/1 model, 453–455
    M/G/1 model, 455–458
    M/M/1 model, 442t, 443–445
    M/M/s/∞/N model, 458–462
    M/M/s model, 450–453
    operating characteristics, 443
    required model parameters,
        identification of, 457
    variety of, 442–443
queuing system
    arrival characteristics, 436–438
    balking, 438
    characteristics of, 436–443
    complex queuing systems, 462
    costs, 433–436
    discipline, 438
    exponential probability distribution,
        439–440, 441f
    Kendall's notation, 441–442
    multiphase queuing system, 439
    multiple-server, with Poisson
        arrivals, exponential service
        times, and finite population
        size (M/M/s/∞/N model),
        450–453, 458–461
    multiple-server queuing
        system, 439
    Nova Scotia Shipping Company
        example, 434–436
    performance measures, 441
    Poisson distribution, 437, 438
    queue characteristics, 438
    reneging, 438
    service costs, 433
    service facility characteristics,
        438–439

service facility configurations,
    438–439, 440 f
service time distribution, 439–440
single-phase queuing system, 439
single-server, with Poisson arrivals
    and constant service times
        (M/D/1 model), 453–455
    and exponential service times
        (M/M/1 model), 442t,
        443–450
    and general service times
        (M/G/1 model), 455
single-server queuing system,
    438–439
waiting costs, 434

R

RAND, 484
RANDBETWEEN, 490, 499
random number intervals, 490, 499
random numbers, 481, 482t,
random variables, 640–641
    continuous, 640, 641, 644–645
    discrete, 640, 641, 642–644
random variations, 555
ranked goals, 282–287
Ray Design, Inc. example, 201–203
realism, criterion of, 382–383
Reduced Cost value, 141
redundant constraint, 47, 48 f
regression analysis, 582–589
regression plots, 586
regret, 383
relative frequency approach, 653
relaxed problem, 231, 237, 238
reneging, 438
reorder point (ROP), 496, 497
replications, 482, 489, 490, 492–494, 507
required profit contribution, 148
resources, 5, 30
revenue management problem,
    modeling, 507–512, 521–525
RHS formula, 54
right-hand-side (RHS) value
    allowable decrease, 139
    allowable increase, 139
    binding constraint, 131–133, 138
    changes in, 129
    constraint RHS, 50, 129
    impact of changes, 131–134, 138–141
    nonbinding constraint, 131, 134–135
    shadow price, 132, 133, 138–139
    simultaneous changes, 146–147
risk avoider, 408
risk neutral, 409

risk preferences, 409f
risk premium, 409
risk seeker, 409
Royal Preston Hospital, 450

S

sales force composite, 554
satisficing, 276
Sawyer Piano House, 577
scale models, 3
scatter diagram, 569–570
Scenario Manager, 501–504
seasonality, 555, 575–577
sensitivity analysis
    alternate optimal solutions, 146
    Answer Report, 136
    binding constraint, change in RHS
        of, 131–133, 138
    constraint coefficients, 129
    described, 9
    graphs, use of, 127–135
    larger maximization example,
        142–146
    in linear programming, 27
    minimization example, 150–154
    nonbinding constraint, change in
        RHS of, 131, 134–135
    objective function coefficients (OFCs),
        128, 129–131, 139–141
    pricing out new variables, 147–150
    right-hand-side (RHS) value, 129
    scarce resources, study of, 126
    Sensitivity Report, 152
    shadow prices, 125
    simultaneous changes, and 100%
        rule, 146–147
    Solver reports, 135–141
    validity of 100% rule, 148
    validity range for shadow
        price, 133–134, 138–139
Sensitivity Report, 136, 137–138
separable programming, 299
sequential decisions, 397
service costs, 433
service facility characteristics, 438–439
service facility configurations,
    438–439, 440f
service time distribution, 439–440
shadow prices, 125, 127, 132, 133–134
shortest-path model
    constraints, 202
    described, 179, 201
    Excel solution, 202–203
    illustration of, 201–202
    linear programming model, 202–203
    objective function, 202

shortest-path problem, 179
Sim, Ken, 197
simplex algorithm, 26
simple probability, 634–635
simplex method, 64–65, 84
simulating future traffic flows, Victoria (BC), 201
simulation modeling
    advantages and disadvantages, 477–478
    best reservation policy, 523–525
    computers, role of, 482–489
    Data Table, 492–494, 507, 511
    described, 476
    discrete-event models, 505
    Excel solution, 484–489, 489t
    expected profit, computation of, 489–495
    flowcharts, 490
    history, 477
    inventory problems, 495–504
    Monte Carlo simulation, 478, 480–482
    operational gaming, 525
    Oracle Crystal Ball add-in, 513–525
    process of simulation, 476
    queuing problem, 504–507
    random generation from probability distributions, 484–489
    random numbers, 481, 482t
    replications, 482, 489, 490, 492–494, 507, 511, 515
    revenue management problem, 507–512, 521–25
    Scenario Manager, 501–504, 511
    systems simulation, 525–526
    water quality management, 475
simulation software packages, 483–484
simultaneous changes, 146–147
simultaneous equations method, 40
single-phase queuing system, 439
single-server queuing time, 438–439
sinking fund problems, 108–112
sinks, 178
slack, 59–60, 65, 131, 154
slack time, 330–332, 331f
smoothing constant, 565
Société des Alcools du Québec, 228–229
software development, 337
solution, 8–9, 27
Solver add-in
    Answer Report, 57, 59f
    assignment model solution, 196
    Assume Linear Model, 56
    Assume Non-Negative, 56
    Big-M method, 252–253

blending problems, 101–103
branch-and-bound (B&B) method, 235, 243, 244
Changing Cells, specifying, 55–56, 563
Changing Cells (decision variables), 52–56
constraint LHS, 54
constraint RHS, 54
constraint type, 54–55
constraints, set up of, 54–55, 563
constraints, specifying, 56, 563
crashing solution, 352
critical path, identification of, 333–335
diet problems, 100–101
entering information, 55–60
fixed-charge problem, 248–254
generalized reduced gradient (GRG) method, 299
goal programming model with ranked goals, 284–287
graphical solution method, 42, 44–46
ingredient problems, 101–103
integer programming models with binary variables, 246–247
integer programming models with general integer variables, 232–237
integer value requirement, 234
labour planning problems, 91–93
larger maximization example, 142
linear programming problems, solution of, 50–61
marketing research problems, 88
Max Time option, 235
maximal-flow model solution, 199–201
media selection LP problem, 84–86
minimization example, 150–154
nonlinear programming models, 290–293, 294, 295–296, 297–298
optimal smoothing constant, determination of, 567–568
optimal weights, determination of, 563–564
options, 56–57, 136
portfolio selection problems, 94–95, 246
Premium Solver for Education, 62
product mix problem, 89–90
production scheduling problems, 103–104
reports. See Solver reports
results window, possible messages in, 57, 58t

shortest-path model solution, 202–203
sinking fund problems, 111–112
slack, 59
solving the model, 50, 57
Target Cell, 53, 55, 563
Thompson Lumber Company, 377
Tolerance option, 235
transportation model, 184
transportation model solution, 184, 185
transshipment model solution, 192, 193
truck loading problem, 96–99
unconstrained optimization, and nonlinear programming models, 290–291
Solver reports
    Answer Report, 57, 59f, 136
    Assume Linear Model, 56, 136
    large maximization example, 142–146
    sensitivity analysis, using, 135–141
    Sensitivity Report, 136, 137–138
sources, 178
special-purpose simulation languages and programs, 484
spreadsheet models, 484
spreadsheets, 4–5
    See also Excel
standard deviation, 644
standard deviation of the regression, 585–586
standard error of the estimate, 585–586, 601
standard evolutionary (Premium Solver), 62
standard normal distribution, 648
standard normal table, 648–649
standard simplex LP (Premium Solver), 62
standard time, 322
state of nature nodes, 378
    See also Outcome node
stationary data, 556
statistically dependent events, 635–637
statistically independent events, 634–635
statistical significance of regression equation, 590–592
stochastic models, 3
stockouts, 495
    See also safety stock
subjective approach, 631–632
SUMPRODUCT function, 53–54
supply constraints, 183–184

surplus, 60
survey results, potential problems with, 405–406
systems simulation, 525–526

T

Target Cell (objective function), 53, 55
tax computation spreadsheet example, 11–13
Taylor, Frederick W., 4
TB drug allocation, 277
Telecommunications network, 204
testing the solution, 9, 18
textbook models, 17
Thompson Lumber Company example, 377–378
time-series forecasting models
    additive decomposition model, 555
    components of a time series, 555, 556f
    cycles, 555
    described, 555
    exponential smoothing, 552, 564–568
    least squares procedure for linear regression, 572–573
    linear trend analysis, 552, 568–577
    moving averages, 552, 556
    multiplicative, decomposition, 552, 577–581
    multiplicative decomposition model, 555
    nonstationary data, 556
    optimal smoothing constant, determination of, 567–568
    optimal weights, determination of, 563–564
    random variations, 555
    scatter diagram, 555, 569–570
    seasonality analysis, 552, 555, 575–577
    stationary data, 556
    trend, 555
    weighted moving averages, 552
tolerance option, 235
toolbars, Excel, 621–633
total cost, 500, 501, 504
total slack time, 332
TransAlta Utilities, 582

transportation model
    alternate Excel layout, 185–186
    balanced problem, 182
    constraints, 183
    demand constraints, 184
    described, 178
    destinations, 178
    Excel solution, 184–185
    facility location analysis, 188–191
    illustration of, 180–184
    linear programming model, 180, 183–184
    multiple optimal solutions, 188
    objective function, 183
    origins, 178
    sinks, 178
    sources, 178
    supply constraints, 183–184
    total requirement exceeds total supply, 187
    total supply exceeds total requirement, 187
    unbalanced problem, 187
transportation problems, 100
transshipment model
    constraints, 192
    described, 178
    Excel solution, 192, 193
    flows, 192
    hub-and-spoke, 178
    illustration of, 193
    linear programming model, 192
    objective function, 192
transshipment points, 179
transshipment problem, 178, 182
TreePlan add-in, 392–397
trend, 555, 577
trial. See replications
truck loading problem, 96–99
two-variable linear programming problem, 34–42

U

unbalanced assignment problems, 196
unbalanced problem, 187
unbounded, 48–49, 49f
university, deciding on, 267–275
unlimited population, 436
unlimited queue length, 438
user involvement, 19

utility assessment, 408–410
utility curve, 407–410
utility theory
    certainty equivalent, 407
    decision-making criterion, 410–412
    lottery ticket example, 406
    measurement of utility, 407–410
    utility curve, 407–410
utilization factor, 407
utility function, 407–410

V

validity range for shadow price, 133–134, 138–139
variables, 8, 229
variance of activity completion time, 338
variance of discrete probability distribution, 643–644
vehicle park management, 287
VIA Rail Canada, 10
Vilpac, 507
Volkswagen, 496
von Neumann, John, 477

W

waiting costs, 434
waiting lines, 444
Wallace Garden Supply example, 556–557, 561, 565
warehousing problems, 188
water quality management, 475
weighted average, 383
weighted goals, 279–282
weighted moving averages, 561–564
weighted sum vector, 273
Weldwood of Canada, 25
what-if analysis, 497
Wilson Doors Company, 277–282
work breakdown structure (WBS), 321, 321f
work packages, 342
worksheets, Excel, 620–621, 624–625, 627–628

Y

yield-management problems, 507

Z

Zero-one variables. See binary variables